CRIME STATE RANKINGS
1999

Crime in the 50 United States

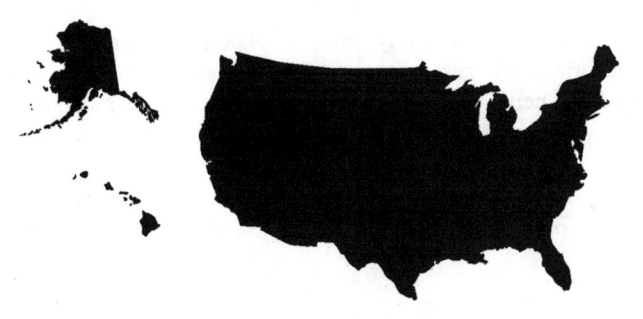

Editors:
Kathleen O'Leary Morgan and Scott Morgan
Associate Editor: Kim Tiffany
Editorial Assistants: Pat Moffet and Emily Davis

MORGAN
QUITNO

Morgan Quitno Press
© Copyright 1999, All Rights Reserved

512 East 9th Street, P.O. Box 1656
Lawrence, KS 66044-8656
USA

800-457-0742 or 785-841-3534
http://www.morganquitno.com

Sixth Edition

D0767572

990184

© Copyright 1999 by
Morgan Quitno Corporation
512 East 9th Street, P.O. Box 1656
Lawrence, Kansas   66044-8656

800-457-0742 or 785-841-3534
http://www.morganquitno.com

ISBN:
1-56692-334-4
ISSN:
1077-4408

Crime State Rankings 1999 sells for $49.95 ($5.00 shipping) and is only available in paper binding. For those who prefer ranking information tailored to a particular state, we also offer *Crime State Perspectives*, state-specific reports for each of the 50 states. These individual guides provide information on a state's data and rank for each of the categories featured in the national *Crime State Rankings* volume. Perspectives sell for $19.00 or $9.50 if ordered with *Crime State Rankings*. If you are interested in city and metropolitan crime data, we offer *City Crime Rankings, 5th Edition* ($37.95 paper). Those interested in health statistics should check out our annual *Health Care State Rankings* ($49.95 paper). If you are interested in a general view of the states, please ask about our annual *State Rankings* ($49.95 paper). We also offer the data in our books on diskette. Shipping is $5.00 per order.

Sixth Edition
Printed in the United States of America
April 1999

PREFACE

How does your state compare in violent crime? What percentage of your state's population is behind bars? Answers to these and hundreds of other crime-related questions are found in *Crime State Rankings 1999*. Now in its sixth edition, this valuable annual reference book offers a wealth of crime-related information in a straightforward, easy-to-understand format.

Important Notes About *Crime State Rankings 1999*

This book is the product of a year-round effort to find and filter basic information regarding crime. Designed with simplicity as its driving force, *Crime State Rankings 1999* is the result of our rigorous annual review process in which we review the previous year's book, examine each table, update most of them, remove others that are no longer pertinent and add new data of interest. With 508 tables of state crime comparisons, this sixth edition is a solid collection of valuable crime and law enforcement information.

While you will find a number of changes and updates, many of the organizational features that have made this book so popular with both reviewers and researchers have not changed. Data are presented in both alphabetical and rank order so that readers may quickly find information for a particular state and then just as quickly learn which states rank above and below that state. Source information and other pertinent footnotes are clearly shown at the bottom of each page and national totals, rates and percentages are prominently displayed at the top of each table. Every other line is shaded in gray for easier reading. In addition, numerous information finding tools are provided: a thorough table of contents, table listings at the beginning of each chapter, a detailed index and a chapter thumb index. Also included is a roster of sources showing addresses, phone numbers and websites.

As in all of our reference books, the numbers shown in *Crime State Rankings 1999* are "complete" numbers, meaning that no additional calculations are required to convert them to thousands, millions, etc. All states are ranked on a high to low basis. Any ties among states are shown alphabetically for a given ranking. Numbers reported in parentheses "( )" are negative numbers. For tables with national totals (as opposed to rates, per capita's, etc.) we include a separate column showing what percent of the national total each individual state's total represents. This column is headed by "% of USA." This percentage figure is particularly interesting when compared with a state's share of the nation's population for a particular year. The appendix contains population tables to aid in these comparisons.

For those interested in focusing on crime information for just one state, we once again are offering our *Crime State Perspective* series of publications. These 21-page, comb-bound reports feature data and ranking information for an individual state pulled from *Crime State Rankings 1999*. (For example, *New York Crime in Perspective* contains crime information about the state of New York only.) When purchased individually, *Crime State Perspectives* sell for $19. When purchased with a copy of *Crime State Rankings 1999*, these handy quick reference guides are just $9.50.

Other Books from Morgan Quitno Press

While *Crime State Rankings* provides crime information for states, our *City Crime Rankings* reference book features up-to-date crime information for cities and metro areas. In its fifth edition, *City Crime Rankings* compares all cities of 75,000 population or more and all metropolitan areas (some as small as 65,000 population) in 40 categories of crime each. Numbers of crimes, crime rates, and crime trends over one and five years are presented for all major crime categories reported by the FBI. This book sells for $37.95 (paper cover; $5 shipping).

Those interested in general state statistics or state health care information may want to check out our *State Rankings* and *Health Care State Rankings* books. *State Rankings* presents statistics for a wide variety of categories including agriculture, transportation, government finance, health, population, crime, education, social welfare, energy and environment. Our annual *Health Care State Rankings* book includes data on health care facilities, providers, insurance and finance, incidence of disease, mortality, physical fitness, natality and reproductive health. *State Rankings* and *Health Care State Rankings* sell for $49.95 each (paper cover) plus $5 shipping. Also available are *State Perspectives* and *Health Care State Perspectives* for each of these books, selling for $19 individually or $9.50 if purchased with their corresponding national volume. Our data is available on diskette (.dbf, Excel or ASCII formats for PC).

New to the Morgan Quitno family of publications is *State Statistical Trends,* a monthly journal that compares changes in life and government for the 50 United States. Each 100-page monthly issue examines a different subject and provides a collection of tables, graphics and commentary showing state multi-year trends. For further information about *Trends* or any of our other publications, please call us toll-free at 1-800-457-0742.

Finally, many thanks to the many hard working librarians and government workers who help us every year with information, explanations and general support. Thanks also to you, our readers. We always welcome your suggestions, so please don't be shy about contacting us. Call us toll-free at 1-800-457-0742, send a letter to P.O. Box 1656, Lawrence, Kansas 66044, or e-mail us through our website: www.morganquitno.com.   - THE EDITORS

WHICH STATE IS THE MOST DANGEROUS?

Nevada, famous for fun, is once again famous for crime. After falling to third place last year, Nevada regains the dubious honor as Morgan Quitno's 1999 Most Dangerous State. In the somewhat more sought after Safest State Award, the appropriately-named Peace Garden State of North Dakota retains its unrelenting hold.

The Methodology

A four step process was followed to determine the Most Dangerous State rankings. First, state rates for six crime categories — murder, rape, robbery, aggravated assault, burglary and motor vehicle theft — were plugged into a formula that measures how a state compares to the national average for a given crime category.

Second, the outcome of this equation was then multiplied by a weight assigned to each crime category. For this year's award, each crime category was given equal weight. In previous years, weights were determined based on a telephone survey which asked Americans which crimes they feared the most in their communities. While the results were always interesting, the telephone survey added an element of subjectivity to the final outcome. By weighting each crime equally, state comparisons are based purely on their crime rates and how these rates stack up to the national average for a given crime category.

Third, the weighted numbers were added together to get a state's score ("SUM.") In the fourth and final step, these composite scores were ranked from highest to lowest to determine which states were the most dangerous and safest. The end result of this process is that the farther below the national average a state's crime rate is, the lower (and safer) it ranked. The farther above the national average, the higher (and more dangerous) a state ranks in the final list.

Morgan Quitno Press takes pride in presenting facts in a nonbiased, objective manner. While a central theme of our books is our clear presentation of data, with the analysis and interpretation left to our readers, we stray from this policy once a year and issue these awards. Annually since 1991 we have named the Most Livable State based on data from our *State Rankings* series. In 1993, we began the Healthiest State Award based on data from our *Health Care State Rankings* series. In 1994, we initiated the annual Safest and Most Dangerous City Award based on data from our *City Crime Rankings* book.

The reaction to our Most Dangerous State announcement ranges from calls for stepped up crime fighting to a "kill the messenger" approach. While it does not affect our rankings, it certainly keeps us on our toes. The vast majority of states are experiencing declining crime rates. Nevada's violent crime rate has fallen more than 8% in five years. Yet with such stiff competition from its fellow states, Nevada will have to work even harder to improve its record.

— THE EDITORS

1999 MOST DANGEROUS STATE

RANK	STATE	SUM	'98	RANK	STATE	SUM	'98
1	Nevada	50.62	3	26	Ohio	(16.48)	27
2	Florida	46.35	2	27	New Jersey	(19.13)	24
3	Louisiana	45.91	1	28	Kansas	(19.75)	30
4	New Mexico	34.80	5	29	Hawaii	(22.23)	31
5	Tennessee	33.04	8	30	Massachusetts	(23.14)	28
6	South Carolina	28.23	6	31	Colorado	(24.51)	29
7	Maryland	28.11	4	32	Minnesota	(25.08)	33
8	Arizona	24.24	9	33	Pennsylvania	(25.41)	34
9	Illinois	19.26	10	34	Utah	(25.74)	35
10	California	19.14	7	35	Connecticut	(29.22)	32
11	Alaska	12.55	13	36	Virginia	(30.93)	37
12	Michigan	10.36	11	37	Kentucky	(33.46)	38
13	Mississippi	7.47	19	38	Rhode Island	(33.64)	36
14	Georgia	6.40	12	39	Nebraska	(38.55)	39
15	Texas	3.19	14	40	Wisconsin	(45.07)	40
16	North Carolina	2.94	17	41	Idaho	(47.67)	41
17	Delaware	1.83	18	42	Iowa	(49.32)	44
18	Oklahoma	1.44	15	43	Wyoming	(51.89)	42
19	Alabama	(0.44)	20	44	South Dakota	(52.72)	46
20	Arkansas	(1.03)	23	45	West Virginia	(53.82)	45
21	Washington	(4.53)	22	46	Montana	(55.05)	43
22	Missouri	(4.84)	21	47	Vermont	(63.81)	47
23	New York	(5.54)	16	48	Maine	(63.95)	48
24	Indiana	(11.04)	26	49	New Hampshire	(64.84)	49
25	Oregon	(12.97)	25	50	North Dakota	(70.86)	50

FACTORS CONSIDERED (all given equal weight):
(all rates per 100,000 population)

1. Murder Rate (Table 328)
2. Rape Rate (Table 347)
3. Robbery Rate (Table 353)
4. Aggravated Assault Rate (Table 368)
5. Burglary Rate (Table 388)
6. Motor Vehicle Theft Rate (Table 398)

TABLE OF CONTENTS

I. Arrests

II. Corrections

TABLE OF CONTENTS (continued)

TABLE OF CONTENTS (continued)

III. Drugs and Alcohol

IV. Finance

TABLE OF CONTENTS (continued)

V. Juveniles

TABLE OF CONTENTS (continued)

VI. Law Enforcement

TABLE OF CONTENTS (continued)

VII. Offenses

TABLE OF CONTENTS (continued)

Urban/Rural Crime

TABLE OF CONTENTS (continued)

1993 Crimes

TABLE OF CONTENTS (continued)

I. ARRESTS

Important Note Regarding Arrest Numbers

The state arrest numbers reported by the FBI and shown in tables 1 to 36 are only from those law enforcement agencies that submitted complete arrests reports for 12 months in 1997. The arrest rates were calculated by the editors using population totals provided by the FBI for those jurisdictions reporting. Reports from law enforcement agencies in Alaska, Delaware, Georgia, Illinois, Kentucky, Mississippi, Montana, Nevada, New York, Pennsylvania, South Dakota and Tennessee represented less than half of their state populations. Thus rates for these states should be interpreted with caution. No arrest data were available for Florida, Kansas, New Hampshire, Vermont and the District of Columbia.

Reported Arrests in 1997

National Total = 10,540,215 Reported Arrests*

ALPHA ORDER

RANK	STATE	ARRESTS	% of USA
16	Alabama	223,057	2.1%
45	Alaska	19,779	0.2%
13	Arizona	275,565	2.6%
20	Arkansas	191,805	1.8%
1	California	1,594,841	15.1%
22	Colorado	181,404	1.7%
23	Connecticut	181,010	1.7%
44	Delaware	23,688	0.2%
NA	Florida**	NA	NA
21	Georgia	187,809	1.8%
35	Hawaii	70,000	0.7%
34	Idaho	73,120	0.7%
11	Illinois	291,338	2.8%
25	Indiana	164,871	1.6%
30	Iowa	98,412	0.9%
NA	Kansas**	NA	NA
39	Kentucky	50,844	0.5%
14	Louisiana	273,715	2.6%
38	Maine	53,028	0.5%
10	Maryland	306,522	2.9%
27	Massachusetts	158,347	1.5%
6	Michigan	366,523	3.5%
18	Minnesota	211,496	2.0%
33	Mississippi	80,698	0.8%
12	Missouri	284,954	2.7%
46	Montana	10,515	0.1%
31	Nebraska	96,236	0.9%
37	Nevada	56,094	0.5%
NA	New Hampshire**	NA	NA
4	New Jersey	414,998	3.9%
32	New Mexico	86,050	0.8%
9	New York	360,463	3.4%
3	North Carolina	520,165	4.9%
42	North Dakota	28,996	0.3%
7	Ohio	361,976	3.4%
26	Oklahoma	158,837	1.5%
28	Oregon	150,369	1.4%
19	Pennsylvania	202,715	1.9%
40	Rhode Island	41,223	0.4%
17	South Carolina	218,788	2.1%
43	South Dakota	25,249	0.2%
24	Tennessee	165,603	1.6%
2	Texas	1,084,247	10.3%
29	Utah	102,541	1.0%
NA	Vermont**	NA	NA
5	Virginia	408,428	3.9%
15	Washington	228,503	2.2%
36	West Virginia	63,439	0.6%
8	Wisconsin	361,333	3.4%
41	Wyoming	35,030	0.3%

RANK ORDER

RANK	STATE	ARRESTS	% of USA
1	California	1,594,841	15.1%
2	Texas	1,084,247	10.3%
3	North Carolina	520,165	4.9%
4	New Jersey	414,998	3.9%
5	Virginia	408,428	3.9%
6	Michigan	366,523	3.5%
7	Ohio	361,976	3.4%
8	Wisconsin	361,333	3.4%
9	New York	360,463	3.4%
10	Maryland	306,522	2.9%
11	Illinois	291,338	2.8%
12	Missouri	284,954	2.7%
13	Arizona	275,565	2.6%
14	Louisiana	273,715	2.6%
15	Washington	228,503	2.2%
16	Alabama	223,057	2.1%
17	South Carolina	218,788	2.1%
18	Minnesota	211,496	2.0%
19	Pennsylvania	202,715	1.9%
20	Arkansas	191,805	1.8%
21	Georgia	187,809	1.8%
22	Colorado	181,404	1.7%
23	Connecticut	181,010	1.7%
24	Tennessee	165,603	1.6%
25	Indiana	164,871	1.6%
26	Oklahoma	158,837	1.5%
27	Massachusetts	158,347	1.5%
28	Oregon	150,369	1.4%
29	Utah	102,541	1.0%
30	Iowa	98,412	0.9%
31	Nebraska	96,236	0.9%
32	New Mexico	86,050	0.8%
33	Mississippi	80,698	0.8%
34	Idaho	73,120	0.7%
35	Hawaii	70,000	0.7%
36	West Virginia	63,439	0.6%
37	Nevada	56,094	0.5%
38	Maine	53,028	0.5%
39	Kentucky	50,844	0.5%
40	Rhode Island	41,223	0.4%
41	Wyoming	35,030	0.3%
42	North Dakota	28,996	0.3%
43	South Dakota	25,249	0.2%
44	Delaware	23,688	0.2%
45	Alaska	19,779	0.2%
46	Montana	10,515	0.1%
NA	Florida**	NA	NA
NA	Kansas**	NA	NA
NA	New Hampshire**	NA	NA
NA	Vermont**	NA	NA
	District of Columbia**	NA	NA

Source: Federal Bureau of Investigation
 "Crime in the United States 1997" (Uniform Crime Reports, November 22, 1998)
*By law enforcement agencies submitting complete reports to the F.B.I. for 12 months in 1997. The F.B.I. estimates 15,284,300 reported and unreported arrests occurred in 1997. See important note at beginning of this chapter.
**Not available.

Reported Arrest Rate in 1997

National Rate = 5,752.1 Reported Arrests per 100,000 Population*

ALPHA ORDER

RANK	STATE	RATE
30	Alabama	5,496.7
14	Alaska	7,298.5
15	Arizona	7,144.5
4	Arkansas	8,539.8
33	California	5,013.2
19	Colorado	6,666.8
21	Connecticut	6,537.0
7	Delaware	7,922.4
NA	Florida**	NA
9	Georgia	7,530.4
25	Hawaii	6,108.2
22	Idaho	6,191.4
1	Illinois	10,532.8
35	Indiana	4,964.5
41	Iowa	4,184.2
NA	Kansas**	NA
17	Kentucky	6,815.5
5	Louisiana	8,005.7
38	Maine	4,528.4
26	Maryland	6,023.2
45	Massachusetts	3,112.2
37	Michigan	4,622.0
39	Minnesota	4,518.2
6	Mississippi	7,982.0
3	Missouri	8,849.5
46	Montana	3,047.8
24	Nebraska	6,153.2
13	Nevada	7,303.9
NA	New Hampshire**	NA
31	New Jersey	5,361.0
12	New Mexico	7,354.7
40	New York	4,297.9
16	North Carolina	7,103.2
34	North Dakota	5,007.9
27	Ohio	5,885.8
36	Oklahoma	4,791.5
32	Oregon	5,330.3
44	Pennsylvania	3,591.7
42	Rhode Island	4,176.6
28	South Carolina	5,862.5
8	South Dakota	7,537.0
11	Tennessee	7,383.1
29	Texas	5,765.7
20	Utah	6,645.6
NA	Vermont**	NA
23	Virginia	6,189.2
18	Washington	6,714.8
43	West Virginia	3,641.7
2	Wisconsin	9,205.9
10	Wyoming	7,469.1

RANK ORDER

RANK	STATE	RATE
1	Illinois	10,532.8
2	Wisconsin	9,205.9
3	Missouri	8,849.5
4	Arkansas	8,539.8
5	Louisiana	8,005.7
6	Mississippi	7,982.0
7	Delaware	7,922.4
8	South Dakota	7,537.0
9	Georgia	7,530.4
10	Wyoming	7,469.1
11	Tennessee	7,383.1
12	New Mexico	7,354.7
13	Nevada	7,303.9
14	Alaska	7,298.5
15	Arizona	7,144.5
16	North Carolina	7,103.2
17	Kentucky	6,815.5
18	Washington	6,714.8
19	Colorado	6,666.8
20	Utah	6,645.6
21	Connecticut	6,537.0
22	Idaho	6,191.4
23	Virginia	6,189.2
24	Nebraska	6,153.2
25	Hawaii	6,108.2
26	Maryland	6,023.2
27	Ohio	5,885.8
28	South Carolina	5,862.5
29	Texas	5,765.7
30	Alabama	5,496.7
31	New Jersey	5,361.0
32	Oregon	5,330.3
33	California	5,013.2
34	North Dakota	5,007.9
35	Indiana	4,964.5
36	Oklahoma	4,791.5
37	Michigan	4,622.0
38	Maine	4,528.4
39	Minnesota	4,518.2
40	New York	4,297.9
41	Iowa	4,184.2
42	Rhode Island	4,176.6
43	West Virginia	3,641.7
44	Pennsylvania	3,591.7
45	Massachusetts	3,112.2
46	Montana	3,047.8
NA	Florida**	NA
NA	Kansas**	NA
NA	New Hampshire**	NA
NA	Vermont**	NA
	District of Columbia**	NA

Source: Morgan Quitno Press using data from Federal Bureau of Investigation
    "Crime in the United States 1997" (Uniform Crime Reports, November 22, 1998)
*By law enforcement agencies submitting complete reports to the F.B.I. for 12 months in 1997. These rates based on population estimates for areas under the jurisdiction of those agencies reporting. Arrest rate based on the F.B.I. estimate of total arrests is 5,710.9 reported and unreported arrests per 100,000 population. See important note at beginning of this chapter. **Not available.

Reported Arrests for Crime Index Offenses in 1997

National Total = 1,910,953 Reported Arrests*

RANK	STATE	ARRESTS	% of USA
20	Alabama	35,503	1.9%
45	Alaska	3,110	0.2%
11	Arizona	53,328	2.8%
28	Arkansas	24,098	1.3%
1	California	367,163	19.2%
27	Colorado	28,336	1.5%
23	Connecticut	33,179	1.7%
41	Delaware	6,524	0.3%
NA	Florida**	NA	NA
18	Georgia	37,647	2.0%
34	Hawaii	12,599	0.7%
35	Idaho	11,325	0.6%
9	Illinois	56,392	3.0%
25	Indiana	32,442	1.7%
30	Iowa	18,200	1.0%
NA	Kansas**	NA	NA
36	Kentucky	11,060	0.6%
10	Louisiana	54,417	2.8%
37	Maine	9,830	0.5%
6	Maryland	58,493	3.1%
21	Massachusetts	34,736	1.8%
7	Michigan	58,231	3.0%
24	Minnesota	32,543	1.7%
33	Mississippi	13,026	0.7%
14	Missouri	47,001	2.5%
46	Montana	1,727	0.1%
32	Nebraska	14,022	0.7%
38	Nevada	8,774	0.5%
NA	New Hampshire**	NA	NA
5	New Jersey	69,633	3.6%
31	New Mexico	15,146	0.8%
4	New York	71,182	3.7%
3	North Carolina	89,327	4.7%
44	North Dakota	3,745	0.2%
12	Ohio	53,308	2.8%
26	Oklahoma	29,472	1.5%
17	Oregon	37,666	2.0%
19	Pennsylvania	35,766	1.9%
40	Rhode Island	7,436	0.4%
16	South Carolina	40,099	2.1%
43	South Dakota	4,188	0.2%
22	Tennessee	33,782	1.8%
2	Texas	169,169	8.9%
29	Utah	20,484	1.1%
NA	Vermont**	NA	NA
8	Virginia	56,482	3.0%
15	Washington	44,838	2.3%
39	West Virginia	8,644	0.5%
13	Wisconsin	52,503	2.7%
42	Wyoming	4,377	0.2%

RANK	STATE	ARRESTS	% of USA
1	California	367,163	19.2%
2	Texas	169,169	8.9%
3	North Carolina	89,327	4.7%
4	New York	71,182	3.7%
5	New Jersey	69,633	3.6%
6	Maryland	58,493	3.1%
7	Michigan	58,231	3.0%
8	Virginia	56,482	3.0%
9	Illinois	56,392	3.0%
10	Louisiana	54,417	2.8%
11	Arizona	53,328	2.8%
12	Ohio	53,308	2.8%
13	Wisconsin	52,503	2.7%
14	Missouri	47,001	2.5%
15	Washington	44,838	2.3%
16	South Carolina	40,099	2.1%
17	Oregon	37,666	2.0%
18	Georgia	37,647	2.0%
19	Pennsylvania	35,766	1.9%
20	Alabama	35,503	1.9%
21	Massachusetts	34,736	1.8%
22	Tennessee	33,782	1.8%
23	Connecticut	33,179	1.7%
24	Minnesota	32,543	1.7%
25	Indiana	32,442	1.7%
26	Oklahoma	29,472	1.5%
27	Colorado	28,336	1.5%
28	Arkansas	24,098	1.3%
29	Utah	20,484	1.1%
30	Iowa	18,200	1.0%
31	New Mexico	15,146	0.8%
32	Nebraska	14,022	0.7%
33	Mississippi	13,026	0.7%
34	Hawaii	12,599	0.7%
35	Idaho	11,325	0.6%
36	Kentucky	11,060	0.6%
37	Maine	9,830	0.5%
38	Nevada	8,774	0.5%
39	West Virginia	8,644	0.5%
40	Rhode Island	7,436	0.4%
41	Delaware	6,524	0.3%
42	Wyoming	4,377	0.2%
43	South Dakota	4,188	0.2%
44	North Dakota	3,745	0.2%
45	Alaska	3,110	0.2%
46	Montana	1,727	0.1%
NA	Florida**	NA	NA
NA	Kansas**	NA	NA
NA	New Hampshire**	NA	NA
NA	Vermont**	NA	NA
	District of Columbia**	NA	NA

Source: Federal Bureau of Investigation
   "Crime in the United States 1997" (Uniform Crime Reports, November 22, 1998)
*By law enforcement agencies submitting complete reports to the F.B.I. for 12 months in 1997. The F.B.I. estimates 2,733,400 reported and unreported arrests for crime index offenses occurred in 1997. Crime index offenses consist of murder, forcible rape, robbery, aggravated assault, burglary, larceny-theft, motor vehicle theft and arson. See important note at beginning of this chapter. **Not available.

Reported Arrest Rate for Crime Index Offenses in 1997

National Rate = 1,042.9 Reported Arrests per 100,000 Population*

<table>
<tr><td colspan="3">ALPHA ORDER</td><td colspan="3">RANK ORDER</td></tr>
<tr><th>RANK</th><th>STATE</th><th>RATE</th><th>RANK</th><th>STATE</th><th>RATE</th></tr>
<tr><td>33</td><td>Alabama</td><td>874.9</td><td>1</td><td>Delaware</td><td>2,181.9</td></tr>
<tr><td>20</td><td>Alaska</td><td>1,147.6</td><td>2</td><td>Illinois</td><td>2,038.8</td></tr>
<tr><td>8</td><td>Arizona</td><td>1,382.6</td><td>3</td><td>Louisiana</td><td>1,591.6</td></tr>
<tr><td>24</td><td>Arkansas</td><td>1,072.9</td><td>4</td><td>Georgia</td><td>1,509.5</td></tr>
<tr><td>18</td><td>California</td><td>1,154.1</td><td>5</td><td>Tennessee</td><td>1,506.1</td></tr>
<tr><td>25</td><td>Colorado</td><td>1,041.4</td><td>6</td><td>Kentucky</td><td>1,482.6</td></tr>
<tr><td>17</td><td>Connecticut</td><td>1,198.2</td><td>7</td><td>Missouri</td><td>1,459.7</td></tr>
<tr><td>1</td><td>Delaware</td><td>2,181.9</td><td>8</td><td>Arizona</td><td>1,382.6</td></tr>
<tr><td>NA</td><td>Florida**</td><td>NA</td><td>9</td><td>Wisconsin</td><td>1,337.7</td></tr>
<tr><td>4</td><td>Georgia</td><td>1,509.5</td><td>10</td><td>Oregon</td><td>1,335.2</td></tr>
<tr><td>22</td><td>Hawaii</td><td>1,099.4</td><td>11</td><td>Utah</td><td>1,327.5</td></tr>
<tr><td>27</td><td>Idaho</td><td>958.9</td><td>12</td><td>Washington</td><td>1,317.6</td></tr>
<tr><td>2</td><td>Illinois</td><td>2,038.8</td><td>13</td><td>New Mexico</td><td>1,294.5</td></tr>
<tr><td>26</td><td>Indiana</td><td>976.9</td><td>14</td><td>Mississippi</td><td>1,288.4</td></tr>
<tr><td>38</td><td>Iowa</td><td>773.8</td><td>15</td><td>South Dakota</td><td>1,250.1</td></tr>
<tr><td>NA</td><td>Kansas**</td><td>NA</td><td>16</td><td>North Carolina</td><td>1,219.8</td></tr>
<tr><td>6</td><td>Kentucky</td><td>1,482.6</td><td>17</td><td>Connecticut</td><td>1,198.2</td></tr>
<tr><td>3</td><td>Louisiana</td><td>1,591.6</td><td>18</td><td>California</td><td>1,154.1</td></tr>
<tr><td>37</td><td>Maine</td><td>839.5</td><td>19</td><td>Maryland</td><td>1,149.4</td></tr>
<tr><td>19</td><td>Maryland</td><td>1,149.4</td><td>20</td><td>Alaska</td><td>1,147.6</td></tr>
<tr><td>42</td><td>Massachusetts</td><td>682.7</td><td>21</td><td>Nevada</td><td>1,142.4</td></tr>
<tr><td>40</td><td>Michigan</td><td>734.3</td><td>22</td><td>Hawaii</td><td>1,099.4</td></tr>
<tr><td>41</td><td>Minnesota</td><td>695.2</td><td>23</td><td>South Carolina</td><td>1,074.5</td></tr>
<tr><td>14</td><td>Mississippi</td><td>1,288.4</td><td>24</td><td>Arkansas</td><td>1,072.9</td></tr>
<tr><td>7</td><td>Missouri</td><td>1,459.7</td><td>25</td><td>Colorado</td><td>1,041.4</td></tr>
<tr><td>45</td><td>Montana</td><td>500.6</td><td>26</td><td>Indiana</td><td>976.9</td></tr>
<tr><td>31</td><td>Nebraska</td><td>896.5</td><td>27</td><td>Idaho</td><td>958.9</td></tr>
<tr><td>21</td><td>Nevada</td><td>1,142.4</td><td>28</td><td>Wyoming</td><td>933.3</td></tr>
<tr><td>NA</td><td>New Hampshire**</td><td>NA</td><td>29</td><td>Texas</td><td>899.6</td></tr>
<tr><td>30</td><td>New Jersey</td><td>899.5</td><td>30</td><td>New Jersey</td><td>899.5</td></tr>
<tr><td>13</td><td>New Mexico</td><td>1,294.5</td><td>31</td><td>Nebraska</td><td>896.5</td></tr>
<tr><td>36</td><td>New York</td><td>848.7</td><td>32</td><td>Oklahoma</td><td>889.0</td></tr>
<tr><td>16</td><td>North Carolina</td><td>1,219.8</td><td>33</td><td>Alabama</td><td>874.9</td></tr>
<tr><td>43</td><td>North Dakota</td><td>646.8</td><td>34</td><td>Ohio</td><td>866.8</td></tr>
<tr><td>34</td><td>Ohio</td><td>866.8</td><td>35</td><td>Virginia</td><td>855.9</td></tr>
<tr><td>32</td><td>Oklahoma</td><td>889.0</td><td>36</td><td>New York</td><td>848.7</td></tr>
<tr><td>10</td><td>Oregon</td><td>1,335.2</td><td>37</td><td>Maine</td><td>839.5</td></tr>
<tr><td>44</td><td>Pennsylvania</td><td>633.7</td><td>38</td><td>Iowa</td><td>773.8</td></tr>
<tr><td>39</td><td>Rhode Island</td><td>753.4</td><td>39</td><td>Rhode Island</td><td>753.4</td></tr>
<tr><td>23</td><td>South Carolina</td><td>1,074.5</td><td>40</td><td>Michigan</td><td>734.3</td></tr>
<tr><td>15</td><td>South Dakota</td><td>1,250.1</td><td>41</td><td>Minnesota</td><td>695.2</td></tr>
<tr><td>5</td><td>Tennessee</td><td>1,506.1</td><td>42</td><td>Massachusetts</td><td>682.7</td></tr>
<tr><td>29</td><td>Texas</td><td>899.6</td><td>43</td><td>North Dakota</td><td>646.8</td></tr>
<tr><td>11</td><td>Utah</td><td>1,327.5</td><td>44</td><td>Pennsylvania</td><td>633.7</td></tr>
<tr><td>NA</td><td>Vermont**</td><td>NA</td><td>45</td><td>Montana</td><td>500.6</td></tr>
<tr><td>35</td><td>Virginia</td><td>855.9</td><td>46</td><td>West Virginia</td><td>496.2</td></tr>
<tr><td>12</td><td>Washington</td><td>1,317.6</td><td>NA</td><td>Florida**</td><td>NA</td></tr>
<tr><td>46</td><td>West Virginia</td><td>496.2</td><td>NA</td><td>Kansas**</td><td>NA</td></tr>
<tr><td>9</td><td>Wisconsin</td><td>1,337.7</td><td>NA</td><td>New Hampshire**</td><td>NA</td></tr>
<tr><td>28</td><td>Wyoming</td><td>933.3</td><td>NA</td><td>Vermont**</td><td>NA</td></tr>
<tr><td></td><td></td><td></td><td></td><td>District of Columbia**</td><td>NA</td></tr>
</table>

Source: Morgan Quitno Press using data from Federal Bureau of Investigation
"Crime in the United States 1997" (Uniform Crime Reports, November 22, 1998)
*By law enforcement agencies submitting complete reports to the F.B.I. for 12 months in 1997. These rates based on population estimates for areas under the jurisdiction of those agencies reporting. Arrest rate based on the F.B.I. estimate of reported and unreported arrests for crime index offenses is 1,021.3 arrests per 100,000 population. See important note at beginning of this chapter. **Not available.

Reported Arrests for Violent Crimes in 1997

National Total = 501,353 Reported Arrests*

ALPHA ORDER

RANK	STATE	ARRESTS	% of USA
16	Alabama	10,095	2.0%
41	Alaska	1,034	0.2%
17	Arizona	8,630	1.7%
25	Arkansas	5,939	1.2%
1	California	150,518	30.0%
26	Colorado	4,921	1.0%
22	Connecticut	7,453	1.5%
36	Delaware	1,540	0.3%
NA	Florida**	NA	NA
13	Georgia	11,277	2.2%
37	Hawaii	1,533	0.3%
40	Idaho	1,304	0.3%
14	Illinois	11,244	2.2%
19	Indiana	8,543	1.7%
29	Iowa	3,785	0.8%
NA	Kansas**	NA	NA
30	Kentucky	3,591	0.7%
8	Louisiana	14,674	2.9%
42	Maine	761	0.2%
10	Maryland	13,631	2.7%
6	Massachusetts	15,468	3.1%
4	Michigan	19,411	3.9%
27	Minnesota	4,099	0.8%
32	Mississippi	2,317	0.5%
15	Missouri	10,138	2.0%
45	Montana	202	0.0%
38	Nebraska	1,487	0.3%
35	Nevada	1,692	0.3%
NA	New Hampshire**	NA	NA
5	New Jersey	19,134	3.8%
31	New Mexico	2,848	0.6%
9	New York	14,459	2.9%
3	North Carolina	28,215	5.6%
46	North Dakota	199	0.0%
7	Ohio	15,143	3.0%
24	Oklahoma	6,079	1.2%
28	Oregon	3,826	0.8%
20	Pennsylvania	8,050	1.6%
33	Rhode Island	2,270	0.5%
11	South Carolina	12,834	2.6%
44	South Dakota	495	0.1%
18	Tennessee	8,574	1.7%
2	Texas	34,137	6.8%
34	Utah	1,832	0.4%
NA	Vermont**	NA	NA
12	Virginia	11,290	2.3%
23	Washington	6,654	1.3%
39	West Virginia	1,364	0.3%
21	Wisconsin	8,001	1.6%
43	Wyoming	662	0.1%

RANK ORDER

RANK	STATE	ARRESTS	% of USA
1	California	150,518	30.0%
2	Texas	34,137	6.8%
3	North Carolina	28,215	5.6%
4	Michigan	19,411	3.9%
5	New Jersey	19,134	3.8%
6	Massachusetts	15,468	3.1%
7	Ohio	15,143	3.0%
8	Louisiana	14,674	2.9%
9	New York	14,459	2.9%
10	Maryland	13,631	2.7%
11	South Carolina	12,834	2.6%
12	Virginia	11,290	2.3%
13	Georgia	11,277	2.2%
14	Illinois	11,244	2.2%
15	Missouri	10,138	2.0%
16	Alabama	10,095	2.0%
17	Arizona	8,630	1.7%
18	Tennessee	8,574	1.7%
19	Indiana	8,543	1.7%
20	Pennsylvania	8,050	1.6%
21	Wisconsin	8,001	1.6%
22	Connecticut	7,453	1.5%
23	Washington	6,654	1.3%
24	Oklahoma	6,079	1.2%
25	Arkansas	5,939	1.2%
26	Colorado	4,921	1.0%
27	Minnesota	4,099	0.8%
28	Oregon	3,826	0.8%
29	Iowa	3,785	0.8%
30	Kentucky	3,591	0.7%
31	New Mexico	2,848	0.6%
32	Mississippi	2,317	0.5%
33	Rhode Island	2,270	0.5%
34	Utah	1,832	0.4%
35	Nevada	1,692	0.3%
36	Delaware	1,540	0.3%
37	Hawaii	1,533	0.3%
38	Nebraska	1,487	0.3%
39	West Virginia	1,364	0.3%
40	Idaho	1,304	0.3%
41	Alaska	1,034	0.2%
42	Maine	761	0.2%
43	Wyoming	662	0.1%
44	South Dakota	495	0.1%
45	Montana	202	0.0%
46	North Dakota	199	0.0%
NA	Florida**	NA	NA
NA	Kansas**	NA	NA
NA	New Hampshire**	NA	NA
NA	Vermont**	NA	NA
	District of Columbia**	NA	NA

Source: Federal Bureau of Investigation
"Crime in the United States 1997" (Uniform Crime Reports, November 22, 1998)

*By law enforcement agencies submitting complete reports to the F.B.I. for 12 months in 1997. The F.B.I. estimates 717,750 reported and unreported arrests for violent crimes occurred in 1997. Violent crimes are offenses of murder, forcible rape, robbery and aggravated assault. See important note at beginning of this chapter.
**Not available.

Reported Arrest Rate for Violent Crime in 1997

National Rate = 273.6 Reported Arrests per 100,000 Population*

ALPHA ORDER

RANK	STATE	RATE
17	Alabama	248.8
9	Alaska	381.5
24	Arizona	223.7
15	Arkansas	264.4
3	California	473.1
30	Colorado	180.9
13	Connecticut	269.2
1	Delaware	515.1
NA	Florida**	NA
4	Georgia	452.2
38	Hawaii	133.8
40	Idaho	110.4
6	Illinois	406.5
16	Indiana	257.2
33	Iowa	160.9
NA	Kansas**	NA
2	Kentucky	481.4
5	Louisiana	429.2
44	Maine	65.0
14	Maryland	267.9
12	Massachusetts	304.0
20	Michigan	244.8
42	Minnesota	87.6
23	Mississippi	229.2
11	Missouri	314.8
45	Montana	58.6
41	Nebraska	95.1
25	Nevada	220.3
NA	New Hampshire**	NA
18	New Jersey	247.2
21	New Mexico	243.4
31	New York	172.4
7	North Carolina	385.3
46	North Dakota	34.4
19	Ohio	246.2
28	Oklahoma	183.4
37	Oregon	135.6
35	Pennsylvania	142.6
22	Rhode Island	230.0
10	South Carolina	343.9
34	South Dakota	147.8
8	Tennessee	382.3
29	Texas	181.5
39	Utah	118.7
NA	Vermont**	NA
32	Virginia	171.1
27	Washington	195.5
43	West Virginia	78.3
26	Wisconsin	203.8
36	Wyoming	141.2

RANK ORDER

RANK	STATE	RATE
1	Delaware	515.1
2	Kentucky	481.4
3	California	473.1
4	Georgia	452.2
5	Louisiana	429.2
6	Illinois	406.5
7	North Carolina	385.3
8	Tennessee	382.3
9	Alaska	381.5
10	South Carolina	343.9
11	Missouri	314.8
12	Massachusetts	304.0
13	Connecticut	269.2
14	Maryland	267.9
15	Arkansas	264.4
16	Indiana	257.2
17	Alabama	248.8
18	New Jersey	247.2
19	Ohio	246.2
20	Michigan	244.8
21	New Mexico	243.4
22	Rhode Island	230.0
23	Mississippi	229.2
24	Arizona	223.7
25	Nevada	220.3
26	Wisconsin	203.8
27	Washington	195.5
28	Oklahoma	183.4
29	Texas	181.5
30	Colorado	180.9
31	New York	172.4
32	Virginia	171.1
33	Iowa	160.9
34	South Dakota	147.8
35	Pennsylvania	142.6
36	Wyoming	141.2
37	Oregon	135.6
38	Hawaii	133.8
39	Utah	118.7
40	Idaho	110.4
41	Nebraska	95.1
42	Minnesota	87.6
43	West Virginia	78.3
44	Maine	65.0
45	Montana	58.6
46	North Dakota	34.4
NA	Florida**	NA
NA	Kansas**	NA
NA	New Hampshire**	NA
NA	Vermont**	NA
	District of Columbia**	NA

*Source: Morgan Quitno Press using data from Federal Bureau of Investigation
"Crime in the United States 1997" (Uniform Crime Reports, November 22, 1998)*
*By law enforcement agencies submitting complete reports to the F.B.I. for 12 months in 1997. These rates based on population estimates for areas under the jurisdiction of those agencies reporting. Arrest rate based on the F.B.I. estimate of reported and unreported arrests for violent crimes is 268.2 arrests per 100,000 population. See important note at beginning of this chapter. **Not available.*

Reported Arrests for Murder in 1997

National Total = 12,764 Reported Arrests*

ALPHA ORDER

RANK ORDER

RANK	STATE	ARRESTS	% of USA
8	Alabama	466	3.7%
41	Alaska	20	0.2%
18	Arizona	227	1.8%
20	Arkansas	204	1.6%
1	California	2,197	17.2%
27	Colorado	108	0.8%
24	Connecticut	143	1.1%
43	Delaware	9	0.1%
NA	Florida**	NA	NA
14	Georgia	298	2.3%
34	Hawaii	42	0.3%
37	Idaho	25	0.2%
5	Illinois	754	5.9%
21	Indiana	179	1.4%
37	Iowa	25	0.2%
NA	Kansas**	NA	NA
28	Kentucky	94	0.7%
6	Louisiana	631	4.9%
42	Maine	12	0.1%
7	Maryland	498	3.9%
29	Massachusetts	78	0.6%
2	Michigan	1,242	9.7%
30	Minnesota	74	0.6%
22	Mississippi	171	1.3%
13	Missouri	311	2.4%
45	Montana	6	0.0%
34	Nebraska	42	0.3%
31	Nevada	68	0.5%
NA	New Hampshire**	NA	NA
11	New Jersey	334	2.6%
32	New Mexico	55	0.4%
17	New York	252	2.0%
4	North Carolina	762	6.0%
46	North Dakota	2	0.0%
15	Ohio	285	2.2%
19	Oklahoma	213	1.7%
26	Oregon	109	0.9%
23	Pennsylvania	161	1.3%
39	Rhode Island	22	0.2%
12	South Carolina	326	2.6%
44	South Dakota	8	0.1%
16	Tennessee	274	2.1%
3	Texas	1,006	7.9%
36	Utah	38	0.3%
NA	Vermont**	NA	NA
9	Virginia	424	3.3%
25	Washington	130	1.0%
33	West Virginia	50	0.4%
10	Wisconsin	368	2.9%
40	Wyoming	21	0.2%

RANK	STATE	ARRESTS	% of USA
1	California	2,197	17.2%
2	Michigan	1,242	9.7%
3	Texas	1,006	7.9%
4	North Carolina	762	6.0%
5	Illinois	754	5.9%
6	Louisiana	631	4.9%
7	Maryland	498	3.9%
8	Alabama	466	3.7%
9	Virginia	424	3.3%
10	Wisconsin	368	2.9%
11	New Jersey	334	2.6%
12	South Carolina	326	2.6%
13	Missouri	311	2.4%
14	Georgia	298	2.3%
15	Ohio	285	2.2%
16	Tennessee	274	2.1%
17	New York	252	2.0%
18	Arizona	227	1.8%
19	Oklahoma	213	1.7%
20	Arkansas	204	1.6%
21	Indiana	179	1.4%
22	Mississippi	171	1.3%
23	Pennsylvania	161	1.3%
24	Connecticut	143	1.1%
25	Washington	130	1.0%
26	Oregon	109	0.9%
27	Colorado	108	0.8%
28	Kentucky	94	0.7%
29	Massachusetts	78	0.6%
30	Minnesota	74	0.6%
31	Nevada	68	0.5%
32	New Mexico	55	0.4%
33	West Virginia	50	0.4%
34	Hawaii	42	0.3%
34	Nebraska	42	0.3%
36	Utah	38	0.3%
37	Idaho	25	0.2%
37	Iowa	25	0.2%
39	Rhode Island	22	0.2%
40	Wyoming	21	0.2%
41	Alaska	20	0.2%
42	Maine	12	0.1%
43	Delaware	9	0.1%
44	South Dakota	8	0.1%
45	Montana	6	0.0%
46	North Dakota	2	0.0%
NA	Florida**	NA	NA
NA	Kansas**	NA	NA
NA	New Hampshire**	NA	NA
NA	Vermont**	NA	NA
	District of Columbia**	NA	NA

Source: Federal Bureau of Investigation
   "Crime in the United States 1997" (Uniform Crime Reports, November 22, 1998)
*By law enforcement agencies submitting complete reports to the F.B.I. for 12 months in 1997. The F.B.I. estimates
18,290 reported and unreported arrests for murder occurred in 1997. Murder includes nonnegligent manslaughter.
See important note at beginning of this chapter.
**Not available.

Reported Arrest Rate for Murder in 1997

National Rate = 7.0 Reported Arrests per 100,000 Population*

ALPHA ORDER

RANK	STATE	RATE
8	Alabama	11.5
16	Alaska	7.4
20	Arizona	5.9
13	Arkansas	9.1
17	California	6.9
28	Colorado	4.0
23	Connecticut	5.2
32	Delaware	3.0
NA	Florida**	NA
7	Georgia	11.9
31	Hawaii	3.7
40	Idaho	2.1
1	Illinois	27.3
21	Indiana	5.4
44	Iowa	1.1
NA	Kansas**	NA
5	Kentucky	12.6
2	Louisiana	18.5
45	Maine	1.0
10	Maryland	9.8
43	Massachusetts	1.5
4	Michigan	15.7
42	Minnesota	1.6
3	Mississippi	16.9
11	Missouri	9.7
41	Montana	1.7
36	Nebraska	2.7
14	Nevada	8.9
NA	New Hampshire**	NA
27	New Jersey	4.3
24	New Mexico	4.7
32	New York	3.0
9	North Carolina	10.4
46	North Dakota	0.3
25	Ohio	4.6
18	Oklahoma	6.4
29	Oregon	3.9
34	Pennsylvania	2.9
39	Rhode Island	2.2
15	South Carolina	8.7
38	South Dakota	2.4
6	Tennessee	12.2
22	Texas	5.3
37	Utah	2.5
NA	Vermont**	NA
18	Virginia	6.4
30	Washington	3.8
34	West Virginia	2.9
12	Wisconsin	9.4
26	Wyoming	4.5

RANK ORDER

RANK	STATE	RATE
1	Illinois	27.3
2	Louisiana	18.5
3	Mississippi	16.9
4	Michigan	15.7
5	Kentucky	12.6
6	Tennessee	12.2
7	Georgia	11.9
8	Alabama	11.5
9	North Carolina	10.4
10	Maryland	9.8
11	Missouri	9.7
12	Wisconsin	9.4
13	Arkansas	9.1
14	Nevada	8.9
15	South Carolina	8.7
16	Alaska	7.4
17	California	6.9
18	Oklahoma	6.4
18	Virginia	6.4
20	Arizona	5.9
21	Indiana	5.4
22	Texas	5.3
23	Connecticut	5.2
24	New Mexico	4.7
25	Ohio	4.6
26	Wyoming	4.5
27	New Jersey	4.3
28	Colorado	4.0
29	Oregon	3.9
30	Washington	3.8
31	Hawaii	3.7
32	Delaware	3.0
32	New York	3.0
34	Pennsylvania	2.9
34	West Virginia	2.9
36	Nebraska	2.7
37	Utah	2.5
38	South Dakota	2.4
39	Rhode Island	2.2
40	Idaho	2.1
41	Montana	1.7
42	Minnesota	1.6
43	Massachusetts	1.5
44	Iowa	1.1
45	Maine	1.0
46	North Dakota	0.3
NA	Florida**	NA
NA	Kansas**	NA
NA	New Hampshire**	NA
NA	Vermont**	NA
	District of Columbia**	NA

Source: Morgan Quitno Press using data from Federal Bureau of Investigation
   "Crime in the United States 1997" (Uniform Crime Reports, November 22, 1998)
*By law enforcement agencies submitting complete reports to the F.B.I. for 12 months in 1997. These rates based on population estimates for areas under the jurisdiction of those agencies reporting. Arrest rate based on the F.B.I. estimate of reported and unreported arrests for murder is 6.8 arrests per 100,000 population. See important note at beginning of this chapter. **Not available.

Reported Arrests for Rape in 1997

National Total = 22,133 Reported Arrests*

RANK	STATE	ARRESTS	% of USA
20	Alabama	444	2.0%
42	Alaska	64	0.3%
27	Arizona	281	1.3%
19	Arkansas	472	2.1%
1	California	3,079	13.9%
17	Colorado	502	2.3%
24	Connecticut	376	1.7%
34	Delaware	128	0.6%
NA	Florida**	NA	NA
23	Georgia	407	1.8%
35	Hawaii	124	0.6%
40	Idaho	80	0.4%
21	Illinois	431	1.9%
30	Indiana	159	0.7%
33	Iowa	130	0.6%
NA	Kansas**	NA	NA
38	Kentucky	88	0.4%
12	Louisiana	623	2.8%
41	Maine	75	0.3%
13	Maryland	601	2.7%
17	Massachusetts	502	2.3%
3	Michigan	1,402	6.3%
8	Minnesota	704	3.2%
28	Mississippi	188	0.8%
15	Missouri	531	2.4%
46	Montana	15	0.1%
29	Nebraska	167	0.8%
39	Nevada	86	0.4%
NA	New Hampshire**	NA	NA
7	New Jersey	799	3.6%
37	New Mexico	99	0.4%
9	New York	695	3.1%
6	North Carolina	805	3.6%
45	North Dakota	21	0.1%
4	Ohio	979	4.4%
22	Oklahoma	416	1.9%
26	Oregon	300	1.4%
15	Pennsylvania	531	2.4%
32	Rhode Island	141	0.6%
10	South Carolina	672	3.0%
43	South Dakota	58	0.3%
25	Tennessee	317	1.4%
2	Texas	2,284	10.3%
31	Utah	155	0.7%
NA	Vermont**	NA	NA
5	Virginia	809	3.7%
11	Washington	670	3.0%
36	West Virginia	100	0.5%
14	Wisconsin	573	2.6%
44	Wyoming	50	0.2%

RANK	STATE	ARRESTS	% of USA
1	California	3,079	13.9%
2	Texas	2,284	10.3%
3	Michigan	1,402	6.3%
4	Ohio	979	4.4%
5	Virginia	809	3.7%
6	North Carolina	805	3.6%
7	New Jersey	799	3.6%
8	Minnesota	704	3.2%
9	New York	695	3.1%
10	South Carolina	672	3.0%
11	Washington	670	3.0%
12	Louisiana	623	2.8%
13	Maryland	601	2.7%
14	Wisconsin	573	2.6%
15	Missouri	531	2.4%
15	Pennsylvania	531	2.4%
17	Colorado	502	2.3%
17	Massachusetts	502	2.3%
19	Arkansas	472	2.1%
20	Alabama	444	2.0%
21	Illinois	431	1.9%
22	Oklahoma	416	1.9%
23	Georgia	407	1.8%
24	Connecticut	376	1.7%
25	Tennessee	317	1.4%
26	Oregon	300	1.4%
27	Arizona	281	1.3%
28	Mississippi	188	0.8%
29	Nebraska	167	0.8%
30	Indiana	159	0.7%
31	Utah	155	0.7%
32	Rhode Island	141	0.6%
33	Iowa	130	0.6%
34	Delaware	128	0.6%
35	Hawaii	124	0.6%
36	West Virginia	100	0.5%
37	New Mexico	99	0.4%
38	Kentucky	88	0.4%
39	Nevada	86	0.4%
40	Idaho	80	0.4%
41	Maine	75	0.3%
42	Alaska	64	0.3%
43	South Dakota	58	0.3%
44	Wyoming	50	0.2%
45	North Dakota	21	0.1%
46	Montana	15	0.1%
NA	Florida**	NA	NA
NA	Kansas**	NA	NA
NA	New Hampshire**	NA	NA
NA	Vermont**	NA	NA
	District of Columbia**	NA	NA

Source: Federal Bureau of Investigation
"Crime in the United States 1997" (Uniform Crime Reports, November 22, 1998)
*By law enforcement agencies submitting complete reports to the F.B.I. for 12 months in 1997. The F.B.I. estimates 32,060 reported and unreported arrests for rape occurred in 1997. Forcible rape is the carnal knowledge of a female forcibly and against her will. Assaults or attempts to commit rape by force or threat of force are included. See important note at beginning of this chapter. **Not available.*

Reported Arrest Rate for Rape in 1997

National Rate = 12.1 Reported Arrests per 100,000 Population*

ALPHA ORDER

RANK	STATE	RATE
27	Alabama	10.9
2	Alaska	23.6
39	Arizona	7.3
3	Arkansas	21.0
35	California	9.7
6	Colorado	18.4
19	Connecticut	13.6
1	Delaware	42.8
NA	Florida**	NA
12	Georgia	16.3
28	Hawaii	10.8
40	Idaho	6.8
14	Illinois	15.6
44	Indiana	4.8
43	Iowa	5.5
NA	Kansas**	NA
23	Kentucky	11.8
7	Louisiana	18.2
41	Maine	6.4
23	Maryland	11.8
34	Massachusetts	9.9
9	Michigan	17.7
15	Minnesota	15.0
5	Mississippi	18.6
11	Missouri	16.5
45	Montana	4.3
29	Nebraska	10.7
25	Nevada	11.2
NA	New Hampshire**	NA
32	New Jersey	10.3
37	New Mexico	8.5
38	New York	8.3
26	North Carolina	11.0
46	North Dakota	3.6
13	Ohio	15.9
20	Oklahoma	12.5
31	Oregon	10.6
36	Pennsylvania	9.4
17	Rhode Island	14.3
8	South Carolina	18.0
10	South Dakota	17.3
18	Tennessee	14.1
22	Texas	12.1
33	Utah	10.0
NA	Vermont**	NA
21	Virginia	12.3
4	Washington	19.7
42	West Virginia	5.7
16	Wisconsin	14.6
29	Wyoming	10.7

RANK ORDER

RANK	STATE	RATE
1	Delaware	42.8
2	Alaska	23.6
3	Arkansas	21.0
4	Washington	19.7
5	Mississippi	18.6
6	Colorado	18.4
7	Louisiana	18.2
8	South Carolina	18.0
9	Michigan	17.7
10	South Dakota	17.3
11	Missouri	16.5
12	Georgia	16.3
13	Ohio	15.9
14	Illinois	15.6
15	Minnesota	15.0
16	Wisconsin	14.6
17	Rhode Island	14.3
18	Tennessee	14.1
19	Connecticut	13.6
20	Oklahoma	12.5
21	Virginia	12.3
22	Texas	12.1
23	Kentucky	11.8
23	Maryland	11.8
25	Nevada	11.2
26	North Carolina	11.0
27	Alabama	10.9
28	Hawaii	10.8
29	Nebraska	10.7
29	Wyoming	10.7
31	Oregon	10.6
32	New Jersey	10.3
33	Utah	10.0
34	Massachusetts	9.9
35	California	9.7
36	Pennsylvania	9.4
37	New Mexico	8.5
38	New York	8.3
39	Arizona	7.3
40	Idaho	6.8
41	Maine	6.4
42	West Virginia	5.7
43	Iowa	5.5
44	Indiana	4.8
45	Montana	4.3
46	North Dakota	3.6
NA	Florida**	NA
NA	Kansas**	NA
NA	New Hampshire**	NA
NA	Vermont**	NA
	District of Columbia**	NA

Source: Morgan Quitno Press using data from Federal Bureau of Investigation
   "Crime in the United States 1997" (Uniform Crime Reports, November 22, 1998)
*By law enforcement agencies submitting complete reports to the F.B.I. for 12 months in 1997. These rates based on population estimates for areas under the jurisdiction of those agencies reporting. Arrest rate based on the F.B.I. estimate of reported and unreported arrests for rape is 12.0 arrests per 100,000 population. See important note at beginning of this chapter. **Not available.

10

Reported Arrests for Robbery in 1997

National Total = 94,034 Reported Arrests*

ALPHA ORDER				RANK ORDER			
RANK	STATE	ARRESTS	% of USA	RANK	STATE	ARRESTS	% of USA
14	Alabama	2,127	2.3%	1	California	23,588	25.1%
43	Alaska	47	0.0%	2	Texas	7,058	7.5%
20	Arizona	1,605	1.7%	3	New Jersey	5,185	5.5%
25	Arkansas	945	1.0%	4	Maryland	4,702	5.0%
1	California	23,588	25.1%	5	North Carolina	4,354	4.6%
31	Colorado	563	0.6%	6	New York	3,779	4.0%
16	Connecticut	1,937	2.1%	7	Michigan	3,442	3.7%
36	Delaware	293	0.3%	8	Ohio	3,290	3.5%
NA	Florida**	NA	NA	9	Illinois	3,058	3.3%
12	Georgia	2,275	2.4%	10	Virginia	2,522	2.7%
28	Hawaii	649	0.7%	11	Louisiana	2,514	2.7%
41	Idaho	98	0.1%	12	Georgia	2,275	2.4%
9	Illinois	3,058	3.3%	13	Missouri	2,262	2.4%
24	Indiana	1,090	1.2%	14	Alabama	2,127	2.3%
35	Iowa	323	0.3%	15	South Carolina	1,981	2.1%
NA	Kansas**	NA	NA	16	Connecticut	1,937	2.1%
27	Kentucky	730	0.8%	17	Wisconsin	1,915	2.0%
11	Louisiana	2,514	2.7%	18	Pennsylvania	1,812	1.9%
40	Maine	171	0.2%	19	Massachusetts	1,777	1.9%
4	Maryland	4,702	5.0%	20	Arizona	1,605	1.7%
19	Massachusetts	1,777	1.9%	21	Washington	1,349	1.4%
7	Michigan	3,442	3.7%	22	Tennessee	1,187	1.3%
29	Minnesota	625	0.7%	23	Oregon	1,185	1.3%
30	Mississippi	615	0.7%	24	Indiana	1,090	1.2%
13	Missouri	2,262	2.4%	25	Arkansas	945	1.0%
46	Montana	9	0.0%	26	Oklahoma	915	1.0%
34	Nebraska	339	0.4%	27	Kentucky	730	0.8%
32	Nevada	478	0.5%	28	Hawaii	649	0.7%
NA	New Hampshire**	NA	NA	29	Minnesota	625	0.7%
3	New Jersey	5,185	5.5%	30	Mississippi	615	0.7%
33	New Mexico	344	0.4%	31	Colorado	563	0.6%
6	New York	3,779	4.0%	32	Nevada	478	0.5%
5	North Carolina	4,354	4.6%	33	New Mexico	344	0.4%
45	North Dakota	27	0.0%	34	Nebraska	339	0.4%
8	Ohio	3,290	3.5%	35	Iowa	323	0.3%
26	Oklahoma	915	1.0%	36	Delaware	293	0.3%
23	Oregon	1,185	1.3%	37	Utah	289	0.3%
18	Pennsylvania	1,812	1.9%	38	West Virginia	239	0.3%
39	Rhode Island	237	0.3%	39	Rhode Island	237	0.3%
15	South Carolina	1,981	2.1%	40	Maine	171	0.2%
42	South Dakota	63	0.1%	41	Idaho	98	0.1%
22	Tennessee	1,187	1.3%	42	South Dakota	63	0.1%
2	Texas	7,058	7.5%	43	Alaska	47	0.0%
37	Utah	289	0.3%	44	Wyoming	41	0.0%
NA	Vermont**	NA	NA	45	North Dakota	27	0.0%
10	Virginia	2,522	2.7%	46	Montana	9	0.0%
21	Washington	1,349	1.4%	NA	Florida**	NA	NA
38	West Virginia	239	0.3%	NA	Kansas**	NA	NA
17	Wisconsin	1,915	2.0%	NA	New Hampshire**	NA	NA
44	Wyoming	41	0.0%	NA	Vermont**	NA	NA
					District of Columbia**	NA	NA

Source: Federal Bureau of Investigation
  "Crime in the United States 1997" (Uniform Crime Reports, November 22, 1998)
*By law enforcement agencies submitting complete reports to the F.B.I. for 12 months in 1997. The F.B.I. estimates 132,450 reported and unreported arrests for robbery occurred in 1997. Robbery is the taking or attempting to take anything of value by force or threat of force. See important note at beginning of this chapter.
**Not available.

Reported Arrest Rate for Robbery in 1997

National Rate = 51.3 Reported Arrests per 100,000 Population*

<table>
<tr><td colspan="3">ALPHA ORDER</td><td colspan="3">RANK ORDER</td></tr>
<tr><th>RANK</th><th>STATE</th><th>RATE</th><th>RANK</th><th>STATE</th><th>RATE</th></tr>
<tr><td>18</td><td>Alabama</td><td>52.4</td><td>1</td><td>Illinois</td><td>110.6</td></tr>
<tr><td>38</td><td>Alaska</td><td>17.3</td><td>2</td><td>Delaware</td><td>98.0</td></tr>
<tr><td>24</td><td>Arizona</td><td>41.6</td><td>3</td><td>Kentucky</td><td>97.9</td></tr>
<tr><td>22</td><td>Arkansas</td><td>42.1</td><td>4</td><td>Maryland</td><td>92.4</td></tr>
<tr><td>6</td><td>California</td><td>74.1</td><td>5</td><td>Georgia</td><td>91.2</td></tr>
<tr><td>35</td><td>Colorado</td><td>20.7</td><td>6</td><td>California</td><td>74.1</td></tr>
<tr><td>9</td><td>Connecticut</td><td>70.0</td><td>7</td><td>Louisiana</td><td>73.5</td></tr>
<tr><td>2</td><td>Delaware</td><td>98.0</td><td>8</td><td>Missouri</td><td>70.2</td></tr>
<tr><td>NA</td><td>Florida**</td><td>NA</td><td>9</td><td>Connecticut</td><td>70.0</td></tr>
<tr><td>5</td><td>Georgia</td><td>91.2</td><td>10</td><td>New Jersey</td><td>67.0</td></tr>
<tr><td>14</td><td>Hawaii</td><td>56.6</td><td>11</td><td>Nevada</td><td>62.2</td></tr>
<tr><td>44</td><td>Idaho</td><td>8.3</td><td>12</td><td>Mississippi</td><td>60.8</td></tr>
<tr><td>1</td><td>Illinois</td><td>110.6</td><td>13</td><td>North Carolina</td><td>59.5</td></tr>
<tr><td>29</td><td>Indiana</td><td>32.8</td><td>14</td><td>Hawaii</td><td>56.6</td></tr>
<tr><td>40</td><td>Iowa</td><td>13.7</td><td>15</td><td>Ohio</td><td>53.5</td></tr>
<tr><td>NA</td><td>Kansas**</td><td>NA</td><td>16</td><td>South Carolina</td><td>53.1</td></tr>
<tr><td>3</td><td>Kentucky</td><td>97.9</td><td>17</td><td>Tennessee</td><td>52.9</td></tr>
<tr><td>7</td><td>Louisiana</td><td>73.5</td><td>18</td><td>Alabama</td><td>52.4</td></tr>
<tr><td>39</td><td>Maine</td><td>14.6</td><td>19</td><td>Wisconsin</td><td>48.8</td></tr>
<tr><td>4</td><td>Maryland</td><td>92.4</td><td>20</td><td>New York</td><td>45.1</td></tr>
<tr><td>28</td><td>Massachusetts</td><td>34.9</td><td>21</td><td>Michigan</td><td>43.4</td></tr>
<tr><td>21</td><td>Michigan</td><td>43.4</td><td>22</td><td>Arkansas</td><td>42.1</td></tr>
<tr><td>42</td><td>Minnesota</td><td>13.4</td><td>23</td><td>Oregon</td><td>42.0</td></tr>
<tr><td>12</td><td>Mississippi</td><td>60.8</td><td>24</td><td>Arizona</td><td>41.6</td></tr>
<tr><td>8</td><td>Missouri</td><td>70.2</td><td>25</td><td>Washington</td><td>39.6</td></tr>
<tr><td>46</td><td>Montana</td><td>2.6</td><td>26</td><td>Virginia</td><td>38.2</td></tr>
<tr><td>34</td><td>Nebraska</td><td>21.7</td><td>27</td><td>Texas</td><td>37.5</td></tr>
<tr><td>11</td><td>Nevada</td><td>62.2</td><td>28</td><td>Massachusetts</td><td>34.9</td></tr>
<tr><td>NA</td><td>New Hampshire**</td><td>NA</td><td>29</td><td>Indiana</td><td>32.8</td></tr>
<tr><td>10</td><td>New Jersey</td><td>67.0</td><td>30</td><td>Pennsylvania</td><td>32.1</td></tr>
<tr><td>31</td><td>New Mexico</td><td>29.4</td><td>31</td><td>New Mexico</td><td>29.4</td></tr>
<tr><td>20</td><td>New York</td><td>45.1</td><td>32</td><td>Oklahoma</td><td>27.6</td></tr>
<tr><td>13</td><td>North Carolina</td><td>59.5</td><td>33</td><td>Rhode Island</td><td>24.0</td></tr>
<tr><td>45</td><td>North Dakota</td><td>4.7</td><td>34</td><td>Nebraska</td><td>21.7</td></tr>
<tr><td>15</td><td>Ohio</td><td>53.5</td><td>35</td><td>Colorado</td><td>20.7</td></tr>
<tr><td>32</td><td>Oklahoma</td><td>27.6</td><td>36</td><td>South Dakota</td><td>18.8</td></tr>
<tr><td>23</td><td>Oregon</td><td>42.0</td><td>37</td><td>Utah</td><td>18.7</td></tr>
<tr><td>30</td><td>Pennsylvania</td><td>32.1</td><td>38</td><td>Alaska</td><td>17.3</td></tr>
<tr><td>33</td><td>Rhode Island</td><td>24.0</td><td>39</td><td>Maine</td><td>14.6</td></tr>
<tr><td>16</td><td>South Carolina</td><td>53.1</td><td>40</td><td>Iowa</td><td>13.7</td></tr>
<tr><td>36</td><td>South Dakota</td><td>18.8</td><td>40</td><td>West Virginia</td><td>13.7</td></tr>
<tr><td>17</td><td>Tennessee</td><td>52.9</td><td>42</td><td>Minnesota</td><td>13.4</td></tr>
<tr><td>27</td><td>Texas</td><td>37.5</td><td>43</td><td>Wyoming</td><td>8.7</td></tr>
<tr><td>37</td><td>Utah</td><td>18.7</td><td>44</td><td>Idaho</td><td>8.3</td></tr>
<tr><td>NA</td><td>Vermont**</td><td>NA</td><td>45</td><td>North Dakota</td><td>4.7</td></tr>
<tr><td>26</td><td>Virginia</td><td>38.2</td><td>46</td><td>Montana</td><td>2.6</td></tr>
<tr><td>25</td><td>Washington</td><td>39.6</td><td>NA</td><td>Florida**</td><td>NA</td></tr>
<tr><td>40</td><td>West Virginia</td><td>13.7</td><td>NA</td><td>Kansas**</td><td>NA</td></tr>
<tr><td>19</td><td>Wisconsin</td><td>48.8</td><td>NA</td><td>New Hampshire**</td><td>NA</td></tr>
<tr><td>43</td><td>Wyoming</td><td>8.7</td><td>NA</td><td>Vermont**</td><td>NA</td></tr>
<tr><td></td><td></td><td></td><td></td><td>District of Columbia**</td><td>NA</td></tr>
</table>

Source: Morgan Quitno Press using data from Federal Bureau of Investigation
   "Crime in the United States 1997" (Uniform Crime Reports, November 22, 1998)
*By law enforcement agencies submitting complete reports to the F.B.I. for 12 months in 1997. These rates based on population estimates for areas under the jurisdiction of those agencies reporting. Arrest rate based on the F.B.I. estimate of reported and unreported arrests for robbery is 49.5 arrests per 100,000 population. See important note at beginning of this chapter. **Not available.

Reported Arrests for Aggravated Assault in 1997

National Total = 372,422 Reported Arrests*

ALPHA ORDER

RANK	STATE	ARRESTS	% of USA
15	Alabama	7,058	1.9%
40	Alaska	903	0.2%
19	Arizona	6,517	1.7%
25	Arkansas	4,318	1.2%
1	California	121,654	32.7%
26	Colorado	3,748	1.0%
22	Connecticut	4,997	1.3%
35	Delaware	1,110	0.3%
NA	Florida**	NA	NA
11	Georgia	8,297	2.2%
41	Hawaii	718	0.2%
36	Idaho	1,101	0.3%
17	Illinois	7,001	1.9%
14	Indiana	7,115	1.9%
27	Iowa	3,307	0.9%
NA	Kansas**	NA	NA
29	Kentucky	2,679	0.7%
7	Louisiana	10,906	2.9%
43	Maine	503	0.1%
12	Maryland	7,830	2.1%
5	Massachusetts	13,111	3.5%
4	Michigan	13,325	3.6%
28	Minnesota	2,696	0.7%
34	Mississippi	1,343	0.4%
16	Missouri	7,034	1.9%
45	Montana	172	0.0%
39	Nebraska	939	0.3%
37	Nevada	1,060	0.3%
NA	New Hampshire**	NA	NA
6	New Jersey	12,816	3.4%
30	New Mexico	2,350	0.6%
10	New York	9,733	2.6%
3	North Carolina	22,294	6.0%
46	North Dakota	149	0.0%
8	Ohio	10,589	2.8%
23	Oklahoma	4,535	1.2%
31	Oregon	2,232	0.6%
20	Pennsylvania	5,546	1.5%
32	Rhode Island	1,870	0.5%
9	South Carolina	9,855	2.6%
44	South Dakota	366	0.1%
18	Tennessee	6,796	1.8%
2	Texas	23,789	6.4%
33	Utah	1,350	0.4%
NA	Vermont**	NA	NA
13	Virginia	7,535	2.0%
24	Washington	4,505	1.2%
38	West Virginia	975	0.3%
21	Wisconsin	5,145	1.4%
42	Wyoming	550	0.1%

RANK ORDER

RANK	STATE	ARRESTS	% of USA
1	California	121,654	32.7%
2	Texas	23,789	6.4%
3	North Carolina	22,294	6.0%
4	Michigan	13,325	3.6%
5	Massachusetts	13,111	3.5%
6	New Jersey	12,816	3.4%
7	Louisiana	10,906	2.9%
8	Ohio	10,589	2.8%
9	South Carolina	9,855	2.6%
10	New York	9,733	2.6%
11	Georgia	8,297	2.2%
12	Maryland	7,830	2.1%
13	Virginia	7,535	2.0%
14	Indiana	7,115	1.9%
15	Alabama	7,058	1.9%
16	Missouri	7,034	1.9%
17	Illinois	7,001	1.9%
18	Tennessee	6,796	1.8%
19	Arizona	6,517	1.7%
20	Pennsylvania	5,546	1.5%
21	Wisconsin	5,145	1.4%
22	Connecticut	4,997	1.3%
23	Oklahoma	4,535	1.2%
24	Washington	4,505	1.2%
25	Arkansas	4,318	1.2%
26	Colorado	3,748	1.0%
27	Iowa	3,307	0.9%
28	Minnesota	2,696	0.7%
29	Kentucky	2,679	0.7%
30	New Mexico	2,350	0.6%
31	Oregon	2,232	0.6%
32	Rhode Island	1,870	0.5%
33	Utah	1,350	0.4%
34	Mississippi	1,343	0.4%
35	Delaware	1,110	0.3%
36	Idaho	1,101	0.3%
37	Nevada	1,060	0.3%
38	West Virginia	975	0.3%
39	Nebraska	939	0.3%
40	Alaska	903	0.2%
41	Hawaii	718	0.2%
42	Wyoming	550	0.1%
43	Maine	503	0.1%
44	South Dakota	366	0.1%
45	Montana	172	0.0%
46	North Dakota	149	0.0%
NA	Florida**	NA	NA
NA	Kansas**	NA	NA
NA	New Hampshire**	NA	NA
NA	Vermont**	NA	NA
	District of Columbia**	NA	NA

Source: Federal Bureau of Investigation
   "Crime in the United States 1997" (Uniform Crime Reports, November 22, 1998)
*By law enforcement agencies submitting complete reports to the F.B.I. for 12 months in 1997. The F.B.I. estimates
534,920 reported and unreported arrests for aggravated assault occurred in 1997. Aggravated assault is an attack
for the purpose of inflicting severe bodily injury. See important note at beginning of this chapter.
**Not available.

Reported Arrest Rate for Aggravated Assault in 1997

National Rate = 203.2 Reported Arrests per 100,000 Population*

ALPHA ORDER				RANK ORDER		
RANK	STATE	RATE		RANK	STATE	RATE
18	Alabama	173.9		1	California	382.4
4	Alaska	333.2		2	Delaware	371.2
20	Arizona	169.0		3	Kentucky	359.1
15	Arkansas	192.3		4	Alaska	333.2
1	California	382.4		5	Georgia	332.7
26	Colorado	137.7		6	Louisiana	319.0
17	Connecticut	180.5		7	North Carolina	304.4
2	Delaware	371.2		8	Tennessee	303.0
NA	Florida**	NA		9	South Carolina	264.1
5	Georgia	332.7		10	Massachusetts	257.7
40	Hawaii	62.7		11	Illinois	253.1
37	Idaho	93.2		12	Missouri	218.4
11	Illinois	253.1		13	Indiana	214.2
13	Indiana	214.2		14	New Mexico	200.9
24	Iowa	140.6		15	Arkansas	192.3
NA	Kansas**	NA		16	Rhode Island	189.5
3	Kentucky	359.1		17	Connecticut	180.5
6	Louisiana	319.0		18	Alabama	173.9
45	Maine	43.0		19	Ohio	172.2
23	Maryland	153.9		20	Arizona	169.0
10	Massachusetts	257.7		21	Michigan	168.0
21	Michigan	168.0		22	New Jersey	165.6
42	Minnesota	57.6		23	Maryland	153.9
28	Mississippi	132.8		24	Iowa	140.6
12	Missouri	218.4		25	Nevada	138.0
44	Montana	49.9		26	Colorado	137.7
41	Nebraska	60.0		27	Oklahoma	136.8
25	Nevada	138.0		28	Mississippi	132.8
NA	New Hampshire**	NA		29	Washington	132.4
22	New Jersey	165.6		30	Wisconsin	131.1
14	New Mexico	200.9		31	Texas	126.5
33	New York	116.0		32	Wyoming	117.3
7	North Carolina	304.4		33	New York	116.0
46	North Dakota	25.7		34	Virginia	114.2
19	Ohio	172.2		35	South Dakota	109.3
27	Oklahoma	136.8		36	Pennsylvania	98.3
39	Oregon	79.1		37	Idaho	93.2
36	Pennsylvania	98.3		38	Utah	87.5
16	Rhode Island	189.5		39	Oregon	79.1
9	South Carolina	264.1		40	Hawaii	62.7
35	South Dakota	109.3		41	Nebraska	60.0
8	Tennessee	303.0		42	Minnesota	57.6
31	Texas	126.5		43	West Virginia	56.0
38	Utah	87.5		44	Montana	49.9
NA	Vermont**	NA		45	Maine	43.0
34	Virginia	114.2		46	North Dakota	25.7
29	Washington	132.4		NA	Florida**	NA
43	West Virginia	56.0		NA	Kansas**	NA
30	Wisconsin	131.1		NA	New Hampshire**	NA
32	Wyoming	117.3		NA	Vermont**	NA
					District of Columbia**	NA

Source: Morgan Quitno Press using data from Federal Bureau of Investigation
    "Crime in the United States 1997" (Uniform Crime Reports, November 22, 1998)
*By law enforcement agencies submitting complete reports to the F.B.I. for 12 months in 1997. These rates based on population estimates for areas under the jurisdiction of those agencies reporting. Arrest rate based on the F.B.I. estimate of reported and unreported arrests for aggravated assault is 199.9 arrests per 100,000 population. See important note at beginning of this chapter. **Not available.

Reported Arrests for Property Crime in 1997

National Total = 1,409,600 Reported Arrests*

ALPHA ORDER

RANK	STATE	ARRESTS	% of USA
22	Alabama	25,408	1.8%
45	Alaska	2,076	0.1%
9	Arizona	44,698	3.2%
29	Arkansas	18,159	1.3%
1	California	216,645	15.4%
25	Colorado	23,415	1.7%
21	Connecticut	25,726	1.8%
41	Delaware	4,984	0.4%
NA	Florida**	NA	NA
20	Georgia	26,370	1.9%
33	Hawaii	11,066	0.8%
35	Idaho	10,021	0.7%
7	Illinois	45,148	3.2%
24	Indiana	23,899	1.7%
30	Iowa	14,415	1.0%
NA	Kansas**	NA	NA
37	Kentucky	7,469	0.5%
11	Louisiana	39,743	2.8%
36	Maine	9,069	0.6%
8	Maryland	44,862	3.2%
27	Massachusetts	19,268	1.4%
12	Michigan	38,820	2.8%
17	Minnesota	28,444	2.0%
34	Mississippi	10,709	0.8%
15	Missouri	36,863	2.6%
46	Montana	1,525	0.1%
31	Nebraska	12,535	0.9%
39	Nevada	7,082	0.5%
NA	New Hampshire**	NA	NA
5	New Jersey	50,499	3.6%
32	New Mexico	12,298	0.9%
4	New York	56,723	4.0%
3	North Carolina	61,112	4.3%
44	North Dakota	3,546	0.3%
14	Ohio	38,165	2.7%
26	Oklahoma	23,393	1.7%
16	Oregon	33,840	2.4%
18	Pennsylvania	27,716	2.0%
40	Rhode Island	5,166	0.4%
19	South Carolina	27,265	1.9%
43	South Dakota	3,693	0.3%
23	Tennessee	25,208	1.8%
2	Texas	135,032	9.6%
28	Utah	18,652	1.3%
NA	Vermont**	NA	NA
6	Virginia	45,192	3.2%
13	Washington	38,184	2.7%
38	West Virginia	7,280	0.5%
10	Wisconsin	44,502	3.2%
42	Wyoming	3,715	0.3%

RANK ORDER

RANK	STATE	ARRESTS	% of USA
1	California	216,645	15.4%
2	Texas	135,032	9.6%
3	North Carolina	61,112	4.3%
4	New York	56,723	4.0%
5	New Jersey	50,499	3.6%
6	Virginia	45,192	3.2%
7	Illinois	45,148	3.2%
8	Maryland	44,862	3.2%
9	Arizona	44,698	3.2%
10	Wisconsin	44,502	3.2%
11	Louisiana	39,743	2.8%
12	Michigan	38,820	2.8%
13	Washington	38,184	2.7%
14	Ohio	38,165	2.7%
15	Missouri	36,863	2.6%
16	Oregon	33,840	2.4%
17	Minnesota	28,444	2.0%
18	Pennsylvania	27,716	2.0%
19	South Carolina	27,265	1.9%
20	Georgia	26,370	1.9%
21	Connecticut	25,726	1.8%
22	Alabama	25,408	1.8%
23	Tennessee	25,208	1.8%
24	Indiana	23,899	1.7%
25	Colorado	23,415	1.7%
26	Oklahoma	23,393	1.7%
27	Massachusetts	19,268	1.4%
28	Utah	18,652	1.3%
29	Arkansas	18,159	1.3%
30	Iowa	14,415	1.0%
31	Nebraska	12,535	0.9%
32	New Mexico	12,298	0.9%
33	Hawaii	11,066	0.8%
34	Mississippi	10,709	0.8%
35	Idaho	10,021	0.7%
36	Maine	9,069	0.6%
37	Kentucky	7,469	0.5%
38	West Virginia	7,280	0.5%
39	Nevada	7,082	0.5%
40	Rhode Island	5,166	0.4%
41	Delaware	4,984	0.4%
42	Wyoming	3,715	0.3%
43	South Dakota	3,693	0.3%
44	North Dakota	3,546	0.3%
45	Alaska	2,076	0.1%
46	Montana	1,525	0.1%
NA	Florida**	NA	NA
NA	Kansas**	NA	NA
NA	New Hampshire**	NA	NA
NA	Vermont**	NA	NA
	District of Columbia**	NA	NA

Source: Federal Bureau of Investigation
"Crime in the United States 1997" (Uniform Crime Reports, November 22, 1998)
*By law enforcement agencies submitting complete reports to the F.B.I. for 12 months in 1997. The F.B.I. estimates 2,015,600 reported and unreported arrests for property crime occurred in 1997. Property crimes are offenses of burglary, larceny-theft, motor vehicle theft and arson. See important note at beginning of this chapter.
**Not available.

Reported Arrest Rate for Property Crime in 1997

National Rate = 769.3 Reported Arrests per 100,000 Population*

ALPHA ORDER

RANK	STATE	RATE
36	Alabama	626.1
27	Alaska	766.1
6	Arizona	1,158.9
23	Arkansas	808.5
33	California	681.0
20	Colorado	860.5
17	Connecticut	929.1
1	Delaware	1,666.9
NA	Florida**	NA
13	Georgia	1,057.3
16	Hawaii	965.6
21	Idaho	848.5
2	Illinois	1,632.2
29	Indiana	719.6
38	Iowa	612.9
NA	Kansas**	NA
15	Kentucky	1,001.2
5	Louisiana	1,162.4
26	Maine	774.5
19	Maryland	881.5
46	Massachusetts	378.7
43	Michigan	489.5
40	Minnesota	607.6
12	Mississippi	1,059.2
7	Missouri	1,144.8
44	Montana	442.0
24	Nebraska	801.5
18	Nevada	922.1
NA	New Hampshire**	NA
35	New Jersey	652.4
14	New Mexico	1,051.1
34	New York	676.3
22	North Carolina	834.5
39	North Dakota	612.4
37	Ohio	620.6
31	Oklahoma	705.7
4	Oregon	1,199.6
42	Pennsylvania	491.1
41	Rhode Island	523.4
28	South Carolina	730.6
11	South Dakota	1,102.4
9	Tennessee	1,123.9
30	Texas	718.1
3	Utah	1,208.8
NA	Vermont**	NA
32	Virginia	684.8
10	Washington	1,122.1
45	West Virginia	417.9
8	Wisconsin	1,133.8
25	Wyoming	792.1

RANK ORDER

RANK	STATE	RATE
1	Delaware	1,666.9
2	Illinois	1,632.2
3	Utah	1,208.8
4	Oregon	1,199.6
5	Louisiana	1,162.4
6	Arizona	1,158.9
7	Missouri	1,144.8
8	Wisconsin	1,133.8
9	Tennessee	1,123.9
10	Washington	1,122.1
11	South Dakota	1,102.4
12	Mississippi	1,059.2
13	Georgia	1,057.3
14	New Mexico	1,051.1
15	Kentucky	1,001.2
16	Hawaii	965.6
17	Connecticut	929.1
18	Nevada	922.1
19	Maryland	881.5
20	Colorado	860.5
21	Idaho	848.5
22	North Carolina	834.5
23	Arkansas	808.5
24	Nebraska	801.5
25	Wyoming	792.1
26	Maine	774.5
27	Alaska	766.1
28	South Carolina	730.6
29	Indiana	719.6
30	Texas	718.1
31	Oklahoma	705.7
32	Virginia	684.8
33	California	681.0
34	New York	676.3
35	New Jersey	652.4
36	Alabama	626.1
37	Ohio	620.6
38	Iowa	612.9
39	North Dakota	612.4
40	Minnesota	607.6
41	Rhode Island	523.4
42	Pennsylvania	491.1
43	Michigan	489.5
44	Montana	442.0
45	West Virginia	417.9
46	Massachusetts	378.7
NA	Florida**	NA
NA	Kansas**	NA
NA	New Hampshire**	NA
NA	Vermont**	NA
	District of Columbia**	NA

Source: Morgan Quitno Press using data from Federal Bureau of Investigation
"Crime in the United States 1997" (Uniform Crime Reports, November 22, 1998)
*By law enforcement agencies submitting complete reports to the F.B.I. for 12 months in 1997. These rates based on population estimates for areas under the jurisdiction of those agencies reporting. Arrest rate based on the F.B.I. estimate of reported and unreported arrests for property crime is 753.1 arrests per 100,000 population. See important note at beginning of this chapter. **Not available.

Reported Arrests for Burglary in 1997

National Total = 245,816 Reported Arrests*

ALPHA ORDER

RANK	STATE	ARRESTS	% of USA
23	Alabama	3,806	1.5%
42	Alaska	536	0.2%
13	Arizona	5,483	2.2%
25	Arkansas	3,188	1.3%
1	California	58,324	23.7%
29	Colorado	2,120	0.9%
21	Connecticut	4,041	1.6%
41	Delaware	730	0.3%
NA	Florida**	NA	NA
17	Georgia	4,219	1.7%
34	Hawaii	1,519	0.6%
39	Idaho	1,264	0.5%
18	Illinois	4,173	1.7%
27	Indiana	2,674	1.1%
30	Iowa	1,979	0.8%
NA	Kansas**	NA	NA
32	Kentucky	1,669	0.7%
7	Louisiana	7,482	3.0%
31	Maine	1,789	0.7%
6	Maryland	8,943	3.6%
20	Massachusetts	4,044	1.6%
8	Michigan	6,920	2.8%
24	Minnesota	3,207	1.3%
28	Mississippi	2,197	0.9%
16	Missouri	4,637	1.9%
46	Montana	185	0.1%
37	Nebraska	1,344	0.5%
33	Nevada	1,552	0.6%
NA	New Hampshire**	NA	NA
5	New Jersey	9,012	3.7%
38	New Mexico	1,325	0.5%
4	New York	9,490	3.9%
3	North Carolina	16,156	6.6%
45	North Dakota	356	0.1%
9	Ohio	6,593	2.7%
19	Oklahoma	4,085	1.7%
22	Oregon	3,955	1.6%
12	Pennsylvania	5,545	2.3%
40	Rhode Island	974	0.4%
11	South Carolina	5,985	2.4%
44	South Dakota	457	0.2%
26	Tennessee	3,134	1.3%
2	Texas	20,881	8.5%
35	Utah	1,428	0.6%
NA	Vermont**	NA	NA
10	Virginia	6,200	2.5%
14	Washington	5,196	2.1%
36	West Virginia	1,403	0.6%
15	Wisconsin	5,099	2.1%
43	Wyoming	517	0.2%

RANK ORDER

RANK	STATE	ARRESTS	% of USA
1	California	58,324	23.7%
2	Texas	20,881	8.5%
3	North Carolina	16,156	6.6%
4	New York	9,490	3.9%
5	New Jersey	9,012	3.7%
6	Maryland	8,943	3.6%
7	Louisiana	7,482	3.0%
8	Michigan	6,920	2.8%
9	Ohio	6,593	2.7%
10	Virginia	6,200	2.5%
11	South Carolina	5,985	2.4%
12	Pennsylvania	5,545	2.3%
13	Arizona	5,483	2.2%
14	Washington	5,196	2.1%
15	Wisconsin	5,099	2.1%
16	Missouri	4,637	1.9%
17	Georgia	4,219	1.7%
18	Illinois	4,173	1.7%
19	Oklahoma	4,085	1.7%
20	Massachusetts	4,044	1.6%
21	Connecticut	4,041	1.6%
22	Oregon	3,955	1.6%
23	Alabama	3,806	1.5%
24	Minnesota	3,207	1.3%
25	Arkansas	3,188	1.3%
26	Tennessee	3,134	1.3%
27	Indiana	2,674	1.1%
28	Mississippi	2,197	0.9%
29	Colorado	2,120	0.9%
30	Iowa	1,979	0.8%
31	Maine	1,789	0.7%
32	Kentucky	1,669	0.7%
33	Nevada	1,552	0.6%
34	Hawaii	1,519	0.6%
35	Utah	1,428	0.6%
36	West Virginia	1,403	0.6%
37	Nebraska	1,344	0.5%
38	New Mexico	1,325	0.5%
39	Idaho	1,264	0.5%
40	Rhode Island	974	0.4%
41	Delaware	730	0.3%
42	Alaska	536	0.2%
43	Wyoming	517	0.2%
44	South Dakota	457	0.2%
45	North Dakota	356	0.1%
46	Montana	185	0.1%
NA	Florida**	NA	NA
NA	Kansas**	NA	NA
NA	New Hampshire**	NA	NA
NA	Vermont**	NA	NA
	District of Columbia**	NA	NA

Source: Federal Bureau of Investigation
    "Crime in the United States 1997" (Uniform Crime Reports, November 22, 1998)
*By law enforcement agencies submitting complete reports to the F.B.I. for 12 months in 1997. The F.B.I. estimates
356,000 reported and unreported arrests for burglary occurred in 1997. Burglary is the unlawful entry of a structure
to commit a felony or theft. Attempts are included. See important note at beginning of this chapter.
**Not available.

Reported Arrest Rate for Burglary in 1997

National Rate = 134.2 Reported Arrests per 100,000 Population*

RANK	STATE	RATE		RANK	STATE	RATE
35	Alabama	93.8		1	Delaware	244.1
7	Alaska	197.8		2	Kentucky	223.7
17	Arizona	142.2		3	North Carolina	220.6
18	Arkansas	141.9		4	Louisiana	218.8
8	California	183.3		5	Mississippi	217.3
43	Colorado	77.9		6	Nevada	202.1
15	Connecticut	145.9		7	Alaska	197.8
1	Delaware	244.1		8	California	183.3
NA	Florida**	NA		9	Maryland	175.7
10	Georgia	169.2		10	Georgia	169.2
22	Hawaii	132.5		11	South Carolina	160.4
31	Idaho	107.0		12	Maine	152.8
14	Illinois	150.9		13	Washington	152.7
40	Indiana	80.5		14	Illinois	150.9
39	Iowa	84.1		15	Connecticut	145.9
NA	Kansas**	NA		16	Missouri	144.0
2	Kentucky	223.7		17	Arizona	142.2
4	Louisiana	218.8		18	Arkansas	141.9
12	Maine	152.8		19	Oregon	140.2
9	Maryland	175.7		20	Tennessee	139.7
42	Massachusetts	79.5		21	South Dakota	136.4
37	Michigan	87.3		22	Hawaii	132.5
44	Minnesota	68.5		23	Wisconsin	129.9
5	Mississippi	217.3		24	Oklahoma	123.2
16	Missouri	144.0		25	New Jersey	116.4
46	Montana	53.6		26	New Mexico	113.2
38	Nebraska	85.9		26	New York	113.2
6	Nevada	202.1		28	Texas	111.0
NA	New Hampshire**	NA		29	Wyoming	110.2
25	New Jersey	116.4		30	Ohio	107.2
26	New Mexico	113.2		31	Idaho	107.0
26	New York	113.2		32	Rhode Island	98.7
3	North Carolina	220.6		33	Pennsylvania	98.2
45	North Dakota	61.5		34	Virginia	94.0
30	Ohio	107.2		35	Alabama	93.8
24	Oklahoma	123.2		36	Utah	92.5
19	Oregon	140.2		37	Michigan	87.3
33	Pennsylvania	98.2		38	Nebraska	85.9
32	Rhode Island	98.7		39	Iowa	84.1
11	South Carolina	160.4		40	Indiana	80.5
21	South Dakota	136.4		40	West Virginia	80.5
20	Tennessee	139.7		42	Massachusetts	79.5
28	Texas	111.0		43	Colorado	77.9
36	Utah	92.5		44	Minnesota	68.5
NA	Vermont**	NA		45	North Dakota	61.5
34	Virginia	94.0		46	Montana	53.6
13	Washington	152.7		NA	Florida**	NA
40	West Virginia	80.5		NA	Kansas**	NA
23	Wisconsin	129.9		NA	New Hampshire**	NA
29	Wyoming	110.2		NA	Vermont**	NA
					District of Columbia**	NA

Source: Morgan Quitno Press using data from Federal Bureau of Investigation
  "Crime in the United States 1997" (Uniform Crime Reports, November 22, 1998)
*By law enforcement agencies submitting complete reports to the F.B.I. for 12 months in 1997. These rates based
on population estimates for areas under the jurisdiction of those agencies reporting. Arrest rate based on the F.B.I.
estimate of reported and unreported arrests for burglary is 133.0 arrests per 100,000 population. See important
note at beginning of this chapter. **Not available.

Reported Arrests for Larceny and Theft in 1997

National Total = 1,033,901 Reported Arrests*

<table>
<tr><td colspan="4">ALPHA ORDER</td><td colspan="4">RANK ORDER</td></tr>
<tr><td>RANK</td><td>STATE</td><td>ARRESTS</td><td>% of USA</td><td>RANK</td><td>STATE</td><td>ARRESTS</td><td>% of USA</td></tr>
<tr><td>19</td><td>Alabama</td><td>20,012</td><td>1.9%</td><td>1</td><td>California</td><td>128,159</td><td>12.4%</td></tr>
<tr><td>45</td><td>Alaska</td><td>1,288</td><td>0.1%</td><td>2</td><td>Texas</td><td>103,142</td><td>10.0%</td></tr>
<tr><td>6</td><td>Arizona</td><td>35,731</td><td>3.5%</td><td>3</td><td>New York</td><td>43,466</td><td>4.2%</td></tr>
<tr><td>28</td><td>Arkansas</td><td>14,395</td><td>1.4%</td><td>4</td><td>North Carolina</td><td>41,972</td><td>4.1%</td></tr>
<tr><td>1</td><td>California</td><td>128,159</td><td>12.4%</td><td>5</td><td>New Jersey</td><td>38,851</td><td>3.8%</td></tr>
<tr><td>22</td><td>Colorado</td><td>19,511</td><td>1.9%</td><td>6</td><td>Arizona</td><td>35,731</td><td>3.5%</td></tr>
<tr><td>20</td><td>Connecticut</td><td>19,734</td><td>1.9%</td><td>7</td><td>Virginia</td><td>35,384</td><td>3.4%</td></tr>
<tr><td>40</td><td>Delaware</td><td>4,101</td><td>0.4%</td><td>8</td><td>Wisconsin</td><td>35,113</td><td>3.4%</td></tr>
<tr><td>NA</td><td>Florida**</td><td>NA</td><td>NA</td><td>9</td><td>Illinois</td><td>32,648</td><td>3.2%</td></tr>
<tr><td>21</td><td>Georgia</td><td>19,729</td><td>1.9%</td><td>10</td><td>Washington</td><td>30,725</td><td>3.0%</td></tr>
<tr><td>33</td><td>Hawaii</td><td>8,119</td><td>0.8%</td><td>11</td><td>Louisiana</td><td>30,492</td><td>3.0%</td></tr>
<tr><td>34</td><td>Idaho</td><td>8,010</td><td>0.8%</td><td>12</td><td>Maryland</td><td>29,794</td><td>2.9%</td></tr>
<tr><td>9</td><td>Illinois</td><td>32,648</td><td>3.2%</td><td>13</td><td>Michigan</td><td>28,712</td><td>2.8%</td></tr>
<tr><td>24</td><td>Indiana</td><td>18,950</td><td>1.8%</td><td>14</td><td>Missouri</td><td>28,623</td><td>2.8%</td></tr>
<tr><td>30</td><td>Iowa</td><td>11,519</td><td>1.1%</td><td>15</td><td>Ohio</td><td>28,182</td><td>2.7%</td></tr>
<tr><td>NA</td><td>Kansas**</td><td>NA</td><td>NA</td><td>16</td><td>Oregon</td><td>26,119</td><td>2.5%</td></tr>
<tr><td>39</td><td>Kentucky</td><td>4,978</td><td>0.5%</td><td>17</td><td>Minnesota</td><td>23,159</td><td>2.2%</td></tr>
<tr><td>11</td><td>Louisiana</td><td>30,492</td><td>3.0%</td><td>18</td><td>South Carolina</td><td>20,077</td><td>1.9%</td></tr>
<tr><td>36</td><td>Maine</td><td>6,642</td><td>0.6%</td><td>19</td><td>Alabama</td><td>20,012</td><td>1.9%</td></tr>
<tr><td>12</td><td>Maryland</td><td>29,794</td><td>2.9%</td><td>20</td><td>Connecticut</td><td>19,734</td><td>1.9%</td></tr>
<tr><td>29</td><td>Massachusetts</td><td>13,565</td><td>1.3%</td><td>21</td><td>Georgia</td><td>19,729</td><td>1.9%</td></tr>
<tr><td>13</td><td>Michigan</td><td>28,712</td><td>2.8%</td><td>22</td><td>Colorado</td><td>19,511</td><td>1.9%</td></tr>
<tr><td>17</td><td>Minnesota</td><td>23,159</td><td>2.2%</td><td>23</td><td>Pennsylvania</td><td>19,290</td><td>1.9%</td></tr>
<tr><td>35</td><td>Mississippi</td><td>7,635</td><td>0.7%</td><td>24</td><td>Indiana</td><td>18,950</td><td>1.8%</td></tr>
<tr><td>14</td><td>Missouri</td><td>28,623</td><td>2.8%</td><td>25</td><td>Tennessee</td><td>18,769</td><td>1.8%</td></tr>
<tr><td>46</td><td>Montana</td><td>1,209</td><td>0.1%</td><td>26</td><td>Oklahoma</td><td>16,611</td><td>1.6%</td></tr>
<tr><td>31</td><td>Nebraska</td><td>10,586</td><td>1.0%</td><td>27</td><td>Utah</td><td>15,708</td><td>1.5%</td></tr>
<tr><td>38</td><td>Nevada</td><td>5,163</td><td>0.5%</td><td>28</td><td>Arkansas</td><td>14,395</td><td>1.4%</td></tr>
<tr><td>NA</td><td>New Hampshire**</td><td>NA</td><td>NA</td><td>29</td><td>Massachusetts</td><td>13,565</td><td>1.3%</td></tr>
<tr><td>5</td><td>New Jersey</td><td>38,851</td><td>3.8%</td><td>30</td><td>Iowa</td><td>11,519</td><td>1.1%</td></tr>
<tr><td>32</td><td>New Mexico</td><td>10,195</td><td>1.0%</td><td>31</td><td>Nebraska</td><td>10,586</td><td>1.0%</td></tr>
<tr><td>3</td><td>New York</td><td>43,466</td><td>4.2%</td><td>32</td><td>New Mexico</td><td>10,195</td><td>1.0%</td></tr>
<tr><td>4</td><td>North Carolina</td><td>41,972</td><td>4.1%</td><td>33</td><td>Hawaii</td><td>8,119</td><td>0.8%</td></tr>
<tr><td>44</td><td>North Dakota</td><td>2,888</td><td>0.3%</td><td>34</td><td>Idaho</td><td>8,010</td><td>0.8%</td></tr>
<tr><td>15</td><td>Ohio</td><td>28,182</td><td>2.7%</td><td>35</td><td>Mississippi</td><td>7,635</td><td>0.7%</td></tr>
<tr><td>26</td><td>Oklahoma</td><td>16,611</td><td>1.6%</td><td>36</td><td>Maine</td><td>6,642</td><td>0.6%</td></tr>
<tr><td>16</td><td>Oregon</td><td>26,119</td><td>2.5%</td><td>37</td><td>West Virginia</td><td>5,284</td><td>0.5%</td></tr>
<tr><td>23</td><td>Pennsylvania</td><td>19,290</td><td>1.9%</td><td>38</td><td>Nevada</td><td>5,163</td><td>0.5%</td></tr>
<tr><td>41</td><td>Rhode Island</td><td>3,641</td><td>0.4%</td><td>39</td><td>Kentucky</td><td>4,978</td><td>0.5%</td></tr>
<tr><td>18</td><td>South Carolina</td><td>20,077</td><td>1.9%</td><td>40</td><td>Delaware</td><td>4,101</td><td>0.4%</td></tr>
<tr><td>42</td><td>South Dakota</td><td>3,045</td><td>0.3%</td><td>41</td><td>Rhode Island</td><td>3,641</td><td>0.4%</td></tr>
<tr><td>25</td><td>Tennessee</td><td>18,769</td><td>1.8%</td><td>42</td><td>South Dakota</td><td>3,045</td><td>0.3%</td></tr>
<tr><td>2</td><td>Texas</td><td>103,142</td><td>10.0%</td><td>43</td><td>Wyoming</td><td>2,975</td><td>0.3%</td></tr>
<tr><td>27</td><td>Utah</td><td>15,708</td><td>1.5%</td><td>44</td><td>North Dakota</td><td>2,888</td><td>0.3%</td></tr>
<tr><td>NA</td><td>Vermont**</td><td>NA</td><td>NA</td><td>45</td><td>Alaska</td><td>1,288</td><td>0.1%</td></tr>
<tr><td>7</td><td>Virginia</td><td>35,384</td><td>3.4%</td><td>46</td><td>Montana</td><td>1,209</td><td>0.1%</td></tr>
<tr><td>10</td><td>Washington</td><td>30,725</td><td>3.0%</td><td>NA</td><td>Florida**</td><td>NA</td><td>NA</td></tr>
<tr><td>37</td><td>West Virginia</td><td>5,284</td><td>0.5%</td><td>NA</td><td>Kansas**</td><td>NA</td><td>NA</td></tr>
<tr><td>8</td><td>Wisconsin</td><td>35,113</td><td>3.4%</td><td>NA</td><td>New Hampshire**</td><td>NA</td><td>NA</td></tr>
<tr><td>43</td><td>Wyoming</td><td>2,975</td><td>0.3%</td><td>NA</td><td>Vermont**</td><td>NA</td><td>NA</td></tr>
<tr><td></td><td></td><td></td><td></td><td></td><td>District of Columbia**</td><td>NA</td><td>NA</td></tr>
</table>

Source: Federal Bureau of Investigation
  "Crime in the United States 1997" (Uniform Crime Reports, November 22, 1998)
*By law enforcement agencies submitting complete reports to the F.B.I. for 12 months in 1997. The F.B.I. estimates 1,472,600 reported and unreported arrests for larceny and theft occurred in 1997. Larceny and theft is the unlawful taking of property without use of force, violence or fraud. Attempts are included. Motor vehicle thefts are excluded. See important note at beginning of this chapter. **Not available.

Reported Arrest Rate for Larceny and Theft in 1997

National Rate = 564.2 Reported Arrests per 100,000 Population*

ALPHA ORDER			RANK ORDER		
RANK	STATE	RATE	RANK	STATE	RATE
36	Alabama	493.1	1	Delaware	1,371.6
38	Alaska	475.3	2	Illinois	1,180.3
4	Arizona	926.4	3	Utah	1,018.0
22	Arkansas	640.9	4	Arizona	926.4
40	California	402.9	5	Oregon	925.9
15	Colorado	717.1	6	South Dakota	909.0
16	Connecticut	712.7	7	Washington	902.9
1	Delaware	1,371.6	8	Wisconsin	894.6
NA	Florida**	NA	9	Louisiana	891.8
13	Georgia	791.1	10	Missouri	888.9
17	Hawaii	708.5	11	New Mexico	871.4
18	Idaho	678.2	12	Tennessee	836.8
2	Illinois	1,180.3	13	Georgia	791.1
26	Indiana	570.6	14	Mississippi	755.2
37	Iowa	489.8	15	Colorado	717.1
NA	Kansas**	NA	16	Connecticut	712.7
21	Kentucky	667.3	17	Hawaii	708.5
9	Louisiana	891.8	18	Idaho	678.2
27	Maine	567.2	19	Nebraska	676.9
24	Maryland	585.5	20	Nevada	672.3
46	Massachusetts	266.6	21	Kentucky	667.3
42	Michigan	362.1	22	Arkansas	640.9
35	Minnesota	494.7	23	Wyoming	634.3
14	Mississippi	755.2	24	Maryland	585.5
10	Missouri	888.9	25	North Carolina	573.2
43	Montana	350.4	26	Indiana	570.6
19	Nebraska	676.9	27	Maine	567.2
20	Nevada	672.3	28	Texas	548.5
NA	New Hampshire**	NA	29	South Carolina	538.0
32	New Jersey	501.9	30	Virginia	536.2
11	New Mexico	871.4	31	New York	518.3
31	New York	518.3	32	New Jersey	501.9
25	North Carolina	573.2	33	Oklahoma	501.1
34	North Dakota	498.8	34	North Dakota	498.8
39	Ohio	458.2	35	Minnesota	494.7
33	Oklahoma	501.1	36	Alabama	493.1
5	Oregon	925.9	37	Iowa	489.8
44	Pennsylvania	341.8	38	Alaska	475.3
41	Rhode Island	368.9	39	Ohio	458.2
29	South Carolina	538.0	40	California	402.9
6	South Dakota	909.0	41	Rhode Island	368.9
12	Tennessee	836.8	42	Michigan	362.1
28	Texas	548.5	43	Montana	350.4
3	Utah	1,018.0	44	Pennsylvania	341.8
NA	Vermont**	NA	45	West Virginia	303.3
30	Virginia	536.2	46	Massachusetts	266.6
7	Washington	902.9	NA	Florida**	NA
45	West Virginia	303.3	NA	Kansas**	NA
8	Wisconsin	894.6	NA	New Hampshire**	NA
23	Wyoming	634.3	NA	Vermont**	NA
				District of Columbia**	NA

Source: Morgan Quitno Press using data from Federal Bureau of Investigation
    "Crime in the United States 1997" (Uniform Crime Reports, November 22, 1998)
*By law enforcement agencies submitting complete reports to the F.B.I. for 12 months in 1997. These rates based
on population estimates for areas under the jurisdiction of those agencies reporting. Arrest rate based on the F.B.I.
estimate of reported and unreported arrests for larceny and theft is 550.2 arrests per 100,000 population. See
important note at beginning of this chapter. **Not available.*

Reported Arrests for Motor Vehicle Theft in 1997

National Total = 116,052 Reported Arrests*

ALPHA ORDER

RANK	STATE	ARRESTS	% of USA
26	Alabama	1,468	1.3%
42	Alaska	233	0.2%
9	Arizona	3,172	2.7%
38	Arkansas	459	0.4%
1	California	28,033	24.2%
23	Colorado	1,598	1.4%
22	Connecticut	1,751	1.5%
45	Delaware	141	0.1%
NA	Florida**	NA	NA
17	Georgia	2,187	1.9%
27	Hawaii	1,387	1.2%
34	Idaho	632	0.5%
3	Illinois	8,112	7.0%
18	Indiana	2,101	1.8%
31	Iowa	790	0.7%
NA	Kansas**	NA	NA
32	Kentucky	745	0.6%
24	Louisiana	1,502	1.3%
35	Maine	506	0.4%
4	Maryland	5,742	4.9%
25	Massachusetts	1,495	1.3%
12	Michigan	2,490	2.1%
21	Minnesota	1,867	1.6%
30	Mississippi	800	0.7%
8	Missouri	3,232	2.8%
46	Montana	123	0.1%
36	Nebraska	495	0.4%
40	Nevada	277	0.2%
NA	New Hampshire**	NA	NA
19	New Jersey	2,020	1.7%
33	New Mexico	726	0.6%
7	New York	3,243	2.8%
13	North Carolina	2,466	2.1%
41	North Dakota	276	0.2%
11	Ohio	2,815	2.4%
15	Oklahoma	2,342	2.0%
6	Oregon	3,429	3.0%
14	Pennsylvania	2,451	2.1%
37	Rhode Island	461	0.4%
29	South Carolina	967	0.8%
44	South Dakota	165	0.1%
16	Tennessee	2,315	2.0%
2	Texas	10,111	8.7%
28	Utah	1,306	1.1%
NA	Vermont**	NA	NA
10	Virginia	3,120	2.7%
20	Washington	1,924	1.7%
39	West Virginia	442	0.4%
5	Wisconsin	3,942	3.4%
43	Wyoming	193	0.2%

RANK ORDER

RANK	STATE	ARRESTS	% of USA
1	California	28,033	24.2%
2	Texas	10,111	8.7%
3	Illinois	8,112	7.0%
4	Maryland	5,742	4.9%
5	Wisconsin	3,942	3.4%
6	Oregon	3,429	3.0%
7	New York	3,243	2.8%
8	Missouri	3,232	2.8%
9	Arizona	3,172	2.7%
10	Virginia	3,120	2.7%
11	Ohio	2,815	2.4%
12	Michigan	2,490	2.1%
13	North Carolina	2,466	2.1%
14	Pennsylvania	2,451	2.1%
15	Oklahoma	2,342	2.0%
16	Tennessee	2,315	2.0%
17	Georgia	2,187	1.9%
18	Indiana	2,101	1.8%
19	New Jersey	2,020	1.7%
20	Washington	1,924	1.7%
21	Minnesota	1,867	1.6%
22	Connecticut	1,751	1.5%
23	Colorado	1,598	1.4%
24	Louisiana	1,502	1.3%
25	Massachusetts	1,495	1.3%
26	Alabama	1,468	1.3%
27	Hawaii	1,387	1.2%
28	Utah	1,306	1.1%
29	South Carolina	967	0.8%
30	Mississippi	800	0.7%
31	Iowa	790	0.7%
32	Kentucky	745	0.6%
33	New Mexico	726	0.6%
34	Idaho	632	0.5%
35	Maine	506	0.4%
36	Nebraska	495	0.4%
37	Rhode Island	461	0.4%
38	Arkansas	459	0.4%
39	West Virginia	442	0.4%
40	Nevada	277	0.2%
41	North Dakota	276	0.2%
42	Alaska	233	0.2%
43	Wyoming	193	0.2%
44	South Dakota	165	0.1%
45	Delaware	141	0.1%
46	Montana	123	0.1%
NA	Florida**	NA	NA
NA	Kansas**	NA	NA
NA	New Hampshire**	NA	NA
NA	Vermont**	NA	NA
	District of Columbia**	NA	NA

Source: Federal Bureau of Investigation
"Crime in the United States 1997" (Uniform Crime Reports, November 22, 1998)
*By law enforcement agencies submitting complete reports to the F.B.I. for 12 months in 1997. The F.B.I. estimates 167,000 reported and unreported arrests for motor vehicle theft occurred in 1997. Motor vehicle theft includes the theft or attempted theft of a self-propelled vehicle. Excludes motorboats, construction equipment, airplanes and farming equipment. See important note at beginning of this chapter. **Not available.*

21

Reported Arrest Rate for Motor Vehicle Theft in 1997

National Rate = 63.3 Reported Arrests per 100,000 Population*

ALPHA ORDER

RANK	STATE	RATE
35	Alabama	36.2
11	Alaska	86.0
13	Arizona	82.2
46	Arkansas	20.4
9	California	88.1
19	Colorado	58.7
17	Connecticut	63.2
26	Delaware	47.2
NA	Florida**	NA
10	Georgia	87.7
3	Hawaii	121.0
22	Idaho	53.5
1	Illinois	293.3
16	Indiana	63.3
39	Iowa	33.6
NA	Kansas**	NA
8	Kentucky	99.9
29	Louisiana	43.9
31	Maine	43.2
4	Maryland	112.8
42	Massachusetts	29.4
41	Michigan	31.4
33	Minnesota	39.9
14	Mississippi	79.1
6	Missouri	100.4
37	Montana	35.7
40	Nebraska	31.6
36	Nevada	36.1
NA	New Hampshire**	NA
43	New Jersey	26.1
18	New Mexico	62.1
34	New York	38.7
38	North Carolina	33.7
24	North Dakota	47.7
28	Ohio	45.8
15	Oklahoma	70.6
2	Oregon	121.6
30	Pennsylvania	43.4
27	Rhode Island	46.7
44	South Carolina	25.9
23	South Dakota	49.3
5	Tennessee	103.2
21	Texas	53.8
12	Utah	84.6
NA	Vermont**	NA
25	Virginia	47.3
20	Washington	56.5
45	West Virginia	25.4
6	Wisconsin	100.4
32	Wyoming	41.2

RANK ORDER

RANK	STATE	RATE
1	Illinois	293.3
2	Oregon	121.6
3	Hawaii	121.0
4	Maryland	112.8
5	Tennessee	103.2
6	Missouri	100.4
6	Wisconsin	100.4
8	Kentucky	99.9
9	California	88.1
10	Georgia	87.7
11	Alaska	86.0
12	Utah	84.6
13	Arizona	82.2
14	Mississippi	79.1
15	Oklahoma	70.6
16	Indiana	63.3
17	Connecticut	63.2
18	New Mexico	62.1
19	Colorado	58.7
20	Washington	56.5
21	Texas	53.8
22	Idaho	53.5
23	South Dakota	49.3
24	North Dakota	47.7
25	Virginia	47.3
26	Delaware	47.2
27	Rhode Island	46.7
28	Ohio	45.8
29	Louisiana	43.9
30	Pennsylvania	43.4
31	Maine	43.2
32	Wyoming	41.2
33	Minnesota	39.9
34	New York	38.7
35	Alabama	36.2
36	Nevada	36.1
37	Montana	35.7
38	North Carolina	33.7
39	Iowa	33.6
40	Nebraska	31.6
41	Michigan	31.4
42	Massachusetts	29.4
43	New Jersey	26.1
44	South Carolina	25.9
45	West Virginia	25.4
46	Arkansas	20.4
NA	Florida**	NA
NA	Kansas**	NA
NA	New Hampshire**	NA
NA	Vermont**	NA
	District of Columbia**	NA

Source: Morgan Quitno Press using data from Federal Bureau of Investigation
   "Crime in the United States 1997" (Uniform Crime Reports, November 22, 1998)
*By law enforcement agencies submitting complete reports to the F.B.I. for 12 months in 1997. These rates based on population estimates for areas under the jurisdiction of those agencies reporting. Arrest rate based on the F.B.I. estimate of reported and unreported arrests for motor vehicle theft is 62.4 arrests per 100,000 population. See important note at beginning of this chapter. **Not available.

Reported Arrests for Arson in 1997

National Total = 13,831 Reported Arrests*

ALPHA ORDER

RANK	STATE	ARRESTS	% of USA
31	Alabama	122	0.9%
44	Alaska	19	0.1%
17	Arizona	312	2.3%
32	Arkansas	117	0.8%
1	California	2,129	15.4%
25	Colorado	186	1.3%
24	Connecticut	200	1.4%
45	Delaware	12	0.1%
NA	Florida**	NA	NA
20	Georgia	235	1.7%
40	Hawaii	41	0.3%
33	Idaho	115	0.8%
21	Illinois	215	1.6%
26	Indiana	174	1.3%
30	Iowa	127	0.9%
NA	Kansas**	NA	NA
37	Kentucky	77	0.6%
18	Louisiana	267	1.9%
29	Maine	132	1.0%
11	Maryland	383	2.8%
27	Massachusetts	164	1.2%
4	Michigan	698	5.0%
22	Minnesota	211	1.5%
37	Mississippi	77	0.6%
12	Missouri	371	2.7%
46	Montana	8	0.1%
34	Nebraska	110	0.8%
35	Nevada	90	0.7%
NA	New Hampshire**	NA	NA
5	New Jersey	616	4.5%
39	New Mexico	52	0.4%
7	New York	524	3.8%
8	North Carolina	518	3.7%
42	North Dakota	26	0.2%
6	Ohio	575	4.2%
13	Oklahoma	355	2.6%
16	Oregon	337	2.4%
10	Pennsylvania	430	3.1%
35	Rhode Island	90	0.7%
19	South Carolina	236	1.7%
42	South Dakota	26	0.2%
2	Tennessee	990	7.2%
3	Texas	898	6.5%
23	Utah	210	1.5%
NA	Vermont**	NA	NA
9	Virginia	488	3.5%
15	Washington	339	2.5%
28	West Virginia	151	1.1%
14	Wisconsin	348	2.5%
41	Wyoming	30	0.2%

RANK ORDER

RANK	STATE	ARRESTS	% of USA
1	California	2,129	15.4%
2	Tennessee	990	7.2%
3	Texas	898	6.5%
4	Michigan	698	5.0%
5	New Jersey	616	4.5%
6	Ohio	575	4.2%
7	New York	524	3.8%
8	North Carolina	518	3.7%
9	Virginia	488	3.5%
10	Pennsylvania	430	3.1%
11	Maryland	383	2.8%
12	Missouri	371	2.7%
13	Oklahoma	355	2.6%
14	Wisconsin	348	2.5%
15	Washington	339	2.5%
16	Oregon	337	2.4%
17	Arizona	312	2.3%
18	Louisiana	267	1.9%
19	South Carolina	236	1.7%
20	Georgia	235	1.7%
21	Illinois	215	1.6%
22	Minnesota	211	1.5%
23	Utah	210	1.5%
24	Connecticut	200	1.4%
25	Colorado	186	1.3%
26	Indiana	174	1.3%
27	Massachusetts	164	1.2%
28	West Virginia	151	1.1%
29	Maine	132	1.0%
30	Iowa	127	0.9%
31	Alabama	122	0.9%
32	Arkansas	117	0.8%
33	Idaho	115	0.8%
34	Nebraska	110	0.8%
35	Nevada	90	0.7%
35	Rhode Island	90	0.7%
37	Kentucky	77	0.6%
37	Mississippi	77	0.6%
39	New Mexico	52	0.4%
40	Hawaii	41	0.3%
41	Wyoming	30	0.2%
42	North Dakota	26	0.2%
42	South Dakota	26	0.2%
44	Alaska	19	0.1%
45	Delaware	12	0.1%
46	Montana	8	0.1%
NA	Florida**	NA	NA
NA	Kansas**	NA	NA
NA	New Hampshire**	NA	NA
NA	Vermont**	NA	NA
	District of Columbia**	NA	NA

Source: Federal Bureau of Investigation
   "Crime in the United States 1997" (Uniform Crime Reports, November 22, 1998)
*By law enforcement agencies submitting complete reports to the F.B.I. for 12 months in 1997. The F.B.I. estimates 20,000 reported and unreported arrests for arson occurred in 1997. Arson is the willful burning of or attempt to burn a building, vehicle or another's personal property. See important note at beginning of this chapter.
**Not available.

Reported Arrest Rate for Arson in 1997

National Rate = 7.5 Reported Arrests per 100,000 Population*

<table>
<tr><td colspan="3">ALPHA ORDER</td><td colspan="3">RANK ORDER</td></tr>
<tr><td>RANK</td><td>STATE</td><td>RATE</td><td>RANK</td><td>STATE</td><td>RATE</td></tr>
<tr><td>45</td><td>Alabama</td><td>3.0</td><td>1</td><td>Tennessee</td><td>44.1</td></tr>
<tr><td>28</td><td>Alaska</td><td>7.0</td><td>2</td><td>Utah</td><td>13.6</td></tr>
<tr><td>17</td><td>Arizona</td><td>8.1</td><td>3</td><td>Oregon</td><td>11.9</td></tr>
<tr><td>36</td><td>Arkansas</td><td>5.2</td><td>4</td><td>Nevada</td><td>11.7</td></tr>
<tr><td>31</td><td>California</td><td>6.7</td><td>5</td><td>Missouri</td><td>11.5</td></tr>
<tr><td>30</td><td>Colorado</td><td>6.8</td><td>6</td><td>Maine</td><td>11.3</td></tr>
<tr><td>26</td><td>Connecticut</td><td>7.2</td><td>7</td><td>Oklahoma</td><td>10.7</td></tr>
<tr><td>42</td><td>Delaware</td><td>4.0</td><td>8</td><td>Kentucky</td><td>10.3</td></tr>
<tr><td>NA</td><td>Florida**</td><td>NA</td><td>9</td><td>Washington</td><td>10.0</td></tr>
<tr><td>11</td><td>Georgia</td><td>9.4</td><td>10</td><td>Idaho</td><td>9.7</td></tr>
<tr><td>43</td><td>Hawaii</td><td>3.6</td><td>11</td><td>Georgia</td><td>9.4</td></tr>
<tr><td>10</td><td>Idaho</td><td>9.7</td><td>12</td><td>Ohio</td><td>9.3</td></tr>
<tr><td>19</td><td>Illinois</td><td>7.8</td><td>13</td><td>Rhode Island</td><td>9.1</td></tr>
<tr><td>36</td><td>Indiana</td><td>5.2</td><td>14</td><td>Wisconsin</td><td>8.9</td></tr>
<tr><td>35</td><td>Iowa</td><td>5.4</td><td>15</td><td>Michigan</td><td>8.8</td></tr>
<tr><td>NA</td><td>Kansas**</td><td>NA</td><td>16</td><td>West Virginia</td><td>8.7</td></tr>
<tr><td>8</td><td>Kentucky</td><td>10.3</td><td>17</td><td>Arizona</td><td>8.1</td></tr>
<tr><td>19</td><td>Louisiana</td><td>7.8</td><td>18</td><td>New Jersey</td><td>8.0</td></tr>
<tr><td>6</td><td>Maine</td><td>11.3</td><td>19</td><td>Illinois</td><td>7.8</td></tr>
<tr><td>24</td><td>Maryland</td><td>7.5</td><td>19</td><td>Louisiana</td><td>7.8</td></tr>
<tr><td>44</td><td>Massachusetts</td><td>3.2</td><td>19</td><td>South Dakota</td><td>7.8</td></tr>
<tr><td>15</td><td>Michigan</td><td>8.8</td><td>22</td><td>Mississippi</td><td>7.6</td></tr>
<tr><td>39</td><td>Minnesota</td><td>4.5</td><td>22</td><td>Pennsylvania</td><td>7.6</td></tr>
<tr><td>22</td><td>Mississippi</td><td>7.6</td><td>24</td><td>Maryland</td><td>7.5</td></tr>
<tr><td>5</td><td>Missouri</td><td>11.5</td><td>25</td><td>Virginia</td><td>7.4</td></tr>
<tr><td>46</td><td>Montana</td><td>2.3</td><td>26</td><td>Connecticut</td><td>7.2</td></tr>
<tr><td>28</td><td>Nebraska</td><td>7.0</td><td>27</td><td>North Carolina</td><td>7.1</td></tr>
<tr><td>4</td><td>Nevada</td><td>11.7</td><td>28</td><td>Alaska</td><td>7.0</td></tr>
<tr><td>NA</td><td>New Hampshire**</td><td>NA</td><td>28</td><td>Nebraska</td><td>7.0</td></tr>
<tr><td>18</td><td>New Jersey</td><td>8.0</td><td>30</td><td>Colorado</td><td>6.8</td></tr>
<tr><td>41</td><td>New Mexico</td><td>4.4</td><td>31</td><td>California</td><td>6.7</td></tr>
<tr><td>34</td><td>New York</td><td>6.2</td><td>32</td><td>Wyoming</td><td>6.4</td></tr>
<tr><td>27</td><td>North Carolina</td><td>7.1</td><td>33</td><td>South Carolina</td><td>6.3</td></tr>
<tr><td>39</td><td>North Dakota</td><td>4.5</td><td>34</td><td>New York</td><td>6.2</td></tr>
<tr><td>12</td><td>Ohio</td><td>9.3</td><td>35</td><td>Iowa</td><td>5.4</td></tr>
<tr><td>7</td><td>Oklahoma</td><td>10.7</td><td>36</td><td>Arkansas</td><td>5.2</td></tr>
<tr><td>3</td><td>Oregon</td><td>11.9</td><td>36</td><td>Indiana</td><td>5.2</td></tr>
<tr><td>22</td><td>Pennsylvania</td><td>7.6</td><td>38</td><td>Texas</td><td>4.8</td></tr>
<tr><td>13</td><td>Rhode Island</td><td>9.1</td><td>39</td><td>Minnesota</td><td>4.5</td></tr>
<tr><td>33</td><td>South Carolina</td><td>6.3</td><td>39</td><td>North Dakota</td><td>4.5</td></tr>
<tr><td>19</td><td>South Dakota</td><td>7.8</td><td>41</td><td>New Mexico</td><td>4.4</td></tr>
<tr><td>1</td><td>Tennessee</td><td>44.1</td><td>42</td><td>Delaware</td><td>4.0</td></tr>
<tr><td>38</td><td>Texas</td><td>4.8</td><td>43</td><td>Hawaii</td><td>3.6</td></tr>
<tr><td>2</td><td>Utah</td><td>13.6</td><td>44</td><td>Massachusetts</td><td>3.2</td></tr>
<tr><td>NA</td><td>Vermont**</td><td>NA</td><td>45</td><td>Alabama</td><td>3.0</td></tr>
<tr><td>25</td><td>Virginia</td><td>7.4</td><td>46</td><td>Montana</td><td>2.3</td></tr>
<tr><td>9</td><td>Washington</td><td>10.0</td><td>NA</td><td>Florida**</td><td>NA</td></tr>
<tr><td>16</td><td>West Virginia</td><td>8.7</td><td>NA</td><td>Kansas**</td><td>NA</td></tr>
<tr><td>14</td><td>Wisconsin</td><td>8.9</td><td>NA</td><td>New Hampshire**</td><td>NA</td></tr>
<tr><td>32</td><td>Wyoming</td><td>6.4</td><td>NA</td><td>Vermont**</td><td>NA</td></tr>
<tr><td></td><td></td><td></td><td></td><td>District of Columbia**</td><td>NA</td></tr>
</table>

Source: Morgan Quitno Press using data from Federal Bureau of Investigation
"Crime in the United States 1997" (Uniform Crime Reports, November 22, 1998)
*By law enforcement agencies submitting complete reports to the F.B.I. for 12 months in 1997. These rates based on population estimates for areas under the jurisdiction of those agencies reporting. Arrest rate based on the F.B.I. estimate of reported and unreported arrests for arson is 7.5 arrests per 100,000 population. See important note at beginning of this chapter. **Not available.

Reported Arrests for Weapons Violations in 1997

National Total = 152,368 Reported Arrests*

<table>
<tr><td colspan="4">ALPHA ORDER</td><td colspan="4">RANK ORDER</td></tr>
<tr><th>RANK</th><th>STATE</th><th>ARRESTS</th><th>% of USA</th><th>RANK</th><th>STATE</th><th>ARRESTS</th><th>% of USA</th></tr>
<tr><td>22</td><td>Alabama</td><td>2,349</td><td>1.5%</td><td>1</td><td>California</td><td>30,931</td><td>20.3%</td></tr>
<tr><td>42</td><td>Alaska</td><td>289</td><td>0.2%</td><td>2</td><td>Texas</td><td>13,793</td><td>9.1%</td></tr>
<tr><td>14</td><td>Arizona</td><td>3,788</td><td>2.5%</td><td>3</td><td>North Carolina</td><td>8,307</td><td>5.5%</td></tr>
<tr><td>20</td><td>Arkansas</td><td>2,473</td><td>1.6%</td><td>4</td><td>Virginia</td><td>7,302</td><td>4.8%</td></tr>
<tr><td>1</td><td>California</td><td>30,931</td><td>20.3%</td><td>5</td><td>Michigan</td><td>6,301</td><td>4.1%</td></tr>
<tr><td>21</td><td>Colorado</td><td>2,392</td><td>1.6%</td><td>6</td><td>Wisconsin</td><td>5,716</td><td>3.8%</td></tr>
<tr><td>23</td><td>Connecticut</td><td>2,168</td><td>1.4%</td><td>7</td><td>New Jersey</td><td>5,661</td><td>3.7%</td></tr>
<tr><td>41</td><td>Delaware</td><td>300</td><td>0.2%</td><td>8</td><td>Illinois</td><td>5,501</td><td>3.6%</td></tr>
<tr><td>NA</td><td>Florida**</td><td>NA</td><td>NA</td><td>9</td><td>Maryland</td><td>4,963</td><td>3.3%</td></tr>
<tr><td>12</td><td>Georgia</td><td>4,182</td><td>2.7%</td><td>10</td><td>Missouri</td><td>4,372</td><td>2.9%</td></tr>
<tr><td>39</td><td>Hawaii</td><td>430</td><td>0.3%</td><td>11</td><td>Ohio</td><td>4,192</td><td>2.8%</td></tr>
<tr><td>36</td><td>Idaho</td><td>699</td><td>0.5%</td><td>12</td><td>Georgia</td><td>4,182</td><td>2.7%</td></tr>
<tr><td>8</td><td>Illinois</td><td>5,501</td><td>3.6%</td><td>13</td><td>New York</td><td>3,908</td><td>2.6%</td></tr>
<tr><td>25</td><td>Indiana</td><td>1,871</td><td>1.2%</td><td>14</td><td>Arizona</td><td>3,788</td><td>2.5%</td></tr>
<tr><td>37</td><td>Iowa</td><td>625</td><td>0.4%</td><td>15</td><td>Tennessee</td><td>3,191</td><td>2.1%</td></tr>
<tr><td>NA</td><td>Kansas**</td><td>NA</td><td>NA</td><td>16</td><td>South Carolina</td><td>3,110</td><td>2.0%</td></tr>
<tr><td>33</td><td>Kentucky</td><td>1,028</td><td>0.7%</td><td>17</td><td>Washington</td><td>3,027</td><td>2.0%</td></tr>
<tr><td>18</td><td>Louisiana</td><td>2,952</td><td>1.9%</td><td>18</td><td>Louisiana</td><td>2,952</td><td>1.9%</td></tr>
<tr><td>40</td><td>Maine</td><td>356</td><td>0.2%</td><td>19</td><td>Oklahoma</td><td>2,744</td><td>1.8%</td></tr>
<tr><td>9</td><td>Maryland</td><td>4,963</td><td>3.3%</td><td>20</td><td>Arkansas</td><td>2,473</td><td>1.6%</td></tr>
<tr><td>31</td><td>Massachusetts</td><td>1,090</td><td>0.7%</td><td>21</td><td>Colorado</td><td>2,392</td><td>1.6%</td></tr>
<tr><td>5</td><td>Michigan</td><td>6,301</td><td>4.1%</td><td>22</td><td>Alabama</td><td>2,349</td><td>1.5%</td></tr>
<tr><td>26</td><td>Minnesota</td><td>1,703</td><td>1.1%</td><td>23</td><td>Connecticut</td><td>2,168</td><td>1.4%</td></tr>
<tr><td>35</td><td>Mississippi</td><td>741</td><td>0.5%</td><td>23</td><td>Oregon</td><td>2,168</td><td>1.4%</td></tr>
<tr><td>10</td><td>Missouri</td><td>4,372</td><td>2.9%</td><td>25</td><td>Indiana</td><td>1,871</td><td>1.2%</td></tr>
<tr><td>46</td><td>Montana</td><td>23</td><td>0.0%</td><td>26</td><td>Minnesota</td><td>1,703</td><td>1.1%</td></tr>
<tr><td>27</td><td>Nebraska</td><td>1,359</td><td>0.9%</td><td>27</td><td>Nebraska</td><td>1,359</td><td>0.9%</td></tr>
<tr><td>32</td><td>Nevada</td><td>1,054</td><td>0.7%</td><td>28</td><td>West Virginia</td><td>1,239</td><td>0.8%</td></tr>
<tr><td>NA</td><td>New Hampshire**</td><td>NA</td><td>NA</td><td>29</td><td>Utah</td><td>1,203</td><td>0.8%</td></tr>
<tr><td>7</td><td>New Jersey</td><td>5,661</td><td>3.7%</td><td>30</td><td>Pennsylvania</td><td>1,147</td><td>0.8%</td></tr>
<tr><td>34</td><td>New Mexico</td><td>757</td><td>0.5%</td><td>31</td><td>Massachusetts</td><td>1,090</td><td>0.7%</td></tr>
<tr><td>13</td><td>New York</td><td>3,908</td><td>2.6%</td><td>32</td><td>Nevada</td><td>1,054</td><td>0.7%</td></tr>
<tr><td>3</td><td>North Carolina</td><td>8,307</td><td>5.5%</td><td>33</td><td>Kentucky</td><td>1,028</td><td>0.7%</td></tr>
<tr><td>45</td><td>North Dakota</td><td>100</td><td>0.1%</td><td>34</td><td>New Mexico</td><td>757</td><td>0.5%</td></tr>
<tr><td>11</td><td>Ohio</td><td>4,192</td><td>2.8%</td><td>35</td><td>Mississippi</td><td>741</td><td>0.5%</td></tr>
<tr><td>19</td><td>Oklahoma</td><td>2,744</td><td>1.8%</td><td>36</td><td>Idaho</td><td>699</td><td>0.5%</td></tr>
<tr><td>23</td><td>Oregon</td><td>2,168</td><td>1.4%</td><td>37</td><td>Iowa</td><td>625</td><td>0.4%</td></tr>
<tr><td>30</td><td>Pennsylvania</td><td>1,147</td><td>0.8%</td><td>38</td><td>Rhode Island</td><td>469</td><td>0.3%</td></tr>
<tr><td>38</td><td>Rhode Island</td><td>469</td><td>0.3%</td><td>39</td><td>Hawaii</td><td>430</td><td>0.3%</td></tr>
<tr><td>16</td><td>South Carolina</td><td>3,110</td><td>2.0%</td><td>40</td><td>Maine</td><td>356</td><td>0.2%</td></tr>
<tr><td>44</td><td>South Dakota</td><td>131</td><td>0.1%</td><td>41</td><td>Delaware</td><td>300</td><td>0.2%</td></tr>
<tr><td>15</td><td>Tennessee</td><td>3,191</td><td>2.1%</td><td>42</td><td>Alaska</td><td>289</td><td>0.2%</td></tr>
<tr><td>2</td><td>Texas</td><td>13,793</td><td>9.1%</td><td>43</td><td>Wyoming</td><td>263</td><td>0.2%</td></tr>
<tr><td>29</td><td>Utah</td><td>1,203</td><td>0.8%</td><td>44</td><td>South Dakota</td><td>131</td><td>0.1%</td></tr>
<tr><td>NA</td><td>Vermont**</td><td>NA</td><td>NA</td><td>45</td><td>North Dakota</td><td>100</td><td>0.1%</td></tr>
<tr><td>4</td><td>Virginia</td><td>7,302</td><td>4.8%</td><td>46</td><td>Montana</td><td>23</td><td>0.0%</td></tr>
<tr><td>17</td><td>Washington</td><td>3,027</td><td>2.0%</td><td>NA</td><td>Florida**</td><td>NA</td><td>NA</td></tr>
<tr><td>28</td><td>West Virginia</td><td>1,239</td><td>0.8%</td><td>NA</td><td>Kansas**</td><td>NA</td><td>NA</td></tr>
<tr><td>6</td><td>Wisconsin</td><td>5,716</td><td>3.8%</td><td>NA</td><td>New Hampshire**</td><td>NA</td><td>NA</td></tr>
<tr><td>43</td><td>Wyoming</td><td>263</td><td>0.2%</td><td>NA</td><td>Vermont**</td><td>NA</td><td>NA</td></tr>
<tr><td></td><td></td><td></td><td></td><td></td><td>District of Columbia**</td><td>NA</td><td>NA</td></tr>
</table>

Source: Federal Bureau of Investigation
   "Crime in the United States 1997" (Uniform Crime Reports, November 22, 1998)
*By law enforcement agencies submitting complete reports to the F.B.I. for 12 months in 1997. The F.B.I. estimates
218,900 reported and unreported arrests for weapons violations occurred in 1997. Weapons violations include
illegal carrying and possession. See important note at beginning of this chapter.
**Not available.

Reported Arrest Rate for Weapons Violations in 1997

National Rate = 83.2 Reported Arrests per 100,000 Population*

ALPHA ORDER

RANK	STATE	RATE
33	Alabama	57.9
11	Alaska	106.6
13	Arizona	98.2
10	Arkansas	110.1
15	California	97.2
17	Colorado	87.9
23	Connecticut	78.3
12	Delaware	100.3
NA	Florida**	NA
2	Georgia	167.7
39	Hawaii	37.5
32	Idaho	59.2
1	Illinois	198.9
34	Indiana	56.3
42	Iowa	26.6
NA	Kansas**	NA
5	Kentucky	137.8
19	Louisiana	86.3
41	Maine	30.4
14	Maryland	97.5
43	Massachusetts	21.4
22	Michigan	79.5
40	Minnesota	36.4
26	Mississippi	73.3
7	Missouri	135.8
46	Montana	6.7
18	Nebraska	86.9
6	Nevada	137.2
NA	New Hampshire**	NA
28	New Jersey	73.1
31	New Mexico	64.7
37	New York	46.6
8	North Carolina	113.4
45	North Dakota	17.3
30	Ohio	68.2
21	Oklahoma	82.8
25	Oregon	76.9
44	Pennsylvania	20.3
36	Rhode Island	47.5
20	South Carolina	83.3
38	South Dakota	39.1
4	Tennessee	142.3
26	Texas	73.3
24	Utah	78.0
NA	Vermont**	NA
9	Virginia	110.7
16	Washington	89.0
29	West Virginia	71.1
3	Wisconsin	145.6
35	Wyoming	56.1

RANK ORDER

RANK	STATE	RATE
1	Illinois	198.9
2	Georgia	167.7
3	Wisconsin	145.6
4	Tennessee	142.3
5	Kentucky	137.8
6	Nevada	137.2
7	Missouri	135.8
8	North Carolina	113.4
9	Virginia	110.7
10	Arkansas	110.1
11	Alaska	106.6
12	Delaware	100.3
13	Arizona	98.2
14	Maryland	97.5
15	California	97.2
16	Washington	89.0
17	Colorado	87.9
18	Nebraska	86.9
19	Louisiana	86.3
20	South Carolina	83.3
21	Oklahoma	82.8
22	Michigan	79.5
23	Connecticut	78.3
24	Utah	78.0
25	Oregon	76.9
26	Mississippi	73.3
26	Texas	73.3
28	New Jersey	73.1
29	West Virginia	71.1
30	Ohio	68.2
31	New Mexico	64.7
32	Idaho	59.2
33	Alabama	57.9
34	Indiana	56.3
35	Wyoming	56.1
36	Rhode Island	47.5
37	New York	46.6
38	South Dakota	39.1
39	Hawaii	37.5
40	Minnesota	36.4
41	Maine	30.4
42	Iowa	26.6
43	Massachusetts	21.4
44	Pennsylvania	20.3
45	North Dakota	17.3
46	Montana	6.7
NA	Florida**	NA
NA	Kansas**	NA
NA	New Hampshire**	NA
NA	Vermont**	NA
	District of Columbia**	NA

Source: Morgan Quitno Press using data from Federal Bureau of Investigation
  "Crime in the United States 1997" (Uniform Crime Reports, November 22, 1998)
*By law enforcement agencies submitting complete reports to the F.B.I. for 12 months in 1997. These rates based on population estimates for areas under the jurisdiction of those agencies reporting. Arrest rate based on the F.B.I. estimate of reported and unreported arrests for weapons violations is 81.8 arrests per 100,000 population. See important note at beginning of this chapter. **Not available.

Reported Arrests for Driving Under the Influence in 1997

National Total = 986,339 Reported Arrests*

ALPHA ORDER

RANK	STATE	ARRESTS	% of USA
16	Alabama	20,290	2.1%
43	Alaska	2,198	0.2%
9	Arizona	28,046	2.8%
18	Arkansas	17,253	1.7%
1	California	190,691	19.3%
19	Colorado	16,393	1.7%
29	Connecticut	10,595	1.1%
46	Delaware	201	0.0%
NA	Florida**	NA	NA
21	Georgia	15,172	1.5%
37	Hawaii	5,145	0.5%
30	Idaho	10,103	1.0%
36	Illinois	5,244	0.5%
22	Indiana	15,124	1.5%
28	Iowa	11,683	1.2%
NA	Kansas**	NA	NA
40	Kentucky	3,787	0.4%
26	Louisiana	13,559	1.4%
34	Maine	7,127	0.7%
13	Maryland	23,695	2.4%
20	Massachusetts	15,297	1.6%
4	Michigan	45,084	4.6%
6	Minnesota	39,274	4.0%
33	Mississippi	8,885	0.9%
17	Missouri	18,360	1.9%
45	Montana	922	0.1%
27	Nebraska	12,866	1.3%
38	Nevada	4,553	0.5%
NA	New Hampshire**	NA	NA
11	New Jersey	24,728	2.5%
32	New Mexico	9,338	0.9%
5	New York	39,428	4.0%
3	North Carolina	66,651	6.8%
41	North Dakota	3,384	0.3%
12	Ohio	24,488	2.5%
15	Oklahoma	20,390	2.1%
24	Oregon	14,230	1.4%
14	Pennsylvania	20,712	2.1%
44	Rhode Island	2,083	0.2%
23	South Carolina	14,439	1.5%
42	South Dakota	3,011	0.3%
25	Tennessee	14,174	1.4%
2	Texas	81,583	8.3%
35	Utah	5,871	0.6%
NA	Vermont**	NA	NA
7	Virginia	30,861	3.1%
8	Washington	30,680	3.1%
31	West Virginia	9,365	0.9%
10	Wisconsin	25,193	2.6%
39	Wyoming	4,183	0.4%

RANK ORDER

RANK	STATE	ARRESTS	% of USA
1	California	190,691	19.3%
2	Texas	81,583	8.3%
3	North Carolina	66,651	6.8%
4	Michigan	45,084	4.6%
5	New York	39,428	4.0%
6	Minnesota	39,274	4.0%
7	Virginia	30,861	3.1%
8	Washington	30,680	3.1%
9	Arizona	28,046	2.8%
10	Wisconsin	25,193	2.6%
11	New Jersey	24,728	2.5%
12	Ohio	24,488	2.5%
13	Maryland	23,695	2.4%
14	Pennsylvania	20,712	2.1%
15	Oklahoma	20,390	2.1%
16	Alabama	20,290	2.1%
17	Missouri	18,360	1.9%
18	Arkansas	17,253	1.7%
19	Colorado	16,393	1.7%
20	Massachusetts	15,297	1.6%
21	Georgia	15,172	1.5%
22	Indiana	15,124	1.5%
23	South Carolina	14,439	1.5%
24	Oregon	14,230	1.4%
25	Tennessee	14,174	1.4%
26	Louisiana	13,559	1.4%
27	Nebraska	12,866	1.3%
28	Iowa	11,683	1.2%
29	Connecticut	10,595	1.1%
30	Idaho	10,103	1.0%
31	West Virginia	9,365	0.9%
32	New Mexico	9,338	0.9%
33	Mississippi	8,885	0.9%
34	Maine	7,127	0.7%
35	Utah	5,871	0.6%
36	Illinois	5,244	0.5%
37	Hawaii	5,145	0.5%
38	Nevada	4,553	0.5%
39	Wyoming	4,183	0.4%
40	Kentucky	3,787	0.4%
41	North Dakota	3,384	0.3%
42	South Dakota	3,011	0.3%
43	Alaska	2,198	0.2%
44	Rhode Island	2,083	0.2%
45	Montana	922	0.1%
46	Delaware	201	0.0%
NA	Florida**	NA	NA
NA	Kansas**	NA	NA
NA	New Hampshire**	NA	NA
NA	Vermont**	NA	NA
	District of Columbia**	NA	NA

Source: Federal Bureau of Investigation
   "Crime in the United States 1997" (Uniform Crime Reports, November 22, 1998)
*By law enforcement agencies submitting complete reports to the F.B.I. for 12 months in 1997. The F.B.I. estimates 1,477,300 reported and unreported arrests for driving under the influence occurred in 1997. Includes driving any vehicle while drunk or under the influence of liquor or narcotics. See important note at beginning of this chapter.
**Not available.

Reported Arrest Rate for Driving Under the Influence in 1997

National Rate = 538.3 Reported Arrests per 100,000 Population*

ALPHA ORDER

RANK	STATE	RATE
27	Alabama	500.0
9	Alaska	811.1
12	Arizona	727.1
11	Arkansas	768.2
19	California	599.4
18	Colorado	602.5
38	Connecticut	382.6
46	Delaware	67.2
NA	Florida**	NA
17	Georgia	608.3
33	Hawaii	449.0
6	Idaho	855.5
45	Illinois	189.6
32	Indiana	455.4
28	Iowa	496.7
NA	Kansas**	NA
25	Kentucky	507.6
36	Louisiana	396.6
16	Maine	608.6
31	Maryland	465.6
42	Massachusetts	300.6
23	Michigan	568.5
7	Minnesota	839.0
5	Mississippi	878.8
22	Missouri	570.2
43	Montana	267.2
8	Nebraska	822.6
20	Nevada	592.8
NA	New Hampshire**	NA
41	New Jersey	319.4
10	New Mexico	798.1
29	New York	470.1
1	North Carolina	910.2
21	North Dakota	584.5
35	Ohio	398.2
15	Oklahoma	615.1
26	Oregon	504.4
40	Pennsylvania	367.0
44	Rhode Island	211.0
37	South Carolina	386.9
3	South Dakota	898.8
14	Tennessee	631.9
34	Texas	433.8
39	Utah	380.5
NA	Vermont**	NA
30	Virginia	467.7
2	Washington	901.6
24	West Virginia	537.6
13	Wisconsin	641.9
4	Wyoming	891.9

RANK ORDER

RANK	STATE	RATE
1	North Carolina	910.2
2	Washington	901.6
3	South Dakota	898.8
4	Wyoming	891.9
5	Mississippi	878.8
6	Idaho	855.5
7	Minnesota	839.0
8	Nebraska	822.6
9	Alaska	811.1
10	New Mexico	798.1
11	Arkansas	768.2
12	Arizona	727.1
13	Wisconsin	641.9
14	Tennessee	631.9
15	Oklahoma	615.1
16	Maine	608.6
17	Georgia	608.3
18	Colorado	602.5
19	California	599.4
20	Nevada	592.8
21	North Dakota	584.5
22	Missouri	570.2
23	Michigan	568.5
24	West Virginia	537.6
25	Kentucky	507.6
26	Oregon	504.4
27	Alabama	500.0
28	Iowa	496.7
29	New York	470.1
30	Virginia	467.7
31	Maryland	465.6
32	Indiana	455.4
33	Hawaii	449.0
34	Texas	433.8
35	Ohio	398.2
36	Louisiana	396.6
37	South Carolina	386.9
38	Connecticut	382.6
39	Utah	380.5
40	Pennsylvania	367.0
41	New Jersey	319.4
42	Massachusetts	300.6
43	Montana	267.2
44	Rhode Island	211.0
45	Illinois	189.6
46	Delaware	67.2
NA	Florida**	NA
NA	Kansas**	NA
NA	New Hampshire**	NA
NA	Vermont**	NA
	District of Columbia**	NA

Source: Morgan Quitno Press using data from Federal Bureau of Investigation
"Crime in the United States 1997" (Uniform Crime Reports, November 22, 1998)
*By law enforcement agencies submitting complete reports to the F.B.I. for 12 months in 1997. These rates based on population estimates for areas under the jurisdiction of those agencies reporting. Arrest rate based on the F.B.I. estimate of reported and unreported arrests for driving under the influence is 552.0 arrests per 100,000 population. See important note at beginning of this chapter. **Not available.

Reported Arrests for Drug Abuse Violations in 1997

National Total = 1,102,335 Reported Arrests*

ALPHA ORDER

RANK	STATE	ARRESTS	% of USA
21	Alabama	15,474	1.4%
45	Alaska	1,095	0.1%
11	Arizona	25,222	2.3%
28	Arkansas	11,857	1.1%
1	California	276,092	25.0%
25	Colorado	13,024	1.2%
17	Connecticut	20,642	1.9%
43	Delaware	1,459	0.1%
NA	Florida**	NA	NA
15	Georgia	23,051	2.1%
39	Hawaii	3,942	0.4%
36	Idaho	4,500	0.4%
4	Illinois	54,534	4.9%
27	Indiana	12,501	1.1%
30	Iowa	8,067	0.7%
NA	Kansas**	NA	NA
33	Kentucky	7,112	0.6%
13	Louisiana	23,597	2.1%
38	Maine	4,049	0.4%
6	Maryland	40,026	3.6%
14	Massachusetts	23,133	2.1%
8	Michigan	31,813	2.9%
24	Minnesota	14,129	1.3%
32	Mississippi	7,243	0.7%
12	Missouri	25,020	2.3%
44	Montana	1,102	0.1%
29	Nebraska	9,097	0.8%
35	Nevada	5,093	0.5%
NA	New Hampshire**	NA	NA
3	New Jersey	60,276	5.5%
34	New Mexico	5,543	0.5%
5	New York	41,504	3.8%
7	North Carolina	39,758	3.6%
46	North Dakota	926	0.1%
9	Ohio	30,421	2.8%
20	Oklahoma	17,194	1.6%
22	Oregon	15,361	1.4%
26	Pennsylvania	12,624	1.1%
37	Rhode Island	4,203	0.4%
16	South Carolina	22,516	2.0%
42	South Dakota	1,470	0.1%
23	Tennessee	14,522	1.3%
2	Texas	95,266	8.6%
31	Utah	7,780	0.7%
NA	Vermont**	NA	NA
10	Virginia	29,178	2.6%
18	Washington	17,924	1.6%
40	West Virginia	3,764	0.3%
19	Wisconsin	17,345	1.6%
41	Wyoming	1,886	0.2%

RANK ORDER

RANK	STATE	ARRESTS	% of USA
1	California	276,092	25.0%
2	Texas	95,266	8.6%
3	New Jersey	60,276	5.5%
4	Illinois	54,534	4.9%
5	New York	41,504	3.8%
6	Maryland	40,026	3.6%
7	North Carolina	39,758	3.6%
8	Michigan	31,813	2.9%
9	Ohio	30,421	2.8%
10	Virginia	29,178	2.6%
11	Arizona	25,222	2.3%
12	Missouri	25,020	2.3%
13	Louisiana	23,597	2.1%
14	Massachusetts	23,133	2.1%
15	Georgia	23,051	2.1%
16	South Carolina	22,516	2.0%
17	Connecticut	20,642	1.9%
18	Washington	17,924	1.6%
19	Wisconsin	17,345	1.6%
20	Oklahoma	17,194	1.6%
21	Alabama	15,474	1.4%
22	Oregon	15,361	1.4%
23	Tennessee	14,522	1.3%
24	Minnesota	14,129	1.3%
25	Colorado	13,024	1.2%
26	Pennsylvania	12,624	1.1%
27	Indiana	12,501	1.1%
28	Arkansas	11,857	1.1%
29	Nebraska	9,097	0.8%
30	Iowa	8,067	0.7%
31	Utah	7,780	0.7%
32	Mississippi	7,243	0.7%
33	Kentucky	7,112	0.6%
34	New Mexico	5,543	0.5%
35	Nevada	5,093	0.5%
36	Idaho	4,500	0.4%
37	Rhode Island	4,203	0.4%
38	Maine	4,049	0.4%
39	Hawaii	3,942	0.4%
40	West Virginia	3,764	0.3%
41	Wyoming	1,886	0.2%
42	South Dakota	1,470	0.1%
43	Delaware	1,459	0.1%
44	Montana	1,102	0.1%
45	Alaska	1,095	0.1%
46	North Dakota	926	0.1%
NA	Florida**	NA	NA
NA	Kansas**	NA	NA
NA	New Hampshire**	NA	NA
NA	Vermont**	NA	NA
	District of Columbia**	NA	NA

Source: Federal Bureau of Investigation
    "Crime in the United States 1997" (Uniform Crime Reports, November 22, 1998)
*By law enforcement agencies submitting complete reports to the F.B.I. for 12 months in 1997. The F.B.I. estimates 1,583,600 reported and unreported arrests for drug abuse violations occurred in 1997. Includes offenses relating to possession, sale, use, growing and manufacturing of narcotic drugs. See important note at beginning of this chapter.
**Not available.

Reported Arrest Rate for Drug Abuse Violations in 1997

National Rate = 601.6 Reported Arrests per 100,000 Population*

ALPHA ORDER

RANK	STATE	RATE
36	Alabama	381.3
33	Alaska	404.1
12	Arizona	653.9
18	Arkansas	527.9
4	California	867.9
26	Colorado	478.6
8	Connecticut	745.5
25	Delaware	488.0
NA	Florida**	NA
3	Georgia	924.3
40	Hawaii	344.0
37	Idaho	381.0
1	Illinois	1,971.6
38	Indiana	376.4
41	Iowa	343.0
NA	Kansas**	NA
2	Kentucky	953.4
10	Louisiana	690.2
39	Maine	345.8
5	Maryland	786.5
28	Massachusetts	454.7
35	Michigan	401.2
43	Minnesota	301.8
9	Mississippi	716.4
7	Missouri	777.0
42	Montana	319.4
15	Nebraska	581.6
11	Nevada	663.2
NA	New Hampshire**	NA
6	New Jersey	778.7
27	New Mexico	473.8
23	New York	494.9
17	North Carolina	542.9
46	North Dakota	159.9
24	Ohio	494.7
20	Oklahoma	518.7
16	Oregon	544.5
44	Pennsylvania	223.7
32	Rhode Island	425.8
14	South Carolina	603.3
31	South Dakota	438.8
13	Tennessee	647.4
21	Texas	506.6
22	Utah	504.2
NA	Vermont**	NA
29	Virginia	442.2
19	Washington	526.7
45	West Virginia	216.1
30	Wisconsin	441.9
34	Wyoming	402.1

RANK ORDER

RANK	STATE	RATE
1	Illinois	1,971.6
2	Kentucky	953.4
3	Georgia	924.3
4	California	867.9
5	Maryland	786.5
6	New Jersey	778.7
7	Missouri	777.0
8	Connecticut	745.5
9	Mississippi	716.4
10	Louisiana	690.2
11	Nevada	663.2
12	Arizona	653.9
13	Tennessee	647.4
14	South Carolina	603.3
15	Nebraska	581.6
16	Oregon	544.5
17	North Carolina	542.9
18	Arkansas	527.9
19	Washington	526.7
20	Oklahoma	518.7
21	Texas	506.6
22	Utah	504.2
23	New York	494.9
24	Ohio	494.7
25	Delaware	488.0
26	Colorado	478.6
27	New Mexico	473.8
28	Massachusetts	454.7
29	Virginia	442.2
30	Wisconsin	441.9
31	South Dakota	438.8
32	Rhode Island	425.8
33	Alaska	404.1
34	Wyoming	402.1
35	Michigan	401.2
36	Alabama	381.3
37	Idaho	381.0
38	Indiana	376.4
39	Maine	345.8
40	Hawaii	344.0
41	Iowa	343.0
42	Montana	319.4
43	Minnesota	301.8
44	Pennsylvania	223.7
45	West Virginia	216.1
46	North Dakota	159.9
NA	Florida**	NA
NA	Kansas**	NA
NA	New Hampshire**	NA
NA	Vermont**	NA
	District of Columbia**	NA

Source: Morgan Quitno Press using data from Federal Bureau of Investigation
   "Crime in the United States 1997" (Uniform Crime Reports, November 22, 1998)
*By law enforcement agencies submitting complete reports to the F.B.I. for 12 months in 1997. These rates based on population estimates for areas under the jurisdiction of those agencies reporting. Arrest rate based on the F.B.I. estimate of reported and unreported arrests for drug abuse violations is 591.7 arrests per 100,000 population. See important note at beginning of this chapter. **Not available.

Reported Arrests for Sex Offenses in 1997

National Total = 70,237 Reported Arrests*

ALPHA ORDER

RANK	STATE	ARRESTS	% of USA
30	Alabama	448	0.6%
39	Alaska	249	0.4%
10	Arizona	2,047	2.9%
29	Arkansas	535	0.8%
1	California	17,215	24.5%
20	Colorado	1,010	1.4%
26	Connecticut	826	1.2%
41	Delaware	203	0.3%
NA	Florida**	NA	NA
6	Georgia	2,479	3.5%
33	Hawaii	379	0.5%
34	Idaho	326	0.5%
11	Illinois	1,966	2.8%
19	Indiana	1,013	1.4%
38	Iowa	270	0.4%
NA	Kansas**	NA	NA
36	Kentucky	282	0.4%
17	Louisiana	1,228	1.7%
37	Maine	280	0.4%
15	Maryland	1,567	2.2%
22	Massachusetts	922	1.3%
12	Michigan	1,907	2.7%
23	Minnesota	901	1.3%
31	Mississippi	422	0.6%
7	Missouri	2,395	3.4%
46	Montana	56	0.1%
27	Nebraska	764	1.1%
32	Nevada	418	0.6%
NA	New Hampshire**	NA	NA
9	New Jersey	2,144	3.1%
43	New Mexico	98	0.1%
3	New York	4,584	6.5%
5	North Carolina	2,681	3.8%
44	North Dakota	94	0.1%
13	Ohio	1,752	2.5%
21	Oklahoma	950	1.4%
18	Oregon	1,183	1.7%
16	Pennsylvania	1,524	2.2%
40	Rhode Island	227	0.3%
25	South Carolina	849	1.2%
45	South Dakota	85	0.1%
28	Tennessee	564	0.8%
2	Texas	4,895	7.0%
24	Utah	858	1.2%
NA	Vermont**	NA	NA
8	Virginia	2,390	3.4%
14	Washington	1,623	2.3%
35	West Virginia	310	0.4%
4	Wisconsin	3,178	4.5%
42	Wyoming	140	0.2%

RANK ORDER

RANK	STATE	ARRESTS	% of USA
1	California	17,215	24.5%
2	Texas	4,895	7.0%
3	New York	4,584	6.5%
4	Wisconsin	3,178	4.5%
5	North Carolina	2,681	3.8%
6	Georgia	2,479	3.5%
7	Missouri	2,395	3.4%
8	Virginia	2,390	3.4%
9	New Jersey	2,144	3.1%
10	Arizona	2,047	2.9%
11	Illinois	1,966	2.8%
12	Michigan	1,907	2.7%
13	Ohio	1,752	2.5%
14	Washington	1,623	2.3%
15	Maryland	1,567	2.2%
16	Pennsylvania	1,524	2.2%
17	Louisiana	1,228	1.7%
18	Oregon	1,183	1.7%
19	Indiana	1,013	1.4%
20	Colorado	1,010	1.4%
21	Oklahoma	950	1.4%
22	Massachusetts	922	1.3%
23	Minnesota	901	1.3%
24	Utah	858	1.2%
25	South Carolina	849	1.2%
26	Connecticut	826	1.2%
27	Nebraska	764	1.1%
28	Tennessee	564	0.8%
29	Arkansas	535	0.8%
30	Alabama	448	0.6%
31	Mississippi	422	0.6%
32	Nevada	418	0.6%
33	Hawaii	379	0.5%
34	Idaho	326	0.5%
35	West Virginia	310	0.4%
36	Kentucky	282	0.4%
37	Maine	280	0.4%
38	Iowa	270	0.4%
39	Alaska	249	0.4%
40	Rhode Island	227	0.3%
41	Delaware	203	0.3%
42	Wyoming	140	0.2%
43	New Mexico	98	0.1%
44	North Dakota	94	0.1%
45	South Dakota	85	0.1%
46	Montana	56	0.1%
NA	Florida**	NA	NA
NA	Kansas**	NA	NA
NA	New Hampshire**	NA	NA
NA	Vermont**	NA	NA
	District of Columbia**	NA	NA

Source: Federal Bureau of Investigation
   "Crime in the United States 1997" (Uniform Crime Reports, November 22, 1998)
*By law enforcement agencies submitting complete reports to the F.B.I. for 12 months in 1997. The F.B.I. estimates 101,900 reported and unreported arrests for sex offenses occurred in 1997. Excludes forcible rape, prostitution and commercialized vice. Includes statutory rape and offenses against chastity, common decency, morals and the like. See important note at beginning of this chapter. **Not available.

Reported Arrest Rate for Sex Offenses in 1997

National Rate = 38.3 Reported Arrests per 100,000 Population*

<table>
<tr><td colspan="3">ALPHA ORDER</td><td colspan="3">RANK ORDER</td></tr>
<tr><td>RANK</td><td>STATE</td><td>RATE</td><td>RANK</td><td>STATE</td><td>RATE</td></tr>
<tr><td>45</td><td>Alabama</td><td>11.0</td><td>1</td><td>Georgia</td><td>99.4</td></tr>
<tr><td>2</td><td>Alaska</td><td>91.9</td><td>2</td><td>Alaska</td><td>91.9</td></tr>
<tr><td>11</td><td>Arizona</td><td>53.1</td><td>3</td><td>Wisconsin</td><td>81.0</td></tr>
<tr><td>36</td><td>Arkansas</td><td>23.8</td><td>4</td><td>Missouri</td><td>74.4</td></tr>
<tr><td>10</td><td>California</td><td>54.1</td><td>5</td><td>Illinois</td><td>71.1</td></tr>
<tr><td>17</td><td>Colorado</td><td>37.1</td><td>6</td><td>Delaware</td><td>67.9</td></tr>
<tr><td>25</td><td>Connecticut</td><td>29.8</td><td>7</td><td>Utah</td><td>55.6</td></tr>
<tr><td>6</td><td>Delaware</td><td>67.9</td><td>8</td><td>New York</td><td>54.7</td></tr>
<tr><td>NA</td><td>Florida**</td><td>NA</td><td>9</td><td>Nevada</td><td>54.4</td></tr>
<tr><td>1</td><td>Georgia</td><td>99.4</td><td>10</td><td>California</td><td>54.1</td></tr>
<tr><td>21</td><td>Hawaii</td><td>33.1</td><td>11</td><td>Arizona</td><td>53.1</td></tr>
<tr><td>29</td><td>Idaho</td><td>27.6</td><td>12</td><td>Nebraska</td><td>48.8</td></tr>
<tr><td>5</td><td>Illinois</td><td>71.1</td><td>13</td><td>Washington</td><td>47.7</td></tr>
<tr><td>23</td><td>Indiana</td><td>30.5</td><td>14</td><td>Oregon</td><td>41.9</td></tr>
<tr><td>44</td><td>Iowa</td><td>11.5</td><td>15</td><td>Mississippi</td><td>41.7</td></tr>
<tr><td>NA</td><td>Kansas**</td><td>NA</td><td>16</td><td>Kentucky</td><td>37.8</td></tr>
<tr><td>16</td><td>Kentucky</td><td>37.8</td><td>17</td><td>Colorado</td><td>37.1</td></tr>
<tr><td>20</td><td>Louisiana</td><td>35.9</td><td>18</td><td>North Carolina</td><td>36.6</td></tr>
<tr><td>35</td><td>Maine</td><td>23.9</td><td>19</td><td>Virginia</td><td>36.2</td></tr>
<tr><td>22</td><td>Maryland</td><td>30.8</td><td>20</td><td>Louisiana</td><td>35.9</td></tr>
<tr><td>40</td><td>Massachusetts</td><td>18.1</td><td>21</td><td>Hawaii</td><td>33.1</td></tr>
<tr><td>34</td><td>Michigan</td><td>24.0</td><td>22</td><td>Maryland</td><td>30.8</td></tr>
<tr><td>39</td><td>Minnesota</td><td>19.2</td><td>23</td><td>Indiana</td><td>30.5</td></tr>
<tr><td>15</td><td>Mississippi</td><td>41.7</td><td>24</td><td>Wyoming</td><td>29.9</td></tr>
<tr><td>4</td><td>Missouri</td><td>74.4</td><td>25</td><td>Connecticut</td><td>29.8</td></tr>
<tr><td>42</td><td>Montana</td><td>16.2</td><td>26</td><td>Oklahoma</td><td>28.7</td></tr>
<tr><td>12</td><td>Nebraska</td><td>48.8</td><td>27</td><td>Ohio</td><td>28.5</td></tr>
<tr><td>9</td><td>Nevada</td><td>54.4</td><td>28</td><td>New Jersey</td><td>27.7</td></tr>
<tr><td>NA</td><td>New Hampshire**</td><td>NA</td><td>29</td><td>Idaho</td><td>27.6</td></tr>
<tr><td>28</td><td>New Jersey</td><td>27.7</td><td>30</td><td>Pennsylvania</td><td>27.0</td></tr>
<tr><td>46</td><td>New Mexico</td><td>8.4</td><td>31</td><td>Texas</td><td>26.0</td></tr>
<tr><td>8</td><td>New York</td><td>54.7</td><td>32</td><td>South Dakota</td><td>25.4</td></tr>
<tr><td>18</td><td>North Carolina</td><td>36.6</td><td>33</td><td>Tennessee</td><td>25.1</td></tr>
<tr><td>42</td><td>North Dakota</td><td>16.2</td><td>34</td><td>Michigan</td><td>24.0</td></tr>
<tr><td>27</td><td>Ohio</td><td>28.5</td><td>35</td><td>Maine</td><td>23.9</td></tr>
<tr><td>26</td><td>Oklahoma</td><td>28.7</td><td>36</td><td>Arkansas</td><td>23.8</td></tr>
<tr><td>14</td><td>Oregon</td><td>41.9</td><td>37</td><td>Rhode Island</td><td>23.0</td></tr>
<tr><td>30</td><td>Pennsylvania</td><td>27.0</td><td>38</td><td>South Carolina</td><td>22.7</td></tr>
<tr><td>37</td><td>Rhode Island</td><td>23.0</td><td>39</td><td>Minnesota</td><td>19.2</td></tr>
<tr><td>38</td><td>South Carolina</td><td>22.7</td><td>40</td><td>Massachusetts</td><td>18.1</td></tr>
<tr><td>32</td><td>South Dakota</td><td>25.4</td><td>41</td><td>West Virginia</td><td>17.8</td></tr>
<tr><td>33</td><td>Tennessee</td><td>25.1</td><td>42</td><td>Montana</td><td>16.2</td></tr>
<tr><td>31</td><td>Texas</td><td>26.0</td><td>42</td><td>North Dakota</td><td>16.2</td></tr>
<tr><td>7</td><td>Utah</td><td>55.6</td><td>44</td><td>Iowa</td><td>11.5</td></tr>
<tr><td>NA</td><td>Vermont**</td><td>NA</td><td>45</td><td>Alabama</td><td>11.0</td></tr>
<tr><td>19</td><td>Virginia</td><td>36.2</td><td>46</td><td>New Mexico</td><td>8.4</td></tr>
<tr><td>13</td><td>Washington</td><td>47.7</td><td>NA</td><td>Florida**</td><td>NA</td></tr>
<tr><td>41</td><td>West Virginia</td><td>17.8</td><td>NA</td><td>Kansas**</td><td>NA</td></tr>
<tr><td>3</td><td>Wisconsin</td><td>81.0</td><td>NA</td><td>New Hampshire**</td><td>NA</td></tr>
<tr><td>24</td><td>Wyoming</td><td>29.9</td><td>NA</td><td>Vermont**</td><td>NA</td></tr>
<tr><td></td><td></td><td></td><td></td><td>District of Columbia**</td><td>NA</td></tr>
</table>

Source: Morgan Quitno Press using data from Federal Bureau of Investigation
"Crime in the United States 1997" (Uniform Crime Reports, November 22, 1998)
*By law enforcement agencies submitting complete reports to the F.B.I. for 12 months in 1997. These rates based on population estimates for areas under the jurisdiction of those agencies reporting. Arrest rate based on the F.B.I. estimate of reported and unreported arrests for sex offenses is 38.1 arrests per 100,000 population. See important note at beginning of this chapter. **Not available.

Reported Arrests for Prostitution and Commercialized Vice in 1997

National Total = 72,385 Reported Arrests*

<table>
<tr><td colspan="4">ALPHA ORDER</td><td colspan="4">RANK ORDER</td></tr>
<tr><td>RANK</td><td>STATE</td><td>ARRESTS</td><td>% of USA</td><td>RANK</td><td>STATE</td><td>ARRESTS</td><td>% of USA</td></tr>
<tr><td>32</td><td>Alabama</td><td>286</td><td>0.4%</td><td>1</td><td>California</td><td>18,133</td><td>25.1%</td></tr>
<tr><td>42</td><td>Alaska</td><td>2</td><td>0.0%</td><td>2</td><td>Illinois</td><td>7,745</td><td>10.7%</td></tr>
<tr><td>11</td><td>Arizona</td><td>2,224</td><td>3.1%</td><td>3</td><td>Texas</td><td>5,624</td><td>7.8%</td></tr>
<tr><td>35</td><td>Arkansas</td><td>165</td><td>0.2%</td><td>4</td><td>Georgia</td><td>3,349</td><td>4.6%</td></tr>
<tr><td>1</td><td>California</td><td>18,133</td><td>25.1%</td><td>5</td><td>Michigan</td><td>3,290</td><td>4.5%</td></tr>
<tr><td>16</td><td>Colorado</td><td>1,117</td><td>1.5%</td><td>6</td><td>New Jersey</td><td>3,024</td><td>4.2%</td></tr>
<tr><td>20</td><td>Connecticut</td><td>991</td><td>1.4%</td><td>7</td><td>Ohio</td><td>2,584</td><td>3.6%</td></tr>
<tr><td>38</td><td>Delaware</td><td>89</td><td>0.1%</td><td>8</td><td>Maryland</td><td>2,537</td><td>3.5%</td></tr>
<tr><td>NA</td><td>Florida**</td><td>NA</td><td>NA</td><td>9</td><td>New York</td><td>2,508</td><td>3.5%</td></tr>
<tr><td>4</td><td>Georgia</td><td>3,349</td><td>4.6%</td><td>10</td><td>Massachusetts</td><td>2,282</td><td>3.2%</td></tr>
<tr><td>28</td><td>Hawaii</td><td>455</td><td>0.6%</td><td>11</td><td>Arizona</td><td>2,224</td><td>3.1%</td></tr>
<tr><td>45</td><td>Idaho</td><td>0</td><td>0.0%</td><td>12</td><td>Wisconsin</td><td>1,898</td><td>2.6%</td></tr>
<tr><td>2</td><td>Illinois</td><td>7,745</td><td>10.7%</td><td>13</td><td>Missouri</td><td>1,569</td><td>2.2%</td></tr>
<tr><td>15</td><td>Indiana</td><td>1,524</td><td>2.1%</td><td>14</td><td>Virginia</td><td>1,530</td><td>2.1%</td></tr>
<tr><td>33</td><td>Iowa</td><td>282</td><td>0.4%</td><td>15</td><td>Indiana</td><td>1,524</td><td>2.1%</td></tr>
<tr><td>NA</td><td>Kansas**</td><td>NA</td><td>NA</td><td>16</td><td>Colorado</td><td>1,117</td><td>1.5%</td></tr>
<tr><td>30</td><td>Kentucky</td><td>339</td><td>0.5%</td><td>17</td><td>Pennsylvania</td><td>1,072</td><td>1.5%</td></tr>
<tr><td>26</td><td>Louisiana</td><td>514</td><td>0.7%</td><td>18</td><td>New Mexico</td><td>1,004</td><td>1.4%</td></tr>
<tr><td>37</td><td>Maine</td><td>99</td><td>0.1%</td><td>19</td><td>Tennessee</td><td>994</td><td>1.4%</td></tr>
<tr><td>8</td><td>Maryland</td><td>2,537</td><td>3.5%</td><td>20</td><td>Connecticut</td><td>991</td><td>1.4%</td></tr>
<tr><td>10</td><td>Massachusetts</td><td>2,282</td><td>3.2%</td><td>21</td><td>North Carolina</td><td>802</td><td>1.1%</td></tr>
<tr><td>5</td><td>Michigan</td><td>3,290</td><td>4.5%</td><td>22</td><td>Washington</td><td>768</td><td>1.1%</td></tr>
<tr><td>36</td><td>Minnesota</td><td>100</td><td>0.1%</td><td>23</td><td>Oregon</td><td>743</td><td>1.0%</td></tr>
<tr><td>39</td><td>Mississippi</td><td>57</td><td>0.1%</td><td>24</td><td>South Carolina</td><td>736</td><td>1.0%</td></tr>
<tr><td>13</td><td>Missouri</td><td>1,569</td><td>2.2%</td><td>25</td><td>Oklahoma</td><td>548</td><td>0.8%</td></tr>
<tr><td>42</td><td>Montana</td><td>2</td><td>0.0%</td><td>26</td><td>Louisiana</td><td>514</td><td>0.7%</td></tr>
<tr><td>27</td><td>Nebraska</td><td>456</td><td>0.6%</td><td>27</td><td>Nebraska</td><td>456</td><td>0.6%</td></tr>
<tr><td>40</td><td>Nevada</td><td>53</td><td>0.1%</td><td>28</td><td>Hawaii</td><td>455</td><td>0.6%</td></tr>
<tr><td>NA</td><td>New Hampshire**</td><td>NA</td><td>NA</td><td>29</td><td>Utah</td><td>396</td><td>0.5%</td></tr>
<tr><td>6</td><td>New Jersey</td><td>3,024</td><td>4.2%</td><td>30</td><td>Kentucky</td><td>339</td><td>0.5%</td></tr>
<tr><td>18</td><td>New Mexico</td><td>1,004</td><td>1.4%</td><td>31</td><td>Rhode Island</td><td>316</td><td>0.4%</td></tr>
<tr><td>9</td><td>New York</td><td>2,508</td><td>3.5%</td><td>32</td><td>Alabama</td><td>286</td><td>0.4%</td></tr>
<tr><td>21</td><td>North Carolina</td><td>802</td><td>1.1%</td><td>33</td><td>Iowa</td><td>282</td><td>0.4%</td></tr>
<tr><td>45</td><td>North Dakota</td><td>0</td><td>0.0%</td><td>34</td><td>West Virginia</td><td>168</td><td>0.2%</td></tr>
<tr><td>7</td><td>Ohio</td><td>2,584</td><td>3.6%</td><td>35</td><td>Arkansas</td><td>165</td><td>0.2%</td></tr>
<tr><td>25</td><td>Oklahoma</td><td>548</td><td>0.8%</td><td>36</td><td>Minnesota</td><td>100</td><td>0.1%</td></tr>
<tr><td>23</td><td>Oregon</td><td>743</td><td>1.0%</td><td>37</td><td>Maine</td><td>99</td><td>0.1%</td></tr>
<tr><td>17</td><td>Pennsylvania</td><td>1,072</td><td>1.5%</td><td>38</td><td>Delaware</td><td>89</td><td>0.1%</td></tr>
<tr><td>31</td><td>Rhode Island</td><td>316</td><td>0.4%</td><td>39</td><td>Mississippi</td><td>57</td><td>0.1%</td></tr>
<tr><td>24</td><td>South Carolina</td><td>736</td><td>1.0%</td><td>40</td><td>Nevada</td><td>53</td><td>0.1%</td></tr>
<tr><td>42</td><td>South Dakota</td><td>2</td><td>0.0%</td><td>41</td><td>Wyoming</td><td>8</td><td>0.0%</td></tr>
<tr><td>19</td><td>Tennessee</td><td>994</td><td>1.4%</td><td>42</td><td>Alaska</td><td>2</td><td>0.0%</td></tr>
<tr><td>3</td><td>Texas</td><td>5,624</td><td>7.8%</td><td>42</td><td>Montana</td><td>2</td><td>0.0%</td></tr>
<tr><td>29</td><td>Utah</td><td>396</td><td>0.5%</td><td>42</td><td>South Dakota</td><td>2</td><td>0.0%</td></tr>
<tr><td>NA</td><td>Vermont**</td><td>NA</td><td>NA</td><td>45</td><td>Idaho</td><td>0</td><td>0.0%</td></tr>
<tr><td>14</td><td>Virginia</td><td>1,530</td><td>2.1%</td><td>45</td><td>North Dakota</td><td>0</td><td>0.0%</td></tr>
<tr><td>22</td><td>Washington</td><td>768</td><td>1.1%</td><td>NA</td><td>Florida**</td><td>NA</td><td>NA</td></tr>
<tr><td>34</td><td>West Virginia</td><td>168</td><td>0.2%</td><td>NA</td><td>Kansas**</td><td>NA</td><td>NA</td></tr>
<tr><td>12</td><td>Wisconsin</td><td>1,898</td><td>2.6%</td><td>NA</td><td>New Hampshire**</td><td>NA</td><td>NA</td></tr>
<tr><td>41</td><td>Wyoming</td><td>8</td><td>0.0%</td><td>NA</td><td>Vermont**</td><td>NA</td><td>NA</td></tr>
<tr><td></td><td></td><td></td><td></td><td></td><td>District of Columbia**</td><td>NA</td><td>NA</td></tr>
</table>

Source: Federal Bureau of Investigation
    "Crime in the United States 1997" (Uniform Crime Reports, November 22, 1998)
*By law enforcement agencies submitting complete reports to the F.B.I. for 12 months in 1997. The F.B.I. estimates 101,600 reported and unreported arrests for prostitution and commercialized vice occurred in 1997. Includes keeping a bawdy house, procuring or transporting women for immoral purposes. Attempts are included. See important note at beginning of this chapter. **Not available.

33

Reported Arrest Rate for Prostitution and Commercialized Vice in 1997

National Rate = 39.5 Reported Arrests per 100,000 Population*

ALPHA ORDER

RANK ORDER

RANK	STATE	RATE		RANK	STATE	RATE
37	Alabama	7.0		1	Illinois	280.0
42	Alaska	0.7		2	Georgia	134.3
4	Arizona	57.7		3	New Mexico	85.8
36	Arkansas	7.3		4	Arizona	57.7
5	California	57.0		5	California	57.0
15	Colorado	41.1		6	Maryland	49.9
18	Connecticut	35.8		7	Missouri	48.7
22	Delaware	29.8		8	Wisconsin	48.4
NA	Florida**	NA		9	Indiana	45.9
2	Georgia	134.3		10	Kentucky	45.4
16	Hawaii	39.7		11	Massachusetts	44.9
45	Idaho	0.0		12	Tennessee	44.3
1	Illinois	280.0		13	Ohio	42.0
9	Indiana	45.9		14	Michigan	41.5
32	Iowa	12.0		15	Colorado	41.1
NA	Kansas**	NA		16	Hawaii	39.7
10	Kentucky	45.4		17	New Jersey	39.1
31	Louisiana	15.0		18	Connecticut	35.8
35	Maine	8.5		19	Rhode Island	32.0
6	Maryland	49.9		20	New York	29.9
11	Massachusetts	44.9		20	Texas	29.9
14	Michigan	41.5		22	Delaware	29.8
40	Minnesota	2.1		23	Nebraska	29.2
39	Mississippi	5.6		24	Oregon	26.3
7	Missouri	48.7		25	Utah	25.7
43	Montana	0.6		26	Virginia	23.2
23	Nebraska	29.2		27	Washington	22.6
38	Nevada	6.9		28	South Carolina	19.7
NA	New Hampshire**	NA		29	Pennsylvania	19.0
17	New Jersey	39.1		30	Oklahoma	16.5
3	New Mexico	85.8		31	Louisiana	15.0
20	New York	29.9		32	Iowa	12.0
33	North Carolina	11.0		33	North Carolina	11.0
45	North Dakota	0.0		34	West Virginia	9.6
13	Ohio	42.0		35	Maine	8.5
30	Oklahoma	16.5		36	Arkansas	7.3
24	Oregon	26.3		37	Alabama	7.0
29	Pennsylvania	19.0		38	Nevada	6.9
19	Rhode Island	32.0		39	Mississippi	5.6
28	South Carolina	19.7		40	Minnesota	2.1
43	South Dakota	0.6		41	Wyoming	1.7
12	Tennessee	44.3		42	Alaska	0.7
20	Texas	29.9		43	Montana	0.6
25	Utah	25.7		43	South Dakota	0.6
NA	Vermont**	NA		45	Idaho	0.0
26	Virginia	23.2		45	North Dakota	0.0
27	Washington	22.6		NA	Florida**	NA
34	West Virginia	9.6		NA	Kansas**	NA
8	Wisconsin	48.4		NA	New Hampshire**	NA
41	Wyoming	1.7		NA	Vermont**	NA
					District of Columbia**	NA

Source: Morgan Quitno Press using data from Federal Bureau of Investigation
    "Crime in the United States 1997" (Uniform Crime Reports, November 22, 1998)
*By law enforcement agencies submitting complete reports to the F.B.I. for 12 months in 1997. These rates based
on population estimates for areas under the jurisdiction of those agencies reporting. Arrest rate based on the F.B.I.
estimate of reported and unreported arrests for prostitution and commercialized vice is 38.0 arrests per 100,000
population. See important note at beginning of this chapter. **Not available.

Reported Arrests for Offenses Against Families and Children in 1997

National Total = 104,997 Reported Arrests*

ALPHA ORDER

RANK	STATE	ARRESTS	% of USA
25	Alabama	1,079	1.0%
42	Alaska	278	0.3%
15	Arizona	1,892	1.8%
17	Arkansas	1,577	1.5%
30	California	683	0.7%
28	Colorado	900	0.9%
11	Connecticut	2,431	2.3%
46	Delaware	98	0.1%
NA	Florida**	NA	NA
27	Georgia	919	0.9%
12	Hawaii	2,095	2.0%
35	Idaho	393	0.4%
34	Illinois	496	0.5%
23	Indiana	1,110	1.1%
38	Iowa	325	0.3%
NA	Kansas**	NA	NA
31	Kentucky	625	0.6%
14	Louisiana	1,992	1.9%
44	Maine	175	0.2%
13	Maryland	2,035	1.9%
8	Massachusetts	3,258	3.1%
6	Michigan	3,630	3.5%
32	Minnesota	616	0.6%
20	Mississippi	1,368	1.3%
7	Missouri	3,518	3.4%
44	Montana	175	0.2%
16	Nebraska	1,578	1.5%
26	Nevada	949	0.9%
NA	New Hampshire**	NA	NA
2	New Jersey	16,712	15.9%
24	New Mexico	1,096	1.0%
9	New York	2,834	2.7%
3	North Carolina	6,602	6.3%
39	North Dakota	310	0.3%
1	Ohio	23,116	22.0%
21	Oklahoma	1,289	1.2%
35	Oregon	393	0.4%
29	Pennsylvania	790	0.8%
33	Rhode Island	553	0.5%
18	South Carolina	1,500	1.4%
41	South Dakota	283	0.3%
19	Tennessee	1,489	1.4%
4	Texas	4,729	4.5%
22	Utah	1,130	1.1%
NA	Vermont**	NA	NA
10	Virginia	2,735	2.6%
37	Washington	338	0.3%
40	West Virginia	295	0.3%
5	Wisconsin	4,372	4.2%
43	Wyoming	236	0.2%

RANK ORDER

RANK	STATE	ARRESTS	% of USA
1	Ohio	23,116	22.0%
2	New Jersey	16,712	15.9%
3	North Carolina	6,602	6.3%
4	Texas	4,729	4.5%
5	Wisconsin	4,372	4.2%
6	Michigan	3,630	3.5%
7	Missouri	3,518	3.4%
8	Massachusetts	3,258	3.1%
9	New York	2,834	2.7%
10	Virginia	2,735	2.6%
11	Connecticut	2,431	2.3%
12	Hawaii	2,095	2.0%
13	Maryland	2,035	1.9%
14	Louisiana	1,992	1.9%
15	Arizona	1,892	1.8%
16	Nebraska	1,578	1.5%
17	Arkansas	1,577	1.5%
18	South Carolina	1,500	1.4%
19	Tennessee	1,489	1.4%
20	Mississippi	1,368	1.3%
21	Oklahoma	1,289	1.2%
22	Utah	1,130	1.1%
23	Indiana	1,110	1.1%
24	New Mexico	1,096	1.0%
25	Alabama	1,079	1.0%
26	Nevada	949	0.9%
27	Georgia	919	0.9%
28	Colorado	900	0.9%
29	Pennsylvania	790	0.8%
30	California	683	0.7%
31	Kentucky	625	0.6%
32	Minnesota	616	0.6%
33	Rhode Island	553	0.5%
34	Illinois	496	0.5%
35	Idaho	393	0.4%
35	Oregon	393	0.4%
37	Washington	338	0.3%
38	Iowa	325	0.3%
39	North Dakota	310	0.3%
40	West Virginia	295	0.3%
41	South Dakota	283	0.3%
42	Alaska	278	0.3%
43	Wyoming	236	0.2%
44	Maine	175	0.2%
44	Montana	175	0.2%
46	Delaware	98	0.1%
NA	Florida**	NA	NA
NA	Kansas**	NA	NA
NA	New Hampshire**	NA	NA
NA	Vermont**	NA	NA
	District of Columbia**	NA	NA

Source: Federal Bureau of Investigation
    "Crime in the United States 1997" (Uniform Crime Reports, November 22, 1998)
*By law enforcement agencies submitting complete reports to the F.B.I. for 12 months in 1997. The F.B.I. estimates
155,800 reported and unreported arrests for offenses against families and children occurred in 1997. Includes
nonsupport, neglect, desertion or abuse of family and children. See important note at beginning of this chapter.
**Not available.

Reported Arrest Rate for Offenses Against Families and Children in 1997

National Rate = 57.3 Reported Arrests per 100,000 Population*

<table>
<tr><td colspan="3">ALPHA ORDER</td><td colspan="3">RANK ORDER</td></tr>
<tr><td>RANK</td><td>STATE</td><td>RATE</td><td>RANK</td><td>STATE</td><td>RATE</td></tr>
<tr><td>36</td><td>Alabama</td><td>26.6</td><td>1</td><td>Ohio</td><td>375.9</td></tr>
<tr><td>8</td><td>Alaska</td><td>102.6</td><td>2</td><td>New Jersey</td><td>215.9</td></tr>
<tr><td>24</td><td>Arizona</td><td>49.1</td><td>3</td><td>Hawaii</td><td>182.8</td></tr>
<tr><td>16</td><td>Arkansas</td><td>70.2</td><td>4</td><td>Mississippi</td><td>135.3</td></tr>
<tr><td>46</td><td>California</td><td>2.1</td><td>5</td><td>Nevada</td><td>123.6</td></tr>
<tr><td>34</td><td>Colorado</td><td>33.1</td><td>6</td><td>Wisconsin</td><td>111.4</td></tr>
<tr><td>12</td><td>Connecticut</td><td>87.8</td><td>7</td><td>Missouri</td><td>109.3</td></tr>
<tr><td>35</td><td>Delaware</td><td>32.8</td><td>8</td><td>Alaska</td><td>102.6</td></tr>
<tr><td>NA</td><td>Florida**</td><td>NA</td><td>9</td><td>Nebraska</td><td>100.9</td></tr>
<tr><td>30</td><td>Georgia</td><td>36.8</td><td>10</td><td>New Mexico</td><td>93.7</td></tr>
<tr><td>3</td><td>Hawaii</td><td>182.8</td><td>11</td><td>North Carolina</td><td>90.2</td></tr>
<tr><td>33</td><td>Idaho</td><td>33.3</td><td>12</td><td>Connecticut</td><td>87.8</td></tr>
<tr><td>38</td><td>Illinois</td><td>17.9</td><td>13</td><td>South Dakota</td><td>84.5</td></tr>
<tr><td>32</td><td>Indiana</td><td>33.4</td><td>14</td><td>Kentucky</td><td>83.8</td></tr>
<tr><td>43</td><td>Iowa</td><td>13.8</td><td>15</td><td>Utah</td><td>73.2</td></tr>
<tr><td>NA</td><td>Kansas**</td><td>NA</td><td>16</td><td>Arkansas</td><td>70.2</td></tr>
<tr><td>14</td><td>Kentucky</td><td>83.8</td><td>17</td><td>Tennessee</td><td>66.4</td></tr>
<tr><td>19</td><td>Louisiana</td><td>58.3</td><td>18</td><td>Massachusetts</td><td>64.0</td></tr>
<tr><td>40</td><td>Maine</td><td>14.9</td><td>19</td><td>Louisiana</td><td>58.3</td></tr>
<tr><td>28</td><td>Maryland</td><td>40.0</td><td>20</td><td>Rhode Island</td><td>56.0</td></tr>
<tr><td>18</td><td>Massachusetts</td><td>64.0</td><td>21</td><td>North Dakota</td><td>53.5</td></tr>
<tr><td>25</td><td>Michigan</td><td>45.8</td><td>22</td><td>Montana</td><td>50.7</td></tr>
<tr><td>44</td><td>Minnesota</td><td>13.2</td><td>23</td><td>Wyoming</td><td>50.3</td></tr>
<tr><td>4</td><td>Mississippi</td><td>135.3</td><td>24</td><td>Arizona</td><td>49.1</td></tr>
<tr><td>7</td><td>Missouri</td><td>109.3</td><td>25</td><td>Michigan</td><td>45.8</td></tr>
<tr><td>22</td><td>Montana</td><td>50.7</td><td>26</td><td>Virginia</td><td>41.4</td></tr>
<tr><td>9</td><td>Nebraska</td><td>100.9</td><td>27</td><td>South Carolina</td><td>40.2</td></tr>
<tr><td>5</td><td>Nevada</td><td>123.6</td><td>28</td><td>Maryland</td><td>40.0</td></tr>
<tr><td>NA</td><td>New Hampshire**</td><td>NA</td><td>29</td><td>Oklahoma</td><td>38.9</td></tr>
<tr><td>2</td><td>New Jersey</td><td>215.9</td><td>30</td><td>Georgia</td><td>36.8</td></tr>
<tr><td>10</td><td>New Mexico</td><td>93.7</td><td>31</td><td>New York</td><td>33.8</td></tr>
<tr><td>31</td><td>New York</td><td>33.8</td><td>32</td><td>Indiana</td><td>33.4</td></tr>
<tr><td>11</td><td>North Carolina</td><td>90.2</td><td>33</td><td>Idaho</td><td>33.3</td></tr>
<tr><td>21</td><td>North Dakota</td><td>53.5</td><td>34</td><td>Colorado</td><td>33.1</td></tr>
<tr><td>1</td><td>Ohio</td><td>375.9</td><td>35</td><td>Delaware</td><td>32.8</td></tr>
<tr><td>29</td><td>Oklahoma</td><td>38.9</td><td>36</td><td>Alabama</td><td>26.6</td></tr>
<tr><td>42</td><td>Oregon</td><td>13.9</td><td>37</td><td>Texas</td><td>25.1</td></tr>
<tr><td>41</td><td>Pennsylvania</td><td>14.0</td><td>38</td><td>Illinois</td><td>17.9</td></tr>
<tr><td>20</td><td>Rhode Island</td><td>56.0</td><td>39</td><td>West Virginia</td><td>16.9</td></tr>
<tr><td>27</td><td>South Carolina</td><td>40.2</td><td>40</td><td>Maine</td><td>14.9</td></tr>
<tr><td>13</td><td>South Dakota</td><td>84.5</td><td>41</td><td>Pennsylvania</td><td>14.0</td></tr>
<tr><td>17</td><td>Tennessee</td><td>66.4</td><td>42</td><td>Oregon</td><td>13.9</td></tr>
<tr><td>37</td><td>Texas</td><td>25.1</td><td>43</td><td>Iowa</td><td>13.8</td></tr>
<tr><td>15</td><td>Utah</td><td>73.2</td><td>44</td><td>Minnesota</td><td>13.2</td></tr>
<tr><td>NA</td><td>Vermont**</td><td>NA</td><td>45</td><td>Washington</td><td>9.9</td></tr>
<tr><td>26</td><td>Virginia</td><td>41.4</td><td>46</td><td>California</td><td>2.1</td></tr>
<tr><td>45</td><td>Washington</td><td>9.9</td><td>NA</td><td>Florida**</td><td>NA</td></tr>
<tr><td>39</td><td>West Virginia</td><td>16.9</td><td>NA</td><td>Kansas**</td><td>NA</td></tr>
<tr><td>6</td><td>Wisconsin</td><td>111.4</td><td>NA</td><td>New Hampshire**</td><td>NA</td></tr>
<tr><td>23</td><td>Wyoming</td><td>50.3</td><td>NA</td><td>Vermont**</td><td>NA</td></tr>
<tr><td></td><td></td><td></td><td></td><td>District of Columbia**</td><td>NA</td></tr>
</table>

*Source: Morgan Quitno Press using data from Federal Bureau of Investigation
"Crime in the United States 1997" (Uniform Crime Reports, November 22, 1998)*
*By law enforcement agencies submitting complete reports to the F.B.I. for 12 months in 1997. These rates based on population estimates for areas under the jurisdiction of those agencies reporting. Arrest rate based on the F.B.I. estimate of reported and unreported arrests for offenses against families and children is 58.2 arrests per 100,000 population. See important note at beginning of this chapter. **Not available.*

Percent of Crimes Cleared in 1996

National Percent = 21.7% Cleared*

ALPHA ORDER				RANK ORDER		
RANK	STATE	PERCENT		RANK	STATE	PERCENT
NA	Alabama**	NA		1	South Dakota	31.8
4	Alaska	28.4		2	Wyoming	29.2
41	Arizona	18.5		3	Delaware	28.7
7	Arkansas	27.5		4	Alaska	28.4
31	California	20.6		5	Nebraska	28.1
20	Colorado	22.8		6	Wisconsin	27.7
35	Connecticut	20.1		7	Arkansas	27.5
3	Delaware	28.7		8	Maine	27.4
NA	Florida**	NA		9	Idaho	26.2
28	Georgia	21.9		10	North Dakota	25.7
43	Hawaii	15.8		11	Kentucky	25.2
9	Idaho	26.2		11	Virginia	25.2
NA	Illinois**	NA		13	Pennsylvania	24.4
38	Indiana	19.4		14	Nevada	24.2
39	Iowa	18.9		15	Tennessee	24.0
NA	Kansas**	NA		16	Minnesota	23.7
11	Kentucky	25.2		17	New York	23.3
29	Louisiana	21.6		18	Massachusetts	23.1
8	Maine	27.4		18	Missouri	23.1
26	Maryland	22.3		20	Colorado	22.8
18	Massachusetts	23.1		21	North Carolina	22.6
44	Michigan	13.9		21	South Carolina	22.6
16	Minnesota	23.7		21	Texas	22.6
31	Mississippi	20.6		24	Oregon	22.5
18	Missouri	23.1		25	Ohio	22.4
NA	Montana**	NA		26	Maryland	22.3
5	Nebraska	28.1		27	West Virginia	22.1
14	Nevada	24.2		28	Georgia	21.9
40	New Hampshire	18.8		29	Louisiana	21.6
33	New Jersey	20.2		30	Washington	21.1
42	New Mexico	16.6		31	California	20.6
17	New York	23.3		31	Mississippi	20.6
21	North Carolina	22.6		33	New Jersey	20.2
10	North Dakota	25.7		33	Rhode Island	20.2
25	Ohio	22.4		35	Connecticut	20.1
37	Oklahoma	19.5		36	Utah	19.7
24	Oregon	22.5		37	Oklahoma	19.5
13	Pennsylvania	24.4		38	Indiana	19.4
33	Rhode Island	20.2		39	Iowa	18.9
21	South Carolina	22.6		40	New Hampshire	18.8
1	South Dakota	31.8		41	Arizona	18.5
15	Tennessee	24.0		42	New Mexico	16.6
21	Texas	22.6		43	Hawaii	15.8
36	Utah	19.7		44	Michigan	13.9
45	Vermont	10.4		45	Vermont	10.4
11	Virginia	25.2		NA	Alabama**	NA
30	Washington	21.1		NA	Florida**	NA
27	West Virginia	22.1		NA	Illinois**	NA
6	Wisconsin	27.7		NA	Kansas**	NA
2	Wyoming	29.2		NA	Montana**	NA
					District of Columbia	7.9

Source: Federal Bureau of Investigation (unpublished data)
*Includes murder, rape, robbery, aggravated assault, burglary, larceny-theft and motor vehicle theft. A crime is considered cleared when at least one person is arrested, charged and turned over to the court for prosecution. Clearances recorded in 1996 may be for crimes which occurred in prior years. Several crimes may be cleared by the arrest of one person while the arrest of many persons may clear only one crime.
**Not available.

Percent of Violent Crimes Cleared in 1996

National Percent = 47.3% Cleared*

ALPHA ORDER

RANK	STATE	PERCENT
NA	Alabama**	NA
4	Alaska	65.1
42	Arizona	39.1
14	Arkansas	54.5
27	California	47.8
11	Colorado	57.7
30	Connecticut	46.7
8	Delaware	59.7
NA	Florida**	NA
32	Georgia	46.1
41	Hawaii	40.2
6	Idaho	61.5
NA	Illinois**	NA
37	Indiana	43.0
16	Iowa	53.5
NA	Kansas**	NA
24	Kentucky	49.8
38	Louisiana	41.4
5	Maine	63.4
35	Maryland	44.8
23	Massachusetts	50.4
45	Michigan	33.3
7	Minnesota	61.2
43	Mississippi	38.8
27	Missouri	47.8
NA	Montana**	NA
1	Nebraska	71.5
40	Nevada	40.5
33	New Hampshire	45.6
34	New Jersey	45.5
44	New Mexico	34.1
36	New York	43.8
18	North Carolina	52.3
14	North Dakota	54.5
29	Ohio	47.4
20	Oklahoma	51.2
31	Oregon	46.6
26	Pennsylvania	48.6
12	Rhode Island	55.7
17	South Carolina	53.4
2	South Dakota	71.2
19	Tennessee	52.2
22	Texas	50.9
39	Utah	40.9
25	Vermont	49.1
9	Virginia	58.9
21	Washington	51.1
13	West Virginia	55.3
10	Wisconsin	58.5
3	Wyoming	69.2

RANK ORDER

RANK	STATE	PERCENT
1	Nebraska	71.5
2	South Dakota	71.2
3	Wyoming	69.2
4	Alaska	65.1
5	Maine	63.4
6	Idaho	61.5
7	Minnesota	61.2
8	Delaware	59.7
9	Virginia	58.9
10	Wisconsin	58.5
11	Colorado	57.7
12	Rhode Island	55.7
13	West Virginia	55.3
14	Arkansas	54.5
14	North Dakota	54.5
16	Iowa	53.5
17	South Carolina	53.4
18	North Carolina	52.3
19	Tennessee	52.2
20	Oklahoma	51.2
21	Washington	51.1
22	Texas	50.9
23	Massachusetts	50.4
24	Kentucky	49.8
25	Vermont	49.1
26	Pennsylvania	48.6
27	California	47.8
27	Missouri	47.8
29	Ohio	47.4
30	Connecticut	46.7
31	Oregon	46.6
32	Georgia	46.1
33	New Hampshire	45.6
34	New Jersey	45.5
35	Maryland	44.8
36	New York	43.8
37	Indiana	43.0
38	Louisiana	41.4
39	Utah	40.9
40	Nevada	40.5
41	Hawaii	40.2
42	Arizona	39.1
43	Mississippi	38.8
44	New Mexico	34.1
45	Michigan	33.3
NA	Alabama**	NA
NA	Florida**	NA
NA	Illinois**	NA
NA	Kansas**	NA
NA	Montana**	NA

District of Columbia 20.7

Source: Federal Bureau of Investigation (unpublished data)
*Includes murder, rape, robbery and aggravated assault. A crime is considered cleared when at least one person is arrested, charged and turned over to the court for prosecution. Clearances recorded in 1996 may be for crimes which occurred in prior years. Several crimes may be cleared by the arrest of one person while the arrest of many persons may clear only one crime.
**Not available.

Percent of Murders Cleared in 1996

National Percent = 66.7% Cleared*

ALPHA ORDER

RANK	STATE	PERCENT
NA	Alabama**	NA
15	Alaska	76.7
39	Arizona	59.0
9	Arkansas	83.0
38	California	59.9
18	Colorado	74.7
24	Connecticut	72.8
31	Delaware	65.5
NA	Florida**	NA
14	Georgia	77.2
3	Hawaii	87.5
6	Idaho	85.0
NA	Illinois**	NA
20	Indiana	74.4
34	Iowa	63.8
NA	Kansas**	NA
30	Kentucky	66.3
42	Louisiana	49.8
11	Maine	80.0
36	Maryland	60.6
35	Massachusetts	63.7
37	Michigan	60.0
18	Minnesota	74.7
27	Mississippi	70.4
17	Missouri	76.1
NA	Montana**	NA
4	Nebraska	87.2
44	Nevada	44.7
1	New Hampshire	105.6
8	New Jersey	83.1
45	New Mexico	42.5
33	New York	64.8
12	North Carolina	78.6
28	North Dakota	70.0
32	Ohio	65.0
7	Oklahoma	84.8
29	Oregon	68.4
21	Pennsylvania	74.2
40	Rhode Island	52.0
10	South Carolina	80.6
2	South Dakota	100.0
23	Tennessee	73.0
25	Texas	72.4
43	Utah	48.4
41	Vermont	50.0
16	Virginia	76.4
13	Washington	78.4
22	West Virginia	73.9
5	Wisconsin	86.8
26	Wyoming	72.2

RANK ORDER

RANK	STATE	PERCENT
1	New Hampshire	105.6
2	South Dakota	100.0
3	Hawaii	87.5
4	Nebraska	87.2
5	Wisconsin	86.8
6	Idaho	85.0
7	Oklahoma	84.8
8	New Jersey	83.1
9	Arkansas	83.0
10	South Carolina	80.6
11	Maine	80.0
12	North Carolina	78.6
13	Washington	78.4
14	Georgia	77.2
15	Alaska	76.7
16	Virginia	76.4
17	Missouri	76.1
18	Colorado	74.7
18	Minnesota	74.7
20	Indiana	74.4
21	Pennsylvania	74.2
22	West Virginia	73.9
23	Tennessee	73.0
24	Connecticut	72.8
25	Texas	72.4
26	Wyoming	72.2
27	Mississippi	70.4
28	North Dakota	70.0
29	Oregon	68.4
30	Kentucky	66.3
31	Delaware	65.5
32	Ohio	65.0
33	New York	64.8
34	Iowa	63.8
35	Massachusetts	63.7
36	Maryland	60.6
37	Michigan	60.0
38	California	59.9
39	Arizona	59.0
40	Rhode Island	52.0
41	Vermont	50.0
42	Louisiana	49.8
43	Utah	48.4
44	Nevada	44.7
45	New Mexico	42.5
NA	Alabama**	NA
NA	Florida**	NA
NA	Illinois**	NA
NA	Kansas**	NA
NA	Montana**	NA
	District of Columbia	23.9

Source: Federal Bureau of Investigation (unpublished data)
Includes nonnegligent manslaughter. A crime is considered cleared when at least one person is arrested, charged and turned over to the court for prosecution. Clearances recorded in 1996 may be for crimes which occurred in prior years. Several crimes may be cleared by the arrest of one person while the arrest of many persons may clear only one crime.
**Not available.*

Percent of Rapes Cleared in 1996

National Percent = 51.8% Cleared*

ALPHA ORDER

RANK	STATE	PERCENT
NA	Alabama**	NA
29	Alaska	48.1
40	Arizona	32.6
6	Arkansas	62.7
23	California	50.2
21	Colorado	51.7
23	Connecticut	50.2
5	Delaware	64.5
NA	Florida**	NA
13	Georgia	56.9
3	Hawaii	66.3
30	Idaho	46.8
NA	Illinois**	NA
27	Indiana	49.0
37	Iowa	38.4
NA	Kansas**	NA
35	Kentucky	41.5
31	Louisiana	44.9
34	Maine	43.2
12	Maryland	57.3
19	Massachusetts	52.7
39	Michigan	34.7
17	Minnesota	55.4
31	Mississippi	44.9
7	Missouri	61.1
NA	Montana**	NA
4	Nebraska	65.6
45	Nevada	25.1
42	New Hampshire	31.7
20	New Jersey	52.2
44	New Mexico	26.8
15	New York	55.9
10	North Carolina	58.7
28	North Dakota	48.5
21	Ohio	51.7
9	Oklahoma	58.8
33	Oregon	44.0
11	Pennsylvania	58.1
38	Rhode Island	36.4
25	South Carolina	49.5
18	South Dakota	54.0
13	Tennessee	56.9
8	Texas	59.8
43	Utah	31.5
40	Vermont	32.6
2	Virginia	69.5
26	Washington	49.3
36	West Virginia	41.3
1	Wisconsin	74.7
16	Wyoming	55.6

RANK ORDER

RANK	STATE	PERCENT
1	Wisconsin	74.7
2	Virginia	69.5
3	Hawaii	66.3
4	Nebraska	65.6
5	Delaware	64.5
6	Arkansas	62.7
7	Missouri	61.1
8	Texas	59.8
9	Oklahoma	58.8
10	North Carolina	58.7
11	Pennsylvania	58.1
12	Maryland	57.3
13	Georgia	56.9
13	Tennessee	56.9
15	New York	55.9
16	Wyoming	55.6
17	Minnesota	55.4
18	South Dakota	54.0
19	Massachusetts	52.7
20	New Jersey	52.2
21	Colorado	51.7
21	Ohio	51.7
23	California	50.2
23	Connecticut	50.2
25	South Carolina	49.5
26	Washington	49.3
27	Indiana	49.0
28	North Dakota	48.5
29	Alaska	48.1
30	Idaho	46.8
31	Louisiana	44.9
31	Mississippi	44.9
33	Oregon	44.0
34	Maine	43.2
35	Kentucky	41.5
36	West Virginia	41.3
37	Iowa	38.4
38	Rhode Island	36.4
39	Michigan	34.7
40	Arizona	32.6
40	Vermont	32.6
42	New Hampshire	31.7
43	Utah	31.5
44	New Mexico	26.8
45	Nevada	25.1
NA	Alabama**	NA
NA	Florida**	NA
NA	Illinois**	NA
NA	Kansas**	NA
NA	Montana**	NA
	District of Columbia	23.8

Source: Federal Bureau of Investigation (unpublished data)
*Forcible rape including attempts. However, statutory rape without force and other sex offenses are excluded. A crime is considered cleared when at least one person is arrested, charged and turned over to the court for prosecution. Clearances recorded in 1996 may be for crimes which occurred in prior years. Several crimes may be cleared by the arrest of one person while the arrest of many persons may clear only one crime.
**Not available.

Percent of Robberies Cleared in 1996

National Percent = 26.8% Cleared*

<table>
<tr><td colspan="3"><u>ALPHA ORDER</u></td><td colspan="3"><u>RANK ORDER</u></td></tr>
<tr><td>RANK</td><td>STATE</td><td>PERCENT</td><td>RANK</td><td>STATE</td><td>PERCENT</td></tr>
<tr><td>NA</td><td>Alabama**</td><td>NA</td><td>1</td><td>South Dakota</td><td>58.3</td></tr>
<tr><td>40</td><td>Alaska</td><td>22.4</td><td>2</td><td>Maine</td><td>44.7</td></tr>
<tr><td>41</td><td>Arizona</td><td>22.3</td><td>3</td><td>Minnesota</td><td>39.9</td></tr>
<tr><td>9</td><td>Arkansas</td><td>34.4</td><td>4</td><td>North Dakota</td><td>39.7</td></tr>
<tr><td>36</td><td>California</td><td>24.9</td><td>5</td><td>Oklahoma</td><td>38.4</td></tr>
<tr><td>14</td><td>Colorado</td><td>32.7</td><td>6</td><td>Idaho</td><td>38.1</td></tr>
<tr><td>34</td><td>Connecticut</td><td>25.1</td><td>6</td><td>Nebraska</td><td>38.1</td></tr>
<tr><td>21</td><td>Delaware</td><td>28.6</td><td>8</td><td>Virginia</td><td>37.2</td></tr>
<tr><td>NA</td><td>Florida**</td><td>NA</td><td>9</td><td>Arkansas</td><td>34.4</td></tr>
<tr><td>19</td><td>Georgia</td><td>29.0</td><td>10</td><td>Oregon</td><td>33.6</td></tr>
<tr><td>23</td><td>Hawaii</td><td>28.1</td><td>11</td><td>North Carolina</td><td>33.5</td></tr>
<tr><td>6</td><td>Idaho</td><td>38.1</td><td>12</td><td>Wisconsin</td><td>33.4</td></tr>
<tr><td>NA</td><td>Illinois**</td><td>NA</td><td>13</td><td>South Carolina</td><td>33.0</td></tr>
<tr><td>38</td><td>Indiana</td><td>24.8</td><td>14</td><td>Colorado</td><td>32.7</td></tr>
<tr><td>29</td><td>Iowa</td><td>25.5</td><td>15</td><td>New Hampshire</td><td>32.5</td></tr>
<tr><td>NA</td><td>Kansas**</td><td>NA</td><td>16</td><td>Ohio</td><td>31.8</td></tr>
<tr><td>27</td><td>Kentucky</td><td>26.5</td><td>17</td><td>Texas</td><td>30.0</td></tr>
<tr><td>43</td><td>Louisiana</td><td>17.8</td><td>18</td><td>New York</td><td>29.8</td></tr>
<tr><td>2</td><td>Maine</td><td>44.7</td><td>19</td><td>Georgia</td><td>29.0</td></tr>
<tr><td>39</td><td>Maryland</td><td>23.5</td><td>20</td><td>Pennsylvania</td><td>28.8</td></tr>
<tr><td>23</td><td>Massachusetts</td><td>28.1</td><td>21</td><td>Delaware</td><td>28.6</td></tr>
<tr><td>44</td><td>Michigan</td><td>13.3</td><td>21</td><td>Washington</td><td>28.6</td></tr>
<tr><td>3</td><td>Minnesota</td><td>39.9</td><td>23</td><td>Hawaii</td><td>28.1</td></tr>
<tr><td>42</td><td>Mississippi</td><td>21.4</td><td>23</td><td>Massachusetts</td><td>28.1</td></tr>
<tr><td>25</td><td>Missouri</td><td>27.6</td><td>25</td><td>Missouri</td><td>27.6</td></tr>
<tr><td>NA</td><td>Montana**</td><td>NA</td><td>26</td><td>Wyoming</td><td>26.6</td></tr>
<tr><td>6</td><td>Nebraska</td><td>38.1</td><td>27</td><td>Kentucky</td><td>26.5</td></tr>
<tr><td>36</td><td>Nevada</td><td>24.9</td><td>28</td><td>New Jersey</td><td>26.2</td></tr>
<tr><td>15</td><td>New Hampshire</td><td>32.5</td><td>29</td><td>Iowa</td><td>25.5</td></tr>
<tr><td>28</td><td>New Jersey</td><td>26.2</td><td>30</td><td>Rhode Island</td><td>25.2</td></tr>
<tr><td>45</td><td>New Mexico</td><td>13.0</td><td>30</td><td>Tennessee</td><td>25.2</td></tr>
<tr><td>18</td><td>New York</td><td>29.8</td><td>30</td><td>Utah</td><td>25.2</td></tr>
<tr><td>11</td><td>North Carolina</td><td>33.5</td><td>30</td><td>West Virginia</td><td>25.2</td></tr>
<tr><td>4</td><td>North Dakota</td><td>39.7</td><td>34</td><td>Connecticut</td><td>25.1</td></tr>
<tr><td>16</td><td>Ohio</td><td>31.8</td><td>35</td><td>Vermont</td><td>25.0</td></tr>
<tr><td>5</td><td>Oklahoma</td><td>38.4</td><td>36</td><td>California</td><td>24.9</td></tr>
<tr><td>10</td><td>Oregon</td><td>33.6</td><td>36</td><td>Nevada</td><td>24.9</td></tr>
<tr><td>20</td><td>Pennsylvania</td><td>28.8</td><td>38</td><td>Indiana</td><td>24.8</td></tr>
<tr><td>30</td><td>Rhode Island</td><td>25.2</td><td>39</td><td>Maryland</td><td>23.5</td></tr>
<tr><td>13</td><td>South Carolina</td><td>33.0</td><td>40</td><td>Alaska</td><td>22.4</td></tr>
<tr><td>1</td><td>South Dakota</td><td>58.3</td><td>41</td><td>Arizona</td><td>22.3</td></tr>
<tr><td>30</td><td>Tennessee</td><td>25.2</td><td>42</td><td>Mississippi</td><td>21.4</td></tr>
<tr><td>17</td><td>Texas</td><td>30.0</td><td>43</td><td>Louisiana</td><td>17.8</td></tr>
<tr><td>30</td><td>Utah</td><td>25.2</td><td>44</td><td>Michigan</td><td>13.3</td></tr>
<tr><td>35</td><td>Vermont</td><td>25.0</td><td>45</td><td>New Mexico</td><td>13.0</td></tr>
<tr><td>8</td><td>Virginia</td><td>37.2</td><td>NA</td><td>Alabama**</td><td>NA</td></tr>
<tr><td>21</td><td>Washington</td><td>28.6</td><td>NA</td><td>Florida**</td><td>NA</td></tr>
<tr><td>30</td><td>West Virginia</td><td>25.2</td><td>NA</td><td>Illinois**</td><td>NA</td></tr>
<tr><td>12</td><td>Wisconsin</td><td>33.4</td><td>NA</td><td>Kansas**</td><td>NA</td></tr>
<tr><td>26</td><td>Wyoming</td><td>26.6</td><td>NA</td><td>Montana**</td><td>NA</td></tr>
<tr><td></td><td></td><td></td><td></td><td>District of Columbia</td><td>7.3</td></tr>
</table>

Source: Federal Bureau of Investigation (unpublished data)
*Robbery is the taking of anything of value by force or threat of force. Attempts are included. A crime is considered cleared when at least one person is arrested, charged and turned over to the court for prosecution. Clearances recorded in 1996 may be for crimes which occurred in prior years. Several crimes may be cleared by the arrest of one person while the arrest of many persons may clear only one crime.
**Not available.

Percent of Aggravated Assaults Cleared in 1996

National Percent = 57.9% Cleared*

RANK	STATE	PERCENT
NA	Alabama**	NA
3	Alaska	77.3
43	Arizona	46.0
26	Arkansas	59.3
22	California	60.3
11	Colorado	67.2
16	Connecticut	62.8
6	Delaware	73.5
NA	Florida**	NA
34	Georgia	53.7
42	Hawaii	47.0
14	Idaho	65.1
NA	Illinois**	NA
39	Indiana	49.7
20	Iowa	60.9
NA	Kansas**	NA
17	Kentucky	62.2
36	Louisiana	53.0
5	Maine	74.0
21	Maryland	60.7
31	Massachusetts	56.2
44	Michigan	41.7
8	Minnesota	72.3
41	Mississippi	47.6
33	Missouri	55.9
NA	Montana**	NA
2	Nebraska	78.0
35	Nevada	53.4
25	New Hampshire	59.6
18	New Jersey	61.3
45	New Mexico	41.6
32	New York	56.1
27	North Carolina	59.2
23	North Dakota	60.1
24	Ohio	59.8
36	Oklahoma	53.0
38	Oregon	51.7
12	Pennsylvania	66.0
10	Rhode Island	69.1
29	South Carolina	58.0
1	South Dakota	78.7
12	Tennessee	66.0
28	Texas	58.1
40	Utah	47.8
30	Vermont	57.5
9	Virginia	71.1
19	Washington	61.0
15	West Virginia	64.9
7	Wisconsin	73.4
4	Wyoming	75.4

RANK	STATE	PERCENT
1	South Dakota	78.7
2	Nebraska	78.0
3	Alaska	77.3
4	Wyoming	75.4
5	Maine	74.0
6	Delaware	73.5
7	Wisconsin	73.4
8	Minnesota	72.3
9	Virginia	71.1
10	Rhode Island	69.1
11	Colorado	67.2
12	Pennsylvania	66.0
12	Tennessee	66.0
14	Idaho	65.1
15	West Virginia	64.9
16	Connecticut	62.8
17	Kentucky	62.2
18	New Jersey	61.3
19	Washington	61.0
20	Iowa	60.9
21	Maryland	60.7
22	California	60.3
23	North Dakota	60.1
24	Ohio	59.8
25	New Hampshire	59.6
26	Arkansas	59.3
27	North Carolina	59.2
28	Texas	58.1
29	South Carolina	58.0
30	Vermont	57.5
31	Massachusetts	56.2
32	New York	56.1
33	Missouri	55.9
34	Georgia	53.7
35	Nevada	53.4
36	Louisiana	53.0
36	Oklahoma	53.0
38	Oregon	51.7
39	Indiana	49.7
40	Utah	47.8
41	Mississippi	47.6
42	Hawaii	47.0
43	Arizona	46.0
44	Michigan	41.7
45	New Mexico	41.6
NA	Alabama**	NA
NA	Florida**	NA
NA	Illinois**	NA
NA	Kansas**	NA
NA	Montana**	NA

	District of Columbia	34.1

Source: Federal Bureau of Investigation (unpublished data)
*Aggravated assault is an attack for the purpose of inflicting severe bodily injury. A crime is considered cleared when at least one person is arrested, charged and turned over to the court for prosecution. Clearances recorded in 1996 may be for crimes which occurred in prior years. Several crimes may be cleared by the arrest of one person while the arrest of many persons may clear only one crime.
**Not available.

Percent of Property Crimes Cleared in 1996

National Percent = 18.1% Cleared*

ALPHA ORDER				RANK ORDER		
RANK	STATE	PERCENT		RANK	STATE	PERCENT
NA	Alabama**	NA		1	South Dakota	29.2
10	Alaska	22.7		2	Wyoming	26.6
37	Arizona	16.4		3	Maine	26.0
6	Arkansas	24.1		4	Wisconsin	25.5
41	California	15.1		5	North Dakota	24.7
17	Colorado	19.8		6	Arkansas	24.1
33	Connecticut	17.2		7	Delaware	23.7
7	Delaware	23.7		7	Idaho	23.7
NA	Florida**	NA		9	Nebraska	23.3
20	Georgia	19.2		10	Alaska	22.7
42	Hawaii	14.7		11	Virginia	22.0
7	Idaho	23.7		12	Nevada	21.6
NA	Illinois**	NA		13	Minnesota	21.5
37	Indiana	16.4		14	Pennsylvania	20.9
39	Iowa	16.2		15	Kentucky	20.8
NA	Kansas**	NA		16	Oregon	20.3
15	Kentucky	20.8		17	Colorado	19.8
28	Louisiana	18.5		17	Missouri	19.8
3	Maine	26.0		19	Ohio	19.4
30	Maryland	18.2		20	Georgia	19.2
32	Massachusetts	17.5		21	New York	19.0
44	Michigan	11.0		21	North Carolina	19.0
13	Minnesota	21.5		21	Tennessee	19.0
27	Mississippi	18.6		21	West Virginia	19.0
17	Missouri	19.8		25	Texas	18.9
NA	Montana**	NA		26	Washington	18.7
9	Nebraska	23.3		27	Mississippi	18.6
12	Nevada	21.6		28	Louisiana	18.5
31	New Hampshire	17.6		29	Utah	18.4
35	New Jersey	16.6		30	Maryland	18.2
43	New Mexico	14.1		31	New Hampshire	17.6
21	New York	19.0		32	Massachusetts	17.5
21	North Carolina	19.0		33	Connecticut	17.2
5	North Dakota	24.7		34	Rhode Island	16.8
19	Ohio	19.4		35	New Jersey	16.6
40	Oklahoma	15.7		35	South Carolina	16.6
16	Oregon	20.3		37	Arizona	16.4
14	Pennsylvania	20.9		37	Indiana	16.4
34	Rhode Island	16.8		39	Iowa	16.2
35	South Carolina	16.6		40	Oklahoma	15.7
1	South Dakota	29.2		41	California	15.1
21	Tennessee	19.0		42	Hawaii	14.7
25	Texas	18.9		43	New Mexico	14.1
29	Utah	18.4		44	Michigan	11.0
45	Vermont	9.0		45	Vermont	9.0
11	Virginia	22.0		NA	Alabama**	NA
26	Washington	18.7		NA	Florida**	NA
21	West Virginia	19.0		NA	Illinois**	NA
4	Wisconsin	25.5		NA	Kansas**	NA
2	Wyoming	26.6		NA	Montana**	NA
					District of Columbia	4.5

Source: Federal Bureau of Investigation (unpublished data)
*Property crimes are offenses of burglary, larceny-theft and motor vehicle theft. A crime is considered cleared when at least one person is arrested, charged and turned over to the court for prosecution. Clearances recorded in 1996 may be for crimes which occurred in prior years. Several crimes may be cleared by the arrest of one person while the arrest of many persons may clear only one crime.
**Not available.

Percent of Burglaries Cleared in 1996

National Percent = 13.7% Cleared*

ALPHA ORDER				RANK ORDER		
RANK	STATE	PERCENT		RANK	STATE	PERCENT
NA	Alabama**	NA		1	South Dakota	21.0
7	Alaska	18.3		1	Virginia	21.0
42	Arizona	8.2		3	Wyoming	20.3
6	Arkansas	19.2		4	Maine	20.2
29	California	12.9		5	Wisconsin	19.5
33	Colorado	12.2		6	Arkansas	19.2
36	Connecticut	11.4		7	Alaska	18.3
10	Delaware	16.8		8	Nevada	17.4
NA	Florida**	NA		9	Massachusetts	17.0
18	Georgia	14.2		10	Delaware	16.8
40	Hawaii	9.9		11	Kentucky	16.6
20	Idaho	14.0		12	Maryland	16.2
NA	Illinois**	NA		12	North Carolina	16.2
39	Indiana	10.7		14	Pennsylvania	16.1
41	Iowa	8.7		15	Missouri	15.7
NA	Kansas**	NA		15	New York	15.7
11	Kentucky	16.6		17	Ohio	14.9
20	Louisiana	14.0		18	Georgia	14.2
4	Maine	20.2		19	Texas	14.1
12	Maryland	16.2		20	Idaho	14.0
9	Massachusetts	17.0		20	Louisiana	14.0
43	Michigan	7.7		22	North Dakota	13.8
32	Minnesota	12.3		23	Nebraska	13.4
26	Mississippi	13.0		24	New Jersey	13.2
15	Missouri	15.7		24	South Carolina	13.2
NA	Montana**	NA		26	Mississippi	13.0
23	Nebraska	13.4		26	Tennessee	13.0
8	Nevada	17.4		26	West Virginia	13.0
33	New Hampshire	12.2		29	California	12.9
24	New Jersey	13.2		30	Oklahoma	12.5
44	New Mexico	7.3		31	Oregon	12.4
15	New York	15.7		32	Minnesota	12.3
12	North Carolina	16.2		33	Colorado	12.2
22	North Dakota	13.8		33	New Hampshire	12.2
17	Ohio	14.9		33	Rhode Island	12.2
30	Oklahoma	12.5		36	Connecticut	11.4
31	Oregon	12.4		37	Utah	11.3
14	Pennsylvania	16.1		38	Washington	11.0
33	Rhode Island	12.2		39	Indiana	10.7
24	South Carolina	13.2		40	Hawaii	9.9
1	South Dakota	21.0		41	Iowa	8.7
26	Tennessee	13.0		42	Arizona	8.2
19	Texas	14.1		43	Michigan	7.7
37	Utah	11.3		44	New Mexico	7.3
45	Vermont	6.8		45	Vermont	6.8
1	Virginia	21.0		NA	Alabama**	NA
38	Washington	11.0		NA	Florida**	NA
26	West Virginia	13.0		NA	Illinois**	NA
5	Wisconsin	19.5		NA	Kansas**	NA
3	Wyoming	20.3		NA	Montana**	NA
					District of Columbia	5.0

Source: Federal Bureau of Investigation (unpublished data)
Burglary is the unlawful entry of a structure to commit a felony or theft. Attempts are included. A crime is considered cleared when at least one person is arrested, charged and turned over to the court for prosecution. Clearances recorded in 1996 may be for crimes which occurred in prior years. Several crimes may be cleared by the arrest of one person while the arrest of many persons may clear only one crime.
**Not available.*

Percent of Larcenies and Thefts Cleared in 1996

National Percent = 20.2% Cleared*

ALPHA ORDER			RANK ORDER		
RANK	STATE	PERCENT	RANK	STATE	PERCENT
NA	Alabama**	NA	1	South Dakota	30.7
11	Alaska	24.4	2	Maine	27.3
30	Arizona	20.0	2	Wisconsin	27.3
10	Arkansas	25.1	2	Wyoming	27.3
41	California	17.6	5	Delaware	27.2
18	Colorado	21.7	6	Idaho	25.7
28	Connecticut	20.2	6	North Dakota	25.7
5	Delaware	27.2	8	Nebraska	25.2
NA	Florida**	NA	8	Nevada	25.2
29	Georgia	20.1	10	Arkansas	25.1
43	Hawaii	16.3	11	Alaska	24.4
6	Idaho	25.7	12	Pennsylvania	23.3
NA	Illinois**	NA	13	Minnesota	23.1
37	Indiana	18.1	14	Oregon	22.6
37	Iowa	18.1	14	Tennessee	22.6
NA	Kansas**	NA	16	Kentucky	22.0
16	Kentucky	22.0	16	New York	22.0
23	Louisiana	21.0	18	Colorado	21.7
2	Maine	27.3	19	Virginia	21.6
32	Maryland	19.7	20	Washington	21.5
36	Massachusetts	18.4	21	West Virginia	21.3
44	Michigan	12.7	22	Missouri	21.2
13	Minnesota	23.1	23	Louisiana	21.0
23	Mississippi	21.0	23	Mississippi	21.0
22	Missouri	21.2	23	Ohio	21.0
NA	Montana**	NA	26	Texas	20.8
8	Nebraska	25.2	27	New Jersey	20.4
8	Nevada	25.2	28	Connecticut	20.2
35	New Hampshire	18.7	29	Georgia	20.1
27	New Jersey	20.4	30	Arizona	20.0
40	New Mexico	17.8	31	Utah	19.9
16	New York	22.0	32	Maryland	19.7
33	North Carolina	19.5	33	North Carolina	19.5
6	North Dakota	25.7	34	Rhode Island	18.9
23	Ohio	21.0	35	New Hampshire	18.7
42	Oklahoma	16.9	36	Massachusetts	18.4
14	Oregon	22.6	37	Indiana	18.1
12	Pennsylvania	23.3	37	Iowa	18.1
34	Rhode Island	18.9	39	South Carolina	18.0
39	South Carolina	18.0	40	New Mexico	17.8
1	South Dakota	30.7	41	California	17.6
14	Tennessee	22.6	42	Oklahoma	16.9
26	Texas	20.8	43	Hawaii	16.3
31	Utah	19.9	44	Michigan	12.7
45	Vermont	9.5	45	Vermont	9.5
19	Virginia	21.6	NA	Alabama**	NA
20	Washington	21.5	NA	Florida**	NA
21	West Virginia	21.3	NA	Illinois**	NA
2	Wisconsin	27.3	NA	Kansas**	NA
2	Wyoming	27.3	NA	Montana**	NA
				District of Columbia	4.7

Source: Federal Bureau of Investigation (unpublished data)
*Larceny and theft is the unlawful taking of property without use of force, violence or fraud. Attempts are included. Motor vehicle thefts are excluded. A crime is considered cleared when at least one person is arrested, charged and turned over to the court for prosecution. Clearances recorded in 1996 may be for crimes which occurred in prior years. Several crimes may be cleared by the arrest of one person while the arrest of many persons may clear only one crime. **Not available.

Percent of Motor Vehicle Thefts Cleared in 1996

National Percent = 14.0% Cleared*

ALPHA ORDER			RANK ORDER		
RANK	STATE	PERCENT	RANK	STATE	PERCENT
NA	Alabama**	NA	1	Wyoming	40.7
15	Alaska	19.3	2	South Dakota	39.8
38	Arizona	11.1	3	Maine	35.1
5	Arkansas	30.6	4	North Dakota	32.0
41	California	9.5	5	Arkansas	30.6
14	Colorado	21.4	6	Idaho	29.5
37	Connecticut	12.1	7	Virginia	27.9
42	Delaware	9.2	8	Minnesota	27.7
NA	Florida**	NA	9	North Carolina	25.6
13	Georgia	22.2	10	Nebraska	24.3
39	Hawaii	10.9	11	Kentucky	23.7
6	Idaho	29.5	12	Wisconsin	22.7
NA	Illinois**	NA	13	Georgia	22.2
26	Indiana	16.0	14	Colorado	21.4
22	Iowa	17.1	15	Alaska	19.3
NA	Kansas**	NA	16	Ohio	18.5
11	Kentucky	23.7	17	Mississippi	18.3
35	Louisiana	12.8	17	Missouri	18.3
3	Maine	35.1	19	Oregon	17.8
33	Maryland	13.8	20	West Virginia	17.6
30	Massachusetts	14.9	21	Utah	17.3
43	Michigan	8.5	22	Iowa	17.1
8	Minnesota	27.7	23	New Hampshire	16.8
17	Mississippi	18.3	24	Vermont	16.7
17	Missouri	18.3	25	Texas	16.6
NA	Montana**	NA	26	Indiana	16.0
10	Nebraska	24.3	27	Oklahoma	15.9
36	Nevada	12.2	28	Pennsylvania	15.7
23	New Hampshire	16.8	29	South Carolina	15.3
45	New Jersey	5.6	30	Massachusetts	14.9
44	New Mexico	7.2	31	Rhode Island	14.3
40	New York	10.4	32	Tennessee	14.0
9	North Carolina	25.6	33	Maryland	13.8
4	North Dakota	32.0	34	Washington	13.1
16	Ohio	18.5	35	Louisiana	12.8
27	Oklahoma	15.9	36	Nevada	12.2
19	Oregon	17.8	37	Connecticut	12.1
28	Pennsylvania	15.7	38	Arizona	11.1
31	Rhode Island	14.3	39	Hawaii	10.9
29	South Carolina	15.3	40	New York	10.4
2	South Dakota	39.8	41	California	9.5
32	Tennessee	14.0	42	Delaware	9.2
25	Texas	16.6	43	Michigan	8.5
21	Utah	17.3	44	New Mexico	7.2
24	Vermont	16.7	45	New Jersey	5.6
7	Virginia	27.9	NA	Alabama**	NA
34	Washington	13.1	NA	Florida**	NA
20	West Virginia	17.6	NA	Illinois**	NA
12	Wisconsin	22.7	NA	Kansas**	NA
1	Wyoming	40.7	NA	Montana**	NA
				District of Columbia	3.3

Source: Federal Bureau of Investigation (unpublished data)
*Motor vehicle theft includes the theft or attempted theft of a self-propelled vehicle. Excludes motorboats, construction equipment, airplanes and farming equipment. A crime is considered cleared when at least one person is arrested, charged and turned over to the court for prosecution. Clearances recorded in 1996 may be for crimes which occurred in prior years. Several crimes may be cleared by the arrest of one person while the arrest of many persons may clear only one crime. **Not available.

II. CORRECTIONS

II. CORRECTIONS (continued)

Prisoners in State Correctional Institutions: Year End 1997

National Total = 1,131,581 State Prisoners*

ALPHA ORDER

RANK	STATE	PRISONERS	% of USA
16	Alabama	22,290	2.0%
39	Alaska	4,220	0.4%
15	Arizona	23,484	2.1%
29	Arkansas	10,021	0.9%
1	California	157,547	13.9%
26	Colorado	13,461	1.2%
20	Connecticut	18,521	1.6%
34	Delaware	5,435	0.5%
4	Florida	64,565	5.7%
8	Georgia	36,450	3.2%
36	Hawaii	4,949	0.4%
40	Idaho	3,946	0.3%
7	Illinois	40,788	3.6%
21	Indiana	17,903	1.6%
33	Iowa	6,938	0.6%
32	Kansas	7,911	0.7%
25	Kentucky	14,600	1.3%
11	Louisiana	29,265	2.6%
47	Maine	1,620	0.1%
17	Maryland	22,232	2.0%
28	Massachusetts	11,947	1.1%
6	Michigan	44,771	4.0%
35	Minnesota	5,326	0.5%
23	Mississippi	15,447	1.4%
14	Missouri	23,998	2.1%
44	Montana	2,242	0.2%
41	Nebraska	3,402	0.3%
30	Nevada	9,024	0.8%
46	New Hampshire	2,164	0.2%
13	New Jersey	28,361	2.5%
37	New Mexico	4,688	0.4%
3	New York	70,026	6.2%
10	North Carolina	31,638	2.8%
50	North Dakota	797	0.1%
5	Ohio	48,002	4.2%
19	Oklahoma	20,542	1.8%
31	Oregon	7,999	0.7%
9	Pennsylvania	34,964	3.1%
42	Rhode Island	3,371	0.3%
18	South Carolina	21,173	1.9%
45	South Dakota	2,239	0.2%
22	Tennessee	16,659	1.5%
2	Texas	140,729	12.4%
38	Utah	4,284	0.4%
49	Vermont	1,270	0.1%
12	Virginia	28,385	2.5%
27	Washington	13,214	1.2%
43	West Virginia	3,172	0.3%
24	Wisconsin	14,682	1.3%
48	Wyoming	1,566	0.1%

RANK ORDER

RANK	STATE	PRISONERS	% of USA
1	California	157,547	13.9%
2	Texas	140,729	12.4%
3	New York	70,026	6.2%
4	Florida	64,565	5.7%
5	Ohio	48,002	4.2%
6	Michigan	44,771	4.0%
7	Illinois	40,788	3.6%
8	Georgia	36,450	3.2%
9	Pennsylvania	34,964	3.1%
10	North Carolina	31,638	2.8%
11	Louisiana	29,265	2.6%
12	Virginia	28,385	2.5%
13	New Jersey	28,361	2.5%
14	Missouri	23,998	2.1%
15	Arizona	23,484	2.1%
16	Alabama	22,290	2.0%
17	Maryland	22,232	2.0%
18	South Carolina	21,173	1.9%
19	Oklahoma	20,542	1.8%
20	Connecticut	18,521	1.6%
21	Indiana	17,903	1.6%
22	Tennessee	16,659	1.5%
23	Mississippi	15,447	1.4%
24	Wisconsin	14,682	1.3%
25	Kentucky	14,600	1.3%
26	Colorado	13,461	1.2%
27	Washington	13,214	1.2%
28	Massachusetts	11,947	1.1%
29	Arkansas	10,021	0.9%
30	Nevada	9,024	0.8%
31	Oregon	7,999	0.7%
32	Kansas	7,911	0.7%
33	Iowa	6,938	0.6%
34	Delaware	5,435	0.5%
35	Minnesota	5,326	0.5%
36	Hawaii	4,949	0.4%
37	New Mexico	4,688	0.4%
38	Utah	4,284	0.4%
39	Alaska	4,220	0.4%
40	Idaho	3,946	0.3%
41	Nebraska	3,402	0.3%
42	Rhode Island	3,371	0.3%
43	West Virginia	3,172	0.3%
44	Montana	2,242	0.2%
45	South Dakota	2,239	0.2%
46	New Hampshire	2,164	0.2%
47	Maine	1,620	0.1%
48	Wyoming	1,566	0.1%
49	Vermont	1,270	0.1%
50	North Dakota	797	0.1%
	District of Columbia	9,353	0.8%

Source: U.S. Department of Justice, Bureau of Justice Statistics
    "Prisoners in 1997" (August 1998, NCJ-170014)
*As of December 31, 1997. Totals reflect all prisoners, including those sentenced to a year or less and those unsentenced.   National total does not include 112,973 prisoners under federal jurisdiction. State and federal prisoners combined total 1,244,554.

Percent Change in Number of State Prisoners: 1996 to 1997

National Percent Change = 5.0% Increase*

ALPHA ORDER				RANK ORDER		
RANK	STATE	PERCENT CHANGE		RANK	STATE	PERCENT CHANGE
41	Alabama	2.4		1	Hawaii	23.4
3	Alaska	13.6		2	West Virginia	15.4
29	Arizona	4.4		3	Alaska	13.6
19	Arkansas	6.5		3	Maine	13.6
15	California	7.9		5	Vermont	13.5
14	Colorado	8.2		6	Kentucky	13.1
31	Connecticut	3.8		7	Wisconsin	13.0
20	Delaware	6.4		8	Mississippi	11.5
43	Florida	1.3		9	North Dakota	10.4
32	Georgia	3.7		10	Iowa	9.4
1	Hawaii	23.4		11	Louisiana	9.3
39	Idaho	3.0		12	Missouri	9.1
25	Illinois	5.0		13	South Dakota	8.5
23	Indiana	5.6		14	Colorado	8.2
10	Iowa	9.4		15	California	7.9
42	Kansas	2.0		15	Utah	7.9
6	Kentucky	13.1		17	Nevada	6.9
11	Louisiana	9.3		18	Tennessee	6.6
3	Maine	13.6		19	Arkansas	6.5
46	Maryland	0.8		20	Delaware	6.4
43	Massachusetts	1.3		21	Texas	6.3
22	Michigan	5.7		22	Michigan	5.7
35	Minnesota	3.3		23	Indiana	5.6
8	Mississippi	11.5		24	Washington	5.5
12	Missouri	9.1		25	Illinois	5.0
49	Montana	(2.2)		26	New Hampshire	4.9
34	Nebraska	3.5		27	Oklahoma	4.8
17	Nevada	6.9		28	Wyoming	4.5
26	New Hampshire	4.9		29	Arizona	4.4
36	New Jersey	3.2		30	Ohio	4.0
48	New Mexico	(0.8)		31	Connecticut	3.8
47	New York	0.5		32	Georgia	3.7
36	North Carolina	3.2		33	South Carolina	3.6
9	North Dakota	10.4		34	Nebraska	3.5
30	Ohio	4.0		35	Minnesota	3.3
27	Oklahoma	4.8		36	New Jersey	3.2
50	Oregon	(7.6)		36	North Carolina	3.2
45	Pennsylvania	1.2		38	Rhode Island	3.1
38	Rhode Island	3.1		39	Idaho	3.0
33	South Carolina	3.6		40	Virginia	2.6
13	South Dakota	8.5		41	Alabama	2.4
18	Tennessee	6.6		42	Kansas	2.0
21	Texas	6.3		43	Florida	1.3
15	Utah	7.9		43	Massachusetts	1.3
5	Vermont	13.5		45	Pennsylvania	1.2
40	Virginia	2.6		46	Maryland	0.8
24	Washington	5.5		47	New York	0.5
2	West Virginia	15.4		48	New Mexico	(0.8)
7	Wisconsin	13.0		49	Montana	(2.2)
28	Wyoming	4.5		50	Oregon	(7.6)
					District of Columbia	(0.2)

Source: U.S. Department of Justice, Bureau of Justice Statistics
    "Prisoners in 1997" (August 1998, NCJ-170014)
*From December 31, 1996 to December 31, 1997. Includes inmates sentenced to more than one year and those
sentenced to a year or less or with no sentence. The percent change in number of prisoners under federal
jurisdiction during the same period was a 7.0% increase. The combined state and federal increase was 5.2%.

State Prisoners Sentenced to More than One Year in 1997

National Total = 1,102,603 State Prisoners*

<table>
<tr><td colspan="4">ALPHA ORDER</td><td colspan="4">RANK ORDER</td></tr>
<tr><th>RANK</th><th>STATE</th><th>PRISONERS</th><th>% of USA</th><th>RANK</th><th>STATE</th><th>PRISONERS</th><th>% of USA</th></tr>
<tr><td>16</td><td>Alabama</td><td>21,680</td><td>2.0%</td><td>1</td><td>California</td><td>154,368</td><td>14.0%</td></tr>
<tr><td>42</td><td>Alaska</td><td>2,571</td><td>0.2%</td><td>2</td><td>Texas</td><td>140,729</td><td>12.8%</td></tr>
<tr><td>15</td><td>Arizona</td><td>22,353</td><td>2.0%</td><td>3</td><td>New York</td><td>70,026</td><td>6.4%</td></tr>
<tr><td>29</td><td>Arkansas</td><td>9,936</td><td>0.9%</td><td>4</td><td>Florida</td><td>64,540</td><td>5.9%</td></tr>
<tr><td>1</td><td>California</td><td>154,368</td><td>14.0%</td><td>5</td><td>Ohio</td><td>48,002</td><td>4.4%</td></tr>
<tr><td>25</td><td>Colorado</td><td>13,461</td><td>1.2%</td><td>6</td><td>Michigan</td><td>44,771</td><td>4.1%</td></tr>
<tr><td>27</td><td>Connecticut</td><td>13,005</td><td>1.2%</td><td>7</td><td>Illinois</td><td>40,788</td><td>3.7%</td></tr>
<tr><td>40</td><td>Delaware</td><td>3,264</td><td>0.3%</td><td>8</td><td>Georgia</td><td>35,722</td><td>3.2%</td></tr>
<tr><td>4</td><td>Florida</td><td>64,540</td><td>5.9%</td><td>9</td><td>Pennsylvania</td><td>34,963</td><td>3.2%</td></tr>
<tr><td>8</td><td>Georgia</td><td>35,722</td><td>3.2%</td><td>10</td><td>Louisiana</td><td>29,265</td><td>2.7%</td></tr>
<tr><td>38</td><td>Hawaii</td><td>3,424</td><td>0.3%</td><td>11</td><td>New Jersey</td><td>28,361</td><td>2.6%</td></tr>
<tr><td>37</td><td>Idaho</td><td>3,946</td><td>0.4%</td><td>12</td><td>North Carolina</td><td>27,726</td><td>2.5%</td></tr>
<tr><td>7</td><td>Illinois</td><td>40,788</td><td>3.7%</td><td>13</td><td>Virginia</td><td>27,524</td><td>2.5%</td></tr>
<tr><td>20</td><td>Indiana</td><td>17,730</td><td>1.6%</td><td>14</td><td>Missouri</td><td>23,980</td><td>2.2%</td></tr>
<tr><td>33</td><td>Iowa</td><td>6,938</td><td>0.6%</td><td>15</td><td>Arizona</td><td>22,353</td><td>2.0%</td></tr>
<tr><td>31</td><td>Kansas</td><td>7,911</td><td>0.7%</td><td>16</td><td>Alabama</td><td>21,680</td><td>2.0%</td></tr>
<tr><td>23</td><td>Kentucky</td><td>14,600</td><td>1.3%</td><td>17</td><td>Maryland</td><td>21,088</td><td>1.9%</td></tr>
<tr><td>10</td><td>Louisiana</td><td>29,265</td><td>2.7%</td><td>18</td><td>Oklahoma</td><td>20,542</td><td>1.9%</td></tr>
<tr><td>48</td><td>Maine</td><td>1,542</td><td>0.1%</td><td>19</td><td>South Carolina</td><td>20,264</td><td>1.8%</td></tr>
<tr><td>17</td><td>Maryland</td><td>21,088</td><td>1.9%</td><td>20</td><td>Indiana</td><td>17,730</td><td>1.6%</td></tr>
<tr><td>28</td><td>Massachusetts</td><td>10,847</td><td>1.0%</td><td>21</td><td>Tennessee</td><td>16,659</td><td>1.5%</td></tr>
<tr><td>6</td><td>Michigan</td><td>44,771</td><td>4.1%</td><td>22</td><td>Wisconsin</td><td>14,682</td><td>1.3%</td></tr>
<tr><td>34</td><td>Minnesota</td><td>5,306</td><td>0.5%</td><td>23</td><td>Kentucky</td><td>14,600</td><td>1.3%</td></tr>
<tr><td>24</td><td>Mississippi</td><td>14,548</td><td>1.3%</td><td>24</td><td>Mississippi</td><td>14,548</td><td>1.3%</td></tr>
<tr><td>14</td><td>Missouri</td><td>23,980</td><td>2.2%</td><td>25</td><td>Colorado</td><td>13,461</td><td>1.2%</td></tr>
<tr><td>43</td><td>Montana</td><td>2,242</td><td>0.2%</td><td>26</td><td>Washington</td><td>13,198</td><td>1.2%</td></tr>
<tr><td>39</td><td>Nebraska</td><td>3,329</td><td>0.3%</td><td>27</td><td>Connecticut</td><td>13,005</td><td>1.2%</td></tr>
<tr><td>30</td><td>Nevada</td><td>8,884</td><td>0.8%</td><td>28</td><td>Massachusetts</td><td>10,847</td><td>1.0%</td></tr>
<tr><td>45</td><td>New Hampshire</td><td>2,164</td><td>0.2%</td><td>29</td><td>Arkansas</td><td>9,936</td><td>0.9%</td></tr>
<tr><td>11</td><td>New Jersey</td><td>28,361</td><td>2.6%</td><td>30</td><td>Nevada</td><td>8,884</td><td>0.8%</td></tr>
<tr><td>35</td><td>New Mexico</td><td>4,450</td><td>0.4%</td><td>31</td><td>Kansas</td><td>7,911</td><td>0.7%</td></tr>
<tr><td>3</td><td>New York</td><td>70,026</td><td>6.4%</td><td>32</td><td>Oregon</td><td>7,589</td><td>0.7%</td></tr>
<tr><td>12</td><td>North Carolina</td><td>27,726</td><td>2.5%</td><td>33</td><td>Iowa</td><td>6,938</td><td>0.6%</td></tr>
<tr><td>50</td><td>North Dakota</td><td>715</td><td>0.1%</td><td>34</td><td>Minnesota</td><td>5,306</td><td>0.5%</td></tr>
<tr><td>5</td><td>Ohio</td><td>48,002</td><td>4.4%</td><td>35</td><td>New Mexico</td><td>4,450</td><td>0.4%</td></tr>
<tr><td>18</td><td>Oklahoma</td><td>20,542</td><td>1.9%</td><td>36</td><td>Utah</td><td>4,263</td><td>0.4%</td></tr>
<tr><td>32</td><td>Oregon</td><td>7,589</td><td>0.7%</td><td>37</td><td>Idaho</td><td>3,946</td><td>0.4%</td></tr>
<tr><td>9</td><td>Pennsylvania</td><td>34,963</td><td>3.2%</td><td>38</td><td>Hawaii</td><td>3,424</td><td>0.3%</td></tr>
<tr><td>46</td><td>Rhode Island</td><td>2,100</td><td>0.2%</td><td>39</td><td>Nebraska</td><td>3,329</td><td>0.3%</td></tr>
<tr><td>19</td><td>South Carolina</td><td>20,264</td><td>1.8%</td><td>40</td><td>Delaware</td><td>3,264</td><td>0.3%</td></tr>
<tr><td>44</td><td>South Dakota</td><td>2,239</td><td>0.2%</td><td>41</td><td>West Virginia</td><td>3,160</td><td>0.3%</td></tr>
<tr><td>21</td><td>Tennessee</td><td>16,659</td><td>1.5%</td><td>42</td><td>Alaska</td><td>2,571</td><td>0.2%</td></tr>
<tr><td>2</td><td>Texas</td><td>140,729</td><td>12.8%</td><td>43</td><td>Montana</td><td>2,242</td><td>0.2%</td></tr>
<tr><td>36</td><td>Utah</td><td>4,263</td><td>0.4%</td><td>44</td><td>South Dakota</td><td>2,239</td><td>0.2%</td></tr>
<tr><td>49</td><td>Vermont</td><td>828</td><td>0.1%</td><td>45</td><td>New Hampshire</td><td>2,164</td><td>0.2%</td></tr>
<tr><td>13</td><td>Virginia</td><td>27,524</td><td>2.5%</td><td>46</td><td>Rhode Island</td><td>2,100</td><td>0.2%</td></tr>
<tr><td>26</td><td>Washington</td><td>13,198</td><td>1.2%</td><td>47</td><td>Wyoming</td><td>1,566</td><td>0.1%</td></tr>
<tr><td>41</td><td>West Virginia</td><td>3,160</td><td>0.3%</td><td>48</td><td>Maine</td><td>1,542</td><td>0.1%</td></tr>
<tr><td>22</td><td>Wisconsin</td><td>14,682</td><td>1.3%</td><td>49</td><td>Vermont</td><td>828</td><td>0.1%</td></tr>
<tr><td>47</td><td>Wyoming</td><td>1,566</td><td>0.1%</td><td>50</td><td>North Dakota</td><td>715</td><td>0.1%</td></tr>
<tr><td></td><td></td><td></td><td></td><td></td><td>District of Columbia</td><td>8,814</td><td>0.8%</td></tr>
</table>

Source: U.S. Department of Justice, Bureau of Justice Statistics
    "Prisoners in 1997" (August 1998, NCJ-170014)
*Advance figures as of December 31, 1997. Does not include 94,987 prisoners under federal jurisdiction sentenced
to more than one year. State and federal prisoners sentenced to more than one year total 1,197,590.

State Prisoner Incarceration Rate in 1997

National Rate = 410 State Prisoners per 100,000 Population*

ALPHA ORDER

RANK	STATE	RATE
7	Alabama	500
16	Alaska	420
8	Arizona	484
20	Arkansas	392
9	California	475
25	Colorado	342
19	Connecticut	397
12	Delaware	443
14	Florida	437
10	Georgia	472
34	Hawaii	288
28	Idaho	323
25	Illinois	342
32	Indiana	301
39	Iowa	243
30	Kansas	304
22	Kentucky	372
2	Louisiana	672
48	Maine	124
17	Maryland	413
36	Massachusetts	278
11	Michigan	457
49	Minnesota	113
5	Mississippi	531
13	Missouri	442
38	Montana	255
44	Nebraska	200
6	Nevada	518
45	New Hampshire	184
24	New Jersey	351
37	New Mexico	256
21	New York	386
23	North Carolina	370
50	North Dakota	112
15	Ohio	429
3	Oklahoma	617
41	Oregon	232
33	Pennsylvania	291
42	Rhode Island	213
4	South Carolina	536
31	South Dakota	303
29	Tennessee	309
1	Texas	717
43	Utah	205
47	Vermont	140
18	Virginia	407
40	Washington	233
46	West Virginia	174
35	Wisconsin	283
27	Wyoming	326

RANK ORDER

RANK	STATE	RATE
1	Texas	717
2	Louisiana	672
3	Oklahoma	617
4	South Carolina	536
5	Mississippi	531
6	Nevada	518
7	Alabama	500
8	Arizona	484
9	California	475
10	Georgia	472
11	Michigan	457
12	Delaware	443
13	Missouri	442
14	Florida	437
15	Ohio	429
16	Alaska	420
17	Maryland	413
18	Virginia	407
19	Connecticut	397
20	Arkansas	392
21	New York	386
22	Kentucky	372
23	North Carolina	370
24	New Jersey	351
25	Colorado	342
25	Illinois	342
27	Wyoming	326
28	Idaho	323
29	Tennessee	309
30	Kansas	304
31	South Dakota	303
32	Indiana	301
33	Pennsylvania	291
34	Hawaii	288
35	Wisconsin	283
36	Massachusetts	278
37	New Mexico	256
38	Montana	255
39	Iowa	243
40	Washington	233
41	Oregon	232
42	Rhode Island	213
43	Utah	205
44	Nebraska	200
45	New Hampshire	184
46	West Virginia	174
47	Vermont	140
48	Maine	124
49	Minnesota	113
50	North Dakota	112
	District of Columbia	1,682

Source: U.S. Department of Justice, Bureau of Justice Statistics
    "Prisoners in 1997" (August 1998, NCJ-170014)

*As of December 31, 1997. Includes only inmates sentenced to more than one year. Does not include federal incarceration rate of 35 prisoners per 100,000 population. State and federal combined incarceration rate is 445 prisoners per 100,000 population.

Percent Change in State Prisoner Incarceration Rate: 1996 to 1997

National Percent Change = 4.1% Increase*

ALPHA ORDER			RANK ORDER		
RANK	STATE	PERCENT CHANGE	RANK	STATE	PERCENT CHANGE
39	Alabama	1.6	1	Connecticut	26.4
7	Alaska	10.8	2	Wisconsin	23.0
45	Arizona	0.6	3	West Virginia	16.0
9	Arkansas	9.8	4	Hawaii	15.7
20	California	5.3	5	Kentucky	12.4
16	Colorado	6.2	6	North Dakota	10.9
1	Connecticut	26.4	7	Alaska	10.8
30	Delaware	3.5	8	Maine	10.7
47	Florida	(0.5)	9	Arkansas	9.8
36	Georgia	2.2	10	Iowa	9.5
4	Hawaii	15.7	11	Louisiana	9.3
40	Idaho	1.3	12	Montana	8.5
22	Illinois	4.6	13	Missouri	8.1
21	Indiana	4.9	14	South Dakota	7.8
10	Iowa	9.5	15	Mississippi	6.6
41	Kansas	1.0	16	Colorado	6.2
5	Kentucky	12.4	16	Wyoming	6.2
11	Louisiana	9.3	18	Tennessee	5.8
8	Maine	10.7	19	Utah	5.7
46	Maryland	0.2	20	California	5.3
50	Massachusetts	(7.9)	21	Indiana	4.9
27	Michigan	3.9	22	Illinois	4.6
33	Minnesota	2.7	23	Texas	4.5
15	Mississippi	6.6	24	Oklahoma	4.4
13	Missouri	8.1	25	New Hampshire	4.0
12	Montana	8.5	25	Washington	4.0
32	Nebraska	3.1	27	Michigan	3.9
31	Nevada	3.2	27	Ohio	3.9
25	New Hampshire	4.0	27	Rhode Island	3.9
35	New Jersey	2.3	30	Delaware	3.5
48	New Mexico	(1.9)	31	Nevada	3.2
42	New York	0.8	32	Nebraska	3.1
49	North Carolina	(2.4)	33	Minnesota	2.7
6	North Dakota	10.9	33	Oregon	2.7
27	Ohio	3.9	35	New Jersey	2.3
24	Oklahoma	4.4	36	Georgia	2.2
33	Oregon	2.7	36	Vermont	2.2
38	Pennsylvania	1.7	38	Pennsylvania	1.7
27	Rhode Island	3.9	39	Alabama	1.6
42	South Carolina	0.8	40	Idaho	1.3
14	South Dakota	7.8	41	Kansas	1.0
18	Tennessee	5.8	42	New York	0.8
23	Texas	4.5	42	South Carolina	0.8
19	Utah	5.7	44	Virginia	0.7
36	Vermont	2.2	45	Arizona	0.6
44	Virginia	0.7	46	Maryland	0.2
25	Washington	4.0	47	Florida	(0.5)
3	West Virginia	16.0	48	New Mexico	(1.9)
2	Wisconsin	23.0	49	North Carolina	(2.4)
16	Wyoming	6.2	50	Massachusetts	(7.9)
				District of Columbia	4.5

Source: Morgan Quitno Press using data from U.S. Department of Justice, Bureau of Justice Statistics
   "Prisoners in 1997" (August 1998, NCJ-170014)
*From December 31, 1996 to December 31, 1997. Includes only inmates sentenced to more than one year. The percent change in rate of prisoners under federal jurisdiction during the same period was a 6.1% increase. The combined state and federal increase was 4.2%.

State Prison Population as a Percent of Highest Capacity in 1997

National Percent = 115% of Highest Capacity*

ALPHA ORDER

RANK	STATE	PERCENT
29	Alabama	100
6	Alaska	147
37	Arizona	97
33	Arkansas	99
1	California	206
19	Colorado	115
NA	Connecticut**	NA
12	Delaware	129
48	Florida	83
29	Georgia	100
5	Hawaii	149
40	Idaho	96
7	Illinois	142
35	Indiana	98
8	Iowa	140
37	Kansas	97
15	Kentucky	124
29	Louisiana	100
27	Maine	102
37	Maryland	97
10	Massachusetts	137
33	Michigan	99
35	Minnesota	98
44	Mississippi	92
23	Missouri	107
16	Montana	117
11	Nebraska	135
27	Nevada	102
21	New Hampshire	110
2	New Jersey	160
49	New Mexico	82
24	New York	106
16	North Carolina	117
14	North Dakota	126
9	Ohio	138
26	Oklahoma	104
25	Oregon	105
4	Pennsylvania	151
46	Rhode Island	89
44	South Carolina	92
40	South Dakota	96
43	Tennessee	94
40	Texas	96
47	Utah	88
20	Vermont	111
3	Virginia	153
22	Washington	108
29	West Virginia	100
12	Wisconsin	129
18	Wyoming	116

RANK ORDER

RANK	STATE	PERCENT
1	California	206
2	New Jersey	160
3	Virginia	153
4	Pennsylvania	151
5	Hawaii	149
6	Alaska	147
7	Illinois	142
8	Iowa	140
9	Ohio	138
10	Massachusetts	137
11	Nebraska	135
12	Delaware	129
12	Wisconsin	129
14	North Dakota	126
15	Kentucky	124
16	Montana	117
16	North Carolina	117
18	Wyoming	116
19	Colorado	115
20	Vermont	111
21	New Hampshire	110
22	Washington	108
23	Missouri	107
24	New York	106
25	Oregon	105
26	Oklahoma	104
27	Maine	102
27	Nevada	102
29	Alabama	100
29	Georgia	100
29	Louisiana	100
29	West Virginia	100
33	Arkansas	99
33	Michigan	99
35	Indiana	98
35	Minnesota	98
37	Arizona	97
37	Kansas	97
37	Maryland	97
40	Idaho	96
40	South Dakota	96
40	Texas	96
43	Tennessee	94
44	Mississippi	92
44	South Carolina	92
46	Rhode Island	89
47	Utah	88
48	Florida	83
49	New Mexico	82
NA	Connecticut**	NA
	District of Columbia	72

Source: U.S. Department of Justice, Bureau of Justice Statistics
    "Prisoners in 1997" (August 1998, NCJ-170014)
*As of December 31, 1997. Federal prison population is at 119% of highest rated capacity.
**Not available.

Female Prisoners in State Correctional Institutions in 1997

National Total = 71,318 State Female Prisoners*

ALPHA ORDER

RANK	STATE	PRISONERS	% of USA
18	Alabama	1,360	1.9%
37	Alaska	304	0.4%
14	Arizona	1,560	2.2%
30	Arkansas	611	0.9%
1	California	11,076	15.5%
24	Colorado	949	1.3%
15	Connecticut	1,550	2.2%
35	Delaware	383	0.5%
4	Florida	3,404	4.8%
7	Georgia	2,258	3.2%
32	Hawaii	505	0.7%
38	Idaho	281	0.4%
6	Illinois	2,430	3.4%
22	Indiana	1,071	1.5%
31	Iowa	528	0.7%
33	Kansas	476	0.7%
23	Kentucky	1,052	1.5%
10	Louisiana	1,868	2.6%
48	Maine	62	0.1%
21	Maryland	1,108	1.6%
28	Massachusetts	733	1.0%
8	Michigan	2,056	2.9%
39	Minnesota	258	0.4%
20	Mississippi	1,131	1.6%
13	Missouri	1,693	2.4%
46	Montana	115	0.2%
40	Nebraska	225	0.3%
29	Nevada	695	1.0%
47	New Hampshire	109	0.2%
17	New Jersey	1,404	2.0%
36	New Mexico	374	0.5%
3	New York	3,584	5.0%
11	North Carolina	1,864	2.6%
48	North Dakota	62	0.1%
5	Ohio	2,843	4.0%
9	Oklahoma	2,053	2.9%
34	Oregon	450	0.6%
16	Pennsylvania	1,414	2.0%
41	Rhode Island	213	0.3%
19	South Carolina	1,302	1.8%
44	South Dakota	169	0.2%
26	Tennessee	798	1.1%
2	Texas	10,549	14.8%
42	Utah	212	0.3%
50	Vermont	53	0.1%
12	Virginia	1,710	2.4%
25	Washington	924	1.3%
43	West Virginia	190	0.3%
27	Wisconsin	761	1.1%
45	Wyoming	131	0.2%

RANK ORDER

RANK	STATE	PRISONERS	% of USA
1	California	11,076	15.5%
2	Texas	10,549	14.8%
3	New York	3,584	5.0%
4	Florida	3,404	4.8%
5	Ohio	2,843	4.0%
6	Illinois	2,430	3.4%
7	Georgia	2,258	3.2%
8	Michigan	2,056	2.9%
9	Oklahoma	2,053	2.9%
10	Louisiana	1,868	2.6%
11	North Carolina	1,864	2.6%
12	Virginia	1,710	2.4%
13	Missouri	1,693	2.4%
14	Arizona	1,560	2.2%
15	Connecticut	1,550	2.2%
16	Pennsylvania	1,414	2.0%
17	New Jersey	1,404	2.0%
18	Alabama	1,360	1.9%
19	South Carolina	1,302	1.8%
20	Mississippi	1,131	1.6%
21	Maryland	1,108	1.6%
22	Indiana	1,071	1.5%
23	Kentucky	1,052	1.5%
24	Colorado	949	1.3%
25	Washington	924	1.3%
26	Tennessee	798	1.1%
27	Wisconsin	761	1.1%
28	Massachusetts	733	1.0%
29	Nevada	695	1.0%
30	Arkansas	611	0.9%
31	Iowa	528	0.7%
32	Hawaii	505	0.7%
33	Kansas	476	0.7%
34	Oregon	450	0.6%
35	Delaware	383	0.5%
36	New Mexico	374	0.5%
37	Alaska	304	0.4%
38	Idaho	281	0.4%
39	Minnesota	258	0.4%
40	Nebraska	225	0.3%
41	Rhode Island	213	0.3%
42	Utah	212	0.3%
43	West Virginia	190	0.3%
44	South Dakota	169	0.2%
45	Wyoming	131	0.2%
46	Montana	115	0.2%
47	New Hampshire	109	0.2%
48	Maine	62	0.1%
48	North Dakota	62	0.1%
50	Vermont	53	0.1%
	District of Columbia	407	0.6%

Source: U.S. Department of Justice, Bureau of Justice Statistics
    "Prisoners in 1997" (August 1998, NCJ-170014)

*As of December 31, 1997. Does not include 8,306 female prisoners under federal jurisdiction. State and federal female prisoners total 79,624.

Female State Prisoner Incarceration Rate in 1997

National Rate = 49 State Female Prisoners per 100,000 Female Population*

<table>
<tr><td colspan="3">ALPHA ORDER</td><td colspan="3">RANK ORDER</td></tr>
<tr><td>RANK</td><td>STATE</td><td>RATE</td><td>RANK</td><td>STATE</td><td>RATE</td></tr>
<tr><td>11</td><td>Alabama</td><td>58</td><td>1</td><td>Oklahoma</td><td>121</td></tr>
<tr><td>14</td><td>Alaska</td><td>54</td><td>2</td><td>Texas</td><td>106</td></tr>
<tr><td>7</td><td>Arizona</td><td>61</td><td>3</td><td>Louisiana</td><td>83</td></tr>
<tr><td>19</td><td>Arkansas</td><td>46</td><td>4</td><td>Nevada</td><td>82</td></tr>
<tr><td>6</td><td>California</td><td>65</td><td>5</td><td>Mississippi</td><td>70</td></tr>
<tr><td>18</td><td>Colorado</td><td>48</td><td>6</td><td>California</td><td>65</td></tr>
<tr><td>14</td><td>Connecticut</td><td>54</td><td>7</td><td>Arizona</td><td>61</td></tr>
<tr><td>24</td><td>Delaware</td><td>42</td><td>7</td><td>Missouri</td><td>61</td></tr>
<tr><td>22</td><td>Florida</td><td>45</td><td>9</td><td>Hawaii</td><td>60</td></tr>
<tr><td>12</td><td>Georgia</td><td>56</td><td>9</td><td>South Carolina</td><td>60</td></tr>
<tr><td>9</td><td>Hawaii</td><td>60</td><td>11</td><td>Alabama</td><td>58</td></tr>
<tr><td>19</td><td>Idaho</td><td>46</td><td>12</td><td>Georgia</td><td>56</td></tr>
<tr><td>26</td><td>Illinois</td><td>40</td><td>13</td><td>Wyoming</td><td>55</td></tr>
<tr><td>33</td><td>Indiana</td><td>35</td><td>14</td><td>Alaska</td><td>54</td></tr>
<tr><td>29</td><td>Iowa</td><td>36</td><td>14</td><td>Connecticut</td><td>54</td></tr>
<tr><td>29</td><td>Kansas</td><td>36</td><td>16</td><td>Kentucky</td><td>52</td></tr>
<tr><td>16</td><td>Kentucky</td><td>52</td><td>17</td><td>Ohio</td><td>49</td></tr>
<tr><td>3</td><td>Louisiana</td><td>83</td><td>18</td><td>Colorado</td><td>48</td></tr>
<tr><td>50</td><td>Maine</td><td>9</td><td>19</td><td>Arkansas</td><td>46</td></tr>
<tr><td>27</td><td>Maryland</td><td>38</td><td>19</td><td>Idaho</td><td>46</td></tr>
<tr><td>47</td><td>Massachusetts</td><td>14</td><td>19</td><td>Virginia</td><td>46</td></tr>
<tr><td>25</td><td>Michigan</td><td>41</td><td>22</td><td>Florida</td><td>45</td></tr>
<tr><td>48</td><td>Minnesota</td><td>11</td><td>22</td><td>South Dakota</td><td>45</td></tr>
<tr><td>5</td><td>Mississippi</td><td>70</td><td>24</td><td>Delaware</td><td>42</td></tr>
<tr><td>7</td><td>Missouri</td><td>61</td><td>25</td><td>Michigan</td><td>41</td></tr>
<tr><td>38</td><td>Montana</td><td>26</td><td>26</td><td>Illinois</td><td>40</td></tr>
<tr><td>39</td><td>Nebraska</td><td>25</td><td>27</td><td>Maryland</td><td>38</td></tr>
<tr><td>4</td><td>Nevada</td><td>82</td><td>27</td><td>New York</td><td>38</td></tr>
<tr><td>44</td><td>New Hampshire</td><td>18</td><td>29</td><td>Iowa</td><td>36</td></tr>
<tr><td>34</td><td>New Jersey</td><td>34</td><td>29</td><td>Kansas</td><td>36</td></tr>
<tr><td>29</td><td>New Mexico</td><td>36</td><td>29</td><td>New Mexico</td><td>36</td></tr>
<tr><td>27</td><td>New York</td><td>38</td><td>29</td><td>North Carolina</td><td>36</td></tr>
<tr><td>29</td><td>North Carolina</td><td>36</td><td>33</td><td>Indiana</td><td>35</td></tr>
<tr><td>45</td><td>North Dakota</td><td>17</td><td>34</td><td>New Jersey</td><td>34</td></tr>
<tr><td>17</td><td>Ohio</td><td>49</td><td>35</td><td>Washington</td><td>32</td></tr>
<tr><td>1</td><td>Oklahoma</td><td>121</td><td>36</td><td>Tennessee</td><td>29</td></tr>
<tr><td>40</td><td>Oregon</td><td>24</td><td>36</td><td>Wisconsin</td><td>29</td></tr>
<tr><td>41</td><td>Pennsylvania</td><td>23</td><td>38</td><td>Montana</td><td>26</td></tr>
<tr><td>46</td><td>Rhode Island</td><td>15</td><td>39</td><td>Nebraska</td><td>25</td></tr>
<tr><td>9</td><td>South Carolina</td><td>60</td><td>40</td><td>Oregon</td><td>24</td></tr>
<tr><td>22</td><td>South Dakota</td><td>45</td><td>41</td><td>Pennsylvania</td><td>23</td></tr>
<tr><td>36</td><td>Tennessee</td><td>29</td><td>42</td><td>Utah</td><td>20</td></tr>
<tr><td>2</td><td>Texas</td><td>106</td><td>42</td><td>West Virginia</td><td>20</td></tr>
<tr><td>42</td><td>Utah</td><td>20</td><td>44</td><td>New Hampshire</td><td>18</td></tr>
<tr><td>48</td><td>Vermont</td><td>11</td><td>45</td><td>North Dakota</td><td>17</td></tr>
<tr><td>19</td><td>Virginia</td><td>46</td><td>46</td><td>Rhode Island</td><td>15</td></tr>
<tr><td>35</td><td>Washington</td><td>32</td><td>47</td><td>Massachusetts</td><td>14</td></tr>
<tr><td>42</td><td>West Virginia</td><td>20</td><td>48</td><td>Minnesota</td><td>11</td></tr>
<tr><td>36</td><td>Wisconsin</td><td>29</td><td>48</td><td>Vermont</td><td>11</td></tr>
<tr><td>13</td><td>Wyoming</td><td>55</td><td>50</td><td>Maine</td><td>9</td></tr>
<tr><td></td><td></td><td></td><td></td><td>District of Columbia</td><td>116</td></tr>
</table>

Source: U.S. Department of Justice, Bureau of Justice Statistics
    "Prisoners in 1997" (August 1998, NCJ-170014)
*As of December 31, 1997. Rate is for female prisoners sentenced to more than one year. National rate does not include federal female inmates. Federal female incarceration rate is five federal female prisoners per 100,000 female population. The combined federal/state female incarceration rate is 54 female prisoners per 100,000 female population.

Female Prisoners in State Correctional Institutions
As a Percent of All State Prisoners in 1997
National Percent = 6.3% of State Prisoners are Female*

ALPHA ORDER

RANK ORDER

RANK	STATE	PERCENT
25	Alabama	6.1
12	Alaska	7.2
20	Arizona	6.6
25	Arkansas	6.1
17	California	7.0
14	Colorado	7.1
3	Connecticut	8.4
17	Delaware	7.0
37	Florida	5.3
24	Georgia	6.2
1	Hawaii	10.2
14	Idaho	7.1
29	Illinois	6.0
29	Indiana	6.0
8	Iowa	7.6
29	Kansas	6.0
12	Kentucky	7.2
22	Louisiana	6.4
50	Maine	3.8
41	Maryland	5.0
25	Massachusetts	6.1
47	Michigan	4.6
45	Minnesota	4.8
11	Mississippi	7.3
14	Missouri	7.1
39	Montana	5.1
20	Nebraska	6.6
7	Nevada	7.7
41	New Hampshire	5.0
41	New Jersey	5.0
5	New Mexico	8.0
39	New York	5.1
34	North Carolina	5.9
6	North Dakota	7.8
34	Ohio	5.9
2	Oklahoma	10.0
36	Oregon	5.6
49	Pennsylvania	4.0
23	Rhode Island	6.3
25	South Carolina	6.1
9	South Dakota	7.5
45	Tennessee	4.8
9	Texas	7.5
44	Utah	4.9
48	Vermont	4.2
29	Virginia	6.0
17	Washington	7.0
29	West Virginia	6.0
38	Wisconsin	5.2
3	Wyoming	8.4

RANK	STATE	PERCENT
1	Hawaii	10.2
2	Oklahoma	10.0
3	Connecticut	8.4
3	Wyoming	8.4
5	New Mexico	8.0
6	North Dakota	7.8
7	Nevada	7.7
8	Iowa	7.6
9	South Dakota	7.5
9	Texas	7.5
11	Mississippi	7.3
12	Alaska	7.2
12	Kentucky	7.2
14	Colorado	7.1
14	Idaho	7.1
14	Missouri	7.1
17	California	7.0
17	Delaware	7.0
17	Washington	7.0
20	Arizona	6.6
20	Nebraska	6.6
22	Louisiana	6.4
23	Rhode Island	6.3
24	Georgia	6.2
25	Alabama	6.1
25	Arkansas	6.1
25	Massachusetts	6.1
25	South Carolina	6.1
29	Illinois	6.0
29	Indiana	6.0
29	Kansas	6.0
29	Virginia	6.0
29	West Virginia	6.0
34	North Carolina	5.9
34	Ohio	5.9
36	Oregon	5.6
37	Florida	5.3
38	Wisconsin	5.2
39	Montana	5.1
39	New York	5.1
41	Maryland	5.0
41	New Hampshire	5.0
41	New Jersey	5.0
44	Utah	4.9
45	Minnesota	4.8
45	Tennessee	4.8
47	Michigan	4.6
48	Vermont	4.2
49	Pennsylvania	4.0
50	Maine	3.8
	District of Columbia	4.4

Source: U.S. Department of Justice, Bureau of Justice Statistics
     "Prisoners in 1997" (August 1998, NCJ-170014)
*As of December 31, 1997. Rate does not include federal female inmates. Federal female inmates constitute 7.4% of federal inmates. The federal/state combined rate is 6.4%.

Percent Change in Female State Prisoner Population: 1996 to 1997

National Percent Change = 6.0% Increase*

ALPHA ORDER				RANK ORDER		
RANK	STATE	PERCENT CHANGE		RANK	STATE	PERCENT CHANGE
40	Alabama	0.2		1	Vermont	65.6
15	Alaska	12.6		2	North Dakota	37.8
32	Arizona	3.0		3	Hawaii	31.2
18	Arkansas	11.5		4	Maine	29.2
20	California	9.6		5	Kentucky	28.3
16	Colorado	12.3		6	West Virginia	27.5
33	Connecticut	1.7		7	Mississippi	26.9
36	Delaware	1.1		8	South Dakota	19.9
31	Florida	3.1		9	Louisiana	19.7
37	Georgia	0.8		10	Wisconsin	18.0
3	Hawaii	31.2		11	Wyoming	17.0
30	Idaho	3.7		12	Nevada	16.2
23	Illinois	8.0		13	Tennessee	16.0
25	Indiana	6.3		14	Missouri	15.6
16	Iowa	12.3		15	Alaska	12.6
41	Kansas	0.0		16	Colorado	12.3
5	Kentucky	28.3		16	Iowa	12.3
9	Louisiana	19.7		18	Arkansas	11.5
4	Maine	29.2		19	Minnesota	10.3
28	Maryland	5.0		20	California	9.6
45	Massachusetts	(2.3)		20	New Jersey	9.6
24	Michigan	7.1		22	South Carolina	8.3
19	Minnesota	10.3		23	Illinois	8.0
7	Mississippi	26.9		24	Michigan	7.1
14	Missouri	15.6		25	Indiana	6.3
50	Montana	(23.8)		26	Texas	6.2
41	Nebraska	0.0		27	Oklahoma	5.8
12	Nevada	16.2		28	Maryland	5.0
29	New Hampshire	3.8		29	New Hampshire	3.8
20	New Jersey	9.6		30	Idaho	3.7
44	New Mexico	(1.1)		31	Florida	3.1
46	New York	(3.9)		32	Arizona	3.0
43	North Carolina	(0.2)		33	Connecticut	1.7
2	North Dakota	37.8		34	Ohio	1.4
34	Ohio	1.4		34	Virginia	1.4
27	Oklahoma	5.8		36	Delaware	1.1
49	Oregon	(21.2)		37	Georgia	0.8
47	Pennsylvania	(4.3)		38	Utah	0.5
48	Rhode Island	(7.0)		39	Washington	0.4
22	South Carolina	8.3		40	Alabama	0.2
8	South Dakota	19.9		41	Kansas	0.0
13	Tennessee	16.0		41	Nebraska	0.0
26	Texas	6.2		43	North Carolina	(0.2)
38	Utah	0.5		44	New Mexico	(1.1)
1	Vermont	65.6		45	Massachusetts	(2.3)
34	Virginia	1.4		46	New York	(3.9)
39	Washington	0.4		47	Pennsylvania	(4.3)
6	West Virginia	27.5		48	Rhode Island	(7.0)
10	Wisconsin	18.0		49	Oregon	(21.2)
11	Wyoming	17.0		50	Montana	(23.8)
					District of Columbia	(11.7)

Source: U.S. Department of Justice, Bureau of Justice Statistics
    "Prisoners in 1997" (August 1998, NCJ-170014)

*As of December 31, 1997.   Rate does not include federal female inmates. Federal female inmates increased by 7.9%. The combined federal/state female prison population grew by 6.2%.

White Prisoners in State Correctional Institutions in 1996

National Total = 416,423 White State Prisoners*

ALPHA ORDER

RANK	STATE	PRISONERS	% of USA
20	Alabama	7,455	1.8%
42	Alaska	1,790	0.4%
6	Arizona	17,831	4.3%
31	Arkansas	4,165	1.0%
1	California	43,336	10.4%
17	Colorado	8,685	2.1%
32	Connecticut	4,010	1.0%
44	Delaware	1,735	0.4%
4	Florida	27,009	6.5%
10	Georgia	11,382	2.7%
48	Hawaii	866	0.2%
36	Idaho	3,108	0.7%
14	Illinois	9,461	2.3%
12	Indiana	9,730	2.3%
30	Iowa	4,387	1.1%
29	Kansas	4,531	1.1%
18	Kentucky	8,090	1.9%
25	Louisiana	6,055	1.5%
NA	Maine**	NA	NA
27	Maryland	4,893	1.2%
26	Massachusetts	5,578	1.3%
7	Michigan	17,362	4.2%
37	Minnesota	2,588	0.6%
34	Mississippi	3,463	0.8%
8	Missouri	11,577	2.8%
43	Montana	1,787	0.4%
39	Nebraska	2,124	0.5%
28	Nevada	4,701	1.1%
41	New Hampshire	1,931	0.5%
21	New Jersey	7,405	1.8%
33	New Mexico	3,929	0.9%
3	New York	30,009	7.2%
13	North Carolina	9,588	2.3%
49	North Dakota	530	0.1%
5	Ohio	20,762	5.0%
11	Oklahoma	10,588	2.5%
22	Oregon	6,438	1.5%
9	Pennsylvania	11,482	2.8%
40	Rhode Island	2,056	0.5%
24	South Carolina	6,081	1.5%
45	South Dakota	1,543	0.4%
19	Tennessee	7,579	1.8%
2	Texas	36,790	8.8%
35	Utah	3,399	0.8%
47	Vermont	1,032	0.2%
15	Virginia	8,900	2.1%
16	Washington	8,837	2.1%
38	West Virginia	2,306	0.6%
23	Wisconsin	6,236	1.5%
46	Wyoming	1,159	0.3%

RANK ORDER

RANK	STATE	PRISONERS	% of USA
1	California	43,336	10.4%
2	Texas	36,790	8.8%
3	New York	30,009	7.2%
4	Florida	27,009	6.5%
5	Ohio	20,762	5.0%
6	Arizona	17,831	4.3%
7	Michigan	17,362	4.2%
8	Missouri	11,577	2.8%
9	Pennsylvania	11,482	2.8%
10	Georgia	11,382	2.7%
11	Oklahoma	10,588	2.5%
12	Indiana	9,730	2.3%
13	North Carolina	9,588	2.3%
14	Illinois	9,461	2.3%
15	Virginia	8,900	2.1%
16	Washington	8,837	2.1%
17	Colorado	8,685	2.1%
18	Kentucky	8,090	1.9%
19	Tennessee	7,579	1.8%
20	Alabama	7,455	1.8%
21	New Jersey	7,405	1.8%
22	Oregon	6,438	1.5%
23	Wisconsin	6,236	1.5%
24	South Carolina	6,081	1.5%
25	Louisiana	6,055	1.5%
26	Massachusetts	5,578	1.3%
27	Maryland	4,893	1.2%
28	Nevada	4,701	1.1%
29	Kansas	4,531	1.1%
30	Iowa	4,387	1.1%
31	Arkansas	4,165	1.0%
32	Connecticut	4,010	1.0%
33	New Mexico	3,929	0.9%
34	Mississippi	3,463	0.8%
35	Utah	3,399	0.8%
36	Idaho	3,108	0.7%
37	Minnesota	2,588	0.6%
38	West Virginia	2,306	0.6%
39	Nebraska	2,124	0.5%
40	Rhode Island	2,056	0.5%
41	New Hampshire	1,931	0.5%
42	Alaska	1,790	0.4%
43	Montana	1,787	0.4%
44	Delaware	1,735	0.4%
45	South Dakota	1,543	0.4%
46	Wyoming	1,159	0.3%
47	Vermont	1,032	0.2%
48	Hawaii	866	0.2%
49	North Dakota	530	0.1%
NA	Maine**	NA	NA
	District of Columbia	144	0.0%

Source: U.S. Department of Justice, Bureau of Justice Statistics
"Correctional Populations in the United States, 1996" (1998)
*As of December 31, 1996. National total does not include 61,885 white federal prisoners.
**Not available.

White State Prisoner Incarceration Rate in 1996

National Rate = 190 White State Prisoners per 100,000 White Population*

ALPHA ORDER

RANK ORDER

RANK	STATE	RATE		RANK	STATE	RATE
11	Alabama	238		1	Arizona	452
2	Alaska	389		2	Alaska	389
1	Arizona	452		3	Oklahoma	386
27	Arkansas	201		4	Nevada	339
36	California	170		5	Delaware	303
10	Colorado	246		6	Idaho	270
40	Connecticut	139		7	New Mexico	264
5	Delaware	303		8	Wyoming	251
16	Florida	226		9	Missouri	247
18	Georgia	222		10	Colorado	246
20	Hawaii	218		11	Alabama	238
6	Idaho	270		11	South Carolina	238
47	Illinois	98		13	South Dakota	230
29	Indiana	184		14	Kentucky	227
38	Iowa	160		14	Texas	227
28	Kansas	192		16	Florida	226
14	Kentucky	227		17	Rhode Island	225
25	Louisiana	210		18	Georgia	222
NA	Maine**	NA		19	Montana	219
39	Maryland	140		20	Hawaii	218
46	Massachusetts	102		21	New York	215
23	Michigan	213		21	Oregon	215
49	Minnesota	59		23	Michigan	213
26	Mississippi	204		23	Ohio	213
9	Missouri	247		25	Louisiana	210
19	Montana	219		26	Mississippi	204
41	Nebraska	137		27	Arkansas	201
4	Nevada	339		28	Kansas	192
36	New Hampshire	170		29	Indiana	184
44	New Jersey	115		30	Vermont	179
7	New Mexico	264		30	Washington	179
21	New York	215		32	Utah	177
33	North Carolina	174		33	North Carolina	174
48	North Dakota	88		33	Virginia	174
23	Ohio	213		35	Tennessee	173
3	Oklahoma	386		36	California	170
21	Oregon	215		36	New Hampshire	170
45	Pennsylvania	108		38	Iowa	160
17	Rhode Island	225		39	Maryland	140
11	South Carolina	238		40	Connecticut	139
13	South Dakota	230		41	Nebraska	137
35	Tennessee	173		42	West Virginia	132
14	Texas	227		43	Wisconsin	131
32	Utah	177		44	New Jersey	115
30	Vermont	179		45	Pennsylvania	108
33	Virginia	174		46	Massachusetts	102
30	Washington	179		47	Illinois	98
42	West Virginia	132		48	North Dakota	88
43	Wisconsin	131		49	Minnesota	59
8	Wyoming	251		NA	Maine**	NA
					District of Columbia	80

Source: Morgan Quitno Press using data from U.S. Department of Justice, Bureau of Justice Statistics
"Correctional Populations in the United States, 1996" (1998)

*As of December 31, 1996. National rate does not include 61,885 white federal prisoners. Federal rate is 28 white prisoners per 100,000 white population. The combined federal/state rate is 218 white prisoners per 100,000 white population.

**Not available.

White Prisoners in State Correctional Institutions
As a Percent of All Prisoners in 1996
National Percent = 38.7% White*

ALPHA ORDER

RANK	STATE	PERCENT
34	Alabama	34.3
26	Alaska	48.2
7	Arizona	79.3
30	Arkansas	44.3
40	California	29.7
14	Colorado	69.8
44	Connecticut	26.7
35	Delaware	34.0
32	Florida	42.4
37	Georgia	32.4
49	Hawaii	21.6
6	Idaho	81.1
46	Illinois	24.4
20	Indiana	57.4
15	Iowa	69.2
19	Kansas	58.4
18	Kentucky	62.7
47	Louisiana	22.6
NA	Maine**	NA
48	Maryland	22.2
28	Massachusetts	47.3
33	Michigan	41.0
24	Minnesota	50.2
45	Mississippi	25.0
23	Missouri	52.6
8	Montana	77.9
16	Nebraska	64.6
21	Nevada	55.7
1	New Hampshire	93.6
43	New Jersey	26.9
5	New Mexico	83.2
31	New York	43.0
39	North Carolina	31.3
12	North Dakota	73.4
29	Ohio	45.0
22	Oklahoma	54.0
11	Oregon	74.3
36	Pennsylvania	33.2
17	Rhode Island	62.9
40	South Carolina	29.7
10	South Dakota	74.8
25	Tennessee	48.5
42	Texas	27.8
3	Utah	85.6
2	Vermont	92.2
38	Virginia	32.2
13	Washington	70.5
4	West Virginia	83.9
27	Wisconsin	48.0
9	Wyoming	77.3

RANK ORDER

RANK	STATE	PERCENT
1	New Hampshire	93.6
2	Vermont	92.2
3	Utah	85.6
4	West Virginia	83.9
5	New Mexico	83.2
6	Idaho	81.1
7	Arizona	79.3
8	Montana	77.9
9	Wyoming	77.3
10	South Dakota	74.8
11	Oregon	74.3
12	North Dakota	73.4
13	Washington	70.5
14	Colorado	69.8
15	Iowa	69.2
16	Nebraska	64.6
17	Rhode Island	62.9
18	Kentucky	62.7
19	Kansas	58.4
20	Indiana	57.4
21	Nevada	55.7
22	Oklahoma	54.0
23	Missouri	52.6
24	Minnesota	50.2
25	Tennessee	48.5
26	Alaska	48.2
27	Wisconsin	48.0
28	Massachusetts	47.3
29	Ohio	45.0
30	Arkansas	44.3
31	New York	43.0
32	Florida	42.4
33	Michigan	41.0
34	Alabama	34.3
35	Delaware	34.0
36	Pennsylvania	33.2
37	Georgia	32.4
38	Virginia	32.2
39	North Carolina	31.3
40	California	29.7
40	South Carolina	29.7
42	Texas	27.8
43	New Jersey	26.9
44	Connecticut	26.7
45	Mississippi	25.0
46	Illinois	24.4
47	Louisiana	22.6
48	Maryland	22.2
49	Hawaii	21.6
NA	Maine**	NA

District of Columbia   1.5

Source: Morgan Quitno Press using data from U.S. Department of Justice, Bureau of Justice Statistics "Correctional Populations in the United States, 1996" (1998)

As of December 31, 1996. National percent does not include white federal prisoners. Federal prison population is 58.6% white. Combined state and federal percentage is 40.5% white.

**Not available.*

Black Prisoners in State Correctional Institutions in 1996

National Total = 525,226 Black State Prisoners*

ALPHA ORDER				RANK ORDER			
RANK	STATE	PRISONERS	% of USA	RANK	STATE	PRISONERS	% of USA
16	Alabama	14,236	2.7%	1	Texas	61,132	11.6%
39	Alaska	529	0.1%	2	California	45,753	8.7%
27	Arizona	3,432	0.7%	3	New York	37,601	7.2%
24	Arkansas	5,147	1.0%	4	Florida	35,461	6.8%
2	California	45,753	8.7%	5	Illinois	25,321	4.8%
29	Colorado	3,022	0.6%	6	Ohio	25,089	4.8%
22	Connecticut	6,882	1.3%	7	Georgia	23,618	4.5%
28	Delaware	3,280	0.6%	8	Michigan	23,586	4.5%
4	Florida	35,461	6.8%	9	Louisiana	20,667	3.9%
7	Georgia	23,618	4.5%	10	North Carolina	20,011	3.8%
42	Hawaii	205	0.0%	11	Pennsylvania	19,565	3.7%
46	Idaho	63	0.0%	12	Virginia	18,539	3.5%
5	Illinois	25,321	4.8%	13	New Jersey	17,857	3.4%
20	Indiana	7,159	1.4%	14	Maryland	17,114	3.3%
34	Iowa	1,568	0.3%	15	South Carolina	14,259	2.7%
30	Kansas	2,974	0.6%	16	Alabama	14,236	2.7%
25	Kentucky	4,790	0.9%	17	Mississippi	10,327	2.0%
9	Louisiana	20,667	3.9%	18	Missouri	10,322	2.0%
NA	Maine**	NA	NA	19	Tennessee	7,973	1.5%
14	Maryland	17,114	3.3%	20	Indiana	7,159	1.4%
26	Massachusetts	3,481	0.7%	21	Oklahoma	6,891	1.3%
8	Michigan	23,586	4.5%	22	Connecticut	6,882	1.3%
33	Minnesota	1,841	0.4%	23	Wisconsin	6,322	1.2%
17	Mississippi	10,327	2.0%	24	Arkansas	5,147	1.0%
18	Missouri	10,322	2.0%	25	Kentucky	4,790	0.9%
47	Montana	51	0.0%	26	Massachusetts	3,481	0.7%
37	Nebraska	1,017	0.2%	27	Arizona	3,432	0.7%
32	Nevada	2,292	0.4%	28	Delaware	3,280	0.6%
43	New Hampshire	115	0.0%	29	Colorado	3,022	0.6%
13	New Jersey	17,857	3.4%	30	Kansas	2,974	0.6%
38	New Mexico	560	0.1%	31	Washington	2,919	0.6%
3	New York	37,601	7.2%	32	Nevada	2,292	0.4%
10	North Carolina	20,011	3.8%	33	Minnesota	1,841	0.4%
48	North Dakota	23	0.0%	34	Iowa	1,568	0.3%
6	Ohio	25,089	4.8%	35	Rhode Island	1,168	0.2%
21	Oklahoma	6,891	1.3%	36	Oregon	1,063	0.2%
36	Oregon	1,063	0.2%	37	Nebraska	1,017	0.2%
11	Pennsylvania	19,565	3.7%	38	New Mexico	560	0.1%
35	Rhode Island	1,168	0.2%	39	Alaska	529	0.1%
15	South Carolina	14,259	2.7%	40	West Virginia	440	0.1%
44	South Dakota	87	0.0%	41	Utah	328	0.1%
19	Tennessee	7,973	1.5%	42	Hawaii	205	0.0%
1	Texas	61,132	11.6%	43	New Hampshire	115	0.0%
41	Utah	328	0.1%	44	South Dakota	87	0.0%
49	Vermont	14	0.0%	45	Wyoming	78	0.0%
12	Virginia	18,539	3.5%	46	Idaho	63	0.0%
31	Washington	2,919	0.6%	47	Montana	51	0.0%
40	West Virginia	440	0.1%	48	North Dakota	23	0.0%
23	Wisconsin	6,322	1.2%	49	Vermont	14	0.0%
45	Wyoming	78	0.0%	NA	Maine**	NA	NA
					District of Columbia	9,054	1.7%

Source: U.S. Department of Justice, Bureau of Justice Statistics
    "Correctional Populations in the United States, 1996" (1998)
*As of December 31, 1996. National total does not include 40,323 black federal prisoners.
**Not available.

Black State Prisoner Incarceration Rate in 1996

National Rate = 1,567 Black State Prisoners per 100,000 Black Population*

ALPHA ORDER

RANK ORDER

RANK	STATE	RATE		RANK	STATE	RATE
35	Alabama	1,285		1	Iowa	2,842
7	Alaska	2,280		2	Oklahoma	2,712
9	Arizona	2,222		3	Texas	2,620
36	Arkansas	1,280		4	Rhode Island	2,503
14	California	1,922		5	Delaware	2,413
17	Colorado	1,837		6	Connecticut	2,318
6	Connecticut	2,318		7	Alaska	2,280
5	Delaware	2,413		8	Wisconsin	2,234
23	Florida	1,621		9	Arizona	2,222
41	Georgia	1,141		10	Ohio	1,984
47	Hawaii	581		11	Utah	1,967
43	Idaho	979		12	Kansas	1,952
32	Illinois	1,403		13	Nevada	1,936
28	Indiana	1,503		14	California	1,922
1	Iowa	2,842		15	Wyoming	1,918
12	Kansas	1,952		16	Oregon	1,853
20	Kentucky	1,707		17	Colorado	1,837
29	Louisiana	1,489		18	South Dakota	1,792
NA	Maine**	NA		19	Missouri	1,726
38	Maryland	1,248		20	Kentucky	1,707
44	Massachusetts	928		21	Michigan	1,702
21	Michigan	1,702		22	Pennsylvania	1,685
30	Minnesota	1,440		23	Florida	1,621
42	Mississippi	1,049		24	Nebraska	1,572
19	Missouri	1,726		25	Montana	1,567
25	Montana	1,567		26	New Jersey	1,543
24	Nebraska	1,572		27	Washington	1,538
13	Nevada	1,936		28	Indiana	1,503
31	New Hampshire	1,417		29	Louisiana	1,489
26	New Jersey	1,543		30	Minnesota	1,440
34	New Mexico	1,304		31	New Hampshire	1,417
40	New York	1,177		32	Illinois	1,403
39	North Carolina	1,236		33	Virginia	1,401
48	North Dakota	556		34	New Mexico	1,304
10	Ohio	1,984		35	Alabama	1,285
2	Oklahoma	2,712		36	Arkansas	1,280
16	Oregon	1,853		37	South Carolina	1,273
22	Pennsylvania	1,685		38	Maryland	1,248
4	Rhode Island	2,503		39	North Carolina	1,236
37	South Carolina	1,273		40	New York	1,177
18	South Dakota	1,792		41	Georgia	1,141
45	Tennessee	914		42	Mississippi	1,049
3	Texas	2,620		43	Idaho	979
11	Utah	1,967		44	Massachusetts	928
49	Vermont	449		45	Tennessee	914
33	Virginia	1,401		46	West Virginia	762
27	Washington	1,538		47	Hawaii	581
46	West Virginia	762		48	North Dakota	556
8	Wisconsin	2,234		49	Vermont	449
15	Wyoming	1,918		NA	Maine**	NA

District of Columbia   2,643

Source: Morgan Quitno Press using data from U.S. Department of Justice, Bureau of Justice Statistics
    "Correctional Populations in the United States, 1996" (1998)
*As of December 31, 1996. National rate does not include 40,323 federal prisoners. Federal rate is 120 black prisoners per 100,000 black population. The combined federal/state rate is 1,687 black prisoners per 100,000 black population.
**Not available.

61

Black Prisoners in State Correctional Institutions
As a Percent of All Prisoners in 1996
National Percent = 48.9% Black*

ALPHA ORDER

RANK	STATE	PERCENT
7	Alabama	65.4
38	Alaska	14.2
37	Arizona	15.3
15	Arkansas	54.7
29	California	31.3
34	Colorado	24.3
22	Connecticut	45.9
11	Delaware	64.2
14	Florida	55.6
5	Georgia	67.2
44	Hawaii	5.1
48	Idaho	1.6
9	Illinois	65.2
23	Indiana	42.2
33	Iowa	24.7
24	Kansas	38.3
25	Kentucky	37.1
2	Louisiana	77.2
NA	Maine**	NA
1	Maryland	77.6
31	Massachusetts	29.5
13	Michigan	55.7
26	Minnesota	35.7
3	Mississippi	74.5
20	Missouri	46.9
47	Montana	2.2
30	Nebraska	30.9
32	Nevada	27.2
42	New Hampshire	5.6
10	New Jersey	65.0
40	New Mexico	11.9
17	New York	53.9
8	North Carolina	65.3
46	North Dakota	3.2
16	Ohio	54.3
28	Oklahoma	35.2
39	Oregon	12.3
12	Pennsylvania	56.6
26	Rhode Island	35.7
4	South Carolina	69.7
45	South Dakota	4.2
18	Tennessee	51.0
21	Texas	46.2
41	Utah	8.3
49	Vermont	1.3
6	Virginia	67.0
35	Washington	23.3
36	West Virginia	16.0
19	Wisconsin	48.7
43	Wyoming	5.2

RANK ORDER

RANK	STATE	PERCENT
1	Maryland	77.6
2	Louisiana	77.2
3	Mississippi	74.5
4	South Carolina	69.7
5	Georgia	67.2
6	Virginia	67.0
7	Alabama	65.4
8	North Carolina	65.3
9	Illinois	65.2
10	New Jersey	65.0
11	Delaware	64.2
12	Pennsylvania	56.6
13	Michigan	55.7
14	Florida	55.6
15	Arkansas	54.7
16	Ohio	54.3
17	New York	53.9
18	Tennessee	51.0
19	Wisconsin	48.7
20	Missouri	46.9
21	Texas	46.2
22	Connecticut	45.9
23	Indiana	42.2
24	Kansas	38.3
25	Kentucky	37.1
26	Minnesota	35.7
26	Rhode Island	35.7
28	Oklahoma	35.2
29	California	31.3
30	Nebraska	30.9
31	Massachusetts	29.5
32	Nevada	27.2
33	Iowa	24.7
34	Colorado	24.3
35	Washington	23.3
36	West Virginia	16.0
37	Arizona	15.3
38	Alaska	14.2
39	Oregon	12.3
40	New Mexico	11.9
41	Utah	8.3
42	New Hampshire	5.6
43	Wyoming	5.2
44	Hawaii	5.1
45	South Dakota	4.2
46	North Dakota	3.2
47	Montana	2.2
48	Idaho	1.6
49	Vermont	1.3
NA	Maine**	NA

District of Columbia	96.6

Source: Morgan Quitno Press using data from U.S. Department of Justice, Bureau of Justice Statistics
    "Correctional Populations in the United States, 1996" (1998)
*As of December 31, 1996. National percent does not include black federal prisoners. Federal prison population
is 38.2% black. Combined state and federal percentage is 47.9% black.
**Not available.

Prisoners Under Sentence of Death in 1997

National Total = 3,320 State Prisoners*

RANK	STATE	PRISONERS	% of USA
7	Alabama	159	4.8%
NA	Alaska**	NA	NA
10	Arizona	120	3.6%
20	Arkansas	38	1.1%
1	California	486	14.6%
31	Colorado	4	0.1%
31	Connecticut	4	0.1%
25	Delaware	15	0.5%
3	Florida	370	11.1%
11	Georgia	115	3.5%
NA	Hawaii**	NA	NA
23	Idaho	19	0.6%
7	Illinois	159	4.8%
18	Indiana	44	1.3%
NA	Iowa**	NA	NA
35	Kansas	0	0.0%
21	Kentucky	30	0.9%
15	Louisiana	70	2.1%
NA	Maine**	NA	NA
24	Maryland	17	0.5%
NA	Massachusetts**	NA	NA
NA	Michigan**	NA	NA
NA	Minnesota**	NA	NA
17	Mississippi	64	1.9%
13	Missouri	88	2.7%
30	Montana	7	0.2%
28	Nebraska	11	0.3%
14	Nevada	87	2.6%
35	New Hampshire	0	0.0%
26	New Jersey	14	0.4%
31	New Mexico	4	0.1%
35	New York	0	0.0%
6	North Carolina	176	5.3%
NA	North Dakota**	NA	NA
5	Ohio	177	5.3%
9	Oklahoma	137	4.1%
22	Oregon	20	0.6%
4	Pennsylvania	214	6.4%
NA	Rhode Island**	NA	NA
16	South Carolina	68	2.0%
34	South Dakota	2	0.1%
12	Tennessee	98	3.0%
2	Texas	438	13.2%
29	Utah	10	0.3%
NA	Vermont**	NA	NA
19	Virginia	43	1.3%
27	Washington	12	0.4%
NA	West Virginia**	NA	NA
NA	Wisconsin**	NA	NA
35	Wyoming	0	0.0%

RANK	STATE	PRISONERS	% of USA
1	California	486	14.6%
2	Texas	438	13.2%
3	Florida	370	11.1%
4	Pennsylvania	214	6.4%
5	Ohio	177	5.3%
6	North Carolina	176	5.3%
7	Alabama	159	4.8%
7	Illinois	159	4.8%
9	Oklahoma	137	4.1%
10	Arizona	120	3.6%
11	Georgia	115	3.5%
12	Tennessee	98	3.0%
13	Missouri	88	2.7%
14	Nevada	87	2.6%
15	Louisiana	70	2.1%
16	South Carolina	68	2.0%
17	Mississippi	64	1.9%
18	Indiana	44	1.3%
19	Virginia	43	1.3%
20	Arkansas	38	1.1%
21	Kentucky	30	0.9%
22	Oregon	20	0.6%
23	Idaho	19	0.6%
24	Maryland	17	0.5%
25	Delaware	15	0.5%
26	New Jersey	14	0.4%
27	Washington	12	0.4%
28	Nebraska	11	0.3%
29	Utah	10	0.3%
30	Montana	7	0.2%
31	Colorado	4	0.1%
31	Connecticut	4	0.1%
31	New Mexico	4	0.1%
34	South Dakota	2	0.1%
35	Kansas	0	0.0%
35	New Hampshire	0	0.0%
35	New York	0	0.0%
35	Wyoming	0	0.0%
NA	Alaska**	NA	NA
NA	Hawaii**	NA	NA
NA	Iowa**	NA	NA
NA	Maine**	NA	NA
NA	Massachusetts**	NA	NA
NA	Michigan**	NA	NA
NA	Minnesota**	NA	NA
NA	North Dakota**	NA	NA
NA	Rhode Island**	NA	NA
NA	Vermont**	NA	NA
NA	West Virginia**	NA	NA
NA	Wisconsin**	NA	NA
	District of Columbia**	NA	NA

Source: U.S. Department of Justice, Bureau of Justice Statistics
   "Capital Punishment 1997" (Bulletin, December 1998, NCJ-172881)
*As of December 31, 1997. Does not include 15 federal prisoners under sentence of death. There were 74
executions in 1997
**No death penalty as of 12/31/97.

Male Prisoners Under Sentence of Death in 1997

National Total = 3,276 Male State Prisoners*

ALPHA ORDER

RANK	STATE	PERCENT	% of USA
8	Alabama	156	4.8%
NA	Alaska**	NA	NA
10	Arizona	119	3.6%
20	Arkansas	38	1.2%
1	California	478	14.6%
31	Colorado	4	0.1%
31	Connecticut	4	0.1%
25	Delaware	15	0.5%
3	Florida	364	11.1%
11	Georgia	115	3.5%
NA	Hawaii**	NA	NA
23	Idaho	18	0.5%
7	Illinois	157	4.8%
18	Indiana	44	1.3%
NA	Iowa**	NA	NA
35	Kansas	0	0.0%
21	Kentucky	30	0.9%
15	Louisiana	70	2.1%
NA	Maine**	NA	NA
24	Maryland	17	0.5%
NA	Massachusetts**	NA	NA
NA	Michigan**	NA	NA
NA	Minnesota**	NA	NA
17	Mississippi	63	1.9%
13	Missouri	87	2.7%
30	Montana	7	0.2%
28	Nebraska	11	0.3%
14	Nevada	86	2.6%
35	New Hampshire	0	0.0%
26	New Jersey	13	0.4%
31	New Mexico	4	0.1%
35	New York	0	0.0%
6	North Carolina	173	5.3%
NA	North Dakota**	NA	NA
5	Ohio	177	5.4%
9	Oklahoma	134	4.1%
22	Oregon	20	0.6%
4	Pennsylvania	210	6.4%
NA	Rhode Island**	NA	NA
16	South Carolina	68	2.1%
34	South Dakota	2	0.1%
12	Tennessee	96	2.9%
2	Texas	431	13.2%
29	Utah	10	0.3%
NA	Vermont**	NA	NA
19	Virginia	43	1.3%
27	Washington	12	0.4%
NA	West Virginia**	NA	NA
NA	Wisconsin**	NA	NA
35	Wyoming	0	0.0%

RANK ORDER

RANK	STATE	PERCENT	% of USA
1	California	478	14.6%
2	Texas	431	13.2%
3	Florida	364	11.1%
4	Pennsylvania	210	6.4%
5	Ohio	177	5.4%
6	North Carolina	173	5.3%
7	Illinois	157	4.8%
8	Alabama	156	4.8%
9	Oklahoma	134	4.1%
10	Arizona	119	3.6%
11	Georgia	115	3.5%
12	Tennessee	96	2.9%
13	Missouri	87	2.7%
14	Nevada	86	2.6%
15	Louisiana	70	2.1%
16	South Carolina	68	2.1%
17	Mississippi	63	1.9%
18	Indiana	44	1.3%
19	Virginia	43	1.3%
20	Arkansas	38	1.2%
21	Kentucky	30	0.9%
22	Oregon	20	0.6%
23	Idaho	18	0.5%
24	Maryland	17	0.5%
25	Delaware	15	0.5%
26	New Jersey	13	0.4%
27	Washington	12	0.4%
28	Nebraska	11	0.3%
29	Utah	10	0.3%
30	Montana	7	0.2%
31	Colorado	4	0.1%
31	Connecticut	4	0.1%
31	New Mexico	4	0.1%
34	South Dakota	2	0.1%
35	Kansas	0	0.0%
35	New Hampshire	0	0.0%
35	New York	0	0.0%
35	Wyoming	0	0.0%
NA	Alaska**	NA	NA
NA	Hawaii**	NA	NA
NA	Iowa**	NA	NA
NA	Maine**	NA	NA
NA	Massachusetts**	NA	NA
NA	Michigan**	NA	NA
NA	Minnesota**	NA	NA
NA	North Dakota**	NA	NA
NA	Rhode Island**	NA	NA
NA	Vermont**	NA	NA
NA	West Virginia**	NA	NA
NA	Wisconsin**	NA	NA
	District of Columbia**	NA	NA

Source: Morgan Quitno Press using data from U.S. Department of Justice, Bureau of Justice Statistics
"Capital Punishment 1997" (Bulletin, December 1998, NCJ-172881)
*As of December 31, 1997. Does not include 15 male federal prisoners under sentence of death. There were 74 executions in 1997. All were male.
**No death penalty as of 12/31/97.

Female Prisoners Under Sentence of Death in 1997

National Total = 44 Female State Prisoners*

ALPHA ORDER					RANK ORDER			
RANK	STATE		PRISONERS	% of USA	RANK	STATE	PRISONERS	% of USA
5	Alabama		3	6.8%	1	California	8	18.2%
NA	Alaska**		NA	NA	2	Texas	7	15.9%
10	Arizona		1	2.3%	3	Florida	6	13.6%
16	Arkansas		0	0.0%	4	Pennsylvania	4	9.1%
1	California		8	18.2%	5	Alabama	3	6.8%
16	Colorado		0	0.0%	5	North Carolina	3	6.8%
16	Connecticut		0	0.0%	5	Oklahoma	3	6.8%
16	Delaware		0	0.0%	8	Illinois	2	4.5%
3	Florida		6	13.6%	8	Tennessee	2	4.5%
16	Georgia		0	0.0%	10	Arizona	1	2.3%
NA	Hawaii**		NA	NA	10	Idaho	1	2.3%
10	Idaho		1	2.3%	10	Mississippi	1	2.3%
8	Illinois		2	4.5%	10	Missouri	1	2.3%
16	Indiana		0	0.0%	10	Nevada	1	2.3%
NA	Iowa**		NA	NA	10	New Jersey	1	2.3%
16	Kansas		0	0.0%	16	Arkansas	0	0.0%
16	Kentucky		0	0.0%	16	Colorado	0	0.0%
16	Louisiana		0	0.0%	16	Connecticut	0	0.0%
NA	Maine**		NA	NA	16	Delaware	0	0.0%
16	Maryland		0	0.0%	16	Georgia	0	0.0%
NA	Massachusetts**		NA	NA	16	Indiana	0	0.0%
NA	Michigan**		NA	NA	16	Kansas	0	0.0%
NA	Minnesota**		NA	NA	16	Kentucky	0	0.0%
10	Mississippi		1	2.3%	16	Louisiana	0	0.0%
10	Missouri		1	2.3%	16	Maryland	0	0.0%
16	Montana		0	0.0%	16	Montana	0	0.0%
16	Nebraska		0	0.0%	16	Nebraska	0	0.0%
10	Nevada		1	2.3%	16	New Hampshire	0	0.0%
16	New Hampshire		0	0.0%	16	New Mexico	0	0.0%
10	New Jersey		1	2.3%	16	New York	0	0.0%
16	New Mexico		0	0.0%	16	Ohio	0	0.0%
16	New York		0	0.0%	16	Oregon	0	0.0%
5	North Carolina		3	6.8%	16	South Carolina	0	0.0%
NA	North Dakota**		NA	NA	16	South Dakota	0	0.0%
16	Ohio		0	0.0%	16	Utah	0	0.0%
5	Oklahoma		3	6.8%	16	Virginia	0	0.0%
16	Oregon		0	0.0%	16	Washington	0	0.0%
4	Pennsylvania		4	9.1%	16	Wyoming	0	0.0%
NA	Rhode Island**		NA	NA	NA	Alaska**	NA	NA
16	South Carolina		0	0.0%	NA	Hawaii**	NA	NA
16	South Dakota		0	0.0%	NA	Iowa**	NA	NA
8	Tennessee		2	4.5%	NA	Maine**	NA	NA
2	Texas		7	15.9%	NA	Massachusetts**	NA	NA
16	Utah		0	0.0%	NA	Michigan**	NA	NA
NA	Vermont**		NA	NA	NA	Minnesota**	NA	NA
16	Virginia		0	0.0%	NA	North Dakota**	NA	NA
16	Washington		0	0.0%	NA	Rhode Island**	NA	NA
NA	West Virginia**		NA	NA	NA	Vermont**	NA	NA
NA	Wisconsin**		NA	NA	NA	West Virginia**	NA	NA
16	Wyoming		0	0.0%	NA	Wisconsin**	NA	NA
						District of Columbia**	NA	NA

Source: U.S. Department of Justice, Bureau of Justice Statistics
    "Capital Punishment 1997" (Bulletin, December 1998, NCJ-172881)
*As of December 31, 1997. There were no federal female prisoners under sentence of death. There were 74 executions in 1997, none of whom was female.
**No death penalty as of 12/31/97.

Percent of Prisoners Under Sentence of Death Who Are Female: 1997

National Percent = 1.3% of State Death Sentence Prisoners*

RANK	STATE	PERCENT
5	Alabama	1.9
NA	Alaska**	NA
15	Arizona	0.8
16	Arkansas	0.0
8	California	1.6
16	Colorado	0.0
16	Connecticut	0.0
16	Delaware	0.0
8	Florida	1.6
16	Georgia	0.0
NA	Hawaii**	NA
2	Idaho	5.3
12	Illinois	1.3
16	Indiana	0.0
NA	Iowa**	NA
16	Kansas	0.0
16	Kentucky	0.0
16	Louisiana	0.0
NA	Maine**	NA
16	Maryland	0.0
NA	Massachusetts**	NA
NA	Michigan**	NA
NA	Minnesota**	NA
8	Mississippi	1.6
13	Missouri	1.1
16	Montana	0.0
16	Nebraska	0.0
13	Nevada	1.1
16	New Hampshire	0.0
1	New Jersey	7.1
16	New Mexico	0.0
16	New York	0.0
7	North Carolina	1.7
NA	North Dakota**	NA
16	Ohio	0.0
3	Oklahoma	2.2
16	Oregon	0.0
5	Pennsylvania	1.9
NA	Rhode Island**	NA
16	South Carolina	0.0
16	South Dakota	0.0
4	Tennessee	2.0
8	Texas	1.6
16	Utah	0.0
NA	Vermont**	NA
16	Virginia	0.0
16	Washington	0.0
NA	West Virginia**	NA
NA	Wisconsin**	NA
16	Wyoming	0.0

RANK	STATE	PERCENT
1	New Jersey	7.1
2	Idaho	5.3
3	Oklahoma	2.2
4	Tennessee	2.0
5	Alabama	1.9
5	Pennsylvania	1.9
7	North Carolina	1.7
8	California	1.6
8	Florida	1.6
8	Mississippi	1.6
8	Texas	1.6
12	Illinois	1.3
13	Missouri	1.1
13	Nevada	1.1
15	Arizona	0.8
16	Arkansas	0.0
16	Colorado	0.0
16	Connecticut	0.0
16	Delaware	0.0
16	Georgia	0.0
16	Indiana	0.0
16	Kansas	0.0
16	Kentucky	0.0
16	Louisiana	0.0
16	Maryland	0.0
16	Montana	0.0
16	Nebraska	0.0
16	New Hampshire	0.0
16	New Mexico	0.0
16	New York	0.0
16	Ohio	0.0
16	Oregon	0.0
16	South Carolina	0.0
16	South Dakota	0.0
16	Utah	0.0
16	Virginia	0.0
16	Washington	0.0
16	Wyoming	0.0
NA	Alaska**	NA
NA	Hawaii**	NA
NA	Iowa**	NA
NA	Maine**	NA
NA	Massachusetts**	NA
NA	Michigan**	NA
NA	Minnesota**	NA
NA	North Dakota**	NA
NA	Rhode Island**	NA
NA	Vermont**	NA
NA	West Virginia**	NA
NA	Wisconsin**	NA
	District of Columbia**	NA

Source: Morgan Quitno Press using data from U.S. Department of Justice, Bureau of Justice Statistics "Capital Punishment 1997" (Bulletin, December 1998, NCJ-172881)

*As of December 31, 1997. There were no federal female prisoners under sentence of death. There were 74 executions in 1997, none of whom was female.

**No death penalty as of 12/31/97.

White Prisoners Under Sentence of Death in 1997

National Total = 1,870 White State Prisoners*

ALPHA ORDER

RANK	STATE	PRISONERS	% of USA
5	Alabama	90	4.8%
NA	Alaska**	NA	NA
4	Arizona	103	5.5%
21	Arkansas	19	1.0%
1	California	295	15.8%
32	Colorado	2	0.1%
34	Connecticut	1	0.1%
26	Delaware	8	0.4%
3	Florida	237	12.7%
11	Georgia	61	3.3%
NA	Hawaii**	NA	NA
21	Idaho	19	1.0%
12	Illinois	60	3.2%
15	Indiana	30	1.6%
NA	Iowa**	NA	NA
35	Kansas	0	0.0%
18	Kentucky	23	1.2%
19	Louisiana	22	1.2%
NA	Maine**	NA	NA
31	Maryland	3	0.2%
NA	Massachusetts**	NA	NA
NA	Michigan**	NA	NA
NA	Minnesota**	NA	NA
15	Mississippi	30	1.6%
14	Missouri	46	2.5%
29	Montana	6	0.3%
24	Nebraska	9	0.5%
13	Nevada	51	2.7%
35	New Hampshire	0	0.0%
26	New Jersey	8	0.4%
30	New Mexico	4	0.2%
35	New York	0	0.0%
8	North Carolina	78	4.2%
NA	North Dakota**	NA	NA
6	Ohio	89	4.8%
7	Oklahoma	82	4.4%
21	Oregon	19	1.0%
9	Pennsylvania	76	4.1%
NA	Rhode Island**	NA	NA
15	South Carolina	30	1.6%
32	South Dakota	2	0.1%
10	Tennessee	66	3.5%
2	Texas	264	14.1%
28	Utah	7	0.4%
NA	Vermont**	NA	NA
20	Virginia	21	1.1%
24	Washington	9	0.5%
NA	West Virginia**	NA	NA
NA	Wisconsin**	NA	NA
35	Wyoming	0	0.0%

RANK ORDER

RANK	STATE	PRISONERS	% of USA
1	California	295	15.8%
2	Texas	264	14.1%
3	Florida	237	12.7%
4	Arizona	103	5.5%
5	Alabama	90	4.8%
6	Ohio	89	4.8%
7	Oklahoma	82	4.4%
8	North Carolina	78	4.2%
9	Pennsylvania	76	4.1%
10	Tennessee	66	3.5%
11	Georgia	61	3.3%
12	Illinois	60	3.2%
13	Nevada	51	2.7%
14	Missouri	46	2.5%
15	Indiana	30	1.6%
15	Mississippi	30	1.6%
15	South Carolina	30	1.6%
18	Kentucky	23	1.2%
19	Louisiana	22	1.2%
20	Virginia	21	1.1%
21	Arkansas	19	1.0%
21	Idaho	19	1.0%
21	Oregon	19	1.0%
24	Nebraska	9	0.5%
24	Washington	9	0.5%
26	Delaware	8	0.4%
26	New Jersey	8	0.4%
28	Utah	7	0.4%
29	Montana	6	0.3%
30	New Mexico	4	0.2%
31	Maryland	3	0.2%
32	Colorado	2	0.1%
32	South Dakota	2	0.1%
34	Connecticut	1	0.1%
35	Kansas	0	0.0%
35	New Hampshire	0	0.0%
35	New York	0	0.0%
35	Wyoming	0	0.0%
NA	Alaska**	NA	NA
NA	Hawaii**	NA	NA
NA	Iowa**	NA	NA
NA	Maine**	NA	NA
NA	Massachusetts**	NA	NA
NA	Michigan**	NA	NA
NA	Minnesota**	NA	NA
NA	North Dakota**	NA	NA
NA	Rhode Island**	NA	NA
NA	Vermont**	NA	NA
NA	West Virginia**	NA	NA
NA	Wisconsin**	NA	NA
	District of Columbia**	NA	NA

Source: U.S. Department of Justice, Bureau of Justice Statistics
   "Capital Punishment 1997" (Bulletin, December 1998, NCJ-172881)
*As of December 31, 1997. Does not include six white federal prisoners under sentence of death. There were
74 executions in 1997, 41 of whom were white prisoners.
**No death penalty as of 12/31/97.

Percent of Prisoners Under Sentence of Death Who Are White: 1997

National Percent = 56.3% of State Death Sentence Prisoners*

ALPHA ORDER

RANK	STATE	PERCENT
19	Alabama	56.6
NA	Alaska**	NA
5	Arizona	85.8
24	Arkansas	50.0
14	California	60.7
24	Colorado	50.0
33	Connecticut	25.0
20	Delaware	53.3
13	Florida	64.1
21	Georgia	53.0
NA	Hawaii**	NA
1	Idaho	100.0
30	Illinois	37.7
11	Indiana	68.2
NA	Iowa**	NA
35	Kansas	0.0
8	Kentucky	76.7
32	Louisiana	31.4
NA	Maine**	NA
34	Maryland	17.6
NA	Massachusetts**	NA
NA	Michigan**	NA
NA	Minnesota**	NA
27	Mississippi	46.9
22	Missouri	52.3
6	Montana	85.7
7	Nebraska	81.8
17	Nevada	58.6
35	New Hampshire	0.0
18	New Jersey	57.1
1	New Mexico	100.0
35	New York	0.0
28	North Carolina	44.3
NA	North Dakota**	NA
23	Ohio	50.3
16	Oklahoma	59.9
4	Oregon	95.0
31	Pennsylvania	35.5
NA	Rhode Island**	NA
29	South Carolina	44.1
1	South Dakota	100.0
12	Tennessee	67.3
15	Texas	60.3
10	Utah	70.0
NA	Vermont**	NA
26	Virginia	48.8
9	Washington	75.0
NA	West Virginia**	NA
NA	Wisconsin**	NA
35	Wyoming	0.0

RANK ORDER

RANK	STATE	PERCENT
1	Idaho	100.0
1	New Mexico	100.0
1	South Dakota	100.0
4	Oregon	95.0
5	Arizona	85.8
6	Montana	85.7
7	Nebraska	81.8
8	Kentucky	76.7
9	Washington	75.0
10	Utah	70.0
11	Indiana	68.2
12	Tennessee	67.3
13	Florida	64.1
14	California	60.7
15	Texas	60.3
16	Oklahoma	59.9
17	Nevada	58.6
18	New Jersey	57.1
19	Alabama	56.6
20	Delaware	53.3
21	Georgia	53.0
22	Missouri	52.3
23	Ohio	50.3
24	Arkansas	50.0
24	Colorado	50.0
26	Virginia	48.8
27	Mississippi	46.9
28	North Carolina	44.3
29	South Carolina	44.1
30	Illinois	37.7
31	Pennsylvania	35.5
32	Louisiana	31.4
33	Connecticut	25.0
34	Maryland	17.6
35	Kansas	0.0
35	New Hampshire	0.0
35	New York	0.0
35	Wyoming	0.0
NA	Alaska**	NA
NA	Hawaii**	NA
NA	Iowa**	NA
NA	Maine**	NA
NA	Massachusetts**	NA
NA	Michigan**	NA
NA	Minnesota**	NA
NA	North Dakota**	NA
NA	Rhode Island**	NA
NA	Vermont**	NA
NA	West Virginia**	NA
NA	Wisconsin**	NA
	District of Columbia**	NA

Source: Morgan Quitno Press using data from U.S. Department of Justice, Bureau of Justice Statistics "Capital Punishment 1997" (Bulletin, December 1998, NCJ-172881)

*As of December 31, 1997. Does not include six white federal prisoners under sentence of death. There were 74 executions in 1997, 41 of whom were white prisoners.

**No death penalty as of 12/31/97.

Black Prisoners Under Sentence of Death in 1997

National Total = 1,397 Black State Prisoners*

<table>
<tr><td colspan="4">ALPHA ORDER</td><td colspan="4">RANK ORDER</td></tr>
<tr><td>RANK</td><td>STATE</td><td>PRISONERS</td><td>% of USA</td><td>RANK</td><td>STATE</td><td>PRISONERS</td><td>% of USA</td></tr>
<tr><td>8</td><td>Alabama</td><td>68</td><td>4.9%</td><td>1</td><td>California</td><td>180</td><td>12.9%</td></tr>
<tr><td>NA</td><td>Alaska**</td><td>NA</td><td>NA</td><td>2</td><td>Texas</td><td>171</td><td>12.2%</td></tr>
<tr><td>21</td><td>Arizona</td><td>10</td><td>0.7%</td><td>3</td><td>Florida</td><td>132</td><td>9.4%</td></tr>
<tr><td>18</td><td>Arkansas</td><td>19</td><td>1.4%</td><td>4</td><td>Pennsylvania</td><td>131</td><td>9.4%</td></tr>
<tr><td>1</td><td>California</td><td>180</td><td>12.9%</td><td>5</td><td>Illinois</td><td>99</td><td>7.1%</td></tr>
<tr><td>27</td><td>Colorado</td><td>2</td><td>0.1%</td><td>6</td><td>North Carolina</td><td>94</td><td>6.7%</td></tr>
<tr><td>25</td><td>Connecticut</td><td>3</td><td>0.2%</td><td>7</td><td>Ohio</td><td>87</td><td>6.2%</td></tr>
<tr><td>22</td><td>Delaware</td><td>7</td><td>0.5%</td><td>8</td><td>Alabama</td><td>68</td><td>4.9%</td></tr>
<tr><td>3</td><td>Florida</td><td>132</td><td>9.4%</td><td>9</td><td>Georgia</td><td>53</td><td>3.8%</td></tr>
<tr><td>9</td><td>Georgia</td><td>53</td><td>3.8%</td><td>10</td><td>Louisiana</td><td>48</td><td>3.4%</td></tr>
<tr><td>NA</td><td>Hawaii**</td><td>NA</td><td>NA</td><td>11</td><td>Oklahoma</td><td>45</td><td>3.2%</td></tr>
<tr><td>30</td><td>Idaho</td><td>0</td><td>0.0%</td><td>12</td><td>Missouri</td><td>42</td><td>3.0%</td></tr>
<tr><td>5</td><td>Illinois</td><td>99</td><td>7.1%</td><td>13</td><td>South Carolina</td><td>38</td><td>2.7%</td></tr>
<tr><td>19</td><td>Indiana</td><td>14</td><td>1.0%</td><td>14</td><td>Nevada</td><td>35</td><td>2.5%</td></tr>
<tr><td>NA</td><td>Iowa**</td><td>NA</td><td>NA</td><td>15</td><td>Mississippi</td><td>34</td><td>2.4%</td></tr>
<tr><td>30</td><td>Kansas</td><td>0</td><td>0.0%</td><td>16</td><td>Tennessee</td><td>30</td><td>2.1%</td></tr>
<tr><td>22</td><td>Kentucky</td><td>7</td><td>0.5%</td><td>17</td><td>Virginia</td><td>22</td><td>1.6%</td></tr>
<tr><td>10</td><td>Louisiana</td><td>48</td><td>3.4%</td><td>18</td><td>Arkansas</td><td>19</td><td>1.4%</td></tr>
<tr><td>NA</td><td>Maine**</td><td>NA</td><td>NA</td><td>19</td><td>Indiana</td><td>14</td><td>1.0%</td></tr>
<tr><td>19</td><td>Maryland</td><td>14</td><td>1.0%</td><td>19</td><td>Maryland</td><td>14</td><td>1.0%</td></tr>
<tr><td>NA</td><td>Massachusetts**</td><td>NA</td><td>NA</td><td>21</td><td>Arizona</td><td>10</td><td>0.7%</td></tr>
<tr><td>NA</td><td>Michigan**</td><td>NA</td><td>NA</td><td>22</td><td>Delaware</td><td>7</td><td>0.5%</td></tr>
<tr><td>NA</td><td>Minnesota**</td><td>NA</td><td>NA</td><td>22</td><td>Kentucky</td><td>7</td><td>0.5%</td></tr>
<tr><td>15</td><td>Mississippi</td><td>34</td><td>2.4%</td><td>24</td><td>New Jersey</td><td>6</td><td>0.4%</td></tr>
<tr><td>12</td><td>Missouri</td><td>42</td><td>3.0%</td><td>25</td><td>Connecticut</td><td>3</td><td>0.2%</td></tr>
<tr><td>30</td><td>Montana</td><td>0</td><td>0.0%</td><td>25</td><td>Washington</td><td>3</td><td>0.2%</td></tr>
<tr><td>29</td><td>Nebraska</td><td>1</td><td>0.1%</td><td>27</td><td>Colorado</td><td>2</td><td>0.1%</td></tr>
<tr><td>14</td><td>Nevada</td><td>35</td><td>2.5%</td><td>27</td><td>Utah</td><td>2</td><td>0.1%</td></tr>
<tr><td>30</td><td>New Hampshire</td><td>0</td><td>0.0%</td><td>29</td><td>Nebraska</td><td>1</td><td>0.1%</td></tr>
<tr><td>24</td><td>New Jersey</td><td>6</td><td>0.4%</td><td>30</td><td>Idaho</td><td>0</td><td>0.0%</td></tr>
<tr><td>30</td><td>New Mexico</td><td>0</td><td>0.0%</td><td>30</td><td>Kansas</td><td>0</td><td>0.0%</td></tr>
<tr><td>30</td><td>New York</td><td>0</td><td>0.0%</td><td>30</td><td>Montana</td><td>0</td><td>0.0%</td></tr>
<tr><td>6</td><td>North Carolina</td><td>94</td><td>6.7%</td><td>30</td><td>New Hampshire</td><td>0</td><td>0.0%</td></tr>
<tr><td>NA</td><td>North Dakota**</td><td>NA</td><td>NA</td><td>30</td><td>New Mexico</td><td>0</td><td>0.0%</td></tr>
<tr><td>7</td><td>Ohio</td><td>87</td><td>6.2%</td><td>30</td><td>New York</td><td>0</td><td>0.0%</td></tr>
<tr><td>11</td><td>Oklahoma</td><td>45</td><td>3.2%</td><td>30</td><td>Oregon</td><td>0</td><td>0.0%</td></tr>
<tr><td>30</td><td>Oregon</td><td>0</td><td>0.0%</td><td>30</td><td>South Dakota</td><td>0</td><td>0.0%</td></tr>
<tr><td>4</td><td>Pennsylvania</td><td>131</td><td>9.4%</td><td>30</td><td>Wyoming</td><td>0</td><td>0.0%</td></tr>
<tr><td>NA</td><td>Rhode Island**</td><td>NA</td><td>NA</td><td>NA</td><td>Alaska**</td><td>NA</td><td>NA</td></tr>
<tr><td>13</td><td>South Carolina</td><td>38</td><td>2.7%</td><td>NA</td><td>Hawaii**</td><td>NA</td><td>NA</td></tr>
<tr><td>30</td><td>South Dakota</td><td>0</td><td>0.0%</td><td>NA</td><td>Iowa**</td><td>NA</td><td>NA</td></tr>
<tr><td>16</td><td>Tennessee</td><td>30</td><td>2.1%</td><td>NA</td><td>Maine**</td><td>NA</td><td>NA</td></tr>
<tr><td>2</td><td>Texas</td><td>171</td><td>12.2%</td><td>NA</td><td>Massachusetts**</td><td>NA</td><td>NA</td></tr>
<tr><td>27</td><td>Utah</td><td>2</td><td>0.1%</td><td>NA</td><td>Michigan**</td><td>NA</td><td>NA</td></tr>
<tr><td>NA</td><td>Vermont**</td><td>NA</td><td>NA</td><td>NA</td><td>Minnesota**</td><td>NA</td><td>NA</td></tr>
<tr><td>17</td><td>Virginia</td><td>22</td><td>1.6%</td><td>NA</td><td>North Dakota**</td><td>NA</td><td>NA</td></tr>
<tr><td>25</td><td>Washington</td><td>3</td><td>0.2%</td><td>NA</td><td>Rhode Island**</td><td>NA</td><td>NA</td></tr>
<tr><td>NA</td><td>West Virginia**</td><td>NA</td><td>NA</td><td>NA</td><td>Vermont**</td><td>NA</td><td>NA</td></tr>
<tr><td>NA</td><td>Wisconsin**</td><td>NA</td><td>NA</td><td>NA</td><td>West Virginia**</td><td>NA</td><td>NA</td></tr>
<tr><td>30</td><td>Wyoming</td><td>0</td><td>0.0%</td><td>NA</td><td>Wisconsin**</td><td>NA</td><td>NA</td></tr>
<tr><td></td><td></td><td></td><td></td><td></td><td>District of Columbia**</td><td>NA</td><td>NA</td></tr>
</table>

Source: U.S. Department of Justice, Bureau of Justice Statistics
    "Capital Punishment 1997" (Bulletin, December 1998, NCJ-172881)
*As of December 31, 1997. Does not include nine black federal prisoners under sentence of death. There were
74 executions in 1997, 26 of whom were black prisoners.
**No death penalty as of 12/31/97.

Percent of Prisoners Under Sentence of Death Who Are Black: 1997

National Percent = 42.1% of State Death Sentence Prisoners*

ALPHA ORDER

RANK	STATE	PERCENT
17	Alabama	42.8
NA	Alaska**	NA
29	Arizona	8.3
10	Arkansas	50.0
20	California	37.0
10	Colorado	50.0
2	Connecticut	75.0
14	Delaware	46.7
21	Florida	35.7
15	Georgia	46.1
NA	Hawaii**	NA
30	Idaho	0.0
4	Illinois	62.3
23	Indiana	31.8
NA	Iowa**	NA
30	Kansas	0.0
26	Kentucky	23.3
3	Louisiana	68.6
NA	Maine**	NA
1	Maryland	82.4
NA	Massachusetts**	NA
NA	Michigan**	NA
NA	Minnesota**	NA
8	Mississippi	53.1
13	Missouri	47.7
30	Montana	0.0
28	Nebraska	9.1
18	Nevada	40.2
30	New Hampshire	0.0
16	New Jersey	42.9
30	New Mexico	0.0
30	New York	0.0
7	North Carolina	53.4
NA	North Dakota**	NA
12	Ohio	49.2
22	Oklahoma	32.8
30	Oregon	0.0
5	Pennsylvania	61.2
NA	Rhode Island**	NA
6	South Carolina	55.9
30	South Dakota	0.0
24	Tennessee	30.6
19	Texas	39.0
27	Utah	20.0
NA	Vermont**	NA
9	Virginia	51.2
25	Washington	25.0
NA	West Virginia**	NA
NA	Wisconsin**	NA
30	Wyoming	0.0

RANK ORDER

RANK	STATE	PERCENT
1	Maryland	82.4
2	Connecticut	75.0
3	Louisiana	68.6
4	Illinois	62.3
5	Pennsylvania	61.2
6	South Carolina	55.9
7	North Carolina	53.4
8	Mississippi	53.1
9	Virginia	51.2
10	Arkansas	50.0
10	Colorado	50.0
12	Ohio	49.2
13	Missouri	47.7
14	Delaware	46.7
15	Georgia	46.1
16	New Jersey	42.9
17	Alabama	42.8
18	Nevada	40.2
19	Texas	39.0
20	California	37.0
21	Florida	35.7
22	Oklahoma	32.8
23	Indiana	31.8
24	Tennessee	30.6
25	Washington	25.0
26	Kentucky	23.3
27	Utah	20.0
28	Nebraska	9.1
29	Arizona	8.3
30	Idaho	0.0
30	Kansas	0.0
30	Montana	0.0
30	New Hampshire	0.0
30	New Mexico	0.0
30	New York	0.0
30	Oregon	0.0
30	South Dakota	0.0
30	Wyoming	0.0
NA	Alaska**	NA
NA	Hawaii**	NA
NA	Iowa**	NA
NA	Maine**	NA
NA	Massachusetts**	NA
NA	Michigan**	NA
NA	Minnesota**	NA
NA	North Dakota**	NA
NA	Rhode Island**	NA
NA	Vermont**	NA
NA	West Virginia**	NA
NA	Wisconsin**	NA
	District of Columbia**	NA

Source: Morgan Quitno Press using data from U.S. Department of Justice, Bureau of Justice Statistics
"Capital Punishment 1997" (Bulletin, December 1998, NCJ-172881)
*As of December 31, 1997. Does not include nine black federal prisoners under sentence of death. There were
74 executions in 1997, 26 of whom were black prisoners.
**No death penalty as of 12/31/97.

Prisoners Executed: 1930 to 1997

National Total = 4,291 Prisoners*

ALPHA ORDER					RANK ORDER			
RANK	STATE		PRISONERS	% of USA	RANK	STATE	PRISONERS	% of USA
12	Alabama		151	3.5%	1	Texas	441	10.3%
43	Alaska		0	0.0%	2	Georgia	388	9.0%
24	Arizona		46	1.1%	3	New York	329	7.7%
14	Arkansas		134	3.1%	4	California	296	6.9%
4	California		296	6.9%	5	North Carolina	271	6.3%
23	Colorado		48	1.1%	6	Florida	209	4.9%
29	Connecticut		21	0.5%	7	South Carolina	175	4.1%
31	Delaware		20	0.5%	8	Ohio	172	4.0%
6	Florida		209	4.9%	9	Mississippi	158	3.7%
2	Georgia		388	9.0%	10	Louisiana	157	3.7%
43	Hawaii		0	0.0%	11	Pennsylvania	154	3.6%
39	Idaho		4	0.1%	12	Alabama	151	3.5%
16	Illinois		100	2.3%	13	Virginia	138	3.2%
24	Indiana		46	1.1%	14	Arkansas	134	3.1%
32	Iowa		18	0.4%	15	Kentucky	104	2.4%
34	Kansas		15	0.3%	16	Illinois	100	2.3%
15	Kentucky		104	2.4%	17	Tennessee	93	2.2%
10	Louisiana		157	3.7%	18	Missouri	91	2.1%
43	Maine		0	0.0%	19	New Jersey	74	1.7%
20	Maryland		70	1.6%	20	Maryland	70	1.6%
28	Massachusetts		27	0.6%	21	Oklahoma	69	1.6%
43	Michigan		0	0.0%	22	Washington	49	1.1%
43	Minnesota		0	0.0%	23	Colorado	48	1.1%
9	Mississippi		158	3.7%	24	Arizona	46	1.1%
18	Missouri		91	2.1%	24	Indiana	46	1.1%
37	Montana		7	0.2%	26	West Virginia	40	0.9%
37	Nebraska		7	0.2%	27	Nevada	35	0.8%
27	Nevada		35	0.8%	28	Massachusetts	27	0.6%
41	New Hampshire		1	0.0%	29	Connecticut	21	0.5%
19	New Jersey		74	1.7%	29	Oregon	21	0.5%
35	New Mexico		8	0.2%	31	Delaware	20	0.5%
3	New York		329	7.7%	32	Iowa	18	0.4%
5	North Carolina		271	6.3%	32	Utah	18	0.4%
43	North Dakota		0	0.0%	34	Kansas	15	0.3%
8	Ohio		172	4.0%	35	New Mexico	8	0.2%
21	Oklahoma		69	1.6%	35	Wyoming	8	0.2%
29	Oregon		21	0.5%	37	Montana	7	0.2%
11	Pennsylvania		154	3.6%	37	Nebraska	7	0.2%
43	Rhode Island		0	0.0%	39	Idaho	4	0.1%
7	South Carolina		175	4.1%	39	Vermont	4	0.1%
41	South Dakota		1	0.0%	41	New Hampshire	1	0.0%
17	Tennessee		93	2.2%	41	South Dakota	1	0.0%
1	Texas		441	10.3%	43	Alaska	0	0.0%
32	Utah		18	0.4%	43	Hawaii	0	0.0%
39	Vermont		4	0.1%	43	Maine	0	0.0%
13	Virginia		138	3.2%	43	Michigan	0	0.0%
22	Washington		49	1.1%	43	Minnesota	0	0.0%
26	West Virginia		40	0.9%	43	North Dakota	0	0.0%
43	Wisconsin		0	0.0%	43	Rhode Island	0	0.0%
35	Wyoming		8	0.2%	43	Wisconsin	0	0.0%
						District of Columbia	40	0.9%

Source: U.S. Department of Justice, Bureau of Justice Statistics
"Capital Punishment 1997" (Bulletin, December 1998, NCJ-172881)
*Includes 33 executions by the federal government. Does not include 160 executions carried out under military authority. There were no executions from 1968 to 1976.

Prisoners Executed: 1977 to 1997

National Total = 432 Prisoners*

<u>ALPHA ORDER</u>

RANK	STATE	PRISONERS	% of USA
7	Alabama	16	3.7%
30	Alaska	0	0.0%
12	Arizona	8	1.9%
7	Arkansas	16	3.7%
18	California	4	0.9%
25	Colorado	1	0.2%
30	Connecticut	0	0.0%
12	Delaware	8	1.9%
3	Florida	39	9.0%
6	Georgia	22	5.1%
30	Hawaii	0	0.0%
25	Idaho	1	0.2%
10	Illinois	10	2.3%
16	Indiana	5	1.2%
30	Iowa	0	0.0%
30	Kansas	0	0.0%
25	Kentucky	1	0.2%
5	Louisiana	24	5.6%
30	Maine	0	0.0%
21	Maryland	2	0.5%
30	Massachusetts	0	0.0%
30	Michigan	0	0.0%
30	Minnesota	0	0.0%
18	Mississippi	4	0.9%
4	Missouri	29	6.7%
25	Montana	1	0.2%
20	Nebraska	3	0.7%
15	Nevada	6	1.4%
30	New Hampshire	0	0.0%
30	New Jersey	0	0.0%
30	New Mexico	0	0.0%
30	New York	0	0.0%
12	North Carolina	8	1.9%
30	North Dakota	0	0.0%
30	Ohio	0	0.0%
11	Oklahoma	9	2.1%
21	Oregon	2	0.5%
21	Pennsylvania	2	0.5%
30	Rhode Island	0	0.0%
9	South Carolina	13	3.0%
30	South Dakota	0	0.0%
30	Tennessee	0	0.0%
1	Texas	144	33.3%
16	Utah	5	1.2%
30	Vermont	0	0.0%
2	Virginia	46	10.6%
21	Washington	2	0.5%
30	West Virginia	0	0.0%
30	Wisconsin	0	0.0%
25	Wyoming	1	0.2%

<u>RANK ORDER</u>

RANK	STATE	PRISONERS	% of USA
1	Texas	144	33.3%
2	Virginia	46	10.6%
3	Florida	39	9.0%
4	Missouri	29	6.7%
5	Louisiana	24	5.6%
6	Georgia	22	5.1%
7	Alabama	16	3.7%
7	Arkansas	16	3.7%
9	South Carolina	13	3.0%
10	Illinois	10	2.3%
11	Oklahoma	9	2.1%
12	Arizona	8	1.9%
12	Delaware	8	1.9%
12	North Carolina	8	1.9%
15	Nevada	6	1.4%
16	Indiana	5	1.2%
16	Utah	5	1.2%
18	California	4	0.9%
18	Mississippi	4	0.9%
20	Nebraska	3	0.7%
21	Maryland	2	0.5%
21	Oregon	2	0.5%
21	Pennsylvania	2	0.5%
21	Washington	2	0.5%
25	Colorado	1	0.2%
25	Idaho	1	0.2%
25	Kentucky	1	0.2%
25	Montana	1	0.2%
25	Wyoming	1	0.2%
30	Alaska	0	0.0%
30	Connecticut	0	0.0%
30	Hawaii	0	0.0%
30	Iowa	0	0.0%
30	Kansas	0	0.0%
30	Maine	0	0.0%
30	Massachusetts	0	0.0%
30	Michigan	0	0.0%
30	Minnesota	0	0.0%
30	New Hampshire	0	0.0%
30	New Jersey	0	0.0%
30	New Mexico	0	0.0%
30	New York	0	0.0%
30	North Dakota	0	0.0%
30	Ohio	0	0.0%
30	Rhode Island	0	0.0%
30	South Dakota	0	0.0%
30	Tennessee	0	0.0%
30	Vermont	0	0.0%
30	West Virginia	0	0.0%
30	Wisconsin	0	0.0%
	District of Columbia	0	0.0%

Source: U.S. Department of Justice, Bureau of Justice Statistics
"Capital Punishment 1997" (Bulletin, December 1998, NCJ-172881)
As of December 31, 1997. All executions since 1977 have been for murder. In this time period, there have been no executions by the federal government. The most common method of executions was lethal injection (284) followed by electrocution (134), lethal gas (9), hanging (3) and firing squad (2).

Prisoners Sentenced to Death: 1973 to 1997

National Total = 6,123 Death Sentences*

ALPHA ORDER

RANK ORDER

RANK	STATE	SENTENCES	% of USA
8	Alabama	276	4.5%
NA	Alaska**	NA	NA
11	Arizona	210	3.4%
20	Arkansas	85	1.4%
3	California	648	10.6%
31	Colorado	16	0.3%
34	Connecticut	6	0.1%
25	Delaware	36	0.6%
1	Florida	777	12.7%
9	Georgia	270	4.4%
NA	Hawaii**	NA	NA
26	Idaho	35	0.6%
10	Illinois	255	4.2%
19	Indiana	87	1.4%
NA	Iowa**	NA	NA
39	Kansas	0	0.0%
21	Kentucky	61	1.0%
13	Louisiana	174	2.8%
NA	Maine**	NA	NA
23	Maryland	45	0.7%
35	Massachusetts	4	0.1%
NA	Michigan**	NA	NA
NA	Minnesota**	NA	NA
14	Mississippi	152	2.5%
16	Missouri	145	2.4%
32	Montana	15	0.2%
30	Nebraska	24	0.4%
17	Nevada	119	1.9%
39	New Hampshire	0	0.0%
22	New Jersey	46	0.8%
28	New Mexico	26	0.4%
36	New York	3	0.0%
4	North Carolina	431	7.0%
NA	North Dakota**	NA	NA
5	Ohio	324	5.3%
7	Oklahoma	278	4.5%
24	Oregon	41	0.7%
6	Pennsylvania	290	4.7%
37	Rhode Island	2	0.0%
15	South Carolina	151	2.5%
37	South Dakota	2	0.0%
12	Tennessee	179	2.9%
2	Texas	738	12.1%
29	Utah	25	0.4%
NA	Vermont**	NA	NA
18	Virginia	107	1.7%
27	Washington	31	0.5%
NA	West Virginia**	NA	NA
NA	Wisconsin**	NA	NA
33	Wyoming	9	0.1%

RANK	STATE	SENTENCES	% of USA
1	Florida	777	12.7%
2	Texas	738	12.1%
3	California	648	10.6%
4	North Carolina	431	7.0%
5	Ohio	324	5.3%
6	Pennsylvania	290	4.7%
7	Oklahoma	278	4.5%
8	Alabama	276	4.5%
9	Georgia	270	4.4%
10	Illinois	255	4.2%
11	Arizona	210	3.4%
12	Tennessee	179	2.9%
13	Louisiana	174	2.8%
14	Mississippi	152	2.5%
15	South Carolina	151	2.5%
16	Missouri	145	2.4%
17	Nevada	119	1.9%
18	Virginia	107	1.7%
19	Indiana	87	1.4%
20	Arkansas	85	1.4%
21	Kentucky	61	1.0%
22	New Jersey	46	0.8%
23	Maryland	45	0.7%
24	Oregon	41	0.7%
25	Delaware	36	0.6%
26	Idaho	35	0.6%
27	Washington	31	0.5%
28	New Mexico	26	0.4%
29	Utah	25	0.4%
30	Nebraska	24	0.4%
31	Colorado	16	0.3%
32	Montana	15	0.2%
33	Wyoming	9	0.1%
34	Connecticut	6	0.1%
35	Massachusetts	4	0.1%
36	New York	3	0.0%
37	Rhode Island	2	0.0%
37	South Dakota	2	0.0%
39	Kansas	0	0.0%
39	New Hampshire	0	0.0%
NA	Alaska**	NA	NA
NA	Hawaii**	NA	NA
NA	Iowa**	NA	NA
NA	Maine**	NA	NA
NA	Michigan**	NA	NA
NA	Minnesota**	NA	NA
NA	North Dakota**	NA	NA
NA	Vermont**	NA	NA
NA	West Virginia**	NA	NA
NA	Wisconsin**	NA	NA
	District of Columbia**	NA	NA

Source: U.S. Department of Justice, Bureau of Justice Statistics
"Capital Punishment 1997" (Bulletin, December 1998, NCJ-172881)
*As of December 31, 1997. Does not includes 16 federal prisoners sentenced to death.
**Not applicable.

Death Sentences Overturned or Commuted: 1973 to 1996

National Total = 2,178 Sentences*

ALPHA ORDER

RANK	STATE	SENTENCES	% of USA
8	Alabama	92	4.2%
NA	Alaska**	NA	NA
12	Arizona	73	3.4%
17	Arkansas	30	1.4%
5	California	130	6.0%
29	Colorado	10	0.5%
36	Connecticut	2	0.1%
28	Delaware	13	0.6%
1	Florida	344	15.8%
7	Georgia	124	5.7%
NA	Hawaii**	NA	NA
26	Idaho	14	0.6%
13	Illinois	72	3.3%
16	Indiana	35	1.6%
NA	Iowa**	NA	NA
38	Kansas	0	0.0%
18	Kentucky	28	1.3%
10	Louisiana	76	3.5%
NA	Maine**	NA	NA
19	Maryland	25	1.1%
34	Massachusetts	4	0.2%
NA	Michigan**	NA	NA
NA	Minnesota**	NA	NA
9	Mississippi	80	3.7%
20	Missouri	22	1.0%
32	Montana	7	0.3%
31	Nebraska	8	0.4%
20	Nevada	22	1.0%
38	New Hampshire	0	0.0%
20	New Jersey	22	1.0%
23	New Mexico	21	1.0%
35	New York	3	0.1%
2	North Carolina	241	11.1%
NA	North Dakota**	NA	NA
3	Ohio	141	6.5%
6	Oklahoma	125	5.7%
24	Oregon	18	0.8%
14	Pennsylvania	66	3.0%
36	Rhode Island	2	0.1%
14	South Carolina	66	3.0%
38	South Dakota	0	0.0%
11	Tennessee	74	3.4%
3	Texas	141	6.5%
29	Utah	10	0.5%
NA	Vermont**	NA	NA
26	Virginia	14	0.6%
25	Washington	16	0.7%
NA	West Virginia**	NA	NA
NA	Wisconsin**	NA	NA
32	Wyoming	7	0.3%

RANK ORDER

RANK	STATE	SENTENCES	% of USA
1	Florida	344	15.8%
2	North Carolina	241	11.1%
3	Ohio	141	6.5%
3	Texas	141	6.5%
5	California	130	6.0%
6	Oklahoma	125	5.7%
7	Georgia	124	5.7%
8	Alabama	92	4.2%
9	Mississippi	80	3.7%
10	Louisiana	76	3.5%
11	Tennessee	74	3.4%
12	Arizona	73	3.4%
13	Illinois	72	3.3%
14	Pennsylvania	66	3.0%
14	South Carolina	66	3.0%
16	Indiana	35	1.6%
17	Arkansas	30	1.4%
18	Kentucky	28	1.3%
19	Maryland	25	1.1%
20	Missouri	22	1.0%
20	Nevada	22	1.0%
20	New Jersey	22	1.0%
23	New Mexico	21	1.0%
24	Oregon	18	0.8%
25	Washington	16	0.7%
26	Idaho	14	0.6%
26	Virginia	14	0.6%
28	Delaware	13	0.6%
29	Colorado	10	0.5%
29	Utah	10	0.5%
31	Nebraska	8	0.4%
32	Montana	7	0.3%
32	Wyoming	7	0.3%
34	Massachusetts	4	0.2%
35	New York	3	0.1%
36	Connecticut	2	0.1%
36	Rhode Island	2	0.1%
38	Kansas	0	0.0%
38	New Hampshire	0	0.0%
38	South Dakota	0	0.0%
NA	Alaska**	NA	NA
NA	Hawaii**	NA	NA
NA	Iowa**	NA	NA
NA	Maine**	NA	NA
NA	Michigan**	NA	NA
NA	Minnesota**	NA	NA
NA	North Dakota**	NA	NA
NA	Vermont**	NA	NA
NA	West Virginia**	NA	NA
NA	Wisconsin**	NA	NA
	District of Columbia**	NA	NA

Source: U.S. Department of Justice, Bureau of Justice Statistics
   "Capital Punishment 1997" (Bulletin, December 1998, NCJ-172881)
*As of December 31, 1997. Does not include one federal prisoner whose sentence was overturned.
**Not applicable.

Percent of Death Penalty Sentences Overturned or Commuted: 1973 to 1997

National Percent = 35.6% of Sentences*

RANK	STATE	PERCENT
28	Alabama	33.3
NA	Alaska**	NA
27	Arizona	34.8
26	Arkansas	35.3
33	California	20.1
6	Colorado	62.5
28	Connecticut	33.3
25	Delaware	36.1
16	Florida	44.3
13	Georgia	45.9
NA	Hawaii**	NA
23	Idaho	40.0
31	Illinois	28.2
22	Indiana	40.2
NA	Iowa**	NA
38	Kansas	0.0
13	Kentucky	45.9
18	Louisiana	43.7
NA	Maine**	NA
8	Maryland	55.6
1	Massachusetts	100.0
NA	Michigan**	NA
NA	Minnesota**	NA
9	Mississippi	52.6
36	Missouri	15.2
12	Montana	46.7
28	Nebraska	33.3
35	Nevada	18.5
38	New Hampshire	0.0
11	New Jersey	47.8
4	New Mexico	80.8
1	New York	100.0
7	North Carolina	55.9
NA	North Dakota**	NA
20	Ohio	43.5
15	Oklahoma	45.0
17	Oregon	43.9
32	Pennsylvania	22.8
1	Rhode Island	100.0
18	South Carolina	43.7
38	South Dakota	0.0
21	Tennessee	41.3
34	Texas	19.1
23	Utah	40.0
NA	Vermont**	NA
37	Virginia	13.1
10	Washington	51.6
NA	West Virginia**	NA
NA	Wisconsin**	NA
5	Wyoming	77.8

RANK	STATE	PERCENT
1	Massachusetts	100.0
1	New York	100.0
1	Rhode Island	100.0
4	New Mexico	80.8
5	Wyoming	77.8
6	Colorado	62.5
7	North Carolina	55.9
8	Maryland	55.6
9	Mississippi	52.6
10	Washington	51.6
11	New Jersey	47.8
12	Montana	46.7
13	Georgia	45.9
13	Kentucky	45.9
15	Oklahoma	45.0
16	Florida	44.3
17	Oregon	43.9
18	Louisiana	43.7
18	South Carolina	43.7
20	Ohio	43.5
21	Tennessee	41.3
22	Indiana	40.2
23	Idaho	40.0
23	Utah	40.0
25	Delaware	36.1
26	Arkansas	35.3
27	Arizona	34.8
28	Alabama	33.3
28	Connecticut	33.3
28	Nebraska	33.3
31	Illinois	28.2
32	Pennsylvania	22.8
33	California	20.1
34	Texas	19.1
35	Nevada	18.5
36	Missouri	15.2
37	Virginia	13.1
38	Kansas	0.0
38	New Hampshire	0.0
38	South Dakota	0.0
NA	Alaska**	NA
NA	Hawaii**	NA
NA	Iowa**	NA
NA	Maine**	NA
NA	Michigan**	NA
NA	Minnesota**	NA
NA	North Dakota**	NA
NA	Vermont**	NA
NA	West Virginia**	NA
NA	Wisconsin**	NA
	District of Columbia**	NA

Source: Morgan Quitno Press using data from U.S. Department of Justice, Bureau of Justice Statistics
    "Capital Punishment 1997" (Bulletin, December 1998, NCJ-172881)

*As of December 31, 1997. Does not include one federal prisoner whose sentence was overturned.
**Not applicable.

Sentenced Prisoners Admitted to State Correctional Institutions in 1996

National Total = 525,711 Prisoners Admitted*

ALPHA ORDER

RANK	STATE	ADMISSIONS	% of USA
15	Alabama	9,750	1.9%
37	Alaska	2,377	0.5%
17	Arizona	9,090	1.7%
27	Arkansas	5,215	1.0%
1	California	123,876	23.6%
25	Colorado	6,098	1.2%
41	Connecticut	1,227	0.2%
40	Delaware	1,481	0.3%
5	Florida	24,209	4.6%
7	Georgia	15,714	3.0%
38	Hawaii	2,356	0.4%
36	Idaho	2,526	0.5%
4	Illinois	24,541	4.7%
18	Indiana	8,847	1.7%
30	Iowa	4,156	0.8%
29	Kansas	4,244	0.8%
21	Kentucky	7,685	1.5%
10	Louisiana	14,175	2.7%
47	Maine	803	0.2%
16	Maryland	9,715	1.8%
32	Massachusetts	3,412	0.6%
11	Michigan	13,731	2.6%
33	Minnesota	3,304	0.6%
26	Mississippi	5,467	1.0%
12	Missouri	13,462	2.6%
45	Montana	1,005	0.2%
39	Nebraska	1,724	0.3%
28	Nevada	4,272	0.8%
46	New Hampshire	996	0.2%
8	New Jersey	15,001	2.9%
34	New Mexico	2,845	0.5%
3	New York	32,152	6.1%
9	North Carolina	14,359	2.7%
50	North Dakota	585	0.1%
6	Ohio	21,727	4.1%
22	Oklahoma	7,433	1.4%
31	Oregon	3,712	0.7%
13	Pennsylvania	9,918	1.9%
44	Rhode Island	1,036	0.2%
20	South Carolina	8,243	1.6%
42	South Dakota	1,143	0.2%
19	Tennessee	8,320	1.6%
2	Texas	38,716	7.4%
35	Utah	2,587	0.5%
47	Vermont	803	0.2%
14	Virginia	9,823	1.9%
24	Washington	6,462	1.2%
43	West Virginia	1,049	0.2%
23	Wisconsin	7,019	1.3%
49	Wyoming	614	0.1%

RANK ORDER

RANK	STATE	ADMISSIONS	% of USA
1	California	123,876	23.6%
2	Texas	38,716	7.4%
3	New York	32,152	6.1%
4	Illinois	24,541	4.7%
5	Florida	24,209	4.6%
6	Ohio	21,727	4.1%
7	Georgia	15,714	3.0%
8	New Jersey	15,001	2.9%
9	North Carolina	14,359	2.7%
10	Louisiana	14,175	2.7%
11	Michigan	13,731	2.6%
12	Missouri	13,462	2.6%
13	Pennsylvania	9,918	1.9%
14	Virginia	9,823	1.9%
15	Alabama	9,750	1.9%
16	Maryland	9,715	1.8%
17	Arizona	9,090	1.7%
18	Indiana	8,847	1.7%
19	Tennessee	8,320	1.6%
20	South Carolina	8,243	1.6%
21	Kentucky	7,685	1.5%
22	Oklahoma	7,433	1.4%
23	Wisconsin	7,019	1.3%
24	Washington	6,462	1.2%
25	Colorado	6,098	1.2%
26	Mississippi	5,467	1.0%
27	Arkansas	5,215	1.0%
28	Nevada	4,272	0.8%
29	Kansas	4,244	0.8%
30	Iowa	4,156	0.8%
31	Oregon	3,712	0.7%
32	Massachusetts	3,412	0.6%
33	Minnesota	3,304	0.6%
34	New Mexico	2,845	0.5%
35	Utah	2,587	0.5%
36	Idaho	2,526	0.5%
37	Alaska	2,377	0.5%
38	Hawaii	2,356	0.4%
39	Nebraska	1,724	0.3%
40	Delaware	1,481	0.3%
41	Connecticut	1,227	0.2%
42	South Dakota	1,143	0.2%
43	West Virginia	1,049	0.2%
44	Rhode Island	1,036	0.2%
45	Montana	1,005	0.2%
46	New Hampshire	996	0.2%
47	Maine	803	0.2%
47	Vermont	803	0.2%
49	Wyoming	614	0.1%
50	North Dakota	585	0.1%
	District of Columbia	6,706	1.3%

Source: U.S. Department of Justice, Bureau of Justice Statistics
   "Correctional Populations in the United States, 1996" (1998)
*Includes sentenced prisoners admitted because of new court commitments, parole violators returned, escapees
returned and others. Does not include 30,281 new federal commitments.

Sentenced Prisoners Admitted to State Correctional Institutions
Through New Court Commitments in 1996
National Total = 326,547 New Prisoners*

RANK	STATE	PRISONERS	% of USA
15	Alabama	7,477	2.3%
36	Alaska	1,549	0.5%
16	Arizona	7,014	2.1%
27	Arkansas	3,234	1.0%
1	California	46,465	14.2%
26	Colorado	4,346	1.3%
49	Connecticut	404	0.1%
40	Delaware	936	0.3%
4	Florida	19,972	6.1%
7	Georgia	12,533	3.8%
38	Hawaii	1,353	0.4%
34	Idaho	1,971	0.6%
5	Illinois	18,290	5.6%
12	Indiana	8,016	2.5%
30	Iowa	2,604	0.8%
29	Kansas	2,859	0.9%
21	Kentucky	5,672	1.7%
18	Louisiana	6,206	1.9%
46	Maine	528	0.2%
13	Maryland	7,974	2.4%
32	Massachusetts	2,201	0.7%
11	Michigan	8,049	2.5%
31	Minnesota	2,478	0.8%
23	Mississippi	4,762	1.5%
14	Missouri	7,916	2.4%
44	Montana	663	0.2%
37	Nebraska	1,370	0.4%
28	Nevada	2,975	0.9%
45	New Hampshire	641	0.2%
9	New Jersey	9,382	2.9%
35	New Mexico	1,642	0.5%
3	New York	21,192	6.5%
8	North Carolina	9,601	2.9%
48	North Dakota	488	0.1%
6	Ohio	17,948	5.5%
17	Oklahoma	6,867	2.1%
33	Oregon	2,141	0.7%
20	Pennsylvania	5,744	1.8%
43	Rhode Island	715	0.2%
19	South Carolina	5,830	1.8%
41	South Dakota	891	0.3%
25	Tennessee	4,578	1.4%
2	Texas	24,468	7.5%
38	Utah	1,353	0.4%
50	Vermont	204	0.1%
10	Virginia	8,191	2.5%
22	Washington	5,532	1.7%
42	West Virginia	876	0.3%
24	Wisconsin	4,619	1.4%
47	Wyoming	523	0.2%

RANK	STATE	PRISONERS	% of USA
1	California	46,465	14.2%
2	Texas	24,468	7.5%
3	New York	21,192	6.5%
4	Florida	19,972	6.1%
5	Illinois	18,290	5.6%
6	Ohio	17,948	5.5%
7	Georgia	12,533	3.8%
8	North Carolina	9,601	2.9%
9	New Jersey	9,382	2.9%
10	Virginia	8,191	2.5%
11	Michigan	8,049	2.5%
12	Indiana	8,016	2.5%
13	Maryland	7,974	2.4%
14	Missouri	7,916	2.4%
15	Alabama	7,477	2.3%
16	Arizona	7,014	2.1%
17	Oklahoma	6,867	2.1%
18	Louisiana	6,206	1.9%
19	South Carolina	5,830	1.8%
20	Pennsylvania	5,744	1.8%
21	Kentucky	5,672	1.7%
22	Washington	5,532	1.7%
23	Mississippi	4,762	1.5%
24	Wisconsin	4,619	1.4%
25	Tennessee	4,578	1.4%
26	Colorado	4,346	1.3%
27	Arkansas	3,234	1.0%
28	Nevada	2,975	0.9%
29	Kansas	2,859	0.9%
30	Iowa	2,604	0.8%
31	Minnesota	2,478	0.8%
32	Massachusetts	2,201	0.7%
33	Oregon	2,141	0.7%
34	Idaho	1,971	0.6%
35	New Mexico	1,642	0.5%
36	Alaska	1,549	0.5%
37	Nebraska	1,370	0.4%
38	Hawaii	1,353	0.4%
38	Utah	1,353	0.4%
40	Delaware	936	0.3%
41	South Dakota	891	0.3%
42	West Virginia	876	0.3%
43	Rhode Island	715	0.2%
44	Montana	663	0.2%
45	New Hampshire	641	0.2%
46	Maine	528	0.2%
47	Wyoming	523	0.2%
48	North Dakota	488	0.1%
49	Connecticut	404	0.1%
50	Vermont	204	0.1%
	District of Columbia	3,304	1.0%

Source: U.S. Department of Justice, Bureau of Justice Statistics
   "Correctional Populations in the United States, 1996" (1998)
*Does not include 27,346 new federal court commitments.

Parole Violators Returned to State Prisons in 1996

National Total = 172,633 Prisoners*

ALPHA ORDER

RANK	STATE	PRISONERS	% of USA
19	Alabama	1,840	1.1%
32	Alaska	782	0.5%
16	Arizona	2,005	1.2%
17	Arkansas	1,878	1.1%
1	California	75,785	43.9%
24	Colorado	1,360	0.8%
45	Connecticut	238	0.1%
37	Delaware	363	0.2%
10	Florida	3,722	2.2%
14	Georgia	3,042	1.8%
28	Hawaii	916	0.5%
36	Idaho	542	0.3%
6	Illinois	5,224	3.0%
34	Indiana	769	0.4%
31	Iowa	792	0.5%
25	Kansas	1,298	0.8%
18	Kentucky	1,854	1.1%
4	Louisiana	7,435	4.3%
43	Maine	267	0.2%
21	Maryland	1,623	0.9%
29	Massachusetts	883	0.5%
12	Michigan	3,606	2.1%
30	Minnesota	826	0.5%
41	Mississippi	322	0.2%
13	Missouri	3,336	1.9%
38	Montana	341	0.2%
40	Nebraska	335	0.2%
35	Nevada	636	0.4%
39	New Hampshire	340	0.2%
5	New Jersey	5,617	3.3%
27	New Mexico	1,153	0.7%
2	New York	8,240	4.8%
7	North Carolina	4,579	2.7%
49	North Dakota	92	0.1%
9	Ohio	3,742	2.2%
46	Oklahoma	225	0.1%
22	Oregon	1,469	0.9%
8	Pennsylvania	3,770	2.2%
42	Rhode Island	283	0.2%
15	South Carolina	2,259	1.3%
47	South Dakota	192	0.1%
11	Tennessee	3,623	2.1%
3	Texas	7,566	4.4%
26	Utah	1,224	0.7%
44	Vermont	249	0.1%
20	Virginia	1,632	0.9%
33	Washington	774	0.4%
48	West Virginia	168	0.1%
23	Wisconsin	1,385	0.8%
50	Wyoming	82	0.0%

RANK ORDER

RANK	STATE	PRISONERS	% of USA
1	California	75,785	43.9%
2	New York	8,240	4.8%
3	Texas	7,566	4.4%
4	Louisiana	7,435	4.3%
5	New Jersey	5,617	3.3%
6	Illinois	5,224	3.0%
7	North Carolina	4,579	2.7%
8	Pennsylvania	3,770	2.2%
9	Ohio	3,742	2.2%
10	Florida	3,722	2.2%
11	Tennessee	3,623	2.1%
12	Michigan	3,606	2.1%
13	Missouri	3,336	1.9%
14	Georgia	3,042	1.8%
15	South Carolina	2,259	1.3%
16	Arizona	2,005	1.2%
17	Arkansas	1,878	1.1%
18	Kentucky	1,854	1.1%
19	Alabama	1,840	1.1%
20	Virginia	1,632	0.9%
21	Maryland	1,623	0.9%
22	Oregon	1,469	0.9%
23	Wisconsin	1,385	0.8%
24	Colorado	1,360	0.8%
25	Kansas	1,298	0.8%
26	Utah	1,224	0.7%
27	New Mexico	1,153	0.7%
28	Hawaii	916	0.5%
29	Massachusetts	883	0.5%
30	Minnesota	826	0.5%
31	Iowa	792	0.5%
32	Alaska	782	0.5%
33	Washington	774	0.4%
34	Indiana	769	0.4%
35	Nevada	636	0.4%
36	Idaho	542	0.3%
37	Delaware	363	0.2%
38	Montana	341	0.2%
39	New Hampshire	340	0.2%
40	Nebraska	335	0.2%
41	Mississippi	322	0.2%
42	Rhode Island	283	0.2%
43	Maine	267	0.2%
44	Vermont	249	0.1%
45	Connecticut	238	0.1%
46	Oklahoma	225	0.1%
47	South Dakota	192	0.1%
48	West Virginia	168	0.1%
49	North Dakota	92	0.1%
50	Wyoming	82	0.0%
	District of Columbia	1,949	1.1%

Source: U.S. Department of Justice, Bureau of Justice Statistics
"Correctional Populations in the United States, 1996" (1998)
Includes other conditional release violators. Does not include 2,672 federal parole violators returned to prison.

Escapees Returned to State Prisons in 1996

National Total = 9,808 Prisoners*

ALPHA ORDER

RANK	STATE	PRISONERS	% of USA
9	Alabama	265	2.7%
25	Alaska	41	0.4%
28	Arizona	30	0.3%
40	Arkansas	7	0.1%
6	California	390	4.0%
7	Colorado	371	3.8%
14	Connecticut	121	1.2%
26	Delaware	39	0.4%
10	Florida	244	2.5%
20	Georgia	79	0.8%
19	Hawaii	80	0.8%
34	Idaho	13	0.1%
3	Illinois	1,012	10.3%
37	Indiana	8	0.1%
5	Iowa	596	6.1%
35	Kansas	12	0.1%
15	Kentucky	117	1.2%
18	Louisiana	84	0.9%
37	Maine	8	0.1%
16	Maryland	103	1.1%
32	Massachusetts	15	0.2%
4	Michigan	1,011	10.3%
46	Minnesota	0	0.0%
26	Mississippi	39	0.4%
2	Missouri	1,215	12.4%
46	Montana	0	0.0%
31	Nebraska	19	0.2%
24	Nevada	42	0.4%
32	New Hampshire	15	0.2%
45	New Jersey	2	0.0%
30	New Mexico	20	0.2%
1	New York	2,091	21.3%
11	North Carolina	179	1.8%
43	North Dakota	5	0.1%
36	Ohio	10	0.1%
8	Oklahoma	341	3.5%
21	Oregon	75	0.8%
13	Pennsylvania	124	1.3%
29	Rhode Island	24	0.2%
22	South Carolina	60	0.6%
40	South Dakota	7	0.1%
17	Tennessee	87	0.9%
46	Texas	0	0.0%
37	Utah	8	0.1%
23	Vermont	50	0.5%
46	Virginia	0	0.0%
12	Washington	132	1.3%
43	West Virginia	5	0.1%
46	Wisconsin	0	0.0%
42	Wyoming	6	0.1%

RANK ORDER

RANK	STATE	PRISONERS	% of USA
1	New York	2,091	21.3%
2	Missouri	1,215	12.4%
3	Illinois	1,012	10.3%
4	Michigan	1,011	10.3%
5	Iowa	596	6.1%
6	California	390	4.0%
7	Colorado	371	3.8%
8	Oklahoma	341	3.5%
9	Alabama	265	2.7%
10	Florida	244	2.5%
11	North Carolina	179	1.8%
12	Washington	132	1.3%
13	Pennsylvania	124	1.3%
14	Connecticut	121	1.2%
15	Kentucky	117	1.2%
16	Maryland	103	1.1%
17	Tennessee	87	0.9%
18	Louisiana	84	0.9%
19	Hawaii	80	0.8%
20	Georgia	79	0.8%
21	Oregon	75	0.8%
22	South Carolina	60	0.6%
23	Vermont	50	0.5%
24	Nevada	42	0.4%
25	Alaska	41	0.4%
26	Delaware	39	0.4%
26	Mississippi	39	0.4%
28	Arizona	30	0.3%
29	Rhode Island	24	0.2%
30	New Mexico	20	0.2%
31	Nebraska	19	0.2%
32	Massachusetts	15	0.2%
32	New Hampshire	15	0.2%
34	Idaho	13	0.1%
35	Kansas	12	0.1%
36	Ohio	10	0.1%
37	Indiana	8	0.1%
37	Maine	8	0.1%
37	Utah	8	0.1%
40	Arkansas	7	0.1%
40	South Dakota	7	0.1%
42	Wyoming	6	0.1%
43	North Dakota	5	0.1%
43	West Virginia	5	0.1%
45	New Jersey	2	0.0%
46	Minnesota	0	0.0%
46	Montana	0	0.0%
46	Texas	0	0.0%
46	Virginia	0	0.0%
46	Wisconsin	0	0.0%
	District of Columbia	606	6.2%

Source: U.S. Department of Justice, Bureau of Justice Statistics
  "Correctional Populations in the United States, 1996" (1998)
*Includes AWOLs returned. Federal data were not reported.

Prisoners Released from State Correctional Institutions in 1996

National Total = 479,344 Prisoners*

<table>
<tr><td colspan="4">ALPHA ORDER</td><td colspan="4">RANK ORDER</td></tr>
<tr><th>RANK</th><th>STATE</th><th>PRISONERS</th><th>% of USA</th><th>RANK</th><th>STATE</th><th>PRISONERS</th><th>% of USA</th></tr>
<tr><td>15</td><td>Alabama</td><td>8,772</td><td>1.8%</td><td>1</td><td>California</td><td>112,756</td><td>23.5%</td></tr>
<tr><td>36</td><td>Alaska</td><td>2,084</td><td>0.4%</td><td>2</td><td>Texas</td><td>34,099</td><td>7.1%</td></tr>
<tr><td>18</td><td>Arizona</td><td>7,858</td><td>1.6%</td><td>3</td><td>New York</td><td>30,929</td><td>6.5%</td></tr>
<tr><td>25</td><td>Arkansas</td><td>4,745</td><td>1.0%</td><td>4</td><td>Florida</td><td>24,329</td><td>5.1%</td></tr>
<tr><td>1</td><td>California</td><td>112,756</td><td>23.5%</td><td>5</td><td>Illinois</td><td>23,347</td><td>4.9%</td></tr>
<tr><td>26</td><td>Colorado</td><td>4,723</td><td>1.0%</td><td>6</td><td>Ohio</td><td>20,216</td><td>4.2%</td></tr>
<tr><td>41</td><td>Connecticut</td><td>1,344</td><td>0.3%</td><td>7</td><td>Georgia</td><td>15,471</td><td>3.2%</td></tr>
<tr><td>40</td><td>Delaware</td><td>1,376</td><td>0.3%</td><td>8</td><td>New Jersey</td><td>14,577</td><td>3.0%</td></tr>
<tr><td>4</td><td>Florida</td><td>24,329</td><td>5.1%</td><td>9</td><td>North Carolina</td><td>14,522</td><td>3.0%</td></tr>
<tr><td>7</td><td>Georgia</td><td>15,471</td><td>3.2%</td><td>10</td><td>Louisiana</td><td>12,591</td><td>2.6%</td></tr>
<tr><td>38</td><td>Hawaii</td><td>1,992</td><td>0.4%</td><td>11</td><td>Michigan</td><td>12,494</td><td>2.6%</td></tr>
<tr><td>37</td><td>Idaho</td><td>2,022</td><td>0.4%</td><td>12</td><td>Missouri</td><td>10,593</td><td>2.2%</td></tr>
<tr><td>5</td><td>Illinois</td><td>23,347</td><td>4.9%</td><td>13</td><td>Virginia</td><td>10,021</td><td>2.1%</td></tr>
<tr><td>16</td><td>Indiana</td><td>8,102</td><td>1.7%</td><td>14</td><td>Maryland</td><td>9,185</td><td>1.9%</td></tr>
<tr><td>28</td><td>Iowa</td><td>3,720</td><td>0.8%</td><td>15</td><td>Alabama</td><td>8,772</td><td>1.8%</td></tr>
<tr><td>30</td><td>Kansas</td><td>3,542</td><td>0.7%</td><td>16</td><td>Indiana</td><td>8,102</td><td>1.7%</td></tr>
<tr><td>21</td><td>Kentucky</td><td>6,835</td><td>1.4%</td><td>17</td><td>Tennessee</td><td>7,900</td><td>1.6%</td></tr>
<tr><td>10</td><td>Louisiana</td><td>12,591</td><td>2.6%</td><td>18</td><td>Arizona</td><td>7,858</td><td>1.6%</td></tr>
<tr><td>45</td><td>Maine</td><td>853</td><td>0.2%</td><td>19</td><td>Pennsylvania</td><td>7,793</td><td>1.6%</td></tr>
<tr><td>14</td><td>Maryland</td><td>9,185</td><td>1.9%</td><td>20</td><td>South Carolina</td><td>7,500</td><td>1.6%</td></tr>
<tr><td>32</td><td>Massachusetts</td><td>2,959</td><td>0.6%</td><td>21</td><td>Kentucky</td><td>6,835</td><td>1.4%</td></tr>
<tr><td>11</td><td>Michigan</td><td>12,494</td><td>2.6%</td><td>22</td><td>Oklahoma</td><td>5,991</td><td>1.2%</td></tr>
<tr><td>31</td><td>Minnesota</td><td>2,992</td><td>0.6%</td><td>23</td><td>Washington</td><td>5,543</td><td>1.2%</td></tr>
<tr><td>27</td><td>Mississippi</td><td>4,575</td><td>1.0%</td><td>24</td><td>Wisconsin</td><td>5,261</td><td>1.1%</td></tr>
<tr><td>12</td><td>Missouri</td><td>10,593</td><td>2.2%</td><td>25</td><td>Arkansas</td><td>4,745</td><td>1.0%</td></tr>
<tr><td>47</td><td>Montana</td><td>815</td><td>0.2%</td><td>26</td><td>Colorado</td><td>4,723</td><td>1.0%</td></tr>
<tr><td>39</td><td>Nebraska</td><td>1,546</td><td>0.3%</td><td>27</td><td>Mississippi</td><td>4,575</td><td>1.0%</td></tr>
<tr><td>29</td><td>Nevada</td><td>3,546</td><td>0.7%</td><td>28</td><td>Iowa</td><td>3,720</td><td>0.8%</td></tr>
<tr><td>44</td><td>New Hampshire</td><td>949</td><td>0.2%</td><td>29</td><td>Nevada</td><td>3,546</td><td>0.7%</td></tr>
<tr><td>8</td><td>New Jersey</td><td>14,577</td><td>3.0%</td><td>30</td><td>Kansas</td><td>3,542</td><td>0.7%</td></tr>
<tr><td>34</td><td>New Mexico</td><td>2,264</td><td>0.5%</td><td>31</td><td>Minnesota</td><td>2,992</td><td>0.6%</td></tr>
<tr><td>3</td><td>New York</td><td>30,929</td><td>6.5%</td><td>32</td><td>Massachusetts</td><td>2,959</td><td>0.6%</td></tr>
<tr><td>9</td><td>North Carolina</td><td>14,522</td><td>3.0%</td><td>33</td><td>Oregon</td><td>2,911</td><td>0.6%</td></tr>
<tr><td>50</td><td>North Dakota</td><td>479</td><td>0.1%</td><td>34</td><td>New Mexico</td><td>2,264</td><td>0.5%</td></tr>
<tr><td>6</td><td>Ohio</td><td>20,216</td><td>4.2%</td><td>35</td><td>Utah</td><td>2,088</td><td>0.4%</td></tr>
<tr><td>22</td><td>Oklahoma</td><td>5,991</td><td>1.2%</td><td>36</td><td>Alaska</td><td>2,084</td><td>0.4%</td></tr>
<tr><td>33</td><td>Oregon</td><td>2,911</td><td>0.6%</td><td>37</td><td>Idaho</td><td>2,022</td><td>0.4%</td></tr>
<tr><td>19</td><td>Pennsylvania</td><td>7,793</td><td>1.6%</td><td>38</td><td>Hawaii</td><td>1,992</td><td>0.4%</td></tr>
<tr><td>46</td><td>Rhode Island</td><td>839</td><td>0.2%</td><td>39</td><td>Nebraska</td><td>1,546</td><td>0.3%</td></tr>
<tr><td>20</td><td>South Carolina</td><td>7,500</td><td>1.6%</td><td>40</td><td>Delaware</td><td>1,376</td><td>0.3%</td></tr>
<tr><td>43</td><td>South Dakota</td><td>951</td><td>0.2%</td><td>41</td><td>Connecticut</td><td>1,344</td><td>0.3%</td></tr>
<tr><td>17</td><td>Tennessee</td><td>7,900</td><td>1.6%</td><td>42</td><td>Vermont</td><td>1,050</td><td>0.2%</td></tr>
<tr><td>2</td><td>Texas</td><td>34,099</td><td>7.1%</td><td>43</td><td>South Dakota</td><td>951</td><td>0.2%</td></tr>
<tr><td>35</td><td>Utah</td><td>2,088</td><td>0.4%</td><td>44</td><td>New Hampshire</td><td>949</td><td>0.2%</td></tr>
<tr><td>42</td><td>Vermont</td><td>1,050</td><td>0.2%</td><td>45</td><td>Maine</td><td>853</td><td>0.2%</td></tr>
<tr><td>13</td><td>Virginia</td><td>10,021</td><td>2.1%</td><td>46</td><td>Rhode Island</td><td>839</td><td>0.2%</td></tr>
<tr><td>23</td><td>Washington</td><td>5,543</td><td>1.2%</td><td>47</td><td>Montana</td><td>815</td><td>0.2%</td></tr>
<tr><td>48</td><td>West Virginia</td><td>807</td><td>0.2%</td><td>48</td><td>West Virginia</td><td>807</td><td>0.2%</td></tr>
<tr><td>24</td><td>Wisconsin</td><td>5,261</td><td>1.1%</td><td>49</td><td>Wyoming</td><td>510</td><td>0.1%</td></tr>
<tr><td>49</td><td>Wyoming</td><td>510</td><td>0.1%</td><td>50</td><td>North Dakota</td><td>479</td><td>0.1%</td></tr>
<tr><td></td><td></td><td></td><td></td><td colspan="2">District of Columbia</td><td>6,977</td><td>1.5%</td></tr>
</table>

Source: U.S. Department of Justice, Bureau of Justice Statistics
"Correctional Populations in the United States, 1996" (1998)
*Includes conditional releases, unconditional releases, escapees, out on appeal, deaths and other releases. Does not include 24,945 federal prisoners released.

State Prisoners Released with Conditions in 1996

National Total = 366,632 Prisoners*

ALPHA ORDER					RANK ORDER			
RANK	STATE	PRISONERS	% of USA		RANK	STATE	PRISONERS	% of USA
19	Alabama	4,745	1.3%		1	California	103,859	28.3%
34	Alaska	1,631	0.4%		2	Texas	28,754	7.8%
16	Arizona	6,777	1.8%		3	New York	26,057	7.1%
22	Arkansas	3,889	1.1%		4	Illinois	21,428	5.8%
1	California	103,859	28.3%		5	Louisiana	11,756	3.2%
26	Colorado	3,106	0.8%		6	North Carolina	11,288	3.1%
48	Connecticut	358	0.1%		7	New Jersey	11,122	3.0%
45	Delaware	538	0.1%		8	Georgia	10,837	3.0%
12	Florida	8,336	2.3%		9	Michigan	9,463	2.6%
8	Georgia	10,837	3.0%		10	Missouri	8,693	2.4%
35	Hawaii	1,488	0.4%		11	Virginia	8,406	2.3%
33	Idaho	1,744	0.5%		12	Florida	8,336	2.3%
4	Illinois	21,428	5.8%		13	Maryland	7,895	2.2%
14	Indiana	7,540	2.1%		14	Indiana	7,540	2.1%
27	Iowa	3,054	0.8%		15	Ohio	7,374	2.0%
25	Kansas	3,292	0.9%		16	Arizona	6,777	1.8%
23	Kentucky	3,783	1.0%		17	Tennessee	5,942	1.6%
5	Louisiana	11,756	3.2%		18	Pennsylvania	5,662	1.5%
46	Maine	467	0.1%		19	Alabama	4,745	1.3%
13	Maryland	7,895	2.2%		20	South Carolina	4,553	1.2%
39	Massachusetts	948	0.3%		21	Wisconsin	4,328	1.2%
9	Michigan	9,463	2.6%		22	Arkansas	3,889	1.1%
30	Minnesota	2,641	0.7%		23	Kentucky	3,783	1.0%
31	Mississippi	1,988	0.5%		24	Washington	3,633	1.0%
10	Missouri	8,693	2.4%		25	Kansas	3,292	0.9%
43	Montana	630	0.2%		26	Colorado	3,106	0.8%
40	Nebraska	819	0.2%		27	Iowa	3,054	0.8%
36	Nevada	1,452	0.4%		28	Oregon	2,780	0.8%
42	New Hampshire	738	0.2%		29	Oklahoma	2,684	0.7%
7	New Jersey	11,122	3.0%		30	Minnesota	2,641	0.7%
37	New Mexico	1,446	0.4%		31	Mississippi	1,988	0.5%
3	New York	26,057	7.1%		32	Utah	1,891	0.5%
6	North Carolina	11,288	3.1%		33	Idaho	1,744	0.5%
49	North Dakota	311	0.1%		34	Alaska	1,631	0.4%
15	Ohio	7,374	2.0%		35	Hawaii	1,488	0.4%
29	Oklahoma	2,684	0.7%		36	Nevada	1,452	0.4%
28	Oregon	2,780	0.8%		37	New Mexico	1,446	0.4%
18	Pennsylvania	5,662	1.5%		38	Vermont	965	0.3%
41	Rhode Island	793	0.2%		39	Massachusetts	948	0.3%
20	South Carolina	4,553	1.2%		40	Nebraska	819	0.2%
44	South Dakota	555	0.2%		41	Rhode Island	793	0.2%
17	Tennessee	5,942	1.6%		42	New Hampshire	738	0.2%
2	Texas	28,754	7.8%		43	Montana	630	0.2%
32	Utah	1,891	0.5%		44	South Dakota	555	0.2%
38	Vermont	965	0.3%		45	Delaware	538	0.1%
11	Virginia	8,406	2.3%		46	Maine	467	0.1%
24	Washington	3,633	1.0%		47	West Virginia	410	0.1%
47	West Virginia	410	0.1%		48	Connecticut	358	0.1%
21	Wisconsin	4,328	1.2%		49	North Dakota	311	0.1%
50	Wyoming	267	0.1%		50	Wyoming	267	0.1%
						District of Columbia	3,516	1.0%

Source: U.S. Department of Justice, Bureau of Justice Statistics
"Correctional Populations in the United States, 1996" (1998)
*Released on parole, probation, supervised mandatory release or other conditions. Does not include 3,176
federal prisoners released with conditions.

State Prisoners Released Conditionally as a Percent of All Releases in 1996

National Percent = 76.5% of Prisoners Released*

ALPHA ORDER				RANK ORDER		
RANK	STATE	PERCENT		RANK	STATE	PERCENT
39	Alabama	54.1		1	Oregon	95.5
21	Alaska	78.3		2	Rhode Island	94.5
12	Arizona	86.2		3	Louisiana	93.4
20	Arkansas	82.0		4	Indiana	93.1
6	California	92.1		5	Kansas	92.9
31	Colorado	65.8		6	California	92.1
50	Connecticut	26.6		7	Vermont	91.9
46	Delaware	39.1		8	Illinois	91.8
48	Florida	34.3		9	Utah	90.6
30	Georgia	70.0		10	Minnesota	88.3
28	Hawaii	74.7		11	Idaho	86.3
11	Idaho	86.3		12	Arizona	86.2
8	Illinois	91.8		13	Maryland	86.0
4	Indiana	93.1		14	Texas	84.3
18	Iowa	82.1		15	New York	84.2
5	Kansas	92.9		16	Virginia	83.9
37	Kentucky	55.3		17	Wisconsin	82.3
3	Louisiana	93.4		18	Iowa	82.1
38	Maine	54.7		18	Missouri	82.1
13	Maryland	86.0		20	Arkansas	82.0
49	Massachusetts	32.0		21	Alaska	78.3
26	Michigan	75.7		22	New Hampshire	77.8
10	Minnesota	88.3		23	North Carolina	77.7
44	Mississippi	43.5		24	Montana	77.3
18	Missouri	82.1		25	New Jersey	76.3
24	Montana	77.3		26	Michigan	75.7
40	Nebraska	53.0		27	Tennessee	75.2
45	Nevada	40.9		28	Hawaii	74.7
22	New Hampshire	77.8		29	Pennsylvania	72.7
25	New Jersey	76.3		30	Georgia	70.0
34	New Mexico	63.9		31	Colorado	65.8
15	New York	84.2		32	Washington	65.5
23	North Carolina	77.7		33	North Dakota	64.9
33	North Dakota	64.9		34	New Mexico	63.9
47	Ohio	36.5		35	South Carolina	60.7
43	Oklahoma	44.8		36	South Dakota	58.4
1	Oregon	95.5		37	Kentucky	55.3
29	Pennsylvania	72.7		38	Maine	54.7
2	Rhode Island	94.5		39	Alabama	54.1
35	South Carolina	60.7		40	Nebraska	53.0
36	South Dakota	58.4		41	Wyoming	52.4
27	Tennessee	75.2		42	West Virginia	50.8
14	Texas	84.3		43	Oklahoma	44.8
9	Utah	90.6		44	Mississippi	43.5
7	Vermont	91.9		45	Nevada	40.9
16	Virginia	83.9		46	Delaware	39.1
32	Washington	65.5		47	Ohio	36.5
42	West Virginia	50.8		48	Florida	34.3
17	Wisconsin	82.3		49	Massachusetts	32.0
41	Wyoming	52.4		50	Connecticut	26.6
					District of Columbia	50.4

Source: Morgan Quitno Press using data from U.S. Department of Justice, Bureau of Justice Statistics
"Correctional Populations in the United States, 1996" (1998)
*Released on parole, probation, supervised mandatory release or other conditions. Does not include federal prisoners released with conditions. Federal percent is 12.7% of releases. The combined state and federal percent is 73.3% of prisoners released are released with conditions.

State Prisoners Released on Parole in 1996

National Total = 141,808 Prisoners*

ALPHA ORDER					RANK ORDER			
RANK	STATE		PRISONERS	% of USA	RANK	STATE	PRISONERS	% of USA
19	Alabama		2,301	1.6%	1	New York	21,330	15.0%
44	Alaska		67	0.0%	2	Texas	11,859	8.4%
27	Arizona		1,002	0.7%	3	North Carolina	11,288	8.0%
11	Arkansas		3,540	2.5%	4	New Jersey	10,621	7.5%
49	California		0	0.0%	5	Michigan	9,463	6.7%
20	Colorado		2,288	1.6%	6	Georgia	9,034	6.4%
39	Connecticut		170	0.1%	7	Pennsylvania	5,662	4.0%
45	Delaware		34	0.0%	8	Missouri	4,615	3.3%
43	Florida		72	0.1%	9	Ohio	4,364	3.1%
6	Georgia		9,034	6.4%	10	Maryland	3,851	2.7%
32	Hawaii		643	0.5%	11	Arkansas	3,540	2.5%
30	Idaho		701	0.5%	12	Virginia	3,492	2.5%
46	Illinois		24	0.0%	13	Wisconsin	3,409	2.4%
49	Indiana		0	0.0%	14	Tennessee	3,232	2.3%
23	Iowa		1,576	1.1%	15	South Carolina	3,190	2.2%
16	Kansas		3,001	2.1%	16	Kansas	3,001	2.1%
17	Kentucky		2,857	2.0%	17	Kentucky	2,857	2.0%
22	Louisiana		1,617	1.1%	18	Oregon	2,780	2.0%
48	Maine		4	0.0%	19	Alabama	2,301	1.6%
10	Maryland		3,851	2.7%	20	Colorado	2,288	1.6%
28	Massachusetts		948	0.7%	21	Utah	1,891	1.3%
5	Michigan		9,463	6.7%	22	Louisiana	1,617	1.1%
47	Minnesota		9	0.0%	23	Iowa	1,576	1.1%
26	Mississippi		1,107	0.8%	24	Nevada	1,452	1.0%
8	Missouri		4,615	3.3%	25	New Mexico	1,407	1.0%
35	Montana		439	0.3%	26	Mississippi	1,107	0.8%
29	Nebraska		819	0.6%	27	Arizona	1,002	0.7%
24	Nevada		1,452	1.0%	28	Massachusetts	948	0.7%
31	New Hampshire		673	0.5%	29	Nebraska	819	0.6%
4	New Jersey		10,621	7.5%	30	Idaho	701	0.5%
25	New Mexico		1,407	1.0%	31	New Hampshire	673	0.5%
1	New York		21,330	15.0%	32	Hawaii	643	0.5%
3	North Carolina		11,288	8.0%	33	South Dakota	478	0.3%
41	North Dakota		154	0.1%	34	Oklahoma	465	0.3%
9	Ohio		4,364	3.1%	35	Montana	439	0.3%
34	Oklahoma		465	0.3%	36	Rhode Island	414	0.3%
18	Oregon		2,780	2.0%	37	West Virginia	381	0.3%
7	Pennsylvania		5,662	4.0%	38	Vermont	338	0.2%
36	Rhode Island		414	0.3%	39	Connecticut	170	0.1%
15	South Carolina		3,190	2.2%	40	Wyoming	168	0.1%
33	South Dakota		478	0.3%	41	North Dakota	154	0.1%
14	Tennessee		3,232	2.3%	42	Washington	88	0.1%
2	Texas		11,859	8.4%	43	Florida	72	0.1%
21	Utah		1,891	1.3%	44	Alaska	67	0.0%
38	Vermont		338	0.2%	45	Delaware	34	0.0%
12	Virginia		3,492	2.5%	46	Illinois	24	0.0%
42	Washington		88	0.1%	47	Minnesota	9	0.0%
37	West Virginia		381	0.3%	48	Maine	4	0.0%
13	Wisconsin		3,409	2.4%	49	California	0	0.0%
40	Wyoming		168	0.1%	49	Indiana	0	0.0%
						District of Columbia	2,490	1.8%

Source: U.S. Department of Justice, Bureau of Justice Statistics
   "Correctional Populations in the United States, 1996" (1998)
*Does not include 1,873 federal prisoners released on parole.

State Prisoners Released on Probation in 1996

National Total = 28,770 Prisoners*

ALPHA ORDER

RANK	STATE	PRISONERS	% of USA
5	Alabama	2,444	8.5%
11	Alaska	916	3.2%
24	Arizona	78	0.3%
29	Arkansas	0	0.0%
29	California	0	0.0%
19	Colorado	266	0.9%
29	Connecticut	0	0.0%
29	Delaware	0	0.0%
1	Florida	3,881	13.5%
26	Georgia	43	0.1%
13	Hawaii	839	2.9%
9	Idaho	1,043	3.6%
29	Illinois	0	0.0%
2	Indiana	3,793	13.2%
14	Iowa	606	2.1%
22	Kansas	132	0.5%
10	Kentucky	926	3.2%
15	Louisiana	483	1.7%
18	Maine	347	1.2%
29	Maryland	0	0.0%
29	Massachusetts	0	0.0%
29	Michigan	0	0.0%
29	Minnesota	0	0.0%
12	Mississippi	880	3.1%
3	Missouri	2,950	10.3%
20	Montana	191	0.7%
29	Nebraska	0	0.0%
29	Nevada	0	0.0%
25	New Hampshire	65	0.2%
29	New Jersey	0	0.0%
29	New Mexico	0	0.0%
29	New York	0	0.0%
29	North Carolina	0	0.0%
21	North Dakota	148	0.5%
4	Ohio	2,650	9.2%
6	Oklahoma	2,051	7.1%
29	Oregon	0	0.0%
29	Pennsylvania	0	0.0%
16	Rhode Island	376	1.3%
8	South Carolina	1,363	4.7%
29	South Dakota	0	0.0%
7	Tennessee	1,784	6.2%
17	Texas	357	1.2%
29	Utah	0	0.0%
27	Vermont	30	0.1%
29	Virginia	0	0.0%
29	Washington	0	0.0%
28	West Virginia	29	0.1%
29	Wisconsin	0	0.0%
23	Wyoming	99	0.3%

RANK ORDER

RANK	STATE	PRISONERS	% of USA
1	Florida	3,881	13.5%
2	Indiana	3,793	13.2%
3	Missouri	2,950	10.3%
4	Ohio	2,650	9.2%
5	Alabama	2,444	8.5%
6	Oklahoma	2,051	7.1%
7	Tennessee	1,784	6.2%
8	South Carolina	1,363	4.7%
9	Idaho	1,043	3.6%
10	Kentucky	926	3.2%
11	Alaska	916	3.2%
12	Mississippi	880	3.1%
13	Hawaii	839	2.9%
14	Iowa	606	2.1%
15	Louisiana	483	1.7%
16	Rhode Island	376	1.3%
17	Texas	357	1.2%
18	Maine	347	1.2%
19	Colorado	266	0.9%
20	Montana	191	0.7%
21	North Dakota	148	0.5%
22	Kansas	132	0.5%
23	Wyoming	99	0.3%
24	Arizona	78	0.3%
25	New Hampshire	65	0.2%
26	Georgia	43	0.1%
27	Vermont	30	0.1%
28	West Virginia	29	0.1%
29	Arkansas	0	0.0%
29	California	0	0.0%
29	Connecticut	0	0.0%
29	Delaware	0	0.0%
29	Illinois	0	0.0%
29	Maryland	0	0.0%
29	Massachusetts	0	0.0%
29	Michigan	0	0.0%
29	Minnesota	0	0.0%
29	Nebraska	0	0.0%
29	Nevada	0	0.0%
29	New Jersey	0	0.0%
29	New Mexico	0	0.0%
29	New York	0	0.0%
29	North Carolina	0	0.0%
29	Oregon	0	0.0%
29	Pennsylvania	0	0.0%
29	South Dakota	0	0.0%
29	Utah	0	0.0%
29	Virginia	0	0.0%
29	Washington	0	0.0%
29	Wisconsin	0	0.0%
	District of Columbia	0	0.0%

Source: U.S. Department of Justice, Bureau of Justice Statistics
   "Correctional Populations in the United States, 1996" (1998)
*Does not include 18 federal prisoners released on probation.

State Prisoners Released on Supervised Mandatory Release in 1996

National Total = 177,321 Prisoners*

ALPHA ORDER

RANK	STATE	PRISONERS	% of USA
17	Alabama	0	0.0%
14	Alaska	245	0.1%
15	Arizona	87	0.0%
17	Arkansas	0	0.0%
1	California	103,859	58.6%
12	Colorado	552	0.3%
17	Connecticut	0	0.0%
13	Delaware	504	0.3%
17	Florida	0	0.0%
17	Georgia	0	0.0%
17	Hawaii	0	0.0%
17	Idaho	0	0.0%
2	Illinois	21,404	12.1%
8	Indiana	3,747	2.1%
17	Iowa	0	0.0%
17	Kansas	0	0.0%
17	Kentucky	0	0.0%
4	Louisiana	9,656	5.4%
17	Maine	0	0.0%
7	Maryland	4,030	2.3%
17	Massachusetts	0	0.0%
17	Michigan	0	0.0%
10	Minnesota	2,446	1.4%
17	Mississippi	0	0.0%
17	Missouri	0	0.0%
17	Montana	0	0.0%
17	Nebraska	0	0.0%
17	Nevada	0	0.0%
17	New Hampshire	0	0.0%
17	New Jersey	0	0.0%
17	New Mexico	0	0.0%
6	New York	4,727	2.7%
17	North Carolina	0	0.0%
17	North Dakota	0	0.0%
17	Ohio	0	0.0%
17	Oklahoma	0	0.0%
17	Oregon	0	0.0%
17	Pennsylvania	0	0.0%
17	Rhode Island	0	0.0%
17	South Carolina	0	0.0%
16	South Dakota	77	0.0%
17	Tennessee	0	0.0%
3	Texas	16,538	9.3%
17	Utah	0	0.0%
17	Vermont	0	0.0%
5	Virginia	4,913	2.8%
9	Washington	3,545	2.0%
17	West Virginia	0	0.0%
11	Wisconsin	919	0.5%
17	Wyoming	0	0.0%

RANK ORDER

RANK	STATE	PRISONERS	% of USA
1	California	103,859	58.6%
2	Illinois	21,404	12.1%
3	Texas	16,538	9.3%
4	Louisiana	9,656	5.4%
5	Virginia	4,913	2.8%
6	New York	4,727	2.7%
7	Maryland	4,030	2.3%
8	Indiana	3,747	2.1%
9	Washington	3,545	2.0%
10	Minnesota	2,446	1.4%
11	Wisconsin	919	0.5%
12	Colorado	552	0.3%
13	Delaware	504	0.3%
14	Alaska	245	0.1%
15	Arizona	87	0.0%
16	South Dakota	77	0.0%
17	Alabama	0	0.0%
17	Arkansas	0	0.0%
17	Connecticut	0	0.0%
17	Florida	0	0.0%
17	Georgia	0	0.0%
17	Hawaii	0	0.0%
17	Idaho	0	0.0%
17	Iowa	0	0.0%
17	Kansas	0	0.0%
17	Kentucky	0	0.0%
17	Maine	0	0.0%
17	Massachusetts	0	0.0%
17	Michigan	0	0.0%
17	Mississippi	0	0.0%
17	Missouri	0	0.0%
17	Montana	0	0.0%
17	Nebraska	0	0.0%
17	Nevada	0	0.0%
17	New Hampshire	0	0.0%
17	New Jersey	0	0.0%
17	New Mexico	0	0.0%
17	North Carolina	0	0.0%
17	North Dakota	0	0.0%
17	Ohio	0	0.0%
17	Oklahoma	0	0.0%
17	Oregon	0	0.0%
17	Pennsylvania	0	0.0%
17	Rhode Island	0	0.0%
17	South Carolina	0	0.0%
17	Tennessee	0	0.0%
17	Utah	0	0.0%
17	Vermont	0	0.0%
17	West Virginia	0	0.0%
17	Wyoming	0	0.0%
	District of Columbia	72	0.0%

Source: U.S. Department of Justice, Bureau of Justice Statistics
"Correctional Populations in the United States, 1996" (1998)
*Does not include 1,285 federal prisoners released on supervised mandatory release.

State Prisoners Released Unconditionally in 1996

National Total = 83,736 Prisoners*

ALPHA ORDER

RANK	STATE	PRISONERS	% of USA
4	Alabama	3,519	4.2%
34	Alaska	406	0.5%
30	Arizona	600	0.7%
26	Arkansas	712	0.9%
17	California	1,535	1.8%
20	Colorado	1,079	1.3%
23	Connecticut	836	1.0%
29	Delaware	611	0.7%
1	Florida	15,380	18.4%
3	Georgia	3,805	4.5%
47	Hawaii	112	0.1%
39	Idaho	262	0.3%
25	Illinois	758	0.9%
33	Indiana	516	0.6%
31	Iowa	558	0.7%
40	Kansas	201	0.2%
7	Kentucky	2,827	3.4%
32	Louisiana	540	0.6%
35	Maine	379	0.5%
21	Maryland	1,050	1.3%
12	Massachusetts	1,971	2.4%
22	Michigan	969	1.2%
38	Minnesota	341	0.4%
10	Mississippi	2,515	3.0%
28	Missouri	672	0.8%
43	Montana	175	0.2%
27	Nebraska	702	0.8%
11	Nevada	2,023	2.4%
41	New Hampshire	194	0.2%
5	New Jersey	3,242	3.9%
24	New Mexico	768	0.9%
14	New York	1,761	2.1%
6	North Carolina	2,851	3.4%
44	North Dakota	160	0.2%
2	Ohio	12,672	15.1%
8	Oklahoma	2,803	3.3%
49	Oregon	8	0.0%
13	Pennsylvania	1,894	2.3%
50	Rhode Island	3	0.0%
9	South Carolina	2,612	3.1%
37	South Dakota	343	0.4%
16	Tennessee	1,692	2.0%
19	Texas	1,383	1.7%
44	Utah	160	0.2%
48	Vermont	79	0.1%
18	Virginia	1,528	1.8%
15	Washington	1,720	2.1%
36	West Virginia	373	0.4%
46	Wisconsin	113	0.1%
42	Wyoming	182	0.2%

RANK ORDER

RANK	STATE	PRISONERS	% of USA
1	Florida	15,380	18.4%
2	Ohio	12,672	15.1%
3	Georgia	3,805	4.5%
4	Alabama	3,519	4.2%
5	New Jersey	3,242	3.9%
6	North Carolina	2,851	3.4%
7	Kentucky	2,827	3.4%
8	Oklahoma	2,803	3.3%
9	South Carolina	2,612	3.1%
10	Mississippi	2,515	3.0%
11	Nevada	2,023	2.4%
12	Massachusetts	1,971	2.4%
13	Pennsylvania	1,894	2.3%
14	New York	1,761	2.1%
15	Washington	1,720	2.1%
16	Tennessee	1,692	2.0%
17	California	1,535	1.8%
18	Virginia	1,528	1.8%
19	Texas	1,383	1.7%
20	Colorado	1,079	1.3%
21	Maryland	1,050	1.3%
22	Michigan	969	1.2%
23	Connecticut	836	1.0%
24	New Mexico	768	0.9%
25	Illinois	758	0.9%
26	Arkansas	712	0.9%
27	Nebraska	702	0.8%
28	Missouri	672	0.8%
29	Delaware	611	0.7%
30	Arizona	600	0.7%
31	Iowa	558	0.7%
32	Louisiana	540	0.6%
33	Indiana	516	0.6%
34	Alaska	406	0.5%
35	Maine	379	0.5%
36	West Virginia	373	0.4%
37	South Dakota	343	0.4%
38	Minnesota	341	0.4%
39	Idaho	262	0.3%
40	Kansas	201	0.2%
41	New Hampshire	194	0.2%
42	Wyoming	182	0.2%
43	Montana	175	0.2%
44	North Dakota	160	0.2%
44	Utah	160	0.2%
46	Wisconsin	113	0.1%
47	Hawaii	112	0.1%
48	Vermont	79	0.1%
49	Oregon	8	0.0%
50	Rhode Island	3	0.0%
	District of Columbia	2,141	2.6%

Source: U.S. Department of Justice, Bureau of Justice Statistics
    "Correctional Populations in the United States, 1996" (1998)
*Does not include 19,699 federal prisoners released without conditions.

State Prisoners Released Unconditionally as a Percent of All Releases in 1996

National Percent = 17.5% of Released Prisoners*

ALPHA ORDER

RANK	STATE	PERCENT
13	Alabama	40.1
28	Alaska	19.5
37	Arizona	7.6
30	Arkansas	15.0
48	California	1.4
22	Colorado	22.8
4	Connecticut	62.2
10	Delaware	44.4
2	Florida	63.2
20	Georgia	24.6
43	Hawaii	5.6
32	Idaho	13.0
46	Illinois	3.2
39	Indiana	6.4
30	Iowa	15.0
41	Kansas	5.7
12	Kentucky	41.4
44	Louisiana	4.3
10	Maine	44.4
33	Maryland	11.4
1	Massachusetts	66.6
35	Michigan	7.8
33	Minnesota	11.4
6	Mississippi	55.0
40	Missouri	6.3
24	Montana	21.5
9	Nebraska	45.4
5	Nevada	57.1
26	New Hampshire	20.4
23	New Jersey	22.2
17	New Mexico	33.9
41	New York	5.7
27	North Carolina	19.6
18	North Dakota	33.4
3	Ohio	62.7
7	Oklahoma	46.8
50	Oregon	0.3
21	Pennsylvania	24.3
49	Rhode Island	0.4
16	South Carolina	34.8
14	South Dakota	36.1
25	Tennessee	21.4
45	Texas	4.1
36	Utah	7.7
38	Vermont	7.5
29	Virginia	15.2
19	Washington	31.0
8	West Virginia	46.2
47	Wisconsin	2.1
15	Wyoming	35.7

RANK ORDER

RANK	STATE	PERCENT
1	Massachusetts	66.6
2	Florida	63.2
3	Ohio	62.7
4	Connecticut	62.2
5	Nevada	57.1
6	Mississippi	55.0
7	Oklahoma	46.8
8	West Virginia	46.2
9	Nebraska	45.4
10	Delaware	44.4
10	Maine	44.4
12	Kentucky	41.4
13	Alabama	40.1
14	South Dakota	36.1
15	Wyoming	35.7
16	South Carolina	34.8
17	New Mexico	33.9
18	North Dakota	33.4
19	Washington	31.0
20	Georgia	24.6
21	Pennsylvania	24.3
22	Colorado	22.8
23	New Jersey	22.2
24	Montana	21.5
25	Tennessee	21.4
26	New Hampshire	20.4
27	North Carolina	19.6
28	Alaska	19.5
29	Virginia	15.2
30	Arkansas	15.0
30	Iowa	15.0
32	Idaho	13.0
33	Maryland	11.4
33	Minnesota	11.4
35	Michigan	7.8
36	Utah	7.7
37	Arizona	7.6
38	Vermont	7.5
39	Indiana	6.4
40	Missouri	6.3
41	Kansas	5.7
41	New York	5.7
43	Hawaii	5.6
44	Louisiana	4.3
45	Texas	4.1
46	Illinois	3.2
47	Wisconsin	2.1
48	California	1.4
49	Rhode Island	0.4
50	Oregon	0.3

District of Columbia — 30.7

Source: Morgan Quitno Press using data from U.S. Department of Justice, Bureau of Justice Statistics
   "Correctional Populations in the United States, 1996" (1998)
*Does not include federal prisoners released without conditions. Federal percent is 79.0% of releases. The
combined state and federal percent is 20.5% of prisoners released are released without conditions.

State Prisoners Released on Appeal or Bond in 1996

National Total = 739 Prisoners*

<table>
<tr><th colspan="4">ALPHA ORDER</th><th colspan="4">RANK ORDER</th></tr>
<tr><th>RANK</th><th>STATE</th><th>PRISONERS</th><th>% of USA</th><th>RANK</th><th>STATE</th><th>PRISONERS</th><th>% of USA</th></tr>
<tr><td>3</td><td>Alabama</td><td>75</td><td>10.1%</td><td>1</td><td>New York</td><td>149</td><td>20.2%</td></tr>
<tr><td>21</td><td>Alaska</td><td>3</td><td>0.4%</td><td>2</td><td>Hawaii</td><td>112</td><td>15.2%</td></tr>
<tr><td>24</td><td>Arizona</td><td>0</td><td>0.0%</td><td>3</td><td>Alabama</td><td>75</td><td>10.1%</td></tr>
<tr><td>16</td><td>Arkansas</td><td>12</td><td>1.6%</td><td>4</td><td>New Jersey</td><td>69</td><td>9.3%</td></tr>
<tr><td>24</td><td>California</td><td>0</td><td>0.0%</td><td>5</td><td>Michigan</td><td>61</td><td>8.3%</td></tr>
<tr><td>14</td><td>Colorado</td><td>13</td><td>1.8%</td><td>6</td><td>Iowa</td><td>39</td><td>5.3%</td></tr>
<tr><td>19</td><td>Connecticut</td><td>7</td><td>0.9%</td><td>7</td><td>Oregon</td><td>31</td><td>4.2%</td></tr>
<tr><td>24</td><td>Delaware</td><td>0</td><td>0.0%</td><td>8</td><td>Ohio</td><td>29</td><td>3.9%</td></tr>
<tr><td>24</td><td>Florida</td><td>0</td><td>0.0%</td><td>9</td><td>Pennsylvania</td><td>26</td><td>3.5%</td></tr>
<tr><td>24</td><td>Georgia</td><td>0</td><td>0.0%</td><td>10</td><td>Illinois</td><td>20</td><td>2.7%</td></tr>
<tr><td>2</td><td>Hawaii</td><td>112</td><td>15.2%</td><td>11</td><td>Utah</td><td>19</td><td>2.6%</td></tr>
<tr><td>24</td><td>Idaho</td><td>0</td><td>0.0%</td><td>11</td><td>Washington</td><td>19</td><td>2.6%</td></tr>
<tr><td>10</td><td>Illinois</td><td>20</td><td>2.7%</td><td>13</td><td>South Carolina</td><td>15</td><td>2.0%</td></tr>
<tr><td>24</td><td>Indiana</td><td>0</td><td>0.0%</td><td>14</td><td>Colorado</td><td>13</td><td>1.8%</td></tr>
<tr><td>6</td><td>Iowa</td><td>39</td><td>5.3%</td><td>14</td><td>Missouri</td><td>13</td><td>1.8%</td></tr>
<tr><td>17</td><td>Kansas</td><td>9</td><td>1.2%</td><td>16</td><td>Arkansas</td><td>12</td><td>1.6%</td></tr>
<tr><td>24</td><td>Kentucky</td><td>0</td><td>0.0%</td><td>17</td><td>Kansas</td><td>9</td><td>1.2%</td></tr>
<tr><td>24</td><td>Louisiana</td><td>0</td><td>0.0%</td><td>18</td><td>West Virginia</td><td>8</td><td>1.1%</td></tr>
<tr><td>24</td><td>Maine</td><td>0</td><td>0.0%</td><td>19</td><td>Connecticut</td><td>7</td><td>0.9%</td></tr>
<tr><td>24</td><td>Maryland</td><td>0</td><td>0.0%</td><td>20</td><td>Rhode Island</td><td>6</td><td>0.8%</td></tr>
<tr><td>24</td><td>Massachusetts</td><td>0</td><td>0.0%</td><td>21</td><td>Alaska</td><td>3</td><td>0.4%</td></tr>
<tr><td>5</td><td>Michigan</td><td>61</td><td>8.3%</td><td>22</td><td>South Dakota</td><td>2</td><td>0.3%</td></tr>
<tr><td>24</td><td>Minnesota</td><td>0</td><td>0.0%</td><td>23</td><td>Nevada</td><td>1</td><td>0.1%</td></tr>
<tr><td>24</td><td>Mississippi</td><td>0</td><td>0.0%</td><td>24</td><td>Arizona</td><td>0</td><td>0.0%</td></tr>
<tr><td>14</td><td>Missouri</td><td>13</td><td>1.8%</td><td>24</td><td>California</td><td>0</td><td>0.0%</td></tr>
<tr><td>24</td><td>Montana</td><td>0</td><td>0.0%</td><td>24</td><td>Delaware</td><td>0</td><td>0.0%</td></tr>
<tr><td>24</td><td>Nebraska</td><td>0</td><td>0.0%</td><td>24</td><td>Florida</td><td>0</td><td>0.0%</td></tr>
<tr><td>23</td><td>Nevada</td><td>1</td><td>0.1%</td><td>24</td><td>Georgia</td><td>0</td><td>0.0%</td></tr>
<tr><td>24</td><td>New Hampshire</td><td>0</td><td>0.0%</td><td>24</td><td>Idaho</td><td>0</td><td>0.0%</td></tr>
<tr><td>4</td><td>New Jersey</td><td>69</td><td>9.3%</td><td>24</td><td>Indiana</td><td>0</td><td>0.0%</td></tr>
<tr><td>24</td><td>New Mexico</td><td>0</td><td>0.0%</td><td>24</td><td>Kentucky</td><td>0</td><td>0.0%</td></tr>
<tr><td>1</td><td>New York</td><td>149</td><td>20.2%</td><td>24</td><td>Louisiana</td><td>0</td><td>0.0%</td></tr>
<tr><td>24</td><td>North Carolina</td><td>0</td><td>0.0%</td><td>24</td><td>Maine</td><td>0</td><td>0.0%</td></tr>
<tr><td>24</td><td>North Dakota</td><td>0</td><td>0.0%</td><td>24</td><td>Maryland</td><td>0</td><td>0.0%</td></tr>
<tr><td>8</td><td>Ohio</td><td>29</td><td>3.9%</td><td>24</td><td>Massachusetts</td><td>0</td><td>0.0%</td></tr>
<tr><td>24</td><td>Oklahoma</td><td>0</td><td>0.0%</td><td>24</td><td>Minnesota</td><td>0</td><td>0.0%</td></tr>
<tr><td>7</td><td>Oregon</td><td>31</td><td>4.2%</td><td>24</td><td>Mississippi</td><td>0</td><td>0.0%</td></tr>
<tr><td>9</td><td>Pennsylvania</td><td>26</td><td>3.5%</td><td>24</td><td>Montana</td><td>0</td><td>0.0%</td></tr>
<tr><td>20</td><td>Rhode Island</td><td>6</td><td>0.8%</td><td>24</td><td>Nebraska</td><td>0</td><td>0.0%</td></tr>
<tr><td>13</td><td>South Carolina</td><td>15</td><td>2.0%</td><td>24</td><td>New Hampshire</td><td>0</td><td>0.0%</td></tr>
<tr><td>22</td><td>South Dakota</td><td>2</td><td>0.3%</td><td>24</td><td>New Mexico</td><td>0</td><td>0.0%</td></tr>
<tr><td>24</td><td>Tennessee</td><td>0</td><td>0.0%</td><td>24</td><td>North Carolina</td><td>0</td><td>0.0%</td></tr>
<tr><td>24</td><td>Texas</td><td>0</td><td>0.0%</td><td>24</td><td>North Dakota</td><td>0</td><td>0.0%</td></tr>
<tr><td>11</td><td>Utah</td><td>19</td><td>2.6%</td><td>24</td><td>Oklahoma</td><td>0</td><td>0.0%</td></tr>
<tr><td>24</td><td>Vermont</td><td>0</td><td>0.0%</td><td>24</td><td>Tennessee</td><td>0</td><td>0.0%</td></tr>
<tr><td>24</td><td>Virginia</td><td>0</td><td>0.0%</td><td>24</td><td>Texas</td><td>0</td><td>0.0%</td></tr>
<tr><td>11</td><td>Washington</td><td>19</td><td>2.6%</td><td>24</td><td>Vermont</td><td>0</td><td>0.0%</td></tr>
<tr><td>18</td><td>West Virginia</td><td>8</td><td>1.1%</td><td>24</td><td>Virginia</td><td>0</td><td>0.0%</td></tr>
<tr><td>24</td><td>Wisconsin</td><td>0</td><td>0.0%</td><td>24</td><td>Wisconsin</td><td>0</td><td>0.0%</td></tr>
<tr><td>24</td><td>Wyoming</td><td>0</td><td>0.0%</td><td>24</td><td>Wyoming</td><td>0</td><td>0.0%</td></tr>
<tr><td></td><td></td><td></td><td></td><td></td><td>District of Columbia</td><td>1</td><td>0.1%</td></tr>
</table>

Source: U.S. Department of Justice, Bureau of Justice Statistics
"Correctional Populations in the United States, 1996" (1998)
*Numbers of federal prisoners released on appeal or bond were not available.

State Prisoners Escaped in 1996

National Total = 9,437 Prisoners*

ALPHA ORDER

RANK	STATE	PRISONERS	% of USA
8	Alabama	276	2.9%
21	Alaska	41	0.4%
26	Arizona	19	0.2%
37	Arkansas	8	0.1%
5	California	588	6.2%
7	Colorado	360	3.8%
18	Connecticut	56	0.6%
47	Delaware	0	0.0%
9	Florida	210	2.2%
17	Georgia	68	0.7%
14	Hawaii	91	1.0%
32	Idaho	13	0.1%
4	Illinois	1,005	10.6%
39	Indiana	7	0.1%
43	Iowa	4	0.0%
25	Kansas	20	0.2%
11	Kentucky	129	1.4%
15	Louisiana	89	0.9%
43	Maine	4	0.0%
13	Maryland	111	1.2%
35	Massachusetts	10	0.1%
2	Michigan	1,405	14.9%
47	Minnesota	0	0.0%
23	Mississippi	28	0.3%
3	Missouri	1,171	12.4%
41	Montana	5	0.1%
27	Nebraska	17	0.2%
22	Nevada	35	0.4%
29	New Hampshire	15	0.2%
46	New Jersey	2	0.0%
29	New Mexico	15	0.2%
1	New York	2,058	21.8%
10	North Carolina	202	2.1%
37	North Dakota	8	0.1%
32	Ohio	13	0.1%
6	Oklahoma	438	4.6%
18	Oregon	56	0.6%
41	Pennsylvania	5	0.1%
28	Rhode Island	16	0.2%
20	South Carolina	46	0.5%
40	South Dakota	6	0.1%
16	Tennessee	73	0.8%
31	Texas	14	0.1%
34	Utah	11	0.1%
47	Vermont	0	0.0%
45	Virginia	3	0.0%
12	Washington	128	1.4%
35	West Virginia	10	0.1%
47	Wisconsin	0	0.0%
24	Wyoming	24	0.3%

RANK ORDER

RANK	STATE	PRISONERS	% of USA
1	New York	2,058	21.8%
2	Michigan	1,405	14.9%
3	Missouri	1,171	12.4%
4	Illinois	1,005	10.6%
5	California	588	6.2%
6	Oklahoma	438	4.6%
7	Colorado	360	3.8%
8	Alabama	276	2.9%
9	Florida	210	2.2%
10	North Carolina	202	2.1%
11	Kentucky	129	1.4%
12	Washington	128	1.4%
13	Maryland	111	1.2%
14	Hawaii	91	1.0%
15	Louisiana	89	0.9%
16	Tennessee	73	0.8%
17	Georgia	68	0.7%
18	Connecticut	56	0.6%
18	Oregon	56	0.6%
20	South Carolina	46	0.5%
21	Alaska	41	0.4%
22	Nevada	35	0.4%
23	Mississippi	28	0.3%
24	Wyoming	24	0.3%
25	Kansas	20	0.2%
26	Arizona	19	0.2%
27	Nebraska	17	0.2%
28	Rhode Island	16	0.2%
29	New Hampshire	15	0.2%
29	New Mexico	15	0.2%
31	Texas	14	0.1%
32	Idaho	13	0.1%
32	Ohio	13	0.1%
34	Utah	11	0.1%
35	Massachusetts	10	0.1%
35	West Virginia	10	0.1%
37	Arkansas	8	0.1%
37	North Dakota	8	0.1%
39	Indiana	7	0.1%
40	South Dakota	6	0.1%
41	Montana	5	0.1%
41	Pennsylvania	5	0.1%
43	Iowa	4	0.0%
43	Maine	4	0.0%
45	Virginia	3	0.0%
46	New Jersey	2	0.0%
47	Delaware	0	0.0%
47	Minnesota	0	0.0%
47	Vermont	0	0.0%
47	Wisconsin	0	0.0%
	District of Columbia	524	5.6%

Source: U.S. Department of Justice, Bureau of Justice Statistics
    "Correctional Populations in the United States, 1996" (1998)
*Includes AWOLs. Numbers of escaped federal prisoners were not available.

State Prisoners Deaths in 1996

National Total = 3,092

ALPHA ORDER

RANK	STATE	DEATHS	% of USA
11	Alabama	89	2.9%
45	Alaska	3	0.1%
17	Arizona	61	2.0%
29	Arkansas	23	0.7%
3	California	253	8.2%
30	Colorado	22	0.7%
19	Connecticut	49	1.6%
31	Delaware	20	0.6%
4	Florida	247	8.0%
9	Georgia	114	3.7%
42	Hawaii	4	0.1%
45	Idaho	3	0.1%
10	Illinois	96	3.1%
21	Indiana	39	1.3%
34	Iowa	10	0.3%
31	Kansas	20	0.6%
27	Kentucky	29	0.9%
12	Louisiana	86	2.8%
45	Maine	3	0.1%
20	Maryland	48	1.6%
26	Massachusetts	30	1.0%
7	Michigan	125	4.0%
34	Minnesota	10	0.3%
25	Mississippi	32	1.0%
22	Missouri	37	1.2%
41	Montana	5	0.2%
36	Nebraska	8	0.3%
23	Nevada	35	1.1%
48	New Hampshire	2	0.1%
5	New Jersey	142	4.6%
42	New Mexico	4	0.1%
2	New York	330	10.7%
15	North Carolina	74	2.4%
49	North Dakota	0	0.0%
8	Ohio	117	3.8%
16	Oklahoma	66	2.1%
28	Oregon	25	0.8%
6	Pennsylvania	126	4.1%
38	Rhode Island	7	0.2%
14	South Carolina	76	2.5%
42	South Dakota	4	0.1%
18	Tennessee	60	1.9%
1	Texas	377	12.2%
38	Utah	7	0.2%
49	Vermont	0	0.0%
13	Virginia	84	2.7%
24	Washington	33	1.1%
40	West Virginia	6	0.2%
33	Wisconsin	14	0.5%
36	Wyoming	8	0.3%

RANK ORDER

RANK	STATE	DEATHS	% of USA
1	Texas	377	12.2%
2	New York	330	10.7%
3	California	253	8.2%
4	Florida	247	8.0%
5	New Jersey	142	4.6%
6	Pennsylvania	126	4.1%
7	Michigan	125	4.0%
8	Ohio	117	3.8%
9	Georgia	114	3.7%
10	Illinois	96	3.1%
11	Alabama	89	2.9%
12	Louisiana	86	2.8%
13	Virginia	84	2.7%
14	South Carolina	76	2.5%
15	North Carolina	74	2.4%
16	Oklahoma	66	2.1%
17	Arizona	61	2.0%
18	Tennessee	60	1.9%
19	Connecticut	49	1.6%
20	Maryland	48	1.6%
21	Indiana	39	1.3%
22	Missouri	37	1.2%
23	Nevada	35	1.1%
24	Washington	33	1.1%
25	Mississippi	32	1.0%
26	Massachusetts	30	1.0%
27	Kentucky	29	0.9%
28	Oregon	25	0.8%
29	Arkansas	23	0.7%
30	Colorado	22	0.7%
31	Delaware	20	0.6%
31	Kansas	20	0.6%
33	Wisconsin	14	0.5%
34	Iowa	10	0.3%
34	Minnesota	10	0.3%
36	Nebraska	8	0.3%
36	Wyoming	8	0.3%
38	Rhode Island	7	0.2%
38	Utah	7	0.2%
40	West Virginia	6	0.2%
41	Montana	5	0.2%
42	Hawaii	4	0.1%
42	New Mexico	4	0.1%
42	South Dakota	4	0.1%
45	Alaska	3	0.1%
45	Idaho	3	0.1%
45	Maine	3	0.1%
48	New Hampshire	2	0.1%
49	North Dakota	0	0.0%
49	Vermont	0	0.0%
	District of Columbia	29	0.9%

Source: U.S. Department of Justice, Bureau of Justice Statistics
"Correctional Populations in the United States, 1996" (1998)

Death Rate of State Prisoners in 1996

National Rate = 287 State Prisoner Deaths per 100,000 Inmates

ALPHA ORDER

RANK	STATE	RATE
5	Alabama	409
47	Alaska	81
19	Arizona	271
25	Arkansas	244
40	California	173
38	Colorado	177
18	Connecticut	274
6	Delaware	391
7	Florida	387
12	Georgia	324
44	Hawaii	100
48	Idaho	78
24	Illinois	247
29	Indiana	230
42	Iowa	158
21	Kansas	258
30	Kentucky	225
13	Louisiana	321
35	Maine	210
31	Maryland	218
22	Massachusetts	254
15	Michigan	295
36	Minnesota	194
28	Mississippi	231
41	Missouri	168
31	Montana	218
26	Nebraska	243
4	Nevada	415
45	New Hampshire	97
2	New Jersey	517
46	New Mexico	85
3	New York	473
27	North Carolina	241
49	North Dakota	0
23	Ohio	253
11	Oklahoma	337
16	Oregon	289
10	Pennsylvania	365
34	Rhode Island	214
9	South Carolina	372
36	South Dakota	194
8	Tennessee	384
17	Texas	285
39	Utah	176
49	Vermont	0
14	Virginia	304
20	Washington	263
31	West Virginia	218
43	Wisconsin	108
1	Wyoming	534

RANK ORDER

RANK	STATE	RATE
1	Wyoming	534
2	New Jersey	517
3	New York	473
4	Nevada	415
5	Alabama	409
6	Delaware	391
7	Florida	387
8	Tennessee	384
9	South Carolina	372
10	Pennsylvania	365
11	Oklahoma	337
12	Georgia	324
13	Louisiana	321
14	Virginia	304
15	Michigan	295
16	Oregon	289
17	Texas	285
18	Connecticut	274
19	Arizona	271
20	Washington	263
21	Kansas	258
22	Massachusetts	254
23	Ohio	253
24	Illinois	247
25	Arkansas	244
26	Nebraska	243
27	North Carolina	241
28	Mississippi	231
29	Indiana	230
30	Kentucky	225
31	Maryland	218
31	Montana	218
31	West Virginia	218
34	Rhode Island	214
35	Maine	210
36	Minnesota	194
36	South Dakota	194
38	Colorado	177
39	Utah	176
40	California	173
41	Missouri	168
42	Iowa	158
43	Wisconsin	108
44	Hawaii	100
45	New Hampshire	97
46	New Mexico	85
47	Alaska	81
48	Idaho	78
49	North Dakota	0
49	Vermont	0
	District of Columbia	309

Source: Morgan Quitno Press using data from U.S. Department of Justice, Bureau of Justice Statistics
"Correctional Populations in the United States, 1996" (1998)

State Prisoner Deaths by Illness or Other Natural Causes in 1996

National Total = 1,715 Deaths*

ALPHA ORDER

RANK	STATE	DEATHS	% of USA
NA	Alabama**	NA	NA
40	Alaska	3	0.2%
10	Arizona	51	3.0%
26	Arkansas	18	1.0%
2	California	154	9.0%
23	Colorado	19	1.1%
31	Connecticut	14	0.8%
30	Delaware	16	0.9%
5	Florida	110	6.4%
8	Georgia	56	3.3%
44	Hawaii	1	0.1%
43	Idaho	2	0.1%
12	Illinois	50	2.9%
18	Indiana	34	2.0%
34	Iowa	7	0.4%
28	Kansas	17	1.0%
19	Kentucky	29	1.7%
9	Louisiana	52	3.0%
44	Maine	1	0.1%
22	Maryland	21	1.2%
23	Massachusetts	19	1.1%
4	Michigan	113	6.6%
33	Minnesota	8	0.5%
21	Mississippi	22	1.3%
26	Missouri	18	1.0%
38	Montana	4	0.2%
34	Nebraska	7	0.4%
23	Nevada	19	1.1%
44	New Hampshire	1	0.1%
15	New Jersey	41	2.4%
NA	New Mexico**	NA	NA
3	New York	116	6.8%
14	North Carolina	44	2.6%
47	North Dakota	0	0.0%
6	Ohio	88	5.1%
13	Oklahoma	48	2.8%
28	Oregon	17	1.0%
7	Pennsylvania	74	4.3%
36	Rhode Island	6	0.3%
17	South Carolina	36	2.1%
40	South Dakota	3	0.2%
10	Tennessee	51	3.0%
1	Texas	220	12.8%
40	Utah	3	0.2%
47	Vermont	0	0.0%
16	Virginia	38	2.2%
20	Washington	23	1.3%
36	West Virginia	6	0.3%
32	Wisconsin	9	0.5%
38	Wyoming	4	0.2%

RANK ORDER

RANK	STATE	DEATHS	% of USA
1	Texas	220	12.8%
2	California	154	9.0%
3	New York	116	6.8%
4	Michigan	113	6.6%
5	Florida	110	6.4%
6	Ohio	88	5.1%
7	Pennsylvania	74	4.3%
8	Georgia	56	3.3%
9	Louisiana	52	3.0%
10	Arizona	51	3.0%
10	Tennessee	51	3.0%
12	Illinois	50	2.9%
13	Oklahoma	48	2.8%
14	North Carolina	44	2.6%
15	New Jersey	41	2.4%
16	Virginia	38	2.2%
17	South Carolina	36	2.1%
18	Indiana	34	2.0%
19	Kentucky	29	1.7%
20	Washington	23	1.3%
21	Mississippi	22	1.3%
22	Maryland	21	1.2%
23	Colorado	19	1.1%
23	Massachusetts	19	1.1%
23	Nevada	19	1.1%
26	Arkansas	18	1.0%
26	Missouri	18	1.0%
28	Kansas	17	1.0%
28	Oregon	17	1.0%
30	Delaware	16	0.9%
31	Connecticut	14	0.8%
32	Wisconsin	9	0.5%
33	Minnesota	8	0.5%
34	Iowa	7	0.4%
34	Nebraska	7	0.4%
36	Rhode Island	6	0.3%
36	West Virginia	6	0.3%
38	Montana	4	0.2%
38	Wyoming	4	0.2%
40	Alaska	3	0.2%
40	South Dakota	3	0.2%
40	Utah	3	0.2%
43	Idaho	2	0.1%
44	Hawaii	1	0.1%
44	Maine	1	0.1%
44	New Hampshire	1	0.1%
47	North Dakota	0	0.0%
47	Vermont	0	0.0%
NA	Alabama**	NA	NA
NA	New Mexico**	NA	NA
	District of Columbia**	NA	NA

Source: U.S. Department of Justice, Bureau of Justice Statistics
"Correctional Populations in the United States, 1996" (1998)
*Excludes AIDS. Federal data were not reported.
**Not available.

Deaths of State Prisoners by Illness or Other Natural Causes
As a Percent of All Prison Deaths in 1996
National Percent = 55.5% of Deaths*

ALPHA ORDER

RANK	STATE	PERCENT
NA	Alabama**	NA
1	Alaska	100.0
11	Arizona	83.6
15	Arkansas	78.3
26	California	60.9
7	Colorado	86.4
45	Connecticut	28.6
12	Delaware	80.0
39	Florida	44.5
35	Georgia	49.1
46	Hawaii	25.0
23	Idaho	66.7
32	Illinois	52.1
6	Indiana	87.2
19	Iowa	70.0
9	Kansas	85.0
1	Kentucky	100.0
27	Louisiana	60.5
43	Maine	33.3
40	Maryland	43.8
25	Massachusetts	63.3
4	Michigan	90.4
12	Minnesota	80.0
21	Mississippi	68.8
36	Missouri	48.6
12	Montana	80.0
5	Nebraska	87.5
31	Nevada	54.3
33	New Hampshire	50.0
44	New Jersey	28.9
NA	New Mexico**	NA
42	New York	35.2
28	North Carolina	59.5
47	North Dakota	0.0
16	Ohio	75.2
18	Oklahoma	72.7
22	Oregon	68.0
29	Pennsylvania	58.7
8	Rhode Island	85.7
37	South Carolina	47.4
17	South Dakota	75.0
9	Tennessee	85.0
30	Texas	58.4
41	Utah	42.9
47	Vermont	0.0
38	Virginia	45.2
20	Washington	69.7
1	West Virginia	100.0
24	Wisconsin	64.3
33	Wyoming	50.0

RANK ORDER

RANK	STATE	PERCENT
1	Alaska	100.0
1	Kentucky	100.0
1	West Virginia	100.0
4	Michigan	90.4
5	Nebraska	87.5
6	Indiana	87.2
7	Colorado	86.4
8	Rhode Island	85.7
9	Kansas	85.0
9	Tennessee	85.0
11	Arizona	83.6
12	Delaware	80.0
12	Minnesota	80.0
12	Montana	80.0
15	Arkansas	78.3
16	Ohio	75.2
17	South Dakota	75.0
18	Oklahoma	72.7
19	Iowa	70.0
20	Washington	69.7
21	Mississippi	68.8
22	Oregon	68.0
23	Idaho	66.7
24	Wisconsin	64.3
25	Massachusetts	63.3
26	California	60.9
27	Louisiana	60.5
28	North Carolina	59.5
29	Pennsylvania	58.7
30	Texas	58.4
31	Nevada	54.3
32	Illinois	52.1
33	New Hampshire	50.0
33	Wyoming	50.0
35	Georgia	49.1
36	Missouri	48.6
37	South Carolina	47.4
38	Virginia	45.2
39	Florida	44.5
40	Maryland	43.8
41	Utah	42.9
42	New York	35.2
43	Maine	33.3
44	New Jersey	28.9
45	Connecticut	28.6
46	Hawaii	25.0
47	North Dakota	0.0
47	Vermont	0.0
NA	Alabama**	NA
NA	New Mexico**	NA
	District of Columbia**	NA

Source: Morgan Quitno Press using data from U.S. Department of Justice, Bureau of Justice Statistics
   "Correctional Populations in the United States, 1996" (1998)
*Excludes AIDS. Federal data were not reported.
**Not available.

Deaths of State Prisoners by AIDS in 1996

National Total = 904 Deaths

ALPHA ORDER

RANK	STATE	DEATHS	% of USA
16	Alabama	13	1.4%
32	Alaska	0	0.0%
32	Arizona	0	0.0%
24	Arkansas	2	0.2%
5	California	49	5.4%
32	Colorado	0	0.0%
7	Connecticut	32	3.5%
32	Delaware	0	0.0%
2	Florida	124	13.7%
6	Georgia	48	5.3%
32	Hawaii	0	0.0%
28	Idaho	1	0.1%
7	Illinois	32	3.5%
24	Indiana	2	0.2%
32	Iowa	0	0.0%
24	Kansas	2	0.2%
32	Kentucky	0	0.0%
13	Louisiana	20	2.2%
32	Maine	0	0.0%
15	Maryland	16	1.8%
20	Massachusetts	7	0.8%
NA	Michigan*	NA	NA
28	Minnesota	1	0.1%
21	Mississippi	5	0.6%
32	Missouri	0	0.0%
32	Montana	0	0.0%
32	Nebraska	0	0.0%
18	Nevada	8	0.9%
32	New Hampshire	0	0.0%
4	New Jersey	74	8.2%
32	New Mexico	0	0.0%
1	New York	182	20.1%
12	North Carolina	26	2.9%
32	North Dakota	0	0.0%
13	Ohio	20	2.2%
22	Oklahoma	4	0.4%
24	Oregon	2	0.2%
9	Pennsylvania	31	3.4%
28	Rhode Island	1	0.1%
11	South Carolina	27	3.0%
32	South Dakota	0	0.0%
18	Tennessee	8	0.9%
3	Texas	122	13.5%
28	Utah	1	0.1%
32	Vermont	0	0.0%
9	Virginia	31	3.4%
17	Washington	9	1.0%
32	West Virginia	0	0.0%
22	Wisconsin	4	0.4%
32	Wyoming	0	0.0%

RANK ORDER

RANK	STATE	DEATHS	% of USA
1	New York	182	20.1%
2	Florida	124	13.7%
3	Texas	122	13.5%
4	New Jersey	74	8.2%
5	California	49	5.4%
6	Georgia	48	5.3%
7	Connecticut	32	3.5%
7	Illinois	32	3.5%
9	Pennsylvania	31	3.4%
9	Virginia	31	3.4%
11	South Carolina	27	3.0%
12	North Carolina	26	2.9%
13	Louisiana	20	2.2%
13	Ohio	20	2.2%
15	Maryland	16	1.8%
16	Alabama	13	1.4%
17	Washington	9	1.0%
18	Nevada	8	0.9%
18	Tennessee	8	0.9%
20	Massachusetts	7	0.8%
21	Mississippi	5	0.6%
22	Oklahoma	4	0.4%
22	Wisconsin	4	0.4%
24	Arkansas	2	0.2%
24	Indiana	2	0.2%
24	Kansas	2	0.2%
24	Oregon	2	0.2%
28	Idaho	1	0.1%
28	Minnesota	1	0.1%
28	Rhode Island	1	0.1%
28	Utah	1	0.1%
32	Alaska	0	0.0%
32	Arizona	0	0.0%
32	Colorado	0	0.0%
32	Delaware	0	0.0%
32	Hawaii	0	0.0%
32	Iowa	0	0.0%
32	Kentucky	0	0.0%
32	Maine	0	0.0%
32	Missouri	0	0.0%
32	Montana	0	0.0%
32	Nebraska	0	0.0%
32	New Hampshire	0	0.0%
32	New Mexico	0	0.0%
32	North Dakota	0	0.0%
32	South Dakota	0	0.0%
32	Vermont	0	0.0%
32	West Virginia	0	0.0%
32	Wyoming	0	0.0%
NA	Michigan*	NA	NA
	District of Columbia*	NA	NA

*Source: U.S. Department of Justice, Bureau of Justice Statistics
"Correctional Populations in the United States, 1996" (1998)*
*Not available.

AIDS-Related Death Rate for State Prisoners in 1996

National Rate = 84 State Prisoner Deaths per 100,000 Inmates

ALPHA ORDER

RANK	STATE	RATE
16	Alabama	60
32	Alaska	0
32	Arizona	0
28	Arkansas	21
21	California	34
32	Colorado	0
4	Connecticut	179
32	Delaware	0
3	Florida	194
5	Georgia	137
32	Hawaii	0
24	Idaho	26
12	Illinois	82
31	Indiana	12
32	Iowa	0
24	Kansas	26
32	Kentucky	0
13	Louisiana	75
32	Maine	0
14	Maryland	73
17	Massachusetts	59
NA	Michigan*	NA
30	Minnesota	19
20	Mississippi	36
32	Missouri	0
32	Montana	0
32	Nebraska	0
8	Nevada	95
32	New Hampshire	0
1	New Jersey	269
32	New Mexico	0
2	New York	261
11	North Carolina	85
32	North Dakota	0
19	Ohio	43
29	Oklahoma	20
27	Oregon	23
10	Pennsylvania	90
22	Rhode Island	31
6	South Carolina	132
32	South Dakota	0
18	Tennessee	51
9	Texas	92
26	Utah	25
32	Vermont	0
7	Virginia	112
15	Washington	72
32	West Virginia	0
22	Wisconsin	31
32	Wyoming	0

RANK ORDER

RANK	STATE	RATE
1	New Jersey	269
2	New York	261
3	Florida	194
4	Connecticut	179
5	Georgia	137
6	South Carolina	132
7	Virginia	112
8	Nevada	95
9	Texas	92
10	Pennsylvania	90
11	North Carolina	85
12	Illinois	82
13	Louisiana	75
14	Maryland	73
15	Washington	72
16	Alabama	60
17	Massachusetts	59
18	Tennessee	51
19	Ohio	43
20	Mississippi	36
21	California	34
22	Rhode Island	31
22	Wisconsin	31
24	Idaho	26
24	Kansas	26
26	Utah	25
27	Oregon	23
28	Arkansas	21
29	Oklahoma	20
30	Minnesota	19
31	Indiana	12
32	Alaska	0
32	Arizona	0
32	Colorado	0
32	Delaware	0
32	Hawaii	0
32	Iowa	0
32	Kentucky	0
32	Maine	0
32	Missouri	0
32	Montana	0
32	Nebraska	0
32	New Hampshire	0
32	New Mexico	0
32	North Dakota	0
32	South Dakota	0
32	Vermont	0
32	West Virginia	0
32	Wyoming	0
NA	Michigan*	NA
	District of Columbia*	NA

Source: Morgan Quitno Press using data from U.S. Department of Justice, Bureau of Justice Statistics
"Correctional Populations in the United States, 1996" (1998)
*Not available.

Deaths of State Prisoners by AIDS as a Percent of All Prison Deaths in 1996

National Percent = 29.2% of Deaths

ALPHA ORDER				RANK ORDER		
RANK	STATE	PERCENT		RANK	STATE	PERCENT
22	Alabama	14.6		1	Connecticut	65.3
32	Alaska	0.0		2	New York	55.2
32	Arizona	0.0		3	New Jersey	52.1
28	Arkansas	8.7		4	Florida	50.2
19	California	19.4		5	Georgia	42.1
32	Colorado	0.0		6	Virginia	36.9
1	Connecticut	65.3		7	South Carolina	35.5
32	Delaware	0.0		8	North Carolina	35.1
4	Florida	50.2		9	Idaho	33.3
5	Georgia	42.1		9	Illinois	33.3
32	Hawaii	0.0		9	Maryland	33.3
9	Idaho	33.3		12	Texas	32.4
9	Illinois	33.3		13	Wisconsin	28.6
31	Indiana	5.1		14	Washington	27.3
32	Iowa	0.0		15	Pennsylvania	24.6
26	Kansas	10.0		16	Louisiana	23.3
32	Kentucky	0.0		16	Massachusetts	23.3
16	Louisiana	23.3		18	Nevada	22.9
32	Maine	0.0		19	California	19.4
9	Maryland	33.3		20	Ohio	17.1
16	Massachusetts	23.3		21	Mississippi	15.6
NA	Michigan*	NA		22	Alabama	14.6
26	Minnesota	10.0		23	Rhode Island	14.3
21	Mississippi	15.6		23	Utah	14.3
32	Missouri	0.0		25	Tennessee	13.3
32	Montana	0.0		26	Kansas	10.0
32	Nebraska	0.0		26	Minnesota	10.0
18	Nevada	22.9		28	Arkansas	8.7
32	New Hampshire	0.0		29	Oregon	8.0
3	New Jersey	52.1		30	Oklahoma	6.1
32	New Mexico	0.0		31	Indiana	5.1
2	New York	55.2		32	Alaska	0.0
8	North Carolina	35.1		32	Arizona	0.0
32	North Dakota	0.0		32	Colorado	0.0
20	Ohio	17.1		32	Delaware	0.0
30	Oklahoma	6.1		32	Hawaii	0.0
29	Oregon	8.0		32	Iowa	0.0
15	Pennsylvania	24.6		32	Kentucky	0.0
23	Rhode Island	14.3		32	Maine	0.0
7	South Carolina	35.5		32	Missouri	0.0
32	South Dakota	0.0		32	Montana	0.0
25	Tennessee	13.3		32	Nebraska	0.0
12	Texas	32.4		32	New Hampshire	0.0
23	Utah	14.3		32	New Mexico	0.0
32	Vermont	0.0		32	North Dakota	0.0
6	Virginia	36.9		32	South Dakota	0.0
14	Washington	27.3		32	Vermont	0.0
32	West Virginia	0.0		32	West Virginia	0.0
13	Wisconsin	28.6		32	Wyoming	0.0
32	Wyoming	0.0		NA	Michigan*	NA
					District of Columbia*	NA

Source: Morgan Quitno Press using data from U.S. Department of Justice, Bureau of Justice Statistics
"Correctional Populations in the United States, 1996" (1998)
*Not available.

State Prisoners Known to be Positive for HIV Infection/AIDS in 1995

National Total = 23,404 Inmates*

ALPHA ORDER

RANK	STATE	INMATES	% of USA
17	Alabama	222	0.95%
43	Alaska	5	0.02%
20	Arizona	140	0.60%
29	Arkansas	83	0.35%
4	California	1,042	4.45%
27	Colorado	93	0.40%
7	Connecticut	755	3.23%
24	Delaware	122	0.52%
2	Florida	2,193	9.37%
6	Georgia	828	3.54%
40	Hawaii	12	0.05%
41	Idaho	11	0.05%
10	Illinois	583	2.49%
NA	Indiana**	NA	NA
38	Iowa	20	0.09%
36	Kansas	24	0.10%
32	Kentucky	41	0.18%
16	Louisiana	314	1.34%
45	Maine	4	0.02%
8	Maryland	724	3.09%
12	Massachusetts	409	1.75%
14	Michigan	379	1.62%
31	Minnesota	46	0.20%
21	Mississippi	138	0.59%
18	Missouri	173	0.74%
45	Montana	4	0.02%
39	Nebraska	19	0.08%
19	Nevada	147	0.63%
33	New Hampshire	31	0.13%
5	New Jersey	847	3.62%
36	New Mexico	24	0.10%
1	New York	9,500	40.59%
11	North Carolina	526	2.25%
48	North Dakota	2	0.01%
15	Ohio	346	1.48%
26	Oklahoma	115	0.49%
35	Oregon	29	0.12%
9	Pennsylvania	590	2.52%
23	Rhode Island	126	0.54%
13	South Carolina	380	1.62%
47	South Dakota	3	0.01%
25	Tennessee	120	0.51%
3	Texas	1,890	8.08%
33	Utah	31	0.13%
49	Vermont	0	0.00%
22	Virginia	134	0.57%
28	Washington	92	0.39%
42	West Virginia	10	0.04%
30	Wisconsin	72	0.31%
43	Wyoming	5	0.02%

RANK ORDER

RANK	STATE	INMATES	% of USA
1	New York	9,500	40.59%
2	Florida	2,193	9.37%
3	Texas	1,890	8.08%
4	California	1,042	4.45%
5	New Jersey	847	3.62%
6	Georgia	828	3.54%
7	Connecticut	755	3.23%
8	Maryland	724	3.09%
9	Pennsylvania	590	2.52%
10	Illinois	583	2.49%
11	North Carolina	526	2.25%
12	Massachusetts	409	1.75%
13	South Carolina	380	1.62%
14	Michigan	379	1.62%
15	Ohio	346	1.48%
16	Louisiana	314	1.34%
17	Alabama	222	0.95%
18	Missouri	173	0.74%
19	Nevada	147	0.63%
20	Arizona	140	0.60%
21	Mississippi	138	0.59%
22	Virginia	134	0.57%
23	Rhode Island	126	0.54%
24	Delaware	122	0.52%
25	Tennessee	120	0.51%
26	Oklahoma	115	0.49%
27	Colorado	93	0.40%
28	Washington	92	0.39%
29	Arkansas	83	0.35%
30	Wisconsin	72	0.31%
31	Minnesota	46	0.20%
32	Kentucky	41	0.18%
33	New Hampshire	31	0.13%
33	Utah	31	0.13%
35	Oregon	29	0.12%
36	Kansas	24	0.10%
36	New Mexico	24	0.10%
38	Iowa	20	0.09%
39	Nebraska	19	0.08%
40	Hawaii	12	0.05%
41	Idaho	11	0.05%
42	West Virginia	10	0.04%
43	Alaska	5	0.02%
43	Wyoming	5	0.02%
45	Maine	4	0.02%
45	Montana	4	0.02%
47	South Dakota	3	0.01%
48	North Dakota	2	0.01%
49	Vermont	0	0.00%
NA	Indiana**	NA	NA
	District of Columbia**	NA	NA

Source: U.S. Department of Justice, Bureau of Justice Statistics
    "HIV in Prisons and Jails, 1995" (Bulletin, April 1997, NCJ-164260)
*Does not include 822 positive federal inmates.
**Not available.

State Prisoners Known to be Positive for HIV Infection/AIDS
As a Percent of Total Prison Population in 1995
National Percent = 2.4% of State Prisoners*

ALPHA ORDER

RANK	STATE	PERCENT
19	Alabama	1.1
46	Alaska	0.2
31	Arizona	0.7
20	Arkansas	1.0
26	California	0.8
20	Colorado	1.0
2	Connecticut	5.1
8	Delaware	2.5
6	Florida	3.4
9	Georgia	2.4
36	Hawaii	0.4
36	Idaho	0.4
15	Illinois	1.5
NA	Indiana**	NA
42	Iowa	0.3
42	Kansas	0.3
36	Kentucky	0.4
13	Louisiana	1.8
42	Maine	0.3
6	Maryland	3.4
4	Massachusetts	3.9
23	Michigan	0.9
20	Minnesota	1.0
18	Mississippi	1.4
23	Missouri	0.9
46	Montana	0.2
32	Nebraska	0.6
11	Nevada	1.9
15	New Hampshire	1.5
5	New Jersey	3.7
32	New Mexico	0.6
1	New York	13.9
11	North Carolina	1.9
42	North Dakota	0.3
26	Ohio	0.8
26	Oklahoma	0.8
36	Oregon	0.4
13	Pennsylvania	1.8
3	Rhode Island	4.4
10	South Carolina	2.0
46	South Dakota	0.2
23	Tennessee	0.9
15	Texas	1.5
26	Utah	0.8
49	Vermont	0.0
32	Virginia	0.6
26	Washington	0.8
36	West Virginia	0.4
32	Wisconsin	0.6
36	Wyoming	0.4

RANK ORDER

RANK	STATE	PERCENT
1	New York	13.9
2	Connecticut	5.1
3	Rhode Island	4.4
4	Massachusetts	3.9
5	New Jersey	3.7
6	Florida	3.4
6	Maryland	3.4
8	Delaware	2.5
9	Georgia	2.4
10	South Carolina	2.0
11	Nevada	1.9
11	North Carolina	1.9
13	Louisiana	1.8
13	Pennsylvania	1.8
15	Illinois	1.5
15	New Hampshire	1.5
15	Texas	1.5
18	Mississippi	1.4
19	Alabama	1.1
20	Arkansas	1.0
20	Colorado	1.0
20	Minnesota	1.0
23	Michigan	0.9
23	Missouri	0.9
23	Tennessee	0.9
26	California	0.8
26	Ohio	0.8
26	Oklahoma	0.8
26	Utah	0.8
26	Washington	0.8
31	Arizona	0.7
32	Nebraska	0.6
32	New Mexico	0.6
32	Virginia	0.6
32	Wisconsin	0.6
36	Hawaii	0.4
36	Idaho	0.4
36	Kentucky	0.4
36	Oregon	0.4
36	West Virginia	0.4
36	Wyoming	0.4
42	Iowa	0.3
42	Kansas	0.3
42	Maine	0.3
42	North Dakota	0.3
46	Alaska	0.2
46	Montana	0.2
46	South Dakota	0.2
49	Vermont	0.0
NA	Indiana**	NA
	District of Columbia**	NA

Source: U.S. Department of Justice, Bureau of Justice Statistics
"HIV in Prisons and Jails, 1995" (Bulletin, April 1997, NCJ-164260)
*Federal rate is 0.9%, combined state and federal rate is 2.3%.
**Not available.

Deaths of State Prisoners by Suicide in 1996

National Total = 154 Suicides

ALPHA ORDER

RANK	STATE	SUICIDES	% of USA
NA	Alabama*	NA	NA
35	Alaska	0	0.0%
21	Arizona	2	1.3%
35	Arkansas	0	0.0%
2	California	18	11.7%
21	Colorado	2	1.3%
16	Connecticut	3	1.9%
26	Delaware	1	0.6%
9	Florida	5	3.2%
16	Georgia	3	1.9%
16	Hawaii	3	1.9%
35	Idaho	0	0.0%
6	Illinois	6	3.9%
21	Indiana	2	1.3%
21	Iowa	2	1.3%
26	Kansas	1	0.6%
35	Kentucky	0	0.0%
26	Louisiana	1	0.6%
35	Maine	0	0.0%
6	Maryland	6	3.9%
16	Massachusetts	3	1.9%
5	Michigan	9	5.8%
26	Minnesota	1	0.6%
16	Mississippi	3	1.9%
6	Missouri	6	3.9%
35	Montana	0	0.0%
35	Nebraska	0	0.0%
12	Nevada	4	2.6%
26	New Hampshire	1	0.6%
35	New Jersey	0	0.0%
NA	New Mexico*	NA	NA
3	New York	13	8.4%
21	North Carolina	2	1.3%
35	North Dakota	0	0.0%
12	Ohio	4	2.6%
12	Oklahoma	4	2.6%
12	Oregon	4	2.6%
4	Pennsylvania	10	6.5%
35	Rhode Island	0	0.0%
9	South Carolina	5	3.2%
26	South Dakota	1	0.6%
35	Tennessee	0	0.0%
1	Texas	20	13.0%
26	Utah	1	0.6%
35	Vermont	0	0.0%
9	Virginia	5	3.2%
26	Washington	1	0.6%
35	West Virginia	0	0.0%
26	Wisconsin	1	0.6%
35	Wyoming	0	0.0%

RANK ORDER

RANK	STATE	SUICIDES	% of USA
1	Texas	20	13.0%
2	California	18	11.7%
3	New York	13	8.4%
4	Pennsylvania	10	6.5%
5	Michigan	9	5.8%
6	Illinois	6	3.9%
6	Maryland	6	3.9%
6	Missouri	6	3.9%
9	Florida	5	3.2%
9	South Carolina	5	3.2%
9	Virginia	5	3.2%
12	Nevada	4	2.6%
12	Ohio	4	2.6%
12	Oklahoma	4	2.6%
12	Oregon	4	2.6%
16	Connecticut	3	1.9%
16	Georgia	3	1.9%
16	Hawaii	3	1.9%
16	Massachusetts	3	1.9%
16	Mississippi	3	1.9%
21	Arizona	2	1.3%
21	Colorado	2	1.3%
21	Indiana	2	1.3%
21	Iowa	2	1.3%
21	North Carolina	2	1.3%
26	Delaware	1	0.6%
26	Kansas	1	0.6%
26	Louisiana	1	0.6%
26	Minnesota	1	0.6%
26	New Hampshire	1	0.6%
26	South Dakota	1	0.6%
26	Utah	1	0.6%
26	Washington	1	0.6%
26	Wisconsin	1	0.6%
35	Alaska	0	0.0%
35	Arkansas	0	0.0%
35	Idaho	0	0.0%
35	Kentucky	0	0.0%
35	Maine	0	0.0%
35	Montana	0	0.0%
35	Nebraska	0	0.0%
35	New Jersey	0	0.0%
35	North Dakota	0	0.0%
35	Rhode Island	0	0.0%
35	Tennessee	0	0.0%
35	Vermont	0	0.0%
35	West Virginia	0	0.0%
35	Wyoming	0	0.0%
NA	Alabama*	NA	NA
NA	New Mexico*	NA	NA
	District of Columbia*	NA	NA

Source: U.S. Department of Justice, Bureau of Justice Statistics
"Correctional Populations in the United States, 1996" (1998)
*Not available.

Deaths of State Prisoners by Suicide as a Percent of All Prison Deaths in 1996

National Percent = 5.0% of Deaths

ALPHA ORDER

RANK	STATE	PERCENT
NA	Alabama*	NA
35	Alaska	0.0
29	Arizona	3.3
35	Arkansas	0.0
16	California	7.1
13	Colorado	9.1
20	Connecticut	6.1
25	Delaware	5.0
33	Florida	2.0
32	Georgia	2.6
1	Hawaii	75.0
35	Idaho	0.0
19	Illinois	6.3
24	Indiana	5.1
4	Iowa	20.0
25	Kansas	5.0
35	Kentucky	0.0
34	Louisiana	1.2
35	Maine	0.0
8	Maryland	12.5
10	Massachusetts	10.0
15	Michigan	7.2
10	Minnesota	10.0
12	Mississippi	9.4
5	Missouri	16.2
35	Montana	0.0
35	Nebraska	0.0
9	Nevada	11.4
2	New Hampshire	50.0
35	New Jersey	0.0
NA	New Mexico*	NA
27	New York	3.9
31	North Carolina	2.7
35	North Dakota	0.0
28	Ohio	3.4
20	Oklahoma	6.1
6	Oregon	16.0
14	Pennsylvania	7.9
35	Rhode Island	0.0
18	South Carolina	6.6
3	South Dakota	25.0
35	Tennessee	0.0
23	Texas	5.3
7	Utah	14.3
35	Vermont	0.0
22	Virginia	6.0
30	Washington	3.0
35	West Virginia	0.0
16	Wisconsin	7.1
35	Wyoming	0.0

RANK ORDER

RANK	STATE	PERCENT
1	Hawaii	75.0
2	New Hampshire	50.0
3	South Dakota	25.0
4	Iowa	20.0
5	Missouri	16.2
6	Oregon	16.0
7	Utah	14.3
8	Maryland	12.5
9	Nevada	11.4
10	Massachusetts	10.0
10	Minnesota	10.0
12	Mississippi	9.4
13	Colorado	9.1
14	Pennsylvania	7.9
15	Michigan	7.2
16	California	7.1
16	Wisconsin	7.1
18	South Carolina	6.6
19	Illinois	6.3
20	Connecticut	6.1
20	Oklahoma	6.1
22	Virginia	6.0
23	Texas	5.3
24	Indiana	5.1
25	Delaware	5.0
25	Kansas	5.0
27	New York	3.9
28	Ohio	3.4
29	Arizona	3.3
30	Washington	3.0
31	North Carolina	2.7
32	Georgia	2.6
33	Florida	2.0
34	Louisiana	1.2
35	Alaska	0.0
35	Arkansas	0.0
35	Idaho	0.0
35	Kentucky	0.0
35	Maine	0.0
35	Montana	0.0
35	Nebraska	0.0
35	New Jersey	0.0
35	North Dakota	0.0
35	Rhode Island	0.0
35	Tennessee	0.0
35	Vermont	0.0
35	West Virginia	0.0
35	Wyoming	0.0
NA	Alabama*	NA
NA	New Mexico*	NA
	District of Columbia*	NA

Source: Morgan Quitno Press using data from U.S. Department of Justice, Bureau of Justice Statistics
"Correctional Populations in the United States, 1996" (1998)
*Not available.

Adults Under State Correctional Supervision in 1993

National Total = 4,711,500 Adults*

ALPHA ORDER					RANK ORDER			
RANK	STATE	ADULTS	% of USA		RANK	STATE	ADULTS	% of USA
22	Alabama	66,400	1.41%		1	Texas	620,000	13.16%
47	Alaska	6,600	0.14%		2	California	557,000	11.82%
24	Arizona	65,700	1.39%		3	Florida	302,800	6.43%
30	Arkansas	31,900	0.68%		4	New York	301,400	6.40%
2	California	557,000	11.82%		5	Georgia	216,400	4.59%
27	Colorado	53,400	1.13%		6	Pennsylvania	205,500	4.36%
25	Connecticut	64,900	1.38%		7	Michigan	205,400	4.36%
35	Delaware	20,600	0.44%		8	New Jersey	180,600	3.83%
3	Florida	302,800	6.43%		9	Ohio	157,100	3.33%
5	Georgia	216,400	4.59%		10	Illinois	148,700	3.16%
39	Hawaii	14,500	0.31%		11	Washington	135,600	2.88%
43	Idaho	9,600	0.20%		12	North Carolina	134,400	2.85%
10	Illinois	148,700	3.16%		13	Maryland	123,300	2.62%
14	Indiana	108,400	2.30%		14	Indiana	108,400	2.30%
33	Iowa	22,800	0.48%		15	Minnesota	83,900	1.78%
29	Kansas	39,700	0.84%		16	Louisiana	78,800	1.67%
31	Kentucky	31,000	0.66%		17	Tennessee	78,000	1.66%
16	Louisiana	78,800	1.67%		18	Massachusetts	69,400	1.47%
41	Maine	10,800	0.23%		19	Virginia	67,900	1.44%
13	Maryland	123,300	2.62%		20	Missouri	67,700	1.44%
18	Massachusetts	69,400	1.47%		21	South Carolina	67,103	1.42%
7	Michigan	205,400	4.36%		22	Alabama	66,400	1.41%
15	Minnesota	83,900	1.78%		23	Wisconsin	66,300	1.41%
32	Mississippi	25,000	0.53%		24	Arizona	65,700	1.39%
20	Missouri	67,700	1.44%		25	Connecticut	64,900	1.38%
46	Montana	7,000	0.15%		26	Oregon	61,900	1.31%
37	Nebraska	19,500	0.41%		27	Colorado	53,400	1.13%
34	Nevada	21,400	0.45%		28	Oklahoma	44,300	0.94%
45	New Hampshire	7,700	0.16%		29	Kansas	39,700	0.84%
8	New Jersey	180,600	3.83%		30	Arkansas	31,900	0.68%
38	New Mexico	15,400	0.33%		31	Kentucky	31,000	0.66%
4	New York	301,400	6.40%		32	Mississippi	25,000	0.53%
12	North Carolina	134,400	2.85%		33	Iowa	22,800	0.48%
50	North Dakota	2,900	0.06%		34	Nevada	21,400	0.45%
9	Ohio	157,100	3.33%		35	Delaware	20,600	0.44%
28	Oklahoma	44,300	0.94%		36	Rhode Island	19,700	0.42%
26	Oregon	61,900	1.31%		37	Nebraska	19,500	0.41%
6	Pennsylvania	205,500	4.36%		38	New Mexico	15,400	0.33%
36	Rhode Island	19,700	0.42%		39	Hawaii	14,500	0.31%
21	South Carolina	67,103	1.42%		39	Utah	14,500	0.31%
47	South Dakota	6,600	0.14%		41	Maine	10,800	0.23%
17	Tennessee	78,000	1.66%		42	West Virginia	10,600	0.22%
1	Texas	620,000	13.16%		43	Idaho	9,600	0.20%
39	Utah	14,500	0.31%		44	Vermont	7,800	0.17%
44	Vermont	7,800	0.17%		45	New Hampshire	7,700	0.16%
19	Virginia	67,900	1.44%		46	Montana	7,000	0.15%
11	Washington	135,600	2.88%		47	Alaska	6,600	0.14%
42	West Virginia	10,600	0.22%		47	South Dakota	6,600	0.14%
23	Wisconsin	66,300	1.41%		49	Wyoming	4,900	0.10%
49	Wyoming	4,900	0.10%		50	North Dakota	2,900	0.06%
						District of Columbia	29,000	0.62%

Source: U.S. Department of Justice, Bureau of Justice Statistics
    "Correctional Populations in the United States, 1993" (October 1995, NCJ-156241)
*Includes adults in prison or jail, on probation or parole. Does not include 168,000 adults under federal correctional supervision.

Percent of Population Under State Correctional Supervision in 1993

National Percent = 2.5% of Adult Population*

ALPHA ORDER

RANK	STATE	PERCENT
22	Alabama	2.1
35	Alaska	1.6
18	Arizona	2.3
28	Arkansas	1.8
16	California	2.5
24	Colorado	2.0
10	Connecticut	2.6
3	Delaware	3.9
8	Florida	2.9
2	Georgia	4.3
32	Hawaii	1.7
40	Idaho	1.3
32	Illinois	1.7
10	Indiana	2.6
46	Iowa	1.1
19	Kansas	2.2
46	Kentucky	1.1
10	Louisiana	2.6
43	Maine	1.2
5	Maryland	3.3
36	Massachusetts	1.5
6	Michigan	3.0
10	Minnesota	2.6
40	Mississippi	1.3
28	Missouri	1.8
43	Montana	1.2
32	Nebraska	1.7
22	Nevada	2.1
48	New Hampshire	0.9
6	New Jersey	3.0
38	New Mexico	1.4
19	New York	2.2
10	North Carolina	2.6
50	North Dakota	0.6
26	Ohio	1.9
26	Oklahoma	1.9
9	Oregon	2.8
19	Pennsylvania	2.2
10	Rhode Island	2.6
16	South Carolina	2.5
40	South Dakota	1.3
24	Tennessee	2.0
1	Texas	4.8
43	Utah	1.2
28	Vermont	1.8
38	Virginia	1.4
4	Washington	3.5
49	West Virginia	0.8
28	Wisconsin	1.8
36	Wyoming	1.5

RANK ORDER

RANK	STATE	PERCENT
1	Texas	4.8
2	Georgia	4.3
3	Delaware	3.9
4	Washington	3.5
5	Maryland	3.3
6	Michigan	3.0
6	New Jersey	3.0
8	Florida	2.9
9	Oregon	2.8
10	Connecticut	2.6
10	Indiana	2.6
10	Louisiana	2.6
10	Minnesota	2.6
10	North Carolina	2.6
10	Rhode Island	2.6
16	California	2.5
16	South Carolina	2.5
18	Arizona	2.3
19	Kansas	2.2
19	New York	2.2
19	Pennsylvania	2.2
22	Alabama	2.1
22	Nevada	2.1
24	Colorado	2.0
24	Tennessee	2.0
26	Ohio	1.9
26	Oklahoma	1.9
28	Arkansas	1.8
28	Missouri	1.8
28	Vermont	1.8
28	Wisconsin	1.8
32	Hawaii	1.7
32	Illinois	1.7
32	Nebraska	1.7
35	Alaska	1.6
36	Massachusetts	1.5
36	Wyoming	1.5
38	New Mexico	1.4
38	Virginia	1.4
40	Idaho	1.3
40	Mississippi	1.3
40	South Dakota	1.3
43	Maine	1.2
43	Montana	1.2
43	Utah	1.2
46	Iowa	1.1
46	Kentucky	1.1
48	New Hampshire	0.9
49	West Virginia	0.8
50	North Dakota	0.6
	District of Columbia	6.3

Source: U.S. Department of Justice, Bureau of Justice Statistics
    "Correctional Populations in the United States, 1993" (October 1995, NCJ-156241)
*Includes adults in prison or jail, on probation or parole. Does not include adults under federal correctional supervision. Federal percent is 0.1% making a combined state and federal percent of 2.6% of adult population is under state or federal correctional supervision.

Adults on State Probation in 1997

National Total = 3,229,261 Adults*

ALPHA ORDER					RANK ORDER			
RANK	STATE	ADULTS	% of USA		RANK	STATE	ADULTS	% of USA
25	Alabama	35,723	1.1%		1	Texas	429,093	13.3%
47	Alaska	4,378	0.1%		2	California	304,531	9.4%
21	Arizona	44,813	1.4%		3	Florida	239,932	7.4%
29	Arkansas	26,392	0.8%		4	New York	185,881	5.8%
2	California	304,531	9.4%		5	Michigan	154,236	4.8%
20	Colorado	45,447	1.4%		6	Georgia	148,420	4.6%
16	Connecticut	55,989	1.7%		7	Washington	132,014	4.1%
31	Delaware	17,872	0.6%		8	New Jersey	130,565	4.0%
3	Florida	239,932	7.4%		9	Illinois	119,481	3.7%
6	Georgia	148,420	4.6%		10	Ohio	118,761	3.7%
34	Hawaii	15,401	0.5%		11	Pennsylvania	112,493	3.5%
43	Idaho	6,367	0.2%		12	North Carolina	105,416	3.3%
9	Illinois	119,481	3.7%		13	Indiana	97,045	3.0%
13	Indiana	97,045	3.0%		14	Minnesota	90,707	2.8%
32	Iowa	16,834	0.5%		15	Maryland	74,612	2.3%
33	Kansas	16,205	0.5%		16	Connecticut	55,989	1.7%
36	Kentucky	12,093	0.4%		17	Wisconsin	49,786	1.5%
26	Louisiana	35,453	1.1%		18	Massachusetts	46,430	1.4%
41	Maine	8,584	0.3%		19	Missouri	46,301	1.4%
15	Maryland	74,612	2.3%		20	Colorado	45,447	1.4%
18	Massachusetts	46,430	1.4%		21	Arizona	44,813	1.4%
5	Michigan	154,236	4.8%		22	Oregon	43,980	1.4%
14	Minnesota	90,707	2.8%		23	South Carolina	42,404	1.3%
37	Mississippi	10,997	0.3%		24	Tennessee	38,251	1.2%
19	Missouri	46,301	1.4%		25	Alabama	35,723	1.1%
46	Montana	4,678	0.1%		26	Louisiana	35,453	1.1%
35	Nebraska	14,525	0.4%		27	Virginia	30,002	0.9%
38	Nevada	10,902	0.3%		28	Oklahoma	28,733	0.9%
45	New Hampshire	4,876	0.2%		29	Arkansas	26,392	0.8%
8	New Jersey	130,565	4.0%		30	Rhode Island	19,648	0.6%
40	New Mexico	8,895	0.3%		31	Delaware	17,872	0.6%
4	New York	185,881	5.8%		32	Iowa	16,834	0.5%
12	North Carolina	105,416	3.3%		33	Kansas	16,205	0.5%
50	North Dakota	2,657	0.1%		34	Hawaii	15,401	0.5%
10	Ohio	118,761	3.7%		35	Nebraska	14,525	0.4%
28	Oklahoma	28,733	0.9%		36	Kentucky	12,093	0.4%
22	Oregon	43,980	1.4%		37	Mississippi	10,997	0.3%
11	Pennsylvania	112,493	3.5%		38	Nevada	10,902	0.3%
30	Rhode Island	19,648	0.6%		39	Utah	9,461	0.3%
23	South Carolina	42,404	1.3%		40	New Mexico	8,895	0.3%
48	South Dakota	3,467	0.1%		41	Maine	8,584	0.3%
24	Tennessee	38,251	1.2%		42	Vermont	8,128	0.3%
1	Texas	429,093	13.3%		43	Idaho	6,367	0.2%
39	Utah	9,461	0.3%		44	West Virginia	6,149	0.2%
42	Vermont	8,128	0.3%		45	New Hampshire	4,876	0.2%
27	Virginia	30,002	0.9%		46	Montana	4,678	0.1%
7	Washington	132,014	4.1%		47	Alaska	4,378	0.1%
44	West Virginia	6,149	0.2%		48	South Dakota	3,467	0.1%
17	Wisconsin	49,786	1.5%		49	Wyoming	3,456	0.1%
49	Wyoming	3,456	0.1%		50	North Dakota	2,657	0.1%
						District of Columbia	10,797	0.3%

Source: U.S. Department of Justice, Bureau of Justice Statistics
 "Nation's Probation and Parole Population Reached New High Last Year" (Press Release, August 16, 1998)
*As of December 31, 1997. Does not include 32,627 adults on federal probation.

Rate of Adults on State Probation in 1997

National Rate = 1,630 Adults on State Probation per 100,000 Adult Population*

ALPHA ORDER			RANK ORDER		
RANK	STATE	RATE	RANK	STATE	RATE
31	Alabama	1,100	1	Delaware	3,225
32	Alaska	1,040	2	Washington	3,177
23	Arizona	1,368	3	Texas	3,095
20	Arkansas	1,419	4	Georgia	2,699
24	California	1,306	5	Minnesota	2,641
17	Colorado	1,580	6	Rhode Island	2,607
7	Connecticut	2,260	7	Connecticut	2,260
1	Delaware	3,225	8	Indiana	2,222
10	Florida	2,146	9	New Jersey	2,153
4	Georgia	2,699	10	Florida	2,146
16	Hawaii	1,742	11	Michigan	2,122
40	Idaho	741	12	Maryland	1,950
21	Illinois	1,370	13	North Carolina	1,899
8	Indiana	2,222	14	Vermont	1,833
39	Iowa	791	15	Oregon	1,808
38	Kansas	850	16	Hawaii	1,742
50	Kentucky	410	17	Colorado	1,580
30	Louisiana	1,122	18	South Carolina	1,512
36	Maine	909	19	Ohio	1,423
12	Maryland	1,950	20	Arkansas	1,419
33	Massachusetts	995	21	Illinois	1,370
11	Michigan	2,122	22	New York	1,369
5	Minnesota	2,641	23	Arizona	1,368
47	Mississippi	556	24	California	1,306
29	Missouri	1,159	25	Wisconsin	1,302
42	Montana	720	26	Pennsylvania	1,229
27	Nebraska	1,198	27	Nebraska	1,198
37	Nevada	884	28	Oklahoma	1,178
47	New Hampshire	556	29	Missouri	1,159
9	New Jersey	2,153	30	Louisiana	1,122
41	New Mexico	723	31	Alabama	1,100
22	New York	1,369	32	Alaska	1,040
13	North Carolina	1,899	33	Massachusetts	995
46	North Dakota	559	34	Wyoming	993
19	Ohio	1,423	35	Tennessee	946
28	Oklahoma	1,178	36	Maine	909
15	Oregon	1,808	37	Nevada	884
26	Pennsylvania	1,229	38	Kansas	850
6	Rhode Island	2,607	39	Iowa	791
18	South Carolina	1,512	40	Idaho	741
44	South Dakota	641	41	New Mexico	723
35	Tennessee	946	42	Montana	720
3	Texas	3,095	43	Utah	690
43	Utah	690	44	South Dakota	641
14	Vermont	1,833	45	Virginia	589
45	Virginia	589	46	North Dakota	559
2	Washington	3,177	47	Mississippi	556
49	West Virginia	438	47	New Hampshire	556
25	Wisconsin	1,302	49	West Virginia	438
34	Wyoming	993	50	Kentucky	410
				District of Columbia	2,560

Source: U.S. Department of Justice, Bureau of Justice Statistics
    "Nation's Probation and Parole Population Reached New High Last Year" (Press Release, August 16, 1998)
*As of December 31, 1997. Federal rate is 16 adults on federal probation per 100,000 adult population.

Adults on State Parole in 1997

National Total = 626,206 Adults*

ALPHA ORDER						RANK ORDER			
RANK	STATE	ADULTS	% of USA			RANK	STATE	ADULTS	% of USA
22	Alabama	4,742	0.8%			1	Texas	109,437	17.5%
42	Alaska	752	0.1%			2	California	104,409	16.7%
27	Arizona	3,378	0.5%			3	Pennsylvania	76,232	12.2%
20	Arkansas	5,867	0.9%			4	New York	59,670	9.5%
2	California	104,409	16.7%			5	Illinois	30,348	4.8%
25	Colorado	4,139	0.7%			6	Georgia	21,915	3.5%
37	Connecticut	996	0.2%			7	Louisiana	19,927	3.2%
45	Delaware	591	0.1%			8	New Jersey	16,903	2.7%
15	Florida	8,477	1.4%			9	Oregon	16,815	2.7%
6	Georgia	21,915	3.5%			10	Maryland	15,763	2.5%
33	Hawaii	1,793	0.3%			11	Michigan	14,351	2.3%
40	Idaho	820	0.1%			12	Missouri	12,514	2.0%
5	Illinois	30,348	4.8%			13	Virginia	10,710	1.7%
26	Indiana	4,044	0.6%			14	Tennessee	8,693	1.4%
31	Iowa	2,051	0.3%			15	Florida	8,477	1.4%
19	Kansas	6,150	1.0%			16	Wisconsin	8,309	1.3%
24	Kentucky	4,233	0.7%			17	North Carolina	8,148	1.3%
7	Louisiana	19,927	3.2%			18	Ohio	6,803	1.1%
50	Maine	59	0.0%			19	Kansas	6,150	1.0%
10	Maryland	15,763	2.5%			20	Arkansas	5,867	0.9%
23	Massachusetts	4,596	0.7%			21	South Carolina	5,010	0.8%
11	Michigan	14,351	2.3%			22	Alabama	4,742	0.8%
30	Minnesota	2,446	0.4%			23	Massachusetts	4,596	0.7%
35	Mississippi	1,378	0.2%			24	Kentucky	4,233	0.7%
12	Missouri	12,514	2.0%			25	Colorado	4,139	0.7%
41	Montana	806	0.1%			26	Indiana	4,044	0.6%
43	Nebraska	688	0.1%			27	Arizona	3,378	0.5%
29	Nevada	3,304	0.5%			28	Utah	3,319	0.5%
36	New Hampshire	1,083	0.2%			29	Nevada	3,304	0.5%
8	New Jersey	16,903	2.7%			30	Minnesota	2,446	0.4%
34	New Mexico	1,626	0.3%			31	Iowa	2,051	0.3%
4	New York	59,670	9.5%			32	Oklahoma	1,928	0.3%
17	North Carolina	8,148	1.3%			33	Hawaii	1,793	0.3%
49	North Dakota	119	0.0%			34	New Mexico	1,626	0.3%
18	Ohio	6,803	1.1%			35	Mississippi	1,378	0.2%
32	Oklahoma	1,928	0.3%			36	New Hampshire	1,083	0.2%
9	Oregon	16,815	2.7%			37	Connecticut	996	0.2%
3	Pennsylvania	76,232	12.2%			38	West Virginia	894	0.1%
46	Rhode Island	531	0.1%			39	South Dakota	860	0.1%
21	South Carolina	5,010	0.8%			40	Idaho	820	0.1%
39	South Dakota	860	0.1%			41	Montana	806	0.1%
14	Tennessee	8,693	1.4%			42	Alaska	752	0.1%
1	Texas	109,437	17.5%			43	Nebraska	688	0.1%
28	Utah	3,319	0.5%			44	Vermont	667	0.1%
44	Vermont	667	0.1%			45	Delaware	591	0.1%
13	Virginia	10,710	1.7%			46	Rhode Island	531	0.1%
47	Washington	480	0.1%			47	Washington	480	0.1%
38	West Virginia	894	0.1%			48	Wyoming	365	0.1%
16	Wisconsin	8,309	1.3%			49	North Dakota	119	0.0%
48	Wyoming	365	0.1%			50	Maine	59	0.0%
							District of Columbia	7,067	1.1%

Source: U.S. Department of Justice, Bureau of Justice Statistics
    "Nation's Probation and Parole Population Reached New High Last Year" (Press Release, August 16, 1998)
*As of December 31, 1997. Does not include 58,827 adults on federal parole.

Rate of Adults on State Parole in 1997

National Rate = 316 Adults on State Parole per 100,000 Adult Population*

ALPHA ORDER

ALPHA ORDER

RANK ORDER

RANK	STATE	RATE	RANK	STATE	RATE
26	Alabama	146	1	Pennsylvania	833
21	Alaska	179	2	Texas	789
34	Arizona	103	3	Oregon	691
11	Arkansas	315	4	Louisiana	630
5	California	448	5	California	448
27	Colorado	144	6	New York	439
47	Connecticut	40	7	Maryland	412
32	Delaware	107	8	Georgia	399
41	Florida	76	9	Illinois	348
8	Georgia	399	10	Kansas	323
19	Hawaii	203	11	Arkansas	315
37	Idaho	95	12	Missouri	313
9	Illinois	348	13	New Jersey	279
38	Indiana	93	14	Nevada	268
36	Iowa	96	15	Utah	242
10	Kansas	323	16	Wisconsin	217
27	Kentucky	144	17	Tennessee	215
4	Louisiana	630	18	Virginia	210
50	Maine	6	19	Hawaii	203
7	Maryland	412	20	Michigan	197
35	Massachusetts	98	21	Alaska	179
20	Michigan	197	21	South Carolina	179
42	Minnesota	71	23	South Dakota	159
43	Mississippi	70	24	Vermont	150
12	Missouri	313	25	North Carolina	147
30	Montana	124	26	Alabama	146
46	Nebraska	57	27	Colorado	144
14	Nevada	268	27	Kentucky	144
30	New Hampshire	124	29	New Mexico	132
13	New Jersey	279	30	Montana	124
29	New Mexico	132	30	New Hampshire	124
6	New York	439	32	Delaware	107
25	North Carolina	147	33	Wyoming	105
48	North Dakota	25	34	Arizona	103
39	Ohio	81	35	Massachusetts	98
40	Oklahoma	79	36	Iowa	96
3	Oregon	691	37	Idaho	95
1	Pennsylvania	833	38	Indiana	93
43	Rhode Island	70	39	Ohio	81
21	South Carolina	179	40	Oklahoma	79
23	South Dakota	159	41	Florida	76
17	Tennessee	215	42	Minnesota	71
2	Texas	789	43	Mississippi	70
15	Utah	242	43	Rhode Island	70
24	Vermont	150	45	West Virginia	64
18	Virginia	210	46	Nebraska	57
49	Washington	12	47	Connecticut	40
45	West Virginia	64	48	North Dakota	25
16	Wisconsin	217	49	Washington	12
33	Wyoming	105	50	Maine	6
				District of Columbia	1,676

Source: U.S. Department of Justice, Bureau of Justice Statistics
   "Nation's Probation and Parole Population Reached New High Last Year" (Press Release, August 16, 1998)
*As of December 31, 1997. Federal rate is 30 adults on federal parole per 100,000 adult population.

State and Local Government Employees in Corrections in 1997

National Total = 648,540 Employees*

ALPHA ORDER

RANK	STATE	EMPLOYEES	% of USA
28	Alabama	6,761	1.0%
45	Alaska	1,309	0.2%
14	Arizona	12,067	1.9%
33	Arkansas	4,972	0.8%
1	California	72,736	11.2%
25	Colorado	7,501	1.2%
24	Connecticut	8,131	1.3%
40	Delaware	2,022	0.3%
4	Florida	51,243	7.9%
7	Georgia	23,434	3.6%
39	Hawaii	2,156	0.3%
38	Idaho	2,381	0.4%
9	Illinois	23,219	3.6%
22	Indiana	10,175	1.6%
36	Iowa	3,280	0.5%
32	Kansas	5,346	0.8%
27	Kentucky	7,183	1.1%
19	Louisiana	11,073	1.7%
41	Maine	1,759	0.3%
13	Maryland	13,250	2.0%
18	Massachusetts	11,401	1.8%
10	Michigan	21,641	3.3%
26	Minnesota	7,388	1.1%
30	Mississippi	5,452	0.8%
17	Missouri	11,518	1.8%
46	Montana	1,280	0.2%
37	Nebraska	2,961	0.5%
34	Nevada	4,395	0.7%
42	New Hampshire	1,653	0.3%
12	New Jersey	14,557	2.2%
31	New Mexico	5,386	0.8%
3	New York	60,128	9.3%
8	North Carolina	23,318	3.6%
50	North Dakota	608	0.1%
6	Ohio	23,999	3.7%
16	Oklahoma	11,540	1.8%
29	Oregon	6,498	1.0%
5	Pennsylvania	25,085	3.9%
43	Rhode Island	1,649	0.3%
21	South Carolina	10,511	1.6%
47	South Dakota	1,148	0.2%
15	Tennessee	11,906	1.8%
2	Texas	63,549	9.8%
35	Utah	3,350	0.5%
49	Vermont	881	0.1%
11	Virginia	19,695	3.0%
20	Washington	10,860	1.7%
44	West Virginia	1,444	0.2%
23	Wisconsin	9,993	1.5%
48	Wyoming	999	0.2%

RANK ORDER

RANK	STATE	EMPLOYEES	% of USA
1	California	72,736	11.2%
2	Texas	63,549	9.8%
3	New York	60,128	9.3%
4	Florida	51,243	7.9%
5	Pennsylvania	25,085	3.9%
6	Ohio	23,999	3.7%
7	Georgia	23,434	3.6%
8	North Carolina	23,318	3.6%
9	Illinois	23,219	3.6%
10	Michigan	21,641	3.3%
11	Virginia	19,695	3.0%
12	New Jersey	14,557	2.2%
13	Maryland	13,250	2.0%
14	Arizona	12,067	1.9%
15	Tennessee	11,906	1.8%
16	Oklahoma	11,540	1.8%
17	Missouri	11,518	1.8%
18	Massachusetts	11,401	1.8%
19	Louisiana	11,073	1.7%
20	Washington	10,860	1.7%
21	South Carolina	10,511	1.6%
22	Indiana	10,175	1.6%
23	Wisconsin	9,993	1.5%
24	Connecticut	8,131	1.3%
25	Colorado	7,501	1.2%
26	Minnesota	7,388	1.1%
27	Kentucky	7,183	1.1%
28	Alabama	6,761	1.0%
29	Oregon	6,498	1.0%
30	Mississippi	5,452	0.8%
31	New Mexico	5,386	0.8%
32	Kansas	5,346	0.8%
33	Arkansas	4,972	0.8%
34	Nevada	4,395	0.7%
35	Utah	3,350	0.5%
36	Iowa	3,280	0.5%
37	Nebraska	2,961	0.5%
38	Idaho	2,381	0.4%
39	Hawaii	2,156	0.3%
40	Delaware	2,022	0.3%
41	Maine	1,759	0.3%
42	New Hampshire	1,653	0.3%
43	Rhode Island	1,649	0.3%
44	West Virginia	1,444	0.2%
45	Alaska	1,309	0.2%
46	Montana	1,280	0.2%
47	South Dakota	1,148	0.2%
48	Wyoming	999	0.2%
49	Vermont	881	0.1%
50	North Dakota	608	0.1%
	District of Columbia	3,749	0.6%

Source: U.S. Bureau of the Census, Governments Division
    "State and Local Employment and Payroll - March 1997" (http://www.census.gov/govs/www/apes97.html)
*As of March 1997.

State and Local Government Employees in Corrections as a Percent of All State and Local Government Employees in 1997
National Percent = 4.6% of Employees*

ALPHA ORDER

ALPHA ORDER

RANK	STATE	PERCENT
44	Alabama	2.6
39	Alaska	2.9
9	Arizona	5.3
27	Arkansas	3.6
15	California	4.8
28	Colorado	3.5
11	Connecticut	5.0
11	Delaware	5.0
1	Florida	7.0
7	Georgia	5.4
32	Hawaii	3.3
28	Idaho	3.5
22	Illinois	3.9
32	Indiana	3.3
48	Iowa	1.9
32	Kansas	3.3
28	Kentucky	3.5
20	Louisiana	4.2
44	Maine	2.6
9	Maryland	5.3
23	Massachusetts	3.8
17	Michigan	4.6
42	Minnesota	2.8
36	Mississippi	3.1
21	Missouri	4.0
47	Montana	2.5
42	Nebraska	2.8
5	Nevada	5.5
38	New Hampshire	3.0
28	New Jersey	3.5
13	New Mexico	4.9
7	New York	5.4
4	North Carolina	5.6
49	North Dakota	1.7
18	Ohio	4.3
2	Oklahoma	5.7
23	Oregon	3.8
13	Pennsylvania	4.9
32	Rhode Island	3.3
16	South Carolina	4.7
39	South Dakota	2.9
18	Tennessee	4.3
2	Texas	5.7
36	Utah	3.1
39	Vermont	2.9
5	Virginia	5.5
26	Washington	3.7
50	West Virginia	1.6
23	Wisconsin	3.8
44	Wyoming	2.6

RANK ORDER

RANK	STATE	PERCENT
1	Florida	7.0
2	Oklahoma	5.7
2	Texas	5.7
4	North Carolina	5.6
5	Nevada	5.5
5	Virginia	5.5
7	Georgia	5.4
7	New York	5.4
9	Arizona	5.3
9	Maryland	5.3
11	Connecticut	5.0
11	Delaware	5.0
13	New Mexico	4.9
13	Pennsylvania	4.9
15	California	4.8
16	South Carolina	4.7
17	Michigan	4.6
18	Ohio	4.3
18	Tennessee	4.3
20	Louisiana	4.2
21	Missouri	4.0
22	Illinois	3.9
23	Massachusetts	3.8
23	Oregon	3.8
23	Wisconsin	3.8
26	Washington	3.7
27	Arkansas	3.6
28	Colorado	3.5
28	Idaho	3.5
28	Kentucky	3.5
28	New Jersey	3.5
32	Hawaii	3.3
32	Indiana	3.3
32	Kansas	3.3
32	Rhode Island	3.3
36	Mississippi	3.1
36	Utah	3.1
38	New Hampshire	3.0
39	Alaska	2.9
39	South Dakota	2.9
39	Vermont	2.9
42	Minnesota	2.8
42	Nebraska	2.8
44	Alabama	2.6
44	Maine	2.6
44	Wyoming	2.6
47	Montana	2.5
48	Iowa	1.9
49	North Dakota	1.7
50	West Virginia	1.6

District of Columbia	8.1

*Source: Morgan Quitno Press using data from U.S. Bureau of the Census, Governments Division
"State and Local Employment and Payroll - March 1997" (http://www.census.gov/govs/www/apes97.html)
Full-time equivalent as of March 1997.

State Government Employees in Corrections in 1997

National Total = 435,655 Employees*

ALPHA ORDER					RANK ORDER			
RANK	STATE	EMPLOYEES	% of USA		RANK	STATE	EMPLOYEES	% of USA
27	Alabama	4,197	1.0%		1	California	44,193	10.1%
42	Alaska	1,272	0.3%		2	Texas	42,986	9.9%
17	Arizona	8,156	1.9%		3	Florida	37,676	8.6%
30	Arkansas	3,601	0.8%		4	New York	34,197	7.8%
1	California	44,193	10.1%		5	North Carolina	19,248	4.4%
26	Colorado	4,551	1.0%		6	Georgia	17,223	4.0%
18	Connecticut	8,131	1.9%		7	Michigan	16,701	3.8%
38	Delaware	2,022	0.5%		8	Ohio	16,290	3.7%
3	Florida	37,676	8.6%		9	Illinois	14,362	3.3%
6	Georgia	17,223	4.0%		10	Pennsylvania	13,828	3.2%
37	Hawaii	2,156	0.5%		11	Virginia	13,154	3.0%
41	Idaho	1,594	0.4%		12	Maryland	10,796	2.5%
9	Illinois	14,362	3.3%		13	Oklahoma	10,590	2.4%
23	Indiana	6,199	1.4%		14	Missouri	9,038	2.1%
36	Iowa	2,399	0.6%		15	South Carolina	8,412	1.9%
33	Kansas	3,504	0.8%		16	New Jersey	8,363	1.9%
25	Kentucky	5,100	1.2%		17	Arizona	8,156	1.9%
22	Louisiana	6,789	1.6%		18	Connecticut	8,131	1.9%
43	Maine	1,152	0.3%		19	Tennessee	7,296	1.7%
12	Maryland	10,796	2.5%		20	Wisconsin	7,188	1.6%
24	Massachusetts	6,114	1.4%		21	Washington	7,071	1.6%
7	Michigan	16,701	3.8%		22	Louisiana	6,789	1.6%
32	Minnesota	3,518	0.8%		23	Indiana	6,199	1.4%
28	Mississippi	4,114	0.9%		24	Massachusetts	6,114	1.4%
14	Missouri	9,038	2.1%		25	Kentucky	5,100	1.2%
47	Montana	827	0.2%		26	Colorado	4,551	1.0%
39	Nebraska	1,958	0.4%		27	Alabama	4,197	1.0%
34	Nevada	3,014	0.7%		28	Mississippi	4,114	0.9%
44	New Hampshire	1,147	0.3%		29	New Mexico	3,955	0.9%
16	New Jersey	8,363	1.9%		30	Arkansas	3,601	0.8%
29	New Mexico	3,955	0.9%		31	Oregon	3,547	0.8%
4	New York	34,197	7.8%		32	Minnesota	3,518	0.8%
5	North Carolina	19,248	4.4%		33	Kansas	3,504	0.8%
50	North Dakota	424	0.1%		34	Nevada	3,014	0.7%
8	Ohio	16,290	3.7%		35	Utah	2,600	0.6%
13	Oklahoma	10,590	2.4%		36	Iowa	2,399	0.6%
31	Oregon	3,547	0.8%		37	Hawaii	2,156	0.5%
10	Pennsylvania	13,828	3.2%		38	Delaware	2,022	0.5%
40	Rhode Island	1,649	0.4%		39	Nebraska	1,958	0.4%
15	South Carolina	8,412	1.9%		40	Rhode Island	1,649	0.4%
48	South Dakota	761	0.2%		41	Idaho	1,594	0.4%
19	Tennessee	7,296	1.7%		42	Alaska	1,272	0.3%
2	Texas	42,986	9.9%		43	Maine	1,152	0.3%
35	Utah	2,600	0.6%		44	New Hampshire	1,147	0.3%
46	Vermont	881	0.2%		45	West Virginia	1,006	0.2%
11	Virginia	13,154	3.0%		46	Vermont	881	0.2%
21	Washington	7,071	1.6%		47	Montana	827	0.2%
45	West Virginia	1,006	0.2%		48	South Dakota	761	0.2%
20	Wisconsin	7,188	1.6%		49	Wyoming	705	0.2%
49	Wyoming	705	0.2%		50	North Dakota	424	0.1%
						District of Columbia**	NA	NA

Source: U.S. Bureau of the Census, Governments Division
   "1997 State Government Employment" (http://www.census.gov/govs/www/apes97.html)
*Full-time equivalent as of March 1997.
**Not applicable.

State Government Employees in Corrections
As a Percent of All State Government Employees in 1997
National Percent = 10.9% of Employees*

RANK	STATE	PERCENT
44	Alabama	5.2
41	Alaska	5.7
9	Arizona	13.3
27	Arkansas	7.4
10	California	13.2
26	Colorado	7.7
7	Connecticut	13.6
20	Delaware	9.2
1	Florida	20.1
4	Georgia	15.5
48	Hawaii	4.2
30	Idaho	7.1
17	Illinois	10.2
28	Indiana	7.2
47	Iowa	4.3
25	Kansas	7.9
30	Kentucky	7.1
28	Louisiana	7.2
41	Maine	5.7
8	Maryland	13.5
33	Massachusetts	6.8
13	Michigan	12.1
45	Minnesota	4.9
24	Mississippi	8.0
17	Missouri	10.2
46	Montana	4.5
36	Nebraska	6.6
11	Nevada	13.1
35	New Hampshire	6.7
33	New Jersey	6.8
19	New Mexico	9.6
6	New York	13.7
3	North Carolina	15.7
50	North Dakota	2.8
14	Ohio	11.6
5	Oklahoma	14.7
36	Oregon	6.6
20	Pennsylvania	9.2
23	Rhode Island	8.2
16	South Carolina	10.8
41	South Dakota	5.7
22	Tennessee	8.9
2	Texas	16.4
40	Utah	5.8
30	Vermont	7.1
12	Virginia	12.5
38	Washington	6.5
49	West Virginia	3.1
15	Wisconsin	11.1
39	Wyoming	6.4

RANK	STATE	PERCENT
1	Florida	20.1
2	Texas	16.4
3	North Carolina	15.7
4	Georgia	15.5
5	Oklahoma	14.7
6	New York	13.7
7	Connecticut	13.6
8	Maryland	13.5
9	Arizona	13.3
10	California	13.2
11	Nevada	13.1
12	Virginia	12.5
13	Michigan	12.1
14	Ohio	11.6
15	Wisconsin	11.1
16	South Carolina	10.8
17	Illinois	10.2
17	Missouri	10.2
19	New Mexico	9.6
20	Delaware	9.2
20	Pennsylvania	9.2
22	Tennessee	8.9
23	Rhode Island	8.2
24	Mississippi	8.0
25	Kansas	7.9
26	Colorado	7.7
27	Arkansas	7.4
28	Indiana	7.2
28	Louisiana	7.2
30	Idaho	7.1
30	Kentucky	7.1
30	Vermont	7.1
33	Massachusetts	6.8
33	New Jersey	6.8
35	New Hampshire	6.7
36	Nebraska	6.6
36	Oregon	6.6
38	Washington	6.5
39	Wyoming	6.4
40	Utah	5.8
41	Alaska	5.7
41	Maine	5.7
41	South Dakota	5.7
44	Alabama	5.2
45	Minnesota	4.9
46	Montana	4.5
47	Iowa	4.3
48	Hawaii	4.2
49	West Virginia	3.1
50	North Dakota	2.8
	District of Columbia**	NA

Source: Morgan Quitno Press using data from U.S. Bureau of the Census, Governments Division
  "1997 State Government Employment" (http://www.census.gov/govs/www/apes97.html)
*Full-time equivalent as of March 1997.
**Not applicable.

State Correctional Officers in 1997

National Total = 225,462 Officers*

RANK	STATE	OFFICERS	% of USA
26	Alabama	2,193	1.0%
40	Alaska	733	0.3%
12	Arizona	5,405	2.4%
28	Arkansas	2,028	0.9%
2	California	22,636	10.0%
25	Colorado	2,257	1.0%
15	Connecticut	4,360	1.9%
37	Delaware	948	0.4%
4	Florida	15,644	6.9%
8	Georgia	8,383	3.7%
36	Hawaii	1,083	0.5%
44	Idaho	615	0.3%
7	Illinois	8,389	3.7%
18	Indiana**	4,006	1.8%
34	Iowa**	1,236	0.5%
29	Kansas	1,786	0.8%
30	Kentucky	1,752	0.8%
19	Louisiana	3,464	1.5%
45	Maine**	611	0.3%
14	Maryland	4,923	2.2%
20	Massachusetts**	3,271	1.5%
5	Michigan	10,540	4.7%
31	Minnesota	1,639	0.7%
24	Mississippi	2,517	1.1%
17	Missouri	4,144	1.8%
41	Montana	716	0.3%
43	Nebraska	677	0.3%
33	Nevada	1,312	0.6%
46	New Hampshire	493	0.2%
13	New Jersey**	5,367	2.4%
35	New Mexico	1,107	0.5%
3	New York	21,597	9.6%
6	North Carolina	10,102	4.5%
50	North Dakota***	139	0.1%
9	Ohio	8,202	3.6%
27	Oklahoma	2,095	0.9%
32	Oregon	1,540	0.7%
10	Pennsylvania	6,879	3.1%
38	Rhode Island	930	0.4%
16	South Carolina	4,158	1.8%
48	South Dakota	361	0.2%
21	Tennessee	3,155	1.4%
1	Texas	24,701	11.0%
39	Utah***	813	0.4%
47	Vermont	416	0.2%
11	Virginia	6,732	3.0%
23	Washington	2,866	1.3%
42	West Virginia	705	0.3%
22	Wisconsin	3,020	1.3%
49	Wyoming	285	0.1%

RANK	STATE	OFFICERS	% of USA
1	Texas	24,701	11.0%
2	California	22,636	10.0%
3	New York	21,597	9.6%
4	Florida	15,644	6.9%
5	Michigan	10,540	4.7%
6	North Carolina	10,102	4.5%
7	Illinois	8,389	3.7%
8	Georgia	8,383	3.7%
9	Ohio	8,202	3.6%
10	Pennsylvania	6,879	3.1%
11	Virginia	6,732	3.0%
12	Arizona	5,405	2.4%
13	New Jersey**	5,367	2.4%
14	Maryland	4,923	2.2%
15	Connecticut	4,360	1.9%
16	South Carolina	4,158	1.8%
17	Missouri	4,144	1.8%
18	Indiana**	4,006	1.8%
19	Louisiana	3,464	1.5%
20	Massachusetts**	3,271	1.5%
21	Tennessee	3,155	1.4%
22	Wisconsin	3,020	1.3%
23	Washington	2,866	1.3%
24	Mississippi	2,517	1.1%
25	Colorado	2,257	1.0%
26	Alabama	2,193	1.0%
27	Oklahoma	2,095	0.9%
28	Arkansas	2,028	0.9%
29	Kansas	1,786	0.8%
30	Kentucky	1,752	0.8%
31	Minnesota	1,639	0.7%
32	Oregon	1,540	0.7%
33	Nevada	1,312	0.6%
34	Iowa**	1,236	0.5%
35	New Mexico	1,107	0.5%
36	Hawaii	1,083	0.5%
37	Delaware	948	0.4%
38	Rhode Island	930	0.4%
39	Utah***	813	0.4%
40	Alaska	733	0.3%
41	Montana	716	0.3%
42	West Virginia	705	0.3%
43	Nebraska	677	0.3%
44	Idaho	615	0.3%
45	Maine**	611	0.3%
46	New Hampshire	493	0.2%
47	Vermont	416	0.2%
48	South Dakota	361	0.2%
49	Wyoming	285	0.1%
50	North Dakota***	139	0.1%
	District of Columbia**	2,531	1.1%

Source: Morgan Quitno Press using data from American Correctional Association (Lanham, MD)
   "1998 Directory of Juvenile and Adult Correctional Departments, Institutions, Agencies and Paroling Authorities"
*As of June 30, 1997. Total does not include federal correctional officers.
**These states' figures are as of June 30, 1995.
***These states' figures are as of June 30, 1996.

Male Correctional Officers in 1997

National Total = 175,163 Male Officers*

RANK	STATE	OFFICERS	% of USA
24	Alabama	1,709	1.0%
41	Alaska	511	0.3%
14	Arizona	4,163	2.4%
28	Arkansas	1,377	0.8%
2	California	17,192	9.8%
23	Colorado	1,717	1.0%
16	Connecticut	3,624	2.1%
36	Delaware	775	0.4%
4	Florida	11,191	6.4%
11	Georgia	6,203	3.5%
43	Hawaii	464	0.3%
42	Idaho	506	0.3%
7	Illinois	7,164	4.1%
8	Indiana**	6,423	3.7%
32	Iowa**	1,056	0.6%
26	Kansas	1,455	0.8%
27	Kentucky	1,419	0.8%
19	Louisiana	2,657	1.5%
39	Maine**	547	0.3%
15	Maryland	3,754	2.1%
NA	Massachusetts***	NA	NA
5	Michigan	8,070	4.6%
30	Minnesota	1,173	0.7%
29	Mississippi	1,369	0.8%
17	Missouri	3,305	1.9%
46	Montana	306	0.2%
40	Nebraska	532	0.3%
33	Nevada	1,054	0.6%
44	New Hampshire	441	0.3%
13	New Jersey**	4,675	2.7%
34	New Mexico	1,019	0.6%
1	New York	19,689	11.2%
6	North Carolina	7,611	4.3%
49	North Dakota**	107	0.1%
10	Ohio	6,297	3.6%
25	Oklahoma	1,549	0.9%
31	Oregon	1,140	0.7%
9	Pennsylvania	6,306	3.6%
35	Rhode Island	852	0.5%
18	South Carolina	2,740	1.6%
47	South Dakota	266	0.2%
21	Tennessee	2,429	1.4%
3	Texas	17,150	9.8%
37	Utah**	732	0.4%
45	Vermont	371	0.2%
12	Virginia	4,832	2.8%
22	Washington	2,190	1.3%
38	West Virginia	600	0.3%
20	Wisconsin	2,443	1.4%
48	Wyoming	227	0.1%

RANK	STATE	OFFICERS	% of USA
1	New York	19,689	11.2%
2	California	17,192	9.8%
3	Texas	17,150	9.8%
4	Florida	11,191	6.4%
5	Michigan	8,070	4.6%
6	North Carolina	7,611	4.3%
7	Illinois	7,164	4.1%
8	Indiana**	6,423	3.7%
9	Pennsylvania	6,306	3.6%
10	Ohio	6,297	3.6%
11	Georgia	6,203	3.5%
12	Virginia	4,832	2.8%
13	New Jersey**	4,675	2.7%
14	Arizona	4,163	2.4%
15	Maryland	3,754	2.1%
16	Connecticut	3,624	2.1%
17	Missouri	3,305	1.9%
18	South Carolina	2,740	1.6%
19	Louisiana	2,657	1.5%
20	Wisconsin	2,443	1.4%
21	Tennessee	2,429	1.4%
22	Washington	2,190	1.3%
23	Colorado	1,717	1.0%
24	Alabama	1,709	1.0%
25	Oklahoma	1,549	0.9%
26	Kansas	1,455	0.8%
27	Kentucky	1,419	0.8%
28	Arkansas	1,377	0.8%
29	Mississippi	1,369	0.8%
30	Minnesota	1,173	0.7%
31	Oregon	1,140	0.7%
32	Iowa**	1,056	0.6%
33	Nevada	1,054	0.6%
34	New Mexico	1,019	0.6%
35	Rhode Island	852	0.5%
36	Delaware	775	0.4%
37	Utah**	732	0.4%
38	West Virginia	600	0.3%
39	Maine**	547	0.3%
40	Nebraska	532	0.3%
41	Alaska	511	0.3%
42	Idaho	506	0.3%
43	Hawaii	464	0.3%
44	New Hampshire	441	0.3%
45	Vermont	371	0.2%
46	Montana	306	0.2%
47	South Dakota	266	0.2%
48	Wyoming	227	0.1%
49	North Dakota**	107	0.1%
NA	Massachusetts***	NA	NA
	District of Columbia**	1,781	1.0%

Source: Morgan Quitno Press using data from American Correctional Association (Lanham, MD)
"1998 Directory of Juvenile and Adult Correctional Departments, Institutions, Agencies and Paroling Authorities"
*As of June 30, 1997 in adult systems. Total does not include male federal correctional officers.
**These states' figures are as of June 30, 1995. North Dakota and Utah are as of June 30, 1996.
***Not available.

Female Correctional Officers in 1997

National Total = 45,690 Female Officers*

ALPHA ORDER					RANK ORDER			

RANK	STATE		OFFICERS	% of USA	RANK	STATE		OFFICERS	% of USA
26	Alabama		472	1.0%	1	Texas		7,354	16.1%
36	Alaska		115	0.3%	2	Florida		4,241	9.3%
14	Arizona		1,114	2.4%	3	California		3,999	8.8%
21	Arkansas		651	1.4%	4	North Carolina		2,271	5.0%
3	California		3,999	8.8%	5	Michigan		2,206	4.8%
25	Colorado		483	1.1%	6	Georgia		2,119	4.6%
18	Connecticut		704	1.5%	7	Virginia		1,888	4.1%
34	Delaware		162	0.4%	8	Ohio		1,879	4.1%
2	Florida		4,241	9.3%	9	New York		1,829	4.0%
6	Georgia		2,119	4.6%	10	South Carolina		1,368	3.0%
40	Hawaii		89	0.2%	11	Illinois		1,168	2.6%
39	Idaho		99	0.2%	12	Maryland		1,162	2.5%
11	Illinois		1,168	2.6%	13	Mississippi		1,141	2.5%
15	Indiana**		908	2.0%	14	Arizona		1,114	2.4%
33	Iowa**		180	0.4%	15	Indiana**		908	2.0%
30	Kansas		301	0.7%	16	Missouri		819	1.8%
28	Kentucky		329	0.7%	17	Louisiana		802	1.8%
17	Louisiana		802	1.8%	18	Connecticut		704	1.5%
44	Maine**		64	0.1%	19	Tennessee		702	1.5%
12	Maryland		1,162	2.5%	20	New Jersey**		692	1.5%
NA	Massachusetts***		NA	NA	21	Arkansas		651	1.4%
5	Michigan		2,206	4.8%	22	Pennsylvania		557	1.2%
27	Minnesota		421	0.9%	23	Washington		545	1.2%
13	Mississippi		1,141	2.5%	24	Wisconsin		532	1.2%
16	Missouri		819	1.8%	25	Colorado		483	1.1%
45	Montana		52	0.1%	26	Alabama		472	1.0%
35	Nebraska		134	0.3%	27	Minnesota		421	0.9%
32	Nevada		210	0.5%	28	Kentucky		329	0.7%
46	New Hampshire		50	0.1%	29	Oklahoma		308	0.7%
20	New Jersey**		692	1.5%	30	Kansas		301	0.7%
42	New Mexico		81	0.2%	31	Oregon		256	0.6%
9	New York		1,829	4.0%	32	Nevada		210	0.5%
4	North Carolina		2,271	5.0%	33	Iowa**		180	0.4%
49	North Dakota**		26	0.1%	34	Delaware		162	0.4%
8	Ohio		1,879	4.1%	35	Nebraska		134	0.3%
29	Oklahoma		308	0.7%	36	Alaska		115	0.3%
31	Oregon		256	0.6%	37	West Virginia		105	0.2%
22	Pennsylvania		557	1.2%	38	Utah**		101	0.2%
43	Rhode Island		74	0.2%	39	Idaho		99	0.2%
10	South Carolina		1,368	3.0%	40	Hawaii		89	0.2%
41	South Dakota		82	0.2%	41	South Dakota		82	0.2%
19	Tennessee		702	1.5%	42	New Mexico		81	0.2%
1	Texas		7,354	16.1%	43	Rhode Island		74	0.2%
38	Utah**		101	0.2%	44	Maine**		64	0.1%
48	Vermont		45	0.1%	45	Montana		52	0.1%
7	Virginia		1,888	4.1%	46	New Hampshire		50	0.1%
23	Washington		545	1.2%	46	Wyoming		50	0.1%
37	West Virginia		105	0.2%	48	Vermont		45	0.1%
24	Wisconsin		532	1.2%	49	North Dakota**		26	0.1%
46	Wyoming		50	0.1%	NA	Massachusetts***		NA	NA
						District of Columbia**		750	1.6%

Source: Morgan Quitno Press using data from American Correctional Association (Lanham, MD)
"1998 Directory of Juvenile and Adult Correctional Departments, Institutions, Agencies and Paroling Authorities"
*As of June 30, 1997 in adult systems. Total does not include female federal correctional officers.
**These states' figures are as of June 30, 1995. North Dakota and Utah are as of June 30, 1996.
***Not available.

State Prisoners per Correctional Officer in 1997

National Rate = 5.1 Prisoners per Officer*

ALPHA ORDER

RANK	STATE	RATE
1	Alabama	9.9
39	Alaska	3.5
34	Arizona	4.1
20	Arkansas	4.9
5	California	6.8
9	Colorado	6.0
46	Connecticut	3.0
40	Delaware	3.4
34	Florida	4.1
31	Georgia	4.3
42	Hawaii	3.2
7	Idaho	6.4
20	Illinois	4.9
37	Indiana**	4.0
26	Iowa**	4.8
29	Kansas	4.4
4	Kentucky	8.3
3	Louisiana	8.4
48	Maine**	2.3
31	Maryland	4.3
41	Massachusetts**	3.3
33	Michigan	4.2
42	Minnesota	3.2
11	Mississippi	5.8
11	Missouri	5.8
45	Montana	3.1
20	Nebraska	4.9
5	Nevada	6.8
29	New Hampshire	4.4
19	New Jersey**	5.0
37	New Mexico	4.0
42	New York	3.2
47	North Carolina	2.7
17	North Dakota**	5.1
10	Ohio	5.9
2	Oklahoma	9.8
20	Oregon	4.9
17	Pennsylvania	5.1
48	Rhode Island	2.3
20	South Carolina	4.9
8	South Dakota	6.2
15	Tennessee	5.3
13	Texas	5.7
16	Utah**	5.2
50	Vermont	2.0
34	Virginia	4.1
27	Washington	4.6
28	West Virginia	4.5
20	Wisconsin	4.9
14	Wyoming	5.5

RANK ORDER

RANK	STATE	RATE
1	Alabama	9.9
2	Oklahoma	9.8
3	Louisiana	8.4
4	Kentucky	8.3
5	California	6.8
5	Nevada	6.8
7	Idaho	6.4
8	South Dakota	6.2
9	Colorado	6.0
10	Ohio	5.9
11	Mississippi	5.8
11	Missouri	5.8
13	Texas	5.7
14	Wyoming	5.5
15	Tennessee	5.3
16	Utah**	5.2
17	North Dakota**	5.1
17	Pennsylvania	5.1
19	New Jersey**	5.0
20	Arkansas	4.9
20	Illinois	4.9
20	Nebraska	4.9
20	Oregon	4.9
20	South Carolina	4.9
20	Wisconsin	4.9
26	Iowa**	4.8
27	Washington	4.6
28	West Virginia	4.5
29	Kansas	4.4
29	New Hampshire	4.4
31	Georgia	4.3
31	Maryland	4.3
33	Michigan	4.2
34	Arizona	4.1
34	Florida	4.1
34	Virginia	4.1
37	Indiana**	4.0
37	New Mexico	4.0
39	Alaska	3.5
40	Delaware	3.4
41	Massachusetts**	3.3
42	Hawaii	3.2
42	Minnesota	3.2
42	New York	3.2
45	Montana	3.1
46	Connecticut	3.0
47	North Carolina	2.7
48	Maine**	2.3
48	Rhode Island	2.3
50	Vermont	2.0

District of Columbia** — 3.6

Source: Morgan Quitno Press using data from American Correctional Association (Lanham, MD)
  "1998 Directory of Juvenile and Adult Correctional Departments, Institutions, Agencies and Paroling Authorities"
*As of June 30, 1997 in adult systems. National rate does not include federal correctional officers or prisoners.
**These states' figures are as of June 30, 1995. North Dakota and Utah are as of June 30, 1996.
***Not available.

Turnover Rate of Correctional Officers in 1997

National Average = 15.03%*

ALPHA ORDER

RANK	STATE	TURNOVER RATE
27	Alabama	12.32
22	Alaska	13.00
8	Arizona	21.10
3	Arkansas	40.00
NA	California**	NA
28	Colorado	10.00
NA	Connecticut**	NA
34	Delaware	6.00
1	Florida	47.00
28	Georgia	10.00
35	Hawaii	5.38
11	Idaho	17.09
1	Illinois	47.00
NA	Indiana**	NA
NA	Iowa**	NA
10	Kansas	18.42
6	Kentucky	28.50
5	Louisiana	30.00
NA	Maine**	NA
12	Maryland	17.00
NA	Massachusetts**	NA
37	Michigan	4.30
24	Minnesota	12.60
NA	Mississippi**	NA
NA	Missouri**	NA
NA	Montana**	NA
18	Nebraska	14.60
31	Nevada	8.20
23	New Hampshire	12.90
NA	New Jersey**	NA
16	New Mexico	15.70
39	New York	3.70
13	North Carolina	16.90
36	North Dakota**	5.00
26	Ohio	12.40
19	Oklahoma	14.40
32	Oregon	7.00
39	Pennsylvania	3.70
38	Rhode Island	4.10
9	South Carolina	20.40
7	South Dakota	28.00
4	Tennessee	32.00
15	Texas	16.00
20	Utah**	14.00
25	Vermont	12.50
14	Virginia	16.66
33	Washington	6.02
28	West Virginia	10.00
17	Wisconsin	15.00
21	Wyoming	13.70

RANK ORDER

RANK	STATE	TURNOVER RATE
1	Florida	47.00
1	Illinois	47.00
3	Arkansas	40.00
4	Tennessee	32.00
5	Louisiana	30.00
6	Kentucky	28.50
7	South Dakota	28.00
8	Arizona	21.10
9	South Carolina	20.40
10	Kansas	18.42
11	Idaho	17.09
12	Maryland	17.00
13	North Carolina	16.90
14	Virginia	16.66
15	Texas	16.00
16	New Mexico	15.70
17	Wisconsin	15.00
18	Nebraska	14.60
19	Oklahoma	14.40
20	Utah**	14.00
21	Wyoming	13.70
22	Alaska	13.00
23	New Hampshire	12.90
24	Minnesota	12.60
25	Vermont	12.50
26	Ohio	12.40
27	Alabama	12.32
28	Colorado	10.00
28	Georgia	10.00
28	West Virginia	10.00
31	Nevada	8.20
32	Oregon	7.00
33	Washington	6.02
34	Delaware	6.00
35	Hawaii	5.38
36	North Dakota**	5.00
37	Michigan	4.30
38	Rhode Island	4.10
39	New York	3.70
39	Pennsylvania	3.70
NA	California**	NA
NA	Connecticut**	NA
NA	Indiana**	NA
NA	Iowa**	NA
NA	Maine**	NA
NA	Massachusetts**	NA
NA	Mississippi**	NA
NA	Missouri**	NA
NA	Montana**	NA
NA	New Jersey**	NA
	District of Columbia**	NA

Source: American Correctional Association (Lanham, MD)
   "1998 Directory of Juvenile and Adult Correctional Departments, Institutions, Agencies and Paroling Authorities"
As of June 30, 1997 in adult systems. North Dakota and Utah are as of June 30, 1996. National rate does not include federal correctional officers.
**Not available.*

Jail and Detention Centers in 1993

National Total = 3,304 Jails*

ALPHA ORDER

RANK	STATE	JAILS	% of USA
4	Alabama	129	3.90%
45	Alaska	5	0.15%
34	Arizona	33	1.00%
19	Arkansas	83	2.51%
3	California	136	4.12%
26	Colorado	61	1.85%
NA	Connecticut**	NA	NA
NA	Delaware**	NA	NA
9	Florida	100	3.03%
2	Georgia	202	6.11%
NA	Hawaii**	NA	NA
32	Idaho	39	1.18%
14	Illinois	93	2.81%
18	Indiana	88	2.66%
16	Iowa	90	2.72%
11	Kansas	96	2.91%
20	Kentucky	81	2.45%
11	Louisiana	96	2.91%
43	Maine	15	0.45%
34	Maryland	33	1.00%
41	Massachusetts	20	0.61%
17	Michigan	89	2.69%
23	Minnesota	75	2.27%
13	Mississippi	95	2.88%
5	Missouri	127	3.84%
29	Montana	44	1.33%
25	Nebraska	64	1.94%
41	Nevada	20	0.61%
44	New Hampshire	11	0.33%
37	New Jersey	25	0.76%
33	New Mexico	34	1.03%
22	New York	78	2.36%
8	North Carolina	104	3.15%
37	North Dakota	25	0.76%
6	Ohio	120	3.63%
9	Oklahoma	100	3.03%
30	Oregon	43	1.30%
21	Pennsylvania	79	2.39%
NA	Rhode Island**	NA	NA
28	South Carolina	55	1.66%
36	South Dakota	28	0.85%
7	Tennessee	111	3.36%
1	Texas	267	8.08%
37	Utah	25	0.76%
NA	Vermont**	NA	NA
14	Virginia	93	2.81%
27	Washington	56	1.69%
31	West Virginia	41	1.24%
24	Wisconsin	72	2.18%
40	Wyoming	22	0.67%

RANK ORDER

RANK	STATE	JAILS	% of USA
1	Texas	267	8.08%
2	Georgia	202	6.11%
3	California	136	4.12%
4	Alabama	129	3.90%
5	Missouri	127	3.84%
6	Ohio	120	3.63%
7	Tennessee	111	3.36%
8	North Carolina	104	3.15%
9	Florida	100	3.03%
9	Oklahoma	100	3.03%
11	Kansas	96	2.91%
11	Louisiana	96	2.91%
13	Mississippi	95	2.88%
14	Illinois	93	2.81%
14	Virginia	93	2.81%
16	Iowa	90	2.72%
17	Michigan	89	2.69%
18	Indiana	88	2.66%
19	Arkansas	83	2.51%
20	Kentucky	81	2.45%
21	Pennsylvania	79	2.39%
22	New York	78	2.36%
23	Minnesota	75	2.27%
24	Wisconsin	72	2.18%
25	Nebraska	64	1.94%
26	Colorado	61	1.85%
27	Washington	56	1.69%
28	South Carolina	55	1.66%
29	Montana	44	1.33%
30	Oregon	43	1.30%
31	West Virginia	41	1.24%
32	Idaho	39	1.18%
33	New Mexico	34	1.03%
34	Arizona	33	1.00%
34	Maryland	33	1.00%
36	South Dakota	28	0.85%
37	New Jersey	25	0.76%
37	North Dakota	25	0.76%
37	Utah	25	0.76%
40	Wyoming	22	0.67%
41	Massachusetts	20	0.61%
41	Nevada	20	0.61%
43	Maine	15	0.45%
44	New Hampshire	11	0.33%
45	Alaska	5	0.15%
NA	Connecticut**	NA	NA
NA	Delaware**	NA	NA
NA	Hawaii**	NA	NA
NA	Rhode Island**	NA	NA
NA	Vermont**	NA	NA
	District of Columbia	1	0.03%

Source: U.S. Department of Justice, Bureau of Justice Statistics
    "Jail and Jail Inmates 1993-94" (Bulletin, April 1995, NCJ-151651)

*As of July 1, 1993. Jails are locally operated correctional facilities that confine persons before or after adjudication. Inmates sentenced to jail usually have a sentence of a year or less.
**These states have combined state and local jail systems and are excluded from this count.

Local Jail Populations as a Percent of Highest Capacity in 1993

National Percent = 96.8% of Highest Capacity*

ALPHA ORDER

RANK	STATE	PERCENT
36	Alabama	76.0
44	Alaska	47.7
11	Arizona	97.8
29	Arkansas	83.4
5	California	112.8
14	Colorado	93.5
NA	Connecticut**	NA
NA	Delaware**	NA
28	Florida	84.0
19	Georgia	89.7
NA	Hawaii**	NA
24	Idaho	88.1
13	Illinois	96.1
12	Indiana	97.1
35	Iowa	76.4
30	Kansas	82.7
18	Kentucky	90.3
31	Louisiana	81.7
38	Maine	71.4
9	Maryland	98.9
6	Massachusetts	105.8
16	Michigan	90.8
32	Minnesota	78.3
17	Mississippi	90.6
34	Missouri	77.4
41	Montana	59.7
40	Nebraska	64.0
33	Nevada	78.2
39	New Hampshire	67.2
3	New Jersey	119.8
15	New Mexico	91.3
25	New York	85.7
23	North Carolina	88.3
45	North Dakota	42.8
10	Ohio	98.0
37	Oklahoma	74.9
27	Oregon	84.3
8	Pennsylvania	100.9
NA	Rhode Island**	NA
2	South Carolina	123.8
42	South Dakota	53.9
21	Tennessee	89.4
4	Texas	114.9
26	Utah	84.8
NA	Vermont**	NA
1	Virginia	160.4
7	Washington	101.6
22	West Virginia	88.4
20	Wisconsin	89.5
43	Wyoming	51.5

RANK ORDER

RANK	STATE	PERCENT
1	Virginia	160.4
2	South Carolina	123.8
3	New Jersey	119.8
4	Texas	114.9
5	California	112.8
6	Massachusetts	105.8
7	Washington	101.6
8	Pennsylvania	100.9
9	Maryland	98.9
10	Ohio	98.0
11	Arizona	97.8
12	Indiana	97.1
13	Illinois	96.1
14	Colorado	93.5
15	New Mexico	91.3
16	Michigan	90.8
17	Mississippi	90.6
18	Kentucky	90.3
19	Georgia	89.7
20	Wisconsin	89.5
21	Tennessee	89.4
22	West Virginia	88.4
23	North Carolina	88.3
24	Idaho	88.1
25	New York	85.7
26	Utah	84.8
27	Oregon	84.3
28	Florida	84.0
29	Arkansas	83.4
30	Kansas	82.7
31	Louisiana	81.7
32	Minnesota	78.3
33	Nevada	78.2
34	Missouri	77.4
35	Iowa	76.4
36	Alabama	76.0
37	Oklahoma	74.9
38	Maine	71.4
39	New Hampshire	67.2
40	Nebraska	64.0
41	Montana	59.7
42	South Dakota	53.9
43	Wyoming	51.5
44	Alaska	47.7
45	North Dakota	42.8
NA	Connecticut**	NA
NA	Delaware**	NA
NA	Hawaii**	NA
NA	Rhode Island**	NA
NA	Vermont**	NA

District of Columbia 121.2

Source: U.S. Department of Justice, Bureau of Justice Statistics
"Jail and Jail Inmates 1993-94" (Bulletin, April 1995, NCJ-151651)
*As of July 1, 1993. Jails are locally operated correctional facilities that confine persons before or after adjudication. Inmates sentenced to jail usually have a sentence of a year or less.
**These states have combined state and local jail systems and are excluded from this count.

Inmates in Local Jails in 1993

National Total = 459,804 Inmates*

ALPHA ORDER

RANK	STATE	INMATES	% of USA
21	Alabama	7,072	1.54%
45	Alaska	31	0.01%
20	Arizona	7,231	1.57%
32	Arkansas	2,846	0.62%
1	California	69,298	15.07%
23	Colorado	6,316	1.37%
NA	Connecticut**	NA	NA
NA	Delaware**	NA	NA
3	Florida	34,183	7.43%
5	Georgia	22,663	4.93%
NA	Hawaii**	NA	NA
38	Idaho	1,485	0.32%
10	Illinois	14,549	3.16%
16	Indiana	8,297	1.80%
37	Iowa	1,602	0.35%
33	Kansas	2,797	0.61%
22	Kentucky	6,813	1.48%
7	Louisiana	16,208	3.52%
40	Maine	704	0.15%
14	Maryland	9,358	2.04%
18	Massachusetts	7,878	1.71%
12	Michigan	12,479	2.71%
29	Minnesota	3,654	0.79%
26	Mississippi	4,851	1.06%
25	Missouri	5,030	1.09%
41	Montana	680	0.15%
36	Nebraska	1,680	0.37%
31	Nevada	2,987	0.65%
39	New Hampshire	1,127	0.25%
8	New Jersey	15,122	3.29%
30	New Mexico	3,058	0.67%
4	New York	29,809	6.48%
15	North Carolina	8,939	1.94%
44	North Dakota	361	0.08%
13	Ohio	11,695	2.54%
27	Oklahoma	4,102	0.89%
28	Oregon	3,777	0.82%
6	Pennsylvania	19,231	4.18%
NA	Rhode Island**	NA	NA
24	South Carolina	5,713	1.24%
42	South Dakota	623	0.14%
11	Tennessee	14,375	3.13%
2	Texas	55,395	12.05%
34	Utah	1,895	0.41%
NA	Vermont**	NA	NA
9	Virginia	14,623	3.18%
19	Washington	7,435	1.62%
35	West Virginia	1,771	0.39%
17	Wisconsin	7,879	1.71%
43	Wyoming	495	0.11%

RANK ORDER

RANK	STATE	INMATES	% of USA
1	California	69,298	15.07%
2	Texas	55,395	12.05%
3	Florida	34,183	7.43%
4	New York	29,809	6.48%
5	Georgia	22,663	4.93%
6	Pennsylvania	19,231	4.18%
7	Louisiana	16,208	3.52%
8	New Jersey	15,122	3.29%
9	Virginia	14,623	3.18%
10	Illinois	14,549	3.16%
11	Tennessee	14,375	3.13%
12	Michigan	12,479	2.71%
13	Ohio	11,695	2.54%
14	Maryland	9,358	2.04%
15	North Carolina	8,939	1.94%
16	Indiana	8,297	1.80%
17	Wisconsin	7,879	1.71%
18	Massachusetts	7,878	1.71%
19	Washington	7,435	1.62%
20	Arizona	7,231	1.57%
21	Alabama	7,072	1.54%
22	Kentucky	6,813	1.48%
23	Colorado	6,316	1.37%
24	South Carolina	5,713	1.24%
25	Missouri	5,030	1.09%
26	Mississippi	4,851	1.06%
27	Oklahoma	4,102	0.89%
28	Oregon	3,777	0.82%
29	Minnesota	3,654	0.79%
30	New Mexico	3,058	0.67%
31	Nevada	2,987	0.65%
32	Arkansas	2,846	0.62%
33	Kansas	2,797	0.61%
34	Utah	1,895	0.41%
35	West Virginia	1,771	0.39%
36	Nebraska	1,680	0.37%
37	Iowa	1,602	0.35%
38	Idaho	1,485	0.32%
39	New Hampshire	1,127	0.25%
40	Maine	704	0.15%
41	Montana	680	0.15%
42	South Dakota	623	0.14%
43	Wyoming	495	0.11%
44	North Dakota	361	0.08%
45	Alaska	31	0.01%
NA	Connecticut**	NA	NA
NA	Delaware**	NA	NA
NA	Hawaii**	NA	NA
NA	Rhode Island**	NA	NA
NA	Vermont**	NA	NA
	District of Columbia	1,687	0.37%

Source: U.S. Department of Justice, Bureau of Justice Statistics
  "Jail and Jail Inmates 1993-94" (Bulletin, April 1995, NCJ-151651)
*As of July 1, 1993. Jails are locally operated correctional facilities that confine persons before or after adjudication. Inmates sentenced to jail usually have a sentence of a year or less.
**These states have combined state and local jail systems and are excluded from this count.

Operating Costs per Inmate in Local Jails: 1993

National Average = $14,667 Per Inmate*

ALPHA ORDER

RANK	STATE	PER INMATE
42	Alabama	$8,297
NA	Alaska**	NA
39	Arizona	8,552
34	Arkansas	11,201
25	California	14,134
9	Colorado	19,177
NA	Connecticut**	NA
NA	Delaware**	NA
13	Florida	17,530
35	Georgia	10,259
NA	Hawaii**	NA
31	Idaho	11,676
26	Illinois	13,766
36	Indiana	10,255
14	Iowa	17,399
10	Kansas	18,972
33	Kentucky	11,416
41	Louisiana	8,404
7	Maine	21,200
16	Maryland	16,812
2	Massachusetts	27,531
17	Michigan	16,451
4	Minnesota	24,238
44	Mississippi	7,014
24	Missouri	14,575
28	Montana	13,121
22	Nebraska	15,198
5	Nevada	23,367
6	New Hampshire	22,993
15	New Jersey	17,259
27	New Mexico	13,273
1	New York	29,297
30	North Carolina	12,620
12	North Dakota	17,607
11	Ohio	18,152
37	Oklahoma	9,397
3	Oregon	24,345
18	Pennsylvania	16,448
NA	Rhode Island**	NA
40	South Carolina	8,438
29	South Dakota	13,109
43	Tennessee	7,675
38	Texas	9,304
19	Utah	16,129
NA	Vermont**	NA
20	Virginia	15,872
21	Washington	15,331
32	West Virginia	11,474
23	Wisconsin	15,057
8	Wyoming	20,130

RANK ORDER

RANK	STATE	PER INMATE
1	New York	$29,297
2	Massachusetts	27,531
3	Oregon	24,345
4	Minnesota	24,238
5	Nevada	23,367
6	New Hampshire	22,993
7	Maine	21,200
8	Wyoming	20,130
9	Colorado	19,177
10	Kansas	18,972
11	Ohio	18,152
12	North Dakota	17,607
13	Florida	17,530
14	Iowa	17,399
15	New Jersey	17,259
16	Maryland	16,812
17	Michigan	16,451
18	Pennsylvania	16,448
19	Utah	16,129
20	Virginia	15,872
21	Washington	15,331
22	Nebraska	15,198
23	Wisconsin	15,057
24	Missouri	14,575
25	California	14,134
26	Illinois	13,766
27	New Mexico	13,273
28	Montana	13,121
29	South Dakota	13,109
30	North Carolina	12,620
31	Idaho	11,676
32	West Virginia	11,474
33	Kentucky	11,416
34	Arkansas	11,201
35	Georgia	10,259
36	Indiana	10,255
37	Oklahoma	9,397
38	Texas	9,304
39	Arizona	8,552
40	South Carolina	8,438
41	Louisiana	8,404
42	Alabama	8,297
43	Tennessee	7,675
44	Mississippi	7,014
NA	Alaska**	NA
NA	Connecticut**	NA
NA	Delaware**	NA
NA	Hawaii**	NA
NA	Rhode Island**	NA
NA	Vermont**	NA
	District of Columbia**	NA

Source: U.S. Department of Justice, Bureau of Justice Statistics
    "Jail and Jail Inmates 1993-94" (Bulletin, April 1995, NCJ-151651)
*As of July 1, 1993. The cost (excluding capital outlays) to keep one jail inmate incarcerated for a year. Jails are locally operated correctional facilities that confine persons before or after adjudication. Inmates sentenced to jail usually have a sentence of a year or less.
**These states have combined state and local jail systems and are excluded from this count.

Male Inmates in Local Jails in 1993

National Total = 415,161 Male Inmates*

ALPHA ORDER

RANK	STATE	INMATES	% of USA
20	Alabama	6,485	1.56%
45	Alaska	30	0.01%
21	Arizona	6,471	1.56%
31	Arkansas	2,632	0.63%
1	California	61,646	14.85%
23	Colorado	5,787	1.39%
NA	Connecticut**	NA	NA
NA	Delaware**	NA	NA
3	Florida	30,500	7.35%
5	Georgia	20,943	5.04%
NA	Hawaii**	NA	NA
38	Idaho	1,383	0.33%
9	Illinois	13,482	3.25%
16	Indiana	7,653	1.84%
37	Iowa	1,477	0.36%
33	Kansas	2,520	0.61%
22	Kentucky	6,198	1.49%
7	Louisiana	14,800	3.56%
40	Maine	658	0.16%
14	Maryland	8,524	2.05%
17	Massachusetts	7,522	1.81%
12	Michigan	11,395	2.74%
29	Minnesota	3,395	0.82%
26	Mississippi	4,459	1.07%
25	Missouri	4,572	1.10%
41	Montana	604	0.15%
36	Nebraska	1,545	0.37%
32	Nevada	2,593	0.62%
39	New Hampshire	990	0.24%
8	New Jersey	14,035	3.38%
30	New Mexico	2,772	0.67%
4	New York	27,156	6.54%
15	North Carolina	7,800	1.88%
44	North Dakota	327	0.08%
13	Ohio	10,332	2.49%
27	Oklahoma	3,589	0.86%
28	Oregon	3,441	0.83%
6	Pennsylvania	17,597	4.24%
NA	Rhode Island**	NA	NA
24	South Carolina	5,242	1.26%
42	South Dakota	557	0.13%
10	Tennessee	13,048	3.14%
2	Texas	48,806	11.76%
34	Utah	1,715	0.41%
NA	Vermont**	NA	NA
11	Virginia	13,042	3.14%
19	Washington	6,663	1.60%
35	West Virginia	1,653	0.40%
18	Wisconsin	7,169	1.73%
43	Wyoming	444	0.11%

RANK ORDER

RANK	STATE	INMATES	% of USA
1	California	61,646	14.85%
2	Texas	48,806	11.76%
3	Florida	30,500	7.35%
4	New York	27,156	6.54%
5	Georgia	20,943	5.04%
6	Pennsylvania	17,597	4.24%
7	Louisiana	14,800	3.56%
8	New Jersey	14,035	3.38%
9	Illinois	13,482	3.25%
10	Tennessee	13,048	3.14%
11	Virginia	13,042	3.14%
12	Michigan	11,395	2.74%
13	Ohio	10,332	2.49%
14	Maryland	8,524	2.05%
15	North Carolina	7,800	1.88%
16	Indiana	7,653	1.84%
17	Massachusetts	7,522	1.81%
18	Wisconsin	7,169	1.73%
19	Washington	6,663	1.60%
20	Alabama	6,485	1.56%
21	Arizona	6,471	1.56%
22	Kentucky	6,198	1.49%
23	Colorado	5,787	1.39%
24	South Carolina	5,242	1.26%
25	Missouri	4,572	1.10%
26	Mississippi	4,459	1.07%
27	Oklahoma	3,589	0.86%
28	Oregon	3,441	0.83%
29	Minnesota	3,395	0.82%
30	New Mexico	2,772	0.67%
31	Arkansas	2,632	0.63%
32	Nevada	2,593	0.62%
33	Kansas	2,520	0.61%
34	Utah	1,715	0.41%
35	West Virginia	1,653	0.40%
36	Nebraska	1,545	0.37%
37	Iowa	1,477	0.36%
38	Idaho	1,383	0.33%
39	New Hampshire	990	0.24%
40	Maine	658	0.16%
41	Montana	604	0.15%
42	South Dakota	557	0.13%
43	Wyoming	444	0.11%
44	North Dakota	327	0.08%
45	Alaska	30	0.01%
NA	Connecticut**	NA	NA
NA	Delaware**	NA	NA
NA	Hawaii**	NA	NA
NA	Rhode Island**	NA	NA
NA	Vermont**	NA	NA
	District of Columbia	1,509	0.36%

Source: U.S. Department of Justice, Bureau of Justice Statistics
   "Correctional Populations in the United States, 1993" (October 1995, NCJ-156241)
*As of July 1, 1993.   Jails are locally operated correctional facilities that confine persons before or after adjudication. Inmates sentenced to jail usually have a sentence of a year or less.
**These states have combined state and local jail systems and are excluded from this count.

Female Inmates in Local Jails in 1993

National Total = 44,184 Female Inmates*

ALPHA ORDER

RANK	STATE	INMATES	% of USA
20	Alabama	587	1.33%
45	Alaska	1	0.00%
16	Arizona	760	1.72%
33	Arkansas	214	0.48%
1	California	7,652	17.32%
22	Colorado	529	1.20%
NA	Connecticut**	NA	NA
NA	Delaware**	NA	NA
3	Florida	3,683	8.34%
5	Georgia	1,720	3.89%
NA	Hawaii**	NA	NA
39	Idaho	102	0.23%
13	Illinois	1,067	2.41%
19	Indiana	644	1.46%
37	Iowa	125	0.28%
31	Kansas	277	0.63%
21	Kentucky	547	1.24%
8	Louisiana	1,408	3.19%
43	Maine	46	0.10%
14	Maryland	834	1.89%
28	Massachusetts	356	0.81%
12	Michigan	1,084	2.45%
32	Minnesota	259	0.59%
27	Mississippi	392	0.89%
25	Missouri	458	1.04%
40	Montana	76	0.17%
36	Nebraska	135	0.31%
26	Nevada	394	0.89%
35	New Hampshire	137	0.31%
11	New Jersey	1,087	2.46%
30	New Mexico	286	0.65%
4	New York	2,653	6.00%
17	North Carolina	748	1.69%
44	North Dakota	34	0.08%
9	Ohio	1,363	3.08%
23	Oklahoma	513	1.16%
29	Oregon	336	0.76%
6	Pennsylvania	1,634	3.70%
NA	Rhode Island**	NA	NA
24	South Carolina	471	1.07%
41	South Dakota	66	0.15%
10	Tennessee	1,327	3.00%
2	Texas	6,589	14.91%
34	Utah	180	0.41%
NA	Vermont**	NA	NA
7	Virginia	1,581	3.58%
15	Washington	772	1.75%
38	West Virginia	118	0.27%
18	Wisconsin	710	1.61%
42	Wyoming	51	0.12%

RANK ORDER

RANK	STATE	INMATES	% of USA
1	California	7,652	17.32%
2	Texas	6,589	14.91%
3	Florida	3,683	8.34%
4	New York	2,653	6.00%
5	Georgia	1,720	3.89%
6	Pennsylvania	1,634	3.70%
7	Virginia	1,581	3.58%
8	Louisiana	1,408	3.19%
9	Ohio	1,363	3.08%
10	Tennessee	1,327	3.00%
11	New Jersey	1,087	2.46%
12	Michigan	1,084	2.45%
13	Illinois	1,067	2.41%
14	Maryland	834	1.89%
15	Washington	772	1.75%
16	Arizona	760	1.72%
17	North Carolina	748	1.69%
18	Wisconsin	710	1.61%
19	Indiana	644	1.46%
20	Alabama	587	1.33%
21	Kentucky	547	1.24%
22	Colorado	529	1.20%
23	Oklahoma	513	1.16%
24	South Carolina	471	1.07%
25	Missouri	458	1.04%
26	Nevada	394	0.89%
27	Mississippi	392	0.89%
28	Massachusetts	356	0.81%
29	Oregon	336	0.76%
30	New Mexico	286	0.65%
31	Kansas	277	0.63%
32	Minnesota	259	0.59%
33	Arkansas	214	0.48%
34	Utah	180	0.41%
35	New Hampshire	137	0.31%
36	Nebraska	135	0.31%
37	Iowa	125	0.28%
38	West Virginia	118	0.27%
39	Idaho	102	0.23%
40	Montana	76	0.17%
41	South Dakota	66	0.15%
42	Wyoming	51	0.12%
43	Maine	46	0.10%
44	North Dakota	34	0.08%
45	Alaska	1	0.00%
NA	Connecticut**	NA	NA
NA	Delaware**	NA	NA
NA	Hawaii**	NA	NA
NA	Rhode Island**	NA	NA
NA	Vermont**	NA	NA
	District of Columbia	178	0.40%

Source: U.S. Department of Justice, Bureau of Justice Statistics
   "Correctional Populations in the United States, 1993" (October 1995, NCJ-156241)
*As of July 1, 1993. Jails are locally operated correctional facilities that confine persons before or after adjudication. Inmates sentenced to jail usually have a sentence of a year or less.
**These states have combined state and local jail systems and are excluded from this count.

White Inmates in Local Jails in 1993

National Total = 153,999 White Inmates*

ALPHA ORDER

RANK	STATE	INMATES	% of USA
24	Alabama	2,147	1.39%
45	Alaska	15	0.01%
18	Arizona	2,980	1.94%
29	Arkansas	1,379	0.90%
1	California	18,471	11.99%
23	Colorado	2,299	1.49%
NA	Connecticut**	NA	NA
NA	Delaware**	NA	NA
3	Florida	14,030	9.11%
7	Georgia	5,368	3.49%
NA	Hawaii**	NA	NA
37	Idaho	832	0.54%
15	Illinois	3,800	2.47%
10	Indiana	4,718	3.06%
34	Iowa	1,016	0.66%
28	Kansas	1,497	0.97%
14	Kentucky	3,812	2.48%
19	Louisiana	2,654	1.72%
39	Maine	577	0.37%
17	Maryland	3,000	1.95%
16	Massachusetts	3,099	2.01%
6	Michigan	5,424	3.52%
24	Minnesota	2,147	1.39%
35	Mississippi	972	0.63%
26	Missouri	2,039	1.32%
41	Montana	408	0.26%
36	Nebraska	928	0.60%
33	Nevada	1,209	0.79%
38	New Hampshire	594	0.39%
21	New Jersey	2,471	1.60%
40	New Mexico	479	0.31%
5	New York	6,419	4.17%
20	North Carolina	2,494	1.62%
44	North Dakota	241	0.16%
12	Ohio	4,126	2.68%
27	Oklahoma	1,899	1.23%
22	Oregon	2,350	1.53%
4	Pennsylvania	8,054	5.23%
NA	Rhode Island**	NA	NA
32	South Carolina	1,248	0.81%
42	South Dakota	376	0.24%
8	Tennessee	5,296	3.44%
2	Texas	16,863	10.95%
31	Utah	1,264	0.82%
NA	Vermont**	NA	NA
11	Virginia	4,659	3.03%
9	Washington	4,735	3.07%
30	West Virginia	1,325	0.86%
13	Wisconsin	3,915	2.54%
43	Wyoming	364	0.24%

RANK ORDER

RANK	STATE	INMATES	% of USA
1	California	18,471	11.99%
2	Texas	16,863	10.95%
3	Florida	14,030	9.11%
4	Pennsylvania	8,054	5.23%
5	New York	6,419	4.17%
6	Michigan	5,424	3.52%
7	Georgia	5,368	3.49%
8	Tennessee	5,296	3.44%
9	Washington	4,735	3.07%
10	Indiana	4,718	3.06%
11	Virginia	4,659	3.03%
12	Ohio	4,126	2.68%
13	Wisconsin	3,915	2.54%
14	Kentucky	3,812	2.48%
15	Illinois	3,800	2.47%
16	Massachusetts	3,099	2.01%
17	Maryland	3,000	1.95%
18	Arizona	2,980	1.94%
19	Louisiana	2,654	1.72%
20	North Carolina	2,494	1.62%
21	New Jersey	2,471	1.60%
22	Oregon	2,350	1.53%
23	Colorado	2,299	1.49%
24	Alabama	2,147	1.39%
24	Minnesota	2,147	1.39%
26	Missouri	2,039	1.32%
27	Oklahoma	1,899	1.23%
28	Kansas	1,497	0.97%
29	Arkansas	1,379	0.90%
30	West Virginia	1,325	0.86%
31	Utah	1,264	0.82%
32	South Carolina	1,248	0.81%
33	Nevada	1,209	0.79%
34	Iowa	1,016	0.66%
35	Mississippi	972	0.63%
36	Nebraska	928	0.60%
37	Idaho	832	0.54%
38	New Hampshire	594	0.39%
39	Maine	577	0.37%
40	New Mexico	479	0.31%
41	Montana	408	0.26%
42	South Dakota	376	0.24%
43	Wyoming	364	0.24%
44	North Dakota	241	0.16%
45	Alaska	15	0.01%
NA	Connecticut**	NA	NA
NA	Delaware**	NA	NA
NA	Hawaii**	NA	NA
NA	Rhode Island**	NA	NA
NA	Vermont**	NA	NA
	District of Columbia***	NA	NA

Source: U.S. Department of Justice, Bureau of Justice Statistics
"Correctional Populations in the United States, 1993" (October 1995, NCJ-156241)

*As of July 1, 1993. Jails are locally operated correctional facilities that confine persons before or after adjudication. Inmates sentenced to jail usually have a sentence of a year or less.

**These states have combined state and local jail systems and are excluded from this count.

***Not available.

White Inmates in Local Jails as a Percent of All Inmates in 1993

National Percent = 33.49% of Inmates*

<table>
<tr><td colspan="3">ALPHA ORDER</td><td colspan="3">RANK ORDER</td></tr>
<tr><th>RANK</th><th>STATE</th><th>PERCENT</th><th>RANK</th><th>STATE</th><th>PERCENT</th></tr>
<tr><td>35</td><td>Alabama</td><td>30.36</td><td>1</td><td>Maine</td><td>81.96</td></tr>
<tr><td>20</td><td>Alaska</td><td>48.39</td><td>2</td><td>West Virginia</td><td>74.82</td></tr>
<tr><td>24</td><td>Arizona</td><td>41.21</td><td>3</td><td>Wyoming</td><td>73.54</td></tr>
<tr><td>19</td><td>Arkansas</td><td>48.45</td><td>4</td><td>North Dakota</td><td>66.76</td></tr>
<tr><td>37</td><td>California</td><td>26.65</td><td>5</td><td>Utah</td><td>66.70</td></tr>
<tr><td>30</td><td>Colorado</td><td>36.40</td><td>6</td><td>Washington</td><td>63.69</td></tr>
<tr><td>NA</td><td>Connecticut**</td><td>NA</td><td>7</td><td>Iowa</td><td>63.42</td></tr>
<tr><td>NA</td><td>Delaware**</td><td>NA</td><td>8</td><td>Oregon</td><td>62.22</td></tr>
<tr><td>25</td><td>Florida</td><td>41.04</td><td>9</td><td>South Dakota</td><td>60.35</td></tr>
<tr><td>39</td><td>Georgia</td><td>23.69</td><td>10</td><td>Montana</td><td>60.00</td></tr>
<tr><td>NA</td><td>Hawaii**</td><td>NA</td><td>11</td><td>Minnesota</td><td>58.76</td></tr>
<tr><td>13</td><td>Idaho</td><td>56.03</td><td>12</td><td>Indiana</td><td>56.86</td></tr>
<tr><td>38</td><td>Illinois</td><td>26.12</td><td>13</td><td>Idaho</td><td>56.03</td></tr>
<tr><td>12</td><td>Indiana</td><td>56.86</td><td>14</td><td>Kentucky</td><td>55.95</td></tr>
<tr><td>7</td><td>Iowa</td><td>63.42</td><td>15</td><td>Nebraska</td><td>55.24</td></tr>
<tr><td>16</td><td>Kansas</td><td>53.52</td><td>16</td><td>Kansas</td><td>53.52</td></tr>
<tr><td>14</td><td>Kentucky</td><td>55.95</td><td>17</td><td>New Hampshire</td><td>52.71</td></tr>
<tr><td>43</td><td>Louisiana</td><td>16.37</td><td>18</td><td>Wisconsin</td><td>49.69</td></tr>
<tr><td>1</td><td>Maine</td><td>81.96</td><td>19</td><td>Arkansas</td><td>48.45</td></tr>
<tr><td>32</td><td>Maryland</td><td>32.06</td><td>20</td><td>Alaska</td><td>48.39</td></tr>
<tr><td>28</td><td>Massachusetts</td><td>39.34</td><td>21</td><td>Oklahoma</td><td>46.29</td></tr>
<tr><td>22</td><td>Michigan</td><td>43.47</td><td>22</td><td>Michigan</td><td>43.47</td></tr>
<tr><td>11</td><td>Minnesota</td><td>58.76</td><td>23</td><td>Pennsylvania</td><td>41.88</td></tr>
<tr><td>42</td><td>Mississippi</td><td>20.04</td><td>24</td><td>Arizona</td><td>41.21</td></tr>
<tr><td>26</td><td>Missouri</td><td>40.54</td><td>25</td><td>Florida</td><td>41.04</td></tr>
<tr><td>10</td><td>Montana</td><td>60.00</td><td>26</td><td>Missouri</td><td>40.54</td></tr>
<tr><td>15</td><td>Nebraska</td><td>55.24</td><td>27</td><td>Nevada</td><td>40.48</td></tr>
<tr><td>27</td><td>Nevada</td><td>40.48</td><td>28</td><td>Massachusetts</td><td>39.34</td></tr>
<tr><td>17</td><td>New Hampshire</td><td>52.71</td><td>29</td><td>Tennessee</td><td>36.84</td></tr>
<tr><td>44</td><td>New Jersey</td><td>16.34</td><td>30</td><td>Colorado</td><td>36.40</td></tr>
<tr><td>45</td><td>New Mexico</td><td>15.66</td><td>31</td><td>Ohio</td><td>35.28</td></tr>
<tr><td>41</td><td>New York</td><td>21.53</td><td>32</td><td>Maryland</td><td>32.06</td></tr>
<tr><td>36</td><td>North Carolina</td><td>27.90</td><td>33</td><td>Virginia</td><td>31.86</td></tr>
<tr><td>4</td><td>North Dakota</td><td>66.76</td><td>34</td><td>Texas</td><td>30.44</td></tr>
<tr><td>31</td><td>Ohio</td><td>35.28</td><td>35</td><td>Alabama</td><td>30.36</td></tr>
<tr><td>21</td><td>Oklahoma</td><td>46.29</td><td>36</td><td>North Carolina</td><td>27.90</td></tr>
<tr><td>8</td><td>Oregon</td><td>62.22</td><td>37</td><td>California</td><td>26.65</td></tr>
<tr><td>23</td><td>Pennsylvania</td><td>41.88</td><td>38</td><td>Illinois</td><td>26.12</td></tr>
<tr><td>NA</td><td>Rhode Island**</td><td>NA</td><td>39</td><td>Georgia</td><td>23.69</td></tr>
<tr><td>40</td><td>South Carolina</td><td>21.84</td><td>40</td><td>South Carolina</td><td>21.84</td></tr>
<tr><td>9</td><td>South Dakota</td><td>60.35</td><td>41</td><td>New York</td><td>21.53</td></tr>
<tr><td>29</td><td>Tennessee</td><td>36.84</td><td>42</td><td>Mississippi</td><td>20.04</td></tr>
<tr><td>34</td><td>Texas</td><td>30.44</td><td>43</td><td>Louisiana</td><td>16.37</td></tr>
<tr><td>5</td><td>Utah</td><td>66.70</td><td>44</td><td>New Jersey</td><td>16.34</td></tr>
<tr><td>NA</td><td>Vermont**</td><td>NA</td><td>45</td><td>New Mexico</td><td>15.66</td></tr>
<tr><td>33</td><td>Virginia</td><td>31.86</td><td>NA</td><td>Connecticut**</td><td>NA</td></tr>
<tr><td>6</td><td>Washington</td><td>63.69</td><td>NA</td><td>Delaware**</td><td>NA</td></tr>
<tr><td>2</td><td>West Virginia</td><td>74.82</td><td>NA</td><td>Hawaii**</td><td>NA</td></tr>
<tr><td>18</td><td>Wisconsin</td><td>49.69</td><td>NA</td><td>Rhode Island**</td><td>NA</td></tr>
<tr><td>3</td><td>Wyoming</td><td>73.54</td><td>NA</td><td>Vermont**</td><td>NA</td></tr>
<tr><td></td><td></td><td></td><td></td><td>District of Columbia***</td><td>NA</td></tr>
</table>

Source: Morgan Quitno Press using data from U.S. Department of Justice, Bureau of Justice Statistics
"Correctional Populations in the United States, 1993" (October 1995, NCJ-156241)
*As of July 1, 1993. Jails are locally operated correctional facilities that confine persons before or after adjudication. Inmates sentenced to jail usually have a sentence of a year or less.
**These states have combined state and local jail systems and are excluded from this count.
***Not available.

Black Inmates in Local Jails in 1993

National Total = 173,193 Black Inmates*

ALPHA ORDER

RANK	STATE	INMATES	% of USA
15	Alabama	3,922	2.26%
45	Alaska	0	0.00%
27	Arizona	921	0.53%
25	Arkansas	1,246	0.72%
3	California	13,887	8.02%
31	Colorado	473	0.27%
NA	Connecticut**	NA	NA
NA	Delaware**	NA	NA
2	Florida	16,426	9.48%
4	Georgia	12,764	7.37%
NA	Hawaii**	NA	NA
41	Idaho	13	0.01%
6	Illinois	8,822	5.09%
23	Indiana	1,650	0.95%
34	Iowa	306	0.18%
28	Kansas	792	0.46%
22	Kentucky	1,810	1.05%
10	Louisiana	6,435	3.72%
42	Maine	11	0.01%
11	Maryland	6,165	3.56%
20	Massachusetts	2,246	1.30%
14	Michigan	4,658	2.69%
29	Minnesota	783	0.45%
18	Mississippi	2,650	1.53%
21	Missouri	2,208	1.27%
40	Montana	14	0.01%
32	Nebraska	415	0.24%
30	Nevada	636	0.37%
42	New Hampshire	11	0.01%
12	New Jersey	5,656	3.27%
37	New Mexico	142	0.08%
5	New York	12,114	6.99%
13	North Carolina	5,443	3.14%
44	North Dakota	10	0.01%
16	Ohio	3,548	2.05%
26	Oklahoma	1,151	0.66%
33	Oregon	389	0.22%
8	Pennsylvania	8,511	4.91%
NA	Rhode Island**	NA	NA
17	South Carolina	3,331	1.92%
38	South Dakota	22	0.01%
7	Tennessee	8,590	4.96%
1	Texas	20,925	12.08%
36	Utah	148	0.09%
NA	Vermont**	NA	NA
9	Virginia	8,183	4.72%
24	Washington	1,299	0.75%
35	West Virginia	217	0.13%
19	Wisconsin	2,587	1.49%
39	Wyoming	20	0.01%

RANK ORDER

RANK	STATE	INMATES	% of USA
1	Texas	20,925	12.08%
2	Florida	16,426	9.48%
3	California	13,887	8.02%
4	Georgia	12,764	7.37%
5	New York	12,114	6.99%
6	Illinois	8,822	5.09%
7	Tennessee	8,590	4.96%
8	Pennsylvania	8,511	4.91%
9	Virginia	8,183	4.72%
10	Louisiana	6,435	3.72%
11	Maryland	6,165	3.56%
12	New Jersey	5,656	3.27%
13	North Carolina	5,443	3.14%
14	Michigan	4,658	2.69%
15	Alabama	3,922	2.26%
16	Ohio	3,548	2.05%
17	South Carolina	3,331	1.92%
18	Mississippi	2,650	1.53%
19	Wisconsin	2,587	1.49%
20	Massachusetts	2,246	1.30%
21	Missouri	2,208	1.27%
22	Kentucky	1,810	1.05%
23	Indiana	1,650	0.95%
24	Washington	1,299	0.75%
25	Arkansas	1,246	0.72%
26	Oklahoma	1,151	0.66%
27	Arizona	921	0.53%
28	Kansas	792	0.46%
29	Minnesota	783	0.45%
30	Nevada	636	0.37%
31	Colorado	473	0.27%
32	Nebraska	415	0.24%
33	Oregon	389	0.22%
34	Iowa	306	0.18%
35	West Virginia	217	0.13%
36	Utah	148	0.09%
37	New Mexico	142	0.08%
38	South Dakota	22	0.01%
39	Wyoming	20	0.01%
40	Montana	14	0.01%
41	Idaho	13	0.01%
42	Maine	11	0.01%
42	New Hampshire	11	0.01%
44	North Dakota	10	0.01%
45	Alaska	0	0.00%
NA	Connecticut**	NA	NA
NA	Delaware**	NA	NA
NA	Hawaii**	NA	NA
NA	Rhode Island**	NA	NA
NA	Vermont**	NA	NA
	District of Columbia***	NA	NA

Source: U.S. Department of Justice, Bureau of Justice Statistics
    "Correctional Populations in the United States, 1993" (October 1995, NCJ-156241)

As of July 1, 1993. Jails are locally operated correctional facilities that confine persons before or after adjudication. Inmates sentenced to jail usually have a sentence of a year or less.

**These states have combined state and local jail systems and are excluded from this count.*

***Not available.*

Black Inmates in Local Jails as a Percent of All Inmates in 1993

National Percent = 37.67% of Inmates*

<table>
<tr><td colspan="3">ALPHA ORDER</td><td colspan="3">RANK ORDER</td></tr>
<tr><td>RANK</td><td>STATE</td><td>PERCENT</td><td>RANK</td><td>STATE</td><td>PERCENT</td></tr>
<tr><td>8</td><td>Alabama</td><td>55.46</td><td>1</td><td>Maryland</td><td>65.88</td></tr>
<tr><td>45</td><td>Alaska</td><td>0.00</td><td>2</td><td>North Carolina</td><td>60.89</td></tr>
<tr><td>32</td><td>Arizona</td><td>12.74</td><td>3</td><td>Illinois</td><td>60.64</td></tr>
<tr><td>13</td><td>Arkansas</td><td>43.78</td><td>4</td><td>Tennessee</td><td>59.76</td></tr>
<tr><td>28</td><td>California</td><td>20.04</td><td>5</td><td>South Carolina</td><td>58.31</td></tr>
<tr><td>36</td><td>Colorado</td><td>7.49</td><td>6</td><td>Georgia</td><td>56.32</td></tr>
<tr><td>NA</td><td>Connecticut**</td><td>NA</td><td>7</td><td>Virginia</td><td>55.96</td></tr>
<tr><td>NA</td><td>Delaware**</td><td>NA</td><td>8</td><td>Alabama</td><td>55.46</td></tr>
<tr><td>10</td><td>Florida</td><td>48.05</td><td>9</td><td>Mississippi</td><td>54.63</td></tr>
<tr><td>6</td><td>Georgia</td><td>56.32</td><td>10</td><td>Florida</td><td>48.05</td></tr>
<tr><td>NA</td><td>Hawaii**</td><td>NA</td><td>11</td><td>Pennsylvania</td><td>44.26</td></tr>
<tr><td>44</td><td>Idaho</td><td>0.88</td><td>12</td><td>Missouri</td><td>43.90</td></tr>
<tr><td>3</td><td>Illinois</td><td>60.64</td><td>13</td><td>Arkansas</td><td>43.78</td></tr>
<tr><td>29</td><td>Indiana</td><td>19.89</td><td>14</td><td>New York</td><td>40.64</td></tr>
<tr><td>30</td><td>Iowa</td><td>19.10</td><td>15</td><td>Louisiana</td><td>39.70</td></tr>
<tr><td>22</td><td>Kansas</td><td>28.32</td><td>16</td><td>Texas</td><td>37.77</td></tr>
<tr><td>24</td><td>Kentucky</td><td>26.57</td><td>17</td><td>New Jersey</td><td>37.40</td></tr>
<tr><td>15</td><td>Louisiana</td><td>39.70</td><td>18</td><td>Michigan</td><td>37.33</td></tr>
<tr><td>42</td><td>Maine</td><td>1.56</td><td>19</td><td>Wisconsin</td><td>32.83</td></tr>
<tr><td>1</td><td>Maryland</td><td>65.88</td><td>20</td><td>Ohio</td><td>30.34</td></tr>
<tr><td>21</td><td>Massachusetts</td><td>28.51</td><td>21</td><td>Massachusetts</td><td>28.51</td></tr>
<tr><td>18</td><td>Michigan</td><td>37.33</td><td>22</td><td>Kansas</td><td>28.32</td></tr>
<tr><td>26</td><td>Minnesota</td><td>21.43</td><td>23</td><td>Oklahoma</td><td>28.06</td></tr>
<tr><td>9</td><td>Mississippi</td><td>54.63</td><td>24</td><td>Kentucky</td><td>26.57</td></tr>
<tr><td>12</td><td>Missouri</td><td>43.90</td><td>25</td><td>Nebraska</td><td>24.70</td></tr>
<tr><td>41</td><td>Montana</td><td>2.06</td><td>26</td><td>Minnesota</td><td>21.43</td></tr>
<tr><td>25</td><td>Nebraska</td><td>24.70</td><td>27</td><td>Nevada</td><td>21.29</td></tr>
<tr><td>27</td><td>Nevada</td><td>21.29</td><td>28</td><td>California</td><td>20.04</td></tr>
<tr><td>43</td><td>New Hampshire</td><td>0.98</td><td>29</td><td>Indiana</td><td>19.89</td></tr>
<tr><td>17</td><td>New Jersey</td><td>37.40</td><td>30</td><td>Iowa</td><td>19.10</td></tr>
<tr><td>37</td><td>New Mexico</td><td>4.64</td><td>31</td><td>Washington</td><td>17.47</td></tr>
<tr><td>14</td><td>New York</td><td>40.64</td><td>32</td><td>Arizona</td><td>12.74</td></tr>
<tr><td>2</td><td>North Carolina</td><td>60.89</td><td>33</td><td>West Virginia</td><td>12.25</td></tr>
<tr><td>40</td><td>North Dakota</td><td>2.77</td><td>34</td><td>Oregon</td><td>10.30</td></tr>
<tr><td>20</td><td>Ohio</td><td>30.34</td><td>35</td><td>Utah</td><td>7.81</td></tr>
<tr><td>23</td><td>Oklahoma</td><td>28.06</td><td>36</td><td>Colorado</td><td>7.49</td></tr>
<tr><td>34</td><td>Oregon</td><td>10.30</td><td>37</td><td>New Mexico</td><td>4.64</td></tr>
<tr><td>11</td><td>Pennsylvania</td><td>44.26</td><td>38</td><td>Wyoming</td><td>4.04</td></tr>
<tr><td>NA</td><td>Rhode Island**</td><td>NA</td><td>39</td><td>South Dakota</td><td>3.53</td></tr>
<tr><td>5</td><td>South Carolina</td><td>58.31</td><td>40</td><td>North Dakota</td><td>2.77</td></tr>
<tr><td>39</td><td>South Dakota</td><td>3.53</td><td>41</td><td>Montana</td><td>2.06</td></tr>
<tr><td>4</td><td>Tennessee</td><td>59.76</td><td>42</td><td>Maine</td><td>1.56</td></tr>
<tr><td>16</td><td>Texas</td><td>37.77</td><td>43</td><td>New Hampshire</td><td>0.98</td></tr>
<tr><td>35</td><td>Utah</td><td>7.81</td><td>44</td><td>Idaho</td><td>0.88</td></tr>
<tr><td>NA</td><td>Vermont**</td><td>NA</td><td>45</td><td>Alaska</td><td>0.00</td></tr>
<tr><td>7</td><td>Virginia</td><td>55.96</td><td>NA</td><td>Connecticut**</td><td>NA</td></tr>
<tr><td>31</td><td>Washington</td><td>17.47</td><td>NA</td><td>Delaware**</td><td>NA</td></tr>
<tr><td>33</td><td>West Virginia</td><td>12.25</td><td>NA</td><td>Hawaii**</td><td>NA</td></tr>
<tr><td>19</td><td>Wisconsin</td><td>32.83</td><td>NA</td><td>Rhode Island**</td><td>NA</td></tr>
<tr><td>38</td><td>Wyoming</td><td>4.04</td><td>NA</td><td>Vermont**</td><td>NA</td></tr>
<tr><td></td><td></td><td></td><td></td><td>District of Columbia***</td><td>NA</td></tr>
</table>

Source: Morgan Quitno Press using data from U.S. Department of Justice, Bureau of Justice Statistics "Correctional Populations in the United States, 1993" (October 1995, NCJ-156241)

*As of July 1, 1993. Jails are locally operated correctional facilities that confine persons before or after adjudication. Inmates sentenced to jail usually have a sentence of a year or less.

**These states have combined state and local jail systems and are excluded from this count.

***Not available.

Hispanic Inmates in Local Jails in 1993

National Total = 58,947 Hispanic Inmates*

ALPHA ORDER

RANK	STATE	INMATES	% of USA
35	Alabama	47	0.08%
45	Alaska	3	0.01%
5	Arizona	1,872	3.18%
39	Arkansas	31	0.05%
1	California	22,110	37.51%
12	Colorado	860	1.46%
NA	Connecticut**	NA	NA
NA	Delaware**	NA	NA
4	Florida	2,764	4.69%
20	Georgia	254	0.43%
NA	Hawaii**	NA	NA
18	Idaho	262	0.44%
9	Illinois	1,274	2.16%
28	Indiana	162	0.27%
32	Iowa	71	0.12%
23	Kansas	204	0.35%
30	Kentucky	80	0.14%
24	Louisiana	190	0.32%
43	Maine	7	0.01%
24	Maryland	190	0.32%
8	Massachusetts	1,324	2.25%
13	Michigan	577	0.98%
27	Minnesota	166	0.28%
37	Mississippi	41	0.07%
31	Missouri	75	0.13%
38	Montana	40	0.07%
26	Nebraska	176	0.30%
21	Nevada	252	0.43%
40	New Hampshire	23	0.04%
6	New Jersey	1,809	3.07%
10	New Mexico	1,229	2.08%
3	New York	6,483	11.00%
29	North Carolina	150	0.25%
40	North Dakota	23	0.04%
22	Ohio	221	0.37%
19	Oklahoma	260	0.44%
14	Oregon	413	0.70%
7	Pennsylvania	1,596	2.71%
NA	Rhode Island**	NA	NA
36	South Carolina	43	0.07%
44	South Dakota	6	0.01%
34	Tennessee	56	0.10%
2	Texas	11,729	19.90%
15	Utah	351	0.60%
NA	Vermont**	NA	NA
16	Virginia	287	0.49%
11	Washington	891	1.51%
42	West Virginia	11	0.02%
17	Wisconsin	272	0.46%
33	Wyoming	58	0.10%

RANK ORDER

RANK	STATE	INMATES	% of USA
1	California	22,110	37.51%
2	Texas	11,729	19.90%
3	New York	6,483	11.00%
4	Florida	2,764	4.69%
5	Arizona	1,872	3.18%
6	New Jersey	1,809	3.07%
7	Pennsylvania	1,596	2.71%
8	Massachusetts	1,324	2.25%
9	Illinois	1,274	2.16%
10	New Mexico	1,229	2.08%
11	Washington	891	1.51%
12	Colorado	860	1.46%
13	Michigan	577	0.98%
14	Oregon	413	0.70%
15	Utah	351	0.60%
16	Virginia	287	0.49%
17	Wisconsin	272	0.46%
18	Idaho	262	0.44%
19	Oklahoma	260	0.44%
20	Georgia	254	0.43%
21	Nevada	252	0.43%
22	Ohio	221	0.37%
23	Kansas	204	0.35%
24	Louisiana	190	0.32%
24	Maryland	190	0.32%
26	Nebraska	176	0.30%
27	Minnesota	166	0.28%
28	Indiana	162	0.27%
29	North Carolina	150	0.25%
30	Kentucky	80	0.14%
31	Missouri	75	0.13%
32	Iowa	71	0.12%
33	Wyoming	58	0.10%
34	Tennessee	56	0.10%
35	Alabama	47	0.08%
36	South Carolina	43	0.07%
37	Mississippi	41	0.07%
38	Montana	40	0.07%
39	Arkansas	31	0.05%
40	New Hampshire	23	0.04%
40	North Dakota	23	0.04%
42	West Virginia	11	0.02%
43	Maine	7	0.01%
44	South Dakota	6	0.01%
45	Alaska	3	0.01%
NA	Connecticut**	NA	NA
NA	Delaware**	NA	NA
NA	Hawaii**	NA	NA
NA	Rhode Island**	NA	NA
NA	Vermont**	NA	NA
	District of Columbia***	NA	NA

Source: U.S. Department of Justice, Bureau of Justice Statistics
"Correctional Populations in the United States, 1993" (October 1995, NCJ-156241)
*As of July 1, 1993. Jails are locally operated correctional facilities that confine persons before or after adjudication. Inmates sentenced to jail usually have a sentence of a year or less.
**These states have combined state and local jail systems and are excluded from this count.
***Not available.

Hispanic Inmates in Local Jails as a Percent of All Inmates in 1993

National Percent = 12.82% of Inmates*

ALPHA ORDER				RANK ORDER		
RANK	STATE	PERCENT		RANK	STATE	PERCENT
43	Alabama	0.66		1	New Mexico	40.19
15	Alaska	9.68		2	California	31.91
3	Arizona	25.89		3	Arizona	25.89
38	Arkansas	1.09		4	New York	21.75
2	California	31.91		5	Texas	21.17
9	Colorado	13.62		6	Utah	18.52
NA	Connecticut**	NA		7	Idaho	17.64
NA	Delaware**	NA		8	Massachusetts	16.81
19	Florida	8.09		9	Colorado	13.62
37	Georgia	1.12		10	Washington	11.98
NA	Hawaii**	NA		11	New Jersey	11.96
7	Idaho	17.64		12	Wyoming	11.72
16	Illinois	8.76		13	Oregon	10.93
31	Indiana	1.95		14	Nebraska	10.48
26	Iowa	4.43		15	Alaska	9.68
20	Kansas	7.29		16	Illinois	8.76
35	Kentucky	1.17		17	Nevada	8.44
35	Louisiana	1.17		18	Pennsylvania	8.30
39	Maine	0.99		19	Florida	8.09
29	Maryland	2.03		20	Kansas	7.29
8	Massachusetts	16.81		21	North Dakota	6.37
24	Michigan	4.62		22	Oklahoma	6.34
25	Minnesota	4.54		23	Montana	5.88
41	Mississippi	0.85		24	Michigan	4.62
34	Missouri	1.49		25	Minnesota	4.54
23	Montana	5.88		26	Iowa	4.43
14	Nebraska	10.48		27	Wisconsin	3.45
17	Nevada	8.44		28	New Hampshire	2.04
28	New Hampshire	2.04		29	Maryland	2.03
11	New Jersey	11.96		30	Virginia	1.96
1	New Mexico	40.19		31	Indiana	1.95
4	New York	21.75		32	Ohio	1.89
33	North Carolina	1.68		33	North Carolina	1.68
21	North Dakota	6.37		34	Missouri	1.49
32	Ohio	1.89		35	Kentucky	1.17
22	Oklahoma	6.34		35	Louisiana	1.17
13	Oregon	10.93		37	Georgia	1.12
18	Pennsylvania	8.30		38	Arkansas	1.09
NA	Rhode Island**	NA		39	Maine	0.99
42	South Carolina	0.75		40	South Dakota	0.96
40	South Dakota	0.96		41	Mississippi	0.85
45	Tennessee	0.39		42	South Carolina	0.75
5	Texas	21.17		43	Alabama	0.66
6	Utah	18.52		44	West Virginia	0.62
NA	Vermont**	NA		45	Tennessee	0.39
30	Virginia	1.96		NA	Connecticut**	NA
10	Washington	11.98		NA	Delaware**	NA
44	West Virginia	0.62		NA	Hawaii**	NA
27	Wisconsin	3.45		NA	Rhode Island**	NA
12	Wyoming	11.72		NA	Vermont**	NA
					District of Columbia***	NA

Source: Morgan Quitno Press using data from U.S. Department of Justice, Bureau of Justice Statistics
   "Correctional Populations in the United States, 1993" (October 1995, NCJ-156241)
*As of July 1, 1993.   Jails are locally operated correctional facilities that confine persons before or after
adjudication. Inmates sentenced to jail usually have a sentence of a year or less.
**These states have combined state and local jail systems and are excluded from this count.
***Not available.

Correctional Officers in Local Jails in 1993

National Total = 117,900 Officers*

<table>
<tr><td colspan="4"><u>ALPHA ORDER</u></td><td colspan="4"><u>RANK ORDER</u></td></tr>
<tr><th>RANK</th><th>STATE</th><th>OFFICERS</th><th>% of USA</th><th>RANK</th><th>STATE</th><th>OFFICERS</th><th>% of USA</th></tr>
<tr><td>23</td><td>Alabama</td><td>1,301</td><td>1.10%</td><td>1</td><td>New York</td><td>12,824</td><td>10.88%</td></tr>
<tr><td>45</td><td>Alaska</td><td>24</td><td>0.02%</td><td>2</td><td>Texas</td><td>11,304</td><td>9.59%</td></tr>
<tr><td>21</td><td>Arizona</td><td>1,489</td><td>1.26%</td><td>3</td><td>California</td><td>10,389</td><td>8.81%</td></tr>
<tr><td>29</td><td>Arkansas</td><td>854</td><td>0.72%</td><td>4</td><td>Florida</td><td>8,547</td><td>7.25%</td></tr>
<tr><td>3</td><td>California</td><td>10,389</td><td>8.81%</td><td>5</td><td>Pennsylvania</td><td>4,937</td><td>4.19%</td></tr>
<tr><td>17</td><td>Colorado</td><td>1,843</td><td>1.56%</td><td>6</td><td>Illinois</td><td>3,843</td><td>3.26%</td></tr>
<tr><td>NA</td><td>Connecticut**</td><td>NA</td><td>NA</td><td>7</td><td>Georgia</td><td>3,815</td><td>3.24%</td></tr>
<tr><td>NA</td><td>Delaware**</td><td>NA</td><td>NA</td><td>8</td><td>Ohio</td><td>3,557</td><td>3.02%</td></tr>
<tr><td>4</td><td>Florida</td><td>8,547</td><td>7.25%</td><td>9</td><td>Tennessee</td><td>3,258</td><td>2.76%</td></tr>
<tr><td>7</td><td>Georgia</td><td>3,815</td><td>3.24%</td><td>10</td><td>Virginia</td><td>3,103</td><td>2.63%</td></tr>
<tr><td>NA</td><td>Hawaii**</td><td>NA</td><td>NA</td><td>11</td><td>New Jersey</td><td>3,065</td><td>2.60%</td></tr>
<tr><td>39</td><td>Idaho</td><td>410</td><td>0.35%</td><td>12</td><td>Michigan</td><td>2,939</td><td>2.49%</td></tr>
<tr><td>6</td><td>Illinois</td><td>3,843</td><td>3.26%</td><td>13</td><td>Massachusetts</td><td>2,851</td><td>2.42%</td></tr>
<tr><td>18</td><td>Indiana</td><td>1,582</td><td>1.34%</td><td>14</td><td>Maryland</td><td>2,272</td><td>1.93%</td></tr>
<tr><td>31</td><td>Iowa</td><td>812</td><td>0.69%</td><td>15</td><td>Louisiana</td><td>2,132</td><td>1.81%</td></tr>
<tr><td>28</td><td>Kansas</td><td>977</td><td>0.83%</td><td>16</td><td>North Carolina</td><td>2,123</td><td>1.80%</td></tr>
<tr><td>22</td><td>Kentucky</td><td>1,412</td><td>1.20%</td><td>17</td><td>Colorado</td><td>1,843</td><td>1.56%</td></tr>
<tr><td>15</td><td>Louisiana</td><td>2,132</td><td>1.81%</td><td>18</td><td>Indiana</td><td>1,582</td><td>1.34%</td></tr>
<tr><td>37</td><td>Maine</td><td>490</td><td>0.42%</td><td>19</td><td>Washington</td><td>1,581</td><td>1.34%</td></tr>
<tr><td>14</td><td>Maryland</td><td>2,272</td><td>1.93%</td><td>20</td><td>Wisconsin</td><td>1,545</td><td>1.31%</td></tr>
<tr><td>13</td><td>Massachusetts</td><td>2,851</td><td>2.42%</td><td>21</td><td>Arizona</td><td>1,489</td><td>1.26%</td></tr>
<tr><td>12</td><td>Michigan</td><td>2,939</td><td>2.49%</td><td>22</td><td>Kentucky</td><td>1,412</td><td>1.20%</td></tr>
<tr><td>24</td><td>Minnesota</td><td>1,248</td><td>1.06%</td><td>23</td><td>Alabama</td><td>1,301</td><td>1.10%</td></tr>
<tr><td>33</td><td>Mississippi</td><td>753</td><td>0.64%</td><td>24</td><td>Minnesota</td><td>1,248</td><td>1.06%</td></tr>
<tr><td>25</td><td>Missouri</td><td>1,093</td><td>0.93%</td><td>25</td><td>Missouri</td><td>1,093</td><td>0.93%</td></tr>
<tr><td>44</td><td>Montana</td><td>208</td><td>0.18%</td><td>26</td><td>South Carolina</td><td>1,046</td><td>0.89%</td></tr>
<tr><td>34</td><td>Nebraska</td><td>709</td><td>0.60%</td><td>27</td><td>Oregon</td><td>1,019</td><td>0.86%</td></tr>
<tr><td>35</td><td>Nevada</td><td>549</td><td>0.47%</td><td>28</td><td>Kansas</td><td>977</td><td>0.83%</td></tr>
<tr><td>40</td><td>New Hampshire</td><td>259</td><td>0.22%</td><td>29</td><td>Arkansas</td><td>854</td><td>0.72%</td></tr>
<tr><td>11</td><td>New Jersey</td><td>3,065</td><td>2.60%</td><td>30</td><td>Oklahoma</td><td>820</td><td>0.70%</td></tr>
<tr><td>32</td><td>New Mexico</td><td>786</td><td>0.67%</td><td>31</td><td>Iowa</td><td>812</td><td>0.69%</td></tr>
<tr><td>1</td><td>New York</td><td>12,824</td><td>10.88%</td><td>32</td><td>New Mexico</td><td>786</td><td>0.67%</td></tr>
<tr><td>16</td><td>North Carolina</td><td>2,123</td><td>1.80%</td><td>33</td><td>Mississippi</td><td>753</td><td>0.64%</td></tr>
<tr><td>41</td><td>North Dakota</td><td>233</td><td>0.20%</td><td>34</td><td>Nebraska</td><td>709</td><td>0.60%</td></tr>
<tr><td>8</td><td>Ohio</td><td>3,557</td><td>3.02%</td><td>35</td><td>Nevada</td><td>549</td><td>0.47%</td></tr>
<tr><td>30</td><td>Oklahoma</td><td>820</td><td>0.70%</td><td>36</td><td>Utah</td><td>499</td><td>0.42%</td></tr>
<tr><td>27</td><td>Oregon</td><td>1,019</td><td>0.86%</td><td>37</td><td>Maine</td><td>490</td><td>0.42%</td></tr>
<tr><td>5</td><td>Pennsylvania</td><td>4,937</td><td>4.19%</td><td>38</td><td>West Virginia</td><td>483</td><td>0.41%</td></tr>
<tr><td>NA</td><td>Rhode Island**</td><td>NA</td><td>NA</td><td>39</td><td>Idaho</td><td>410</td><td>0.35%</td></tr>
<tr><td>26</td><td>South Carolina</td><td>1,046</td><td>0.89%</td><td>40</td><td>New Hampshire</td><td>259</td><td>0.22%</td></tr>
<tr><td>43</td><td>South Dakota</td><td>220</td><td>0.19%</td><td>41</td><td>North Dakota</td><td>233</td><td>0.20%</td></tr>
<tr><td>9</td><td>Tennessee</td><td>3,258</td><td>2.76%</td><td>42</td><td>Wyoming</td><td>223</td><td>0.19%</td></tr>
<tr><td>2</td><td>Texas</td><td>11,304</td><td>9.59%</td><td>43</td><td>South Dakota</td><td>220</td><td>0.19%</td></tr>
<tr><td>36</td><td>Utah</td><td>499</td><td>0.42%</td><td>44</td><td>Montana</td><td>208</td><td>0.18%</td></tr>
<tr><td>NA</td><td>Vermont**</td><td>NA</td><td>NA</td><td>45</td><td>Alaska</td><td>24</td><td>0.02%</td></tr>
<tr><td>10</td><td>Virginia</td><td>3,103</td><td>2.63%</td><td>NA</td><td>Connecticut**</td><td>NA</td><td>NA</td></tr>
<tr><td>19</td><td>Washington</td><td>1,581</td><td>1.34%</td><td>NA</td><td>Delaware**</td><td>NA</td><td>NA</td></tr>
<tr><td>38</td><td>West Virginia</td><td>483</td><td>0.41%</td><td>NA</td><td>Hawaii**</td><td>NA</td><td>NA</td></tr>
<tr><td>20</td><td>Wisconsin</td><td>1,545</td><td>1.31%</td><td>NA</td><td>Rhode Island**</td><td>NA</td><td>NA</td></tr>
<tr><td>42</td><td>Wyoming</td><td>223</td><td>0.19%</td><td>NA</td><td>Vermont**</td><td>NA</td><td>NA</td></tr>
<tr><td></td><td></td><td></td><td></td><td></td><td>District of Columbia</td><td>512</td><td>0.43%</td></tr>
</table>

Source: U.S. Department of Justice, Bureau of Justice Statistics
"Correctional Populations in the United States, 1993" (October 1995, NCJ-156241)
*National total includes estimates for units that did not provide data. Includes 113,300 full-time and 4,600 part-time officers.
**These states have combined state and local jail systems and are excluded from this count.

Number of Local Jail Inmates per Correctional Officer in 1993

National Rate = 3.9 Inmates per Officer*

ALPHA ORDER

RANK	STATE	RATE
6	Alabama	4.8
NA	Alaska**	NA
7	Arizona	4.7
28	Arkansas	3.2
1	California	6.6
33	Colorado	2.8
NA	Connecticut**	NA
NA	Delaware**	NA
22	Florida	3.5
4	Georgia	5.1
NA	Hawaii**	NA
24	Idaho	3.4
20	Illinois	3.6
4	Indiana	5.1
41	Iowa	2.0
34	Kansas	2.7
14	Kentucky	4.2
9	Louisiana	4.6
44	Maine	1.4
16	Maryland	4.1
38	Massachusetts	2.5
18	Michigan	3.9
34	Minnesota	2.7
2	Mississippi	5.7
25	Missouri	3.3
32	Montana	2.9
39	Nebraska	2.2
3	Nevada	5.3
36	New Hampshire	2.6
22	New Jersey	3.5
25	New Mexico	3.3
41	New York	2.0
17	North Carolina	4.0
43	North Dakota	1.5
30	Ohio	3.1
20	Oklahoma	3.6
25	Oregon	3.3
31	Pennsylvania	3.0
NA	Rhode Island**	NA
12	South Carolina	4.3
36	South Dakota	2.6
14	Tennessee	4.2
9	Texas	4.6
19	Utah	3.8
NA	Vermont**	NA
12	Virginia	4.3
7	Washington	4.7
28	West Virginia	3.2
9	Wisconsin	4.6
39	Wyoming	2.2

RANK ORDER

RANK	STATE	RATE
1	California	6.6
2	Mississippi	5.7
3	Nevada	5.3
4	Georgia	5.1
4	Indiana	5.1
6	Alabama	4.8
7	Arizona	4.7
7	Washington	4.7
9	Louisiana	4.6
9	Texas	4.6
9	Wisconsin	4.6
12	South Carolina	4.3
12	Virginia	4.3
14	Kentucky	4.2
14	Tennessee	4.2
16	Maryland	4.1
17	North Carolina	4.0
18	Michigan	3.9
19	Utah	3.8
20	Illinois	3.6
20	Oklahoma	3.6
22	Florida	3.5
22	New Jersey	3.5
24	Idaho	3.4
25	Missouri	3.3
25	New Mexico	3.3
25	Oregon	3.3
28	Arkansas	3.2
28	West Virginia	3.2
30	Ohio	3.1
31	Pennsylvania	3.0
32	Montana	2.9
33	Colorado	2.8
34	Kansas	2.7
34	Minnesota	2.7
36	New Hampshire	2.6
36	South Dakota	2.6
38	Massachusetts	2.5
39	Nebraska	2.2
39	Wyoming	2.2
41	Iowa	2.0
41	New York	2.0
43	North Dakota	1.5
44	Maine	1.4
NA	Alaska**	NA
NA	Connecticut**	NA
NA	Delaware**	NA
NA	Hawaii**	NA
NA	Rhode Island**	NA
NA	Vermont**	NA
	District of Columbia	3.3

Source: U.S. Department of Justice, Bureau of Justice Statistics
  "Correctional Populations in the United States, 1993" (October 1995, NCJ-156241)
*Inmate-to-staff ratios were calculated by dividing the reported number of inmates by the reported number of staff.
**These states have combined state and local jail systems and are excluded from this count.

III. DRUGS AND ALCOHOL

Alcohol and Other Drug Treatment Units in 1995

National Total = 7,064 Units*

ALPHA ORDER				RANK ORDER			
RANK	STATE	UNITS	% of USA	RANK	STATE	UNITS	% of USA
37	Alabama	38	0.54%	1	California	889	12.58%
31	Alaska	56	0.79%	2	Pennsylvania	773	10.94%
25	Arizona	69	0.98%	3	New York	722	10.22%
43	Arkansas	25	0.35%	4	Ohio	529	7.49%
1	California	889	12.58%	5	Texas	347	4.91%
14	Colorado	141	2.00%	6	Illinois	312	4.42%
16	Connecticut	126	1.78%	7	Michigan	251	3.55%
41	Delaware	29	0.41%	8	Massachusetts	248	3.51%
NA	Florida**	NA	NA	9	Virginia	217	3.07%
19	Georgia	95	1.34%	10	Kentucky	201	2.85%
45	Hawaii	22	0.31%	11	Washington	167	2.36%
23	Idaho	71	1.01%	12	New Jersey	153	2.17%
6	Illinois	312	4.42%	13	Wisconsin	142	2.01%
27	Indiana	65	0.92%	14	Colorado	141	2.00%
40	Iowa	35	0.50%	15	Maryland	132	1.87%
32	Kansas	53	0.75%	16	Connecticut	126	1.78%
10	Kentucky	201	2.85%	16	Nebraska	126	1.78%
20	Louisiana	89	1.26%	18	Oregon	101	1.43%
28	Maine	62	0.88%	19	Georgia	95	1.34%
15	Maryland	132	1.87%	20	Louisiana	89	1.26%
8	Massachusetts	248	3.51%	21	Missouri	79	1.12%
7	Michigan	251	3.55%	22	Mississippi	77	1.09%
NA	Minnesota**	NA	NA	23	Idaho	71	1.01%
22	Mississippi	77	1.09%	24	Utah	70	0.99%
21	Missouri	79	1.12%	25	Arizona	69	0.98%
44	Montana	24	0.34%	25	New Mexico	69	0.98%
16	Nebraska	126	1.78%	27	Indiana	65	0.92%
35	Nevada	44	0.62%	28	Maine	62	0.88%
38	New Hampshire	36	0.51%	29	Oklahoma	61	0.86%
12	New Jersey	153	2.17%	30	Tennessee	60	0.85%
25	New Mexico	69	0.98%	31	Alaska	56	0.79%
3	New York	722	10.22%	32	Kansas	53	0.75%
35	North Carolina	44	0.62%	33	Rhode Island	45	0.64%
47	North Dakota	8	0.11%	33	South Dakota	45	0.64%
4	Ohio	529	7.49%	35	Nevada	44	0.62%
29	Oklahoma	61	0.86%	35	North Carolina	44	0.62%
18	Oregon	101	1.43%	37	Alabama	38	0.54%
2	Pennsylvania	773	10.94%	38	New Hampshire	36	0.51%
33	Rhode Island	45	0.64%	38	South Carolina	36	0.51%
38	South Carolina	36	0.51%	40	Iowa	35	0.50%
33	South Dakota	45	0.64%	41	Delaware	29	0.41%
30	Tennessee	60	0.85%	41	West Virginia	29	0.41%
5	Texas	347	4.91%	43	Arkansas	25	0.35%
24	Utah	70	0.99%	44	Montana	24	0.34%
46	Vermont	20	0.28%	45	Hawaii	22	0.31%
9	Virginia	217	3.07%	46	Vermont	20	0.28%
11	Washington	167	2.36%	47	North Dakota	8	0.11%
41	West Virginia	29	0.41%	NA	Florida**	NA	NA
13	Wisconsin	142	2.01%	NA	Minnesota**	NA	NA
NA	Wyoming**	NA	NA	NA	Wyoming**	NA	NA
					District of Columbia	31	0.44%

Source: U.S. Department of Health and Human Services, Substance Abuse and Mental Health Services Administration
"State Resources and Services Related to Alcohol and Other Drug Problems-Fiscal Year 1995" (July 1997)
*Does not include 44 units in U.S. territories. Data are only from treatment units that received at least some funds administered by a state's alcohol/drug agency in fiscal year 1995.
**Not available.

Alcohol and Other Drug Treatment Admissions in 1995

National Total = 1,876,363 Admissions*

ALPHA ORDER

RANK	STATE	ADMISSIONS	% of USA
31	Alabama	14,782	0.79%
38	Alaska	9,098	0.48%
25	Arizona	22,149	1.18%
32	Arkansas	13,950	0.74%
1	California	190,496	10.15%
12	Colorado	52,684	2.81%
17	Connecticut	42,716	2.28%
41	Delaware	6,842	0.36%
4	Florida	104,571	5.57%
10	Georgia	60,788	3.24%
46	Hawaii	4,483	0.24%
45	Idaho	5,521	0.29%
3	Illinois	121,552	6.48%
21	Indiana	27,663	1.47%
24	Iowa	23,986	1.28%
28	Kansas	19,142	1.02%
27	Kentucky	19,692	1.05%
22	Louisiana	27,259	1.45%
39	Maine	9,052	0.48%
19	Maryland	34,454	1.84%
5	Massachusetts	99,864	5.32%
6	Michigan	84,795	4.52%
NA	Minnesota**	NA	NA
33	Mississippi	13,702	0.73%
20	Missouri	33,960	1.81%
44	Montana	5,707	0.30%
26	Nebraska	21,438	1.14%
43	Nevada	6,481	0.35%
47	New Hampshire	3,888	0.21%
13	New Jersey	50,704	2.70%
34	New Mexico	12,840	0.68%
2	New York	156,172	8.32%
14	North Carolina	50,578	2.70%
48	North Dakota	3,277	0.17%
7	Ohio	74,123	3.95%
40	Oklahoma	7,690	0.41%
15	Oregon	46,456	2.48%
9	Pennsylvania	68,659	3.66%
36	Rhode Island	11,204	0.60%
23	South Carolina	26,728	1.42%
35	South Dakota	12,379	0.66%
37	Tennessee	10,670	0.57%
11	Texas	56,039	2.99%
29	Utah	16,624	0.89%
42	Vermont	6,735	0.36%
18	Virginia	35,799	1.91%
16	Washington	45,764	2.44%
30	West Virginia	15,972	0.85%
8	Wisconsin	72,689	3.87%
NA	Wyoming**	NA	NA

RANK ORDER

RANK	STATE	ADMISSIONS	% of USA
1	California	190,496	10.15%
2	New York	156,172	8.32%
3	Illinois	121,552	6.48%
4	Florida	104,571	5.57%
5	Massachusetts	99,864	5.32%
6	Michigan	84,795	4.52%
7	Ohio	74,123	3.95%
8	Wisconsin	72,689	3.87%
9	Pennsylvania	68,659	3.66%
10	Georgia	60,788	3.24%
11	Texas	56,039	2.99%
12	Colorado	52,684	2.81%
13	New Jersey	50,704	2.70%
14	North Carolina	50,578	2.70%
15	Oregon	46,456	2.48%
16	Washington	45,764	2.44%
17	Connecticut	42,716	2.28%
18	Virginia	35,799	1.91%
19	Maryland	34,454	1.84%
20	Missouri	33,960	1.81%
21	Indiana	27,663	1.47%
22	Louisiana	27,259	1.45%
23	South Carolina	26,728	1.42%
24	Iowa	23,986	1.28%
25	Arizona	22,149	1.18%
26	Nebraska	21,438	1.14%
27	Kentucky	19,692	1.05%
28	Kansas	19,142	1.02%
29	Utah	16,624	0.89%
30	West Virginia	15,972	0.85%
31	Alabama	14,782	0.79%
32	Arkansas	13,950	0.74%
33	Mississippi	13,702	0.73%
34	New Mexico	12,840	0.68%
35	South Dakota	12,379	0.66%
36	Rhode Island	11,204	0.60%
37	Tennessee	10,670	0.57%
38	Alaska	9,098	0.48%
39	Maine	9,052	0.48%
40	Oklahoma	7,690	0.41%
41	Delaware	6,842	0.36%
42	Vermont	6,735	0.36%
43	Nevada	6,481	0.35%
44	Montana	5,707	0.30%
45	Idaho	5,521	0.29%
46	Hawaii	4,483	0.24%
47	New Hampshire	3,888	0.21%
48	North Dakota	3,277	0.17%
NA	Minnesota**	NA	NA
NA	Wyoming**	NA	NA
	District of Columbia	14,546	0.78%

Source: U.S. Department of Health and Human Services, Substance Abuse and Mental Health Services Administration
   "State Resources and Services Related to Alcohol and Other Drug Problems-Fiscal Year 1995" (July 1997)
*Does not include 22,638 admissions in U.S. territories. Data are only from treatment units that received at least some funds administered by a state's alcohol/drug agency in fiscal year 1995. National total is only for reporting states.
**Not available.

Male Admissions to Alcohol and Other Drug Treatment Programs in 1995

National Total = 1,290,044 Admissions*

ALPHA ORDER

RANK	STATE	ADMISSIONS	% of USA
33	Alabama	9,937	0.77%
39	Alaska	6,242	0.48%
25	Arizona	15,070	1.17%
31	Arkansas	10,836	0.84%
1	California	121,168	9.39%
13	Colorado	36,251	2.81%
17	Connecticut	30,665	2.38%
42	Delaware	4,898	0.38%
9	Florida	43,863	3.40%
10	Georgia	42,901	3.33%
46	Hawaii	2,940	0.23%
45	Idaho	3,767	0.29%
3	Illinois	85,465	6.62%
22	Indiana	19,858	1.54%
23	Iowa	17,501	1.36%
27	Kansas	14,044	1.09%
26	Kentucky	14,355	1.11%
28	Louisiana	13,444	1.04%
38	Maine	6,789	0.53%
20	Maryland	23,811	1.85%
4	Massachusetts	71,868	5.57%
5	Michigan	59,252	4.59%
NA	Minnesota**	NA	NA
32	Mississippi	10,706	0.83%
19	Missouri	23,933	1.86%
44	Montana	3,910	0.30%
24	Nebraska	16,822	1.30%
43	Nevada	4,260	0.33%
47	New Hampshire	2,876	0.22%
14	New Jersey	35,504	2.75%
34	New Mexico	9,272	0.72%
2	New York	116,952	9.07%
12	North Carolina	36,815	2.85%
48	North Dakota	2,259	0.18%
7	Ohio	52,026	4.03%
40	Oklahoma	5,002	0.39%
15	Oregon	31,216	2.42%
8	Pennsylvania	49,605	3.85%
37	Rhode Island	7,306	0.57%
21	South Carolina	20,451	1.59%
35	South Dakota	8,927	0.69%
36	Tennessee	7,611	0.59%
11	Texas	41,392	3.21%
30	Utah	12,221	0.95%
41	Vermont	4,952	0.38%
18	Virginia	24,774	1.92%
16	Washington	30,900	2.40%
29	West Virginia	12,579	0.98%
6	Wisconsin	52,716	4.09%
NA	Wyoming**	NA	NA

RANK ORDER

RANK	STATE	ADMISSIONS	% of USA
1	California	121,168	9.39%
2	New York	116,952	9.07%
3	Illinois	85,465	6.62%
4	Massachusetts	71,868	5.57%
5	Michigan	59,252	4.59%
6	Wisconsin	52,716	4.09%
7	Ohio	52,026	4.03%
8	Pennsylvania	49,605	3.85%
9	Florida	43,863	3.40%
10	Georgia	42,901	3.33%
11	Texas	41,392	3.21%
12	North Carolina	36,815	2.85%
13	Colorado	36,251	2.81%
14	New Jersey	35,504	2.75%
15	Oregon	31,216	2.42%
16	Washington	30,900	2.40%
17	Connecticut	30,665	2.38%
18	Virginia	24,774	1.92%
19	Missouri	23,933	1.86%
20	Maryland	23,811	1.85%
21	South Carolina	20,451	1.59%
22	Indiana	19,858	1.54%
23	Iowa	17,501	1.36%
24	Nebraska	16,822	1.30%
25	Arizona	15,070	1.17%
26	Kentucky	14,355	1.11%
27	Kansas	14,044	1.09%
28	Louisiana	13,444	1.04%
29	West Virginia	12,579	0.98%
30	Utah	12,221	0.95%
31	Arkansas	10,836	0.84%
32	Mississippi	10,706	0.83%
33	Alabama	9,937	0.77%
34	New Mexico	9,272	0.72%
35	South Dakota	8,927	0.69%
36	Tennessee	7,611	0.59%
37	Rhode Island	7,306	0.57%
38	Maine	6,789	0.53%
39	Alaska	6,242	0.48%
40	Oklahoma	5,002	0.39%
41	Vermont	4,952	0.38%
42	Delaware	4,898	0.38%
43	Nevada	4,260	0.33%
44	Montana	3,910	0.30%
45	Idaho	3,767	0.29%
46	Hawaii	2,940	0.23%
47	New Hampshire	2,876	0.22%
48	North Dakota	2,259	0.18%
NA	Minnesota**	NA	NA
NA	Wyoming**	NA	NA
	District of Columbia	10,132	0.79%

Source: U.S. Department of Health and Human Services, Substance Abuse and Mental Health Services Administration "State Resources and Services Related to Alcohol and Other Drug Problems-Fiscal Year 1995" (July 1997)
*Does not include 20,696 male admissions in U.S. territories. Data are only from treatment units that received at least some funds administered by a state's alcohol/drug agency in fiscal year 1995. An additional 58,931 admissions were not reported by sex. National total is only other reporting states.
**Not available.

Male Admissions to Alcohol and Drug Treatment Programs
As a Percent of All Admissions in 1995
National Percent = 68.8% Males*

ALPHA ORDER

RANK	STATE	PERCENT
40	Alabama	67.2
35	Alaska	68.6
38	Arizona	68.0
4	Arkansas	77.7
46	California	63.6
34	Colorado	68.8
21	Connecticut	71.8
23	Delaware	71.6
48	Florida	41.9
25	Georgia	70.6
43	Hawaii	65.6
37	Idaho	68.2
27	Illinois	70.3
21	Indiana	71.8
13	Iowa	73.0
12	Kansas	73.4
14	Kentucky	72.9
47	Louisiana	49.3
6	Maine	75.0
32	Maryland	69.1
20	Massachusetts	72.0
30	Michigan	69.9
NA	Minnesota**	NA
3	Mississippi	78.1
26	Missouri	70.5
36	Montana	68.5
2	Nebraska	78.5
42	Nevada	65.7
8	New Hampshire	74.0
29	New Jersey	70.0
17	New Mexico	72.2
7	New York	74.9
15	North Carolina	72.8
33	North Dakota	68.9
28	Ohio	70.2
45	Oklahoma	65.0
40	Oregon	67.2
17	Pennsylvania	72.2
44	Rhode Island	65.2
5	South Carolina	76.5
19	South Dakota	72.1
24	Tennessee	71.3
9	Texas	73.9
10	Utah	73.5
10	Vermont	73.5
31	Virginia	69.2
39	Washington	67.5
1	West Virginia	78.8
16	Wisconsin	72.5
NA	Wyoming**	NA

RANK ORDER

RANK	STATE	PERCENT
1	West Virginia	78.8
2	Nebraska	78.5
3	Mississippi	78.1
4	Arkansas	77.7
5	South Carolina	76.5
6	Maine	75.0
7	New York	74.9
8	New Hampshire	74.0
9	Texas	73.9
10	Utah	73.5
10	Vermont	73.5
12	Kansas	73.4
13	Iowa	73.0
14	Kentucky	72.9
15	North Carolina	72.8
16	Wisconsin	72.5
17	New Mexico	72.2
17	Pennsylvania	72.2
19	South Dakota	72.1
20	Massachusetts	72.0
21	Connecticut	71.8
21	Indiana	71.8
23	Delaware	71.6
24	Tennessee	71.3
25	Georgia	70.6
26	Missouri	70.5
27	Illinois	70.3
28	Ohio	70.2
29	New Jersey	70.0
30	Michigan	69.9
31	Virginia	69.2
32	Maryland	69.1
33	North Dakota	68.9
34	Colorado	68.8
35	Alaska	68.6
36	Montana	68.5
37	Idaho	68.2
38	Arizona	68.0
39	Washington	67.5
40	Alabama	67.2
40	Oregon	67.2
42	Nevada	65.7
43	Hawaii	65.6
44	Rhode Island	65.2
45	Oklahoma	65.0
46	California	63.6
47	Louisiana	49.3
48	Florida	41.9
NA	Minnesota**	NA
NA	Wyoming**	NA

	District of Columbia	69.7

Source: Morgan Quitno Press using data from U.S. Department of Health and Human Services, Substance Abuse and Mental Health Services Administration
"State Resources and Services Related to Alcohol and Other Drug Problems-Fiscal Year 1995" (July 1997)
*Does not include admissions in U.S. territories. Data are only from treatment units that received at least some funds administered by a state's alcohol/drug agency in fiscal year 1995. An additional 58,931 admissions were not reported by sex. **Not available.

Female Admissions to Alcohol and Other Drug Treatment Programs in 1995

National Total = 527,388 Female Admissions*

ALPHA ORDER

RANK	STATE	ADMISSIONS	% of USA
31	Alabama	3,711	0.70%
38	Alaska	2,856	0.54%
22	Arizona	7,079	1.34%
35	Arkansas	3,114	0.59%
1	California	69,328	13.15%
17	Colorado	11,261	2.14%
16	Connecticut	12,051	2.29%
42	Delaware	1,944	0.37%
9	Florida	18,248	3.46%
10	Georgia	17,887	3.39%
46	Hawaii	1,539	0.29%
45	Idaho	1,754	0.33%
3	Illinois	36,087	6.84%
21	Indiana	7,805	1.48%
23	Iowa	6,485	1.23%
26	Kansas	5,098	0.97%
25	Kentucky	5,337	1.01%
29	Louisiana	4,240	0.80%
39	Maine	2,263	0.43%
19	Maryland	10,643	2.02%
4	Massachusetts	27,996	5.31%
5	Michigan	25,523	4.84%
NA	Minnesota**	NA	NA
37	Mississippi	2,996	0.57%
20	Missouri	10,027	1.90%
43	Montana	1,797	0.34%
27	Nebraska	4,610	0.87%
40	Nevada	2,221	0.42%
48	New Hampshire	1,012	0.19%
12	New Jersey	15,200	2.88%
32	New Mexico	3,568	0.68%
2	New York	39,220	7.44%
15	North Carolina	13,727	2.60%
47	North Dakota	1,018	0.19%
6	Ohio	22,097	4.19%
41	Oklahoma	2,205	0.42%
11	Oregon	15,240	2.89%
8	Pennsylvania	19,054	3.61%
30	Rhode Island	3,898	0.74%
24	South Carolina	6,277	1.19%
33	South Dakota	3,452	0.65%
36	Tennessee	3,059	0.58%
14	Texas	14,642	2.78%
28	Utah	4,375	0.83%
44	Vermont	1,775	0.34%
18	Virginia	11,025	2.09%
13	Washington	14,864	2.82%
34	West Virginia	3,393	0.64%
7	Wisconsin	19,973	3.79%
NA	Wyoming**	NA	NA

RANK ORDER

RANK	STATE	ADMISSIONS	% of USA
1	California	69,328	13.15%
2	New York	39,220	7.44%
3	Illinois	36,087	6.84%
4	Massachusetts	27,996	5.31%
5	Michigan	25,523	4.84%
6	Ohio	22,097	4.19%
7	Wisconsin	19,973	3.79%
8	Pennsylvania	19,054	3.61%
9	Florida	18,248	3.46%
10	Georgia	17,887	3.39%
11	Oregon	15,240	2.89%
12	New Jersey	15,200	2.88%
13	Washington	14,864	2.82%
14	Texas	14,642	2.78%
15	North Carolina	13,727	2.60%
16	Connecticut	12,051	2.29%
17	Colorado	11,261	2.14%
18	Virginia	11,025	2.09%
19	Maryland	10,643	2.02%
20	Missouri	10,027	1.90%
21	Indiana	7,805	1.48%
22	Arizona	7,079	1.34%
23	Iowa	6,485	1.23%
24	South Carolina	6,277	1.19%
25	Kentucky	5,337	1.01%
26	Kansas	5,098	0.97%
27	Nebraska	4,610	0.87%
28	Utah	4,375	0.83%
29	Louisiana	4,240	0.80%
30	Rhode Island	3,898	0.74%
31	Alabama	3,711	0.70%
32	New Mexico	3,568	0.68%
33	South Dakota	3,452	0.65%
34	West Virginia	3,393	0.64%
35	Arkansas	3,114	0.59%
36	Tennessee	3,059	0.58%
37	Mississippi	2,996	0.57%
38	Alaska	2,856	0.54%
39	Maine	2,263	0.43%
40	Nevada	2,221	0.42%
41	Oklahoma	2,205	0.42%
42	Delaware	1,944	0.37%
43	Montana	1,797	0.34%
44	Vermont	1,775	0.34%
45	Idaho	1,754	0.33%
46	Hawaii	1,539	0.29%
47	North Dakota	1,018	0.19%
48	New Hampshire	1,012	0.19%
NA	Minnesota**	NA	NA
NA	Wyoming**	NA	NA
	District of Columbia	4,414	0.84%

Source: U.S. Department of Health and Human Services, Substance Abuse and Mental Health Services Administration "State Resources and Services Related to Alcohol and Other Drug Problems-Fiscal Year 1995" (July 1997)
*Does not include 1,942 female admissions in U.S. territories. Data are only from treatment units that received at least some funds administered by a state's alcohol/drug agency in fiscal year 1995. An additional 58,931 admissions were not reported by sex. National total is only for reporting states.
**Not available.

Female Admissions to Alcohol and Other Drug Treatment Programs
As a Percent of All Admissions in 1995
National Percent = 28.1% Female*

ALPHA ORDER

RANK ORDER

RANK	STATE	PERCENT		RANK	STATE	PERCENT
38	Alabama	25.1		1	California	36.4
10	Alaska	31.4		2	Rhode Island	34.8
7	Arizona	32.0		3	Hawaii	34.3
42	Arkansas	22.3		3	Nevada	34.3
1	California	36.4		5	Oregon	32.8
45	Colorado	21.4		6	Washington	32.5
23	Connecticut	28.2		7	Arizona	32.0
22	Delaware	28.4		8	Idaho	31.8
47	Florida	17.5		9	Montana	31.5
19	Georgia	29.4		10	Alaska	31.4
3	Hawaii	34.3		11	North Dakota	31.1
8	Idaho	31.8		12	Maryland	30.9
17	Illinois	29.7		13	Virginia	30.8
23	Indiana	28.2		14	Michigan	30.1
32	Iowa	27.0		15	New Jersey	30.0
33	Kansas	26.6		16	Ohio	29.8
30	Kentucky	27.1		17	Illinois	29.7
48	Louisiana	15.6		18	Missouri	29.5
40	Maine	25.0		19	Georgia	29.4
12	Maryland	30.9		20	Oklahoma	28.7
25	Massachusetts	28.0		20	Tennessee	28.7
14	Michigan	30.1		22	Delaware	28.4
NA	Minnesota**	NA		23	Connecticut	28.2
43	Mississippi	21.9		23	Indiana	28.2
18	Missouri	29.5		25	Massachusetts	28.0
9	Montana	31.5		26	South Dakota	27.9
44	Nebraska	21.5		27	New Mexico	27.8
3	Nevada	34.3		27	Pennsylvania	27.8
37	New Hampshire	26.0		29	Wisconsin	27.5
15	New Jersey	30.0		30	Kentucky	27.1
27	New Mexico	27.8		30	North Carolina	27.1
38	New York	25.1		32	Iowa	27.0
30	North Carolina	27.1		33	Kansas	26.6
11	North Dakota	31.1		34	Vermont	26.4
16	Ohio	29.8		35	Utah	26.3
20	Oklahoma	28.7		36	Texas	26.1
5	Oregon	32.8		37	New Hampshire	26.0
27	Pennsylvania	27.8		38	Alabama	25.1
2	Rhode Island	34.8		38	New York	25.1
41	South Carolina	23.5		40	Maine	25.0
26	South Dakota	27.9		41	South Carolina	23.5
20	Tennessee	28.7		42	Arkansas	22.3
36	Texas	26.1		43	Mississippi	21.9
35	Utah	26.3		44	Nebraska	21.5
34	Vermont	26.4		45	Colorado	21.4
13	Virginia	30.8		46	West Virginia	21.2
6	Washington	32.5		47	Florida	17.5
46	West Virginia	21.2		48	Louisiana	15.6
29	Wisconsin	27.5		NA	Minnesota**	NA
NA	Wyoming**	NA		NA	Wyoming**	NA

District of Columbia 30.3

Source: Morgan Quitno Press using data from U.S. Department of Health and Human Services, Substance Abuse and Mental Health Services Administration
"State Resources and Services Related to Alcohol and Other Drug Problems-Fiscal Year 1995" (July 1997)
*Does not include admissions in U.S. territories. Data are only from treatment units that received at least some funds administered by a state's alcohol/drug agency in fiscal year 1995. An additional 58,931 admissions were not reported by sex. **Not available.

White Admissions to Alcohol and Other Drug Treatment Programs in 1995

National Total = 1,062,509 White Admissions*

<table>
<tr><td colspan="4">ALPHA ORDER</td><td colspan="4">RANK ORDER</td></tr>
<tr><td>RANK</td><td>STATE</td><td>ADMISSIONS</td><td>% of USA</td><td>RANK</td><td>STATE</td><td>ADMISSIONS</td><td>% of USA</td></tr>
<tr><td>35</td><td>Alabama</td><td>7,594</td><td>0.71%</td><td>1</td><td>California</td><td>98,410</td><td>9.26%</td></tr>
<tr><td>43</td><td>Alaska</td><td>4,135</td><td>0.39%</td><td>2</td><td>New York</td><td>72,649</td><td>6.84%</td></tr>
<tr><td>28</td><td>Arizona</td><td>13,300</td><td>1.25%</td><td>3</td><td>Massachusetts</td><td>68,602</td><td>6.46%</td></tr>
<tr><td>30</td><td>Arkansas</td><td>9,262</td><td>0.87%</td><td>4</td><td>Wisconsin</td><td>60,545</td><td>5.70%</td></tr>
<tr><td>1</td><td>California</td><td>98,410</td><td>9.26%</td><td>5</td><td>Michigan</td><td>55,289</td><td>5.20%</td></tr>
<tr><td>13</td><td>Colorado</td><td>28,885</td><td>2.72%</td><td>6</td><td>Ohio</td><td>48,801</td><td>4.59%</td></tr>
<tr><td>16</td><td>Connecticut</td><td>23,495</td><td>2.21%</td><td>7</td><td>Illinois</td><td>42,543</td><td>4.00%</td></tr>
<tr><td>45</td><td>Delaware</td><td>3,790</td><td>0.36%</td><td>8</td><td>Pennsylvania</td><td>39,006</td><td>3.67%</td></tr>
<tr><td>10</td><td>Florida</td><td>36,636</td><td>3.45%</td><td>9</td><td>Oregon</td><td>37,347</td><td>3.51%</td></tr>
<tr><td>12</td><td>Georgia</td><td>33,008</td><td>3.11%</td><td>10</td><td>Florida</td><td>36,636</td><td>3.45%</td></tr>
<tr><td>48</td><td>Hawaii</td><td>1,827</td><td>0.17%</td><td>11</td><td>Washington</td><td>33,449</td><td>3.15%</td></tr>
<tr><td>40</td><td>Idaho</td><td>4,763</td><td>0.45%</td><td>12</td><td>Georgia</td><td>33,008</td><td>3.11%</td></tr>
<tr><td>7</td><td>Illinois</td><td>42,543</td><td>4.00%</td><td>13</td><td>Colorado</td><td>28,885</td><td>2.72%</td></tr>
<tr><td>21</td><td>Indiana</td><td>18,484</td><td>1.74%</td><td>14</td><td>North Carolina</td><td>26,408</td><td>2.49%</td></tr>
<tr><td>19</td><td>Iowa</td><td>21,330</td><td>2.01%</td><td>15</td><td>New Jersey</td><td>24,450</td><td>2.30%</td></tr>
<tr><td>27</td><td>Kansas</td><td>13,323</td><td>1.25%</td><td>16</td><td>Connecticut</td><td>23,495</td><td>2.21%</td></tr>
<tr><td>23</td><td>Kentucky</td><td>16,698</td><td>1.57%</td><td>17</td><td>Texas</td><td>23,064</td><td>2.17%</td></tr>
<tr><td>34</td><td>Louisiana</td><td>8,035</td><td>0.76%</td><td>18</td><td>Missouri</td><td>22,215</td><td>2.09%</td></tr>
<tr><td>31</td><td>Maine</td><td>8,755</td><td>0.82%</td><td>19</td><td>Iowa</td><td>21,330</td><td>2.01%</td></tr>
<tr><td>22</td><td>Maryland</td><td>17,466</td><td>1.64%</td><td>20</td><td>Virginia</td><td>19,764</td><td>1.86%</td></tr>
<tr><td>3</td><td>Massachusetts</td><td>68,602</td><td>6.46%</td><td>21</td><td>Indiana</td><td>18,484</td><td>1.74%</td></tr>
<tr><td>5</td><td>Michigan</td><td>55,289</td><td>5.20%</td><td>22</td><td>Maryland</td><td>17,466</td><td>1.64%</td></tr>
<tr><td>NA</td><td>Minnesota**</td><td>NA</td><td>NA</td><td>23</td><td>Kentucky</td><td>16,698</td><td>1.57%</td></tr>
<tr><td>38</td><td>Mississippi</td><td>6,098</td><td>0.57%</td><td>24</td><td>South Carolina</td><td>15,495</td><td>1.46%</td></tr>
<tr><td>18</td><td>Missouri</td><td>22,215</td><td>2.09%</td><td>25</td><td>Nebraska</td><td>15,055</td><td>1.42%</td></tr>
<tr><td>42</td><td>Montana</td><td>4,329</td><td>0.41%</td><td>26</td><td>West Virginia</td><td>14,751</td><td>1.39%</td></tr>
<tr><td>25</td><td>Nebraska</td><td>15,055</td><td>1.42%</td><td>27</td><td>Kansas</td><td>13,323</td><td>1.25%</td></tr>
<tr><td>41</td><td>Nevada</td><td>4,597</td><td>0.43%</td><td>28</td><td>Arizona</td><td>13,300</td><td>1.25%</td></tr>
<tr><td>46</td><td>New Hampshire</td><td>3,697</td><td>0.35%</td><td>29</td><td>Utah</td><td>12,319</td><td>1.16%</td></tr>
<tr><td>15</td><td>New Jersey</td><td>24,450</td><td>2.30%</td><td>30</td><td>Arkansas</td><td>9,262</td><td>0.87%</td></tr>
<tr><td>44</td><td>New Mexico</td><td>3,944</td><td>0.37%</td><td>31</td><td>Maine</td><td>8,755</td><td>0.82%</td></tr>
<tr><td>2</td><td>New York</td><td>72,649</td><td>6.84%</td><td>32</td><td>South Dakota</td><td>8,718</td><td>0.82%</td></tr>
<tr><td>14</td><td>North Carolina</td><td>26,408</td><td>2.49%</td><td>33</td><td>Rhode Island</td><td>8,458</td><td>0.80%</td></tr>
<tr><td>47</td><td>North Dakota</td><td>2,416</td><td>0.23%</td><td>34</td><td>Louisiana</td><td>8,035</td><td>0.76%</td></tr>
<tr><td>6</td><td>Ohio</td><td>48,801</td><td>4.59%</td><td>35</td><td>Alabama</td><td>7,594</td><td>0.71%</td></tr>
<tr><td>39</td><td>Oklahoma</td><td>5,144</td><td>0.48%</td><td>36</td><td>Tennessee</td><td>7,258</td><td>0.68%</td></tr>
<tr><td>9</td><td>Oregon</td><td>37,347</td><td>3.51%</td><td>37</td><td>Vermont</td><td>6,466</td><td>0.61%</td></tr>
<tr><td>8</td><td>Pennsylvania</td><td>39,006</td><td>3.67%</td><td>38</td><td>Mississippi</td><td>6,098</td><td>0.57%</td></tr>
<tr><td>33</td><td>Rhode Island</td><td>8,458</td><td>0.80%</td><td>39</td><td>Oklahoma</td><td>5,144</td><td>0.48%</td></tr>
<tr><td>24</td><td>South Carolina</td><td>15,495</td><td>1.46%</td><td>40</td><td>Idaho</td><td>4,763</td><td>0.45%</td></tr>
<tr><td>32</td><td>South Dakota</td><td>8,718</td><td>0.82%</td><td>41</td><td>Nevada</td><td>4,597</td><td>0.43%</td></tr>
<tr><td>36</td><td>Tennessee</td><td>7,258</td><td>0.68%</td><td>42</td><td>Montana</td><td>4,329</td><td>0.41%</td></tr>
<tr><td>17</td><td>Texas</td><td>23,064</td><td>2.17%</td><td>43</td><td>Alaska</td><td>4,135</td><td>0.39%</td></tr>
<tr><td>29</td><td>Utah</td><td>12,319</td><td>1.16%</td><td>44</td><td>New Mexico</td><td>3,944</td><td>0.37%</td></tr>
<tr><td>37</td><td>Vermont</td><td>6,466</td><td>0.61%</td><td>45</td><td>Delaware</td><td>3,790</td><td>0.36%</td></tr>
<tr><td>20</td><td>Virginia</td><td>19,764</td><td>1.86%</td><td>46</td><td>New Hampshire</td><td>3,697</td><td>0.35%</td></tr>
<tr><td>11</td><td>Washington</td><td>33,449</td><td>3.15%</td><td>47</td><td>North Dakota</td><td>2,416</td><td>0.23%</td></tr>
<tr><td>26</td><td>West Virginia</td><td>14,751</td><td>1.39%</td><td>48</td><td>Hawaii</td><td>1,827</td><td>0.17%</td></tr>
<tr><td>4</td><td>Wisconsin</td><td>60,545</td><td>5.70%</td><td>NA</td><td>Minnesota**</td><td>NA</td><td>NA</td></tr>
<tr><td>NA</td><td>Wyoming**</td><td>NA</td><td>NA</td><td>NA</td><td>Wyoming**</td><td>NA</td><td>NA</td></tr>
<tr><td></td><td></td><td></td><td></td><td></td><td>District of Columbia</td><td>436</td><td>0.04%</td></tr>
</table>

Source: U.S. Department of Health and Human Services, Substance Abuse and Mental Health Services Administration
"State Resources and Services Related to Alcohol and Other Drug Problems-Fiscal Year 1995" (July 1997)
*Data are only from treatment units that received at least some funds administered by a state's alcohol/drug agency in fiscal year 1995. An additional 95,039 admissions were not reported by race.
**Not available.

White Admissions to Alcohol and Other Drug Treatment Programs
As a Percent of All Admissions in 1995
National Percent = 56.6% of Admissions*

ALPHA ORDER

RANK	STATE	PERCENT
37	Alabama	51.4
41	Alaska	45.4
27	Arizona	60.0
23	Arkansas	66.4
36	California	51.7
33	Colorado	54.8
32	Connecticut	55.0
30	Delaware	55.4
45	Florida	35.0
34	Georgia	54.3
44	Hawaii	40.8
6	Idaho	86.3
45	Illinois	35.0
22	Indiana	66.8
5	Iowa	88.9
18	Kansas	69.6
7	Kentucky	84.8
48	Louisiana	29.5
1	Maine	96.7
38	Maryland	50.7
19	Massachusetts	68.7
26	Michigan	65.2
NA	Minnesota**	NA
42	Mississippi	44.5
25	Missouri	65.4
10	Montana	75.9
17	Nebraska	70.2
15	Nevada	70.9
3	New Hampshire	95.1
39	New Jersey	48.2
47	New Mexico	30.7
40	New York	46.5
35	North Carolina	52.2
13	North Dakota	73.7
24	Ohio	65.8
21	Oklahoma	66.9
9	Oregon	80.4
29	Pennsylvania	56.8
11	Rhode Island	75.5
28	South Carolina	58.0
16	South Dakota	70.4
20	Tennessee	68.0
43	Texas	41.2
12	Utah	74.1
2	Vermont	96.0
31	Virginia	55.2
14	Washington	73.1
4	West Virginia	92.4
8	Wisconsin	83.3
NA	Wyoming**	NA

RANK ORDER

RANK	STATE	PERCENT
1	Maine	96.7
2	Vermont	96.0
3	New Hampshire	95.1
4	West Virginia	92.4
5	Iowa	88.9
6	Idaho	86.3
7	Kentucky	84.8
8	Wisconsin	83.3
9	Oregon	80.4
10	Montana	75.9
11	Rhode Island	75.5
12	Utah	74.1
13	North Dakota	73.7
14	Washington	73.1
15	Nevada	70.9
16	South Dakota	70.4
17	Nebraska	70.2
18	Kansas	69.6
19	Massachusetts	68.7
20	Tennessee	68.0
21	Oklahoma	66.9
22	Indiana	66.8
23	Arkansas	66.4
24	Ohio	65.8
25	Missouri	65.4
26	Michigan	65.2
27	Arizona	60.0
28	South Carolina	58.0
29	Pennsylvania	56.8
30	Delaware	55.4
31	Virginia	55.2
32	Connecticut	55.0
33	Colorado	54.8
34	Georgia	54.3
35	North Carolina	52.2
36	California	51.7
37	Alabama	51.4
38	Maryland	50.7
39	New Jersey	48.2
40	New York	46.5
41	Alaska	45.4
42	Mississippi	44.5
43	Texas	41.2
44	Hawaii	40.8
45	Florida	35.0
45	Illinois	35.0
47	New Mexico	30.7
48	Louisiana	29.5
NA	Minnesota**	NA
NA	Wyoming**	NA
	District of Columbia	3.0

Source: Morgan Quitno Press using data from U.S. Department of Health and Human Services, Substance Abuse
and Mental Health Services Administration
"State Resources and Services Related to Alcohol and Other Drug Problems-Fiscal Year 1995" (July 1997)
*Data are only from treatment units that received at least some funds administered by a state's alcohol/drug agency
in fiscal year 1995. An additional 95,039 admissions were not reported by race.
**Not available.

Black Admissions to Alcohol and Other Drug Treatment Programs in 1995

National Total = 493,101 Black Admissions*

ALPHA ORDER

RANK	STATE	ADMISSIONS	% of USA
22	Alabama	5,882	1.19%
39	Alaska	376	0.08%
32	Arizona	1,719	0.35%
24	Arkansas	4,516	0.92%
3	California	37,274	7.56%
25	Colorado	4,260	0.86%
15	Connecticut	11,890	2.41%
29	Delaware	2,737	0.56%
8	Florida	19,698	3.99%
4	Georgia	27,240	5.52%
41	Hawaii	160	0.03%
47	Idaho	44	0.01%
2	Illinois	51,315	10.41%
19	Indiana	8,093	1.64%
33	Iowa	1,674	0.34%
26	Kansas	3,485	0.71%
30	Kentucky	2,690	0.55%
18	Louisiana	9,488	1.92%
45	Maine	77	0.02%
12	Maryland	15,940	3.23%
13	Massachusetts	15,656	3.18%
5	Michigan	26,267	5.33%
NA	Minnesota**	NA	NA
21	Mississippi	7,505	1.52%
16	Missouri	11,225	2.28%
46	Montana	52	0.01%
31	Nebraska	2,514	0.51%
37	Nevada	945	0.19%
43	New Hampshire	99	0.02%
11	New Jersey	17,975	3.65%
40	New Mexico	272	0.06%
1	New York	57,204	11.60%
7	North Carolina	22,297	4.52%
48	North Dakota	10	0.00%
6	Ohio	23,531	4.77%
36	Oklahoma	1,083	0.22%
28	Oregon	2,797	0.57%
10	Pennsylvania	18,001	3.65%
34	Rhode Island	1,230	0.25%
17	South Carolina	10,943	2.22%
42	South Dakota	159	0.03%
27	Tennessee	3,122	0.63%
9	Texas	18,721	3.80%
38	Utah	569	0.12%
44	Vermont	80	0.02%
14	Virginia	14,734	2.99%
23	Washington	4,803	0.97%
35	West Virginia	1,121	0.23%
20	Wisconsin	7,909	1.60%
NA	Wyoming**	NA	NA

RANK ORDER

RANK	STATE	ADMISSIONS	% of USA
1	New York	57,204	11.60%
2	Illinois	51,315	10.41%
3	California	37,274	7.56%
4	Georgia	27,240	5.52%
5	Michigan	26,267	5.33%
6	Ohio	23,531	4.77%
7	North Carolina	22,297	4.52%
8	Florida	19,698	3.99%
9	Texas	18,721	3.80%
10	Pennsylvania	18,001	3.65%
11	New Jersey	17,975	3.65%
12	Maryland	15,940	3.23%
13	Massachusetts	15,656	3.18%
14	Virginia	14,734	2.99%
15	Connecticut	11,890	2.41%
16	Missouri	11,225	2.28%
17	South Carolina	10,943	2.22%
18	Louisiana	9,488	1.92%
19	Indiana	8,093	1.64%
20	Wisconsin	7,909	1.60%
21	Mississippi	7,505	1.52%
22	Alabama	5,882	1.19%
23	Washington	4,803	0.97%
24	Arkansas	4,516	0.92%
25	Colorado	4,260	0.86%
26	Kansas	3,485	0.71%
27	Tennessee	3,122	0.63%
28	Oregon	2,797	0.57%
29	Delaware	2,737	0.56%
30	Kentucky	2,690	0.55%
31	Nebraska	2,514	0.51%
32	Arizona	1,719	0.35%
33	Iowa	1,674	0.34%
34	Rhode Island	1,230	0.25%
35	West Virginia	1,121	0.23%
36	Oklahoma	1,083	0.22%
37	Nevada	945	0.19%
38	Utah	569	0.12%
39	Alaska	376	0.08%
40	New Mexico	272	0.06%
41	Hawaii	160	0.03%
42	South Dakota	159	0.03%
43	New Hampshire	99	0.02%
44	Vermont	80	0.02%
45	Maine	77	0.02%
46	Montana	52	0.01%
47	Idaho	44	0.01%
48	North Dakota	10	0.00%
NA	Minnesota**	NA	NA
NA	Wyoming**	NA	NA
	District of Columbia	13,719	2.78%

Source: U.S. Department of Health and Human Services, Substance Abuse and Mental Health Services Administration
"State Resources and Services Related to Alcohol and Other Drug Problems-Fiscal Year 1995" (July 1997)
*Data are only from treatment units that received at least some funds administered by a state's alcohol/drug agency
in fiscal year 1995. An additional 95,039 admissions were not reported by race.
**Not available.

Black Admissions to Alcohol and Other Drug Treatment Programs
As a Percent of All Admissions in 1995
National Percent = 26.3% of Admissions*

ALPHA ORDER

RANK	STATE	PERCENT	RANK	STATE	PERCENT
9	Alabama	39.8	1	Mississippi	54.8
38	Alaska	4.1	2	Maryland	46.3
34	Arizona	7.8	3	Georgia	44.8
15	Arkansas	32.4	4	North Carolina	44.1
22	California	19.6	5	Illinois	42.2
33	Colorado	8.1	6	Virginia	41.2
20	Connecticut	27.8	7	South Carolina	40.9
8	Delaware	40.0	8	Delaware	40.0
23	Florida	18.8	9	Alabama	39.8
3	Georgia	44.8	10	New York	36.6
39	Hawaii	3.6	11	New Jersey	35.5
47	Idaho	0.8	12	Louisiana	34.8
5	Illinois	42.2	13	Texas	33.4
18	Indiana	29.3	14	Missouri	33.1
35	Iowa	7.0	15	Arkansas	32.4
24	Kansas	18.2	16	Ohio	31.7
28	Kentucky	13.7	17	Michigan	31.0
12	Louisiana	34.8	18	Indiana	29.3
45	Maine	0.9	18	Tennessee	29.3
2	Maryland	46.3	20	Connecticut	27.8
25	Massachusetts	15.7	21	Pennsylvania	26.2
17	Michigan	31.0	22	California	19.6
NA	Minnesota**	NA	23	Florida	18.8
1	Mississippi	54.8	24	Kansas	18.2
14	Missouri	33.1	25	Massachusetts	15.7
45	Montana	0.9	26	Nevada	14.6
29	Nebraska	11.7	27	Oklahoma	14.1
26	Nevada	14.6	28	Kentucky	13.7
41	New Hampshire	2.5	29	Nebraska	11.7
11	New Jersey	35.5	30	Rhode Island	11.0
42	New Mexico	2.1	31	Wisconsin	10.9
10	New York	36.6	32	Washington	10.5
4	North Carolina	44.1	33	Colorado	8.1
48	North Dakota	0.3	34	Arizona	7.8
16	Ohio	31.7	35	Iowa	7.0
27	Oklahoma	14.1	35	West Virginia	7.0
37	Oregon	6.0	37	Oregon	6.0
21	Pennsylvania	26.2	38	Alaska	4.1
30	Rhode Island	11.0	39	Hawaii	3.6
7	South Carolina	40.9	40	Utah	3.4
43	South Dakota	1.3	41	New Hampshire	2.5
18	Tennessee	29.3	42	New Mexico	2.1
13	Texas	33.4	43	South Dakota	1.3
40	Utah	3.4	44	Vermont	1.2
44	Vermont	1.2	45	Maine	0.9
6	Virginia	41.2	45	Montana	0.9
32	Washington	10.5	47	Idaho	0.8
35	West Virginia	7.0	48	North Dakota	0.3
31	Wisconsin	10.9	NA	Minnesota**	NA
NA	Wyoming**	NA	NA	Wyoming**	NA

District of Columbia 94.3

Source: Morgan Quitno Press using data from U.S. Department of Health and Human Services, Substance Abuse
and Mental Health Services Administration
"State Resources and Services Related to Alcohol and Other Drug Problems-Fiscal Year 1995" (July 1997)
*Data are only from treatment units that received at least some funds administered by a state's alcohol/drug agency
in fiscal year 1995. An additional 95,039 admissions were not reported by race.
**Not available.

Hispanic Admissions to Alcohol and Other Drug Treatment Programs in 1995

National Total = 124,079 Hispanic Admissions*

ALPHA ORDER

RANK	STATE	ADMISSIONS	% of USA
NA	Alabama**	NA	NA
NA	Alaska**	NA	NA
8	Arizona	4,842	3.90%
20	Arkansas	106	0.09%
1	California	45,678	36.81%
NA	Colorado**	NA	NA
5	Connecticut	7,023	5.66%
NA	Delaware**	NA	NA
NA	Florida**	NA	NA
17	Georgia	178	0.14%
NA	Hawaii**	NA	NA
NA	Idaho**	NA	NA
6	Illinois	6,786	5.47%
15	Indiana	309	0.25%
NA	Iowa**	NA	NA
10	Kansas	1,734	1.40%
21	Kentucky	100	0.08%
24	Louisiana	0	0.00%
NA	Maine**	NA	NA
16	Maryland	183	0.15%
3	Massachusetts	12,517	10.09%
NA	Michigan**	NA	NA
NA	Minnesota**	NA	NA
24	Mississippi	0	0.00%
22	Missouri	98	0.08%
18	Montana	147	0.12%
24	Nebraska	0	0.00%
14	Nevada	567	0.46%
NA	New Hampshire**	NA	NA
4	New Jersey	7,678	6.19%
7	New Mexico	6,181	4.98%
2	New York	23,369	18.83%
24	North Carolina	0	0.00%
24	North Dakota	0	0.00%
NA	Ohio**	NA	NA
24	Oklahoma	0	0.00%
NA	Oregon**	NA	NA
9	Pennsylvania	2,292	1.85%
13	Rhode Island	995	0.80%
NA	South Carolina**	NA	NA
19	South Dakota	114	0.09%
NA	Tennessee**	NA	NA
NA	Texas**	NA	NA
11	Utah	1,725	1.39%
23	Vermont	22	0.02%
NA	Virginia**	NA	NA
NA	Washington**	NA	NA
24	West Virginia	0	0.00%
12	Wisconsin	1,234	0.99%
NA	Wyoming**	NA	NA

RANK ORDER

RANK	STATE	ADMISSIONS	% of USA
1	California	45,678	36.81%
2	New York	23,369	18.83%
3	Massachusetts	12,517	10.09%
4	New Jersey	7,678	6.19%
5	Connecticut	7,023	5.66%
6	Illinois	6,786	5.47%
7	New Mexico	6,181	4.98%
8	Arizona	4,842	3.90%
9	Pennsylvania	2,292	1.85%
10	Kansas	1,734	1.40%
11	Utah	1,725	1.39%
12	Wisconsin	1,234	0.99%
13	Rhode Island	995	0.80%
14	Nevada	567	0.46%
15	Indiana	309	0.25%
16	Maryland	183	0.15%
17	Georgia	178	0.14%
18	Montana	147	0.12%
19	South Dakota	114	0.09%
20	Arkansas	106	0.09%
21	Kentucky	100	0.08%
22	Missouri	98	0.08%
23	Vermont	22	0.02%
24	Louisiana	0	0.00%
24	Mississippi	0	0.00%
24	Nebraska	0	0.00%
24	North Carolina	0	0.00%
24	North Dakota	0	0.00%
24	Oklahoma	0	0.00%
24	West Virginia	0	0.00%
NA	Alabama**	NA	NA
NA	Alaska**	NA	NA
NA	Colorado**	NA	NA
NA	Delaware**	NA	NA
NA	Florida**	NA	NA
NA	Hawaii**	NA	NA
NA	Idaho**	NA	NA
NA	Iowa**	NA	NA
NA	Maine**	NA	NA
NA	Michigan**	NA	NA
NA	Minnesota**	NA	NA
NA	New Hampshire**	NA	NA
NA	Ohio**	NA	NA
NA	Oregon**	NA	NA
NA	South Carolina**	NA	NA
NA	Tennessee**	NA	NA
NA	Texas**	NA	NA
NA	Virginia**	NA	NA
NA	Washington**	NA	NA
NA	Wyoming**	NA	NA
	District of Columbia	201	0.16%

Source: U.S. Department of Health and Human Services, Substance Abuse and Mental Health Services Administration "State Resources and Services Related to Alcohol and Other Drug Problems-Fiscal Year 1995" (July 1997)

*Does not include 22,581 Hispanic admissions in U.S. territories. Data are only from treatment units that received at least some funds administered by a state's alcohol/drug agency in fiscal year 1995. An additional 95,039 admissions were not reported by race.

**Not available.

Hispanic Admissions to Alcohol and Other Drug Treatment Programs
As a Percent of All Admissions in 1995
National Percent = 6.6% of Admissions*

RANK	STATE	PERCENT
NA	Alabama**	NA
NA	Alaska**	NA
3	Arizona	21.9
18	Arkansas	0.8
2	California	24.0
NA	Colorado**	NA
4	Connecticut	16.4
NA	Delaware**	NA
NA	Florida**	NA
21	Georgia	0.3
NA	Hawaii**	NA
NA	Idaho**	NA
12	Illinois	5.6
16	Indiana	1.1
NA	Iowa**	NA
9	Kansas	9.1
19	Kentucky	0.5
24	Louisiana	0.0
NA	Maine**	NA
19	Maryland	0.5
7	Massachusetts	12.5
NA	Michigan**	NA
NA	Minnesota**	NA
24	Mississippi	0.0
21	Missouri	0.3
14	Montana	2.6
24	Nebraska	0.0
11	Nevada	8.7
NA	New Hampshire**	NA
5	New Jersey	15.1
1	New Mexico	48.1
6	New York	15.0
24	North Carolina	0.0
24	North Dakota	0.0
NA	Ohio**	NA
24	Oklahoma	0.0
NA	Oregon**	NA
13	Pennsylvania	3.3
10	Rhode Island	8.9
NA	South Carolina**	NA
17	South Dakota	0.9
NA	Tennessee**	NA
NA	Texas**	NA
8	Utah	10.4
21	Vermont	0.3
NA	Virginia**	NA
NA	Washington**	NA
24	West Virginia	0.0
15	Wisconsin	1.7
NA	Wyoming**	NA

RANK	STATE	PERCENT
1	New Mexico	48.1
2	California	24.0
3	Arizona	21.9
4	Connecticut	16.4
5	New Jersey	15.1
6	New York	15.0
7	Massachusetts	12.5
8	Utah	10.4
9	Kansas	9.1
10	Rhode Island	8.9
11	Nevada	8.7
12	Illinois	5.6
13	Pennsylvania	3.3
14	Montana	2.6
15	Wisconsin	1.7
16	Indiana	1.1
17	South Dakota	0.9
18	Arkansas	0.8
19	Kentucky	0.5
19	Maryland	0.5
21	Georgia	0.3
21	Missouri	0.3
21	Vermont	0.3
24	Louisiana	0.0
24	Mississippi	0.0
24	Nebraska	0.0
24	North Carolina	0.0
24	North Dakota	0.0
24	Oklahoma	0.0
24	West Virginia	0.0
NA	Alabama**	NA
NA	Alaska**	NA
NA	Colorado**	NA
NA	Delaware**	NA
NA	Florida**	NA
NA	Hawaii**	NA
NA	Idaho**	NA
NA	Iowa**	NA
NA	Maine**	NA
NA	Michigan**	NA
NA	Minnesota**	NA
NA	New Hampshire**	NA
NA	Ohio**	NA
NA	Oregon**	NA
NA	South Carolina**	NA
NA	Tennessee**	NA
NA	Texas**	NA
NA	Virginia**	NA
NA	Washington**	NA
NA	Wyoming**	NA

District of Columbia   1.4

Source: Morgan Quitno Press using data from U.S. Department of Health and Human Services, Substance Abuse
and Mental Health Services Administration
"State Resources and Services Related to Alcohol and Other Drug Problems-Fiscal Year 1995" (July 1997)
*Data are only from treatment units that received at least some funds administered by a state's alcohol/drug agency
in fiscal year 1995. An additional 95,039 admissions were not reported by race.
**Not available.

Expenditures for State-Supported Alcohol and Other Drug Abuse Services: 1995

National Total = $4,032,786,784*

ALPHA ORDER

RANK	STATE	EXPENDITURES	% of USA
32	Alabama	$22,694,860	0.56%
33	Alaska	22,450,175	0.56%
26	Arizona	32,458,699	0.80%
37	Arkansas	15,264,992	0.38%
2	California	544,851,000	13.51%
20	Colorado	51,124,582	1.27%
9	Connecticut	102,525,662	2.54%
44	Delaware	8,887,347	0.22%
5	Florida	192,020,229	4.76%
16	Georgia	69,501,022	1.72%
35	Hawaii	17,841,224	0.44%
47	Idaho	6,781,249	0.17%
4	Illinois	204,960,979	5.08%
19	Indiana	52,527,820	1.30%
21	Iowa	50,111,156	1.24%
34	Kansas	18,156,687	0.45%
28	Kentucky	25,715,370	0.64%
25	Louisiana	34,964,571	0.87%
38	Maine	15,232,636	0.38%
13	Maryland	76,283,076	1.89%
14	Massachusetts	76,212,460	1.89%
8	Michigan	151,573,606	3.76%
NA	Minnesota**	NA	NA
40	Mississippi	14,915,278	0.37%
23	Missouri	44,744,508	1.11%
42	Montana	12,263,980	0.30%
39	Nebraska	15,085,068	0.37%
43	Nevada	10,564,331	0.26%
46	New Hampshire	7,290,076	0.18%
10	New Jersey	102,089,567	2.53%
30	New Mexico	23,833,597	0.59%
1	New York	840,056,882	20.83%
17	North Carolina	60,466,422	1.50%
48	North Dakota	4,213,000	0.10%
6	Ohio	177,308,445	4.40%
31	Oklahoma	23,480,541	0.58%
12	Oregon	82,778,742	2.05%
3	Pennsylvania	223,120,406	5.53%
29	Rhode Island	24,044,163	0.60%
22	South Carolina	45,362,123	1.12%
41	South Dakota	12,892,649	0.32%
27	Tennessee	28,812,282	0.71%
7	Texas	174,713,730	4.33%
24	Utah	36,816,506	0.91%
45	Vermont	7,542,924	0.19%
11	Virginia	89,194,350	2.21%
15	Washington	72,165,460	1.79%
36	West Virginia	17,350,261	0.43%
18	Wisconsin	59,067,626	1.46%
NA	Wyoming**	NA	NA

RANK ORDER

RANK	STATE	EXPENDITURES	% of USA
1	New York	$840,056,882	20.83%
2	California	544,851,000	13.51%
3	Pennsylvania	223,120,406	5.53%
4	Illinois	204,960,979	5.08%
5	Florida	192,020,229	4.76%
6	Ohio	177,308,445	4.40%
7	Texas	174,713,730	4.33%
8	Michigan	151,573,606	3.76%
9	Connecticut	102,525,662	2.54%
10	New Jersey	102,089,567	2.53%
11	Virginia	89,194,350	2.21%
12	Oregon	82,778,742	2.05%
13	Maryland	76,283,076	1.89%
14	Massachusetts	76,212,460	1.89%
15	Washington	72,165,460	1.79%
16	Georgia	69,501,022	1.72%
17	North Carolina	60,466,422	1.50%
18	Wisconsin	59,067,626	1.46%
19	Indiana	52,527,820	1.30%
20	Colorado	51,124,582	1.27%
21	Iowa	50,111,156	1.24%
22	South Carolina	45,362,123	1.12%
23	Missouri	44,744,508	1.11%
24	Utah	36,816,506	0.91%
25	Louisiana	34,964,571	0.87%
26	Arizona	32,458,699	0.80%
27	Tennessee	28,812,282	0.71%
28	Kentucky	25,715,370	0.64%
29	Rhode Island	24,044,163	0.60%
30	New Mexico	23,833,597	0.59%
31	Oklahoma	23,480,541	0.58%
32	Alabama	22,694,860	0.56%
33	Alaska	22,450,175	0.56%
34	Kansas	18,156,687	0.45%
35	Hawaii	17,841,224	0.44%
36	West Virginia	17,350,261	0.43%
37	Arkansas	15,264,992	0.38%
38	Maine	15,232,636	0.38%
39	Nebraska	15,085,068	0.37%
40	Mississippi	14,915,278	0.37%
41	South Dakota	12,892,649	0.32%
42	Montana	12,263,980	0.30%
43	Nevada	10,564,331	0.26%
44	Delaware	8,887,347	0.22%
45	Vermont	7,542,924	0.19%
46	New Hampshire	7,290,076	0.18%
47	Idaho	6,781,249	0.17%
48	North Dakota	4,213,000	0.10%
NA	Minnesota**	NA	NA
NA	Wyoming**	NA	NA
	District of Columbia	30,474,465	0.76%

Source: U.S. Department of Health and Human Services, Substance Abuse and Mental Health Services Administration
"State Resources and Services Related to Alcohol and Other Drug Problems-Fiscal Year 1995" (July 1997)
*Funds for treatment and prevention programs as well as "other" costs (e.g. administration, capital construction and research.) Total does not include $49,009,302 in U.S. territories.
**Not available.

Per Capita Expenditures for State-Supported Alcohol and Other Drug Abuse Services in 1995
National Per Capita = $15.35*

ALPHA ORDER

RANK	STATE	PER CAPITA
48	Alabama	$5.32
2	Alaska	37.31
37	Arizona	7.53
44	Arkansas	6.15
11	California	17.26
18	Colorado	13.66
3	Connecticut	31.38
25	Delaware	12.42
19	Florida	13.54
29	Georgia	9.66
15	Hawaii	15.13
45	Idaho	5.82
10	Illinois	17.38
33	Indiana	9.08
8	Iowa	17.64
39	Kansas	7.07
41	Kentucky	6.67
36	Louisiana	8.08
26	Maine	12.34
14	Maryland	15.17
24	Massachusetts	12.58
13	Michigan	15.70
NA	Minnesota**	NA
46	Mississippi	5.54
35	Missouri	8.40
17	Montana	14.12
32	Nebraska	9.22
40	Nevada	6.91
43	New Hampshire	6.36
23	New Jersey	12.83
16	New Mexico	14.13
1	New York	46.29
34	North Carolina	8.41
42	North Dakota	6.57
12	Ohio	15.93
38	Oklahoma	7.18
4	Oregon	26.34
7	Pennsylvania	18.52
5	Rhode Island	24.29
27	South Carolina	12.32
9	South Dakota	17.54
47	Tennessee	5.50
31	Texas	9.32
6	Utah	18.65
22	Vermont	12.94
20	Virginia	13.51
21	Washington	13.28
30	West Virginia	9.52
28	Wisconsin	11.55
NA	Wyoming**	NA

RANK ORDER

RANK	STATE	PER CAPITA
1	New York	$46.29
2	Alaska	37.31
3	Connecticut	31.38
4	Oregon	26.34
5	Rhode Island	24.29
6	Utah	18.65
7	Pennsylvania	18.52
8	Iowa	17.64
9	South Dakota	17.54
10	Illinois	17.38
11	California	17.26
12	Ohio	15.93
13	Michigan	15.70
14	Maryland	15.17
15	Hawaii	15.13
16	New Mexico	14.13
17	Montana	14.12
18	Colorado	13.66
19	Florida	13.54
20	Virginia	13.51
21	Washington	13.28
22	Vermont	12.94
23	New Jersey	12.83
24	Massachusetts	12.58
25	Delaware	12.42
26	Maine	12.34
27	South Carolina	12.32
28	Wisconsin	11.55
29	Georgia	9.66
30	West Virginia	9.52
31	Texas	9.32
32	Nebraska	9.22
33	Indiana	9.08
34	North Carolina	8.41
35	Missouri	8.40
36	Louisiana	8.08
37	Arizona	7.53
38	Oklahoma	7.18
39	Kansas	7.07
40	Nevada	6.91
41	Kentucky	6.67
42	North Dakota	6.57
43	New Hampshire	6.36
44	Arkansas	6.15
45	Idaho	5.82
46	Mississippi	5.54
47	Tennessee	5.50
48	Alabama	5.32
NA	Minnesota**	NA
NA	Wyoming**	NA
	District of Columbia	55.18

Source: Morgan Quitno Press using data from U.S. Department of Health and Human Services, Substance Abuse and Mental Health Services Administration
   "State Resources and Services Related to Alcohol and Other Drug Problems-Fiscal Year 1995" (July 1997)
*Funds for treatment and prevention programs as well as "other" costs (e.g. administration, capital construction and research.) National per capita does not include expenditures in U.S. territories.
**Not available.

Expenditures for State-Supported Alcohol and Other Drug Abuse Treatment Programs in 1995
National Total = $3,179,369,701*

ALPHA ORDER

RANK	STATE	EXPENDITURES	% of USA
33	Alabama	$17,644,108	0.55%
27	Alaska	21,156,174	0.67%
26	Arizona	27,847,817	0.88%
38	Arkansas	11,900,546	0.37%
2	California	362,879,000	11.41%
18	Colorado	44,267,973	1.39%
9	Connecticut	89,533,115	2.82%
43	Delaware	7,797,288	0.25%
3	Florida	178,522,719	5.62%
13	Georgia	63,861,566	2.01%
36	Hawaii	13,766,703	0.43%
47	Idaho	4,597,259	0.14%
4	Illinois	177,595,268	5.59%
19	Indiana	43,195,735	1.36%
21	Iowa	39,769,960	1.25%
35	Kansas	14,323,206	0.45%
28	Kentucky	20,982,223	0.66%
24	Louisiana	29,878,770	0.94%
42	Maine	8,995,047	0.28%
14	Maryland	63,032,310	1.98%
12	Massachusetts	66,353,841	2.09%
8	Michigan	118,015,662	3.71%
NA	Minnesota**	NA	NA
37	Mississippi	11,972,336	0.38%
22	Missouri	37,855,303	1.19%
40	Montana	11,196,526	0.35%
39	Nebraska	11,634,884	0.37%
44	Nevada	7,120,951	0.22%
46	New Hampshire	5,317,451	0.17%
10	New Jersey	86,592,262	2.72%
30	New Mexico	18,232,995	0.57%
1	New York	678,399,295	21.34%
15	North Carolina	53,416,441	1.68%
48	North Dakota	3,787,000	0.12%
6	Ohio	134,404,251	4.23%
29	Oklahoma	18,442,305	0.58%
20	Oregon	40,527,240	1.27%
5	Pennsylvania	177,347,885	5.58%
32	Rhode Island	18,064,415	0.57%
23	South Carolina	35,053,946	1.10%
41	South Dakota	9,531,053	0.30%
31	Tennessee	18,091,874	0.57%
7	Texas	124,247,222	3.91%
25	Utah	28,276,967	0.89%
45	Vermont	6,011,659	0.19%
11	Virginia	77,888,617	2.45%
16	Washington	51,246,222	1.61%
34	West Virginia	15,313,725	0.48%
17	Wisconsin	46,539,757	1.46%
NA	Wyoming**	NA	NA

RANK ORDER

RANK	STATE	EXPENDITURES	% of USA
1	New York	$678,399,295	21.34%
2	California	362,879,000	11.41%
3	Florida	178,522,719	5.62%
4	Illinois	177,595,268	5.59%
5	Pennsylvania	177,347,885	5.58%
6	Ohio	134,404,251	4.23%
7	Texas	124,247,222	3.91%
8	Michigan	118,015,662	3.71%
9	Connecticut	89,533,115	2.82%
10	New Jersey	86,592,262	2.72%
11	Virginia	77,888,617	2.45%
12	Massachusetts	66,353,841	2.09%
13	Georgia	63,861,566	2.01%
14	Maryland	63,032,310	1.98%
15	North Carolina	53,416,441	1.68%
16	Washington	51,246,222	1.61%
17	Wisconsin	46,539,757	1.46%
18	Colorado	44,267,973	1.39%
19	Indiana	43,195,735	1.36%
20	Oregon	40,527,240	1.27%
21	Iowa	39,769,960	1.25%
22	Missouri	37,855,303	1.19%
23	South Carolina	35,053,946	1.10%
24	Louisiana	29,878,770	0.94%
25	Utah	28,276,967	0.89%
26	Arizona	27,847,817	0.88%
27	Alaska	21,156,174	0.67%
28	Kentucky	20,982,223	0.66%
29	Oklahoma	18,442,305	0.58%
30	New Mexico	18,232,995	0.57%
31	Tennessee	18,091,874	0.57%
32	Rhode Island	18,064,415	0.57%
33	Alabama	17,644,108	0.55%
34	West Virginia	15,313,725	0.48%
35	Kansas	14,323,206	0.45%
36	Hawaii	13,766,703	0.43%
37	Mississippi	11,972,336	0.38%
38	Arkansas	11,900,546	0.37%
39	Nebraska	11,634,884	0.37%
40	Montana	11,196,526	0.35%
41	South Dakota	9,531,053	0.30%
42	Maine	8,995,047	0.28%
43	Delaware	7,797,288	0.25%
44	Nevada	7,120,951	0.22%
45	Vermont	6,011,659	0.19%
46	New Hampshire	5,317,451	0.17%
47	Idaho	4,597,259	0.14%
48	North Dakota	3,787,000	0.12%
NA	Minnesota**	NA	NA
NA	Wyoming**	NA	NA
	District of Columbia	26,940,829	0.85%

*Source: U.S. Department of Health and Human Services, Substance Abuse and Mental Health Services Administration
"State Resources and Services Related to Alcohol and Other Drug Problems-Fiscal Year 1995" (July 1997)*
Total does not include $24,502,015 in U.S. territories.
**Not available.*

Expenditures per Alcohol and Other Drug Treatment Admission in 1995

National Rate = $1,694 in Treatment Expenditures per Admission*

ALPHA ORDER

RANK	STATE	RATE
26	Alabama	$1,194
5	Alaska	2,325
25	Arizona	1,257
41	Arkansas	853
10	California	1,905
42	Colorado	840
8	Connecticut	2,096
28	Delaware	1,140
14	Florida	1,707
35	Georgia	1,051
2	Hawaii	3,071
43	Idaho	833
20	Illinois	1,461
19	Indiana	1,561
17	Iowa	1,658
45	Kansas	748
33	Kentucky	1,066
32	Louisiana	1,096
36	Maine	994
11	Maryland	1,829
46	Massachusetts	664
22	Michigan	1,392
NA	Minnesota**	NA
39	Mississippi	874
30	Missouri	1,115
9	Montana	1,962
48	Nebraska	543
31	Nevada	1,099
23	New Hampshire	1,368
13	New Jersey	1,708
21	New Mexico	1,420
1	New York	4,344
34	North Carolina	1,056
27	North Dakota	1,156
12	Ohio	1,813
4	Oklahoma	2,398
40	Oregon	872
3	Pennsylvania	2,583
18	Rhode Island	1,612
24	South Carolina	1,312
44	South Dakota	770
16	Tennessee	1,696
6	Texas	2,217
15	Utah	1,701
38	Vermont	893
7	Virginia	2,176
29	Washington	1,120
37	West Virginia	959
47	Wisconsin	640
NA	Wyoming**	NA

RANK ORDER

RANK	STATE	RATE
1	New York	$4,344
2	Hawaii	3,071
3	Pennsylvania	2,583
4	Oklahoma	2,398
5	Alaska	2,325
6	Texas	2,217
7	Virginia	2,176
8	Connecticut	2,096
9	Montana	1,962
10	California	1,905
11	Maryland	1,829
12	Ohio	1,813
13	New Jersey	1,708
14	Florida	1,707
15	Utah	1,701
16	Tennessee	1,696
17	Iowa	1,658
18	Rhode Island	1,612
19	Indiana	1,561
20	Illinois	1,461
21	New Mexico	1,420
22	Michigan	1,392
23	New Hampshire	1,368
24	South Carolina	1,312
25	Arizona	1,257
26	Alabama	1,194
27	North Dakota	1,156
28	Delaware	1,140
29	Washington	1,120
30	Missouri	1,115
31	Nevada	1,099
32	Louisiana	1,096
33	Kentucky	1,066
34	North Carolina	1,056
35	Georgia	1,051
36	Maine	994
37	West Virginia	959
38	Vermont	893
39	Mississippi	874
40	Oregon	872
41	Arkansas	853
42	Colorado	840
43	Idaho	833
44	South Dakota	770
45	Kansas	748
46	Massachusetts	664
47	Wisconsin	640
48	Nebraska	543
NA	Minnesota**	NA
NA	Wyoming**	NA
	District of Columbia	1,852

Source: Morgan Quitno Press using data from U.S. Department of Health and Human Services, Substance Abuse and Mental Health Services Administration
"State Resources and Services Related to Alcohol and Other Drug Problems-Fiscal Year 1994" (March 1996)
Does not include admissions in U.S. territories. Data are only from treatment units that received at least some funds administered by a state's alcohol/drug agency in fiscal year 1995.
***Not available.*

Per Capita Expenditures for State-Supported Alcohol and Other Drug Abuse Treatment Programs in 1995
National Per Capita = $12.10*

ALPHA ORDER

RANK	STATE	PER CAPITA
46	Alabama	$4.14
2	Alaska	35.16
37	Arizona	6.46
42	Arkansas	4.80
19	California	11.50
16	Colorado	11.83
3	Connecticut	27.41
21	Delaware	10.89
12	Florida	12.59
28	Georgia	8.88
18	Hawaii	11.68
47	Idaho	3.95
5	Illinois	15.06
30	Indiana	7.46
8	Iowa	14.00
40	Kansas	5.57
41	Kentucky	5.44
35	Louisiana	6.90
32	Maine	7.29
13	Maryland	12.54
20	Massachusetts	10.95
14	Michigan	12.22
NA	Minnesota**	NA
45	Mississippi	4.45
33	Missouri	7.11
10	Montana	12.89
33	Nebraska	7.11
43	Nevada	4.66
44	New Hampshire	4.64
22	New Jersey	10.88
23	New Mexico	10.81
1	New York	37.39
31	North Carolina	7.43
38	North Dakota	5.90
15	Ohio	12.07
39	Oklahoma	5.64
10	Oregon	12.89
6	Pennsylvania	14.72
4	Rhode Island	18.25
25	South Carolina	9.52
9	South Dakota	12.97
48	Tennessee	3.46
36	Texas	6.63
7	Utah	14.32
24	Vermont	10.31
17	Virginia	11.80
26	Washington	9.43
29	West Virginia	8.41
27	Wisconsin	9.10
NA	Wyoming**	NA

RANK ORDER

RANK	STATE	PER CAPITA
1	New York	$37.39
2	Alaska	35.16
3	Connecticut	27.41
4	Rhode Island	18.25
5	Illinois	15.06
6	Pennsylvania	14.72
7	Utah	14.32
8	Iowa	14.00
9	South Dakota	12.97
10	Montana	12.89
10	Oregon	12.89
12	Florida	12.59
13	Maryland	12.54
14	Michigan	12.22
15	Ohio	12.07
16	Colorado	11.83
17	Virginia	11.80
18	Hawaii	11.68
19	California	11.50
20	Massachusetts	10.95
21	Delaware	10.89
22	New Jersey	10.88
23	New Mexico	10.81
24	Vermont	10.31
25	South Carolina	9.52
26	Washington	9.43
27	Wisconsin	9.10
28	Georgia	8.88
29	West Virginia	8.41
30	Indiana	7.46
31	North Carolina	7.43
32	Maine	7.29
33	Missouri	7.11
33	Nebraska	7.11
35	Louisiana	6.90
36	Texas	6.63
37	Arizona	6.46
38	North Dakota	5.90
39	Oklahoma	5.64
40	Kansas	5.57
41	Kentucky	5.44
42	Arkansas	4.80
43	Nevada	4.66
44	New Hampshire	4.64
45	Mississippi	4.45
46	Alabama	4.14
47	Idaho	3.95
48	Tennessee	3.46
NA	Minnesota**	NA
NA	Wyoming**	NA

District of Columbia   48.78

Source: Morgan Quitno Press using data from U.S. Department of Health and Human Services, Substance Abuse and Mental Health Services Administration
"State Resources and Services Related to Alcohol and Other Drug Problems-Fiscal Year 1995" (July 1997)
*National per capita does not include expenditures in U.S. territories.
**Not available.

Expenditures for State-Supported Alcohol and Other Drug Abuse Prevention Programs in 1995
National Total = $576,142,644*

ALPHA ORDER

RANK	STATE	EXPENDITURES	% of USA
33	Alabama	$3,642,937	0.63%
46	Alaska	943,605	0.16%
32	Arizona	3,882,555	0.67%
38	Arkansas	2,326,465	0.40%
1	California	119,152,000	20.68%
31	Colorado	3,956,240	0.69%
18	Connecticut	7,456,762	1.29%
43	Delaware	1,064,899	0.18%
13	Florida	9,830,077	1.71%
22	Georgia	5,639,456	0.98%
35	Hawaii	2,629,038	0.46%
44	Idaho	1,013,273	0.18%
8	Illinois	17,928,187	3.11%
16	Indiana	7,984,381	1.39%
10	Iowa	10,341,196	1.79%
36	Kansas	2,591,227	0.45%
27	Kentucky	4,733,147	0.82%
30	Louisiana	4,006,535	0.70%
25	Maine	5,155,423	0.89%
19	Maryland	7,060,626	1.23%
15	Massachusetts	8,140,164	1.41%
6	Michigan	24,201,032	4.20%
NA	Minnesota**	NA	NA
40	Mississippi	1,997,767	0.35%
23	Missouri	5,341,447	0.93%
47	Montana	646,625	0.11%
37	Nebraska	2,587,590	0.45%
39	Nevada	2,117,379	0.37%
42	New Hampshire	1,355,911	0.24%
9	New Jersey	12,020,819	2.09%
28	New Mexico	4,310,717	0.75%
2	New York	106,321,122	18.45%
20	North Carolina	7,049,981	1.22%
48	North Dakota	426,000	0.07%
4	Ohio	28,884,391	5.01%
29	Oklahoma	4,230,534	0.73%
7	Oregon	19,536,178	3.39%
5	Pennsylvania	24,728,681	4.29%
24	Rhode Island	5,304,590	0.92%
14	South Carolina	9,594,501	1.67%
34	South Dakota	2,787,324	0.48%
21	Tennessee	6,591,154	1.14%
3	Texas	39,626,828	6.88%
17	Utah	7,724,756	1.34%
45	Vermont	954,933	0.17%
12	Virginia	9,888,321	1.72%
26	Washington	5,020,210	0.87%
41	West Virginia	1,512,363	0.26%
11	Wisconsin	10,079,205	1.75%
NA	Wyoming**	NA	NA

RANK ORDER

RANK	STATE	EXPENDITURES	% of USA
1	California	$119,152,000	20.68%
2	New York	106,321,122	18.45%
3	Texas	39,626,828	6.88%
4	Ohio	28,884,391	5.01%
5	Pennsylvania	24,728,681	4.29%
6	Michigan	24,201,032	4.20%
7	Oregon	19,536,178	3.39%
8	Illinois	17,928,187	3.11%
9	New Jersey	12,020,819	2.09%
10	Iowa	10,341,196	1.79%
11	Wisconsin	10,079,205	1.75%
12	Virginia	9,888,321	1.72%
13	Florida	9,830,077	1.71%
14	South Carolina	9,594,501	1.67%
15	Massachusetts	8,140,164	1.41%
16	Indiana	7,984,381	1.39%
17	Utah	7,724,756	1.34%
18	Connecticut	7,456,762	1.29%
19	Maryland	7,060,626	1.23%
20	North Carolina	7,049,981	1.22%
21	Tennessee	6,591,154	1.14%
22	Georgia	5,639,456	0.98%
23	Missouri	5,341,447	0.93%
24	Rhode Island	5,304,590	0.92%
25	Maine	5,155,423	0.89%
26	Washington	5,020,210	0.87%
27	Kentucky	4,733,147	0.82%
28	New Mexico	4,310,717	0.75%
29	Oklahoma	4,230,534	0.73%
30	Louisiana	4,006,535	0.70%
31	Colorado	3,956,240	0.69%
32	Arizona	3,882,555	0.67%
33	Alabama	3,642,937	0.63%
34	South Dakota	2,787,324	0.48%
35	Hawaii	2,629,038	0.46%
36	Kansas	2,591,227	0.45%
37	Nebraska	2,587,590	0.45%
38	Arkansas	2,326,465	0.40%
39	Nevada	2,117,379	0.37%
40	Mississippi	1,997,767	0.35%
41	West Virginia	1,512,363	0.26%
42	New Hampshire	1,355,911	0.24%
43	Delaware	1,064,899	0.18%
44	Idaho	1,013,273	0.18%
45	Vermont	954,933	0.17%
46	Alaska	943,605	0.16%
47	Montana	646,625	0.11%
48	North Dakota	426,000	0.07%
NA	Minnesota**	NA	NA
NA	Wyoming**	NA	NA
	District of Columbia	1,824,092	0.32%

Source: U.S. Department of Health and Human Services, Substance Abuse and Mental Health Services Administration
"State Resources and Services Related to Alcohol and Other Drug Problems-Fiscal Year 1995" (July 1997)
*Total does not include $7,056,729 in U.S. territories.
**Not available.

Per Capita Expenditures for State-Supported Alcohol and Other Drug Abuse Prevention Programs in 1995
National Per Capita = $2.19*

ALPHA ORDER

RANK	STATE	PER CAPITA
42	Alabama	$0.85
20	Alaska	1.57
40	Arizona	0.90
37	Arkansas	0.94
7	California	3.78
33	Colorado	1.06
13	Connecticut	2.28
24	Delaware	1.49
47	Florida	0.69
44	Georgia	0.78
14	Hawaii	2.23
41	Idaho	0.87
21	Illinois	1.52
26	Indiana	1.38
8	Iowa	3.64
34	Kansas	1.01
31	Kentucky	1.23
38	Louisiana	0.93
4	Maine	4.18
25	Maryland	1.40
28	Massachusetts	1.34
12	Michigan	2.51
NA	Minnesota**	NA
45	Mississippi	0.74
35	Missouri	1.00
45	Montana	0.74
19	Nebraska	1.58
26	Nevada	1.38
32	New Hampshire	1.18
22	New Jersey	1.51
11	New Mexico	2.56
2	New York	5.86
36	North Carolina	0.98
48	North Dakota	0.66
10	Ohio	2.59
29	Oklahoma	1.29
1	Oregon	6.22
16	Pennsylvania	2.05
3	Rhode Island	5.36
9	South Carolina	2.60
6	South Dakota	3.79
30	Tennessee	1.26
15	Texas	2.11
5	Utah	3.91
18	Vermont	1.64
23	Virginia	1.50
39	Washington	0.92
43	West Virginia	0.83
17	Wisconsin	1.97
NA	Wyoming**	NA

RANK ORDER

RANK	STATE	PER CAPITA
1	Oregon	$6.22
2	New York	5.86
3	Rhode Island	5.36
4	Maine	4.18
5	Utah	3.91
6	South Dakota	3.79
7	California	3.78
8	Iowa	3.64
9	South Carolina	2.60
10	Ohio	2.59
11	New Mexico	2.56
12	Michigan	2.51
13	Connecticut	2.28
14	Hawaii	2.23
15	Texas	2.11
16	Pennsylvania	2.05
17	Wisconsin	1.97
18	Vermont	1.64
19	Nebraska	1.58
20	Alaska	1.57
21	Illinois	1.52
22	New Jersey	1.51
23	Virginia	1.50
24	Delaware	1.49
25	Maryland	1.40
26	Indiana	1.38
26	Nevada	1.38
28	Massachusetts	1.34
29	Oklahoma	1.29
30	Tennessee	1.26
31	Kentucky	1.23
32	New Hampshire	1.18
33	Colorado	1.06
34	Kansas	1.01
35	Missouri	1.00
36	North Carolina	0.98
37	Arkansas	0.94
38	Louisiana	0.93
39	Washington	0.92
40	Arizona	0.90
41	Idaho	0.87
42	Alabama	0.85
43	West Virginia	0.83
44	Georgia	0.78
45	Mississippi	0.74
45	Montana	0.74
47	Florida	0.69
48	North Dakota	0.66
NA	Minnesota**	NA
NA	Wyoming**	NA
	District of Columbia	3.30

Source: Morgan Quitno Press using data from U.S. Department of Health and Human Services, Substance Abuse and Mental Health Services Administration
"State Resources and Services Related to Alcohol and Other Drug Problems-Fiscal Year 1995" (July 1997)
*National per capita does not include expenditures in U.S. territories.
**Not available.

IV. FINANCE

State and Local Government Expenditures for Justice Activities in 1995

National Total = $96,079,539,000*

ALPHA ORDER

RANK	STATE	EXPENDITURES	% of USA
26	Alabama	998,971,000	1.0%
37	Alaska	466,441,000	0.5%
17	Arizona	1,657,057,000	1.7%
36	Arkansas	503,547,000	0.5%
1	California	15,609,419,000	16.2%
22	Colorado	1,272,001,000	1.3%
23	Connecticut	1,263,588,000	1.3%
44	Delaware	293,434,000	0.3%
4	Florida	6,432,681,000	6.7%
11	Georgia	2,242,422,000	2.3%
38	Hawaii	452,981,000	0.5%
41	Idaho	321,271,000	0.3%
5	Illinois	3,968,770,000	4.1%
24	Indiana	1,245,070,000	1.3%
32	Iowa	700,505,000	0.7%
31	Kansas	710,027,000	0.7%
28	Kentucky	828,749,000	0.9%
20	Louisiana	1,319,789,000	1.4%
45	Maine	259,902,000	0.3%
14	Maryland	2,058,791,000	2.1%
12	Massachusetts	2,141,992,000	2.2%
9	Michigan	3,555,016,000	3.7%
19	Minnesota	1,331,485,000	1.4%
35	Mississippi	507,568,000	0.5%
21	Missouri	1,282,767,000	1.3%
46	Montana	194,366,000	0.2%
39	Nebraska	367,429,000	0.4%
30	Nevada	722,650,000	0.8%
43	New Hampshire	295,624,000	0.3%
6	New Jersey	3,731,148,000	3.9%
33	New Mexico	587,885,000	0.6%
2	New York	9,988,564,000	10.4%
10	North Carolina	2,308,154,000	2.4%
50	North Dakota	110,913,000	0.1%
7	Ohio	3,721,293,000	3.9%
29	Oklahoma	780,477,000	0.8%
25	Oregon	1,046,710,000	1.1%
8	Pennsylvania	3,670,586,000	3.8%
40	Rhode Island	355,765,000	0.4%
27	South Carolina	978,541,000	1.0%
47	South Dakota	161,350,000	0.2%
18	Tennessee	1,348,566,000	1.4%
3	Texas	6,674,247,000	6.9%
34	Utah	558,863,000	0.6%
49	Vermont	135,225,000	0.1%
13	Virginia	2,089,243,000	2.2%
15	Washington	1,891,048,000	2.0%
42	West Virginia	307,415,000	0.3%
16	Wisconsin	1,796,976,000	1.9%
48	Wyoming	154,320,000	0.2%

RANK ORDER

RANK	STATE	EXPENDITURES	% of USA
1	California	15,609,419,000	16.2%
2	New York	9,988,564,000	10.4%
3	Texas	6,674,247,000	6.9%
4	Florida	6,432,681,000	6.7%
5	Illinois	3,968,770,000	4.1%
6	New Jersey	3,731,148,000	3.9%
7	Ohio	3,721,293,000	3.9%
8	Pennsylvania	3,670,586,000	3.8%
9	Michigan	3,555,016,000	3.7%
10	North Carolina	2,308,154,000	2.4%
11	Georgia	2,242,422,000	2.3%
12	Massachusetts	2,141,992,000	2.2%
13	Virginia	2,089,243,000	2.2%
14	Maryland	2,058,791,000	2.1%
15	Washington	1,891,048,000	2.0%
16	Wisconsin	1,796,976,000	1.9%
17	Arizona	1,657,057,000	1.7%
18	Tennessee	1,348,566,000	1.4%
19	Minnesota	1,331,485,000	1.4%
20	Louisiana	1,319,789,000	1.4%
21	Missouri	1,282,767,000	1.3%
22	Colorado	1,272,001,000	1.3%
23	Connecticut	1,263,588,000	1.3%
24	Indiana	1,245,070,000	1.3%
25	Oregon	1,046,710,000	1.1%
26	Alabama	998,971,000	1.0%
27	South Carolina	978,541,000	1.0%
28	Kentucky	828,749,000	0.9%
29	Oklahoma	780,477,000	0.8%
30	Nevada	722,650,000	0.8%
31	Kansas	710,027,000	0.7%
32	Iowa	700,505,000	0.7%
33	New Mexico	587,885,000	0.6%
34	Utah	558,863,000	0.6%
35	Mississippi	507,568,000	0.5%
36	Arkansas	503,547,000	0.5%
37	Alaska	466,441,000	0.5%
38	Hawaii	452,981,000	0.5%
39	Nebraska	367,429,000	0.4%
40	Rhode Island	355,765,000	0.4%
41	Idaho	321,271,000	0.3%
42	West Virginia	307,415,000	0.3%
43	New Hampshire	295,624,000	0.3%
44	Delaware	293,434,000	0.3%
45	Maine	259,902,000	0.3%
46	Montana	194,366,000	0.2%
47	South Dakota	161,350,000	0.2%
48	Wyoming	154,320,000	0.2%
49	Vermont	135,225,000	0.1%
50	North Dakota	110,913,000	0.1%
	District of Columbia	677,937,000	0.7%

Source: Morgan Quitno Press using data from U.S. Bureau of the Census
"Government Finances: 1994-1995" (1998) (http://www.census.gov/govs/www/esti95.html)
*Direct general expenditures. Includes Police Protection, Corrections and Judicial and Legal Services.

Per Capita State & Local Government Expenditures for Justice Activities: 1995

National Per Capita = $366*

ALPHA ORDER

RANK	STATE	PER CAPITA
39	Alabama	$234
1	Alaska	775
10	Arizona	385
47	Arkansas	203
3	California	496
19	Colorado	340
9	Connecticut	387
8	Delaware	408
6	Florida	454
26	Georgia	312
11	Hawaii	383
31	Idaho	276
20	Illinois	334
44	Indiana	215
36	Iowa	247
31	Kansas	276
44	Kentucky	215
27	Louisiana	305
46	Maine	211
7	Maryland	410
15	Massachusetts	354
12	Michigan	368
29	Minnesota	289
48	Mississippi	189
37	Missouri	240
42	Montana	224
41	Nebraska	225
4	Nevada	473
34	New Hampshire	258
5	New Jersey	469
17	New Mexico	349
2	New York	550
24	North Carolina	321
49	North Dakota	173
20	Ohio	334
38	Oklahoma	239
22	Oregon	333
27	Pennsylvania	305
13	Rhode Island	360
33	South Carolina	265
43	South Dakota	220
34	Tennessee	258
14	Texas	357
30	Utah	281
40	Vermont	232
25	Virginia	316
18	Washington	348
50	West Virginia	169
16	Wisconsin	350
23	Wyoming	323

RANK ORDER

RANK	STATE	PER CAPITA
1	Alaska	$775
2	New York	550
3	California	496
4	Nevada	473
5	New Jersey	469
6	Florida	454
7	Maryland	410
8	Delaware	408
9	Connecticut	387
10	Arizona	385
11	Hawaii	383
12	Michigan	368
13	Rhode Island	360
14	Texas	357
15	Massachusetts	354
16	Wisconsin	350
17	New Mexico	349
18	Washington	348
19	Colorado	340
20	Illinois	334
20	Ohio	334
22	Oregon	333
23	Wyoming	323
24	North Carolina	321
25	Virginia	316
26	Georgia	312
27	Louisiana	305
27	Pennsylvania	305
29	Minnesota	289
30	Utah	281
31	Idaho	276
31	Kansas	276
33	South Carolina	265
34	New Hampshire	258
34	Tennessee	258
36	Iowa	247
37	Missouri	240
38	Oklahoma	239
39	Alabama	234
40	Vermont	232
41	Nebraska	225
42	Montana	224
43	South Dakota	220
44	Indiana	215
44	Kentucky	215
46	Maine	211
47	Arkansas	203
48	Mississippi	189
49	North Dakota	173
50	West Virginia	169
	District of Columbia	1,227

Source: Morgan Quitno Press using data from U.S. Bureau of the Census
"Government Finances: 1994-1995" (1998) (http://www.census.gov/govs/www/esti95.html)
*Direct general expenditures. Includes Police Protection, Corrections and Judicial and Legal Services.

State and Local Government Expenditures for Justice Activities
As a Percent of All Direct General Expenditures in 1995
National Percent = 8.4% of Direct General Expenditures*

ALPHA ORDER

RANK	STATE	PERCENT
36	Alabama	6.3
19	Alaska	7.5
4	Arizona	10.5
36	Arkansas	6.3
3	California	10.7
14	Colorado	8.1
20	Connecticut	7.4
10	Delaware	8.4
2	Florida	11.1
18	Georgia	7.7
34	Hawaii	6.7
20	Idaho	7.4
14	Illinois	8.1
39	Indiana	5.9
39	Iowa	5.9
32	Kansas	6.9
38	Kentucky	6.1
29	Louisiana	7.1
48	Maine	5.0
6	Maryland	9.7
26	Massachusetts	7.2
8	Michigan	8.6
43	Minnesota	5.6
47	Mississippi	5.3
26	Missouri	7.2
44	Montana	5.5
44	Nebraska	5.5
1	Nevada	11.2
35	New Hampshire	6.6
7	New Jersey	8.8
16	New Mexico	8.0
10	New York	8.4
10	North Carolina	8.4
50	North Dakota	4.0
9	Ohio	8.5
31	Oklahoma	7.0
22	Oregon	7.3
22	Pennsylvania	7.3
22	Rhode Island	7.3
33	South Carolina	6.8
42	South Dakota	5.7
29	Tennessee	7.1
5	Texas	9.8
22	Utah	7.3
46	Vermont	5.4
13	Virginia	8.3
26	Washington	7.2
49	West Virginia	4.3
17	Wisconsin	7.8
39	Wyoming	5.9

RANK ORDER

RANK	STATE	PERCENT
1	Nevada	11.2
2	Florida	11.1
3	California	10.7
4	Arizona	10.5
5	Texas	9.8
6	Maryland	9.7
7	New Jersey	8.8
8	Michigan	8.6
9	Ohio	8.5
10	Delaware	8.4
10	New York	8.4
10	North Carolina	8.4
13	Virginia	8.3
14	Colorado	8.1
14	Illinois	8.1
16	New Mexico	8.0
17	Wisconsin	7.8
18	Georgia	7.7
19	Alaska	7.5
20	Connecticut	7.4
20	Idaho	7.4
22	Oregon	7.3
22	Pennsylvania	7.3
22	Rhode Island	7.3
22	Utah	7.3
26	Massachusetts	7.2
26	Missouri	7.2
26	Washington	7.2
29	Louisiana	7.1
29	Tennessee	7.1
31	Oklahoma	7.0
32	Kansas	6.9
33	South Carolina	6.8
34	Hawaii	6.7
35	New Hampshire	6.6
36	Alabama	6.3
36	Arkansas	6.3
38	Kentucky	6.1
39	Indiana	5.9
39	Iowa	5.9
39	Wyoming	5.9
42	South Dakota	5.7
43	Minnesota	5.6
44	Montana	5.5
44	Nebraska	5.5
46	Vermont	5.4
47	Mississippi	5.3
48	Maine	5.0
49	West Virginia	4.3
50	North Dakota	4.0

	District of Columbia	15.8

Source: Morgan Quitno Press using data from U.S. Bureau of the Census
"Government Finances: 1994-1995" (1998) (http://www.census.gov/govs/www/esti95.html)
*Includes Police Protection, Corrections and Judicial and Legal Services.

State Government Expenditures for Justice Activities in 1995

National Total = $37,359,746,000*

ALPHA ORDER

RANK	STATE	EXPENDITURES	% of USA
26	Alabama	$441,217,000	1.2%
30	Alaska	356,789,000	1.0%
18	Arizona	562,162,000	1.5%
36	Arkansas	234,989,000	0.6%
1	California	4,718,387,000	12.6%
23	Colorado	478,320,000	1.3%
15	Connecticut	814,593,000	2.2%
38	Delaware	215,107,000	0.6%
4	Florida	2,335,595,000	6.3%
13	Georgia	935,438,000	2.5%
35	Hawaii	244,437,000	0.7%
44	Idaho	139,546,000	0.4%
10	Illinois	1,221,525,000	3.3%
21	Indiana	496,380,000	1.3%
31	Iowa	318,650,000	0.9%
33	Kansas	307,818,000	0.8%
25	Kentucky	457,725,000	1.2%
22	Louisiana	494,535,000	1.3%
45	Maine	131,342,000	0.4%
11	Maryland	1,123,661,000	3.0%
12	Massachusetts	1,053,006,000	2.8%
5	Michigan	1,540,057,000	4.1%
28	Minnesota	409,213,000	1.1%
39	Mississippi	214,926,000	0.6%
24	Missouri	471,515,000	1.3%
47	Montana	89,683,000	0.2%
42	Nebraska	151,069,000	0.4%
40	Nevada	194,130,000	0.5%
43	New Hampshire	144,032,000	0.4%
7	New Jersey	1,318,900,000	3.5%
32	New Mexico	308,431,000	0.8%
2	New York	3,514,174,000	9.4%
8	North Carolina	1,311,083,000	3.5%
50	North Dakota	45,654,000	0.1%
9	Ohio	1,292,654,000	3.5%
29	Oklahoma	386,181,000	1.0%
27	Oregon	432,827,000	1.2%
6	Pennsylvania	1,429,650,000	3.8%
37	Rhode Island	219,522,000	0.6%
20	South Carolina	502,137,000	1.3%
48	South Dakota	76,731,000	0.2%
19	Tennessee	535,377,000	1.4%
3	Texas	2,855,105,000	7.6%
34	Utah	269,383,000	0.7%
46	Vermont	99,683,000	0.3%
14	Virginia	925,746,000	2.5%
16	Washington	661,740,000	1.8%
41	West Virginia	173,750,000	0.5%
17	Wisconsin	642,135,000	1.7%
49	Wyoming	63,036,000	0.2%

RANK ORDER

RANK	STATE	EXPENDITURES	% of USA
1	California	$4,718,387,000	12.6%
2	New York	3,514,174,000	9.4%
3	Texas	2,855,105,000	7.6%
4	Florida	2,335,595,000	6.3%
5	Michigan	1,540,057,000	4.1%
6	Pennsylvania	1,429,650,000	3.8%
7	New Jersey	1,318,900,000	3.5%
8	North Carolina	1,311,083,000	3.5%
9	Ohio	1,292,654,000	3.5%
10	Illinois	1,221,525,000	3.3%
11	Maryland	1,123,661,000	3.0%
12	Massachusetts	1,053,006,000	2.8%
13	Georgia	935,438,000	2.5%
14	Virginia	925,746,000	2.5%
15	Connecticut	814,593,000	2.2%
16	Washington	661,740,000	1.8%
17	Wisconsin	642,135,000	1.7%
18	Arizona	562,162,000	1.5%
19	Tennessee	535,377,000	1.4%
20	South Carolina	502,137,000	1.3%
21	Indiana	496,380,000	1.3%
22	Louisiana	494,535,000	1.3%
23	Colorado	478,320,000	1.3%
24	Missouri	471,515,000	1.3%
25	Kentucky	457,725,000	1.2%
26	Alabama	441,217,000	1.2%
27	Oregon	432,827,000	1.2%
28	Minnesota	409,213,000	1.1%
29	Oklahoma	386,181,000	1.0%
30	Alaska	356,789,000	1.0%
31	Iowa	318,650,000	0.9%
32	New Mexico	308,431,000	0.8%
33	Kansas	307,818,000	0.8%
34	Utah	269,383,000	0.7%
35	Hawaii	244,437,000	0.7%
36	Arkansas	234,989,000	0.6%
37	Rhode Island	219,522,000	0.6%
38	Delaware	215,107,000	0.6%
39	Mississippi	214,926,000	0.6%
40	Nevada	194,130,000	0.5%
41	West Virginia	173,750,000	0.5%
42	Nebraska	151,069,000	0.4%
43	New Hampshire	144,032,000	0.4%
44	Idaho	139,546,000	0.4%
45	Maine	131,342,000	0.4%
46	Vermont	99,683,000	0.3%
47	Montana	89,683,000	0.2%
48	South Dakota	76,731,000	0.2%
49	Wyoming	63,036,000	0.2%
50	North Dakota	45,654,000	0.1%
	District of Columbia**	NA	NA

Source: Morgan Quitno Press using data from U.S. Bureau of the Census
"Government Finances: 1994-1995" (1998) (http://www.census.gov/govs/www/esti95.html)
*Direct general expenditures. Includes Police Protection, Corrections and Judicial and Legal Services.
**Not applicable.

Per Capita State Government Expenditures for Justice Activities in 1995

National Per Capita = $142.18*

ALPHA ORDER

RANK	STATE	PER CAPITA
39	Alabama	$103.32
1	Alaska	593.09
22	Arizona	130.52
44	Arkansas	94.75
16	California	149.92
24	Colorado	127.95
3	Connecticut	249.74
2	Delaware	299.30
13	Florida	164.71
23	Georgia	130.13
6	Hawaii	206.61
29	Idaho	119.93
41	Illinois	102.94
48	Indiana	85.78
36	Iowa	112.18
30	Kansas	119.56
32	Kentucky	118.70
35	Louisiana	114.26
37	Maine	106.51
4	Maryland	223.68
10	Massachusetts	173.82
14	Michigan	159.38
46	Minnesota	88.86
49	Mississippi	79.88
47	Missouri	88.34
40	Montana	103.26
45	Nebraska	92.37
25	Nevada	127.02
26	New Hampshire	125.66
12	New Jersey	165.64
8	New Mexico	183.18
7	New York	193.67
9	North Carolina	182.45
50	North Dakota	71.18
34	Ohio	116.06
33	Oklahoma	118.05
18	Oregon	137.79
31	Pennsylvania	118.74
5	Rhode Island	221.90
19	South Carolina	135.74
38	South Dakota	104.46
42	Tennessee	102.27
15	Texas	152.73
20	Utah	135.27
11	Vermont	171.15
17	Virginia	140.23
28	Washington	121.80
43	West Virginia	95.38
27	Wisconsin	125.00
21	Wyoming	131.77

RANK ORDER

RANK	STATE	PER CAPITA
1	Alaska	$593.09
2	Delaware	299.30
3	Connecticut	249.74
4	Maryland	223.68
5	Rhode Island	221.90
6	Hawaii	206.61
7	New York	193.67
8	New Mexico	183.18
9	North Carolina	182.45
10	Massachusetts	173.82
11	Vermont	171.15
12	New Jersey	165.64
13	Florida	164.71
14	Michigan	159.38
15	Texas	152.73
16	California	149.92
17	Virginia	140.23
18	Oregon	137.79
19	South Carolina	135.74
20	Utah	135.27
21	Wyoming	131.77
22	Arizona	130.52
23	Georgia	130.13
24	Colorado	127.95
25	Nevada	127.02
26	New Hampshire	125.66
27	Wisconsin	125.00
28	Washington	121.80
29	Idaho	119.93
30	Kansas	119.56
31	Pennsylvania	118.74
32	Kentucky	118.70
33	Oklahoma	118.05
34	Ohio	116.06
35	Louisiana	114.26
36	Iowa	112.18
37	Maine	106.51
38	South Dakota	104.46
39	Alabama	103.32
40	Montana	103.26
41	Illinois	102.94
42	Tennessee	102.27
43	West Virginia	95.38
44	Arkansas	94.75
45	Nebraska	92.37
46	Minnesota	88.86
47	Missouri	88.34
48	Indiana	85.78
49	Mississippi	79.88
50	North Dakota	71.18
	District of Columbia**	NA

Source: Morgan Quitno Press using data from U.S. Bureau of the Census
   "Government Finances: 1994-1995" (1998) (http://www.census.gov/govs/www/esti95.html)
*Direct general expenditures. Includes Police Protection, Corrections and Judicial and Legal Services.
**Not applicable.

State Government Expenditures for Justice Activities
As a Percent of All Direct General Expenditures in 1995
National Percent = 7.6% of Direct General Expenditures*

RANK	STATE	PERCENT
36	Alabama	5.6
8	Alaska	9.0
7	Arizona	9.2
41	Arkansas	5.2
6	California	9.6
12	Colorado	8.3
9	Connecticut	8.9
5	Delaware	9.8
2	Florida	11.0
18	Georgia	7.2
46	Hawaii	4.7
22	Idaho	7.0
32	Illinois	5.9
38	Indiana	5.4
31	Iowa	6.0
18	Kansas	7.2
28	Kentucky	6.2
43	Louisiana	4.9
47	Maine	4.5
1	Maryland	11.4
29	Massachusetts	6.1
9	Michigan	8.9
47	Minnesota	4.5
43	Mississippi	4.9
32	Missouri	5.9
45	Montana	4.8
42	Nebraska	5.1
11	Nevada	8.5
29	New Hampshire	6.1
21	New Jersey	7.1
15	New Mexico	7.9
13	New York	8.2
3	North Carolina	10.9
50	North Dakota	2.8
22	Ohio	7.0
16	Oklahoma	7.5
26	Oregon	6.6
34	Pennsylvania	5.8
18	Rhode Island	7.2
25	South Carolina	6.7
40	South Dakota	5.3
35	Tennessee	5.7
4	Texas	10.0
22	Utah	7.0
27	Vermont	6.4
14	Virginia	8.1
38	Washington	5.4
49	West Virginia	4.2
17	Wisconsin	7.3
36	Wyoming	5.6

RANK	STATE	PERCENT
1	Maryland	11.4
2	Florida	11.0
3	North Carolina	10.9
4	Texas	10.0
5	Delaware	9.8
6	California	9.6
7	Arizona	9.2
8	Alaska	9.0
9	Connecticut	8.9
9	Michigan	8.9
11	Nevada	8.5
12	Colorado	8.3
13	New York	8.2
14	Virginia	8.1
15	New Mexico	7.9
16	Oklahoma	7.5
17	Wisconsin	7.3
18	Georgia	7.2
18	Kansas	7.2
18	Rhode Island	7.2
21	New Jersey	7.1
22	Idaho	7.0
22	Ohio	7.0
22	Utah	7.0
25	South Carolina	6.7
26	Oregon	6.6
27	Vermont	6.4
28	Kentucky	6.2
29	Massachusetts	6.1
29	New Hampshire	6.1
31	Iowa	6.0
32	Illinois	5.9
32	Missouri	5.9
34	Pennsylvania	5.8
35	Tennessee	5.7
36	Alabama	5.6
36	Wyoming	5.6
38	Indiana	5.4
38	Washington	5.4
40	South Dakota	5.3
41	Arkansas	5.2
42	Nebraska	5.1
43	Louisiana	4.9
43	Mississippi	4.9
45	Montana	4.8
46	Hawaii	4.7
47	Maine	4.5
47	Minnesota	4.5
49	West Virginia	4.2
50	North Dakota	2.8
	District of Columbia**	NA

Source: Morgan Quitno Press using data from U.S. Bureau of the Census
"Government Finances: 1994-1995" (1998) (http://www.census.gov/govs/www/esti95.html)
*Includes Police Protection, Corrections and Judicial and Legal Services.
**Not applicable.

Local Government Expenditures for Justice Activities in 1995

National Total = $58,719,793,000*

ALPHA ORDER				RANK ORDER			
RANK	STATE	EXPENDITURES	% of USA	RANK	STATE	EXPENDITURES	% of USA
25	Alabama	$557,754,000	0.9%	1	California	$10,891,032,000	18.5%
44	Alaska	109,652,000	0.2%	2	New York	6,474,390,000	11.0%
14	Arizona	1,094,895,000	1.9%	3	Florida	4,097,086,000	7.0%
36	Arkansas	268,558,000	0.5%	4	Texas	3,819,142,000	6.5%
1	California	10,891,032,000	18.5%	5	Illinois	2,747,245,000	4.7%
22	Colorado	793,681,000	1.4%	6	Ohio	2,428,639,000	4.1%
28	Connecticut	448,995,000	0.8%	7	New Jersey	2,412,248,000	4.1%
48	Delaware	78,327,000	0.1%	8	Pennsylvania	2,240,936,000	3.8%
3	Florida	4,097,086,000	7.0%	9	Michigan	2,014,959,000	3.4%
10	Georgia	1,306,984,000	2.2%	10	Georgia	1,306,984,000	2.2%
38	Hawaii	208,544,000	0.4%	11	Washington	1,229,308,000	2.1%
39	Idaho	181,725,000	0.3%	12	Virginia	1,163,497,000	2.0%
5	Illinois	2,747,245,000	4.7%	13	Wisconsin	1,154,841,000	2.0%
23	Indiana	748,690,000	1.3%	14	Arizona	1,094,895,000	1.9%
31	Iowa	381,855,000	0.7%	15	Massachusetts	1,088,986,000	1.9%
29	Kansas	402,209,000	0.7%	16	North Carolina	997,071,000	1.7%
32	Kentucky	371,024,000	0.6%	17	Maryland	935,130,000	1.6%
19	Louisiana	825,254,000	1.4%	18	Minnesota	922,272,000	1.6%
43	Maine	128,560,000	0.2%	19	Louisiana	825,254,000	1.4%
17	Maryland	935,130,000	1.6%	20	Tennessee	813,189,000	1.4%
15	Massachusetts	1,088,986,000	1.9%	21	Missouri	811,252,000	1.4%
9	Michigan	2,014,959,000	3.4%	22	Colorado	793,681,000	1.4%
18	Minnesota	922,272,000	1.6%	23	Indiana	748,690,000	1.3%
33	Mississippi	292,642,000	0.5%	24	Oregon	613,883,000	1.0%
21	Missouri	811,252,000	1.4%	25	Alabama	557,754,000	0.9%
45	Montana	104,683,000	0.2%	26	Nevada	528,520,000	0.9%
37	Nebraska	216,360,000	0.4%	27	South Carolina	476,404,000	0.8%
26	Nevada	528,520,000	0.9%	28	Connecticut	448,995,000	0.8%
40	New Hampshire	151,592,000	0.3%	29	Kansas	402,209,000	0.7%
7	New Jersey	2,412,248,000	4.1%	30	Oklahoma	394,296,000	0.7%
35	New Mexico	279,454,000	0.5%	31	Iowa	381,855,000	0.7%
2	New York	6,474,390,000	11.0%	32	Kentucky	371,024,000	0.6%
16	North Carolina	997,071,000	1.7%	33	Mississippi	292,642,000	0.5%
49	North Dakota	65,259,000	0.1%	34	Utah	289,480,000	0.5%
6	Ohio	2,428,639,000	4.1%	35	New Mexico	279,454,000	0.5%
30	Oklahoma	394,296,000	0.7%	36	Arkansas	268,558,000	0.5%
24	Oregon	613,883,000	1.0%	37	Nebraska	216,360,000	0.4%
8	Pennsylvania	2,240,936,000	3.8%	38	Hawaii	208,544,000	0.4%
41	Rhode Island	136,243,000	0.2%	39	Idaho	181,725,000	0.3%
27	South Carolina	476,404,000	0.8%	40	New Hampshire	151,592,000	0.3%
47	South Dakota	84,619,000	0.1%	41	Rhode Island	136,243,000	0.2%
20	Tennessee	813,189,000	1.4%	42	West Virginia	133,665,000	0.2%
4	Texas	3,819,142,000	6.5%	43	Maine	128,560,000	0.2%
34	Utah	289,480,000	0.5%	44	Alaska	109,652,000	0.2%
50	Vermont	35,542,000	0.1%	45	Montana	104,683,000	0.2%
12	Virginia	1,163,497,000	2.0%	46	Wyoming	91,284,000	0.2%
11	Washington	1,229,308,000	2.1%	47	South Dakota	84,619,000	0.1%
42	West Virginia	133,665,000	0.2%	48	Delaware	78,327,000	0.1%
13	Wisconsin	1,154,841,000	2.0%	49	North Dakota	65,259,000	0.1%
46	Wyoming	91,284,000	0.2%	50	Vermont	35,542,000	0.1%
					District of Columbia	677,937,000	1.2%

Source: Morgan Quitno Press using data from U.S. Bureau of the Census
   "Government Finances: 1994-1995" (1998) (http://www.census.gov/govs/www/esti95.html)
*Direct general expenditures. Includes Police Protection, Corrections and Judicial and Legal Services.

Per Capita Local Government Expenditures for Justice Activities in 1995

National Per Capita = $223.47*

ALPHA ORDER

RANK	STATE	PER CAPITA
37	Alabama	$130.61
20	Alaska	182.27
6	Arizona	254.21
45	Arkansas	108.29
2	California	346.05
11	Colorado	212.31
33	Connecticut	137.65
43	Delaware	108.98
5	Florida	288.93
21	Georgia	181.82
23	Hawaii	176.27
27	Idaho	156.18
7	Illinois	231.52
38	Indiana	129.38
34	Iowa	134.43
26	Kansas	156.22
48	Kentucky	96.22
17	Louisiana	190.67
46	Maine	104.25
18	Maryland	186.15
22	Massachusetts	179.76
12	Michigan	208.53
14	Minnesota	200.28
44	Mississippi	108.77
29	Missouri	152.00
40	Montana	120.54
35	Nebraska	132.30
3	Nevada	345.81
36	New Hampshire	132.26
4	New Jersey	302.96
25	New Mexico	165.97
1	New York	356.81
31	North Carolina	138.75
47	North Dakota	101.75
10	Ohio	218.06
41	Oklahoma	120.53
15	Oregon	195.43
19	Pennsylvania	186.13
32	Rhode Island	137.72
39	South Carolina	128.78
42	South Dakota	115.20
28	Tennessee	155.33
13	Texas	204.30
30	Utah	145.36
50	Vermont	61.02
24	Virginia	176.24
8	Washington	226.26
49	West Virginia	73.38
9	Wisconsin	224.81
16	Wyoming	190.83

RANK ORDER

RANK	STATE	PER CAPITA
1	New York	$356.81
2	California	346.05
3	Nevada	345.81
4	New Jersey	302.96
5	Florida	288.93
6	Arizona	254.21
7	Illinois	231.52
8	Washington	226.26
9	Wisconsin	224.81
10	Ohio	218.06
11	Colorado	212.31
12	Michigan	208.53
13	Texas	204.30
14	Minnesota	200.28
15	Oregon	195.43
16	Wyoming	190.83
17	Louisiana	190.67
18	Maryland	186.15
19	Pennsylvania	186.13
20	Alaska	182.27
21	Georgia	181.82
22	Massachusetts	179.76
23	Hawaii	176.27
24	Virginia	176.24
25	New Mexico	165.97
26	Kansas	156.22
27	Idaho	156.18
28	Tennessee	155.33
29	Missouri	152.00
30	Utah	145.36
31	North Carolina	138.75
32	Rhode Island	137.72
33	Connecticut	137.65
34	Iowa	134.43
35	Nebraska	132.30
36	New Hampshire	132.26
37	Alabama	130.61
38	Indiana	129.38
39	South Carolina	128.78
40	Montana	120.54
41	Oklahoma	120.53
42	South Dakota	115.20
43	Delaware	108.98
44	Mississippi	108.77
45	Arkansas	108.29
46	Maine	104.25
47	North Dakota	101.75
48	Kentucky	96.22
49	West Virginia	73.38
50	Vermont	61.02
	District of Columbia	1,227.11

Source: Morgan Quitno Press using data from U.S. Bureau of the Census
"Government Finances: 1994-1995" (1998) (http://www.census.gov/govs/www/esti95.html)
*Direct general expenditures. Includes Police Protection, Corrections and Judicial and Legal Services.

Local Government Expenditures for Justice Activities
As a Percent of All Direct General Expenditures in 1995
National Percent = 9.0% of Direct General Expenditures*

ALPHA ORDER

RANK	STATE	PERCENT
29	Alabama	7.1
48	Alaska	4.8
4	Arizona	11.2
26	Arkansas	7.6
3	California	11.3
23	Colorado	8.0
43	Connecticut	5.8
38	Delaware	6.1
4	Florida	11.2
20	Georgia	8.1
1	Hawaii	14.0
24	Idaho	7.8
7	Illinois	9.9
35	Indiana	6.3
43	Iowa	5.8
32	Kansas	6.7
41	Kentucky	5.9
8	Louisiana	9.7
46	Maine	5.6
19	Maryland	8.2
13	Massachusetts	8.6
16	Michigan	8.3
35	Minnesota	6.3
46	Mississippi	5.6
16	Missouri	8.3
35	Montana	6.3
41	Nebraska	5.9
2	Nevada	12.8
30	New Hampshire	7.0
6	New Jersey	10.2
20	New Mexico	8.1
13	New York	8.6
33	North Carolina	6.5
45	North Dakota	5.7
10	Ohio	9.5
33	Oklahoma	6.5
24	Oregon	7.8
11	Pennsylvania	8.7
28	Rhode Island	7.5
30	South Carolina	7.0
38	South Dakota	6.1
16	Tennessee	8.3
8	Texas	9.7
26	Utah	7.6
50	Vermont	3.7
15	Virginia	8.5
11	Washington	8.7
49	West Virginia	4.5
20	Wisconsin	8.1
38	Wyoming	6.1

RANK ORDER

RANK	STATE	PERCENT
1	Hawaii	14.0
2	Nevada	12.8
3	California	11.3
4	Arizona	11.2
4	Florida	11.2
6	New Jersey	10.2
7	Illinois	9.9
8	Louisiana	9.7
8	Texas	9.7
10	Ohio	9.5
11	Pennsylvania	8.7
11	Washington	8.7
13	Massachusetts	8.6
13	New York	8.6
15	Virginia	8.5
16	Michigan	8.3
16	Missouri	8.3
16	Tennessee	8.3
19	Maryland	8.2
20	Georgia	8.1
20	New Mexico	8.1
20	Wisconsin	8.1
23	Colorado	8.0
24	Idaho	7.8
24	Oregon	7.8
26	Arkansas	7.6
26	Utah	7.6
28	Rhode Island	7.5
29	Alabama	7.1
30	New Hampshire	7.0
30	South Carolina	7.0
32	Kansas	6.7
33	North Carolina	6.5
33	Oklahoma	6.5
35	Indiana	6.3
35	Minnesota	6.3
35	Montana	6.3
38	Delaware	6.1
38	South Dakota	6.1
38	Wyoming	6.1
41	Kentucky	5.9
41	Nebraska	5.9
43	Connecticut	5.8
43	Iowa	5.8
45	North Dakota	5.7
46	Maine	5.6
46	Mississippi	5.6
48	Alaska	4.8
49	West Virginia	4.5
50	Vermont	3.7

District of Columbia   15.8

Source: Morgan Quitno Press using data from U.S. Bureau of the Census
      "Government Finances: 1994-1995" (1998) (http://www.census.gov/govs/www/esti95.html)
*Includes Police Protection, Corrections and Judicial and Legal Services.

State and Local Government Expenditures for Police Protection in 1995

National Total = $41,054,532,000*

ALPHA ORDER

RANK	STATE	EXPENDITURES	% of USA
25	Alabama	$478,062,000	1.2%
40	Alaska	148,729,000	0.4%
17	Arizona	712,639,000	1.7%
36	Arkansas	230,747,000	0.6%
1	California	6,411,663,000	15.6%
22	Colorado	569,411,000	1.4%
24	Connecticut	521,593,000	1.3%
45	Delaware	116,334,000	0.3%
3	Florida	2,871,260,000	7.0%
12	Georgia	902,064,000	2.2%
37	Hawaii	192,855,000	0.5%
41	Idaho	145,292,000	0.4%
5	Illinois	2,109,244,000	5.1%
23	Indiana	553,031,000	1.3%
30	Iowa	348,514,000	0.8%
31	Kansas	344,243,000	0.8%
29	Kentucky	354,526,000	0.9%
19	Louisiana	629,702,000	1.5%
44	Maine	119,692,000	0.3%
15	Maryland	816,841,000	2.0%
10	Massachusetts	1,001,450,000	2.4%
8	Michigan	1,397,322,000	3.4%
20	Minnesota	611,048,000	1.5%
33	Mississippi	264,883,000	0.6%
18	Missouri	664,251,000	1.6%
46	Montana	88,000,000	0.2%
38	Nebraska	172,783,000	0.4%
32	Nevada	304,551,000	0.7%
42	New Hampshire	139,881,000	0.3%
6	New Jersey	1,765,305,000	4.3%
34	New Mexico	253,994,000	0.6%
2	New York	4,270,526,000	10.4%
11	North Carolina	917,997,000	2.2%
50	North Dakota	50,282,000	0.1%
7	Ohio	1,593,981,000	3.9%
28	Oklahoma	373,681,000	0.9%
26	Oregon	467,687,000	1.1%
9	Pennsylvania	1,392,650,000	3.4%
39	Rhode Island	155,700,000	0.4%
27	South Carolina	404,381,000	1.0%
47	South Dakota	73,546,000	0.2%
21	Tennessee	589,397,000	1.4%
4	Texas	2,357,577,000	5.7%
35	Utah	237,814,000	0.6%
49	Vermont	60,439,000	0.1%
13	Virginia	851,784,000	2.1%
16	Washington	759,912,000	1.9%
43	West Virginia	123,576,000	0.3%
14	Wisconsin	823,822,000	2.0%
48	Wyoming	71,462,000	0.2%

RANK ORDER

RANK	STATE	EXPENDITURES	% of USA
1	California	$6,411,663,000	15.6%
2	New York	4,270,526,000	10.4%
3	Florida	2,871,260,000	7.0%
4	Texas	2,357,577,000	5.7%
5	Illinois	2,109,244,000	5.1%
6	New Jersey	1,765,305,000	4.3%
7	Ohio	1,593,981,000	3.9%
8	Michigan	1,397,322,000	3.4%
9	Pennsylvania	1,392,650,000	3.4%
10	Massachusetts	1,001,450,000	2.4%
11	North Carolina	917,997,000	2.2%
12	Georgia	902,064,000	2.2%
13	Virginia	851,784,000	2.1%
14	Wisconsin	823,822,000	2.0%
15	Maryland	816,841,000	2.0%
16	Washington	759,912,000	1.9%
17	Arizona	712,639,000	1.7%
18	Missouri	664,251,000	1.6%
19	Louisiana	629,702,000	1.5%
20	Minnesota	611,048,000	1.5%
21	Tennessee	589,397,000	1.4%
22	Colorado	569,411,000	1.4%
23	Indiana	553,031,000	1.3%
24	Connecticut	521,593,000	1.3%
25	Alabama	478,062,000	1.2%
26	Oregon	467,687,000	1.1%
27	South Carolina	404,381,000	1.0%
28	Oklahoma	373,681,000	0.9%
29	Kentucky	354,526,000	0.9%
30	Iowa	348,514,000	0.8%
31	Kansas	344,243,000	0.8%
32	Nevada	304,551,000	0.7%
33	Mississippi	264,883,000	0.6%
34	New Mexico	253,994,000	0.6%
35	Utah	237,814,000	0.6%
36	Arkansas	230,747,000	0.6%
37	Hawaii	192,855,000	0.5%
38	Nebraska	172,783,000	0.4%
39	Rhode Island	155,700,000	0.4%
40	Alaska	148,729,000	0.4%
41	Idaho	145,292,000	0.4%
42	New Hampshire	139,881,000	0.3%
43	West Virginia	123,576,000	0.3%
44	Maine	119,692,000	0.3%
45	Delaware	116,334,000	0.3%
46	Montana	88,000,000	0.2%
47	South Dakota	73,546,000	0.2%
48	Wyoming	71,462,000	0.2%
49	Vermont	60,439,000	0.1%
50	North Dakota	50,282,000	0.1%
	District of Columbia	238,408,000	0.6%

Source: Morgan Quitno Press using data from U.S. Bureau of the Census
"Government Finances: 1994-1995" (1998) (http://www.census.gov/govs/www/esti95.html)
Direct general expenditures.

Per Capita State & Local Government Expenditures for Police Protection: 1995

National Per Capita = $156.24*

ALPHA ORDER

ALPHA ORDER

RANK	STATE	PER CAPITA
38	Alabama	$111.95
1	Alaska	247.23
8	Arizona	165.46
47	Arkansas	93.04
4	California	203.72
16	Colorado	152.32
14	Connecticut	159.91
12	Delaware	161.87
5	Florida	202.48
29	Georgia	125.49
10	Hawaii	163.01
30	Idaho	124.87
7	Illinois	177.76
46	Indiana	95.57
32	Iowa	122.69
24	Kansas	133.71
48	Kentucky	91.94
20	Louisiana	145.49
45	Maine	97.06
11	Maryland	162.61
9	Massachusetts	165.31
21	Michigan	144.61
25	Minnesota	132.69
44	Mississippi	98.45
31	Missouri	124.45
42	Montana	101.33
40	Nebraska	105.65
6	Nevada	199.27
33	New Hampshire	122.04
3	New Jersey	221.71
17	New Mexico	150.85
2	New York	235.36
27	North Carolina	127.75
49	North Dakota	78.40
22	Ohio	143.12
36	Oklahoma	114.23
19	Oregon	148.89
35	Pennsylvania	115.67
15	Rhode Island	157.38
39	South Carolina	109.31
43	South Dakota	100.13
37	Tennessee	112.59
28	Texas	126.11
34	Utah	119.41
41	Vermont	103.77
26	Virginia	129.03
23	Washington	139.87
50	West Virginia	67.84
13	Wisconsin	160.37
18	Wyoming	149.39

RANK ORDER

RANK	STATE	PER CAPITA
1	Alaska	$247.23
2	New York	235.36
3	New Jersey	221.71
4	California	203.72
5	Florida	202.48
6	Nevada	199.27
7	Illinois	177.76
8	Arizona	165.46
9	Massachusetts	165.31
10	Hawaii	163.01
11	Maryland	162.61
12	Delaware	161.87
13	Wisconsin	160.37
14	Connecticut	159.91
15	Rhode Island	157.38
16	Colorado	152.32
17	New Mexico	150.85
18	Wyoming	149.39
19	Oregon	148.89
20	Louisiana	145.49
21	Michigan	144.61
22	Ohio	143.12
23	Washington	139.87
24	Kansas	133.71
25	Minnesota	132.69
26	Virginia	129.03
27	North Carolina	127.75
28	Texas	126.11
29	Georgia	125.49
30	Idaho	124.87
31	Missouri	124.45
32	Iowa	122.69
33	New Hampshire	122.04
34	Utah	119.41
35	Pennsylvania	115.67
36	Oklahoma	114.23
37	Tennessee	112.59
38	Alabama	111.95
39	South Carolina	109.31
40	Nebraska	105.65
41	Vermont	103.77
42	Montana	101.33
43	South Dakota	100.13
44	Mississippi	98.45
45	Maine	97.06
46	Indiana	95.57
47	Arkansas	93.04
48	Kentucky	91.94
49	North Dakota	78.40
50	West Virginia	67.84
	District of Columbia	431.53

Source: Morgan Quitno Press using data from U.S. Bureau of the Census
"Government Finances: 1994-1995" (1998) (http://www.census.gov/govs/www/esti95.html)
*Direct general expenditures.

State and Local Government Expenditures for Police Protection As a Percent of All Direct General Expenditures in 1995
National Percent = 3.6% of Direct General Expenditures

ALPHA ORDER

RANK	STATE	PERCENT
31	Alabama	3.0
46	Alaska	2.4
3	Arizona	4.5
32	Arkansas	2.9
4	California	4.4
9	Colorado	3.6
26	Connecticut	3.1
21	Delaware	3.3
1	Florida	5.0
26	Georgia	3.1
32	Hawaii	2.9
14	Idaho	3.4
5	Illinois	4.3
40	Indiana	2.6
32	Iowa	2.9
14	Kansas	3.4
40	Kentucky	2.6
14	Louisiana	3.4
48	Maine	2.3
7	Maryland	3.9
14	Massachusetts	3.4
14	Michigan	3.4
40	Minnesota	2.6
38	Mississippi	2.7
8	Missouri	3.7
45	Montana	2.5
40	Nebraska	2.6
2	Nevada	4.7
26	New Hampshire	3.1
6	New Jersey	4.2
14	New Mexico	3.4
9	New York	3.6
21	North Carolina	3.3
49	North Dakota	1.8
9	Ohio	3.6
21	Oklahoma	3.3
24	Oregon	3.2
36	Pennsylvania	2.8
24	Rhode Island	3.2
36	South Carolina	2.8
40	South Dakota	2.6
26	Tennessee	3.1
13	Texas	3.5
26	Utah	3.1
46	Vermont	2.4
14	Virginia	3.4
32	Washington	2.9
50	West Virginia	1.7
9	Wisconsin	3.6
38	Wyoming	2.7

RANK ORDER

RANK	STATE	PERCENT
1	Florida	5.0
2	Nevada	4.7
3	Arizona	4.5
4	California	4.4
5	Illinois	4.3
6	New Jersey	4.2
7	Maryland	3.9
8	Missouri	3.7
9	Colorado	3.6
9	New York	3.6
9	Ohio	3.6
9	Wisconsin	3.6
13	Texas	3.5
14	Idaho	3.4
14	Kansas	3.4
14	Louisiana	3.4
14	Massachusetts	3.4
14	Michigan	3.4
14	New Mexico	3.4
14	Virginia	3.4
21	Delaware	3.3
21	North Carolina	3.3
21	Oklahoma	3.3
24	Oregon	3.2
24	Rhode Island	3.2
26	Connecticut	3.1
26	Georgia	3.1
26	New Hampshire	3.1
26	Tennessee	3.1
26	Utah	3.1
31	Alabama	3.0
32	Arkansas	2.9
32	Hawaii	2.9
32	Iowa	2.9
32	Washington	2.9
36	Pennsylvania	2.8
36	South Carolina	2.8
38	Mississippi	2.7
38	Wyoming	2.7
40	Indiana	2.6
40	Kentucky	2.6
40	Minnesota	2.6
40	Nebraska	2.6
40	South Dakota	2.6
45	Montana	2.5
46	Alaska	2.4
46	Vermont	2.4
48	Maine	2.3
49	North Dakota	1.8
50	West Virginia	1.7

| | District of Columbia | 5.5 |

Source: Morgan Quitno Press using data from U.S. Bureau of the Census
"Government Finances: 1994-1995" (1998) (http://www.census.gov/govs/www/esti95.html)

State Government Expenditures for Police Protection in 1995

National Total = $5,734,937,000*

ALPHA ORDER

RANK	STATE	EXPENDITURES	% of USA
25	Alabama	$72,879,000	1.3%
32	Alaska	48,931,000	0.9%
19	Arizona	105,703,000	1.8%
29	Arkansas	49,435,000	0.9%
1	California	811,625,000	14.2%
30	Colorado	49,039,000	0.9%
20	Connecticut	105,522,000	1.8%
35	Delaware	45,148,000	0.8%
4	Florida	278,535,000	4.9%
14	Georgia	134,868,000	2.4%
48	Hawaii	15,660,000	0.3%
42	Idaho	27,908,000	0.5%
7	Illinois	236,350,000	4.1%
15	Indiana	116,109,000	2.0%
28	Iowa	53,816,000	0.9%
36	Kansas	41,428,000	0.7%
21	Kentucky	101,363,000	1.8%
18	Louisiana	110,172,000	1.9%
41	Maine	28,525,000	0.5%
12	Maryland	161,569,000	2.8%
8	Massachusetts	210,649,000	3.7%
9	Michigan	199,395,000	3.5%
26	Minnesota	70,813,000	1.2%
33	Mississippi	48,820,000	0.9%
22	Missouri	98,325,000	1.7%
46	Montana	20,794,000	0.4%
39	Nebraska	34,095,000	0.6%
40	Nevada	32,678,000	0.6%
45	New Hampshire	25,991,000	0.5%
5	New Jersey	249,879,000	4.4%
31	New Mexico	48,972,000	0.9%
3	New York	337,207,000	5.9%
10	North Carolina	193,349,000	3.4%
50	North Dakota	6,636,000	0.1%
11	Ohio	178,102,000	3.1%
34	Oklahoma	47,727,000	0.8%
23	Oregon	89,706,000	1.6%
2	Pennsylvania	341,375,000	6.0%
43	Rhode Island	27,774,000	0.5%
16	South Carolina	115,146,000	2.0%
47	South Dakota	15,695,000	0.3%
24	Tennessee	80,422,000	1.4%
6	Texas	239,658,000	4.2%
38	Utah	36,543,000	0.6%
44	Vermont	26,842,000	0.5%
13	Virginia	148,714,000	2.6%
17	Washington	113,033,000	2.0%
37	West Virginia	37,160,000	0.6%
27	Wisconsin	54,514,000	1.0%
49	Wyoming	10,338,000	0.2%

RANK ORDER

RANK	STATE	EXPENDITURES	% of USA
1	California	$811,625,000	14.2%
2	Pennsylvania	341,375,000	6.0%
3	New York	337,207,000	5.9%
4	Florida	278,535,000	4.9%
5	New Jersey	249,879,000	4.4%
6	Texas	239,658,000	4.2%
7	Illinois	236,350,000	4.1%
8	Massachusetts	210,649,000	3.7%
9	Michigan	199,395,000	3.5%
10	North Carolina	193,349,000	3.4%
11	Ohio	178,102,000	3.1%
12	Maryland	161,569,000	2.8%
13	Virginia	148,714,000	2.6%
14	Georgia	134,868,000	2.4%
15	Indiana	116,109,000	2.0%
16	South Carolina	115,146,000	2.0%
17	Washington	113,033,000	2.0%
18	Louisiana	110,172,000	1.9%
19	Arizona	105,703,000	1.8%
20	Connecticut	105,522,000	1.8%
21	Kentucky	101,363,000	1.8%
22	Missouri	98,325,000	1.7%
23	Oregon	89,706,000	1.6%
24	Tennessee	80,422,000	1.4%
25	Alabama	72,879,000	1.3%
26	Minnesota	70,813,000	1.2%
27	Wisconsin	54,514,000	1.0%
28	Iowa	53,816,000	0.9%
29	Arkansas	49,435,000	0.9%
30	Colorado	49,039,000	0.9%
31	New Mexico	48,972,000	0.9%
32	Alaska	48,931,000	0.9%
33	Mississippi	48,820,000	0.9%
34	Oklahoma	47,727,000	0.8%
35	Delaware	45,148,000	0.8%
36	Kansas	41,428,000	0.7%
37	West Virginia	37,160,000	0.6%
38	Utah	36,543,000	0.6%
39	Nebraska	34,095,000	0.6%
40	Nevada	32,678,000	0.6%
41	Maine	28,525,000	0.5%
42	Idaho	27,908,000	0.5%
43	Rhode Island	27,774,000	0.5%
44	Vermont	26,842,000	0.5%
45	New Hampshire	25,991,000	0.5%
46	Montana	20,794,000	0.4%
47	South Dakota	15,695,000	0.3%
48	Hawaii	15,660,000	0.3%
49	Wyoming	10,338,000	0.2%
50	North Dakota	6,636,000	0.1%

District of Columbia** NA NA

Source: Morgan Quitno Press using data from U.S. Bureau of the Census
    "Government Finances: 1994-1995" (1998) (http://www.census.gov/govs/www/esti95.html)
*Direct general expenditures.
**Not applicable.

Per Capita State Government Expenditures for Police Protection in 1995

National Per Capita = $21.83*

ALPHA ORDER

ALPHA ORDER

RANK	STATE	PER CAPITA
40	Alabama	$17.07
1	Alaska	81.34
17	Arizona	24.54
31	Arkansas	19.93
15	California	25.79
47	Colorado	13.12
5	Connecticut	32.35
2	Delaware	62.82
33	Florida	19.64
35	Georgia	18.76
46	Hawaii	13.24
18	Idaho	23.99
32	Illinois	19.92
30	Indiana	20.07
34	Iowa	18.95
41	Kansas	16.09
14	Kentucky	26.29
16	Louisiana	25.45
20	Maine	23.13
6	Maryland	32.16
4	Massachusetts	34.77
28	Michigan	20.64
43	Minnesota	15.38
39	Mississippi	18.15
37	Missouri	18.42
19	Montana	23.94
26	Nebraska	20.85
24	Nevada	21.38
21	New Hampshire	22.68
7	New Jersey	31.38
9	New Mexico	29.08
36	New York	18.58
13	North Carolina	26.91
50	North Dakota	10.35
42	Ohio	15.99
45	Oklahoma	14.59
10	Oregon	28.56
11	Pennsylvania	28.35
12	Rhode Island	28.07
8	South Carolina	31.13
25	South Dakota	21.37
44	Tennessee	15.36
48	Texas	12.82
38	Utah	18.35
3	Vermont	46.09
22	Virginia	22.53
27	Washington	20.80
29	West Virginia	20.40
49	Wisconsin	10.61
23	Wyoming	21.61

RANK ORDER

RANK	STATE	PER CAPITA
1	Alaska	$81.34
2	Delaware	62.82
3	Vermont	46.09
4	Massachusetts	34.77
5	Connecticut	32.35
6	Maryland	32.16
7	New Jersey	31.38
8	South Carolina	31.13
9	New Mexico	29.08
10	Oregon	28.56
11	Pennsylvania	28.35
12	Rhode Island	28.07
13	North Carolina	26.91
14	Kentucky	26.29
15	California	25.79
16	Louisiana	25.45
17	Arizona	24.54
18	Idaho	23.99
19	Montana	23.94
20	Maine	23.13
21	New Hampshire	22.68
22	Virginia	22.53
23	Wyoming	21.61
24	Nevada	21.38
25	South Dakota	21.37
26	Nebraska	20.85
27	Washington	20.80
28	Michigan	20.64
29	West Virginia	20.40
30	Indiana	20.07
31	Arkansas	19.93
32	Illinois	19.92
33	Florida	19.64
34	Iowa	18.95
35	Georgia	18.76
36	New York	18.58
37	Missouri	18.42
38	Utah	18.35
39	Mississippi	18.15
40	Alabama	17.07
41	Kansas	16.09
42	Ohio	15.99
43	Minnesota	15.38
44	Tennessee	15.36
45	Oklahoma	14.59
46	Hawaii	13.24
47	Colorado	13.12
48	Texas	12.82
49	Wisconsin	10.61
50	North Dakota	10.35

District of Columbia**   NA

Source: Morgan Quitno Press using data from U.S. Bureau of the Census
"Government Finances: 1994-1995" (1998) (http://www.census.gov/govs/www/esti95.html)
*Direct general expenditures.
**Not applicable.

State Government Expenditures for Police Protection
As a Percent of All Direct General Expenditures in 1995
National Percent = 1.2% of Direct General Expenditures

ALPHA ORDER

RANK	STATE	PERCENT
37	Alabama	0.9
18	Alaska	1.2
2	Arizona	1.7
23	Arkansas	1.1
2	California	1.7
37	Colorado	0.9
23	Connecticut	1.1
1	Delaware	2.1
13	Florida	1.3
31	Georgia	1.0
50	Hawaii	0.3
8	Idaho	1.4
23	Illinois	1.1
13	Indiana	1.3
31	Iowa	1.0
31	Kansas	1.0
8	Kentucky	1.4
23	Louisiana	1.1
31	Maine	1.0
5	Maryland	1.6
18	Massachusetts	1.2
18	Michigan	1.2
45	Minnesota	0.8
23	Mississippi	1.1
18	Missouri	1.2
23	Montana	1.1
18	Nebraska	1.2
8	Nevada	1.4
23	New Hampshire	1.1
13	New Jersey	1.3
13	New Mexico	1.3
45	New York	0.8
5	North Carolina	1.6
49	North Dakota	0.4
31	Ohio	1.0
37	Oklahoma	0.9
8	Oregon	1.4
8	Pennsylvania	1.4
37	Rhode Island	0.9
7	South Carolina	1.5
23	South Dakota	1.1
37	Tennessee	0.9
45	Texas	0.8
31	Utah	1.0
2	Vermont	1.7
13	Virginia	1.3
37	Washington	0.9
37	West Virginia	0.9
48	Wisconsin	0.6
37	Wyoming	0.9

RANK ORDER

RANK	STATE	PERCENT
1	Delaware	2.1
2	Arizona	1.7
2	California	1.7
2	Vermont	1.7
5	Maryland	1.6
5	North Carolina	1.6
7	South Carolina	1.5
8	Idaho	1.4
8	Kentucky	1.4
8	Nevada	1.4
8	Oregon	1.4
8	Pennsylvania	1.4
13	Florida	1.3
13	Indiana	1.3
13	New Jersey	1.3
13	New Mexico	1.3
13	Virginia	1.3
18	Alaska	1.2
18	Massachusetts	1.2
18	Michigan	1.2
18	Missouri	1.2
18	Nebraska	1.2
23	Arkansas	1.1
23	Connecticut	1.1
23	Illinois	1.1
23	Louisiana	1.1
23	Mississippi	1.1
23	Montana	1.1
23	New Hampshire	1.1
23	South Dakota	1.1
31	Georgia	1.0
31	Iowa	1.0
31	Kansas	1.0
31	Maine	1.0
31	Ohio	1.0
31	Utah	1.0
37	Alabama	0.9
37	Colorado	0.9
37	Oklahoma	0.9
37	Rhode Island	0.9
37	Tennessee	0.9
37	Washington	0.9
37	West Virginia	0.9
37	Wyoming	0.9
45	Minnesota	0.8
45	New York	0.8
45	Texas	0.8
48	Wisconsin	0.6
49	North Dakota	0.4
50	Hawaii	0.3
	District of Columbia*	NA

Source: Morgan Quitno Press using data from U.S. Bureau of the Census
    "Government Finances: 1994-1995" (1998) (http://www.census.gov/govs/www/esti95.html)
*Not applicable.

Local Government Expenditures for Police Protection in 1995

National Total = $35,319,595,000*

ALPHA ORDER

RANK	STATE	EXPENDITURES	% of USA
25	Alabama	$405,183,000	1.1%
42	Alaska	99,798,000	0.3%
17	Arizona	606,936,000	1.7%
36	Arkansas	181,312,000	0.5%
1	California	5,600,038,000	15.9%
20	Colorado	520,372,000	1.5%
24	Connecticut	416,071,000	1.2%
45	Delaware	71,186,000	0.2%
3	Florida	2,592,725,000	7.3%
12	Georgia	767,196,000	2.2%
37	Hawaii	177,195,000	0.5%
40	Idaho	117,384,000	0.3%
5	Illinois	1,872,894,000	5.3%
23	Indiana	436,922,000	1.2%
29	Iowa	294,698,000	0.8%
28	Kansas	302,815,000	0.9%
32	Kentucky	253,163,000	0.7%
21	Louisiana	519,530,000	1.5%
43	Maine	91,167,000	0.3%
15	Maryland	655,272,000	1.9%
10	Massachusetts	790,801,000	2.2%
8	Michigan	1,197,927,000	3.4%
19	Minnesota	540,235,000	1.5%
33	Mississippi	216,063,000	0.6%
18	Missouri	565,926,000	1.6%
46	Montana	67,206,000	0.2%
38	Nebraska	138,688,000	0.4%
31	Nevada	271,873,000	0.8%
41	New Hampshire	113,890,000	0.3%
6	New Jersey	1,515,426,000	4.3%
34	New Mexico	205,022,000	0.6%
2	New York	3,933,319,000	11.1%
13	North Carolina	724,648,000	2.1%
49	North Dakota	43,646,000	0.1%
7	Ohio	1,415,879,000	4.0%
27	Oklahoma	325,954,000	0.9%
26	Oregon	377,981,000	1.1%
9	Pennsylvania	1,051,275,000	3.0%
39	Rhode Island	127,926,000	0.4%
30	South Carolina	289,235,000	0.8%
48	South Dakota	57,851,000	0.2%
22	Tennessee	508,975,000	1.4%
4	Texas	2,117,919,000	6.0%
35	Utah	201,271,000	0.6%
50	Vermont	33,597,000	0.1%
14	Virginia	703,070,000	2.0%
16	Washington	646,879,000	1.8%
44	West Virginia	86,416,000	0.2%
11	Wisconsin	769,308,000	2.2%
47	Wyoming	61,124,000	0.2%

RANK ORDER

RANK	STATE	EXPENDITURES	% of USA
1	California	$5,600,038,000	15.9%
2	New York	3,933,319,000	11.1%
3	Florida	2,592,725,000	7.3%
4	Texas	2,117,919,000	6.0%
5	Illinois	1,872,894,000	5.3%
6	New Jersey	1,515,426,000	4.3%
7	Ohio	1,415,879,000	4.0%
8	Michigan	1,197,927,000	3.4%
9	Pennsylvania	1,051,275,000	3.0%
10	Massachusetts	790,801,000	2.2%
11	Wisconsin	769,308,000	2.2%
12	Georgia	767,196,000	2.2%
13	North Carolina	724,648,000	2.1%
14	Virginia	703,070,000	2.0%
15	Maryland	655,272,000	1.9%
16	Washington	646,879,000	1.8%
17	Arizona	606,936,000	1.7%
18	Missouri	565,926,000	1.6%
19	Minnesota	540,235,000	1.5%
20	Colorado	520,372,000	1.5%
21	Louisiana	519,530,000	1.5%
22	Tennessee	508,975,000	1.4%
23	Indiana	436,922,000	1.2%
24	Connecticut	416,071,000	1.2%
25	Alabama	405,183,000	1.1%
26	Oregon	377,981,000	1.1%
27	Oklahoma	325,954,000	0.9%
28	Kansas	302,815,000	0.9%
29	Iowa	294,698,000	0.8%
30	South Carolina	289,235,000	0.8%
31	Nevada	271,873,000	0.8%
32	Kentucky	253,163,000	0.7%
33	Mississippi	216,063,000	0.6%
34	New Mexico	205,022,000	0.6%
35	Utah	201,271,000	0.6%
36	Arkansas	181,312,000	0.5%
37	Hawaii	177,195,000	0.5%
38	Nebraska	138,688,000	0.4%
39	Rhode Island	127,926,000	0.4%
40	Idaho	117,384,000	0.3%
41	New Hampshire	113,890,000	0.3%
42	Alaska	99,798,000	0.3%
43	Maine	91,167,000	0.3%
44	West Virginia	86,416,000	0.2%
45	Delaware	71,186,000	0.2%
46	Montana	67,206,000	0.2%
47	Wyoming	61,124,000	0.2%
48	South Dakota	57,851,000	0.2%
49	North Dakota	43,646,000	0.1%
50	Vermont	33,597,000	0.1%
	District of Columbia	238,408,000	0.7%

Source: Morgan Quitno Press using data from U.S. Bureau of the Census
"Government Finances: 1994-1995" (1998) (http://www.census.gov/govs/www/esti95.html)
*Direct general expenditures.

Per Capita Local Government Expenditures for Police Protection in 1995

National Per Capita = $134.42*

ALPHA ORDER

RANK	STATE	PER CAPITA
37	Alabama	$94.88
6	Alaska	165.89
10	Arizona	140.92
46	Arkansas	73.11
4	California	177.94
11	Colorado	139.20
16	Connecticut	127.56
35	Delaware	99.05
3	Florida	182.84
26	Georgia	106.73
8	Hawaii	149.78
31	Idaho	100.89
7	Illinois	157.84
44	Indiana	75.51
29	Iowa	103.74
23	Kansas	117.62
48	Kentucky	65.65
21	Louisiana	120.03
45	Maine	73.93
13	Maryland	130.44
12	Massachusetts	130.54
18	Michigan	123.97
24	Minnesota	117.32
40	Mississippi	80.31
28	Missouri	106.03
43	Montana	77.38
39	Nebraska	84.80
5	Nevada	177.89
34	New Hampshire	99.36
2	New Jersey	190.33
19	New Mexico	121.76
1	New York	216.77
32	North Carolina	100.84
47	North Dakota	68.05
17	Ohio	127.13
33	Oklahoma	99.64
20	Oregon	120.33
38	Pennsylvania	87.32
14	Rhode Island	129.31
42	South Carolina	78.19
41	South Dakota	78.76
36	Tennessee	97.22
25	Texas	113.29
30	Utah	101.07
49	Vermont	57.68
27	Virginia	106.50
22	Washington	119.06
50	West Virginia	47.44
9	Wisconsin	149.76
15	Wyoming	127.78

RANK ORDER

RANK	STATE	PER CAPITA
1	New York	$216.77
2	New Jersey	190.33
3	Florida	182.84
4	California	177.94
5	Nevada	177.89
6	Alaska	165.89
7	Illinois	157.84
8	Hawaii	149.78
9	Wisconsin	149.76
10	Arizona	140.92
11	Colorado	139.20
12	Massachusetts	130.54
13	Maryland	130.44
14	Rhode Island	129.31
15	Wyoming	127.78
16	Connecticut	127.56
17	Ohio	127.13
18	Michigan	123.97
19	New Mexico	121.76
20	Oregon	120.33
21	Louisiana	120.03
22	Washington	119.06
23	Kansas	117.62
24	Minnesota	117.32
25	Texas	113.29
26	Georgia	106.73
27	Virginia	106.50
28	Missouri	106.03
29	Iowa	103.74
30	Utah	101.07
31	Idaho	100.89
32	North Carolina	100.84
33	Oklahoma	99.64
34	New Hampshire	99.36
35	Delaware	99.05
36	Tennessee	97.22
37	Alabama	94.88
38	Pennsylvania	87.32
39	Nebraska	84.80
40	Mississippi	80.31
41	South Dakota	78.76
42	South Carolina	78.19
43	Montana	77.38
44	Indiana	75.51
45	Maine	73.93
46	Arkansas	73.11
47	North Dakota	68.05
48	Kentucky	65.65
49	Vermont	57.68
50	West Virginia	47.44
	District of Columbia	431.53

Source: Morgan Quitno Press using data from U.S. Bureau of the Census
    "Government Finances: 1994-1995" (1998) (http://www.census.gov/govs/www/esti95.html)
*Direct general expenditures.

Local Government Expenditures for Police Protection
As a Percent of All Direct General Expenditures in 1995
National Percent = 5.4% of Direct General Expenditures

RANK	STATE	PERCENT
22	Alabama	5.2
36	Alaska	4.3
7	Arizona	6.2
26	Arkansas	5.1
11	California	5.8
22	Colorado	5.2
18	Connecticut	5.3
15	Delaware	5.5
2	Florida	7.1
32	Georgia	4.7
1	Hawaii	11.9
29	Idaho	5.0
4	Illinois	6.7
47	Indiana	3.7
35	Iowa	4.4
26	Kansas	5.1
43	Kentucky	4.0
9	Louisiana	6.1
43	Maine	4.0
11	Maryland	5.8
7	Massachusetts	6.2
30	Michigan	4.9
47	Minnesota	3.7
38	Mississippi	4.2
11	Missouri	5.8
40	Montana	4.1
45	Nebraska	3.8
5	Nevada	6.6
18	New Hampshire	5.3
6	New Jersey	6.4
10	New Mexico	5.9
22	New York	5.2
32	North Carolina	4.7
45	North Dakota	3.8
14	Ohio	5.6
18	Oklahoma	5.3
31	Oregon	4.8
40	Pennsylvania	4.1
2	Rhode Island	7.1
36	South Carolina	4.3
38	South Dakota	4.2
22	Tennessee	5.2
16	Texas	5.4
18	Utah	5.3
49	Vermont	3.5
26	Virginia	5.1
34	Washington	4.6
50	West Virginia	2.9
16	Wisconsin	5.4
40	Wyoming	4.1

RANK	STATE	PERCENT
1	Hawaii	11.9
2	Florida	7.1
2	Rhode Island	7.1
4	Illinois	6.7
5	Nevada	6.6
6	New Jersey	6.4
7	Arizona	6.2
7	Massachusetts	6.2
9	Louisiana	6.1
10	New Mexico	5.9
11	California	5.8
11	Maryland	5.8
11	Missouri	5.8
14	Ohio	5.6
15	Delaware	5.5
16	Texas	5.4
16	Wisconsin	5.4
18	Connecticut	5.3
18	New Hampshire	5.3
18	Oklahoma	5.3
18	Utah	5.3
22	Alabama	5.2
22	Colorado	5.2
22	New York	5.2
22	Tennessee	5.2
26	Arkansas	5.1
26	Kansas	5.1
26	Virginia	5.1
29	Idaho	5.0
30	Michigan	4.9
31	Oregon	4.8
32	Georgia	4.7
32	North Carolina	4.7
34	Washington	4.6
35	Iowa	4.4
36	Alaska	4.3
36	South Carolina	4.3
38	Mississippi	4.2
38	South Dakota	4.2
40	Montana	4.1
40	Pennsylvania	4.1
40	Wyoming	4.1
43	Kentucky	4.0
43	Maine	4.0
45	Nebraska	3.8
45	North Dakota	3.8
47	Indiana	3.7
47	Minnesota	3.7
49	Vermont	3.5
50	West Virginia	2.9
	District of Columbia	5.5

Source: Morgan Quitno Press using data from U.S. Bureau of the Census
"Government Finances: 1994-1995" (1998) (http://www.census.gov/govs/www/esti95.html)

State and Local Government Expenditures for Corrections in 1995

National Total = $35,856,854,000*

ALPHA ORDER

RANK	STATE	EXPENDITURES	% of USA
27	Alabama	$307,356,000	0.9%
37	Alaska	143,114,000	0.4%
17	Arizona	561,472,000	1.6%
33	Arkansas	188,933,000	0.5%
1	California	5,781,687,000	16.1%
21	Colorado	449,371,000	1.3%
19	Connecticut	481,266,000	1.3%
41	Delaware	110,072,000	0.3%
4	Florida	2,450,761,000	6.8%
11	Georgia	996,102,000	2.8%
40	Hawaii	110,238,000	0.3%
42	Idaho	104,270,000	0.3%
8	Illinois	1,146,203,000	3.2%
20	Indiana	470,401,000	1.3%
35	Iowa	175,867,000	0.5%
32	Kansas	214,068,000	0.6%
28	Kentucky	297,387,000	0.8%
23	Louisiana	424,232,000	1.2%
44	Maine	91,460,000	0.3%
13	Maryland	871,853,000	2.4%
15	Massachusetts	688,362,000	1.9%
6	Michigan	1,460,331,000	4.1%
25	Minnesota	395,991,000	1.1%
36	Mississippi	151,654,000	0.4%
24	Missouri	404,443,000	1.1%
46	Montana	55,828,000	0.2%
38	Nebraska	120,395,000	0.3%
30	Nevada	258,432,000	0.7%
45	New Hampshire	83,474,000	0.2%
9	New Jersey	1,107,576,000	3.1%
31	New Mexico	216,842,000	0.6%
2	New York	3,807,067,000	10.6%
10	North Carolina	1,017,405,000	2.8%
50	North Dakota	24,582,000	0.1%
7	Ohio	1,323,233,000	3.7%
29	Oklahoma	260,904,000	0.7%
26	Oregon	340,322,000	0.9%
5	Pennsylvania	1,482,748,000	4.1%
39	Rhode Island	114,371,000	0.3%
22	South Carolina	437,863,000	1.2%
47	South Dakota	52,818,000	0.1%
18	Tennessee	497,242,000	1.4%
3	Texas	3,291,275,000	9.2%
34	Utah	188,754,000	0.5%
49	Vermont	41,193,000	0.1%
12	Virginia	891,330,000	2.5%
14	Washington	713,291,000	2.0%
43	West Virginia	95,655,000	0.3%
16	Wisconsin	621,687,000	1.7%
48	Wyoming	43,292,000	0.1%

RANK ORDER

RANK	STATE	EXPENDITURES	% of USA
1	California	$5,781,687,000	16.1%
2	New York	3,807,067,000	10.6%
3	Texas	3,291,275,000	9.2%
4	Florida	2,450,761,000	6.8%
5	Pennsylvania	1,482,748,000	4.1%
6	Michigan	1,460,331,000	4.1%
7	Ohio	1,323,233,000	3.7%
8	Illinois	1,146,203,000	3.2%
9	New Jersey	1,107,576,000	3.1%
10	North Carolina	1,017,405,000	2.8%
11	Georgia	996,102,000	2.8%
12	Virginia	891,330,000	2.5%
13	Maryland	871,853,000	2.4%
14	Washington	713,291,000	2.0%
15	Massachusetts	688,362,000	1.9%
16	Wisconsin	621,687,000	1.7%
17	Arizona	561,472,000	1.6%
18	Tennessee	497,242,000	1.4%
19	Connecticut	481,266,000	1.3%
20	Indiana	470,401,000	1.3%
21	Colorado	449,371,000	1.3%
22	South Carolina	437,863,000	1.2%
23	Louisiana	424,232,000	1.2%
24	Missouri	404,443,000	1.1%
25	Minnesota	395,991,000	1.1%
26	Oregon	340,322,000	0.9%
27	Alabama	307,356,000	0.9%
28	Kentucky	297,387,000	0.8%
29	Oklahoma	260,904,000	0.7%
30	Nevada	258,432,000	0.7%
31	New Mexico	216,842,000	0.6%
32	Kansas	214,068,000	0.6%
33	Arkansas	188,933,000	0.5%
34	Utah	188,754,000	0.5%
35	Iowa	175,867,000	0.5%
36	Mississippi	151,654,000	0.4%
37	Alaska	143,114,000	0.4%
38	Nebraska	120,395,000	0.3%
39	Rhode Island	114,371,000	0.3%
40	Hawaii	110,238,000	0.3%
41	Delaware	110,072,000	0.3%
42	Idaho	104,270,000	0.3%
43	West Virginia	95,655,000	0.3%
44	Maine	91,460,000	0.3%
45	New Hampshire	83,474,000	0.2%
46	Montana	55,828,000	0.2%
47	South Dakota	52,818,000	0.1%
48	Wyoming	43,292,000	0.1%
49	Vermont	41,193,000	0.1%
50	North Dakota	24,582,000	0.1%
	District of Columbia	292,381,000	0.8%

Source: Morgan Quitno Press using data from U.S. Bureau of the Census
   "Government Finances: 1994-1995" (1998) (http://www.census.gov/govs/www/esti95.html)
*Direct general expenditures.

Per Capita State and Local Government Expenditures for Corrections in 1995

National Per Capita = $136.46*

ALPHA ORDER

RANK	STATE	PER CAPITA
43	Alabama	$71.97
1	Alaska	237.90
16	Arizona	130.36
38	Arkansas	76.18
3	California	183.71
20	Colorado	120.21
10	Connecticut	147.55
8	Delaware	153.15
6	Florida	172.83
13	Georgia	138.57
30	Hawaii	93.18
32	Idaho	89.61
27	Illinois	96.60
35	Indiana	81.29
47	Iowa	61.91
34	Kansas	83.15
37	Kentucky	77.12
26	Louisiana	98.02
40	Maine	74.17
5	Maryland	173.56
24	Massachusetts	113.63
9	Michigan	151.13
33	Minnesota	85.99
48	Mississippi	56.37
39	Missouri	75.78
46	Montana	64.28
41	Nebraska	73.62
7	Nevada	169.09
42	New Hampshire	72.83
12	New Jersey	139.10
17	New Mexico	128.78
2	New York	209.81
11	North Carolina	141.58
50	North Dakota	38.33
21	Ohio	118.81
36	Oklahoma	79.76
25	Oregon	108.34
18	Pennsylvania	123.15
23	Rhode Island	115.61
22	South Carolina	118.36
44	South Dakota	71.91
28	Tennessee	94.98
4	Texas	176.06
29	Utah	94.78
45	Vermont	70.72
14	Virginia	135.02
15	Washington	131.29
49	West Virginia	52.51
19	Wisconsin	121.02
31	Wyoming	90.50

RANK ORDER

RANK	STATE	PER CAPITA
1	Alaska	$237.90
2	New York	209.81
3	California	183.71
4	Texas	176.06
5	Maryland	173.56
6	Florida	172.83
7	Nevada	169.09
8	Delaware	153.15
9	Michigan	151.13
10	Connecticut	147.55
11	North Carolina	141.58
12	New Jersey	139.10
13	Georgia	138.57
14	Virginia	135.02
15	Washington	131.29
16	Arizona	130.36
17	New Mexico	128.78
18	Pennsylvania	123.15
19	Wisconsin	121.02
20	Colorado	120.21
21	Ohio	118.81
22	South Carolina	118.36
23	Rhode Island	115.61
24	Massachusetts	113.63
25	Oregon	108.34
26	Louisiana	98.02
27	Illinois	96.60
28	Tennessee	94.98
29	Utah	94.78
30	Hawaii	93.18
31	Wyoming	90.50
32	Idaho	89.61
33	Minnesota	85.99
34	Kansas	83.15
35	Indiana	81.29
36	Oklahoma	79.76
37	Kentucky	77.12
38	Arkansas	76.18
39	Missouri	75.78
40	Maine	74.17
41	Nebraska	73.62
42	New Hampshire	72.83
43	Alabama	71.97
44	South Dakota	71.91
45	Vermont	70.72
46	Montana	64.28
47	Iowa	61.91
48	Mississippi	56.37
49	West Virginia	52.51
50	North Dakota	38.33
	District of Columbia	529.23

Source: Morgan Quitno Press using data from U.S. Bureau of the Census
    "Government Finances: 1994-1995" (1998) (http://www.census.gov/govs/www/esti95.html)
*Direct general expenditures.

State and Local Government Expenditures for Corrections
As a Percent of All Direct General Expenditures in 1995
National Percent = 3.1% of Direct General Expenditures

ALPHA ORDER

RANK	STATE	PERCENT
37	Alabama	2.0
29	Alaska	2.3
8	Arizona	3.5
24	Arkansas	2.4
4	California	4.0
15	Colorado	2.9
18	Connecticut	2.8
11	Delaware	3.2
2	Florida	4.2
10	Georgia	3.4
44	Hawaii	1.6
24	Idaho	2.4
24	Illinois	2.4
34	Indiana	2.2
48	Iowa	1.5
36	Kansas	2.1
34	Kentucky	2.2
29	Louisiana	2.3
40	Maine	1.8
3	Maryland	4.1
29	Massachusetts	2.3
8	Michigan	3.5
42	Minnesota	1.7
44	Mississippi	1.6
29	Missouri	2.3
44	Montana	1.6
40	Nebraska	1.8
4	Nevada	4.0
38	New Hampshire	1.9
21	New Jersey	2.6
15	New Mexico	2.9
11	New York	3.2
6	North Carolina	3.7
50	North Dakota	0.9
14	Ohio	3.0
29	Oklahoma	2.3
24	Oregon	2.4
15	Pennsylvania	2.9
24	Rhode Island	2.4
13	South Carolina	3.1
38	South Dakota	1.9
21	Tennessee	2.6
1	Texas	4.8
23	Utah	2.5
44	Vermont	1.6
7	Virginia	3.6
19	Washington	2.7
49	West Virginia	1.3
19	Wisconsin	2.7
42	Wyoming	1.7

RANK ORDER

RANK	STATE	PERCENT
1	Texas	4.8
2	Florida	4.2
3	Maryland	4.1
4	California	4.0
4	Nevada	4.0
6	North Carolina	3.7
7	Virginia	3.6
8	Arizona	3.5
8	Michigan	3.5
10	Georgia	3.4
11	Delaware	3.2
11	New York	3.2
13	South Carolina	3.1
14	Ohio	3.0
15	Colorado	2.9
15	New Mexico	2.9
15	Pennsylvania	2.9
18	Connecticut	2.8
19	Washington	2.7
19	Wisconsin	2.7
21	New Jersey	2.6
21	Tennessee	2.6
23	Utah	2.5
24	Arkansas	2.4
24	Idaho	2.4
24	Illinois	2.4
24	Oregon	2.4
24	Rhode Island	2.4
29	Alaska	2.3
29	Louisiana	2.3
29	Massachusetts	2.3
29	Missouri	2.3
29	Oklahoma	2.3
34	Indiana	2.2
34	Kentucky	2.2
36	Kansas	2.1
37	Alabama	2.0
38	New Hampshire	1.9
38	South Dakota	1.9
40	Maine	1.8
40	Nebraska	1.8
42	Minnesota	1.7
42	Wyoming	1.7
44	Hawaii	1.6
44	Mississippi	1.6
44	Montana	1.6
44	Vermont	1.6
48	Iowa	1.5
49	West Virginia	1.3
50	North Dakota	0.9
	District of Columbia	6.8

Source: Morgan Quitno Press using data from U.S. Bureau of the Census
"Government Finances: 1994-1995" (1998) (http://www.census.gov/govs/www/esti95.html)

State Government Expenditures for Corrections in 1995

National Total = $24,091,069,000*

<table>
<tr><td colspan="4">ALPHA ORDER</td><td colspan="4">RANK ORDER</td></tr>
<tr><th>RANK</th><th>STATE</th><th>EXPENDITURES</th><th>% of USA</th><th>RANK</th><th>STATE</th><th>EXPENDITURES</th><th>% of USA</th></tr>
<tr><td>26</td><td>Alabama</td><td>$226,536,000</td><td>0.9%</td><td>1</td><td>California</td><td>$3,561,507,000</td><td>14.8%</td></tr>
<tr><td>34</td><td>Alaska</td><td>142,585,000</td><td>0.6%</td><td>2</td><td>Texas</td><td>2,325,446,000</td><td>9.7%</td></tr>
<tr><td>18</td><td>Arizona</td><td>385,618,000</td><td>1.6%</td><td>3</td><td>New York</td><td>2,028,558,000</td><td>8.4%</td></tr>
<tr><td>32</td><td>Arkansas</td><td>149,404,000</td><td>0.6%</td><td>4</td><td>Florida</td><td>1,599,250,000</td><td>6.6%</td></tr>
<tr><td>1</td><td>California</td><td>3,561,507,000</td><td>14.8%</td><td>5</td><td>Michigan</td><td>1,172,931,000</td><td>4.9%</td></tr>
<tr><td>22</td><td>Colorado</td><td>297,605,000</td><td>1.2%</td><td>6</td><td>Ohio</td><td>973,277,000</td><td>4.0%</td></tr>
<tr><td>15</td><td>Connecticut</td><td>481,266,000</td><td>2.0%</td><td>7</td><td>Pennsylvania</td><td>875,225,000</td><td>3.6%</td></tr>
<tr><td>40</td><td>Delaware</td><td>110,072,000</td><td>0.5%</td><td>8</td><td>North Carolina</td><td>801,797,000</td><td>3.3%</td></tr>
<tr><td>4</td><td>Florida</td><td>1,599,250,000</td><td>6.6%</td><td>9</td><td>Illinois</td><td>778,060,000</td><td>3.2%</td></tr>
<tr><td>10</td><td>Georgia</td><td>739,632,000</td><td>3.1%</td><td>10</td><td>Georgia</td><td>739,632,000</td><td>3.1%</td></tr>
<tr><td>39</td><td>Hawaii</td><td>110,238,000</td><td>0.5%</td><td>11</td><td>Maryland</td><td>733,828,000</td><td>3.0%</td></tr>
<tr><td>42</td><td>Idaho</td><td>75,654,000</td><td>0.3%</td><td>12</td><td>New Jersey</td><td>723,636,000</td><td>3.0%</td></tr>
<tr><td>9</td><td>Illinois</td><td>778,060,000</td><td>3.2%</td><td>13</td><td>Virginia</td><td>596,771,000</td><td>2.5%</td></tr>
<tr><td>21</td><td>Indiana</td><td>324,219,000</td><td>1.3%</td><td>14</td><td>Washington</td><td>482,756,000</td><td>2.0%</td></tr>
<tr><td>36</td><td>Iowa</td><td>135,109,000</td><td>0.6%</td><td>15</td><td>Connecticut</td><td>481,266,000</td><td>2.0%</td></tr>
<tr><td>30</td><td>Kansas</td><td>173,748,000</td><td>0.7%</td><td>16</td><td>Massachusetts</td><td>434,270,000</td><td>1.8%</td></tr>
<tr><td>28</td><td>Kentucky</td><td>205,993,000</td><td>0.9%</td><td>17</td><td>Wisconsin</td><td>426,954,000</td><td>1.8%</td></tr>
<tr><td>23</td><td>Louisiana</td><td>285,980,000</td><td>1.2%</td><td>18</td><td>Arizona</td><td>385,618,000</td><td>1.6%</td></tr>
<tr><td>44</td><td>Maine</td><td>63,155,000</td><td>0.3%</td><td>19</td><td>South Carolina</td><td>348,052,000</td><td>1.4%</td></tr>
<tr><td>11</td><td>Maryland</td><td>733,828,000</td><td>3.0%</td><td>20</td><td>Tennessee</td><td>342,430,000</td><td>1.4%</td></tr>
<tr><td>16</td><td>Massachusetts</td><td>434,270,000</td><td>1.8%</td><td>21</td><td>Indiana</td><td>324,219,000</td><td>1.3%</td></tr>
<tr><td>5</td><td>Michigan</td><td>1,172,931,000</td><td>4.9%</td><td>22</td><td>Colorado</td><td>297,605,000</td><td>1.2%</td></tr>
<tr><td>27</td><td>Minnesota</td><td>210,045,000</td><td>0.9%</td><td>23</td><td>Louisiana</td><td>285,980,000</td><td>1.2%</td></tr>
<tr><td>37</td><td>Mississippi</td><td>126,278,000</td><td>0.5%</td><td>24</td><td>Missouri</td><td>265,242,000</td><td>1.1%</td></tr>
<tr><td>24</td><td>Missouri</td><td>265,242,000</td><td>1.1%</td><td>25</td><td>Oklahoma</td><td>242,391,000</td><td>1.0%</td></tr>
<tr><td>46</td><td>Montana</td><td>49,635,000</td><td>0.2%</td><td>26</td><td>Alabama</td><td>226,536,000</td><td>0.9%</td></tr>
<tr><td>41</td><td>Nebraska</td><td>84,987,000</td><td>0.4%</td><td>27</td><td>Minnesota</td><td>210,045,000</td><td>0.9%</td></tr>
<tr><td>35</td><td>Nevada</td><td>135,591,000</td><td>0.6%</td><td>28</td><td>Kentucky</td><td>205,993,000</td><td>0.9%</td></tr>
<tr><td>45</td><td>New Hampshire</td><td>58,300,000</td><td>0.2%</td><td>29</td><td>Oregon</td><td>185,828,000</td><td>0.8%</td></tr>
<tr><td>12</td><td>New Jersey</td><td>723,636,000</td><td>3.0%</td><td>30</td><td>Kansas</td><td>173,748,000</td><td>0.7%</td></tr>
<tr><td>31</td><td>New Mexico</td><td>159,981,000</td><td>0.7%</td><td>31</td><td>New Mexico</td><td>159,981,000</td><td>0.7%</td></tr>
<tr><td>3</td><td>New York</td><td>2,028,558,000</td><td>8.4%</td><td>32</td><td>Arkansas</td><td>149,404,000</td><td>0.6%</td></tr>
<tr><td>8</td><td>North Carolina</td><td>801,797,000</td><td>3.3%</td><td>33</td><td>Utah</td><td>144,326,000</td><td>0.6%</td></tr>
<tr><td>50</td><td>North Dakota</td><td>17,647,000</td><td>0.1%</td><td>34</td><td>Alaska</td><td>142,585,000</td><td>0.6%</td></tr>
<tr><td>6</td><td>Ohio</td><td>973,277,000</td><td>4.0%</td><td>35</td><td>Nevada</td><td>135,591,000</td><td>0.6%</td></tr>
<tr><td>25</td><td>Oklahoma</td><td>242,391,000</td><td>1.0%</td><td>36</td><td>Iowa</td><td>135,109,000</td><td>0.6%</td></tr>
<tr><td>29</td><td>Oregon</td><td>185,828,000</td><td>0.8%</td><td>37</td><td>Mississippi</td><td>126,278,000</td><td>0.5%</td></tr>
<tr><td>7</td><td>Pennsylvania</td><td>875,225,000</td><td>3.6%</td><td>38</td><td>Rhode Island</td><td>114,371,000</td><td>0.5%</td></tr>
<tr><td>38</td><td>Rhode Island</td><td>114,371,000</td><td>0.5%</td><td>39</td><td>Hawaii</td><td>110,238,000</td><td>0.5%</td></tr>
<tr><td>19</td><td>South Carolina</td><td>348,052,000</td><td>1.4%</td><td>40</td><td>Delaware</td><td>110,072,000</td><td>0.5%</td></tr>
<tr><td>48</td><td>South Dakota</td><td>40,388,000</td><td>0.2%</td><td>41</td><td>Nebraska</td><td>84,987,000</td><td>0.4%</td></tr>
<tr><td>20</td><td>Tennessee</td><td>342,430,000</td><td>1.4%</td><td>42</td><td>Idaho</td><td>75,654,000</td><td>0.3%</td></tr>
<tr><td>2</td><td>Texas</td><td>2,325,446,000</td><td>9.7%</td><td>43</td><td>West Virginia</td><td>73,889,000</td><td>0.3%</td></tr>
<tr><td>33</td><td>Utah</td><td>144,326,000</td><td>0.6%</td><td>44</td><td>Maine</td><td>63,155,000</td><td>0.3%</td></tr>
<tr><td>47</td><td>Vermont</td><td>41,159,000</td><td>0.2%</td><td>45</td><td>New Hampshire</td><td>58,300,000</td><td>0.2%</td></tr>
<tr><td>13</td><td>Virginia</td><td>596,771,000</td><td>2.5%</td><td>46</td><td>Montana</td><td>49,635,000</td><td>0.2%</td></tr>
<tr><td>14</td><td>Washington</td><td>482,756,000</td><td>2.0%</td><td>47</td><td>Vermont</td><td>41,159,000</td><td>0.2%</td></tr>
<tr><td>43</td><td>West Virginia</td><td>73,889,000</td><td>0.3%</td><td>48</td><td>South Dakota</td><td>40,388,000</td><td>0.2%</td></tr>
<tr><td>17</td><td>Wisconsin</td><td>426,954,000</td><td>1.8%</td><td>49</td><td>Wyoming</td><td>29,449,000</td><td>0.1%</td></tr>
<tr><td>49</td><td>Wyoming</td><td>29,449,000</td><td>0.1%</td><td>50</td><td>North Dakota</td><td>17,647,000</td><td>0.1%</td></tr>
<tr><td></td><td></td><td></td><td></td><td colspan="2">District of Columbia**</td><td>NA</td><td>NA</td></tr>
</table>

Source: Morgan Quitno Press using data from U.S. Bureau of the Census
"Government Finances: 1994-1995" (1998) (http://www.census.gov/govs/www/esti95.html)
Direct general expenditures.
**Not applicable.*

Per Capita State Government Expenditures for Corrections in 1995

National Per Capita = $91.68*

ALPHA ORDER

RANK	STATE	PER CAPITA
41	Alabama	$53.05
1	Alaska	237.02
18	Arizona	89.53
35	Arkansas	60.24
8	California	113.16
23	Colorado	79.61
3	Connecticut	147.55
2	Delaware	153.15
9	Florida	112.78
12	Georgia	102.89
15	Hawaii	93.18
33	Idaho	65.02
31	Illinois	65.57
38	Indiana	56.03
46	Iowa	47.56
29	Kansas	67.49
40	Kentucky	53.42
30	Louisiana	66.07
43	Maine	51.21
4	Maryland	146.08
27	Massachusetts	71.69
6	Michigan	121.39
48	Minnesota	45.61
47	Mississippi	46.94
45	Missouri	49.70
37	Montana	57.15
42	Nebraska	51.97
20	Nevada	88.72
44	New Hampshire	50.86
16	New Jersey	90.88
13	New Mexico	95.01
10	New York	111.80
11	North Carolina	111.58
50	North Dakota	27.51
21	Ohio	87.39
24	Oklahoma	74.10
36	Oregon	59.16
25	Pennsylvania	72.69
7	Rhode Island	115.61
14	South Carolina	94.09
39	South Dakota	54.98
32	Tennessee	65.41
5	Texas	124.39
26	Utah	72.47
28	Vermont	70.67
17	Virginia	90.40
19	Washington	88.86
49	West Virginia	40.56
22	Wisconsin	83.11
34	Wyoming	61.56

RANK ORDER

RANK	STATE	PER CAPITA
1	Alaska	$237.02
2	Delaware	153.15
3	Connecticut	147.55
4	Maryland	146.08
5	Texas	124.39
6	Michigan	121.39
7	Rhode Island	115.61
8	California	113.16
9	Florida	112.78
10	New York	111.80
11	North Carolina	111.58
12	Georgia	102.89
13	New Mexico	95.01
14	South Carolina	94.09
15	Hawaii	93.18
16	New Jersey	90.88
17	Virginia	90.40
18	Arizona	89.53
19	Washington	88.86
20	Nevada	88.72
21	Ohio	87.39
22	Wisconsin	83.11
23	Colorado	79.61
24	Oklahoma	74.10
25	Pennsylvania	72.69
26	Utah	72.47
27	Massachusetts	71.69
28	Vermont	70.67
29	Kansas	67.49
30	Louisiana	66.07
31	Illinois	65.57
32	Tennessee	65.41
33	Idaho	65.02
34	Wyoming	61.56
35	Arkansas	60.24
36	Oregon	59.16
37	Montana	57.15
38	Indiana	56.03
39	South Dakota	54.98
40	Kentucky	53.42
41	Alabama	53.05
42	Nebraska	51.97
43	Maine	51.21
44	New Hampshire	50.86
45	Missouri	49.70
46	Iowa	47.56
47	Mississippi	46.94
48	Minnesota	45.61
49	West Virginia	40.56
50	North Dakota	27.51

District of Columbia** NA

Source: Morgan Quitno Press using data from U.S. Bureau of the Census
   "Government Finances: 1994-1995" (1998) (http://www.census.gov/govs/www/esti95.html)
*Direct general expenditures.
**Not applicable.

State Government Expenditures for Corrections
As a Percent of All Direct General Expenditures in 1995
National Percent = 4.9% of Direct General Expenditures

RANK	STATE	PERCENT
33	Alabama	2.9
28	Alaska	3.6
7	Arizona	6.3
31	Arkansas	3.3
4	California	7.3
10	Colorado	5.2
10	Connecticut	5.2
14	Delaware	5.0
2	Florida	7.5
9	Georgia	5.7
48	Hawaii	2.1
23	Idaho	3.8
26	Illinois	3.7
30	Indiana	3.5
43	Iowa	2.5
19	Kansas	4.1
36	Kentucky	2.8
36	Louisiana	2.8
47	Maine	2.2
2	Maryland	7.5
43	Massachusetts	2.5
5	Michigan	6.8
46	Minnesota	2.3
33	Mississippi	2.9
31	Missouri	3.3
41	Montana	2.6
33	Nebraska	2.9
8	Nevada	5.9
43	New Hampshire	2.5
22	New Jersey	3.9
19	New Mexico	4.1
16	New York	4.7
6	North Carolina	6.6
50	North Dakota	1.1
10	Ohio	5.2
16	Oklahoma	4.7
36	Oregon	2.8
28	Pennsylvania	3.6
23	Rhode Island	3.8
18	South Carolina	4.6
36	South Dakota	2.8
26	Tennessee	3.7
1	Texas	8.1
23	Utah	3.8
40	Vermont	2.7
10	Virginia	5.2
21	Washington	4.0
49	West Virginia	1.8
15	Wisconsin	4.8
41	Wyoming	2.6

RANK	STATE	PERCENT
1	Texas	8.1
2	Florida	7.5
2	Maryland	7.5
4	California	7.3
5	Michigan	6.8
6	North Carolina	6.6
7	Arizona	6.3
8	Nevada	5.9
9	Georgia	5.7
10	Colorado	5.2
10	Connecticut	5.2
10	Ohio	5.2
10	Virginia	5.2
14	Delaware	5.0
15	Wisconsin	4.8
16	New York	4.7
16	Oklahoma	4.7
18	South Carolina	4.6
19	Kansas	4.1
19	New Mexico	4.1
21	Washington	4.0
22	New Jersey	3.9
23	Idaho	3.8
23	Rhode Island	3.8
23	Utah	3.8
26	Illinois	3.7
26	Tennessee	3.7
28	Alaska	3.6
28	Pennsylvania	3.6
30	Indiana	3.5
31	Arkansas	3.3
31	Missouri	3.3
33	Alabama	2.9
33	Mississippi	2.9
33	Nebraska	2.9
36	Kentucky	2.8
36	Louisiana	2.8
36	Oregon	2.8
36	South Dakota	2.8
40	Vermont	2.7
41	Montana	2.6
41	Wyoming	2.6
43	Iowa	2.5
43	Massachusetts	2.5
43	New Hampshire	2.5
46	Minnesota	2.3
47	Maine	2.2
48	Hawaii	2.1
49	West Virginia	1.8
50	North Dakota	1.1
	District of Columbia*	NA

Source: Morgan Quitno Press using data from U.S. Bureau of the Census
"Government Finances: 1994-1995" (1998) (http://www.census.gov/govs/www/esti95.html)
*Not applicable.

Local Government Expenditures for Corrections in 1995

National Total = $11,765,785,000*

ALPHA ORDER

ALPHA ORDER

RANK	STATE	EXPENDITURES	% of USA
28	Alabama	$80,820,000	0.7%
45	Alaska	529,000	0.0%
17	Arizona	175,854,000	1.5%
33	Arkansas	39,529,000	0.3%
1	California	2,220,180,000	18.9%
20	Colorado	151,766,000	1.3%
47	Connecticut	0	0.0%
47	Delaware	0	0.0%
4	Florida	851,511,000	7.2%
11	Georgia	256,470,000	2.2%
47	Hawaii	0	0.0%
35	Idaho	28,616,000	0.2%
7	Illinois	368,143,000	3.1%
21	Indiana	146,182,000	1.2%
31	Iowa	40,758,000	0.3%
32	Kansas	40,320,000	0.3%
26	Kentucky	91,394,000	0.8%
23	Louisiana	138,252,000	1.2%
36	Maine	28,305,000	0.2%
24	Maryland	138,025,000	1.2%
12	Massachusetts	254,092,000	2.2%
10	Michigan	287,400,000	2.4%
16	Minnesota	185,946,000	1.6%
37	Mississippi	25,376,000	0.2%
22	Missouri	139,201,000	1.2%
44	Montana	6,193,000	0.1%
34	Nebraska	35,408,000	0.3%
25	Nevada	122,841,000	1.0%
38	New Hampshire	25,174,000	0.2%
6	New Jersey	383,940,000	3.3%
29	New Mexico	56,861,000	0.5%
2	New York	1,778,509,000	15.1%
14	North Carolina	215,608,000	1.8%
43	North Dakota	6,935,000	0.1%
8	Ohio	349,956,000	3.0%
40	Oklahoma	18,513,000	0.2%
19	Oregon	154,494,000	1.3%
5	Pennsylvania	607,523,000	5.2%
47	Rhode Island	0	0.0%
27	South Carolina	89,811,000	0.8%
42	South Dakota	12,430,000	0.1%
18	Tennessee	154,812,000	1.3%
3	Texas	965,829,000	8.2%
30	Utah	44,428,000	0.4%
46	Vermont	34,000	0.0%
9	Virginia	294,559,000	2.5%
13	Washington	230,535,000	2.0%
39	West Virginia	21,766,000	0.2%
15	Wisconsin	194,733,000	1.7%
41	Wyoming	13,843,000	0.1%

RANK ORDER

RANK	STATE	EXPENDITURES	% of USA
1	California	$2,220,180,000	18.9%
2	New York	1,778,509,000	15.1%
3	Texas	965,829,000	8.2%
4	Florida	851,511,000	7.2%
5	Pennsylvania	607,523,000	5.2%
6	New Jersey	383,940,000	3.3%
7	Illinois	368,143,000	3.1%
8	Ohio	349,956,000	3.0%
9	Virginia	294,559,000	2.5%
10	Michigan	287,400,000	2.4%
11	Georgia	256,470,000	2.2%
12	Massachusetts	254,092,000	2.2%
13	Washington	230,535,000	2.0%
14	North Carolina	215,608,000	1.8%
15	Wisconsin	194,733,000	1.7%
16	Minnesota	185,946,000	1.6%
17	Arizona	175,854,000	1.5%
18	Tennessee	154,812,000	1.3%
19	Oregon	154,494,000	1.3%
20	Colorado	151,766,000	1.3%
21	Indiana	146,182,000	1.2%
22	Missouri	139,201,000	1.2%
23	Louisiana	138,252,000	1.2%
24	Maryland	138,025,000	1.2%
25	Nevada	122,841,000	1.0%
26	Kentucky	91,394,000	0.8%
27	South Carolina	89,811,000	0.8%
28	Alabama	80,820,000	0.7%
29	New Mexico	56,861,000	0.5%
30	Utah	44,428,000	0.4%
31	Iowa	40,758,000	0.3%
32	Kansas	40,320,000	0.3%
33	Arkansas	39,529,000	0.3%
34	Nebraska	35,408,000	0.3%
35	Idaho	28,616,000	0.2%
36	Maine	28,305,000	0.2%
37	Mississippi	25,376,000	0.2%
38	New Hampshire	25,174,000	0.2%
39	West Virginia	21,766,000	0.2%
40	Oklahoma	18,513,000	0.2%
41	Wyoming	13,843,000	0.1%
42	South Dakota	12,430,000	0.1%
43	North Dakota	6,935,000	0.1%
44	Montana	6,193,000	0.1%
45	Alaska	529,000	0.0%
46	Vermont	34,000	0.0%
47	Connecticut	0	0.0%
47	Delaware	0	0.0%
47	Hawaii	0	0.0%
47	Rhode Island	0	0.0%
	District of Columbia	292,381,000	2.5%

Source: Morgan Quitno Press using data from U.S. Bureau of the Census
"Government Finances: 1994-1995" (1998) (http://www.census.gov/govs/www/esti95.html)
*Direct general expenditures.

Per Capita Local Government Expenditures for Corrections in 1995

National Per Capita = $44.78*

ALPHA ORDER

RANK	STATE	PER CAPITA
35	Alabama	$18.93
45	Alaska	0.88
12	Arizona	40.83
37	Arkansas	15.94
3	California	70.54
13	Colorado	40.60
47	Connecticut	0.00
47	Delaware	0.00
4	Florida	60.05
16	Georgia	35.68
47	Hawaii	0.00
28	Idaho	24.59
20	Illinois	31.03
27	Indiana	25.26
39	Iowa	14.35
38	Kansas	15.66
30	Kentucky	23.70
18	Louisiana	31.94
31	Maine	22.95
25	Maryland	27.48
11	Massachusetts	41.94
22	Michigan	29.74
14	Minnesota	40.38
42	Mississippi	9.43
26	Missouri	26.08
43	Montana	7.13
34	Nebraska	21.65
2	Nevada	80.37
33	New Hampshire	21.96
8	New Jersey	48.22
17	New Mexico	33.77
1	New York	98.02
21	North Carolina	30.00
41	North Dakota	10.81
19	Ohio	31.42
44	Oklahoma	5.66
7	Oregon	49.18
6	Pennsylvania	50.46
47	Rhode Island	0.00
29	South Carolina	24.28
36	South Dakota	16.92
23	Tennessee	29.57
5	Texas	51.66
32	Utah	22.31
46	Vermont	0.06
9	Virginia	44.62
10	Washington	42.43
40	West Virginia	11.95
15	Wisconsin	37.91
24	Wyoming	28.94

RANK ORDER

RANK	STATE	PER CAPITA
1	New York	$98.02
2	Nevada	80.37
3	California	70.54
4	Florida	60.05
5	Texas	51.66
6	Pennsylvania	50.46
7	Oregon	49.18
8	New Jersey	48.22
9	Virginia	44.62
10	Washington	42.43
11	Massachusetts	41.94
12	Arizona	40.83
13	Colorado	40.60
14	Minnesota	40.38
15	Wisconsin	37.91
16	Georgia	35.68
17	New Mexico	33.77
18	Louisiana	31.94
19	Ohio	31.42
20	Illinois	31.03
21	North Carolina	30.00
22	Michigan	29.74
23	Tennessee	29.57
24	Wyoming	28.94
25	Maryland	27.48
26	Missouri	26.08
27	Indiana	25.26
28	Idaho	24.59
29	South Carolina	24.28
30	Kentucky	23.70
31	Maine	22.95
32	Utah	22.31
33	New Hampshire	21.96
34	Nebraska	21.65
35	Alabama	18.93
36	South Dakota	16.92
37	Arkansas	15.94
38	Kansas	15.66
39	Iowa	14.35
40	West Virginia	11.95
41	North Dakota	10.81
42	Mississippi	9.43
43	Montana	7.13
44	Oklahoma	5.66
45	Alaska	0.88
46	Vermont	0.06
47	Connecticut	0.00
47	Delaware	0.00
47	Hawaii	0.00
47	Rhode Island	0.00
	District of Columbia	529.23

Source: Morgan Quitno Press using data from U.S. Bureau of the Census
"Government Finances: 1994-1995" (1998) (http://www.census.gov/govs/www/esti95.html)
*Direct general expenditures.

Local Government Expenditures for Corrections
As a Percent of All Direct General Expenditures in 1995
National Percent = 1.8% of Direct General Expenditures

ALPHA ORDER

RANK	STATE	PERCENT
34	Alabama	1.0
45	Alaska	0.0
10	Arizona	1.8
33	Arkansas	1.1
5	California	2.3
17	Colorado	1.5
45	Connecticut	0.0
45	Delaware	0.0
5	Florida	2.3
11	Georgia	1.6
45	Hawaii	0.0
26	Idaho	1.2
23	Illinois	1.3
26	Indiana	1.2
40	Iowa	0.6
38	Kansas	0.7
17	Kentucky	1.5
11	Louisiana	1.6
26	Maine	1.2
26	Maryland	1.2
8	Massachusetts	2.0
26	Michigan	1.2
23	Minnesota	1.3
42	Mississippi	0.5
19	Missouri	1.4
43	Montana	0.4
34	Nebraska	1.0
1	Nevada	3.0
26	New Hampshire	1.2
11	New Jersey	1.6
11	New Mexico	1.6
3	New York	2.4
19	North Carolina	1.4
40	North Dakota	0.6
19	Ohio	1.4
44	Oklahoma	0.3
8	Oregon	2.0
3	Pennsylvania	2.4
45	Rhode Island	0.0
23	South Carolina	1.3
36	South Dakota	0.9
11	Tennessee	1.6
2	Texas	2.5
26	Utah	1.2
45	Vermont	0.0
7	Virginia	2.1
11	Washington	1.6
38	West Virginia	0.7
19	Wisconsin	1.4
36	Wyoming	0.9

RANK ORDER

RANK	STATE	PERCENT
1	Nevada	3.0
2	Texas	2.5
3	New York	2.4
3	Pennsylvania	2.4
5	California	2.3
5	Florida	2.3
7	Virginia	2.1
8	Massachusetts	2.0
8	Oregon	2.0
10	Arizona	1.8
11	Georgia	1.6
11	Louisiana	1.6
11	New Jersey	1.6
11	New Mexico	1.6
11	Tennessee	1.6
11	Washington	1.6
17	Colorado	1.5
17	Kentucky	1.5
19	Missouri	1.4
19	North Carolina	1.4
19	Ohio	1.4
19	Wisconsin	1.4
23	Illinois	1.3
23	Minnesota	1.3
23	South Carolina	1.3
26	Idaho	1.2
26	Indiana	1.2
26	Maine	1.2
26	Maryland	1.2
26	Michigan	1.2
26	New Hampshire	1.2
26	Utah	1.2
33	Arkansas	1.1
34	Alabama	1.0
34	Nebraska	1.0
36	South Dakota	0.9
36	Wyoming	0.9
38	Kansas	0.7
38	West Virginia	0.7
40	Iowa	0.6
40	North Dakota	0.6
42	Mississippi	0.5
43	Montana	0.4
44	Oklahoma	0.3
45	Alaska	0.0
45	Connecticut	0.0
45	Delaware	0.0
45	Hawaii	0.0
45	Rhode Island	0.0
45	Vermont	0.0
	District of Columbia	6.8

Source: Morgan Quitno Press using data from U.S. Bureau of the Census
"Government Finances: 1994-1995" (1998) (http://www.census.gov/govs/www/esti95.html)

State and Local Government Expenditures for Judicial and Legal Services: 1995

National Total = $19,168,153,000*

ALPHA ORDER					RANK ORDER			

RANK	STATE	EXPENDITURES	% of USA		RANK	STATE	EXPENDITURES	% of USA
26	Alabama	$213,553,000	1.1%		1	California	$3,416,069,000	17.8%
29	Alaska	174,598,000	0.9%		2	New York	1,910,971,000	10.0%
12	Arizona	382,946,000	2.0%		3	Florida	1,110,660,000	5.8%
40	Arkansas	83,867,000	0.4%		4	Texas	1,025,395,000	5.3%
1	California	3,416,069,000	17.8%		5	New Jersey	858,267,000	4.5%
22	Colorado	253,219,000	1.3%		6	Ohio	804,079,000	4.2%
21	Connecticut	260,729,000	1.4%		7	Pennsylvania	795,188,000	4.1%
44	Delaware	67,028,000	0.3%		8	Illinois	713,323,000	3.7%
3	Florida	1,110,660,000	5.8%		9	Michigan	697,363,000	3.6%
17	Georgia	344,256,000	1.8%		10	Massachusetts	452,180,000	2.4%
32	Hawaii	149,888,000	0.8%		11	Washington	417,845,000	2.2%
43	Idaho	71,709,000	0.4%		12	Arizona	382,946,000	2.0%
8	Illinois	713,323,000	3.7%		13	North Carolina	372,752,000	1.9%
24	Indiana	221,638,000	1.2%		14	Maryland	370,097,000	1.9%
28	Iowa	176,124,000	0.9%		15	Wisconsin	351,467,000	1.8%
31	Kansas	151,716,000	0.8%		16	Virginia	346,129,000	1.8%
27	Kentucky	176,836,000	0.9%		17	Georgia	344,256,000	1.8%
19	Louisiana	265,855,000	1.4%		18	Minnesota	324,446,000	1.7%
46	Maine	48,750,000	0.3%		19	Louisiana	265,855,000	1.4%
14	Maryland	370,097,000	1.9%		20	Tennessee	261,927,000	1.4%
10	Massachusetts	452,180,000	2.4%		21	Connecticut	260,729,000	1.4%
9	Michigan	697,363,000	3.6%		22	Colorado	253,219,000	1.3%
18	Minnesota	324,446,000	1.7%		23	Oregon	238,701,000	1.2%
37	Mississippi	91,031,000	0.5%		24	Indiana	221,638,000	1.2%
25	Missouri	214,073,000	1.1%		25	Missouri	214,073,000	1.1%
45	Montana	50,538,000	0.3%		26	Alabama	213,553,000	1.1%
41	Nebraska	74,251,000	0.4%		27	Kentucky	176,836,000	0.9%
30	Nevada	159,667,000	0.8%		28	Iowa	176,124,000	0.9%
42	New Hampshire	72,269,000	0.4%		29	Alaska	174,598,000	0.9%
5	New Jersey	858,267,000	4.5%		30	Nevada	159,667,000	0.8%
36	New Mexico	117,049,000	0.6%		31	Kansas	151,716,000	0.8%
2	New York	1,910,971,000	10.0%		32	Hawaii	149,888,000	0.8%
13	North Carolina	372,752,000	1.9%		33	Oklahoma	145,892,000	0.8%
48	North Dakota	36,049,000	0.2%		34	South Carolina	136,297,000	0.7%
6	Ohio	804,079,000	4.2%		35	Utah	132,295,000	0.7%
33	Oklahoma	145,892,000	0.8%		36	New Mexico	117,049,000	0.6%
23	Oregon	238,701,000	1.2%		37	Mississippi	91,031,000	0.5%
7	Pennsylvania	795,188,000	4.1%		38	West Virginia	88,184,000	0.5%
39	Rhode Island	85,694,000	0.4%		39	Rhode Island	85,694,000	0.4%
34	South Carolina	136,297,000	0.7%		40	Arkansas	83,867,000	0.4%
49	South Dakota	34,986,000	0.2%		41	Nebraska	74,251,000	0.4%
20	Tennessee	261,927,000	1.4%		42	New Hampshire	72,269,000	0.4%
4	Texas	1,025,395,000	5.3%		43	Idaho	71,709,000	0.4%
35	Utah	132,295,000	0.7%		44	Delaware	67,028,000	0.3%
50	Vermont	33,593,000	0.2%		45	Montana	50,538,000	0.3%
16	Virginia	346,129,000	1.8%		46	Maine	48,750,000	0.3%
11	Washington	417,845,000	2.2%		47	Wyoming	39,566,000	0.2%
38	West Virginia	88,184,000	0.5%		48	North Dakota	36,049,000	0.2%
15	Wisconsin	351,467,000	1.8%		49	South Dakota	34,986,000	0.2%
47	Wyoming	39,566,000	0.2%		50	Vermont	33,593,000	0.2%
						District of Columbia	147,148,000	0.8%

Source: Morgan Quitno Press using data from U.S. Bureau of the Census
   "Government Finances: 1994-1995" (1998) (http://www.census.gov/govs/www/esti95.html)
*Direct general expenditures. Includes Courts, Prosecution and Legal Services and Public Defense.

Per Capita State and Local Government Expenditures
For Judicial and Legal Services in 1995
National Per Capita = $72.95*

ALPHA ORDER

RANK	STATE	PER CAPITA
38	Alabama	$50.01
1	Alaska	290.23
8	Arizona	88.91
50	Arkansas	33.82
3	California	108.54
22	Colorado	67.74
11	Connecticut	79.93
7	Delaware	93.26
12	Florida	78.32
40	Georgia	47.89
2	Hawaii	126.69
27	Idaho	61.63
29	Illinois	60.11
47	Indiana	38.30
26	Iowa	62.00
30	Kansas	58.93
42	Kentucky	45.86
28	Louisiana	61.42
46	Maine	39.53
16	Maryland	73.67
15	Massachusetts	74.64
18	Michigan	72.17
19	Minnesota	70.46
49	Mississippi	33.83
45	Missouri	40.11
31	Montana	58.19
43	Nebraska	45.40
6	Nevada	104.47
25	New Hampshire	63.05
4	New Jersey	107.79
20	New Mexico	69.52
5	New York	105.32
36	North Carolina	51.87
33	North Dakota	56.21
17	Ohio	72.19
44	Oklahoma	44.60
14	Oregon	75.99
24	Pennsylvania	66.05
9	Rhode Island	86.62
48	South Carolina	36.84
41	South Dakota	47.63
37	Tennessee	50.03
34	Texas	54.85
23	Utah	66.43
32	Vermont	57.68
35	Virginia	52.43
13	Washington	76.91
39	West Virginia	48.41
21	Wisconsin	68.42
10	Wyoming	82.71

RANK ORDER

RANK	STATE	PER CAPITA
1	Alaska	$290.23
2	Hawaii	126.69
3	California	108.54
4	New Jersey	107.79
5	New York	105.32
6	Nevada	104.47
7	Delaware	93.26
8	Arizona	88.91
9	Rhode Island	86.62
10	Wyoming	82.71
11	Connecticut	79.93
12	Florida	78.32
13	Washington	76.91
14	Oregon	75.99
15	Massachusetts	74.64
16	Maryland	73.67
17	Ohio	72.19
18	Michigan	72.17
19	Minnesota	70.46
20	New Mexico	69.52
21	Wisconsin	68.42
22	Colorado	67.74
23	Utah	66.43
24	Pennsylvania	66.05
25	New Hampshire	63.05
26	Iowa	62.00
27	Idaho	61.63
28	Louisiana	61.42
29	Illinois	60.11
30	Kansas	58.93
31	Montana	58.19
32	Vermont	57.68
33	North Dakota	56.21
34	Texas	54.85
35	Virginia	52.43
36	North Carolina	51.87
37	Tennessee	50.03
38	Alabama	50.01
39	West Virginia	48.41
40	Georgia	47.89
41	South Dakota	47.63
42	Kentucky	45.86
43	Nebraska	45.40
44	Oklahoma	44.60
45	Missouri	40.11
46	Maine	39.53
47	Indiana	38.30
48	South Carolina	36.84
49	Mississippi	33.83
50	Arkansas	33.82
	District of Columbia	266.35

Source: Morgan Quitno Press using data from U.S. Bureau of the Census
"Government Finances: 1994-1995" (1998) (http://www.census.gov/govs/www/esti95.html)
*Direct general expenditures. Includes Courts, Prosecution and Legal Services and Public Defense.

State and Local Government Expenditures for Judicial and Legal Services As a Percent of All Direct General Expenditures in 1995
National Percent = 1.7% of Direct General Expenditures*

ALPHA ORDER				RANK ORDER		
RANK	STATE	PERCENT		RANK	STATE	PERCENT
30	Alabama	1.4		1	Alaska	2.8
1	Alaska	2.8		2	Nevada	2.5
3	Arizona	2.4		3	Arizona	2.4
46	Arkansas	1.0		4	California	2.3
4	California	2.3		5	Hawaii	2.2
16	Colorado	1.6		6	New Jersey	2.0
22	Connecticut	1.5		7	Delaware	1.9
7	Delaware	1.9		7	Florida	1.9
7	Florida	1.9		9	Ohio	1.8
41	Georgia	1.2		9	Rhode Island	1.8
5	Hawaii	2.2		11	Idaho	1.7
11	Idaho	1.7		11	Maryland	1.7
22	Illinois	1.5		11	Michigan	1.7
46	Indiana	1.0		11	Oregon	1.7
22	Iowa	1.5		11	Utah	1.7
22	Kansas	1.5		16	Colorado	1.6
37	Kentucky	1.3		16	New Hampshire	1.6
30	Louisiana	1.4		16	New Mexico	1.6
49	Maine	0.9		16	New York	1.6
11	Maryland	1.7		16	Pennsylvania	1.6
22	Massachusetts	1.5		16	Washington	1.6
11	Michigan	1.7		22	Connecticut	1.5
30	Minnesota	1.4		22	Illinois	1.5
49	Mississippi	0.9		22	Iowa	1.5
41	Missouri	1.2		22	Kansas	1.5
30	Montana	1.4		22	Massachusetts	1.5
45	Nebraska	1.1		22	Texas	1.5
2	Nevada	2.5		22	Wisconsin	1.5
16	New Hampshire	1.6		22	Wyoming	1.5
6	New Jersey	2.0		30	Alabama	1.4
16	New Mexico	1.6		30	Louisiana	1.4
16	New York	1.6		30	Minnesota	1.4
30	North Carolina	1.4		30	Montana	1.4
37	North Dakota	1.3		30	North Carolina	1.4
9	Ohio	1.8		30	Tennessee	1.4
37	Oklahoma	1.3		30	Virginia	1.4
11	Oregon	1.7		37	Kentucky	1.3
16	Pennsylvania	1.6		37	North Dakota	1.3
9	Rhode Island	1.8		37	Oklahoma	1.3
46	South Carolina	1.0		37	Vermont	1.3
41	South Dakota	1.2		41	Georgia	1.2
30	Tennessee	1.4		41	Missouri	1.2
22	Texas	1.5		41	South Dakota	1.2
11	Utah	1.7		41	West Virginia	1.2
37	Vermont	1.3		45	Nebraska	1.1
30	Virginia	1.4		46	Arkansas	1.0
16	Washington	1.6		46	Indiana	1.0
41	West Virginia	1.2		46	South Carolina	1.0
22	Wisconsin	1.5		49	Maine	0.9
22	Wyoming	1.5		49	Mississippi	0.9
					District of Columbia	3.4

Source: Morgan Quitno Press using data from U.S. Bureau of the Census
"Government Finances: 1994-1995" (1998) (http://www.census.gov/govs/www/esti95.html)
*Includes Courts, Prosecution and Legal Services and Public Defense.

State Government Expenditures for Judicial and Legal Services in 1995

National Total = $7,533,740,000*

ALPHA ORDER

RANK	STATE	EXPENDITURES	% of USA
18	Alabama	$141,802,000	1.9%
14	Alaska	165,273,000	2.2%
32	Arizona	70,841,000	0.9%
42	Arkansas	36,150,000	0.5%
5	California	345,255,000	4.6%
20	Colorado	131,676,000	1.7%
9	Connecticut	227,805,000	3.0%
36	Delaware	59,887,000	0.8%
2	Florida	457,810,000	6.1%
35	Georgia	60,938,000	0.8%
23	Hawaii	118,539,000	1.6%
43	Idaho	35,984,000	0.5%
11	Illinois	207,115,000	2.7%
38	Indiana	56,052,000	0.7%
21	Iowa	129,725,000	1.7%
29	Kansas	92,642,000	1.2%
17	Kentucky	150,369,000	2.0%
27	Louisiana	98,383,000	1.3%
40	Maine	39,662,000	0.5%
8	Maryland	228,264,000	3.0%
3	Massachusetts	408,087,000	5.4%
13	Michigan	167,731,000	2.2%
22	Minnesota	128,355,000	1.7%
39	Mississippi	39,828,000	0.5%
25	Missouri	107,948,000	1.4%
50	Montana	19,254,000	0.3%
44	Nebraska	31,987,000	0.4%
46	Nevada	25,861,000	0.3%
37	New Hampshire	59,741,000	0.8%
4	New Jersey	345,385,000	4.6%
26	New Mexico	99,478,000	1.3%
1	New York	1,148,409,000	15.2%
6	North Carolina	315,937,000	4.2%
48	North Dakota	21,371,000	0.3%
19	Ohio	141,275,000	1.9%
28	Oklahoma	96,063,000	1.3%
16	Oregon	157,293,000	2.1%
10	Pennsylvania	213,050,000	2.8%
31	Rhode Island	77,377,000	1.0%
41	South Carolina	38,939,000	0.5%
49	South Dakota	20,648,000	0.3%
24	Tennessee	112,525,000	1.5%
7	Texas	290,001,000	3.8%
30	Utah	88,514,000	1.2%
45	Vermont	31,682,000	0.4%
12	Virginia	180,261,000	2.4%
33	Washington	65,951,000	0.9%
34	West Virginia	62,701,000	0.8%
15	Wisconsin	160,667,000	2.1%
47	Wyoming	23,249,000	0.3%

RANK ORDER

RANK	STATE	EXPENDITURES	% of USA
1	New York	$1,148,409,000	15.2%
2	Florida	457,810,000	6.1%
3	Massachusetts	408,087,000	5.4%
4	New Jersey	345,385,000	4.6%
5	California	345,255,000	4.6%
6	North Carolina	315,937,000	4.2%
7	Texas	290,001,000	3.8%
8	Maryland	228,264,000	3.0%
9	Connecticut	227,805,000	3.0%
10	Pennsylvania	213,050,000	2.8%
11	Illinois	207,115,000	2.7%
12	Virginia	180,261,000	2.4%
13	Michigan	167,731,000	2.2%
14	Alaska	165,273,000	2.2%
15	Wisconsin	160,667,000	2.1%
16	Oregon	157,293,000	2.1%
17	Kentucky	150,369,000	2.0%
18	Alabama	141,802,000	1.9%
19	Ohio	141,275,000	1.9%
20	Colorado	131,676,000	1.7%
21	Iowa	129,725,000	1.7%
22	Minnesota	128,355,000	1.7%
23	Hawaii	118,539,000	1.6%
24	Tennessee	112,525,000	1.5%
25	Missouri	107,948,000	1.4%
26	New Mexico	99,478,000	1.3%
27	Louisiana	98,383,000	1.3%
28	Oklahoma	96,063,000	1.3%
29	Kansas	92,642,000	1.2%
30	Utah	88,514,000	1.2%
31	Rhode Island	77,377,000	1.0%
32	Arizona	70,841,000	0.9%
33	Washington	65,951,000	0.9%
34	West Virginia	62,701,000	0.8%
35	Georgia	60,938,000	0.8%
36	Delaware	59,887,000	0.8%
37	New Hampshire	59,741,000	0.8%
38	Indiana	56,052,000	0.7%
39	Mississippi	39,828,000	0.5%
40	Maine	39,662,000	0.5%
41	South Carolina	38,939,000	0.5%
42	Arkansas	36,150,000	0.5%
43	Idaho	35,984,000	0.5%
44	Nebraska	31,987,000	0.4%
45	Vermont	31,682,000	0.4%
46	Nevada	25,861,000	0.3%
47	Wyoming	23,249,000	0.3%
48	North Dakota	21,371,000	0.3%
49	South Dakota	20,648,000	0.3%
50	Montana	19,254,000	0.3%
	District of Columbia**	NA	NA

Source: Morgan Quitno Press using data from U.S. Bureau of the Census
    "Government Finances: 1994-1995" (1998) (http://www.census.gov/govs/www/esti95.html)
*Direct general expenditures. Includes Courts, Prosecution and Legal Services and Public Defense.
**Not applicable.

Per Capita State Government Expenditures for Judicial and Legal Services: 1995

National Per Capita = $28.67*

<table>
<tr><td colspan="3">ALPHA ORDER</td><td colspan="3">RANK ORDER</td></tr>
<tr><td>RANK</td><td>STATE</td><td>PER CAPITA</td><td>RANK</td><td>STATE</td><td>PER CAPITA</td></tr>
<tr><td>23</td><td>Alabama</td><td>$33.21</td><td>1</td><td>Alaska</td><td>$274.73</td></tr>
<tr><td>1</td><td>Alaska</td><td>274.73</td><td>2</td><td>Hawaii</td><td>100.20</td></tr>
<tr><td>41</td><td>Arizona</td><td>16.45</td><td>3</td><td>Delaware</td><td>83.33</td></tr>
<tr><td>44</td><td>Arkansas</td><td>14.58</td><td>4</td><td>Rhode Island</td><td>78.21</td></tr>
<tr><td>47</td><td>California</td><td>10.97</td><td>5</td><td>Connecticut</td><td>69.84</td></tr>
<tr><td>20</td><td>Colorado</td><td>35.22</td><td>6</td><td>Massachusetts</td><td>67.36</td></tr>
<tr><td>5</td><td>Connecticut</td><td>69.84</td><td>7</td><td>New York</td><td>63.29</td></tr>
<tr><td>3</td><td>Delaware</td><td>83.33</td><td>8</td><td>New Mexico</td><td>59.08</td></tr>
<tr><td>24</td><td>Florida</td><td>32.29</td><td>9</td><td>Vermont</td><td>54.40</td></tr>
<tr><td>50</td><td>Georgia</td><td>8.48</td><td>10</td><td>New Hampshire</td><td>52.12</td></tr>
<tr><td>2</td><td>Hawaii</td><td>100.20</td><td>11</td><td>Oregon</td><td>50.07</td></tr>
<tr><td>27</td><td>Idaho</td><td>30.93</td><td>12</td><td>Wyoming</td><td>48.60</td></tr>
<tr><td>38</td><td>Illinois</td><td>17.45</td><td>13</td><td>Iowa</td><td>45.67</td></tr>
<tr><td>49</td><td>Indiana</td><td>9.69</td><td>14</td><td>Maryland</td><td>45.44</td></tr>
<tr><td>13</td><td>Iowa</td><td>45.67</td><td>15</td><td>Utah</td><td>44.45</td></tr>
<tr><td>19</td><td>Kansas</td><td>35.98</td><td>16</td><td>North Carolina</td><td>43.97</td></tr>
<tr><td>18</td><td>Kentucky</td><td>39.00</td><td>17</td><td>New Jersey</td><td>43.38</td></tr>
<tr><td>32</td><td>Louisiana</td><td>22.73</td><td>18</td><td>Kentucky</td><td>39.00</td></tr>
<tr><td>25</td><td>Maine</td><td>32.16</td><td>19</td><td>Kansas</td><td>35.98</td></tr>
<tr><td>14</td><td>Maryland</td><td>45.44</td><td>20</td><td>Colorado</td><td>35.22</td></tr>
<tr><td>6</td><td>Massachusetts</td><td>67.36</td><td>21</td><td>West Virginia</td><td>34.42</td></tr>
<tr><td>39</td><td>Michigan</td><td>17.36</td><td>22</td><td>North Dakota</td><td>33.32</td></tr>
<tr><td>30</td><td>Minnesota</td><td>27.87</td><td>23</td><td>Alabama</td><td>33.21</td></tr>
<tr><td>43</td><td>Mississippi</td><td>14.80</td><td>24</td><td>Florida</td><td>32.29</td></tr>
<tr><td>35</td><td>Missouri</td><td>20.22</td><td>25</td><td>Maine</td><td>32.16</td></tr>
<tr><td>33</td><td>Montana</td><td>22.17</td><td>26</td><td>Wisconsin</td><td>31.28</td></tr>
<tr><td>36</td><td>Nebraska</td><td>19.56</td><td>27</td><td>Idaho</td><td>30.93</td></tr>
<tr><td>40</td><td>Nevada</td><td>16.92</td><td>28</td><td>Oklahoma</td><td>29.37</td></tr>
<tr><td>10</td><td>New Hampshire</td><td>52.12</td><td>29</td><td>South Dakota</td><td>28.11</td></tr>
<tr><td>17</td><td>New Jersey</td><td>43.38</td><td>30</td><td>Minnesota</td><td>27.87</td></tr>
<tr><td>8</td><td>New Mexico</td><td>59.08</td><td>31</td><td>Virginia</td><td>27.31</td></tr>
<tr><td>7</td><td>New York</td><td>63.29</td><td>32</td><td>Louisiana</td><td>22.73</td></tr>
<tr><td>16</td><td>North Carolina</td><td>43.97</td><td>33</td><td>Montana</td><td>22.17</td></tr>
<tr><td>22</td><td>North Dakota</td><td>33.32</td><td>34</td><td>Tennessee</td><td>21.49</td></tr>
<tr><td>45</td><td>Ohio</td><td>12.68</td><td>35</td><td>Missouri</td><td>20.22</td></tr>
<tr><td>28</td><td>Oklahoma</td><td>29.37</td><td>36</td><td>Nebraska</td><td>19.56</td></tr>
<tr><td>11</td><td>Oregon</td><td>50.07</td><td>37</td><td>Pennsylvania</td><td>17.70</td></tr>
<tr><td>37</td><td>Pennsylvania</td><td>17.70</td><td>38</td><td>Illinois</td><td>17.45</td></tr>
<tr><td>4</td><td>Rhode Island</td><td>78.21</td><td>39</td><td>Michigan</td><td>17.36</td></tr>
<tr><td>48</td><td>South Carolina</td><td>10.53</td><td>40</td><td>Nevada</td><td>16.92</td></tr>
<tr><td>29</td><td>South Dakota</td><td>28.11</td><td>41</td><td>Arizona</td><td>16.45</td></tr>
<tr><td>34</td><td>Tennessee</td><td>21.49</td><td>42</td><td>Texas</td><td>15.51</td></tr>
<tr><td>42</td><td>Texas</td><td>15.51</td><td>43</td><td>Mississippi</td><td>14.80</td></tr>
<tr><td>15</td><td>Utah</td><td>44.45</td><td>44</td><td>Arkansas</td><td>14.58</td></tr>
<tr><td>9</td><td>Vermont</td><td>54.40</td><td>45</td><td>Ohio</td><td>12.68</td></tr>
<tr><td>31</td><td>Virginia</td><td>27.31</td><td>46</td><td>Washington</td><td>12.14</td></tr>
<tr><td>46</td><td>Washington</td><td>12.14</td><td>47</td><td>California</td><td>10.97</td></tr>
<tr><td>21</td><td>West Virginia</td><td>34.42</td><td>48</td><td>South Carolina</td><td>10.53</td></tr>
<tr><td>26</td><td>Wisconsin</td><td>31.28</td><td>49</td><td>Indiana</td><td>9.69</td></tr>
<tr><td>12</td><td>Wyoming</td><td>48.60</td><td>50</td><td>Georgia</td><td>8.48</td></tr>
<tr><td colspan="3"></td><td colspan="2">District of Columbia**</td><td>NA</td></tr>
</table>

Source: Morgan Quitno Press using data from U.S. Bureau of the Census
"Government Finances: 1994-1995" (1998) (http://www.census.gov/govs/www/esti95.html)
*Direct general expenditures. Includes Courts, Prosecution and Legal Services and Public Defense.
**Not applicable.

State Government Expenditures for Judicial and Legal Services
As a Percent of All Direct General Expenditures in 1995
National Percent = 1.5% of Direct General Expenditures*

ALPHA ORDER

RANK ORDER

RANK	STATE	PERCENT		RANK	STATE	PERCENT
23	Alabama	1.8		1	Alaska	4.2
1	Alaska	4.2		2	Delaware	2.7
33	Arizona	1.2		2	New York	2.7
44	Arkansas	0.8		4	New Mexico	2.6
46	California	0.7		4	North Carolina	2.6
12	Colorado	2.3		6	Connecticut	2.5
6	Connecticut	2.5		6	New Hampshire	2.5
2	Delaware	2.7		6	Rhode Island	2.5
16	Florida	2.2		9	Iowa	2.4
48	Georgia	0.5		9	Massachusetts	2.4
12	Hawaii	2.3		9	Oregon	2.4
23	Idaho	1.8		12	Colorado	2.3
37	Illinois	1.0		12	Hawaii	2.3
47	Indiana	0.6		12	Maryland	2.3
9	Iowa	2.4		12	Utah	2.3
16	Kansas	2.2		16	Florida	2.2
19	Kentucky	2.0		16	Kansas	2.2
37	Louisiana	1.0		18	Wyoming	2.1
28	Maine	1.4		19	Kentucky	2.0
12	Maryland	2.3		19	Vermont	2.0
9	Massachusetts	2.4		21	New Jersey	1.9
37	Michigan	1.0		21	Oklahoma	1.9
28	Minnesota	1.4		23	Alabama	1.8
42	Mississippi	0.9		23	Idaho	1.8
28	Missouri	1.4		23	Wisconsin	1.8
37	Montana	1.0		26	Virginia	1.6
35	Nebraska	1.1		27	West Virginia	1.5
35	Nevada	1.1		28	Maine	1.4
6	New Hampshire	2.5		28	Minnesota	1.4
21	New Jersey	1.9		28	Missouri	1.4
4	New Mexico	2.6		28	South Dakota	1.4
2	New York	2.7		32	North Dakota	1.3
4	North Carolina	2.6		33	Arizona	1.2
32	North Dakota	1.3		33	Tennessee	1.2
44	Ohio	0.8		35	Nebraska	1.1
21	Oklahoma	1.9		35	Nevada	1.1
9	Oregon	2.4		37	Illinois	1.0
42	Pennsylvania	0.9		37	Louisiana	1.0
6	Rhode Island	2.5		37	Michigan	1.0
48	South Carolina	0.5		37	Montana	1.0
28	South Dakota	1.4		37	Texas	1.0
33	Tennessee	1.2		42	Mississippi	0.9
37	Texas	1.0		42	Pennsylvania	0.9
12	Utah	2.3		44	Arkansas	0.8
19	Vermont	2.0		44	Ohio	0.8
26	Virginia	1.6		46	California	0.7
48	Washington	0.5		47	Indiana	0.6
27	West Virginia	1.5		48	Georgia	0.5
23	Wisconsin	1.8		48	South Carolina	0.5
18	Wyoming	2.1		48	Washington	0.5
					District of Columbia**	NA

Source: Morgan Quitno Press using data from U.S. Bureau of the Census
   "Government Finances: 1994-1995" (1998) (http://www.census.gov/govs/www/esti95.html)
*Includes Courts, Prosecution and Legal Services and Public Defense.
**Not applicable.

Local Government Expenditures for Judicial and Legal Services in 1995

National Total = $11,634,413,000*

RANK	STATE	EXPENDITURES	% of USA
25	Alabama	$71,751,000	0.6%
46	Alaska	9,325,000	0.1%
11	Arizona	312,105,000	2.7%
30	Arkansas	47,717,000	0.4%
1	California	3,070,814,000	26.4%
21	Colorado	121,543,000	1.0%
36	Connecticut	32,924,000	0.3%
49	Delaware	7,141,000	0.1%
5	Florida	652,850,000	5.6%
12	Georgia	283,318,000	2.4%
37	Hawaii	31,349,000	0.3%
35	Idaho	35,725,000	0.3%
9	Illinois	506,208,000	4.4%
17	Indiana	165,586,000	1.4%
31	Iowa	46,399,000	0.4%
26	Kansas	59,074,000	0.5%
39	Kentucky	26,467,000	0.2%
15	Louisiana	167,472,000	1.4%
47	Maine	9,088,000	0.1%
19	Maryland	141,833,000	1.2%
32	Massachusetts	44,093,000	0.4%
7	Michigan	529,632,000	4.6%
13	Minnesota	196,091,000	1.7%
28	Mississippi	51,203,000	0.4%
22	Missouri	106,125,000	0.9%
38	Montana	31,284,000	0.3%
34	Nebraska	42,264,000	0.4%
20	Nevada	133,806,000	1.2%
45	New Hampshire	12,528,000	0.1%
8	New Jersey	512,882,000	4.4%
41	New Mexico	17,571,000	0.2%
2	New York	762,562,000	6.6%
27	North Carolina	56,815,000	0.5%
43	North Dakota	14,678,000	0.1%
4	Ohio	662,804,000	5.7%
29	Oklahoma	49,829,000	0.4%
24	Oregon	81,408,000	0.7%
6	Pennsylvania	582,138,000	5.0%
48	Rhode Island	8,317,000	0.1%
23	South Carolina	97,358,000	0.8%
44	South Dakota	14,338,000	0.1%
18	Tennessee	149,402,000	1.3%
3	Texas	735,394,000	6.3%
33	Utah	43,781,000	0.4%
50	Vermont	1,911,000	0.0%
16	Virginia	165,868,000	1.4%
10	Washington	351,894,000	3.0%
40	West Virginia	25,483,000	0.2%
14	Wisconsin	190,800,000	1.6%
42	Wyoming	16,317,000	0.1%

RANK	STATE	EXPENDITURES	% of USA
1	California	$3,070,814,000	26.4%
2	New York	762,562,000	6.6%
3	Texas	735,394,000	6.3%
4	Ohio	662,804,000	5.7%
5	Florida	652,850,000	5.6%
6	Pennsylvania	582,138,000	5.0%
7	Michigan	529,632,000	4.6%
8	New Jersey	512,882,000	4.4%
9	Illinois	506,208,000	4.4%
10	Washington	351,894,000	3.0%
11	Arizona	312,105,000	2.7%
12	Georgia	283,318,000	2.4%
13	Minnesota	196,091,000	1.7%
14	Wisconsin	190,800,000	1.6%
15	Louisiana	167,472,000	1.4%
16	Virginia	165,868,000	1.4%
17	Indiana	165,586,000	1.4%
18	Tennessee	149,402,000	1.3%
19	Maryland	141,833,000	1.2%
20	Nevada	133,806,000	1.2%
21	Colorado	121,543,000	1.0%
22	Missouri	106,125,000	0.9%
23	South Carolina	97,358,000	0.8%
24	Oregon	81,408,000	0.7%
25	Alabama	71,751,000	0.6%
26	Kansas	59,074,000	0.5%
27	North Carolina	56,815,000	0.5%
28	Mississippi	51,203,000	0.4%
29	Oklahoma	49,829,000	0.4%
30	Arkansas	47,717,000	0.4%
31	Iowa	46,399,000	0.4%
32	Massachusetts	44,093,000	0.4%
33	Utah	43,781,000	0.4%
34	Nebraska	42,264,000	0.4%
35	Idaho	35,725,000	0.3%
36	Connecticut	32,924,000	0.3%
37	Hawaii	31,349,000	0.3%
38	Montana	31,284,000	0.3%
39	Kentucky	26,467,000	0.2%
40	West Virginia	25,483,000	0.2%
41	New Mexico	17,571,000	0.2%
42	Wyoming	16,317,000	0.1%
43	North Dakota	14,678,000	0.1%
44	South Dakota	14,338,000	0.1%
45	New Hampshire	12,528,000	0.1%
46	Alaska	9,325,000	0.1%
47	Maine	9,088,000	0.1%
48	Rhode Island	8,317,000	0.1%
49	Delaware	7,141,000	0.1%
50	Vermont	1,911,000	0.0%
	District of Columbia	147,148,000	1.3%

Source: Morgan Quitno Press using data from U.S. Bureau of the Census
"Government Finances: 1994-1995" (1998) (http://www.census.gov/govs/www/esti95.html)
*Direct general expenditures. Includes Courts, Prosecution and Legal Services and Public Defense.

Per Capita Local Government Expenditures for Judicial & Legal Services: 1995

National Per Capita = $44.28*

ALPHA ORDER			RANK ORDER		
RANK	STATE	PER CAPITA	RANK	STATE	PER CAPITA
36	Alabama	$16.80	1	California	$97.57
38	Alaska	15.50	2	Nevada	87.55
3	Arizona	72.46	3	Arizona	72.46
34	Arkansas	19.24	4	Washington	64.77
1	California	97.57	5	New Jersey	64.41
19	Colorado	32.51	6	Ohio	59.51
43	Connecticut	10.09	7	Michigan	54.81
44	Delaware	9.94	8	Pennsylvania	48.35
9	Florida	46.04	9	Florida	46.04
13	Georgia	39.41	10	Illinois	42.66
24	Hawaii	26.50	11	Minnesota	42.58
20	Idaho	30.70	12	New York	42.03
10	Illinois	42.66	13	Georgia	39.41
21	Indiana	28.62	14	Texas	39.34
37	Iowa	16.33	15	Louisiana	38.69
29	Kansas	22.95	16	Wisconsin	37.14
49	Kentucky	6.86	17	Montana	36.02
15	Louisiana	38.69	18	Wyoming	34.11
47	Maine	7.37	19	Colorado	32.51
23	Maryland	28.23	20	Idaho	30.70
48	Massachusetts	7.28	21	Indiana	28.62
7	Michigan	54.81	22	Tennessee	28.54
11	Minnesota	42.58	23	Maryland	28.23
35	Mississippi	19.03	24	Hawaii	26.50
32	Missouri	19.88	25	South Carolina	26.32
17	Montana	36.02	26	Oregon	25.92
27	Nebraska	25.84	27	Nebraska	25.84
2	Nevada	87.55	28	Virginia	25.13
41	New Hampshire	10.93	29	Kansas	22.95
5	New Jersey	64.41	30	North Dakota	22.89
42	New Mexico	10.44	31	Utah	21.98
12	New York	42.03	32	Missouri	19.88
46	North Carolina	7.91	33	South Dakota	19.52
30	North Dakota	22.89	34	Arkansas	19.24
6	Ohio	59.51	35	Mississippi	19.03
39	Oklahoma	15.23	36	Alabama	16.80
26	Oregon	25.92	37	Iowa	16.33
8	Pennsylvania	48.35	38	Alaska	15.50
45	Rhode Island	8.41	39	Oklahoma	15.23
25	South Carolina	26.32	40	West Virginia	13.99
33	South Dakota	19.52	41	New Hampshire	10.93
22	Tennessee	28.54	42	New Mexico	10.44
14	Texas	39.34	43	Connecticut	10.09
31	Utah	21.98	44	Delaware	9.94
50	Vermont	3.28	45	Rhode Island	8.41
28	Virginia	25.13	46	North Carolina	7.91
4	Washington	64.77	47	Maine	7.37
40	West Virginia	13.99	48	Massachusetts	7.28
16	Wisconsin	37.14	49	Kentucky	6.86
18	Wyoming	34.11	50	Vermont	3.28
				District of Columbia	266.35

Source: Morgan Quitno Press using data from U.S. Bureau of the Census
   "Government Finances: 1994-1995" (1998) (http://www.census.gov/govs/www/esti95.html)
*Direct general expenditures. Includes Courts, Prosecution and Legal Services and Public Defense.

Local Government Expenditures for Judicial and Legal Services
As a Percent of All Direct General Expenditures in 1995
National Percent = 1.8% of Direct General Expenditures*

RANK	STATE	PERCENT
36	Alabama	0.9
44	Alaska	0.4
1	Arizona	3.2
20	Arkansas	1.3
1	California	3.2
24	Colorado	1.2
44	Connecticut	0.4
40	Delaware	0.6
13	Florida	1.8
13	Georgia	1.8
9	Hawaii	2.1
16	Idaho	1.5
13	Illinois	1.8
18	Indiana	1.4
39	Iowa	0.7
31	Kansas	1.0
44	Kentucky	0.4
10	Louisiana	2.0
44	Maine	0.4
24	Maryland	1.2
49	Massachusetts	0.3
7	Michigan	2.2
20	Minnesota	1.3
31	Mississippi	1.0
27	Missouri	1.1
11	Montana	1.9
27	Nebraska	1.1
1	Nevada	3.2
40	New Hampshire	0.6
7	New Jersey	2.2
42	New Mexico	0.5
31	New York	1.0
44	North Carolina	0.4
20	North Dakota	1.3
4	Ohio	2.6
38	Oklahoma	0.8
31	Oregon	1.0
6	Pennsylvania	2.3
42	Rhode Island	0.5
18	South Carolina	1.4
31	South Dakota	1.0
16	Tennessee	1.5
11	Texas	1.9
27	Utah	1.1
50	Vermont	0.2
24	Virginia	1.2
5	Washington	2.5
36	West Virginia	0.9
20	Wisconsin	1.3
27	Wyoming	1.1

RANK	STATE	PERCENT
1	Arizona	3.2
1	California	3.2
1	Nevada	3.2
4	Ohio	2.6
5	Washington	2.5
6	Pennsylvania	2.3
7	Michigan	2.2
7	New Jersey	2.2
9	Hawaii	2.1
10	Louisiana	2.0
11	Montana	1.9
11	Texas	1.9
13	Florida	1.8
13	Georgia	1.8
13	Illinois	1.8
16	Idaho	1.5
16	Tennessee	1.5
18	Indiana	1.4
18	South Carolina	1.4
20	Arkansas	1.3
20	Minnesota	1.3
20	North Dakota	1.3
20	Wisconsin	1.3
24	Colorado	1.2
24	Maryland	1.2
24	Virginia	1.2
27	Missouri	1.1
27	Nebraska	1.1
27	Utah	1.1
27	Wyoming	1.1
31	Kansas	1.0
31	Mississippi	1.0
31	New York	1.0
31	Oregon	1.0
31	South Dakota	1.0
36	Alabama	0.9
36	West Virginia	0.9
38	Oklahoma	0.8
39	Iowa	0.7
40	Delaware	0.6
40	New Hampshire	0.6
42	New Mexico	0.5
42	Rhode Island	0.5
44	Alaska	0.4
44	Connecticut	0.4
44	Kentucky	0.4
44	Maine	0.4
44	North Carolina	0.4
49	Massachusetts	0.3
50	Vermont	0.2
	District of Columbia	3.4

Source: Morgan Quitno Press using data from U.S. Bureau of the Census
"Government Finances: 1994-1995" (1998) (http://www.census.gov/govs/www/esti95.html)
*Includes Courts, Prosecution and Legal Services and Public Defense.

State and Local Government Judicial and Legal Payroll in 1995

National Total = $11,924,751,660*

ALPHA ORDER

RANK	STATE	PAYROLL	% of USA
23	Alabama	$136,609,260	1.15%
37	Alaska	58,151,856	0.49%
12	Arizona	245,938,836	2.06%
38	Arkansas	55,487,316	0.47%
1	California	1,916,338,068	16.07%
19	Colorado	186,187,284	1.56%
26	Connecticut	126,396,336	1.06%
41	Delaware	46,992,924	0.39%
3	Florida	813,111,000	6.82%
13	Georgia	244,023,120	2.05%
30	Hawaii	99,645,480	0.84%
43	Idaho	45,426,360	0.38%
6	Illinois	555,710,100	4.66%
22	Indiana	142,154,568	1.19%
29	Iowa	109,295,808	0.92%
32	Kansas	92,129,556	0.77%
25	Kentucky	128,047,236	1.07%
21	Louisiana	162,227,952	1.36%
49	Maine	23,020,140	0.19%
15	Maryland	205,762,068	1.73%
11	Massachusetts	256,005,612	2.15%
9	Michigan	390,378,708	3.27%
14	Minnesota	209,025,216	1.75%
35	Mississippi	72,642,252	0.61%
27	Missouri	116,000,448	0.97%
45	Montana	24,283,176	0.20%
39	Nebraska	49,630,356	0.42%
28	Nevada	114,713,940	0.96%
44	New Hampshire	29,859,672	0.25%
4	New Jersey	690,990,684	5.79%
34	New Mexico	75,371,292	0.63%
2	New York	1,297,945,668	10.88%
17	North Carolina	197,217,888	1.65%
47	North Dakota	23,449,176	0.20%
7	Ohio	462,723,648	3.88%
31	Oklahoma	94,243,584	0.79%
24	Oregon	132,095,664	1.11%
8	Pennsylvania	457,367,124	3.84%
40	Rhode Island	48,118,512	0.40%
33	South Carolina	87,819,792	0.74%
48	South Dakota	23,225,280	0.19%
20	Tennessee	163,223,520	1.37%
5	Texas	622,286,160	5.22%
36	Utah	67,056,696	0.56%
50	Vermont	18,484,524	0.16%
16	Virginia	203,910,960	1.71%
10	Washington	264,309,684	2.22%
42	West Virginia	46,740,480	0.39%
18	Wisconsin	192,772,296	1.62%
46	Wyoming	23,834,184	0.20%

RANK ORDER

RANK	STATE	PAYROLL	% of USA
1	California	$1,916,338,068	16.07%
2	New York	1,297,945,668	10.88%
3	Florida	813,111,000	6.82%
4	New Jersey	690,990,684	5.79%
5	Texas	622,286,160	5.22%
6	Illinois	555,710,100	4.66%
7	Ohio	462,723,648	3.88%
8	Pennsylvania	457,367,124	3.84%
9	Michigan	390,378,708	3.27%
10	Washington	264,309,684	2.22%
11	Massachusetts	256,005,612	2.15%
12	Arizona	245,938,836	2.06%
13	Georgia	244,023,120	2.05%
14	Minnesota	209,025,216	1.75%
15	Maryland	205,762,068	1.73%
16	Virginia	203,910,960	1.71%
17	North Carolina	197,217,888	1.65%
18	Wisconsin	192,772,296	1.62%
19	Colorado	186,187,284	1.56%
20	Tennessee	163,223,520	1.37%
21	Louisiana	162,227,952	1.36%
22	Indiana	142,154,568	1.19%
23	Alabama	136,609,260	1.15%
24	Oregon	132,095,664	1.11%
25	Kentucky	128,047,236	1.07%
26	Connecticut	126,396,336	1.06%
27	Missouri	116,000,448	0.97%
28	Nevada	114,713,940	0.96%
29	Iowa	109,295,808	0.92%
30	Hawaii	99,645,480	0.84%
31	Oklahoma	94,243,584	0.79%
32	Kansas	92,129,556	0.77%
33	South Carolina	87,819,792	0.74%
34	New Mexico	75,371,292	0.63%
35	Mississippi	72,642,252	0.61%
36	Utah	67,056,696	0.56%
37	Alaska	58,151,856	0.49%
38	Arkansas	55,487,316	0.47%
39	Nebraska	49,630,356	0.42%
40	Rhode Island	48,118,512	0.40%
41	Delaware	46,992,924	0.39%
42	West Virginia	46,740,480	0.39%
43	Idaho	45,426,360	0.38%
44	New Hampshire	29,859,672	0.25%
45	Montana	24,283,176	0.20%
46	Wyoming	23,834,184	0.20%
47	North Dakota	23,449,176	0.20%
48	South Dakota	23,225,280	0.19%
49	Maine	23,020,140	0.19%
50	Vermont	18,484,524	0.16%
	District of Columbia	76,370,196	0.64%

Source: U.S. Bureau of the Census, Governments Division
"1995 State and Local Government Employment" (http://www.census.gov/govs/www/apes95sl.html)
*Twelve times the October 1995 full and part time payroll. Includes court and court related activities (except probation and parole which are part of corrections), court activities of sheriffs' offices, prosecuting attorneys' and public defenders' offices, legal departments and attorneys providing government-wide legal service.

State and Local Government Police Protection Payroll in 1995

National Total = $29,721,280,788*

ALPHA ORDER

RANK	STATE	PAYROLL	% of USA
25	Alabama	$316,179,984	1.06%
41	Alaska	103,855,968	0.35%
18	Arizona	475,795,944	1.60%
34	Arkansas	150,816,096	0.51%
1	California	4,540,096,860	15.28%
22	Colorado	392,179,392	1.32%
19	Connecticut	445,772,820	1.50%
44	Delaware	82,874,736	0.28%
4	Florida	1,797,400,944	6.05%
12	Georgia	586,015,716	1.97%
37	Hawaii	137,704,272	0.46%
42	Idaho	102,618,192	0.35%
3	Illinois	1,860,497,208	6.26%
20	Indiana	405,456,396	1.36%
31	Iowa	211,549,116	0.71%
29	Kansas	226,843,860	0.76%
30	Kentucky	216,768,888	0.73%
24	Louisiana	337,949,256	1.14%
43	Maine	86,218,728	0.29%
11	Maryland	586,045,872	1.97%
10	Massachusetts	735,335,484	2.47%
9	Michigan	920,579,340	3.10%
21	Minnesota	397,646,148	1.34%
33	Mississippi	176,300,196	0.59%
17	Missouri	490,154,832	1.65%
46	Montana	59,009,604	0.20%
38	Nebraska	134,608,272	0.45%
32	Nevada	206,638,200	0.70%
40	New Hampshire	111,408,444	0.37%
6	New Jersey	1,539,200,352	5.18%
36	New Mexico	139,406,604	0.47%
2	New York	3,632,610,312	12.22%
14	North Carolina	562,082,532	1.89%
50	North Dakota	36,806,724	0.12%
8	Ohio	1,075,130,676	3.62%
28	Oklahoma	264,462,984	0.89%
26	Oregon	306,612,192	1.03%
7	Pennsylvania	1,159,610,976	3.90%
39	Rhode Island	121,935,756	0.41%
27	South Carolina	283,304,280	0.95%
49	South Dakota	43,354,188	0.15%
23	Tennessee	383,887,140	1.29%
5	Texas	1,746,122,184	5.87%
35	Utah	148,653,048	0.50%
47	Vermont	48,216,804	0.16%
13	Virginia	577,816,608	1.94%
15	Washington	537,328,572	1.81%
45	West Virginia	81,149,364	0.27%
16	Wisconsin	498,652,128	1.68%
48	Wyoming	46,084,428	0.16%

RANK ORDER

RANK	STATE	PAYROLL	% of USA
1	California	$4,540,096,860	15.28%
2	New York	3,632,610,312	12.22%
3	Illinois	1,860,497,208	6.26%
4	Florida	1,797,400,944	6.05%
5	Texas	1,746,122,184	5.87%
6	New Jersey	1,539,200,352	5.18%
7	Pennsylvania	1,159,610,976	3.90%
8	Ohio	1,075,130,676	3.62%
9	Michigan	920,579,340	3.10%
10	Massachusetts	735,335,484	2.47%
11	Maryland	586,045,872	1.97%
12	Georgia	586,015,716	1.97%
13	Virginia	577,816,608	1.94%
14	North Carolina	562,082,532	1.89%
15	Washington	537,328,572	1.81%
16	Wisconsin	498,652,128	1.68%
17	Missouri	490,154,832	1.65%
18	Arizona	475,795,944	1.60%
19	Connecticut	445,772,820	1.50%
20	Indiana	405,456,396	1.36%
21	Minnesota	397,646,148	1.34%
22	Colorado	392,179,392	1.32%
23	Tennessee	383,887,140	1.29%
24	Louisiana	337,949,256	1.14%
25	Alabama	316,179,984	1.06%
26	Oregon	306,612,192	1.03%
27	South Carolina	283,304,280	0.95%
28	Oklahoma	264,462,984	0.89%
29	Kansas	226,843,860	0.76%
30	Kentucky	216,768,888	0.73%
31	Iowa	211,549,116	0.71%
32	Nevada	206,638,200	0.70%
33	Mississippi	176,300,196	0.59%
34	Arkansas	150,816,096	0.51%
35	Utah	148,653,048	0.50%
36	New Mexico	139,406,604	0.47%
37	Hawaii	137,704,272	0.46%
38	Nebraska	134,608,272	0.45%
39	Rhode Island	121,935,756	0.41%
40	New Hampshire	111,408,444	0.37%
41	Alaska	103,855,968	0.35%
42	Idaho	102,618,192	0.35%
43	Maine	86,218,728	0.29%
44	Delaware	82,874,736	0.28%
45	West Virginia	81,149,364	0.27%
46	Montana	59,009,604	0.20%
47	Vermont	48,216,804	0.16%
48	Wyoming	46,084,428	0.16%
49	South Dakota	43,354,188	0.15%
50	North Dakota	36,806,724	0.12%
	District of Columbia	194,532,168	0.65%

Source: U.S. Bureau of the Census, Governments Division
    "1995 State and Local Government Employment" (http://www.census.gov/govs/www/apes95sl.html)
*Twelve times the October 1995 full and part time payroll. Includes all activities concerned with the enforcement of law and order, including coroners' offices, police training academies, investigation bureaus and local jails.

State and Local Government Corrections Payroll in 1995

National Total = $19,443,945,636*

RANK	STATE	PAYROLL	% of USA
27	Alabama	$179,046,504	0.92%
41	Alaska	58,018,464	0.30%
15	Arizona	327,658,428	1.69%
35	Arkansas	97,267,572	0.50%
1	California	2,919,221,748	15.01%
22	Colorado	241,428,108	1.24%
19	Connecticut	263,064,168	1.35%
42	Delaware	57,044,472	0.29%
4	Florida	1,318,425,780	6.78%
10	Georgia	621,128,820	3.19%
40	Hawaii	61,536,360	0.32%
39	Idaho	61,732,776	0.32%
7	Illinois	741,396,912	3.81%
21	Indiana	249,254,796	1.28%
33	Iowa	100,929,012	0.52%
31	Kansas	144,409,296	0.74%
28	Kentucky	172,818,684	0.89%
24	Louisiana	213,230,148	1.10%
44	Maine	50,443,068	0.26%
12	Maryland	422,674,608	2.17%
13	Massachusetts	382,681,596	1.97%
5	Michigan	797,417,808	4.10%
20	Minnesota	254,291,352	1.31%
34	Mississippi	98,979,600	0.51%
26	Missouri	188,918,436	0.97%
45	Montana	29,358,372	0.15%
38	Nebraska	66,723,744	0.34%
29	Nevada	160,492,728	0.83%
43	New Hampshire	52,194,264	0.27%
9	New Jersey	670,403,772	3.45%
32	New Mexico	141,342,744	0.73%
2	New York	2,463,290,892	12.67%
14	North Carolina	382,080,360	1.97%
50	North Dakota	17,214,744	0.09%
8	Ohio	702,146,580	3.61%
30	Oklahoma	152,703,732	0.79%
25	Oregon	192,517,752	0.99%
6	Pennsylvania	741,553,380	3.81%
36	Rhode Island	89,568,288	0.46%
23	South Carolina	226,021,572	1.16%
46	South Dakota	23,046,996	0.12%
17	Tennessee	276,832,620	1.42%
3	Texas	1,565,311,728	8.05%
37	Utah	88,006,656	0.45%
48	Vermont	21,105,384	0.11%
11	Virginia	548,900,436	2.82%
16	Washington	315,152,688	1.62%
47	West Virginia	22,791,948	0.12%
18	Wisconsin	274,563,528	1.41%
49	Wyoming	18,417,636	0.09%

RANK	STATE	PAYROLL	% of USA
1	California	$2,919,221,748	15.01%
2	New York	2,463,290,892	12.67%
3	Texas	1,565,311,728	8.05%
4	Florida	1,318,425,780	6.78%
5	Michigan	797,417,808	4.10%
6	Pennsylvania	741,553,380	3.81%
7	Illinois	741,396,912	3.81%
8	Ohio	702,146,580	3.61%
9	New Jersey	670,403,772	3.45%
10	Georgia	621,128,820	3.19%
11	Virginia	548,900,436	2.82%
12	Maryland	422,674,608	2.17%
13	Massachusetts	382,681,596	1.97%
14	North Carolina	382,080,360	1.97%
15	Arizona	327,658,428	1.69%
16	Washington	315,152,688	1.62%
17	Tennessee	276,832,620	1.42%
18	Wisconsin	274,563,528	1.41%
19	Connecticut	263,064,168	1.35%
20	Minnesota	254,291,352	1.31%
21	Indiana	249,254,796	1.28%
22	Colorado	241,428,108	1.24%
23	South Carolina	226,021,572	1.16%
24	Louisiana	213,230,148	1.10%
25	Oregon	192,517,752	0.99%
26	Missouri	188,918,436	0.97%
27	Alabama	179,046,504	0.92%
28	Kentucky	172,818,684	0.89%
29	Nevada	160,492,728	0.83%
30	Oklahoma	152,703,732	0.79%
31	Kansas	144,409,296	0.74%
32	New Mexico	141,342,744	0.73%
33	Iowa	100,929,012	0.52%
34	Mississippi	98,979,600	0.51%
35	Arkansas	97,267,572	0.50%
36	Rhode Island	89,568,288	0.46%
37	Utah	88,006,656	0.45%
38	Nebraska	66,723,744	0.34%
39	Idaho	61,732,776	0.32%
40	Hawaii	61,536,360	0.32%
41	Alaska	58,018,464	0.30%
42	Delaware	57,044,472	0.29%
43	New Hampshire	52,194,264	0.27%
44	Maine	50,443,068	0.26%
45	Montana	29,358,372	0.15%
46	South Dakota	23,046,996	0.12%
47	West Virginia	22,791,948	0.12%
48	Vermont	21,105,384	0.11%
49	Wyoming	18,417,636	0.09%
50	North Dakota	17,214,744	0.09%
	District of Columbia	179,184,576	0.92%

Source: U.S. Bureau of the Census, Governments Division
    "1995 State and Local Government Employment" (http://www.census.gov/govs/www/apes95sl.html)
Twelve times the October 1995 full and part time payroll. Includes all activities pertaining to the confinement and correction of adults and minors accused or convicted of criminal offenses. Includes any pardon, probation or parole activity.

Base Salary for Justices of States' Highest Courts in 1998

National Average = $105,058

ALPHA ORDER

RANK	STATE	SALARY
11	Alabama	$115,695
16	Alaska	111,552
14	Arizona	114,257
26	Arkansas	105,507
3	California	131,085
38	Colorado	94,000
12	Connecticut	115,303
9	Delaware	121,200
1	Florida	137,314
8	Georgia	124,310
39	Hawaii	93,780
42	Idaho	86,468
4	Illinois	130,250
13	Indiana	115,000
28	Iowa	103,600
35	Kansas	96,489
32	Kentucky	98,800
29	Louisiana	103,336
41	Maine	90,909
23	Maryland	107,300
22	Massachusetts	107,730
7	Michigan	124,770
30	Minnesota	103,080
33	Mississippi	98,300
20	Missouri	108,903
50	Montana	77,092
37	Nebraska	94,892
44	Nevada	85,000
36	New Hampshire	95,623
2	New Jersey	132,250
47	New Mexico	83,593
6	New York	125,000
27	North Carolina	104,333
49	North Dakota	79,771
18	Ohio	110,550
34	Oklahoma	97,807
40	Oregon	93,600
5	Pennsylvania	125,936
17	Rhode Island	110,776
25	South Carolina	106,712
48	South Dakota	82,700
21	Tennessee	107,820
19	Texas	109,000
31	Utah	99,500
43	Vermont	86,436
10	Virginia	116,526
15	Washington	112,078
44	West Virginia	85,000
24	Wisconsin	106,967
44	Wyoming	85,000

RANK ORDER

RANK	STATE	SALARY
1	Florida	$137,314
2	New Jersey	132,250
3	California	131,085
4	Illinois	130,250
5	Pennsylvania	125,936
6	New York	125,000
7	Michigan	124,770
8	Georgia	124,310
9	Delaware	121,200
10	Virginia	116,526
11	Alabama	115,695
12	Connecticut	115,303
13	Indiana	115,000
14	Arizona	114,257
15	Washington	112,078
16	Alaska	111,552
17	Rhode Island	110,776
18	Ohio	110,550
19	Texas	109,000
20	Missouri	108,903
21	Tennessee	107,820
22	Massachusetts	107,730
23	Maryland	107,300
24	Wisconsin	106,967
25	South Carolina	106,712
26	Arkansas	105,507
27	North Carolina	104,333
28	Iowa	103,600
29	Louisiana	103,336
30	Minnesota	103,080
31	Utah	99,500
32	Kentucky	98,800
33	Mississippi	98,300
34	Oklahoma	97,807
35	Kansas	96,489
36	New Hampshire	95,623
37	Nebraska	94,892
38	Colorado	94,000
39	Hawaii	93,780
40	Oregon	93,600
41	Maine	90,909
42	Idaho	86,468
43	Vermont	86,436
44	Nevada	85,000
44	West Virginia	85,000
44	Wyoming	85,000
47	New Mexico	83,593
48	South Dakota	82,700
49	North Dakota	79,771
50	Montana	77,092
	District of Columbia	145,500

Source: National Center for State Courts
  "Survey of Judicial Salaries-Winter 1998" (Volume 23, Number 1)

Base Salary of Judges of Intermediate Appellate Courts in 1998

National Average = $103,703

ALPHA ORDER

RANK	STATE	SALARY
9	Alabama	$114,615
15	Alaska	105,384
10	Arizona	111,536
20	Arkansas	102,171
4	California	122,893
37	Colorado	89,500
13	Connecticut	107,214
NA	Delaware*	NA
2	Florida	123,583
3	Georgia	123,522
36	Hawaii	89,780
38	Idaho	85,468
5	Illinois	122,588
12	Indiana	110,000
26	Iowa	99,600
32	Kansas	93,044
30	Kentucky	94,767
27	Louisiana	97,928
NA	Maine*	NA
23	Maryland	100,300
25	Massachusetts	99,690
8	Michigan	114,788
28	Minnesota	97,128
33	Mississippi	91,500
21	Missouri	101,711
NA	Montana*	NA
35	Nebraska	90,148
NA	Nevada*	NA
NA	New Hampshire*	NA
1	New Jersey	124,200
39	New Mexico	79,413
7	New York	119,000
24	North Carolina	99,986
NA	North Dakota*	NA
17	Ohio	102,950
31	Oklahoma	94,349
33	Oregon	91,500
6	Pennsylvania	121,992
NA	Rhode Island*	NA
19	South Carolina	102,711
NA	South Dakota*	NA
18	Tennessee	102,804
16	Texas	103,550
29	Utah	94,950
NA	Vermont*	NA
11	Virginia	110,700
14	Washington	106,537
NA	West Virginia*	NA
22	Wisconsin	100,911
NA	Wyoming*	NA

RANK ORDER

RANK	STATE	SALARY
1	New Jersey	$124,200
2	Florida	123,583
3	Georgia	123,522
4	California	122,893
5	Illinois	122,588
6	Pennsylvania	121,992
7	New York	119,000
8	Michigan	114,788
9	Alabama	114,615
10	Arizona	111,536
11	Virginia	110,700
12	Indiana	110,000
13	Connecticut	107,214
14	Washington	106,537
15	Alaska	105,384
16	Texas	103,550
17	Ohio	102,950
18	Tennessee	102,804
19	South Carolina	102,711
20	Arkansas	102,171
21	Missouri	101,711
22	Wisconsin	100,911
23	Maryland	100,300
24	North Carolina	99,986
25	Massachusetts	99,690
26	Iowa	99,600
27	Louisiana	97,928
28	Minnesota	97,128
29	Utah	94,950
30	Kentucky	94,767
31	Oklahoma	94,349
32	Kansas	93,044
33	Mississippi	91,500
33	Oregon	91,500
35	Nebraska	90,148
36	Hawaii	89,780
37	Colorado	89,500
38	Idaho	85,468
39	New Mexico	79,413
NA	Delaware*	NA
NA	Maine*	NA
NA	Montana*	NA
NA	Nevada*	NA
NA	New Hampshire*	NA
NA	North Dakota*	NA
NA	Rhode Island*	NA
NA	South Dakota*	NA
NA	Vermont*	NA
NA	West Virginia*	NA
NA	Wyoming*	NA
	District of Columbia*	NA

Source: National Center for State Courts
"Survey of Judicial Salaries-Winter 1998" (Volume 23, Number 1)
*No intermediate court.

Base Salaries of Judges of General Trial Courts in 1998

National Average = $94,041

ALPHA ORDER

RANK	STATE	SALARY
43	Alabama	$80,615
12	Alaska	103,152
8	Arizona	108,816
17	Arkansas	98,828
10	California	107,390
39	Colorado	85,000
13	Connecticut	102,420
1	Delaware	115,300
5	Florida	110,754
11	Georgia	106,664
36	Hawaii	86,780
42	Idaho	81,043
4	Illinois	112,491
32	Indiana	90,000
23	Iowa	94,800
40	Kansas	83,883
29	Kentucky	90,734
27	Louisiana	92,520
37	Maine	85,976
20	Maryland	96,500
21	Massachusetts	95,710
7	Michigan	109,257
28	Minnesota	91,176
34	Mississippi	88,700
26	Missouri	94,235
50	Montana	72,042
31	Nebraska	90,408
45	Nevada	79,000
33	New Hampshire	89,646
2	New Jersey	115,000
48	New Mexico	75,443
3	New York	113,000
25	North Carolina	94,552
49	North Dakota	73,616
24	Ohio	94,700
35	Oklahoma	88,511
38	Oregon	85,300
6	Pennsylvania	109,372
16	Rhode Island	99,722
14	South Carolina	101,377
46	South Dakota	77,234
18	Tennessee	98,364
19	Texas	98,100
30	Utah	90,450
41	Vermont	82,105
9	Virginia	108,175
15	Washington	100,995
44	West Virginia	80,000
22	Wisconsin	95,199
47	Wyoming	77,000

RANK ORDER

RANK	STATE	SALARY
1	Delaware	$115,300
2	New Jersey	115,000
3	New York	113,000
4	Illinois	112,491
5	Florida	110,754
6	Pennsylvania	109,372
7	Michigan	109,257
8	Arizona	108,816
9	Virginia	108,175
10	California	107,390
11	Georgia	106,664
12	Alaska	103,152
13	Connecticut	102,420
14	South Carolina	101,377
15	Washington	100,995
16	Rhode Island	99,722
17	Arkansas	98,828
18	Tennessee	98,364
19	Texas	98,100
20	Maryland	96,500
21	Massachusetts	95,710
22	Wisconsin	95,199
23	Iowa	94,800
24	Ohio	94,700
25	North Carolina	94,552
26	Missouri	94,235
27	Louisiana	92,520
28	Minnesota	91,176
29	Kentucky	90,734
30	Utah	90,450
31	Nebraska	90,408
32	Indiana	90,000
33	New Hampshire	89,646
34	Mississippi	88,700
35	Oklahoma	88,511
36	Hawaii	86,780
37	Maine	85,976
38	Oregon	85,300
39	Colorado	85,000
40	Kansas	83,883
41	Vermont	82,105
42	Idaho	81,043
43	Alabama	80,615
44	West Virginia	80,000
45	Nevada	79,000
46	South Dakota	77,234
47	Wyoming	77,000
48	New Mexico	75,443
49	North Dakota	73,616
50	Montana	72,042
	District of Columbia	136,700

Source: National Center for State Courts
"Survey of Judicial Salaries-Winter 1998" (Volume 23, Number 1)

V. JUVENILES

V. JUVENILES (continued)

Important Note Regarding Juvenile Arrest Rates

The juvenile arrest rates shown in tables 192 to 243 were calculated by the editors as follows:

The state arrest numbers reported by the FBI are only from those law enforcement agencies that submitted complete arrests reports for 12 months in 1997. Included in the FBI report are population totals of these reporting jurisdictions by state. Using these FBI population figures, we first determined what percentage the FBI numbers represented of each state's total resident population. Next, using 1997 US Census Bureau state estimates for 10 to 17 year olds, we multiplied the percentages derived from the FBI population figures into the Census Bureau's total juvenile population estimates. The resulting juvenile population is the base that was used to determine juvenile arrests per 100,000 juvenile population. The national rate was calculated in the same manner.

Reports from law enforcement agencies in Alaska, Delaware, Georgia, Illinois, Kentucky, Mississippi, Montana, Nevada, New York, Pennsylvania, South Dakota and Tennessee represented less than half of their state populations. Thus rates for these states should be interpreted with caution. No arrest data were available for Florida, Kansas, New Hampshire, Vermont and the District of Columbia.

Reported Arrests of Juveniles in 1997

National Total = 1,969,407 Reported Arrests*

ALPHA ORDER

ALPHA ORDER | | | | RANK ORDER | | |

RANK	STATE	ARRESTS	% of USA	RANK	STATE	ARRESTS	% of USA
32	Alabama	18,234	0.9%	1	California	273,012	13.9%
45	Alaska	3,554	0.2%	2	Texas	223,039	11.3%
7	Arizona	63,287	3.2%	3	Wisconsin	112,549	5.7%
31	Arkansas	20,047	1.0%	4	New Jersey	81,101	4.1%
1	California	273,012	13.9%	5	Ohio	66,672	3.4%
18	Colorado	39,653	2.0%	6	Minnesota	63,937	3.2%
23	Connecticut	31,059	1.6%	7	Arizona	63,287	3.2%
44	Delaware	4,499	0.2%	8	New York	63,225	3.2%
NA	Florida**	NA	NA	9	Illinois	62,501	3.2%
25	Georgia	25,675	1.3%	10	Virginia	58,401	3.0%
33	Hawaii	16,840	0.9%	11	Maryland	57,865	2.9%
27	Idaho	22,517	1.1%	12	North Carolina	57,727	2.9%
9	Illinois	62,501	3.2%	13	Michigan	52,635	2.7%
20	Indiana	37,183	1.9%	14	Louisiana	49,150	2.5%
29	Iowa	21,046	1.1%	15	Pennsylvania	48,499	2.5%
NA	Kansas**	NA	NA	16	Washington	47,499	2.4%
42	Kentucky	7,918	0.4%	17	Oregon	42,274	2.1%
14	Louisiana	49,150	2.5%	18	Colorado	39,653	2.0%
37	Maine	12,223	0.6%	19	Missouri	38,932	2.0%
11	Maryland	57,865	2.9%	20	Indiana	37,183	1.9%
28	Massachusetts	22,513	1.1%	21	Oklahoma	32,279	1.6%
13	Michigan	52,635	2.7%	22	Utah	31,206	1.6%
6	Minnesota	63,937	3.2%	23	Connecticut	31,059	1.6%
36	Mississippi	12,387	0.6%	24	South Carolina	30,226	1.5%
19	Missouri	38,932	2.0%	25	Georgia	25,675	1.3%
46	Montana	3,011	0.2%	26	Tennessee	23,851	1.2%
30	Nebraska	20,051	1.0%	27	Idaho	22,517	1.1%
35	Nevada	13,674	0.7%	28	Massachusetts	22,513	1.1%
NA	New Hampshire**	NA	NA	29	Iowa	21,046	1.1%
4	New Jersey	81,101	4.1%	30	Nebraska	20,051	1.0%
34	New Mexico	15,504	0.8%	31	Arkansas	20,047	1.0%
8	New York	63,225	3.2%	32	Alabama	18,234	0.9%
12	North Carolina	57,727	2.9%	33	Hawaii	16,840	0.9%
40	North Dakota	8,643	0.4%	34	New Mexico	15,504	0.8%
5	Ohio	66,672	3.4%	35	Nevada	13,674	0.7%
21	Oklahoma	32,279	1.6%	36	Mississippi	12,387	0.6%
17	Oregon	42,274	2.1%	37	Maine	12,223	0.6%
15	Pennsylvania	48,499	2.5%	38	Rhode Island	8,833	0.4%
38	Rhode Island	8,833	0.4%	39	Wyoming	8,664	0.4%
24	South Carolina	30,226	1.5%	40	North Dakota	8,643	0.4%
41	South Dakota	8,204	0.4%	41	South Dakota	8,204	0.4%
26	Tennessee	23,851	1.2%	42	Kentucky	7,918	0.4%
2	Texas	223,039	11.3%	43	West Virginia	7,608	0.4%
22	Utah	31,206	1.6%	44	Delaware	4,499	0.2%
NA	Vermont**	NA	NA	45	Alaska	3,554	0.2%
10	Virginia	58,401	3.0%	46	Montana	3,011	0.2%
16	Washington	47,499	2.4%	NA	Florida**	NA	NA
43	West Virginia	7,608	0.4%	NA	Kansas**	NA	NA
3	Wisconsin	112,549	5.7%	NA	New Hampshire**	NA	NA
39	Wyoming	8,664	0.4%	NA	Vermont**	NA	NA
					District of Columbia**	NA	NA

Source: Federal Bureau of Investigation
"Crime in the United States 1997" (Uniform Crime Reports, November 22, 1998)
*Arrests of youths 17 years and younger by law enforcement agencies submitting complete reports to the F.B.I. for 12 months in 1997. See important note at beginning of this chapter.
**Not available.

Reported Juvenile Arrest Rate in 1997

National Rate = 9,387.4 Reported Arrests per 100,000 Juvenile Population*

ALPHA ORDER

RANK	STATE	RATE
44	Alabama	4,013.3
26	Alaska	9,485.9
6	Arizona	13,782.3
36	Arkansas	7,388.6
35	California	7,642.8
11	Colorado	12,308.4
16	Connecticut	10,714.1
4	Delaware	14,244.6
NA	Florida**	NA
30	Georgia	8,878.1
7	Hawaii	13,770.4
5	Idaho	13,855.8
NA	Illinois**	NA
22	Indiana	9,669.5
37	Iowa	7,361.1
NA	Kansas**	NA
27	Kentucky	9,358.5
14	Louisiana	11,282.8
29	Maine	8,971.3
17	Maryland	10,540.1
43	Massachusetts	4,330.6
42	Michigan	5,689.8
15	Minnesota	10,848.6
23	Mississippi	9,651.2
20	Missouri	10,065.7
41	Montana	6,744.6
18	Nebraska	10,113.6
3	Nevada	16,010.4
NA	New Hampshire**	NA
21	New Jersey	9,975.6
19	New Mexico	10,089.9
39	New York	7,146.4
38	North Carolina	7,181.0
13	North Dakota	11,822.1
28	Ohio	9,334.7
34	Oklahoma	7,825.4
10	Oregon	12,945.5
33	Pennsylvania	7,869.4
31	Rhode Island	8,545.9
40	South Carolina	7,110.9
2	South Dakota	19,022.4
24	Tennessee	9,641.1
25	Texas	9,510.3
8	Utah	13,415.3
NA	Vermont**	NA
32	Virginia	8,254.6
12	Washington	11,839.1
45	West Virginia	3,990.6
1	Wisconsin	23,052.4
9	Wyoming	13,320.6

RANK ORDER

RANK	STATE	RATE
1	Wisconsin	23,052.4
2	South Dakota	19,022.4
3	Nevada	16,010.4
4	Delaware	14,244.6
5	Idaho	13,855.8
6	Arizona	13,782.3
7	Hawaii	13,770.4
8	Utah	13,415.3
9	Wyoming	13,320.6
10	Oregon	12,945.5
11	Colorado	12,308.4
12	Washington	11,839.1
13	North Dakota	11,822.1
14	Louisiana	11,282.8
15	Minnesota	10,848.6
16	Connecticut	10,714.1
17	Maryland	10,540.1
18	Nebraska	10,113.6
19	New Mexico	10,089.9
20	Missouri	10,065.7
21	New Jersey	9,975.6
22	Indiana	9,669.5
23	Mississippi	9,651.2
24	Tennessee	9,641.1
25	Texas	9,510.3
26	Alaska	9,485.9
27	Kentucky	9,358.5
28	Ohio	9,334.7
29	Maine	8,971.3
30	Georgia	8,878.1
31	Rhode Island	8,545.9
32	Virginia	8,254.6
33	Pennsylvania	7,869.4
34	Oklahoma	7,825.4
35	California	7,642.8
36	Arkansas	7,388.6
37	Iowa	7,361.1
38	North Carolina	7,181.0
39	New York	7,146.4
40	South Carolina	7,110.9
41	Montana	6,744.6
42	Michigan	5,689.8
43	Massachusetts	4,330.6
44	Alabama	4,013.3
45	West Virginia	3,990.6
NA	Florida**	NA
NA	Illinois**	NA
NA	Kansas**	NA
NA	New Hampshire**	NA
NA	Vermont**	NA
	District of Columbia**	NA

Source: Morgan Quitno Press using data from Federal Bureau of Investigation
 "Crime in the United States 1997" (Uniform Crime Reports, November 22, 1998)
*By law enforcement agencies submitting complete reports to the F.B.I. for 12 months in 1997. Arrests of youths 17 years and younger divided into population of 10 to 17 year olds. See important note at beginning of this chapter.
**Not available.

Reported Arrests of Juveniles as a Percent of All Arrests in 1997

National Percent = 18.7% of Reported Arrests*

ALPHA ORDER

RANK	STATE	PERCENT
46	Alabama	8.2
28	Alaska	18.0
14	Arizona	23.0
45	Arkansas	10.5
33	California	17.1
16	Colorado	21.9
32	Connecticut	17.2
25	Delaware	19.0
NA	Florida**	NA
41	Georgia	13.7
11	Hawaii	24.1
3	Idaho	30.8
17	Illinois	21.5
15	Indiana	22.6
18	Iowa	21.4
NA	Kansas**	NA
34	Kentucky	15.6
28	Louisiana	18.0
13	Maine	23.1
26	Maryland	18.9
39	Massachusetts	14.2
36	Michigan	14.4
5	Minnesota	30.2
35	Mississippi	15.3
41	Missouri	13.7
7	Montana	28.6
20	Nebraska	20.8
10	Nevada	24.4
NA	New Hampshire**	NA
24	New Jersey	19.5
28	New Mexico	18.0
31	New York	17.5
44	North Carolina	11.1
6	North Dakota	29.8
27	Ohio	18.4
23	Oklahoma	20.3
8	Oregon	28.1
12	Pennsylvania	23.9
18	Rhode Island	21.4
40	South Carolina	13.8
1	South Dakota	32.5
36	Tennessee	14.4
22	Texas	20.6
4	Utah	30.4
NA	Vermont**	NA
38	Virginia	14.3
20	Washington	20.8
43	West Virginia	12.0
2	Wisconsin	31.1
9	Wyoming	24.7

RANK ORDER

RANK	STATE	PERCENT
1	South Dakota	32.5
2	Wisconsin	31.1
3	Idaho	30.8
4	Utah	30.4
5	Minnesota	30.2
6	North Dakota	29.8
7	Montana	28.6
8	Oregon	28.1
9	Wyoming	24.7
10	Nevada	24.4
11	Hawaii	24.1
12	Pennsylvania	23.9
13	Maine	23.1
14	Arizona	23.0
15	Indiana	22.6
16	Colorado	21.9
17	Illinois	21.5
18	Iowa	21.4
18	Rhode Island	21.4
20	Nebraska	20.8
20	Washington	20.8
22	Texas	20.6
23	Oklahoma	20.3
24	New Jersey	19.5
25	Delaware	19.0
26	Maryland	18.9
27	Ohio	18.4
28	Alaska	18.0
28	Louisiana	18.0
28	New Mexico	18.0
31	New York	17.5
32	Connecticut	17.2
33	California	17.1
34	Kentucky	15.6
35	Mississippi	15.3
36	Michigan	14.4
36	Tennessee	14.4
38	Virginia	14.3
39	Massachusetts	14.2
40	South Carolina	13.8
41	Georgia	13.7
41	Missouri	13.7
43	West Virginia	12.0
44	North Carolina	11.1
45	Arkansas	10.5
46	Alabama	8.2
NA	Florida**	NA
NA	Kansas**	NA
NA	New Hampshire**	NA
NA	Vermont**	NA
	District of Columbia**	NA

Source: Morgan Quitno Press using data from Federal Bureau of Investigation
    "Crime in the United States 1997" (Uniform Crime Reports, November 22, 1998)
*Arrests of youths 17 years and younger by law enforcement agencies submitting complete reports to the F.B.I. for 12 months in 1997.
**Not available.

Reported Arrests of Juveniles for Crime Index Offenses in 1997

National Total = 576,848 Reported Arrests*

ALPHA ORDER

RANK	STATE	ARRESTS	% of USA
28	Alabama	7,286	1.3%
45	Alaska	1,209	0.2%
10	Arizona	17,046	3.0%
31	Arkansas	6,312	1.1%
1	California	95,413	16.5%
22	Colorado	9,974	1.7%
24	Connecticut	8,687	1.5%
44	Delaware	1,795	0.3%
NA	Florida**	NA	NA
25	Georgia	8,406	1.5%
35	Hawaii	4,289	0.7%
32	Idaho	6,062	1.1%
15	Illinois	12,679	2.2%
21	Indiana	10,668	1.8%
29	Iowa	7,256	1.3%
NA	Kansas**	NA	NA
37	Kentucky	3,292	0.6%
14	Louisiana	13,823	2.4%
34	Maine	4,597	0.8%
6	Maryland	19,385	3.4%
26	Massachusetts	7,822	1.4%
9	Michigan	17,531	3.0%
11	Minnesota	15,963	2.8%
36	Mississippi	3,501	0.6%
16	Missouri	12,449	2.2%
46	Montana	765	0.1%
30	Nebraska	6,376	1.1%
38	Nevada	3,274	0.6%
NA	New Hampshire**	NA	NA
4	New Jersey	20,480	3.6%
33	New Mexico	5,026	0.9%
5	New York	20,062	3.5%
8	North Carolina	18,529	3.2%
41	North Dakota	2,096	0.4%
12	Ohio	15,743	2.7%
18	Oklahoma	12,193	2.1%
17	Oregon	12,279	2.1%
19	Pennsylvania	11,913	2.1%
39	Rhode Island	2,565	0.4%
20	South Carolina	10,734	1.9%
42	South Dakota	1,986	0.3%
27	Tennessee	7,340	1.3%
2	Texas	58,782	10.2%
23	Utah	9,702	1.7%
NA	Vermont**	NA	NA
13	Virginia	15,060	2.6%
7	Washington	18,756	3.3%
40	West Virginia	2,319	0.4%
3	Wisconsin	23,598	4.1%
43	Wyoming	1,825	0.3%

RANK ORDER

RANK	STATE	ARRESTS	% of USA
1	California	95,413	16.5%
2	Texas	58,782	10.2%
3	Wisconsin	23,598	4.1%
4	New Jersey	20,480	3.6%
5	New York	20,062	3.5%
6	Maryland	19,385	3.4%
7	Washington	18,756	3.3%
8	North Carolina	18,529	3.2%
9	Michigan	17,531	3.0%
10	Arizona	17,046	3.0%
11	Minnesota	15,963	2.8%
12	Ohio	15,743	2.7%
13	Virginia	15,060	2.6%
14	Louisiana	13,823	2.4%
15	Illinois	12,679	2.2%
16	Missouri	12,449	2.2%
17	Oregon	12,279	2.1%
18	Oklahoma	12,193	2.1%
19	Pennsylvania	11,913	2.1%
20	South Carolina	10,734	1.9%
21	Indiana	10,668	1.8%
22	Colorado	9,974	1.7%
23	Utah	9,702	1.7%
24	Connecticut	8,687	1.5%
25	Georgia	8,406	1.5%
26	Massachusetts	7,822	1.4%
27	Tennessee	7,340	1.3%
28	Alabama	7,286	1.3%
29	Iowa	7,256	1.3%
30	Nebraska	6,376	1.1%
31	Arkansas	6,312	1.1%
32	Idaho	6,062	1.1%
33	New Mexico	5,026	0.9%
34	Maine	4,597	0.8%
35	Hawaii	4,289	0.7%
36	Mississippi	3,501	0.6%
37	Kentucky	3,292	0.6%
38	Nevada	3,274	0.6%
39	Rhode Island	2,565	0.4%
40	West Virginia	2,319	0.4%
41	North Dakota	2,096	0.4%
42	South Dakota	1,986	0.3%
43	Wyoming	1,825	0.3%
44	Delaware	1,795	0.3%
45	Alaska	1,209	0.2%
46	Montana	765	0.1%
NA	Florida**	NA	NA
NA	Kansas**	NA	NA
NA	New Hampshire**	NA	NA
NA	Vermont**	NA	NA
	District of Columbia**	NA	NA

Source: Federal Bureau of Investigation
"Crime in the United States 1997" (Uniform Crime Reports, November 22, 1998)
*Arrests of youths 17 years and younger by law enforcement agencies submitting complete reports to the F.B.I. for 12 months in 1997. Crime index offenses consist of murder, forcible rape, robbery, aggravated assault, burglary, larceny-theft, motor vehicle theft and arson. See important note at beginning of this chapter.
**Not available.

Reported Juvenile Arrest Rate for Crime Index Offenses in 1997

National Rate = 2,749.6 Reported Arrests per 100,000 Juvenile Population*

ALPHA ORDER

RANK	STATE	RATE
43	Alabama	1,603.6
15	Alaska	3,226.9
10	Arizona	3,712.2
35	Arkansas	2,326.4
29	California	2,671.0
19	Colorado	3,095.9
20	Connecticut	2,996.7
1	Delaware	5,683.3
NA	Florida**	NA
23	Georgia	2,906.7
12	Hawaii	3,507.2
9	Idaho	3,730.2
NA	Illinois**	NA
26	Indiana	2,774.2
30	Iowa	2,537.9
NA	Kansas**	NA
6	Kentucky	3,890.9
18	Louisiana	3,173.2
13	Maine	3,374.1
11	Maryland	3,531.0
44	Massachusetts	1,504.6
41	Michigan	1,895.1
28	Minnesota	2,708.5
27	Mississippi	2,727.8
16	Missouri	3,218.7
42	Montana	1,713.6
17	Nebraska	3,216.0
7	Nevada	3,833.4
NA	New Hampshire**	NA
32	New Jersey	2,519.1
14	New Mexico	3,270.9
37	New York	2,267.6
36	North Carolina	2,304.9
24	North Dakota	2,867.0
38	Ohio	2,204.2
22	Oklahoma	2,956.0
8	Oregon	3,760.2
40	Pennsylvania	1,933.0
34	Rhode Island	2,481.6
31	South Carolina	2,525.3
4	South Dakota	4,604.9
21	Tennessee	2,967.0
33	Texas	2,506.4
5	Utah	4,170.8
NA	Vermont**	NA
39	Virginia	2,128.6
3	Washington	4,674.9
45	West Virginia	1,216.4
2	Wisconsin	4,833.4
25	Wyoming	2,805.9

RANK ORDER

RANK	STATE	RATE
1	Delaware	5,683.3
2	Wisconsin	4,833.4
3	Washington	4,674.9
4	South Dakota	4,604.9
5	Utah	4,170.8
6	Kentucky	3,890.9
7	Nevada	3,833.4
8	Oregon	3,760.2
9	Idaho	3,730.2
10	Arizona	3,712.2
11	Maryland	3,531.0
12	Hawaii	3,507.2
13	Maine	3,374.1
14	New Mexico	3,270.9
15	Alaska	3,226.9
16	Missouri	3,218.7
17	Nebraska	3,216.0
18	Louisiana	3,173.2
19	Colorado	3,095.9
20	Connecticut	2,996.7
21	Tennessee	2,967.0
22	Oklahoma	2,956.0
23	Georgia	2,906.7
24	North Dakota	2,867.0
25	Wyoming	2,805.9
26	Indiana	2,774.2
27	Mississippi	2,727.8
28	Minnesota	2,708.5
29	California	2,671.0
30	Iowa	2,537.9
31	South Carolina	2,525.3
32	New Jersey	2,519.1
33	Texas	2,506.4
34	Rhode Island	2,481.6
35	Arkansas	2,326.4
36	North Carolina	2,304.9
37	New York	2,267.6
38	Ohio	2,204.2
39	Virginia	2,128.6
40	Pennsylvania	1,933.0
41	Michigan	1,895.1
42	Montana	1,713.6
43	Alabama	1,603.6
44	Massachusetts	1,504.6
45	West Virginia	1,216.4
NA	Florida**	NA
NA	Illinois**	NA
NA	Kansas**	NA
NA	New Hampshire**	NA
NA	Vermont**	NA
	District of Columbia**	NA

Source: Morgan Quitno Press using data from Federal Bureau of Investigation
    "Crime in the United States 1997" (Uniform Crime Reports, November 22, 1998)
Arrests of youths 17 years and younger by law enforcement agencies submitting complete reports to the F.B.I. for 12 months in 1997. Crime index offenses consist of murder, forcible rape, robbery, aggravated assault, burglary, larceny-theft, motor vehicle theft and arson.
**Not available.*

Reported Arrests of Juveniles for Crime Index Offenses
As a Percent of All Such Arrests in 1997
National Percent = 30.2% of Reported Arrests for Crime Index Offenses*

ALPHA ORDER

RANK	STATE	PERCENT
46	Alabama	20.5
14	Alaska	38.9
25	Arizona	32.0
37	Arkansas	26.2
39	California	26.0
16	Colorado	35.2
37	Connecticut	26.2
31	Delaware	27.5
NA	Florida**	NA
43	Georgia	22.3
19	Hawaii	34.0
2	Idaho	53.5
41	Illinois	22.5
23	Indiana	32.9
13	Iowa	39.9
NA	Kansas**	NA
27	Kentucky	29.8
40	Louisiana	25.4
6	Maine	46.8
22	Maryland	33.1
41	Massachusetts	22.5
26	Michigan	30.1
3	Minnesota	49.1
32	Mississippi	26.9
36	Missouri	26.5
9	Montana	44.3
7	Nebraska	45.5
15	Nevada	37.3
NA	New Hampshire**	NA
29	New Jersey	29.4
21	New Mexico	33.2
30	New York	28.2
45	North Carolina	20.7
1	North Dakota	56.0
28	Ohio	29.5
12	Oklahoma	41.4
24	Oregon	32.6
20	Pennsylvania	33.3
18	Rhode Island	34.5
33	South Carolina	26.8
4	South Dakota	47.4
44	Tennessee	21.7
17	Texas	34.7
4	Utah	47.4
NA	Vermont**	NA
35	Virginia	26.7
10	Washington	41.8
33	West Virginia	26.8
8	Wisconsin	44.9
11	Wyoming	41.7

RANK ORDER

RANK	STATE	PERCENT
1	North Dakota	56.0
2	Idaho	53.5
3	Minnesota	49.1
4	South Dakota	47.4
4	Utah	47.4
6	Maine	46.8
7	Nebraska	45.5
8	Wisconsin	44.9
9	Montana	44.3
10	Washington	41.8
11	Wyoming	41.7
12	Oklahoma	41.4
13	Iowa	39.9
14	Alaska	38.9
15	Nevada	37.3
16	Colorado	35.2
17	Texas	34.7
18	Rhode Island	34.5
19	Hawaii	34.0
20	Pennsylvania	33.3
21	New Mexico	33.2
22	Maryland	33.1
23	Indiana	32.9
24	Oregon	32.6
25	Arizona	32.0
26	Michigan	30.1
27	Kentucky	29.8
28	Ohio	29.5
29	New Jersey	29.4
30	New York	28.2
31	Delaware	27.5
32	Mississippi	26.9
33	South Carolina	26.8
33	West Virginia	26.8
35	Virginia	26.7
36	Missouri	26.5
37	Arkansas	26.2
37	Connecticut	26.2
39	California	26.0
40	Louisiana	25.4
41	Illinois	22.5
41	Massachusetts	22.5
43	Georgia	22.3
44	Tennessee	21.7
45	North Carolina	20.7
46	Alabama	20.5
NA	Florida**	NA
NA	Kansas**	NA
NA	New Hampshire**	NA
NA	Vermont**	NA
	District of Columbia**	NA

Source: Morgan Quitno Press using data from Federal Bureau of Investigation
   "Crime in the United States 1997" (Uniform Crime Reports, November 22, 1998)
Arrests of youths 17 years and younger by law enforcement agencies submitting complete reports to the F.B.I. for 12 months in 1997. Crime index offenses consist of murder, forcible rape, robbery, aggravated assault, burglary, larceny-theft, motor vehicle theft and arson.
**Not available.*

Reported Arrests of Juveniles for Violent Crimes in 1997

National Total = 86,462 Reported Arrests*

ALPHA ORDER

RANK	STATE	ARRESTS	% of USA
24	Alabama	992	1.1%
41	Alaska	171	0.2%
12	Arizona	2,013	2.3%
28	Arkansas	781	0.9%
1	California	20,552	23.8%
27	Colorado	832	1.0%
21	Connecticut	1,464	1.7%
38	Delaware	301	0.3%
NA	Florida**	NA	NA
20	Georgia	1,494	1.7%
34	Hawaii	424	0.5%
35	Idaho	367	0.4%
6	Illinois	3,234	3.7%
14	Indiana	1,888	2.2%
29	Iowa	733	0.8%
NA	Kansas**	NA	NA
31	Kentucky	636	0.7%
11	Louisiana	2,286	2.6%
40	Maine	181	0.2%
4	Maryland	4,057	4.7%
9	Massachusetts	2,818	3.3%
8	Michigan	2,855	3.3%
22	Minnesota	1,222	1.4%
36	Mississippi	363	0.4%
19	Missouri	1,570	1.8%
45	Montana	47	0.1%
39	Nebraska	262	0.3%
37	Nevada	357	0.4%
NA	New Hampshire**	NA	NA
3	New Jersey	4,685	5.4%
32	New Mexico	463	0.5%
7	New York	2,938	3.4%
5	North Carolina	3,457	4.0%
45	North Dakota	47	0.1%
10	Ohio	2,618	3.0%
23	Oklahoma	1,194	1.4%
26	Oregon	877	1.0%
15	Pennsylvania	1,854	2.1%
33	Rhode Island	425	0.5%
16	South Carolina	1,835	2.1%
43	South Dakota	98	0.1%
25	Tennessee	935	1.1%
2	Texas	6,932	8.0%
30	Utah	679	0.8%
NA	Vermont**	NA	NA
18	Virginia	1,646	1.9%
17	Washington	1,670	1.9%
42	West Virginia	150	0.2%
13	Wisconsin	1,974	2.3%
44	Wyoming	85	0.1%

RANK ORDER

RANK	STATE	ARRESTS	% of USA
1	California	20,552	23.8%
2	Texas	6,932	8.0%
3	New Jersey	4,685	5.4%
4	Maryland	4,057	4.7%
5	North Carolina	3,457	4.0%
6	Illinois	3,234	3.7%
7	New York	2,938	3.4%
8	Michigan	2,855	3.3%
9	Massachusetts	2,818	3.3%
10	Ohio	2,618	3.0%
11	Louisiana	2,286	2.6%
12	Arizona	2,013	2.3%
13	Wisconsin	1,974	2.3%
14	Indiana	1,888	2.2%
15	Pennsylvania	1,854	2.1%
16	South Carolina	1,835	2.1%
17	Washington	1,670	1.9%
18	Virginia	1,646	1.9%
19	Missouri	1,570	1.8%
20	Georgia	1,494	1.7%
21	Connecticut	1,464	1.7%
22	Minnesota	1,222	1.4%
23	Oklahoma	1,194	1.4%
24	Alabama	992	1.1%
25	Tennessee	935	1.1%
26	Oregon	877	1.0%
27	Colorado	832	1.0%
28	Arkansas	781	0.9%
29	Iowa	733	0.8%
30	Utah	679	0.8%
31	Kentucky	636	0.7%
32	New Mexico	463	0.5%
33	Rhode Island	425	0.5%
34	Hawaii	424	0.5%
35	Idaho	367	0.4%
36	Mississippi	363	0.4%
37	Nevada	357	0.4%
38	Delaware	301	0.3%
39	Nebraska	262	0.3%
40	Maine	181	0.2%
41	Alaska	171	0.2%
42	West Virginia	150	0.2%
43	South Dakota	98	0.1%
44	Wyoming	85	0.1%
45	Montana	47	0.1%
45	North Dakota	47	0.1%
NA	Florida**	NA	NA
NA	Kansas**	NA	NA
NA	New Hampshire**	NA	NA
NA	Vermont**	NA	NA
	District of Columbia**	NA	NA

Source: Federal Bureau of Investigation
"Crime in the United States 1997" (Uniform Crime Reports, November 22, 1998)
*Arrests of youths 17 years and younger by law enforcement agencies submitting complete reports to the F.B.I. for 12 months in 1997. Violent crimes are offenses of murder, forcible rape, robbery and aggravated assault. See important note at beginning of this chapter.
**Not available.

197

Reported Juvenile Arrest Rate for Violent Crime in 1997

National Rate = 412.1 Reported Arrests per 100,000 Juvenile Population*

ALPHA ORDER

RANK ORDER

RANK	STATE	RATE	RANK	STATE	RATE
38	Alabama	218.3	1	Delaware	953.0
11	Alaska	456.4	2	Kentucky	751.7
12	Arizona	438.4	3	Maryland	739.0
30	Arkansas	287.8	4	New Jersey	576.3
5	California	575.3	5	California	575.3
33	Colorado	258.3	6	Massachusetts	542.1
9	Connecticut	505.0	7	Louisiana	524.8
1	Delaware	953.0	8	Georgia	516.6
NA	Florida**	NA	9	Connecticut	505.0
8	Georgia	516.6	10	Indiana	491.0
22	Hawaii	346.7	11	Alaska	456.4
37	Idaho	225.8	12	Arizona	438.4
NA	Illinois**	NA	13	South Carolina	431.7
10	Indiana	491.0	14	North Carolina	430.0
34	Iowa	256.4	15	Nevada	418.0
NA	Kansas**	NA	16	Washington	416.2
2	Kentucky	751.7	17	Rhode Island	411.2
7	Louisiana	524.8	18	Missouri	405.9
40	Maine	132.8	19	Wisconsin	404.3
3	Maryland	739.0	20	Tennessee	377.9
6	Massachusetts	542.1	21	Ohio	366.5
24	Michigan	308.6	22	Hawaii	346.7
39	Minnesota	207.3	23	New York	332.1
31	Mississippi	282.8	24	Michigan	308.6
18	Missouri	405.9	25	New Mexico	301.3
43	Montana	105.3	26	Pennsylvania	300.8
41	Nebraska	132.2	27	Texas	295.6
15	Nevada	418.0	28	Utah	291.9
NA	New Hampshire**	NA	29	Oklahoma	289.5
4	New Jersey	576.3	30	Arkansas	287.8
25	New Mexico	301.3	31	Mississippi	282.8
23	New York	332.1	32	Oregon	268.6
14	North Carolina	430.0	33	Colorado	258.3
45	North Dakota	64.3	34	Iowa	256.4
21	Ohio	366.5	35	Virginia	232.7
29	Oklahoma	289.5	36	South Dakota	227.2
32	Oregon	268.6	37	Idaho	225.8
26	Pennsylvania	300.8	38	Alabama	218.3
17	Rhode Island	411.2	39	Minnesota	207.3
13	South Carolina	431.7	40	Maine	132.8
36	South Dakota	227.2	41	Nebraska	132.2
20	Tennessee	377.9	42	Wyoming	130.7
27	Texas	295.6	43	Montana	105.3
28	Utah	291.9	44	West Virginia	78.7
NA	Vermont**	NA	45	North Dakota	64.3
35	Virginia	232.7	NA	Florida**	NA
16	Washington	416.2	NA	Illinois**	NA
44	West Virginia	78.7	NA	Kansas**	NA
19	Wisconsin	404.3	NA	New Hampshire**	NA
42	Wyoming	130.7	NA	Vermont**	NA
				District of Columbia**	NA

Source: Morgan Quitno Press using data from Federal Bureau of Investigation
  "Crime in the United States 1997" (Uniform Crime Reports, November 22, 1998)
*By law enforcement agencies submitting complete reports to the F.B.I. for 12 months in 1997. Arrests of youths 17 years and younger divided into population of 10 to 17 year olds. See important note at beginning of this chapter. Violent crimes are offenses of murder, forcible rape, robbery and aggravated assault.
**Not available.

Reported Arrests of Juveniles for Violent Crime
As a Percent of All Such Arrests in 1997
National Percent = 17.2% of Reported Arrests for Violent Crime*

ALPHA ORDER

RANK ORDER

RANK	STATE	PERCENT		RANK	STATE	PERCENT
46	Alabama	9.8		1	Utah	37.1
31	Alaska	16.5		2	Maryland	29.8
12	Arizona	23.3		2	Minnesota	29.8
40	Arkansas	13.2		4	Illinois	28.8
39	California	13.7		5	Idaho	28.1
30	Colorado	16.9		6	Hawaii	27.7
21	Connecticut	19.6		7	Washington	25.1
23	Delaware	19.5		8	Wisconsin	24.7
NA	Florida**	NA		9	New Jersey	24.5
40	Georgia	13.2		10	Maine	23.8
6	Hawaii	27.7		11	North Dakota	23.6
5	Idaho	28.1		12	Arizona	23.3
4	Illinois	28.8		12	Montana	23.3
16	Indiana	22.1		14	Pennsylvania	23.0
24	Iowa	19.4		15	Oregon	22.9
NA	Kansas**	NA		16	Indiana	22.1
27	Kentucky	17.7		17	Nevada	21.1
34	Louisiana	15.6		18	New York	20.3
10	Maine	23.8		18	Texas	20.3
2	Maryland	29.8		20	South Dakota	19.8
26	Massachusetts	18.2		21	Connecticut	19.6
36	Michigan	14.7		21	Oklahoma	19.6
2	Minnesota	29.8		23	Delaware	19.5
33	Mississippi	15.7		24	Iowa	19.4
35	Missouri	15.5		25	Rhode Island	18.7
12	Montana	23.3		26	Massachusetts	18.2
28	Nebraska	17.6		27	Kentucky	17.7
17	Nevada	21.1		28	Nebraska	17.6
NA	New Hampshire**	NA		29	Ohio	17.3
9	New Jersey	24.5		30	Colorado	16.9
32	New Mexico	16.3		31	Alaska	16.5
18	New York	20.3		32	New Mexico	16.3
43	North Carolina	12.3		33	Mississippi	15.7
11	North Dakota	23.6		34	Louisiana	15.6
29	Ohio	17.3		35	Missouri	15.5
21	Oklahoma	19.6		36	Michigan	14.7
15	Oregon	22.9		37	Virginia	14.6
14	Pennsylvania	23.0		38	South Carolina	14.3
25	Rhode Island	18.7		39	California	13.7
38	South Carolina	14.3		40	Arkansas	13.2
20	South Dakota	19.8		40	Georgia	13.2
45	Tennessee	10.9		42	Wyoming	12.8
18	Texas	20.3		43	North Carolina	12.3
1	Utah	37.1		44	West Virginia	11.0
NA	Vermont**	NA		45	Tennessee	10.9
37	Virginia	14.6		46	Alabama	9.8
7	Washington	25.1		NA	Florida**	NA
44	West Virginia	11.0		NA	Kansas**	NA
8	Wisconsin	24.7		NA	New Hampshire**	NA
42	Wyoming	12.8		NA	Vermont**	NA
					District of Columbia**	NA

Source: Morgan Quitno Press using data from Federal Bureau of Investigation
   "Crime in the United States 1997" (Uniform Crime Reports, November 22, 1998)
*Arrests of youths 17 years and younger by law enforcement agencies submitting complete reports to the F.B.I. for
12 months in 1997. Violent crimes are offenses of murder, forcible rape, robbery and aggravated assault.
**Not available.

Reported Arrests of Juveniles for Murder in 1997

National Total = 1,731 Reported Arrests*

RANK	STATE	ARRESTS	% of USA
11	Alabama	55	3.2%
36	Alaska	3	0.2%
15	Arizona	32	1.8%
24	Arkansas	16	0.9%
1	California	354	20.5%
25	Colorado	14	0.8%
28	Connecticut	12	0.7%
41	Delaware	0	0.0%
NA	Florida**	NA	NA
19	Georgia	24	1.4%
41	Hawaii	0	0.0%
36	Idaho	3	0.2%
3	Illinois	137	7.9%
25	Indiana	14	0.8%
40	Iowa	1	0.1%
NA	Kansas**	NA	NA
20	Kentucky	22	1.3%
6	Louisiana	81	4.7%
39	Maine	2	0.1%
4	Maryland	110	6.4%
30	Massachusetts	10	0.6%
5	Michigan	103	6.0%
30	Minnesota	10	0.6%
23	Mississippi	18	1.0%
14	Missouri	44	2.5%
41	Montana	0	0.0%
33	Nebraska	5	0.3%
34	Nevada	4	0.2%
NA	New Hampshire**	NA	NA
13	New Jersey	45	2.6%
32	New Mexico	7	0.4%
17	New York	26	1.5%
8	North Carolina	70	4.0%
41	North Dakota	0	0.0%
16	Ohio	30	1.7%
18	Oklahoma	25	1.4%
27	Oregon	13	0.8%
22	Pennsylvania	19	1.1%
36	Rhode Island	3	0.2%
9	South Carolina	57	3.3%
41	South Dakota	0	0.0%
12	Tennessee	53	3.1%
2	Texas	142	8.2%
28	Utah	12	0.7%
NA	Vermont**	NA	NA
9	Virginia	57	3.3%
20	Washington	22	1.3%
34	West Virginia	4	0.2%
7	Wisconsin	72	4.2%
41	Wyoming	0	0.0%

RANK	STATE	ARRESTS	% of USA
1	California	354	20.5%
2	Texas	142	8.2%
3	Illinois	137	7.9%
4	Maryland	110	6.4%
5	Michigan	103	6.0%
6	Louisiana	81	4.7%
7	Wisconsin	72	4.2%
8	North Carolina	70	4.0%
9	South Carolina	57	3.3%
9	Virginia	57	3.3%
11	Alabama	55	3.2%
12	Tennessee	53	3.1%
13	New Jersey	45	2.6%
14	Missouri	44	2.5%
15	Arizona	32	1.8%
16	Ohio	30	1.7%
17	New York	26	1.5%
18	Oklahoma	25	1.4%
19	Georgia	24	1.4%
20	Kentucky	22	1.3%
20	Washington	22	1.3%
22	Pennsylvania	19	1.1%
23	Mississippi	18	1.0%
24	Arkansas	16	0.9%
25	Colorado	14	0.8%
25	Indiana	14	0.8%
27	Oregon	13	0.8%
28	Connecticut	12	0.7%
28	Utah	12	0.7%
30	Massachusetts	10	0.6%
30	Minnesota	10	0.6%
32	New Mexico	7	0.4%
33	Nebraska	5	0.3%
34	Nevada	4	0.2%
34	West Virginia	4	0.2%
36	Alaska	3	0.2%
36	Idaho	3	0.2%
36	Rhode Island	3	0.2%
39	Maine	2	0.1%
40	Iowa	1	0.1%
41	Delaware	0	0.0%
41	Hawaii	0	0.0%
41	Montana	0	0.0%
41	North Dakota	0	0.0%
41	South Dakota	0	0.0%
41	Wyoming	0	0.0%
NA	Florida**	NA	NA
NA	Kansas**	NA	NA
NA	New Hampshire**	NA	NA
NA	Vermont**	NA	NA
	District of Columbia**	NA	NA

Source: Federal Bureau of Investigation
   "Crime in the United States 1997" (Uniform Crime Reports, November 22, 1998)
*Arrests of youths 17 years and younger by law enforcement agencies submitting complete reports to the F.B.I. for 12 months in 1997. Includes nonnegligent manslaughter. See important note at beginning of this chapter.
**Not available.

Reported Juvenile Arrest Rate for Murder in 1997

National Rate = 8.3 Reported Arrests per 100,000 Juvenile Population*

ALPHA ORDER

RANK	STATE	RATE
8	Alabama	12.1
15	Alaska	8.0
16	Arizona	7.0
19	Arkansas	5.9
11	California	9.9
25	Colorado	4.3
27	Connecticut	4.1
40	Delaware	0.0
NA	Florida**	NA
13	Georgia	8.3
40	Hawaii	0.0
36	Idaho	1.8
NA	Illinois**	NA
29	Indiana	3.6
39	Iowa	0.3
NA	Kansas**	NA
1	Kentucky	26.0
4	Louisiana	18.6
38	Maine	1.5
3	Maryland	20.0
35	Massachusetts	1.9
10	Michigan	11.1
37	Minnesota	1.7
6	Mississippi	14.0
9	Missouri	11.4
40	Montana	0.0
33	Nebraska	2.5
23	Nevada	4.7
NA	New Hampshire**	NA
20	New Jersey	5.5
24	New Mexico	4.6
31	New York	2.9
12	North Carolina	8.7
40	North Dakota	0.0
26	Ohio	4.2
17	Oklahoma	6.1
28	Oregon	4.0
30	Pennsylvania	3.1
31	Rhode Island	2.9
7	South Carolina	13.4
40	South Dakota	0.0
2	Tennessee	21.4
17	Texas	6.1
22	Utah	5.2
NA	Vermont**	NA
14	Virginia	8.1
20	Washington	5.5
34	West Virginia	2.1
5	Wisconsin	14.7
40	Wyoming	0.0

RANK ORDER

RANK	STATE	RATE
1	Kentucky	26.0
2	Tennessee	21.4
3	Maryland	20.0
4	Louisiana	18.6
5	Wisconsin	14.7
6	Mississippi	14.0
7	South Carolina	13.4
8	Alabama	12.1
9	Missouri	11.4
10	Michigan	11.1
11	California	9.9
12	North Carolina	8.7
13	Georgia	8.3
14	Virginia	8.1
15	Alaska	8.0
16	Arizona	7.0
17	Oklahoma	6.1
17	Texas	6.1
19	Arkansas	5.9
20	New Jersey	5.5
20	Washington	5.5
22	Utah	5.2
23	Nevada	4.7
24	New Mexico	4.6
25	Colorado	4.3
26	Ohio	4.2
27	Connecticut	4.1
28	Oregon	4.0
29	Indiana	3.6
30	Pennsylvania	3.1
31	New York	2.9
31	Rhode Island	2.9
33	Nebraska	2.5
34	West Virginia	2.1
35	Massachusetts	1.9
36	Idaho	1.8
37	Minnesota	1.7
38	Maine	1.5
39	Iowa	0.3
40	Delaware	0.0
40	Hawaii	0.0
40	Montana	0.0
40	North Dakota	0.0
40	South Dakota	0.0
40	Wyoming	0.0
NA	Florida**	NA
NA	Illinois**	NA
NA	Kansas**	NA
NA	New Hampshire**	NA
NA	Vermont**	NA
	District of Columbia**	NA

Source: Morgan Quitno Press using data from Federal Bureau of Investigation
"Crime in the United States 1997" (Uniform Crime Reports, November 22, 1998)
*By law enforcement agencies submitting complete reports to the F.B.I. for 12 months in 1997. Includes nonnegligent manslaughter. Arrests of youths 17 years and younger divided into population of 10 to 17 year olds. See important note at beginning of this chapter.
**Not available.

Reported Arrests of Juveniles for Murder
As a Percent of All Such Arrests in 1997
National Percent = 13.6% of Reported Arrests for Murder*

ALPHA ORDER

RANK	STATE	PERCENT
26	Alabama	11.8
11	Alaska	15.0
12	Arizona	14.1
37	Arkansas	7.8
10	California	16.1
19	Colorado	13.0
33	Connecticut	8.4
41	Delaware	0.0
NA	Florida**	NA
35	Georgia	8.1
41	Hawaii	0.0
23	Idaho	12.0
6	Illinois	18.2
37	Indiana	7.8
40	Iowa	4.0
NA	Kansas**	NA
2	Kentucky	23.4
20	Louisiana	12.8
9	Maine	16.7
3	Maryland	22.1
20	Massachusetts	12.8
34	Michigan	8.3
16	Minnesota	13.5
29	Mississippi	10.5
12	Missouri	14.1
41	Montana	0.0
24	Nebraska	11.9
39	Nevada	5.9
NA	New Hampshire**	NA
16	New Jersey	13.5
22	New Mexico	12.7
31	New York	10.3
32	North Carolina	9.2
41	North Dakota	0.0
29	Ohio	10.5
28	Oklahoma	11.7
24	Oregon	11.9
26	Pennsylvania	11.8
15	Rhode Island	13.6
7	South Carolina	17.5
41	South Dakota	0.0
5	Tennessee	19.3
12	Texas	14.1
1	Utah	31.6
NA	Vermont**	NA
18	Virginia	13.4
8	Washington	16.9
36	West Virginia	8.0
4	Wisconsin	19.6
41	Wyoming	0.0

RANK ORDER

RANK	STATE	PERCENT
1	Utah	31.6
2	Kentucky	23.4
3	Maryland	22.1
4	Wisconsin	19.6
5	Tennessee	19.3
6	Illinois	18.2
7	South Carolina	17.5
8	Washington	16.9
9	Maine	16.7
10	California	16.1
11	Alaska	15.0
12	Arizona	14.1
12	Missouri	14.1
12	Texas	14.1
15	Rhode Island	13.6
16	Minnesota	13.5
16	New Jersey	13.5
18	Virginia	13.4
19	Colorado	13.0
20	Louisiana	12.8
20	Massachusetts	12.8
22	New Mexico	12.7
23	Idaho	12.0
24	Nebraska	11.9
24	Oregon	11.9
26	Alabama	11.8
26	Pennsylvania	11.8
28	Oklahoma	11.7
29	Mississippi	10.5
29	Ohio	10.5
31	New York	10.3
32	North Carolina	9.2
33	Connecticut	8.4
34	Michigan	8.3
35	Georgia	8.1
36	West Virginia	8.0
37	Arkansas	7.8
37	Indiana	7.8
39	Nevada	5.9
40	Iowa	4.0
41	Delaware	0.0
41	Hawaii	0.0
41	Montana	0.0
41	North Dakota	0.0
41	South Dakota	0.0
41	Wyoming	0.0
NA	Florida**	NA
NA	Kansas**	NA
NA	New Hampshire**	NA
NA	Vermont**	NA
	District of Columbia**	NA

Source: Morgan Quitno Press using data from Federal Bureau of Investigation
"Crime in the United States 1997" (Uniform Crime Reports, November 22, 1998)
*Arrests of youths 17 years and younger by law enforcement agencies submitting complete reports to the F.B.I. for 12 months in 1997. Includes nonnegligent manslaughter.
**Not available.

Reported Arrests of Juveniles for Rape in 1997

National Total = 3,792 Reported Arrests*

ALPHA ORDER

RANK	STATE	ARRESTS	% of USA
26	Alabama	43	1.1%
40	Alaska	13	0.3%
25	Arizona	54	1.4%
23	Arkansas	59	1.6%
1	California	444	11.7%
12	Colorado	99	2.6%
24	Connecticut	56	1.5%
31	Delaware	27	0.7%
NA	Florida**	NA	NA
19	Georgia	83	2.2%
37	Hawaii	16	0.4%
37	Idaho	16	0.4%
6	Illinois	152	4.0%
28	Indiana	31	0.8%
33	Iowa	22	0.6%
NA	Kansas**	NA	NA
40	Kentucky	13	0.3%
10	Louisiana	122	3.2%
39	Maine	15	0.4%
11	Maryland	102	2.7%
20	Massachusetts	69	1.8%
4	Michigan	235	6.2%
5	Minnesota	166	4.4%
34	Mississippi	18	0.5%
18	Missouri	84	2.2%
46	Montana	1	0.0%
34	Nebraska	18	0.5%
32	Nevada	25	0.7%
NA	New Hampshire**	NA	NA
6	New Jersey	152	4.0%
34	New Mexico	18	0.5%
12	New York	99	2.6%
17	North Carolina	86	2.3%
45	North Dakota	4	0.1%
3	Ohio	240	6.3%
21	Oklahoma	64	1.7%
22	Oregon	61	1.6%
15	Pennsylvania	94	2.5%
30	Rhode Island	28	0.7%
16	South Carolina	90	2.4%
42	South Dakota	12	0.3%
29	Tennessee	30	0.8%
2	Texas	424	11.2%
27	Utah	37	1.0%
NA	Vermont**	NA	NA
14	Virginia	98	2.6%
8	Washington	136	3.6%
43	West Virginia	8	0.2%
9	Wisconsin	123	3.2%
44	Wyoming	5	0.1%

RANK ORDER

RANK	STATE	ARRESTS	% of USA
1	California	444	11.7%
2	Texas	424	11.2%
3	Ohio	240	6.3%
4	Michigan	235	6.2%
5	Minnesota	166	4.4%
6	Illinois	152	4.0%
6	New Jersey	152	4.0%
8	Washington	136	3.6%
9	Wisconsin	123	3.2%
10	Louisiana	122	3.2%
11	Maryland	102	2.7%
12	Colorado	99	2.6%
12	New York	99	2.6%
14	Virginia	98	2.6%
15	Pennsylvania	94	2.5%
16	South Carolina	90	2.4%
17	North Carolina	86	2.3%
18	Missouri	84	2.2%
19	Georgia	83	2.2%
20	Massachusetts	69	1.8%
21	Oklahoma	64	1.7%
22	Oregon	61	1.6%
23	Arkansas	59	1.6%
24	Connecticut	56	1.5%
25	Arizona	54	1.4%
26	Alabama	43	1.1%
27	Utah	37	1.0%
28	Indiana	31	0.8%
29	Tennessee	30	0.8%
30	Rhode Island	28	0.7%
31	Delaware	27	0.7%
32	Nevada	25	0.7%
33	Iowa	22	0.6%
34	Mississippi	18	0.5%
34	Nebraska	18	0.5%
34	New Mexico	18	0.5%
37	Hawaii	16	0.4%
37	Idaho	16	0.4%
39	Maine	15	0.4%
40	Alaska	13	0.3%
40	Kentucky	13	0.3%
42	South Dakota	12	0.3%
43	West Virginia	8	0.2%
44	Wyoming	5	0.1%
45	North Dakota	4	0.1%
46	Montana	1	0.0%
NA	Florida**	NA	NA
NA	Kansas**	NA	NA
NA	New Hampshire**	NA	NA
NA	Vermont**	NA	NA
	District of Columbia**	NA	NA

Source: Federal Bureau of Investigation
   "Crime in the United States 1997" (Uniform Crime Reports, November 22, 1998)
*Arrests of youths 17 years and younger by law enforcement agencies submitting complete reports to the F.B.I. for 12 months in 1997. Forcible rape is the carnal knowledge of a female forcibly and against her will. Assaults or attempts to commit rape by force or threat of force are included. However, statutory rape without force and other sex offenses are excluded. See important note at beginning of this chapter. **Not available.

Reported Juvenile Arrest Rate for Rape in 1997

National Rate = 18.1 Arrests per 100,000 Population*

ALPHA ORDER

RANK ORDER

RANK	STATE	RATE		RANK	STATE	RATE
38	Alabama	9.5		1	Delaware	85.5
2	Alaska	34.7		2	Alaska	34.7
32	Arizona	11.8		3	Washington	33.9
14	Arkansas	21.7		4	Ohio	33.6
30	California	12.4		5	Colorado	30.7
5	Colorado	30.7		6	Nevada	29.3
17	Connecticut	19.3		7	Georgia	28.7
1	Delaware	85.5		8	Minnesota	28.2
NA	Florida**	NA		9	Louisiana	28.0
7	Georgia	28.7		10	South Dakota	27.8
29	Hawaii	13.1		11	Rhode Island	27.1
37	Idaho	9.8		12	Michigan	25.4
NA	Illinois**	NA		13	Wisconsin	25.2
40	Indiana	8.1		14	Arkansas	21.7
41	Iowa	7.7		14	Missouri	21.7
NA	Kansas**	NA		16	South Carolina	21.2
24	Kentucky	15.4		17	Connecticut	19.3
9	Louisiana	28.0		18	New Jersey	18.7
35	Maine	11.0		18	Oregon	18.7
20	Maryland	18.6		20	Maryland	18.6
28	Massachusetts	13.3		21	Texas	18.1
12	Michigan	25.4		22	Utah	15.9
8	Minnesota	28.2		23	Oklahoma	15.5
26	Mississippi	14.0		24	Kentucky	15.4
14	Missouri	21.7		25	Pennsylvania	15.3
45	Montana	2.2		26	Mississippi	14.0
39	Nebraska	9.1		27	Virginia	13.9
6	Nevada	29.3		28	Massachusetts	13.3
NA	New Hampshire**	NA		29	Hawaii	13.1
18	New Jersey	18.7		30	California	12.4
33	New Mexico	11.7		31	Tennessee	12.1
34	New York	11.2		32	Arizona	11.8
36	North Carolina	10.7		33	New Mexico	11.7
43	North Dakota	5.5		34	New York	11.2
4	Ohio	33.6		35	Maine	11.0
23	Oklahoma	15.5		36	North Carolina	10.7
18	Oregon	18.7		37	Idaho	9.8
25	Pennsylvania	15.3		38	Alabama	9.5
11	Rhode Island	27.1		39	Nebraska	9.1
16	South Carolina	21.2		40	Indiana	8.1
10	South Dakota	27.8		41	Iowa	7.7
31	Tennessee	12.1		41	Wyoming	7.7
21	Texas	18.1		43	North Dakota	5.5
22	Utah	15.9		44	West Virginia	4.2
NA	Vermont**	NA		45	Montana	2.2
27	Virginia	13.9		NA	Florida**	NA
3	Washington	33.9		NA	Illinois**	NA
44	West Virginia	4.2		NA	Kansas**	NA
13	Wisconsin	25.2		NA	New Hampshire**	NA
41	Wyoming	7.7		NA	Vermont**	NA
					District of Columbia**	NA

Source: Morgan Quitno Press using data from Federal Bureau of Investigation
    "Crime in the United States 1997" (Uniform Crime Reports, November 22, 1998)
*By law enforcement agencies submitting complete reports to the F.B.I. for 12 months in 1997. Arrests of youths 17
years and younger divided into population of 10 to 17 year olds. See important note at beginning of this chapter.
Forcible rape is the carnal knowledge of a female forcibly and against her will. Assaults or attempts to commit rape
by force or threat of force are included. **Not available.

Reported Arrests of Juveniles for Rape
As a Percent of All Such Arrests in 1997
National Percent = 17.1% of Reported Arrests for Rape*

ALPHA ORDER

RANK ORDER

RANK	STATE	PERCENT		RANK	STATE	PERCENT
42	Alabama	9.7		1	Illinois	35.3
10	Alaska	20.3		2	Nevada	29.1
19	Arizona	19.2		3	Ohio	24.5
37	Arkansas	12.5		4	Utah	23.9
32	California	14.4		5	Minnesota	23.6
16	Colorado	19.7		6	Wisconsin	21.5
30	Connecticut	14.9		7	Delaware	21.1
7	Delaware	21.1		8	South Dakota	20.7
NA	Florida**	NA		9	Georgia	20.4
9	Georgia	20.4		10	Alaska	20.3
36	Hawaii	12.9		10	Oregon	20.3
13	Idaho	20.0		10	Washington	20.3
1	Illinois	35.3		13	Idaho	20.0
18	Indiana	19.5		13	Maine	20.0
26	Iowa	16.9		15	Rhode Island	19.9
NA	Kansas**	NA		16	Colorado	19.7
31	Kentucky	14.8		17	Louisiana	19.6
17	Louisiana	19.6		18	Indiana	19.5
13	Maine	20.0		19	Arizona	19.2
25	Maryland	17.0		20	New Jersey	19.0
34	Massachusetts	13.7		20	North Dakota	19.0
27	Michigan	16.8		22	Texas	18.6
5	Minnesota	23.6		23	New Mexico	18.2
43	Mississippi	9.6		24	Pennsylvania	17.7
28	Missouri	15.8		25	Maryland	17.0
46	Montana	6.7		26	Iowa	16.9
39	Nebraska	10.8		27	Michigan	16.8
2	Nevada	29.1		28	Missouri	15.8
NA	New Hampshire**	NA		29	Oklahoma	15.4
20	New Jersey	19.0		30	Connecticut	14.9
23	New Mexico	18.2		31	Kentucky	14.8
33	New York	14.2		32	California	14.4
40	North Carolina	10.7		33	New York	14.2
20	North Dakota	19.0		34	Massachusetts	13.7
3	Ohio	24.5		35	South Carolina	13.4
29	Oklahoma	15.4		36	Hawaii	12.9
10	Oregon	20.3		37	Arkansas	12.5
24	Pennsylvania	17.7		38	Virginia	12.1
15	Rhode Island	19.9		39	Nebraska	10.8
35	South Carolina	13.4		40	North Carolina	10.7
8	South Dakota	20.7		41	Wyoming	10.0
44	Tennessee	9.5		42	Alabama	9.7
22	Texas	18.6		43	Mississippi	9.6
4	Utah	23.9		44	Tennessee	9.5
NA	Vermont**	NA		45	West Virginia	8.0
38	Virginia	12.1		46	Montana	6.7
10	Washington	20.3		NA	Florida**	NA
45	West Virginia	8.0		NA	Kansas**	NA
6	Wisconsin	21.5		NA	New Hampshire**	NA
41	Wyoming	10.0		NA	Vermont**	NA
					District of Columbia**	NA

Source: Morgan Quitno Press using data from Federal Bureau of Investigation
"Crime in the United States 1997" (Uniform Crime Reports, November 22, 1998)
*Arrests of youths 17 years and younger by law enforcement agencies submitting complete reports to the F.B.I. for 12 months in 1997. Forcible rape is the carnal knowledge of a female forcibly and against her will. Assaults or attempts to commit rape by force or threat of force are included. However, statutory rape without force and other sex offenses are excluded. **Not available.

Reported Arrests of Juveniles for Robbery in 1997

National Total = 28,069 Reported Arrests*

ALPHA ORDER

RANK	STATE	ARRESTS	% of USA
21	Alabama	401	1.4%
42	Alaska	20	0.1%
20	Arizona	428	1.5%
27	Arkansas	222	0.8%
1	California	7,957	28.3%
30	Colorado	162	0.6%
16	Connecticut	490	1.7%
38	Delaware	79	0.3%
NA	Florida**	NA	NA
18	Georgia	467	1.7%
24	Hawaii	288	1.0%
41	Idaho	40	0.1%
5	Illinois	1,175	4.2%
26	Indiana	257	0.9%
34	Iowa	110	0.4%
NA	Kansas**	NA	NA
29	Kentucky	187	0.7%
11	Louisiana	615	2.2%
39	Maine	61	0.2%
4	Maryland	1,666	5.9%
14	Massachusetts	563	2.0%
9	Michigan	810	2.9%
23	Minnesota	314	1.1%
31	Mississippi	146	0.5%
12	Missouri	590	2.1%
46	Montana	0	0.0%
33	Nebraska	111	0.4%
32	Nevada	143	0.5%
NA	New Hampshire**	NA	NA
3	New Jersey	1,787	6.4%
35	New Mexico	99	0.4%
6	New York	1,106	3.9%
7	North Carolina	983	3.5%
45	North Dakota	11	0.0%
8	Ohio	950	3.4%
22	Oklahoma	333	1.2%
25	Oregon	273	1.0%
15	Pennsylvania	524	1.9%
37	Rhode Island	82	0.3%
19	South Carolina	448	1.6%
43	South Dakota	15	0.1%
28	Tennessee	210	0.7%
2	Texas	2,076	7.4%
36	Utah	87	0.3%
NA	Vermont**	NA	NA
13	Virginia	570	2.0%
17	Washington	473	1.7%
40	West Virginia	53	0.2%
10	Wisconsin	675	2.4%
44	Wyoming	12	0.0%

RANK ORDER

RANK	STATE	ARRESTS	% of USA
1	California	7,957	28.3%
2	Texas	2,076	7.4%
3	New Jersey	1,787	6.4%
4	Maryland	1,666	5.9%
5	Illinois	1,175	4.2%
6	New York	1,106	3.9%
7	North Carolina	983	3.5%
8	Ohio	950	3.4%
9	Michigan	810	2.9%
10	Wisconsin	675	2.4%
11	Louisiana	615	2.2%
12	Missouri	590	2.1%
13	Virginia	570	2.0%
14	Massachusetts	563	2.0%
15	Pennsylvania	524	1.9%
16	Connecticut	490	1.7%
17	Washington	473	1.7%
18	Georgia	467	1.7%
19	South Carolina	448	1.6%
20	Arizona	428	1.5%
21	Alabama	401	1.4%
22	Oklahoma	333	1.2%
23	Minnesota	314	1.1%
24	Hawaii	288	1.0%
25	Oregon	273	1.0%
26	Indiana	257	0.9%
27	Arkansas	222	0.8%
28	Tennessee	210	0.7%
29	Kentucky	187	0.7%
30	Colorado	162	0.6%
31	Mississippi	146	0.5%
32	Nevada	143	0.5%
33	Nebraska	111	0.4%
34	Iowa	110	0.4%
35	New Mexico	99	0.4%
36	Utah	87	0.3%
37	Rhode Island	82	0.3%
38	Delaware	79	0.3%
39	Maine	61	0.2%
40	West Virginia	53	0.2%
41	Idaho	40	0.1%
42	Alaska	20	0.1%
43	South Dakota	15	0.1%
44	Wyoming	12	0.0%
45	North Dakota	11	0.0%
46	Montana	0	0.0%
NA	Florida**	NA	NA
NA	Kansas**	NA	NA
NA	New Hampshire**	NA	NA
NA	Vermont**	NA	NA
	District of Columbia**	NA	NA

Source: Federal Bureau of Investigation
    "Crime in the United States 1997" (Uniform Crime Reports, November 22, 1998)
*Arrests of youths 17 years and younger by law enforcement agencies submitting complete reports to the F.B.I. for 12 months in 1997. Robbery is the taking or attempting to take anything of value by force or threat of force. See important note at beginning of this chapter. **Not available.

Reported Juvenile Arrest Rate for Robbery in 1997

National Rate = 133.8 Reported Arrests per 100,000 Juvenile Population*

ALPHA ORDER

RANK ORDER

RANK	STATE	RATE		RANK	STATE	RATE
22	Alabama	88.3		1	Maryland	303.5
34	Alaska	53.4		2	Delaware	250.1
20	Arizona	93.2		3	Hawaii	235.5
27	Arkansas	81.8		4	California	222.8
4	California	222.8		5	Kentucky	221.0
36	Colorado	50.3		6	New Jersey	219.8
7	Connecticut	169.0		7	Connecticut	169.0
2	Delaware	250.1		8	Nevada	167.4
NA	Florida**	NA		9	Georgia	161.5
9	Georgia	161.5		10	Missouri	152.5
3	Hawaii	235.5		11	Louisiana	141.2
42	Idaho	24.6		12	Wisconsin	138.3
NA	Illinois**	NA		13	Ohio	133.0
31	Indiana	66.8		14	New York	125.0
38	Iowa	38.5		15	North Carolina	122.3
NA	Kansas**	NA		16	Washington	117.9
5	Kentucky	221.0		17	Mississippi	113.8
11	Louisiana	141.2		18	Massachusetts	108.3
37	Maine	44.8		19	South Carolina	105.4
1	Maryland	303.5		20	Arizona	93.2
18	Massachusetts	108.3		21	Texas	88.5
23	Michigan	87.6		22	Alabama	88.3
35	Minnesota	53.3		23	Michigan	87.6
17	Mississippi	113.8		24	Pennsylvania	85.0
10	Missouri	152.5		25	Tennessee	84.9
45	Montana	0.0		26	Oregon	83.6
33	Nebraska	56.0		27	Arkansas	81.8
8	Nevada	167.4		28	Oklahoma	80.7
NA	New Hampshire**	NA		29	Virginia	80.6
6	New Jersey	219.8		30	Rhode Island	79.3
32	New Mexico	64.4		31	Indiana	66.8
14	New York	125.0		32	New Mexico	64.4
15	North Carolina	122.3		33	Nebraska	56.0
44	North Dakota	15.0		34	Alaska	53.4
13	Ohio	133.0		35	Minnesota	53.3
28	Oklahoma	80.7		36	Colorado	50.3
26	Oregon	83.6		37	Maine	44.8
24	Pennsylvania	85.0		38	Iowa	38.5
30	Rhode Island	79.3		39	Utah	37.4
19	South Carolina	105.4		40	South Dakota	34.8
40	South Dakota	34.8		41	West Virginia	27.8
25	Tennessee	84.9		42	Idaho	24.6
21	Texas	88.5		43	Wyoming	18.4
39	Utah	37.4		44	North Dakota	15.0
NA	Vermont**	NA		45	Montana	0.0
29	Virginia	80.6		NA	Florida**	NA
16	Washington	117.9		NA	Illinois**	NA
41	West Virginia	27.8		NA	Kansas**	NA
12	Wisconsin	138.3		NA	New Hampshire**	NA
43	Wyoming	18.4		NA	Vermont**	NA
					District of Columbia**	NA

Source: Morgan Quitno Press using data from Federal Bureau of Investigation
    "Crime in the United States 1997" (Uniform Crime Reports, November 22, 1998)
*By law enforcement agencies submitting complete reports to the F.B.I. for 12 months in 1997. Arrests of youths 17 years and younger divided into population of 10 to 17 year olds. See important note at beginning of this chapter. Robbery is the taking or attempting to take anything of value by force or threat of force.
**Not available.

Reported Arrests of Juveniles for Robbery
As a Percent of All Such Arrests in 1997
National Percent = 29.8% of Reported Arrests for Robbery*

ALPHA ORDER

RANK	STATE	PERCENT
44	Alabama	18.9
3	Alaska	42.6
28	Arizona	26.7
36	Arkansas	23.5
15	California	33.7
25	Colorado	28.8
31	Connecticut	25.3
27	Delaware	27.0
NA	Florida**	NA
43	Georgia	20.5
2	Hawaii	44.4
4	Idaho	40.8
6	Illinois	38.4
35	Indiana	23.6
14	Iowa	34.1
NA	Kansas**	NA
30	Kentucky	25.6
32	Louisiana	24.5
8	Maine	35.7
9	Maryland	35.4
17	Massachusetts	31.7
36	Michigan	23.5
1	Minnesota	50.2
34	Mississippi	23.7
29	Missouri	26.1
46	Montana	0.0
16	Nebraska	32.7
19	Nevada	29.9
NA	New Hampshire**	NA
13	New Jersey	34.5
25	New Mexico	28.8
21	New York	29.3
39	North Carolina	22.6
5	North Dakota	40.7
23	Ohio	28.9
7	Oklahoma	36.4
38	Oregon	23.0
23	Pennsylvania	28.9
12	Rhode Island	34.6
39	South Carolina	22.6
33	South Dakota	23.8
45	Tennessee	17.7
20	Texas	29.4
18	Utah	30.1
NA	Vermont**	NA
39	Virginia	22.6
11	Washington	35.1
42	West Virginia	22.2
10	Wisconsin	35.2
21	Wyoming	29.3

RANK ORDER

RANK	STATE	PERCENT
1	Minnesota	50.2
2	Hawaii	44.4
3	Alaska	42.6
4	Idaho	40.8
5	North Dakota	40.7
6	Illinois	38.4
7	Oklahoma	36.4
8	Maine	35.7
9	Maryland	35.4
10	Wisconsin	35.2
11	Washington	35.1
12	Rhode Island	34.6
13	New Jersey	34.5
14	Iowa	34.1
15	California	33.7
16	Nebraska	32.7
17	Massachusetts	31.7
18	Utah	30.1
19	Nevada	29.9
20	Texas	29.4
21	New York	29.3
21	Wyoming	29.3
23	Ohio	28.9
23	Pennsylvania	28.9
25	Colorado	28.8
25	New Mexico	28.8
27	Delaware	27.0
28	Arizona	26.7
29	Missouri	26.1
30	Kentucky	25.6
31	Connecticut	25.3
32	Louisiana	24.5
33	South Dakota	23.8
34	Mississippi	23.7
35	Indiana	23.6
36	Arkansas	23.5
36	Michigan	23.5
38	Oregon	23.0
39	North Carolina	22.6
39	South Carolina	22.6
39	Virginia	22.6
42	West Virginia	22.2
43	Georgia	20.5
44	Alabama	18.9
45	Tennessee	17.7
46	Montana	0.0
NA	Florida**	NA
NA	Kansas**	NA
NA	New Hampshire**	NA
NA	Vermont**	NA
	District of Columbia**	NA

Source: Morgan Quitno Press using data from Federal Bureau of Investigation
   "Crime in the United States 1997" (Uniform Crime Reports, November 22, 1998)
*Arrests of youths 17 years and younger by law enforcement agencies submitting complete reports to the F.B.I. for 12 months in 1997. Robbery is the taking or attempting to take anything of value by force or threat of force.
**Not available.

Reported Arrests of Juveniles for Aggravated Assault in 1997

National Total = 52,870 Reported Arrests*

ALPHA ORDER

RANK	STATE	ARRESTS	% of USA
29	Alabama	493	0.9%
38	Alaska	135	0.3%
11	Arizona	1,499	2.8%
30	Arkansas	484	0.9%
1	California	11,797	22.3%
26	Colorado	557	1.1%
20	Connecticut	906	1.7%
35	Delaware	195	0.4%
NA	Florida**	NA	NA
19	Georgia	920	1.7%
40	Hawaii	120	0.2%
34	Idaho	308	0.6%
7	Illinois	1,770	3.3%
10	Indiana	1,586	3.0%
25	Iowa	600	1.1%
NA	Kansas**	NA	NA
31	Kentucky	414	0.8%
12	Louisiana	1,468	2.8%
41	Maine	103	0.2%
5	Maryland	2,179	4.1%
6	Massachusetts	2,176	4.1%
8	Michigan	1,707	3.2%
23	Minnesota	732	1.4%
37	Mississippi	181	0.3%
21	Missouri	852	1.6%
45	Montana	46	0.1%
39	Nebraska	128	0.2%
36	Nevada	185	0.3%
NA	New Hampshire**	NA	NA
3	New Jersey	2,701	5.1%
32	New Mexico	339	0.6%
8	New York	1,707	3.2%
4	North Carolina	2,318	4.4%
46	North Dakota	32	0.1%
13	Ohio	1,398	2.6%
22	Oklahoma	772	1.5%
28	Oregon	530	1.0%
15	Pennsylvania	1,217	2.3%
33	Rhode Island	312	0.6%
14	South Carolina	1,240	2.3%
43	South Dakota	71	0.1%
24	Tennessee	642	1.2%
2	Texas	4,290	8.1%
27	Utah	543	1.0%
NA	Vermont**	NA	NA
18	Virginia	921	1.7%
17	Washington	1,039	2.0%
42	West Virginia	85	0.2%
16	Wisconsin	1,104	2.1%
44	Wyoming	68	0.1%

RANK ORDER

RANK	STATE	ARRESTS	% of USA
1	California	11,797	22.3%
2	Texas	4,290	8.1%
3	New Jersey	2,701	5.1%
4	North Carolina	2,318	4.4%
5	Maryland	2,179	4.1%
6	Massachusetts	2,176	4.1%
7	Illinois	1,770	3.3%
8	Michigan	1,707	3.2%
8	New York	1,707	3.2%
10	Indiana	1,586	3.0%
11	Arizona	1,499	2.8%
12	Louisiana	1,468	2.8%
13	Ohio	1,398	2.6%
14	South Carolina	1,240	2.3%
15	Pennsylvania	1,217	2.3%
16	Wisconsin	1,104	2.1%
17	Washington	1,039	2.0%
18	Virginia	921	1.7%
19	Georgia	920	1.7%
20	Connecticut	906	1.7%
21	Missouri	852	1.6%
22	Oklahoma	772	1.5%
23	Minnesota	732	1.4%
24	Tennessee	642	1.2%
25	Iowa	600	1.1%
26	Colorado	557	1.1%
27	Utah	543	1.0%
28	Oregon	530	1.0%
29	Alabama	493	0.9%
30	Arkansas	484	0.9%
31	Kentucky	414	0.8%
32	New Mexico	339	0.6%
33	Rhode Island	312	0.6%
34	Idaho	308	0.6%
35	Delaware	195	0.4%
36	Nevada	185	0.3%
37	Mississippi	181	0.3%
38	Alaska	135	0.3%
39	Nebraska	128	0.2%
40	Hawaii	120	0.2%
41	Maine	103	0.2%
42	West Virginia	85	0.2%
43	South Dakota	71	0.1%
44	Wyoming	68	0.1%
45	Montana	46	0.1%
46	North Dakota	32	0.1%
NA	Florida**	NA	NA
NA	Kansas**	NA	NA
NA	New Hampshire**	NA	NA
NA	Vermont**	NA	NA
	District of Columbia**	NA	NA

Source: Federal Bureau of Investigation
"Crime in the United States 1997" (Uniform Crime Reports, November 22, 1998)
Arrests of youths 17 years and younger by law enforcement agencies submitting complete reports to the F.B.I. for 12 months in 1997. Aggravated assault is an attack for the purpose of inflicting severe bodily injury. See important note at beginning of this chapter.
***Not available.*

Reported Juvenile Arrest Rate for Aggravated Assault in 1997

National Rate = 252.0 Reported Arrests per 100,000 Juvenile Population*

ALPHA ORDER

RANK	STATE	RATE
38	Alabama	108.5
6	Alaska	360.3
10	Arizona	326.4
31	Arkansas	178.4
9	California	330.2
32	Colorado	172.9
12	Connecticut	312.5
1	Delaware	617.4
NA	Florida**	NA
11	Georgia	318.1
41	Hawaii	98.1
27	Idaho	189.5
NA	Illinois**	NA
4	Indiana	412.4
23	Iowa	209.9
NA	Kansas**	NA
2	Kentucky	489.3
7	Louisiana	337.0
42	Maine	75.6
5	Maryland	396.9
3	Massachusetts	418.6
29	Michigan	184.5
37	Minnesota	124.2
35	Mississippi	141.0
21	Missouri	220.3
40	Montana	103.0
43	Nebraska	64.6
22	Nevada	216.6
NA	New Hampshire**	NA
8	New Jersey	332.2
20	New Mexico	220.6
26	New York	192.9
15	North Carolina	288.3
45	North Dakota	43.8
25	Ohio	195.7
28	Oklahoma	187.2
34	Oregon	162.3
24	Pennsylvania	197.5
13	Rhode Island	301.9
14	South Carolina	291.7
33	South Dakota	164.6
16	Tennessee	259.5
30	Texas	182.9
18	Utah	233.4
NA	Vermont**	NA
36	Virginia	130.2
17	Washington	259.0
44	West Virginia	44.6
19	Wisconsin	226.1
39	Wyoming	104.5

RANK ORDER

RANK	STATE	RATE
1	Delaware	617.4
2	Kentucky	489.3
3	Massachusetts	418.6
4	Indiana	412.4
5	Maryland	396.9
6	Alaska	360.3
7	Louisiana	337.0
8	New Jersey	332.2
9	California	330.2
10	Arizona	326.4
11	Georgia	318.1
12	Connecticut	312.5
13	Rhode Island	301.9
14	South Carolina	291.7
15	North Carolina	288.3
16	Tennessee	259.5
17	Washington	259.0
18	Utah	233.4
19	Wisconsin	226.1
20	New Mexico	220.6
21	Missouri	220.3
22	Nevada	216.6
23	Iowa	209.9
24	Pennsylvania	197.5
25	Ohio	195.7
26	New York	192.9
27	Idaho	189.5
28	Oklahoma	187.2
29	Michigan	184.5
30	Texas	182.9
31	Arkansas	178.4
32	Colorado	172.9
33	South Dakota	164.6
34	Oregon	162.3
35	Mississippi	141.0
36	Virginia	130.2
37	Minnesota	124.2
38	Alabama	108.5
39	Wyoming	104.5
40	Montana	103.0
41	Hawaii	98.1
42	Maine	75.6
43	Nebraska	64.6
44	West Virginia	44.6
45	North Dakota	43.8
NA	Florida**	NA
NA	Illinois**	NA
NA	Kansas**	NA
NA	New Hampshire**	NA
NA	Vermont**	NA
	District of Columbia**	NA

Source: Morgan Quitno Press using data from Federal Bureau of Investigation
   "Crime in the United States 1997" (Uniform Crime Reports, November 22, 1998)
*By law enforcement agencies submitting complete reports to the F.B.I. for 12 months in 1997. Arrests of youths 17 years and younger divided into population of 10 to 17 year olds. See important note at beginning of this chapter. Aggravated assault is an attack for the purpose of inflicting severe bodily injury.
**Not available.

Reported Arrests of Juveniles for Aggravated Assault
As a Percent of All Such Arrests in 1997
National Percent = 14.2% of Reported Arrests for Aggravated Assault*

ALPHA ORDER

RANK	STATE	PERCENT
46	Alabama	7.0
28	Alaska	15.0
9	Arizona	23.0
40	Arkansas	11.2
43	California	9.7
29	Colorado	14.9
17	Connecticut	18.1
20	Delaware	17.6
NA	Florida**	NA
41	Georgia	11.1
24	Hawaii	16.7
2	Idaho	28.0
6	Illinois	25.3
10	Indiana	22.3
17	Iowa	18.1
NA	Kansas**	NA
27	Kentucky	15.5
32	Louisiana	13.5
15	Maine	20.5
3	Maryland	27.8
26	Massachusetts	16.6
35	Michigan	12.8
4	Minnesota	27.2
32	Mississippi	13.5
39	Missouri	12.1
5	Montana	26.7
31	Nebraska	13.6
21	Nevada	17.5
NA	New Hampshire**	NA
14	New Jersey	21.1
30	New Mexico	14.4
21	New York	17.5
42	North Carolina	10.4
12	North Dakota	21.5
34	Ohio	13.2
23	Oklahoma	17.0
7	Oregon	23.7
11	Pennsylvania	21.9
24	Rhode Island	16.7
36	South Carolina	12.6
16	South Dakota	19.4
44	Tennessee	9.4
19	Texas	18.0
1	Utah	40.2
NA	Vermont**	NA
38	Virginia	12.2
8	Washington	23.1
45	West Virginia	8.7
12	Wisconsin	21.5
37	Wyoming	12.4

RANK ORDER

RANK	STATE	PERCENT
1	Utah	40.2
2	Idaho	28.0
3	Maryland	27.8
4	Minnesota	27.2
5	Montana	26.7
6	Illinois	25.3
7	Oregon	23.7
8	Washington	23.1
9	Arizona	23.0
10	Indiana	22.3
11	Pennsylvania	21.9
12	North Dakota	21.5
12	Wisconsin	21.5
14	New Jersey	21.1
15	Maine	20.5
16	South Dakota	19.4
17	Connecticut	18.1
17	Iowa	18.1
19	Texas	18.0
20	Delaware	17.6
21	Nevada	17.5
21	New York	17.5
23	Oklahoma	17.0
24	Hawaii	16.7
24	Rhode Island	16.7
26	Massachusetts	16.6
27	Kentucky	15.5
28	Alaska	15.0
29	Colorado	14.9
30	New Mexico	14.4
31	Nebraska	13.6
32	Louisiana	13.5
32	Mississippi	13.5
34	Ohio	13.2
35	Michigan	12.8
36	South Carolina	12.6
37	Wyoming	12.4
38	Virginia	12.2
39	Missouri	12.1
40	Arkansas	11.2
41	Georgia	11.1
42	North Carolina	10.4
43	California	9.7
44	Tennessee	9.4
45	West Virginia	8.7
46	Alabama	7.0
NA	Florida**	NA
NA	Kansas**	NA
NA	New Hampshire**	NA
NA	Vermont**	NA
	District of Columbia**	NA

Source: Morgan Quitno Press using data from Federal Bureau of Investigation
   "Crime in the United States 1997" (Uniform Crime Reports, November 22, 1998)
*Arrests of youths 17 years and younger by law enforcement agencies submitting complete reports to the F.B.I. for 12 months in 1997. Aggravated assault is an attack for the purpose of inflicting severe bodily injury.
**Not available.

Reported Arrests of Juveniles for Property Crimes in 1997

National Total = 490,386 Reported Arrests*

ALPHA ORDER					RANK ORDER			
RANK	STATE		ARRESTS	% of USA	RANK	STATE	ARRESTS	% of USA
28	Alabama		6,294	1.3%	1	California	74,861	15.3%
45	Alaska		1,038	0.2%	2	Texas	51,850	10.6%
9	Arizona		15,033	3.1%	3	Wisconsin	21,624	4.4%
31	Arkansas		5,531	1.1%	4	New York	17,124	3.5%
1	California		74,861	15.3%	5	Washington	17,086	3.5%
20	Colorado		9,142	1.9%	6	New Jersey	15,795	3.2%
24	Connecticut		7,223	1.5%	7	Maryland	15,328	3.1%
44	Delaware		1,494	0.3%	8	North Carolina	15,072	3.1%
NA	Florida**		NA	NA	9	Arizona	15,033	3.1%
25	Georgia		6,912	1.4%	10	Minnesota	14,741	3.0%
35	Hawaii		3,865	0.8%	11	Michigan	14,676	3.0%
30	Idaho		5,695	1.2%	12	Virginia	13,414	2.7%
19	Illinois		9,445	1.9%	13	Ohio	13,125	2.7%
23	Indiana		8,780	1.8%	14	Louisiana	11,537	2.4%
26	Iowa		6,523	1.3%	15	Oregon	11,402	2.3%
NA	Kansas**		NA	NA	16	Oklahoma	10,999	2.2%
38	Kentucky		2,656	0.5%	17	Missouri	10,879	2.2%
14	Louisiana		11,537	2.4%	18	Pennsylvania	10,059	2.1%
34	Maine		4,416	0.9%	19	Illinois	9,445	1.9%
7	Maryland		15,328	3.1%	20	Colorado	9,142	1.9%
32	Massachusetts		5,004	1.0%	21	Utah	9,023	1.8%
11	Michigan		14,676	3.0%	22	South Carolina	8,899	1.8%
10	Minnesota		14,741	3.0%	23	Indiana	8,780	1.8%
36	Mississippi		3,138	0.6%	24	Connecticut	7,223	1.5%
17	Missouri		10,879	2.2%	25	Georgia	6,912	1.4%
46	Montana		718	0.1%	26	Iowa	6,523	1.3%
29	Nebraska		6,114	1.2%	27	Tennessee	6,405	1.3%
37	Nevada		2,917	0.6%	28	Alabama	6,294	1.3%
NA	New Hampshire**		NA	NA	29	Nebraska	6,114	1.2%
6	New Jersey		15,795	3.2%	30	Idaho	5,695	1.2%
33	New Mexico		4,563	0.9%	31	Arkansas	5,531	1.1%
4	New York		17,124	3.5%	32	Massachusetts	5,004	1.0%
8	North Carolina		15,072	3.1%	33	New Mexico	4,563	0.9%
41	North Dakota		2,049	0.4%	34	Maine	4,416	0.9%
13	Ohio		13,125	2.7%	35	Hawaii	3,865	0.8%
16	Oklahoma		10,999	2.2%	36	Mississippi	3,138	0.6%
15	Oregon		11,402	2.3%	37	Nevada	2,917	0.6%
18	Pennsylvania		10,059	2.1%	38	Kentucky	2,656	0.5%
40	Rhode Island		2,140	0.4%	39	West Virginia	2,169	0.4%
22	South Carolina		8,899	1.8%	40	Rhode Island	2,140	0.4%
42	South Dakota		1,888	0.4%	41	North Dakota	2,049	0.4%
27	Tennessee		6,405	1.3%	42	South Dakota	1,888	0.4%
2	Texas		51,850	10.6%	43	Wyoming	1,740	0.4%
21	Utah		9,023	1.8%	44	Delaware	1,494	0.3%
NA	Vermont**		NA	NA	45	Alaska	1,038	0.2%
12	Virginia		13,414	2.7%	46	Montana	718	0.1%
5	Washington		17,086	3.5%	NA	Florida**	NA	NA
39	West Virginia		2,169	0.4%	NA	Kansas**	NA	NA
3	Wisconsin		21,624	4.4%	NA	New Hampshire**	NA	NA
43	Wyoming		1,740	0.4%	NA	Vermont**	NA	NA
						District of Columbia**	NA	NA

Source: Federal Bureau of Investigation
   "Crime in the United States 1997" (Uniform Crime Reports, November 22, 1998)
*Arrests of youths 17 years and younger by law enforcement agencies submitting complete reports to the F.B.I. for 12 months in 1997. Property crimes are offenses of burglary, larceny-theft, motor vehicle theft and arson. See important note at beginning of this chapter.
**Not available.

Reported Juvenile Arrest Rate for Property Crime in 1997

National Rate = 2,337.5 Reported Arrests per 100,000 Juvenile Population*

ALPHA ORDER

RANK	STATE	RATE
43	Alabama	1,385.3
19	Alaska	2,770.5
9	Arizona	3,273.8
34	Arkansas	2,038.5
31	California	2,095.7
15	Colorado	2,837.7
25	Connecticut	2,491.6
1	Delaware	4,730.2
NA	Florida**	NA
27	Georgia	2,390.1
11	Hawaii	3,160.5
6	Idaho	3,504.4
NA	Illinois**	NA
28	Indiana	2,283.3
29	Iowa	2,281.5
NA	Kansas**	NA
12	Kentucky	3,139.2
22	Louisiana	2,648.4
10	Maine	3,241.2
18	Maryland	2,792.0
45	Massachusetts	962.6
42	Michigan	1,586.5
24	Minnesota	2,501.2
26	Mississippi	2,444.9
16	Missouri	2,812.7
41	Montana	1,608.3
13	Nebraska	3,083.9
8	Nevada	3,415.4
NA	New Hampshire**	NA
35	New Jersey	1,942.8
14	New Mexico	2,969.6
36	New York	1,935.6
38	North Carolina	1,874.9
17	North Dakota	2,802.7
39	Ohio	1,837.6
21	Oklahoma	2,666.5
7	Oregon	3,491.6
40	Pennsylvania	1,632.2
33	Rhode Island	2,070.4
32	South Carolina	2,093.6
3	South Dakota	4,377.7
23	Tennessee	2,589.0
30	Texas	2,210.9
5	Utah	3,878.9
NA	Vermont**	NA
37	Virginia	1,896.0
4	Washington	4,258.7
44	West Virginia	1,137.7
2	Wisconsin	4,429.1
20	Wyoming	2,675.2

RANK ORDER

RANK	STATE	RATE
1	Delaware	4,730.2
2	Wisconsin	4,429.1
3	South Dakota	4,377.7
4	Washington	4,258.7
5	Utah	3,878.9
6	Idaho	3,504.4
7	Oregon	3,491.6
8	Nevada	3,415.4
9	Arizona	3,273.8
10	Maine	3,241.2
11	Hawaii	3,160.5
12	Kentucky	3,139.2
13	Nebraska	3,083.9
14	New Mexico	2,969.6
15	Colorado	2,837.7
16	Missouri	2,812.7
17	North Dakota	2,802.7
18	Maryland	2,792.0
19	Alaska	2,770.5
20	Wyoming	2,675.2
21	Oklahoma	2,666.5
22	Louisiana	2,648.4
23	Tennessee	2,589.0
24	Minnesota	2,501.2
25	Connecticut	2,491.6
26	Mississippi	2,444.9
27	Georgia	2,390.1
28	Indiana	2,283.3
29	Iowa	2,281.5
30	Texas	2,210.9
31	California	2,095.7
32	South Carolina	2,093.6
33	Rhode Island	2,070.4
34	Arkansas	2,038.5
35	New Jersey	1,942.8
36	New York	1,935.6
37	Virginia	1,896.0
38	North Carolina	1,874.9
39	Ohio	1,837.6
40	Pennsylvania	1,632.2
41	Montana	1,608.3
42	Michigan	1,586.5
43	Alabama	1,385.3
44	West Virginia	1,137.7
45	Massachusetts	962.6
NA	Florida**	NA
NA	Illinois**	NA
NA	Kansas**	NA
NA	New Hampshire**	NA
NA	Vermont**	NA
	District of Columbia**	NA

Source: Morgan Quitno Press using data from Federal Bureau of Investigation
"Crime in the United States 1997" (Uniform Crime Reports, November 22, 1998)
By law enforcement agencies submitting complete reports to the F.B.I. for 12 months in 1997. Arrests of youths 17 years and younger divided into population of 10 to 17 year olds. See important note at beginning of this chapter. Property crimes are offenses of burglary, larceny-theft, motor vehicle theft and arson.
***Not available.*

Reported Arrests of Juveniles for Property Crime
As a Percent of All Such Arrests in 1997
National Percent = 34.8% of Reported Arrests for Property Crime*

ALPHA ORDER

RANK	STATE	PERCENT
44	Alabama	24.8
5	Alaska	50.0
29	Arizona	33.6
32	Arkansas	30.5
25	California	34.6
17	Colorado	39.0
40	Connecticut	28.1
34	Delaware	30.0
NA	Florida**	NA
41	Georgia	26.2
24	Hawaii	34.9
2	Idaho	56.8
46	Illinois	20.9
21	Indiana	36.7
13	Iowa	45.3
NA	Kansas**	NA
23	Kentucky	35.6
39	Louisiana	29.0
7	Maine	48.7
27	Maryland	34.2
42	Massachusetts	26.0
19	Michigan	37.8
3	Minnesota	51.8
38	Mississippi	29.3
37	Missouri	29.5
10	Montana	47.1
6	Nebraska	48.8
16	Nevada	41.2
NA	New Hampshire**	NA
31	New Jersey	31.3
20	New Mexico	37.1
33	New York	30.2
45	North Carolina	24.7
1	North Dakota	57.8
26	Ohio	34.4
11	Oklahoma	47.0
28	Oregon	33.7
22	Pennsylvania	36.3
15	Rhode Island	41.4
30	South Carolina	32.6
4	South Dakota	51.1
43	Tennessee	25.4
18	Texas	38.4
9	Utah	48.4
NA	Vermont**	NA
36	Virginia	29.7
14	Washington	44.7
35	West Virginia	29.8
8	Wisconsin	48.6
12	Wyoming	46.8

RANK ORDER

RANK	STATE	PERCENT
1	North Dakota	57.8
2	Idaho	56.8
3	Minnesota	51.8
4	South Dakota	51.1
5	Alaska	50.0
6	Nebraska	48.8
7	Maine	48.7
8	Wisconsin	48.6
9	Utah	48.4
10	Montana	47.1
11	Oklahoma	47.0
12	Wyoming	46.8
13	Iowa	45.3
14	Washington	44.7
15	Rhode Island	41.4
16	Nevada	41.2
17	Colorado	39.0
18	Texas	38.4
19	Michigan	37.8
20	New Mexico	37.1
21	Indiana	36.7
22	Pennsylvania	36.3
23	Kentucky	35.6
24	Hawaii	34.9
25	California	34.6
26	Ohio	34.4
27	Maryland	34.2
28	Oregon	33.7
29	Arizona	33.6
30	South Carolina	32.6
31	New Jersey	31.3
32	Arkansas	30.5
33	New York	30.2
34	Delaware	30.0
35	West Virginia	29.8
36	Virginia	29.7
37	Missouri	29.5
38	Mississippi	29.3
39	Louisiana	29.0
40	Connecticut	28.1
41	Georgia	26.2
42	Massachusetts	26.0
43	Tennessee	25.4
44	Alabama	24.8
45	North Carolina	24.7
46	Illinois	20.9
NA	Florida**	NA
NA	Kansas**	NA
NA	New Hampshire**	NA
NA	Vermont**	NA
	District of Columbia**	NA

Source: Morgan Quitno Press using data from Federal Bureau of Investigation
   "Crime in the United States 1997" (Uniform Crime Reports, November 22, 1998)
Arrests of youths 17 years and younger by law enforcement agencies submitting complete reports to the F.B.I. for 12 months in 1997. Property crimes are offenses of burglary, larceny-theft, motor vehicle theft and arson.
**Not available.*

Reported Arrests of Juveniles for Burglary in 1997

National Total = 90,445 Reported Arrests*

ALPHA ORDER

RANK	STATE	ARRESTS	% of USA
25	Alabama	1,022	1.1%
41	Alaska	276	0.3%
10	Arizona	2,493	2.8%
24	Arkansas	1,145	1.3%
1	California	20,706	22.9%
27	Colorado	919	1.0%
21	Connecticut	1,221	1.3%
42	Delaware	273	0.3%
NA	Florida**	NA	NA
20	Georgia	1,285	1.4%
37	Hawaii	573	0.6%
32	Idaho	733	0.8%
22	Illinois	1,186	1.3%
26	Indiana	968	1.1%
29	Iowa	855	0.9%
NA	Kansas**	NA	NA
34	Kentucky	635	0.7%
12	Louisiana	2,300	2.5%
28	Maine	875	1.0%
5	Maryland	3,077	3.4%
23	Massachusetts	1,157	1.3%
8	Michigan	2,505	2.8%
18	Minnesota	1,570	1.7%
31	Mississippi	754	0.8%
19	Missouri	1,416	1.6%
46	Montana	107	0.1%
36	Nebraska	598	0.7%
35	Nevada	631	0.7%
NA	New Hampshire**	NA	NA
6	New Jersey	2,825	3.1%
38	New Mexico	553	0.6%
4	New York	3,770	4.2%
3	North Carolina	3,970	4.4%
44	North Dakota	194	0.2%
9	Ohio	2,504	2.8%
16	Oklahoma	1,750	1.9%
17	Oregon	1,619	1.8%
13	Pennsylvania	2,286	2.5%
40	Rhode Island	412	0.5%
14	South Carolina	2,256	2.5%
43	South Dakota	252	0.3%
30	Tennessee	791	0.9%
2	Texas	9,568	10.6%
33	Utah	683	0.8%
NA	Vermont**	NA	NA
15	Virginia	1,987	2.2%
11	Washington	2,439	2.7%
39	West Virginia	441	0.5%
7	Wisconsin	2,695	3.0%
45	Wyoming	170	0.2%

RANK ORDER

RANK	STATE	ARRESTS	% of USA
1	California	20,706	22.9%
2	Texas	9,568	10.6%
3	North Carolina	3,970	4.4%
4	New York	3,770	4.2%
5	Maryland	3,077	3.4%
6	New Jersey	2,825	3.1%
7	Wisconsin	2,695	3.0%
8	Michigan	2,505	2.8%
9	Ohio	2,504	2.8%
10	Arizona	2,493	2.8%
11	Washington	2,439	2.7%
12	Louisiana	2,300	2.5%
13	Pennsylvania	2,286	2.5%
14	South Carolina	2,256	2.5%
15	Virginia	1,987	2.2%
16	Oklahoma	1,750	1.9%
17	Oregon	1,619	1.8%
18	Minnesota	1,570	1.7%
19	Missouri	1,416	1.6%
20	Georgia	1,285	1.4%
21	Connecticut	1,221	1.3%
22	Illinois	1,186	1.3%
23	Massachusetts	1,157	1.3%
24	Arkansas	1,145	1.3%
25	Alabama	1,022	1.1%
26	Indiana	968	1.1%
27	Colorado	919	1.0%
28	Maine	875	1.0%
29	Iowa	855	0.9%
30	Tennessee	791	0.9%
31	Mississippi	754	0.8%
32	Idaho	733	0.8%
33	Utah	683	0.8%
34	Kentucky	635	0.7%
35	Nevada	631	0.7%
36	Nebraska	598	0.7%
37	Hawaii	573	0.6%
38	New Mexico	553	0.6%
39	West Virginia	441	0.5%
40	Rhode Island	412	0.5%
41	Alaska	276	0.3%
42	Delaware	273	0.3%
43	South Dakota	252	0.3%
44	North Dakota	194	0.2%
45	Wyoming	170	0.2%
46	Montana	107	0.1%
NA	Florida**	NA	NA
NA	Kansas**	NA	NA
NA	New Hampshire**	NA	NA
NA	Vermont**	NA	NA
	District of Columbia**	NA	NA

Source: Federal Bureau of Investigation
   "Crime in the United States 1997" (Uniform Crime Reports, November 22, 1998)
*Arrests of youths 17 years and younger by law enforcement agencies submitting complete reports to the F.B.I. for 12 months in 1997. Burglary is the unlawful entry of a structure to commit a felony or theft. Attempts are included. See important note at beginning of this chapter.
**Not available.

Reported Juvenile Arrest Rate for Burglary in 1997

National Rate = 431.1 Reported Arrests per 100,000 Juvenile Population*

RANK	STATE	RATE
44	Alabama	224.9
4	Alaska	736.7
12	Arizona	542.9
22	Arkansas	422.0
9	California	579.6
35	Colorado	285.3
23	Connecticut	421.2
1	Delaware	864.4
NA	Florida**	NA
19	Georgia	444.3
17	Hawaii	468.6
18	Idaho	451.0
NA	Illinois**	NA
41	Indiana	251.7
33	Iowa	299.0
NA	Kansas**	NA
2	Kentucky	750.5
14	Louisiana	528.0
5	Maine	642.2
10	Maryland	560.5
45	Massachusetts	222.6
37	Michigan	270.8
38	Minnesota	266.4
7	Mississippi	587.5
27	Missouri	366.1
42	Montana	239.7
32	Nebraska	301.6
3	Nevada	738.8
NA	New Hampshire**	NA
30	New Jersey	347.5
28	New Mexico	359.9
20	New York	426.1
16	North Carolina	493.8
39	North Dakota	265.4
29	Ohio	350.6
21	Oklahoma	424.3
15	Oregon	495.8
26	Pennsylvania	370.9
25	Rhode Island	398.6
13	South Carolina	530.7
8	South Dakota	584.3
31	Tennessee	319.7
24	Texas	408.0
34	Utah	293.6
NA	Vermont**	NA
36	Virginia	280.8
6	Washington	607.9
43	West Virginia	231.3
11	Wisconsin	552.0
40	Wyoming	261.4

RANK	STATE	RATE
1	Delaware	864.4
2	Kentucky	750.5
3	Nevada	738.8
4	Alaska	736.7
5	Maine	642.2
6	Washington	607.9
7	Mississippi	587.5
8	South Dakota	584.3
9	California	579.6
10	Maryland	560.5
11	Wisconsin	552.0
12	Arizona	542.9
13	South Carolina	530.7
14	Louisiana	528.0
15	Oregon	495.8
16	North Carolina	493.8
17	Hawaii	468.6
18	Idaho	451.0
19	Georgia	444.3
20	New York	426.1
21	Oklahoma	424.3
22	Arkansas	422.0
23	Connecticut	421.2
24	Texas	408.0
25	Rhode Island	398.6
26	Pennsylvania	370.9
27	Missouri	366.1
28	New Mexico	359.9
29	Ohio	350.6
30	New Jersey	347.5
31	Tennessee	319.7
32	Nebraska	301.6
33	Iowa	299.0
34	Utah	293.6
35	Colorado	285.3
36	Virginia	280.8
37	Michigan	270.8
38	Minnesota	266.4
39	North Dakota	265.4
40	Wyoming	261.4
41	Indiana	251.7
42	Montana	239.7
43	West Virginia	231.3
44	Alabama	224.9
45	Massachusetts	222.6
NA	Florida**	NA
NA	Illinois**	NA
NA	Kansas**	NA
NA	New Hampshire**	NA
NA	Vermont**	NA
	District of Columbia**	NA

*Source: Morgan Quitno Press using data from Federal Bureau of Investigation
"Crime in the United States 1997" (Uniform Crime Reports, November 22, 1998)*
By law enforcement agencies submitting complete reports to the F.B.I. for 12 months in 1997. Arrests of youths 17 years and younger divided into population of 10 to 17 year olds. See important note at beginning of this chapter. Burglary is the unlawful entry of a structure to commit a felony or theft. Attempts are included.
***Not available.*

Reported Arrests of Juveniles for Burglary
As a Percent of All Such Arrests in 1997
National Percent = 36.8% of Reported Burglary Arrests*

ALPHA ORDER

RANK	STATE	PERCENT
44	Alabama	26.9
6	Alaska	51.5
12	Arizona	45.5
30	Arkansas	35.9
31	California	35.5
14	Colorado	43.3
41	Connecticut	30.2
27	Delaware	37.4
NA	Florida**	NA
39	Georgia	30.5
25	Hawaii	37.7
1	Idaho	58.0
43	Illinois	28.4
28	Indiana	36.2
15	Iowa	43.2
NA	Kansas**	NA
23	Kentucky	38.0
38	Louisiana	30.7
8	Maine	48.9
32	Maryland	34.4
42	Massachusetts	28.6
28	Michigan	36.2
7	Minnesota	49.0
33	Mississippi	34.3
39	Missouri	30.5
2	Montana	57.8
13	Nebraska	44.5
21	Nevada	40.7
NA	New Hampshire**	NA
37	New Jersey	31.3
18	New Mexico	41.7
22	New York	39.7
46	North Carolina	24.6
4	North Dakota	54.5
23	Ohio	38.0
16	Oklahoma	42.8
20	Oregon	40.9
19	Pennsylvania	41.2
17	Rhode Island	42.3
25	South Carolina	37.7
3	South Dakota	55.1
45	Tennessee	25.2
11	Texas	45.8
9	Utah	47.8
NA	Vermont**	NA
35	Virginia	32.0
10	Washington	46.9
36	West Virginia	31.4
5	Wisconsin	52.9
34	Wyoming	32.9

RANK ORDER

RANK	STATE	PERCENT
1	Idaho	58.0
2	Montana	57.8
3	South Dakota	55.1
4	North Dakota	54.5
5	Wisconsin	52.9
6	Alaska	51.5
7	Minnesota	49.0
8	Maine	48.9
9	Utah	47.8
10	Washington	46.9
11	Texas	45.8
12	Arizona	45.5
13	Nebraska	44.5
14	Colorado	43.3
15	Iowa	43.2
16	Oklahoma	42.8
17	Rhode Island	42.3
18	New Mexico	41.7
19	Pennsylvania	41.2
20	Oregon	40.9
21	Nevada	40.7
22	New York	39.7
23	Kentucky	38.0
23	Ohio	38.0
25	Hawaii	37.7
25	South Carolina	37.7
27	Delaware	37.4
28	Indiana	36.2
28	Michigan	36.2
30	Arkansas	35.9
31	California	35.5
32	Maryland	34.4
33	Mississippi	34.3
34	Wyoming	32.9
35	Virginia	32.0
36	West Virginia	31.4
37	New Jersey	31.3
38	Louisiana	30.7
39	Georgia	30.5
39	Missouri	30.5
41	Connecticut	30.2
42	Massachusetts	28.6
43	Illinois	28.4
44	Alabama	26.9
45	Tennessee	25.2
46	North Carolina	24.6
NA	Florida**	NA
NA	Kansas**	NA
NA	New Hampshire**	NA
NA	Vermont**	NA
	District of Columbia**	NA

Source: Morgan Quitno Press using data from Federal Bureau of Investigation
   "Crime in the United States 1997" (Uniform Crime Reports, November 22, 1998)
*Arrests of youths 17 years and younger by law enforcement agencies submitting complete reports to the F.B.I. for
12 months in 1997. Burglary is the unlawful entry of a structure to commit a felony or theft. Attempts are included.
**Not available.

Reported Arrests of Juveniles for Larceny and Theft in 1997

National Total = 346,753 Reported Arrests*

ALPHA ORDER					RANK ORDER			
RANK	STATE	ARRESTS	% of USA		RANK	STATE	ARRESTS	% of USA
28	Alabama	4,914	1.4%		1	California	42,751	12.3%
45	Alaska	654	0.2%		2	Texas	37,685	10.9%
8	Arizona	10,902	3.1%		3	Wisconsin	16,464	4.7%
31	Arkansas	4,174	1.2%		4	Washington	13,370	3.9%
1	California	42,751	12.3%		5	Minnesota	12,052	3.5%
19	Colorado	7,456	2.2%		6	New York	11,848	3.4%
26	Connecticut	5,113	1.5%		7	New Jersey	11,655	3.4%
44	Delaware	1,159	0.3%		8	Arizona	10,902	3.1%
NA	Florida**	NA	NA		9	Michigan	10,824	3.1%
29	Georgia	4,762	1.4%		10	North Carolina	10,118	2.9%
35	Hawaii	2,927	0.8%		11	Virginia	9,746	2.8%
30	Idaho	4,499	1.3%		12	Maryland	9,412	2.7%
23	Illinois	5,436	1.6%		13	Ohio	9,019	2.6%
20	Indiana	6,798	2.0%		14	Louisiana	8,655	2.5%
24	Iowa	5,174	1.5%		15	Oregon	8,583	2.5%
NA	Kansas**	NA	NA		16	Missouri	8,237	2.4%
38	Kentucky	1,666	0.5%		17	Oklahoma	7,931	2.3%
14	Louisiana	8,655	2.5%		18	Utah	7,593	2.2%
34	Maine	3,177	0.9%		19	Colorado	7,456	2.2%
12	Maryland	9,412	2.7%		20	Indiana	6,798	2.0%
33	Massachusetts	3,198	0.9%		21	Pennsylvania	6,532	1.9%
9	Michigan	10,824	3.1%		22	South Carolina	6,120	1.8%
5	Minnesota	12,052	3.5%		23	Illinois	5,436	1.6%
36	Mississippi	2,142	0.6%		24	Iowa	5,174	1.5%
16	Missouri	8,237	2.4%		25	Nebraska	5,172	1.5%
46	Montana	540	0.2%		26	Connecticut	5,113	1.5%
25	Nebraska	5,172	1.5%		27	Tennessee	4,926	1.4%
37	Nevada	2,099	0.6%		28	Alabama	4,914	1.4%
NA	New Hampshire**	NA	NA		29	Georgia	4,762	1.4%
7	New Jersey	11,655	3.4%		30	Idaho	4,499	1.3%
32	New Mexico	3,667	1.1%		31	Arkansas	4,174	1.2%
6	New York	11,848	3.4%		32	New Mexico	3,667	1.1%
10	North Carolina	10,118	2.9%		33	Massachusetts	3,198	0.9%
39	North Dakota	1,646	0.5%		34	Maine	3,177	0.9%
13	Ohio	9,019	2.6%		35	Hawaii	2,927	0.8%
17	Oklahoma	7,931	2.3%		36	Mississippi	2,142	0.6%
15	Oregon	8,583	2.5%		37	Nevada	2,099	0.6%
21	Pennsylvania	6,532	1.9%		38	Kentucky	1,666	0.5%
41	Rhode Island	1,496	0.4%		39	North Dakota	1,646	0.5%
22	South Carolina	6,120	1.8%		40	South Dakota	1,520	0.4%
40	South Dakota	1,520	0.4%		41	Rhode Island	1,496	0.4%
27	Tennessee	4,926	1.4%		42	West Virginia	1,486	0.4%
2	Texas	37,685	10.9%		43	Wyoming	1,455	0.4%
18	Utah	7,593	2.2%		44	Delaware	1,159	0.3%
NA	Vermont**	NA	NA		45	Alaska	654	0.2%
11	Virginia	9,746	2.8%		46	Montana	540	0.2%
4	Washington	13,370	3.9%		NA	Florida**	NA	NA
42	West Virginia	1,486	0.4%		NA	Kansas**	NA	NA
3	Wisconsin	16,464	4.7%		NA	New Hampshire**	NA	NA
43	Wyoming	1,455	0.4%		NA	Vermont**	NA	NA
						District of Columbia**	NA	NA

Source: Federal Bureau of Investigation
   "Crime in the United States 1997" (Uniform Crime Reports, November 22, 1998)
*Arrests of youths 17 years and younger by law enforcement agencies submitting complete reports to the F.B.I. for 12 months in 1997. Larceny and theft is the unlawful taking of property without use of force, violence or fraud. Attempts are included. Motor vehicle thefts are excluded. See important note at beginning of this chapter.
**Not available.

Reported Arrest Rate for Juveniles for Larceny and Theft in 1997

National Rate = 1,652.8 Reported Arrests per 100,000 Juvenile Population*

ALPHA ORDER

RANK	STATE	RATE
42	Alabama	1,081.6
26	Alaska	1,745.6
12	Arizona	2,374.2
31	Arkansas	1,538.4
40	California	1,196.8
14	Colorado	2,314.4
25	Connecticut	1,763.8
1	Delaware	3,669.6
NA	Florida**	NA
29	Georgia	1,646.6
10	Hawaii	2,393.5
6	Idaho	2,768.4
NA	Illinois**	NA
24	Indiana	1,767.8
23	Iowa	1,809.7
NA	Kansas**	NA
21	Kentucky	1,969.1
20	Louisiana	1,986.8
13	Maine	2,331.8
27	Maryland	1,714.4
45	Massachusetts	615.2
41	Michigan	1,170.1
18	Minnesota	2,044.9
28	Mississippi	1,668.9
17	Missouri	2,129.7
39	Montana	1,209.6
8	Nebraska	2,608.7
9	Nevada	2,457.6
NA	New Hampshire**	NA
34	New Jersey	1,433.6
11	New Mexico	2,386.5
36	New York	1,339.2
38	North Carolina	1,258.6
15	North Dakota	2,251.4
37	Ohio	1,262.7
22	Oklahoma	1,922.7
7	Oregon	2,628.4
43	Pennsylvania	1,059.9
32	Rhode Island	1,447.4
33	South Carolina	1,439.8
2	South Dakota	3,524.4
19	Tennessee	1,991.2
30	Texas	1,606.9
5	Utah	3,264.2
NA	Vermont**	NA
35	Virginia	1,377.5
4	Washington	3,332.5
44	West Virginia	779.5
3	Wisconsin	3,372.2
16	Wyoming	2,237.0

RANK ORDER

RANK	STATE	RATE
1	Delaware	3,669.6
2	South Dakota	3,524.4
3	Wisconsin	3,372.2
4	Washington	3,332.5
5	Utah	3,264.2
6	Idaho	2,768.4
7	Oregon	2,628.4
8	Nebraska	2,608.7
9	Nevada	2,457.6
10	Hawaii	2,393.5
11	New Mexico	2,386.5
12	Arizona	2,374.2
13	Maine	2,331.8
14	Colorado	2,314.4
15	North Dakota	2,251.4
16	Wyoming	2,237.0
17	Missouri	2,129.7
18	Minnesota	2,044.9
19	Tennessee	1,991.2
20	Louisiana	1,986.8
21	Kentucky	1,969.1
22	Oklahoma	1,922.7
23	Iowa	1,809.7
24	Indiana	1,767.8
25	Connecticut	1,763.8
26	Alaska	1,745.6
27	Maryland	1,714.4
28	Mississippi	1,668.9
29	Georgia	1,646.6
30	Texas	1,606.9
31	Arkansas	1,538.4
32	Rhode Island	1,447.4
33	South Carolina	1,439.8
34	New Jersey	1,433.6
35	Virginia	1,377.5
36	New York	1,339.2
37	Ohio	1,262.7
38	North Carolina	1,258.6
39	Montana	1,209.6
40	California	1,196.8
41	Michigan	1,170.1
42	Alabama	1,081.6
43	Pennsylvania	1,059.9
44	West Virginia	779.5
45	Massachusetts	615.2
NA	Florida**	NA
NA	Illinois**	NA
NA	Kansas**	NA
NA	New Hampshire**	NA
NA	Vermont**	NA
	District of Columbia**	NA

Source: Morgan Quitno Press using data from Federal Bureau of Investigation
"Crime in the United States 1997" (Uniform Crime Reports, November 22, 1998)
*By law enforcement agencies submitting complete reports to the F.B.I. for 12 months in 1997. Arrests of youths 17 years and younger divided into population of 10 to 17 year olds. See important note at beginning of this chapter. Larceny and theft is the unlawful taking of property without use of force, violence or fraud. Attempts are included. Motor vehicle thefts are excluded. **Not available.

219

Reported Arrests of Juveniles for Larceny and Theft
As a Percent of All Such Arrests in 1997
National Percent = 33.5% of Reported Larceny and Theft Arrests*

ALPHA ORDER

RANK ORDER

RANK	STATE	PERCENT		RANK	STATE	PERCENT
42	Alabama	24.6		1	North Dakota	57.0
4	Alaska	50.8		2	Idaho	56.2
29	Arizona	30.5		3	Minnesota	52.0
32	Arkansas	29.0		4	Alaska	50.8
25	California	33.4		5	South Dakota	49.9
17	Colorado	38.2		6	Nebraska	48.9
41	Connecticut	25.9		6	Wyoming	48.9
35	Delaware	28.3		8	Utah	48.3
NA	Florida**	NA		9	Maine	47.8
43	Georgia	24.1		10	Oklahoma	47.7
20	Hawaii	36.1		11	Wisconsin	46.9
2	Idaho	56.2		12	Iowa	44.9
46	Illinois	16.7		13	Montana	44.7
22	Indiana	35.9		14	Washington	43.5
12	Iowa	44.9		15	Rhode Island	41.1
NA	Kansas**	NA		16	Nevada	40.7
24	Kentucky	33.5		17	Colorado	38.2
34	Louisiana	28.4		18	Michigan	37.7
9	Maine	47.8		19	Texas	36.5
28	Maryland	31.6		20	Hawaii	36.1
45	Massachusetts	23.6		21	New Mexico	36.0
18	Michigan	37.7		22	Indiana	35.9
3	Minnesota	52.0		23	Pennsylvania	33.9
36	Mississippi	28.1		24	Kentucky	33.5
33	Missouri	28.8		25	California	33.4
13	Montana	44.7		26	Oregon	32.9
6	Nebraska	48.9		27	Ohio	32.0
16	Nevada	40.7		28	Maryland	31.6
NA	New Hampshire**	NA		29	Arizona	30.5
31	New Jersey	30.0		29	South Carolina	30.5
21	New Mexico	36.0		31	New Jersey	30.0
39	New York	27.3		32	Arkansas	29.0
43	North Carolina	24.1		33	Missouri	28.8
1	North Dakota	57.0		34	Louisiana	28.4
27	Ohio	32.0		35	Delaware	28.3
10	Oklahoma	47.7		36	Mississippi	28.1
26	Oregon	32.9		36	West Virginia	28.1
23	Pennsylvania	33.9		38	Virginia	27.5
15	Rhode Island	41.1		39	New York	27.3
29	South Carolina	30.5		40	Tennessee	26.2
5	South Dakota	49.9		41	Connecticut	25.9
40	Tennessee	26.2		42	Alabama	24.6
19	Texas	36.5		43	Georgia	24.1
8	Utah	48.3		43	North Carolina	24.1
NA	Vermont**	NA		45	Massachusetts	23.6
38	Virginia	27.5		46	Illinois	16.7
14	Washington	43.5		NA	Florida**	NA
36	West Virginia	28.1		NA	Kansas**	NA
11	Wisconsin	46.9		NA	New Hampshire**	NA
6	Wyoming	48.9		NA	Vermont**	NA
					District of Columbia**	NA

Source: Morgan Quitno Press using data from Federal Bureau of Investigation
   "Crime in the United States 1997" (Uniform Crime Reports, November 22, 1998)
*Arrests of youths 17 years and younger by law enforcement agencies submitting complete reports to the F.B.I. for 12 months in 1997. Larceny and theft is the unlawful taking of property without use of force, violence or fraud. Attempts are included. Motor vehicle thefts are excluded.
**Not available.

Reported Arrests of Juveniles for Motor Vehicle Theft in 1997

National Total = 46,274 Reported Arrests*

<table>
<tr><td colspan="4">ALPHA ORDER</td><td colspan="4">RANK ORDER</td></tr>
<tr><td>RANK</td><td>STATE</td><td>ARRESTS</td><td>% of USA</td><td>RANK</td><td>STATE</td><td>ARRESTS</td><td>% of USA</td></tr>
<tr><td>31</td><td>Alabama</td><td>337</td><td>0.7%</td><td>1</td><td>California</td><td>10,093</td><td>21.8%</td></tr>
<tr><td>42</td><td>Alaska</td><td>99</td><td>0.2%</td><td>2</td><td>Texas</td><td>4,134</td><td>8.9%</td></tr>
<tr><td>6</td><td>Arizona</td><td>1,449</td><td>3.1%</td><td>3</td><td>Illinois</td><td>2,739</td><td>5.9%</td></tr>
<tr><td>38</td><td>Arkansas</td><td>181</td><td>0.4%</td><td>4</td><td>Maryland</td><td>2,630</td><td>5.7%</td></tr>
<tr><td>1</td><td>California</td><td>10,093</td><td>21.8%</td><td>5</td><td>Wisconsin</td><td>2,243</td><td>4.8%</td></tr>
<tr><td>23</td><td>Colorado</td><td>646</td><td>1.4%</td><td>6</td><td>Arizona</td><td>1,449</td><td>3.1%</td></tr>
<tr><td>19</td><td>Connecticut</td><td>802</td><td>1.7%</td><td>7</td><td>Virginia</td><td>1,443</td><td>3.1%</td></tr>
<tr><td>46</td><td>Delaware</td><td>60</td><td>0.1%</td><td>8</td><td>Ohio</td><td>1,285</td><td>2.8%</td></tr>
<tr><td>NA</td><td>Florida**</td><td>NA</td><td>NA</td><td>9</td><td>New York</td><td>1,192</td><td>2.6%</td></tr>
<tr><td>20</td><td>Georgia</td><td>764</td><td>1.7%</td><td>10</td><td>Oklahoma</td><td>1,118</td><td>2.4%</td></tr>
<tr><td>30</td><td>Hawaii</td><td>339</td><td>0.7%</td><td>11</td><td>Michigan</td><td>1,112</td><td>2.4%</td></tr>
<tr><td>29</td><td>Idaho</td><td>375</td><td>0.8%</td><td>12</td><td>Missouri</td><td>1,085</td><td>2.3%</td></tr>
<tr><td>3</td><td>Illinois</td><td>2,739</td><td>5.9%</td><td>13</td><td>Washington</td><td>1,064</td><td>2.3%</td></tr>
<tr><td>18</td><td>Indiana</td><td>919</td><td>2.0%</td><td>14</td><td>Pennsylvania</td><td>1,037</td><td>2.2%</td></tr>
<tr><td>28</td><td>Iowa</td><td>422</td><td>0.9%</td><td>15</td><td>Minnesota</td><td>995</td><td>2.2%</td></tr>
<tr><td>NA</td><td>Kansas**</td><td>NA</td><td>NA</td><td>16</td><td>Oregon</td><td>957</td><td>2.1%</td></tr>
<tr><td>32</td><td>Kentucky</td><td>322</td><td>0.7%</td><td>17</td><td>New Jersey</td><td>951</td><td>2.1%</td></tr>
<tr><td>26</td><td>Louisiana</td><td>492</td><td>1.1%</td><td>18</td><td>Indiana</td><td>919</td><td>2.0%</td></tr>
<tr><td>35</td><td>Maine</td><td>257</td><td>0.6%</td><td>19</td><td>Connecticut</td><td>802</td><td>1.7%</td></tr>
<tr><td>4</td><td>Maryland</td><td>2,630</td><td>5.7%</td><td>20</td><td>Georgia</td><td>764</td><td>1.7%</td></tr>
<tr><td>25</td><td>Massachusetts</td><td>578</td><td>1.2%</td><td>21</td><td>North Carolina</td><td>760</td><td>1.6%</td></tr>
<tr><td>11</td><td>Michigan</td><td>1,112</td><td>2.4%</td><td>22</td><td>Utah</td><td>652</td><td>1.4%</td></tr>
<tr><td>15</td><td>Minnesota</td><td>995</td><td>2.2%</td><td>23</td><td>Colorado</td><td>646</td><td>1.4%</td></tr>
<tr><td>36</td><td>Mississippi</td><td>220</td><td>0.5%</td><td>24</td><td>Tennessee</td><td>594</td><td>1.3%</td></tr>
<tr><td>12</td><td>Missouri</td><td>1,085</td><td>2.3%</td><td>25</td><td>Massachusetts</td><td>578</td><td>1.2%</td></tr>
<tr><td>45</td><td>Montana</td><td>67</td><td>0.1%</td><td>26</td><td>Louisiana</td><td>492</td><td>1.1%</td></tr>
<tr><td>34</td><td>Nebraska</td><td>279</td><td>0.6%</td><td>27</td><td>South Carolina</td><td>428</td><td>0.9%</td></tr>
<tr><td>41</td><td>Nevada</td><td>126</td><td>0.3%</td><td>28</td><td>Iowa</td><td>422</td><td>0.9%</td></tr>
<tr><td>NA</td><td>New Hampshire**</td><td>NA</td><td>NA</td><td>29</td><td>Idaho</td><td>375</td><td>0.8%</td></tr>
<tr><td>17</td><td>New Jersey</td><td>951</td><td>2.1%</td><td>30</td><td>Hawaii</td><td>339</td><td>0.7%</td></tr>
<tr><td>33</td><td>New Mexico</td><td>309</td><td>0.7%</td><td>31</td><td>Alabama</td><td>337</td><td>0.7%</td></tr>
<tr><td>9</td><td>New York</td><td>1,192</td><td>2.6%</td><td>32</td><td>Kentucky</td><td>322</td><td>0.7%</td></tr>
<tr><td>21</td><td>North Carolina</td><td>760</td><td>1.6%</td><td>33</td><td>New Mexico</td><td>309</td><td>0.7%</td></tr>
<tr><td>37</td><td>North Dakota</td><td>186</td><td>0.4%</td><td>34</td><td>Nebraska</td><td>279</td><td>0.6%</td></tr>
<tr><td>8</td><td>Ohio</td><td>1,285</td><td>2.8%</td><td>35</td><td>Maine</td><td>257</td><td>0.6%</td></tr>
<tr><td>10</td><td>Oklahoma</td><td>1,118</td><td>2.4%</td><td>36</td><td>Mississippi</td><td>220</td><td>0.5%</td></tr>
<tr><td>16</td><td>Oregon</td><td>957</td><td>2.1%</td><td>37</td><td>North Dakota</td><td>186</td><td>0.4%</td></tr>
<tr><td>14</td><td>Pennsylvania</td><td>1,037</td><td>2.2%</td><td>38</td><td>Arkansas</td><td>181</td><td>0.4%</td></tr>
<tr><td>40</td><td>Rhode Island</td><td>167</td><td>0.4%</td><td>39</td><td>West Virginia</td><td>179</td><td>0.4%</td></tr>
<tr><td>27</td><td>South Carolina</td><td>428</td><td>0.9%</td><td>40</td><td>Rhode Island</td><td>167</td><td>0.4%</td></tr>
<tr><td>44</td><td>South Dakota</td><td>92</td><td>0.2%</td><td>41</td><td>Nevada</td><td>126</td><td>0.3%</td></tr>
<tr><td>24</td><td>Tennessee</td><td>594</td><td>1.3%</td><td>42</td><td>Alaska</td><td>99</td><td>0.2%</td></tr>
<tr><td>2</td><td>Texas</td><td>4,134</td><td>8.9%</td><td>43</td><td>Wyoming</td><td>95</td><td>0.2%</td></tr>
<tr><td>22</td><td>Utah</td><td>652</td><td>1.4%</td><td>44</td><td>South Dakota</td><td>92</td><td>0.2%</td></tr>
<tr><td>NA</td><td>Vermont**</td><td>NA</td><td>NA</td><td>45</td><td>Montana</td><td>67</td><td>0.1%</td></tr>
<tr><td>7</td><td>Virginia</td><td>1,443</td><td>3.1%</td><td>46</td><td>Delaware</td><td>60</td><td>0.1%</td></tr>
<tr><td>13</td><td>Washington</td><td>1,064</td><td>2.3%</td><td>NA</td><td>Florida**</td><td>NA</td><td>NA</td></tr>
<tr><td>39</td><td>West Virginia</td><td>179</td><td>0.4%</td><td>NA</td><td>Kansas**</td><td>NA</td><td>NA</td></tr>
<tr><td>5</td><td>Wisconsin</td><td>2,243</td><td>4.8%</td><td>NA</td><td>New Hampshire**</td><td>NA</td><td>NA</td></tr>
<tr><td>43</td><td>Wyoming</td><td>95</td><td>0.2%</td><td>NA</td><td>Vermont**</td><td>NA</td><td>NA</td></tr>
<tr><td></td><td></td><td></td><td></td><td></td><td>District of Columbia**</td><td>NA</td><td>NA</td></tr>
</table>

Source: Federal Bureau of Investigation
"Crime in the United States 1997" (Uniform Crime Reports, November 22, 1998)
*Arrests of youths 17 years and younger by law enforcement agencies submitting complete reports to the F.B.I. for 12 months in 1997. Motor vehicle theft includes the theft or attempted theft of a self-propelled vehicle. Excludes motorboats, construction equipment, airplanes and farming equipment. See important note at beginning of this chapter. **Not available.

Reported Arrest Rate of Juveniles for Motor Vehicle Theft in 1997

National Rate = 220.6 Reported Arrests per 100,000 Juvenile Population*

ALPHA ORDER

RANK	STATE	RATE
44	Alabama	74.2
13	Alaska	264.2
4	Arizona	315.6
45	Arkansas	66.7
6	California	282.5
22	Colorado	200.5
10	Connecticut	276.7
23	Delaware	190.0
NA	Florida**	NA
13	Georgia	264.2
9	Hawaii	277.2
18	Idaho	230.8
NA	Illinois**	NA
17	Indiana	239.0
32	Iowa	147.6
NA	Kansas**	NA
3	Kentucky	380.6
39	Louisiana	112.9
24	Maine	188.6
1	Maryland	479.1
40	Massachusetts	111.2
37	Michigan	120.2
28	Minnesota	168.8
27	Mississippi	171.4
7	Missouri	280.5
31	Montana	150.1
35	Nebraska	140.7
33	Nevada	147.5
NA	New Hampshire**	NA
38	New Jersey	117.0
21	New Mexico	201.1
36	New York	134.7
42	North Carolina	94.5
15	North Dakota	254.4
25	Ohio	179.9
11	Oklahoma	271.0
5	Oregon	293.1
29	Pennsylvania	168.3
30	Rhode Island	161.6
41	South Carolina	100.7
19	South Dakota	213.3
16	Tennessee	240.1
26	Texas	176.3
8	Utah	280.3
NA	Vermont**	NA
20	Virginia	204.0
12	Washington	265.2
43	West Virginia	93.9
2	Wisconsin	459.4
34	Wyoming	146.1

RANK ORDER

RANK	STATE	RATE
1	Maryland	479.1
2	Wisconsin	459.4
3	Kentucky	380.6
4	Arizona	315.6
5	Oregon	293.1
6	California	282.5
7	Missouri	280.5
8	Utah	280.3
9	Hawaii	277.2
10	Connecticut	276.7
11	Oklahoma	271.0
12	Washington	265.2
13	Alaska	264.2
13	Georgia	264.2
15	North Dakota	254.4
16	Tennessee	240.1
17	Indiana	239.0
18	Idaho	230.8
19	South Dakota	213.3
20	Virginia	204.0
21	New Mexico	201.1
22	Colorado	200.5
23	Delaware	190.0
24	Maine	188.6
25	Ohio	179.9
26	Texas	176.3
27	Mississippi	171.4
28	Minnesota	168.8
29	Pennsylvania	168.3
30	Rhode Island	161.6
31	Montana	150.1
32	Iowa	147.6
33	Nevada	147.5
34	Wyoming	146.1
35	Nebraska	140.7
36	New York	134.7
37	Michigan	120.2
38	New Jersey	117.0
39	Louisiana	112.9
40	Massachusetts	111.2
41	South Carolina	100.7
42	North Carolina	94.5
43	West Virginia	93.9
44	Alabama	74.2
45	Arkansas	66.7
NA	Florida**	NA
NA	Illinois**	NA
NA	Kansas**	NA
NA	New Hampshire**	NA
NA	Vermont**	NA
	District of Columbia**	NA

Source: Morgan Quitno Press using data from Federal Bureau of Investigation
"Crime in the United States 1997" (Uniform Crime Reports, November 22, 1998)
*By law enforcement agencies submitting complete reports to the F.B.I. for 12 months in 1997. Arrests of youths 17 years and younger divided into population of 10 to 17 year olds. See important note at beginning of this chapter. Motor vehicle theft includes the theft or attempted theft of a self-propelled vehicle. Excludes motorboats, construction equipment, airplanes and farming equipment. **Not available.

Reported Arrests of Juveniles for Motor Vehicle Theft
As a Percent of All Such Arrests in 1997
National Percent = 39.9% of Reported Motor Vehicle Theft Arrests*

ALPHA ORDER

RANK	STATE	PERCENT
46	Alabama	23.0
27	Alaska	42.5
18	Arizona	45.7
32	Arkansas	39.4
36	California	36.0
31	Colorado	40.4
16	Connecticut	45.8
25	Delaware	42.6
NA	Florida**	NA
37	Georgia	34.9
45	Hawaii	24.4
2	Idaho	59.3
38	Illinois	33.8
23	Indiana	43.7
8	Iowa	53.4
NA	Kansas**	NA
24	Kentucky	43.2
40	Louisiana	32.8
10	Maine	50.8
16	Maryland	45.8
33	Massachusetts	38.7
21	Michigan	44.7
9	Minnesota	53.3
43	Mississippi	27.5
39	Missouri	33.6
7	Montana	54.5
4	Nebraska	56.4
20	Nevada	45.5
NA	New Hampshire**	NA
14	New Jersey	47.1
25	New Mexico	42.6
34	New York	36.8
41	North Carolina	30.8
1	North Dakota	67.4
19	Ohio	45.6
13	Oklahoma	47.7
42	Oregon	27.9
28	Pennsylvania	42.3
35	Rhode Island	36.2
22	South Carolina	44.3
5	South Dakota	55.8
44	Tennessee	25.7
29	Texas	40.9
11	Utah	49.9
NA	Vermont**	NA
15	Virginia	46.3
6	Washington	55.3
30	West Virginia	40.5
3	Wisconsin	56.9
12	Wyoming	49.2

RANK ORDER

RANK	STATE	PERCENT
1	North Dakota	67.4
2	Idaho	59.3
3	Wisconsin	56.9
4	Nebraska	56.4
5	South Dakota	55.8
6	Washington	55.3
7	Montana	54.5
8	Iowa	53.4
9	Minnesota	53.3
10	Maine	50.8
11	Utah	49.9
12	Wyoming	49.2
13	Oklahoma	47.7
14	New Jersey	47.1
15	Virginia	46.3
16	Connecticut	45.8
16	Maryland	45.8
18	Arizona	45.7
19	Ohio	45.6
20	Nevada	45.5
21	Michigan	44.7
22	South Carolina	44.3
23	Indiana	43.7
24	Kentucky	43.2
25	Delaware	42.6
25	New Mexico	42.6
27	Alaska	42.5
28	Pennsylvania	42.3
29	Texas	40.9
30	West Virginia	40.5
31	Colorado	40.4
32	Arkansas	39.4
33	Massachusetts	38.7
34	New York	36.8
35	Rhode Island	36.2
36	California	36.0
37	Georgia	34.9
38	Illinois	33.8
39	Missouri	33.6
40	Louisiana	32.8
41	North Carolina	30.8
42	Oregon	27.9
43	Mississippi	27.5
44	Tennessee	25.7
45	Hawaii	24.4
46	Alabama	23.0
NA	Florida**	NA
NA	Kansas**	NA
NA	New Hampshire**	NA
NA	Vermont**	NA
	District of Columbia**	NA

Source: Morgan Quitno Press using data from Federal Bureau of Investigation
  "Crime in the United States 1997" (Uniform Crime Reports, November 22, 1998)
*Arrests of youths 17 years and younger by law enforcement agencies submitting complete reports to the F.B.I. for 12 months in 1997. Motor vehicle theft includes the theft or attempted theft of a self-propelled vehicle. Excludes motorboats, construction equipment, airplanes and farming equipment.
**Not available.

Reported Arrests of Juveniles for Arson in 1997

National Total = 6,914 Reported Arrests*

ALPHA ORDER

RANK	STATE	ARRESTS	% of USA
42	Alabama	21	0.3%
44	Alaska	9	0.1%
15	Arizona	189	2.7%
37	Arkansas	31	0.4%
1	California	1,311	19.0%
18	Colorado	121	1.8%
27	Connecticut	87	1.3%
46	Delaware	2	0.0%
NA	Florida**	NA	NA
20	Georgia	101	1.5%
38	Hawaii	26	0.4%
26	Idaho	88	1.3%
28	Illinois	84	1.2%
21	Indiana	95	1.4%
29	Iowa	72	1.0%
NA	Kansas**	NA	NA
36	Kentucky	33	0.5%
25	Louisiana	90	1.3%
19	Maine	107	1.5%
12	Maryland	209	3.0%
30	Massachusetts	71	1.0%
8	Michigan	235	3.4%
17	Minnesota	124	1.8%
41	Mississippi	22	0.3%
16	Missouri	141	2.0%
45	Montana	4	0.1%
31	Nebraska	65	0.9%
34	Nevada	61	0.9%
NA	New Hampshire**	NA	NA
3	New Jersey	364	5.3%
35	New Mexico	34	0.5%
5	New York	314	4.5%
9	North Carolina	224	3.2%
40	North Dakota	23	0.3%
4	Ohio	317	4.6%
14	Oklahoma	200	2.9%
6	Oregon	243	3.5%
13	Pennsylvania	204	3.0%
31	Rhode Island	65	0.9%
21	South Carolina	95	1.4%
39	South Dakota	24	0.3%
24	Tennessee	94	1.4%
2	Texas	463	6.7%
21	Utah	95	1.4%
NA	Vermont**	NA	NA
7	Virginia	238	3.4%
11	Washington	213	3.1%
33	West Virginia	63	0.9%
10	Wisconsin	222	3.2%
43	Wyoming	20	0.3%

RANK ORDER

RANK	STATE	ARRESTS	% of USA
1	California	1,311	19.0%
2	Texas	463	6.7%
3	New Jersey	364	5.3%
4	Ohio	317	4.6%
5	New York	314	4.5%
6	Oregon	243	3.5%
7	Virginia	238	3.4%
8	Michigan	235	3.4%
9	North Carolina	224	3.2%
10	Wisconsin	222	3.2%
11	Washington	213	3.1%
12	Maryland	209	3.0%
13	Pennsylvania	204	3.0%
14	Oklahoma	200	2.9%
15	Arizona	189	2.7%
16	Missouri	141	2.0%
17	Minnesota	124	1.8%
18	Colorado	121	1.8%
19	Maine	107	1.5%
20	Georgia	101	1.5%
21	Indiana	95	1.4%
21	South Carolina	95	1.4%
21	Utah	95	1.4%
24	Tennessee	94	1.4%
25	Louisiana	90	1.3%
26	Idaho	88	1.3%
27	Connecticut	87	1.3%
28	Illinois	84	1.2%
29	Iowa	72	1.0%
30	Massachusetts	71	1.0%
31	Nebraska	65	0.9%
31	Rhode Island	65	0.9%
33	West Virginia	63	0.9%
34	Nevada	61	0.9%
35	New Mexico	34	0.5%
36	Kentucky	33	0.5%
37	Arkansas	31	0.4%
38	Hawaii	26	0.4%
39	South Dakota	24	0.3%
40	North Dakota	23	0.3%
41	Mississippi	22	0.3%
42	Alabama	21	0.3%
43	Wyoming	20	0.3%
44	Alaska	9	0.1%
45	Montana	4	0.1%
46	Delaware	2	0.0%
NA	Florida**	NA	NA
NA	Kansas**	NA	NA
NA	New Hampshire**	NA	NA
NA	Vermont**	NA	NA
	District of Columbia**	NA	NA

Source: Federal Bureau of Investigation
   "Crime in the United States 1997" (Uniform Crime Reports, November 22, 1998)
Arrests of youths 17 years and younger by law enforcement agencies submitting complete reports to the F.B.I. for 12 months in 1997. Arson is the willful burning of or attempt to burn a building, vehicle or another's personal property. See important note at beginning of this chapter.
**Not available.*

Reported Juvenile Arrest Rate for Arson in 1997

National Rate = 33.0 Reported Arrests per 100,000 Juvenile Population*

ALPHA ORDER

RANK	STATE	RATE
45	Alabama	4.6
33	Alaska	24.0
12	Arizona	41.2
42	Arkansas	11.4
18	California	36.7
17	Colorado	37.6
28	Connecticut	30.0
44	Delaware	6.3
NA	Florida**	NA
21	Georgia	34.9
36	Hawaii	21.3
6	Idaho	54.2
NA	Illinois**	NA
32	Indiana	24.7
31	Iowa	25.2
NA	Kansas**	NA
14	Kentucky	39.0
38	Louisiana	20.7
1	Maine	78.5
15	Maryland	38.1
41	Massachusetts	13.7
30	Michigan	25.4
37	Minnesota	21.0
40	Mississippi	17.1
19	Missouri	36.5
43	Montana	9.0
25	Nebraska	32.8
3	Nevada	71.4
NA	New Hampshire**	NA
10	New Jersey	44.8
35	New Mexico	22.1
20	New York	35.5
29	North Carolina	27.9
26	North Dakota	31.5
11	Ohio	44.4
8	Oklahoma	48.5
2	Oregon	74.4
23	Pennsylvania	33.1
4	Rhode Island	62.9
34	South Carolina	22.3
5	South Dakota	55.6
16	Tennessee	38.0
39	Texas	19.7
13	Utah	40.8
NA	Vermont**	NA
22	Virginia	33.6
7	Washington	53.1
24	West Virginia	33.0
9	Wisconsin	45.5
27	Wyoming	30.7

RANK ORDER

RANK	STATE	RATE
1	Maine	78.5
2	Oregon	74.4
3	Nevada	71.4
4	Rhode Island	62.9
5	South Dakota	55.6
6	Idaho	54.2
7	Washington	53.1
8	Oklahoma	48.5
9	Wisconsin	45.5
10	New Jersey	44.8
11	Ohio	44.4
12	Arizona	41.2
13	Utah	40.8
14	Kentucky	39.0
15	Maryland	38.1
16	Tennessee	38.0
17	Colorado	37.6
18	California	36.7
19	Missouri	36.5
20	New York	35.5
21	Georgia	34.9
22	Virginia	33.6
23	Pennsylvania	33.1
24	West Virginia	33.0
25	Nebraska	32.8
26	North Dakota	31.5
27	Wyoming	30.7
28	Connecticut	30.0
29	North Carolina	27.9
30	Michigan	25.4
31	Iowa	25.2
32	Indiana	24.7
33	Alaska	24.0
34	South Carolina	22.3
35	New Mexico	22.1
36	Hawaii	21.3
37	Minnesota	21.0
38	Louisiana	20.7
39	Texas	19.7
40	Mississippi	17.1
41	Massachusetts	13.7
42	Arkansas	11.4
43	Montana	9.0
44	Delaware	6.3
45	Alabama	4.6
NA	Florida**	NA
NA	Illinois**	NA
NA	Kansas**	NA
NA	New Hampshire**	NA
NA	Vermont**	NA
	District of Columbia**	NA

Source: Morgan Quitno Press using data from Federal Bureau of Investigation
   "Crime in the United States 1997" (Uniform Crime Reports, November 22, 1998)
*By law enforcement agencies submitting complete reports to the F.B.I. for 12 months in 1997. Arrests of youths 17 years and younger divided into population of 10 to 17 year olds. See important note at beginning of this chapter. Arson is the willful burning of or attempt to burn a building, vehicle or another's personal property.
**Not available.

Reported Arrests of Juveniles for Arson
As a Percent of All Such Arrests in 1997
National Percent = 50.0% of Reported Arson Arrests*

ALPHA ORDER

RANK ORDER

RANK	STATE	PERCENT		RANK	STATE	PERCENT
44	Alabama	17.2		1	South Dakota	92.3
28	Alaska	47.4		2	North Dakota	88.5
15	Arizona	60.6		3	Maine	81.1
43	Arkansas	26.5		4	Idaho	76.5
14	California	61.6		5	Rhode Island	72.2
10	Colorado	65.1		6	Oregon	72.1
31	Connecticut	43.5		7	Nevada	67.8
45	Delaware	16.7		8	Wyoming	66.7
NA	Florida**	NA		9	New Mexico	65.4
34	Georgia	43.0		10	Colorado	65.1
12	Hawaii	63.4		11	Wisconsin	63.8
4	Idaho	76.5		12	Hawaii	63.4
38	Illinois	39.1		13	Washington	62.8
23	Indiana	54.6		14	California	61.6
20	Iowa	56.7		15	Arizona	60.6
NA	Kansas**	NA		16	New York	59.9
35	Kentucky	42.9		17	Nebraska	59.1
40	Louisiana	33.7		17	New Jersey	59.1
3	Maine	81.1		19	Minnesota	58.8
23	Maryland	54.6		20	Iowa	56.7
32	Massachusetts	43.3		21	Oklahoma	56.3
40	Michigan	33.7		22	Ohio	55.1
19	Minnesota	58.8		23	Indiana	54.6
42	Mississippi	28.6		23	Maryland	54.6
39	Missouri	38.0		25	Texas	51.6
26	Montana	50.0		26	Montana	50.0
17	Nebraska	59.1		27	Virginia	48.8
7	Nevada	67.8		28	Alaska	47.4
NA	New Hampshire**	NA		28	Pennsylvania	47.4
17	New Jersey	59.1		30	Utah	45.2
9	New Mexico	65.4		31	Connecticut	43.5
16	New York	59.9		32	Massachusetts	43.3
33	North Carolina	43.2		33	North Carolina	43.2
2	North Dakota	88.5		34	Georgia	43.0
22	Ohio	55.1		35	Kentucky	42.9
21	Oklahoma	56.3		36	West Virginia	41.7
6	Oregon	72.1		37	South Carolina	40.3
28	Pennsylvania	47.4		38	Illinois	39.1
5	Rhode Island	72.2		39	Missouri	38.0
37	South Carolina	40.3		40	Louisiana	33.7
1	South Dakota	92.3		40	Michigan	33.7
46	Tennessee	9.5		42	Mississippi	28.6
25	Texas	51.6		43	Arkansas	26.5
30	Utah	45.2		44	Alabama	17.2
NA	Vermont**	NA		45	Delaware	16.7
27	Virginia	48.8		46	Tennessee	9.5
13	Washington	62.8		NA	Florida**	NA
36	West Virginia	41.7		NA	Kansas**	NA
11	Wisconsin	63.8		NA	New Hampshire**	NA
8	Wyoming	66.7		NA	Vermont**	NA
					District of Columbia**	NA

Source: Morgan Quitno Press using data from Federal Bureau of Investigation
    "Crime in the United States 1997" (Uniform Crime Reports, November 22, 1998)
*Arrests of youths 17 years and younger by law enforcement agencies submitting complete reports to the F.B.I. for 12 months in 1997. Arson is the willful burning of or attempt to burn a building, vehicle or another's personal property.
**Not available.

Reported Arrests of Juveniles for Weapons Violations in 1997

National Total = 36,345 Reported Arrests*

<table>
<tr><td colspan="4">ALPHA ORDER</td><td colspan="4">RANK ORDER</td></tr>
<tr><td>RANK</td><td>STATE</td><td>ARRESTS</td><td>% of USA</td><td>RANK</td><td>STATE</td><td>ARRESTS</td><td>% of USA</td></tr>
<tr><td>23</td><td>Alabama</td><td>473</td><td>1.3%</td><td>1</td><td>California</td><td>8,719</td><td>24.0%</td></tr>
<tr><td>44</td><td>Alaska</td><td>41</td><td>0.1%</td><td>2</td><td>Texas</td><td>2,854</td><td>7.9%</td></tr>
<tr><td>15</td><td>Arizona</td><td>711</td><td>2.0%</td><td>3</td><td>Wisconsin</td><td>1,839</td><td>5.1%</td></tr>
<tr><td>28</td><td>Arkansas</td><td>322</td><td>0.9%</td><td>4</td><td>Illinois</td><td>1,783</td><td>4.9%</td></tr>
<tr><td>1</td><td>California</td><td>8,719</td><td>24.0%</td><td>5</td><td>New Jersey</td><td>1,761</td><td>4.8%</td></tr>
<tr><td>18</td><td>Colorado</td><td>626</td><td>1.7%</td><td>6</td><td>North Carolina</td><td>1,607</td><td>4.4%</td></tr>
<tr><td>20</td><td>Connecticut</td><td>601</td><td>1.7%</td><td>7</td><td>Maryland</td><td>1,597</td><td>4.4%</td></tr>
<tr><td>42</td><td>Delaware</td><td>62</td><td>0.2%</td><td>8</td><td>Virginia</td><td>1,200</td><td>3.3%</td></tr>
<tr><td>NA</td><td>Florida**</td><td>NA</td><td>NA</td><td>9</td><td>Michigan</td><td>978</td><td>2.7%</td></tr>
<tr><td>19</td><td>Georgia</td><td>622</td><td>1.7%</td><td>10</td><td>New York</td><td>887</td><td>2.4%</td></tr>
<tr><td>40</td><td>Hawaii</td><td>87</td><td>0.2%</td><td>11</td><td>Ohio</td><td>838</td><td>2.3%</td></tr>
<tr><td>33</td><td>Idaho</td><td>240</td><td>0.7%</td><td>12</td><td>South Carolina</td><td>787</td><td>2.2%</td></tr>
<tr><td>4</td><td>Illinois</td><td>1,783</td><td>4.9%</td><td>13</td><td>Washington</td><td>784</td><td>2.2%</td></tr>
<tr><td>29</td><td>Indiana</td><td>290</td><td>0.8%</td><td>14</td><td>Minnesota</td><td>776</td><td>2.1%</td></tr>
<tr><td>38</td><td>Iowa</td><td>135</td><td>0.4%</td><td>15</td><td>Arizona</td><td>711</td><td>2.0%</td></tr>
<tr><td>NA</td><td>Kansas**</td><td>NA</td><td>NA</td><td>16</td><td>Louisiana</td><td>658</td><td>1.8%</td></tr>
<tr><td>37</td><td>Kentucky</td><td>161</td><td>0.4%</td><td>17</td><td>Missouri</td><td>652</td><td>1.8%</td></tr>
<tr><td>16</td><td>Louisiana</td><td>658</td><td>1.8%</td><td>18</td><td>Colorado</td><td>626</td><td>1.7%</td></tr>
<tr><td>41</td><td>Maine</td><td>70</td><td>0.2%</td><td>19</td><td>Georgia</td><td>622</td><td>1.7%</td></tr>
<tr><td>7</td><td>Maryland</td><td>1,597</td><td>4.4%</td><td>20</td><td>Connecticut</td><td>601</td><td>1.7%</td></tr>
<tr><td>31</td><td>Massachusetts</td><td>249</td><td>0.7%</td><td>21</td><td>Utah</td><td>493</td><td>1.4%</td></tr>
<tr><td>9</td><td>Michigan</td><td>978</td><td>2.7%</td><td>22</td><td>Oregon</td><td>486</td><td>1.3%</td></tr>
<tr><td>14</td><td>Minnesota</td><td>776</td><td>2.1%</td><td>23</td><td>Alabama</td><td>473</td><td>1.3%</td></tr>
<tr><td>35</td><td>Mississippi</td><td>176</td><td>0.5%</td><td>24</td><td>Oklahoma</td><td>467</td><td>1.3%</td></tr>
<tr><td>17</td><td>Missouri</td><td>652</td><td>1.8%</td><td>25</td><td>Tennessee</td><td>466</td><td>1.3%</td></tr>
<tr><td>46</td><td>Montana</td><td>6</td><td>0.0%</td><td>26</td><td>Pennsylvania</td><td>424</td><td>1.2%</td></tr>
<tr><td>32</td><td>Nebraska</td><td>242</td><td>0.7%</td><td>27</td><td>Nevada</td><td>343</td><td>0.9%</td></tr>
<tr><td>27</td><td>Nevada</td><td>343</td><td>0.9%</td><td>28</td><td>Arkansas</td><td>322</td><td>0.9%</td></tr>
<tr><td>NA</td><td>New Hampshire**</td><td>NA</td><td>NA</td><td>29</td><td>Indiana</td><td>290</td><td>0.8%</td></tr>
<tr><td>5</td><td>New Jersey</td><td>1,761</td><td>4.8%</td><td>30</td><td>New Mexico</td><td>286</td><td>0.8%</td></tr>
<tr><td>30</td><td>New Mexico</td><td>286</td><td>0.8%</td><td>31</td><td>Massachusetts</td><td>249</td><td>0.7%</td></tr>
<tr><td>10</td><td>New York</td><td>887</td><td>2.4%</td><td>32</td><td>Nebraska</td><td>242</td><td>0.7%</td></tr>
<tr><td>6</td><td>North Carolina</td><td>1,607</td><td>4.4%</td><td>33</td><td>Idaho</td><td>240</td><td>0.7%</td></tr>
<tr><td>45</td><td>North Dakota</td><td>26</td><td>0.1%</td><td>34</td><td>Rhode Island</td><td>183</td><td>0.5%</td></tr>
<tr><td>11</td><td>Ohio</td><td>838</td><td>2.3%</td><td>35</td><td>Mississippi</td><td>176</td><td>0.5%</td></tr>
<tr><td>24</td><td>Oklahoma</td><td>467</td><td>1.3%</td><td>36</td><td>Wyoming</td><td>166</td><td>0.5%</td></tr>
<tr><td>22</td><td>Oregon</td><td>486</td><td>1.3%</td><td>37</td><td>Kentucky</td><td>161</td><td>0.4%</td></tr>
<tr><td>26</td><td>Pennsylvania</td><td>424</td><td>1.2%</td><td>38</td><td>Iowa</td><td>135</td><td>0.4%</td></tr>
<tr><td>34</td><td>Rhode Island</td><td>183</td><td>0.5%</td><td>39</td><td>West Virginia</td><td>114</td><td>0.3%</td></tr>
<tr><td>12</td><td>South Carolina</td><td>787</td><td>2.2%</td><td>40</td><td>Hawaii</td><td>87</td><td>0.2%</td></tr>
<tr><td>43</td><td>South Dakota</td><td>57</td><td>0.2%</td><td>41</td><td>Maine</td><td>70</td><td>0.2%</td></tr>
<tr><td>25</td><td>Tennessee</td><td>466</td><td>1.3%</td><td>42</td><td>Delaware</td><td>62</td><td>0.2%</td></tr>
<tr><td>2</td><td>Texas</td><td>2,854</td><td>7.9%</td><td>43</td><td>South Dakota</td><td>57</td><td>0.2%</td></tr>
<tr><td>21</td><td>Utah</td><td>493</td><td>1.4%</td><td>44</td><td>Alaska</td><td>41</td><td>0.1%</td></tr>
<tr><td>NA</td><td>Vermont**</td><td>NA</td><td>NA</td><td>45</td><td>North Dakota</td><td>26</td><td>0.1%</td></tr>
<tr><td>8</td><td>Virginia</td><td>1,200</td><td>3.3%</td><td>46</td><td>Montana</td><td>6</td><td>0.0%</td></tr>
<tr><td>13</td><td>Washington</td><td>784</td><td>2.2%</td><td>NA</td><td>Florida**</td><td>NA</td><td>NA</td></tr>
<tr><td>39</td><td>West Virginia</td><td>114</td><td>0.3%</td><td>NA</td><td>Kansas**</td><td>NA</td><td>NA</td></tr>
<tr><td>3</td><td>Wisconsin</td><td>1,839</td><td>5.1%</td><td>NA</td><td>New Hampshire**</td><td>NA</td><td>NA</td></tr>
<tr><td>36</td><td>Wyoming</td><td>166</td><td>0.5%</td><td>NA</td><td>Vermont**</td><td>NA</td><td>NA</td></tr>
<tr><td></td><td></td><td></td><td></td><td></td><td>District of Columbia**</td><td>NA</td><td>NA</td></tr>
</table>

Source: Federal Bureau of Investigation
  "Crime in the United States 1997" (Uniform Crime Reports, November 22, 1998)
*Arrests of youths 17 years and younger by law enforcement agencies submitting complete reports to the F.B.I. for 12 months in 1997. Weapons violations include illegal carrying and possession. See important note at beginning of this chapter.
**Not available.

Reported Arrest Rate of Juveniles for Weapons Violations in 1997

National Rate = 173.2 Reported Arrests per 100,000 Juvenile Population*

ALPHA ORDER

RANK ORDER

RANK	STATE	RATE
35	Alabama	104.1
33	Alaska	109.4
21	Arizona	154.8
30	Arkansas	118.7
5	California	244.1
13	Colorado	194.3
9	Connecticut	207.3
11	Delaware	196.3
NA	Florida**	NA
7	Georgia	215.1
38	Hawaii	71.1
24	Idaho	147.7
NA	Illinois**	NA
37	Indiana	75.4
43	Iowa	47.2
NA	Kansas**	NA
14	Kentucky	190.3
22	Louisiana	151.0
41	Maine	51.4
3	Maryland	290.9
42	Massachusetts	47.9
34	Michigan	105.7
27	Minnesota	131.7
25	Mississippi	137.1
20	Missouri	168.6
45	Montana	13.4
28	Nebraska	122.1
1	Nevada	401.6
NA	New Hampshire**	NA
6	New Jersey	216.6
16	New Mexico	186.1
36	New York	100.3
10	North Carolina	199.9
44	North Dakota	35.6
31	Ohio	117.3
32	Oklahoma	113.2
23	Oregon	148.8
39	Pennsylvania	68.8
18	Rhode Island	177.1
17	South Carolina	185.1
26	South Dakota	132.2
15	Tennessee	188.4
29	Texas	121.7
8	Utah	211.9
NA	Vermont**	NA
19	Virginia	169.6
12	Washington	195.4
40	West Virginia	59.8
2	Wisconsin	376.7
4	Wyoming	255.2

RANK	STATE	RATE
1	Nevada	401.6
2	Wisconsin	376.7
3	Maryland	290.9
4	Wyoming	255.2
5	California	244.1
6	New Jersey	216.6
7	Georgia	215.1
8	Utah	211.9
9	Connecticut	207.3
10	North Carolina	199.9
11	Delaware	196.3
12	Washington	195.4
13	Colorado	194.3
14	Kentucky	190.3
15	Tennessee	188.4
16	New Mexico	186.1
17	South Carolina	185.1
18	Rhode Island	177.1
19	Virginia	169.6
20	Missouri	168.6
21	Arizona	154.8
22	Louisiana	151.0
23	Oregon	148.8
24	Idaho	147.7
25	Mississippi	137.1
26	South Dakota	132.2
27	Minnesota	131.7
28	Nebraska	122.1
29	Texas	121.7
30	Arkansas	118.7
31	Ohio	117.3
32	Oklahoma	113.2
33	Alaska	109.4
34	Michigan	105.7
35	Alabama	104.1
36	New York	100.3
37	Indiana	75.4
38	Hawaii	71.1
39	Pennsylvania	68.8
40	West Virginia	59.8
41	Maine	51.4
42	Massachusetts	47.9
43	Iowa	47.2
44	North Dakota	35.6
45	Montana	13.4
NA	Florida**	NA
NA	Illinois**	NA
NA	Kansas**	NA
NA	New Hampshire**	NA
NA	Vermont**	NA
	District of Columbia**	NA

Source: Morgan Quitno Press using data from Federal Bureau of Investigation
    "Crime in the United States 1997" (Uniform Crime Reports, November 22, 1998)
*By law enforcement agencies submitting complete reports to the F.B.I. for 12 months in 1997. Arrests of youths 17 years and younger divided into population of 10 to 17 year olds. See important note at beginning of this chapter. Weapons violations include illegal carrying and possession.
**Not available.

228

Reported Arrests of Juveniles for Weapons Violations
As a Percent of All Such Arrests in 1997
National Percent = 23.9% of Reported Arrests for Weapons Violations*

ALPHA ORDER

RANK	STATE	PERCENT
30	Alabama	20.1
44	Alaska	14.2
34	Arizona	18.8
45	Arkansas	13.0
14	California	28.2
16	Colorado	26.2
15	Connecticut	27.7
27	Delaware	20.7
NA	Florida**	NA
41	Georgia	14.9
29	Hawaii	20.2
8	Idaho	34.3
10	Illinois	32.4
39	Indiana	15.5
26	Iowa	21.6
NA	Kansas**	NA
38	Kentucky	15.7
25	Louisiana	22.3
32	Maine	19.7
11	Maryland	32.2
22	Massachusetts	22.8
39	Michigan	15.5
2	Minnesota	45.6
21	Mississippi	23.8
41	Missouri	14.9
17	Montana	26.1
35	Nebraska	17.8
9	Nevada	32.5
NA	New Hampshire**	NA
13	New Jersey	31.1
6	New Mexico	37.8
23	New York	22.7
33	North Carolina	19.3
18	North Dakota	26.0
31	Ohio	20.0
36	Oklahoma	17.0
24	Oregon	22.4
7	Pennsylvania	37.0
5	Rhode Island	39.0
20	South Carolina	25.3
3	South Dakota	43.5
43	Tennessee	14.6
27	Texas	20.7
4	Utah	41.0
NA	Vermont**	NA
37	Virginia	16.4
19	Washington	25.9
46	West Virginia	9.2
11	Wisconsin	32.2
1	Wyoming	63.1

RANK ORDER

RANK	STATE	PERCENT
1	Wyoming	63.1
2	Minnesota	45.6
3	South Dakota	43.5
4	Utah	41.0
5	Rhode Island	39.0
6	New Mexico	37.8
7	Pennsylvania	37.0
8	Idaho	34.3
9	Nevada	32.5
10	Illinois	32.4
11	Maryland	32.2
11	Wisconsin	32.2
13	New Jersey	31.1
14	California	28.2
15	Connecticut	27.7
16	Colorado	26.2
17	Montana	26.1
18	North Dakota	26.0
19	Washington	25.9
20	South Carolina	25.3
21	Mississippi	23.8
22	Massachusetts	22.8
23	New York	22.7
24	Oregon	22.4
25	Louisiana	22.3
26	Iowa	21.6
27	Delaware	20.7
27	Texas	20.7
29	Hawaii	20.2
30	Alabama	20.1
31	Ohio	20.0
32	Maine	19.7
33	North Carolina	19.3
34	Arizona	18.8
35	Nebraska	17.8
36	Oklahoma	17.0
37	Virginia	16.4
38	Kentucky	15.7
39	Indiana	15.5
39	Michigan	15.5
41	Georgia	14.9
41	Missouri	14.9
43	Tennessee	14.6
44	Alaska	14.2
45	Arkansas	13.0
46	West Virginia	9.2
NA	Florida**	NA
NA	Kansas**	NA
NA	New Hampshire**	NA
NA	Vermont**	NA
	District of Columbia**	NA

Source: Morgan Quitno Press using data from Federal Bureau of Investigation
   "Crime in the United States 1997" (Uniform Crime Reports, November 22, 1998)
*Arrests of youths 17 years and younger by law enforcement agencies submitting complete reports to the F.B.I. for
12 months in 1997. Weapons violations include illegal carrying and possession.
**Not available.

Reported Arrests of Juveniles for Driving Under the Influence in 1997

National Total = 13,085 Reported Arrests*

ALPHA ORDER

RANK	STATE	ARRESTS	% of USA
25	Alabama	206	1.6%
43	Alaska	40	0.3%
8	Arizona	406	3.1%
18	Arkansas	269	2.1%
1	California	1,705	13.0%
16	Colorado	289	2.2%
35	Connecticut	105	0.8%
46	Delaware	0	0.0%
NA	Florida**	NA	NA
22	Georgia	234	1.8%
36	Hawaii	80	0.6%
21	Idaho	247	1.9%
41	Illinois	44	0.3%
33	Indiana	114	0.9%
15	Iowa	292	2.2%
NA	Kansas**	NA	NA
42	Kentucky	41	0.3%
27	Louisiana	176	1.3%
31	Maine	151	1.2%
19	Maryland	268	2.0%
26	Massachusetts	185	1.4%
5	Michigan	632	4.8%
4	Minnesota	770	5.9%
34	Mississippi	111	0.8%
20	Missouri	250	1.9%
44	Montana	22	0.2%
12	Nebraska	359	2.7%
40	Nevada	56	0.4%
NA	New Hampshire**	NA	NA
17	New Jersey	286	2.2%
23	New Mexico	229	1.8%
14	New York	326	2.5%
2	North Carolina	940	7.2%
37	North Dakota	66	0.5%
13	Ohio	342	2.6%
9	Oklahoma	404	3.1%
24	Oregon	209	1.6%
11	Pennsylvania	380	2.9%
45	Rhode Island	17	0.1%
29	South Carolina	166	1.3%
38	South Dakota	62	0.5%
28	Tennessee	171	1.3%
3	Texas	827	6.3%
30	Utah	163	1.2%
NA	Vermont**	NA	NA
7	Virginia	412	3.1%
6	Washington	468	3.6%
32	West Virginia	116	0.9%
10	Wisconsin	390	3.0%
39	Wyoming	59	0.5%

RANK ORDER

RANK	STATE	ARRESTS	% of USA
1	California	1,705	13.0%
2	North Carolina	940	7.2%
3	Texas	827	6.3%
4	Minnesota	770	5.9%
5	Michigan	632	4.8%
6	Washington	468	3.6%
7	Virginia	412	3.1%
8	Arizona	406	3.1%
9	Oklahoma	404	3.1%
10	Wisconsin	390	3.0%
11	Pennsylvania	380	2.9%
12	Nebraska	359	2.7%
13	Ohio	342	2.6%
14	New York	326	2.5%
15	Iowa	292	2.2%
16	Colorado	289	2.2%
17	New Jersey	286	2.2%
18	Arkansas	269	2.1%
19	Maryland	268	2.0%
20	Missouri	250	1.9%
21	Idaho	247	1.9%
22	Georgia	234	1.8%
23	New Mexico	229	1.8%
24	Oregon	209	1.6%
25	Alabama	206	1.6%
26	Massachusetts	185	1.4%
27	Louisiana	176	1.3%
28	Tennessee	171	1.3%
29	South Carolina	166	1.3%
30	Utah	163	1.2%
31	Maine	151	1.2%
32	West Virginia	116	0.9%
33	Indiana	114	0.9%
34	Mississippi	111	0.8%
35	Connecticut	105	0.8%
36	Hawaii	80	0.6%
37	North Dakota	66	0.5%
38	South Dakota	62	0.5%
39	Wyoming	59	0.5%
40	Nevada	56	0.4%
41	Illinois	44	0.3%
42	Kentucky	41	0.3%
43	Alaska	40	0.3%
44	Montana	22	0.2%
45	Rhode Island	17	0.1%
46	Delaware	0	0.0%
NA	Florida**	NA	NA
NA	Kansas**	NA	NA
NA	New Hampshire**	NA	NA
NA	Vermont**	NA	NA
	District of Columbia**	NA	NA

Source: Federal Bureau of Investigation
   "Crime in the United States 1997" (Uniform Crime Reports, November 22, 1998)

*Arrests of youths 17 years and younger by law enforcement agencies submitting complete reports to the F.B.I. for 12 months in 1997. Includes driving any vehicle while drunk or under the influence of liquor or narcotics. See important note at beginning of this chapter.
**Not available.

Reported Juvenile Arrest Rate for Driving Under the Influence in 1997

National Rate = 62.4 Reported Arrests per 100,000 Juvenile Population*

ALPHA ORDER

RANK ORDER

RANK	STATE	RATE		RANK	STATE	RATE
35	Alabama	45.3		1	Nebraska	181.1
9	Alaska	106.8		2	Idaho	152.0
16	Arizona	88.4		3	New Mexico	149.0
11	Arkansas	99.1		4	South Dakota	143.8
34	California	47.7		5	Minnesota	130.7
15	Colorado	89.7		6	North Carolina	116.9
39	Connecticut	36.2		7	Washington	116.6
45	Delaware	0.0		8	Maine	110.8
NA	Florida**	NA		9	Alaska	106.8
18	Georgia	80.9		10	Iowa	102.1
24	Hawaii	65.4		11	Arkansas	99.1
2	Idaho	152.0		12	Oklahoma	97.9
NA	Illinois**	NA		13	Wyoming	90.7
43	Indiana	29.6		14	North Dakota	90.3
10	Iowa	102.1		15	Colorado	89.7
NA	Kansas**	NA		16	Arizona	88.4
32	Kentucky	48.5		17	Mississippi	86.5
36	Louisiana	40.4		18	Georgia	80.9
8	Maine	110.8		19	Wisconsin	79.9
31	Maryland	48.8		20	Utah	70.1
40	Massachusetts	35.6		21	Tennessee	69.1
22	Michigan	68.3		22	Michigan	68.3
5	Minnesota	130.7		23	Nevada	65.6
17	Mississippi	86.5		24	Hawaii	65.4
25	Missouri	64.6		25	Missouri	64.6
30	Montana	49.3		26	Oregon	64.0
1	Nebraska	181.1		27	Pennsylvania	61.7
23	Nevada	65.6		28	West Virginia	60.8
NA	New Hampshire**	NA		29	Virginia	58.2
42	New Jersey	35.2		30	Montana	49.3
3	New Mexico	149.0		31	Maryland	48.8
38	New York	36.8		32	Kentucky	48.5
6	North Carolina	116.9		33	Ohio	47.9
14	North Dakota	90.3		34	California	47.7
33	Ohio	47.9		35	Alabama	45.3
12	Oklahoma	97.9		36	Louisiana	40.4
26	Oregon	64.0		37	South Carolina	39.1
27	Pennsylvania	61.7		38	New York	36.8
44	Rhode Island	16.4		39	Connecticut	36.2
37	South Carolina	39.1		40	Massachusetts	35.6
4	South Dakota	143.8		41	Texas	35.3
21	Tennessee	69.1		42	New Jersey	35.2
41	Texas	35.3		43	Indiana	29.6
20	Utah	70.1		44	Rhode Island	16.4
NA	Vermont**	NA		45	Delaware	0.0
29	Virginia	58.2		NA	Florida**	NA
7	Washington	116.6		NA	Illinois**	NA
28	West Virginia	60.8		NA	Kansas**	NA
19	Wisconsin	79.9		NA	New Hampshire**	NA
13	Wyoming	90.7		NA	Vermont**	NA
					District of Columbia**	NA

Source: Morgan Quitno Press using data from Federal Bureau of Investigation
  "Crime in the United States 1997" (Uniform Crime Reports, November 22, 1998)
*By law enforcement agencies submitting complete reports to the F.B.I. for 12 months in 1997. Arrests of youths 17 years and younger divided into population of 10 to 17 year olds. See important note at beginning of this chapter. Includes driving any vehicle while drunk or under the influence of liquor or narcotics.
**Not available.

Reported Arrests of Juveniles for Driving Under the Influence
As a Percent of All Such Arrests in 1997
National Percent = 1.3% of Reported Arrests for Driving Under the Influence*

ALPHA ORDER

RANK ORDER

RANK	STATE	PERCENT		RANK	STATE	PERCENT
38	Alabama	1.0		1	Maryland	3.9
13	Alaska	1.8		2	Nebraska	2.8
22	Arizona	1.4		2	Utah	2.8
16	Arkansas	1.6		4	Iowa	2.5
41	California	0.9		4	New Mexico	2.5
13	Colorado	1.8		6	Idaho	2.4
38	Connecticut	1.0		6	Montana	2.4
46	Delaware	0.0		8	Maine	2.1
NA	Florida**	NA		8	South Dakota	2.1
18	Georgia	1.5		10	Minnesota	2.0
16	Hawaii	1.6		10	North Dakota	2.0
6	Idaho	2.4		10	Oklahoma	2.0
42	Illinois	0.8		13	Alaska	1.8
42	Indiana	0.8		13	Colorado	1.8
4	Iowa	2.5		13	Pennsylvania	1.8
NA	Kansas**	NA		16	Arkansas	1.6
36	Kentucky	1.1		16	Hawaii	1.6
28	Louisiana	1.3		18	Georgia	1.5
8	Maine	2.1		18	Oregon	1.5
1	Maryland	3.9		18	Washington	1.5
30	Massachusetts	1.2		18	Wisconsin	1.5
22	Michigan	1.4		22	Arizona	1.4
10	Minnesota	2.0		22	Michigan	1.4
30	Mississippi	1.2		22	Missouri	1.4
22	Missouri	1.4		22	North Carolina	1.4
6	Montana	2.4		22	Ohio	1.4
2	Nebraska	2.8		22	Wyoming	1.4
30	Nevada	1.2		28	Louisiana	1.3
NA	New Hampshire**	NA		28	Virginia	1.3
30	New Jersey	1.2		30	Massachusetts	1.2
4	New Mexico	2.5		30	Mississippi	1.2
42	New York	0.8		30	Nevada	1.2
22	North Carolina	1.4		30	New Jersey	1.2
10	North Dakota	2.0		30	Tennessee	1.2
22	Ohio	1.4		30	West Virginia	1.2
10	Oklahoma	2.0		36	Kentucky	1.1
18	Oregon	1.5		36	South Carolina	1.1
13	Pennsylvania	1.8		38	Alabama	1.0
42	Rhode Island	0.8		38	Connecticut	1.0
36	South Carolina	1.1		38	Texas	1.0
8	South Dakota	2.1		41	California	0.9
30	Tennessee	1.2		42	Illinois	0.8
38	Texas	1.0		42	Indiana	0.8
2	Utah	2.8		42	New York	0.8
NA	Vermont**	NA		42	Rhode Island	0.8
28	Virginia	1.3		46	Delaware	0.0
18	Washington	1.5		NA	Florida**	NA
30	West Virginia	1.2		NA	Kansas**	NA
18	Wisconsin	1.5		NA	New Hampshire**	NA
22	Wyoming	1.4		NA	Vermont**	NA
					District of Columbia**	NA

Source: Morgan Quitno Press using data from Federal Bureau of Investigation
   "Crime in the United States 1997" (Uniform Crime Reports, November 22, 1998)
*Arrests of youths 17 years and younger by law enforcement agencies submitting complete reports to the F.B.I. for
12 months in 1997. Includes driving any vehicle while drunk or under the influence of liquor or narcotics.
**Not available.

Reported Arrests of Juveniles for Drug Abuse Violations in 1997

National Total = 153,600 Reported Arrests*

RANK	STATE	ARRESTS	% of USA
28	Alabama	1,496	1.0%
45	Alaska	198	0.1%
7	Arizona	5,045	3.3%
31	Arkansas	1,117	0.7%
1	California	26,125	17.0%
21	Colorado	2,345	1.5%
14	Connecticut	3,303	2.2%
43	Delaware	275	0.2%
NA	Florida**	NA	NA
18	Georgia	2,726	1.8%
37	Hawaii	724	0.5%
34	Idaho	877	0.6%
3	Illinois	10,387	6.8%
25	Indiana	1,890	1.2%
32	Iowa	1,033	0.7%
NA	Kansas**	NA	NA
36	Kentucky	838	0.5%
16	Louisiana	3,075	2.0%
39	Maine	677	0.4%
5	Maryland	9,191	6.0%
19	Massachusetts	2,711	1.8%
12	Michigan	3,620	2.4%
11	Minnesota	3,682	2.4%
35	Mississippi	867	0.6%
17	Missouri	2,893	1.9%
44	Montana	208	0.1%
30	Nebraska	1,167	0.8%
33	Nevada	932	0.6%
NA	New Hampshire**	NA	NA
4	New Jersey	9,973	6.5%
29	New Mexico	1,315	0.9%
6	New York	5,523	3.6%
8	North Carolina	4,649	3.0%
46	North Dakota	187	0.1%
9	Ohio	4,283	2.8%
24	Oklahoma	1,919	1.2%
22	Oregon	2,081	1.4%
23	Pennsylvania	2,056	1.3%
38	Rhode Island	694	0.5%
15	South Carolina	3,174	2.1%
42	South Dakota	288	0.2%
26	Tennessee	1,803	1.2%
2	Texas	15,706	10.2%
27	Utah	1,662	1.1%
NA	Vermont**	NA	NA
13	Virginia	3,543	2.3%
20	Washington	2,631	1.7%
40	West Virginia	444	0.3%
10	Wisconsin	3,863	2.5%
41	Wyoming	404	0.3%

RANK	STATE	ARRESTS	% of USA
1	California	26,125	17.0%
2	Texas	15,706	10.2%
3	Illinois	10,387	6.8%
4	New Jersey	9,973	6.5%
5	Maryland	9,191	6.0%
6	New York	5,523	3.6%
7	Arizona	5,045	3.3%
8	North Carolina	4,649	3.0%
9	Ohio	4,283	2.8%
10	Wisconsin	3,863	2.5%
11	Minnesota	3,682	2.4%
12	Michigan	3,620	2.4%
13	Virginia	3,543	2.3%
14	Connecticut	3,303	2.2%
15	South Carolina	3,174	2.1%
16	Louisiana	3,075	2.0%
17	Missouri	2,893	1.9%
18	Georgia	2,726	1.8%
19	Massachusetts	2,711	1.8%
20	Washington	2,631	1.7%
21	Colorado	2,345	1.5%
22	Oregon	2,081	1.4%
23	Pennsylvania	2,056	1.3%
24	Oklahoma	1,919	1.2%
25	Indiana	1,890	1.2%
26	Tennessee	1,803	1.2%
27	Utah	1,662	1.1%
28	Alabama	1,496	1.0%
29	New Mexico	1,315	0.9%
30	Nebraska	1,167	0.8%
31	Arkansas	1,117	0.7%
32	Iowa	1,033	0.7%
33	Nevada	932	0.6%
34	Idaho	877	0.6%
35	Mississippi	867	0.6%
36	Kentucky	838	0.5%
37	Hawaii	724	0.5%
38	Rhode Island	694	0.5%
39	Maine	677	0.4%
40	West Virginia	444	0.3%
41	Wyoming	404	0.3%
42	South Dakota	288	0.2%
43	Delaware	275	0.2%
44	Montana	208	0.1%
45	Alaska	198	0.1%
46	North Dakota	187	0.1%
NA	Florida**	NA	NA
NA	Kansas**	NA	NA
NA	New Hampshire**	NA	NA
NA	Vermont**	NA	NA
	District of Columbia**	NA	NA

Source: Federal Bureau of Investigation
   "Crime in the United States 1997" (Uniform Crime Reports, November 22, 1998)
*Arrests of youths 17 years and younger by law enforcement agencies submitting complete reports to the F.B.I. for 12 months in 1997. Includes offenses relating to possession, sale, use, growing and manufacturing of narcotic drugs. See important note at beginning of this chapter.
**Not available.

Reported Arrest Rate of Juveniles for Drug Abuse Violations in 1997

National Rate = 732.2 Reported Arrests per 100,000 Juvenile Population*

ALPHA ORDER

RANK	STATE	RATE
43	Alabama	329.3
32	Alaska	528.5
4	Arizona	1,098.7
39	Arkansas	411.7
13	California	731.3
15	Colorado	727.9
3	Connecticut	1,139.4
8	Delaware	870.7
NA	Florida**	NA
7	Georgia	942.6
28	Hawaii	592.0
31	Idaho	539.7
NA	Illinois**	NA
36	Indiana	491.5
41	Iowa	361.3
NA	Kansas**	NA
6	Kentucky	990.5
17	Louisiana	705.9
35	Maine	496.9
1	Maryland	1,674.1
33	Massachusetts	521.5
40	Michigan	391.3
24	Minnesota	624.7
18	Mississippi	675.5
11	Missouri	748.0
37	Montana	465.9
29	Nebraska	588.6
5	Nevada	1,091.2
NA	New Hampshire**	NA
2	New Jersey	1,226.7
9	New Mexico	855.8
25	New York	624.3
30	North Carolina	578.3
44	North Dakota	255.8
27	Ohio	599.7
38	Oklahoma	465.2
23	Oregon	637.3
42	Pennsylvania	333.6
19	Rhode Island	671.4
12	South Carolina	746.7
21	South Dakota	667.8
14	Tennessee	728.8
20	Texas	669.7
16	Utah	714.5
NA	Vermont**	NA
34	Virginia	500.8
22	Washington	655.8
45	West Virginia	232.9
10	Wisconsin	791.2
26	Wyoming	621.1

RANK ORDER

RANK	STATE	RATE
1	Maryland	1,674.1
2	New Jersey	1,226.7
3	Connecticut	1,139.4
4	Arizona	1,098.7
5	Nevada	1,091.2
6	Kentucky	990.5
7	Georgia	942.6
8	Delaware	870.7
9	New Mexico	855.8
10	Wisconsin	791.2
11	Missouri	748.0
12	South Carolina	746.7
13	California	731.3
14	Tennessee	728.8
15	Colorado	727.9
16	Utah	714.5
17	Louisiana	705.9
18	Mississippi	675.5
19	Rhode Island	671.4
20	Texas	669.7
21	South Dakota	667.8
22	Washington	655.8
23	Oregon	637.3
24	Minnesota	624.7
25	New York	624.3
26	Wyoming	621.1
27	Ohio	599.7
28	Hawaii	592.0
29	Nebraska	588.6
30	North Carolina	578.3
31	Idaho	539.7
32	Alaska	528.5
33	Massachusetts	521.5
34	Virginia	500.8
35	Maine	496.9
36	Indiana	491.5
37	Montana	465.9
38	Oklahoma	465.2
39	Arkansas	411.7
40	Michigan	391.3
41	Iowa	361.3
42	Pennsylvania	333.6
43	Alabama	329.3
44	North Dakota	255.8
45	West Virginia	232.9
NA	Florida**	NA
NA	Illinois**	NA
NA	Kansas**	NA
NA	New Hampshire**	NA
NA	Vermont**	NA
	District of Columbia**	NA

Source: Morgan Quitno Press using data from Federal Bureau of Investigation
   "Crime in the United States 1997" (Uniform Crime Reports, November 22, 1998)
*By law enforcement agencies submitting complete reports to the F.B.I. for 12 months in 1997. Arrests of youths 17 years and younger divided into population of 10 to 17 year olds. See important note at beginning of this chapter. Includes offenses relating to possession, sale, use, growing and manufacturing of narcotic drugs.
**Not available.

Reported Arrests of Juveniles for Drug Abuse Violations
As a Percent of All Such Arrests in 1997
National Percent = 13.9% of Reported Drug Abuse Violation Arrests*

ALPHA ORDER

RANK ORDER

RANK	STATE	PERCENT	RANK	STATE	PERCENT
44	Alabama	9.7	1	Minnesota	26.1
16	Alaska	18.1	2	New Mexico	23.7
8	Arizona	20.0	3	Maryland	23.0
46	Arkansas	9.4	4	Wisconsin	22.3
45	California	9.5	5	Utah	21.4
17	Colorado	18.0	5	Wyoming	21.4
23	Connecticut	16.0	7	North Dakota	20.2
13	Delaware	18.8	8	Arizona	20.0
NA	Florida**	NA	9	South Dakota	19.6
36	Georgia	11.8	10	Idaho	19.5
14	Hawaii	18.4	11	Illinois	19.0
10	Idaho	19.5	12	Montana	18.9
11	Illinois	19.0	13	Delaware	18.8
24	Indiana	15.1	14	Hawaii	18.4
31	Iowa	12.8	15	Nevada	18.3
NA	Kansas**	NA	16	Alaska	18.1
36	Kentucky	11.8	17	Colorado	18.0
30	Louisiana	13.0	18	Maine	16.7
18	Maine	16.7	19	New Jersey	16.5
3	Maryland	23.0	19	Rhode Island	16.5
39	Massachusetts	11.7	19	Texas	16.5
42	Michigan	11.4	22	Pennsylvania	16.3
1	Minnesota	26.1	23	Connecticut	16.0
35	Mississippi	12.0	24	Indiana	15.1
41	Missouri	11.6	25	Washington	14.7
12	Montana	18.9	26	Ohio	14.1
31	Nebraska	12.8	26	South Carolina	14.1
15	Nevada	18.3	28	Oregon	13.5
NA	New Hampshire**	NA	29	New York	13.3
19	New Jersey	16.5	30	Louisiana	13.0
2	New Mexico	23.7	31	Iowa	12.8
29	New York	13.3	31	Nebraska	12.8
39	North Carolina	11.7	33	Tennessee	12.4
7	North Dakota	20.2	34	Virginia	12.1
26	Ohio	14.1	35	Mississippi	12.0
43	Oklahoma	11.2	36	Georgia	11.8
28	Oregon	13.5	36	Kentucky	11.8
22	Pennsylvania	16.3	36	West Virginia	11.8
19	Rhode Island	16.5	39	Massachusetts	11.7
26	South Carolina	14.1	39	North Carolina	11.7
9	South Dakota	19.6	41	Missouri	11.6
33	Tennessee	12.4	42	Michigan	11.4
19	Texas	16.5	43	Oklahoma	11.2
5	Utah	21.4	44	Alabama	9.7
NA	Vermont**	NA	45	California	9.5
34	Virginia	12.1	46	Arkansas	9.4
25	Washington	14.7	NA	Florida**	NA
36	West Virginia	11.8	NA	Kansas**	NA
4	Wisconsin	22.3	NA	New Hampshire**	NA
5	Wyoming	21.4	NA	Vermont**	NA
			NA	District of Columbia**	NA

Source: Morgan Quitno Press using data from Federal Bureau of Investigation
   "Crime in the United States 1997" (Uniform Crime Reports, November 22, 1998)
Arrests of youths 17 years and younger by law enforcement agencies submitting complete reports to the F.B.I. for 12 months in 1997. Includes offenses relating to possession, sale, use, growing and manufacturing of narcotic drugs.
**Not available.*

Reported Arrests of Juveniles for Sex Offenses in 1997

National Total = 12,775 Reported Arrests*

ALPHA ORDER

RANK	STATE	ARRESTS	% of USA
40	Alabama	36	0.3%
36	Alaska	48	0.4%
12	Arizona	321	2.5%
34	Arkansas	64	0.5%
1	California	2,434	19.1%
22	Colorado	188	1.5%
20	Connecticut	237	1.9%
35	Delaware	52	0.4%
NA	Florida**	NA	NA
22	Georgia	188	1.5%
31	Hawaii	68	0.5%
25	Idaho	123	1.0%
14	Illinois	289	2.3%
24	Indiana	165	1.3%
27	Iowa	88	0.7%
NA	Kansas**	NA	NA
39	Kentucky	41	0.3%
19	Louisiana	246	1.9%
33	Maine	65	0.5%
8	Maryland	415	3.2%
32	Massachusetts	67	0.5%
7	Michigan	425	3.3%
16	Minnesota	274	2.1%
30	Mississippi	75	0.6%
6	Missouri	432	3.4%
42	Montana	23	0.2%
26	Nebraska	107	0.8%
29	Nevada	82	0.6%
NA	New Hampshire**	NA	NA
5	New Jersey	452	3.5%
45	New Mexico	18	0.1%
3	New York	917	7.2%
11	North Carolina	342	2.7%
41	North Dakota	28	0.2%
13	Ohio	298	2.3%
28	Oklahoma	84	0.7%
18	Oregon	254	2.0%
15	Pennsylvania	276	2.2%
38	Rhode Island	42	0.3%
21	South Carolina	221	1.7%
46	South Dakota	15	0.1%
37	Tennessee	46	0.4%
4	Texas	833	6.5%
10	Utah	353	2.8%
NA	Vermont**	NA	NA
9	Virginia	360	2.8%
17	Washington	269	2.1%
44	West Virginia	21	0.2%
2	Wisconsin	1,371	10.7%
43	Wyoming	22	0.2%

RANK ORDER

RANK	STATE	ARRESTS	% of USA
1	California	2,434	19.1%
2	Wisconsin	1,371	10.7%
3	New York	917	7.2%
4	Texas	833	6.5%
5	New Jersey	452	3.5%
6	Missouri	432	3.4%
7	Michigan	425	3.3%
8	Maryland	415	3.2%
9	Virginia	360	2.8%
10	Utah	353	2.8%
11	North Carolina	342	2.7%
12	Arizona	321	2.5%
13	Ohio	298	2.3%
14	Illinois	289	2.3%
15	Pennsylvania	276	2.2%
16	Minnesota	274	2.1%
17	Washington	269	2.1%
18	Oregon	254	2.0%
19	Louisiana	246	1.9%
20	Connecticut	237	1.9%
21	South Carolina	221	1.7%
22	Colorado	188	1.5%
22	Georgia	188	1.5%
24	Indiana	165	1.3%
25	Idaho	123	1.0%
26	Nebraska	107	0.8%
27	Iowa	88	0.7%
28	Oklahoma	84	0.7%
29	Nevada	82	0.6%
30	Mississippi	75	0.6%
31	Hawaii	68	0.5%
32	Massachusetts	67	0.5%
33	Maine	65	0.5%
34	Arkansas	64	0.5%
35	Delaware	52	0.4%
36	Alaska	48	0.4%
37	Tennessee	46	0.4%
38	Rhode Island	42	0.3%
39	Kentucky	41	0.3%
40	Alabama	36	0.3%
41	North Dakota	28	0.2%
42	Montana	23	0.2%
43	Wyoming	22	0.2%
44	West Virginia	21	0.2%
45	New Mexico	18	0.1%
46	South Dakota	15	0.1%
NA	Florida**	NA	NA
NA	Kansas**	NA	NA
NA	New Hampshire**	NA	NA
NA	Vermont**	NA	NA
	District of Columbia**	NA	NA

Source: Federal Bureau of Investigation
   "Crime in the United States 1997" (Uniform Crime Reports, November 22, 1998)
*Arrests of youths 17 years and younger by law enforcement agencies submitting complete reports to the F.B.I. for 12 months in 1997. Excludes forcible rape, prostitution and commercialized vice. Includes statutory rape and offenses against chastity, common decency, morals and the like. See important note at beginning of this chapter.
**Not available.

Reported Arrest Rate of Juveniles for Sex Offenses in 1997

National Rate = 60.9 Reported Arrests per 100,000 Population*

ALPHA ORDER

RANK ORDER

RANK	STATE	RATE
45	Alabama	7.9
4	Alaska	128.1
12	Arizona	69.9
39	Arkansas	23.6
13	California	68.1
16	Colorado	58.4
8	Connecticut	81.8
2	Delaware	164.6
NA	Florida**	NA
15	Georgia	65.0
19	Hawaii	55.6
10	Idaho	75.7
NA	Illinois**	NA
30	Indiana	42.9
38	Iowa	30.8
NA	Kansas**	NA
25	Kentucky	48.5
18	Louisiana	56.5
26	Maine	47.7
11	Maryland	75.6
42	Massachusetts	12.9
28	Michigan	45.9
27	Minnesota	46.5
16	Mississippi	58.4
5	Missouri	111.7
23	Montana	51.5
21	Nebraska	54.0
7	Nevada	96.0
NA	New Hampshire**	NA
19	New Jersey	55.6
43	New Mexico	11.7
6	New York	103.7
31	North Carolina	42.5
34	North Dakota	38.3
32	Ohio	41.7
40	Oklahoma	20.4
9	Oregon	77.8
29	Pennsylvania	44.8
33	Rhode Island	40.6
22	South Carolina	52.0
36	South Dakota	34.8
41	Tennessee	18.6
35	Texas	35.5
3	Utah	151.8
NA	Vermont**	NA
24	Virginia	50.9
14	Washington	67.0
44	West Virginia	11.0
1	Wisconsin	280.8
37	Wyoming	33.8

RANK	STATE	RATE
1	Wisconsin	280.8
2	Delaware	164.6
3	Utah	151.8
4	Alaska	128.1
5	Missouri	111.7
6	New York	103.7
7	Nevada	96.0
8	Connecticut	81.8
9	Oregon	77.8
10	Idaho	75.7
11	Maryland	75.6
12	Arizona	69.9
13	California	68.1
14	Washington	67.0
15	Georgia	65.0
16	Colorado	58.4
16	Mississippi	58.4
18	Louisiana	56.5
19	Hawaii	55.6
19	New Jersey	55.6
21	Nebraska	54.0
22	South Carolina	52.0
23	Montana	51.5
24	Virginia	50.9
25	Kentucky	48.5
26	Maine	47.7
27	Minnesota	46.5
28	Michigan	45.9
29	Pennsylvania	44.8
30	Indiana	42.9
31	North Carolina	42.5
32	Ohio	41.7
33	Rhode Island	40.6
34	North Dakota	38.3
35	Texas	35.5
36	South Dakota	34.8
37	Wyoming	33.8
38	Iowa	30.8
39	Arkansas	23.6
40	Oklahoma	20.4
41	Tennessee	18.6
42	Massachusetts	12.9
43	New Mexico	11.7
44	West Virginia	11.0
45	Alabama	7.9
NA	Florida**	NA
NA	Illinois**	NA
NA	Kansas**	NA
NA	New Hampshire**	NA
NA	Vermont**	NA
	District of Columbia**	NA

Source: Morgan Quitno Press using data from Federal Bureau of Investigation
    "Crime in the United States 1997" (Uniform Crime Reports, November 22, 1998)
*By law enforcement agencies submitting complete reports to the F.B.I. for 12 months in 1997. Arrests of youths 17
years and younger divided into population of 10 to 17 year olds. See important note at beginning of this chapter.
Excludes forcible rape, prostitution and commercialized vice. Includes statutory rape and offenses against chastity,
common decency, morals and the like. **Not available.

Reported Arrests of Juveniles for Sex Offenses
As a Percent of All Such Arrests in 1997
National Percent = 18.2% of Reported Sex Offenses Arrests*

ALPHA ORDER   RANK ORDER

RANK	STATE	PERCENT		RANK	STATE	PERCENT
43	Alabama	8.0		1	Wisconsin	43.1
19	Alaska	19.3		2	Montana	41.1
32	Arizona	15.7		2	Utah	41.1
40	Arkansas	12.0		4	Idaho	37.7
37	California	14.1		5	Iowa	32.6
20	Colorado	18.6		6	Minnesota	30.4
8	Connecticut	28.7		7	North Dakota	29.8
11	Delaware	25.6		8	Connecticut	28.7
NA	Florida**	NA		9	Maryland	26.5
44	Georgia	7.6		10	South Carolina	26.0
25	Hawaii	17.9		11	Delaware	25.6
4	Idaho	37.7		12	Maine	23.2
35	Illinois	14.7		13	Michigan	22.3
31	Indiana	16.3		14	Oregon	21.5
5	Iowa	32.6		15	New Jersey	21.1
NA	Kansas**	NA		16	Louisiana	20.0
36	Kentucky	14.5		16	New York	20.0
16	Louisiana	20.0		18	Nevada	19.6
12	Maine	23.2		19	Alaska	19.3
9	Maryland	26.5		20	Colorado	18.6
45	Massachusetts	7.3		21	Rhode Island	18.5
13	Michigan	22.3		22	New Mexico	18.4
6	Minnesota	30.4		23	Pennsylvania	18.1
26	Mississippi	17.8		24	Missouri	18.0
24	Missouri	18.0		25	Hawaii	17.9
2	Montana	41.1		26	Mississippi	17.8
38	Nebraska	14.0		27	South Dakota	17.6
18	Nevada	19.6		28	Ohio	17.0
NA	New Hampshire**	NA		28	Texas	17.0
15	New Jersey	21.1		30	Washington	16.6
22	New Mexico	18.4		31	Indiana	16.3
16	New York	20.0		32	Arizona	15.7
39	North Carolina	12.8		32	Wyoming	15.7
7	North Dakota	29.8		34	Virginia	15.1
28	Ohio	17.0		35	Illinois	14.7
41	Oklahoma	8.8		36	Kentucky	14.5
14	Oregon	21.5		37	California	14.1
23	Pennsylvania	18.1		38	Nebraska	14.0
21	Rhode Island	18.5		39	North Carolina	12.8
10	South Carolina	26.0		40	Arkansas	12.0
27	South Dakota	17.6		41	Oklahoma	8.8
42	Tennessee	8.2		42	Tennessee	8.2
28	Texas	17.0		43	Alabama	8.0
2	Utah	41.1		44	Georgia	7.6
NA	Vermont**	NA		45	Massachusetts	7.3
34	Virginia	15.1		46	West Virginia	6.8
30	Washington	16.6		NA	Florida**	NA
46	West Virginia	6.8		NA	Kansas**	NA
1	Wisconsin	43.1		NA	New Hampshire**	NA
32	Wyoming	15.7		NA	Vermont**	NA
					District of Columbia**	NA

Source: Morgan Quitno Press using data from Federal Bureau of Investigation
    "Crime in the United States 1997" (Uniform Crime Reports, November 22, 1998)
*Arrests of youths 17 years and younger by law enforcement agencies submitting complete reports to the F.B.I. for 12 months in 1997. Excludes forcible rape, prostitution and commercialized vice. Includes statutory rape and offenses against chastity, common decency, morals and the like.
**Not available.

Reported Arrests of Juveniles for Prostitution and Commercialized Vice in 1997

National Total = 992 Reported Arrests*

RANK	STATE	ARRESTS	% of USA
34	Alabama	2	0.2%
39	Alaska	0	0.0%
10	Arizona	25	2.5%
35	Arkansas	1	0.1%
1	California	296	29.8%
31	Colorado	5	0.5%
20	Connecticut	9	0.9%
39	Delaware	0	0.0%
NA	Florida**	NA	NA
5	Georgia	58	5.8%
15	Hawaii	15	1.5%
39	Idaho	0	0.0%
2	Illinois	96	9.7%
23	Indiana	7	0.7%
29	Iowa	6	0.6%
NA	Kansas**	NA	NA
17	Kentucky	12	1.2%
20	Louisiana	9	0.9%
39	Maine	0	0.0%
4	Maryland	66	6.7%
12	Massachusetts	22	2.2%
9	Michigan	26	2.6%
23	Minnesota	7	0.7%
35	Mississippi	1	0.1%
13	Missouri	18	1.8%
39	Montana	0	0.0%
18	Nebraska	10	1.0%
35	Nevada	1	0.1%
NA	New Hampshire**	NA	NA
8	New Jersey	28	2.8%
18	New Mexico	10	1.0%
7	New York	29	2.9%
23	North Carolina	7	0.7%
39	North Dakota	0	0.0%
11	Ohio	23	2.3%
6	Oklahoma	32	3.2%
16	Oregon	14	1.4%
20	Pennsylvania	9	0.9%
31	Rhode Island	5	0.5%
33	South Carolina	3	0.3%
39	South Dakota	0	0.0%
23	Tennessee	7	0.7%
3	Texas	95	9.6%
23	Utah	7	0.7%
NA	Vermont**	NA	NA
29	Virginia	6	0.6%
14	Washington	17	1.7%
35	West Virginia	1	0.1%
23	Wisconsin	7	0.7%
39	Wyoming	0	0.0%

RANK	STATE	ARRESTS	% of USA
1	California	296	29.8%
2	Illinois	96	9.7%
3	Texas	95	9.6%
4	Maryland	66	6.7%
5	Georgia	58	5.8%
6	Oklahoma	32	3.2%
7	New York	29	2.9%
8	New Jersey	28	2.8%
9	Michigan	26	2.6%
10	Arizona	25	2.5%
11	Ohio	23	2.3%
12	Massachusetts	22	2.2%
13	Missouri	18	1.8%
14	Washington	17	1.7%
15	Hawaii	15	1.5%
16	Oregon	14	1.4%
17	Kentucky	12	1.2%
18	Nebraska	10	1.0%
18	New Mexico	10	1.0%
20	Connecticut	9	0.9%
20	Louisiana	9	0.9%
20	Pennsylvania	9	0.9%
23	Indiana	7	0.7%
23	Minnesota	7	0.7%
23	North Carolina	7	0.7%
23	Tennessee	7	0.7%
23	Utah	7	0.7%
23	Wisconsin	7	0.7%
29	Iowa	6	0.6%
29	Virginia	6	0.6%
31	Colorado	5	0.5%
31	Rhode Island	5	0.5%
33	South Carolina	3	0.3%
34	Alabama	2	0.2%
35	Arkansas	1	0.1%
35	Mississippi	1	0.1%
35	Nevada	1	0.1%
35	West Virginia	1	0.1%
39	Alaska	0	0.0%
39	Delaware	0	0.0%
39	Idaho	0	0.0%
39	Maine	0	0.0%
39	Montana	0	0.0%
39	North Dakota	0	0.0%
39	South Dakota	0	0.0%
39	Wyoming	0	0.0%
NA	Florida**	NA	NA
NA	Kansas**	NA	NA
NA	New Hampshire**	NA	NA
NA	Vermont**	NA	NA
	District of Columbia**	NA	NA

Source: Federal Bureau of Investigation
    "Crime in the United States 1997" (Uniform Crime Reports, November 22, 1998)
*Arrests of youths 17 years and younger by law enforcement agencies submitting complete reports to the F.B.I. for 12 months in 1997. Includes keeping a bawdy house, procuring or transporting women for immoral purposes. Attempts are included. See important note at beginning of this chapter.
**Not available.

Reported Juvenile Arrest Rate for Prostitution and Commercialized Vice in 1997

National Rate = 4.7 Reported Arrests per 100,000 Population*

<table>
<tr><td colspan="3">ALPHA ORDER</td><td colspan="3">RANK ORDER</td></tr>
<tr><td>RANK</td><td>STATE</td><td>RATE</td><td>RANK</td><td>STATE</td><td>RATE</td></tr>
<tr><td>36</td><td>Alabama</td><td>0.4</td><td>1</td><td>Georgia</td><td>20.1</td></tr>
<tr><td>38</td><td>Alaska</td><td>0.0</td><td>2</td><td>Kentucky</td><td>14.2</td></tr>
<tr><td>8</td><td>Arizona</td><td>5.4</td><td>3</td><td>Hawaii</td><td>12.3</td></tr>
<tr><td>36</td><td>Arkansas</td><td>0.4</td><td>4</td><td>Maryland</td><td>12.0</td></tr>
<tr><td>5</td><td>California</td><td>8.3</td><td>5</td><td>California</td><td>8.3</td></tr>
<tr><td>26</td><td>Colorado</td><td>1.6</td><td>6</td><td>Oklahoma</td><td>7.8</td></tr>
<tr><td>19</td><td>Connecticut</td><td>3.1</td><td>7</td><td>New Mexico</td><td>6.5</td></tr>
<tr><td>38</td><td>Delaware</td><td>0.0</td><td>8</td><td>Arizona</td><td>5.4</td></tr>
<tr><td>NA</td><td>Florida**</td><td>NA</td><td>9</td><td>Nebraska</td><td>5.0</td></tr>
<tr><td>1</td><td>Georgia</td><td>20.1</td><td>10</td><td>Rhode Island</td><td>4.8</td></tr>
<tr><td>3</td><td>Hawaii</td><td>12.3</td><td>11</td><td>Missouri</td><td>4.7</td></tr>
<tr><td>38</td><td>Idaho</td><td>0.0</td><td>12</td><td>Oregon</td><td>4.3</td></tr>
<tr><td>NA</td><td>Illinois**</td><td>NA</td><td>13</td><td>Massachusetts</td><td>4.2</td></tr>
<tr><td>25</td><td>Indiana</td><td>1.8</td><td>13</td><td>Washington</td><td>4.2</td></tr>
<tr><td>23</td><td>Iowa</td><td>2.1</td><td>15</td><td>Texas</td><td>4.1</td></tr>
<tr><td>NA</td><td>Kansas**</td><td>NA</td><td>16</td><td>New Jersey</td><td>3.4</td></tr>
<tr><td>2</td><td>Kentucky</td><td>14.2</td><td>17</td><td>New York</td><td>3.3</td></tr>
<tr><td>23</td><td>Louisiana</td><td>2.1</td><td>18</td><td>Ohio</td><td>3.2</td></tr>
<tr><td>38</td><td>Maine</td><td>0.0</td><td>19</td><td>Connecticut</td><td>3.1</td></tr>
<tr><td>4</td><td>Maryland</td><td>12.0</td><td>20</td><td>Utah</td><td>3.0</td></tr>
<tr><td>13</td><td>Massachusetts</td><td>4.2</td><td>21</td><td>Michigan</td><td>2.8</td></tr>
<tr><td>21</td><td>Michigan</td><td>2.8</td><td>21</td><td>Tennessee</td><td>2.8</td></tr>
<tr><td>29</td><td>Minnesota</td><td>1.2</td><td>23</td><td>Iowa</td><td>2.1</td></tr>
<tr><td>32</td><td>Mississippi</td><td>0.8</td><td>23</td><td>Louisiana</td><td>2.1</td></tr>
<tr><td>11</td><td>Missouri</td><td>4.7</td><td>25</td><td>Indiana</td><td>1.8</td></tr>
<tr><td>38</td><td>Montana</td><td>0.0</td><td>26</td><td>Colorado</td><td>1.6</td></tr>
<tr><td>9</td><td>Nebraska</td><td>5.0</td><td>27</td><td>Pennsylvania</td><td>1.5</td></tr>
<tr><td>29</td><td>Nevada</td><td>1.2</td><td>28</td><td>Wisconsin</td><td>1.4</td></tr>
<tr><td>NA</td><td>New Hampshire**</td><td>NA</td><td>29</td><td>Minnesota</td><td>1.2</td></tr>
<tr><td>16</td><td>New Jersey</td><td>3.4</td><td>29</td><td>Nevada</td><td>1.2</td></tr>
<tr><td>7</td><td>New Mexico</td><td>6.5</td><td>31</td><td>North Carolina</td><td>0.9</td></tr>
<tr><td>17</td><td>New York</td><td>3.3</td><td>32</td><td>Mississippi</td><td>0.8</td></tr>
<tr><td>31</td><td>North Carolina</td><td>0.9</td><td>32</td><td>Virginia</td><td>0.8</td></tr>
<tr><td>38</td><td>North Dakota</td><td>0.0</td><td>34</td><td>South Carolina</td><td>0.7</td></tr>
<tr><td>18</td><td>Ohio</td><td>3.2</td><td>35</td><td>West Virginia</td><td>0.5</td></tr>
<tr><td>6</td><td>Oklahoma</td><td>7.8</td><td>36</td><td>Alabama</td><td>0.4</td></tr>
<tr><td>12</td><td>Oregon</td><td>4.3</td><td>36</td><td>Arkansas</td><td>0.4</td></tr>
<tr><td>27</td><td>Pennsylvania</td><td>1.5</td><td>38</td><td>Alaska</td><td>0.0</td></tr>
<tr><td>10</td><td>Rhode Island</td><td>4.8</td><td>38</td><td>Delaware</td><td>0.0</td></tr>
<tr><td>34</td><td>South Carolina</td><td>0.7</td><td>38</td><td>Idaho</td><td>0.0</td></tr>
<tr><td>38</td><td>South Dakota</td><td>0.0</td><td>38</td><td>Maine</td><td>0.0</td></tr>
<tr><td>21</td><td>Tennessee</td><td>2.8</td><td>38</td><td>Montana</td><td>0.0</td></tr>
<tr><td>15</td><td>Texas</td><td>4.1</td><td>38</td><td>North Dakota</td><td>0.0</td></tr>
<tr><td>20</td><td>Utah</td><td>3.0</td><td>38</td><td>South Dakota</td><td>0.0</td></tr>
<tr><td>NA</td><td>Vermont**</td><td>NA</td><td>38</td><td>Wyoming</td><td>0.0</td></tr>
<tr><td>32</td><td>Virginia</td><td>0.8</td><td>NA</td><td>Florida**</td><td>NA</td></tr>
<tr><td>13</td><td>Washington</td><td>4.2</td><td>NA</td><td>Illinois**</td><td>NA</td></tr>
<tr><td>35</td><td>West Virginia</td><td>0.5</td><td>NA</td><td>Kansas**</td><td>NA</td></tr>
<tr><td>28</td><td>Wisconsin</td><td>1.4</td><td>NA</td><td>New Hampshire**</td><td>NA</td></tr>
<tr><td>38</td><td>Wyoming</td><td>0.0</td><td>NA</td><td>Vermont**</td><td>NA</td></tr>
<tr><td></td><td></td><td></td><td></td><td>District of Columbia**</td><td>NA</td></tr>
</table>

Source: Morgan Quitno Press using data from Federal Bureau of Investigation
   "Crime in the United States 1997" (Uniform Crime Reports, November 22, 1998)
*By law enforcement agencies submitting complete reports to the F.B.I. for 12 months in 1997. Arrests of youths 17 years and younger divided into population of 10 to 17 year olds. See important note at beginning of this chapter. Includes keeping a bawdy house, procuring or transporting women for immoral purposes. Attempts are included.
**Not available.

Reported Arrests of Juveniles for Prostitution and Commercialized Vice
As a Percent of All Such Arrests in 1997
National Percent = 1.4% of Reported Prostitution/Commercialized Vice Arrests*

ALPHA ORDER

RANK	STATE	PERCENT
30	Alabama	0.7
39	Alaska	0.0
20	Arizona	1.1
32	Arkansas	0.6
16	California	1.6
35	Colorado	0.4
24	Connecticut	0.9
39	Delaware	0.0
NA	Florida**	NA
14	Georgia	1.7
4	Hawaii	3.3
39	Idaho	0.0
18	Illinois	1.2
34	Indiana	0.5
8	Iowa	2.1
NA	Kansas**	NA
3	Kentucky	3.5
11	Louisiana	1.8
39	Maine	0.0
5	Maryland	2.6
22	Massachusetts	1.0
28	Michigan	0.8
1	Minnesota	7.0
11	Mississippi	1.8
20	Missouri	1.1
39	Montana	0.0
6	Nebraska	2.2
9	Nevada	1.9
NA	New Hampshire**	NA
24	New Jersey	0.9
22	New Mexico	1.0
18	New York	1.2
24	North Carolina	0.9
39	North Dakota	0.0
24	Ohio	0.9
2	Oklahoma	5.8
9	Oregon	1.9
28	Pennsylvania	0.8
16	Rhode Island	1.6
35	South Carolina	0.4
39	South Dakota	0.0
30	Tennessee	0.7
14	Texas	1.7
11	Utah	1.8
NA	Vermont**	NA
35	Virginia	0.4
6	Washington	2.2
32	West Virginia	0.6
35	Wisconsin	0.4
39	Wyoming	0.0

RANK ORDER

RANK	STATE	PERCENT
1	Minnesota	7.0
2	Oklahoma	5.8
3	Kentucky	3.5
4	Hawaii	3.3
5	Maryland	2.6
6	Nebraska	2.2
6	Washington	2.2
8	Iowa	2.1
9	Nevada	1.9
9	Oregon	1.9
11	Louisiana	1.8
11	Mississippi	1.8
11	Utah	1.8
14	Georgia	1.7
14	Texas	1.7
16	California	1.6
16	Rhode Island	1.6
18	Illinois	1.2
18	New York	1.2
20	Arizona	1.1
20	Missouri	1.1
22	Massachusetts	1.0
22	New Mexico	1.0
24	Connecticut	0.9
24	New Jersey	0.9
24	North Carolina	0.9
24	Ohio	0.9
28	Michigan	0.8
28	Pennsylvania	0.8
30	Alabama	0.7
30	Tennessee	0.7
32	Arkansas	0.6
32	West Virginia	0.6
34	Indiana	0.5
35	Colorado	0.4
35	South Carolina	0.4
35	Virginia	0.4
35	Wisconsin	0.4
39	Alaska	0.0
39	Delaware	0.0
39	Idaho	0.0
39	Maine	0.0
39	Montana	0.0
39	North Dakota	0.0
39	South Dakota	0.0
39	Wyoming	0.0
NA	Florida**	NA
NA	Kansas**	NA
NA	New Hampshire**	NA
NA	Vermont**	NA
	District of Columbia**	NA

Source: Morgan Quitno Press using data from Federal Bureau of Investigation
    "Crime in the United States 1997" (Uniform Crime Reports, November 22, 1998)

*Arrests of youths 17 years and younger by law enforcement agencies submitting complete reports to the F.B.I. for 12 months in 1997. Includes keeping a bawdy house, procuring or transporting women for immoral purposes. Attempts are included.
**Not available.

Reported Arrests of Juveniles for Offenses Against Families & Children in 1997

National Total = 6,843 Reported Arrests*

<u>ALPHA ORDER</u>

RANK	STATE	ARRESTS	% of USA
21	Alabama	75	1.1%
36	Alaska	12	0.2%
14	Arizona	136	2.0%
25	Arkansas	53	0.8%
38	California	11	0.2%
23	Colorado	57	0.8%
8	Connecticut	187	2.7%
46	Delaware	1	0.0%
NA	Florida**	NA	NA
35	Georgia	13	0.2%
7	Hawaii	201	2.9%
33	Idaho	16	0.2%
26	Illinois	47	0.7%
5	Indiana	317	4.6%
42	Iowa	5	0.1%
NA	Kansas**	NA	NA
41	Kentucky	7	0.1%
3	Louisiana	364	5.3%
45	Maine	3	0.0%
19	Maryland	87	1.3%
11	Massachusetts	174	2.5%
39	Michigan	9	0.1%
32	Minnesota	22	0.3%
22	Mississippi	64	0.9%
9	Missouri	184	2.7%
44	Montana	4	0.1%
31	Nebraska	25	0.4%
16	Nevada	101	1.5%
NA	New Hampshire**	NA	NA
29	New Jersey	30	0.4%
20	New Mexico	86	1.3%
2	New York	477	7.0%
15	North Carolina	128	1.9%
17	North Dakota	94	1.4%
1	Ohio	2,466	36.0%
18	Oklahoma	92	1.3%
39	Oregon	9	0.1%
27	Pennsylvania	38	0.6%
12	Rhode Island	165	2.4%
30	South Carolina	29	0.4%
10	South Dakota	177	2.6%
28	Tennessee	33	0.5%
13	Texas	162	2.4%
23	Utah	57	0.8%
NA	Vermont**	NA	NA
6	Virginia	268	3.9%
34	Washington	15	0.2%
36	West Virginia	12	0.2%
4	Wisconsin	325	4.7%
42	Wyoming	5	0.1%

<u>RANK ORDER</u>

RANK	STATE	ARRESTS	% of USA
1	Ohio	2,466	36.0%
2	New York	477	7.0%
3	Louisiana	364	5.3%
4	Wisconsin	325	4.7%
5	Indiana	317	4.6%
6	Virginia	268	3.9%
7	Hawaii	201	2.9%
8	Connecticut	187	2.7%
9	Missouri	184	2.7%
10	South Dakota	177	2.6%
11	Massachusetts	174	2.5%
12	Rhode Island	165	2.4%
13	Texas	162	2.4%
14	Arizona	136	2.0%
15	North Carolina	128	1.9%
16	Nevada	101	1.5%
17	North Dakota	94	1.4%
18	Oklahoma	92	1.3%
19	Maryland	87	1.3%
20	New Mexico	86	1.3%
21	Alabama	75	1.1%
22	Mississippi	64	0.9%
23	Colorado	57	0.8%
23	Utah	57	0.8%
25	Arkansas	53	0.8%
26	Illinois	47	0.7%
27	Pennsylvania	38	0.6%
28	Tennessee	33	0.5%
29	New Jersey	30	0.4%
30	South Carolina	29	0.4%
31	Nebraska	25	0.4%
32	Minnesota	22	0.3%
33	Idaho	16	0.2%
34	Washington	15	0.2%
35	Georgia	13	0.2%
36	Alaska	12	0.2%
36	West Virginia	12	0.2%
38	California	11	0.2%
39	Michigan	9	0.1%
39	Oregon	9	0.1%
41	Kentucky	7	0.1%
42	Iowa	5	0.1%
42.	Wyoming	5	0.1%
44	Montana	4	0.1%
45	Maine	3	0.0%
46	Delaware	1	0.0%
NA	Florida**	NA	NA
NA	Kansas**	NA	NA
NA	New Hampshire**	NA	NA
NA	Vermont**	NA	NA
	District of Columbia**	NA	NA

Source: Federal Bureau of Investigation
   "Crime in the United States 1997" (Uniform Crime Reports, November 22, 1998)
*Arrests of youths 17 years and younger by law enforcement agencies submitting complete reports to the F.B.I. for 12 months in 1997. Includes nonsupport, neglect, desertion or abuse of family and children. See important note at beginning of this chapter.
**Not available.

Reported Juvenile Arrest Rate for Offenses Against Families & Children in 1997

National Rate = 32.6 Reported Arrests per 100,000 Juvenile Population*

ALPHA ORDER

RANK	STATE	RATE
23	Alabama	16.5
17	Alaska	32.0
18	Arizona	29.6
21	Arkansas	19.5
45	California	0.3
22	Colorado	17.7
10	Connecticut	64.5
40	Delaware	3.2
NA	Florida**	NA
36	Georgia	4.5
3	Hawaii	164.4
28	Idaho	9.8
NA	Illinois**	NA
8	Indiana	82.4
43	Iowa	1.7
NA	Kansas**	NA
30	Kentucky	8.3
7	Louisiana	83.6
42	Maine	2.2
25	Maryland	15.8
16	Massachusetts	33.5
44	Michigan	1.0
37	Minnesota	3.7
13	Mississippi	49.9
14	Missouri	47.6
29	Montana	9.0
27	Nebraska	12.6
6	Nevada	118.3
NA	New Hampshire**	NA
37	New Jersey	3.7
11	New Mexico	56.0
12	New York	53.9
24	North Carolina	15.9
5	North Dakota	128.6
2	Ohio	345.3
20	Oklahoma	22.3
41	Oregon	2.8
35	Pennsylvania	6.2
4	Rhode Island	159.6
33	South Carolina	6.8
1	South Dakota	410.4
26	Tennessee	13.3
32	Texas	6.9
19	Utah	24.5
NA	Vermont**	NA
15	Virginia	37.9
37	Washington	3.7
34	West Virginia	6.3
9	Wisconsin	66.6
31	Wyoming	7.7

RANK ORDER

RANK	STATE	RATE
1	South Dakota	410.4
2	Ohio	345.3
3	Hawaii	164.4
4	Rhode Island	159.6
5	North Dakota	128.6
6	Nevada	118.3
7	Louisiana	83.6
8	Indiana	82.4
9	Wisconsin	66.6
10	Connecticut	64.5
11	New Mexico	56.0
12	New York	53.9
13	Mississippi	49.9
14	Missouri	47.6
15	Virginia	37.9
16	Massachusetts	33.5
17	Alaska	32.0
18	Arizona	29.6
19	Utah	24.5
20	Oklahoma	22.3
21	Arkansas	19.5
22	Colorado	17.7
23	Alabama	16.5
24	North Carolina	15.9
25	Maryland	15.8
26	Tennessee	13.3
27	Nebraska	12.6
28	Idaho	9.8
29	Montana	9.0
30	Kentucky	8.3
31	Wyoming	7.7
32	Texas	6.9
33	South Carolina	6.8
34	West Virginia	6.3
35	Pennsylvania	6.2
36	Georgia	4.5
37	Minnesota	3.7
37	New Jersey	3.7
37	Washington	3.7
40	Delaware	3.2
41	Oregon	2.8
42	Maine	2.2
43	Iowa	1.7
44	Michigan	1.0
45	California	0.3
NA	Florida**	NA
NA	Illinois**	NA
NA	Kansas**	NA
NA	New Hampshire**	NA
NA	Vermont**	NA

District of Columbia**   NA

Source: Morgan Quitno Press using data from Federal Bureau of Investigation
 "Crime in the United States 1997" (Uniform Crime Reports, November 22, 1998)
*By law enforcement agencies submitting complete reports to the F.B.I. for 12 months in 1997. Arrests of youths 17 years and younger divided into population of 10 to 17 year olds. See important note at beginning of this chapter. Includes nonsupport, neglect, desertion or abuse of family and children.
**Not available.

Reported Arrests of Juveniles for Offenses Against Families and Children As a Percent of All Such Arrests in 1997
National Percent = 6.5% of Offenses Against Families and Children Arrests*

	ALPHA ORDER			RANK ORDER	
RANK	STATE	PERCENT	RANK	STATE	PERCENT
17	Alabama	7.0	1	South Dakota	62.5
25	Alaska	4.3	2	North Dakota	30.3
15	Arizona	7.2	3	Rhode Island	29.8
30	Arkansas	3.4	4	Indiana	28.6
39	California	1.6	5	Louisiana	18.3
18	Colorado	6.3	6	New York	16.8
13	Connecticut	7.7	7	Ohio	10.7
44	Delaware	1.0	8	Nevada	10.6
NA	Florida**	NA	9	Virginia	9.8
42	Georgia	1.4	10	Hawaii	9.6
10	Hawaii	9.6	11	Illinois	9.5
27	Idaho	4.1	12	New Mexico	7.8
11	Illinois	9.5	13	Connecticut	7.7
4	Indiana	28.6	14	Wisconsin	7.4
41	Iowa	1.5	15	Arizona	7.2
NA	Kansas**	NA	16	Oklahoma	7.1
43	Kentucky	1.1	17	Alabama	7.0
5	Louisiana	18.3	18	Colorado	6.3
38	Maine	1.7	19	Massachusetts	5.3
25	Maryland	4.3	20	Missouri	5.2
19	Massachusetts	5.3	21	Utah	5.0
45	Michigan	0.2	22	Pennsylvania	4.8
29	Minnesota	3.6	23	Mississippi	4.7
23	Mississippi	4.7	24	Washington	4.4
20	Missouri	5.2	25	Alaska	4.3
32	Montana	2.3	25	Maryland	4.3
39	Nebraska	1.6	27	Idaho	4.1
NA	New Hampshire**	NA	27	West Virginia	4.1
45	New Jersey	0.2	29	Minnesota	3.6
12	New Mexico	7.8	30	Arkansas	3.4
6	New York	16.8	30	Texas	3.4
36	North Carolina	1.9	32	Montana	2.3
2	North Dakota	30.3	32	Oregon	2.3
7	Ohio	10.7	34	Tennessee	2.2
16	Oklahoma	7.1	35	Wyoming	2.1
32	Oregon	2.3	36	North Carolina	1.9
22	Pennsylvania	4.8	36	South Carolina	1.9
3	Rhode Island	29.8	38	Maine	1.7
36	South Carolina	1.9	39	California	1.6
1	South Dakota	62.5	39	Nebraska	1.6
34	Tennessee	2.2	41	Iowa	1.5
30	Texas	3.4	42	Georgia	1.4
21	Utah	5.0	43	Kentucky	1.1
NA	Vermont**	NA	44	Delaware	1.0
9	Virginia	9.8	45	Michigan	0.2
24	Washington	4.4	45	New Jersey	0.2
27	West Virginia	4.1	NA	Florida**	NA
14	Wisconsin	7.4	NA	Kansas**	NA
35	Wyoming	2.1	NA	New Hampshire**	NA
			NA	Vermont**	NA
				District of Columbia**	NA

Source: Morgan Quitno Press using data from Federal Bureau of Investigation
"Crime in the United States 1997" (Uniform Crime Reports, November 22, 1998)
*Arrests of youths 17 years and younger by law enforcement agencies submitting complete reports to the F.B.I. for 12 months in 1997. Includes nonsupport, neglect, desertion or abuse of family and children.
**Not available.

Juveniles in Public Facilities in 1995

National Total = 69,075 Juveniles*

ALPHA ORDER					RANK ORDER			

RANK	STATE	JUVENILES	% of USA
21	Alabama	908	1.31%
40	Alaska	223	0.32%
16	Arizona	1,083	1.57%
38	Arkansas	275	0.40%
1	California	19,567	28.33%
25	Colorado	776	1.12%
35	Connecticut	371	0.54%
41	Delaware	164	0.24%
5	Florida	2,674	3.87%
7	Georgia	2,337	3.38%
48	Hawaii	101	0.15%
44	Idaho	154	0.22%
6	Illinois	2,641	3.82%
12	Indiana	1,704	2.47%
32	Iowa	461	0.67%
23	Kansas	808	1.17%
30	Kentucky	593	0.86%
13	Louisiana	1,509	2.18%
36	Maine	369	0.53%
26	Maryland	715	1.04%
37	Massachusetts	331	0.48%
11	Michigan	1,778	2.57%
24	Minnesota	803	1.16%
29	Mississippi	641	0.93%
19	Missouri	1,037	1.50%
46	Montana	140	0.20%
33	Nebraska	419	0.61%
28	Nevada	660	0.96%
47	New Hampshire	125	0.18%
9	New Jersey	1,999	2.89%
27	New Mexico	662	0.96%
4	New York	2,862	4.14%
18	North Carolina	1,051	1.52%
49	North Dakota	97	0.14%
2	Ohio	3,551	5.14%
34	Oklahoma	392	0.57%
22	Oregon	902	1.31%
14	Pennsylvania	1,487	2.15%
43	Rhode Island	155	0.22%
17	South Carolina	1,062	1.54%
39	South Dakota	261	0.38%
20	Tennessee	974	1.41%
3	Texas	3,505	5.07%
31	Utah	465	0.67%
50	Vermont	24	0.03%
8	Virginia	2,211	3.20%
10	Washington	1,870	2.71%
45	West Virginia	148	0.21%
15	Wisconsin	1,450	2.10%
41	Wyoming	164	0.24%

RANK	STATE	JUVENILES	% of USA
1	California	19,567	28.33%
2	Ohio	3,551	5.14%
3	Texas	3,505	5.07%
4	New York	2,862	4.14%
5	Florida	2,674	3.87%
6	Illinois	2,641	3.82%
7	Georgia	2,337	3.38%
8	Virginia	2,211	3.20%
9	New Jersey	1,999	2.89%
10	Washington	1,870	2.71%
11	Michigan	1,778	2.57%
12	Indiana	1,704	2.47%
13	Louisiana	1,509	2.18%
14	Pennsylvania	1,487	2.15%
15	Wisconsin	1,450	2.10%
16	Arizona	1,083	1.57%
17	South Carolina	1,062	1.54%
18	North Carolina	1,051	1.52%
19	Missouri	1,037	1.50%
20	Tennessee	974	1.41%
21	Alabama	908	1.31%
22	Oregon	902	1.31%
23	Kansas	808	1.17%
24	Minnesota	803	1.16%
25	Colorado	776	1.12%
26	Maryland	715	1.04%
27	New Mexico	662	0.96%
28	Nevada	660	0.96%
29	Mississippi	641	0.93%
30	Kentucky	593	0.86%
31	Utah	465	0.67%
32	Iowa	461	0.67%
33	Nebraska	419	0.61%
34	Oklahoma	392	0.57%
35	Connecticut	371	0.54%
36	Maine	369	0.53%
37	Massachusetts	331	0.48%
38	Arkansas	275	0.40%
39	South Dakota	261	0.38%
40	Alaska	223	0.32%
41	Delaware	164	0.24%
41	Wyoming	164	0.24%
43	Rhode Island	155	0.22%
44	Idaho	154	0.22%
45	West Virginia	148	0.21%
46	Montana	140	0.20%
47	New Hampshire	125	0.18%
48	Hawaii	101	0.15%
49	North Dakota	97	0.14%
50	Vermont	24	0.03%
	District of Columbia	251	0.36%

Source: U.S. Department of Justice, Office of Juvenile Justice and Delinquency Prevention
"States at a Glance: Juveniles in Public Facilities, 1995" (Fact Sheet #69, November 1997)

*Juveniles in residential custody on February 15, 1995. Includes 66,236 held because of delinquent offenses (offenses that would also be illegal if they were adults), 1,785 for status offenses (offenses that would not be illegal if they were adult, such as truancy), 889 for other offenses and 165 whose offenses were unknown.

245

Rate of Juveniles in Public Facilities in 1995

National Rate = 100.8 Juveniles per 100,000 Population Under 18*

ALPHA ORDER				RANK ORDER		
RANK	STATE	RATE		RANK	STATE	RATE
24	Alabama	84.2		1	California	223.1
12	Alaska	119.6		2	Nevada	166.1
19	Arizona	95.1		3	Virginia	136.7
46	Arkansas	42.1		4	New Mexico	133.3
1	California	223.1		5	Washington	131.9
26	Colorado	79.3		6	South Dakota	127.2
42	Connecticut	46.9		7	Ohio	124.6
21	Delaware	93.1		8	Louisiana	122.3
25	Florida	79.7		9	Maine	122.1
10	Georgia	121.6		10	Georgia	121.6
48	Hawaii	33.1		11	Wyoming	121.5
44	Idaho	44.7		12	Alaska	119.6
23	Illinois	84.5		13	Kansas	117.7
14	Indiana	114.4		14	Indiana	114.4
34	Iowa	63.7		15	Oregon	113.1
13	Kansas	117.7		16	South Carolina	112.8
36	Kentucky	61.1		17	Wisconsin	108.0
8	Louisiana	122.3		18	New Jersey	101.7
9	Maine	122.1		19	Arizona	95.1
40	Maryland	56.2		20	Nebraska	95.0
49	Massachusetts	23.3		21	Delaware	93.1
29	Michigan	70.3		22	Mississippi	84.6
33	Minnesota	64.8		23	Illinois	84.5
22	Mississippi	84.6		24	Alabama	84.2
27	Missouri	75.0		25	Florida	79.7
37	Montana	60.0		26	Colorado	79.3
20	Nebraska	95.0		27	Missouri	75.0
2	Nevada	166.1		28	Tennessee	74.3
45	New Hampshire	42.6		29	Michigan	70.3
18	New Jersey	101.7		30	Utah	68.8
4	New Mexico	133.3		31	Rhode Island	65.9
35	New York	63.2		32	Texas	65.3
38	North Carolina	58.4		33	Minnesota	64.8
39	North Dakota	57.2		34	Iowa	63.7
7	Ohio	124.6		35	New York	63.2
43	Oklahoma	44.8		36	Kentucky	61.1
15	Oregon	113.1		37	Montana	60.0
41	Pennsylvania	51.4		38	North Carolina	58.4
31	Rhode Island	65.9		39	North Dakota	57.2
16	South Carolina	112.8		40	Maryland	56.2
6	South Dakota	127.2		41	Pennsylvania	51.4
28	Tennessee	74.3		42	Connecticut	46.9
32	Texas	65.3		43	Oklahoma	44.8
30	Utah	68.8		44	Idaho	44.7
50	Vermont	16.4		45	New Hampshire	42.6
3	Virginia	136.7		46	Arkansas	42.1
5	Washington	131.9		47	West Virginia	34.8
47	West Virginia	34.8		48	Hawaii	33.1
17	Wisconsin	108.0		49	Massachusetts	23.3
11	Wyoming	121.5		50	Vermont	16.4
					District of Columbia	222.5

Source: Morgan Quitno Press using data from U.S. Dept. of Justice, Office of Juvenile Justice and Delinquency Prevention
"States at a Glance: Juveniles in Public Facilities, 1995" (Fact Sheet #69, November 1997)
*Juveniles in residential custody on February 15, 1995. Includes 66,236 held because of delinquent offenses
(offenses that would also be illegal if they were adults), 1,785 for status offenses (offenses that would not be
illegal if they were adult, such as truancy), 889 for other offenses and 165 whose offenses were unknown.

Public Juvenile Facilities Administered by State and Local Governments in 1993

National Total = 1,025 Facilities*

	ALPHA ORDER					RANK ORDER		
RANK	STATE	FACILITIES	% of USA		RANK	STATE	FACILITIES	% of USA
19	Alabama	16	1.56%		1	California	103	10.05%
39	Alaska	5	0.49%		2	New York	65	6.34%
23	Arizona	14	1.37%		3	Ohio	62	6.05%
30	Arkansas	10	0.98%		4	Virginia	58	5.66%
1	California	103	10.05%		5	Texas	55	5.37%
32	Colorado	9	0.88%		6	Florida	49	4.78%
40	Connecticut	4	0.39%		7	New Jersey	46	4.49%
42	Delaware	3	0.29%		8	Missouri	45	4.39%
6	Florida	49	4.78%		9	Michigan	43	4.20%
13	Georgia	28	2.73%		10	Pennsylvania	34	3.32%
45	Hawaii	2	0.20%		11	Indiana	31	3.02%
42	Idaho	3	0.29%		12	Washington	30	2.93%
17	Illinois	19	1.85%		13	Georgia	28	2.73%
11	Indiana	31	3.02%		14	Kentucky	27	2.63%
25	Iowa	13	1.27%		15	North Carolina	24	2.34%
25	Kansas	13	1.27%		16	Tennessee	23	2.24%
14	Kentucky	27	2.63%		17	Illinois	19	1.85%
22	Louisiana	15	1.46%		18	Minnesota	18	1.76%
48	Maine	1	0.10%		19	Alabama	16	1.56%
25	Maryland	13	1.27%		19	Oklahoma	16	1.56%
30	Massachusetts	10	0.98%		19	Utah	16	1.56%
9	Michigan	43	4.20%		22	Louisiana	15	1.46%
18	Minnesota	18	1.76%		23	Arizona	14	1.37%
32	Mississippi	9	0.88%		23	New Mexico	14	1.37%
8	Missouri	45	4.39%		25	Iowa	13	1.27%
36	Montana	6	0.59%		25	Kansas	13	1.27%
40	Nebraska	4	0.39%		25	Maryland	13	1.27%
32	Nevada	9	0.88%		25	Oregon	13	1.27%
45	New Hampshire	2	0.20%		25	Wisconsin	13	1.27%
7	New Jersey	46	4.49%		30	Arkansas	10	0.98%
23	New Mexico	14	1.37%		30	Massachusetts	10	0.98%
2	New York	65	6.34%		32	Colorado	9	0.88%
15	North Carolina	24	2.34%		32	Mississippi	9	0.88%
42	North Dakota	3	0.29%		32	Nevada	9	0.88%
3	Ohio	62	6.05%		32	South Carolina	9	0.88%
19	Oklahoma	16	1.56%		36	Montana	6	0.59%
25	Oregon	13	1.27%		36	South Dakota	6	0.59%
10	Pennsylvania	34	3.32%		36	West Virginia	6	0.59%
48	Rhode Island	1	0.10%		39	Alaska	5	0.49%
32	South Carolina	9	0.88%		40	Connecticut	4	0.39%
36	South Dakota	6	0.59%		40	Nebraska	4	0.39%
16	Tennessee	23	2.24%		42	Delaware	3	0.29%
5	Texas	55	5.37%		42	Idaho	3	0.29%
19	Utah	16	1.56%		42	North Dakota	3	0.29%
48	Vermont	1	0.10%		45	Hawaii	2	0.20%
4	Virginia	58	5.66%		45	New Hampshire	2	0.20%
12	Washington	30	2.93%		45	Wyoming	2	0.20%
36	West Virginia	6	0.59%		48	Maine	1	0.10%
25	Wisconsin	13	1.27%		48	Rhode Island	1	0.10%
45	Wyoming	2	0.20%		48	Vermont	1	0.10%
						District of Columbia	4	0.39%

Source: U.S. Department of Justice, Office of Juvenile Justice and Delinquency Prevention
   "Juveniles in Public Facilities, 1993" (Fact Sheet #25, May 1995)
*Public facilities available to hold delinquent and status offenders.

Admissions of Juveniles to Alcohol and Other Drug Treatment Programs in 1995

National Total = 121,149 Juvenile Admissions*

ALPHA ORDER

RANK	STATE	ADMISSIONS	% of USA
31	Alabama	1,054	0.87%
34	Alaska	681	0.56%
46	Arizona	51	0.04%
30	Arkansas	1,070	0.88%
2	California	9,950	8.21%
12	Colorado	3,683	3.04%
39	Connecticut	509	0.42%
47	Delaware	14	0.01%
1	Florida	11,140	9.20%
20	Georgia	1,830	1.51%
29	Hawaii	1,118	0.92%
26	Idaho	1,225	1.01%
5	Illinois	6,986	5.77%
33	Indiana	773	0.64%
14	Iowa	3,029	2.50%
23	Kansas	1,635	1.35%
27	Kentucky	1,202	0.99%
28	Louisiana	1,155	0.95%
35	Maine	583	0.48%
8	Maryland	5,145	4.25%
17	Massachusetts	2,396	1.98%
9	Michigan	4,495	3.71%
NA	Minnesota**	NA	NA
36	Mississippi	570	0.47%
24	Missouri	1,552	1.28%
45	Montana	270	0.22%
19	Nebraska	1,910	1.58%
43	Nevada	343	0.28%
40	New Hampshire	424	0.35%
15	New Jersey	2,884	2.38%
41	New Mexico	389	0.32%
4	New York	8,714	7.19%
16	North Carolina	2,733	2.26%
44	North Dakota	326	0.27%
3	Ohio	8,799	7.26%
42	Oklahoma	344	0.28%
10	Oregon	4,338	3.58%
6	Pennsylvania	6,495	5.36%
37	Rhode Island	563	0.46%
25	South Carolina	1,541	1.27%
18	South Dakota	2,058	1.70%
NA	Tennessee**	NA	NA
13	Texas	3,115	2.57%
22	Utah	1,682	1.39%
38	Vermont	537	0.44%
21	Virginia	1,807	1.49%
7	Washington	5,353	4.42%
32	West Virginia	795	0.66%
11	Wisconsin	3,799	3.14%
NA	Wyoming**	NA	NA

RANK ORDER

RANK	STATE	ADMISSIONS	% of USA
1	Florida	11,140	9.20%
2	California	9,950	8.21%
3	Ohio	8,799	7.26%
4	New York	8,714	7.19%
5	Illinois	6,986	5.77%
6	Pennsylvania	6,495	5.36%
7	Washington	5,353	4.42%
8	Maryland	5,145	4.25%
9	Michigan	4,495	3.71%
10	Oregon	4,338	3.58%
11	Wisconsin	3,799	3.14%
12	Colorado	3,683	3.04%
13	Texas	3,115	2.57%
14	Iowa	3,029	2.50%
15	New Jersey	2,884	2.38%
16	North Carolina	2,733	2.26%
17	Massachusetts	2,396	1.98%
18	South Dakota	2,058	1.70%
19	Nebraska	1,910	1.58%
20	Georgia	1,830	1.51%
21	Virginia	1,807	1.49%
22	Utah	1,682	1.39%
23	Kansas	1,635	1.35%
24	Missouri	1,552	1.28%
25	South Carolina	1,541	1.27%
26	Idaho	1,225	1.01%
27	Kentucky	1,202	0.99%
28	Louisiana	1,155	0.95%
29	Hawaii	1,118	0.92%
30	Arkansas	1,070	0.88%
31	Alabama	1,054	0.87%
32	West Virginia	795	0.66%
33	Indiana	773	0.64%
34	Alaska	681	0.56%
35	Maine	583	0.48%
36	Mississippi	570	0.47%
37	Rhode Island	563	0.46%
38	Vermont	537	0.44%
39	Connecticut	509	0.42%
40	New Hampshire	424	0.35%
41	New Mexico	389	0.32%
42	Oklahoma	344	0.28%
43	Nevada	343	0.28%
44	North Dakota	326	0.27%
45	Montana	270	0.22%
46	Arizona	51	0.04%
47	Delaware	14	0.01%
NA	Minnesota**	NA	NA
NA	Tennessee**	NA	NA
NA	Wyoming**	NA	NA

District of Columbia	84	0.07%

Source: U.S. Department of Health and Human Services, Substance Abuse and Mental Health Services Administration "State Resources and Services Related to Alcohol and Other Drug Problems-Fiscal Year 1995" (July 1997)
Youths 17 years and younger. Does not include 2,361 admissions of juveniles in U.S. territories. Data are only from treatment units that received at least some funds administered by a state's alcohol/drug agency in fiscal year 1995. An additional 87,857 admissions were not reported by age.
***Not available.*

Admissions of Juveniles to Alcohol and Other Drug Treatment Programs As a Percent of All Admissions in 1995
National Percent = 6.5% of Admissions*

<table>
<tr><td colspan="3">ALPHA ORDER</td><td colspan="3">RANK ORDER</td></tr>
<tr><th>RANK</th><th>STATE</th><th>PERCENT</th><th>RANK</th><th>STATE</th><th>PERCENT</th></tr>
<tr><td>19</td><td>Alabama</td><td>7.1</td><td>1</td><td>Hawaii</td><td>24.9</td></tr>
<tr><td>18</td><td>Alaska</td><td>7.5</td><td>2</td><td>Idaho</td><td>22.2</td></tr>
<tr><td>46</td><td>Arizona</td><td>0.2</td><td>3</td><td>South Dakota</td><td>16.6</td></tr>
<tr><td>17</td><td>Arkansas</td><td>7.7</td><td>4</td><td>Maryland</td><td>14.9</td></tr>
<tr><td>31</td><td>California</td><td>5.2</td><td>5</td><td>Iowa</td><td>12.6</td></tr>
<tr><td>20</td><td>Colorado</td><td>7.0</td><td>6</td><td>Ohio</td><td>11.9</td></tr>
<tr><td>45</td><td>Connecticut</td><td>1.2</td><td>7</td><td>Washington</td><td>11.7</td></tr>
<tr><td>46</td><td>Delaware</td><td>0.2</td><td>8</td><td>New Hampshire</td><td>10.9</td></tr>
<tr><td>9</td><td>Florida</td><td>10.7</td><td>9</td><td>Florida</td><td>10.7</td></tr>
<tr><td>41</td><td>Georgia</td><td>3.0</td><td>10</td><td>Utah</td><td>10.1</td></tr>
<tr><td>1</td><td>Hawaii</td><td>24.9</td><td>11</td><td>North Dakota</td><td>9.9</td></tr>
<tr><td>2</td><td>Idaho</td><td>22.2</td><td>12</td><td>Pennsylvania</td><td>9.5</td></tr>
<tr><td>24</td><td>Illinois</td><td>5.7</td><td>13</td><td>Oregon</td><td>9.3</td></tr>
<tr><td>43</td><td>Indiana</td><td>2.8</td><td>14</td><td>Nebraska</td><td>8.9</td></tr>
<tr><td>5</td><td>Iowa</td><td>12.6</td><td>15</td><td>Kansas</td><td>8.5</td></tr>
<tr><td>15</td><td>Kansas</td><td>8.5</td><td>16</td><td>Vermont</td><td>8.0</td></tr>
<tr><td>22</td><td>Kentucky</td><td>6.1</td><td>17</td><td>Arkansas</td><td>7.7</td></tr>
<tr><td>39</td><td>Louisiana</td><td>4.2</td><td>18</td><td>Alaska</td><td>7.5</td></tr>
<tr><td>21</td><td>Maine</td><td>6.4</td><td>19</td><td>Alabama</td><td>7.1</td></tr>
<tr><td>4</td><td>Maryland</td><td>14.9</td><td>20</td><td>Colorado</td><td>7.0</td></tr>
<tr><td>44</td><td>Massachusetts</td><td>2.4</td><td>21</td><td>Maine</td><td>6.4</td></tr>
<tr><td>29</td><td>Michigan</td><td>5.3</td><td>22</td><td>Kentucky</td><td>6.1</td></tr>
<tr><td>NA</td><td>Minnesota**</td><td>NA</td><td>23</td><td>South Carolina</td><td>5.8</td></tr>
<tr><td>39</td><td>Mississippi</td><td>4.2</td><td>24</td><td>Illinois</td><td>5.7</td></tr>
<tr><td>37</td><td>Missouri</td><td>4.6</td><td>24</td><td>New Jersey</td><td>5.7</td></tr>
<tr><td>36</td><td>Montana</td><td>4.7</td><td>26</td><td>New York</td><td>5.6</td></tr>
<tr><td>14</td><td>Nebraska</td><td>8.9</td><td>26</td><td>Texas</td><td>5.6</td></tr>
<tr><td>29</td><td>Nevada</td><td>5.3</td><td>28</td><td>North Carolina</td><td>5.4</td></tr>
<tr><td>8</td><td>New Hampshire</td><td>10.9</td><td>29</td><td>Michigan</td><td>5.3</td></tr>
<tr><td>24</td><td>New Jersey</td><td>5.7</td><td>29</td><td>Nevada</td><td>5.3</td></tr>
<tr><td>41</td><td>New Mexico</td><td>3.0</td><td>31</td><td>California</td><td>5.2</td></tr>
<tr><td>26</td><td>New York</td><td>5.6</td><td>31</td><td>Wisconsin</td><td>5.2</td></tr>
<tr><td>28</td><td>North Carolina</td><td>5.4</td><td>33</td><td>Rhode Island</td><td>5.0</td></tr>
<tr><td>11</td><td>North Dakota</td><td>9.9</td><td>33</td><td>Virginia</td><td>5.0</td></tr>
<tr><td>6</td><td>Ohio</td><td>11.9</td><td>33</td><td>West Virginia</td><td>5.0</td></tr>
<tr><td>38</td><td>Oklahoma</td><td>4.5</td><td>36</td><td>Montana</td><td>4.7</td></tr>
<tr><td>13</td><td>Oregon</td><td>9.3</td><td>37</td><td>Missouri</td><td>4.6</td></tr>
<tr><td>12</td><td>Pennsylvania</td><td>9.5</td><td>38</td><td>Oklahoma</td><td>4.5</td></tr>
<tr><td>33</td><td>Rhode Island</td><td>5.0</td><td>39</td><td>Louisiana</td><td>4.2</td></tr>
<tr><td>23</td><td>South Carolina</td><td>5.8</td><td>39</td><td>Mississippi</td><td>4.2</td></tr>
<tr><td>3</td><td>South Dakota</td><td>16.6</td><td>41</td><td>Georgia</td><td>3.0</td></tr>
<tr><td>NA</td><td>Tennessee**</td><td>NA</td><td>41</td><td>New Mexico</td><td>3.0</td></tr>
<tr><td>26</td><td>Texas</td><td>5.6</td><td>43</td><td>Indiana</td><td>2.8</td></tr>
<tr><td>10</td><td>Utah</td><td>10.1</td><td>44</td><td>Massachusetts</td><td>2.4</td></tr>
<tr><td>16</td><td>Vermont</td><td>8.0</td><td>45</td><td>Connecticut</td><td>1.2</td></tr>
<tr><td>33</td><td>Virginia</td><td>5.0</td><td>46</td><td>Arizona</td><td>0.2</td></tr>
<tr><td>7</td><td>Washington</td><td>11.7</td><td>46</td><td>Delaware</td><td>0.2</td></tr>
<tr><td>33</td><td>West Virginia</td><td>5.0</td><td>NA</td><td>Minnesota**</td><td>NA</td></tr>
<tr><td>31</td><td>Wisconsin</td><td>5.2</td><td>NA</td><td>Tennessee**</td><td>NA</td></tr>
<tr><td>NA</td><td>Wyoming**</td><td>NA</td><td>NA</td><td>Wyoming**</td><td>NA</td></tr>
<tr><td></td><td></td><td></td><td></td><td>District of Columbia</td><td>0.6</td></tr>
</table>

Source: Morgan Quitno Press using data from U.S. Department of Health and Human Services, Substance Abuse and Mental Health Services Administration
"State Resources and Services Related to Alcohol and Other Drug Problems-Fiscal Year 1995" (July 1997)
*Youths 17 years and younger. Does not include admissions in U.S. territories. Data are only from treatment units that received at least some funds administered by a state's alcohol/drug agency in fiscal year 1995. An additional 87,857 admissions were not reported by age. **Not available.

Victims of Child Abuse and Neglect in 1996

National Total = 1,105,253 Children*

<table>
<tr><td colspan="4">ALPHA ORDER</td><td colspan="4">RANK ORDER</td></tr>
<tr><td>RANK</td><td>STATE</td><td>CHILDREN</td><td>% of USA</td><td>RANK</td><td>STATE</td><td>CHILDREN</td><td>% of USA</td></tr>
<tr><td>16</td><td>Alabama</td><td>21,205</td><td>1.9%</td><td>1</td><td>California</td><td>182,160</td><td>16.5%</td></tr>
<tr><td>35</td><td>Alaska</td><td>6,117</td><td>0.6%</td><td>2</td><td>New York</td><td>103,919</td><td>9.4%</td></tr>
<tr><td>17</td><td>Arizona</td><td>20,633</td><td>1.9%</td><td>3</td><td>Florida</td><td>91,462</td><td>8.3%</td></tr>
<tr><td>33</td><td>Arkansas</td><td>7,567</td><td>0.7%</td><td>4</td><td>Ohio</td><td>60,395</td><td>5.5%</td></tr>
<tr><td>1</td><td>California</td><td>182,160</td><td>16.5%</td><td>5</td><td>Texas</td><td>52,649</td><td>4.8%</td></tr>
<tr><td>29</td><td>Colorado</td><td>9,122</td><td>0.8%</td><td>6</td><td>Illinois</td><td>50,952</td><td>4.6%</td></tr>
<tr><td>8</td><td>Connecticut</td><td>43,194</td><td>3.9%</td><td>7</td><td>Georgia</td><td>48,572</td><td>4.4%</td></tr>
<tr><td>43</td><td>Delaware</td><td>2,337</td><td>0.2%</td><td>8</td><td>Connecticut</td><td>43,194</td><td>3.9%</td></tr>
<tr><td>3</td><td>Florida</td><td>91,462</td><td>8.3%</td><td>9</td><td>North Carolina</td><td>33,135</td><td>3.0%</td></tr>
<tr><td>7</td><td>Georgia</td><td>48,572</td><td>4.4%</td><td>10</td><td>Washington</td><td>32,309</td><td>2.9%</td></tr>
<tr><td>40</td><td>Hawaii</td><td>3,623</td><td>0.3%</td><td>11</td><td>Massachusetts</td><td>30,880</td><td>2.8%</td></tr>
<tr><td>30</td><td>Idaho</td><td>8,867</td><td>0.8%</td><td>12</td><td>Kentucky</td><td>27,296</td><td>2.5%</td></tr>
<tr><td>6</td><td>Illinois</td><td>50,952</td><td>4.6%</td><td>13</td><td>Indiana</td><td>22,861</td><td>2.1%</td></tr>
<tr><td>13</td><td>Indiana</td><td>22,861</td><td>2.1%</td><td>14</td><td>Michigan</td><td>21,933</td><td>2.0%</td></tr>
<tr><td>23</td><td>Iowa</td><td>11,840</td><td>1.1%</td><td>15</td><td>Missouri</td><td>21,834</td><td>2.0%</td></tr>
<tr><td>41</td><td>Kansas</td><td>3,264</td><td>0.3%</td><td>16</td><td>Alabama</td><td>21,205</td><td>1.9%</td></tr>
<tr><td>12</td><td>Kentucky</td><td>27,296</td><td>2.5%</td><td>17</td><td>Arizona</td><td>20,633</td><td>1.9%</td></tr>
<tr><td>20</td><td>Louisiana</td><td>14,911</td><td>1.3%</td><td>18</td><td>Wisconsin</td><td>19,624</td><td>1.8%</td></tr>
<tr><td>36</td><td>Maine</td><td>4,656</td><td>0.4%</td><td>19</td><td>Oklahoma</td><td>18,678</td><td>1.7%</td></tr>
<tr><td>NA</td><td>Maryland**</td><td>NA</td><td>NA</td><td>20</td><td>Louisiana</td><td>14,911</td><td>1.3%</td></tr>
<tr><td>11</td><td>Massachusetts</td><td>30,880</td><td>2.8%</td><td>21</td><td>South Carolina</td><td>13,839</td><td>1.3%</td></tr>
<tr><td>14</td><td>Michigan</td><td>21,933</td><td>2.0%</td><td>22</td><td>Virginia</td><td>12,239</td><td>1.1%</td></tr>
<tr><td>26</td><td>Minnesota</td><td>11,263</td><td>1.0%</td><td>23</td><td>Iowa</td><td>11,840</td><td>1.1%</td></tr>
<tr><td>NA</td><td>Mississippi**</td><td>NA</td><td>NA</td><td>24</td><td>Tennessee</td><td>11,439</td><td>1.0%</td></tr>
<tr><td>15</td><td>Missouri</td><td>21,834</td><td>2.0%</td><td>25</td><td>Oregon</td><td>11,354</td><td>1.0%</td></tr>
<tr><td>39</td><td>Montana</td><td>3,664</td><td>0.3%</td><td>26</td><td>Minnesota</td><td>11,263</td><td>1.0%</td></tr>
<tr><td>38</td><td>Nebraska</td><td>3,671</td><td>0.3%</td><td>27</td><td>Nevada</td><td>10,568</td><td>1.0%</td></tr>
<tr><td>27</td><td>Nevada</td><td>10,568</td><td>1.0%</td><td>28</td><td>New Jersey</td><td>10,537</td><td>1.0%</td></tr>
<tr><td>44</td><td>New Hampshire</td><td>1,280</td><td>0.1%</td><td>29</td><td>Colorado</td><td>9,122</td><td>0.8%</td></tr>
<tr><td>28</td><td>New Jersey</td><td>10,537</td><td>1.0%</td><td>30</td><td>Idaho</td><td>8,867</td><td>0.8%</td></tr>
<tr><td>31</td><td>New Mexico</td><td>8,845</td><td>0.8%</td><td>31</td><td>New Mexico</td><td>8,845</td><td>0.8%</td></tr>
<tr><td>2</td><td>New York</td><td>103,919</td><td>9.4%</td><td>32</td><td>Utah</td><td>8,538</td><td>0.8%</td></tr>
<tr><td>9</td><td>North Carolina</td><td>33,135</td><td>3.0%</td><td>33</td><td>Arkansas</td><td>7,567</td><td>0.7%</td></tr>
<tr><td>NA</td><td>North Dakota**</td><td>NA</td><td>NA</td><td>34</td><td>Pennsylvania</td><td>6,371</td><td>0.6%</td></tr>
<tr><td>4</td><td>Ohio</td><td>60,395</td><td>5.5%</td><td>35</td><td>Alaska</td><td>6,117</td><td>0.6%</td></tr>
<tr><td>19</td><td>Oklahoma</td><td>18,678</td><td>1.7%</td><td>36</td><td>Maine</td><td>4,656</td><td>0.4%</td></tr>
<tr><td>25</td><td>Oregon</td><td>11,354</td><td>1.0%</td><td>37</td><td>Rhode Island</td><td>4,626</td><td>0.4%</td></tr>
<tr><td>34</td><td>Pennsylvania</td><td>6,371</td><td>0.6%</td><td>38</td><td>Nebraska</td><td>3,671</td><td>0.3%</td></tr>
<tr><td>37</td><td>Rhode Island</td><td>4,626</td><td>0.4%</td><td>39</td><td>Montana</td><td>3,664</td><td>0.3%</td></tr>
<tr><td>21</td><td>South Carolina</td><td>13,839</td><td>1.3%</td><td>40</td><td>Hawaii</td><td>3,623</td><td>0.3%</td></tr>
<tr><td>42</td><td>South Dakota</td><td>2,935</td><td>0.3%</td><td>41</td><td>Kansas</td><td>3,264</td><td>0.3%</td></tr>
<tr><td>24</td><td>Tennessee</td><td>11,439</td><td>1.0%</td><td>42</td><td>South Dakota</td><td>2,935</td><td>0.3%</td></tr>
<tr><td>5</td><td>Texas</td><td>52,649</td><td>4.8%</td><td>43</td><td>Delaware</td><td>2,337</td><td>0.2%</td></tr>
<tr><td>32</td><td>Utah</td><td>8,538</td><td>0.8%</td><td>44</td><td>New Hampshire</td><td>1,280</td><td>0.1%</td></tr>
<tr><td>45</td><td>Vermont</td><td>1,194</td><td>0.1%</td><td>45</td><td>Vermont</td><td>1,194</td><td>0.1%</td></tr>
<tr><td>22</td><td>Virginia</td><td>12,239</td><td>1.1%</td><td>46</td><td>Wyoming</td><td>1,028</td><td>0.1%</td></tr>
<tr><td>10</td><td>Washington</td><td>32,309</td><td>2.9%</td><td>NA</td><td>Maryland**</td><td>NA</td><td>NA</td></tr>
<tr><td>NA</td><td>West Virginia**</td><td>NA</td><td>NA</td><td>NA</td><td>Mississippi**</td><td>NA</td><td>NA</td></tr>
<tr><td>18</td><td>Wisconsin</td><td>19,624</td><td>1.8%</td><td>NA</td><td>North Dakota**</td><td>NA</td><td>NA</td></tr>
<tr><td>46</td><td>Wyoming</td><td>1,028</td><td>0.1%</td><td>NA</td><td>West Virginia**</td><td>NA</td><td>NA</td></tr>
<tr><td></td><td></td><td></td><td></td><td></td><td>District of Columbia</td><td>5,867</td><td>0.5%</td></tr>
</table>

Source: U.S. Department of Health and Human Services, Children's Bureau
"Child Maltreatment 1996: Reports from the States to the National Child Abuse and Neglect Data System"
*State-substantiated or indicated incidents. Some children may be counted twice if they were victims of multiple types of abuse. Fifty-two percent of maltreated children suffered neglect, 24% physical abuse, 12% sexual abuse, 6% emotional maltreatment, 3% medical neglect and 16% other forms of maltreatment. More than half of the abused or neglected children were 7 years old or younger, with about 28% younger than four years old. **Not available.

Rate of Abuse and Neglect in 1996

National Rate = 16.6 Abused Children per 1,000 Population Under 18*

<table>
<tr><td colspan="3">ALPHA ORDER</td><td colspan="3">RANK ORDER</td></tr>
<tr><th>RANK</th><th>STATE</th><th>RATE</th><th>RANK</th><th>STATE</th><th>RATE</th></tr>
<tr><td>15</td><td>Alabama</td><td>19.7</td><td>1</td><td>Connecticut</td><td>54.7</td></tr>
<tr><td>2</td><td>Alaska</td><td>32.8</td><td>2</td><td>Alaska</td><td>32.8</td></tr>
<tr><td>18</td><td>Arizona</td><td>16.8</td><td>3</td><td>Kentucky</td><td>28.3</td></tr>
<tr><td>33</td><td>Arkansas</td><td>11.5</td><td>4</td><td>Florida</td><td>26.8</td></tr>
<tr><td>13</td><td>California</td><td>20.5</td><td>5</td><td>Idaho</td><td>25.5</td></tr>
<tr><td>35</td><td>Colorado</td><td>9.2</td><td>6</td><td>Nevada</td><td>25.2</td></tr>
<tr><td>1</td><td>Connecticut</td><td>54.7</td><td>7</td><td>Georgia</td><td>24.9</td></tr>
<tr><td>29</td><td>Delaware</td><td>13.2</td><td>8</td><td>New York</td><td>22.9</td></tr>
<tr><td>4</td><td>Florida</td><td>26.8</td><td>9</td><td>Washington</td><td>22.5</td></tr>
<tr><td>7</td><td>Georgia</td><td>24.9</td><td>10</td><td>Massachusetts</td><td>21.5</td></tr>
<tr><td>32</td><td>Hawaii</td><td>11.9</td><td>11</td><td>Oklahoma</td><td>21.4</td></tr>
<tr><td>5</td><td>Idaho</td><td>25.5</td><td>12</td><td>Ohio</td><td>21.3</td></tr>
<tr><td>20</td><td>Illinois</td><td>16.2</td><td>13</td><td>California</td><td>20.5</td></tr>
<tr><td>24</td><td>Indiana</td><td>15.3</td><td>14</td><td>Rhode Island</td><td>19.8</td></tr>
<tr><td>19</td><td>Iowa</td><td>16.4</td><td>15</td><td>Alabama</td><td>19.7</td></tr>
<tr><td>44</td><td>Kansas</td><td>4.8</td><td>16</td><td>North Carolina</td><td>18.1</td></tr>
<tr><td>3</td><td>Kentucky</td><td>28.3</td><td>17</td><td>New Mexico</td><td>17.8</td></tr>
<tr><td>31</td><td>Louisiana</td><td>12.3</td><td>18</td><td>Arizona</td><td>16.8</td></tr>
<tr><td>23</td><td>Maine</td><td>15.6</td><td>19</td><td>Iowa</td><td>16.4</td></tr>
<tr><td>NA</td><td>Maryland**</td><td>NA</td><td>20</td><td>Illinois</td><td>16.2</td></tr>
<tr><td>10</td><td>Massachusetts</td><td>21.5</td><td>21</td><td>Montana</td><td>15.9</td></tr>
<tr><td>37</td><td>Michigan</td><td>8.7</td><td>22</td><td>Missouri</td><td>15.7</td></tr>
<tr><td>36</td><td>Minnesota</td><td>9.1</td><td>23</td><td>Maine</td><td>15.6</td></tr>
<tr><td>NA</td><td>Mississippi**</td><td>NA</td><td>24</td><td>Indiana</td><td>15.3</td></tr>
<tr><td>22</td><td>Missouri</td><td>15.7</td><td>25</td><td>South Carolina</td><td>14.6</td></tr>
<tr><td>21</td><td>Montana</td><td>15.9</td><td>25</td><td>South Dakota</td><td>14.6</td></tr>
<tr><td>39</td><td>Nebraska</td><td>8.3</td><td>25</td><td>Wisconsin</td><td>14.6</td></tr>
<tr><td>6</td><td>Nevada</td><td>25.2</td><td>28</td><td>Oregon</td><td>14.1</td></tr>
<tr><td>45</td><td>New Hampshire</td><td>4.4</td><td>29</td><td>Delaware</td><td>13.2</td></tr>
<tr><td>43</td><td>New Jersey</td><td>5.3</td><td>30</td><td>Utah</td><td>12.5</td></tr>
<tr><td>17</td><td>New Mexico</td><td>17.8</td><td>31</td><td>Louisiana</td><td>12.3</td></tr>
<tr><td>8</td><td>New York</td><td>22.9</td><td>32</td><td>Hawaii</td><td>11.9</td></tr>
<tr><td>16</td><td>North Carolina</td><td>18.1</td><td>33</td><td>Arkansas</td><td>11.5</td></tr>
<tr><td>NA</td><td>North Dakota**</td><td>NA</td><td>34</td><td>Texas</td><td>9.6</td></tr>
<tr><td>12</td><td>Ohio</td><td>21.3</td><td>35</td><td>Colorado</td><td>9.2</td></tr>
<tr><td>11</td><td>Oklahoma</td><td>21.4</td><td>36</td><td>Minnesota</td><td>9.1</td></tr>
<tr><td>28</td><td>Oregon</td><td>14.1</td><td>37</td><td>Michigan</td><td>8.7</td></tr>
<tr><td>46</td><td>Pennsylvania</td><td>2.2</td><td>37</td><td>Tennessee</td><td>8.7</td></tr>
<tr><td>14</td><td>Rhode Island</td><td>19.8</td><td>39</td><td>Nebraska</td><td>8.3</td></tr>
<tr><td>25</td><td>South Carolina</td><td>14.6</td><td>40</td><td>Vermont</td><td>8.2</td></tr>
<tr><td>25</td><td>South Dakota</td><td>14.6</td><td>41</td><td>Wyoming</td><td>7.7</td></tr>
<tr><td>37</td><td>Tennessee</td><td>8.7</td><td>42</td><td>Virginia</td><td>7.5</td></tr>
<tr><td>34</td><td>Texas</td><td>9.6</td><td>43</td><td>New Jersey</td><td>5.3</td></tr>
<tr><td>30</td><td>Utah</td><td>12.5</td><td>44</td><td>Kansas</td><td>4.8</td></tr>
<tr><td>40</td><td>Vermont</td><td>8.2</td><td>45</td><td>New Hampshire</td><td>4.4</td></tr>
<tr><td>42</td><td>Virginia</td><td>7.5</td><td>46</td><td>Pennsylvania</td><td>2.2</td></tr>
<tr><td>9</td><td>Washington</td><td>22.5</td><td>NA</td><td>Maryland**</td><td>NA</td></tr>
<tr><td>NA</td><td>West Virginia**</td><td>NA</td><td>NA</td><td>Mississippi**</td><td>NA</td></tr>
<tr><td>25</td><td>Wisconsin</td><td>14.6</td><td>NA</td><td>North Dakota**</td><td>NA</td></tr>
<tr><td>41</td><td>Wyoming</td><td>7.7</td><td>NA</td><td>West Virginia**</td><td>NA</td></tr>
<tr><td></td><td></td><td></td><td></td><td>District of Columbia</td><td>53.6</td></tr>
</table>

Source: Morgan Quitno Press using data from U.S. Department of Health and Human Services, Children's Bureau
"Child Maltreatment 1996: Reports from the States to the National Child Abuse and Neglect Data System"
*State-substantiated or indicated incidents. National total is for reporting states only. Fifty-two percent of maltreated children suffered neglect, 24% physical abuse, 12% sexual abuse, 6% emotional maltreatment, 3% medical neglect and 16% other forms of maltreatment. More than half of the abused or neglected children were 7 years old or younger, with about 28% younger than four years old. **Not available.

Physically Abused Children in 1996

National Total = 229,264 Children*

<u>ALPHA ORDER</u>

RANK	STATE	CHILDREN	% of USA
8	Alabama	6,653	2.9%
30	Alaska	1,930	0.8%
14	Arizona	4,400	1.9%
34	Arkansas	1,369	0.6%
1	California	57,745	25.2%
27	Colorado	2,234	1.0%
15	Connecticut	4,351	1.9%
44	Delaware	303	0.1%
2	Florida	15,865	6.9%
6	Georgia	8,499	3.7%
40	Hawaii	682	0.3%
20	Idaho	3,014	1.3%
11	Illinois	4,713	2.1%
12	Indiana	4,647	2.0%
17	Iowa	3,525	1.5%
38	Kansas	838	0.4%
7	Kentucky	7,132	3.1%
21	Louisiana	2,966	1.3%
39	Maine	712	0.3%
NA	Maryland**	NA	NA
9	Massachusetts	6,650	2.9%
13	Michigan	4,611	2.0%
19	Minnesota	3,240	1.4%
NA	Mississippi**	NA	NA
18	Missouri	3,409	1.5%
41	Montana	553	0.2%
37	Nebraska	937	0.4%
35	Nevada	1,339	0.6%
43	New Hampshire	374	0.2%
25	New Jersey	2,644	1.2%
28	New Mexico	2,010	0.9%
5	New York	13,455	5.9%
33	North Carolina	1,514	0.7%
NA	North Dakota**	NA	NA
4	Ohio	13,825	6.0%
22	Oklahoma	2,835	1.2%
32	Oregon	1,658	0.7%
23	Pennsylvania	2,777	1.2%
36	Rhode Island	1,271	0.6%
29	South Carolina	1,973	0.9%
42	South Dakota	529	0.2%
26	Tennessee	2,257	1.0%
3	Texas	14,329	6.3%
31	Utah	1,818	0.8%
45	Vermont	273	0.1%
24	Virginia	2,765	1.2%
10	Washington	6,080	2.7%
NA	West Virginia**	NA	NA
16	Wisconsin	3,851	1.7%
46	Wyoming	243	0.1%

<u>RANK ORDER</u>

RANK	STATE	CHILDREN	% of USA
1	California	57,745	25.2%
2	Florida	15,865	6.9%
3	Texas	14,329	6.3%
4	Ohio	13,825	6.0%
5	New York	13,455	5.9%
6	Georgia	8,499	3.7%
7	Kentucky	7,132	3.1%
8	Alabama	6,653	2.9%
9	Massachusetts	6,650	2.9%
10	Washington	6,080	2.7%
11	Illinois	4,713	2.1%
12	Indiana	4,647	2.0%
13	Michigan	4,611	2.0%
14	Arizona	4,400	1.9%
15	Connecticut	4,351	1.9%
16	Wisconsin	3,851	1.7%
17	Iowa	3,525	1.5%
18	Missouri	3,409	1.5%
19	Minnesota	3,240	1.4%
20	Idaho	3,014	1.3%
21	Louisiana	2,966	1.3%
22	Oklahoma	2,835	1.2%
23	Pennsylvania	2,777	1.2%
24	Virginia	2,765	1.2%
25	New Jersey	2,644	1.2%
26	Tennessee	2,257	1.0%
27	Colorado	2,234	1.0%
28	New Mexico	2,010	0.9%
29	South Carolina	1,973	0.9%
30	Alaska	1,930	0.8%
31	Utah	1,818	0.8%
32	Oregon	1,658	0.7%
33	North Carolina	1,514	0.7%
34	Arkansas	1,369	0.6%
35	Nevada	1,339	0.6%
36	Rhode Island	1,271	0.6%
37	Nebraska	937	0.4%
38	Kansas	838	0.4%
39	Maine	712	0.3%
40	Hawaii	682	0.3%
41	Montana	553	0.2%
42	South Dakota	529	0.2%
43	New Hampshire	374	0.2%
44	Delaware	303	0.1%
45	Vermont	273	0.1%
46	Wyoming	243	0.1%
NA	Maryland**	NA	NA
NA	Mississippi**	NA	NA
NA	North Dakota**	NA	NA
NA	West Virginia**	NA	NA
	District of Columbia	466	0.2%

Source: U.S. Department of Health and Human Services, Children's Bureau
"Child Maltreatment 1996: Reports from the States to the National Child Abuse and Neglect Data System"
*State-substantiated or indicated incidents. National total is for reporting states only. Fifty-two percent of maltreated children suffered neglect, 24% physical abuse, 12% sexual abuse, 6% emotional maltreatment, 3% medical neglect and 16% other forms of maltreatment. More than half of the abused or neglected children were 7 years old or younger, with about 28% younger than four years old. **Not available.*

Rate of Physically Abused Children in 1996

National Rate = 3.5 Physically Abused Children per 1,000 Population Under 18*

ALPHA ORDER				RANK ORDER		
RANK	**STATE**	**RATE**		**RANK**	**STATE**	**RATE**
5	Alabama	6.2		1	Alaska	10.4
1	Alaska	10.4		2	Idaho	8.7
15	Arizona	3.6		3	Kentucky	7.4
31	Arkansas	2.1		4	California	6.5
4	California	6.5		5	Alabama	6.2
29	Colorado	2.2		6	Connecticut	5.5
6	Connecticut	5.5		7	Rhode Island	5.4
38	Delaware	1.7		8	Iowa	4.9
10	Florida	4.7		8	Ohio	4.9
12	Georgia	4.4		10	Florida	4.7
29	Hawaii	2.2		11	Massachusetts	4.6
2	Idaho	8.7		12	Georgia	4.4
41	Illinois	1.5		13	Washington	4.2
18	Indiana	3.1		14	New Mexico	4.0
8	Iowa	4.9		15	Arizona	3.6
44	Kansas	1.2		16	Nevada	3.2
3	Kentucky	7.4		16	Oklahoma	3.2
25	Louisiana	2.4		18	Indiana	3.1
25	Maine	2.4		19	New York	3.0
NA	Maryland**	NA		20	Wisconsin	2.9
11	Massachusetts	4.6		21	Utah	2.7
36	Michigan	1.8		22	Minnesota	2.6
22	Minnesota	2.6		22	South Dakota	2.6
NA	Mississippi**	NA		22	Texas	2.6
25	Missouri	2.4		25	Louisiana	2.4
25	Montana	2.4		25	Maine	2.4
31	Nebraska	2.1		25	Missouri	2.4
16	Nevada	3.2		25	Montana	2.4
42	New Hampshire	1.3		29	Colorado	2.2
42	New Jersey	1.3		29	Hawaii	2.2
14	New Mexico	4.0		31	Arkansas	2.1
19	New York	3.0		31	Nebraska	2.1
46	North Carolina	0.8		31	Oregon	2.1
NA	North Dakota**	NA		31	South Carolina	2.1
8	Ohio	4.9		35	Vermont	1.9
16	Oklahoma	3.2		36	Michigan	1.8
31	Oregon	2.1		36	Wyoming	1.8
45	Pennsylvania	1.0		38	Delaware	1.7
7	Rhode Island	5.4		38	Tennessee	1.7
31	South Carolina	2.1		38	Virginia	1.7
22	South Dakota	2.6		41	Illinois	1.5
38	Tennessee	1.7		42	New Hampshire	1.3
22	Texas	2.6		42	New Jersey	1.3
21	Utah	2.7		44	Kansas	1.2
35	Vermont	1.9		45	Pennsylvania	1.0
38	Virginia	1.7		46	North Carolina	0.8
13	Washington	4.2		NA	Maryland**	NA
NA	West Virginia**	NA		NA	Mississippi**	NA
20	Wisconsin	2.9		NA	North Dakota**	NA
36	Wyoming	1.8		NA	West Virginia**	NA
					District of Columbia	4.3

*Source: Morgan Quitno Press using data from U.S. Department of Health and Human Services, Children's Bureau "Child Maltreatment 1996: Reports from the States to the National Child Abuse and Neglect Data System" *State-substantiated or indicated incidents. National total is for reporting states only. Fifty-two percent of maltreated children suffered neglect, 24% physical abuse, 12% sexual abuse, 6% emotional maltreatment, 3% medical neglect and 16% other forms of maltreatment. More than half of the abused or neglected children were 7 years old or younger, with about 28% younger than four years old. **Not available.*

Sexually Abused Children in 1996

National Total = 119,357 Children*

ALPHA ORDER

RANK	STATE	CHILDREN	% of USA
9	Alabama	3,975	3.3%
31	Alaska	893	0.7%
28	Arizona	1,017	0.9%
26	Arkansas	1,107	0.9%
1	California	28,963	24.3%
27	Colorado	1,056	0.9%
25	Connecticut	1,196	1.0%
45	Delaware	170	0.1%
5	Florida	6,363	5.3%
6	Georgia	4,497	3.8%
43	Hawaii	216	0.2%
17	Idaho	1,697	1.4%
7	Illinois	4,301	3.6%
8	Indiana	4,181	3.5%
22	Iowa	1,382	1.2%
30	Kansas	957	0.8%
16	Kentucky	2,042	1.7%
33	Louisiana	796	0.7%
39	Maine	377	0.3%
NA	Maryland**	NA	NA
21	Massachusetts	1,415	1.2%
19	Michigan	1,621	1.4%
32	Minnesota	852	0.7%
NA	Mississippi**	NA	NA
13	Missouri	2,695	2.3%
40	Montana	301	0.3%
37	Nebraska	441	0.4%
42	Nevada	221	0.2%
41	New Hampshire	250	0.2%
34	New Jersey	784	0.7%
35	New Mexico	604	0.5%
10	New York	3,357	2.8%
23	North Carolina	1,378	1.2%
NA	North Dakota**	NA	NA
2	Ohio	9,123	7.6%
24	Oklahoma	1,330	1.1%
20	Oregon	1,496	1.3%
11	Pennsylvania	2,722	2.3%
38	Rhode Island	383	0.3%
29	South Carolina	968	0.8%
44	South Dakota	210	0.2%
14	Tennessee	2,380	2.0%
3	Texas	7,567	6.3%
15	Utah	2,128	1.8%
36	Vermont	588	0.5%
18	Virginia	1,626	1.4%
12	Washington	2,700	2.3%
NA	West Virginia**	NA	NA
4	Wisconsin	6,834	5.7%
46	Wyoming	84	0.1%

RANK ORDER

RANK	STATE	CHILDREN	% of USA
1	California	28,963	24.3%
2	Ohio	9,123	7.6%
3	Texas	7,567	6.3%
4	Wisconsin	6,834	5.7%
5	Florida	6,363	5.3%
6	Georgia	4,497	3.8%
7	Illinois	4,301	3.6%
8	Indiana	4,181	3.5%
9	Alabama	3,975	3.3%
10	New York	3,357	2.8%
11	Pennsylvania	2,722	2.3%
12	Washington	2,700	2.3%
13	Missouri	2,695	2.3%
14	Tennessee	2,380	2.0%
15	Utah	2,128	1.8%
16	Kentucky	2,042	1.7%
17	Idaho	1,697	1.4%
18	Virginia	1,626	1.4%
19	Michigan	1,621	1.4%
20	Oregon	1,496	1.3%
21	Massachusetts	1,415	1.2%
22	Iowa	1,382	1.2%
23	North Carolina	1,378	1.2%
24	Oklahoma	1,330	1.1%
25	Connecticut	1,196	1.0%
26	Arkansas	1,107	0.9%
27	Colorado	1,056	0.9%
28	Arizona	1,017	0.9%
29	South Carolina	968	0.8%
30	Kansas	957	0.8%
31	Alaska	893	0.7%
32	Minnesota	852	0.7%
33	Louisiana	796	0.7%
34	New Jersey	784	0.7%
35	New Mexico	604	0.5%
36	Vermont	588	0.5%
37	Nebraska	441	0.4%
38	Rhode Island	383	0.3%
39	Maine	377	0.3%
40	Montana	301	0.3%
41	New Hampshire	250	0.2%
42	Nevada	221	0.2%
43	Hawaii	216	0.2%
44	South Dakota	210	0.2%
45	Delaware	170	0.1%
46	Wyoming	84	0.1%
NA	Maryland**	NA	NA
NA	Mississippi**	NA	NA
NA	North Dakota**	NA	NA
NA	West Virginia**	NA	NA
	District of Columbia	113	0.1%

Source: U.S. Department of Health and Human Services, Children's Bureau
"Child Maltreatment 1996: Reports from the States to the National Child Abuse and Neglect Data System"
*State-substantiated or indicated incidents. National total is for reporting states only. Fifty-two percent of maltreated children suffered neglect, 24% physical abuse, 12% sexual abuse, 6% emotional maltreatment, 3% medical neglect and 16% other forms of maltreatment. More than half of the abused or neglected children were 7 years old or younger, with about 28% younger than four years old. **Not available.*

Rate of Sexually Abused Children in 1996

National Rate = 1.8 Sexually Abused Children per 1,000 Population Under 18*

ALPHA ORDER				RANK ORDER		
RANK	STATE	RATE		RANK	STATE	RATE
5	Alabama	3.7		1	Wisconsin	5.1
3	Alaska	4.8		2	Idaho	4.9
37	Arizona	0.8		3	Alaska	4.8
18	Arkansas	1.7		4	Vermont	4.0
6	California	3.3		5	Alabama	3.7
28	Colorado	1.1		6	California	3.3
20	Connecticut	1.5		7	Ohio	3.2
29	Delaware	1.0		8	Utah	3.1
12	Florida	1.9		9	Indiana	2.8
10	Georgia	2.3		10	Georgia	2.3
39	Hawaii	0.7		11	Kentucky	2.1
2	Idaho	4.9		12	Florida	1.9
22	Illinois	1.4		12	Iowa	1.9
9	Indiana	2.8		12	Missouri	1.9
12	Iowa	1.9		12	Oregon	1.9
22	Kansas	1.4		12	Washington	1.9
11	Kentucky	2.1		17	Tennessee	1.8
39	Louisiana	0.7		18	Arkansas	1.7
25	Maine	1.3		19	Rhode Island	1.6
NA	Maryland**	NA		20	Connecticut	1.5
29	Massachusetts	1.0		20	Oklahoma	1.5
43	Michigan	0.6		22	Illinois	1.4
39	Minnesota	0.7		22	Kansas	1.4
NA	Mississippi**	NA		22	Texas	1.4
12	Missouri	1.9		25	Maine	1.3
25	Montana	1.3		25	Montana	1.3
29	Nebraska	1.0		27	New Mexico	1.2
45	Nevada	0.5		28	Colorado	1.1
35	New Hampshire	0.9		29	Delaware	1.0
46	New Jersey	0.4		29	Massachusetts	1.0
27	New Mexico	1.2		29	Nebraska	1.0
39	New York	0.7		29	South Carolina	1.0
37	North Carolina	0.8		29	South Dakota	1.0
NA	North Dakota**	NA		29	Virginia	1.0
7	Ohio	3.2		35	New Hampshire	0.9
20	Oklahoma	1.5		35	Pennsylvania	0.9
12	Oregon	1.9		37	Arizona	0.8
35	Pennsylvania	0.9		37	North Carolina	0.8
19	Rhode Island	1.6		39	Hawaii	0.7
29	South Carolina	1.0		39	Louisiana	0.7
29	South Dakota	1.0		39	Minnesota	0.7
17	Tennessee	1.8		39	New York	0.7
22	Texas	1.4		43	Michigan	0.6
8	Utah	3.1		43	Wyoming	0.6
4	Vermont	4.0		45	Nevada	0.5
29	Virginia	1.0		46	New Jersey	0.4
12	Washington	1.9		NA	Maryland**	NA
NA	West Virginia**	NA		NA	Mississippi**	NA
1	Wisconsin	5.1		NA	North Dakota**	NA
43	Wyoming	0.6		NA	West Virginia**	NA

District of Columbia   1.0

Source: Morgan Quitno Press using data from U.S. Department of Health and Human Services, Children's Bureau "Child Maltreatment 1996: Reports from the States to the National Child Abuse and Neglect Data System" *State-substantiated or indicated incidents. National total is for reporting states only. Fifty-two percent of maltreated children suffered neglect, 24% physical abuse, 12% sexual abuse, 6% emotional maltreatment, 3% medical neglect and 16% other forms of maltreatment. More than half of the abused or neglected children were 7 years old or younger, with about 28% younger than four years old. **Not available.

Emotionally Abused Children in 1996

National Total = 55,430 Children*

ALPHA ORDER

RANK	STATE	CHILDREN	% of USA
9	Alabama	1,385	2.5%
34	Alaska	142	0.3%
23	Arizona	471	0.8%
NA	Arkansas**	NA	NA
1	California	10,747	19.4%
14	Colorado	887	1.6%
2	Connecticut	10,214	18.4%
25	Delaware	377	0.7%
5	Florida	2,974	5.4%
7	Georgia	2,190	4.0%
33	Hawaii	146	0.3%
NA	Idaho**	NA	NA
20	Illinois	549	1.0%
NA	Indiana**	NA	NA
31	Iowa	163	0.3%
36	Kansas	111	0.2%
NA	Kentucky**	NA	NA
19	Louisiana	557	1.0%
8	Maine	1,938	3.5%
NA	Maryland**	NA	NA
18	Massachusetts	588	1.1%
17	Michigan	594	1.1%
28	Minnesota	215	0.4%
NA	Mississippi**	NA	NA
4	Missouri	3,409	6.2%
16	Montana	734	1.3%
NA	Nebraska**	NA	NA
21	Nevada	494	0.9%
38	New Hampshire	38	0.1%
27	New Jersey	237	0.4%
NA	New Mexico**	NA	NA
13	New York	969	1.7%
30	North Carolina	168	0.3%
NA	North Dakota**	NA	NA
3	Ohio	5,660	10.2%
15	Oklahoma	856	1.5%
12	Oregon	1,003	1.8%
35	Pennsylvania	118	0.2%
NA	Rhode Island**	NA	NA
32	South Carolina	153	0.3%
26	South Dakota	282	0.5%
22	Tennessee	480	0.9%
6	Texas	2,726	4.9%
10	Utah	1,295	2.3%
39	Vermont	7	0.0%
24	Virginia	420	0.8%
11	Washington	1,260	2.3%
NA	West Virginia**	NA	NA
29	Wisconsin	184	0.3%
37	Wyoming	39	0.1%

RANK ORDER

RANK	STATE	CHILDREN	% of USA
1	California	10,747	19.4%
2	Connecticut	10,214	18.4%
3	Ohio	5,660	10.2%
4	Missouri	3,409	6.2%
5	Florida	2,974	5.4%
6	Texas	2,726	4.9%
7	Georgia	2,190	4.0%
8	Maine	1,938	3.5%
9	Alabama	1,385	2.5%
10	Utah	1,295	2.3%
11	Washington	1,260	2.3%
12	Oregon	1,003	1.8%
13	New York	969	1.7%
14	Colorado	887	1.6%
15	Oklahoma	856	1.5%
16	Montana	734	1.3%
17	Michigan	594	1.1%
18	Massachusetts	588	1.1%
19	Louisiana	557	1.0%
20	Illinois	549	1.0%
21	Nevada	494	0.9%
22	Tennessee	480	0.9%
23	Arizona	471	0.8%
24	Virginia	420	0.8%
25	Delaware	377	0.7%
26	South Dakota	282	0.5%
27	New Jersey	237	0.4%
28	Minnesota	215	0.4%
29	Wisconsin	184	0.3%
30	North Carolina	168	0.3%
31	Iowa	163	0.3%
32	South Carolina	153	0.3%
33	Hawaii	146	0.3%
34	Alaska	142	0.3%
35	Pennsylvania	118	0.2%
36	Kansas	111	0.2%
37	Wyoming	39	0.1%
38	New Hampshire	38	0.1%
39	Vermont	7	0.0%
NA	Arkansas**	NA	NA
NA	Idaho**	NA	NA
NA	Indiana**	NA	NA
NA	Kentucky**	NA	NA
NA	Maryland**	NA	NA
NA	Mississippi**	NA	NA
NA	Nebraska**	NA	NA
NA	New Mexico**	NA	NA
NA	North Dakota**	NA	NA
NA	Rhode Island**	NA	NA
NA	West Virginia**	NA	NA
	District of Columbia	650	1.2%

Source: U.S. Department of Health and Human Services, Children's Bureau
"Child Maltreatment 1996: Reports from the States to the National Child Abuse and Neglect Data System"
*State-substantiated or indicated incidents. National total is for reporting states only. Fifty-two percent of maltreated children suffered neglect, 24% physical abuse, 12% sexual abuse, 6% emotional maltreatment, 3% medical neglect and 16% other forms of maltreatment. More than half of the abused or neglected children were 7 years old or younger, with about 28% younger than four years old. **Not available.

Rate of Emotionally Abused Children in 1996

National Rate = 0.9 Emotionally Abused Children per 1,000 Population Under 18*

ALPHA ORDER				RANK ORDER		
RANK	STATE	RATE		RANK	STATE	RATE
9	Alabama	1.3		1	Connecticut	12.9
18	Alaska	0.8		2	Maine	6.5
22	Arizona	0.4		3	Montana	3.2
NA	Arkansas**	NA		4	Missouri	2.4
10	California	1.2		5	Delaware	2.1
15	Colorado	0.9		6	Ohio	2.0
1	Connecticut	12.9		7	Utah	1.9
5	Delaware	2.1		8	South Dakota	1.4
15	Florida	0.9		9	Alabama	1.3
13	Georgia	1.1		10	California	1.2
19	Hawaii	0.5		10	Nevada	1.2
NA	Idaho**	NA		10	Oregon	1.2
27	Illinois	0.2		13	Georgia	1.1
NA	Indiana**	NA		14	Oklahoma	1.0
27	Iowa	0.2		15	Colorado	0.9
27	Kansas	0.2		15	Florida	0.9
NA	Kentucky**	NA		15	Washington	0.9
19	Louisiana	0.5		18	Alaska	0.8
2	Maine	6.5		19	Hawaii	0.5
NA	Maryland**	NA		19	Louisiana	0.5
22	Massachusetts	0.4		19	Texas	0.5
27	Michigan	0.2		22	Arizona	0.4
27	Minnesota	0.2		22	Massachusetts	0.4
NA	Mississippi**	NA		22	Tennessee	0.4
4	Missouri	2.4		25	Virginia	0.3
3	Montana	3.2		25	Wyoming	0.3
NA	Nebraska**	NA		27	Illinois	0.2
10	Nevada	1.2		27	Iowa	0.2
34	New Hampshire	0.1		27	Kansas	0.2
34	New Jersey	0.1		27	Michigan	0.2
NA	New Mexico**	NA		27	Minnesota	0.2
27	New York	0.2		27	New York	0.2
34	North Carolina	0.1		27	South Carolina	0.2
NA	North Dakota**	NA		34	New Hampshire	0.1
6	Ohio	2.0		34	New Jersey	0.1
14	Oklahoma	1.0		34	North Carolina	0.1
10	Oregon	1.2		34	Wisconsin	0.1
38	Pennsylvania	0.0		38	Pennsylvania	0.0
NA	Rhode Island**	NA		38	Vermont	0.0
27	South Carolina	0.2		NA	Arkansas**	NA
8	South Dakota	1.4		NA	Idaho**	NA
22	Tennessee	0.4		NA	Indiana**	NA
19	Texas	0.5		NA	Kentucky**	NA
7	Utah	1.9		NA	Maryland**	NA
38	Vermont	0.0		NA	Mississippi**	NA
25	Virginia	0.3		NA	Nebraska**	NA
15	Washington	0.9		NA	New Mexico**	NA
NA	West Virginia**	NA		NA	North Dakota**	NA
34	Wisconsin	0.1		NA	Rhode Island**	NA
25	Wyoming	0.3		NA	West Virginia**	NA

District of Columbia   5.9

Source: Morgan Quitno Press using data from U.S. Department of Health and Human Services, Children's Bureau
"Child Maltreatment 1996: Reports from the States to the National Child Abuse and Neglect Data System"
*State-substantiated or indicated incidents. National rate is for reporting states only. Fifty-two percent of maltreated children suffered neglect, 24% physical abuse, 12% sexual abuse, 6% emotional maltreatment, 3% medical neglect and 16% other forms of maltreatment. More than half of the abused or neglected children were 7 years old or younger, with about 28% younger than four years old. **Not available.

Neglected Children in 1996

National Total = 499,871 Children*

ALPHA ORDER				RANK ORDER			
RANK	STATE	CHILDREN	% of USA	RANK	STATE	CHILDREN	% of USA
17	Alabama	9,192	1.8%	1	California	84,158	16.8%
31	Alaska	3,144	0.6%	2	Florida	36,839	7.4%
21	Arizona	6,397	1.3%	3	Ohio	31,775	6.4%
35	Arkansas	2,146	0.4%	4	Georgia	29,226	5.8%
1	California	84,158	16.8%	5	North Carolina	28,867	5.8%
29	Colorado	4,440	0.9%	6	Texas	24,318	4.9%
11	Connecticut	15,344	3.1%	7	New York	22,971	4.6%
40	Delaware	845	0.2%	8	Massachusetts	22,148	4.4%
2	Florida	36,839	7.4%	9	Illinois	17,266	3.5%
4	Georgia	29,226	5.8%	10	Kentucky	16,994	3.4%
42	Hawaii	699	0.1%	11	Connecticut	15,344	3.1%
30	Idaho	3,741	0.7%	12	Indiana	12,799	2.6%
9	Illinois	17,266	3.5%	13	Oklahoma	11,844	2.4%
12	Indiana	12,799	2.6%	14	Michigan	11,605	2.3%
24	Iowa	6,069	1.2%	15	Louisiana	10,505	2.1%
41	Kansas	808	0.2%	16	Missouri	9,740	1.9%
10	Kentucky	16,994	3.4%	17	Alabama	9,192	1.8%
15	Louisiana	10,505	2.1%	18	Washington	8,706	1.7%
38	Maine	1,629	0.3%	19	Virginia	6,884	1.4%
NA	Maryland**	NA	NA	20	Minnesota	6,476	1.3%
8	Massachusetts	22,148	4.4%	21	Arizona	6,397	1.3%
14	Michigan	11,605	2.3%	22	New Mexico	6,231	1.2%
20	Minnesota	6,476	1.3%	23	Wisconsin	6,111	1.2%
NA	Mississippi**	NA	NA	24	Iowa	6,069	1.2%
16	Missouri	9,740	1.9%	25	New Jersey	5,824	1.2%
37	Montana	1,793	0.4%	26	South Carolina	5,627	1.1%
34	Nebraska	2,293	0.5%	27	Tennessee	4,874	1.0%
28	Nevada	4,464	0.9%	28	Nevada	4,464	0.9%
43	New Hampshire	618	0.1%	29	Colorado	4,440	0.9%
25	New Jersey	5,824	1.2%	30	Idaho	3,741	0.7%
22	New Mexico	6,231	1.2%	31	Alaska	3,144	0.6%
7	New York	22,971	4.6%	32	Rhode Island	2,865	0.6%
5	North Carolina	28,867	5.8%	33	Oregon	2,652	0.5%
NA	North Dakota**	NA	NA	34	Nebraska	2,293	0.5%
3	Ohio	31,775	6.4%	35	Arkansas	2,146	0.4%
13	Oklahoma	11,844	2.4%	36	South Dakota	1,914	0.4%
33	Oregon	2,652	0.5%	37	Montana	1,793	0.4%
46	Pennsylvania	239	0.0%	38	Maine	1,629	0.3%
32	Rhode Island	2,865	0.6%	39	Utah	1,442	0.3%
26	South Carolina	5,627	1.1%	40	Delaware	845	0.2%
36	South Dakota	1,914	0.4%	41	Kansas	808	0.2%
27	Tennessee	4,874	1.0%	42	Hawaii	699	0.1%
6	Texas	24,318	4.9%	43	New Hampshire	618	0.1%
39	Utah	1,442	0.3%	44	Wyoming	411	0.1%
45	Vermont	300	0.1%	45	Vermont	300	0.1%
19	Virginia	6,884	1.4%	46	Pennsylvania	239	0.0%
18	Washington	8,706	1.7%	NA	Maryland**	NA	NA
NA	West Virginia**	NA	NA	NA	Mississippi**	NA	NA
23	Wisconsin	6,111	1.2%	NA	North Dakota**	NA	NA
44	Wyoming	411	0.1%	NA	West Virginia**	NA	NA
					District of Columbia	4,638	0.9%

Source: U.S. Department of Health and Human Services, Children's Bureau
   "Child Maltreatment 1996: Reports from the States to the National Child Abuse and Neglect Data System"
*State-substantiated or indicated incidents. National total is for reporting states only. Fifty-two percent of maltreated children suffered neglect, 24% physical abuse, 12% sexual abuse, 6% emotional maltreatment, 3% medical neglect and 16% other forms of maltreatment. More than half of the abused or neglected children were 7 years old or younger, with about 28% younger than four years old. **Not available.

Rate of Neglected Children in 1996

National Rate = 7.5 Neglected Children per 1,000 Population Under 18*

ALPHA ORDER

RANK	STATE	RATE
18	Alabama	8.5
3	Alaska	16.9
26	Arizona	5.2
37	Arkansas	3.3
14	California	9.5
33	Colorado	4.5
1	Connecticut	19.4
30	Delaware	4.8
11	Florida	10.8
6	Georgia	15.0
41	Hawaii	2.3
11	Idaho	10.8
24	Illinois	5.5
17	Indiana	8.6
19	Iowa	8.4
45	Kansas	1.2
2	Kentucky	17.6
16	Louisiana	8.7
24	Maine	5.5
NA	Maryland**	NA
5	Massachusetts	15.4
31	Michigan	4.6
26	Minnesota	5.2
NA	Mississippi**	NA
21	Missouri	7.0
20	Montana	7.8
26	Nebraska	5.2
13	Nevada	10.7
42	New Hampshire	2.1
40	New Jersey	2.9
8	New Mexico	12.5
29	New York	5.1
4	North Carolina	15.8
NA	North Dakota**	NA
10	Ohio	11.2
7	Oklahoma	13.5
37	Oregon	3.3
46	Pennsylvania	0.1
9	Rhode Island	12.2
23	South Carolina	5.9
14	South Dakota	9.5
36	Tennessee	3.7
34	Texas	4.4
42	Utah	2.1
42	Vermont	2.1
35	Virginia	4.2
22	Washington	6.1
NA	West Virginia**	NA
31	Wisconsin	4.6
39	Wyoming	3.1

RANK ORDER

RANK	STATE	RATE
1	Connecticut	19.4
2	Kentucky	17.6
3	Alaska	16.9
4	North Carolina	15.8
5	Massachusetts	15.4
6	Georgia	15.0
7	Oklahoma	13.5
8	New Mexico	12.5
9	Rhode Island	12.2
10	Ohio	11.2
11	Florida	10.8
11	Idaho	10.8
13	Nevada	10.7
14	California	9.5
14	South Dakota	9.5
16	Louisiana	8.7
17	Indiana	8.6
18	Alabama	8.5
19	Iowa	8.4
20	Montana	7.8
21	Missouri	7.0
22	Washington	6.1
23	South Carolina	5.9
24	Illinois	5.5
24	Maine	5.5
26	Arizona	5.2
26	Minnesota	5.2
26	Nebraska	5.2
29	New York	5.1
30	Delaware	4.8
31	Michigan	4.6
31	Wisconsin	4.6
33	Colorado	4.5
34	Texas	4.4
35	Virginia	4.2
36	Tennessee	3.7
37	Arkansas	3.3
37	Oregon	3.3
39	Wyoming	3.1
40	New Jersey	2.9
41	Hawaii	2.3
42	New Hampshire	2.1
42	Utah	2.1
42	Vermont	2.1
45	Kansas	1.2
46	Pennsylvania	0.1
NA	Maryland**	NA
NA	Mississippi**	NA
NA	North Dakota**	NA
NA	West Virginia**	NA

District of Columbia	42.3

Source: Morgan Quitno Press using data from U.S. Department of Health and Human Services, Children's Bureau
"Child Maltreatment 1996: Reports from the States to the National Child Abuse and Neglect Data System"
*State-substantiated or indicated incidents. National total is for reporting states only. Fifty-two percent of maltreated children suffered neglect, 24% physical abuse, 12% sexual abuse, 6% emotional maltreatment, 3% medical neglect and 16% other forms of maltreatment. More than half of the abused or neglected children were 7 years old or younger, with about 28% younger than four years old. **Not available.*

Child Abuse and Neglect Fatalities in 1995

National Total = 996 Fatalities*

RANK	STATE	DEATHS	% of USA
13	Alabama	26	2.61%
NA	Alaska**	NA	NA
18	Arizona	16	1.61%
38	Arkansas	3	0.30%
5	California	66	6.63%
16	Colorado	23	2.31%
33	Connecticut	5	0.50%
31	Delaware	6	0.60%
3	Florida	68	6.83%
18	Georgia	16	1.61%
31	Hawaii	6	0.60%
22	Idaho	15	1.51%
2	Illinois	89	8.94%
11	Indiana	29	2.91%
25	Iowa	13	1.31%
35	Kansas	4	0.40%
14	Kentucky	24	2.41%
18	Louisiana	16	1.61%
40	Maine	2	0.20%
NA	Maryland**	NA	NA
27	Massachusetts	9	0.90%
NA	Michigan**	NA	NA
23	Minnesota	14	1.41%
26	Mississippi	12	1.20%
7	Missouri	43	4.32%
44	Montana	0	0.00%
43	Nebraska	1	0.10%
35	Nevada	4	0.40%
33	New Hampshire	5	0.50%
12	New Jersey	28	2.81%
29	New Mexico	7	0.70%
3	New York	68	6.83%
17	North Carolina	17	1.71%
40	North Dakota	2	0.20%
NA	Ohio**	NA	NA
9	Oklahoma	34	3.41%
8	Oregon	36	3.61%
6	Pennsylvania	61	6.12%
35	Rhode Island	4	0.40%
29	South Carolina	7	0.70%
40	South Dakota	2	0.20%
9	Tennessee	34	3.41%
1	Texas	96	9.64%
23	Utah	14	1.41%
44	Vermont	0	0.00%
14	Virginia	24	2.41%
27	Washington	9	0.90%
NA	West Virginia**	NA	NA
18	Wisconsin	16	1.61%
38	Wyoming	3	0.30%

RANK	STATE	DEATHS	% of USA
1	Texas	96	9.64%
2	Illinois	89	8.94%
3	Florida	68	6.83%
3	New York	68	6.83%
5	California	66	6.63%
6	Pennsylvania	61	6.12%
7	Missouri	43	4.32%
8	Oregon	36	3.61%
9	Oklahoma	34	3.41%
9	Tennessee	34	3.41%
11	Indiana	29	2.91%
12	New Jersey	28	2.81%
13	Alabama	26	2.61%
14	Kentucky	24	2.41%
14	Virginia	24	2.41%
16	Colorado	23	2.31%
17	North Carolina	17	1.71%
18	Arizona	16	1.61%
18	Georgia	16	1.61%
18	Louisiana	16	1.61%
18	Wisconsin	16	1.61%
22	Idaho	15	1.51%
23	Minnesota	14	1.41%
23	Utah	14	1.41%
25	Iowa	13	1.31%
26	Mississippi	12	1.20%
27	Massachusetts	9	0.90%
27	Washington	9	0.90%
29	New Mexico	7	0.70%
29	South Carolina	7	0.70%
31	Delaware	6	0.60%
31	Hawaii	6	0.60%
33	Connecticut	5	0.50%
33	New Hampshire	5	0.50%
35	Kansas	4	0.40%
35	Nevada	4	0.40%
35	Rhode Island	4	0.40%
38	Arkansas	3	0.30%
38	Wyoming	3	0.30%
40	Maine	2	0.20%
40	North Dakota	2	0.20%
40	South Dakota	2	0.20%
43	Nebraska	1	0.10%
44	Montana	0	0.00%
44	Vermont	0	0.00%
NA	Alaska**	NA	NA
NA	Maryland**	NA	NA
NA	Michigan**	NA	NA
NA	Ohio**	NA	NA
NA	West Virginia**	NA	NA
	District of Columbia**	NA	NA

Source: U.S. Department of Health and Human Services, National Center on Child Abuse and Neglect
"Child Maltreatment 1995: Reports from the States to the National Center on Child Abuse and Neglect"
*State-substantiated incidents. There were reports of 2,960,000 children abused leading to 1,110,000 cases confirmed. Fifty-two percent of maltreated children suffered neglect, 25% physical abuse, 13% sexual abuse, 5% emotional maltreatment, 3% medical neglect and 14% other forms of maltreatment. More than half of the abused or neglected children were 7 years old or younger, with about 26% younger than four years old. **Not available.*

Rate of Child Abuse and Neglect Fatalities in 1995

National Rate = 1.6 Fatalities per 100,000 Population Under 18*

RANK	STATE	RATE
11	Alabama	2.1
NA	Alaska**	NA
26	Arizona	1.3
42	Arkansas	0.4
35	California	0.7
8	Colorado	2.3
38	Connecticut	0.6
5	Delaware	3.4
15	Florida	1.9
34	Georgia	0.8
15	Hawaii	1.9
1	Idaho	4.7
6	Illinois	2.8
11	Indiana	2.1
22	Iowa	1.5
38	Kansas	0.6
7	Kentucky	2.4
23	Louisiana	1.4
35	Maine	0.7
NA	Maryland**	NA
38	Massachusetts	0.6
NA	Michigan**	NA
28	Minnesota	1.1
20	Mississippi	1.6
4	Missouri	3.5
44	Montana	0.0
43	Nebraska	0.2
31	Nevada	1.0
18	New Hampshire	1.7
23	New Jersey	1.4
27	New Mexico	1.2
23	New York	1.4
28	North Carolina	1.1
28	North Dakota	1.1
NA	Ohio**	NA
3	Oklahoma	4.0
2	Oregon	4.3
13	Pennsylvania	2.0
18	Rhode Island	1.7
35	South Carolina	0.7
31	South Dakota	1.0
8	Tennessee	2.3
17	Texas	1.8
13	Utah	2.0
44	Vermont	0.0
20	Virginia	1.6
38	Washington	0.6
NA	West Virginia**	NA
31	Wisconsin	1.0
10	Wyoming	2.2

RANK ORDER

RANK	STATE	RATE
1	Idaho	4.7
2	Oregon	4.3
3	Oklahoma	4.0
4	Missouri	3.5
5	Delaware	3.4
6	Illinois	2.8
7	Kentucky	2.4
8	Colorado	2.3
8	Tennessee	2.3
10	Wyoming	2.2
11	Alabama	2.1
11	Indiana	2.1
13	Pennsylvania	2.0
13	Utah	2.0
15	Florida	1.9
15	Hawaii	1.9
17	Texas	1.8
18	New Hampshire	1.7
18	Rhode Island	1.7
20	Mississippi	1.6
20	Virginia	1.6
22	Iowa	1.5
23	Louisiana	1.4
23	New Jersey	1.4
23	New York	1.4
26	Arizona	1.3
27	New Mexico	1.2
28	Minnesota	1.1
28	North Carolina	1.1
28	North Dakota	1.1
31	Nevada	1.0
31	South Dakota	1.0
31	Wisconsin	1.0
34	Georgia	0.8
35	California	0.7
35	Maine	0.7
35	South Carolina	0.7
38	Connecticut	0.6
38	Kansas	0.6
38	Massachusetts	0.6
38	Washington	0.6
42	Arkansas	0.4
43	Nebraska	0.2
44	Montana	0.0
44	Vermont	0.0
NA	Alaska**	NA
NA	Maryland**	NA
NA	Michigan**	NA
NA	Ohio**	NA
NA	West Virginia**	NA
	District of Columbia**	NA

Source: U.S. Department of Health and Human Services, National Center on Child Abuse and Neglect
"Child Maltreatment 1995: Reports from the States to the National Center on Child Abuse and Neglect"
*State-substantiated incidents for reporting states. Fifty-two percent of maltreated children suffered neglect, 25% physical abuse, 13% sexual abuse, 5% emotional maltreatment, 3% medical neglect and 14% other forms of maltreatment. More than half of the abused or neglected children were 7 years old or younger, with about 26% younger than four years old. **Not available.

VI. LAW ENFORCEMENT

Federal Law Enforcement Officers in 1996

National Total = 74,493 Officers*

ALPHA ORDER

RANK	STATE	OFFICERS	% of USA
25	Alabama	696	0.93%
38	Alaska	325	0.44%
7	Arizona	2,608	3.50%
36	Arkansas	351	0.47%
1	California	10,469	14.05%
12	Colorado	1,442	1.94%
33	Connecticut	412	0.55%
46	Delaware	149	0.20%
4	Florida	4,980	6.69%
10	Georgia	1,869	2.51%
28	Hawaii	511	0.69%
43	Idaho	178	0.24%
6	Illinois	2,652	3.56%
27	Indiana	629	0.84%
47	Iowa	133	0.18%
34	Kansas	390	0.52%
21	Kentucky	851	1.14%
14	Louisiana	1,178	1.58%
40	Maine	284	0.38%
15	Maryland	1,142	1.53%
17	Massachusetts	1,053	1.41%
11	Michigan	1,541	2.07%
22	Minnesota	804	1.08%
39	Mississippi	305	0.41%
16	Missouri	1,100	1.48%
37	Montana	330	0.44%
42	Nebraska	206	0.28%
31	Nevada	459	0.62%
50	New Hampshire	58	0.08%
8	New Jersey	1,997	2.68%
23	New Mexico	775	1.04%
3	New York	6,556	8.80%
18	North Carolina	972	1.30%
41	North Dakota	226	0.30%
20	Ohio	883	1.19%
24	Oklahoma	757	1.02%
26	Oregon	649	0.87%
5	Pennsylvania	2,853	3.83%
49	Rhode Island	94	0.13%
29	South Carolina	486	0.65%
45	South Dakota	155	0.21%
19	Tennessee	935	1.26%
2	Texas	8,836	11.86%
35	Utah	376	0.50%
44	Vermont	162	0.22%
9	Virginia	1,891	2.54%
13	Washington	1,246	1.67%
29	West Virginia	486	0.65%
32	Wisconsin	421	0.57%
47	Wyoming	133	0.18%

RANK ORDER

RANK	STATE	OFFICERS	% of USA
1	California	10,469	14.05%
2	Texas	8,836	11.86%
3	New York	6,556	8.80%
4	Florida	4,980	6.69%
5	Pennsylvania	2,853	3.83%
6	Illinois	2,652	3.56%
7	Arizona	2,608	3.50%
8	New Jersey	1,997	2.68%
9	Virginia	1,891	2.54%
10	Georgia	1,869	2.51%
11	Michigan	1,541	2.07%
12	Colorado	1,442	1.94%
13	Washington	1,246	1.67%
14	Louisiana	1,178	1.58%
15	Maryland	1,142	1.53%
16	Missouri	1,100	1.48%
17	Massachusetts	1,053	1.41%
18	North Carolina	972	1.30%
19	Tennessee	935	1.26%
20	Ohio	883	1.19%
21	Kentucky	851	1.14%
22	Minnesota	804	1.08%
23	New Mexico	775	1.04%
24	Oklahoma	757	1.02%
25	Alabama	696	0.93%
26	Oregon	649	0.87%
27	Indiana	629	0.84%
28	Hawaii	511	0.69%
29	South Carolina	486	0.65%
29	West Virginia	486	0.65%
31	Nevada	459	0.62%
32	Wisconsin	421	0.57%
33	Connecticut	412	0.55%
34	Kansas	390	0.52%
35	Utah	376	0.50%
36	Arkansas	351	0.47%
37	Montana	330	0.44%
38	Alaska	325	0.44%
39	Mississippi	305	0.41%
40	Maine	284	0.38%
41	North Dakota	226	0.30%
42	Nebraska	206	0.28%
43	Idaho	178	0.24%
44	Vermont	162	0.22%
45	South Dakota	155	0.21%
46	Delaware	149	0.20%
47	Iowa	133	0.18%
47	Wyoming	133	0.18%
49	Rhode Island	94	0.13%
50	New Hampshire	58	0.08%
	District of Columbia	6,508	8.74%

Source: U.S. Department of Justice, Bureau of Justice Statistics
   "Federal Law Enforcement Officers, 1996" (NCJ-164617, January 1998)
*Full-time officers authorized to carry firearms and make arrests.   Includes F.B.I., Customs Service, Immigration and Naturalization Service, I.R.S., Postal Inspection, Drug Enforcement Administration, Secret Service, National Park Service, Bureau of Alcohol, Tobacco and Firearms, Capitol Police, U.S. Courts, Federal Bureau of Prisons, Tennessee Valley Authority, and U.S. Forest Service.

Rate of Federal Law Enforcement Officers in 1996

National Rate = 28 Officers per 100,000 Population*

<table>
<tr><td colspan="3">ALPHA ORDER</td><td colspan="3">RANK ORDER</td></tr>
<tr><td>RANK</td><td>STATE</td><td>RATE</td><td>RANK</td><td>STATE</td><td>RATE</td></tr>
<tr><td>35</td><td>Alabama</td><td>16</td><td>1</td><td>Arizona</td><td>59</td></tr>
<tr><td>2</td><td>Alaska</td><td>54</td><td>2</td><td>Alaska</td><td>54</td></tr>
<tr><td>1</td><td>Arizona</td><td>59</td><td>3</td><td>Texas</td><td>46</td></tr>
<tr><td>39</td><td>Arkansas</td><td>14</td><td>4</td><td>New Mexico</td><td>45</td></tr>
<tr><td>11</td><td>California</td><td>33</td><td>5</td><td>Hawaii</td><td>43</td></tr>
<tr><td>6</td><td>Colorado</td><td>38</td><td>6</td><td>Colorado</td><td>38</td></tr>
<tr><td>40</td><td>Connecticut</td><td>13</td><td>6</td><td>Montana</td><td>38</td></tr>
<tr><td>27</td><td>Delaware</td><td>21</td><td>8</td><td>New York</td><td>36</td></tr>
<tr><td>9</td><td>Florida</td><td>35</td><td>9</td><td>Florida</td><td>35</td></tr>
<tr><td>18</td><td>Georgia</td><td>25</td><td>9</td><td>North Dakota</td><td>35</td></tr>
<tr><td>5</td><td>Hawaii</td><td>43</td><td>11</td><td>California</td><td>33</td></tr>
<tr><td>37</td><td>Idaho</td><td>15</td><td>12</td><td>Nevada</td><td>29</td></tr>
<tr><td>25</td><td>Illinois</td><td>22</td><td>13</td><td>Vermont</td><td>28</td></tr>
<tr><td>44</td><td>Indiana</td><td>11</td><td>13</td><td>Virginia</td><td>28</td></tr>
<tr><td>49</td><td>Iowa</td><td>5</td><td>13</td><td>Wyoming</td><td>28</td></tr>
<tr><td>37</td><td>Kansas</td><td>15</td><td>16</td><td>Louisiana</td><td>27</td></tr>
<tr><td>25</td><td>Kentucky</td><td>22</td><td>16</td><td>West Virginia</td><td>27</td></tr>
<tr><td>16</td><td>Louisiana</td><td>27</td><td>18</td><td>Georgia</td><td>25</td></tr>
<tr><td>21</td><td>Maine</td><td>23</td><td>18</td><td>New Jersey</td><td>25</td></tr>
<tr><td>21</td><td>Maryland</td><td>23</td><td>20</td><td>Pennsylvania</td><td>24</td></tr>
<tr><td>33</td><td>Massachusetts</td><td>17</td><td>21</td><td>Maine</td><td>23</td></tr>
<tr><td>35</td><td>Michigan</td><td>16</td><td>21</td><td>Maryland</td><td>23</td></tr>
<tr><td>33</td><td>Minnesota</td><td>17</td><td>21</td><td>Oklahoma</td><td>23</td></tr>
<tr><td>44</td><td>Mississippi</td><td>11</td><td>21</td><td>Washington</td><td>23</td></tr>
<tr><td>27</td><td>Missouri</td><td>21</td><td>25</td><td>Illinois</td><td>22</td></tr>
<tr><td>6</td><td>Montana</td><td>38</td><td>25</td><td>Kentucky</td><td>22</td></tr>
<tr><td>43</td><td>Nebraska</td><td>12</td><td>27</td><td>Delaware</td><td>21</td></tr>
<tr><td>12</td><td>Nevada</td><td>29</td><td>27</td><td>Missouri</td><td>21</td></tr>
<tr><td>49</td><td>New Hampshire</td><td>5</td><td>27</td><td>South Dakota</td><td>21</td></tr>
<tr><td>18</td><td>New Jersey</td><td>25</td><td>30</td><td>Oregon</td><td>20</td></tr>
<tr><td>4</td><td>New Mexico</td><td>45</td><td>31</td><td>Utah</td><td>19</td></tr>
<tr><td>8</td><td>New York</td><td>36</td><td>32</td><td>Tennessee</td><td>18</td></tr>
<tr><td>40</td><td>North Carolina</td><td>13</td><td>33</td><td>Massachusetts</td><td>17</td></tr>
<tr><td>9</td><td>North Dakota</td><td>35</td><td>33</td><td>Minnesota</td><td>17</td></tr>
<tr><td>47</td><td>Ohio</td><td>8</td><td>35</td><td>Alabama</td><td>16</td></tr>
<tr><td>21</td><td>Oklahoma</td><td>23</td><td>35</td><td>Michigan</td><td>16</td></tr>
<tr><td>30</td><td>Oregon</td><td>20</td><td>37</td><td>Idaho</td><td>15</td></tr>
<tr><td>20</td><td>Pennsylvania</td><td>24</td><td>37</td><td>Kansas</td><td>15</td></tr>
<tr><td>46</td><td>Rhode Island</td><td>9</td><td>39</td><td>Arkansas</td><td>14</td></tr>
<tr><td>40</td><td>South Carolina</td><td>13</td><td>40</td><td>Connecticut</td><td>13</td></tr>
<tr><td>27</td><td>South Dakota</td><td>21</td><td>40</td><td>North Carolina</td><td>13</td></tr>
<tr><td>32</td><td>Tennessee</td><td>18</td><td>40</td><td>South Carolina</td><td>13</td></tr>
<tr><td>3</td><td>Texas</td><td>46</td><td>43</td><td>Nebraska</td><td>12</td></tr>
<tr><td>31</td><td>Utah</td><td>19</td><td>44</td><td>Indiana</td><td>11</td></tr>
<tr><td>13</td><td>Vermont</td><td>28</td><td>44</td><td>Mississippi</td><td>11</td></tr>
<tr><td>13</td><td>Virginia</td><td>28</td><td>46</td><td>Rhode Island</td><td>9</td></tr>
<tr><td>21</td><td>Washington</td><td>23</td><td>47</td><td>Ohio</td><td>8</td></tr>
<tr><td>16</td><td>West Virginia</td><td>27</td><td>47</td><td>Wisconsin</td><td>8</td></tr>
<tr><td>47</td><td>Wisconsin</td><td>8</td><td>49</td><td>Iowa</td><td>5</td></tr>
<tr><td>13</td><td>Wyoming</td><td>28</td><td>49</td><td>New Hampshire</td><td>5</td></tr>
<tr><td colspan="3"></td><td colspan="2">District of Columbia</td><td>1,198</td></tr>
</table>

Source: U.S. Department of Justice, Bureau of Justice Statistics
    "Federal Law Enforcement Officers, 1996" (NCJ-164617, January 1998)
*Full-time officers authorized to carry firearms and make arrests.   Includes F.B.I., Customs Service, Immigration and
Naturalization Service, I.R.S., Postal Inspection, Drug Enforcement Administration, Secret Service, National Park
Service, Bureau of Alcohol, Tobacco and Firearms, Capitol Police, U.S. Courts, Federal Bureau of Prisons,
Tennessee Valley Authority, and U.S. Forest Service.

State and Local Justice System Employment in 1995

National Total = 1,724,927 Employees*

ALPHA ORDER

RANK	STATE	EMPLOYEES	% of USA
25	Alabama	21,894	1.27%
45	Alaska	4,296	0.25%
15	Arizona	32,282	1.87%
32	Arkansas	12,996	0.75%
1	California	199,819	11.58%
23	Colorado	22,508	1.30%
27	Connecticut	20,723	1.20%
44	Delaware	5,301	0.31%
4	Florida	115,783	6.71%
10	Georgia	54,506	3.16%
38	Hawaii	8,118	0.47%
39	Idaho	7,166	0.42%
5	Illinois	80,619	4.67%
17	Indiana	30,411	1.76%
33	Iowa	12,868	0.75%
30	Kansas	16,262	0.94%
28	Kentucky	20,014	1.16%
20	Louisiana	29,172	1.69%
43	Maine	5,327	0.31%
14	Maryland	35,011	2.03%
13	Massachusetts	36,183	2.10%
9	Michigan	55,039	3.19%
24	Minnesota	22,196	1.29%
31	Mississippi	14,805	0.86%
16	Missouri	30,461	1.77%
46	Montana	4,141	0.24%
37	Nebraska	8,458	0.49%
35	Nevada	11,577	0.67%
42	New Hampshire	5,558	0.32%
7	New Jersey	68,714	3.98%
34	New Mexico	12,416	0.72%
2	New York	162,219	9.40%
11	North Carolina	41,811	2.42%
49	North Dakota	2,791	0.16%
8	Ohio	68,005	3.94%
26	Oklahoma	21,704	1.26%
29	Oregon	17,009	0.99%
6	Pennsylvania	70,322	4.08%
41	Rhode Island	5,805	0.34%
22	South Carolina	24,067	1.40%
47	South Dakota	3,337	0.19%
18	Tennessee	29,984	1.74%
3	Texas	141,399	8.20%
36	Utah	9,842	0.57%
50	Vermont	2,697	0.16%
12	Virginia	41,260	2.39%
19	Washington	29,915	1.73%
40	West Virginia	6,188	0.36%
21	Wisconsin	28,253	1.64%
48	Wyoming	3,184	0.18%

RANK ORDER

RANK	STATE	EMPLOYEES	% of USA
1	California	199,819	11.58%
2	New York	162,219	9.40%
3	Texas	141,399	8.20%
4	Florida	115,783	6.71%
5	Illinois	80,619	4.67%
6	Pennsylvania	70,322	4.08%
7	New Jersey	68,714	3.98%
8	Ohio	68,005	3.94%
9	Michigan	55,039	3.19%
10	Georgia	54,506	3.16%
11	North Carolina	41,811	2.42%
12	Virginia	41,260	2.39%
13	Massachusetts	36,183	2.10%
14	Maryland	35,011	2.03%
15	Arizona	32,282	1.87%
16	Missouri	30,461	1.77%
17	Indiana	30,411	1.76%
18	Tennessee	29,984	1.74%
19	Washington	29,915	1.73%
20	Louisiana	29,172	1.69%
21	Wisconsin	28,253	1.64%
22	South Carolina	24,067	1.40%
23	Colorado	22,508	1.30%
24	Minnesota	22,196	1.29%
25	Alabama	21,894	1.27%
26	Oklahoma	21,704	1.26%
27	Connecticut	20,723	1.20%
28	Kentucky	20,014	1.16%
29	Oregon	17,009	0.99%
30	Kansas	16,262	0.94%
31	Mississippi	14,805	0.86%
32	Arkansas	12,996	0.75%
33	Iowa	12,868	0.75%
34	New Mexico	12,416	0.72%
35	Nevada	11,577	0.67%
36	Utah	9,842	0.57%
37	Nebraska	8,458	0.49%
38	Hawaii	8,118	0.47%
39	Idaho	7,166	0.42%
40	West Virginia	6,188	0.36%
41	Rhode Island	5,805	0.34%
42	New Hampshire	5,558	0.32%
43	Maine	5,327	0.31%
44	Delaware	5,301	0.31%
45	Alaska	4,296	0.25%
46	Montana	4,141	0.24%
47	South Dakota	3,337	0.19%
48	Wyoming	3,184	0.18%
49	North Dakota	2,791	0.16%
50	Vermont	2,697	0.16%
	District of Columbia	10,511	0.61%

Source: Morgan Quitno Press using data from U.S. Bureau of the Census, Governments Division
"1995 State and Local Government Employment" (http://www.census.gov/govs/www/apes95sl.html)
*Full-time equivalent as of October 1995. Includes police, courts, prosecution, public defense and corrections.

Rate of State and Local Justice System Employment in 1995

National Rate = 65.7 Employees per 10,000 Population*

ALPHA ORDER			RANK ORDER		
RANK	STATE	RATE	RANK	STATE	RATE
40	Alabama	51.5	1	New York	89.2
10	Alaska	71.3	2	New Jersey	86.5
7	Arizona	75.0	3	Florida	81.6
37	Arkansas	52.3	4	Georgia	75.6
20	California	63.3	4	Nevada	75.6
24	Colorado	60.2	6	Texas	75.2
18	Connecticut	63.5	7	Arizona	75.0
8	Delaware	74.0	8	Delaware	74.0
3	Florida	81.6	9	New Mexico	73.5
4	Georgia	75.6	10	Alaska	71.3
12	Hawaii	69.0	11	Maryland	69.4
22	Idaho	61.5	12	Hawaii	69.0
13	Illinois	68.5	13	Illinois	68.5
36	Indiana	52.5	14	Louisiana	67.2
47	Iowa	45.3	15	Wyoming	66.4
19	Kansas	63.4	16	Oklahoma	66.3
38	Kentucky	51.9	17	South Carolina	65.7
14	Louisiana	67.2	18	Connecticut	63.5
49	Maine	43.1	19	Kansas	63.4
11	Maryland	69.4	20	California	63.3
25	Massachusetts	59.6	21	Virginia	62.4
29	Michigan	57.8	22	Idaho	61.5
43	Minnesota	48.1	23	Ohio	61.1
33	Mississippi	54.9	24	Colorado	60.2
30	Missouri	57.3	25	Massachusetts	59.6
44	Montana	47.6	26	Rhode Island	58.5
39	Nebraska	51.6	27	Pennsylvania	58.3
4	Nevada	75.6	28	North Carolina	58.0
42	New Hampshire	48.4	29	Michigan	57.8
2	New Jersey	86.5	30	Missouri	57.3
9	New Mexico	73.5	31	Tennessee	57.1
1	New York	89.2	32	Wisconsin	55.3
28	North Carolina	58.0	33	Mississippi	54.9
48	North Dakota	43.5	33	Washington	54.9
23	Ohio	61.1	35	Oregon	54.0
16	Oklahoma	66.3	36	Indiana	52.5
35	Oregon	54.0	37	Arkansas	52.3
27	Pennsylvania	58.3	38	Kentucky	51.9
26	Rhode Island	58.5	39	Nebraska	51.6
17	South Carolina	65.7	40	Alabama	51.5
46	South Dakota	45.7	41	Utah	50.2
31	Tennessee	57.1	42	New Hampshire	48.4
6	Texas	75.2	43	Minnesota	48.1
41	Utah	50.2	44	Montana	47.6
45	Vermont	46.0	45	Vermont	46.0
21	Virginia	62.4	46	South Dakota	45.7
33	Washington	54.9	47	Iowa	45.3
50	West Virginia	33.9	48	North Dakota	43.5
32	Wisconsin	55.3	49	Maine	43.1
15	Wyoming	66.4	50	West Virginia	33.9
				District of Columbia	189.6

Source: Morgan Quitno Press using data from U.S. Bureau of the Census, Governments Division
"1995 State and Local Government Employment" (http://www.census.gov/govs/www/apes95sl.html)
*Full-time equivalent as of October 1995. Includes police, courts, prosecution, public defense and corrections.

State and Local Judicial and Legal System Employment in 1995

National Total = 331,196 Employees*

ALPHA ORDER

RANK	STATE	EMPLOYEES	% of USA
25	Alabama	4,243	1.28%
43	Alaska	1,228	0.37%
11	Arizona	7,207	2.18%
36	Arkansas	2,076	0.63%
1	California	38,481	11.62%
24	Colorado	4,792	1.45%
27	Connecticut	3,655	1.10%
41	Delaware	1,461	0.44%
3	Florida	22,799	6.88%
10	Georgia	8,000	2.42%
33	Hawaii	2,696	0.81%
40	Idaho	1,490	0.45%
7	Illinois	15,742	4.75%
17	Indiana	5,855	1.77%
31	Iowa	3,001	0.91%
30	Kansas	3,200	0.97%
23	Kentucky	4,801	1.45%
14	Louisiana	6,359	1.92%
49	Maine	691	0.21%
15	Maryland	6,158	1.86%
12	Massachusetts	6,766	2.04%
9	Michigan	10,475	3.16%
20	Minnesota	5,166	1.56%
34	Mississippi	2,560	0.77%
19	Missouri	5,194	1.57%
45	Montana	841	0.25%
39	Nebraska	1,590	0.48%
32	Nevada	2,724	0.82%
44	New Hampshire	972	0.29%
5	New Jersey	20,404	6.16%
35	New Mexico	2,274	0.69%
2	New York	27,559	8.32%
16	North Carolina	6,062	1.83%
48	North Dakota	736	0.22%
6	Ohio	16,155	4.88%
28	Oklahoma	3,281	0.99%
26	Oregon	3,904	1.18%
8	Pennsylvania	15,338	4.63%
42	Rhode Island	1,271	0.38%
29	South Carolina	3,222	0.97%
47	South Dakota	762	0.23%
22	Tennessee	5,090	1.54%
4	Texas	20,688	6.25%
37	Utah	1,983	0.60%
50	Vermont	551	0.17%
18	Virginia	5,624	1.70%
13	Washington	6,561	1.98%
38	West Virginia	1,744	0.53%
21	Wisconsin	5,164	1.56%
46	Wyoming	764	0.23%

RANK ORDER

RANK	STATE	EMPLOYEES	% of USA
1	California	38,481	11.62%
2	New York	27,559	8.32%
3	Florida	22,799	6.88%
4	Texas	20,688	6.25%
5	New Jersey	20,404	6.16%
6	Ohio	16,155	4.88%
7	Illinois	15,742	4.75%
8	Pennsylvania	15,338	4.63%
9	Michigan	10,475	3.16%
10	Georgia	8,000	2.42%
11	Arizona	7,207	2.18%
12	Massachusetts	6,766	2.04%
13	Washington	6,561	1.98%
14	Louisiana	6,359	1.92%
15	Maryland	6,158	1.86%
16	North Carolina	6,062	1.83%
17	Indiana	5,855	1.77%
18	Virginia	5,624	1.70%
19	Missouri	5,194	1.57%
20	Minnesota	5,166	1.56%
21	Wisconsin	5,164	1.56%
22	Tennessee	5,090	1.54%
23	Kentucky	4,801	1.45%
24	Colorado	4,792	1.45%
25	Alabama	4,243	1.28%
26	Oregon	3,904	1.18%
27	Connecticut	3,655	1.10%
28	Oklahoma	3,281	0.99%
29	South Carolina	3,222	0.97%
30	Kansas	3,200	0.97%
31	Iowa	3,001	0.91%
32	Nevada	2,724	0.82%
33	Hawaii	2,696	0.81%
34	Mississippi	2,560	0.77%
35	New Mexico	2,274	0.69%
36	Arkansas	2,076	0.63%
37	Utah	1,983	0.60%
38	West Virginia	1,744	0.53%
39	Nebraska	1,590	0.48%
40	Idaho	1,490	0.45%
41	Delaware	1,461	0.44%
42	Rhode Island	1,271	0.38%
43	Alaska	1,228	0.37%
44	New Hampshire	972	0.29%
45	Montana	841	0.25%
46	Wyoming	764	0.23%
47	South Dakota	762	0.23%
48	North Dakota	736	0.22%
49	Maine	691	0.21%
50	Vermont	551	0.17%
	District of Columbia	1,836	0.55%

Source: U.S. Bureau of the Census, Governments Division
     "1995 State and Local Government Employment" (http://www.census.gov/govs/www/apes95sl.html)
*Full-time equivalent as of October 1995. Includes courts, prosecution and public defense.

Rate of State and Local Judicial and Legal System Employment in 1995

National Rate = 12.6 Employees per 10,000 Population*

ALPHA ORDER

RANK	STATE	RATE
36	Alabama	10.0
3	Alaska	20.4
6	Arizona	16.7
48	Arkansas	8.4
21	California	12.2
14	Colorado	12.8
25	Connecticut	11.2
3	Delaware	20.4
7	Florida	16.1
27	Georgia	11.1
2	Hawaii	22.9
14	Idaho	12.8
13	Illinois	13.4
33	Indiana	10.1
31	Iowa	10.6
18	Kansas	12.5
19	Kentucky	12.4
10	Louisiana	14.7
50	Maine	5.6
21	Maryland	12.2
27	Massachusetts	11.1
29	Michigan	11.0
25	Minnesota	11.2
43	Mississippi	9.5
38	Missouri	9.8
39	Montana	9.7
39	Nebraska	9.7
5	Nevada	17.8
46	New Hampshire	8.5
1	New Jersey	25.7
12	New Mexico	13.5
9	New York	15.2
48	North Carolina	8.4
24	North Dakota	11.5
11	Ohio	14.5
36	Oklahoma	10.0
19	Oregon	12.4
17	Pennsylvania	12.7
14	Rhode Island	12.8
45	South Carolina	8.8
32	South Dakota	10.4
39	Tennessee	9.7
29	Texas	11.0
33	Utah	10.1
44	Vermont	9.4
46	Virginia	8.5
23	Washington	12.0
42	West Virginia	9.6
33	Wisconsin	10.1
8	Wyoming	15.9

RANK ORDER

RANK	STATE	RATE
1	New Jersey	25.7
2	Hawaii	22.9
3	Alaska	20.4
3	Delaware	20.4
5	Nevada	17.8
6	Arizona	16.7
7	Florida	16.1
8	Wyoming	15.9
9	New York	15.2
10	Louisiana	14.7
11	Ohio	14.5
12	New Mexico	13.5
13	Illinois	13.4
14	Colorado	12.8
14	Idaho	12.8
14	Rhode Island	12.8
17	Pennsylvania	12.7
18	Kansas	12.5
19	Kentucky	12.4
19	Oregon	12.4
21	California	12.2
21	Maryland	12.2
23	Washington	12.0
24	North Dakota	11.5
25	Connecticut	11.2
25	Minnesota	11.2
27	Georgia	11.1
27	Massachusetts	11.1
29	Michigan	11.0
29	Texas	11.0
31	Iowa	10.6
32	South Dakota	10.4
33	Indiana	10.1
33	Utah	10.1
33	Wisconsin	10.1
36	Alabama	10.0
36	Oklahoma	10.0
38	Missouri	9.8
39	Montana	9.7
39	Nebraska	9.7
39	Tennessee	9.7
42	West Virginia	9.6
43	Mississippi	9.5
44	Vermont	9.4
45	South Carolina	8.8
46	New Hampshire	8.5
46	Virginia	8.5
48	Arkansas	8.4
48	North Carolina	8.4
50	Maine	5.6
	District of Columbia	33.1

Source: U.S. Bureau of the Census, Governments Division
   "1995 State and Local Government Employment" (http://www.census.gov/govs/www/apes95sl.html)
*Full-time equivalent as of October 1995. Includes courts, prosecution and public defense.

State and Local Police Officers in 1995

National Total = 585,156 Officers*

ALPHA ORDER				RANK ORDER			
RANK	STATE	OFFICERS	% of USA	RANK	STATE	OFFICERS	% of USA
22	Alabama	8,427	1.44%	1	New York	66,280	11.33%
46	Alaska	1,193	0.20%	2	California	63,713	10.89%
21	Arizona	8,637	1.48%	3	Texas	41,976	7.17%
33	Arkansas	4,841	0.83%	4	Illinois	32,274	5.52%
2	California	63,713	10.89%	5	Florida	32,156	5.50%
23	Colorado	8,039	1.37%	6	Pennsylvania	24,814	4.24%
25	Connecticut	7,445	1.27%	7	New Jersey	22,628	3.87%
44	Delaware	1,460	0.25%	8	Ohio	22,022	3.76%
5	Florida	32,156	5.50%	9	Michigan	18,389	3.14%
10	Georgia	16,084	2.75%	10	Georgia	16,084	2.75%
39	Hawaii	2,542	0.43%	11	North Carolina	15,846	2.71%
40	Idaho	2,325	0.40%	12	Massachusetts	15,165	2.59%
4	Illinois	32,274	5.52%	13	Virginia	12,816	2.19%
17	Indiana	10,473	1.79%	14	Maryland	12,671	2.17%
32	Iowa	4,959	0.85%	15	Missouri	11,544	1.97%
31	Kansas	5,365	0.92%	16	Wisconsin	11,095	1.90%
28	Kentucky	5,549	0.95%	17	Indiana	10,473	1.79%
18	Louisiana	10,433	1.78%	18	Louisiana	10,433	1.78%
43	Maine	2,155	0.37%	19	Tennessee	10,362	1.77%
14	Maryland	12,671	2.17%	20	Washington	8,874	1.52%
12	Massachusetts	15,165	2.59%	21	Arizona	8,637	1.48%
9	Michigan	18,389	3.14%	22	Alabama	8,427	1.44%
26	Minnesota	7,397	1.26%	23	Colorado	8,039	1.37%
29	Mississippi	5,490	0.94%	24	South Carolina	7,998	1.37%
15	Missouri	11,544	1.97%	25	Connecticut	7,445	1.27%
45	Montana	1,455	0.25%	26	Minnesota	7,397	1.26%
37	Nebraska	3,060	0.52%	27	Oklahoma	6,872	1.17%
36	Nevada	3,159	0.54%	28	Kentucky	5,549	0.95%
41	New Hampshire	2,291	0.39%	29	Mississippi	5,490	0.94%
7	New Jersey	22,628	3.87%	30	Oregon	5,412	0.92%
34	New Mexico	3,556	0.61%	31	Kansas	5,365	0.92%
1	New York	66,280	11.33%	32	Iowa	4,959	0.85%
11	North Carolina	15,846	2.71%	33	Arkansas	4,841	0.83%
49	North Dakota	1,008	0.17%	34	New Mexico	3,556	0.61%
8	Ohio	22,022	3.76%	35	Utah	3,171	0.54%
27	Oklahoma	6,872	1.17%	36	Nevada	3,159	0.54%
30	Oregon	5,412	0.92%	37	Nebraska	3,060	0.52%
6	Pennsylvania	24,814	4.24%	38	West Virginia	2,545	0.43%
42	Rhode Island	2,254	0.39%	39	Hawaii	2,542	0.43%
24	South Carolina	7,998	1.37%	40	Idaho	2,325	0.40%
47	South Dakota	1,190	0.20%	41	New Hampshire	2,291	0.39%
19	Tennessee	10,362	1.77%	42	Rhode Island	2,254	0.39%
3	Texas	41,976	7.17%	43	Maine	2,155	0.37%
35	Utah	3,171	0.54%	44	Delaware	1,460	0.25%
50	Vermont	897	0.15%	45	Montana	1,455	0.25%
13	Virginia	12,816	2.19%	46	Alaska	1,193	0.20%
20	Washington	8,874	1.52%	47	South Dakota	1,190	0.20%
38	West Virginia	2,545	0.43%	48	Wyoming	1,095	0.19%
16	Wisconsin	11,095	1.90%	49	North Dakota	1,008	0.17%
48	Wyoming	1,095	0.19%	50	Vermont	897	0.15%
					District of Columbia	3,754	0.64%

Source: U.S. Bureau of the Census, Governments Division
"1995 State and Local Government Employment" (http://www.census.gov/govs/www/apes95sl.html)
*Full-time equivalent as of October 1995. Does not include employees of police departments who are not officers.

Rate of State and Local Police Officers in 1995

National Rate = 22.3 Officers per 10,000 Population*

ALPHA ORDER

RANK	STATE	RATE
30	Alabama	19.8
30	Alaska	19.8
27	Arizona	20.1
34	Arkansas	19.5
26	California	20.2
18	Colorado	21.5
8	Connecticut	22.8
24	Delaware	20.4
9	Florida	22.7
11	Georgia	22.3
17	Hawaii	21.6
29	Idaho	19.9
3	Illinois	27.4
38	Indiana	18.1
39	Iowa	17.4
21	Kansas	20.9
49	Kentucky	14.4
6	Louisiana	24.0
39	Maine	17.4
4	Maryland	25.1
5	Massachusetts	25.0
36	Michigan	19.3
46	Minnesota	16.0
24	Mississippi	20.4
15	Missouri	21.7
42	Montana	16.7
37	Nebraska	18.7
22	Nevada	20.6
28	New Hampshire	20.0
2	New Jersey	28.5
19	New Mexico	21.0
1	New York	36.4
13	North Carolina	22.0
47	North Dakota	15.7
30	Ohio	19.8
19	Oklahoma	21.0
41	Oregon	17.2
22	Pennsylvania	20.6
9	Rhode Island	22.7
14	South Carolina	21.8
43	South Dakota	16.3
33	Tennessee	19.7
11	Texas	22.3
45	Utah	16.2
48	Vermont	15.3
35	Virginia	19.4
43	Washington	16.3
50	West Virginia	13.9
15	Wisconsin	21.7
7	Wyoming	22.9

RANK ORDER

RANK	STATE	RATE
1	New York	36.4
2	New Jersey	28.5
3	Illinois	27.4
4	Maryland	25.1
5	Massachusetts	25.0
6	Louisiana	24.0
7	Wyoming	22.9
8	Connecticut	22.8
9	Florida	22.7
9	Rhode Island	22.7
11	Georgia	22.3
11	Texas	22.3
13	North Carolina	22.0
14	South Carolina	21.8
15	Missouri	21.7
15	Wisconsin	21.7
17	Hawaii	21.6
18	Colorado	21.5
19	New Mexico	21.0
19	Oklahoma	21.0
21	Kansas	20.9
22	Nevada	20.6
22	Pennsylvania	20.6
24	Delaware	20.4
24	Mississippi	20.4
26	California	20.2
27	Arizona	20.1
28	New Hampshire	20.0
29	Idaho	19.9
30	Alabama	19.8
30	Alaska	19.8
30	Ohio	19.8
33	Tennessee	19.7
34	Arkansas	19.5
35	Virginia	19.4
36	Michigan	19.3
37	Nebraska	18.7
38	Indiana	18.1
39	Iowa	17.4
39	Maine	17.4
41	Oregon	17.2
42	Montana	16.7
43	South Dakota	16.3
43	Washington	16.3
45	Utah	16.2
46	Minnesota	16.0
47	North Dakota	15.7
48	Vermont	15.3
49	Kentucky	14.4
50	West Virginia	13.9
	District of Columbia	67.7

Source: U.S. Bureau of the Census, Governments Division
   "1995 State and Local Government Employment" (http://www.census.gov/govs/www/apes95sl.html)
*Full-time equivalent as of October 1995. Does not include employees of police departments who are not officers.

Law Enforcement Agencies in 1996

National Total = 18,769 Agencies*

ALPHA ORDER

RANK	STATE	AGENCIES	% of USA
16	Alabama	432	2.3%
45	Alaska	69	0.4%
40	Arizona	130	0.7%
24	Arkansas	360	1.9%
12	California	524	2.8%
31	Colorado	247	1.3%
41	Connecticut	129	0.7%
49	Delaware	45	0.2%
20	Florida	385	2.1%
8	Georgia	581	3.1%
50	Hawaii	7	0.0%
43	Idaho	124	0.7%
3	Illinois	963	5.1%
11	Indiana	547	2.9%
17	Iowa	426	2.3%
22	Kansas	369	2.0%
18	Kentucky	391	2.1%
23	Louisiana	365	1.9%
37	Maine	141	0.8%
35	Maryland	147	0.8%
19	Massachusetts	390	2.1%
7	Michigan	588	3.1%
14	Minnesota	486	2.6%
26	Mississippi	317	1.7%
5	Missouri	647	3.4%
41	Montana	129	0.7%
28	Nebraska	266	1.4%
47	Nevada	58	0.3%
32	New Hampshire	233	1.2%
10	New Jersey	554	3.0%
38	New Mexico	140	0.7%
6	New York	598	3.2%
13	North Carolina	503	2.7%
36	North Dakota	142	0.8%
4	Ohio	938	5.0%
15	Oklahoma	459	2.4%
34	Oregon	184	1.0%
2	Pennsylvania	1,298	6.9%
48	Rhode Island	51	0.3%
29	South Carolina	264	1.4%
33	South Dakota	191	1.0%
21	Tennessee	374	2.0%
1	Texas	1,861	9.9%
39	Utah	138	0.7%
45	Vermont	69	0.4%
25	Virginia	330	1.8%
27	Washington	277	1.5%
30	West Virginia	250	1.3%
9	Wisconsin	567	3.0%
44	Wyoming	82	0.4%

RANK ORDER

RANK	STATE	AGENCIES	% of USA
1	Texas	1,861	9.9%
2	Pennsylvania	1,298	6.9%
3	Illinois	963	5.1%
4	Ohio	938	5.0%
5	Missouri	647	3.4%
6	New York	598	3.2%
7	Michigan	588	3.1%
8	Georgia	581	3.1%
9	Wisconsin	567	3.0%
10	New Jersey	554	3.0%
11	Indiana	547	2.9%
12	California	524	2.8%
13	North Carolina	503	2.7%
14	Minnesota	486	2.6%
15	Oklahoma	459	2.4%
16	Alabama	432	2.3%
17	Iowa	426	2.3%
18	Kentucky	391	2.1%
19	Massachusetts	390	2.1%
20	Florida	385	2.1%
21	Tennessee	374	2.0%
22	Kansas	369	2.0%
23	Louisiana	365	1.9%
24	Arkansas	360	1.9%
25	Virginia	330	1.8%
26	Mississippi	317	1.7%
27	Washington	277	1.5%
28	Nebraska	266	1.4%
29	South Carolina	264	1.4%
30	West Virginia	250	1.3%
31	Colorado	247	1.3%
32	New Hampshire	233	1.2%
33	South Dakota	191	1.0%
34	Oregon	184	1.0%
35	Maryland	147	0.8%
36	North Dakota	142	0.8%
37	Maine	141	0.8%
38	New Mexico	140	0.7%
39	Utah	138	0.7%
40	Arizona	130	0.7%
41	Connecticut	129	0.7%
41	Montana	129	0.7%
43	Idaho	124	0.7%
44	Wyoming	82	0.4%
45	Alaska	69	0.4%
45	Vermont	69	0.4%
47	Nevada	58	0.3%
48	Rhode Island	51	0.3%
49	Delaware	45	0.2%
50	Hawaii	7	0.0%
	District of Columbia	3	0.0%

Source: U.S. Department of Justice, Bureau of Justice Statistics
"Census of State and Local Law Enforcement Agencies, 1996" (Bulletin, June 1998, NCJ-164618)
*Includes state and local police, sheriffs' departments and special police agencies.

Population per Law Enforcement Agency in 1996

National Rate = 14,134 Population per Agency*

ALPHA ORDER				RANK ORDER		
RANK	STATE	RATE		RANK	STATE	RATE
30	Alabama	9,891		1	Hawaii	169,103
36	Alaska	8,797		2	California	60,836
5	Arizona	34,062		3	Florida	37,403
42	Arkansas	6,972		4	Maryland	34,501
2	California	60,836		5	Arizona	34,062
16	Colorado	15,476		6	New York	30,409
8	Connecticut	25,382		7	Nevada	27,641
14	Delaware	16,108		8	Connecticut	25,382
3	Florida	37,403		9	Virginia	20,229
22	Georgia	12,656		10	Washington	19,975
1	Hawaii	169,103		11	Rhode Island	19,416
31	Idaho	9,591		12	Oregon	17,412
23	Illinois	12,302		13	Michigan	16,317
27	Indiana	10,677		14	Delaware	16,108
45	Iowa	6,694		15	Massachusetts	15,621
43	Kansas	6,971		16	Colorado	15,476
29	Kentucky	9,933		17	North Carolina	14,558
25	Louisiana	11,919		18	Utah	14,496
35	Maine	8,818		19	New Jersey	14,419
4	Maryland	34,501		20	Tennessee	14,224
15	Massachusetts	15,621		21	South Carolina	14,010
13	Michigan	16,317		22	Georgia	12,656
32	Minnesota	9,584		23	Illinois	12,302
37	Mississippi	8,568		24	New Mexico	12,239
39	Missouri	8,282		25	Louisiana	11,919
44	Montana	6,817		26	Ohio	11,911
46	Nebraska	6,211		27	Indiana	10,677
7	Nevada	27,641		28	Texas	10,278
48	New Hampshire	4,989		29	Kentucky	9,933
19	New Jersey	14,419		30	Alabama	9,891
24	New Mexico	12,239		31	Idaho	9,591
6	New York	30,409		32	Minnesota	9,584
17	North Carolina	14,558		33	Pennsylvania	9,288
49	North Dakota	4,532		34	Wisconsin	9,100
26	Ohio	11,911		35	Maine	8,818
41	Oklahoma	7,192		36	Alaska	8,797
12	Oregon	17,412		37	Mississippi	8,568
33	Pennsylvania	9,288		38	Vermont	8,531
11	Rhode Island	19,416		39	Missouri	8,282
21	South Carolina	14,010		40	West Virginia	7,303
50	South Dakota	3,835		41	Oklahoma	7,192
20	Tennessee	14,224		42	Arkansas	6,972
28	Texas	10,278		43	Kansas	6,971
18	Utah	14,496		44	Montana	6,817
38	Vermont	8,531		45	Iowa	6,694
9	Virginia	20,229		46	Nebraska	6,211
10	Washington	19,975		47	Wyoming	5,871
40	West Virginia	7,303		48	New Hampshire	4,989
34	Wisconsin	9,100		49	North Dakota	4,532
47	Wyoming	5,871		50	South Dakota	3,835
					District of Columbia	181,071

Source: Morgan Quitno Press using data from U.S. Department of Justice, Bureau of Justice Statistics
"Census of State and Local Law Enforcement Agencies, 1996" (Bulletin, June 1998, NCJ-164618)
Includes state and local police, sheriffs' departments and special police agencies.

Law Enforcement Agencies per 1,000 Square Miles in 1996

National Rate = 5.0 Agencies per 1,000 Square Miles*

ALPHA ORDER				RANK ORDER		
RANK	STATE	RATE		RANK	STATE	RATE
21	Alabama	8.3		1	New Jersey	67.4
50	Alaska	0.1		2	Massachusetts	42.2
45	Arizona	1.1		3	Rhode Island	41.4
27	Arkansas	6.8		4	Pennsylvania	28.2
37	California	3.3		5	New Hampshire	25.1
39	Colorado	2.4		6	Connecticut	23.3
6	Connecticut	23.3		7	Ohio	20.9
8	Delaware	18.8		8	Delaware	18.8
30	Florida	6.4		9	Illinois	16.6
14	Georgia	9.9		10	Indiana	15.0
45	Hawaii	1.1		11	Maryland	12.0
43	Idaho	1.5		12	New York	11.1
9	Illinois	16.6		13	West Virginia	10.3
10	Indiana	15.0		14	Georgia	9.9
23	Iowa	7.6		15	Kentucky	9.7
33	Kansas	4.5		16	North Carolina	9.5
15	Kentucky	9.7		17	Missouri	9.3
24	Louisiana	7.4		18	Tennessee	8.9
34	Maine	4.2		19	Wisconsin	8.7
11	Maryland	12.0		20	South Carolina	8.5
2	Massachusetts	42.2		21	Alabama	8.3
31	Michigan	6.1		22	Virginia	7.8
32	Minnesota	5.6		23	Iowa	7.6
28	Mississippi	6.6		24	Louisiana	7.4
17	Missouri	9.3		25	Vermont	7.2
47	Montana	0.9		26	Texas	7.0
36	Nebraska	3.4		27	Arkansas	6.8
49	Nevada	0.5		28	Mississippi	6.6
5	New Hampshire	25.1		28	Oklahoma	6.6
1	New Jersey	67.4		30	Florida	6.4
44	New Mexico	1.2		31	Michigan	6.1
12	New York	11.1		32	Minnesota	5.6
16	North Carolina	9.5		33	Kansas	4.5
40	North Dakota	2.0		34	Maine	4.2
7	Ohio	20.9		35	Washington	3.9
28	Oklahoma	6.6		36	Nebraska	3.4
41	Oregon	1.9		37	California	3.3
4	Pennsylvania	28.2		38	South Dakota	2.5
3	Rhode Island	41.4		39	Colorado	2.4
20	South Carolina	8.5		40	North Dakota	2.0
38	South Dakota	2.5		41	Oregon	1.9
18	Tennessee	8.9		42	Utah	1.6
26	Texas	7.0		43	Idaho	1.5
42	Utah	1.6		44	New Mexico	1.2
25	Vermont	7.2		45	Arizona	1.1
22	Virginia	7.8		45	Hawaii	1.1
35	Washington	3.9		47	Montana	0.9
13	West Virginia	10.3		48	Wyoming	0.8
19	Wisconsin	8.7		49	Nevada	0.5
48	Wyoming	0.8		50	Alaska	0.1
					District of Columbia**	NA

Source: Morgan Quitno Press using data from U.S. Department of Justice, Bureau of Justice Statistics
   "Census of State and Local Law Enforcement Agencies, 1996" (Bulletin, June 1998, NCJ-164618)
*Includes state and local police, sheriffs' departments and special police agencies.
**The District of Columbia has three agencies for its 68 square miles.

Full-Time Sworn Officers in Law Enforcement Agencies in 1996

National Total = 663,535 Officers*

ALPHA ORDER

RANK	STATE	OFFICERS	% of USA
22	Alabama	9,767	1.5%
48	Alaska	1,254	0.2%
20	Arizona	10,088	1.5%
31	Arkansas	5,819	0.9%
2	California	69,134	10.4%
21	Colorado	9,896	1.5%
25	Connecticut	8,525	1.3%
45	Delaware	1,660	0.3%
5	Florida	37,395	5.6%
10	Georgia	19,115	2.9%
38	Hawaii	2,989	0.5%
40	Idaho	2,524	0.4%
4	Illinois	38,192	5.8%
19	Indiana	10,931	1.6%
33	Iowa	5,043	0.8%
29	Kansas	6,183	0.9%
28	Kentucky	6,466	1.0%
14	Louisiana	16,125	2.4%
42	Maine	2,318	0.3%
15	Maryland	13,828	2.1%
12	Massachusetts	17,935	2.7%
9	Michigan	20,568	3.1%
26	Minnesota	7,994	1.2%
32	Mississippi	5,813	0.9%
16	Missouri	12,998	2.0%
44	Montana	1,682	0.3%
37	Nebraska	3,297	0.5%
34	Nevada	4,363	0.7%
43	New Hampshire	2,305	0.3%
6	New Jersey	28,058	4.2%
35	New Mexico	4,134	0.6%
1	New York	71,221	10.7%
13	North Carolina	16,953	2.6%
49	North Dakota	1,141	0.2%
8	Ohio	23,811	3.6%
27	Oklahoma	7,232	1.1%
30	Oregon	6,064	0.9%
7	Pennsylvania	24,873	3.7%
41	Rhode Island	2,422	0.4%
24	South Carolina	8,675	1.3%
46	South Dakota	1,464	0.2%
18	Tennessee	12,152	1.8%
3	Texas	47,767	7.2%
36	Utah	3,699	0.6%
50	Vermont	981	0.1%
11	Virginia	18,448	2.8%
23	Washington	9,292	1.4%
39	West Virginia	2,977	0.4%
17	Wisconsin	12,678	1.9%
47	Wyoming	1,377	0.2%

RANK ORDER

RANK	STATE	OFFICERS	% of USA
1	New York	71,221	10.7%
2	California	69,134	10.4%
3	Texas	47,767	7.2%
4	Illinois	38,192	5.8%
5	Florida	37,395	5.6%
6	New Jersey	28,058	4.2%
7	Pennsylvania	24,873	3.7%
8	Ohio	23,811	3.6%
9	Michigan	20,568	3.1%
10	Georgia	19,115	2.9%
11	Virginia	18,448	2.8%
12	Massachusetts	17,935	2.7%
13	North Carolina	16,953	2.6%
14	Louisiana	16,125	2.4%
15	Maryland	13,828	2.1%
16	Missouri	12,998	2.0%
17	Wisconsin	12,678	1.9%
18	Tennessee	12,152	1.8%
19	Indiana	10,931	1.6%
20	Arizona	10,088	1.5%
21	Colorado	9,896	1.5%
22	Alabama	9,767	1.5%
23	Washington	9,292	1.4%
24	South Carolina	8,675	1.3%
25	Connecticut	8,525	1.3%
26	Minnesota	7,994	1.2%
27	Oklahoma	7,232	1.1%
28	Kentucky	6,466	1.0%
29	Kansas	6,183	0.9%
30	Oregon	6,064	0.9%
31	Arkansas	5,819	0.9%
32	Mississippi	5,813	0.9%
33	Iowa	5,043	0.8%
34	Nevada	4,363	0.7%
35	New Mexico	4,134	0.6%
36	Utah	3,699	0.6%
37	Nebraska	3,297	0.5%
38	Hawaii	2,989	0.5%
39	West Virginia	2,977	0.4%
40	Idaho	2,524	0.4%
41	Rhode Island	2,422	0.4%
42	Maine	2,318	0.3%
43	New Hampshire	2,305	0.3%
44	Montana	1,682	0.3%
45	Delaware	1,660	0.3%
46	South Dakota	1,464	0.2%
47	Wyoming	1,377	0.2%
48	Alaska	1,254	0.2%
49	North Dakota	1,141	0.2%
50	Vermont	981	0.1%
	District of Columbia	3,909	0.6%

Source: U.S. Department of Justice, Bureau of Justice Statistics
   "Census of State and Local Law Enforcement Agencies, 1996" (Bulletin, June 1998, NCJ-164618)
*Includes state and local police, sheriffs' departments and special police agencies.

Percent of Full-Time Law Enforcement Agency Employees
Who are Sworn Officers: 1996
National Percent = 72.0% of Employees are Sworn Officers*

ALPHA ORDER

RANK	STATE	PERCENT
34	Alabama	67.9
40	Alaska	66.6
50	Arizona	59.9
22	Arkansas	73.1
41	California	66.5
29	Colorado	70.7
2	Connecticut	82.6
10	Delaware	77.8
49	Florida	61.5
36	Georgia	67.8
6	Hawaii	79.8
33	Idaho	68.7
12	Illinois	76.0
39	Indiana	66.7
17	Iowa	74.2
28	Kansas	70.8
13	Kentucky	75.7
3	Louisiana	81.4
44	Maine	65.6
15	Maryland	75.2
19	Massachusetts	73.4
16	Michigan	74.8
30	Minnesota	70.6
37	Mississippi	67.7
27	Missouri	72.7
42	Montana	66.2
25	Nebraska	72.8
31	Nevada	70.0
9	New Hampshire	78.0
5	New Jersey	80.3
38	New Mexico	66.9
4	New York	80.6
24	North Carolina	72.9
17	North Dakota	74.2
25	Ohio	72.8
32	Oklahoma	68.9
34	Oregon	67.9
1	Pennsylvania	84.3
8	Rhode Island	78.2
14	South Carolina	75.5
48	South Dakota	62.0
46	Tennessee	64.8
45	Texas	65.3
21	Utah	73.2
19	Vermont	73.4
6	Virginia	79.8
43	Washington	66.1
22	West Virginia	73.1
11	Wisconsin	76.9
47	Wyoming	64.1

RANK ORDER

RANK	STATE	PERCENT
1	Pennsylvania	84.3
2	Connecticut	82.6
3	Louisiana	81.4
4	New York	80.6
5	New Jersey	80.3
6	Hawaii	79.8
6	Virginia	79.8
8	Rhode Island	78.2
9	New Hampshire	78.0
10	Delaware	77.8
11	Wisconsin	76.9
12	Illinois	76.0
13	Kentucky	75.7
14	South Carolina	75.5
15	Maryland	75.2
16	Michigan	74.8
17	Iowa	74.2
17	North Dakota	74.2
19	Massachusetts	73.4
19	Vermont	73.4
21	Utah	73.2
22	Arkansas	73.1
22	West Virginia	73.1
24	North Carolina	72.9
25	Nebraska	72.8
25	Ohio	72.8
27	Missouri	72.7
28	Kansas	70.8
29	Colorado	70.7
30	Minnesota	70.6
31	Nevada	70.0
32	Oklahoma	68.9
33	Idaho	68.7
34	Alabama	67.9
34	Oregon	67.9
36	Georgia	67.8
37	Mississippi	67.7
38	New Mexico	66.9
39	Indiana	66.7
40	Alaska	66.6
41	California	66.5
42	Montana	66.2
43	Washington	66.1
44	Maine	65.6
45	Texas	65.3
46	Tennessee	64.8
47	Wyoming	64.1
48	South Dakota	62.0
49	Florida	61.5
50	Arizona	59.9

District of Columbia   84.0

Source: Morgan Quitno Press using data from U.S. Department of Justice, Bureau of Justice Statistics
  "Census of State and Local Law Enforcement Agencies, 1996" (Bulletin, June 1998, NCJ-164618)
*Includes state and local police, sheriffs' departments and special police agencies.

Rate of Full-Time Sworn Officers in Law Enforcement Agencies in 1996

National Rate = 25 Officers per 10,000 Population*

ALPHA ORDER				RANK ORDER		
RANK	STATE	RATE		RANK	STATE	RATE
21	Alabama	23		1	New York	39
30	Alaska	21		2	Louisiana	37
21	Arizona	23		3	New Jersey	35
21	Arkansas	23		4	Illinois	32
28	California	22		5	Massachusetts	29
10	Colorado	26		5	Wyoming	29
10	Connecticut	26		7	Virginia	28
21	Delaware	23		8	Maryland	27
10	Florida	26		8	Nevada	27
10	Georgia	26		10	Colorado	26
14	Hawaii	25		10	Connecticut	26
30	Idaho	21		10	Florida	26
4	Illinois	32		10	Georgia	26
39	Indiana	19		14	Hawaii	25
43	Iowa	18		14	Texas	25
17	Kansas	24		14	Wisconsin	25
46	Kentucky	17		17	Kansas	24
2	Louisiana	37		17	Missouri	24
39	Maine	19		17	New Mexico	24
8	Maryland	27		17	Rhode Island	24
5	Massachusetts	29		21	Alabama	23
30	Michigan	21		21	Arizona	23
46	Minnesota	17		21	Arkansas	23
30	Mississippi	21		21	Delaware	23
17	Missouri	24		21	North Carolina	23
39	Montana	19		21	South Carolina	23
36	Nebraska	20		21	Tennessee	23
8	Nevada	27		28	California	22
36	New Hampshire	20		28	Oklahoma	22
3	New Jersey	35		30	Alaska	21
17	New Mexico	24		30	Idaho	21
1	New York	39		30	Michigan	21
21	North Carolina	23		30	Mississippi	21
43	North Dakota	18		30	Ohio	21
30	Ohio	21		30	Pennsylvania	21
28	Oklahoma	22		36	Nebraska	20
39	Oregon	19		36	New Hampshire	20
30	Pennsylvania	21		36	South Dakota	20
17	Rhode Island	24		39	Indiana	19
21	South Carolina	23		39	Maine	19
36	South Dakota	20		39	Montana	19
21	Tennessee	23		39	Oregon	19
14	Texas	25		43	Iowa	18
43	Utah	18		43	North Dakota	18
46	Vermont	17		43	Utah	18
7	Virginia	28		46	Kentucky	17
46	Washington	17		46	Minnesota	17
50	West Virginia	16		46	Vermont	17
14	Wisconsin	25		46	Washington	17
5	Wyoming	29		50	West Virginia	16
					District of Columbia	72

Source: Morgan Quitno Press using data from U.S. Department of Justice, Bureau of Justice Statistics
"Census of State and Local Law Enforcement Agencies, 1996" (Bulletin, June 1998, NCJ-164618)
*Includes state and local police, sheriffs' departments and special police agencies.

Full-Time Sworn Law Enforcement Officers per 1,000 Square Miles in 1996

National Rate = 178 Officers per 1,000 Square Miles*

<table>
<tr><td colspan="3">ALPHA ORDER</td><td colspan="3">RANK ORDER</td></tr>
<tr><td>RANK</td><td>STATE</td><td>RATE</td><td>RANK</td><td>STATE</td><td>RATE</td></tr>
<tr><td>24</td><td>Alabama</td><td>187</td><td>1</td><td>New Jersey</td><td>3,415</td></tr>
<tr><td>50</td><td>Alaska</td><td>2</td><td>2</td><td>Rhode Island</td><td>1,968</td></tr>
<tr><td>37</td><td>Arizona</td><td>88</td><td>3</td><td>Massachusetts</td><td>1,941</td></tr>
<tr><td>31</td><td>Arkansas</td><td>109</td><td>4</td><td>Connecticut</td><td>1,538</td></tr>
<tr><td>14</td><td>California</td><td>435</td><td>5</td><td>New York</td><td>1,319</td></tr>
<tr><td>34</td><td>Colorado</td><td>95</td><td>6</td><td>Maryland</td><td>1,125</td></tr>
<tr><td>4</td><td>Connecticut</td><td>1,538</td><td>7</td><td>Delaware</td><td>693</td></tr>
<tr><td>7</td><td>Delaware</td><td>693</td><td>8</td><td>Illinois</td><td>659</td></tr>
<tr><td>9</td><td>Florida</td><td>624</td><td>9</td><td>Florida</td><td>624</td></tr>
<tr><td>16</td><td>Georgia</td><td>324</td><td>10</td><td>Pennsylvania</td><td>540</td></tr>
<tr><td>12</td><td>Hawaii</td><td>463</td><td>11</td><td>Ohio</td><td>531</td></tr>
<tr><td>45</td><td>Idaho</td><td>30</td><td>12</td><td>Hawaii</td><td>463</td></tr>
<tr><td>8</td><td>Illinois</td><td>659</td><td>13</td><td>Virginia</td><td>436</td></tr>
<tr><td>18</td><td>Indiana</td><td>300</td><td>14</td><td>California</td><td>435</td></tr>
<tr><td>36</td><td>Iowa</td><td>90</td><td>15</td><td>Louisiana</td><td>325</td></tr>
<tr><td>38</td><td>Kansas</td><td>75</td><td>16</td><td>Georgia</td><td>324</td></tr>
<tr><td>27</td><td>Kentucky</td><td>160</td><td>17</td><td>North Carolina</td><td>322</td></tr>
<tr><td>15</td><td>Louisiana</td><td>325</td><td>18</td><td>Indiana</td><td>300</td></tr>
<tr><td>39</td><td>Maine</td><td>69</td><td>19</td><td>Tennessee</td><td>288</td></tr>
<tr><td>6</td><td>Maryland</td><td>1,125</td><td>20</td><td>South Carolina</td><td>278</td></tr>
<tr><td>3</td><td>Massachusetts</td><td>1,941</td><td>21</td><td>New Hampshire</td><td>248</td></tr>
<tr><td>22</td><td>Michigan</td><td>213</td><td>22</td><td>Michigan</td><td>213</td></tr>
<tr><td>35</td><td>Minnesota</td><td>92</td><td>23</td><td>Wisconsin</td><td>194</td></tr>
<tr><td>30</td><td>Mississippi</td><td>120</td><td>24</td><td>Alabama</td><td>187</td></tr>
<tr><td>25</td><td>Missouri</td><td>186</td><td>25</td><td>Missouri</td><td>186</td></tr>
<tr><td>49</td><td>Montana</td><td>11</td><td>26</td><td>Texas</td><td>179</td></tr>
<tr><td>42</td><td>Nebraska</td><td>43</td><td>27</td><td>Kentucky</td><td>160</td></tr>
<tr><td>43</td><td>Nevada</td><td>39</td><td>28</td><td>Washington</td><td>132</td></tr>
<tr><td>21</td><td>New Hampshire</td><td>248</td><td>29</td><td>West Virginia</td><td>123</td></tr>
<tr><td>1</td><td>New Jersey</td><td>3,415</td><td>30</td><td>Mississippi</td><td>120</td></tr>
<tr><td>44</td><td>New Mexico</td><td>34</td><td>31</td><td>Arkansas</td><td>109</td></tr>
<tr><td>5</td><td>New York</td><td>1,319</td><td>32</td><td>Oklahoma</td><td>103</td></tr>
<tr><td>17</td><td>North Carolina</td><td>322</td><td>33</td><td>Vermont</td><td>102</td></tr>
<tr><td>47</td><td>North Dakota</td><td>16</td><td>34</td><td>Colorado</td><td>95</td></tr>
<tr><td>11</td><td>Ohio</td><td>531</td><td>35</td><td>Minnesota</td><td>92</td></tr>
<tr><td>32</td><td>Oklahoma</td><td>103</td><td>36</td><td>Iowa</td><td>90</td></tr>
<tr><td>40</td><td>Oregon</td><td>62</td><td>37</td><td>Arizona</td><td>88</td></tr>
<tr><td>10</td><td>Pennsylvania</td><td>540</td><td>38</td><td>Kansas</td><td>75</td></tr>
<tr><td>2</td><td>Rhode Island</td><td>1,968</td><td>39</td><td>Maine</td><td>69</td></tr>
<tr><td>20</td><td>South Carolina</td><td>278</td><td>40</td><td>Oregon</td><td>62</td></tr>
<tr><td>46</td><td>South Dakota</td><td>19</td><td>41</td><td>Utah</td><td>44</td></tr>
<tr><td>19</td><td>Tennessee</td><td>288</td><td>42</td><td>Nebraska</td><td>43</td></tr>
<tr><td>26</td><td>Texas</td><td>179</td><td>43</td><td>Nevada</td><td>39</td></tr>
<tr><td>41</td><td>Utah</td><td>44</td><td>44</td><td>New Mexico</td><td>34</td></tr>
<tr><td>33</td><td>Vermont</td><td>102</td><td>45</td><td>Idaho</td><td>30</td></tr>
<tr><td>13</td><td>Virginia</td><td>436</td><td>46</td><td>South Dakota</td><td>19</td></tr>
<tr><td>28</td><td>Washington</td><td>132</td><td>47</td><td>North Dakota</td><td>16</td></tr>
<tr><td>29</td><td>West Virginia</td><td>123</td><td>48</td><td>Wyoming</td><td>14</td></tr>
<tr><td>23</td><td>Wisconsin</td><td>194</td><td>49</td><td>Montana</td><td>11</td></tr>
<tr><td>48</td><td>Wyoming</td><td>14</td><td>50</td><td>Alaska</td><td>2</td></tr>
<tr><td></td><td></td><td></td><td></td><td>District of Columbia**</td><td>NA</td></tr>
</table>

Source: Morgan Quitno Press using data from U.S. Department of Justice, Bureau of Justice Statistics
"Census of State and Local Law Enforcement Agencies, 1996" (Bulletin, June 1998, NCJ-164618)
*Includes state and local police, sheriffs' departments and special police agencies.
**The District of Columbia has 3,909 sworn officers for its 68 square miles.

Full-Time Employees in Law Enforcement Agencies in 1996

National Total = 921,978 Employees*

<table>
<tr><td colspan="4">ALPHA ORDER</td><td colspan="4">RANK ORDER</td></tr>
<tr><td>RANK</td><td>STATE</td><td>EMPLOYEES</td><td>% of USA</td><td>RANK</td><td>STATE</td><td>EMPLOYEES</td><td>% of USA</td></tr>
<tr><td>21</td><td>Alabama</td><td>14,389</td><td>1.6%</td><td>1</td><td>California</td><td>103,967</td><td>11.3%</td></tr>
<tr><td>48</td><td>Alaska</td><td>1,884</td><td>0.2%</td><td>2</td><td>New York</td><td>88,348</td><td>9.6%</td></tr>
<tr><td>18</td><td>Arizona</td><td>16,828</td><td>1.8%</td><td>3</td><td>Texas</td><td>73,112</td><td>7.9%</td></tr>
<tr><td>32</td><td>Arkansas</td><td>7,958</td><td>0.9%</td><td>4</td><td>Florida</td><td>60,808</td><td>6.6%</td></tr>
<tr><td>1</td><td>California</td><td>103,967</td><td>11.3%</td><td>5</td><td>Illinois</td><td>50,255</td><td>5.5%</td></tr>
<tr><td>23</td><td>Colorado</td><td>14,002</td><td>1.5%</td><td>6</td><td>New Jersey</td><td>34,940</td><td>3.8%</td></tr>
<tr><td>27</td><td>Connecticut</td><td>10,319</td><td>1.1%</td><td>7</td><td>Ohio</td><td>32,719</td><td>3.5%</td></tr>
<tr><td>47</td><td>Delaware</td><td>2,134</td><td>0.2%</td><td>8</td><td>Pennsylvania</td><td>29,506</td><td>3.2%</td></tr>
<tr><td>4</td><td>Florida</td><td>60,808</td><td>6.6%</td><td>9</td><td>Georgia</td><td>28,204</td><td>3.1%</td></tr>
<tr><td>9</td><td>Georgia</td><td>28,204</td><td>3.1%</td><td>10</td><td>Michigan</td><td>27,490</td><td>3.0%</td></tr>
<tr><td>39</td><td>Hawaii</td><td>3,745</td><td>0.4%</td><td>11</td><td>Massachusetts</td><td>24,434</td><td>2.7%</td></tr>
<tr><td>40</td><td>Idaho</td><td>3,674</td><td>0.4%</td><td>12</td><td>North Carolina</td><td>23,263</td><td>2.5%</td></tr>
<tr><td>5</td><td>Illinois</td><td>50,255</td><td>5.5%</td><td>13</td><td>Virginia</td><td>23,108</td><td>2.5%</td></tr>
<tr><td>20</td><td>Indiana</td><td>16,378</td><td>1.8%</td><td>14</td><td>Louisiana</td><td>19,817</td><td>2.1%</td></tr>
<tr><td>33</td><td>Iowa</td><td>6,799</td><td>0.7%</td><td>15</td><td>Tennessee</td><td>18,746</td><td>2.0%</td></tr>
<tr><td>29</td><td>Kansas</td><td>8,736</td><td>0.9%</td><td>16</td><td>Maryland</td><td>18,382</td><td>2.0%</td></tr>
<tr><td>31</td><td>Kentucky</td><td>8,544</td><td>0.9%</td><td>17</td><td>Missouri</td><td>17,889</td><td>1.9%</td></tr>
<tr><td>14</td><td>Louisiana</td><td>19,817</td><td>2.1%</td><td>18</td><td>Arizona</td><td>16,828</td><td>1.8%</td></tr>
<tr><td>41</td><td>Maine</td><td>3,534</td><td>0.4%</td><td>19</td><td>Wisconsin</td><td>16,490</td><td>1.8%</td></tr>
<tr><td>16</td><td>Maryland</td><td>18,382</td><td>2.0%</td><td>20</td><td>Indiana</td><td>16,378</td><td>1.8%</td></tr>
<tr><td>11</td><td>Massachusetts</td><td>24,434</td><td>2.7%</td><td>21</td><td>Alabama</td><td>14,389</td><td>1.6%</td></tr>
<tr><td>10</td><td>Michigan</td><td>27,490</td><td>3.0%</td><td>22</td><td>Washington</td><td>14,061</td><td>1.5%</td></tr>
<tr><td>25</td><td>Minnesota</td><td>11,317</td><td>1.2%</td><td>23</td><td>Colorado</td><td>14,002</td><td>1.5%</td></tr>
<tr><td>30</td><td>Mississippi</td><td>8,583</td><td>0.9%</td><td>24</td><td>South Carolina</td><td>11,494</td><td>1.2%</td></tr>
<tr><td>17</td><td>Missouri</td><td>17,889</td><td>1.9%</td><td>25</td><td>Minnesota</td><td>11,317</td><td>1.2%</td></tr>
<tr><td>44</td><td>Montana</td><td>2,541</td><td>0.3%</td><td>26</td><td>Oklahoma</td><td>10,491</td><td>1.1%</td></tr>
<tr><td>37</td><td>Nebraska</td><td>4,529</td><td>0.5%</td><td>27</td><td>Connecticut</td><td>10,319</td><td>1.1%</td></tr>
<tr><td>34</td><td>Nevada</td><td>6,231</td><td>0.7%</td><td>28</td><td>Oregon</td><td>8,933</td><td>1.0%</td></tr>
<tr><td>43</td><td>New Hampshire</td><td>2,957</td><td>0.3%</td><td>29</td><td>Kansas</td><td>8,736</td><td>0.9%</td></tr>
<tr><td>6</td><td>New Jersey</td><td>34,940</td><td>3.8%</td><td>30</td><td>Mississippi</td><td>8,583</td><td>0.9%</td></tr>
<tr><td>35</td><td>New Mexico</td><td>6,182</td><td>0.7%</td><td>31</td><td>Kentucky</td><td>8,544</td><td>0.9%</td></tr>
<tr><td>2</td><td>New York</td><td>88,348</td><td>9.6%</td><td>32</td><td>Arkansas</td><td>7,958</td><td>0.9%</td></tr>
<tr><td>12</td><td>North Carolina</td><td>23,263</td><td>2.5%</td><td>33</td><td>Iowa</td><td>6,799</td><td>0.7%</td></tr>
<tr><td>49</td><td>North Dakota</td><td>1,537</td><td>0.2%</td><td>34</td><td>Nevada</td><td>6,231</td><td>0.7%</td></tr>
<tr><td>7</td><td>Ohio</td><td>32,719</td><td>3.5%</td><td>35</td><td>New Mexico</td><td>6,182</td><td>0.7%</td></tr>
<tr><td>26</td><td>Oklahoma</td><td>10,491</td><td>1.1%</td><td>36</td><td>Utah</td><td>5,052</td><td>0.5%</td></tr>
<tr><td>28</td><td>Oregon</td><td>8,933</td><td>1.0%</td><td>37</td><td>Nebraska</td><td>4,529</td><td>0.5%</td></tr>
<tr><td>8</td><td>Pennsylvania</td><td>29,506</td><td>3.2%</td><td>38</td><td>West Virginia</td><td>4,074</td><td>0.4%</td></tr>
<tr><td>42</td><td>Rhode Island</td><td>3,098</td><td>0.3%</td><td>39</td><td>Hawaii</td><td>3,745</td><td>0.4%</td></tr>
<tr><td>24</td><td>South Carolina</td><td>11,494</td><td>1.2%</td><td>40</td><td>Idaho</td><td>3,674</td><td>0.4%</td></tr>
<tr><td>45</td><td>South Dakota</td><td>2,360</td><td>0.3%</td><td>41</td><td>Maine</td><td>3,534</td><td>0.4%</td></tr>
<tr><td>15</td><td>Tennessee</td><td>18,746</td><td>2.0%</td><td>42</td><td>Rhode Island</td><td>3,098</td><td>0.3%</td></tr>
<tr><td>3</td><td>Texas</td><td>73,112</td><td>7.9%</td><td>43</td><td>New Hampshire</td><td>2,957</td><td>0.3%</td></tr>
<tr><td>36</td><td>Utah</td><td>5,052</td><td>0.5%</td><td>44</td><td>Montana</td><td>2,541</td><td>0.3%</td></tr>
<tr><td>50</td><td>Vermont</td><td>1,336</td><td>0.1%</td><td>45</td><td>South Dakota</td><td>2,360</td><td>0.3%</td></tr>
<tr><td>13</td><td>Virginia</td><td>23,108</td><td>2.5%</td><td>46</td><td>Wyoming</td><td>2,149</td><td>0.2%</td></tr>
<tr><td>22</td><td>Washington</td><td>14,061</td><td>1.5%</td><td>47</td><td>Delaware</td><td>2,134</td><td>0.2%</td></tr>
<tr><td>38</td><td>West Virginia</td><td>4,074</td><td>0.4%</td><td>48</td><td>Alaska</td><td>1,884</td><td>0.2%</td></tr>
<tr><td>19</td><td>Wisconsin</td><td>16,490</td><td>1.8%</td><td>49</td><td>North Dakota</td><td>1,537</td><td>0.2%</td></tr>
<tr><td>46</td><td>Wyoming</td><td>2,149</td><td>0.2%</td><td>50</td><td>Vermont</td><td>1,336</td><td>0.1%</td></tr>
<tr><td></td><td></td><td></td><td></td><td></td><td>District of Columbia</td><td>4,651</td><td>0.5%</td></tr>
</table>

Source: U.S. Department of Justice, Bureau of Justice Statistics
"Census of State and Local Law Enforcement Agencies, 1996" (Bulletin, June 1998, NCJ-164618)
*Includes state and local police, sheriffs' departments and special police agencies.

Rate of Full-Time Employees in Law Enforcement Agencies in 1996

National Rate = 35 Employees per 10,000 Population*

ALPHA ORDER

RANK	STATE	RATE
17	Alabama	34
29	Alaska	31
9	Arizona	38
21	Arkansas	32
19	California	33
12	Colorado	37
21	Connecticut	32
33	Delaware	29
5	Florida	42
9	Georgia	38
21	Hawaii	32
29	Idaho	31
5	Illinois	42
37	Indiana	28
44	Iowa	24
17	Kansas	34
49	Kentucky	22
2	Louisiana	46
37	Maine	28
13	Maryland	36
7	Massachusetts	40
33	Michigan	29
44	Minnesota	24
21	Mississippi	32
19	Missouri	33
33	Montana	29
40	Nebraska	27
8	Nevada	39
41	New Hampshire	25
4	New Jersey	44
13	New Mexico	36
1	New York	49
21	North Carolina	32
44	North Dakota	24
33	Ohio	29
21	Oklahoma	32
37	Oregon	28
44	Pennsylvania	24
29	Rhode Island	31
29	South Carolina	31
21	South Dakota	32
15	Tennessee	35
9	Texas	38
41	Utah	25
48	Vermont	23
15	Virginia	35
41	Washington	25
49	West Virginia	22
21	Wisconsin	32
3	Wyoming	45

RANK ORDER

RANK	STATE	RATE
1	New York	49
2	Louisiana	46
3	Wyoming	45
4	New Jersey	44
5	Florida	42
5	Illinois	42
7	Massachusetts	40
8	Nevada	39
9	Arizona	38
9	Georgia	38
9	Texas	38
12	Colorado	37
13	Maryland	36
13	New Mexico	36
15	Tennessee	35
15	Virginia	35
17	Alabama	34
17	Kansas	34
19	California	33
19	Missouri	33
21	Arkansas	32
21	Connecticut	32
21	Hawaii	32
21	Mississippi	32
21	North Carolina	32
21	Oklahoma	32
21	South Dakota	32
21	Wisconsin	32
29	Alaska	31
29	Idaho	31
29	Rhode Island	31
29	South Carolina	31
33	Delaware	29
33	Michigan	29
33	Montana	29
33	Ohio	29
37	Indiana	28
37	Maine	28
37	Oregon	28
40	Nebraska	27
41	New Hampshire	25
41	Utah	25
41	Washington	25
44	Iowa	24
44	Minnesota	24
44	North Dakota	24
44	Pennsylvania	24
48	Vermont	23
49	Kentucky	22
49	West Virginia	22
	District of Columbia	86

Source: U.S. Department of Justice, Bureau of Justice Statistics
"Census of State and Local Law Enforcement Agencies, 1996" (Bulletin, June 1998, NCJ-164618)
*Includes state and local police, sheriffs' departments and special police agencies.

Full-Time Sworn Officers in State Police Departments in 1996

National Total = 54,587 Officers*

ALPHA ORDER

RANK	STATE	OFFICERS	% of USA
27	Alabama	581	1.1%
41	Alaska	290	0.5%
18	Arizona	952	1.7%
32	Arkansas	522	1.0%
1	California	6,219	11.4%
27	Colorado	581	1.1%
15	Connecticut	1,022	1.9%
30	Delaware	540	1.0%
9	Florida	1,740	3.2%
21	Georgia	878	1.6%
50	Hawaii	0	0.0%
46	Idaho	192	0.4%
8	Illinois	1,988	3.6%
14	Indiana	1,207	2.2%
37	Iowa	433	0.8%
29	Kansas	552	1.0%
17	Kentucky	984	1.8%
22	Louisiana	873	1.6%
40	Maine	337	0.6%
11	Maryland	1,625	3.0%
6	Massachusetts	2,565	4.7%
7	Michigan	2,164	4.0%
34	Minnesota	484	0.9%
31	Mississippi	535	1.0%
16	Missouri	996	1.8%
44	Montana	212	0.4%
35	Nebraska	464	0.9%
38	Nevada	375	0.7%
43	New Hampshire	245	0.4%
5	New Jersey	2,702	4.9%
36	New Mexico	435	0.8%
3	New York	3,972	7.3%
13	North Carolina	1,380	2.5%
49	North Dakota	120	0.2%
12	Ohio	1,391	2.5%
25	Oklahoma	756	1.4%
23	Oregon	824	1.5%
2	Pennsylvania	4,114	7.5%
45	Rhode Island	193	0.4%
20	South Carolina	892	1.6%
47	South Dakota	155	0.3%
24	Tennessee	768	1.4%
4	Texas	2,873	5.3%
39	Utah	355	0.7%
41	Vermont	290	0.5%
10	Virginia	1,662	3.0%
19	Washington	906	1.7%
26	West Virginia	595	1.1%
33	Wisconsin	497	0.9%
48	Wyoming	151	0.3%

RANK ORDER

RANK	STATE	OFFICERS	% of USA
1	California	6,219	11.4%
2	Pennsylvania	4,114	7.5%
3	New York	3,972	7.3%
4	Texas	2,873	5.3%
5	New Jersey	2,702	4.9%
6	Massachusetts	2,565	4.7%
7	Michigan	2,164	4.0%
8	Illinois	1,988	3.6%
9	Florida	1,740	3.2%
10	Virginia	1,662	3.0%
11	Maryland	1,625	3.0%
12	Ohio	1,391	2.5%
13	North Carolina	1,380	2.5%
14	Indiana	1,207	2.2%
15	Connecticut	1,022	1.9%
16	Missouri	996	1.8%
17	Kentucky	984	1.8%
18	Arizona	952	1.7%
19	Washington	906	1.7%
20	South Carolina	892	1.6%
21	Georgia	878	1.6%
22	Louisiana	873	1.6%
23	Oregon	824	1.5%
24	Tennessee	768	1.4%
25	Oklahoma	756	1.4%
26	West Virginia	595	1.1%
27	Alabama	581	1.1%
27	Colorado	581	1.1%
29	Kansas	552	1.0%
30	Delaware	540	1.0%
31	Mississippi	535	1.0%
32	Arkansas	522	1.0%
33	Wisconsin	497	0.9%
34	Minnesota	484	0.9%
35	Nebraska	464	0.9%
36	New Mexico	435	0.8%
37	Iowa	433	0.8%
38	Nevada	375	0.7%
39	Utah	355	0.7%
40	Maine	337	0.6%
41	Alaska	290	0.5%
41	Vermont	290	0.5%
43	New Hampshire	245	0.4%
44	Montana	212	0.4%
45	Rhode Island	193	0.4%
46	Idaho	192	0.4%
47	South Dakota	155	0.3%
48	Wyoming	151	0.3%
49	North Dakota	120	0.2%
50	Hawaii	0	0.0%
	District of Columbia	0	0.0%

Source: U.S. Department of Justice, Bureau of Justice Statistics
   "Census of State and Local Law Enforcement Agencies, 1996" (Bulletin, June 1998, NCJ-164618)
*All states except Hawaii and the District of Columbia have a state police department.

Percent of Full-Time State Police Department Employees Who are Sworn Officers: 1996
National Percent = 65.2% of Employees*

ALPHA ORDER

RANK	STATE	PERCENT
45	Alabama	48.9
34	Alaska	64.7
39	Arizona	56.8
14	Arkansas	73.3
27	California	68.1
19	Colorado	71.9
31	Connecticut	66.1
22	Delaware	71.1
7	Florida	78.8
49	Georgia	30.5
NA	Hawaii**	NA
17	Idaho	73.0
41	Illinois	55.5
36	Indiana	64.0
1	Iowa	92.5
15	Kansas	73.2
37	Kentucky	58.4
21	Louisiana	71.2
22	Maine	71.1
29	Maryland	67.0
2	Massachusetts	88.9
24	Michigan	69.0
25	Minnesota	68.8
26	Mississippi	68.4
46	Missouri	47.8
10	Montana	76.5
18	Nebraska	72.7
20	Nevada	71.4
13	New Hampshire	73.6
11	New Jersey	74.1
42	New Mexico	52.6
4	New York	85.2
8	North Carolina	78.7
35	North Dakota	64.5
38	Ohio	58.2
40	Oklahoma	56.6
30	Oregon	66.2
9	Pennsylvania	77.6
5	Rhode Island	81.8
6	South Carolina	80.9
28	South Dakota	67.7
44	Tennessee	49.3
48	Texas	42.6
3	Utah	88.3
33	Vermont	65.2
12	Virginia	73.9
47	Washington	43.9
32	West Virginia	65.4
16	Wisconsin	73.1
43	Wyoming	50.2

RANK ORDER

RANK	STATE	PERCENT
1	Iowa	92.5
2	Massachusetts	88.9
3	Utah	88.3
4	New York	85.2
5	Rhode Island	81.8
6	South Carolina	80.9
7	Florida	78.8
8	North Carolina	78.7
9	Pennsylvania	77.6
10	Montana	76.5
11	New Jersey	74.1
12	Virginia	73.9
13	New Hampshire	73.6
14	Arkansas	73.3
15	Kansas	73.2
16	Wisconsin	73.1
17	Idaho	73.0
18	Nebraska	72.7
19	Colorado	71.9
20	Nevada	71.4
21	Louisiana	71.2
22	Delaware	71.1
22	Maine	71.1
24	Michigan	69.0
25	Minnesota	68.8
26	Mississippi	68.4
27	California	68.1
28	South Dakota	67.7
29	Maryland	67.0
30	Oregon	66.2
31	Connecticut	66.1
32	West Virginia	65.4
33	Vermont	65.2
34	Alaska	64.7
35	North Dakota	64.5
36	Indiana	64.0
37	Kentucky	58.4
38	Ohio	58.2
39	Arizona	56.8
40	Oklahoma	56.6
41	Illinois	55.5
42	New Mexico	52.6
43	Wyoming	50.2
44	Tennessee	49.3
45	Alabama	48.9
46	Missouri	47.8
47	Washington	43.9
48	Texas	42.6
49	Georgia	30.5
NA	Hawaii**	NA
	District of Columbia**	NA

Source: Morgan Quitno Press using data from U.S. Department of Justice, Bureau of Justice Statistics
    "Census of State and Local Law Enforcement Agencies, 1996" (Bulletin, June 1998, NCJ-164618)
*All states except Hawaii and the District of Columbia have a state police department.
**Not applicable.

Rate of Full-Time Sworn Officers in State Police Departments in 1996

National Rate = 2.1 Officers per 10,000 Population*

ALPHA ORDER

RANK ORDER

RANK	STATE	RATE		RANK	STATE	RATE
43	Alabama	1.4		1	Delaware	7.4
3	Alaska	4.8		2	Vermont	4.9
23	Arizona	2.1		3	Alaska	4.8
23	Arkansas	2.1		4	Massachusetts	4.2
29	California	2.0		5	New Jersey	3.4
40	Colorado	1.5		5	Pennsylvania	3.4
9	Connecticut	3.1		7	West Virginia	3.3
1	Delaware	7.4		8	Maryland	3.2
45	Florida	1.2		9	Connecticut	3.1
45	Georgia	1.2		9	Wyoming	3.1
50	Hawaii*	0.0		11	Nebraska	2.8
38	Idaho	1.6		12	Maine	2.7
37	Illinois	1.7		13	Oregon	2.6
23	Indiana	2.1		14	Kentucky	2.5
40	Iowa	1.5		14	New Mexico	2.5
23	Kansas	2.1		14	Virginia	2.5
14	Kentucky	2.5		17	Montana	2.4
29	Louisiana	2.0		17	South Carolina	2.4
12	Maine	2.7		19	Michigan	2.3
8	Maryland	3.2		19	Nevada	2.3
4	Massachusetts	4.2		19	Oklahoma	2.3
19	Michigan	2.3		22	New York	2.2
48	Minnesota	1.0		23	Arizona	2.1
29	Mississippi	2.0		23	Arkansas	2.1
32	Missouri	1.9		23	Indiana	2.1
17	Montana	2.4		23	Kansas	2.1
11	Nebraska	2.8		23	New Hampshire	2.1
19	Nevada	2.3		23	South Dakota	2.1
23	New Hampshire	2.1		29	California	2.0
5	New Jersey	3.4		29	Louisiana	2.0
14	New Mexico	2.5		29	Mississippi	2.0
22	New York	2.2		32	Missouri	1.9
32	North Carolina	1.9		32	North Carolina	1.9
32	North Dakota	1.9		32	North Dakota	1.9
45	Ohio	1.2		32	Rhode Island	1.9
19	Oklahoma	2.3		36	Utah	1.8
13	Oregon	2.6		37	Illinois	1.7
5	Pennsylvania	3.4		38	Idaho	1.6
32	Rhode Island	1.9		38	Washington	1.6
17	South Carolina	2.4		40	Colorado	1.5
23	South Dakota	2.1		40	Iowa	1.5
43	Tennessee	1.4		40	Texas	1.5
40	Texas	1.5		43	Alabama	1.4
36	Utah	1.8		43	Tennessee	1.4
2	Vermont	4.9		45	Florida	1.2
14	Virginia	2.5		45	Georgia	1.2
38	Washington	1.6		45	Ohio	1.2
7	West Virginia	3.3		48	Minnesota	1.0
48	Wisconsin	1.0		48	Wisconsin	1.0
9	Wyoming	3.1		50	Hawaii*	0.0
					District of Columbia*	0.0

Source: Morgan Quitno Press using data from U.S. Department of Justice, Bureau of Justice Statistics
"Census of State and Local Law Enforcement Agencies, 1996" (Bulletin, June 1998, NCJ-164618)
*All states except Hawaii and the District of Columbia have a state police department.

State Government Law Enforcement Officers in 1997

National Total = 62,225 Officers*

<table>
<tr><td colspan="4"><u>ALPHA ORDER</u></td><td colspan="4"><u>RANK ORDER</u></td></tr>
<tr><th>RANK</th><th>STATE</th><th>OFFICERS</th><th>% of USA</th><th>RANK</th><th>STATE</th><th>OFFICERS</th><th>% of USA</th></tr>
<tr><td>25</td><td>Alabama</td><td>888</td><td>1.4%</td><td>1</td><td>California</td><td>7,390</td><td>11.9%</td></tr>
<tr><td>42</td><td>Alaska</td><td>321</td><td>0.5%</td><td>2</td><td>Pennsylvania</td><td>4,165</td><td>6.7%</td></tr>
<tr><td>20</td><td>Arizona</td><td>1,004</td><td>1.6%</td><td>3</td><td>New York</td><td>3,995</td><td>6.4%</td></tr>
<tr><td>33</td><td>Arkansas</td><td>543</td><td>0.9%</td><td>4</td><td>Texas</td><td>2,807</td><td>4.5%</td></tr>
<tr><td>1</td><td>California</td><td>7,390</td><td>11.9%</td><td>5</td><td>New Jersey</td><td>2,652</td><td>4.3%</td></tr>
<tr><td>22</td><td>Colorado</td><td>939</td><td>1.5%</td><td>6</td><td>Illinois</td><td>2,651</td><td>4.3%</td></tr>
<tr><td>21</td><td>Connecticut</td><td>991</td><td>1.6%</td><td>7</td><td>Maryland</td><td>2,627</td><td>4.2%</td></tr>
<tr><td>31</td><td>Delaware</td><td>670</td><td>1.1%</td><td>8</td><td>Massachusetts</td><td>2,259</td><td>3.6%</td></tr>
<tr><td>13</td><td>Florida</td><td>1,688</td><td>2.7%</td><td>9</td><td>Michigan</td><td>2,121</td><td>3.4%</td></tr>
<tr><td>12</td><td>Georgia</td><td>1,814</td><td>2.9%</td><td>10</td><td>North Carolina</td><td>2,019</td><td>3.2%</td></tr>
<tr><td>50</td><td>Hawaii</td><td>0</td><td>0.0%</td><td>11</td><td>Virginia</td><td>1,916</td><td>3.1%</td></tr>
<tr><td>45</td><td>Idaho</td><td>235</td><td>0.4%</td><td>12</td><td>Georgia</td><td>1,814</td><td>2.9%</td></tr>
<tr><td>6</td><td>Illinois</td><td>2,651</td><td>4.3%</td><td>13</td><td>Florida</td><td>1,688</td><td>2.7%</td></tr>
<tr><td>17</td><td>Indiana</td><td>1,252</td><td>2.0%</td><td>14</td><td>South Carolina</td><td>1,373</td><td>2.2%</td></tr>
<tr><td>32</td><td>Iowa</td><td>618</td><td>1.0%</td><td>15</td><td>Kentucky</td><td>1,370</td><td>2.2%</td></tr>
<tr><td>30</td><td>Kansas</td><td>718</td><td>1.2%</td><td>16</td><td>Ohio</td><td>1,337</td><td>2.1%</td></tr>
<tr><td>15</td><td>Kentucky</td><td>1,370</td><td>2.2%</td><td>17</td><td>Indiana</td><td>1,252</td><td>2.0%</td></tr>
<tr><td>26</td><td>Louisiana</td><td>856</td><td>1.4%</td><td>18</td><td>Missouri</td><td>1,117</td><td>1.8%</td></tr>
<tr><td>41</td><td>Maine</td><td>363</td><td>0.6%</td><td>19</td><td>Tennessee</td><td>1,114</td><td>1.8%</td></tr>
<tr><td>7</td><td>Maryland</td><td>2,627</td><td>4.2%</td><td>20</td><td>Arizona</td><td>1,004</td><td>1.6%</td></tr>
<tr><td>8</td><td>Massachusetts</td><td>2,259</td><td>3.6%</td><td>21</td><td>Connecticut</td><td>991</td><td>1.6%</td></tr>
<tr><td>9</td><td>Michigan</td><td>2,121</td><td>3.4%</td><td>22</td><td>Colorado</td><td>939</td><td>1.5%</td></tr>
<tr><td>36</td><td>Minnesota</td><td>461</td><td>0.7%</td><td>23</td><td>Washington</td><td>929</td><td>1.5%</td></tr>
<tr><td>34</td><td>Mississippi</td><td>520</td><td>0.8%</td><td>24</td><td>Oregon</td><td>909</td><td>1.5%</td></tr>
<tr><td>18</td><td>Missouri</td><td>1,117</td><td>1.8%</td><td>25</td><td>Alabama</td><td>888</td><td>1.4%</td></tr>
<tr><td>37</td><td>Montana</td><td>460</td><td>0.7%</td><td>26</td><td>Louisiana</td><td>856</td><td>1.4%</td></tr>
<tr><td>35</td><td>Nebraska</td><td>475</td><td>0.8%</td><td>27</td><td>Oklahoma</td><td>769</td><td>1.2%</td></tr>
<tr><td>40</td><td>Nevada</td><td>371</td><td>0.6%</td><td>28</td><td>West Virginia</td><td>734</td><td>1.2%</td></tr>
<tr><td>43</td><td>New Hampshire</td><td>304</td><td>0.5%</td><td>29</td><td>Wisconsin</td><td>722</td><td>1.2%</td></tr>
<tr><td>5</td><td>New Jersey</td><td>2,652</td><td>4.3%</td><td>30</td><td>Kansas</td><td>718</td><td>1.2%</td></tr>
<tr><td>39</td><td>New Mexico</td><td>403</td><td>0.6%</td><td>31</td><td>Delaware</td><td>670</td><td>1.1%</td></tr>
<tr><td>3</td><td>New York</td><td>3,995</td><td>6.4%</td><td>32</td><td>Iowa</td><td>618</td><td>1.0%</td></tr>
<tr><td>10</td><td>North Carolina</td><td>2,019</td><td>3.2%</td><td>33</td><td>Arkansas</td><td>543</td><td>0.9%</td></tr>
<tr><td>49</td><td>North Dakota</td><td>130</td><td>0.2%</td><td>34</td><td>Mississippi</td><td>520</td><td>0.8%</td></tr>
<tr><td>16</td><td>Ohio</td><td>1,337</td><td>2.1%</td><td>35</td><td>Nebraska</td><td>475</td><td>0.8%</td></tr>
<tr><td>27</td><td>Oklahoma</td><td>769</td><td>1.2%</td><td>36</td><td>Minnesota</td><td>461</td><td>0.7%</td></tr>
<tr><td>24</td><td>Oregon</td><td>909</td><td>1.5%</td><td>37</td><td>Montana</td><td>460</td><td>0.7%</td></tr>
<tr><td>2</td><td>Pennsylvania</td><td>4,165</td><td>6.7%</td><td>38</td><td>Utah</td><td>420</td><td>0.7%</td></tr>
<tr><td>46</td><td>Rhode Island</td><td>218</td><td>0.4%</td><td>39</td><td>New Mexico</td><td>403</td><td>0.6%</td></tr>
<tr><td>14</td><td>South Carolina</td><td>1,373</td><td>2.2%</td><td>40</td><td>Nevada</td><td>371</td><td>0.6%</td></tr>
<tr><td>47</td><td>South Dakota</td><td>162</td><td>0.3%</td><td>41</td><td>Maine</td><td>363</td><td>0.6%</td></tr>
<tr><td>19</td><td>Tennessee</td><td>1,114</td><td>1.8%</td><td>42</td><td>Alaska</td><td>321</td><td>0.5%</td></tr>
<tr><td>4</td><td>Texas</td><td>2,807</td><td>4.5%</td><td>43</td><td>New Hampshire</td><td>304</td><td>0.5%</td></tr>
<tr><td>38</td><td>Utah</td><td>420</td><td>0.7%</td><td>44</td><td>Vermont</td><td>280</td><td>0.4%</td></tr>
<tr><td>44</td><td>Vermont</td><td>280</td><td>0.4%</td><td>45</td><td>Idaho</td><td>235</td><td>0.4%</td></tr>
<tr><td>11</td><td>Virginia</td><td>1,916</td><td>3.1%</td><td>46</td><td>Rhode Island</td><td>218</td><td>0.4%</td></tr>
<tr><td>23</td><td>Washington</td><td>929</td><td>1.5%</td><td>47</td><td>South Dakota</td><td>162</td><td>0.3%</td></tr>
<tr><td>28</td><td>West Virginia</td><td>734</td><td>1.2%</td><td>48</td><td>Wyoming</td><td>145</td><td>0.2%</td></tr>
<tr><td>29</td><td>Wisconsin</td><td>722</td><td>1.2%</td><td>49</td><td>North Dakota</td><td>130</td><td>0.2%</td></tr>
<tr><td>48</td><td>Wyoming</td><td>145</td><td>0.2%</td><td>50</td><td>Hawaii</td><td>0</td><td>0.0%</td></tr>
<tr><td></td><td></td><td></td><td></td><td></td><td>District of Columbia</td><td>0</td><td>0.0%</td></tr>
</table>

Source: Federal Bureau of Investigation
"Crime in the United States 1997" (Uniform Crime Reports, November 22, 1998)
*Includes state police agencies and other agencies with law enforcement powers. Hawaii and the District of Columbia do not have a state police agency.

Male State Government Law Enforcement Officers in 1997

National Total = 57,988 Male Officers*

ALPHA ORDER					RANK ORDER				
RANK	STATE		OFFICERS	% of USA	RANK	STATE		OFFICERS	% of USA
24	Alabama		864	1.5%	1	California		6,658	11.5%
42	Alaska		304	0.5%	2	Pennsylvania		4,004	6.9%
20	Arizona		936	1.6%	3	New York		3,673	6.3%
33	Arkansas		515	0.9%	4	Texas		2,673	4.6%
1	California		6,658	11.5%	5	New Jersey		2,573	4.4%
23	Colorado		881	1.5%	6	Illinois		2,430	4.2%
21	Connecticut		923	1.6%	7	Maryland		2,318	4.0%
31	Delaware		615	1.1%	8	Massachusetts		2,036	3.5%
13	Florida		1,497	2.6%	9	North Carolina		1,925	3.3%
12	Georgia		1,681	2.9%	10	Michigan		1,862	3.2%
50	Hawaii		0	0.0%	11	Virginia		1,829	3.2%
45	Idaho		225	0.4%	12	Georgia		1,681	2.9%
6	Illinois		2,430	4.2%	13	Florida		1,497	2.6%
17	Indiana		1,188	2.0%	14	Kentucky		1,322	2.3%
32	Iowa		583	1.0%	15	South Carolina		1,284	2.2%
29	Kansas		678	1.2%	16	Ohio		1,224	2.1%
14	Kentucky		1,322	2.3%	17	Indiana		1,188	2.0%
26	Louisiana		837	1.4%	18	Missouri		1,079	1.9%
41	Maine		342	0.6%	19	Tennessee		1,058	1.8%
7	Maryland		2,318	4.0%	20	Arizona		936	1.6%
8	Massachusetts		2,036	3.5%	21	Connecticut		923	1.6%
10	Michigan		1,862	3.2%	22	Washington		886	1.5%
37	Minnesota		428	0.7%	23	Colorado		881	1.5%
34	Mississippi		512	0.9%	24	Alabama		864	1.5%
18	Missouri		1,079	1.9%	25	Oregon		838	1.4%
36	Montana		430	0.7%	26	Louisiana		837	1.4%
35	Nebraska		454	0.8%	27	Oklahoma		756	1.3%
40	Nevada		348	0.6%	28	West Virginia		720	1.2%
43	New Hampshire		277	0.5%	29	Kansas		678	1.2%
5	New Jersey		2,573	4.4%	30	Wisconsin		636	1.1%
39	New Mexico		393	0.7%	31	Delaware		615	1.1%
3	New York		3,673	6.3%	32	Iowa		583	1.0%
9	North Carolina		1,925	3.3%	33	Arkansas		515	0.9%
49	North Dakota		125	0.2%	34	Mississippi		512	0.9%
16	Ohio		1,224	2.1%	35	Nebraska		454	0.8%
27	Oklahoma		756	1.3%	36	Montana		430	0.7%
25	Oregon		838	1.4%	37	Minnesota		428	0.7%
2	Pennsylvania		4,004	6.9%	38	Utah		400	0.7%
46	Rhode Island		201	0.3%	39	New Mexico		393	0.7%
15	South Carolina		1,284	2.2%	40	Nevada		348	0.6%
47	South Dakota		160	0.3%	41	Maine		342	0.6%
19	Tennessee		1,058	1.8%	42	Alaska		304	0.5%
4	Texas		2,673	4.6%	43	New Hampshire		277	0.5%
38	Utah		400	0.7%	44	Vermont		264	0.5%
44	Vermont		264	0.5%	45	Idaho		225	0.4%
11	Virginia		1,829	3.2%	46	Rhode Island		201	0.3%
22	Washington		886	1.5%	47	South Dakota		160	0.3%
28	West Virginia		720	1.2%	48	Wyoming		143	0.2%
30	Wisconsin		636	1.1%	49	North Dakota		125	0.2%
48	Wyoming		143	0.2%	50	Hawaii		0	0.0%
						District of Columbia		0	0.0%

Source: Federal Bureau of Investigation
   "Crime in the United States 1997" (Uniform Crime Reports, November 22, 1998)
*Includes state police agencies and other agencies with law enforcement powers. Hawaii and the District of Columbia do not have a state police agency.

Female State Government Law Enforcement Officers in 1997

National Total = 4,237 Female Officers*

ALPHA ORDER

RANK ORDER

RANK	STATE	OFFICERS	% of USA
33	Alabama	24	0.6%
39	Alaska	17	0.4%
18	Arizona	68	1.6%
31	Arkansas	28	0.7%
1	California	732	17.3%
21	Colorado	58	1.4%
18	Connecticut	68	1.6%
23	Delaware	55	1.3%
7	Florida	191	4.5%
10	Georgia	133	3.1%
50	Hawaii	0	0.0%
44	Idaho	10	0.2%
6	Illinois	221	5.2%
20	Indiana	64	1.5%
28	Iowa	35	0.8%
26	Kansas	40	0.9%
24	Kentucky	48	1.1%
38	Louisiana	19	0.4%
35	Maine	21	0.5%
3	Maryland	309	7.3%
5	Massachusetts	223	5.3%
4	Michigan	259	6.1%
29	Minnesota	33	0.8%
46	Mississippi	8	0.2%
27	Missouri	38	0.9%
30	Montana	30	0.7%
35	Nebraska	21	0.5%
34	Nevada	23	0.5%
32	New Hampshire	27	0.6%
16	New Jersey	79	1.9%
44	New Mexico	10	0.2%
2	New York	322	7.6%
12	North Carolina	94	2.2%
47	North Dakota	5	0.1%
11	Ohio	113	2.7%
43	Oklahoma	13	0.3%
17	Oregon	71	1.7%
8	Pennsylvania	161	3.8%
39	Rhode Island	17	0.4%
13	South Carolina	89	2.1%
48	South Dakota	2	0.0%
22	Tennessee	56	1.3%
9	Texas	134	3.2%
37	Utah	20	0.5%
41	Vermont	16	0.4%
14	Virginia	87	2.1%
25	Washington	43	1.0%
42	West Virginia	14	0.3%
15	Wisconsin	86	2.0%
48	Wyoming	2	0.0%

RANK	STATE	OFFICERS	% of USA
1	California	732	17.3%
2	New York	322	7.6%
3	Maryland	309	7.3%
4	Michigan	259	6.1%
5	Massachusetts	223	5.3%
6	Illinois	221	5.2%
7	Florida	191	4.5%
8	Pennsylvania	161	3.8%
9	Texas	134	3.2%
10	Georgia	133	3.1%
11	Ohio	113	2.7%
12	North Carolina	94	2.2%
13	South Carolina	89	2.1%
14	Virginia	87	2.1%
15	Wisconsin	86	2.0%
16	New Jersey	79	1.9%
17	Oregon	71	1.7%
18	Arizona	68	1.6%
18	Connecticut	68	1.6%
20	Indiana	64	1.5%
21	Colorado	58	1.4%
22	Tennessee	56	1.3%
23	Delaware	55	1.3%
24	Kentucky	48	1.1%
25	Washington	43	1.0%
26	Kansas	40	0.9%
27	Missouri	38	0.9%
28	Iowa	35	0.8%
29	Minnesota	33	0.8%
30	Montana	30	0.7%
31	Arkansas	28	0.7%
32	New Hampshire	27	0.6%
33	Alabama	24	0.6%
34	Nevada	23	0.5%
35	Maine	21	0.5%
35	Nebraska	21	0.5%
37	Utah	20	0.5%
38	Louisiana	19	0.4%
39	Alaska	17	0.4%
39	Rhode Island	17	0.4%
41	Vermont	16	0.4%
42	West Virginia	14	0.3%
43	Oklahoma	13	0.3%
44	Idaho	10	0.2%
44	New Mexico	10	0.2%
46	Mississippi	8	0.2%
47	North Dakota	5	0.1%
48	South Dakota	2	0.0%
48	Wyoming	2	0.0%
50	Hawaii	0	0.0%
	District of Columbia	0	0.0%

Source: Federal Bureau of Investigation
   "Crime in the United States 1997" (Uniform Crime Reports, November 22, 1998)
*Includes state police agencies and other agencies with law enforcement powers. Hawaii and the District of Columbia do not have a state police agency.

Female State Government Law Enforcement Officers
As a Percent of All Officers: 1997
National Percent = 6.8% of Officers*

ALPHA ORDER

RANK ORDER

RANK	STATE	PERCENT		RANK	STATE	PERCENT
42	Alabama	2.7		1	Michigan	12.2
26	Alaska	5.3		2	Wisconsin	11.9
17	Arizona	6.8		3	Maryland	11.8
27	Arkansas	5.2		4	Florida	11.3
5	California	9.9		5	California	9.9
20	Colorado	6.2		5	Massachusetts	9.9
16	Connecticut	6.9		7	New Hampshire	8.9
10	Delaware	8.2		8	Ohio	8.5
4	Florida	11.3		9	Illinois	8.3
14	Georgia	7.3		10	Delaware	8.2
NA	Hawaii**	NA		11	New York	8.1
36	Idaho	4.3		12	Oregon	7.8
9	Illinois	8.3		12	Rhode Island	7.8
28	Indiana	5.1		14	Georgia	7.3
23	Iowa	5.7		15	Minnesota	7.2
25	Kansas	5.6		16	Connecticut	6.9
39	Kentucky	3.5		17	Arizona	6.8
44	Louisiana	2.2		18	Montana	6.5
22	Maine	5.8		18	South Carolina	6.5
3	Maryland	11.8		20	Colorado	6.2
5	Massachusetts	9.9		20	Nevada	6.2
1	Michigan	12.2		22	Maine	5.8
15	Minnesota	7.2		23	Iowa	5.7
47	Mississippi	1.5		23	Vermont	5.7
40	Missouri	3.4		25	Kansas	5.6
18	Montana	6.5		26	Alaska	5.3
35	Nebraska	4.4		27	Arkansas	5.2
20	Nevada	6.2		28	Indiana	5.1
7	New Hampshire	8.9		29	Tennessee	5.0
41	New Jersey	3.0		30	Texas	4.8
43	New Mexico	2.5		30	Utah	4.8
11	New York	8.1		32	North Carolina	4.7
32	North Carolina	4.7		33	Washington	4.6
38	North Dakota	3.8		34	Virginia	4.5
8	Ohio	8.5		35	Nebraska	4.4
46	Oklahoma	1.7		36	Idaho	4.3
12	Oregon	7.8		37	Pennsylvania	3.9
37	Pennsylvania	3.9		38	North Dakota	3.8
12	Rhode Island	7.8		39	Kentucky	3.5
18	South Carolina	6.5		40	Missouri	3.4
49	South Dakota	1.2		41	New Jersey	3.0
29	Tennessee	5.0		42	Alabama	2.7
30	Texas	4.8		43	New Mexico	2.5
30	Utah	4.8		44	Louisiana	2.2
23	Vermont	5.7		45	West Virginia	1.9
34	Virginia	4.5		46	Oklahoma	1.7
33	Washington	4.6		47	Mississippi	1.5
45	West Virginia	1.9		48	Wyoming	1.4
2	Wisconsin	11.9		49	South Dakota	1.2
48	Wyoming	1.4		NA	Hawaii**	NA
					District of Columbia**	NA

Source: Morgan Quitno Press using data from Federal Bureau of Investigation
     "Crime in the United States 1997" (Uniform Crime Reports, November 22, 1998)
*Includes state police agencies and other agencies with law enforcement powers.
**Hawaii and the District of Columbia do not have a state police agency.

Local Police Departments in 1996

National Total = 13,578 Departments*

ALPHA ORDER

RANK	STATE	DEPARTMENTS	% of USA
17	Alabama	331	2.4%
44	Alaska	61	0.4%
39	Arizona	88	0.6%
21	Arkansas	261	1.9%
15	California	344	2.5%
32	Colorado	163	1.2%
36	Connecticut	107	0.8%
48	Delaware	35	0.3%
19	Florida	289	2.1%
12	Georgia	377	2.8%
50	Hawaii	4	0.0%
42	Idaho	76	0.6%
2	Illinois	809	6.0%
10	Indiana	432	3.2%
18	Iowa	318	2.3%
24	Kansas	245	1.8%
23	Kentucky	254	1.9%
20	Louisiana	271	2.0%
35	Maine	115	0.8%
41	Maryland	78	0.6%
16	Massachusetts	341	2.5%
8	Michigan	475	3.5%
11	Minnesota	384	2.8%
27	Mississippi	205	1.5%
5	Missouri	509	3.7%
43	Montana	65	0.5%
31	Nebraska	168	1.2%
49	Nevada	26	0.2%
26	New Hampshire	219	1.6%
6	New Jersey	487	3.6%
38	New Mexico	91	0.7%
7	New York	476	3.5%
13	North Carolina	370	2.7%
40	North Dakota	81	0.6%
3	Ohio	808	6.0%
14	Oklahoma	347	2.6%
33	Oregon	142	1.0%
1	Pennsylvania	1,141	8.4%
47	Rhode Island	40	0.3%
28	South Carolina	192	1.4%
34	South Dakota	119	0.9%
22	Tennessee	255	1.9%
4	Texas	735	5.4%
37	Utah	95	0.7%
46	Vermont	52	0.4%
30	Virginia	170	1.3%
25	Washington	223	1.6%
29	West Virginia	179	1.3%
9	Wisconsin	471	3.5%
45	Wyoming	53	0.4%

RANK ORDER

RANK	STATE	DEPARTMENTS	% of USA
1	Pennsylvania	1,141	8.4%
2	Illinois	809	6.0%
3	Ohio	808	6.0%
4	Texas	735	5.4%
5	Missouri	509	3.7%
6	New Jersey	487	3.6%
7	New York	476	3.5%
8	Michigan	475	3.5%
9	Wisconsin	471	3.5%
10	Indiana	432	3.2%
11	Minnesota	384	2.8%
12	Georgia	377	2.8%
13	North Carolina	370	2.7%
14	Oklahoma	347	2.6%
15	California	344	2.5%
16	Massachusetts	341	2.5%
17	Alabama	331	2.4%
18	Iowa	318	2.3%
19	Florida	289	2.1%
20	Louisiana	271	2.0%
21	Arkansas	261	1.9%
22	Tennessee	255	1.9%
23	Kentucky	254	1.9%
24	Kansas	245	1.8%
25	Washington	223	1.6%
26	New Hampshire	219	1.6%
27	Mississippi	205	1.5%
28	South Carolina	192	1.4%
29	West Virginia	179	1.3%
30	Virginia	170	1.3%
31	Nebraska	168	1.2%
32	Colorado	163	1.2%
33	Oregon	142	1.0%
34	South Dakota	119	0.9%
35	Maine	115	0.8%
36	Connecticut	107	0.8%
37	Utah	95	0.7%
38	New Mexico	91	0.7%
39	Arizona	88	0.6%
40	North Dakota	81	0.6%
41	Maryland	78	0.6%
42	Idaho	76	0.6%
43	Montana	65	0.5%
44	Alaska	61	0.4%
45	Wyoming	53	0.4%
46	Vermont	52	0.4%
47	Rhode Island	40	0.3%
48	Delaware	35	0.3%
49	Nevada	26	0.2%
50	Hawaii	4	0.0%
	District of Columbia	1	0.0%

Source: U.S. Department of Justice, Bureau of Justice Statistics
   "Census of State and Local Law Enforcement Agencies, 1996" (Bulletin, June 1998, NCJ-164618)
*Includes consolidated police-sheriffs' departments.

Full-Time Officers in Local Police Departments in 1996

National Total = 410,956 Officers*

<table>
<tr><td colspan="4">ALPHA ORDER</td><td colspan="4">RANK ORDER</td></tr>
<tr><th>RANK</th><th>STATE</th><th>OFFICERS</th><th>% of USA</th><th>RANK</th><th>STATE</th><th>OFFICERS</th><th>% of USA</th></tr>
<tr><td>19</td><td>Alabama</td><td>6,484</td><td>1.6%</td><td>1</td><td>New York</td><td>54,657</td><td>13.3%</td></tr>
<tr><td>46</td><td>Alaska</td><td>740</td><td>0.2%</td><td>2</td><td>California</td><td>35,939</td><td>8.7%</td></tr>
<tr><td>18</td><td>Arizona</td><td>6,967</td><td>1.7%</td><td>3</td><td>Texas</td><td>28,269</td><td>6.9%</td></tr>
<tr><td>32</td><td>Arkansas</td><td>3,244</td><td>0.8%</td><td>4</td><td>Illinois</td><td>26,151</td><td>6.4%</td></tr>
<tr><td>2</td><td>California</td><td>35,939</td><td>8.7%</td><td>5</td><td>New Jersey</td><td>19,891</td><td>4.8%</td></tr>
<tr><td>23</td><td>Colorado</td><td>5,451</td><td>1.3%</td><td>6</td><td>Florida</td><td>19,652</td><td>4.8%</td></tr>
<tr><td>21</td><td>Connecticut</td><td>6,411</td><td>1.6%</td><td>7</td><td>Pennsylvania</td><td>17,655</td><td>4.3%</td></tr>
<tr><td>44</td><td>Delaware</td><td>923</td><td>0.2%</td><td>8</td><td>Ohio</td><td>15,932</td><td>3.9%</td></tr>
<tr><td>6</td><td>Florida</td><td>19,652</td><td>4.8%</td><td>9</td><td>Michigan</td><td>13,288</td><td>3.2%</td></tr>
<tr><td>11</td><td>Georgia</td><td>10,241</td><td>2.5%</td><td>10</td><td>Massachusetts</td><td>13,068</td><td>3.2%</td></tr>
<tr><td>34</td><td>Hawaii</td><td>2,746</td><td>0.7%</td><td>11</td><td>Georgia</td><td>10,241</td><td>2.5%</td></tr>
<tr><td>43</td><td>Idaho</td><td>1,142</td><td>0.3%</td><td>12</td><td>North Carolina</td><td>9,505</td><td>2.3%</td></tr>
<tr><td>4</td><td>Illinois</td><td>26,151</td><td>6.4%</td><td>13</td><td>Maryland</td><td>8,923</td><td>2.2%</td></tr>
<tr><td>20</td><td>Indiana</td><td>6,426</td><td>1.6%</td><td>14</td><td>Virginia</td><td>8,911</td><td>2.2%</td></tr>
<tr><td>33</td><td>Iowa</td><td>3,037</td><td>0.7%</td><td>15</td><td>Missouri</td><td>8,836</td><td>2.2%</td></tr>
<tr><td>29</td><td>Kansas</td><td>3,616</td><td>0.9%</td><td>16</td><td>Wisconsin</td><td>7,640</td><td>1.9%</td></tr>
<tr><td>27</td><td>Kentucky</td><td>4,089</td><td>1.0%</td><td>17</td><td>Tennessee</td><td>7,076</td><td>1.7%</td></tr>
<tr><td>22</td><td>Louisiana</td><td>5,733</td><td>1.4%</td><td>18</td><td>Arizona</td><td>6,967</td><td>1.7%</td></tr>
<tr><td>41</td><td>Maine</td><td>1,426</td><td>0.3%</td><td>19</td><td>Alabama</td><td>6,484</td><td>1.6%</td></tr>
<tr><td>13</td><td>Maryland</td><td>8,923</td><td>2.2%</td><td>20</td><td>Indiana</td><td>6,426</td><td>1.6%</td></tr>
<tr><td>10</td><td>Massachusetts</td><td>13,068</td><td>3.2%</td><td>21</td><td>Connecticut</td><td>6,411</td><td>1.6%</td></tr>
<tr><td>9</td><td>Michigan</td><td>13,288</td><td>3.2%</td><td>22</td><td>Louisiana</td><td>5,733</td><td>1.4%</td></tr>
<tr><td>25</td><td>Minnesota</td><td>5,006</td><td>1.2%</td><td>23</td><td>Colorado</td><td>5,451</td><td>1.3%</td></tr>
<tr><td>30</td><td>Mississippi</td><td>3,326</td><td>0.8%</td><td>24</td><td>Washington</td><td>5,430</td><td>1.3%</td></tr>
<tr><td>15</td><td>Missouri</td><td>8,836</td><td>2.2%</td><td>25</td><td>Minnesota</td><td>5,006</td><td>1.2%</td></tr>
<tr><td>47</td><td>Montana</td><td>690</td><td>0.2%</td><td>26</td><td>Oklahoma</td><td>4,951</td><td>1.2%</td></tr>
<tr><td>38</td><td>Nebraska</td><td>1,929</td><td>0.5%</td><td>27</td><td>Kentucky</td><td>4,089</td><td>1.0%</td></tr>
<tr><td>35</td><td>Nevada</td><td>2,565</td><td>0.6%</td><td>28</td><td>South Carolina</td><td>4,004</td><td>1.0%</td></tr>
<tr><td>40</td><td>New Hampshire</td><td>1,862</td><td>0.5%</td><td>29</td><td>Kansas</td><td>3,616</td><td>0.9%</td></tr>
<tr><td>5</td><td>New Jersey</td><td>19,891</td><td>4.8%</td><td>30</td><td>Mississippi</td><td>3,326</td><td>0.8%</td></tr>
<tr><td>36</td><td>New Mexico</td><td>2,462</td><td>0.6%</td><td>31</td><td>Oregon</td><td>3,245</td><td>0.8%</td></tr>
<tr><td>1</td><td>New York</td><td>54,657</td><td>13.3%</td><td>32</td><td>Arkansas</td><td>3,244</td><td>0.8%</td></tr>
<tr><td>12</td><td>North Carolina</td><td>9,505</td><td>2.3%</td><td>33</td><td>Iowa</td><td>3,037</td><td>0.7%</td></tr>
<tr><td>49</td><td>North Dakota</td><td>561</td><td>0.1%</td><td>34</td><td>Hawaii</td><td>2,746</td><td>0.7%</td></tr>
<tr><td>8</td><td>Ohio</td><td>15,932</td><td>3.9%</td><td>35</td><td>Nevada</td><td>2,565</td><td>0.6%</td></tr>
<tr><td>26</td><td>Oklahoma</td><td>4,951</td><td>1.2%</td><td>36</td><td>New Mexico</td><td>2,462</td><td>0.6%</td></tr>
<tr><td>31</td><td>Oregon</td><td>3,245</td><td>0.8%</td><td>37</td><td>Rhode Island</td><td>1,958</td><td>0.5%</td></tr>
<tr><td>7</td><td>Pennsylvania</td><td>17,655</td><td>4.3%</td><td>38</td><td>Nebraska</td><td>1,929</td><td>0.5%</td></tr>
<tr><td>37</td><td>Rhode Island</td><td>1,958</td><td>0.5%</td><td>39</td><td>Utah</td><td>1,882</td><td>0.5%</td></tr>
<tr><td>28</td><td>South Carolina</td><td>4,004</td><td>1.0%</td><td>40</td><td>New Hampshire</td><td>1,862</td><td>0.5%</td></tr>
<tr><td>45</td><td>South Dakota</td><td>847</td><td>0.2%</td><td>41</td><td>Maine</td><td>1,426</td><td>0.3%</td></tr>
<tr><td>17</td><td>Tennessee</td><td>7,076</td><td>1.7%</td><td>42</td><td>West Virginia</td><td>1,416</td><td>0.3%</td></tr>
<tr><td>3</td><td>Texas</td><td>28,269</td><td>6.9%</td><td>43</td><td>Idaho</td><td>1,142</td><td>0.3%</td></tr>
<tr><td>39</td><td>Utah</td><td>1,882</td><td>0.5%</td><td>44</td><td>Delaware</td><td>923</td><td>0.2%</td></tr>
<tr><td>50</td><td>Vermont</td><td>548</td><td>0.1%</td><td>45</td><td>South Dakota</td><td>847</td><td>0.2%</td></tr>
<tr><td>14</td><td>Virginia</td><td>8,911</td><td>2.2%</td><td>46</td><td>Alaska</td><td>740</td><td>0.2%</td></tr>
<tr><td>24</td><td>Washington</td><td>5,430</td><td>1.3%</td><td>47</td><td>Montana</td><td>690</td><td>0.2%</td></tr>
<tr><td>42</td><td>West Virginia</td><td>1,416</td><td>0.3%</td><td>48</td><td>Wyoming</td><td>618</td><td>0.2%</td></tr>
<tr><td>16</td><td>Wisconsin</td><td>7,640</td><td>1.9%</td><td>49</td><td>North Dakota</td><td>561</td><td>0.1%</td></tr>
<tr><td>48</td><td>Wyoming</td><td>618</td><td>0.2%</td><td>50</td><td>Vermont</td><td>548</td><td>0.1%</td></tr>
<tr><td></td><td></td><td></td><td></td><td></td><td>District of Columbia</td><td>3,587</td><td>0.9%</td></tr>
</table>

Source: U.S. Department of Justice, Bureau of Justice Statistics
"Census of State and Local Law Enforcement Agencies, 1996" (Bulletin, June 1998, NCJ-164618)
*Includes consolidated police-sheriffs' departments.

Percent of Full-Time Local Police Department Employees
Who Are Sworn Officers: 1996
National Percent = 78.7% of Employees*

RANK	STATE	PERCENT	RANK	STATE	PERCENT
35	Alabama	76.7	1	Pennsylvania	86.4
50	Alaska	63.9	2	Delaware	86.1
45	Arizona	71.9	3	West Virginia	85.7
27	Arkansas	78.7	4	Michigan	84.4
46	California	71.2	5	Massachusetts	84.3
42	Colorado	74.8	6	Connecticut	84.1
6	Connecticut	84.1	7	New Jersey	83.5
2	Delaware	86.1	8	New York	83.0
47	Florida	70.0	9	Iowa	82.9
25	Georgia	79.1	10	Minnesota	82.7
25	Hawaii	79.1	11	North Carolina	82.3
21	Idaho	80.0	12	Wisconsin	82.2
19	Illinois	80.4	13	South Carolina	82.0
17	Indiana	80.7	14	Louisiana	81.9
9	Iowa	82.9	15	North Dakota	81.8
36	Kansas	76.4	16	Maryland	81.0
23	Kentucky	79.3	17	Indiana	80.7
14	Louisiana	81.9	18	Ohio	80.5
29	Maine	78.1	19	Illinois	80.4
16	Maryland	81.0	20	Nebraska	80.1
5	Massachusetts	84.3	21	Idaho	80.0
4	Michigan	84.4	22	Utah	79.6
10	Minnesota	82.7	23	Kentucky	79.3
44	Mississippi	73.7	24	New Hampshire	79.2
37	Missouri	76.2	25	Georgia	79.1
31	Montana	77.9	25	Hawaii	79.1
20	Nebraska	80.1	27	Arkansas	78.7
49	Nevada	67.3	28	Vermont	78.3
24	New Hampshire	79.2	29	Maine	78.1
7	New Jersey	83.5	30	Oklahoma	78.0
48	New Mexico	68.5	31	Montana	77.9
8	New York	83.0	32	Rhode Island	77.5
11	North Carolina	82.3	32	Virginia	77.5
15	North Dakota	81.8	34	Tennessee	76.9
18	Ohio	80.5	35	Alabama	76.7
30	Oklahoma	78.0	36	Kansas	76.4
38	Oregon	75.4	37	Missouri	76.2
1	Pennsylvania	86.4	38	Oregon	75.4
32	Rhode Island	77.5	38	Texas	75.4
13	South Carolina	82.0	40	Wyoming	75.2
43	South Dakota	74.0	41	Washington	74.9
34	Tennessee	76.9	42	Colorado	74.8
38	Texas	75.4	43	South Dakota	74.0
22	Utah	79.6	44	Mississippi	73.7
28	Vermont	78.3	45	Arizona	71.9
32	Virginia	77.5	46	California	71.2
41	Washington	74.9	47	Florida	70.0
3	West Virginia	85.7	48	New Mexico	68.5
12	Wisconsin	82.2	49	Nevada	67.3
40	Wyoming	75.2	50	Alaska	63.9
				District of Columbia	84.9

Source: Morgan Quitno Press using data from U.S. Department of Justice, Bureau of Justice Statistics
"Census of State and Local Law Enforcement Agencies, 1996" (Bulletin, June 1998, NCJ-164618)
*Includes consolidated police-sheriffs' departments.

Rate of Full-Time Officers in Local Police Departments in 1996

National Rate = 15 Officers per 10,000 Population*

ALPHA ORDER

RANK	STATE	RATE
13	Alabama	15
32	Alaska	12
9	Arizona	16
25	Arkansas	13
36	California	11
18	Colorado	14
6	Connecticut	20
25	Delaware	13
18	Florida	14
18	Georgia	14
3	Hawaii	23
43	Idaho	10
4	Illinois	22
36	Indiana	11
36	Iowa	11
18	Kansas	14
36	Kentucky	11
25	Louisiana	13
36	Maine	11
8	Maryland	18
5	Massachusetts	21
18	Michigan	14
36	Minnesota	11
32	Mississippi	12
9	Missouri	16
49	Montana	8
32	Nebraska	12
9	Nevada	16
9	New Hampshire	16
2	New Jersey	25
18	New Mexico	14
1	New York	30
25	North Carolina	13
46	North Dakota	9
18	Ohio	14
13	Oklahoma	15
43	Oregon	10
13	Pennsylvania	15
6	Rhode Island	20
36	South Carolina	11
32	South Dakota	12
25	Tennessee	13
13	Texas	15
46	Utah	9
46	Vermont	9
25	Virginia	13
43	Washington	10
49	West Virginia	8
13	Wisconsin	15
25	Wyoming	13

RANK ORDER

RANK	STATE	RATE
1	New York	30
2	New Jersey	25
3	Hawaii	23
4	Illinois	22
5	Massachusetts	21
6	Connecticut	20
6	Rhode Island	20
8	Maryland	18
9	Arizona	16
9	Missouri	16
9	Nevada	16
9	New Hampshire	16
13	Alabama	15
13	Oklahoma	15
13	Pennsylvania	15
13	Texas	15
13	Wisconsin	15
18	Colorado	14
18	Florida	14
18	Georgia	14
18	Kansas	14
18	Michigan	14
18	New Mexico	14
18	Ohio	14
25	Arkansas	13
25	Delaware	13
25	Louisiana	13
25	North Carolina	13
25	Tennessee	13
25	Virginia	13
25	Wyoming	13
32	Alaska	12
32	Mississippi	12
32	Nebraska	12
32	South Dakota	12
36	California	11
36	Indiana	11
36	Iowa	11
36	Kentucky	11
36	Maine	11
36	Minnesota	11
36	South Carolina	11
43	Idaho	10
43	Oregon	10
43	Washington	10
46	North Dakota	9
46	Utah	9
46	Vermont	9
49	Montana	8
49	West Virginia	8
	District of Columbia	66

Source: U.S. Department of Justice, Bureau of Justice Statistics
    "Census of State and Local Law Enforcement Agencies, 1996" (Bulletin, June 1998, NCJ-164618)
*Includes consolidated police-sheriffs' departments.

Full-Time Employees in Local Police Departments in 1996

National Total = 521,985 Employees*

ALPHA ORDER

RANK	STATE	EMPLOYEES	% of USA
19	Alabama	8,454	1.6%
44	Alaska	1,158	0.2%
16	Arizona	9,686	1.9%
32	Arkansas	4,124	0.8%
2	California	50,491	9.7%
22	Colorado	7,283	1.4%
21	Connecticut	7,625	1.5%
46	Delaware	1,072	0.2%
5	Florida	28,075	5.4%
11	Georgia	12,954	2.5%
36	Hawaii	3,471	0.7%
43	Idaho	1,428	0.3%
4	Illinois	32,522	6.2%
20	Indiana	7,965	1.5%
34	Iowa	3,664	0.7%
29	Kansas	4,732	0.9%
27	Kentucky	5,157	1.0%
24	Louisiana	7,001	1.3%
41	Maine	1,826	0.3%
15	Maryland	11,015	2.1%
10	Massachusetts	15,506	3.0%
9	Michigan	15,735	3.0%
26	Minnesota	6,053	1.2%
30	Mississippi	4,511	0.9%
12	Missouri	11,594	2.2%
47	Montana	886	0.2%
38	Nebraska	2,409	0.5%
33	Nevada	3,809	0.7%
40	New Hampshire	2,351	0.5%
6	New Jersey	23,829	4.6%
35	New Mexico	3,593	0.7%
1	New York	65,854	12.6%
13	North Carolina	11,546	2.2%
50	North Dakota	686	0.1%
8	Ohio	19,799	3.8%
25	Oklahoma	6,348	1.2%
31	Oregon	4,305	0.8%
7	Pennsylvania	20,427	3.9%
37	Rhode Island	2,527	0.5%
28	South Carolina	4,884	0.9%
45	South Dakota	1,144	0.2%
18	Tennessee	9,206	1.8%
3	Texas	37,472	7.2%
39	Utah	2,363	0.5%
49	Vermont	700	0.1%
14	Virginia	11,502	2.2%
23	Washington	7,246	1.4%
42	West Virginia	1,652	0.3%
17	Wisconsin	9,298	1.8%
48	Wyoming	822	0.2%

RANK ORDER

RANK	STATE	EMPLOYEES	% of USA
1	New York	65,854	12.6%
2	California	50,491	9.7%
3	Texas	37,472	7.2%
4	Illinois	32,522	6.2%
5	Florida	28,075	5.4%
6	New Jersey	23,829	4.6%
7	Pennsylvania	20,427	3.9%
8	Ohio	19,799	3.8%
9	Michigan	15,735	3.0%
10	Massachusetts	15,506	3.0%
11	Georgia	12,954	2.5%
12	Missouri	11,594	2.2%
13	North Carolina	11,546	2.2%
14	Virginia	11,502	2.2%
15	Maryland	11,015	2.1%
16	Arizona	9,686	1.9%
17	Wisconsin	9,298	1.8%
18	Tennessee	9,206	1.8%
19	Alabama	8,454	1.6%
20	Indiana	7,965	1.5%
21	Connecticut	7,625	1.5%
22	Colorado	7,283	1.4%
23	Washington	7,246	1.4%
24	Louisiana	7,001	1.3%
25	Oklahoma	6,348	1.2%
26	Minnesota	6,053	1.2%
27	Kentucky	5,157	1.0%
28	South Carolina	4,884	0.9%
29	Kansas	4,732	0.9%
30	Mississippi	4,511	0.9%
31	Oregon	4,305	0.8%
32	Arkansas	4,124	0.8%
33	Nevada	3,809	0.7%
34	Iowa	3,664	0.7%
35	New Mexico	3,593	0.7%
36	Hawaii	3,471	0.7%
37	Rhode Island	2,527	0.5%
38	Nebraska	2,409	0.5%
39	Utah	2,363	0.5%
40	New Hampshire	2,351	0.5%
41	Maine	1,826	0.3%
42	West Virginia	1,652	0.3%
43	Idaho	1,428	0.3%
44	Alaska	1,158	0.2%
45	South Dakota	1,144	0.2%
46	Delaware	1,072	0.2%
47	Montana	886	0.2%
48	Wyoming	822	0.2%
49	Vermont	700	0.1%
50	North Dakota	686	0.1%
	District of Columbia	4,225	0.8%

Source: U.S. Department of Justice, Bureau of Justice Statistics
    "Census of State and Local Law Enforcement Agencies, 1996" (Bulletin, June 1998, NCJ-164618)
*Includes consolidated police-sheriffs' departments.

Sheriffs' Departments in 1996

National Total = 3,088 Departments*

ALPHA ORDER					RANK ORDER			
RANK	STATE	DEPARTMENTS	% of USA		RANK	STATE	DEPARTMENTS	% of USA
20	Alabama	67	2.2%		1	Texas	254	8.2%
49	Alaska	0	0.0%		2	Georgia	159	5.1%
42	Arizona	15	0.5%		3	Virginia	125	4.0%
18	Arkansas	75	2.4%		4	Kentucky	120	3.9%
26	California	58	1.9%		5	Missouri	115	3.7%
25	Colorado	63	2.0%		6	Kansas	104	3.4%
46	Connecticut	8	0.3%		7	Illinois	102	3.3%
48	Delaware	3	0.1%		8	North Carolina	100	3.2%
23	Florida	65	2.1%		9	Iowa	99	3.2%
2	Georgia	159	5.1%		10	Tennessee	95	3.1%
49	Hawaii	0	0.0%		11	Nebraska	93	3.0%
32	Idaho	44	1.4%		12	Indiana	92	3.0%
7	Illinois	102	3.3%		13	Ohio	88	2.8%
12	Indiana	92	3.0%		14	Minnesota	87	2.8%
9	Iowa	99	3.2%		15	Michigan	83	2.7%
6	Kansas	104	3.4%		16	Mississippi	82	2.7%
4	Kentucky	120	3.9%		17	Oklahoma	77	2.5%
24	Louisiana	64	2.1%		18	Arkansas	75	2.4%
40	Maine	16	0.5%		19	Wisconsin	72	2.3%
37	Maryland	24	0.8%		20	Alabama	67	2.2%
43	Massachusetts	14	0.5%		20	Pennsylvania	67	2.2%
15	Michigan	83	2.7%		22	South Dakota	66	2.1%
14	Minnesota	87	2.8%		23	Florida	65	2.1%
16	Mississippi	82	2.7%		24	Louisiana	64	2.1%
5	Missouri	115	3.7%		25	Colorado	63	2.0%
28	Montana	55	1.8%		26	California	58	1.9%
11	Nebraska	93	3.0%		27	New York	57	1.8%
40	Nevada	16	0.5%		28	Montana	55	1.8%
45	New Hampshire	10	0.3%		28	West Virginia	55	1.8%
39	New Jersey	21	0.7%		30	North Dakota	53	1.7%
35	New Mexico	33	1.1%		31	South Carolina	46	1.5%
27	New York	57	1.8%		32	Idaho	44	1.4%
8	North Carolina	100	3.2%		33	Washington	39	1.3%
30	North Dakota	53	1.7%		34	Oregon	36	1.2%
13	Ohio	88	2.8%		35	New Mexico	33	1.1%
17	Oklahoma	77	2.5%		36	Utah	29	0.9%
34	Oregon	36	1.2%		37	Maryland	24	0.8%
20	Pennsylvania	67	2.2%		38	Wyoming	23	0.7%
47	Rhode Island	5	0.2%		39	New Jersey	21	0.7%
31	South Carolina	46	1.5%		40	Maine	16	0.5%
22	South Dakota	66	2.1%		40	Nevada	16	0.5%
10	Tennessee	95	3.1%		42	Arizona	15	0.5%
1	Texas	254	8.2%		43	Massachusetts	14	0.5%
36	Utah	29	0.9%		43	Vermont	14	0.5%
43	Vermont	14	0.5%		45	New Hampshire	10	0.3%
3	Virginia	125	4.0%		46	Connecticut	8	0.3%
33	Washington	39	1.3%		47	Rhode Island	5	0.2%
28	West Virginia	55	1.8%		48	Delaware	3	0.1%
19	Wisconsin	72	2.3%		49	Alaska	0	0.0%
38	Wyoming	23	0.7%		49	Hawaii	0	0.0%
						District of Columbia	0	0.0%

Source: U.S. Department of Justice, Bureau of Justice Statistics
"Census of State and Local Law Enforcement Agencies, 1996" (Bulletin, June 1998, NCJ-164618)
*Sheriffs' departments generally operate at the county level.

Full-Time Officers in Sheriffs' Departments in 1996

National Total = 152,922 Officers*

ALPHA ORDER

RANK	STATE	OFFICERS	% of USA
21	Alabama	1,963	1.3%
49	Alaska	0	0.0%
24	Arizona	1,563	1.0%
28	Arkansas	1,410	0.9%
1	California	22,869	15.0%
14	Colorado	3,324	2.2%
37	Connecticut	886	0.6%
48	Delaware	24	0.0%
2	Florida	14,124	9.2%
6	Georgia	6,752	4.4%
49	Hawaii	0	0.0%
33	Idaho	1,053	0.7%
5	Illinois	8,426	5.5%
17	Indiana	2,618	1.7%
29	Iowa	1,343	0.9%
23	Kansas	1,683	1.1%
32	Kentucky	1,113	0.7%
4	Louisiana	8,720	5.7%
44	Maine	321	0.2%
27	Maryland	1,438	0.9%
25	Massachusetts	1,540	1.0%
11	Michigan	4,435	2.9%
20	Minnesota	2,139	1.4%
26	Mississippi	1,474	1.0%
19	Missouri	2,421	1.6%
40	Montana	616	0.4%
38	Nebraska	794	0.5%
35	Nevada	935	0.6%
46	New Hampshire	129	0.1%
15	New Jersey	3,145	2.1%
36	New Mexico	889	0.6%
8	New York	5,852	3.8%
9	North Carolina	5,264	3.4%
42	North Dakota	364	0.2%
10	Ohio	5,179	3.4%
34	Oklahoma	1,014	0.7%
22	Oregon	1,921	1.3%
30	Pennsylvania	1,239	0.8%
45	Rhode Island	153	0.1%
16	South Carolina	3,037	2.0%
43	South Dakota	344	0.2%
13	Tennessee	3,520	2.3%
3	Texas	11,326	7.4%
31	Utah	1,198	0.8%
47	Vermont	87	0.1%
7	Virginia	6,605	4.3%
18	Washington	2,553	1.7%
39	West Virginia	726	0.5%
12	Wisconsin	3,886	2.5%
41	Wyoming	507	0.3%

RANK ORDER

RANK	STATE	OFFICERS	% of USA
1	California	22,869	15.0%
2	Florida	14,124	9.2%
3	Texas	11,326	7.4%
4	Louisiana	8,720	5.7%
5	Illinois	8,426	5.5%
6	Georgia	6,752	4.4%
7	Virginia	6,605	4.3%
8	New York	5,852	3.8%
9	North Carolina	5,264	3.4%
10	Ohio	5,179	3.4%
11	Michigan	4,435	2.9%
12	Wisconsin	3,886	2.5%
13	Tennessee	3,520	2.3%
14	Colorado	3,324	2.2%
15	New Jersey	3,145	2.1%
16	South Carolina	3,037	2.0%
17	Indiana	2,618	1.7%
18	Washington	2,553	1.7%
19	Missouri	2,421	1.6%
20	Minnesota	2,139	1.4%
21	Alabama	1,963	1.3%
22	Oregon	1,921	1.3%
23	Kansas	1,683	1.1%
24	Arizona	1,563	1.0%
25	Massachusetts	1,540	1.0%
26	Mississippi	1,474	1.0%
27	Maryland	1,438	0.9%
28	Arkansas	1,410	0.9%
29	Iowa	1,343	0.9%
30	Pennsylvania	1,239	0.8%
31	Utah	1,198	0.8%
32	Kentucky	1,113	0.7%
33	Idaho	1,053	0.7%
34	Oklahoma	1,014	0.7%
35	Nevada	935	0.6%
36	New Mexico	889	0.6%
37	Connecticut	886	0.6%
38	Nebraska	794	0.5%
39	West Virginia	726	0.5%
40	Montana	616	0.4%
41	Wyoming	507	0.3%
42	North Dakota	364	0.2%
43	South Dakota	344	0.2%
44	Maine	321	0.2%
45	Rhode Island	153	0.1%
46	New Hampshire	129	0.1%
47	Vermont	87	0.1%
48	Delaware	24	0.0%
49	Alaska	0	0.0%
49	Hawaii	0	0.0%
	District of Columbia	0	0.0%

Source: U.S. Department of Justice, Bureau of Justice Statistics
"Census of State and Local Law Enforcement Agencies, 1996" (Bulletin, June 1998, NCJ-164618)
*Sheriffs' departments generally operate at the county level.

Percent of Full-Time Sheriffs' Department Employees
Who Are Sworn Officers: 1996
National Percent = 59.3% of Employees*

ALPHA ORDER

RANK	STATE	PERCENT
39	Alabama	51.7
NA	Alaska**	NA
47	Arizona	33.9
22	Arkansas	59.5
23	California	59.2
17	Colorado	64.3
1	Connecticut	99.7
43	Delaware	46.2
40	Florida	50.6
18	Georgia	64.1
NA	Hawaii**	NA
31	Idaho	57.9
13	Illinois	69.0
44	Indiana	45.8
33	Iowa	56.8
21	Kansas	59.7
3	Kentucky	87.6
5	Louisiana	81.9
46	Maine	34.2
25	Maryland	58.8
48	Massachusetts	30.5
24	Michigan	59.1
38	Minnesota	52.0
34	Mississippi	55.5
7	Missouri	74.5
36	Montana	54.0
25	Nebraska	58.8
8	Nevada	74.1
11	New Hampshire	70.5
10	New Jersey	70.7
16	New Mexico	66.2
32	New York	57.7
25	North Carolina	58.8
15	North Dakota	67.7
28	Ohio	58.5
42	Oklahoma	47.4
28	Oregon	58.5
6	Pennsylvania	77.6
2	Rhode Island	99.4
9	South Carolina	72.9
45	South Dakota	40.4
41	Tennessee	50.4
37	Texas	52.6
19	Utah	61.0
12	Vermont	69.6
4	Virginia	84.5
20	Washington	60.5
28	West Virginia	58.5
14	Wisconsin	67.9
34	Wyoming	55.5

RANK ORDER

RANK	STATE	PERCENT
1	Connecticut	99.7
2	Rhode Island	99.4
3	Kentucky	87.6
4	Virginia	84.5
5	Louisiana	81.9
6	Pennsylvania	77.6
7	Missouri	74.5
8	Nevada	74.1
9	South Carolina	72.9
10	New Jersey	70.7
11	New Hampshire	70.5
12	Vermont	69.6
13	Illinois	69.0
14	Wisconsin	67.9
15	North Dakota	67.7
16	New Mexico	66.2
17	Colorado	64.3
18	Georgia	64.1
19	Utah	61.0
20	Washington	60.5
21	Kansas	59.7
22	Arkansas	59.5
23	California	59.2
24	Michigan	59.1
25	Maryland	58.8
25	Nebraska	58.8
25	North Carolina	58.8
28	Ohio	58.5
28	Oregon	58.5
28	West Virginia	58.5
31	Idaho	57.9
32	New York	57.7
33	Iowa	56.8
34	Mississippi	55.5
34	Wyoming	55.5
36	Montana	54.0
37	Texas	52.6
38	Minnesota	52.0
39	Alabama	51.7
40	Florida	50.6
41	Tennessee	50.4
42	Oklahoma	47.4
43	Delaware	46.2
44	Indiana	45.8
45	South Dakota	40.4
46	Maine	34.2
47	Arizona	33.9
48	Massachusetts	30.5
NA	Alaska**	NA
NA	Hawaii**	NA
	District of Columbia**	NA

Source: Morgan Quitno Press using data from U.S. Department of Justice, Bureau of Justice Statistics
    "Census of State and Local Law Enforcement Agencies, 1996" (Bulletin, June 1998, NCJ-164618)
*Sheriffs' departments generally operate at the county level.
**Not applicable.

Rate of Full-Time Sworn Officers in Sheriffs' Departments in 1996

National Rate = 5.8 Officers per 10,000 Population*

RANK	STATE	RATE
27	Alabama	4.6
49	Alaska	0.0
36	Arizona	3.5
21	Arkansas	5.6
10	California	7.2
7	Colorado	8.7
41	Connecticut	2.7
48	Delaware	0.3
4	Florida	9.8
5	Georgia	9.2
49	Hawaii	0.0
6	Idaho	8.9
12	Illinois	7.1
32	Indiana	4.5
25	Iowa	4.7
15	Kansas	6.5
39	Kentucky	2.9
1	Louisiana	20.0
42	Maine	2.6
40	Maryland	2.8
43	Massachusetts	2.5
27	Michigan	4.6
27	Minnesota	4.6
22	Mississippi	5.4
32	Missouri	4.5
13	Montana	7.0
24	Nebraska	4.8
19	Nevada	5.8
46	New Hampshire	1.1
35	New Jersey	3.9
23	New Mexico	5.2
37	New York	3.2
10	North Carolina	7.2
20	North Dakota	5.7
27	Ohio	4.6
38	Oklahoma	3.1
16	Oregon	6.0
47	Pennsylvania	1.0
44	Rhode Island	1.5
8	South Carolina	8.2
25	South Dakota	4.7
14	Tennessee	6.6
18	Texas	5.9
16	Utah	6.0
44	Vermont	1.5
3	Virginia	9.9
27	Washington	4.6
34	West Virginia	4.0
9	Wisconsin	7.5
2	Wyoming	10.5

RANK	STATE	RATE
1	Louisiana	20.0
2	Wyoming	10.5
3	Virginia	9.9
4	Florida	9.8
5	Georgia	9.2
6	Idaho	8.9
7	Colorado	8.7
8	South Carolina	8.2
9	Wisconsin	7.5
10	California	7.2
10	North Carolina	7.2
12	Illinois	7.1
13	Montana	7.0
14	Tennessee	6.6
15	Kansas	6.5
16	Oregon	6.0
16	Utah	6.0
18	Texas	5.9
19	Nevada	5.8
20	North Dakota	5.7
21	Arkansas	5.6
22	Mississippi	5.4
23	New Mexico	5.2
24	Nebraska	4.8
25	Iowa	4.7
25	South Dakota	4.7
27	Alabama	4.6
27	Michigan	4.6
27	Minnesota	4.6
27	Ohio	4.6
27	Washington	4.6
32	Indiana	4.5
32	Missouri	4.5
34	West Virginia	4.0
35	New Jersey	3.9
36	Arizona	3.5
37	New York	3.2
38	Oklahoma	3.1
39	Kentucky	2.9
40	Maryland	2.8
41	Connecticut	2.7
42	Maine	2.6
43	Massachusetts	2.5
44	Rhode Island	1.5
44	Vermont	1.5
46	New Hampshire	1.1
47	Pennsylvania	1.0
48	Delaware	0.3
49	Alaska	0.0
49	Hawaii	0.0
	District of Columbia	0.0

Source: U.S. Department of Justice, Bureau of Justice Statistics
  "Census of State and Local Law Enforcement Agencies, 1996" (Bulletin, June 1998, NCJ-164618)
*Sheriffs' departments generally operate at the county level.

Full-Time Employees in Sheriffs' Departments in 1996

National Total = 257,712 Employees*

ALPHA ORDER

RANK	STATE	EMPLOYEES	% of USA
22	Alabama	3,796	1.5%
49	Alaska	0	0.0%
17	Arizona	4,604	1.8%
28	Arkansas	2,370	0.9%
1	California	38,603	15.0%
15	Colorado	5,168	2.0%
42	Connecticut	889	0.3%
48	Delaware	52	0.0%
2	Florida	27,928	10.8%
6	Georgia	10,537	4.1%
49	Hawaii	0	0.0%
32	Idaho	1,820	0.7%
4	Illinois	12,212	4.7%
14	Indiana	5,721	2.2%
29	Iowa	2,364	0.9%
25	Kansas	2,817	1.1%
36	Kentucky	1,270	0.5%
5	Louisiana	10,652	4.1%
40	Maine	939	0.4%
27	Maryland	2,445	0.9%
16	Massachusetts	5,047	2.0%
11	Michigan	7,508	2.9%
21	Minnesota	4,115	1.6%
26	Mississippi	2,657	1.0%
24	Missouri	3,250	1.3%
39	Montana	1,141	0.4%
34	Nebraska	1,351	0.5%
37	Nevada	1,261	0.5%
45	New Hampshire	183	0.1%
18	New Jersey	4,451	1.7%
35	New Mexico	1,343	0.5%
7	New York	10,150	3.9%
8	North Carolina	8,948	3.5%
44	North Dakota	538	0.2%
9	Ohio	8,855	3.4%
30	Oklahoma	2,138	0.8%
23	Oregon	3,285	1.3%
33	Pennsylvania	1,596	0.6%
46	Rhode Island	154	0.1%
20	South Carolina	4,167	1.6%
43	South Dakota	851	0.3%
12	Tennessee	6,981	2.7%
3	Texas	21,548	8.4%
31	Utah	1,965	0.8%
47	Vermont	125	0.0%
10	Virginia	7,816	3.0%
19	Washington	4,223	1.6%
38	West Virginia	1,242	0.5%
13	Wisconsin	5,723	2.2%
41	Wyoming	913	0.4%

RANK ORDER

RANK	STATE	EMPLOYEES	% of USA
1	California	38,603	15.0%
2	Florida	27,928	10.8%
3	Texas	21,548	8.4%
4	Illinois	12,212	4.7%
5	Louisiana	10,652	4.1%
6	Georgia	10,537	4.1%
7	New York	10,150	3.9%
8	North Carolina	8,948	3.5%
9	Ohio	8,855	3.4%
10	Virginia	7,816	3.0%
11	Michigan	7,508	2.9%
12	Tennessee	6,981	2.7%
13	Wisconsin	5,723	2.2%
14	Indiana	5,721	2.2%
15	Colorado	5,168	2.0%
16	Massachusetts	5,047	2.0%
17	Arizona	4,604	1.8%
18	New Jersey	4,451	1.7%
19	Washington	4,223	1.6%
20	South Carolina	4,167	1.6%
21	Minnesota	4,115	1.6%
22	Alabama	3,796	1.5%
23	Oregon	3,285	1.3%
24	Missouri	3,250	1.3%
25	Kansas	2,817	1.1%
26	Mississippi	2,657	1.0%
27	Maryland	2,445	0.9%
28	Arkansas	2,370	0.9%
29	Iowa	2,364	0.9%
30	Oklahoma	2,138	0.8%
31	Utah	1,965	0.8%
32	Idaho	1,820	0.7%
33	Pennsylvania	1,596	0.6%
34	Nebraska	1,351	0.5%
35	New Mexico	1,343	0.5%
36	Kentucky	1,270	0.5%
37	Nevada	1,261	0.5%
38	West Virginia	1,242	0.5%
39	Montana	1,141	0.4%
40	Maine	939	0.4%
41	Wyoming	913	0.4%
42	Connecticut	889	0.3%
43	South Dakota	851	0.3%
44	North Dakota	538	0.2%
45	New Hampshire	183	0.1%
46	Rhode Island	154	0.1%
47	Vermont	125	0.0%
48	Delaware	52	0.0%
49	Alaska	0	0.0%
49	Hawaii	0	0.0%
	District of Columbia	0	0.0%

Source: U.S. Department of Justice, Bureau of Justice Statistics
"Census of State and Local Law Enforcement Agencies, 1996" (Bulletin, June 1998, NCJ-164618)
Sheriffs' departments generally operate at the county level.

Special Police Agencies in 1996

National Total = 1,316 Agencies*

ALPHA ORDER

RANK	STATE	AGENCIES	% of USA
13	Alabama	33	2.5%
39	Alaska	7	0.5%
19	Arizona	26	2.0%
21	Arkansas	23	1.7%
2	California	121	9.2%
26	Colorado	20	1.5%
34	Connecticut	13	1.0%
41	Delaware	6	0.5%
15	Florida	30	2.3%
7	Georgia	44	3.3%
47	Hawaii	3	0.2%
47	Idaho	3	0.2%
5	Illinois	51	3.9%
24	Indiana	22	1.7%
37	Iowa	8	0.6%
27	Kansas	19	1.4%
28	Kentucky	16	1.2%
16	Louisiana	29	2.2%
36	Maine	9	0.7%
7	Maryland	44	3.3%
10	Massachusetts	34	2.6%
16	Michigan	29	2.2%
32	Minnesota	14	1.1%
16	Mississippi	29	2.2%
24	Missouri	22	1.7%
37	Montana	8	0.6%
46	Nebraska	4	0.3%
29	Nevada	15	1.1%
47	New Hampshire	3	0.2%
6	New Jersey	45	3.4%
29	New Mexico	15	1.1%
4	New York	64	4.9%
14	North Carolina	32	2.4%
39	North Dakota	7	0.5%
9	Ohio	41	3.1%
10	Oklahoma	34	2.6%
42	Oregon	5	0.4%
3	Pennsylvania	89	6.8%
42	Rhode Island	5	0.4%
20	South Carolina	25	1.9%
42	South Dakota	5	0.4%
21	Tennessee	23	1.7%
1	Texas	133	10.1%
34	Utah	13	1.0%
50	Vermont	2	0.2%
10	Virginia	34	2.6%
32	Washington	14	1.1%
29	West Virginia	15	1.1%
21	Wisconsin	23	1.7%
42	Wyoming	5	0.4%

RANK ORDER

RANK	STATE	AGENCIES	% of USA
1	Texas	133	10.1%
2	California	121	9.2%
3	Pennsylvania	89	6.8%
4	New York	64	4.9%
5	Illinois	51	3.9%
6	New Jersey	45	3.4%
7	Georgia	44	3.3%
7	Maryland	44	3.3%
9	Ohio	41	3.1%
10	Massachusetts	34	2.6%
10	Oklahoma	34	2.6%
10	Virginia	34	2.6%
13	Alabama	33	2.5%
14	North Carolina	32	2.4%
15	Florida	30	2.3%
16	Louisiana	29	2.2%
16	Michigan	29	2.2%
16	Mississippi	29	2.2%
19	Arizona	26	2.0%
20	South Carolina	25	1.9%
21	Arkansas	23	1.7%
21	Tennessee	23	1.7%
21	Wisconsin	23	1.7%
24	Indiana	22	1.7%
24	Missouri	22	1.7%
26	Colorado	20	1.5%
27	Kansas	19	1.4%
28	Kentucky	16	1.2%
29	Nevada	15	1.1%
29	New Mexico	15	1.1%
29	West Virginia	15	1.1%
32	Minnesota	14	1.1%
32	Washington	14	1.1%
34	Connecticut	13	1.0%
34	Utah	13	1.0%
36	Maine	9	0.7%
37	Iowa	8	0.6%
37	Montana	8	0.6%
39	Alaska	7	0.5%
39	North Dakota	7	0.5%
41	Delaware	6	0.5%
42	Oregon	5	0.4%
42	Rhode Island	5	0.4%
42	South Dakota	5	0.4%
42	Wyoming	5	0.4%
46	Nebraska	4	0.3%
47	Hawaii	3	0.2%
47	Idaho	3	0.2%
47	New Hampshire	3	0.2%
50	Vermont	2	0.2%
	District of Columbia	2	0.2%

Source: U.S. Department of Justice, Bureau of Justice Statistics
    "Census of State and Local Law Enforcement Agencies, 1996" (Bulletin, June 1998, NCJ-164618)
*Agencies with special jurisdictions or special enforcement responsibilities.

Full-Time Sworn Officers in Special Police Departments in 1996

National Total = 43,082 Officers*

ALPHA ORDER

RANK	STATE	OFFICERS	% of USA
18	Alabama	739	1.7%
38	Alaska	224	0.5%
23	Arizona	606	1.4%
22	Arkansas	643	1.5%
2	California	4,107	9.5%
24	Colorado	540	1.3%
39	Connecticut	206	0.5%
40	Delaware	173	0.4%
5	Florida	1,879	4.4%
11	Georgia	1,244	2.9%
34	Hawaii	243	0.6%
42	Idaho	137	0.3%
8	Illinois	1,627	3.8%
20	Indiana	680	1.6%
37	Iowa	230	0.5%
31	Kansas	332	0.8%
32	Kentucky	280	0.6%
13	Louisiana	799	1.9%
36	Maine	234	0.5%
7	Maryland	1,842	4.3%
15	Massachusetts	762	1.8%
19	Michigan	681	1.6%
29	Minnesota	365	0.8%
27	Mississippi	478	1.1%
16	Missouri	745	1.7%
41	Montana	164	0.4%
45	Nebraska	110	0.3%
26	Nevada	488	1.1%
49	New Hampshire	69	0.2%
4	New Jersey	2,320	5.4%
30	New Mexico	348	0.8%
1	New York	6,740	15.6%
12	North Carolina	804	1.9%
47	North Dakota	96	0.2%
9	Ohio	1,309	3.0%
25	Oklahoma	511	1.2%
48	Oregon	74	0.2%
6	Pennsylvania	1,865	4.3%
43	Rhode Island	118	0.3%
17	South Carolina	742	1.7%
43	South Dakota	118	0.3%
14	Tennessee	788	1.8%
3	Texas	3,311	7.7%
33	Utah	264	0.6%
50	Vermont	56	0.1%
10	Virginia	1,270	2.9%
28	Washington	403	0.9%
35	West Virginia	240	0.6%
21	Wisconsin	655	1.5%
46	Wyoming	101	0.2%

RANK ORDER

RANK	STATE	OFFICERS	% of USA
1	New York	6,740	15.6%
2	California	4,107	9.5%
3	Texas	3,311	7.7%
4	New Jersey	2,320	5.4%
5	Florida	1,879	4.4%
6	Pennsylvania	1,865	4.3%
7	Maryland	1,842	4.3%
8	Illinois	1,627	3.8%
9	Ohio	1,309	3.0%
10	Virginia	1,270	2.9%
11	Georgia	1,244	2.9%
12	North Carolina	804	1.9%
13	Louisiana	799	1.9%
14	Tennessee	788	1.8%
15	Massachusetts	762	1.8%
16	Missouri	745	1.7%
17	South Carolina	742	1.7%
18	Alabama	739	1.7%
19	Michigan	681	1.6%
20	Indiana	680	1.6%
21	Wisconsin	655	1.5%
22	Arkansas	643	1.5%
23	Arizona	606	1.4%
24	Colorado	540	1.3%
25	Oklahoma	511	1.2%
26	Nevada	488	1.1%
27	Mississippi	478	1.1%
28	Washington	403	0.9%
29	Minnesota	365	0.8%
30	New Mexico	348	0.8%
31	Kansas	332	0.8%
32	Kentucky	280	0.6%
33	Utah	264	0.6%
34	Hawaii	243	0.6%
35	West Virginia	240	0.6%
36	Maine	234	0.5%
37	Iowa	230	0.5%
38	Alaska	224	0.5%
39	Connecticut	206	0.5%
40	Delaware	173	0.4%
41	Montana	164	0.4%
42	Idaho	137	0.3%
43	Rhode Island	118	0.3%
43	South Dakota	118	0.3%
45	Nebraska	110	0.3%
46	Wyoming	101	0.2%
47	North Dakota	96	0.2%
48	Oregon	74	0.2%
49	New Hampshire	69	0.2%
50	Vermont	56	0.1%
	District of Columbia	322	0.7%

Source: U.S. Department of Justice, Bureau of Justice Statistics
"Census of State and Local Law Enforcement Agencies, 1996" (Bulletin, June 1998, NCJ-164618)
*Agencies with special jurisdictions or special enforcement responsibilities.

Percent of Full-Time Special Police Department Employees
Who Are Sworn Officers: 1996
National Percent = 76.6% of Employees*

ALPHA ORDER

RANK	STATE	PERCENT
25	Alabama	77.7
19	Alaska	80.6
42	Arizona	70.2
6	Arkansas	85.5
41	California	71.5
39	Colorado	72.7
20	Connecticut	79.8
43	Delaware	69.2
40	Florida	72.3
45	Georgia	67.8
3	Hawaii	88.7
11	Idaho	84.0
13	Illinois	83.8
10	Indiana	84.4
34	Iowa	75.9
28	Kansas	76.7
48	Kentucky	64.8
8	Louisiana	85.2
21	Maine	79.3
38	Maryland	73.7
31	Massachusetts	76.6
49	Michigan	61.2
18	Minnesota	81.8
36	Mississippi	75.5
26	Missouri	77.4
43	Montana	69.2
11	Nebraska	84.0
28	Nevada	76.7
28	New Hampshire	76.7
27	New Jersey	76.9
14	New Mexico	83.1
4	New York	87.7
22	North Carolina	79.1
35	North Dakota	75.6
24	Ohio	78.1
33	Oklahoma	76.4
37	Oregon	74.7
6	Pennsylvania	85.5
47	Rhode Island	65.2
50	South Carolina	55.4
5	South Dakota	86.8
23	Tennessee	78.7
46	Texas	65.7
17	Utah	82.0
9	Vermont	84.8
16	Virginia	82.4
32	Washington	76.5
2	West Virginia	88.9
15	Wisconsin	83.0
1	Wyoming	89.4

RANK ORDER

RANK	STATE	PERCENT
1	Wyoming	89.4
2	West Virginia	88.9
3	Hawaii	88.7
4	New York	87.7
5	South Dakota	86.8
6	Arkansas	85.5
6	Pennsylvania	85.5
8	Louisiana	85.2
9	Vermont	84.8
10	Indiana	84.4
11	Idaho	84.0
11	Nebraska	84.0
13	Illinois	83.8
14	New Mexico	83.1
15	Wisconsin	83.0
16	Virginia	82.4
17	Utah	82.0
18	Minnesota	81.8
19	Alaska	80.6
20	Connecticut	79.8
21	Maine	79.3
22	North Carolina	79.1
23	Tennessee	78.7
24	Ohio	78.1
25	Alabama	77.7
26	Missouri	77.4
27	New Jersey	76.9
28	Kansas	76.7
28	Nevada	76.7
28	New Hampshire	76.7
31	Massachusetts	76.6
32	Washington	76.5
33	Oklahoma	76.4
34	Iowa	75.9
35	North Dakota	75.6
36	Mississippi	75.5
37	Oregon	74.7
38	Maryland	73.7
39	Colorado	72.7
40	Florida	72.3
41	California	71.5
42	Arizona	70.2
43	Delaware	69.2
43	Montana	69.2
45	Georgia	67.8
46	Texas	65.7
47	Rhode Island	65.2
48	Kentucky	64.8
49	Michigan	61.2
50	South Carolina	55.4
	District of Columbia	75.6

Source: Morgan Quitno Press using data from U.S. Department of Justice, Bureau of Justice Statistics
"Census of State and Local Law Enforcement Agencies, 1996" (Bulletin, June 1998, NCJ-164618)
*Agencies with special jurisdictions or special enforcement responsibilities.

298

Rate of Full-Time Sworn Officers in Special Police Departments in 1996

National Rate = 1.6 Officers per 10,000 Population*

ALPHA ORDER				RANK ORDER		
RANK	STATE	RATE		RANK	STATE	RATE
17	Alabama	1.7		1	Alaska	3.7
1	Alaska	3.7		1	New York	3.7
25	Arizona	1.4		3	Maryland	3.6
6	Arkansas	2.6		4	Nevada	3.0
29	California	1.3		5	New Jersey	2.9
25	Colorado	1.4		6	Arkansas	2.6
48	Connecticut	0.6		7	Delaware	2.4
7	Delaware	2.4		8	Hawaii	2.1
29	Florida	1.3		8	Wyoming	2.1
17	Georgia	1.7		10	New Mexico	2.0
8	Hawaii	2.1		10	South Carolina	2.0
36	Idaho	1.2		12	Maine	1.9
25	Illinois	1.4		12	Montana	1.9
36	Indiana	1.2		12	Virginia	1.9
42	Iowa	0.8		15	Louisiana	1.8
29	Kansas	1.3		15	Mississippi	1.8
44	Kentucky	0.7		17	Alabama	1.7
15	Louisiana	1.8		17	Georgia	1.7
12	Maine	1.9		17	Texas	1.7
3	Maryland	3.6		20	South Dakota	1.6
29	Massachusetts	1.3		21	North Dakota	1.5
44	Michigan	0.7		21	Oklahoma	1.5
42	Minnesota	0.8		21	Pennsylvania	1.5
15	Mississippi	1.8		21	Tennessee	1.5
25	Missouri	1.4		25	Arizona	1.4
12	Montana	1.9		25	Colorado	1.4
44	Nebraska	0.7		25	Illinois	1.4
4	Nevada	3.0		25	Missouri	1.4
48	New Hampshire	0.6		29	California	1.3
5	New Jersey	2.9		29	Florida	1.3
10	New Mexico	2.0		29	Kansas	1.3
1	New York	3.7		29	Massachusetts	1.3
40	North Carolina	1.1		29	Utah	1.3
21	North Dakota	1.5		29	West Virginia	1.3
36	Ohio	1.2		29	Wisconsin	1.3
21	Oklahoma	1.5		36	Idaho	1.2
50	Oregon	0.2		36	Indiana	1.2
21	Pennsylvania	1.5		36	Ohio	1.2
36	Rhode Island	1.2		36	Rhode Island	1.2
10	South Carolina	2.0		40	North Carolina	1.1
20	South Dakota	1.6		41	Vermont	1.0
21	Tennessee	1.5		42	Iowa	0.8
17	Texas	1.7		42	Minnesota	0.8
29	Utah	1.3		44	Kentucky	0.7
41	Vermont	1.0		44	Michigan	0.7
12	Virginia	1.9		44	Nebraska	0.7
44	Washington	0.7		44	Washington	0.7
29	West Virginia	1.3		48	Connecticut	0.6
29	Wisconsin	1.3		48	New Hampshire	0.6
8	Wyoming	2.1		50	Oregon	0.2
					District of Columbia	5.9

Source: U.S. Department of Justice, Bureau of Justice Statistics
   "Census of State and Local Law Enforcement Agencies, 1996" (Bulletin, June 1998, NCJ-164618)
*Agencies with special jurisdictions or special enforcement responsibilities.

Full-Time Employees in Special Police Departments in 1996

National Total = 56,229 Employees*

RANK	STATE	EMPLOYEES	% of USA
18	Alabama	951	1.7%
36	Alaska	278	0.5%
20	Arizona	863	1.5%
23	Arkansas	752	1.3%
2	California	5,741	10.2%
24	Colorado	743	1.3%
39	Connecticut	258	0.5%
40	Delaware	250	0.4%
5	Florida	2,598	4.6%
9	Georgia	1,835	3.3%
37	Hawaii	274	0.5%
43	Idaho	163	0.3%
8	Illinois	1,942	3.5%
21	Indiana	806	1.4%
34	Iowa	303	0.5%
30	Kansas	433	0.8%
31	Kentucky	432	0.8%
19	Louisiana	938	1.7%
35	Maine	295	0.5%
6	Maryland	2,498	4.4%
16	Massachusetts	995	1.8%
13	Michigan	1,113	2.0%
29	Minnesota	446	0.8%
27	Mississippi	633	1.1%
17	Missouri	962	1.7%
41	Montana	237	0.4%
45	Nebraska	131	0.2%
26	Nevada	636	1.1%
49	New Hampshire	90	0.2%
4	New Jersey	3,016	5.4%
32	New Mexico	419	0.7%
1	New York	7,681	13.7%
14	North Carolina	1,016	1.8%
46	North Dakota	127	0.2%
10	Ohio	1,675	3.0%
25	Oklahoma	669	1.2%
48	Oregon	99	0.2%
7	Pennsylvania	2,182	3.9%
42	Rhode Island	181	0.3%
12	South Carolina	1,340	2.4%
44	South Dakota	136	0.2%
15	Tennessee	1,001	1.8%
3	Texas	5,037	9.0%
33	Utah	322	0.6%
50	Vermont	66	0.1%
11	Virginia	1,541	2.7%
28	Washington	527	0.9%
38	West Virginia	270	0.5%
22	Wisconsin	789	1.4%
47	Wyoming	113	0.2%

RANK	STATE	EMPLOYEES	% of USA
1	New York	7,681	13.7%
2	California	5,741	10.2%
3	Texas	5,037	9.0%
4	New Jersey	3,016	5.4%
5	Florida	2,598	4.6%
6	Maryland	2,498	4.4%
7	Pennsylvania	2,182	3.9%
8	Illinois	1,942	3.5%
9	Georgia	1,835	3.3%
10	Ohio	1,675	3.0%
11	Virginia	1,541	2.7%
12	South Carolina	1,340	2.4%
13	Michigan	1,113	2.0%
14	North Carolina	1,016	1.8%
15	Tennessee	1,001	1.8%
16	Massachusetts	995	1.8%
17	Missouri	962	1.7%
18	Alabama	951	1.7%
19	Louisiana	938	1.7%
20	Arizona	863	1.5%
21	Indiana	806	1.4%
22	Wisconsin	789	1.4%
23	Arkansas	752	1.3%
24	Colorado	743	1.3%
25	Oklahoma	669	1.2%
26	Nevada	636	1.1%
27	Mississippi	633	1.1%
28	Washington	527	0.9%
29	Minnesota	446	0.8%
30	Kansas	433	0.8%
31	Kentucky	432	0.8%
32	New Mexico	419	0.7%
33	Utah	322	0.6%
34	Iowa	303	0.5%
35	Maine	295	0.5%
36	Alaska	278	0.5%
37	Hawaii	274	0.5%
38	West Virginia	270	0.5%
39	Connecticut	258	0.5%
40	Delaware	250	0.4%
41	Montana	237	0.4%
42	Rhode Island	181	0.3%
43	Idaho	163	0.3%
44	South Dakota	136	0.2%
45	Nebraska	131	0.2%
46	North Dakota	127	0.2%
47	Wyoming	113	0.2%
48	Oregon	99	0.2%
49	New Hampshire	90	0.2%
50	Vermont	66	0.1%
	District of Columbia	426	0.8%

Source: U.S. Department of Justice, Bureau of Justice Statistics
"Census of State and Local Law Enforcement Agencies, 1996" (Bulletin, June 1998, NCJ-164618)
*Agencies with special jurisdictions or special enforcement responsibilities.

Law Enforcement Officers Feloniously Killed in 1997

National Total = 65 Officers

ALPHA ORDER					RANK ORDER			
RANK	STATE		OFFICERS	% of USA	RANK	STATE	OFFICERS	% of USA
10	Alabama		2	3.1%	1	California	7	10.8%
15	Alaska		1	1.5%	2	Mississippi	5	7.7%
15	Arizona		1	1.5%	2	North Carolina	5	7.7%
6	Arkansas		3	4.6%	4	Indiana	4	6.2%
1	California		7	10.8%	4	Ohio	4	6.2%
15	Colorado		1	1.5%	6	Arkansas	3	4.6%
30	Connecticut		0	0.0%	6	New Hampshire	3	4.6%
30	Delaware		0	0.0%	6	Tennessee	3	4.6%
15	Florida		1	1.5%	6	Texas	3	4.6%
10	Georgia		2	3.1%	10	Alabama	2	3.1%
30	Hawaii		0	0.0%	10	Georgia	2	3.1%
15	Idaho		1	1.5%	10	New Jersey	2	3.1%
15	Illinois		1	1.5%	10	New York	2	3.1%
4	Indiana		4	6.2%	10	South Carolina	2	3.1%
30	Iowa		0	0.0%	15	Alaska	1	1.5%
15	Kansas		1	1.5%	15	Arizona	1	1.5%
15	Kentucky		1	1.5%	15	Colorado	1	1.5%
15	Louisiana		1	1.5%	15	Florida	1	1.5%
30	Maine		0	0.0%	15	Idaho	1	1.5%
15	Maryland		1	1.5%	15	Illinois	1	1.5%
30	Massachusetts		0	0.0%	15	Kansas	1	1.5%
30	Michigan		0	0.0%	15	Kentucky	1	1.5%
15	Minnesota		1	1.5%	15	Louisiana	1	1.5%
2	Mississippi		5	7.7%	15	Maryland	1	1.5%
30	Missouri		0	0.0%	15	Minnesota	1	1.5%
30	Montana		0	0.0%	15	Nevada	1	1.5%
30	Nebraska		0	0.0%	15	New Mexico	1	1.5%
15	Nevada		1	1.5%	15	Oregon	1	1.5%
6	New Hampshire		3	4.6%	15	Washington	1	1.5%
10	New Jersey		2	3.1%	30	Connecticut	0	0.0%
15	New Mexico		1	1.5%	30	Delaware	0	0.0%
10	New York		2	3.1%	30	Hawaii	0	0.0%
2	North Carolina		5	7.7%	30	Iowa	0	0.0%
30	North Dakota		0	0.0%	30	Maine	0	0.0%
4	Ohio		4	6.2%	30	Massachusetts	0	0.0%
30	Oklahoma		0	0.0%	30	Michigan	0	0.0%
15	Oregon		1	1.5%	30	Missouri	0	0.0%
30	Pennsylvania		0	0.0%	30	Montana	0	0.0%
30	Rhode Island		0	0.0%	30	Nebraska	0	0.0%
10	South Carolina		2	3.1%	30	North Dakota	0	0.0%
30	South Dakota		0	0.0%	30	Oklahoma	0	0.0%
6	Tennessee		3	4.6%	30	Pennsylvania	0	0.0%
6	Texas		3	4.6%	30	Rhode Island	0	0.0%
30	Utah		0	0.0%	30	South Dakota	0	0.0%
30	Vermont		0	0.0%	30	Utah	0	0.0%
30	Virginia		0	0.0%	30	Vermont	0	0.0%
15	Washington		1	1.5%	30	Virginia	0	0.0%
30	West Virginia		0	0.0%	30	West Virginia	0	0.0%
30	Wisconsin		0	0.0%	30	Wisconsin	0	0.0%
30	Wyoming		0	0.0%	30	Wyoming	0	0.0%
						District of Columbia	3	4.6%

Source: Federal Bureau of Investigation
"Law Enforcement Officers Killed and Assaulted 1997" (http://www.fbi.gov/ucr/97leokap.pdf)

Law Enforcement Officers Feloniously Killed: 1988 to 1997

National Total = 638 Officers*

<table>
<tr><td colspan="4">ALPHA ORDER</td><td colspan="4">RANK ORDER</td></tr>
<tr><td>RANK</td><td>STATE</td><td>OFFICERS</td><td>% of USA</td><td>RANK</td><td>STATE</td><td>OFFICERS</td><td>% of USA</td></tr>
<tr><td>24</td><td>Alabama</td><td>10</td><td>1.6%</td><td>1</td><td>California</td><td>66</td><td>10.3%</td></tr>
<tr><td>32</td><td>Alaska</td><td>4</td><td>0.6%</td><td>2</td><td>Texas</td><td>59</td><td>9.2%</td></tr>
<tr><td>12</td><td>Arizona</td><td>18</td><td>2.8%</td><td>3</td><td>New York</td><td>36</td><td>5.6%</td></tr>
<tr><td>18</td><td>Arkansas</td><td>12</td><td>1.9%</td><td>4</td><td>Florida</td><td>33</td><td>5.2%</td></tr>
<tr><td>1</td><td>California</td><td>66</td><td>10.3%</td><td>5</td><td>Georgia</td><td>25</td><td>3.9%</td></tr>
<tr><td>24</td><td>Colorado</td><td>10</td><td>1.6%</td><td>6</td><td>Mississippi</td><td>24</td><td>3.8%</td></tr>
<tr><td>41</td><td>Connecticut</td><td>2</td><td>0.3%</td><td>7</td><td>North Carolina</td><td>23</td><td>3.6%</td></tr>
<tr><td>47</td><td>Delaware</td><td>0</td><td>0.0%</td><td>8</td><td>Illinois</td><td>22</td><td>3.4%</td></tr>
<tr><td>4</td><td>Florida</td><td>33</td><td>5.2%</td><td>8</td><td>Louisiana</td><td>22</td><td>3.4%</td></tr>
<tr><td>5</td><td>Georgia</td><td>25</td><td>3.9%</td><td>8</td><td>Pennsylvania</td><td>22</td><td>3.4%</td></tr>
<tr><td>44</td><td>Hawaii</td><td>1</td><td>0.2%</td><td>11</td><td>Michigan</td><td>20</td><td>3.1%</td></tr>
<tr><td>32</td><td>Idaho</td><td>4</td><td>0.6%</td><td>12</td><td>Arizona</td><td>18</td><td>2.8%</td></tr>
<tr><td>8</td><td>Illinois</td><td>22</td><td>3.4%</td><td>12</td><td>Tennessee</td><td>18</td><td>2.8%</td></tr>
<tr><td>17</td><td>Indiana</td><td>13</td><td>2.0%</td><td>14</td><td>Ohio</td><td>17</td><td>2.7%</td></tr>
<tr><td>47</td><td>Iowa</td><td>0</td><td>0.0%</td><td>14</td><td>South Carolina</td><td>17</td><td>2.7%</td></tr>
<tr><td>29</td><td>Kansas</td><td>7</td><td>1.1%</td><td>16</td><td>Missouri</td><td>15</td><td>2.4%</td></tr>
<tr><td>18</td><td>Kentucky</td><td>12</td><td>1.9%</td><td>17</td><td>Indiana</td><td>13</td><td>2.0%</td></tr>
<tr><td>8</td><td>Louisiana</td><td>22</td><td>3.4%</td><td>18</td><td>Arkansas</td><td>12</td><td>1.9%</td></tr>
<tr><td>41</td><td>Maine</td><td>2</td><td>0.3%</td><td>18</td><td>Kentucky</td><td>12</td><td>1.9%</td></tr>
<tr><td>26</td><td>Maryland</td><td>9</td><td>1.4%</td><td>18</td><td>Minnesota</td><td>12</td><td>1.9%</td></tr>
<tr><td>26</td><td>Massachusetts</td><td>9</td><td>1.4%</td><td>18</td><td>Oklahoma</td><td>12</td><td>1.9%</td></tr>
<tr><td>11</td><td>Michigan</td><td>20</td><td>3.1%</td><td>18</td><td>Virginia</td><td>12</td><td>1.9%</td></tr>
<tr><td>18</td><td>Minnesota</td><td>12</td><td>1.9%</td><td>18</td><td>Wisconsin</td><td>12</td><td>1.9%</td></tr>
<tr><td>6</td><td>Mississippi</td><td>24</td><td>3.8%</td><td>24</td><td>Alabama</td><td>10</td><td>1.6%</td></tr>
<tr><td>16</td><td>Missouri</td><td>15</td><td>2.4%</td><td>24</td><td>Colorado</td><td>10</td><td>1.6%</td></tr>
<tr><td>32</td><td>Montana</td><td>4</td><td>0.6%</td><td>26</td><td>Maryland</td><td>9</td><td>1.4%</td></tr>
<tr><td>37</td><td>Nebraska</td><td>3</td><td>0.5%</td><td>26</td><td>Massachusetts</td><td>9</td><td>1.4%</td></tr>
<tr><td>30</td><td>Nevada</td><td>6</td><td>0.9%</td><td>28</td><td>New Jersey</td><td>8</td><td>1.3%</td></tr>
<tr><td>32</td><td>New Hampshire</td><td>4</td><td>0.6%</td><td>29</td><td>Kansas</td><td>7</td><td>1.1%</td></tr>
<tr><td>28</td><td>New Jersey</td><td>8</td><td>1.3%</td><td>30</td><td>Nevada</td><td>6</td><td>0.9%</td></tr>
<tr><td>30</td><td>New Mexico</td><td>6</td><td>0.9%</td><td>30</td><td>New Mexico</td><td>6</td><td>0.9%</td></tr>
<tr><td>3</td><td>New York</td><td>36</td><td>5.6%</td><td>32</td><td>Alaska</td><td>4</td><td>0.6%</td></tr>
<tr><td>7</td><td>North Carolina</td><td>23</td><td>3.6%</td><td>32</td><td>Idaho</td><td>4</td><td>0.6%</td></tr>
<tr><td>41</td><td>North Dakota</td><td>2</td><td>0.3%</td><td>32</td><td>Montana</td><td>4</td><td>0.6%</td></tr>
<tr><td>14</td><td>Ohio</td><td>17</td><td>2.7%</td><td>32</td><td>New Hampshire</td><td>4</td><td>0.6%</td></tr>
<tr><td>18</td><td>Oklahoma</td><td>12</td><td>1.9%</td><td>32</td><td>Washington</td><td>4</td><td>0.6%</td></tr>
<tr><td>37</td><td>Oregon</td><td>3</td><td>0.5%</td><td>37</td><td>Nebraska</td><td>3</td><td>0.5%</td></tr>
<tr><td>8</td><td>Pennsylvania</td><td>22</td><td>3.4%</td><td>37</td><td>Oregon</td><td>3</td><td>0.5%</td></tr>
<tr><td>44</td><td>Rhode Island</td><td>1</td><td>0.2%</td><td>37</td><td>Utah</td><td>3</td><td>0.5%</td></tr>
<tr><td>14</td><td>South Carolina</td><td>17</td><td>2.7%</td><td>37</td><td>West Virginia</td><td>3</td><td>0.5%</td></tr>
<tr><td>47</td><td>South Dakota</td><td>0</td><td>0.0%</td><td>41</td><td>Connecticut</td><td>2</td><td>0.3%</td></tr>
<tr><td>12</td><td>Tennessee</td><td>18</td><td>2.8%</td><td>41</td><td>Maine</td><td>2</td><td>0.3%</td></tr>
<tr><td>2</td><td>Texas</td><td>59</td><td>9.2%</td><td>41</td><td>North Dakota</td><td>2</td><td>0.3%</td></tr>
<tr><td>37</td><td>Utah</td><td>3</td><td>0.5%</td><td>44</td><td>Hawaii</td><td>1</td><td>0.2%</td></tr>
<tr><td>47</td><td>Vermont</td><td>0</td><td>0.0%</td><td>44</td><td>Rhode Island</td><td>1</td><td>0.2%</td></tr>
<tr><td>18</td><td>Virginia</td><td>12</td><td>1.9%</td><td>44</td><td>Wyoming</td><td>1</td><td>0.2%</td></tr>
<tr><td>32</td><td>Washington</td><td>4</td><td>0.6%</td><td>47</td><td>Delaware</td><td>0</td><td>0.0%</td></tr>
<tr><td>37</td><td>West Virginia</td><td>3</td><td>0.5%</td><td>47</td><td>Iowa</td><td>0</td><td>0.0%</td></tr>
<tr><td>18</td><td>Wisconsin</td><td>12</td><td>1.9%</td><td>47</td><td>South Dakota</td><td>0</td><td>0.0%</td></tr>
<tr><td>44</td><td>Wyoming</td><td>1</td><td>0.2%</td><td>47</td><td>Vermont</td><td>0</td><td>0.0%</td></tr>
<tr><td></td><td></td><td></td><td></td><td></td><td>District of Columbia</td><td>10</td><td>1.6%</td></tr>
</table>

Source: Federal Bureau of Investigation
   "Law Enforcement Officers Killed and Assaulted 1997" (http://www.fbi.gov/ucr/97leokap.pdf)
*Total does not include 50 officers killed in U.S. territories (47 officers killed in Puerto Rico, one in American Samoa, one in the U.S. Virgin Islands and one in the Mariana Islands).

U.S. District Court Judges in 1997

National Total = 647 Judges*

<table>
<tr><td colspan="4">ALPHA ORDER</td><td colspan="4">RANK ORDER</td></tr>
<tr><td>RANK</td><td>STATE</td><td>JUDGES</td><td>% of USA</td><td>RANK</td><td>STATE</td><td>JUDGES</td><td>% of USA</td></tr>
<tr><td>15</td><td>Alabama</td><td>13</td><td>2.0%</td><td>1</td><td>California</td><td>56</td><td>8.7%</td></tr>
<tr><td>41</td><td>Alaska</td><td>3</td><td>0.5%</td><td>2</td><td>New York</td><td>52</td><td>8.0%</td></tr>
<tr><td>25</td><td>Arizona</td><td>8</td><td>1.2%</td><td>3</td><td>Texas</td><td>47</td><td>7.3%</td></tr>
<tr><td>25</td><td>Arkansas</td><td>8</td><td>1.2%</td><td>4</td><td>Pennsylvania</td><td>39</td><td>6.0%</td></tr>
<tr><td>1</td><td>California</td><td>56</td><td>8.7%</td><td>5</td><td>Florida</td><td>31</td><td>4.8%</td></tr>
<tr><td>29</td><td>Colorado</td><td>7</td><td>1.1%</td><td>6</td><td>Illinois</td><td>30</td><td>4.6%</td></tr>
<tr><td>25</td><td>Connecticut</td><td>8</td><td>1.2%</td><td>7</td><td>Louisiana</td><td>22</td><td>3.4%</td></tr>
<tr><td>37</td><td>Delaware</td><td>4</td><td>0.6%</td><td>8</td><td>Ohio</td><td>20</td><td>3.1%</td></tr>
<tr><td>5</td><td>Florida</td><td>31</td><td>4.8%</td><td>9</td><td>Michigan</td><td>19</td><td>2.9%</td></tr>
<tr><td>10</td><td>Georgia</td><td>18</td><td>2.8%</td><td>10</td><td>Georgia</td><td>18</td><td>2.8%</td></tr>
<tr><td>37</td><td>Hawaii</td><td>4</td><td>0.6%</td><td>11</td><td>New Jersey</td><td>17</td><td>2.6%</td></tr>
<tr><td>48</td><td>Idaho</td><td>2</td><td>0.3%</td><td>12</td><td>Missouri</td><td>14</td><td>2.2%</td></tr>
<tr><td>6</td><td>Illinois</td><td>30</td><td>4.6%</td><td>12</td><td>Tennessee</td><td>14</td><td>2.2%</td></tr>
<tr><td>20</td><td>Indiana</td><td>10</td><td>1.5%</td><td>12</td><td>Virginia</td><td>14</td><td>2.2%</td></tr>
<tr><td>34</td><td>Iowa</td><td>5</td><td>0.8%</td><td>15</td><td>Alabama</td><td>13</td><td>2.0%</td></tr>
<tr><td>31</td><td>Kansas</td><td>6</td><td>0.9%</td><td>15</td><td>Massachusetts</td><td>13</td><td>2.0%</td></tr>
<tr><td>22</td><td>Kentucky</td><td>9</td><td>1.4%</td><td>17</td><td>North Carolina</td><td>11</td><td>1.7%</td></tr>
<tr><td>7</td><td>Louisiana</td><td>22</td><td>3.4%</td><td>17</td><td>Oklahoma</td><td>11</td><td>1.7%</td></tr>
<tr><td>41</td><td>Maine</td><td>3</td><td>0.5%</td><td>17</td><td>Washington</td><td>11</td><td>1.7%</td></tr>
<tr><td>20</td><td>Maryland</td><td>10</td><td>1.5%</td><td>20</td><td>Indiana</td><td>10</td><td>1.5%</td></tr>
<tr><td>15</td><td>Massachusetts</td><td>13</td><td>2.0%</td><td>20</td><td>Maryland</td><td>10</td><td>1.5%</td></tr>
<tr><td>9</td><td>Michigan</td><td>19</td><td>2.9%</td><td>22</td><td>Kentucky</td><td>9</td><td>1.4%</td></tr>
<tr><td>29</td><td>Minnesota</td><td>7</td><td>1.1%</td><td>22</td><td>Mississippi</td><td>9</td><td>1.4%</td></tr>
<tr><td>22</td><td>Mississippi</td><td>9</td><td>1.4%</td><td>22</td><td>South Carolina</td><td>9</td><td>1.4%</td></tr>
<tr><td>12</td><td>Missouri</td><td>14</td><td>2.2%</td><td>25</td><td>Arizona</td><td>8</td><td>1.2%</td></tr>
<tr><td>41</td><td>Montana</td><td>3</td><td>0.5%</td><td>25</td><td>Arkansas</td><td>8</td><td>1.2%</td></tr>
<tr><td>37</td><td>Nebraska</td><td>4</td><td>0.6%</td><td>25</td><td>Connecticut</td><td>8</td><td>1.2%</td></tr>
<tr><td>37</td><td>Nevada</td><td>4</td><td>0.6%</td><td>25</td><td>West Virginia</td><td>8</td><td>1.2%</td></tr>
<tr><td>41</td><td>New Hampshire</td><td>3</td><td>0.5%</td><td>29</td><td>Colorado</td><td>7</td><td>1.1%</td></tr>
<tr><td>11</td><td>New Jersey</td><td>17</td><td>2.6%</td><td>29</td><td>Minnesota</td><td>7</td><td>1.1%</td></tr>
<tr><td>34</td><td>New Mexico</td><td>5</td><td>0.8%</td><td>31</td><td>Kansas</td><td>6</td><td>0.9%</td></tr>
<tr><td>2</td><td>New York</td><td>52</td><td>8.0%</td><td>31</td><td>Oregon</td><td>6</td><td>0.9%</td></tr>
<tr><td>17</td><td>North Carolina</td><td>11</td><td>1.7%</td><td>31</td><td>Wisconsin</td><td>6</td><td>0.9%</td></tr>
<tr><td>48</td><td>North Dakota</td><td>2</td><td>0.3%</td><td>34</td><td>Iowa</td><td>5</td><td>0.8%</td></tr>
<tr><td>8</td><td>Ohio</td><td>20</td><td>3.1%</td><td>34</td><td>New Mexico</td><td>5</td><td>0.8%</td></tr>
<tr><td>17</td><td>Oklahoma</td><td>11</td><td>1.7%</td><td>34</td><td>Utah</td><td>5</td><td>0.8%</td></tr>
<tr><td>31</td><td>Oregon</td><td>6</td><td>0.9%</td><td>37</td><td>Delaware</td><td>4</td><td>0.6%</td></tr>
<tr><td>4</td><td>Pennsylvania</td><td>39</td><td>6.0%</td><td>37</td><td>Hawaii</td><td>4</td><td>0.6%</td></tr>
<tr><td>41</td><td>Rhode Island</td><td>3</td><td>0.5%</td><td>37</td><td>Nebraska</td><td>4</td><td>0.6%</td></tr>
<tr><td>22</td><td>South Carolina</td><td>9</td><td>1.4%</td><td>37</td><td>Nevada</td><td>4</td><td>0.6%</td></tr>
<tr><td>41</td><td>South Dakota</td><td>3</td><td>0.5%</td><td>41</td><td>Alaska</td><td>3</td><td>0.5%</td></tr>
<tr><td>12</td><td>Tennessee</td><td>14</td><td>2.2%</td><td>41</td><td>Maine</td><td>3</td><td>0.5%</td></tr>
<tr><td>3</td><td>Texas</td><td>47</td><td>7.3%</td><td>41</td><td>Montana</td><td>3</td><td>0.5%</td></tr>
<tr><td>34</td><td>Utah</td><td>5</td><td>0.8%</td><td>41</td><td>New Hampshire</td><td>3</td><td>0.5%</td></tr>
<tr><td>48</td><td>Vermont</td><td>2</td><td>0.3%</td><td>41</td><td>Rhode Island</td><td>3</td><td>0.5%</td></tr>
<tr><td>12</td><td>Virginia</td><td>14</td><td>2.2%</td><td>41</td><td>South Dakota</td><td>3</td><td>0.5%</td></tr>
<tr><td>17</td><td>Washington</td><td>11</td><td>1.7%</td><td>41</td><td>Wyoming</td><td>3</td><td>0.5%</td></tr>
<tr><td>25</td><td>West Virginia</td><td>8</td><td>1.2%</td><td>48</td><td>Idaho</td><td>2</td><td>0.3%</td></tr>
<tr><td>31</td><td>Wisconsin</td><td>6</td><td>0.9%</td><td>48</td><td>North Dakota</td><td>2</td><td>0.3%</td></tr>
<tr><td>41</td><td>Wyoming</td><td>3</td><td>0.5%</td><td>48</td><td>Vermont</td><td>2</td><td>0.3%</td></tr>
<tr><td></td><td></td><td></td><td></td><td></td><td>District of Columbia</td><td>15</td><td>2.3%</td></tr>
</table>

Source: Administrative Office of the United States Courts
   "1997 Federal Court Management Statistics" (March 1998)
*Total includes 11 judgeships in U.S. territories.

Rate of U.S. District Court Judges in 1997

National Rate = 0.24 Judges per 100,000 Population*

ALPHA ORDER				RANK ORDER		
RANK	STATE	RATE		RANK	STATE	RATE
15	Alabama	0.30		1	Wyoming	0.62
4	Alaska	0.49		2	Delaware	0.54
40	Arizona	0.18		3	Louisiana	0.51
12	Arkansas	0.32		4	Alaska	0.49
45	California	0.17		5	West Virginia	0.44
40	Colorado	0.18		6	South Dakota	0.41
23	Connecticut	0.24		7	Hawaii	0.34
2	Delaware	0.54		7	Montana	0.34
33	Florida	0.21		7	Vermont	0.34
23	Georgia	0.24		10	Mississippi	0.33
7	Hawaii	0.34		10	Oklahoma	0.33
45	Idaho	0.17		12	Arkansas	0.32
22	Illinois	0.25		12	Pennsylvania	0.32
45	Indiana	0.17		14	North Dakota	0.31
40	Iowa	0.18		15	Alabama	0.30
31	Kansas	0.23		15	Rhode Island	0.30
31	Kentucky	0.23		17	New Mexico	0.29
3	Louisiana	0.51		17	New York	0.29
23	Maine	0.24		19	Missouri	0.26
37	Maryland	0.20		19	New Hampshire	0.26
33	Massachusetts	0.21		19	Tennessee	0.26
39	Michigan	0.19		22	Illinois	0.25
48	Minnesota	0.15		23	Connecticut	0.24
10	Mississippi	0.33		23	Georgia	0.24
19	Missouri	0.26		23	Maine	0.24
7	Montana	0.34		23	Nebraska	0.24
23	Nebraska	0.24		23	Nevada	0.24
23	Nevada	0.24		23	South Carolina	0.24
19	New Hampshire	0.26		23	Texas	0.24
33	New Jersey	0.21		23	Utah	0.24
17	New Mexico	0.29		31	Kansas	0.23
17	New York	0.29		31	Kentucky	0.23
48	North Carolina	0.15		33	Florida	0.21
14	North Dakota	0.31		33	Massachusetts	0.21
40	Ohio	0.18		33	New Jersey	0.21
10	Oklahoma	0.33		33	Virginia	0.21
40	Oregon	0.18		37	Maryland	0.20
12	Pennsylvania	0.32		37	Washington	0.20
15	Rhode Island	0.30		39	Michigan	0.19
23	South Carolina	0.24		40	Arizona	0.18
6	South Dakota	0.41		40	Colorado	0.18
19	Tennessee	0.26		40	Iowa	0.18
23	Texas	0.24		40	Ohio	0.18
23	Utah	0.24		40	Oregon	0.18
7	Vermont	0.34		45	California	0.17
33	Virginia	0.21		45	Idaho	0.17
37	Washington	0.20		45	Indiana	0.17
5	West Virginia	0.44		48	Minnesota	0.15
50	Wisconsin	0.12		48	North Carolina	0.15
1	Wyoming	0.62		50	Wisconsin	0.12
					District of Columbia	2.83

Source: Morgan Quitno Press using data from Administrative Office of the United States Courts "1997 Federal Court Management Statistics" (March 1998)

National rate does not include judgeships or population in U.S. territories.

Felony Criminal Cases Filed in U.S. District Courts in 1997

National Total = 37,831 Felony Criminal Cases*

ALPHA ORDER

RANK	STATE	CASES	% of USA
16	Alabama	661	1.7%
45	Alaska	101	0.3%
5	Arizona	1,470	3.9%
34	Arkansas	306	0.8%
1	California	5,597	14.8%
25	Colorado	388	1.0%
40	Connecticut	214	0.6%
46	Delaware	96	0.3%
4	Florida	2,624	6.9%
8	Georgia	902	2.4%
41	Hawaii	188	0.5%
50	Idaho	83	0.2%
11	Illinois	780	2.1%
26	Indiana	372	1.0%
32	Iowa	307	0.8%
35	Kansas	300	0.8%
22	Kentucky	440	1.2%
21	Louisiana	532	1.4%
44	Maine	130	0.3%
23	Maryland	421	1.1%
29	Massachusetts	334	0.9%
10	Michigan	786	2.1%
36	Minnesota	297	0.8%
31	Mississippi	322	0.9%
15	Missouri	674	1.8%
37	Montana	275	0.7%
38	Nebraska	268	0.7%
39	Nevada	264	0.7%
43	New Hampshire	143	0.4%
17	New Jersey	627	1.7%
12	New Mexico	723	1.9%
3	New York	2,731	7.2%
9	North Carolina	872	2.3%
42	North Dakota	150	0.4%
14	Ohio	682	1.8%
24	Oklahoma	408	1.1%
20	Oregon	544	1.4%
7	Pennsylvania	1,097	2.9%
46	Rhode Island	96	0.3%
18	South Carolina	613	1.6%
27	South Dakota	364	1.0%
13	Tennessee	705	1.9%
2	Texas	4,915	13.0%
28	Utah	343	0.9%
49	Vermont	85	0.2%
6	Virginia	1,183	3.1%
19	Washington	596	1.6%
30	West Virginia	325	0.9%
32	Wisconsin	307	0.8%
48	Wyoming	95	0.3%

RANK ORDER

RANK	STATE	CASES	% of USA
1	California	5,597	14.8%
2	Texas	4,915	13.0%
3	New York	2,731	7.2%
4	Florida	2,624	6.9%
5	Arizona	1,470	3.9%
6	Virginia	1,183	3.1%
7	Pennsylvania	1,097	2.9%
8	Georgia	902	2.4%
9	North Carolina	872	2.3%
10	Michigan	786	2.1%
11	Illinois	780	2.1%
12	New Mexico	723	1.9%
13	Tennessee	705	1.9%
14	Ohio	682	1.8%
15	Missouri	674	1.8%
16	Alabama	661	1.7%
17	New Jersey	627	1.7%
18	South Carolina	613	1.6%
19	Washington	596	1.6%
20	Oregon	544	1.4%
21	Louisiana	532	1.4%
22	Kentucky	440	1.2%
23	Maryland	421	1.1%
24	Oklahoma	408	1.1%
25	Colorado	388	1.0%
26	Indiana	372	1.0%
27	South Dakota	364	1.0%
28	Utah	343	0.9%
29	Massachusetts	334	0.9%
30	West Virginia	325	0.9%
31	Mississippi	322	0.9%
32	Iowa	307	0.8%
32	Wisconsin	307	0.8%
34	Arkansas	306	0.8%
35	Kansas	300	0.8%
36	Minnesota	297	0.8%
37	Montana	275	0.7%
38	Nebraska	268	0.7%
39	Nevada	264	0.7%
40	Connecticut	214	0.6%
41	Hawaii	188	0.5%
42	North Dakota	150	0.4%
43	New Hampshire	143	0.4%
44	Maine	130	0.3%
45	Alaska	101	0.3%
46	Delaware	96	0.3%
46	Rhode Island	96	0.3%
48	Wyoming	95	0.3%
49	Vermont	85	0.2%
50	Idaho	83	0.2%
	District of Columbia	526	1.4%

Source: Morgan Quitno Press using data from Administrative Office of the United States Courts
    "1997 Federal Court Management Statistics" (March 1998)
*National total includes 572 cases in U.S. territories. Does not include transfers from one district to another.

Felony Criminal Cases Filed per U.S. District Judge in 1997

National Rate = 58 Felony Criminal Cases per Judge*

ALPHA ORDER

RANK	STATE	RATE
20	Alabama	51
41	Alaska	34
1	Arizona	184
36	Arkansas	38
5	California	100
17	Colorado	55
46	Connecticut	27
49	Delaware	24
8	Florida	85
22	Georgia	50
28	Hawaii	47
31	Idaho	42
47	Illinois	26
37	Indiana	37
16	Iowa	61
22	Kansas	50
25	Kentucky	49
49	Louisiana	24
29	Maine	43
31	Maryland	42
47	Massachusetts	26
34	Michigan	41
31	Minnesota	42
40	Mississippi	36
26	Missouri	48
6	Montana	92
14	Nebraska	67
15	Nevada	66
26	New Hampshire	48
37	New Jersey	37
2	New Mexico	145
19	New York	53
10	North Carolina	79
11	North Dakota	75
41	Ohio	34
37	Oklahoma	37
7	Oregon	91
45	Pennsylvania	28
43	Rhode Island	32
13	South Carolina	68
3	South Dakota	121
22	Tennessee	50
4	Texas	105
12	Utah	69
29	Vermont	43
8	Virginia	85
18	Washington	54
34	West Virginia	41
20	Wisconsin	51
43	Wyoming	32

RANK ORDER

RANK	STATE	RATE
1	Arizona	184
2	New Mexico	145
3	South Dakota	121
4	Texas	105
5	California	100
6	Montana	92
7	Oregon	91
8	Florida	85
8	Virginia	85
10	North Carolina	79
11	North Dakota	75
12	Utah	69
13	South Carolina	68
14	Nebraska	67
15	Nevada	66
16	Iowa	61
17	Colorado	55
18	Washington	54
19	New York	53
20	Alabama	51
20	Wisconsin	51
22	Georgia	50
22	Kansas	50
22	Tennessee	50
25	Kentucky	49
26	Missouri	48
26	New Hampshire	48
28	Hawaii	47
29	Maine	43
29	Vermont	43
31	Idaho	42
31	Maryland	42
31	Minnesota	42
34	Michigan	41
34	West Virginia	41
36	Arkansas	38
37	Indiana	37
37	New Jersey	37
37	Oklahoma	37
40	Mississippi	36
41	Alaska	34
41	Ohio	34
43	Rhode Island	32
43	Wyoming	32
45	Pennsylvania	28
46	Connecticut	27
47	Illinois	26
47	Massachusetts	26
49	Delaware	24
49	Louisiana	24

District of Columbia 35

Source: Morgan Quitno Press using data from Administrative Office of the United States Courts
"1997 Federal Court Management Statistics" (March 1998)
*National rate includes cases and judges in U.S. territories. Does not include transfers from one district to another.

Median Length of Federal Criminal Cases in 1997

National Median = 6.6 Month*

ALPHA ORDER

RANK	STATE	MONTHS
38	Alabama	5.9
49	Alaska	5.0
45	Arizona	5.4
22	Arkansas	7.1
34	California	6.3
41	Colorado	5.7
4	Connecticut	11.0
40	Delaware	5.8
26	Florida	6.7
14	Georgia	7.8
7	Hawaii	9.3
28	Idaho	6.6
11	Illinois	8.5
28	Indiana	6.6
17	Iowa	7.4
12	Kansas	7.9
25	Kentucky	6.8
28	Louisiana	6.6
41	Maine	5.7
16	Maryland	7.5
5	Massachusetts	9.8
8	Michigan	8.8
23	Minnesota	7.0
37	Mississippi	6.0
15	Missouri	7.6
18	Montana	7.3
6	Nebraska	9.4
2	Nevada	11.2
28	New Hampshire	6.6
8	New Jersey	8.8
21	New Mexico	7.2
2	New York	11.2
12	North Carolina	7.9
50	North Dakota	4.8
23	Ohio	7.0
45	Oklahoma	5.4
43	Oregon	5.5
18	Pennsylvania	7.3
35	Rhode Island	6.2
18	South Carolina	7.3
45	South Dakota	5.4
10	Tennessee	8.7
43	Texas	5.5
35	Utah	6.2
1	Vermont	11.9
28	Virginia	6.6
45	Washington	5.4
38	West Virginia	5.9
33	Wisconsin	6.4
26	Wyoming	6.7

RANK ORDER

RANK	STATE	MONTHS
1	Vermont	11.9
2	Nevada	11.2
2	New York	11.2
4	Connecticut	11.0
5	Massachusetts	9.8
6	Nebraska	9.4
7	Hawaii	9.3
8	Michigan	8.8
8	New Jersey	8.8
10	Tennessee	8.7
11	Illinois	8.5
12	Kansas	7.9
12	North Carolina	7.9
14	Georgia	7.8
15	Missouri	7.6
16	Maryland	7.5
17	Iowa	7.4
18	Montana	7.3
18	Pennsylvania	7.3
18	South Carolina	7.3
21	New Mexico	7.2
22	Arkansas	7.1
23	Minnesota	7.0
23	Ohio	7.0
25	Kentucky	6.8
26	Florida	6.7
26	Wyoming	6.7
28	Idaho	6.6
28	Indiana	6.6
28	Louisiana	6.6
28	New Hampshire	6.6
28	Virginia	6.6
33	Wisconsin	6.4
34	California	6.3
35	Rhode Island	6.2
35	Utah	6.2
37	Mississippi	6.0
38	Alabama	5.9
38	West Virginia	5.9
40	Delaware	5.8
41	Colorado	5.7
41	Maine	5.7
43	Oregon	5.5
43	Texas	5.5
45	Arizona	5.4
45	Oklahoma	5.4
45	South Dakota	5.4
45	Washington	5.4
49	Alaska	5.0
50	North Dakota	4.8
	District of Columbia	6.4

Source: Morgan Quitno Press using data from Administrative Office of the United States Courts
   "1997 Federal Court Management Statistics" (March 1998)
*Felony criminal cases. National rate includes cases U.S. territories. Does not include transfers from one district to another.

Authorized Wiretaps in 1997

National Total = 617 State Authorized Wiretaps*

ALPHA ORDER					RANK ORDER			
RANK	STATE		WIRETAPS	% of USA	RANK	STATE	WIRETAPS	% of USA
NA	Alabama**		NA	NA	1	New York	304	49.3%
24	Alaska		0	0.0%	2	New Jersey	70	11.3%
11	Arizona		6	1.0%	3	Florida	57	9.2%
NA	Arkansas**		NA	NA	4	Pennsylvania	42	6.8%
5	California		28	4.5%	5	California	28	4.5%
12	Colorado		4	0.6%	6	Maryland	27	4.4%
10	Connecticut		8	1.3%	7	Georgia	18	2.9%
24	Delaware		0	0.0%	8	Illinois	17	2.8%
3	Florida		57	9.2%	9	Nevada	10	1.6%
7	Georgia		18	2.9%	10	Connecticut	8	1.3%
24	Hawaii		0	0.0%	11	Arizona	6	1.0%
24	Idaho		0	0.0%	12	Colorado	4	0.6%
8	Illinois		17	2.8%	12	Mississippi	4	0.6%
24	Indiana		0	0.0%	12	Nebraska	4	0.6%
24	Iowa		0	0.0%	12	New Hampshire	4	0.6%
24	Kansas		0	0.0%	16	Wisconsin	3	0.5%
NA	Kentucky**		NA	NA	17	Louisiana	2	0.3%
17	Louisiana		2	0.3%	17	Massachusetts	2	0.3%
NA	Maine**		NA	NA	17	Ohio	2	0.3%
6	Maryland		27	4.4%	17	Rhode Island	2	0.3%
17	Massachusetts		2	0.3%	21	New Mexico	1	0.2%
NA	Michigan**		NA	NA	21	Oregon	1	0.2%
24	Minnesota		0	0.0%	21	Virginia	1	0.2%
12	Mississippi		4	0.6%	24	Alaska	0	0.0%
24	Missouri		0	0.0%	24	Delaware	0	0.0%
NA	Montana**		NA	NA	24	Hawaii	0	0.0%
12	Nebraska		4	0.6%	24	Idaho	0	0.0%
9	Nevada		10	1.6%	24	Indiana	0	0.0%
12	New Hampshire		4	0.6%	24	Iowa	0	0.0%
2	New Jersey		70	11.3%	24	Kansas	0	0.0%
21	New Mexico		1	0.2%	24	Minnesota	0	0.0%
1	New York		304	49.3%	24	Missouri	0	0.0%
24	North Carolina		0	0.0%	24	North Carolina	0	0.0%
24	North Dakota		0	0.0%	24	North Dakota	0	0.0%
17	Ohio		2	0.3%	24	Oklahoma	0	0.0%
24	Oklahoma		0	0.0%	24	South Dakota	0	0.0%
21	Oregon		1	0.2%	24	Tennessee	0	0.0%
4	Pennsylvania		42	6.8%	24	Texas	0	0.0%
17	Rhode Island		2	0.3%	24	Utah	0	0.0%
NA	South Carolina**		NA	NA	24	Washington	0	0.0%
24	South Dakota		0	0.0%	24	West Virginia	0	0.0%
24	Tennessee		0	0.0%	24	Wyoming	0	0.0%
24	Texas		0	0.0%	NA	Alabama**	NA	NA
24	Utah		0	0.0%	NA	Arkansas**	NA	NA
NA	Vermont**		NA	NA	NA	Kentucky**	NA	NA
21	Virginia		1	0.2%	NA	Maine**	NA	NA
24	Washington		0	0.0%	NA	Michigan**	NA	NA
24	West Virginia		0	0.0%	NA	Montana**	NA	NA
16	Wisconsin		3	0.5%	NA	South Carolina**	NA	NA
24	Wyoming		0	0.0%	NA	Vermont**	NA	NA
						District of Columbia	0	0.0%

Source: Administrative Office of the United States Courts
   "1997 Wiretap Report" (April 1998)
*Total does not include 569 wiretaps authorized under federal statute.
**No state statute authorizing wiretaps.

VII. OFFENSES

VII. OFFENSES (continued)

Urban/Rural Crime

VII. OFFENSES (continued)

1993 Crimes

VII. OFFENSES (continued)

Crimes in 1997

National Total = 13,175,070 Crimes*

ALPHA ORDER

RANK	STATE	CRIMES	% of USA
22	Alabama	211,188	1.6%
45	Alaska	32,110	0.2%
12	Arizona	327,734	2.5%
33	Arkansas	119,052	0.9%
1	California	1,569,949	11.9%
27	Colorado	181,041	1.4%
28	Connecticut	130,286	1.0%
43	Delaware	37,612	0.3%
2	Florida	1,065,609	8.1%
8	Georgia	433,563	3.3%
37	Hawaii	71,492	0.5%
39	Idaho	47,495	0.4%
5	Illinois	611,589	4.6%
17	Indiana	261,902	2.0%
35	Iowa	108,827	0.8%
34	Kansas	118,422	0.9%
31	Kentucky	122,205	0.9%
16	Louisiana	280,671	2.1%
41	Maine	38,896	0.3%
15	Maryland	287,969	2.2%
21	Massachusetts	224,848	1.7%
7	Michigan	480,579	3.6%
23	Minnesota	206,833	1.6%
29	Mississippi	126,452	1.0%
19	Missouri	260,081	2.0%
42	Montana	38,753	0.3%
38	Nebraska	70,982	0.5%
36	Nevada	101,702	0.8%
46	New Hampshire	30,963	0.2%
13	New Jersey	326,711	2.5%
32	New Mexico	119,483	0.9%
4	New York	709,328	5.4%
10	North Carolina	407,743	3.1%
49	North Dakota	17,380	0.1%
6	Ohio	505,005	3.8%
26	Oklahoma	182,258	1.4%
24	Oregon	203,328	1.5%
9	Pennsylvania	412,463	3.1%
44	Rhode Island	36,069	0.3%
20	South Carolina	230,637	1.8%
47	South Dakota	23,948	0.2%
14	Tennessee	295,873	2.2%
3	Texas	1,065,357	8.1%
30	Utah	123,447	0.9%
50	Vermont	16,658	0.1%
18	Virginia	261,022	2.0%
11	Washington	332,466	2.5%
40	West Virginia	44,839	0.3%
25	Wisconsin	190,133	1.4%
48	Wyoming	20,068	0.2%

RANK ORDER

RANK	STATE	CRIMES	% of USA
1	California	1,569,949	11.9%
2	Florida	1,065,609	8.1%
3	Texas	1,065,357	8.1%
4	New York	709,328	5.4%
5	Illinois	611,589	4.6%
6	Ohio	505,005	3.8%
7	Michigan	480,579	3.6%
8	Georgia	433,563	3.3%
9	Pennsylvania	412,463	3.1%
10	North Carolina	407,743	3.1%
11	Washington	332,466	2.5%
12	Arizona	327,734	2.5%
13	New Jersey	326,711	2.5%
14	Tennessee	295,873	2.2%
15	Maryland	287,969	2.2%
16	Louisiana	280,671	2.1%
17	Indiana	261,902	2.0%
18	Virginia	261,022	2.0%
19	Missouri	260,081	2.0%
20	South Carolina	230,637	1.8%
21	Massachusetts	224,848	1.7%
22	Alabama	211,188	1.6%
23	Minnesota	206,833	1.6%
24	Oregon	203,328	1.5%
25	Wisconsin	190,133	1.4%
26	Oklahoma	182,258	1.4%
27	Colorado	181,041	1.4%
28	Connecticut	130,286	1.0%
29	Mississippi	126,452	1.0%
30	Utah	123,447	0.9%
31	Kentucky	122,205	0.9%
32	New Mexico	119,483	0.9%
33	Arkansas	119,052	0.9%
34	Kansas	118,422	0.9%
35	Iowa	108,827	0.8%
36	Nevada	101,702	0.8%
37	Hawaii	71,492	0.5%
38	Nebraska	70,982	0.5%
39	Idaho	47,495	0.4%
40	West Virginia	44,839	0.3%
41	Maine	38,896	0.3%
42	Montana	38,753	0.3%
43	Delaware	37,612	0.3%
44	Rhode Island	36,069	0.3%
45	Alaska	32,110	0.2%
46	New Hampshire	30,963	0.2%
47	South Dakota	23,948	0.2%
48	Wyoming	20,068	0.2%
49	North Dakota	17,380	0.1%
50	Vermont	16,658	0.1%
	District of Columbia	52,049	0.4%

Source: Federal Bureau of Investigation
"Crime in the United States 1997" (Uniform Crime Reports, November 22, 1998)
*Includes murder, rape, robbery, aggravated assault, burglary, larceny-theft and motor vehicle theft.

Average Time Between Crimes in 1997

National Rate = A Crime Occurs Every 2 Seconds*

ALPHA ORDER				RANK ORDER		
RANK	**STATE**	**MINUTES.SECONDS**		**RANK**	**STATE**	**MINUTES.SECONDS**
29	Alabama	2.29		1	Vermont	31.33
6	Alaska	16.22		2	North Dakota	30.14
39	Arizona	1.36		3	Wyoming	26.11
18	Arkansas	4.25		4	South Dakota	21.57
50	California	0.20		5	New Hampshire	16.59
24	Colorado	2.54		6	Alaska	16.22
23	Connecticut	4.02		7	Rhode Island	14.34
8	Delaware	13.58		8	Delaware	13.58
48	Florida	0.29		9	Montana	13.34
43	Georgia	1.13		10	Maine	13.31
14	Hawaii	7.21		11	West Virginia	11.43
12	Idaho	11.04		12	Idaho	11.04
46	Illinois	0.52		13	Nebraska	7.24
32	Indiana	2.01		14	Hawaii	7.21
16	Iowa	4.50		15	Nevada	5.10
17	Kansas	4.26		16	Iowa	4.50
20	Kentucky	4.18		17	Kansas	4.26
35	Louisiana	1.52		18	Arkansas	4.25
10	Maine	13.31		19	New Mexico	4.24
36	Maryland	1.50		20	Kentucky	4.18
30	Massachusetts	2.20		21	Utah	4.16
44	Michigan	1.05		22	Mississippi	4.10
28	Minnesota	2.32		23	Connecticut	4.02
22	Mississippi	4.10		24	Colorado	2.54
32	Missouri	2.01		25	Oklahoma	2.53
9	Montana	13.34		26	Wisconsin	2.46
13	Nebraska	7.24		27	Oregon	2.35
15	Nevada	5.10		28	Minnesota	2.32
5	New Hampshire	16.59		29	Alabama	2.29
38	New Jersey	1.37		30	Massachusetts	2.20
19	New Mexico	4.24		31	South Carolina	2.17
47	New York	0.44		32	Indiana	2.01
41	North Carolina	1.17		32	Missouri	2.01
2	North Dakota	30.14		32	Virginia	2.01
45	Ohio	1.02		35	Louisiana	1.52
25	Oklahoma	2.53		36	Maryland	1.50
27	Oregon	2.35		37	Tennessee	1.47
42	Pennsylvania	1.16		38	New Jersey	1.37
7	Rhode Island	14.34		39	Arizona	1.36
31	South Carolina	2.17		40	Washington	1.35
4	South Dakota	21.57		41	North Carolina	1.17
37	Tennessee	1.47		42	Pennsylvania	1.16
48	Texas	0.29		43	Georgia	1.13
21	Utah	4.16		44	Michigan	1.05
1	Vermont	31.33		45	Ohio	1.02
32	Virginia	2.01		46	Illinois	0.52
40	Washington	1.35		47	New York	0.44
11	West Virginia	11.43		48	Florida	0.29
26	Wisconsin	2.46		48	Texas	0.29
3	Wyoming	26.11		50	California	0.20
					District of Columbia	10.06

Source: Morgan Quitno Press using data from Federal Bureau of Investigation
"Crime in the United States 1997" (Uniform Crime Reports, November 22, 1998)
Includes murder, rape, robbery, aggravated assault, burglary, larceny-theft and motor vehicle theft.

Crimes per Square Mile in 1997

National Rate = 3.5 Crimes per Square Mile*

ALPHA ORDER

RANK	STATE	RATE
23	Alabama	4.0
50	Alaska	0.1
28	Arizona	2.9
33	Arkansas	2.2
12	California	9.9
37	Colorado	1.7
4	Connecticut	23.5
7	Delaware	15.7
6	Florida	17.8
15	Georgia	7.4
10	Hawaii	11.1
45	Idaho	0.6
11	Illinois	10.6
17	Indiana	7.2
35	Iowa	1.9
40	Kansas	1.4
27	Kentucky	3.0
20	Louisiana	5.7
41	Maine	1.2
5	Maryland	23.4
3	Massachusetts	24.3
21	Michigan	5.0
32	Minnesota	2.4
30	Mississippi	2.6
25	Missouri	3.7
46	Montana	0.3
43	Nebraska	0.9
43	Nevada	0.9
26	New Hampshire	3.3
1	New Jersey	39.8
42	New Mexico	1.0
8	New York	13.1
14	North Carolina	7.7
48	North Dakota	0.2
9	Ohio	11.3
30	Oklahoma	2.6
34	Oregon	2.1
13	Pennsylvania	9.0
2	Rhode Island	29.3
15	South Carolina	7.4
46	South Dakota	0.3
18	Tennessee	7.0
23	Texas	4.0
39	Utah	1.5
37	Vermont	1.7
19	Virginia	6.2
22	Washington	4.7
35	West Virginia	1.9
28	Wisconsin	2.9
48	Wyoming	0.2

RANK ORDER

RANK	STATE	RATE
1	New Jersey	39.8
2	Rhode Island	29.3
3	Massachusetts	24.3
4	Connecticut	23.5
5	Maryland	23.4
6	Florida	17.8
7	Delaware	15.7
8	New York	13.1
9	Ohio	11.3
10	Hawaii	11.1
11	Illinois	10.6
12	California	9.9
13	Pennsylvania	9.0
14	North Carolina	7.7
15	Georgia	7.4
15	South Carolina	7.4
17	Indiana	7.2
18	Tennessee	7.0
19	Virginia	6.2
20	Louisiana	5.7
21	Michigan	5.0
22	Washington	4.7
23	Alabama	4.0
23	Texas	4.0
25	Missouri	3.7
26	New Hampshire	3.3
27	Kentucky	3.0
28	Arizona	2.9
28	Wisconsin	2.9
30	Mississippi	2.6
30	Oklahoma	2.6
32	Minnesota	2.4
33	Arkansas	2.2
34	Oregon	2.1
35	Iowa	1.9
35	West Virginia	1.9
37	Colorado	1.7
37	Vermont	1.7
39	Utah	1.5
40	Kansas	1.4
41	Maine	1.2
42	New Mexico	1.0
43	Nebraska	0.9
43	Nevada	0.9
45	Idaho	0.6
46	Montana	0.3
46	South Dakota	0.3
48	North Dakota	0.2
48	Wyoming	0.2
50	Alaska	0.1

District of Columbia	765.4

Source: Morgan Quitno Press using data from Federal Bureau of Investigation
     "Crime in the United States 1997" (Uniform Crime Reports, November 22, 1998)
*Includes murder, rape, robbery, aggravated assault, burglary, larceny-theft and motor vehicle theft.

Percent Change in Number of Crimes: 1996 to 1997

National Percent Change = 2.4% Decrease*

ALPHA ORDER

ALPHA ORDER

RANK	STATE	PERCENT CHANGE
10	Alabama	2.5
31	Alaska	(2.9)
6	Arizona	4.7
15	Arkansas	0.9
38	California	(5.4)
47	Colorado	(7.5)
44	Connecticut	(5.9)
2	Delaware	6.0
23	Florida	(1.3)
46	Georgia	(6.6)
49	Hawaii	(8.3)
19	Idaho	(0.4)
32	Illinois	(3.0)
18	Indiana	(0.3)
7	Iowa	4.6
25	Kansas	(1.7)
21	Kentucky	(0.6)
42	Louisiana	(5.7)
48	Maine	(7.8)
45	Maryland	(6.3)
35	Massachusetts	(3.8)
28	Michigan	(2.1)
20	Minnesota	(0.5)
9	Mississippi	2.9
37	Missouri	(4.5)
26	Montana	(1.9)
33	Nebraska	(3.2)
3	Nevada	5.9
39	New Hampshire	(5.6)
39	New Jersey	(5.6)
5	New Mexico	5.6
39	New York	(5.6)
16	North Carolina	0.8
14	North Dakota	1.1
13	Ohio	1.4
29	Oklahoma	(2.3)
4	Oregon	5.8
35	Pennsylvania	(3.8)
50	Rhode Island	(8.8)
17	South Carolina	0.3
1	South Dakota	10.2
11	Tennessee	2.1
30	Texas	(2.4)
8	Utah	3.1
43	Vermont	(5.8)
24	Virginia	(1.5)
12	Washington	1.7
22	West Virginia	(1.1)
34	Wisconsin	(3.6)
26	Wyoming	(1.9)

RANK ORDER

RANK	STATE	PERCENT CHANGE
1	South Dakota	10.2
2	Delaware	6.0
3	Nevada	5.9
4	Oregon	5.8
5	New Mexico	5.6
6	Arizona	4.7
7	Iowa	4.6
8	Utah	3.1
9	Mississippi	2.9
10	Alabama	2.5
11	Tennessee	2.1
12	Washington	1.7
13	Ohio	1.4
14	North Dakota	1.1
15	Arkansas	0.9
16	North Carolina	0.8
17	South Carolina	0.3
18	Indiana	(0.3)
19	Idaho	(0.4)
20	Minnesota	(0.5)
21	Kentucky	(0.6)
22	West Virginia	(1.1)
23	Florida	(1.3)
24	Virginia	(1.5)
25	Kansas	(1.7)
26	Montana	(1.9)
26	Wyoming	(1.9)
28	Michigan	(2.1)
29	Oklahoma	(2.3)
30	Texas	(2.4)
31	Alaska	(2.9)
32	Illinois	(3.0)
33	Nebraska	(3.2)
34	Wisconsin	(3.6)
35	Massachusetts	(3.8)
35	Pennsylvania	(3.8)
37	Missouri	(4.5)
38	California	(5.4)
39	New Hampshire	(5.6)
39	New Jersey	(5.6)
39	New York	(5.6)
42	Louisiana	(5.7)
43	Vermont	(5.8)
44	Connecticut	(5.9)
45	Maryland	(6.3)
46	Georgia	(6.6)
47	Colorado	(7.5)
48	Maine	(7.8)
49	Hawaii	(8.3)
50	Rhode Island	(8.8)

	District of Columbia	(19.4)

Source: Federal Bureau of Investigation
"Crime in the United States 1997" (Uniform Crime Reports, November 22, 1998)
Includes murder, rape, robbery, aggravated assault, burglary, larceny-theft and motor vehicle theft.

Crime Rate in 1997

National Rate = 4,922.7 Crimes per 100,000 Population*

ALPHA ORDER

RANK	STATE	RATE
21	Alabama	4,889.7
17	Alaska	5,272.6
2	Arizona	7,195.0
24	Arkansas	4,718.7
22	California	4,865.3
25	Colorado	4,650.4
35	Connecticut	3,984.3
19	Delaware	5,138.3
1	Florida	7,271.8
11	Georgia	5,791.7
8	Hawaii	6,022.9
36	Idaho	3,925.2
18	Illinois	5,141.1
29	Indiana	4,466.3
39	Iowa	3,815.8
27	Kansas	4,563.5
46	Kentucky	3,127.0
4	Louisiana	6,449.2
45	Maine	3,131.7
12	Maryland	5,653.1
41	Massachusetts	3,675.2
20	Michigan	4,916.9
30	Minnesota	4,413.8
26	Mississippi	4,630.2
23	Missouri	4,814.5
31	Montana	4,408.8
32	Nebraska	4,283.8
7	Nevada	6,064.5
49	New Hampshire	2,639.6
34	New Jersey	4,057.0
3	New Mexico	6,906.5
37	New York	3,910.9
15	North Carolina	5,491.5
48	North Dakota	2,711.4
28	Ohio	4,514.6
14	Oklahoma	5,494.7
5	Oregon	6,269.8
43	Pennsylvania	3,431.5
42	Rhode Island	3,654.4
6	South Carolina	6,134.0
44	South Dakota	3,245.0
13	Tennessee	5,511.8
16	Texas	5,480.5
9	Utah	5,995.5
47	Vermont	2,828.2
38	Virginia	3,876.2
10	Washington	5,926.3
50	West Virginia	2,469.1
40	Wisconsin	3,677.6
33	Wyoming	4,180.8

RANK ORDER

RANK	STATE	RATE
1	Florida	7,271.8
2	Arizona	7,195.0
3	New Mexico	6,906.5
4	Louisiana	6,449.2
5	Oregon	6,269.8
6	South Carolina	6,134.0
7	Nevada	6,064.5
8	Hawaii	6,022.9
9	Utah	5,995.5
10	Washington	5,926.3
11	Georgia	5,791.7
12	Maryland	5,653.1
13	Tennessee	5,511.8
14	Oklahoma	5,494.7
15	North Carolina	5,491.5
16	Texas	5,480.5
17	Alaska	5,272.6
18	Illinois	5,141.1
19	Delaware	5,138.3
20	Michigan	4,916.9
21	Alabama	4,889.7
22	California	4,865.3
23	Missouri	4,814.5
24	Arkansas	4,718.7
25	Colorado	4,650.4
26	Mississippi	4,630.2
27	Kansas	4,563.5
28	Ohio	4,514.6
29	Indiana	4,466.3
30	Minnesota	4,413.8
31	Montana	4,408.8
32	Nebraska	4,283.8
33	Wyoming	4,180.8
34	New Jersey	4,057.0
35	Connecticut	3,984.3
36	Idaho	3,925.2
37	New York	3,910.9
38	Virginia	3,876.2
39	Iowa	3,815.8
40	Wisconsin	3,677.6
41	Massachusetts	3,675.2
42	Rhode Island	3,654.4
43	Pennsylvania	3,431.5
44	South Dakota	3,245.0
45	Maine	3,131.7
46	Kentucky	3,127.0
47	Vermont	2,828.2
48	North Dakota	2,711.4
49	New Hampshire	2,639.6
50	West Virginia	2,469.1
	District of Columbia	9,839.1

Source: Federal Bureau of Investigation
   "Crime in the United States 1997" (Uniform Crime Reports, November 22, 1998)
*Includes murder, rape, robbery, aggravated assault, burglary, larceny-theft and motor vehicle theft.

Percent Change in Crime Rate: 1996 to 1997

National Percent Change = 3.2% Decrease*

RANK	STATE	PERCENT CHANGE		RANK	STATE	PERCENT CHANGE
ALPHA ORDER				RANK ORDER		
9	Alabama	1.4		1	South Dakota	9.3
29	Alaska	(3.3)		2	Delaware	5.0
7	Arizona	1.8		3	Iowa	4.6
13	Arkansas	0.4		3	New Mexico	4.6
44	California	(6.6)		3	Oregon	4.6
50	Colorado	(9.1)		6	Mississippi	2.4
40	Connecticut	(5.8)		7	Arizona	1.8
2	Delaware	5.0		8	North Dakota	1.6
28	Florida	(3.0)		9	Alabama	1.4
47	Georgia	(8.2)		10	Ohio	1.3
48	Hawaii	(8.5)		11	Nevada	1.2
24	Idaho	(2.2)		12	Tennessee	1.1
30	Illinois	(3.4)		13	Arkansas	0.4
18	Indiana	(0.7)		14	Washington	0.3
3	Iowa	4.6		15	Utah	0.2
26	Kansas	(2.5)		16	North Carolina	(0.6)
20	Kentucky	(1.2)		16	West Virginia	(0.6)
39	Louisiana	(5.7)		18	Indiana	(0.7)
46	Maine	(7.7)		19	Minnesota	(1.1)
45	Maryland	(6.7)		20	Kentucky	(1.2)
36	Massachusetts	(4.2)		21	South Carolina	(1.3)
34	Michigan	(3.9)		22	Wyoming	(1.7)
19	Minnesota	(1.1)		23	Montana	(1.9)
6	Mississippi	2.4		24	Idaho	(2.2)
37	Missouri	(5.3)		25	Virginia	(2.3)
23	Montana	(1.9)		26	Kansas	(2.5)
30	Nebraska	(3.4)		27	Oklahoma	(2.8)
11	Nevada	1.2		28	Florida	(3.0)
43	New Hampshire	(6.5)		29	Alaska	(3.3)
42	New Jersey	(6.4)		30	Illinois	(3.4)
3	New Mexico	4.6		30	Nebraska	(3.4)
38	New York	(5.4)		32	Pennsylvania	(3.5)
16	North Carolina	(0.6)		33	Wisconsin	(3.8)
8	North Dakota	1.6		34	Michigan	(3.9)
10	Ohio	1.3		35	Texas	(4.0)
27	Oklahoma	(2.8)		36	Massachusetts	(4.2)
3	Oregon	4.6		37	Missouri	(5.3)
32	Pennsylvania	(3.5)		38	New York	(5.4)
48	Rhode Island	(8.5)		39	Louisiana	(5.7)
21	South Carolina	(1.3)		40	Connecticut	(5.8)
1	South Dakota	9.3		40	Vermont	(5.8)
12	Tennessee	1.1		42	New Jersey	(6.4)
35	Texas	(4.0)		43	New Hampshire	(6.5)
15	Utah	0.2		44	California	(6.6)
40	Vermont	(5.8)		45	Maryland	(6.7)
25	Virginia	(2.3)		46	Maine	(7.7)
14	Washington	0.3		47	Georgia	(8.2)
16	West Virginia	(0.6)		48	Hawaii	(8.5)
33	Wisconsin	(3.8)		48	Rhode Island	(8.5)
22	Wyoming	(1.7)		50	Colorado	(9.1)
					District of Columbia	(17.3)

Source: Federal Bureau of Investigation
   "Crime in the United States 1997" (Uniform Crime Reports, November 22, 1998)
*Includes murder, rape, robbery, aggravated assault, burglary, larceny-theft and motor vehicle theft.

Violent Crimes in 1997

National Total = 1,634,773 Violent Crimes*

ALPHA ORDER

RANK	STATE	CRIMES	% of USA
21	Alabama	24,379	1.5%
39	Alaska	4,270	0.3%
19	Arizona	28,411	1.7%
30	Arkansas	13,293	0.8%
1	California	257,582	15.8%
27	Colorado	14,139	0.9%
32	Connecticut	12,781	0.8%
38	Delaware	4,962	0.3%
2	Florida	149,996	9.2%
9	Georgia	45,408	2.8%
41	Hawaii	3,299	0.2%
43	Idaho	3,107	0.2%
5	Illinois	102,476	6.3%
18	Indiana	30,179	1.8%
35	Iowa	8,841	0.5%
34	Kansas	10,619	0.6%
33	Kentucky	12,386	0.8%
15	Louisiana	37,248	2.3%
44	Maine	1,500	0.1%
11	Maryland	43,127	2.6%
14	Massachusetts	39,411	2.4%
6	Michigan	57,663	3.5%
24	Minnesota	15,827	1.0%
31	Mississippi	12,808	0.8%
17	Missouri	31,192	1.9%
48	Montana	1,161	0.1%
36	Nebraska	7,265	0.4%
29	Nevada	13,395	0.8%
46	New Hampshire	1,328	0.1%
13	New Jersey	39,673	2.4%
25	New Mexico	14,762	0.9%
3	New York	124,890	7.6%
10	North Carolina	45,071	2.8%
50	North Dakota	559	0.0%
8	Ohio	48,706	3.0%
23	Oklahoma	18,560	1.1%
26	Oregon	14,412	0.9%
7	Pennsylvania	53,140	3.3%
42	Rhode Island	3,292	0.2%
16	South Carolina	37,235	2.3%
45	South Dakota	1,457	0.1%
12	Tennessee	42,389	2.6%
4	Texas	117,126	7.2%
37	Utah	6,878	0.4%
49	Vermont	705	0.0%
22	Virginia	23,249	1.4%
20	Washington	24,724	1.5%
40	West Virginia	3,971	0.2%
28	Wisconsin	13,988	0.9%
47	Wyoming	1,225	0.1%

RANK ORDER

RANK	STATE	CRIMES	% of USA
1	California	257,582	15.8%
2	Florida	149,996	9.2%
3	New York	124,890	7.6%
4	Texas	117,126	7.2%
5	Illinois	102,476	6.3%
6	Michigan	57,663	3.5%
7	Pennsylvania	53,140	3.3%
8	Ohio	48,706	3.0%
9	Georgia	45,408	2.8%
10	North Carolina	45,071	2.8%
11	Maryland	43,127	2.6%
12	Tennessee	42,389	2.6%
13	New Jersey	39,673	2.4%
14	Massachusetts	39,411	2.4%
15	Louisiana	37,248	2.3%
16	South Carolina	37,235	2.3%
17	Missouri	31,192	1.9%
18	Indiana	30,179	1.8%
19	Arizona	28,411	1.7%
20	Washington	24,724	1.5%
21	Alabama	24,379	1.5%
22	Virginia	23,249	1.4%
23	Oklahoma	18,560	1.1%
24	Minnesota	15,827	1.0%
25	New Mexico	14,762	0.9%
26	Oregon	14,412	0.9%
27	Colorado	14,139	0.9%
28	Wisconsin	13,988	0.9%
29	Nevada	13,395	0.8%
30	Arkansas	13,293	0.8%
31	Mississippi	12,808	0.8%
32	Connecticut	12,781	0.8%
33	Kentucky	12,386	0.8%
34	Kansas	10,619	0.6%
35	Iowa	8,841	0.5%
36	Nebraska	7,265	0.4%
37	Utah	6,878	0.4%
38	Delaware	4,962	0.3%
39	Alaska	4,270	0.3%
40	West Virginia	3,971	0.2%
41	Hawaii	3,299	0.2%
42	Rhode Island	3,292	0.2%
43	Idaho	3,107	0.2%
44	Maine	1,500	0.1%
45	South Dakota	1,457	0.1%
46	New Hampshire	1,328	0.1%
47	Wyoming	1,225	0.1%
48	Montana	1,161	0.1%
49	Vermont	705	0.0%
50	North Dakota	559	0.0%
	District of Columbia	10,708	0.7%

Source: Federal Bureau of Investigation
    "Crime in the United States 1997" (Uniform Crime Reports, November 22, 1998)
*Violent crimes are offenses of murder, forcible rape, robbery and aggravated assault.

Average Time Between Violent Crimes in 1997

National Rate = A Violent Crime Occurs Every 19 Seconds*

ALPHA ORDER

RANK	STATE	MINUTES.SECONDS
30	Alabama	21.34
12	Alaska	123.05
32	Arizona	18.30
21	Arkansas	39.32
50	California	2.02
24	Colorado	37.10
19	Connecticut	41.07
13	Delaware	105.56
49	Florida	3.30
42	Georgia	11.35
10	Hawaii	159.19
8	Idaho	169.10
46	Illinois	5.08
33	Indiana	17.25
16	Iowa	59.27
17	Kansas	49.30
18	Kentucky	42.26
35	Louisiana	14.07
7	Maine	350.24
40	Maryland	12.11
37	Massachusetts	13.20
45	Michigan	9.07
27	Minnesota	33.13
20	Mississippi	41.02
34	Missouri	16.51
3	Montana	452.43
15	Nebraska	72.21
22	Nevada	39.14
5	New Hampshire	395.47
38	New Jersey	13.15
26	New Mexico	35.37
48	New York	4.13
41	North Carolina	11.40
1	North Dakota	940.15
43	Ohio	10.47
28	Oklahoma	28.19
25	Oregon	36.28
44	Pennsylvania	9.53
9	Rhode Island	159.40
35	South Carolina	14.07
6	South Dakota	360.44
39	Tennessee	12.24
47	Texas	4.29
14	Utah	76.25
2	Vermont	745.32
29	Virginia	22.37
31	Washington	21.16
11	West Virginia	132.22
23	Wisconsin	37.35
4	Wyoming	429.04

RANK ORDER

RANK	STATE	MINUTES.SECONDS
1	North Dakota	940.15
2	Vermont	745.32
3	Montana	452.43
4	Wyoming	429.04
5	New Hampshire	395.47
6	South Dakota	360.44
7	Maine	350.24
8	Idaho	169.10
9	Rhode Island	159.40
10	Hawaii	159.19
11	West Virginia	132.22
12	Alaska	123.05
13	Delaware	105.56
14	Utah	76.25
15	Nebraska	72.21
16	Iowa	59.27
17	Kansas	49.30
18	Kentucky	42.26
19	Connecticut	41.07
20	Mississippi	41.02
21	Arkansas	39.32
22	Nevada	39.14
23	Wisconsin	37.35
24	Colorado	37.10
25	Oregon	36.28
26	New Mexico	35.37
27	Minnesota	33.13
28	Oklahoma	28.19
29	Virginia	22.37
30	Alabama	21.34
31	Washington	21.16
32	Arizona	18.30
33	Indiana	17.25
34	Missouri	16.51
35	Louisiana	14.07
35	South Carolina	14.07
37	Massachusetts	13.20
38	New Jersey	13.15
39	Tennessee	12.24
40	Maryland	12.11
41	North Carolina	11.40
42	Georgia	11.35
43	Ohio	10.47
44	Pennsylvania	9.53
45	Michigan	9.07
46	Illinois	5.08
47	Texas	4.29
48	New York	4.13
49	Florida	3.30
50	California	2.02
	District of Columbia	49.05

Source: Morgan Quitno Press using data from Federal Bureau of Investigation
  "Crime in the United States 1997" (Uniform Crime Reports, November 22, 1998)
*Violent crimes are offenses of murder, forcible rape, robbery and aggravated assault.

Violent Crimes per Square Mile in 1997

National Rate = 0.44 Violent Crimes per Square Mile*

RANK	STATE	RATE
22	Alabama	0.47
47	Alaska	0.01
29	Arizona	0.25
29	Arkansas	0.25
10	California	1.62
36	Colorado	0.14
6	Connecticut	2.31
8	Delaware	2.07
5	Florida	2.50
17	Georgia	0.77
21	Hawaii	0.51
44	Idaho	0.04
9	Illinois	1.77
16	Indiana	0.83
33	Iowa	0.16
38	Kansas	0.13
26	Kentucky	0.31
18	Louisiana	0.75
44	Maine	0.04
3	Maryland	3.51
2	Massachusetts	4.26
19	Michigan	0.60
32	Minnesota	0.18
27	Mississippi	0.27
23	Missouri	0.45
47	Montana	0.01
41	Nebraska	0.09
39	Nevada	0.12
36	New Hampshire	0.14
1	New Jersey	4.83
39	New Mexico	0.12
6	New York	2.31
15	North Carolina	0.86
47	North Dakota	0.01
13	Ohio	1.09
27	Oklahoma	0.27
35	Oregon	0.15
12	Pennsylvania	1.15
4	Rhode Island	2.67
11	South Carolina	1.19
46	South Dakota	0.02
14	Tennessee	1.01
24	Texas	0.44
42	Utah	0.08
43	Vermont	0.07
20	Virginia	0.55
25	Washington	0.35
33	West Virginia	0.16
31	Wisconsin	0.21
47	Wyoming	0.01

RANK	STATE	RATE
1	New Jersey	4.83
2	Massachusetts	4.26
3	Maryland	3.51
4	Rhode Island	2.67
5	Florida	2.50
6	Connecticut	2.31
6	New York	2.31
8	Delaware	2.07
9	Illinois	1.77
10	California	1.62
11	South Carolina	1.19
12	Pennsylvania	1.15
13	Ohio	1.09
14	Tennessee	1.01
15	North Carolina	0.86
16	Indiana	0.83
17	Georgia	0.77
18	Louisiana	0.75
19	Michigan	0.60
20	Virginia	0.55
21	Hawaii	0.51
22	Alabama	0.47
23	Missouri	0.45
24	Texas	0.44
25	Washington	0.35
26	Kentucky	0.31
27	Mississippi	0.27
27	Oklahoma	0.27
29	Arizona	0.25
29	Arkansas	0.25
31	Wisconsin	0.21
32	Minnesota	0.18
33	Iowa	0.16
33	West Virginia	0.16
35	Oregon	0.15
36	Colorado	0.14
36	New Hampshire	0.14
38	Kansas	0.13
39	Nevada	0.12
39	New Mexico	0.12
41	Nebraska	0.09
42	Utah	0.08
43	Vermont	0.07
44	Idaho	0.04
44	Maine	0.04
46	South Dakota	0.02
47	Alaska	0.01
47	Montana	0.01
47	North Dakota	0.01
47	Wyoming	0.01

| | District of Columbia | 157.47 |

Source: Morgan Quitno Press using data from Federal Bureau of Investigation
"Crime in the United States 1997" (Uniform Crime Reports, November 22, 1998)
*Violent crimes are offenses of murder, forcible rape, robbery and aggravated assault.

Percent Change in Number of Violent Crimes: 1996 to 1997

National Percent Change = 3.2% Decrease*

ALPHA ORDER				RANK ORDER		
RANK	STATE	PERCENT CHANGE		RANK	STATE	PERCENT CHANGE
20	Alabama	0.9		1	Iowa	13.8
32	Alaska	(3.3)		2	South Dakota	12.3
16	Arizona	1.6		3	Wisconsin	7.3
18	Arkansas	1.0		4	North Carolina	4.7
44	California	(6.3)		5	Utah	3.6
48	Colorado	(8.6)		5	Washington	3.6
40	Connecticut	(5.3)		7	West Virginia	3.5
12	Delaware	2.4		8	North Dakota	3.3
26	Florida	(0.9)		9	Nevada	3.0
32	Georgia	(3.3)		10	Tennessee	2.9
25	Hawaii	(0.7)		11	New Mexico	2.5
29	Idaho	(2.2)		12	Delaware	2.4
30	Illinois	(2.8)		13	Virginia	2.0
37	Indiana	(3.8)		13	Wyoming	2.0
1	Iowa	13.8		15	Ohio	1.7
23	Kansas	(0.2)		16	Arizona	1.6
24	Kentucky	(0.5)		17	Nebraska	1.2
46	Louisiana	(7.9)		18	Arkansas	1.0
35	Maine	(3.4)		18	South Carolina	1.0
49	Maryland	(8.7)		20	Alabama	0.9
21	Massachusetts	0.7		21	Massachusetts	0.7
41	Michigan	(5.4)		22	Minnesota	0.3
22	Minnesota	0.3		23	Kansas	(0.2)
35	Mississippi	(3.4)		24	Kentucky	(0.5)
28	Missouri	(1.5)		25	Hawaii	(0.7)
50	Montana	(18.0)		26	Florida	(0.9)
17	Nebraska	1.2		27	Vermont	(1.3)
9	Nevada	3.0		28	Missouri	(1.5)
32	New Hampshire	(3.3)		29	Idaho	(2.2)
45	New Jersey	(6.6)		30	Illinois	(2.8)
11	New Mexico	2.5		31	Oregon	(2.9)
42	New York	(5.5)		32	Alaska	(3.3)
4	North Carolina	4.7		32	Georgia	(3.3)
8	North Dakota	3.3		32	New Hampshire	(3.3)
15	Ohio	1.7		35	Maine	(3.4)
43	Oklahoma	(5.8)		35	Mississippi	(3.4)
31	Oregon	(2.9)		37	Indiana	(3.8)
47	Pennsylvania	(8.2)		38	Rhode Island	(4.2)
38	Rhode Island	(4.2)		39	Texas	(5.0)
18	South Carolina	1.0		40	Connecticut	(5.3)
2	South Dakota	12.3		41	Michigan	(5.4)
10	Tennessee	2.9		42	New York	(5.5)
39	Texas	(5.0)		43	Oklahoma	(5.8)
5	Utah	3.6		44	California	(6.3)
27	Vermont	(1.3)		45	New Jersey	(6.6)
13	Virginia	2.0		46	Louisiana	(7.9)
5	Washington	3.6		47	Pennsylvania	(8.2)
7	West Virginia	3.5		48	Colorado	(8.6)
3	Wisconsin	7.3		49	Maryland	(8.7)
13	Wyoming	2.0		50	Montana	(18.0)
					District of Columbia	(20.2)

Source: Federal Bureau of Investigation
   "Crime in the United States 1997" (Uniform Crime Reports, November 22, 1998)
*Violent crimes are offenses of murder, forcible rape, robbery and aggravated assault.

Violent Crime Rate in 1997

National Rate = 610.8 Violent Crimes per 100,000 Population*

ALPHA ORDER

RANK	STATE	RATE
20	Alabama	564.5
10	Alaska	701.1
14	Arizona	623.7
22	Arkansas	526.9
8	California	798.3
33	Colorado	363.2
32	Connecticut	390.9
12	Delaware	677.9
1	Florida	1,023.6
16	Georgia	606.6
40	Hawaii	277.9
42	Idaho	256.8
3	Illinois	861.4
23	Indiana	514.6
39	Iowa	310.0
31	Kansas	409.2
38	Kentucky	316.9
4	Louisiana	855.9
47	Maine	120.8
6	Maryland	846.6
13	Massachusetts	644.2
18	Michigan	590.0
35	Minnesota	337.8
25	Mississippi	469.0
19	Missouri	577.4
46	Montana	132.1
29	Nebraska	438.4
7	Nevada	798.7
49	New Hampshire	113.2
24	New Jersey	492.6
5	New Mexico	853.3
11	New York	688.6
15	North Carolina	607.0
50	North Dakota	87.2
30	Ohio	435.4
21	Oklahoma	559.5
26	Oregon	444.4
27	Pennsylvania	442.1
37	Rhode Island	333.5
2	South Carolina	990.3
45	South Dakota	197.4
9	Tennessee	789.7
17	Texas	602.5
36	Utah	334.0
48	Vermont	119.7
34	Virginia	345.2
28	Washington	440.7
44	West Virginia	218.7
41	Wisconsin	270.6
43	Wyoming	255.2

RANK ORDER

RANK	STATE	RATE
1	Florida	1,023.6
2	South Carolina	990.3
3	Illinois	861.4
4	Louisiana	855.9
5	New Mexico	853.3
6	Maryland	846.6
7	Nevada	798.7
8	California	798.3
9	Tennessee	789.7
10	Alaska	701.1
11	New York	688.6
12	Delaware	677.9
13	Massachusetts	644.2
14	Arizona	623.7
15	North Carolina	607.0
16	Georgia	606.6
17	Texas	602.5
18	Michigan	590.0
19	Missouri	577.4
20	Alabama	564.5
21	Oklahoma	559.5
22	Arkansas	526.9
23	Indiana	514.6
24	New Jersey	492.6
25	Mississippi	469.0
26	Oregon	444.4
27	Pennsylvania	442.1
28	Washington	440.7
29	Nebraska	438.4
30	Ohio	435.4
31	Kansas	409.2
32	Connecticut	390.9
33	Colorado	363.2
34	Virginia	345.2
35	Minnesota	337.8
36	Utah	334.0
37	Rhode Island	333.5
38	Kentucky	316.9
39	Iowa	310.0
40	Hawaii	277.9
41	Wisconsin	270.6
42	Idaho	256.8
43	Wyoming	255.2
44	West Virginia	218.7
45	South Dakota	197.4
46	Montana	132.1
47	Maine	120.8
48	Vermont	119.7
49	New Hampshire	113.2
50	North Dakota	87.2
	District of Columbia	2,024.2

Source: Federal Bureau of Investigation
    "Crime in the United States 1997" (Uniform Crime Reports, November 22, 1998)
*Violent crimes are offenses of murder, forcible rape, robbery and aggravated assault.

Percent Change in Violent Crime Rate: 1996 to 1997

National Percent Change = 4.0% Decrease*

ALPHA ORDER

RANK ORDER

RANK	STATE	PERCENT CHANGE	RANK	STATE	PERCENT CHANGE
18	Alabama	(0.2)	1	Iowa	13.8
31	Alaska	(3.7)	2	South Dakota	11.4
24	Arizona	(1.2)	3	Wisconsin	7.1
16	Arkansas	0.5	4	West Virginia	4.1
45	California	(7.5)	5	North Dakota	3.8
49	Colorado	(10.2)	6	North Carolina	3.2
39	Connecticut	(5.1)	7	Washington	2.2
12	Delaware	1.4	7	Wyoming	2.2
28	Florida	(2.6)	9	Tennessee	2.0
38	Georgia	(5.0)	10	Ohio	1.6
21	Hawaii	(1.0)	11	New Mexico	1.5
32	Idaho	(3.9)	12	Delaware	1.4
29	Illinois	(3.3)	13	Virginia	1.1
36	Indiana	(4.2)	14	Nebraska	0.9
1	Iowa	13.8	15	Utah	0.6
22	Kansas	(1.1)	16	Arkansas	0.5
22	Kentucky	(1.1)	17	Massachusetts	0.3
46	Louisiana	(7.9)	18	Alabama	(0.2)
29	Maine	(3.3)	19	Minnesota	(0.3)
48	Maryland	(9.1)	20	South Carolina	(0.7)
17	Massachusetts	0.3	21	Hawaii	(1.0)
43	Michigan	(7.1)	22	Kansas	(1.1)
19	Minnesota	(0.3)	22	Kentucky	(1.1)
34	Mississippi	(4.0)	24	Arizona	(1.2)
27	Missouri	(2.3)	24	Vermont	(1.2)
50	Montana	(18.0)	26	Nevada	(1.6)
14	Nebraska	0.9	27	Missouri	(2.3)
26	Nevada	(1.6)	28	Florida	(2.6)
36	New Hampshire	(4.2)	29	Illinois	(3.3)
44	New Jersey	(7.3)	29	Maine	(3.3)
11	New Mexico	1.5	31	Alaska	(3.7)
40	New York	(5.3)	32	Idaho	(3.9)
6	North Carolina	3.2	32	Rhode Island	(3.9)
5	North Dakota	3.8	34	Mississippi	(4.0)
10	Ohio	1.6	34	Oregon	(4.0)
41	Oklahoma	(6.3)	36	Indiana	(4.2)
34	Oregon	(4.0)	36	New Hampshire	(4.2)
47	Pennsylvania	(8.0)	38	Georgia	(5.0)
32	Rhode Island	(3.9)	39	Connecticut	(5.1)
20	South Carolina	(0.7)	40	New York	(5.3)
2	South Dakota	11.4	41	Oklahoma	(6.3)
9	Tennessee	2.0	42	Texas	(6.5)
42	Texas	(6.5)	43	Michigan	(7.1)
15	Utah	0.6	44	New Jersey	(7.3)
24	Vermont	(1.2)	45	California	(7.5)
13	Virginia	1.1	46	Louisiana	(7.9)
7	Washington	2.2	47	Pennsylvania	(8.0)
4	West Virginia	4.1	48	Maryland	(9.1)
3	Wisconsin	7.1	49	Colorado	(10.2)
7	Wyoming	2.2	50	Montana	(18.0)
				District of Columbia	(18.0)

Source: Federal Bureau of Investigation
"Crime in the United States 1997" (Uniform Crime Reports, November 22, 1998)
*Violent crimes are offenses of murder, forcible rape, robbery and aggravated assault.

Violent Crimes with Firearms in 1997

National Total = 367,478 Violent Crimes*

ALPHA ORDER

RANK	STATE	CRIMES	% of USA
16	Alabama	6,857	1.9%
34	Alaska	869	0.2%
13	Arizona	8,552	2.3%
22	Arkansas	3,727	1.0%
1	California	58,748	16.0%
30	Colorado	2,533	0.7%
26	Connecticut	2,930	0.8%
38	Delaware	721	0.2%
NA	Florida**	NA	NA
8	Georgia	13,369	3.6%
40	Hawaii	373	0.1%
37	Idaho	798	0.2%
3	Illinois	21,981	6.0%
17	Indiana	6,778	1.8%
35	Iowa	849	0.2%
NA	Kansas**	NA	NA
NA	Kentucky**	NA	NA
10	Louisiana	12,398	3.4%
43	Maine	94	0.0%
7	Maryland	13,384	3.6%
25	Massachusetts	3,010	0.8%
6	Michigan	14,538	4.0%
28	Minnesota	2,713	0.7%
29	Mississippi	2,566	0.7%
12	Missouri	8,713	2.4%
44	Montana	92	0.0%
32	Nebraska	1,109	0.3%
33	Nevada	1,102	0.3%
NA	New Hampshire**	NA	NA
14	New Jersey	8,001	2.2%
23	New Mexico	3,676	1.0%
4	New York	18,940	5.2%
5	North Carolina	15,018	4.1%
45	North Dakota	32	0.0%
15	Ohio	7,863	2.1%
20	Oklahoma	4,361	1.2%
27	Oregon	2,801	0.8%
24	Pennsylvania	3,636	1.0%
39	Rhode Island	404	0.1%
11	South Carolina	9,252	2.5%
42	South Dakota	113	0.0%
9	Tennessee	13,225	3.6%
2	Texas	30,711	8.4%
31	Utah	1,307	0.4%
NA	Vermont**	NA	NA
18	Virginia	5,978	1.6%
19	Washington	4,691	1.3%
36	West Virginia	823	0.2%
21	Wisconsin	3,975	1.1%
41	Wyoming	155	0.0%

RANK ORDER

RANK	STATE	CRIMES	% of USA
1	California	58,748	16.0%
2	Texas	30,711	8.4%
3	Illinois	21,981	6.0%
4	New York	18,940	5.2%
5	North Carolina	15,018	4.1%
6	Michigan	14,538	4.0%
7	Maryland	13,384	3.6%
8	Georgia	13,369	3.6%
9	Tennessee	13,225	3.6%
10	Louisiana	12,398	3.4%
11	South Carolina	9,252	2.5%
12	Missouri	8,713	2.4%
13	Arizona	8,552	2.3%
14	New Jersey	8,001	2.2%
15	Ohio	7,863	2.1%
16	Alabama	6,857	1.9%
17	Indiana	6,778	1.8%
18	Virginia	5,978	1.6%
19	Washington	4,691	1.3%
20	Oklahoma	4,361	1.2%
21	Wisconsin	3,975	1.1%
22	Arkansas	3,727	1.0%
23	New Mexico	3,676	1.0%
24	Pennsylvania	3,636	1.0%
25	Massachusetts	3,010	0.8%
26	Connecticut	2,930	0.8%
27	Oregon	2,801	0.8%
28	Minnesota	2,713	0.7%
29	Mississippi	2,566	0.7%
30	Colorado	2,533	0.7%
31	Utah	1,307	0.4%
32	Nebraska	1,109	0.3%
33	Nevada	1,102	0.3%
34	Alaska	869	0.2%
35	Iowa	849	0.2%
36	West Virginia	823	0.2%
37	Idaho	798	0.2%
38	Delaware	721	0.2%
39	Rhode Island	404	0.1%
40	Hawaii	373	0.1%
41	Wyoming	155	0.0%
42	South Dakota	113	0.0%
43	Maine	94	0.0%
44	Montana	92	0.0%
45	North Dakota	32	0.0%
NA	Florida**	NA	NA
NA	Kansas**	NA	NA
NA	Kentucky**	NA	NA
NA	New Hampshire**	NA	NA
NA	Vermont**	NA	NA
	District of Columbia	3,040	0.8%

Source: Morgan Quitno Press using data from Federal Bureau of Investigation
   "Crime in the United States 1997" (Uniform Crime Reports, November 22, 1998)
*Includes murder, robbery and aggravated assault. Does not include rape. National total reflects only those violent crimes for which the type of weapon was known and reported. There were an additional 182,065 violent crimes (excluding rape) for which the type of weapon was not reported to the F.B.I.
**Not available.

Violent Crime Rate with Firearms in 1997

National Rate = 170.6 Violent Crimes per 100,000 Population*

ALPHA ORDER

RANK	STATE	RATE
13	Alabama	189.1
17	Alaska	164.6
10	Arizona	213.6
19	Arkansas	158.2
16	California	182.4
27	Colorado	91.6
24	Connecticut	105.8
8	Delaware	241.2
NA	Florida**	NA
5	Georgia	271.4
42	Hawaii	32.5
34	Idaho	66.8
1	Illinois	656.5
14	Indiana	184.1
39	Iowa	36.5
NA	Kansas**	NA
NA	Kentucky**	NA
3	Louisiana	344.1
44	Maine	7.7
6	Maryland	262.9
35	Massachusetts	60.4
14	Michigan	184.1
30	Minnesota	89.3
9	Mississippi	225.7
12	Missouri	203.6
43	Montana	26.7
32	Nebraska	73.3
20	Nevada	136.5
NA	New Hampshire**	NA
25	New Jersey	99.3
4	New Mexico	308.7
22	New York	120.1
11	North Carolina	205.0
45	North Dakota	5.5
23	Ohio	116.3
21	Oklahoma	131.6
26	Oregon	94.7
36	Pennsylvania	59.9
38	Rhode Island	40.9
7	South Carolina	261.5
40	South Dakota	34.6
2	Tennessee	403.1
18	Texas	158.3
33	Utah	68.0
NA	Vermont**	NA
29	Virginia	90.5
28	Washington	91.3
37	West Virginia	45.2
31	Wisconsin	83.3
41	Wyoming	33.1

RANK ORDER

RANK	STATE	RATE
1	Illinois	656.5
2	Tennessee	403.1
3	Louisiana	344.1
4	New Mexico	308.7
5	Georgia	271.4
6	Maryland	262.9
7	South Carolina	261.5
8	Delaware	241.2
9	Mississippi	225.7
10	Arizona	213.6
11	North Carolina	205.0
12	Missouri	203.6
13	Alabama	189.1
14	Indiana	184.1
14	Michigan	184.1
16	California	182.4
17	Alaska	164.6
18	Texas	158.3
19	Arkansas	158.2
20	Nevada	136.5
21	Oklahoma	131.6
22	New York	120.1
23	Ohio	116.3
24	Connecticut	105.8
25	New Jersey	99.3
26	Oregon	94.7
27	Colorado	91.6
28	Washington	91.3
29	Virginia	90.5
30	Minnesota	89.3
31	Wisconsin	83.3
32	Nebraska	73.3
33	Utah	68.0
34	Idaho	66.8
35	Massachusetts	60.4
36	Pennsylvania	59.9
37	West Virginia	45.2
38	Rhode Island	40.9
39	Iowa	36.5
40	South Dakota	34.6
41	Wyoming	33.1
42	Hawaii	32.5
43	Montana	26.7
44	Maine	7.7
45	North Dakota	5.5
NA	Florida**	NA
NA	Kansas**	NA
NA	Kentucky**	NA
NA	New Hampshire**	NA
NA	Vermont**	NA

District of Columbia — 574.7

Source: Morgan Quitno Press using data from Federal Bureau of Investigation
"Crime in the United States 1997" (Uniform Crime Reports, November 22, 1998)
*Based only on population of reporting jurisdictions. Includes murder, robbery and aggravated assault. Does not include rape. National rate reflects only those violent crimes for which the type of weapon was known and reported. Illinois' rate is especially affected by number of nonreporting jurisdictions.
**Not available.

Percent of Violent Crimes Involving Firearms in 1997

National Percent = 27.1% of Violent Crimes*

ALPHA ORDER			RANK ORDER		
RANK	STATE	PERCENT	RANK	STATE	PERCENT
7	Alabama	35.0	1	Mississippi	44.9
20	Alaska	27.6	2	Tennessee	42.2
8	Arizona	34.3	3	Louisiana	40.4
14	Arkansas	31.4	4	Georgia	39.4
29	California	23.8	5	North Carolina	35.6
23	Colorado	26.3	6	New Mexico	35.2
28	Connecticut	24.4	7	Alabama	35.0
27	Delaware	25.4	8	Arizona	34.3
NA	Florida**	NA	9	Illinois	32.6
4	Georgia	39.4	9	Missouri	32.6
42	Hawaii	12.7	11	Maryland	32.5
16	Idaho	29.1	12	Michigan	31.7
9	Illinois	32.6	12	Wisconsin	31.7
15	Indiana	30.5	14	Arkansas	31.4
41	Iowa	13.2	15	Indiana	30.5
NA	Kansas**	NA	16	Idaho	29.1
NA	Kentucky**	NA	17	Texas	28.2
3	Louisiana	40.4	17	Virginia	28.2
45	Maine	8.0	19	South Carolina	27.7
11	Maryland	32.5	20	Alaska	27.6
43	Massachusetts	9.2	21	Ohio	27.2
12	Michigan	31.7	22	Nevada	26.8
25	Minnesota	25.6	23	Colorado	26.3
1	Mississippi	44.9	24	Montana	26.1
9	Missouri	32.6	25	Minnesota	25.6
24	Montana	26.1	25	Oklahoma	25.6
36	Nebraska	16.6	27	Delaware	25.4
22	Nevada	26.8	28	Connecticut	24.4
NA	New Hampshire**	NA	29	California	23.8
35	New Jersey	21.1	30	Utah	23.4
6	New Mexico	35.2	31	Washington	23.3
37	New York	16.5	32	West Virginia	22.8
5	North Carolina	35.6	33	Oregon	22.5
44	North Dakota	8.4	34	Pennsylvania	21.9
21	Ohio	27.2	35	New Jersey	21.1
25	Oklahoma	25.6	36	Nebraska	16.6
33	Oregon	22.5	37	New York	16.5
34	Pennsylvania	21.9	38	South Dakota	15.3
40	Rhode Island	13.8	39	Wyoming	14.7
19	South Carolina	27.7	40	Rhode Island	13.8
38	South Dakota	15.3	41	Iowa	13.2
2	Tennessee	42.2	42	Hawaii	12.7
17	Texas	28.2	43	Massachusetts	9.2
30	Utah	23.4	44	North Dakota	8.4
NA	Vermont**	NA	45	Maine	8.0
17	Virginia	28.2	NA	Florida**	NA
31	Washington	23.3	NA	Kansas**	NA
32	West Virginia	22.8	NA	Kentucky**	NA
12	Wisconsin	31.7	NA	New Hampshire**	NA
39	Wyoming	14.7	NA	Vermont**	NA
				District of Columbia	29.0

Source: Morgan Quitno Press using data from Federal Bureau of Investigation
   "Crime in the United States 1997" (Uniform Crime Reports, November 22, 1998)
*Includes murder, robbery and aggravated assault. Does not include rape. National percent reflects only those violent crimes for which the type of weapon was known and reported. There were an additional 182,065 violent crimes (excluding rape) for which the type of weapon was not reported to the F.B.I.
**Not available.

Bombings in 1996

National Total = 1,865 Bombings*

ALPHA ORDER					RANK ORDER			
RANK	**STATE**	**BOMBINGS**	**% of USA**		**RANK**	**STATE**	**BOMBINGS**	**% of USA**
31	Alabama	14	0.8%		1	California	342	18.3%
44	Alaska	3	0.2%		2	Illinois	208	11.2%
4	Arizona	101	5.4%		3	Florida	182	9.8%
31	Arkansas	14	0.8%		4	Arizona	101	5.4%
1	California	342	18.3%		5	Texas	75	4.0%
8	Colorado	60	3.2%		6	Ohio	63	3.4%
38	Connecticut	9	0.5%		7	Maryland	62	3.3%
39	Delaware	8	0.4%		8	Colorado	60	3.2%
3	Florida	182	9.8%		9	Minnesota	52	2.8%
27	Georgia	18	1.0%		9	New York	52	2.8%
49	Hawaii	0	0.0%		11	Washington	51	2.7%
16	Idaho	27	1.4%		12	Utah	48	2.6%
2	Illinois	208	11.2%		13	Tennessee	35	1.9%
25	Indiana	20	1.1%		14	Oregon	34	1.8%
21	Iowa	22	1.2%		15	Missouri	32	1.7%
29	Kansas	16	0.9%		16	Idaho	27	1.4%
39	Kentucky	8	0.4%		16	Michigan	27	1.4%
21	Louisiana	22	1.2%		16	Pennsylvania	27	1.4%
43	Maine	4	0.2%		19	Oklahoma	25	1.3%
7	Maryland	62	3.3%		19	Virginia	25	1.3%
34	Massachusetts	13	0.7%		21	Iowa	22	1.2%
16	Michigan	27	1.4%		21	Louisiana	22	1.2%
9	Minnesota	52	2.8%		21	New Mexico	22	1.2%
34	Mississippi	13	0.7%		24	New Jersey	21	1.1%
15	Missouri	32	1.7%		25	Indiana	20	1.1%
37	Montana	10	0.5%		26	North Carolina	19	1.0%
41	Nebraska	5	0.3%		27	Georgia	18	1.0%
34	Nevada	13	0.7%		27	Wisconsin	18	1.0%
46	New Hampshire	2	0.1%		29	Kansas	16	0.9%
24	New Jersey	21	1.1%		30	North Dakota	15	0.8%
21	New Mexico	22	1.2%		31	Alabama	14	0.8%
9	New York	52	2.8%		31	Arkansas	14	0.8%
26	North Carolina	19	1.0%		31	West Virginia	14	0.8%
30	North Dakota	15	0.8%		34	Massachusetts	13	0.7%
6	Ohio	63	3.4%		34	Mississippi	13	0.7%
19	Oklahoma	25	1.3%		34	Nevada	13	0.7%
14	Oregon	34	1.8%		37	Montana	10	0.5%
16	Pennsylvania	27	1.4%		38	Connecticut	9	0.5%
46	Rhode Island	2	0.1%		39	Delaware	8	0.4%
44	South Carolina	3	0.2%		39	Kentucky	8	0.4%
46	South Dakota	2	0.1%		41	Nebraska	5	0.3%
13	Tennessee	35	1.9%		41	Wyoming	5	0.3%
5	Texas	75	4.0%		43	Maine	4	0.2%
12	Utah	48	2.6%		44	Alaska	3	0.2%
49	Vermont	0	0.0%		44	South Carolina	3	0.2%
19	Virginia	25	1.3%		46	New Hampshire	2	0.1%
11	Washington	51	2.7%		46	Rhode Island	2	0.1%
31	West Virginia	14	0.8%		46	South Dakota	2	0.1%
27	Wisconsin	18	1.0%		49	Hawaii	0	0.0%
41	Wyoming	5	0.3%		49	Vermont	0	0.0%
						District of Columbia	2	0.1%

Source: Federal Bureau of Investigation, Bomb Data Center
  "1996 Bombing Incidents" (General Information Bulletin 96-1)
*Includes explosive and incendiary bombings and excludes bombing attempts. Total does not include 18 bombings in Puerto Rico or 1 in Guam. There were 23 deaths and 336 injuries from bombings in 1996.

Murders in 1997

National Total = 18,209 Murders*

ALPHA ORDER

RANK	STATE	MURDERS	% of USA
16	Alabama	426	2.3%
36	Alaska	54	0.3%
18	Arizona	375	2.1%
22	Arkansas	250	1.4%
1	California	2,579	14.2%
28	Colorado	157	0.9%
32	Connecticut	124	0.7%
45	Delaware	18	0.1%
5	Florida	1,012	5.6%
10	Georgia	563	3.1%
40	Hawaii	47	0.3%
42	Idaho	39	0.2%
3	Illinois	1,096	6.0%
15	Indiana	430	2.4%
37	Iowa	52	0.3%
29	Kansas	155	0.9%
25	Kentucky	228	1.3%
8	Louisiana	682	3.7%
43	Maine	25	0.1%
13	Maryland	502	2.8%
33	Massachusetts	119	0.7%
6	Michigan	759	4.2%
31	Minnesota	129	0.7%
19	Mississippi	358	2.0%
16	Missouri	426	2.3%
41	Montana	42	0.2%
38	Nebraska	50	0.3%
27	Nevada	187	1.0%
47	New Hampshire	16	0.1%
20	New Jersey	337	1.9%
30	New Mexico	134	0.7%
4	New York	1,093	6.0%
9	North Carolina	614	3.4%
50	North Dakota	6	0.0%
11	Ohio	523	2.9%
24	Oklahoma	229	1.3%
34	Oregon	95	0.5%
7	Pennsylvania	705	3.9%
43	Rhode Island	25	0.1%
21	South Carolina	314	1.7%
48	South Dakota	10	0.1%
12	Tennessee	511	2.8%
2	Texas	1,327	7.3%
38	Utah	50	0.3%
49	Vermont	9	0.0%
14	Virginia	488	2.7%
23	Washington	241	1.3%
35	West Virginia	75	0.4%
26	Wisconsin	205	1.1%
46	Wyoming	17	0.1%

RANK ORDER

RANK	STATE	MURDERS	% of USA
1	California	2,579	14.2%
2	Texas	1,327	7.3%
3	Illinois	1,096	6.0%
4	New York	1,093	6.0%
5	Florida	1,012	5.6%
6	Michigan	759	4.2%
7	Pennsylvania	705	3.9%
8	Louisiana	682	3.7%
9	North Carolina	614	3.4%
10	Georgia	563	3.1%
11	Ohio	523	2.9%
12	Tennessee	511	2.8%
13	Maryland	502	2.8%
14	Virginia	488	2.7%
15	Indiana	430	2.4%
16	Alabama	426	2.3%
16	Missouri	426	2.3%
18	Arizona	375	2.1%
19	Mississippi	358	2.0%
20	New Jersey	337	1.9%
21	South Carolina	314	1.7%
22	Arkansas	250	1.4%
23	Washington	241	1.3%
24	Oklahoma	229	1.3%
25	Kentucky	228	1.3%
26	Wisconsin	205	1.1%
27	Nevada	187	1.0%
28	Colorado	157	0.9%
29	Kansas	155	0.9%
30	New Mexico	134	0.7%
31	Minnesota	129	0.7%
32	Connecticut	124	0.7%
33	Massachusetts	119	0.7%
34	Oregon	95	0.5%
35	West Virginia	75	0.4%
36	Alaska	54	0.3%
37	Iowa	52	0.3%
38	Nebraska	50	0.3%
38	Utah	50	0.3%
40	Hawaii	47	0.3%
41	Montana	42	0.2%
42	Idaho	39	0.2%
43	Maine	25	0.1%
43	Rhode Island	25	0.1%
45	Delaware	18	0.1%
46	Wyoming	17	0.1%
47	New Hampshire	16	0.1%
48	South Dakota	10	0.1%
49	Vermont	9	0.0%
50	North Dakota	6	0.0%
	District of Columbia	301	1.7%

Source: Federal Bureau of Investigation
"Crime in the United States 1997" (Uniform Crime Reports, November 22, 1998)
*Includes nonnegligent manslaughter.

Average Time Between Murders in 1997

National Rate = A Murder Occurs Every 29 Minutes*

ALPHA ORDER

RANK	STATE	HOURS.MINUTES
34	Alabama	20.34
15	Alaska	162.13
33	Arizona	23.22
29	Arkansas	35.02
50	California	3.24
23	Colorado	55.48
19	Connecticut	70.39
6	Delaware	486.40
46	Florida	8.40
41	Georgia	15.34
11	Hawaii	186.23
9	Idaho	224.37
48	Illinois	7.59
36	Indiana	20.22
14	Iowa	168.28
22	Kansas	56.31
26	Kentucky	38.25
43	Louisiana	12.50
7	Maine	350.24
38	Maryland	17.27
18	Massachusetts	73.37
45	Michigan	11.32
20	Minnesota	67.55
32	Mississippi	24.28
34	Missouri	20.34
10	Montana	208.34
12	Nebraska	175.12
24	Nevada	46.51
4	New Hampshire	547.30
31	New Jersey	25.59
21	New Mexico	65.22
47	New York	8.01
42	North Carolina	14.16
1	North Dakota	1,460.00
40	Ohio	16.45
27	Oklahoma	38.15
17	Oregon	92.13
44	Pennsylvania	12.26
7	Rhode Island	350.24
30	South Carolina	27.54
3	South Dakota	876.00
39	Tennessee	17.08
49	Texas	6.36
12	Utah	175.12
2	Vermont	973.20
37	Virginia	17.57
28	Washington	36.21
16	West Virginia	116.48
25	Wisconsin	42.44
5	Wyoming	515.17

RANK ORDER

RANK	STATE	HOURS.MINUTES
1	North Dakota	1,460.00
2	Vermont	973.20
3	South Dakota	876.00
4	New Hampshire	547.30
5	Wyoming	515.17
6	Delaware	486.40
7	Maine	350.24
7	Rhode Island	350.24
9	Idaho	224.37
10	Montana	208.34
11	Hawaii	186.23
12	Nebraska	175.12
12	Utah	175.12
14	Iowa	168.28
15	Alaska	162.13
16	West Virginia	116.48
17	Oregon	92.13
18	Massachusetts	73.37
19	Connecticut	70.39
20	Minnesota	67.55
21	New Mexico	65.22
22	Kansas	56.31
23	Colorado	55.48
24	Nevada	46.51
25	Wisconsin	42.44
26	Kentucky	38.25
27	Oklahoma	38.15
28	Washington	36.21
29	Arkansas	35.02
30	South Carolina	27.54
31	New Jersey	25.59
32	Mississippi	24.28
33	Arizona	23.22
34	Alabama	20.34
34	Missouri	20.34
36	Indiana	20.22
37	Virginia	17.57
38	Maryland	17.27
39	Tennessee	17.08
40	Ohio	16.45
41	Georgia	15.34
42	North Carolina	14.16
43	Louisiana	12.50
44	Pennsylvania	12.26
45	Michigan	11.32
46	Florida	8.40
47	New York	8.01
48	Illinois	7.59
49	Texas	6.36
50	California	3.24
	District of Columbia	29.06

Source: Morgan Quitno Press using data from Federal Bureau of Investigation
   "Crime in the United States 1997" (Uniform Crime Reports, November 22, 1998)
*Includes nonnegligent manslaughter.

Percent Change in Number of Murders: 1996 to 1997

National Percent Change = 7.3% Decrease*

ALPHA ORDER

RANK	STATE	PERCENT CHANGE
26	Alabama	(4.1)
2	Alaska	20.0
20	Arizona	(0.5)
5	Arkansas	14.2
36	California	(11.6)
37	Colorado	(12.8)
44	Connecticut	(21.5)
49	Delaware	(41.9)
29	Florida	(6.0)
35	Georgia	(10.6)
4	Hawaii	17.5
32	Idaho	(9.3)
30	Illinois	(7.0)
13	Indiana	2.4
23	Iowa	(1.9)
31	Kansas	(8.8)
16	Kentucky	0.0
34	Louisiana	(10.5)
16	Maine	0.0
38	Maryland	(14.6)
46	Massachusetts	(24.2)
9	Michigan	5.1
45	Minnesota	(22.8)
3	Mississippi	18.9
22	Missouri	(1.6)
1	Montana	23.5
10	Nebraska	4.2
39	Nevada	(15.0)
42	New Hampshire	(20.0)
19	New Jersey	(0.3)
48	New Mexico	(32.0)
41	New York	(19.2)
21	North Carolina	(0.8)
50	North Dakota	(57.1)
25	Ohio	(2.8)
12	Oklahoma	2.7
47	Oregon	(26.4)
11	Pennsylvania	2.8
16	Rhode Island	0.0
27	South Carolina	(5.4)
6	South Dakota	11.1
14	Tennessee	1.6
33	Texas	(10.2)
43	Utah	(20.6)
40	Vermont	(18.2)
24	Virginia	(2.4)
28	Washington	(5.5)
7	West Virginia	8.7
15	Wisconsin	0.5
8	Wyoming	6.3

RANK ORDER

RANK	STATE	PERCENT CHANGE
1	Montana	23.5
2	Alaska	20.0
3	Mississippi	18.9
4	Hawaii	17.5
5	Arkansas	14.2
6	South Dakota	11.1
7	West Virginia	8.7
8	Wyoming	6.3
9	Michigan	5.1
10	Nebraska	4.2
11	Pennsylvania	2.8
12	Oklahoma	2.7
13	Indiana	2.4
14	Tennessee	1.6
15	Wisconsin	0.5
16	Kentucky	0.0
16	Maine	0.0
16	Rhode Island	0.0
19	New Jersey	(0.3)
20	Arizona	(0.5)
21	North Carolina	(0.8)
22	Missouri	(1.6)
23	Iowa	(1.9)
24	Virginia	(2.4)
25	Ohio	(2.8)
26	Alabama	(4.1)
27	South Carolina	(5.4)
28	Washington	(5.5)
29	Florida	(6.0)
30	Illinois	(7.0)
31	Kansas	(8.8)
32	Idaho	(9.3)
33	Texas	(10.2)
34	Louisiana	(10.5)
35	Georgia	(10.6)
36	California	(11.6)
37	Colorado	(12.8)
38	Maryland	(14.6)
39	Nevada	(15.0)
40	Vermont	(18.2)
41	New York	(19.2)
42	New Hampshire	(20.0)
43	Utah	(20.6)
44	Connecticut	(21.5)
45	Minnesota	(22.8)
46	Massachusetts	(24.2)
47	Oregon	(26.4)
48	New Mexico	(32.0)
49	Delaware	(41.9)
50	North Dakota	(57.1)
	District of Columbia	(24.2)

Source: Federal Bureau of Investigation
    "Crime in the United States 1997" (Uniform Crime Reports, November 22, 1998)
Includes nonnegligent manslaughter.

Murder Rate in 1997

National Rate = 6.8 Murders Per 100,000 Population*

ALPHA ORDER

RANK	STATE	RATE
4	Alabama	9.9
9	Alaska	8.9
12	Arizona	8.2
4	Arkansas	9.9
13	California	8.0
32	Colorado	4.0
35	Connecticut	3.8
41	Delaware	2.5
20	Florida	6.9
17	Georgia	7.5
32	Hawaii	4.0
37	Idaho	3.2
8	Illinois	9.2
18	Indiana	7.3
46	Iowa	1.8
23	Kansas	6.0
26	Kentucky	5.8
1	Louisiana	15.7
44	Maine	2.0
4	Maryland	9.9
45	Massachusetts	1.9
15	Michigan	7.8
40	Minnesota	2.8
2	Mississippi	13.1
14	Missouri	7.9
27	Montana	4.8
38	Nebraska	3.0
3	Nevada	11.2
48	New Hampshire	1.4
30	New Jersey	4.2
16	New Mexico	7.7
23	New York	6.0
11	North Carolina	8.3
50	North Dakota	0.9
28	Ohio	4.7
20	Oklahoma	6.9
39	Oregon	2.9
25	Pennsylvania	5.9
41	Rhode Island	2.5
10	South Carolina	8.4
48	South Dakota	1.4
7	Tennessee	9.5
22	Texas	6.8
43	Utah	2.4
47	Vermont	1.5
19	Virginia	7.2
29	Washington	4.3
31	West Virginia	4.1
32	Wisconsin	4.0
36	Wyoming	3.5

RANK ORDER

RANK	STATE	RATE
1	Louisiana	15.7
2	Mississippi	13.1
3	Nevada	11.2
4	Alabama	9.9
4	Arkansas	9.9
4	Maryland	9.9
7	Tennessee	9.5
8	Illinois	9.2
9	Alaska	8.9
10	South Carolina	8.4
11	North Carolina	8.3
12	Arizona	8.2
13	California	8.0
14	Missouri	7.9
15	Michigan	7.8
16	New Mexico	7.7
17	Georgia	7.5
18	Indiana	7.3
19	Virginia	7.2
20	Florida	6.9
20	Oklahoma	6.9
22	Texas	6.8
23	Kansas	6.0
23	New York	6.0
25	Pennsylvania	5.9
26	Kentucky	5.8
27	Montana	4.8
28	Ohio	4.7
29	Washington	4.3
30	New Jersey	4.2
31	West Virginia	4.1
32	Colorado	4.0
32	Hawaii	4.0
32	Wisconsin	4.0
35	Connecticut	3.8
36	Wyoming	3.5
37	Idaho	3.2
38	Nebraska	3.0
39	Oregon	2.9
40	Minnesota	2.8
41	Delaware	2.5
41	Rhode Island	2.5
43	Utah	2.4
44	Maine	2.0
45	Massachusetts	1.9
46	Iowa	1.8
47	Vermont	1.5
48	New Hampshire	1.4
48	South Dakota	1.4
50	North Dakota	0.9
	District of Columbia	56.9

Source: Federal Bureau of Investigation
   "Crime in the United States 1997" (Uniform Crime Reports, November 22, 1998)
*Includes nonnegligent manslaughter.

Percent Change in Murder Rate: 1996 to 1997

National Percent Change = 8.1% Decrease*

ALPHA ORDER				RANK ORDER		
RANK	STATE	PERCENT CHANGE		RANK	STATE	PERCENT CHANGE
25	Alabama	(4.8)		1	Montana	23.1
2	Alaska	20.3		2	Alaska	20.3
23	Arizona	(3.5)		3	Mississippi	18.0
6	Arkansas	13.8		4	Hawaii	17.6
35	California	(12.1)		5	South Dakota	16.7
38	Colorado	(14.9)		6	Arkansas	13.8
42	Connecticut	(20.8)		7	West Virginia	7.9
49	Delaware	(41.9)		8	Wyoming	6.1
29	Florida	(8.0)		9	Michigan	4.0
36	Georgia	(12.8)		10	Pennsylvania	3.5
4	Hawaii	17.6		11	Nebraska	3.4
33	Idaho	(11.1)		12	Oklahoma	1.5
29	Illinois	(8.0)		13	Indiana	1.4
13	Indiana	1.4		14	Maine	0.0
26	Iowa	(5.3)		14	New Jersey	0.0
31	Kansas	(9.1)		14	Rhode Island	0.0
19	Kentucky	(1.7)		14	Tennessee	0.0
32	Louisiana	(10.3)		14	Wisconsin	0.0
14	Maine	0.0		19	Kentucky	(1.7)
37	Maryland	(14.7)		20	Ohio	(2.1)
46	Massachusetts	(26.9)		21	North Carolina	(2.4)
9	Michigan	4.0		22	Missouri	(2.5)
44	Minnesota	(22.2)		23	Arizona	(3.5)
3	Mississippi	18.0		24	Virginia	(4.0)
22	Missouri	(2.5)		25	Alabama	(4.8)
1	Montana	23.1		26	Iowa	(5.3)
11	Nebraska	3.4		27	Washington	(6.5)
40	Nevada	(18.2)		28	South Carolina	(6.7)
39	New Hampshire	(17.6)		29	Florida	(8.0)
14	New Jersey	0.0		29	Illinois	(8.0)
48	New Mexico	(33.0)		31	Kansas	(9.1)
41	New York	(18.9)		32	Louisiana	(10.3)
21	North Carolina	(2.4)		33	Idaho	(11.1)
50	North Dakota	(59.1)		34	Texas	(11.7)
20	Ohio	(2.1)		35	California	(12.1)
12	Oklahoma	1.5		36	Georgia	(12.8)
47	Oregon	(27.5)		37	Maryland	(14.7)
10	Pennsylvania	3.5		38	Colorado	(14.9)
14	Rhode Island	0.0		39	New Hampshire	(17.6)
28	South Carolina	(6.7)		40	Nevada	(18.2)
5	South Dakota	16.7		41	New York	(18.9)
14	Tennessee	0.0		42	Connecticut	(20.8)
34	Texas	(11.7)		43	Vermont	(21.1)
45	Utah	(25.0)		44	Minnesota	(22.2)
43	Vermont	(21.1)		45	Utah	(25.0)
24	Virginia	(4.0)		46	Massachusetts	(26.9)
27	Washington	(6.5)		47	Oregon	(27.5)
7	West Virginia	7.9		48	New Mexico	(33.0)
14	Wisconsin	0.0		49	Delaware	(41.9)
8	Wyoming	6.1		50	North Dakota	(59.1)
					District of Columbia	(22.2)

Source: Federal Bureau of Investigation
    "Crime in the United States 1997" (Uniform Crime Reports, November 22, 1998)
*Includes nonnegligent manslaughter.

Murders with Firearms in 1997

National Total = 10,068 Murders*

ALPHA ORDER

RANK	STATE	MURDERS	% of USA
13	Alabama	280	2.8%
33	Alaska	26	0.3%
14	Arizona	257	2.6%
20	Arkansas	168	1.7%
1	California	1,832	18.2%
28	Colorado	75	0.7%
26	Connecticut	80	0.8%
43	Delaware	5	0.0%
NA	Florida**	NA	NA
11	Georgia	311	3.1%
36	Hawaii	15	0.1%
35	Idaho	18	0.2%
3	Illinois	560	5.6%
16	Indiana	230	2.3%
38	Iowa	11	0.1%
NA	Kansas**	NA	NA
NA	Kentucky**	NA	NA
4	Louisiana	497	4.9%
38	Maine	11	0.1%
8	Maryland	389	3.9%
30	Massachusetts	60	0.6%
5	Michigan	477	4.7%
27	Minnesota	78	0.8%
22	Mississippi	143	1.4%
15	Missouri	254	2.5%
42	Montana	9	0.1%
40	Nebraska	10	0.1%
24	Nevada	120	1.2%
NA	New Hampshire**	NA	NA
19	New Jersey	176	1.7%
32	New Mexico	55	0.5%
7	New York	408	4.1%
9	North Carolina	366	3.6%
45	North Dakota	1	0.0%
17	Ohio	229	2.3%
21	Oklahoma	151	1.5%
29	Oregon	63	0.6%
6	Pennsylvania	417	4.1%
37	Rhode Island	14	0.1%
18	South Carolina	209	2.1%
44	South Dakota	3	0.0%
12	Tennessee	283	2.8%
2	Texas	876	8.7%
33	Utah	26	0.3%
NA	Vermont**	NA	NA
10	Virginia	346	3.4%
23	Washington	135	1.3%
31	West Virginia	57	0.6%
25	Wisconsin	85	0.8%
40	Wyoming	10	0.1%

RANK ORDER

RANK	STATE	MURDERS	% of USA
1	California	1,832	18.2%
2	Texas	876	8.7%
3	Illinois	560	5.6%
4	Louisiana	497	4.9%
5	Michigan	477	4.7%
6	Pennsylvania	417	4.1%
7	New York	408	4.1%
8	Maryland	389	3.9%
9	North Carolina	366	3.6%
10	Virginia	346	3.4%
11	Georgia	311	3.1%
12	Tennessee	283	2.8%
13	Alabama	280	2.8%
14	Arizona	257	2.6%
15	Missouri	254	2.5%
16	Indiana	230	2.3%
17	Ohio	229	2.3%
18	South Carolina	209	2.1%
19	New Jersey	176	1.7%
20	Arkansas	168	1.7%
21	Oklahoma	151	1.5%
22	Mississippi	143	1.4%
23	Washington	135	1.3%
24	Nevada	120	1.2%
25	Wisconsin	85	0.8%
26	Connecticut	80	0.8%
27	Minnesota	78	0.8%
28	Colorado	75	0.7%
29	Oregon	63	0.6%
30	Massachusetts	60	0.6%
31	West Virginia	57	0.6%
32	New Mexico	55	0.5%
33	Alaska	26	0.3%
33	Utah	26	0.3%
35	Idaho	18	0.2%
36	Hawaii	15	0.1%
37	Rhode Island	14	0.1%
38	Iowa	11	0.1%
38	Maine	11	0.1%
40	Nebraska	10	0.1%
40	Wyoming	10	0.1%
42	Montana	9	0.1%
43	Delaware	5	0.0%
44	South Dakota	3	0.0%
45	North Dakota	1	0.0%
NA	Florida**	NA	NA
NA	Kansas**	NA	NA
NA	Kentucky**	NA	NA
NA	New Hampshire**	NA	NA
NA	Vermont**	NA	NA
	District of Columbia	242	2.4%

Source: Federal Bureau of Investigation
   "Crime in the United States 1997" (Uniform Crime Reports, November 22, 1998)

*Of the 14,913 murders in 1997 for which supplemental data were received by the F.B.I. There were an additional 3,296 murders for which the type of murder weapon was not reported to the F.B.I. Includes nonnegligent manslaughter. Numbers are for reporting jurisdictions only.

**Not available.

Murder Rate with Firearms in 1997

National Rate = 5.0 Murders per 100,000 Population*

ALPHA ORDER				RANK ORDER		
RANK	STATE	RATE		RANK	STATE	RATE
6	Alabama	7.7		1	Illinois	16.7
19	Alaska	4.9		2	Nevada	14.9
10	Arizona	6.4		3	Louisiana	13.8
8	Arkansas	7.1		4	Mississippi	12.6
16	California	5.7		5	Tennessee	8.6
26	Colorado	2.7		6	Alabama	7.7
25	Connecticut	2.9		7	Maryland	7.6
35	Delaware	1.7		8	Arkansas	7.1
NA	Florida**	NA		9	Pennsylvania	6.9
11	Georgia	6.3		10	Arizona	6.4
39	Hawaii	1.3		11	Georgia	6.3
36	Idaho	1.5		12	Indiana	6.2
1	Illinois	16.7		13	Michigan	6.0
12	Indiana	6.2		14	Missouri	5.9
44	Iowa	0.5		14	South Carolina	5.9
NA	Kansas**	NA		16	California	5.7
NA	Kentucky**	NA		17	Virginia	5.2
3	Louisiana	13.8		18	North Carolina	5.0
41	Maine	0.9		19	Alaska	4.9
7	Maryland	7.6		20	New Mexico	4.6
40	Massachusetts	1.2		20	Oklahoma	4.6
13	Michigan	6.0		22	Texas	4.5
27	Minnesota	2.6		23	Ohio	3.4
4	Mississippi	12.6		24	West Virginia	3.1
14	Missouri	5.9		25	Connecticut	2.9
27	Montana	2.6		26	Colorado	2.7
43	Nebraska	0.7		27	Minnesota	2.6
2	Nevada	14.9		27	Montana	2.6
NA	New Hampshire**	NA		27	New York	2.6
31	New Jersey	2.2		27	Washington	2.6
20	New Mexico	4.6		31	New Jersey	2.2
27	New York	2.6		32	Oregon	2.1
18	North Carolina	5.0		32	Wyoming	2.1
45	North Dakota	0.2		34	Wisconsin	1.8
23	Ohio	3.4		35	Delaware	1.7
20	Oklahoma	4.6		36	Idaho	1.5
32	Oregon	2.1		37	Rhode Island	1.4
9	Pennsylvania	6.9		37	Utah	1.4
37	Rhode Island	1.4		39	Hawaii	1.3
14	South Carolina	5.9		40	Massachusetts	1.2
41	South Dakota	0.9		41	Maine	0.9
5	Tennessee	8.6		41	South Dakota	0.9
22	Texas	4.5		43	Nebraska	0.7
37	Utah	1.4		44	Iowa	0.5
NA	Vermont**	NA		45	North Dakota	0.2
17	Virginia	5.2		NA	Florida**	NA
27	Washington	2.6		NA	Kansas**	NA
24	West Virginia	3.1		NA	Kentucky**	NA
34	Wisconsin	1.8		NA	New Hampshire**	NA
32	Wyoming	2.1		NA	Vermont**	NA
					District of Columbia	45.7

Source: Morgan Quitno Press using data from Federal Bureau of Investigation
   "Crime in the United States 1997" (Uniform Crime Reports, November 22, 1998)
*Of the 14,913 murders in 1997 for which supplemental data were received by the F.B.I. There were an additional 3,296 murders for which the type of murder weapon was not reported to the F.B.I. Includes nonnegligent manslaughter. National and state rates based on population for reporting jurisdictions only.
**Not available.

Percent of Murders Involving Firearms in 1997

National Percent = 67.5% of Murders*

ALPHA ORDER

RANK ORDER

RANK	STATE	PERCENT		RANK	STATE	PERCENT
12	Alabama	68.3		1	Mississippi	78.6
32	Alaska	55.3		2	Louisiana	78.3
9	Arizona	71.2		3	Maryland	77.5
13	Arkansas	68.0		4	West Virginia	76.0
10	California	71.0		5	Tennessee	75.5
36	Colorado	51.4		6	Illinois	75.4
21	Connecticut	64.5		7	Indiana	74.0
44	Delaware	31.3		8	Pennsylvania	71.6
NA	Florida**	NA		9	Arizona	71.2
14	Georgia	67.3		10	California	71.0
42	Hawaii	32.6		11	Virginia	70.9
39	Idaho	48.6		12	Alabama	68.3
6	Illinois	75.4		13	Arkansas	68.0
7	Indiana	74.0		14	Georgia	67.3
43	Iowa	31.4		15	Oregon	67.0
NA	Kansas**	NA		16	Missouri	66.8
NA	Kentucky**	NA		17	South Carolina	66.6
2	Louisiana	78.3		18	Michigan	66.5
38	Maine	50.0		19	Oklahoma	66.2
3	Maryland	77.5		20	Texas	66.0
37	Massachusetts	51.3		21	Connecticut	64.5
18	Michigan	66.5		22	Montana	64.3
24	Minnesota	63.9		23	Nevada	64.2
1	Mississippi	78.6		24	Minnesota	63.9
16	Missouri	66.8		25	Ohio	62.4
22	Montana	64.3		26	South Dakota	60.0
40	Nebraska	47.6		27	North Carolina	59.8
23	Nevada	64.2		28	Washington	59.0
NA	New Hampshire**	NA		29	Wyoming	58.8
34	New Jersey	52.2		30	New York	57.5
33	New Mexico	52.9		31	Rhode Island	56.0
30	New York	57.5		32	Alaska	55.3
27	North Carolina	59.8		33	New Mexico	52.9
45	North Dakota	16.7		34	New Jersey	52.2
25	Ohio	62.4		35	Utah	52.0
19	Oklahoma	66.2		36	Colorado	51.4
15	Oregon	67.0		37	Massachusetts	51.3
8	Pennsylvania	71.6		38	Maine	50.0
31	Rhode Island	56.0		39	Idaho	48.6
17	South Carolina	66.6		40	Nebraska	47.6
26	South Dakota	60.0		41	Wisconsin	41.7
5	Tennessee	75.5		42	Hawaii	32.6
20	Texas	66.0		43	Iowa	31.4
35	Utah	52.0		44	Delaware	31.3
NA	Vermont**	NA		45	North Dakota	16.7
11	Virginia	70.9		NA	Florida**	NA
28	Washington	59.0		NA	Kansas**	NA
4	West Virginia	76.0		NA	Kentucky**	NA
41	Wisconsin	41.7		NA	New Hampshire**	NA
29	Wyoming	58.8		NA	Vermont**	NA

District of Columbia 80.4

Source: Morgan Quitno Press using data from Federal Bureau of Investigation
"Crime in the United States 1997" (Uniform Crime Reports, November 22, 1998)
Of the 14,913 murders in 1997 for which supplemental data were received by the F.B.I. There were an additional 3,296 murders for which the type of murder weapon was not reported to the F.B.I. There were also 991 murders that were reported as murders by "firearms, type unknown." Murder includes nonnegligent manslaughter.
**Not available.*

Murders with Handguns in 1997

National Total = 7,838 Murders*

ALPHA ORDER

RANK	STATE	MURDERS	% of USA
11	Alabama	251	3.2%
34	Alaska	13	0.2%
14	Arizona	205	2.6%
23	Arkansas	95	1.2%
1	California	1,631	20.8%
28	Colorado	51	0.7%
26	Connecticut	70	0.9%
43	Delaware	4	0.1%
NA	Florida**	NA	NA
9	Georgia	256	3.3%
37	Hawaii	10	0.1%
36	Idaho	11	0.1%
3	Illinois	471	6.0%
16	Indiana	185	2.4%
40	Iowa	7	0.1%
NA	Kansas**	NA	NA
NA	Kentucky**	NA	NA
4	Louisiana	390	5.0%
38	Maine	8	0.1%
6	Maryland	354	4.5%
31	Massachusetts	33	0.4%
12	Michigan	235	3.0%
27	Minnesota	65	0.8%
21	Mississippi	112	1.4%
16	Missouri	185	2.4%
42	Montana	6	0.1%
38	Nebraska	8	0.1%
22	Nevada	105	1.3%
NA	New Hampshire**	NA	NA
19	New Jersey	159	2.0%
30	New Mexico	38	0.5%
7	New York	346	4.4%
8	North Carolina	288	3.7%
44	North Dakota	0	0.0%
15	Ohio	198	2.5%
20	Oklahoma	114	1.5%
29	Oregon	50	0.6%
5	Pennsylvania	372	4.7%
34	Rhode Island	13	0.2%
18	South Carolina	163	2.1%
44	South Dakota	0	0.0%
13	Tennessee	217	2.8%
2	Texas	630	8.0%
33	Utah	21	0.3%
NA	Vermont**	NA	NA
10	Virginia	255	3.3%
23	Washington	95	1.2%
32	West Virginia	31	0.4%
25	Wisconsin	73	0.9%
40	Wyoming	7	0.1%

RANK ORDER

RANK	STATE	MURDERS	% of USA
1	California	1,631	20.8%
2	Texas	630	8.0%
3	Illinois	471	6.0%
4	Louisiana	390	5.0%
5	Pennsylvania	372	4.7%
6	Maryland	354	4.5%
7	New York	346	4.4%
8	North Carolina	288	3.7%
9	Georgia	256	3.3%
10	Virginia	255	3.3%
11	Alabama	251	3.2%
12	Michigan	235	3.0%
13	Tennessee	217	2.8%
14	Arizona	205	2.6%
15	Ohio	198	2.5%
16	Indiana	185	2.4%
16	Missouri	185	2.4%
18	South Carolina	163	2.1%
19	New Jersey	159	2.0%
20	Oklahoma	114	1.5%
21	Mississippi	112	1.4%
22	Nevada	105	1.3%
23	Arkansas	95	1.2%
23	Washington	95	1.2%
25	Wisconsin	73	0.9%
26	Connecticut	70	0.9%
27	Minnesota	65	0.8%
28	Colorado	51	0.7%
29	Oregon	50	0.6%
30	New Mexico	38	0.5%
31	Massachusetts	33	0.4%
32	West Virginia	31	0.4%
33	Utah	21	0.3%
34	Alaska	13	0.2%
34	Rhode Island	13	0.2%
36	Idaho	11	0.1%
37	Hawaii	10	0.1%
38	Maine	8	0.1%
38	Nebraska	8	0.1%
40	Iowa	7	0.1%
40	Wyoming	7	0.1%
42	Montana	6	0.1%
43	Delaware	4	0.1%
44	North Dakota	0	0.0%
44	South Dakota	0	0.0%
NA	Florida**	NA	NA
NA	Kansas**	NA	NA
NA	Kentucky**	NA	NA
NA	New Hampshire**	NA	NA
NA	Vermont**	NA	NA
	District of Columbia**	NA	NA

Source: Federal Bureau of Investigation
"Crime in the United States 1997" (Uniform Crime Reports, November 22, 1998)
*Of the 14,913 murders in 1997 for which supplemental data were received by the F.B.I. There were an additional 3,296 murders for which the type of murder weapon was not reported to the F.B.I. There were also 991 murders that were reported as murders by "firearms, type unknown." Murder includes nonnegligent manslaughter. Numbers are for reporting jurisdictions only. **Not available.

Murder Rate with Handguns in 1997

National Rate = 3.9 Murders per 100,000 Population*

ALPHA ORDER

RANK	STATE	RATE
6	Alabama	6.9
23	Alaska	2.5
10	Arizona	5.1
15	Arkansas	4.0
10	California	5.1
29	Colorado	1.8
23	Connecticut	2.5
35	Delaware	1.3
NA	Florida**	NA
9	Georgia	5.2
38	Hawaii	0.9
38	Idaho	0.9
1	Illinois	14.1
12	Indiana	5.0
43	Iowa	0.3
NA	Kansas**	NA
NA	Kentucky**	NA
3	Louisiana	10.8
40	Maine	0.7
5	Maryland	7.0
40	Massachusetts	0.7
21	Michigan	3.0
26	Minnesota	2.1
4	Mississippi	9.9
14	Missouri	4.3
30	Montana	1.7
42	Nebraska	0.5
2	Nevada	13.0
NA	New Hampshire**	NA
27	New Jersey	2.0
19	New Mexico	3.2
25	New York	2.2
16	North Carolina	3.9
44	North Dakota	0.0
22	Ohio	2.9
18	Oklahoma	3.4
30	Oregon	1.7
8	Pennsylvania	6.1
35	Rhode Island	1.3
13	South Carolina	4.6
44	South Dakota	0.0
7	Tennessee	6.6
19	Texas	3.2
37	Utah	1.1
NA	Vermont**	NA
16	Virginia	3.9
28	Washington	1.9
30	West Virginia	1.7
33	Wisconsin	1.5
33	Wyoming	1.5

RANK ORDER

RANK	STATE	RATE
1	Illinois	14.1
2	Nevada	13.0
3	Louisiana	10.8
4	Mississippi	9.9
5	Maryland	7.0
6	Alabama	6.9
7	Tennessee	6.6
8	Pennsylvania	6.1
9	Georgia	5.2
10	Arizona	5.1
10	California	5.1
12	Indiana	5.0
13	South Carolina	4.6
14	Missouri	4.3
15	Arkansas	4.0
16	North Carolina	3.9
16	Virginia	3.9
18	Oklahoma	3.4
19	New Mexico	3.2
19	Texas	3.2
21	Michigan	3.0
22	Ohio	2.9
23	Alaska	2.5
23	Connecticut	2.5
25	New York	2.2
26	Minnesota	2.1
27	New Jersey	2.0
28	Washington	1.9
29	Colorado	1.8
30	Montana	1.7
30	Oregon	1.7
30	West Virginia	1.7
33	Wisconsin	1.5
33	Wyoming	1.5
35	Delaware	1.3
35	Rhode Island	1.3
37	Utah	1.1
38	Hawaii	0.9
38	Idaho	0.9
40	Maine	0.7
40	Massachusetts	0.7
42	Nebraska	0.5
43	Iowa	0.3
44	North Dakota	0.0
44	South Dakota	0.0
NA	Florida**	NA
NA	Kansas**	NA
NA	Kentucky**	NA
NA	New Hampshire**	NA
NA	Vermont**	NA
	District of Columbia**	NA

Source: Morgan Quitno Press using data from Federal Bureau of Investigation
   "Crime in the United States 1997" (Uniform Crime Reports, November 22, 1998)
*Of the 14,913 murders in 1997 for which supplemental data were received by the F.B.I. There were an additional
3,296 murders for which the type of murder weapon was not reported to the F.B.I. There were also 991 murders that
were reported as murders by "firearms, type unknown." Murder includes nonnegligent manslaughter.
**Not available.

Percent of Murders Involving Handguns in 1997

National Percent = 52.6% of Murders*

RANK	STATE	PERCENT
7	Alabama	61.2
40	Alaska	27.7
10	Arizona	56.8
31	Arkansas	38.5
4	California	63.2
36	Colorado	34.9
11	Connecticut	56.5
41	Delaware	25.0
NA	Florida**	NA
13	Georgia	55.4
42	Hawaii	21.7
38	Idaho	29.7
3	Illinois	63.4
8	Indiana	59.5
43	Iowa	20.0
NA	Kansas**	NA
NA	Kentucky**	NA
6	Louisiana	61.4
34	Maine	36.4
1	Maryland	70.5
39	Massachusetts	28.2
37	Michigan	32.8
15	Minnesota	53.3
5	Mississippi	61.5
21	Missouri	48.7
26	Montana	42.9
32	Nebraska	38.1
12	Nevada	56.1
NA	New Hampshire**	NA
24	New Jersey	47.2
33	New Mexico	36.5
21	New York	48.7
25	North Carolina	47.1
44	North Dakota	0.0
14	Ohio	54.0
20	Oklahoma	50.0
16	Oregon	53.2
2	Pennsylvania	63.9
18	Rhode Island	52.0
19	South Carolina	51.9
44	South Dakota	0.0
9	Tennessee	57.9
23	Texas	47.5
27	Utah	42.0
NA	Vermont**	NA
17	Virginia	52.3
28	Washington	41.5
29	West Virginia	41.3
35	Wisconsin	35.8
30	Wyoming	41.2

RANK	STATE	PERCENT
1	Maryland	70.5
2	Pennsylvania	63.9
3	Illinois	63.4
4	California	63.2
5	Mississippi	61.5
6	Louisiana	61.4
7	Alabama	61.2
8	Indiana	59.5
9	Tennessee	57.9
10	Arizona	56.8
11	Connecticut	56.5
12	Nevada	56.1
13	Georgia	55.4
14	Ohio	54.0
15	Minnesota	53.3
16	Oregon	53.2
17	Virginia	52.3
18	Rhode Island	52.0
19	South Carolina	51.9
20	Oklahoma	50.0
21	Missouri	48.7
21	New York	48.7
23	Texas	47.5
24	New Jersey	47.2
25	North Carolina	47.1
26	Montana	42.9
27	Utah	42.0
28	Washington	41.5
29	West Virginia	41.3
30	Wyoming	41.2
31	Arkansas	38.5
32	Nebraska	38.1
33	New Mexico	36.5
34	Maine	36.4
35	Wisconsin	35.8
36	Colorado	34.9
37	Michigan	32.8
38	Idaho	29.7
39	Massachusetts	28.2
40	Alaska	27.7
41	Delaware	25.0
42	Hawaii	21.7
43	Iowa	20.0
44	North Dakota	0.0
44	South Dakota	0.0
NA	Florida**	NA
NA	Kansas**	NA
NA	Kentucky**	NA
NA	New Hampshire**	NA
NA	Vermont**	NA
	District of Columbia**	NA

Source: Morgan Quitno Press using data from Federal Bureau of Investigation
   "Crime in the United States 1997" (Uniform Crime Reports, November 22, 1998)
*Of the 14,913 murders in 1997 for which supplemental data were received by the F.B.I. There were an additional 3,296 murders for which the type of murder weapon was not reported to the F.B.I. There were also 991 murders that were reported as murders by "firearms, type unknown." Murder includes nonnegligent manslaughter.
**Not available.

Murders with Rifles in 1997

National Total = 613 Murders*

ALPHA ORDER					RANK ORDER			
RANK	STATE		MURDERS	% of USA	RANK	STATE	MURDERS	% of USA
13	Alabama		15	2.4%	1	California	114	18.6%
22	Alaska		7	1.1%	2	Texas	65	10.6%
6	Arizona		25	4.1%	3	North Carolina	38	6.2%
16	Arkansas		13	2.1%	4	Michigan	36	5.9%
1	California		114	18.6%	5	Louisiana	27	4.4%
28	Colorado		4	0.7%	6	Arizona	25	4.1%
26	Connecticut		5	0.8%	7	Missouri	23	3.8%
40	Delaware		0	0.0%	8	Pennsylvania	22	3.6%
NA	Florida**		NA	NA	9	Georgia	21	3.4%
9	Georgia		21	3.4%	9	Oklahoma	21	3.4%
32	Hawaii		3	0.5%	11	Virginia	20	3.3%
28	Idaho		4	0.7%	12	Washington	18	2.9%
16	Illinois		13	2.1%	13	Alabama	15	2.4%
15	Indiana		14	2.3%	13	New York	15	2.4%
38	Iowa		1	0.2%	15	Indiana	14	2.3%
NA	Kansas**		NA	NA	16	Arkansas	13	2.1%
NA	Kentucky**		NA	NA	16	Illinois	13	2.1%
5	Louisiana		27	4.4%	16	South Carolina	13	2.1%
40	Maine		0	0.0%	19	Tennessee	12	2.0%
22	Maryland		7	1.1%	20	West Virginia	10	1.6%
35	Massachusetts		2	0.3%	21	Mississippi	9	1.5%
4	Michigan		36	5.9%	22	Alaska	7	1.1%
24	Minnesota		6	1.0%	22	Maryland	7	1.1%
21	Mississippi		9	1.5%	24	Minnesota	6	1.0%
7	Missouri		23	3.8%	24	Oregon	6	1.0%
32	Montana		3	0.5%	26	Connecticut	5	0.8%
40	Nebraska		0	0.0%	26	New Jersey	5	0.8%
35	Nevada		2	0.3%	28	Colorado	4	0.7%
NA	New Hampshire**		NA	NA	28	Idaho	4	0.7%
26	New Jersey		5	0.8%	28	New Mexico	4	0.7%
28	New Mexico		4	0.7%	28	Wisconsin	4	0.7%
13	New York		15	2.4%	32	Hawaii	3	0.5%
3	North Carolina		38	6.2%	32	Montana	3	0.5%
40	North Dakota		0	0.0%	32	Ohio	3	0.5%
32	Ohio		3	0.5%	35	Massachusetts	2	0.3%
9	Oklahoma		21	3.4%	35	Nevada	2	0.3%
24	Oregon		6	1.0%	35	Wyoming	2	0.3%
8	Pennsylvania		22	3.6%	38	Iowa	1	0.2%
40	Rhode Island		0	0.0%	38	Utah	1	0.2%
16	South Carolina		13	2.1%	40	Delaware	0	0.0%
40	South Dakota		0	0.0%	40	Maine	0	0.0%
19	Tennessee		12	2.0%	40	Nebraska	0	0.0%
2	Texas		65	10.6%	40	North Dakota	0	0.0%
38	Utah		1	0.2%	40	Rhode Island	0	0.0%
NA	Vermont**		NA	NA	40	South Dakota	0	0.0%
11	Virginia		20	3.3%	NA	Florida**	NA	NA
12	Washington		18	2.9%	NA	Kansas**	NA	NA
20	West Virginia		10	1.6%	NA	Kentucky**	NA	NA
28	Wisconsin		4	0.7%	NA	New Hampshire**	NA	NA
35	Wyoming		2	0.3%	NA	Vermont**	NA	NA
						District of Columbia	0	0.0%

Source: Federal Bureau of Investigation
   "Crime in the United States 1997" (Uniform Crime Reports, November 22, .1998)
*Of the 14,913 murders in 1997 for which supplemental data were received by the F.B.I. There were an additional 3,296 murders for which the type of murder weapon was not reported to the F.B.I. There were also 991 murders that were reported as murders by "firearms, type unknown." Murder includes nonnegligent manslaughter. Numbers are for reporting jurisdictions only. **Not available.*

Percent of Murders Involving Rifles in 1997

National Percent = 4.1% of Murders*

ALPHA ORDER				RANK ORDER		
RANK	STATE	PERCENT		RANK	STATE	PERCENT
27	Alabama	3.7		1	Montana	21.4
2	Alaska	14.9		2	Alaska	14.9
8	Arizona	6.9		3	West Virginia	13.3
13	Arkansas	5.3		4	Wyoming	11.8
20	California	4.4		5	Idaho	10.8
30	Colorado	2.7		6	Oklahoma	9.2
24	Connecticut	4.0		7	Washington	7.9
40	Delaware	0.0		8	Arizona	6.9
NA	Florida**	NA		9	Hawaii	6.5
18	Georgia	4.5		10	Oregon	6.4
9	Hawaii	6.5		11	North Carolina	6.2
5	Idaho	10.8		12	Missouri	6.1
34	Illinois	1.7		13	Arkansas	5.3
18	Indiana	4.5		14	Michigan	5.0
29	Iowa	2.9		15	Minnesota	4.9
NA	Kansas**	NA		15	Mississippi	4.9
NA	Kentucky**	NA		15	Texas	4.9
21	Louisiana	4.3		18	Georgia	4.5
40	Maine	0.0		18	Indiana	4.5
37	Maryland	1.4		20	California	4.4
34	Massachusetts	1.7		21	Louisiana	4.3
14	Michigan	5.0		22	South Carolina	4.1
15	Minnesota	4.9		22	Virginia	4.1
15	Mississippi	4.9		24	Connecticut	4.0
12	Missouri	6.1		25	New Mexico	3.8
1	Montana	21.4		25	Pennsylvania	3.8
40	Nebraska	0.0		27	Alabama	3.7
38	Nevada	1.1		28	Tennessee	3.2
NA	New Hampshire**	NA		29	Iowa	2.9
36	New Jersey	1.5		30	Colorado	2.7
25	New Mexico	3.8		31	New York	2.1
31	New York	2.1		32	Utah	2.0
11	North Carolina	6.2		32	Wisconsin	2.0
40	North Dakota	0.0		34	Illinois	1.7
39	Ohio	0.8		34	Massachusetts	1.7
6	Oklahoma	9.2		36	New Jersey	1.5
10	Oregon	6.4		37	Maryland	1.4
25	Pennsylvania	3.8		38	Nevada	1.1
40	Rhode Island	0.0		39	Ohio	0.8
22	South Carolina	4.1		40	Delaware	0.0
40	South Dakota	0.0		40	Maine	0.0
28	Tennessee	3.2		40	Nebraska	0.0
15	Texas	4.9		40	North Dakota	0.0
32	Utah	2.0		40	Rhode Island	0.0
NA	Vermont**	NA		40	South Dakota	0.0
22	Virginia	4.1		NA	Florida**	NA
7	Washington	7.9		NA	Kansas**	NA
3	West Virginia	13.3		NA	Kentucky**	NA
32	Wisconsin	2.0		NA	New Hampshire**	NA
4	Wyoming	11.8		NA	Vermont**	NA
					District of Columbia	0.0

Source: Morgan Quitno Press using data from Federal Bureau of Investigation
    "Crime in the United States 1997" (Uniform Crime Reports, November 22, 1998)
*Of the 14,913 murders in 1997 for which supplemental data were received by the F.B.I. There were an additional
3,296 murders for which the type of murder weapon was not reported to the F.B.I. There were also 991 murders that
were reported as murders by "firearms, type unknown." Murder includes nonnegligent manslaughter.
**Not available.

Murders with Shotguns in 1997

National Total = 626 Murders*

ALPHA ORDER				RANK ORDER			
RANK	STATE	MURDERS	% of USA	RANK	STATE	MURDERS	% of USA
16	Alabama	14	2.2%	1	Texas	75	12.0%
31	Alaska	4	0.6%	2	California	72	11.5%
21	Arizona	11	1.8%	3	Michigan	42	6.7%
11	Arkansas	18	2.9%	4	New York	39	6.2%
2	California	72	11.5%	5	North Carolina	31	5.0%
24	Colorado	8	1.3%	5	Tennessee	31	5.0%
40	Connecticut	0	0.0%	7	Louisiana	25	4.0%
37	Delaware	1	0.2%	8	Pennsylvania	22	3.5%
NA	Florida**	NA	NA	8	Virginia	22	3.5%
14	Georgia	15	2.4%	10	South Carolina	20	3.2%
40	Hawaii	0	0.0%	11	Arkansas	18	2.9%
37	Idaho	1	0.2%	11	Mississippi	18	2.9%
24	Illinois	8	1.3%	13	Missouri	16	2.6%
20	Indiana	12	1.9%	14	Georgia	15	2.4%
34	Iowa	2	0.3%	14	West Virginia	15	2.4%
NA	Kansas**	NA	NA	16	Alabama	14	2.2%
NA	Kentucky**	NA	NA	16	Maryland	14	2.2%
7	Louisiana	25	4.0%	16	Oklahoma	14	2.2%
37	Maine	1	0.2%	19	Washington	13	2.1%
16	Maryland	14	2.2%	20	Indiana	12	1.9%
31	Massachusetts	4	0.6%	21	Arizona	11	1.8%
3	Michigan	42	6.7%	22	Ohio	10	1.6%
27	Minnesota	6	1.0%	23	New Jersey	9	1.4%
11	Mississippi	18	2.9%	24	Colorado	8	1.3%
13	Missouri	16	2.6%	24	Illinois	8	1.3%
40	Montana	0	0.0%	24	New Mexico	8	1.3%
34	Nebraska	2	0.3%	27	Minnesota	6	1.0%
27	Nevada	6	1.0%	27	Nevada	6	1.0%
NA	New Hampshire**	NA	NA	27	Oregon	6	1.0%
23	New Jersey	9	1.4%	30	Wisconsin	5	0.8%
24	New Mexico	8	1.3%	31	Alaska	4	0.6%
4	New York	39	6.2%	31	Massachusetts	4	0.6%
5	North Carolina	31	5.0%	33	Utah	3	0.5%
40	North Dakota	0	0.0%	34	Iowa	2	0.3%
22	Ohio	10	1.6%	34	Nebraska	2	0.3%
16	Oklahoma	14	2.2%	34	South Dakota	2	0.3%
27	Oregon	6	1.0%	37	Delaware	1	0.2%
8	Pennsylvania	22	3.5%	37	Idaho	1	0.2%
40	Rhode Island	0	0.0%	37	Maine	1	0.2%
10	South Carolina	20	3.2%	40	Connecticut	0	0.0%
34	South Dakota	2	0.3%	40	Hawaii	0	0.0%
5	Tennessee	31	5.0%	40	Montana	0	0.0%
1	Texas	75	12.0%	40	North Dakota	0	0.0%
33	Utah	3	0.5%	40	Rhode Island	0	0.0%
NA	Vermont**	NA	NA	40	Wyoming	0	0.0%
8	Virginia	22	3.5%	NA	Florida**	NA	NA
19	Washington	13	2.1%	NA	Kansas**	NA	NA
14	West Virginia	15	2.4%	NA	Kentucky**	NA	NA
30	Wisconsin	5	0.8%	NA	New Hampshire**	NA	NA
40	Wyoming	0	0.0%	NA	Vermont**	NA	NA
					District of Columbia	1	0.2%

Source: Federal Bureau of Investigation
  "Crime in the United States 1997" (Uniform Crime Reports, November 22, 1998)
*Of the 14,913 murders in 1997 for which supplemental data were received by the F.B.I. There were an additional 3,296 murders for which the type of murder weapon was not reported to the F.B.I. There were also 991 murders that were reported as murders by "firearms, type unknown." Murder includes nonnegligent manslaughter. Numbers are for reporting jurisdictions only. **Not available.*

Percent of Murders Involving Shotguns in 1997

National Percent = 4.2% of Murders*

ALPHA ORDER

RANK	STATE	PERCENT
28	Alabama	3.4
5	Alaska	8.5
32	Arizona	3.0
8	Arkansas	7.3
33	California	2.8
18	Colorado	5.5
40	Connecticut	0.0
11	Delaware	6.3
NA	Florida**	NA
30	Georgia	3.2
40	Hawaii	0.0
35	Idaho	2.7
39	Illinois	1.1
25	Indiana	3.9
15	Iowa	5.7
NA	Kansas**	NA
NA	Kentucky**	NA
25	Louisiana	3.9
22	Maine	4.5
33	Maryland	2.8
28	Massachusetts	3.4
14	Michigan	5.9
21	Minnesota	4.9
3	Mississippi	9.9
24	Missouri	4.2
40	Montana	0.0
4	Nebraska	9.5
30	Nevada	3.2
NA	New Hampshire**	NA
35	New Jersey	2.7
7	New Mexico	7.7
18	New York	5.5
20	North Carolina	5.1
40	North Dakota	0.0
35	Ohio	2.7
12	Oklahoma	6.1
9	Oregon	6.4
27	Pennsylvania	3.8
40	Rhode Island	0.0
9	South Carolina	6.4
1	South Dakota	40.0
6	Tennessee	8.3
15	Texas	5.7
13	Utah	6.0
NA	Vermont**	NA
22	Virginia	4.5
15	Washington	5.7
2	West Virginia	20.0
38	Wisconsin	2.5
40	Wyoming	0.0

RANK ORDER

RANK	STATE	PERCENT
1	South Dakota	40.0
2	West Virginia	20.0
3	Mississippi	9.9
4	Nebraska	9.5
5	Alaska	8.5
6	Tennessee	8.3
7	New Mexico	7.7
8	Arkansas	7.3
9	Oregon	6.4
9	South Carolina	6.4
11	Delaware	6.3
12	Oklahoma	6.1
13	Utah	6.0
14	Michigan	5.9
15	Iowa	5.7
15	Texas	5.7
15	Washington	5.7
18	Colorado	5.5
18	New York	5.5
20	North Carolina	5.1
21	Minnesota	4.9
22	Maine	4.5
22	Virginia	4.5
24	Missouri	4.2
25	Indiana	3.9
25	Louisiana	3.9
27	Pennsylvania	3.8
28	Alabama	3.4
28	Massachusetts	3.4
30	Georgia	3.2
30	Nevada	3.2
32	Arizona	3.0
33	California	2.8
33	Maryland	2.8
35	Idaho	2.7
35	New Jersey	2.7
35	Ohio	2.7
38	Wisconsin	2.5
39	Illinois	1.1
40	Connecticut	0.0
40	Hawaii	0.0
40	Montana	0.0
40	North Dakota	0.0
40	Rhode Island	0.0
40	Wyoming	0.0
NA	Florida**	NA
NA	Kansas**	NA
NA	Kentucky**	NA
NA	New Hampshire**	NA
NA	Vermont**	NA
	District of Columbia	0.3

Source: Morgan Quitno Press using data from Federal Bureau of Investigation
   "Crime in the United States 1997" (Uniform Crime Reports, November 22, 1998)
*Of the 14,913 murders in 1997 for which supplemental data were received by the F.B.I. There were an additional 3,296 murders for which the type of murder weapon was not reported to the F.B.I. There were also 991 murders that were reported as murders by "firearms, type unknown." Murder includes nonnegligent manslaughter.
**Not available.

Murders with Knives or Cutting Instruments in 1997

National Total = 1,938 Murders*

<table>
<tr><td colspan="4"><u>ALPHA ORDER</u></td><td colspan="4"><u>RANK ORDER</u></td></tr>
<tr><td>RANK</td><td>STATE</td><td>MURDERS</td><td>% of USA</td><td>RANK</td><td>STATE</td><td>MURDERS</td><td>% of USA</td></tr>
<tr><td>9</td><td>Alabama</td><td>58</td><td>3.0%</td><td>1</td><td>California</td><td>306</td><td>15.8%</td></tr>
<tr><td>34</td><td>Alaska</td><td>7</td><td>0.4%</td><td>2</td><td>Texas</td><td>195</td><td>10.1%</td></tr>
<tr><td>17</td><td>Arizona</td><td>41</td><td>2.1%</td><td>3</td><td>New York</td><td>138</td><td>7.1%</td></tr>
<tr><td>17</td><td>Arkansas</td><td>41</td><td>2.1%</td><td>4</td><td>Michigan</td><td>85</td><td>4.4%</td></tr>
<tr><td>1</td><td>California</td><td>306</td><td>15.8%</td><td>5</td><td>North Carolina</td><td>81</td><td>4.2%</td></tr>
<tr><td>26</td><td>Colorado</td><td>22</td><td>1.1%</td><td>6</td><td>Georgia</td><td>73</td><td>3.8%</td></tr>
<tr><td>29</td><td>Connecticut</td><td>18</td><td>0.9%</td><td>6</td><td>Illinois</td><td>73</td><td>3.8%</td></tr>
<tr><td>34</td><td>Delaware</td><td>7</td><td>0.4%</td><td>8</td><td>Louisiana</td><td>65</td><td>3.4%</td></tr>
<tr><td>NA</td><td>Florida**</td><td>NA</td><td>NA</td><td>9</td><td>Alabama</td><td>58</td><td>3.0%</td></tr>
<tr><td>6</td><td>Georgia</td><td>73</td><td>3.8%</td><td>10</td><td>Pennsylvania</td><td>57</td><td>2.9%</td></tr>
<tr><td>31</td><td>Hawaii</td><td>13</td><td>0.7%</td><td>11</td><td>Missouri</td><td>56</td><td>2.9%</td></tr>
<tr><td>39</td><td>Idaho</td><td>3</td><td>0.2%</td><td>11</td><td>New Jersey</td><td>56</td><td>2.9%</td></tr>
<tr><td>6</td><td>Illinois</td><td>73</td><td>3.8%</td><td>13</td><td>Virginia</td><td>52</td><td>2.7%</td></tr>
<tr><td>21</td><td>Indiana</td><td>33</td><td>1.7%</td><td>14</td><td>Maryland</td><td>46</td><td>2.4%</td></tr>
<tr><td>32</td><td>Iowa</td><td>11</td><td>0.6%</td><td>15</td><td>South Carolina</td><td>45</td><td>2.3%</td></tr>
<tr><td>NA</td><td>Kansas**</td><td>NA</td><td>NA</td><td>15</td><td>Tennessee</td><td>45</td><td>2.3%</td></tr>
<tr><td>NA</td><td>Kentucky**</td><td>NA</td><td>NA</td><td>17</td><td>Arizona</td><td>41</td><td>2.1%</td></tr>
<tr><td>8</td><td>Louisiana</td><td>65</td><td>3.4%</td><td>17</td><td>Arkansas</td><td>41</td><td>2.1%</td></tr>
<tr><td>39</td><td>Maine</td><td>3</td><td>0.2%</td><td>19</td><td>Washington</td><td>36</td><td>1.9%</td></tr>
<tr><td>14</td><td>Maryland</td><td>46</td><td>2.4%</td><td>20</td><td>Ohio</td><td>34</td><td>1.8%</td></tr>
<tr><td>23</td><td>Massachusetts</td><td>32</td><td>1.7%</td><td>21</td><td>Indiana</td><td>33</td><td>1.7%</td></tr>
<tr><td>4</td><td>Michigan</td><td>85</td><td>4.4%</td><td>21</td><td>Wisconsin</td><td>33</td><td>1.7%</td></tr>
<tr><td>30</td><td>Minnesota</td><td>16</td><td>0.8%</td><td>23</td><td>Massachusetts</td><td>32</td><td>1.7%</td></tr>
<tr><td>28</td><td>Mississippi</td><td>21</td><td>1.1%</td><td>24</td><td>Oklahoma</td><td>28</td><td>1.4%</td></tr>
<tr><td>11</td><td>Missouri</td><td>56</td><td>2.9%</td><td>25</td><td>New Mexico</td><td>23</td><td>1.2%</td></tr>
<tr><td>42</td><td>Montana</td><td>2</td><td>0.1%</td><td>26</td><td>Colorado</td><td>22</td><td>1.1%</td></tr>
<tr><td>43</td><td>Nebraska</td><td>1</td><td>0.1%</td><td>26</td><td>Nevada</td><td>22</td><td>1.1%</td></tr>
<tr><td>26</td><td>Nevada</td><td>22</td><td>1.1%</td><td>28</td><td>Mississippi</td><td>21</td><td>1.1%</td></tr>
<tr><td>NA</td><td>New Hampshire**</td><td>NA</td><td>NA</td><td>29</td><td>Connecticut</td><td>18</td><td>0.9%</td></tr>
<tr><td>11</td><td>New Jersey</td><td>56</td><td>2.9%</td><td>30</td><td>Minnesota</td><td>16</td><td>0.8%</td></tr>
<tr><td>25</td><td>New Mexico</td><td>23</td><td>1.2%</td><td>31</td><td>Hawaii</td><td>13</td><td>0.7%</td></tr>
<tr><td>3</td><td>New York</td><td>138</td><td>7.1%</td><td>32</td><td>Iowa</td><td>11</td><td>0.6%</td></tr>
<tr><td>5</td><td>North Carolina</td><td>81</td><td>4.2%</td><td>33</td><td>West Virginia</td><td>9</td><td>0.5%</td></tr>
<tr><td>43</td><td>North Dakota</td><td>1</td><td>0.1%</td><td>34</td><td>Alaska</td><td>7</td><td>0.4%</td></tr>
<tr><td>20</td><td>Ohio</td><td>34</td><td>1.8%</td><td>34</td><td>Delaware</td><td>7</td><td>0.4%</td></tr>
<tr><td>24</td><td>Oklahoma</td><td>28</td><td>1.4%</td><td>34</td><td>Oregon</td><td>7</td><td>0.4%</td></tr>
<tr><td>34</td><td>Oregon</td><td>7</td><td>0.4%</td><td>37</td><td>Rhode Island</td><td>5</td><td>0.3%</td></tr>
<tr><td>10</td><td>Pennsylvania</td><td>57</td><td>2.9%</td><td>37</td><td>Utah</td><td>5</td><td>0.3%</td></tr>
<tr><td>37</td><td>Rhode Island</td><td>5</td><td>0.3%</td><td>39</td><td>Idaho</td><td>3</td><td>0.2%</td></tr>
<tr><td>15</td><td>South Carolina</td><td>45</td><td>2.3%</td><td>39</td><td>Maine</td><td>3</td><td>0.2%</td></tr>
<tr><td>43</td><td>South Dakota</td><td>1</td><td>0.1%</td><td>39</td><td>Wyoming</td><td>3</td><td>0.2%</td></tr>
<tr><td>15</td><td>Tennessee</td><td>45</td><td>2.3%</td><td>42</td><td>Montana</td><td>2</td><td>0.1%</td></tr>
<tr><td>2</td><td>Texas</td><td>195</td><td>10.1%</td><td>43</td><td>Nebraska</td><td>1</td><td>0.1%</td></tr>
<tr><td>37</td><td>Utah</td><td>5</td><td>0.3%</td><td>43</td><td>North Dakota</td><td>1</td><td>0.1%</td></tr>
<tr><td>NA</td><td>Vermont**</td><td>NA</td><td>NA</td><td>43</td><td>South Dakota</td><td>1</td><td>0.1%</td></tr>
<tr><td>13</td><td>Virginia</td><td>52</td><td>2.7%</td><td>NA</td><td>Florida**</td><td>NA</td><td>NA</td></tr>
<tr><td>19</td><td>Washington</td><td>36</td><td>1.9%</td><td>NA</td><td>Kansas**</td><td>NA</td><td>NA</td></tr>
<tr><td>33</td><td>West Virginia</td><td>9</td><td>0.5%</td><td>NA</td><td>Kentucky**</td><td>NA</td><td>NA</td></tr>
<tr><td>21</td><td>Wisconsin</td><td>33</td><td>1.7%</td><td>NA</td><td>New Hampshire**</td><td>NA</td><td>NA</td></tr>
<tr><td>39</td><td>Wyoming</td><td>3</td><td>0.2%</td><td>NA</td><td>Vermont**</td><td>NA</td><td>NA</td></tr>
<tr><td></td><td></td><td></td><td></td><td></td><td>District of Columbia</td><td>29</td><td>1.5%</td></tr>
</table>

Source: Federal Bureau of Investigation
   "Crime in the United States 1997" (Uniform Crime Reports, November 22, 1998)
*Of the 14,913 murders in 1997 for which supplemental data were received by the F.B.I. There were an additional 3,296 murders for which the type of murder weapon was not reported to the F.B.I. There were also 991 murders that were reported as murders by "firearms, type unknown." Murder includes nonnegligent manslaughter. Numbers are for reporting jurisdictions only. **Not available.

Percent of Murders Involving Knives or Cutting Instruments in 1997

National Percent = 13.0% of Murders*

<table>
<tr><td colspan="3">ALPHA ORDER</td><td colspan="3">RANK ORDER</td></tr>
<tr><td>RANK</td><td>STATE</td><td>PERCENT</td><td>RANK</td><td>STATE</td><td>PERCENT</td></tr>
<tr><td>23</td><td>Alabama</td><td>14.1</td><td>1</td><td>Delaware</td><td>43.8</td></tr>
<tr><td>17</td><td>Alaska</td><td>14.9</td><td>2</td><td>Iowa</td><td>31.4</td></tr>
<tr><td>34</td><td>Arizona</td><td>11.4</td><td>3</td><td>Hawaii</td><td>28.3</td></tr>
<tr><td>11</td><td>Arkansas</td><td>16.6</td><td>4</td><td>Massachusetts</td><td>27.4</td></tr>
<tr><td>30</td><td>California</td><td>11.9</td><td>5</td><td>New Mexico</td><td>22.1</td></tr>
<tr><td>16</td><td>Colorado</td><td>15.1</td><td>6</td><td>Rhode Island</td><td>20.0</td></tr>
<tr><td>20</td><td>Connecticut</td><td>14.5</td><td>6</td><td>South Dakota</td><td>20.0</td></tr>
<tr><td>1</td><td>Delaware</td><td>43.8</td><td>8</td><td>New York</td><td>19.4</td></tr>
<tr><td>NA</td><td>Florida**</td><td>NA</td><td>9</td><td>Wyoming</td><td>17.6</td></tr>
<tr><td>14</td><td>Georgia</td><td>15.8</td><td>10</td><td>North Dakota</td><td>16.7</td></tr>
<tr><td>3</td><td>Hawaii</td><td>28.3</td><td>11</td><td>Arkansas</td><td>16.6</td></tr>
<tr><td>43</td><td>Idaho</td><td>8.1</td><td>11</td><td>New Jersey</td><td>16.6</td></tr>
<tr><td>39</td><td>Illinois</td><td>9.8</td><td>13</td><td>Wisconsin</td><td>16.2</td></tr>
<tr><td>36</td><td>Indiana</td><td>10.6</td><td>14</td><td>Georgia</td><td>15.8</td></tr>
<tr><td>2</td><td>Iowa</td><td>31.4</td><td>15</td><td>Washington</td><td>15.7</td></tr>
<tr><td>NA</td><td>Kansas**</td><td>NA</td><td>16</td><td>Colorado</td><td>15.1</td></tr>
<tr><td>NA</td><td>Kentucky**</td><td>NA</td><td>17</td><td>Alaska</td><td>14.9</td></tr>
<tr><td>37</td><td>Louisiana</td><td>10.2</td><td>18</td><td>Missouri</td><td>14.7</td></tr>
<tr><td>24</td><td>Maine</td><td>13.6</td><td>18</td><td>Texas</td><td>14.7</td></tr>
<tr><td>42</td><td>Maryland</td><td>9.2</td><td>20</td><td>Connecticut</td><td>14.5</td></tr>
<tr><td>4</td><td>Massachusetts</td><td>27.4</td><td>21</td><td>Montana</td><td>14.3</td></tr>
<tr><td>30</td><td>Michigan</td><td>11.9</td><td>21</td><td>South Carolina</td><td>14.3</td></tr>
<tr><td>26</td><td>Minnesota</td><td>13.1</td><td>23</td><td>Alabama</td><td>14.1</td></tr>
<tr><td>33</td><td>Mississippi</td><td>11.5</td><td>24</td><td>Maine</td><td>13.6</td></tr>
<tr><td>18</td><td>Missouri</td><td>14.7</td><td>25</td><td>North Carolina</td><td>13.2</td></tr>
<tr><td>21</td><td>Montana</td><td>14.3</td><td>26</td><td>Minnesota</td><td>13.1</td></tr>
<tr><td>45</td><td>Nebraska</td><td>4.8</td><td>27</td><td>Oklahoma</td><td>12.3</td></tr>
<tr><td>32</td><td>Nevada</td><td>11.8</td><td>28</td><td>Tennessee</td><td>12.0</td></tr>
<tr><td>NA</td><td>New Hampshire**</td><td>NA</td><td>28</td><td>West Virginia</td><td>12.0</td></tr>
<tr><td>11</td><td>New Jersey</td><td>16.6</td><td>30</td><td>California</td><td>11.9</td></tr>
<tr><td>5</td><td>New Mexico</td><td>22.1</td><td>30</td><td>Michigan</td><td>11.9</td></tr>
<tr><td>8</td><td>New York</td><td>19.4</td><td>32</td><td>Nevada</td><td>11.8</td></tr>
<tr><td>25</td><td>North Carolina</td><td>13.2</td><td>33</td><td>Mississippi</td><td>11.5</td></tr>
<tr><td>10</td><td>North Dakota</td><td>16.7</td><td>34</td><td>Arizona</td><td>11.4</td></tr>
<tr><td>41</td><td>Ohio</td><td>9.3</td><td>35</td><td>Virginia</td><td>10.7</td></tr>
<tr><td>27</td><td>Oklahoma</td><td>12.3</td><td>36</td><td>Indiana</td><td>10.6</td></tr>
<tr><td>44</td><td>Oregon</td><td>7.4</td><td>37</td><td>Louisiana</td><td>10.2</td></tr>
<tr><td>39</td><td>Pennsylvania</td><td>9.8</td><td>38</td><td>Utah</td><td>10.0</td></tr>
<tr><td>6</td><td>Rhode Island</td><td>20.0</td><td>39</td><td>Illinois</td><td>9.8</td></tr>
<tr><td>21</td><td>South Carolina</td><td>14.3</td><td>39</td><td>Pennsylvania</td><td>9.8</td></tr>
<tr><td>6</td><td>South Dakota</td><td>20.0</td><td>41</td><td>Ohio</td><td>9.3</td></tr>
<tr><td>28</td><td>Tennessee</td><td>12.0</td><td>42</td><td>Maryland</td><td>9.2</td></tr>
<tr><td>18</td><td>Texas</td><td>14.7</td><td>43</td><td>Idaho</td><td>8.1</td></tr>
<tr><td>38</td><td>Utah</td><td>10.0</td><td>44</td><td>Oregon</td><td>7.4</td></tr>
<tr><td>NA</td><td>Vermont**</td><td>NA</td><td>45</td><td>Nebraska</td><td>4.8</td></tr>
<tr><td>35</td><td>Virginia</td><td>10.7</td><td>NA</td><td>Florida**</td><td>NA</td></tr>
<tr><td>15</td><td>Washington</td><td>15.7</td><td>NA</td><td>Kansas**</td><td>NA</td></tr>
<tr><td>28</td><td>West Virginia</td><td>12.0</td><td>NA</td><td>Kentucky**</td><td>NA</td></tr>
<tr><td>13</td><td>Wisconsin</td><td>16.2</td><td>NA</td><td>New Hampshire**</td><td>NA</td></tr>
<tr><td>9</td><td>Wyoming</td><td>17.6</td><td>NA</td><td>Vermont**</td><td>NA</td></tr>
<tr><td></td><td></td><td></td><td></td><td>District of Columbia</td><td>9.6</td></tr>
</table>

Source: Morgan Quitno Press using data from Federal Bureau of Investigation
   "Crime in the United States 1997" (Uniform Crime Reports, November 22, 1998)
*Of the 14,913 murders in 1997 for which supplemental data were received by the F.B.I. There were an additional
3,296 murders for which the type of murder weapon was not reported to the F.B.I. There were also 991 murders that
were reported as murders by "firearms, type unknown." Murder includes nonnegligent manslaughter.
**Not available.

Murders by Hands, Fists or Feet in 1997

National Total = 944 Murders*

ALPHA ORDER

RANK	STATE	MURDERS	% of USA
11	Alabama	23	2.4%
29	Alaska	7	0.7%
15	Arizona	20	2.1%
25	Arkansas	12	1.3%
1	California	150	15.9%
23	Colorado	15	1.6%
30	Connecticut	6	0.6%
42	Delaware	1	0.1%
NA	Florida**	NA	NA
13	Georgia	22	2.3%
27	Hawaii	11	1.2%
35	Idaho	4	0.4%
5	Illinois	48	5.1%
24	Indiana	13	1.4%
31	Iowa	5	0.5%
NA	Kansas**	NA	NA
NA	Kentucky**	NA	NA
10	Louisiana	25	2.6%
31	Maine	5	0.5%
11	Maryland	23	2.4%
31	Massachusetts	5	0.5%
9	Michigan	35	3.7%
25	Minnesota	12	1.3%
35	Mississippi	4	0.4%
15	Missouri	20	2.1%
40	Montana	2	0.2%
31	Nebraska	5	0.5%
22	Nevada	16	1.7%
NA	New Hampshire**	NA	NA
7	New Jersey	45	4.8%
28	New Mexico	9	1.0%
4	New York	56	5.9%
3	North Carolina	57	6.0%
44	North Dakota	0	0.0%
6	Ohio	46	4.9%
19	Oklahoma	19	2.0%
35	Oregon	4	0.4%
8	Pennsylvania	40	4.2%
40	Rhode Island	2	0.2%
19	South Carolina	19	2.0%
44	South Dakota	0	0.0%
15	Tennessee	20	2.1%
2	Texas	65	6.9%
35	Utah	4	0.4%
NA	Vermont**	NA	NA
15	Virginia	20	2.1%
13	Washington	22	2.3%
35	West Virginia	4	0.4%
21	Wisconsin	17	1.8%
42	Wyoming	1	0.1%

RANK ORDER

RANK	STATE	MURDERS	% of USA
1	California	150	15.9%
2	Texas	65	6.9%
3	North Carolina	57	6.0%
4	New York	56	5.9%
5	Illinois	48	5.1%
6	Ohio	46	4.9%
7	New Jersey	45	4.8%
8	Pennsylvania	40	4.2%
9	Michigan	35	3.7%
10	Louisiana	25	2.6%
11	Alabama	23	2.4%
11	Maryland	23	2.4%
13	Georgia	22	2.3%
13	Washington	22	2.3%
15	Arizona	20	2.1%
15	Missouri	20	2.1%
15	Tennessee	20	2.1%
15	Virginia	20	2.1%
19	Oklahoma	19	2.0%
19	South Carolina	19	2.0%
21	Wisconsin	17	1.8%
22	Nevada	16	1.7%
23	Colorado	15	1.6%
24	Indiana	13	1.4%
25	Arkansas	12	1.3%
25	Minnesota	12	1.3%
27	Hawaii	11	1.2%
28	New Mexico	9	1.0%
29	Alaska	7	0.7%
30	Connecticut	6	0.6%
31	Iowa	5	0.5%
31	Maine	5	0.5%
31	Massachusetts	5	0.5%
31	Nebraska	5	0.5%
35	Idaho	4	0.4%
35	Mississippi	4	0.4%
35	Oregon	4	0.4%
35	Utah	4	0.4%
35	West Virginia	4	0.4%
40	Montana	2	0.2%
40	Rhode Island	2	0.2%
42	Delaware	1	0.1%
42	Wyoming	1	0.1%
44	North Dakota	0	0.0%
44	South Dakota	0	0.0%
NA	Florida**	NA	NA
NA	Kansas**	NA	NA
NA	Kentucky**	NA	NA
NA	New Hampshire**	NA	NA
NA	Vermont**	NA	NA
	District of Columbia	5	0.5%

Source: Federal Bureau of Investigation
  "Crime in the United States 1997" (Uniform Crime Reports, November 22, 1998)
*Of the 14,913 murders in 1997 for which supplemental data were received by the F.B.I. There were an additional 3,296 murders for which the type of murder weapon was not reported to the F.B.I. There were also 991 murders that were reported as murders by "firearms, type unknown." Murder includes nonnegligent manslaughter. Numbers are for reporting jurisdictions only. **Not available.*

Percent of Murders Involving Hands, Fists or Feet in 1997

National Percent = 6.3% of Murders*

<table>
<tr><td colspan="3"><u>ALPHA ORDER</u></td><td colspan="3"><u>RANK ORDER</u></td></tr>
<tr><th>RANK</th><th>STATE</th><th>PERCENT</th><th>RANK</th><th>STATE</th><th>PERCENT</th></tr>
<tr><td>27</td><td>Alabama</td><td>5.6</td><td>1</td><td>Hawaii</td><td>23.9</td></tr>
<tr><td>4</td><td>Alaska</td><td>14.9</td><td>2</td><td>Nebraska</td><td>23.8</td></tr>
<tr><td>28</td><td>Arizona</td><td>5.5</td><td>3</td><td>Maine</td><td>22.7</td></tr>
<tr><td>32</td><td>Arkansas</td><td>4.9</td><td>4</td><td>Alaska</td><td>14.9</td></tr>
<tr><td>26</td><td>California</td><td>5.8</td><td>5</td><td>Iowa</td><td>14.3</td></tr>
<tr><td>10</td><td>Colorado</td><td>10.3</td><td>5</td><td>Montana</td><td>14.3</td></tr>
<tr><td>35</td><td>Connecticut</td><td>4.8</td><td>7</td><td>New Jersey</td><td>13.4</td></tr>
<tr><td>23</td><td>Delaware</td><td>6.3</td><td>8</td><td>Ohio</td><td>12.5</td></tr>
<tr><td>NA</td><td>Florida**</td><td>NA</td><td>9</td><td>Idaho</td><td>10.8</td></tr>
<tr><td>35</td><td>Georgia</td><td>4.8</td><td>10</td><td>Colorado</td><td>10.3</td></tr>
<tr><td>1</td><td>Hawaii</td><td>23.9</td><td>11</td><td>Minnesota</td><td>9.8</td></tr>
<tr><td>9</td><td>Idaho</td><td>10.8</td><td>12</td><td>Washington</td><td>9.6</td></tr>
<tr><td>22</td><td>Illinois</td><td>6.5</td><td>13</td><td>North Carolina</td><td>9.3</td></tr>
<tr><td>40</td><td>Indiana</td><td>4.2</td><td>14</td><td>New Mexico</td><td>8.7</td></tr>
<tr><td>5</td><td>Iowa</td><td>14.3</td><td>15</td><td>Nevada</td><td>8.6</td></tr>
<tr><td>NA</td><td>Kansas**</td><td>NA</td><td>16</td><td>Oklahoma</td><td>8.3</td></tr>
<tr><td>NA</td><td>Kentucky**</td><td>NA</td><td>16</td><td>Wisconsin</td><td>8.3</td></tr>
<tr><td>42</td><td>Louisiana</td><td>3.9</td><td>18</td><td>Rhode Island</td><td>8.0</td></tr>
<tr><td>3</td><td>Maine</td><td>22.7</td><td>18</td><td>Utah</td><td>8.0</td></tr>
<tr><td>37</td><td>Maryland</td><td>4.6</td><td>20</td><td>New York</td><td>7.9</td></tr>
<tr><td>38</td><td>Massachusetts</td><td>4.3</td><td>21</td><td>Pennsylvania</td><td>6.9</td></tr>
<tr><td>32</td><td>Michigan</td><td>4.9</td><td>22</td><td>Illinois</td><td>6.5</td></tr>
<tr><td>11</td><td>Minnesota</td><td>9.8</td><td>23</td><td>Delaware</td><td>6.3</td></tr>
<tr><td>43</td><td>Mississippi</td><td>2.2</td><td>24</td><td>South Carolina</td><td>6.1</td></tr>
<tr><td>29</td><td>Missouri</td><td>5.3</td><td>25</td><td>Wyoming</td><td>5.9</td></tr>
<tr><td>5</td><td>Montana</td><td>14.3</td><td>26</td><td>California</td><td>5.8</td></tr>
<tr><td>2</td><td>Nebraska</td><td>23.8</td><td>27</td><td>Alabama</td><td>5.6</td></tr>
<tr><td>15</td><td>Nevada</td><td>8.6</td><td>28</td><td>Arizona</td><td>5.5</td></tr>
<tr><td>NA</td><td>New Hampshire**</td><td>NA</td><td>29</td><td>Missouri</td><td>5.3</td></tr>
<tr><td>7</td><td>New Jersey</td><td>13.4</td><td>29</td><td>Tennessee</td><td>5.3</td></tr>
<tr><td>14</td><td>New Mexico</td><td>8.7</td><td>29</td><td>West Virginia</td><td>5.3</td></tr>
<tr><td>20</td><td>New York</td><td>7.9</td><td>32</td><td>Arkansas</td><td>4.9</td></tr>
<tr><td>13</td><td>North Carolina</td><td>9.3</td><td>32</td><td>Michigan</td><td>4.9</td></tr>
<tr><td>44</td><td>North Dakota</td><td>0.0</td><td>32</td><td>Texas</td><td>4.9</td></tr>
<tr><td>8</td><td>Ohio</td><td>12.5</td><td>35</td><td>Connecticut</td><td>4.8</td></tr>
<tr><td>16</td><td>Oklahoma</td><td>8.3</td><td>35</td><td>Georgia</td><td>4.8</td></tr>
<tr><td>38</td><td>Oregon</td><td>4.3</td><td>37</td><td>Maryland</td><td>4.6</td></tr>
<tr><td>21</td><td>Pennsylvania</td><td>6.9</td><td>38</td><td>Massachusetts</td><td>4.3</td></tr>
<tr><td>18</td><td>Rhode Island</td><td>8.0</td><td>38</td><td>Oregon</td><td>4.3</td></tr>
<tr><td>24</td><td>South Carolina</td><td>6.1</td><td>40</td><td>Indiana</td><td>4.2</td></tr>
<tr><td>44</td><td>South Dakota</td><td>0.0</td><td>41</td><td>Virginia</td><td>4.1</td></tr>
<tr><td>29</td><td>Tennessee</td><td>5.3</td><td>42</td><td>Louisiana</td><td>3.9</td></tr>
<tr><td>32</td><td>Texas</td><td>4.9</td><td>43</td><td>Mississippi</td><td>2.2</td></tr>
<tr><td>18</td><td>Utah</td><td>8.0</td><td>44</td><td>North Dakota</td><td>0.0</td></tr>
<tr><td>NA</td><td>Vermont**</td><td>NA</td><td>44</td><td>South Dakota</td><td>0.0</td></tr>
<tr><td>41</td><td>Virginia</td><td>4.1</td><td>NA</td><td>Florida**</td><td>NA</td></tr>
<tr><td>12</td><td>Washington</td><td>9.6</td><td>NA</td><td>Kansas**</td><td>NA</td></tr>
<tr><td>29</td><td>West Virginia</td><td>5.3</td><td>NA</td><td>Kentucky**</td><td>NA</td></tr>
<tr><td>16</td><td>Wisconsin</td><td>8.3</td><td>NA</td><td>New Hampshire**</td><td>NA</td></tr>
<tr><td>25</td><td>Wyoming</td><td>5.9</td><td>NA</td><td>Vermont**</td><td>NA</td></tr>
<tr><td></td><td></td><td></td><td></td><td>District of Columbia</td><td>1.7</td></tr>
</table>

Source: Morgan Quitno Press using data from Federal Bureau of Investigation
   "Crime in the United States 1997" (Uniform Crime Reports, November 22, 1998)
*Of the 14,913 murders in 1997 for which supplemental data were received by the F.B.I. There were an additional
3,296 murders for which the type of murder weapon was not reported to the F.B.I. There were also 991 murders that
were reported as murders by "firearms, type unknown." Murder includes nonnegligent manslaughter.
**Not available.

Rapes in 1997

National Total = 96,122 Rapes*

ALPHA ORDER

RANK	STATE	RAPES	% of USA
25	Alabama	1,396	1.5%
39	Alaska	403	0.4%
24	Arizona	1,492	1.6%
29	Arkansas	1,098	1.1%
1	California	10,189	10.6%
20	Colorado	1,677	1.7%
35	Connecticut	740	0.8%
37	Delaware	476	0.5%
3	Florida	7,599	7.9%
13	Georgia	2,328	2.4%
41	Hawaii	371	0.4%
45	Idaho	350	0.4%
6	Illinois	4,415	4.6%
14	Indiana	1,928	2.0%
36	Iowa	579	0.6%
28	Kansas	1,100	1.1%
27	Kentucky	1,304	1.4%
18	Louisiana	1,799	1.9%
46	Maine	254	0.3%
17	Maryland	1,814	1.9%
21	Massachusetts	1,647	1.7%
4	Michigan	5,070	5.3%
11	Minnesota	2,446	2.5%
30	Mississippi	1,065	1.1%
22	Missouri	1,525	1.6%
47	Montana	171	0.2%
38	Nebraska	406	0.4%
32	Nevada	1,005	1.0%
40	New Hampshire	395	0.4%
19	New Jersey	1,729	1.8%
34	New Mexico	872	0.9%
7	New York	4,075	4.2%
12	North Carolina	2,348	2.4%
48	North Dakota	159	0.2%
5	Ohio	4,566	4.8%
23	Oklahoma	1,517	1.6%
26	Oregon	1,306	1.4%
8	Pennsylvania	3,289	3.4%
42	Rhode Island	363	0.4%
15	South Carolina	1,837	1.9%
43	South Dakota	357	0.4%
9	Tennessee	3,056	3.2%
2	Texas	8,011	8.3%
33	Utah	977	1.0%
49	Vermont	156	0.2%
16	Virginia	1,819	1.9%
10	Washington	2,885	3.0%
44	West Virginia	355	0.4%
31	Wisconsin	1,048	1.1%
50	Wyoming	137	0.1%

RANK ORDER

RANK	STATE	RAPES	% of USA
1	California	10,189	10.6%
2	Texas	8,011	8.3%
3	Florida	7,599	7.9%
4	Michigan	5,070	5.3%
5	Ohio	4,566	4.8%
6	Illinois	4,415	4.6%
7	New York	4,075	4.2%
8	Pennsylvania	3,289	3.4%
9	Tennessee	3,056	3.2%
10	Washington	2,885	3.0%
11	Minnesota	2,446	2.5%
12	North Carolina	2,348	2.4%
13	Georgia	2,328	2.4%
14	Indiana	1,928	2.0%
15	South Carolina	1,837	1.9%
16	Virginia	1,819	1.9%
17	Maryland	1,814	1.9%
18	Louisiana	1,799	1.9%
19	New Jersey	1,729	1.8%
20	Colorado	1,677	1.7%
21	Massachusetts	1,647	1.7%
22	Missouri	1,525	1.6%
23	Oklahoma	1,517	1.6%
24	Arizona	1,492	1.6%
25	Alabama	1,396	1.5%
26	Oregon	1,306	1.4%
27	Kentucky	1,304	1.4%
28	Kansas	1,100	1.1%
29	Arkansas	1,098	1.1%
30	Mississippi	1,065	1.1%
31	Wisconsin	1,048	1.1%
32	Nevada	1,005	1.0%
33	Utah	977	1.0%
34	New Mexico	872	0.9%
35	Connecticut	740	0.8%
36	Iowa	579	0.6%
37	Delaware	476	0.5%
38	Nebraska	406	0.4%
39	Alaska	403	0.4%
40	New Hampshire	395	0.4%
41	Hawaii	371	0.4%
42	Rhode Island	363	0.4%
43	South Dakota	357	0.4%
44	West Virginia	355	0.4%
45	Idaho	350	0.4%
46	Maine	254	0.3%
47	Montana	171	0.2%
48	North Dakota	159	0.2%
49	Vermont	156	0.2%
50	Wyoming	137	0.1%
	District of Columbia	218	0.2%

Source: Federal Bureau of Investigation
"Crime in the United States 1997" (Uniform Crime Reports, November 22, 1998)
Forcible rape is the carnal knowledge of a female forcibly and against her will. Assaults or attempts to commit rape by force or threat of force are included. However, statutory rape without force and other sex offenses are excluded.

Average Time Between Rapes in 1997

National Rate = A Rape Occurs Every 5 Minutes*

ALPHA ORDER

RANK ORDER

RANK	STATE	HOURS.MINUTES
26	Alabama	6.17
12	Alaska	21.44
27	Arizona	5.52
22	Arkansas	7.59
50	California	0.52
31	Colorado	5.13
16	Connecticut	11.50
14	Delaware	18.24
48	Florida	1.09
38	Georgia	3.46
10	Hawaii	23.37
6	Idaho	25.02
45	Illinois	1.59
37	Indiana	4.32
15	Iowa	15.08
23	Kansas	7.58
24	Kentucky	6.43
33	Louisiana	4.52
5	Maine	34.29
34	Maryland	4.50
30	Massachusetts	5.19
47	Michigan	1.44
40	Minnesota	3.35
21	Mississippi	8.14
29	Missouri	5.44
4	Montana	51.14
13	Nebraska	21.35
19	Nevada	8.43
11	New Hampshire	22.11
32	New Jersey	5.04
17	New Mexico	10.03
44	New York	2.09
39	North Carolina	3.44
3	North Dakota	55.05
46	Ohio	1.55
28	Oklahoma	5.46
24	Oregon	6.43
43	Pennsylvania	2.40
9	Rhode Island	24.08
36	South Carolina	4.46
8	South Dakota	24.32
42	Tennessee	2.52
49	Texas	1.05
18	Utah	8.58
2	Vermont	56.09
35	Virginia	4.49
41	Washington	3.02
7	West Virginia	24.41
20	Wisconsin	8.22
1	Wyoming	63.56

RANK	STATE	HOURS.MINUTES
1	Wyoming	63.56
2	Vermont	56.09
3	North Dakota	55.05
4	Montana	51.14
5	Maine	34.29
6	Idaho	25.02
7	West Virginia	24.41
8	South Dakota	24.32
9	Rhode Island	24.08
10	Hawaii	23.37
11	New Hampshire	22.11
12	Alaska	21.44
13	Nebraska	21.35
14	Delaware	18.24
15	Iowa	15.08
16	Connecticut	11.50
17	New Mexico	10.03
18	Utah	8.58
19	Nevada	8.43
20	Wisconsin	8.22
21	Mississippi	8.14
22	Arkansas	7.59
23	Kansas	7.58
24	Kentucky	6.43
24	Oregon	6.43
26	Alabama	6.17
27	Arizona	5.52
28	Oklahoma	5.46
29	Missouri	5.44
30	Massachusetts	5.19
31	Colorado	5.13
32	New Jersey	5.04
33	Louisiana	4.52
34	Maryland	4.50
35	Virginia	4.49
36	South Carolina	4.46
37	Indiana	4.32
38	Georgia	3.46
39	North Carolina	3.44
40	Minnesota	3.35
41	Washington	3.02
42	Tennessee	2.52
43	Pennsylvania	2.40
44	New York	2.09
45	Illinois	1.59
46	Ohio	1.55
47	Michigan	1.44
48	Florida	1.09
49	Texas	1.05
50	California	0.52
	District of Columbia	40.11

Source: Morgan Quitno Press using data from Federal Bureau of Investigation
"Crime in the United States 1997" (Uniform Crime Reports, November 22, 1998)
*Forcible rape is the carnal knowledge of a female forcibly and against her will. Assaults or attempts to commit rape by force or threat of force are included. However, statutory rape without force and other sex offenses are excluded.

Percent Change in Number of Rapes: 1996 to 1997

National Percent Change = 0.1% Decrease*

ALPHA ORDER				RANK ORDER		
RANK	STATE	PERCENT CHANGE		RANK	STATE	PERCENT CHANGE
25	Alabama	(0.1)		1	Rhode Island	26.5
21	Alaska	1.3		2	Tennessee	23.5
10	Arizona	8.0		3	South Dakota	19.0
13	Arkansas	5.0		4	Nevada	17.4
27	California	(0.5)		5	Utah	16.9
44	Colorado	(5.0)		6	Hawaii	13.8
33	Connecticut	(2.0)		7	Idaho	11.8
14	Delaware	4.8		8	Mississippi	8.6
22	Florida	1.2		9	Pennsylvania	8.4
30	Georgia	(1.2)		10	Arizona	8.0
6	Hawaii	13.8		11	Kentucky	6.0
7	Idaho	11.8		12	Minnesota	5.1
39	Illinois	(2.9)		13	Arkansas	5.0
40	Indiana	(3.2)		14	Delaware	4.8
15	Iowa	3.2		15	Iowa	3.2
24	Kansas	0.4		16	Oregon	2.7
11	Kentucky	6.0		17	North Carolina	2.6
26	Louisiana	(0.3)		17	North Dakota	2.6
36	Maine	(2.3)		19	Virginia	2.0
43	Maryland	(4.8)		19	Washington	2.0
45	Massachusetts	(6.8)		21	Alaska	1.3
46	Michigan	(7.2)		22	Florida	1.2
12	Minnesota	5.1		23	South Carolina	0.9
8	Mississippi	8.6		24	Kansas	0.4
38	Missouri	(2.6)		25	Alabama	(0.1)
50	Montana	(28.2)		26	Louisiana	(0.3)
47	Nebraska	(9.2)		27	California	(0.5)
4	Nevada	17.4		28	West Virginia	(0.8)
35	New Hampshire	(2.2)		29	Ohio	(1.1)
48	New Jersey	(12.5)		30	Georgia	(1.2)
49	New Mexico	(19.9)		31	Oklahoma	(1.8)
37	New York	(2.4)		32	Vermont	(1.9)
17	North Carolina	2.6		33	Connecticut	(2.0)
17	North Dakota	2.6		34	Wyoming	(2.1)
29	Ohio	(1.1)		35	New Hampshire	(2.2)
31	Oklahoma	(1.8)		36	Maine	(2.3)
16	Oregon	2.7		37	New York	(2.4)
9	Pennsylvania	8.4		38	Missouri	(2.6)
1	Rhode Island	26.5		39	Illinois	(2.9)
23	South Carolina	0.9		40	Indiana	(3.2)
3	South Dakota	19.0		41	Wisconsin	(3.5)
2	Tennessee	23.5		42	Texas	(4.4)
42	Texas	(4.4)		43	Maryland	(4.8)
5	Utah	16.9		44	Colorado	(5.0)
32	Vermont	(1.9)		45	Massachusetts	(6.8)
19	Virginia	2.0		46	Michigan	(7.2)
19	Washington	2.0		47	Nebraska	(9.2)
28	West Virginia	(0.8)		48	New Jersey	(12.5)
41	Wisconsin	(3.5)		49	New Mexico	(19.9)
34	Wyoming	(2.1)		50	Montana	(28.2)
					District of Columbia	(16.2)

Source: Federal Bureau of Investigation
    "Crime in the United States 1997" (Uniform Crime Reports, November 22, 1998)
*Forcible rape is the carnal knowledge of a female forcibly and against her will. Assaults or attempts to commit rape by force or threat of force are included. However, statutory rape without force and other sex offenses are excluded.

Rape Rate in 1997

National Rate = 35.9 Rapes per 100,000 Population*

ALPHA ORDER

RANK	STATE	RATE
29	Alabama	32.3
1	Alaska	66.2
28	Arizona	32.8
14	Arkansas	43.5
30	California	31.6
15	Colorado	43.1
43	Connecticut	22.6
2	Delaware	65.0
6	Florida	51.9
33	Georgia	31.1
32	Hawaii	31.3
34	Idaho	28.9
22	Illinois	37.1
27	Indiana	32.9
47	Iowa	20.3
16	Kansas	42.4
26	Kentucky	33.4
17	Louisiana	41.3
46	Maine	20.5
24	Maryland	35.6
39	Massachusetts	26.9
6	Michigan	51.9
5	Minnesota	52.2
21	Mississippi	39.0
36	Missouri	28.2
49	Montana	19.5
42	Nebraska	24.5
3	Nevada	59.9
25	New Hampshire	33.7
45	New Jersey	21.5
9	New Mexico	50.4
44	New York	22.5
30	North Carolina	31.6
41	North Dakota	24.8
19	Ohio	40.8
13	Oklahoma	45.7
20	Oregon	40.3
37	Pennsylvania	27.4
23	Rhode Island	36.8
10	South Carolina	48.9
11	South Dakota	48.4
4	Tennessee	56.9
18	Texas	41.2
12	Utah	47.5
40	Vermont	26.5
38	Virginia	27.0
8	Washington	51.4
49	West Virginia	19.5
47	Wisconsin	20.3
35	Wyoming	28.5

RANK ORDER

RANK	STATE	RATE
1	Alaska	66.2
2	Delaware	65.0
3	Nevada	59.9
4	Tennessee	56.9
5	Minnesota	52.2
6	Florida	51.9
6	Michigan	51.9
8	Washington	51.4
9	New Mexico	50.4
10	South Carolina	48.9
11	South Dakota	48.4
12	Utah	47.5
13	Oklahoma	45.7
14	Arkansas	43.5
15	Colorado	43.1
16	Kansas	42.4
17	Louisiana	41.3
18	Texas	41.2
19	Ohio	40.8
20	Oregon	40.3
21	Mississippi	39.0
22	Illinois	37.1
23	Rhode Island	36.8
24	Maryland	35.6
25	New Hampshire	33.7
26	Kentucky	33.4
27	Indiana	32.9
28	Arizona	32.8
29	Alabama	32.3
30	California	31.6
30	North Carolina	31.6
32	Hawaii	31.3
33	Georgia	31.1
34	Idaho	28.9
35	Wyoming	28.5
36	Missouri	28.2
37	Pennsylvania	27.4
38	Virginia	27.0
39	Massachusetts	26.9
40	Vermont	26.5
41	North Dakota	24.8
42	Nebraska	24.5
43	Connecticut	22.6
44	New York	22.5
45	New Jersey	21.5
46	Maine	20.5
47	Iowa	20.3
47	Wisconsin	20.3
49	Montana	19.5
49	West Virginia	19.5
	District of Columbia	41.2

Source: Federal Bureau of Investigation
   "Crime in the United States 1997" (Uniform Crime Reports, November 22, 1998)
*Forcible rape is the carnal knowledge of a female forcibly and against her will. Assaults or attempts to commit rape by force or threat of force are included. However, statutory rape without force and other sex offenses are excluded.

Percent Change in Rape Rate: 1996 to 1997

National Percent Change = 1.1% Decrease*

ALPHA ORDER

RANK	STATE	PERCENT CHANGE
27	Alabama	(1.2)
20	Alaska	0.9
11	Arizona	5.1
13	Arkansas	4.3
29	California	(1.6)
44	Colorado	(6.7)
33	Connecticut	(2.2)
14	Delaware	3.8
22	Florida	(0.4)
36	Georgia	(3.1)
4	Hawaii	13.8
7	Idaho	9.9
39	Illinois	(3.4)
41	Indiana	(3.5)
15	Iowa	3.0
23	Kansas	(0.5)
10	Kentucky	5.4
23	Louisiana	(0.5)
30	Maine	(1.9)
42	Maryland	(5.3)
45	Massachusetts	(7.2)
46	Michigan	(8.9)
12	Minnesota	4.4
9	Mississippi	8.0
39	Missouri	(3.4)
50	Montana	(28.0)
47	Nebraska	(9.6)
6	Nevada	12.2
37	New Hampshire	(3.2)
48	New Jersey	(13.0)
49	New Mexico	(20.6)
33	New York	(2.2)
19	North Carolina	1.0
16	North Dakota	2.9
27	Ohio	(1.2)
35	Oklahoma	(2.4)
17	Oregon	1.5
8	Pennsylvania	8.7
1	Rhode Island	26.9
26	South Carolina	(0.6)
3	South Dakota	18.0
2	Tennessee	22.4
43	Texas	(5.9)
5	Utah	13.6
30	Vermont	(1.9)
18	Virginia	1.1
21	Washington	0.6
23	West Virginia	(0.5)
38	Wisconsin	(3.3)
32	Wyoming	(2.1)

RANK ORDER

RANK	STATE	PERCENT CHANGE
1	Rhode Island	26.9
2	Tennessee	22.4
3	South Dakota	18.0
4	Hawaii	13.8
5	Utah	13.6
6	Nevada	12.2
7	Idaho	9.9
8	Pennsylvania	8.7
9	Mississippi	8.0
10	Kentucky	5.4
11	Arizona	5.1
12	Minnesota	4.4
13	Arkansas	4.3
14	Delaware	3.8
15	Iowa	3.0
16	North Dakota	2.9
17	Oregon	1.5
18	Virginia	1.1
19	North Carolina	1.0
20	Alaska	0.9
21	Washington	0.6
22	Florida	(0.4)
23	Kansas	(0.5)
23	Louisiana	(0.5)
23	West Virginia	(0.5)
26	South Carolina	(0.6)
27	Alabama	(1.2)
27	Ohio	(1.2)
29	California	(1.6)
30	Maine	(1.9)
30	Vermont	(1.9)
32	Wyoming	(2.1)
33	Connecticut	(2.2)
33	New York	(2.2)
35	Oklahoma	(2.4)
36	Georgia	(3.1)
37	New Hampshire	(3.2)
38	Wisconsin	(3.3)
39	Illinois	(3.4)
39	Missouri	(3.4)
41	Indiana	(3.5)
42	Maryland	(5.3)
43	Texas	(5.9)
44	Colorado	(6.7)
45	Massachusetts	(7.2)
46	Michigan	(8.9)
47	Nebraska	(9.6)
48	New Jersey	(13.0)
49	New Mexico	(20.6)
50	Montana	(28.0)
	District of Columbia	(14.0)

Source: Federal Bureau of Investigation
   "Crime in the United States 1997" (Uniform Crime Reports, November 22, 1998)
*Forcible rape is the carnal knowledge of a female forcibly and against her will. Assaults or attempts to commit rape by force or threat of force are included. However, statutory rape without force and other sex offenses are excluded.

Rape Rate per 100,000 Female Population in 1997

National Rate = 70.4 Rapes per 100,000 Females*

ALPHA ORDER

RANK	STATE	RATE
31	Alabama	62.3
1	Alaska	139.4
26	Arizona	65.0
15	Arkansas	84.4
29	California	63.3
14	Colorado	85.5
43	Connecticut	44.0
2	Delaware	126.9
8	Florida	100.9
33	Georgia	60.7
30	Hawaii	62.9
34	Idaho	57.9
22	Illinois	72.6
28	Indiana	64.2
48	Iowa	39.6
16	Kansas	83.5
27	Kentucky	64.9
18	Louisiana	79.8
46	Maine	40.0
24	Maryland	69.4
40	Massachusetts	52.1
7	Michigan	101.2
5	Minnesota	103.1
21	Mississippi	75.1
36	Missouri	54.8
49	Montana	38.8
42	Nebraska	48.1
3	Nevada	122.3
25	New Hampshire	66.4
45	New Jersey	41.7
9	New Mexico	99.4
44	New York	43.4
32	North Carolina	61.6
41	North Dakota	49.5
20	Ohio	79.2
13	Oklahoma	89.6
19	Oregon	79.7
38	Pennsylvania	52.8
23	Rhode Island	70.9
11	South Carolina	94.5
10	South Dakota	95.4
4	Tennessee	110.2
17	Texas	81.5
11	Utah	94.5
39	Vermont	52.2
37	Virginia	52.9
6	Washington	102.5
50	West Virginia	37.8
47	Wisconsin	39.9
35	Wyoming	57.5

RANK ORDER

RANK	STATE	RATE
1	Alaska	139.4
2	Delaware	126.9
3	Nevada	122.3
4	Tennessee	110.2
5	Minnesota	103.1
6	Washington	102.5
7	Michigan	101.2
8	Florida	100.9
9	New Mexico	99.4
10	South Dakota	95.4
11	South Carolina	94.5
11	Utah	94.5
13	Oklahoma	89.6
14	Colorado	85.5
15	Arkansas	84.4
16	Kansas	83.5
17	Texas	81.5
18	Louisiana	79.8
19	Oregon	79.7
20	Ohio	79.2
21	Mississippi	75.1
22	Illinois	72.6
23	Rhode Island	70.9
24	Maryland	69.4
25	New Hampshire	66.4
26	Arizona	65.0
27	Kentucky	64.9
28	Indiana	64.2
29	California	63.3
30	Hawaii	62.9
31	Alabama	62.3
32	North Carolina	61.6
33	Georgia	60.7
34	Idaho	57.9
35	Wyoming	57.5
36	Missouri	54.8
37	Virginia	52.9
38	Pennsylvania	52.8
39	Vermont	52.2
40	Massachusetts	52.1
41	North Dakota	49.5
42	Nebraska	48.1
43	Connecticut	44.0
44	New York	43.4
45	New Jersey	41.7
46	Maine	40.0
47	Wisconsin	39.9
48	Iowa	39.6
49	Montana	38.8
50	West Virginia	37.8
	District of Columbia	77.6

Source: Morgan Quitno Press using data from Federal Bureau of Investigation
    "Crime in the United States 1997" (Uniform Crime Reports, November 22, 1998)
*Forcible rape is the carnal knowledge of a female forcibly and against her will. Assaults or attempts to commit rape by force or threat of force are included. However, statutory rape without force and other sex offenses are excluded.

Robberies in 1997

National Total = 497,950 Robberies*

ALPHA ORDER

RANK	STATE	ROBBERIES	% of USA
19	Alabama	6,931	1.4%
42	Alaska	648	0.1%
18	Arizona	7,547	1.5%
33	Arkansas	2,814	0.6%
1	California	81,468	16.4%
31	Colorado	3,242	0.7%
26	Connecticut	4,999	1.0%
38	Delaware	1,314	0.3%
3	Florida	40,459	8.1%
10	Georgia	15,473	3.1%
37	Hawaii	1,403	0.3%
45	Idaho	237	0.0%
4	Illinois	33,123	6.7%
17	Indiana	7,763	1.6%
35	Iowa	1,593	0.3%
34	Kansas	2,420	0.5%
29	Kentucky	3,546	0.7%
14	Louisiana	10,407	2.1%
44	Maine	257	0.1%
8	Maryland	17,157	3.4%
21	Massachusetts	6,676	1.3%
11	Michigan	14,934	3.0%
23	Minnesota	5,373	1.1%
28	Mississippi	3,741	0.8%
15	Missouri	8,430	1.7%
46	Montana	179	0.0%
39	Nebraska	1,097	0.2%
25	Nevada	5,071	1.0%
43	New Hampshire	274	0.1%
9	New Jersey	16,957	3.4%
32	New Mexico	2,966	0.6%
2	New York	56,094	11.3%
12	North Carolina	12,817	2.6%
50	North Dakota	41	0.0%
7	Ohio	17,755	3.6%
30	Oklahoma	3,446	0.7%
27	Oregon	3,811	0.8%
6	Pennsylvania	18,788	3.8%
41	Rhode Island	707	0.1%
22	South Carolina	6,624	1.3%
47	South Dakota	172	0.0%
13	Tennessee	11,487	2.3%
5	Texas	30,522	6.1%
36	Utah	1,408	0.3%
49	Vermont	79	0.0%
16	Virginia	8,384	1.7%
20	Washington	6,734	1.4%
40	West Virginia	782	0.2%
24	Wisconsin	5,214	1.0%
48	Wyoming	85	0.0%

RANK ORDER

RANK	STATE	ROBBERIES	% of USA
1	California	81,468	16.4%
2	New York	56,094	11.3%
3	Florida	40,459	8.1%
4	Illinois	33,123	6.7%
5	Texas	30,522	6.1%
6	Pennsylvania	18,788	3.8%
7	Ohio	17,755	3.6%
8	Maryland	17,157	3.4%
9	New Jersey	16,957	3.4%
10	Georgia	15,473	3.1%
11	Michigan	14,934	3.0%
12	North Carolina	12,817	2.6%
13	Tennessee	11,487	2.3%
14	Louisiana	10,407	2.1%
15	Missouri	8,430	1.7%
16	Virginia	8,384	1.7%
17	Indiana	7,763	1.6%
18	Arizona	7,547	1.5%
19	Alabama	6,931	1.4%
20	Washington	6,734	1.4%
21	Massachusetts	6,676	1.3%
22	South Carolina	6,624	1.3%
23	Minnesota	5,373	1.1%
24	Wisconsin	5,214	1.0%
25	Nevada	5,071	1.0%
26	Connecticut	4,999	1.0%
27	Oregon	3,811	0.8%
28	Mississippi	3,741	0.8%
29	Kentucky	3,546	0.7%
30	Oklahoma	3,446	0.7%
31	Colorado	3,242	0.7%
32	New Mexico	2,966	0.6%
33	Arkansas	2,814	0.6%
34	Kansas	2,420	0.5%
35	Iowa	1,593	0.3%
36	Utah	1,408	0.3%
37	Hawaii	1,403	0.3%
38	Delaware	1,314	0.3%
39	Nebraska	1,097	0.2%
40	West Virginia	782	0.2%
41	Rhode Island	707	0.1%
42	Alaska	648	0.1%
43	New Hampshire	274	0.1%
44	Maine	257	0.1%
45	Idaho	237	0.0%
46	Montana	179	0.0%
47	South Dakota	172	0.0%
48	Wyoming	85	0.0%
49	Vermont	79	0.0%
50	North Dakota	41	0.0%
	District of Columbia	4,501	0.9%

Source: Federal Bureau of Investigation
"Crime in the United States 1997" (Uniform Crime Reports, November 22, 1998)
*Robbery is the taking or attempting to take anything of value by force or threat of force.

Average Time Between Robberies in 1997

National Rate = A Robbery Occurs Every 1 Minute*

ALPHA ORDER			
RANK	STATE	HOURS.MINUTES	% of USA
32	Alabama	1	0.0%
9	Alaska	13	0.0%
33	Arizona	1	0.0%
18	Arkansas	3	0.0%
50	California	0	0.0%
20	Colorado	2	0.0%
25	Connecticut	1	0.0%
13	Delaware	6	0.0%
48	Florida	0	0.0%
41	Georgia	0	0.0%
14	Hawaii	6	0.0%
6	Idaho	37	0.0%
47	Illinois	0	0.0%
34	Indiana	1	0.0%
16	Iowa	5	0.0%
17	Kansas	3	0.0%
22	Kentucky	2	0.0%
37	Louisiana	1	0.0%
7	Maine	34	0.0%
42	Maryland	0	0.0%
29	Massachusetts	1	0.0%
40	Michigan	0	0.0%
28	Minnesota	1	0.0%
23	Mississippi	2	0.0%
35	Missouri	1	0.0%
5	Montana	49	0.0%
12	Nebraska	8	0.0%
26	Nevada	1	0.0%
8	New Hampshire	32	0.0%
42	New Jersey	0	0.0%
19	New Mexico	3	0.0%
49	New York	0	0.0%
39	North Carolina	0	0.0%
1	North Dakota	213	0.0%
44	Ohio	0	0.0%
21	Oklahoma	2	0.0%
24	Oregon	2	0.0%
45	Pennsylvania	0	0.0%
10	Rhode Island	12	0.0%
29	South Carolina	1	0.0%
4	South Dakota	51	0.0%
38	Tennessee	0	0.0%
46	Texas	0	0.0%
15	Utah	6	0.0%
2	Vermont	111	0.0%
35	Virginia	1	0.0%
31	Washington	1	0.0%
11	West Virginia	11	0.0%
27	Wisconsin	1	0.0%
3	Wyoming	103	0.0%

RANK ORDER			
RANK	STATE	HOURS.MINUTES	% of USA
1	North Dakota	213	0.0%
2	Vermont	111	0.0%
3	Wyoming	103	0.0%
4	South Dakota	51	0.0%
5	Montana	49	0.0%
6	Idaho	37	0.0%
7	Maine	34	0.0%
8	New Hampshire	32	0.0%
9	Alaska	13	0.0%
10	Rhode Island	12	0.0%
11	West Virginia	11	0.0%
12	Nebraska	8	0.0%
13	Delaware	6	0.0%
14	Hawaii	6	0.0%
15	Utah	6	0.0%
16	Iowa	5	0.0%
17	Kansas	3	0.0%
18	Arkansas	3	0.0%
19	New Mexico	3	0.0%
20	Colorado	2	0.0%
21	Oklahoma	2	0.0%
22	Kentucky	2	0.0%
23	Mississippi	2	0.0%
24	Oregon	2	0.0%
25	Connecticut	1	0.0%
26	Nevada	1	0.0%
27	Wisconsin	1	0.0%
28	Minnesota	1	0.0%
29	Massachusetts	1	0.0%
29	South Carolina	1	0.0%
31	Washington	1	0.0%
32	Alabama	1	0.0%
33	Arizona	1	0.0%
34	Indiana	1	0.0%
35	Missouri	1	0.0%
35	Virginia	1	0.0%
37	Louisiana	1	0.0%
38	Tennessee	0	0.0%
39	North Carolina	0	0.0%
40	Michigan	0	0.0%
41	Georgia	0	0.0%
42	Maryland	0	0.0%
42	New Jersey	0	0.0%
44	Ohio	0	0.0%
45	Pennsylvania	0	0.0%
46	Texas	0	0.0%
47	Illinois	0	0.0%
48	Florida	0	0.0%
49	New York	0	0.0%
50	California	0	0.0%
	District of Columbia	2	0.0%

Source: Morgan Quitno Press using data from Federal Bureau of Investigation
"Crime in the United States 1997" (Uniform Crime Reports, November 22, 1998)
*Robbery is the taking or attempting to take anything of value by force or threat of force.

Percent Change in Number of Robberies: 1996 to 1997

National Percent Change = 7.0% Decrease*

ALPHA ORDER				RANK ORDER		
RANK	STATE	PERCENT CHANGE		RANK	STATE	PERCENT CHANGE
25	Alabama	(2.7)		1	South Dakota	24.6
32	Alaska	(8.7)		2	Iowa	23.9
16	Arizona	1.6		3	Indiana	7.1
20	Arkansas	(1.7)		4	North Carolina	6.8
41	California	(13.5)		5	New Mexico	6.6
44	Colorado	(13.7)		6	West Virginia	6.1
34	Connecticut	(10.0)		7	Wisconsin	4.7
17	Delaware	0.8		8	Nebraska	4.3
27	Florida	(2.8)		9	South Carolina	4.1
12	Georgia	2.5		10	Nevada	2.8
38	Hawaii	(12.6)		11	Mississippi	2.6
20	Idaho	(1.7)		12	Georgia	2.5
18	Illinois	0.1		12	Virginia	2.5
3	Indiana	7.1		14	Utah	2.3
2	Iowa	23.9		15	Washington	2.2
23	Kansas	(2.3)		16	Arizona	1.6
25	Kentucky	(2.7)		17	Delaware	0.8
42	Louisiana	(13.5)		18	Illinois	0.1
37	Maine	(12.0)		19	Minnesota	(0.2)
45	Maryland	(14.0)		20	Arkansas	(1.7)
46	Massachusetts	(14.2)		20	Idaho	(1.7)
36	Michigan	(11.7)		22	Oklahoma	(2.1)
19	Minnesota	(0.2)		23	Kansas	(2.3)
11	Mississippi	2.6		24	Oregon	(2.6)
31	Missouri	(7.8)		25	Alabama	(2.7)
49	Montana	(31.4)		25	Kentucky	(2.7)
8	Nebraska	4.3		27	Florida	(2.8)
10	Nevada	2.8		28	Ohio	(3.2)
43	New Hampshire	(13.6)		29	Tennessee	(3.5)
34	New Jersey	(10.0)		30	Texas	(7.0)
5	New Mexico	6.6		31	Missouri	(7.8)
33	New York	(9.3)		32	Alaska	(8.7)
4	North Carolina	6.8		33	New York	(9.3)
50	North Dakota	(42.3)		34	Connecticut	(10.0)
28	Ohio	(3.2)		34	New Jersey	(10.0)
22	Oklahoma	(2.1)		36	Michigan	(11.7)
24	Oregon	(2.6)		37	Maine	(12.0)
48	Pennsylvania	(17.5)		38	Hawaii	(12.6)
46	Rhode Island	(14.2)		39	Vermont	(13.2)
9	South Carolina	4.1		40	Wyoming	(13.3)
1	South Dakota	24.6		41	California	(13.5)
29	Tennessee	(3.5)		42	Louisiana	(13.5)
30	Texas	(7.0)		43	New Hampshire	(13.6)
14	Utah	2.3		44	Colorado	(13.7)
39	Vermont	(13.2)		45	Maryland	(14.0)
12	Virginia	2.5		46	Massachusetts	(14.2)
15	Washington	2.2		46	Rhode Island	(14.2)
6	West Virginia	6.1		48	Pennsylvania	(17.5)
7	Wisconsin	4.7		49	Montana	(31.4)
40	Wyoming	(13.3)		50	North Dakota	(42.3)
					District of Columbia	(30.2)

Source: Federal Bureau of Investigation
   "Crime in the United States 1997" (Uniform Crime Reports, November 22, 1998)
*Robbery is the taking or attempting to take anything of value by force or threat of force.

Robbery Rate in 1997

National Rate = 186.1 Robberies per 100,000 Population*

ALPHA ORDER				RANK ORDER		
RANK	**STATE**	**RATE**		**RANK**	**STATE**	**RATE**
16	Alabama	160.5		1	Maryland	336.8
32	Alaska	106.4		2	New York	309.3
15	Arizona	165.7		3	Nevada	302.4
30	Arkansas	111.5		4	Illinois	278.4
6	California	252.5		5	Florida	276.1
37	Colorado	83.3		6	California	252.5
21	Connecticut	152.9		7	Louisiana	239.1
11	Delaware	179.5		8	Tennessee	214.0
5	Florida	276.1		9	New Jersey	210.6
10	Georgia	206.7		10	Georgia	206.7
27	Hawaii	118.2		11	Delaware	179.5
47	Idaho	19.6		12	South Carolina	176.2
4	Illinois	278.4		13	North Carolina	172.6
24	Indiana	132.4		14	New Mexico	171.4
41	Iowa	55.9		15	Arizona	165.7
35	Kansas	93.3		16	Alabama	160.5
36	Kentucky	90.7		17	Ohio	158.7
7	Louisiana	239.1		18	Texas	157.0
45	Maine	20.7		19	Pennsylvania	156.3
1	Maryland	336.8		20	Missouri	156.1
31	Massachusetts	109.1		21	Connecticut	152.9
22	Michigan	152.8		22	Michigan	152.8
29	Minnesota	114.7		23	Mississippi	137.0
23	Mississippi	137.0		24	Indiana	132.4
20	Missouri	156.1		25	Virginia	124.5
46	Montana	20.4		26	Washington	120.0
40	Nebraska	66.2		27	Hawaii	118.2
3	Nevada	302.4		28	Oregon	117.5
43	New Hampshire	23.4		29	Minnesota	114.7
9	New Jersey	210.6		30	Arkansas	111.5
14	New Mexico	171.4		31	Massachusetts	109.1
2	New York	309.3		32	Alaska	106.4
13	North Carolina	172.6		33	Oklahoma	103.9
50	North Dakota	6.4		34	Wisconsin	100.9
17	Ohio	158.7		35	Kansas	93.3
33	Oklahoma	103.9		36	Kentucky	90.7
28	Oregon	117.5		37	Colorado	83.3
19	Pennsylvania	156.3		38	Rhode Island	71.6
38	Rhode Island	71.6		39	Utah	68.4
12	South Carolina	176.2		40	Nebraska	66.2
44	South Dakota	23.3		41	Iowa	55.9
8	Tennessee	214.0		42	West Virginia	43.1
18	Texas	157.0		43	New Hampshire	23.4
39	Utah	68.4		44	South Dakota	23.3
49	Vermont	13.4		45	Maine	20.7
25	Virginia	124.5		46	Montana	20.4
26	Washington	120.0		47	Idaho	19.6
42	West Virginia	43.1		48	Wyoming	17.7
34	Wisconsin	100.9		49	Vermont	13.4
48	Wyoming	17.7		50	North Dakota	6.4
					District of Columbia	850.9

Source: Federal Bureau of Investigation
  "Crime in the United States 1997" (Uniform Crime Reports, November 22, 1998)
*Robbery is the taking or attempting to take anything of value by force or threat of force.

Percent Change in Robbery Rate: 1996 to 1997

National Percent Change = 7.8% Decrease*

ALPHA ORDER				RANK ORDER		
RANK	STATE	PERCENT CHANGE		RANK	STATE	PERCENT CHANGE
26	Alabama	(3.7)		1	Iowa	23.9
33	Alaska	(9.1)		2	South Dakota	23.3
18	Arizona	(1.3)		3	Indiana	6.7
20	Arkansas	(2.3)		3	West Virginia	6.7
45	California	(14.6)		5	New Mexico	5.5
47	Colorado	(15.2)		6	North Carolina	5.3
34	Connecticut	(9.8)		7	Wisconsin	4.5
14	Delaware	(0.2)		8	Nebraska	3.9
29	Florida	(4.5)		9	South Carolina	2.4
13	Georgia	0.6		10	Mississippi	2.1
37	Hawaii	(12.8)		11	Virginia	1.5
25	Idaho	(3.4)		12	Washington	0.8
15	Illinois	(0.4)		13	Georgia	0.6
3	Indiana	6.7		14	Delaware	(0.2)
1	Iowa	23.9		15	Illinois	(0.4)
22	Kansas	(3.1)		16	Utah	(0.7)
23	Kentucky	(3.3)		17	Minnesota	(0.8)
41	Louisiana	(13.6)		18	Arizona	(1.3)
36	Maine	(11.9)		19	Nevada	(1.7)
43	Maryland	(14.3)		20	Arkansas	(2.3)
45	Massachusetts	(14.6)		21	Oklahoma	(2.5)
40	Michigan	(13.3)		22	Kansas	(3.1)
17	Minnesota	(0.8)		23	Kentucky	(3.3)
10	Mississippi	2.1		23	Ohio	(3.3)
30	Missouri	(8.5)		25	Idaho	(3.4)
49	Montana	(31.3)		26	Alabama	(3.7)
8	Nebraska	3.9		27	Oregon	(3.8)
19	Nevada	(1.7)		28	Tennessee	(4.3)
43	New Hampshire	(14.3)		29	Florida	(4.5)
35	New Jersey	(10.7)		30	Missouri	(8.5)
5	New Mexico	5.5		30	Texas	(8.5)
32	New York	(9.0)		32	New York	(9.0)
6	North Carolina	5.3		33	Alaska	(9.1)
50	North Dakota	(41.8)		34	Connecticut	(9.8)
23	Ohio	(3.3)		35	New Jersey	(10.7)
21	Oklahoma	(2.5)		36	Maine	(11.9)
27	Oregon	(3.8)		37	Hawaii	(12.8)
48	Pennsylvania	(17.3)		38	Vermont	(13.0)
42	Rhode Island	(13.9)		39	Wyoming	(13.2)
9	South Carolina	2.4		40	Michigan	(13.3)
2	South Dakota	23.3		41	Louisiana	(13.6)
28	Tennessee	(4.3)		42	Rhode Island	(13.9)
30	Texas	(8.5)		43	Maryland	(14.3)
16	Utah	(0.7)		43	New Hampshire	(14.3)
38	Vermont	(13.0)		45	California	(14.6)
11	Virginia	1.5		45	Massachusetts	(14.6)
12	Washington	0.8		47	Colorado	(15.2)
3	West Virginia	6.7		48	Pennsylvania	(17.3)
7	Wisconsin	4.5		49	Montana	(31.3)
39	Wyoming	(13.2)		50	North Dakota	(41.8)
					District of Columbia	(28.3)

Source: Federal Bureau of Investigation
"Crime in the United States 1997" (Uniform Crime Reports, November 22, 1998)
*Robbery is the taking or attempting to take anything of value by force or threat of force.

Robberies with Firearms in 1997

National Total = 178,710 Robberies*

ALPHA ORDER

RANK	STATE	ROBBERIES	% of USA
17	Alabama	2,958	1.7%
40	Alaska	249	0.1%
18	Arizona	2,906	1.6%
26	Arkansas	1,373	0.8%
1	California	31,173	17.4%
32	Colorado	880	0.5%
22	Connecticut	1,916	1.1%
37	Delaware	389	0.2%
2	Florida	16,456	9.2%
7	Georgia	7,249	4.1%
42	Hawaii	165	0.1%
43	Idaho	78	0.0%
5	Illinois	11,119	6.2%
16	Indiana	3,292	1.8%
38	Iowa	280	0.2%
33	Kansas	570	0.3%
31	Kentucky	1,054	0.6%
11	Louisiana	6,103	3.4%
44	Maine	44	0.0%
6	Maryland	8,480	4.7%
24	Massachusetts	1,515	0.8%
8	Michigan	6,220	3.5%
28	Minnesota	1,236	0.7%
27	Mississippi	1,294	0.7%
15	Missouri	3,355	1.9%
47	Montana	12	0.0%
35	Nebraska	441	0.2%
36	Nevada	424	0.2%
NA	New Hampshire**	NA	NA
12	New Jersey	5,021	2.8%
29	New Mexico	1,230	0.7%
4	New York	12,459	7.0%
10	North Carolina	6,118	3.4%
48	North Dakota	5	0.0%
13	Ohio	4,983	2.8%
25	Oklahoma	1,496	0.8%
30	Oregon	1,176	0.7%
21	Pennsylvania	1,969	1.1%
41	Rhode Island	170	0.1%
20	South Carolina	2,559	1.4%
45	South Dakota	30	0.0%
9	Tennessee	6,188	3.5%
3	Texas	12,962	7.3%
34	Utah	449	0.3%
NA	Vermont**	NA	NA
14	Virginia	3,882	2.2%
23	Washington	1,887	1.1%
39	West Virginia	266	0.1%
19	Wisconsin	2,764	1.5%
46	Wyoming	20	0.0%

RANK ORDER

RANK	STATE	ROBBERIES	% of USA
1	California	31,173	17.4%
2	Florida	16,456	9.2%
3	Texas	12,962	7.3%
4	New York	12,459	7.0%
5	Illinois	11,119	6.2%
6	Maryland	8,480	4.7%
7	Georgia	7,249	4.1%
8	Michigan	6,220	3.5%
9	Tennessee	6,188	3.5%
10	North Carolina	6,118	3.4%
11	Louisiana	6,103	3.4%
12	New Jersey	5,021	2.8%
13	Ohio	4,983	2.8%
14	Virginia	3,882	2.2%
15	Missouri	3,355	1.9%
16	Indiana	3,292	1.8%
17	Alabama	2,958	1.7%
18	Arizona	2,906	1.6%
19	Wisconsin	2,764	1.5%
20	South Carolina	2,559	1.4%
21	Pennsylvania	1,969	1.1%
22	Connecticut	1,916	1.1%
23	Washington	1,887	1.1%
24	Massachusetts	1,515	0.8%
25	Oklahoma	1,496	0.8%
26	Arkansas	1,373	0.8%
27	Mississippi	1,294	0.7%
28	Minnesota	1,236	0.7%
29	New Mexico	1,230	0.7%
30	Oregon	1,176	0.7%
31	Kentucky	1,054	0.6%
32	Colorado	880	0.5%
33	Kansas	570	0.3%
34	Utah	449	0.3%
35	Nebraska	441	0.2%
36	Nevada	424	0.2%
37	Delaware	389	0.2%
38	Iowa	280	0.2%
39	West Virginia	266	0.1%
40	Alaska	249	0.1%
41	Rhode Island	170	0.1%
42	Hawaii	165	0.1%
43	Idaho	78	0.0%
44	Maine	44	0.0%
45	South Dakota	30	0.0%
46	Wyoming	20	0.0%
47	Montana	12	0.0%
48	North Dakota	5	0.0%
NA	New Hampshire**	NA	NA
NA	Vermont**	NA	NA
	District of Columbia	1,845	1.0%

Source: Federal Bureau of Investigation
  "Crime in the United States 1997" (Uniform Crime Reports, November 22, 1998)
*Of the 450,126 robberies in 1997 for which supplemental data were received by the F.B.I. There were an additional 47,824 robberies for which the type of weapon was not reported to the F.B.I. Robbery is the taking or attempting to take anything of value by force or threat of force.
**Not available.

Robbery Rate with Firearms in 1997

National Rate = 82.8 Robberies per 100,000 Population*

ALPHA ORDER				RANK ORDER		
RANK	STATE	RATE		RANK	STATE	RATE
15	Alabama	81.6		1	Illinois*	332.1
29	Alaska	47.2		2	Tennessee	188.6
20	Arizona	72.6		3	Louisiana	169.4
26	Arkansas	58.3		4	Maryland	166.6
12	California	96.8		5	Georgia	147.2
35	Colorado	31.8		6	Kentucky	135.1
22	Connecticut	69.2		7	Delaware	130.1
7	Delaware	130.1		7	Kansas	130.1
10	Florida	112.5		9	Mississippi	113.8
5	Georgia	147.2		10	Florida	112.5
41	Hawaii	14.4		11	New Mexico	103.3
44	Idaho	6.5		12	California	96.8
1	Illinois*	332.1		13	Indiana	89.4
13	Indiana	89.4		14	North Carolina	83.5
42	Iowa	12.0		15	Alabama	81.6
7	Kansas	130.1		16	New York	79.0
6	Kentucky	135.1		17	Michigan	78.8
3	Louisiana	169.4		18	Missouri	78.4
46	Maine	3.6		19	Ohio	73.7
4	Maryland	166.6		20	Arizona	72.6
36	Massachusetts	30.4		21	South Carolina	72.3
17	Michigan	78.8		22	Connecticut	69.2
31	Minnesota	40.7		23	Texas	66.8
9	Mississippi	113.8		24	New Jersey	62.3
18	Missouri	78.4		25	Virginia	58.8
47	Montana	3.5		26	Arkansas	58.3
37	Nebraska	29.1		27	Wisconsin	57.9
28	Nevada	52.5		28	Nevada	52.5
NA	New Hampshire**	NA		29	Alaska	47.2
24	New Jersey	62.3		30	Oklahoma	45.1
11	New Mexico	103.3		31	Minnesota	40.7
16	New York	79.0		32	Oregon	39.8
14	North Carolina	83.5		33	Washington	36.7
48	North Dakota	0.9		34	Pennsylvania	32.4
19	Ohio	73.7		35	Colorado	31.8
30	Oklahoma	45.1		36	Massachusetts	30.4
32	Oregon	39.8		37	Nebraska	29.1
34	Pennsylvania	32.4		38	Utah	23.3
39	Rhode Island	17.2		39	Rhode Island	17.2
21	South Carolina	72.3		40	West Virginia	14.6
43	South Dakota	9.2		41	Hawaii	14.4
2	Tennessee	188.6		42	Iowa	12.0
23	Texas	66.8		43	South Dakota	9.2
38	Utah	23.3		44	Idaho	6.5
NA	Vermont**	NA		45	Wyoming	4.3
25	Virginia	58.8		46	Maine	3.6
33	Washington	36.7		47	Montana	3.5
40	West Virginia	14.6		48	North Dakota	0.9
27	Wisconsin	57.9		NA	New Hampshire**	NA
45	Wyoming	4.3		NA	Vermont**	NA
					District of Columbia	348.8

Source: Morgan Quitno Press using data from Federal Bureau of Investigation
"Crime in the United States 1997" (Uniform Crime Reports, November 22, 1998)
Based only on population of reporting jurisdictions. Robbery is the taking or attempting to take anything of value by force or threat of force. National rate reflects only those robberies for which the type of weapon was known and reported. Illinois' rate is especially affected by number of nonreporting jurisdictions.
**Not available.*

Percent of Robberies Involving Firearms in 1997

National Percent = 39.7% of Robberies*

ALPHA ORDER				RANK ORDER		
RANK	STATE	PERCENT		RANK	STATE	PERCENT
11	Alabama	47.4		1	Louisiana	62.7
18	Alaska	42.1		2	Tennessee	61.2
24	Arizona	40.8		3	Georgia	54.4
8	Arkansas	49.8		4	Wisconsin	53.3
28	California	38.3		5	Mississippi	53.1
31	Colorado	35.1		6	Indiana	51.6
28	Connecticut	38.3		7	New Mexico	51.0
12	Delaware	46.8		8	Arkansas	49.8
24	Florida	40.8		9	Maryland	49.5
3	Georgia	54.4		10	North Carolina	48.2
48	Hawaii	11.8		11	Alabama	47.4
34	Idaho	33.2		12	Delaware	46.8
23	Illinois	41.1		13	Virginia	46.4
6	Indiana	51.6		14	Michigan	46.0
40	Iowa	26.0		15	Oklahoma	43.4
20	Kansas	41.5		16	Kentucky	43.0
16	Kentucky	43.0		17	Texas	42.5
1	Louisiana	62.7		18	Alaska	42.1
46	Maine	17.2		18	South Carolina	42.1
9	Maryland	49.5		20	Kansas	41.5
42	Massachusetts	23.9		21	Missouri	41.2
14	Michigan	46.0		21	Nebraska	41.2
39	Minnesota	27.1		23	Illinois	41.1
5	Mississippi	53.1		24	Arizona	40.8
21	Missouri	41.2		24	Florida	40.8
27	Montana	38.7		26	Ohio	39.1
21	Nebraska	41.2		27	Montana	38.7
36	Nevada	31.5		28	California	38.3
NA	New Hampshire**	NA		28	Connecticut	38.3
38	New Jersey	29.6		30	Pennsylvania	35.2
7	New Mexico	51.0		31	Colorado	35.1
44	New York	23.1		32	West Virginia	34.0
10	North Carolina	48.2		33	Utah	33.4
47	North Dakota	12.5		34	Idaho	33.2
26	Ohio	39.1		35	Oregon	32.3
15	Oklahoma	43.4		36	Nevada	31.5
35	Oregon	32.3		37	Washington	30.3
30	Pennsylvania	35.2		38	New Jersey	29.6
41	Rhode Island	24.0		39	Minnesota	27.1
18	South Carolina	42.1		40	Iowa	26.0
45	South Dakota	21.6		41	Rhode Island	24.0
2	Tennessee	61.2		42	Massachusetts	23.9
17	Texas	42.5		43	Wyoming	23.8
33	Utah	33.4		44	New York	23.1
NA	Vermont**	NA		45	South Dakota	21.6
13	Virginia	46.4		46	Maine	17.2
37	Washington	30.3		47	North Dakota	12.5
32	West Virginia	34.0		48	Hawaii	11.8
4	Wisconsin	53.3		NA	New Hampshire**	NA
43	Wyoming	23.8		NA	Vermont**	NA
					District of Columbia	41.0

Source: Morgan Quitno Press using data from Federal Bureau of Investigation
  "Crime in the United States 1997" (Uniform Crime Reports, November 22, 1998)
*Of the 450,126 robberies in 1997 for which supplemental data were received by the F.B.I. There were an
additional 47,824 robberies for which the type of weapon was not reported to the F.B.I. Robbery is the taking or
attempting to take anything of value by force or threat of force.
**Not available.

Robberies with Knives or Cutting Instruments in 1997

National Total = 38,354 Robberies*

ALPHA ORDER

RANK	STATE	ROBBERIES	% of USA
19	Alabama	496	1.3%
41	Alaska	72	0.2%
11	Arizona	710	1.9%
30	Arkansas	207	0.5%
1	California	7,786	20.3%
29	Colorado	237	0.6%
22	Connecticut	439	1.1%
42	Delaware	53	0.1%
3	Florida	2,937	7.7%
16	Georgia	570	1.5%
36	Hawaii	109	0.3%
44	Idaho	27	0.1%
4	Illinois	2,828	7.4%
21	Indiana	443	1.2%
35	Iowa	126	0.3%
37	Kansas	104	0.3%
31	Kentucky	165	0.4%
20	Louisiana	457	1.2%
43	Maine	31	0.1%
7	Maryland	1,364	3.6%
8	Massachusetts	1,151	3.0%
10	Michigan	814	2.1%
24	Minnesota	379	1.0%
33	Mississippi	139	0.4%
14	Missouri	579	1.5%
48	Montana	5	0.0%
38	Nebraska	86	0.2%
32	Nevada	164	0.4%
NA	New Hampshire**	NA	NA
6	New Jersey	1,613	4.2%
27	New Mexico	301	0.8%
2	New York	5,398	14.1%
9	North Carolina	891	2.3%
47	North Dakota	7	0.0%
12	Ohio	675	1.8%
28	Oklahoma	250	0.7%
26	Oregon	333	0.9%
23	Pennsylvania	398	1.0%
39	Rhode Island	82	0.2%
17	South Carolina	543	1.4%
45	South Dakota	26	0.1%
13	Tennessee	655	1.7%
5	Texas	2,724	7.1%
33	Utah	139	0.4%
NA	Vermont**	NA	NA
18	Virginia	510	1.3%
15	Washington	578	1.5%
40	West Virginia	76	0.2%
25	Wisconsin	356	0.9%
46	Wyoming	17	0.0%

RANK ORDER

RANK	STATE	ROBBERIES	% of USA
1	California	7,786	20.3%
2	New York	5,398	14.1%
3	Florida	2,937	7.7%
4	Illinois	2,828	7.4%
5	Texas	2,724	7.1%
6	New Jersey	1,613	4.2%
7	Maryland	1,364	3.6%
8	Massachusetts	1,151	3.0%
9	North Carolina	891	2.3%
10	Michigan	814	2.1%
11	Arizona	710	1.9%
12	Ohio	675	1.8%
13	Tennessee	655	1.7%
14	Missouri	579	1.5%
15	Washington	578	1.5%
16	Georgia	570	1.5%
17	South Carolina	543	1.4%
18	Virginia	510	1.3%
19	Alabama	496	1.3%
20	Louisiana	457	1.2%
21	Indiana	443	1.2%
22	Connecticut	439	1.1%
23	Pennsylvania	398	1.0%
24	Minnesota	379	1.0%
25	Wisconsin	356	0.9%
26	Oregon	333	0.9%
27	New Mexico	301	0.8%
28	Oklahoma	250	0.7%
29	Colorado	237	0.6%
30	Arkansas	207	0.5%
31	Kentucky	165	0.4%
32	Nevada	164	0.4%
33	Mississippi	139	0.4%
33	Utah	139	0.4%
35	Iowa	126	0.3%
36	Hawaii	109	0.3%
37	Kansas	104	0.3%
38	Nebraska	86	0.2%
39	Rhode Island	82	0.2%
40	West Virginia	76	0.2%
41	Alaska	72	0.2%
42	Delaware	53	0.1%
43	Maine	31	0.1%
44	Idaho	27	0.1%
45	South Dakota	26	0.1%
46	Wyoming	17	0.0%
47	North Dakota	7	0.0%
48	Montana	5	0.0%
NA	New Hampshire**	NA	NA
NA	Vermont**	NA	NA
	District of Columbia	304	0.8%

Source: Federal Bureau of Investigation
"Crime in the United States 1997" (Uniform Crime Reports, November 22, 1998)
*Of the 450,126 robberies in 1997 for which supplemental data were received by the F.B.I. There were an additional 47,824 robberies for which the type of weapon was not reported to the F.B.I. Robbery is the taking or attempting to take anything of value by force or threat of force.
**Not available.

Percent of Robberies Involving Knives or Cutting Instruments in 1997

National Percent = 8.5% of Robberies*

<table>
<tr><td colspan="3">ALPHA ORDER</td><td colspan="3">RANK ORDER</td></tr>
<tr><th>RANK</th><th>STATE</th><th>PERCENT</th><th>RANK</th><th>STATE</th><th>PERCENT</th></tr>
<tr><td>29</td><td>Alabama</td><td>7.9</td><td>1</td><td>Wyoming</td><td>20.2</td></tr>
<tr><td>7</td><td>Alaska</td><td>12.2</td><td>2</td><td>South Dakota</td><td>18.7</td></tr>
<tr><td>15</td><td>Arizona</td><td>10.0</td><td>3</td><td>Massachusetts</td><td>18.2</td></tr>
<tr><td>32</td><td>Arkansas</td><td>7.5</td><td>4</td><td>North Dakota</td><td>17.5</td></tr>
<tr><td>18</td><td>California</td><td>9.6</td><td>5</td><td>Montana</td><td>16.1</td></tr>
<tr><td>19</td><td>Colorado</td><td>9.5</td><td>6</td><td>New Mexico</td><td>12.5</td></tr>
<tr><td>25</td><td>Connecticut</td><td>8.8</td><td>7</td><td>Alaska</td><td>12.2</td></tr>
<tr><td>42</td><td>Delaware</td><td>6.4</td><td>7</td><td>Nevada</td><td>12.2</td></tr>
<tr><td>33</td><td>Florida</td><td>7.3</td><td>9</td><td>Maine</td><td>12.1</td></tr>
<tr><td>48</td><td>Georgia</td><td>4.3</td><td>10</td><td>Iowa</td><td>11.7</td></tr>
<tr><td>30</td><td>Hawaii</td><td>7.8</td><td>11</td><td>Rhode Island</td><td>11.6</td></tr>
<tr><td>12</td><td>Idaho</td><td>11.5</td><td>12</td><td>Idaho</td><td>11.5</td></tr>
<tr><td>13</td><td>Illinois</td><td>10.5</td><td>13</td><td>Illinois</td><td>10.5</td></tr>
<tr><td>38</td><td>Indiana</td><td>6.9</td><td>14</td><td>Utah</td><td>10.3</td></tr>
<tr><td>10</td><td>Iowa</td><td>11.7</td><td>15</td><td>Arizona</td><td>10.0</td></tr>
<tr><td>31</td><td>Kansas</td><td>7.6</td><td>15</td><td>New York</td><td>10.0</td></tr>
<tr><td>40</td><td>Kentucky</td><td>6.7</td><td>17</td><td>West Virginia</td><td>9.7</td></tr>
<tr><td>47</td><td>Louisiana</td><td>4.7</td><td>18</td><td>California</td><td>9.6</td></tr>
<tr><td>9</td><td>Maine</td><td>12.1</td><td>19</td><td>Colorado</td><td>9.5</td></tr>
<tr><td>27</td><td>Maryland</td><td>8.0</td><td>19</td><td>New Jersey</td><td>9.5</td></tr>
<tr><td>3</td><td>Massachusetts</td><td>18.2</td><td>21</td><td>Washington</td><td>9.3</td></tr>
<tr><td>44</td><td>Michigan</td><td>6.0</td><td>22</td><td>Oregon</td><td>9.1</td></tr>
<tr><td>26</td><td>Minnesota</td><td>8.3</td><td>23</td><td>South Carolina</td><td>8.9</td></tr>
<tr><td>45</td><td>Mississippi</td><td>5.7</td><td>23</td><td>Texas</td><td>8.9</td></tr>
<tr><td>35</td><td>Missouri</td><td>7.1</td><td>25</td><td>Connecticut</td><td>8.8</td></tr>
<tr><td>5</td><td>Montana</td><td>16.1</td><td>26</td><td>Minnesota</td><td>8.3</td></tr>
<tr><td>27</td><td>Nebraska</td><td>8.0</td><td>27</td><td>Maryland</td><td>8.0</td></tr>
<tr><td>7</td><td>Nevada</td><td>12.2</td><td>27</td><td>Nebraska</td><td>8.0</td></tr>
<tr><td>NA</td><td>New Hampshire**</td><td>NA</td><td>29</td><td>Alabama</td><td>7.9</td></tr>
<tr><td>19</td><td>New Jersey</td><td>9.5</td><td>30</td><td>Hawaii</td><td>7.8</td></tr>
<tr><td>6</td><td>New Mexico</td><td>12.5</td><td>31</td><td>Kansas</td><td>7.6</td></tr>
<tr><td>15</td><td>New York</td><td>10.0</td><td>32</td><td>Arkansas</td><td>7.5</td></tr>
<tr><td>37</td><td>North Carolina</td><td>7.0</td><td>33</td><td>Florida</td><td>7.3</td></tr>
<tr><td>4</td><td>North Dakota</td><td>17.5</td><td>33</td><td>Oklahoma</td><td>7.3</td></tr>
<tr><td>46</td><td>Ohio</td><td>5.3</td><td>35</td><td>Missouri</td><td>7.1</td></tr>
<tr><td>33</td><td>Oklahoma</td><td>7.3</td><td>35</td><td>Pennsylvania</td><td>7.1</td></tr>
<tr><td>22</td><td>Oregon</td><td>9.1</td><td>37</td><td>North Carolina</td><td>7.0</td></tr>
<tr><td>35</td><td>Pennsylvania</td><td>7.1</td><td>38</td><td>Indiana</td><td>6.9</td></tr>
<tr><td>11</td><td>Rhode Island</td><td>11.6</td><td>38</td><td>Wisconsin</td><td>6.9</td></tr>
<tr><td>23</td><td>South Carolina</td><td>8.9</td><td>40</td><td>Kentucky</td><td>6.7</td></tr>
<tr><td>2</td><td>South Dakota</td><td>18.7</td><td>41</td><td>Tennessee</td><td>6.5</td></tr>
<tr><td>41</td><td>Tennessee</td><td>6.5</td><td>42</td><td>Delaware</td><td>6.4</td></tr>
<tr><td>23</td><td>Texas</td><td>8.9</td><td>43</td><td>Virginia</td><td>6.1</td></tr>
<tr><td>14</td><td>Utah</td><td>10.3</td><td>44</td><td>Michigan</td><td>6.0</td></tr>
<tr><td>NA</td><td>Vermont**</td><td>NA</td><td>45</td><td>Mississippi</td><td>5.7</td></tr>
<tr><td>43</td><td>Virginia</td><td>6.1</td><td>46</td><td>Ohio</td><td>5.3</td></tr>
<tr><td>21</td><td>Washington</td><td>9.3</td><td>47</td><td>Louisiana</td><td>4.7</td></tr>
<tr><td>17</td><td>West Virginia</td><td>9.7</td><td>48</td><td>Georgia</td><td>4.3</td></tr>
<tr><td>38</td><td>Wisconsin</td><td>6.9</td><td>NA</td><td>New Hampshire**</td><td>NA</td></tr>
<tr><td>1</td><td>Wyoming</td><td>20.2</td><td>NA</td><td>Vermont**</td><td>NA</td></tr>
<tr><td></td><td></td><td></td><td></td><td>District of Columbia</td><td>6.8</td></tr>
</table>

Source: Morgan Quitno Press using data from Federal Bureau of Investigation
   "Crime in the United States 1997" (Uniform Crime Reports, November 22, 1998)
*Of the 450,126 robberies in 1997 for which supplemental data were received by the F.B.I. There were an additional 47,824 robberies for which the type of weapon was not reported to the F.B.I. Robbery is the taking or attempting to take anything of value by force or threat of force.
**Not available.

Robberies with Blunt Objects and Other Dangerous Weapons in 1997

National Total = 60,168 Robberies*

ALPHA ORDER

RANK	STATE	ROBBERIES	% of USA
19	Alabama	520	0.9%
42	Alaska	29	0.0%
17	Arizona	672	1.1%
30	Arkansas	197	0.3%
2	California	7,318	12.2%
22	Colorado	383	0.6%
21	Connecticut	457	0.8%
39	Delaware	57	0.1%
3	Florida	3,874	6.4%
7	Georgia	1,734	2.9%
41	Hawaii	35	0.1%
43	Idaho	28	0.0%
4	Illinois	3,540	5.9%
23	Indiana	376	0.6%
34	Iowa	158	0.3%
32	Kansas	166	0.3%
35	Kentucky	132	0.2%
18	Louisiana	596	1.0%
43	Maine	28	0.0%
10	Maryland	1,279	2.1%
13	Massachusetts	847	1.4%
6	Michigan	2,734	4.5%
24	Minnesota	359	0.6%
28	Mississippi	233	0.4%
16	Missouri	719	1.2%
48	Montana	3	0.0%
37	Nebraska	74	0.1%
36	Nevada	94	0.2%
NA	New Hampshire**	NA	NA
8	New Jersey	1,401	2.3%
33	New Mexico	162	0.3%
1	New York	21,420	35.6%
9	North Carolina	1,307	2.2%
46	North Dakota	16	0.0%
12	Ohio	996	1.7%
29	Oklahoma	224	0.4%
27	Oregon	278	0.5%
26	Pennsylvania	308	0.5%
40	Rhode Island	55	0.1%
15	South Carolina	766	1.3%
45	South Dakota	17	0.0%
14	Tennessee	770	1.3%
5	Texas	3,285	5.5%
31	Utah	169	0.3%
NA	Vermont**	NA	NA
11	Virginia	1,235	2.1%
20	Washington	509	0.8%
38	West Virginia	66	0.1%
25	Wisconsin	323	0.5%
47	Wyoming	10	0.0%

RANK ORDER

RANK	STATE	ROBBERIES	% of USA
1	New York	21,420	35.6%
2	California	7,318	12.2%
3	Florida	3,874	6.4%
4	Illinois	3,540	5.9%
5	Texas	3,285	5.5%
6	Michigan	2,734	4.5%
7	Georgia	1,734	2.9%
8	New Jersey	1,401	2.3%
9	North Carolina	1,307	2.2%
10	Maryland	1,279	2.1%
11	Virginia	1,235	2.1%
12	Ohio	996	1.7%
13	Massachusetts	847	1.4%
14	Tennessee	770	1.3%
15	South Carolina	766	1.3%
16	Missouri	719	1.2%
17	Arizona	672	1.1%
18	Louisiana	596	1.0%
19	Alabama	520	0.9%
20	Washington	509	0.8%
21	Connecticut	457	0.8%
22	Colorado	383	0.6%
23	Indiana	376	0.6%
24	Minnesota	359	0.6%
25	Wisconsin	323	0.5%
26	Pennsylvania	308	0.5%
27	Oregon	278	0.5%
28	Mississippi	233	0.4%
29	Oklahoma	224	0.4%
30	Arkansas	197	0.3%
31	Utah	169	0.3%
32	Kansas	166	0.3%
33	New Mexico	162	0.3%
34	Iowa	158	0.3%
35	Kentucky	132	0.2%
36	Nevada	94	0.2%
37	Nebraska	74	0.1%
38	West Virginia	66	0.1%
39	Delaware	57	0.1%
40	Rhode Island	55	0.1%
41	Hawaii	35	0.1%
42	Alaska	29	0.0%
43	Idaho	28	0.0%
43	Maine	28	0.0%
45	South Dakota	17	0.0%
46	North Dakota	16	0.0%
47	Wyoming	10	0.0%
48	Montana	3	0.0%
NA	New Hampshire**	NA	NA
NA	Vermont**	NA	NA
	District of Columbia	209	0.3%

Source: Federal Bureau of Investigation
"Crime in the United States 1997" (Uniform Crime Reports, November 22, 1998)
*Of the 450,126 robberies in 1997 for which supplemental data were received by the F.B.I. There were an additional 47,824 robberies for which the type of weapon was not reported to the F.B.I. Robbery is the taking or attempting to take anything of value by force or threat of force.
**Not available.

Percent of Robberies Involving Blunt Objects
And Other Dangerous Weapons in 1997
National Percent = 13.4% of Robberies*

<table>
<tr><td colspan="3">ALPHA ORDER</td><td colspan="3">RANK ORDER</td></tr>
<tr><td>RANK</td><td>STATE</td><td>PERCENT</td><td>RANK</td><td>STATE</td><td>PERCENT</td></tr>
<tr><td>27</td><td>Alabama</td><td>8.3</td><td>1</td><td>North Dakota</td><td>40.0</td></tr>
<tr><td>47</td><td>Alaska</td><td>4.9</td><td>2</td><td>New York</td><td>39.6</td></tr>
<tr><td>22</td><td>Arizona</td><td>9.4</td><td>3</td><td>Michigan</td><td>20.2</td></tr>
<tr><td>36</td><td>Arkansas</td><td>7.1</td><td>4</td><td>Colorado</td><td>15.3</td></tr>
<tr><td>24</td><td>California</td><td>9.0</td><td>5</td><td>Virginia</td><td>14.8</td></tr>
<tr><td>4</td><td>Colorado</td><td>15.3</td><td>6</td><td>Iowa</td><td>14.7</td></tr>
<tr><td>23</td><td>Connecticut</td><td>9.1</td><td>7</td><td>Massachusetts</td><td>13.4</td></tr>
<tr><td>38</td><td>Delaware</td><td>6.9</td><td>8</td><td>Illinois</td><td>13.1</td></tr>
<tr><td>20</td><td>Florida</td><td>9.6</td><td>9</td><td>Georgia</td><td>13.0</td></tr>
<tr><td>9</td><td>Georgia</td><td>13.0</td><td>10</td><td>South Carolina</td><td>12.6</td></tr>
<tr><td>48</td><td>Hawaii</td><td>2.5</td><td>10</td><td>Utah</td><td>12.6</td></tr>
<tr><td>14</td><td>Idaho</td><td>11.9</td><td>12</td><td>South Dakota</td><td>12.2</td></tr>
<tr><td>8</td><td>Illinois</td><td>13.1</td><td>13</td><td>Kansas</td><td>12.1</td></tr>
<tr><td>44</td><td>Indiana</td><td>5.9</td><td>14</td><td>Idaho</td><td>11.9</td></tr>
<tr><td>6</td><td>Iowa</td><td>14.7</td><td>14</td><td>Wyoming</td><td>11.9</td></tr>
<tr><td>13</td><td>Kansas</td><td>12.1</td><td>16</td><td>Maine</td><td>10.9</td></tr>
<tr><td>46</td><td>Kentucky</td><td>5.4</td><td>17</td><td>Texas</td><td>10.8</td></tr>
<tr><td>43</td><td>Louisiana</td><td>6.1</td><td>18</td><td>North Carolina</td><td>10.3</td></tr>
<tr><td>16</td><td>Maine</td><td>10.9</td><td>19</td><td>Montana</td><td>9.7</td></tr>
<tr><td>35</td><td>Maryland</td><td>7.5</td><td>20</td><td>Florida</td><td>9.6</td></tr>
<tr><td>7</td><td>Massachusetts</td><td>13.4</td><td>20</td><td>Mississippi</td><td>9.6</td></tr>
<tr><td>3</td><td>Michigan</td><td>20.2</td><td>22</td><td>Arizona</td><td>9.4</td></tr>
<tr><td>30</td><td>Minnesota</td><td>7.9</td><td>23</td><td>Connecticut</td><td>9.1</td></tr>
<tr><td>20</td><td>Mississippi</td><td>9.6</td><td>24</td><td>California</td><td>9.0</td></tr>
<tr><td>25</td><td>Missouri</td><td>8.8</td><td>25</td><td>Missouri</td><td>8.8</td></tr>
<tr><td>19</td><td>Montana</td><td>9.7</td><td>26</td><td>West Virginia</td><td>8.4</td></tr>
<tr><td>38</td><td>Nebraska</td><td>6.9</td><td>27</td><td>Alabama</td><td>8.3</td></tr>
<tr><td>37</td><td>Nevada</td><td>7.0</td><td>27</td><td>New Jersey</td><td>8.3</td></tr>
<tr><td>NA</td><td>New Hampshire**</td><td>NA</td><td>29</td><td>Washington</td><td>8.2</td></tr>
<tr><td>27</td><td>New Jersey</td><td>8.3</td><td>30</td><td>Minnesota</td><td>7.9</td></tr>
<tr><td>40</td><td>New Mexico</td><td>6.7</td><td>31</td><td>Ohio</td><td>7.8</td></tr>
<tr><td>2</td><td>New York</td><td>39.6</td><td>31</td><td>Rhode Island</td><td>7.8</td></tr>
<tr><td>18</td><td>North Carolina</td><td>10.3</td><td>33</td><td>Oregon</td><td>7.6</td></tr>
<tr><td>1</td><td>North Dakota</td><td>40.0</td><td>33</td><td>Tennessee</td><td>7.6</td></tr>
<tr><td>31</td><td>Ohio</td><td>7.8</td><td>35</td><td>Maryland</td><td>7.5</td></tr>
<tr><td>41</td><td>Oklahoma</td><td>6.5</td><td>36</td><td>Arkansas</td><td>7.1</td></tr>
<tr><td>33</td><td>Oregon</td><td>7.6</td><td>37</td><td>Nevada</td><td>7.0</td></tr>
<tr><td>45</td><td>Pennsylvania</td><td>5.5</td><td>38</td><td>Delaware</td><td>6.9</td></tr>
<tr><td>31</td><td>Rhode Island</td><td>7.8</td><td>38</td><td>Nebraska</td><td>6.9</td></tr>
<tr><td>10</td><td>South Carolina</td><td>12.6</td><td>40</td><td>New Mexico</td><td>6.7</td></tr>
<tr><td>12</td><td>South Dakota</td><td>12.2</td><td>41</td><td>Oklahoma</td><td>6.5</td></tr>
<tr><td>33</td><td>Tennessee</td><td>7.6</td><td>42</td><td>Wisconsin</td><td>6.2</td></tr>
<tr><td>17</td><td>Texas</td><td>10.8</td><td>43</td><td>Louisiana</td><td>6.1</td></tr>
<tr><td>10</td><td>Utah</td><td>12.6</td><td>44</td><td>Indiana</td><td>5.9</td></tr>
<tr><td>NA</td><td>Vermont**</td><td>NA</td><td>45</td><td>Pennsylvania</td><td>5.5</td></tr>
<tr><td>5</td><td>Virginia</td><td>14.8</td><td>46</td><td>Kentucky</td><td>5.4</td></tr>
<tr><td>29</td><td>Washington</td><td>8.2</td><td>47</td><td>Alaska</td><td>4.9</td></tr>
<tr><td>26</td><td>West Virginia</td><td>8.4</td><td>48</td><td>Hawaii</td><td>2.5</td></tr>
<tr><td>42</td><td>Wisconsin</td><td>6.2</td><td>NA</td><td>New Hampshire**</td><td>NA</td></tr>
<tr><td>14</td><td>Wyoming</td><td>11.9</td><td>NA</td><td>Vermont**</td><td>NA</td></tr>
<tr><td></td><td></td><td></td><td></td><td>District of Columbia</td><td>4.6</td></tr>
</table>

Source: Morgan Quitno Press using data from Federal Bureau of Investigation
"Crime in the United States 1997" (Uniform Crime Reports, November 22, 1998)
*Of the 450,126 robberies in 1997 for which supplemental data were received by the F.B.I. There were an additional 47,824 robberies for which the type of weapon was not reported to the F.B.I. Robbery is the taking or attempting to take anything of value by force or threat of force.
**Not available.

Robberies Committed with Hands, Fists or Feet in 1997

National Total = 172,894 Robberies*

RANK	STATE	ROBBERIES	% of USA
21	Alabama	2,272	1.3%
42	Alaska	241	0.1%
15	Arizona	2,838	1.6%
31	Arkansas	979	0.6%
1	California	35,043	20.3%
30	Colorado	1,007	0.6%
24	Connecticut	2,186	1.3%
41	Delaware	332	0.2%
2	Florida	17,113	9.9%
10	Georgia	3,770	2.2%
29	Hawaii	1,094	0.6%
44	Idaho	102	0.1%
5	Illinois	9,545	5.5%
21	Indiana	2,272	1.3%
37	Iowa	514	0.3%
36	Kansas	534	0.3%
28	Kentucky	1,103	0.6%
19	Louisiana	2,573	1.5%
43	Maine	153	0.1%
8	Maryland	6,002	3.5%
16	Massachusetts	2,815	1.6%
11	Michigan	3,741	2.2%
18	Minnesota	2,594	1.5%
32	Mississippi	772	0.4%
12	Missouri	3,492	2.0%
48	Montana	11	0.0%
38	Nebraska	470	0.3%
34	Nevada	662	0.4%
NA	New Hampshire**	NA	NA
6	New Jersey	8,922	5.2%
33	New Mexico	720	0.4%
3	New York	14,766	8.5%
9	North Carolina	4,367	2.5%
47	North Dakota	12	0.0%
7	Ohio	6,085	3.5%
27	Oklahoma	1,475	0.9%
25	Oregon	1,859	1.1%
14	Pennsylvania	2,912	1.7%
39	Rhode Island	400	0.2%
23	South Carolina	2,212	1.3%
45	South Dakota	66	0.0%
20	Tennessee	2,495	1.4%
4	Texas	11,508	6.7%
35	Utah	589	0.3%
NA	Vermont**	NA	NA
17	Virginia	2,731	1.6%
13	Washington	3,252	1.9%
40	West Virginia	374	0.2%
26	Wisconsin	1,739	1.0%
46	Wyoming	37	0.0%

RANK	STATE	ROBBERIES	% of USA
1	California	35,043	20.3%
2	Florida	17,113	9.9%
3	New York	14,766	8.5%
4	Texas	11,508	6.7%
5	Illinois	9,545	5.5%
6	New Jersey	8,922	5.2%
7	Ohio	6,085	3.5%
8	Maryland	6,002	3.5%
9	North Carolina	4,367	2.5%
10	Georgia	3,770	2.2%
11	Michigan	3,741	2.2%
12	Missouri	3,492	2.0%
13	Washington	3,252	1.9%
14	Pennsylvania	2,912	1.7%
15	Arizona	2,838	1.6%
16	Massachusetts	2,815	1.6%
17	Virginia	2,731	1.6%
18	Minnesota	2,594	1.5%
19	Louisiana	2,573	1.5%
20	Tennessee	2,495	1.4%
21	Alabama	2,272	1.3%
21	Indiana	2,272	1.3%
23	South Carolina	2,212	1.3%
24	Connecticut	2,186	1.3%
25	Oregon	1,859	1.1%
26	Wisconsin	1,739	1.0%
27	Oklahoma	1,475	0.9%
28	Kentucky	1,103	0.6%
29	Hawaii	1,094	0.6%
30	Colorado	1,007	0.6%
31	Arkansas	979	0.6%
32	Mississippi	772	0.4%
33	New Mexico	720	0.4%
34	Nevada	662	0.4%
35	Utah	589	0.3%
36	Kansas	534	0.3%
37	Iowa	514	0.3%
38	Nebraska	470	0.3%
39	Rhode Island	400	0.2%
40	West Virginia	374	0.2%
41	Delaware	332	0.2%
42	Alaska	241	0.1%
43	Maine	153	0.1%
44	Idaho	102	0.1%
45	South Dakota	66	0.0%
46	Wyoming	37	0.0%
47	North Dakota	12	0.0%
48	Montana	11	0.0%
NA	New Hampshire**	NA	NA
NA	Vermont**	NA	NA
	District of Columbia	2,143	1.2%

Source: Federal Bureau of Investigation
   "Crime in the United States 1997" (Uniform Crime Reports, November 22, 1998)
*Also called strong-armed robberies. Of the 450,126 robberies in 1997 for which supplemental data were received
by the F.B.I. There were an additional 47,824 robberies for which the type of weapon was not reported to the F.B.I.
 Robbery is the taking or attempting to take anything of value by force or threat of force.
**Not available.

Percent of Robberies Committed with Hands, Fists or Feet in 1997

National Percent = 38.4% of Robberies*

ALPHA ORDER				RANK ORDER		
RANK	STATE	PERCENT		RANK	STATE	PERCENT
31	Alabama	36.4		1	Hawaii	78.0
25	Alaska	40.8		2	Maine	59.8
28	Arizona	39.8		3	Minnesota	56.8
34	Arkansas	35.5		4	Rhode Island	56.6
21	California	43.1		5	New Jersey	52.6
26	Colorado	40.2		6	Washington	52.2
19	Connecticut	43.7		7	Pennsylvania	52.1
27	Delaware	40.0		8	Oregon	51.0
24	Florida	42.4		9	Nevada	49.3
44	Georgia	28.3		10	Ohio	47.8
1	Hawaii	78.0		10	West Virginia	47.8
20	Idaho	43.4		12	Iowa	47.7
36	Illinois	35.3		13	South Dakota	47.5
33	Indiana	35.6		14	Kentucky	44.9
12	Iowa	47.7		15	Massachusetts	44.5
29	Kansas	38.9		16	Wyoming	44.0
14	Kentucky	44.9		17	Nebraska	43.9
47	Louisiana	26.4		18	Utah	43.8
2	Maine	59.8		19	Connecticut	43.7
37	Maryland	35.0		20	Idaho	43.4
15	Massachusetts	44.5		21	California	43.1
45	Michigan	27.7		22	Missouri	42.9
3	Minnesota	56.8		23	Oklahoma	42.8
41	Mississippi	31.7		24	Florida	42.4
22	Missouri	42.9		25	Alaska	40.8
34	Montana	35.5		26	Colorado	40.2
17	Nebraska	43.9		27	Delaware	40.0
9	Nevada	49.3		28	Arizona	39.8
NA	New Hampshire**	NA		29	Kansas	38.9
5	New Jersey	52.6		30	Texas	37.8
43	New Mexico	29.8		31	Alabama	36.4
46	New York	27.3		31	South Carolina	36.4
38	North Carolina	34.4		33	Indiana	35.6
42	North Dakota	30.0		34	Arkansas	35.5
10	Ohio	47.8		34	Montana	35.5
23	Oklahoma	42.8		36	Illinois	35.3
8	Oregon	51.0		37	Maryland	35.0
7	Pennsylvania	52.1		38	North Carolina	34.4
4	Rhode Island	56.6		39	Wisconsin	33.6
31	South Carolina	36.4		40	Virginia	32.7
13	South Dakota	47.5		41	Mississippi	31.7
48	Tennessee	24.7		42	North Dakota	30.0
30	Texas	37.8		43	New Mexico	29.8
18	Utah	43.8		44	Georgia	28.3
NA	Vermont**	NA		45	Michigan	27.7
40	Virginia	32.7		46	New York	27.3
6	Washington	52.2		47	Louisiana	26.4
10	West Virginia	47.8		48	Tennessee	24.7
39	Wisconsin	33.6		NA	New Hampshire**	NA
16	Wyoming	44.0		NA	Vermont**	NA
					District of Columbia	47.6

Source: Morgan Quitno Press using data from Federal Bureau of Investigation
   "Crime in the United States 1997" (Uniform Crime Reports, November 22, 1998)
*Also called strong-armed robberies. Of the 450,126 robberies in 1997 for which supplemental data were received
by the F.B.I. There were an additional 47,824 robberies for which the type of weapon was not reported to the F.B.I.
Robbery is the taking or attempting to take anything of value by force or threat of force.
**Not available.

Bank Robberies in 1997

National Total = 7,853 Robberies*

ALPHA ORDER

RANK	STATE	ROBBERIES	% of USA
22	Alabama	104	1.3%
41	Alaska	12	0.2%
9	Arizona	251	3.2%
35	Arkansas	31	0.4%
1	California	1,565	19.9%
20	Colorado	119	1.5%
32	Connecticut	48	0.6%
38	Delaware	24	0.3%
2	Florida	707	9.0%
14	Georgia	176	2.2%
33	Hawaii	43	0.5%
42	Idaho	11	0.1%
15	Illinois	165	2.1%
18	Indiana	143	1.8%
34	Iowa	39	0.5%
37	Kansas	26	0.3%
28	Kentucky	76	1.0%
22	Louisiana	104	1.3%
48	Maine	2	0.0%
4	Maryland	370	4.7%
17	Massachusetts	150	1.9%
5	Michigan	340	4.3%
24	Minnesota	101	1.3%
30	Mississippi	52	0.7%
26	Missouri	90	1.1%
47	Montana	3	0.0%
39	Nebraska	22	0.3%
25	Nevada	100	1.3%
44	New Hampshire	8	0.1%
27	New Jersey	87	1.1%
29	New Mexico	65	0.8%
3	New York	453	5.8%
13	North Carolina	209	2.7%
46	North Dakota	4	0.1%
8	Ohio	271	3.5%
36	Oklahoma	30	0.4%
11	Oregon	230	2.9%
10	Pennsylvania	240	3.1%
43	Rhode Island	9	0.1%
21	South Carolina	109	1.4%
48	South Dakota	2	0.0%
16	Tennessee	161	2.1%
7	Texas	306	3.9%
31	Utah	50	0.6%
48	Vermont	2	0.0%
12	Virginia	219	2.8%
6	Washington	321	4.1%
40	West Virginia	17	0.2%
19	Wisconsin	134	1.7%
45	Wyoming	5	0.1%

RANK ORDER

RANK	STATE	ROBBERIES	% of USA
1	California	1,565	19.9%
2	Florida	707	9.0%
3	New York	453	5.8%
4	Maryland	370	4.7%
5	Michigan	340	4.3%
6	Washington	321	4.1%
7	Texas	306	3.9%
8	Ohio	271	3.5%
9	Arizona	251	3.2%
10	Pennsylvania	240	3.1%
11	Oregon	230	2.9%
12	Virginia	219	2.8%
13	North Carolina	209	2.7%
14	Georgia	176	2.2%
15	Illinois	165	2.1%
16	Tennessee	161	2.1%
17	Massachusetts	150	1.9%
18	Indiana	143	1.8%
19	Wisconsin	134	1.7%
20	Colorado	119	1.5%
21	South Carolina	109	1.4%
22	Alabama	104	1.3%
22	Louisiana	104	1.3%
24	Minnesota	101	1.3%
25	Nevada	100	1.3%
26	Missouri	90	1.1%
27	New Jersey	87	1.1%
28	Kentucky	76	1.0%
29	New Mexico	65	0.8%
30	Mississippi	52	0.7%
31	Utah	50	0.6%
32	Connecticut	48	0.6%
33	Hawaii	43	0.5%
34	Iowa	39	0.5%
35	Arkansas	31	0.4%
36	Oklahoma	30	0.4%
37	Kansas	26	0.3%
38	Delaware	24	0.3%
39	Nebraska	22	0.3%
40	West Virginia	17	0.2%
41	Alaska	12	0.2%
42	Idaho	11	0.1%
43	Rhode Island	9	0.1%
44	New Hampshire	8	0.1%
45	Wyoming	5	0.1%
46	North Dakota	4	0.1%
47	Montana	3	0.0%
48	Maine	2	0.0%
48	South Dakota	2	0.0%
48	Vermont	2	0.0%
	District of Columbia	47	0.6%

Source: Federal Bureau of Investigation
    "Bank Crime Statistics, Federally Insured Financial Institutions, January 1, 1997 - December 31, 1997"
*Does not include 23 robberies in Puerto Rico. In addition, there were 413 bank burglaries, 83 bank larcenies and 42 extortions. Of these 8,372 bank crimes, loot valued at $103,072,136 was taken in 7,630 cases. Of this, $28,790,618 was recovered.

Aggravated Assaults in 1997

National Total = 1,022,492 Aggravated Assaults*

ALPHA ORDER

RANK	STATE	ASSAULTS	% of USA
20	Alabama	15,626	1.5%
38	Alaska	3,165	0.3%
19	Arizona	18,997	1.9%
26	Arkansas	9,131	0.9%
1	California	163,346	16.0%
27	Colorado	9,063	0.9%
34	Connecticut	6,918	0.7%
39	Delaware	3,154	0.3%
2	Florida	100,926	9.9%
12	Georgia	27,044	2.6%
43	Hawaii	1,478	0.1%
41	Idaho	2,481	0.2%
4	Illinois	63,842	6.2%
18	Indiana	20,058	2.0%
35	Iowa	6,617	0.6%
33	Kansas	6,944	0.7%
31	Kentucky	7,308	0.7%
14	Louisiana	24,360	2.4%
45	Maine	964	0.1%
15	Maryland	23,654	2.3%
7	Massachusetts	30,969	3.0%
6	Michigan	36,900	3.6%
28	Minnesota	7,879	0.8%
29	Mississippi	7,644	0.7%
16	Missouri	20,811	2.0%
47	Montana	769	0.1%
36	Nebraska	5,712	0.6%
32	Nevada	7,132	0.7%
48	New Hampshire	643	0.1%
17	New Jersey	20,650	2.0%
24	New Mexico	10,790	1.1%
5	New York	63,628	6.2%
9	North Carolina	29,292	2.9%
50	North Dakota	353	0.0%
13	Ohio	25,862	2.5%
22	Oklahoma	13,368	1.3%
25	Oregon	9,200	0.9%
8	Pennsylvania	30,358	3.0%
42	Rhode Island	2,197	0.2%
10	South Carolina	28,460	2.8%
46	South Dakota	918	0.1%
11	Tennessee	27,335	2.7%
3	Texas	77,266	7.6%
37	Utah	4,443	0.4%
49	Vermont	461	0.0%
23	Virginia	12,558	1.2%
21	Washington	14,864	1.5%
40	West Virginia	2,759	0.3%
30	Wisconsin	7,521	0.7%
44	Wyoming	986	0.1%

RANK ORDER

RANK	STATE	ASSAULTS	% of USA
1	California	163,346	16.0%
2	Florida	100,926	9.9%
3	Texas	77,266	7.6%
4	Illinois	63,842	6.2%
5	New York	63,628	6.2%
6	Michigan	36,900	3.6%
7	Massachusetts	30,969	3.0%
8	Pennsylvania	30,358	3.0%
9	North Carolina	29,292	2.9%
10	South Carolina	28,460	2.8%
11	Tennessee	27,335	2.7%
12	Georgia	27,044	2.6%
13	Ohio	25,862	2.5%
14	Louisiana	24,360	2.4%
15	Maryland	23,654	2.3%
16	Missouri	20,811	2.0%
17	New Jersey	20,650	2.0%
18	Indiana	20,058	2.0%
19	Arizona	18,997	1.9%
20	Alabama	15,626	1.5%
21	Washington	14,864	1.5%
22	Oklahoma	13,368	1.3%
23	Virginia	12,558	1.2%
24	New Mexico	10,790	1.1%
25	Oregon	9,200	0.9%
26	Arkansas	9,131	0.9%
27	Colorado	9,063	0.9%
28	Minnesota	7,879	0.8%
29	Mississippi	7,644	0.7%
30	Wisconsin	7,521	0.7%
31	Kentucky	7,308	0.7%
32	Nevada	7,132	0.7%
33	Kansas	6,944	0.7%
34	Connecticut	6,918	0.7%
35	Iowa	6,617	0.6%
36	Nebraska	5,712	0.6%
37	Utah	4,443	0.4%
38	Alaska	3,165	0.3%
39	Delaware	3,154	0.3%
40	West Virginia	2,759	0.3%
41	Idaho	2,481	0.2%
42	Rhode Island	2,197	0.2%
43	Hawaii	1,478	0.1%
44	Wyoming	986	0.1%
45	Maine	964	0.1%
46	South Dakota	918	0.1%
47	Montana	769	0.1%
48	New Hampshire	643	0.1%
49	Vermont	461	0.0%
50	North Dakota	353	0.0%
	District of Columbia	5,688	0.6%

Source: Federal Bureau of Investigation
"Crime in the United States 1997" (Uniform Crime Reports, November 22, 1998)
*Aggravated assault is an attack for the purpose of inflicting severe bodily injury.

Average Time Between Aggravated Assaults in 1997

National Rate = An Aggravated Assault Occurs Every 31 Seconds*

ALPHA ORDER

ALPHA ORDER

RANK	STATE	MINUTES.SECONDS	RANK	STATE	MINUTES.SECONDS
31	Alabama	33.38	1	North Dakota	1,488.57
13	Alaska	166.04	2	Vermont	1,140.08
32	Arizona	27.40	3	New Hampshire	817.25
25	Arkansas	57.34	4	Montana	683.29
50	California	3.13	5	South Dakota	572.33
24	Colorado	57.59	6	Maine	545.14
17	Connecticut	75.59	7	Wyoming	533.04
12	Delaware	166.39	8	Hawaii	355.37
49	Florida	5.13	9	Rhode Island	239.14
39	Georgia	19.26	10	Idaho	211.51
8	Hawaii	355.37	11	West Virginia	190.30
10	Idaho	211.51	12	Delaware	166.39
47	Illinois	8.14	13	Alaska	166.04
33	Indiana	26.12	14	Utah	118.18
16	Iowa	79.26	15	Nebraska	92.01
18	Kansas	75.41	16	Iowa	79.26
20	Kentucky	71.55	17	Connecticut	75.59
37	Louisiana	21.35	18	Kansas	75.41
6	Maine	545.14	19	Nevada	73.42
36	Maryland	22.13	20	Kentucky	71.55
44	Massachusetts	16.58	21	Wisconsin	69.53
45	Michigan	14.14	22	Mississippi	68.46
23	Minnesota	66.43	23	Minnesota	66.43
22	Mississippi	68.46	24	Colorado	57.59
35	Missouri	25.16	25	Arkansas	57.34
4	Montana	683.29	26	Oregon	57.08
15	Nebraska	92.01	27	New Mexico	48.43
19	Nevada	73.42	28	Virginia	41.51
3	New Hampshire	817.25	29	Oklahoma	39.19
34	New Jersey	25.27	30	Washington	35.22
27	New Mexico	48.43	31	Alabama	33.38
46	New York	8.16	32	Arizona	27.40
42	North Carolina	17.56	33	Indiana	26.12
1	North Dakota	1,488.57	34	New Jersey	25.27
38	Ohio	20.19	35	Missouri	25.16
29	Oklahoma	39.19	36	Maryland	22.13
26	Oregon	57.08	37	Louisiana	21.35
43	Pennsylvania	17.19	38	Ohio	20.19
9	Rhode Island	239.14	39	Georgia	19.26
41	South Carolina	18.28	40	Tennessee	19.14
5	South Dakota	572.33	41	South Carolina	18.28
40	Tennessee	19.14	42	North Carolina	17.56
48	Texas	6.48	43	Pennsylvania	17.19
14	Utah	118.18	44	Massachusetts	16.58
2	Vermont	1,140.08	45	Michigan	14.14
28	Virginia	41.51	46	New York	8.16
30	Washington	35.22	47	Illinois	8.14
11	West Virginia	190.30	48	Texas	6.48
21	Wisconsin	69.53	49	Florida	5.13
7	Wyoming	533.04	50	California	3.13
				District of Columbia	92.25

Source: Morgan Quitno Press using data from Federal Bureau of Investigation
   "Crime in the United States 1997" (Uniform Crime Reports, November 22, 1998)
*Aggravated assault is an attack for the purpose of inflicting severe bodily injury.

Percent Change in Number of Aggravated Assaults: 1996 to 1997

National Percent Change = 1.4% Decrease*

ALPHA ORDER

RANK	STATE	PERCENT CHANGE
15	Alabama	2.8
35	Alaska	(3.0)
23	Arizona	1.2
24	Arkansas	1.1
33	California	(2.5)
46	Colorado	(7.2)
31	Connecticut	(1.5)
14	Delaware	3.2
27	Florida	(0.2)
45	Georgia	(6.4)
4	Hawaii	9.5
39	Idaho	(3.8)
40	Illinois	(4.2)
48	Indiana	(7.6)
2	Iowa	12.7
25	Kansas	0.6
29	Kentucky	(0.5)
44	Louisiana	(5.7)
30	Maine	(1.2)
43	Maryland	(4.6)
7	Massachusetts	5.3
33	Michigan	(2.5)
28	Minnesota	(0.3)
49	Mississippi	(8.3)
21	Missouri	1.4
50	Montana	(12.8)
21	Nebraska	1.4
16	Nevada	1.9
20	New Hampshire	1.7
36	New Jersey	(3.1)
9	New Mexico	4.4
32	New York	(1.9)
11	North Carolina	4.0
1	North Dakota	17.3
6	Ohio	6.0
47	Oklahoma	(7.3)
38	Oregon	(3.4)
37	Pennsylvania	(3.3)
42	Rhode Island	(4.5)
26	South Carolina	0.3
5	South Dakota	8.0
11	Tennessee	4.0
40	Texas	(4.2)
16	Utah	1.9
19	Vermont	1.8
16	Virginia	1.9
8	Washington	4.8
13	West Virginia	3.3
3	Wisconsin	11.1
10	Wyoming	4.1

RANK ORDER

RANK	STATE	PERCENT CHANGE
1	North Dakota	17.3
2	Iowa	12.7
3	Wisconsin	11.1
4	Hawaii	9.5
5	South Dakota	8.0
6	Ohio	6.0
7	Massachusetts	5.3
8	Washington	4.8
9	New Mexico	4.4
10	Wyoming	4.1
11	North Carolina	4.0
11	Tennessee	4.0
13	West Virginia	3.3
14	Delaware	3.2
15	Alabama	2.8
16	Nevada	1.9
16	Utah	1.9
16	Virginia	1.9
19	Vermont	1.8
20	New Hampshire	1.7
21	Missouri	1.4
21	Nebraska	1.4
23	Arizona	1.2
24	Arkansas	1.1
25	Kansas	0.6
26	South Carolina	0.3
27	Florida	(0.2)
28	Minnesota	(0.3)
29	Kentucky	(0.5)
30	Maine	(1.2)
31	Connecticut	(1.5)
32	New York	(1.9)
33	California	(2.5)
33	Michigan	(2.5)
35	Alaska	(3.0)
36	New Jersey	(3.1)
37	Pennsylvania	(3.3)
38	Oregon	(3.4)
39	Idaho	(3.8)
40	Illinois	(4.2)
40	Texas	(4.2)
42	Rhode Island	(4.5)
43	Maryland	(4.6)
44	Louisiana	(5.7)
45	Georgia	(6.4)
46	Colorado	(7.2)
47	Oklahoma	(7.3)
48	Indiana	(7.6)
49	Mississippi	(8.3)
50	Montana	(12.8)

District of Columbia (9.9)

Source: Federal Bureau of Investigation
    "Crime in the United States 1997" (Uniform Crime Reports, November 22, 1998)
*Aggravated assault is an attack for the purpose of inflicting severe bodily injury.

Aggravated Assault Rate in 1997

National Rate = 382.0 Aggravated Assaults per 100,000 Population*

ALPHA ORDER

RANK	STATE	ASSAULTS
20	Alabama	361.8
6	Alaska	519.7
13	Arizona	417.1
19	Arkansas	361.9
8	California	506.2
31	Colorado	232.8
36	Connecticut	211.6
11	Delaware	430.9
2	Florida	688.7
21	Georgia	361.3
44	Hawaii	124.5
38	Idaho	205.0
5	Illinois	536.7
24	Indiana	342.1
32	Iowa	232.0
27	Kansas	267.6
39	Kentucky	187.0
4	Louisiana	559.7
48	Maine	77.6
10	Maryland	464.4
8	Massachusetts	506.2
18	Michigan	377.5
41	Minnesota	168.1
26	Mississippi	279.9
17	Missouri	385.2
46	Montana	87.5
23	Nebraska	344.7
12	Nevada	425.3
50	New Hampshire	54.8
29	New Jersey	256.4
3	New Mexico	623.7
22	New York	350.8
16	North Carolina	394.5
49	North Dakota	55.1
33	Ohio	231.2
14	Oklahoma	403.0
25	Oregon	283.7
30	Pennsylvania	252.6
34	Rhode Island	222.6
1	South Carolina	756.9
45	South Dakota	124.4
7	Tennessee	509.2
15	Texas	397.5
35	Utah	215.8
47	Vermont	78.3
40	Virginia	186.5
28	Washington	265.0
42	West Virginia	151.9
43	Wisconsin	145.5
37	Wyoming	205.4

RANK ORDER

RANK	STATE	ASSAULTS
1	South Carolina	756.9
2	Florida	688.7
3	New Mexico	623.7
4	Louisiana	559.7
5	Illinois	536.7
6	Alaska	519.7
7	Tennessee	509.2
8	California	506.2
8	Massachusetts	506.2
10	Maryland	464.4
11	Delaware	430.9
12	Nevada	425.3
13	Arizona	417.1
14	Oklahoma	403.0
15	Texas	397.5
16	North Carolina	394.5
17	Missouri	385.2
18	Michigan	377.5
19	Arkansas	361.9
20	Alabama	361.8
21	Georgia	361.3
22	New York	350.8
23	Nebraska	344.7
24	Indiana	342.1
25	Oregon	283.7
26	Mississippi	279.9
27	Kansas	267.6
28	Washington	265.0
29	New Jersey	256.4
30	Pennsylvania	252.6
31	Colorado	232.8
32	Iowa	232.0
33	Ohio	231.2
34	Rhode Island	222.6
35	Utah	215.8
36	Connecticut	211.6
37	Wyoming	205.4
38	Idaho	205.0
39	Kentucky	187.0
40	Virginia	186.5
41	Minnesota	168.1
42	West Virginia	151.9
43	Wisconsin	145.5
44	Hawaii	124.5
45	South Dakota	124.4
46	Montana	87.5
47	Vermont	78.3
48	Maine	77.6
49	North Dakota	55.1
50	New Hampshire	54.8
	District of Columbia	1,075.2

Source: Federal Bureau of Investigation
"Crime in the United States 1997" (Uniform Crime Reports, November 22, 1998)
*Aggravated assault is an attack for the purpose of inflicting severe bodily injury.

Percent Change in Aggravated Assault Rate: 1996 to 1997

National Percent Change = 2.3% Decrease*

ALPHA ORDER

RANK ORDER

RANK	STATE	PERCENT CHANGE
16	Alabama	1.7
34	Alaska	(3.3)
29	Arizona	(1.6)
20	Arkansas	0.6
35	California	(3.7)
48	Colorado	(8.8)
28	Connecticut	(1.4)
14	Delaware	2.2
31	Florida	(1.9)
47	Georgia	(8.0)
4	Hawaii	9.2
42	Idaho	(5.5)
40	Illinois	(4.6)
46	Indiana	(7.9)
2	Iowa	12.7
22	Kansas	(0.3)
26	Kentucky	(1.2)
43	Louisiana	(5.7)
24	Maine	(1.1)
41	Maryland	(5.0)
7	Massachusetts	4.8
38	Michigan	(4.3)
23	Minnesota	(0.9)
48	Mississippi	(8.8)
21	Missouri	0.5
50	Montana	(12.8)
17	Nebraska	1.1
32	Nevada	(2.6)
19	New Hampshire	0.7
36	New Jersey	(3.9)
10	New Mexico	3.4
30	New York	(1.7)
13	North Carolina	2.6
1	North Dakota	18.0
6	Ohio	5.9
45	Oklahoma	(7.8)
39	Oregon	(4.5)
33	Pennsylvania	(3.0)
37	Rhode Island	(4.2)
27	South Carolina	(1.3)
5	South Dakota	7.1
12	Tennessee	3.0
43	Texas	(5.7)
24	Utah	(1.1)
15	Vermont	1.8
17	Virginia	1.1
10	Washington	3.4
9	West Virginia	3.8
3	Wisconsin	11.0
8	Wyoming	4.3

RANK	STATE	PERCENT CHANGE
1	North Dakota	18.0
2	Iowa	12.7
3	Wisconsin	11.0
4	Hawaii	9.2
5	South Dakota	7.1
6	Ohio	5.9
7	Massachusetts	4.8
8	Wyoming	4.3
9	West Virginia	3.8
10	New Mexico	3.4
10	Washington	3.4
12	Tennessee	3.0
13	North Carolina	2.6
14	Delaware	2.2
15	Vermont	1.8
16	Alabama	1.7
17	Nebraska	1.1
17	Virginia	1.1
19	New Hampshire	0.7
20	Arkansas	0.6
21	Missouri	0.5
22	Kansas	(0.3)
23	Minnesota	(0.9)
24	Maine	(1.1)
24	Utah	(1.1)
26	Kentucky	(1.2)
27	South Carolina	(1.3)
28	Connecticut	(1.4)
29	Arizona	(1.6)
30	New York	(1.7)
31	Florida	(1.9)
32	Nevada	(2.6)
33	Pennsylvania	(3.0)
34	Alaska	(3.3)
35	California	(3.7)
36	New Jersey	(3.9)
37	Rhode Island	(4.2)
38	Michigan	(4.3)
39	Oregon	(4.5)
40	Illinois	(4.6)
41	Maryland	(5.0)
42	Idaho	(5.5)
43	Louisiana	(5.7)
43	Texas	(5.7)
45	Oklahoma	(7.8)
46	Indiana	(7.9)
47	Georgia	(8.0)
48	Colorado	(8.8)
48	Mississippi	(8.8)
50	Montana	(12.8)

District of Columbia (7.5)

Source: Federal Bureau of Investigation
"Crime in the United States 1997" (Uniform Crime Reports, November 22, 1998)
*Aggravated assault is an attack for the purpose of inflicting severe bodily injury.

Aggravated Assaults with Firearms in 1997

National Total = 178,700 Aggravated Assaults*

ALPHA ORDER

RANK	STATE	ASSAULTS	% of USA
15	Alabama	3,619	2.0%
37	Alaska	594	0.3%
12	Arizona	5,389	3.0%
22	Arkansas	2,186	1.2%
1	California	25,743	14.4%
24	Colorado	1,578	0.9%
32	Connecticut	934	0.5%
41	Delaware	327	0.2%
2	Florida	20,846	11.7%
10	Georgia	5,809	3.3%
43	Hawaii	193	0.1%
35	Idaho	702	0.4%
4	Illinois	10,302	5.8%
16	Indiana	3,256	1.8%
38	Iowa	558	0.3%
34	Kansas	734	0.4%
31	Kentucky	1,012	0.6%
11	Louisiana	5,798	3.2%
47	Maine	39	0.0%
14	Maryland	4,515	2.5%
26	Massachusetts	1,435	0.8%
6	Michigan	7,841	4.4%
27	Minnesota	1,399	0.8%
29	Mississippi	1,129	0.6%
13	Missouri	5,104	2.9%
46	Montana	71	0.0%
36	Nebraska	658	0.4%
38	Nevada	558	0.3%
NA	New Hampshire**	NA	NA
17	New Jersey	2,804	1.6%
21	New Mexico	2,391	1.3%
9	New York	6,073	3.4%
5	North Carolina	8,534	4.8%
48	North Dakota	26	0.0%
20	Ohio	2,651	1.5%
18	Oklahoma	2,714	1.5%
25	Oregon	1,562	0.9%
28	Pennsylvania	1,250	0.7%
42	Rhode Island	220	0.1%
8	South Carolina	6,484	3.6%
45	South Dakota	80	0.0%
7	Tennessee	6,754	3.8%
3	Texas	16,873	9.4%
33	Utah	832	0.5%
NA	Vermont**	NA	NA
23	Virginia	1,750	1.0%
19	Washington	2,669	1.5%
40	West Virginia	500	0.3%
30	Wisconsin	1,126	0.6%
44	Wyoming	125	0.1%

RANK ORDER

RANK	STATE	ASSAULTS	% of USA
1	California	25,743	14.4%
2	Florida	20,846	11.7%
3	Texas	16,873	9.4%
4	Illinois	10,302	5.8%
5	North Carolina	8,534	4.8%
6	Michigan	7,841	4.4%
7	Tennessee	6,754	3.8%
8	South Carolina	6,484	3.6%
9	New York	6,073	3.4%
10	Georgia	5,809	3.3%
11	Louisiana	5,798	3.2%
12	Arizona	5,389	3.0%
13	Missouri	5,104	2.9%
14	Maryland	4,515	2.5%
15	Alabama	3,619	2.0%
16	Indiana	3,256	1.8%
17	New Jersey	2,804	1.6%
18	Oklahoma	2,714	1.5%
19	Washington	2,669	1.5%
20	Ohio	2,651	1.5%
21	New Mexico	2,391	1.3%
22	Arkansas	2,186	1.2%
23	Virginia	1,750	1.0%
24	Colorado	1,578	0.9%
25	Oregon	1,562	0.9%
26	Massachusetts	1,435	0.8%
27	Minnesota	1,399	0.8%
28	Pennsylvania	1,250	0.7%
29	Mississippi	1,129	0.6%
30	Wisconsin	1,126	0.6%
31	Kentucky	1,012	0.6%
32	Connecticut	934	0.5%
33	Utah	832	0.5%
34	Kansas	734	0.4%
35	Idaho	702	0.4%
36	Nebraska	658	0.4%
37	Alaska	594	0.3%
38	Iowa	558	0.3%
38	Nevada	558	0.3%
40	West Virginia	500	0.3%
41	Delaware	327	0.2%
42	Rhode Island	220	0.1%
43	Hawaii	193	0.1%
44	Wyoming	125	0.1%
45	South Dakota	80	0.0%
46	Montana	71	0.0%
47	Maine	39	0.0%
48	North Dakota	26	0.0%
NA	New Hampshire**	NA	NA
NA	Vermont**	NA	NA
	District of Columbia	953	0.5%

Source: Federal Bureau of Investigation
    "Crime in the United States 1997" (Uniform Crime Reports, November 22, 1998)
*Of the 891,547 aggravated assaults in 1997 for which supplemental data were received by the F.B.I. There were an additional 130,945 aggravated assaults for which the type of weapon was not reported to the F.B.I. Aggravated assault is an attack for the purpose of inflicting severe bodily injury.
**Not available.

Aggravated Assault Rate with Firearms in 1997

National Rate = 82.8 Aggravated Assaults per 100,000 Population*

ALPHA ORDER

RANK	STATE	RATE
15	Alabama	99.8
13	Alaska	112.5
8	Arizona	134.6
18	Arkansas	92.8
23	California	79.9
26	Colorado	57.1
35	Connecticut	33.7
14	Delaware	109.4
7	Florida	142.5
11	Georgia	117.9
46	Hawaii	16.8
25	Idaho	58.8
1	Illinois	307.7
20	Indiana	88.5
41	Iowa	24.0
5	Kansas	167.6
9	Kentucky	129.7
6	Louisiana	160.9
48	Maine	3.2
19	Maryland	88.7
36	Massachusetts	28.8
16	Michigan	99.3
29	Minnesota	46.0
16	Mississippi	99.3
10	Missouri	119.3
44	Montana	20.6
30	Nebraska	43.5
24	Nevada	69.1
NA	New Hampshire**	NA
34	New Jersey	34.8
3	New Mexico	200.8
33	New York	38.5
12	North Carolina	116.5
47	North Dakota	4.4
32	Ohio	39.2
22	Oklahoma	81.9
27	Oregon	52.8
44	Pennsylvania	20.6
43	Rhode Island	22.3
4	South Carolina	183.3
40	South Dakota	24.5
2	Tennessee	205.9
21	Texas	87.0
31	Utah	43.3
NA	Vermont**	NA
39	Virginia	26.5
28	Washington	52.0
37	West Virginia	27.5
42	Wisconsin	23.6
38	Wyoming	26.7

RANK ORDER

RANK	STATE	RATE
1	Illinois	307.7
2	Tennessee	205.9
3	New Mexico	200.8
4	South Carolina	183.3
5	Kansas	167.6
6	Louisiana	160.9
7	Florida	142.5
8	Arizona	134.6
9	Kentucky	129.7
10	Missouri	119.3
11	Georgia	117.9
12	North Carolina	116.5
13	Alaska	112.5
14	Delaware	109.4
15	Alabama	99.8
16	Michigan	99.3
16	Mississippi	99.3
18	Arkansas	92.8
19	Maryland	88.7
20	Indiana	88.5
21	Texas	87.0
22	Oklahoma	81.9
23	California	79.9
24	Nevada	69.1
25	Idaho	58.8
26	Colorado	57.1
27	Oregon	52.8
28	Washington	52.0
29	Minnesota	46.0
30	Nebraska	43.5
31	Utah	43.3
32	Ohio	39.2
33	New York	38.5
34	New Jersey	34.8
35	Connecticut	33.7
36	Massachusetts	28.8
37	West Virginia	27.5
38	Wyoming	26.7
39	Virginia	26.5
40	South Dakota	24.5
41	Iowa	24.0
42	Wisconsin	23.6
43	Rhode Island	22.3
44	Montana	20.6
44	Pennsylvania	20.6
46	Hawaii	16.8
47	North Dakota	4.4
48	Maine	3.2
NA	New Hampshire**	NA
NA	Vermont**	NA
	District of Columbia	180.2

Source: Morgan Quitno Press using data from Federal Bureau of Investigation
"Crime in the United States 1997" (Uniform Crime Reports, November 22, 1998)
*Based only on population of reporting jurisdictions. Aggravated assault is an attack for the purpose of inflicting severe bodily injury. National rate reflects only those robberies for which the type of weapon was known and reported. Illinois' rate is especially affected by number of nonreporting jurisdictions.
**Not available.

Percent of Aggravated Assaults Involving Firearms in 1997

National Percent = 20.0% of Aggravated Assaults*

<table>
<tr><td colspan="3">ALPHA ORDER</td><td colspan="3">RANK ORDER</td></tr>
<tr><th>RANK</th><th>STATE</th><th>PERCENT</th><th>RANK</th><th>STATE</th><th>PERCENT</th></tr>
<tr><td>11</td><td>Alabama</td><td>28.0</td><td>1</td><td>Mississippi</td><td>36.5</td></tr>
<tr><td>18</td><td>Alaska</td><td>23.6</td><td>2</td><td>Tennessee</td><td>32.4</td></tr>
<tr><td>3</td><td>Arizona</td><td>30.9</td><td>3</td><td>Arizona</td><td>30.9</td></tr>
<tr><td>15</td><td>Arkansas</td><td>24.6</td><td>4</td><td>New Mexico</td><td>30.2</td></tr>
<tr><td>33</td><td>California</td><td>15.8</td><td>5</td><td>Kansas</td><td>29.8</td></tr>
<tr><td>20</td><td>Colorado</td><td>22.6</td><td>6</td><td>North Carolina</td><td>29.5</td></tr>
<tr><td>37</td><td>Connecticut</td><td>13.5</td><td>7</td><td>Georgia</td><td>28.8</td></tr>
<tr><td>32</td><td>Delaware</td><td>16.5</td><td>8</td><td>Idaho</td><td>28.5</td></tr>
<tr><td>24</td><td>Florida</td><td>20.7</td><td>8</td><td>Louisiana</td><td>28.5</td></tr>
<tr><td>7</td><td>Georgia</td><td>28.8</td><td>10</td><td>Missouri</td><td>28.1</td></tr>
<tr><td>39</td><td>Hawaii</td><td>13.1</td><td>11</td><td>Alabama</td><td>28.0</td></tr>
<tr><td>8</td><td>Idaho</td><td>28.5</td><td>12</td><td>Kentucky</td><td>27.5</td></tr>
<tr><td>13</td><td>Illinois</td><td>26.0</td><td>13</td><td>Illinois</td><td>26.0</td></tr>
<tr><td>23</td><td>Indiana</td><td>20.9</td><td>14</td><td>Michigan</td><td>24.7</td></tr>
<tr><td>43</td><td>Iowa</td><td>10.5</td><td>15</td><td>Arkansas</td><td>24.6</td></tr>
<tr><td>5</td><td>Kansas</td><td>29.8</td><td>16</td><td>South Carolina</td><td>24.0</td></tr>
<tr><td>12</td><td>Kentucky</td><td>27.5</td><td>17</td><td>Minnesota</td><td>23.7</td></tr>
<tr><td>8</td><td>Louisiana</td><td>28.5</td><td>18</td><td>Alaska</td><td>23.6</td></tr>
<tr><td>48</td><td>Maine</td><td>4.3</td><td>19</td><td>Montana</td><td>23.1</td></tr>
<tr><td>28</td><td>Maryland</td><td>19.2</td><td>20</td><td>Colorado</td><td>22.6</td></tr>
<tr><td>47</td><td>Massachusetts</td><td>5.4</td><td>21</td><td>Texas</td><td>21.9</td></tr>
<tr><td>14</td><td>Michigan</td><td>24.7</td><td>22</td><td>Nevada</td><td>21.6</td></tr>
<tr><td>17</td><td>Minnesota</td><td>23.7</td><td>23</td><td>Indiana</td><td>20.9</td></tr>
<tr><td>1</td><td>Mississippi</td><td>36.5</td><td>24</td><td>Florida</td><td>20.7</td></tr>
<tr><td>10</td><td>Missouri</td><td>28.1</td><td>25</td><td>Oklahoma</td><td>20.3</td></tr>
<tr><td>19</td><td>Montana</td><td>23.1</td><td>26</td><td>Utah</td><td>19.9</td></tr>
<tr><td>42</td><td>Nebraska</td><td>11.8</td><td>27</td><td>Washington</td><td>19.5</td></tr>
<tr><td>22</td><td>Nevada</td><td>21.6</td><td>28</td><td>Maryland</td><td>19.2</td></tr>
<tr><td>NA</td><td>New Hampshire**</td><td>NA</td><td>29</td><td>West Virginia</td><td>18.1</td></tr>
<tr><td>36</td><td>New Jersey</td><td>13.6</td><td>30</td><td>Oregon</td><td>17.9</td></tr>
<tr><td>4</td><td>New Mexico</td><td>30.2</td><td>31</td><td>Ohio</td><td>16.8</td></tr>
<tr><td>44</td><td>New York</td><td>10.1</td><td>32</td><td>Delaware</td><td>16.5</td></tr>
<tr><td>6</td><td>North Carolina</td><td>29.5</td><td>33</td><td>California</td><td>15.8</td></tr>
<tr><td>46</td><td>North Dakota</td><td>7.7</td><td>34</td><td>Wisconsin</td><td>15.7</td></tr>
<tr><td>31</td><td>Ohio</td><td>16.8</td><td>35</td><td>Virginia</td><td>14.2</td></tr>
<tr><td>25</td><td>Oklahoma</td><td>20.3</td><td>36</td><td>New Jersey</td><td>13.6</td></tr>
<tr><td>30</td><td>Oregon</td><td>17.9</td><td>37</td><td>Connecticut</td><td>13.5</td></tr>
<tr><td>41</td><td>Pennsylvania</td><td>12.0</td><td>37</td><td>South Dakota</td><td>13.5</td></tr>
<tr><td>45</td><td>Rhode Island</td><td>10.0</td><td>39</td><td>Hawaii</td><td>13.1</td></tr>
<tr><td>16</td><td>South Carolina</td><td>24.0</td><td>39</td><td>Wyoming</td><td>13.1</td></tr>
<tr><td>37</td><td>South Dakota</td><td>13.5</td><td>41</td><td>Pennsylvania</td><td>12.0</td></tr>
<tr><td>2</td><td>Tennessee</td><td>32.4</td><td>42</td><td>Nebraska</td><td>11.8</td></tr>
<tr><td>21</td><td>Texas</td><td>21.9</td><td>43</td><td>Iowa</td><td>10.5</td></tr>
<tr><td>26</td><td>Utah</td><td>19.9</td><td>44</td><td>New York</td><td>10.1</td></tr>
<tr><td>NA</td><td>Vermont**</td><td>NA</td><td>45</td><td>Rhode Island</td><td>10.0</td></tr>
<tr><td>35</td><td>Virginia</td><td>14.2</td><td>46</td><td>North Dakota</td><td>7.7</td></tr>
<tr><td>27</td><td>Washington</td><td>19.5</td><td>47</td><td>Massachusetts</td><td>5.4</td></tr>
<tr><td>29</td><td>West Virginia</td><td>18.1</td><td>48</td><td>Maine</td><td>4.3</td></tr>
<tr><td>34</td><td>Wisconsin</td><td>15.7</td><td>NA</td><td>New Hampshire**</td><td>NA</td></tr>
<tr><td>39</td><td>Wyoming</td><td>13.1</td><td>NA</td><td>Vermont**</td><td>NA</td></tr>
<tr><td></td><td></td><td></td><td></td><td>District of Columbia</td><td>16.8</td></tr>
</table>

Source: Morgan Quitno Press using data from Federal Bureau of Investigation
    "Crime in the United States 1997" (Uniform Crime Reports, November 22, 1998)
*Of the 891,547 aggravated assaults in 1997 for which supplemental data were received by the F.B.I. There
were an additional 130,945 aggravated assaults for which the type of weapon was not reported to the F.B.I.
Aggravated assault is an attack for the purpose of inflicting severe bodily injury.
**Not available.

Aggravated Assaults with Knives or Cutting Instruments in 1997

National Total = 159,995 Aggravated Assaults*

ALPHA ORDER

RANK	STATE	ASSAULTS	% of USA
19	Alabama	2,292	1.4%
34	Alaska	591	0.4%
16	Arizona	2,686	1.7%
24	Arkansas	1,446	0.9%
1	California	20,735	13.0%
25	Colorado	1,431	0.9%
28	Connecticut	1,155	0.7%
40	Delaware	423	0.3%
2	Florida	18,477	11.5%
12	Georgia	3,966	2.5%
43	Hawaii	179	0.1%
37	Idaho	547	0.3%
5	Illinois	8,576	5.4%
23	Indiana	1,534	1.0%
31	Iowa	847	0.5%
42	Kansas	331	0.2%
38	Kentucky	537	0.3%
11	Louisiana	4,138	2.6%
46	Maine	121	0.1%
9	Maryland	5,195	3.2%
14	Massachusetts	3,732	2.3%
7	Michigan	6,056	3.8%
22	Minnesota	1,660	1.0%
33	Mississippi	669	0.4%
15	Missouri	3,057	1.9%
48	Montana	47	0.0%
35	Nebraska	581	0.4%
36	Nevada	572	0.4%
NA	New Hampshire**	NA	NA
10	New Jersey	4,265	2.7%
27	New Mexico	1,341	0.8%
4	New York	14,242	8.9%
8	North Carolina	5,471	3.4%
47	North Dakota	48	0.0%
17	Ohio	2,601	1.6%
21	Oklahoma	2,077	1.3%
26	Oregon	1,360	0.9%
30	Pennsylvania	1,096	0.7%
41	Rhode Island	413	0.3%
6	South Carolina	6,252	3.9%
45	South Dakota	159	0.1%
13	Tennessee	3,901	2.4%
3	Texas	16,626	10.4%
32	Utah	799	0.5%
NA	Vermont**	NA	NA
20	Virginia	2,168	1.4%
18	Washington	2,499	1.6%
39	West Virginia	431	0.3%
29	Wisconsin	1,097	0.7%
44	Wyoming	171	0.1%

RANK ORDER

RANK	STATE	ASSAULTS	% of USA
1	California	20,735	13.0%
2	Florida	18,477	11.5%
3	Texas	16,626	10.4%
4	New York	14,242	8.9%
5	Illinois	8,576	5.4%
6	South Carolina	6,252	3.9%
7	Michigan	6,056	3.8%
8	North Carolina	5,471	3.4%
9	Maryland	5,195	3.2%
10	New Jersey	4,265	2.7%
11	Louisiana	4,138	2.6%
12	Georgia	3,966	2.5%
13	Tennessee	3,901	2.4%
14	Massachusetts	3,732	2.3%
15	Missouri	3,057	1.9%
16	Arizona	2,686	1.7%
17	Ohio	2,601	1.6%
18	Washington	2,499	1.6%
19	Alabama	2,292	1.4%
20	Virginia	2,168	1.4%
21	Oklahoma	2,077	1.3%
22	Minnesota	1,660	1.0%
23	Indiana	1,534	1.0%
24	Arkansas	1,446	0.9%
25	Colorado	1,431	0.9%
26	Oregon	1,360	0.9%
27	New Mexico	1,341	0.8%
28	Connecticut	1,155	0.7%
29	Wisconsin	1,097	0.7%
30	Pennsylvania	1,096	0.7%
31	Iowa	847	0.5%
32	Utah	799	0.5%
33	Mississippi	669	0.4%
34	Alaska	591	0.4%
35	Nebraska	581	0.4%
36	Nevada	572	0.4%
37	Idaho	547	0.3%
38	Kentucky	537	0.3%
39	West Virginia	431	0.3%
40	Delaware	423	0.3%
41	Rhode Island	413	0.3%
42	Kansas	331	0.2%
43	Hawaii	179	0.1%
44	Wyoming	171	0.1%
45	South Dakota	159	0.1%
46	Maine	121	0.1%
47	North Dakota	48	0.0%
48	Montana	47	0.0%
NA	New Hampshire**	NA	NA
NA	Vermont**	NA	NA
	District of Columbia	1,397	0.9%

Source: Federal Bureau of Investigation
   "Crime in the United States 1997" (Uniform Crime Reports, November 22, 1998)
*Of the 891,547 aggravated assaults in 1997 for which supplemental data were received by the F.B.I. There were an additional 130,945 aggravated assaults for which the type of weapon was not reported to the F.B.I. Aggravated assault is an attack for the purpose of inflicting severe bodily injury.
**Not available.

373

Percent of Aggravated Assaults Involving Knives or Cutting Instruments in 1997

National Percent = 17.9% of Aggravated Assaults*

<table>
<tr><td colspan="3">ALPHA ORDER</td><td colspan="3">RANK ORDER</td></tr>
<tr><td>RANK</td><td>STATE</td><td>PERCENT</td><td>RANK</td><td>STATE</td><td>PERCENT</td></tr>
<tr><td>25</td><td>Alabama</td><td>17.7</td><td>1</td><td>Minnesota</td><td>28.1</td></tr>
<tr><td>4</td><td>Alaska</td><td>23.5</td><td>2</td><td>South Dakota</td><td>26.8</td></tr>
<tr><td>36</td><td>Arizona</td><td>15.4</td><td>3</td><td>New York</td><td>23.7</td></tr>
<tr><td>31</td><td>Arkansas</td><td>16.3</td><td>4</td><td>Alaska</td><td>23.5</td></tr>
<tr><td>44</td><td>California</td><td>12.7</td><td>5</td><td>South Carolina</td><td>23.1</td></tr>
<tr><td>14</td><td>Colorado</td><td>20.5</td><td>6</td><td>Idaho</td><td>22.2</td></tr>
<tr><td>29</td><td>Connecticut</td><td>16.7</td><td>7</td><td>Nevada</td><td>22.1</td></tr>
<tr><td>12</td><td>Delaware</td><td>21.3</td><td>8</td><td>Maryland</td><td>22.0</td></tr>
<tr><td>22</td><td>Florida</td><td>18.3</td><td>9</td><td>Illinois</td><td>21.6</td></tr>
<tr><td>16</td><td>Georgia</td><td>19.7</td><td>9</td><td>Mississippi</td><td>21.6</td></tr>
<tr><td>45</td><td>Hawaii</td><td>12.1</td><td>9</td><td>Texas</td><td>21.6</td></tr>
<tr><td>6</td><td>Idaho</td><td>22.2</td><td>12</td><td>Delaware</td><td>21.3</td></tr>
<tr><td>9</td><td>Illinois</td><td>21.6</td><td>13</td><td>New Jersey</td><td>20.6</td></tr>
<tr><td>48</td><td>Indiana</td><td>9.9</td><td>14</td><td>Colorado</td><td>20.5</td></tr>
<tr><td>32</td><td>Iowa</td><td>15.9</td><td>15</td><td>Louisiana</td><td>20.4</td></tr>
<tr><td>42</td><td>Kansas</td><td>13.5</td><td>16</td><td>Georgia</td><td>19.7</td></tr>
<tr><td>39</td><td>Kentucky</td><td>14.6</td><td>17</td><td>Michigan</td><td>19.1</td></tr>
<tr><td>15</td><td>Louisiana</td><td>20.4</td><td>17</td><td>Utah</td><td>19.1</td></tr>
<tr><td>43</td><td>Maine</td><td>13.4</td><td>19</td><td>North Carolina</td><td>18.9</td></tr>
<tr><td>8</td><td>Maryland</td><td>22.0</td><td>20</td><td>Rhode Island</td><td>18.8</td></tr>
<tr><td>41</td><td>Massachusetts</td><td>14.1</td><td>21</td><td>Tennessee</td><td>18.7</td></tr>
<tr><td>17</td><td>Michigan</td><td>19.1</td><td>22</td><td>Florida</td><td>18.3</td></tr>
<tr><td>1</td><td>Minnesota</td><td>28.1</td><td>23</td><td>Washington</td><td>18.2</td></tr>
<tr><td>9</td><td>Mississippi</td><td>21.6</td><td>24</td><td>Wyoming</td><td>17.9</td></tr>
<tr><td>28</td><td>Missouri</td><td>16.8</td><td>25</td><td>Alabama</td><td>17.7</td></tr>
<tr><td>37</td><td>Montana</td><td>15.3</td><td>26</td><td>Virginia</td><td>17.5</td></tr>
<tr><td>47</td><td>Nebraska</td><td>10.4</td><td>27</td><td>New Mexico</td><td>16.9</td></tr>
<tr><td>7</td><td>Nevada</td><td>22.1</td><td>28</td><td>Missouri</td><td>16.8</td></tr>
<tr><td>NA</td><td>New Hampshire**</td><td>NA</td><td>29</td><td>Connecticut</td><td>16.7</td></tr>
<tr><td>13</td><td>New Jersey</td><td>20.6</td><td>30</td><td>Ohio</td><td>16.5</td></tr>
<tr><td>27</td><td>New Mexico</td><td>16.9</td><td>31</td><td>Arkansas</td><td>16.3</td></tr>
<tr><td>3</td><td>New York</td><td>23.7</td><td>32</td><td>Iowa</td><td>15.9</td></tr>
<tr><td>19</td><td>North Carolina</td><td>18.9</td><td>33</td><td>Oregon</td><td>15.6</td></tr>
<tr><td>40</td><td>North Dakota</td><td>14.2</td><td>33</td><td>West Virginia</td><td>15.6</td></tr>
<tr><td>30</td><td>Ohio</td><td>16.5</td><td>35</td><td>Oklahoma</td><td>15.5</td></tr>
<tr><td>35</td><td>Oklahoma</td><td>15.5</td><td>36</td><td>Arizona</td><td>15.4</td></tr>
<tr><td>33</td><td>Oregon</td><td>15.6</td><td>37</td><td>Montana</td><td>15.3</td></tr>
<tr><td>46</td><td>Pennsylvania</td><td>10.5</td><td>37</td><td>Wisconsin</td><td>15.3</td></tr>
<tr><td>20</td><td>Rhode Island</td><td>18.8</td><td>39</td><td>Kentucky</td><td>14.6</td></tr>
<tr><td>5</td><td>South Carolina</td><td>23.1</td><td>40</td><td>North Dakota</td><td>14.2</td></tr>
<tr><td>2</td><td>South Dakota</td><td>26.8</td><td>41</td><td>Massachusetts</td><td>14.1</td></tr>
<tr><td>21</td><td>Tennessee</td><td>18.7</td><td>42</td><td>Kansas</td><td>13.5</td></tr>
<tr><td>9</td><td>Texas</td><td>21.6</td><td>43</td><td>Maine</td><td>13.4</td></tr>
<tr><td>17</td><td>Utah</td><td>19.1</td><td>44</td><td>California</td><td>12.7</td></tr>
<tr><td>NA</td><td>Vermont**</td><td>NA</td><td>45</td><td>Hawaii</td><td>12.1</td></tr>
<tr><td>26</td><td>Virginia</td><td>17.5</td><td>46</td><td>Pennsylvania</td><td>10.5</td></tr>
<tr><td>23</td><td>Washington</td><td>18.2</td><td>47</td><td>Nebraska</td><td>10.4</td></tr>
<tr><td>33</td><td>West Virginia</td><td>15.6</td><td>48</td><td>Indiana</td><td>9.9</td></tr>
<tr><td>37</td><td>Wisconsin</td><td>15.3</td><td>NA</td><td>New Hampshire**</td><td>NA</td></tr>
<tr><td>24</td><td>Wyoming</td><td>17.9</td><td>NA</td><td>Vermont**</td><td>NA</td></tr>
<tr><td></td><td></td><td></td><td></td><td>District of Columbia</td><td>24.6</td></tr>
</table>

Source: Morgan Quitno Press using data from Federal Bureau of Investigation
"Crime in the United States 1997" (Uniform Crime Reports, November 22, 1998)
*Of the 891,547 aggravated assaults in 1997 for which supplemental data were received by the F.B.I. There were an additional 130,945 aggravated assaults for which the type of weapon was not reported to the F.B.I. Aggravated assault is an attack for the purpose of inflicting severe bodily injury.
**Not available.

Aggravated Assaults with Blunt Objects and Other Dangerous Weapons In 1997

National Total = 314,943 Aggravated Assaults*

ALPHA ORDER

RANK	STATE	ASSAULTS	% of USA
21	Alabama	3,900	1.2%
41	Alaska	642	0.2%
16	Arizona	4,973	1.6%
28	Arkansas	1,929	0.6%
1	California	50,869	16.2%
25	Colorado	2,402	0.8%
27	Connecticut	2,237	0.7%
36	Delaware	1,007	0.3%
2	Florida	42,896	13.6%
12	Georgia	7,152	2.3%
43	Hawaii	374	0.1%
39	Idaho	865	0.3%
6	Illinois	13,803	4.4%
20	Indiana	4,043	1.3%
32	Iowa	1,395	0.4%
35	Kansas	1,106	0.4%
34	Kentucky	1,313	0.4%
13	Louisiana	6,718	2.1%
44	Maine	299	0.1%
8	Maryland	10,402	3.3%
7	Massachusetts	10,586	3.4%
5	Michigan	14,766	4.7%
33	Minnesota	1,325	0.4%
40	Mississippi	748	0.2%
15	Missouri	6,317	2.0%
48	Montana	84	0.0%
31	Nebraska	1,458	0.5%
37	Nevada	909	0.3%
NA	New Hampshire**	NA	NA
14	New Jersey	6,605	2.1%
24	New Mexico	2,443	0.8%
3	New York	29,393	9.3%
10	North Carolina	8,625	2.7%
47	North Dakota	119	0.0%
18	Ohio	4,722	1.5%
17	Oklahoma	4,832	1.5%
23	Oregon	3,014	1.0%
26	Pennsylvania	2,383	0.8%
38	Rhode Island	901	0.3%
9	South Carolina	9,203	2.9%
46	South Dakota	168	0.1%
11	Tennessee	7,183	2.3%
4	Texas	26,365	8.4%
30	Utah	1,488	0.5%
NA	Vermont**	NA	NA
22	Virginia	3,408	1.1%
19	Washington	4,428	1.4%
42	West Virginia	573	0.2%
29	Wisconsin	1,635	0.5%
45	Wyoming	294	0.1%

RANK ORDER

RANK	STATE	ASSAULTS	% of USA
1	California	50,869	16.2%
2	Florida	42,896	13.6%
3	New York	29,393	9.3%
4	Texas	26,365	8.4%
5	Michigan	14,766	4.7%
6	Illinois	13,803	4.4%
7	Massachusetts	10,586	3.4%
8	Maryland	10,402	3.3%
9	South Carolina	9,203	2.9%
10	North Carolina	8,625	2.7%
11	Tennessee	7,183	2.3%
12	Georgia	7,152	2.3%
13	Louisiana	6,718	2.1%
14	New Jersey	6,605	2.1%
15	Missouri	6,317	2.0%
16	Arizona	4,973	1.6%
17	Oklahoma	4,832	1.5%
18	Ohio	4,722	1.5%
19	Washington	4,428	1.4%
20	Indiana	4,043	1.3%
21	Alabama	3,900	1.2%
22	Virginia	3,408	1.1%
23	Oregon	3,014	1.0%
24	New Mexico	2,443	0.8%
25	Colorado	2,402	0.8%
26	Pennsylvania	2,383	0.8%
27	Connecticut	2,237	0.7%
28	Arkansas	1,929	0.6%
29	Wisconsin	1,635	0.5%
30	Utah	1,488	0.5%
31	Nebraska	1,458	0.5%
32	Iowa	1,395	0.4%
33	Minnesota	1,325	0.4%
34	Kentucky	1,313	0.4%
35	Kansas	1,106	0.4%
36	Delaware	1,007	0.3%
37	Nevada	909	0.3%
38	Rhode Island	901	0.3%
39	Idaho	865	0.3%
40	Mississippi	748	0.2%
41	Alaska	642	0.2%
42	West Virginia	573	0.2%
43	Hawaii	374	0.1%
44	Maine	299	0.1%
45	Wyoming	294	0.1%
46	South Dakota	168	0.1%
47	North Dakota	119	0.0%
48	Montana	84	0.0%
NA	New Hampshire**	NA	NA
NA	Vermont**	NA	NA
	District of Columbia	2,643	0.8%

Source: Federal Bureau of Investigation
   "Crime in the United States 1997" (Uniform Crime Reports, November 22, 1998)
*Of the 891,547 aggravated assaults in 1997 for which supplemental data were received by the F.B.I. There were an additional 130,945 aggravated assaults for which the type of weapon was not reported to the F.B.I. Aggravated assault is an attack for the purpose of inflicting severe bodily injury.
**Not available.

Percent of Aggravated Assaults Involving Blunt Objects
And Other Dangerous Weapons in 1997
National Percent = 35.3% of Aggravated Assaults*

ALPHA ORDER

RANK	STATE	PERCENT
31	Alabama	30.2
41	Alaska	25.5
34	Arizona	28.5
47	Arkansas	21.7
28	California	31.2
20	Colorado	34.4
25	Connecticut	32.4
1	Delaware	50.7
6	Florida	42.6
11	Georgia	35.5
42	Hawaii	25.3
15	Idaho	35.1
16	Illinois	34.8
40	Indiana	26.0
38	Iowa	26.2
4	Kansas	45.0
10	Kentucky	35.7
23	Louisiana	33.1
23	Maine	33.1
5	Maryland	44.1
8	Massachusetts	40.1
3	Michigan	46.6
46	Minnesota	22.4
43	Mississippi	24.2
16	Missouri	34.8
37	Montana	27.4
38	Nebraska	26.2
14	Nevada	35.2
NA	New Hampshire**	NA
27	New Jersey	32.0
29	New Mexico	30.9
2	New York	48.9
33	North Carolina	29.8
13	North Dakota	35.3
32	Ohio	29.9
9	Oklahoma	36.2
18	Oregon	34.5
44	Pennsylvania	22.9
7	Rhode Island	41.0
22	South Carolina	34.1
35	South Dakota	28.3
18	Tennessee	34.5
21	Texas	34.2
11	Utah	35.5
NA	Vermont**	NA
36	Virginia	27.6
26	Washington	32.3
48	West Virginia	20.8
45	Wisconsin	22.8
30	Wyoming	30.7

RANK ORDER

RANK	STATE	PERCENT
1	Delaware	50.7
2	New York	48.9
3	Michigan	46.6
4	Kansas	45.0
5	Maryland	44.1
6	Florida	42.6
7	Rhode Island	41.0
8	Massachusetts	40.1
9	Oklahoma	36.2
10	Kentucky	35.7
11	Georgia	35.5
11	Utah	35.5
13	North Dakota	35.3
14	Nevada	35.2
15	Idaho	35.1
16	Illinois	34.8
16	Missouri	34.8
18	Oregon	34.5
18	Tennessee	34.5
20	Colorado	34.4
21	Texas	34.2
22	South Carolina	34.1
23	Louisiana	33.1
23	Maine	33.1
25	Connecticut	32.4
26	Washington	32.3
27	New Jersey	32.0
28	California	31.2
29	New Mexico	30.9
30	Wyoming	30.7
31	Alabama	30.2
32	Ohio	29.9
33	North Carolina	29.8
34	Arizona	28.5
35	South Dakota	28.3
36	Virginia	27.6
37	Montana	27.4
38	Iowa	26.2
38	Nebraska	26.2
40	Indiana	26.0
41	Alaska	25.5
42	Hawaii	25.3
43	Mississippi	24.2
44	Pennsylvania	22.9
45	Wisconsin	22.8
46	Minnesota	22.4
47	Arkansas	21.7
48	West Virginia	20.8
NA	New Hampshire**	NA
NA	Vermont**	NA
	District of Columbia	46.5

Source: Morgan Quitno Press using data from Federal Bureau of Investigation
   "Crime in the United States 1997" (Uniform Crime Reports, November 22, 1998)
*Of the 891,547 aggravated assaults in 1997 for which supplemental data were received by the F.B.I. There were an additional 130,945 aggravated assaults for which the type of weapon was not reported to the F.B.I. Aggravated assault is an attack for the purpose of inflicting severe bodily injury.
**Not available.

Aggravated Assaults Committed with Hands, Fists or Feet in 1997

National Total = 237,909 Aggravated Assaults*

ALPHA ORDER

RANK	STATE	ASSAULTS	% of USA
23	Alabama	3,124	1.3%
37	Alaska	686	0.3%
14	Arizona	4,396	1.8%
20	Arkansas	3,321	1.4%
1	California	65,672	27.6%
31	Colorado	1,575	0.7%
28	Connecticut	2,582	1.1%
45	Delaware	230	0.1%
2	Florida	18,537	7.8%
22	Georgia	3,222	1.4%
36	Hawaii	732	0.3%
43	Idaho	352	0.1%
6	Illinois	6,994	2.9%
8	Indiana	6,723	2.8%
29	Iowa	2,534	1.1%
44	Kansas	289	0.1%
35	Kentucky	816	0.3%
18	Louisiana	3,672	1.5%
41	Maine	444	0.2%
19	Maryland	3,464	1.5%
4	Massachusetts	10,659	4.5%
24	Michigan	3,030	1.3%
32	Minnesota	1,524	0.6%
39	Mississippi	549	0.2%
17	Missouri	3,698	1.6%
48	Montana	105	0.0%
26	Nebraska	2,876	1.2%
40	Nevada	545	0.2%
NA	New Hampshire**	NA	NA
7	New Jersey	6,986	2.9%
30	New Mexico	1,743	0.7%
5	New York	10,382	4.4%
9	North Carolina	6,312	2.7%
47	North Dakota	144	0.1%
10	Ohio	5,827	2.4%
16	Oklahoma	3,738	1.6%
27	Oregon	2,792	1.2%
11	Pennsylvania	5,669	2.4%
38	Rhode Island	663	0.3%
12	South Carolina	5,077	2.1%
46	South Dakota	186	0.1%
25	Tennessee	2,981	1.3%
3	Texas	17,241	7.2%
34	Utah	1,069	0.4%
NA	Vermont**	NA	NA
13	Virginia	5,032	2.1%
15	Washington	4,099	1.7%
33	West Virginia	1,255	0.5%
21	Wisconsin	3,300	1.4%
42	Wyoming	367	0.2%

RANK ORDER

RANK	STATE	ASSAULTS	% of USA
1	California	65,672	27.6%
2	Florida	18,537	7.8%
3	Texas	17,241	7.2%
4	Massachusetts	10,659	4.5%
5	New York	10,382	4.4%
6	Illinois	6,994	2.9%
7	New Jersey	6,986	2.9%
8	Indiana	6,723	2.8%
9	North Carolina	6,312	2.7%
10	Ohio	5,827	2.4%
11	Pennsylvania	5,669	2.4%
12	South Carolina	5,077	2.1%
13	Virginia	5,032	2.1%
14	Arizona	4,396	1.8%
15	Washington	4,099	1.7%
16	Oklahoma	3,738	1.6%
17	Missouri	3,698	1.6%
18	Louisiana	3,672	1.5%
19	Maryland	3,464	1.5%
20	Arkansas	3,321	1.4%
21	Wisconsin	3,300	1.4%
22	Georgia	3,222	1.4%
23	Alabama	3,124	1.3%
24	Michigan	3,030	1.3%
25	Tennessee	2,981	1.3%
26	Nebraska	2,876	1.2%
27	Oregon	2,792	1.2%
28	Connecticut	2,582	1.1%
29	Iowa	2,534	1.1%
30	New Mexico	1,743	0.7%
31	Colorado	1,575	0.7%
32	Minnesota	1,524	0.6%
33	West Virginia	1,255	0.5%
34	Utah	1,069	0.4%
35	Kentucky	816	0.3%
36	Hawaii	732	0.3%
37	Alaska	686	0.3%
38	Rhode Island	663	0.3%
39	Mississippi	549	0.2%
40	Nevada	545	0.2%
41	Maine	444	0.2%
42	Wyoming	367	0.2%
43	Idaho	352	0.1%
44	Kansas	289	0.1%
45	Delaware	230	0.1%
46	South Dakota	186	0.1%
47	North Dakota	144	0.1%
48	Montana	105	0.0%
NA	New Hampshire**	NA	NA
NA	Vermont**	NA	NA
	District of Columbia	695	0.3%

Source: Federal Bureau of Investigation
"Crime in the United States 1997" (Uniform Crime Reports, November 22, 1998)
*Of the 891,547 aggravated assaults in 1997 for which supplemental data were received by the F.B.I. There were an additional 130,945 aggravated assaults for which the type of weapon was not reported to the F.B.I. Aggravated assault is an attack for the purpose of inflicting severe bodily injury.
**Not available.

Percent of Aggravated Assaults Committed with Hands, Fists or Feet in 1997

National Percent = 26.7% of Aggravated Assaults*

ALPHA ORDER			RANK ORDER		
RANK	STATE	PERCENT	RANK	STATE	PERCENT
28	Alabama	24.2	1	Pennsylvania	54.5
24	Alaska	27.3	2	Nebraska	51.6
27	Arizona	25.2	3	Hawaii	49.5
14	Arkansas	37.4	4	Maine	49.2
12	California	40.3	5	Iowa	47.5
29	Colorado	22.5	6	Wisconsin	46.1
14	Connecticut	37.4	7	West Virginia	45.5
47	Delaware	11.6	8	Indiana	43.2
37	Florida	18.4	9	North Dakota	42.7
42	Georgia	16.0	10	Virginia	40.7
3	Hawaii	49.5	11	Massachusetts	40.4
44	Idaho	14.3	12	California	40.3
40	Illinois	17.6	13	Wyoming	38.3
8	Indiana	43.2	14	Arkansas	37.4
5	Iowa	47.5	14	Connecticut	37.4
46	Kansas	11.7	16	Ohio	36.9
31	Kentucky	22.2	17	Montana	34.2
38	Louisiana	18.1	18	New Jersey	33.8
4	Maine	49.2	19	Oregon	32.0
43	Maryland	14.7	20	South Dakota	31.4
11	Massachusetts	40.4	21	Rhode Island	30.2
48	Michigan	9.6	22	Washington	29.9
25	Minnesota	25.8	23	Oklahoma	28.0
39	Mississippi	17.7	24	Alaska	27.3
35	Missouri	20.3	25	Minnesota	25.8
17	Montana	34.2	26	Utah	25.5
2	Nebraska	51.6	27	Arizona	25.2
34	Nevada	21.1	28	Alabama	24.2
NA	New Hampshire**	NA	29	Colorado	22.5
18	New Jersey	33.8	30	Texas	22.4
32	New Mexico	22.0	31	Kentucky	22.2
41	New York	17.3	32	New Mexico	22.0
33	North Carolina	21.8	33	North Carolina	21.8
9	North Dakota	42.7	34	Nevada	21.1
16	Ohio	36.9	35	Missouri	20.3
23	Oklahoma	28.0	36	South Carolina	18.8
19	Oregon	32.0	37	Florida	18.4
1	Pennsylvania	54.5	38	Louisiana	18.1
21	Rhode Island	30.2	39	Mississippi	17.7
36	South Carolina	18.8	40	Illinois	17.6
20	South Dakota	31.4	41	New York	17.3
44	Tennessee	14.3	42	Georgia	16.0
30	Texas	22.4	43	Maryland	14.7
26	Utah	25.5	44	Idaho	14.3
NA	Vermont**	NA	44	Tennessee	14.3
10	Virginia	40.7	46	Kansas	11.7
22	Washington	29.9	47	Delaware	11.6
7	West Virginia	45.5	48	Michigan	9.6
6	Wisconsin	46.1	NA	New Hampshire**	NA
13	Wyoming	38.3	NA	Vermont**	NA
				District of Columbia	12.2

Source: Morgan Quitno Press using data from Federal Bureau of Investigation
    "Crime in the United States 1997" (Uniform Crime Reports, November 22, 1998)
*Of the 891,547 aggravated assaults in 1997 for which supplemental data were received by the F.B.I. There were an additional 130,945 aggravated assaults for which the type of weapon was not reported to the F.B.I. Aggravated assault is an attack for the purpose of inflicting severe bodily injury.
**Not available.

Property Crimes in 1997

National Total = 11,540,297 Property Crimes*

ALPHA ORDER

RANK	STATE	CRIMES	% of USA
23	Alabama	186,809	1.6%
46	Alaska	27,840	0.2%
12	Arizona	299,323	2.6%
33	Arkansas	105,759	0.9%
1	California	1,312,367	11.4%
26	Colorado	166,902	1.4%
28	Connecticut	117,505	1.0%
44	Delaware	32,650	0.3%
3	Florida	915,613	7.9%
8	Georgia	388,155	3.4%
37	Hawaii	68,193	0.6%
39	Idaho	44,388	0.4%
5	Illinois	509,113	4.4%
18	Indiana	231,723	2.0%
35	Iowa	99,986	0.9%
32	Kansas	107,803	0.9%
31	Kentucky	109,819	1.0%
16	Louisiana	243,423	2.1%
42	Maine	37,396	0.3%
15	Maryland	244,842	2.1%
24	Massachusetts	185,437	1.6%
7	Michigan	422,916	3.7%
21	Minnesota	191,006	1.7%
30	Mississippi	113,644	1.0%
19	Missouri	228,889	2.0%
41	Montana	37,592	0.3%
38	Nebraska	63,717	0.6%
36	Nevada	88,307	0.8%
45	New Hampshire	29,635	0.3%
13	New Jersey	287,038	2.5%
34	New Mexico	104,721	0.9%
4	New York	584,438	5.1%
9	North Carolina	362,672	3.1%
49	North Dakota	16,821	0.1%
6	Ohio	456,299	4.0%
27	Oklahoma	163,698	1.4%
22	Oregon	188,916	1.6%
10	Pennsylvania	359,323	3.1%
43	Rhode Island	32,777	0.3%
20	South Carolina	193,402	1.7%
47	South Dakota	22,491	0.2%
14	Tennessee	253,484	2.2%
2	Texas	948,231	8.2%
29	Utah	116,569	1.0%
50	Vermont	15,953	0.1%
17	Virginia	237,773	2.1%
11	Washington	307,742	2.7%
40	West Virginia	40,868	0.4%
25	Wisconsin	176,145	1.5%
48	Wyoming	18,843	0.2%

RANK ORDER

RANK	STATE	CRIMES	% of USA
1	California	1,312,367	11.4%
2	Texas	948,231	8.2%
3	Florida	915,613	7.9%
4	New York	584,438	5.1%
5	Illinois	509,113	4.4%
6	Ohio	456,299	4.0%
7	Michigan	422,916	3.7%
8	Georgia	388,155	3.4%
9	North Carolina	362,672	3.1%
10	Pennsylvania	359,323	3.1%
11	Washington	307,742	2.7%
12	Arizona	299,323	2.6%
13	New Jersey	287,038	2.5%
14	Tennessee	253,484	2.2%
15	Maryland	244,842	2.1%
16	Louisiana	243,423	2.1%
17	Virginia	237,773	2.1%
18	Indiana	231,723	2.0%
19	Missouri	228,889	2.0%
20	South Carolina	193,402	1.7%
21	Minnesota	191,006	1.7%
22	Oregon	188,916	1.6%
23	Alabama	186,809	1.6%
24	Massachusetts	185,437	1.6%
25	Wisconsin	176,145	1.5%
26	Colorado	166,902	1.4%
27	Oklahoma	163,698	1.4%
28	Connecticut	117,505	1.0%
29	Utah	116,569	1.0%
30	Mississippi	113,644	1.0%
31	Kentucky	109,819	1.0%
32	Kansas	107,803	0.9%
33	Arkansas	105,759	0.9%
34	New Mexico	104,721	0.9%
35	Iowa	99,986	0.9%
36	Nevada	88,307	0.8%
37	Hawaii	68,193	0.6%
38	Nebraska	63,717	0.6%
39	Idaho	44,388	0.4%
40	West Virginia	40,868	0.4%
41	Montana	37,592	0.3%
42	Maine	37,396	0.3%
43	Rhode Island	32,777	0.3%
44	Delaware	32,650	0.3%
45	New Hampshire	29,635	0.3%
46	Alaska	27,840	0.2%
47	South Dakota	22,491	0.2%
48	Wyoming	18,843	0.2%
49	North Dakota	16,821	0.1%
50	Vermont	15,953	0.1%
	District of Columbia	41,341	0.4%

Source: Federal Bureau of Investigation
    "Crime in the United States 1997" (Uniform Crime Reports, November 22, 1998)
*Property crimes are offenses of burglary, larceny-theft and motor vehicle theft.

Average Time Between Property Crimes in 1997

National Rate = A Property Crime Occurs Every 3 Seconds*

ALPHA ORDER			RANK ORDER		
RANK	STATE	MINUTES.SECONDS	RANK	STATE	MINUTES.SECONDS
28	Alabama	2.49	1	Vermont	32.57
5	Alaska	18.53	2	North Dakota	31.15
39	Arizona	1.46	3	Wyoming	27.53
18	Arkansas	4.58	4	South Dakota	23.22
50	California	0.24	5	Alaska	18.53
25	Colorado	3.09	6	New Hampshire	17.44
23	Connecticut	4.28	7	Delaware	16.06
7	Delaware	16.06	8	Rhode Island	16.02
48	Florida	0.34	9	Maine	14.04
43	Georgia	1.21	10	Montana	13.59
14	Hawaii	7.43	11	West Virginia	12.52
12	Idaho	11.50	12	Idaho	11.50
46	Illinois	1.02	13	Nebraska	8.15
33	Indiana	2.16	14	Hawaii	7.43
16	Iowa	5.16	15	Nevada	5.57
19	Kansas	4.53	16	Iowa	5.16
20	Kentucky	4.47	17	New Mexico	5.01
35	Louisiana	2.10	18	Arkansas	4.58
9	Maine	14.04	19	Kansas	4.53
36	Maryland	2.09	20	Kentucky	4.47
27	Massachusetts	2.50	21	Mississippi	4.38
44	Michigan	1.14	22	Utah	4.31
30	Minnesota	2.45	23	Connecticut	4.28
21	Mississippi	4.38	24	Oklahoma	3.13
32	Missouri	2.18	25	Colorado	3.09
10	Montana	13.59	26	Wisconsin	2.59
13	Nebraska	8.15	27	Massachusetts	2.50
15	Nevada	5.57	28	Alabama	2.49
6	New Hampshire	17.44	29	Oregon	2.47
38	New Jersey	1.50	30	Minnesota	2.45
17	New Mexico	5.01	31	South Carolina	2.43
47	New York	0.54	32	Missouri	2.18
42	North Carolina	1.27	33	Indiana	2.16
2	North Dakota	31.15	34	Virginia	2.13
45	Ohio	1.09	35	Louisiana	2.10
24	Oklahoma	3.13	36	Maryland	2.09
29	Oregon	2.47	37	Tennessee	2.04
41	Pennsylvania	1.28	38	New Jersey	1.50
8	Rhode Island	16.02	39	Arizona	1.46
31	South Carolina	2.43	40	Washington	1.43
4	South Dakota	23.22	41	Pennsylvania	1.28
37	Tennessee	2.04	42	North Carolina	1.27
49	Texas	0.33	43	Georgia	1.21
22	Utah	4.31	44	Michigan	1.14
1	Vermont	32.57	45	Ohio	1.09
34	Virginia	2.13	46	Illinois	1.02
40	Washington	1.43	47	New York	0.54
11	West Virginia	12.52	48	Florida	0.34
26	Wisconsin	2.59	49	Texas	0.33
3	Wyoming	27.53	50	California	0.24
				District of Columbia	12.43

Source: Morgan Quitno Press using data from Federal Bureau of Investigation
"Crime in the United States 1997" (Uniform Crime Reports, November 22, 1998)
*Property crimes are offenses of burglary, larceny-theft and motor vehicle theft.

Property Crimes per Square Mile in 1997

National Rate = 3.1 Property Crimes per Square Mile*

ALPHA ORDER

RANK	STATE	RATE
23	Alabama	3.6
50	Alaska	0.0
29	Arizona	2.6
33	Arkansas	2.0
12	California	8.3
38	Colorado	1.6
3	Connecticut	21.2
7	Delaware	13.6
6	Florida	15.3
15	Georgia	6.6
9	Hawaii	10.6
45	Idaho	0.5
11	Illinois	8.8
16	Indiana	6.4
35	Iowa	1.8
40	Kansas	1.3
27	Kentucky	2.7
20	Louisiana	4.9
41	Maine	1.1
5	Maryland	19.9
4	Massachusetts	20.1
21	Michigan	4.4
32	Minnesota	2.2
30	Mississippi	2.4
25	Missouri	3.3
46	Montana	0.3
43	Nebraska	0.8
43	Nevada	0.8
26	New Hampshire	3.2
1	New Jersey	34.9
42	New Mexico	0.9
8	New York	10.8
14	North Carolina	6.9
48	North Dakota	0.2
10	Ohio	10.2
31	Oklahoma	2.3
34	Oregon	1.9
13	Pennsylvania	7.8
2	Rhode Island	26.6
17	South Carolina	6.2
46	South Dakota	0.3
18	Tennessee	6.0
24	Texas	3.5
39	Utah	1.4
36	Vermont	1.7
19	Virginia	5.6
21	Washington	4.4
36	West Virginia	1.7
27	Wisconsin	2.7
48	Wyoming	0.2

RANK ORDER

RANK	STATE	RATE
1	New Jersey	34.9
2	Rhode Island	26.6
3	Connecticut	21.2
4	Massachusetts	20.1
5	Maryland	19.9
6	Florida	15.3
7	Delaware	13.6
8	New York	10.8
9	Hawaii	10.6
10	Ohio	10.2
11	Illinois	8.8
12	California	8.3
13	Pennsylvania	7.8
14	North Carolina	6.9
15	Georgia	6.6
16	Indiana	6.4
17	South Carolina	6.2
18	Tennessee	6.0
19	Virginia	5.6
20	Louisiana	4.9
21	Michigan	4.4
21	Washington	4.4
23	Alabama	3.6
24	Texas	3.5
25	Missouri	3.3
26	New Hampshire	3.2
27	Kentucky	2.7
27	Wisconsin	2.7
29	Arizona	2.6
30	Mississippi	2.4
31	Oklahoma	2.3
32	Minnesota	2.2
33	Arkansas	2.0
34	Oregon	1.9
35	Iowa	1.8
36	Vermont	1.7
36	West Virginia	1.7
38	Colorado	1.6
39	Utah	1.4
40	Kansas	1.3
41	Maine	1.1
42	New Mexico	0.9
43	Nebraska	0.8
43	Nevada	0.8
45	Idaho	0.5
46	Montana	0.3
46	South Dakota	0.3
48	North Dakota	0.2
48	Wyoming	0.2
50	Alaska	0.0
	District of Columbia	608.0

Source: Morgan Quitno Press using data from Federal Bureau of Investigation
"Crime in the United States 1997" (Uniform Crime Reports, November 22, 1998)
*Property crimes are offenses of burglary, larceny-theft and motor vehicle theft.

Percent Change in Number of Property Crimes: 1996 to 1997

National Percent Change = 2.2% Decrease*

ALPHA ORDER			RANK ORDER		
RANK	STATE	PERCENT CHANGE	RANK	STATE	PERCENT CHANGE
10	Alabama	2.8	1	South Dakota	10.0
31	Alaska	(2.9)	2	Oregon	6.6
6	Arizona	5.0	3	Delaware	6.5
15	Arkansas	0.9	4	Nevada	6.3
38	California	(5.3)	5	New Mexico	6.1
47	Colorado	(7.4)	6	Arizona	5.0
43	Connecticut	(5.9)	7	Iowa	3.8
3	Delaware	6.5	8	Mississippi	3.7
23	Florida	(1.4)	9	Utah	3.1
46	Georgia	(6.9)	10	Alabama	2.8
49	Hawaii	(8.6)	11	Tennessee	1.9
19	Idaho	(0.3)	12	Washington	1.5
32	Illinois	(3.0)	13	Ohio	1.4
18	Indiana	0.1	14	North Dakota	1.0
7	Iowa	3.8	15	Arkansas	0.9
26	Kansas	(1.8)	16	North Carolina	0.3
20	Kentucky	(0.6)	17	South Carolina	0.2
38	Louisiana	(5.3)	18	Indiana	0.1
48	Maine	(8.0)	19	Idaho	(0.3)
43	Maryland	(5.9)	20	Kentucky	(0.6)
36	Massachusetts	(4.7)	20	Minnesota	(0.6)
25	Michigan	(1.7)	22	Montana	(1.3)
20	Minnesota	(0.6)	23	Florida	(1.4)
8	Mississippi	3.7	24	West Virginia	(1.5)
37	Missouri	(4.9)	25	Michigan	(1.7)
22	Montana	(1.3)	26	Kansas	(1.8)
34	Nebraska	(3.6)	26	Virginia	(1.8)
4	Nevada	6.3	28	Oklahoma	(1.9)
42	New Hampshire	(5.7)	29	Texas	(2.1)
40	New Jersey	(5.5)	30	Wyoming	(2.2)
5	New Mexico	6.1	31	Alaska	(2.9)
41	New York	(5.6)	32	Illinois	(3.0)
16	North Carolina	0.3	33	Pennsylvania	(3.1)
14	North Dakota	1.0	34	Nebraska	(3.6)
13	Ohio	1.4	35	Wisconsin	(4.3)
28	Oklahoma	(1.9)	36	Massachusetts	(4.7)
2	Oregon	6.6	37	Missouri	(4.9)
33	Pennsylvania	(3.1)	38	California	(5.3)
50	Rhode Island	(9.2)	38	Louisiana	(5.3)
17	South Carolina	0.2	40	New Jersey	(5.5)
1	South Dakota	10.0	41	New York	(5.6)
11	Tennessee	1.9	42	New Hampshire	(5.7)
29	Texas	(2.1)	43	Connecticut	(5.9)
9	Utah	3.1	43	Maryland	(5.9)
45	Vermont	(6.0)	45	Vermont	(6.0)
26	Virginia	(1.8)	46	Georgia	(6.9)
12	Washington	1.5	47	Colorado	(7.4)
24	West Virginia	(1.5)	48	Maine	(8.0)
35	Wisconsin	(4.3)	49	Hawaii	(8.6)
30	Wyoming	(2.2)	50	Rhode Island	(9.2)
				District of Columbia	(19.2)

Source: Federal Bureau of Investigation
   "Crime in the United States 1997" (Uniform Crime Reports, November 22, 1998)
*Property crimes are offenses of burglary, larceny-theft and motor vehicle theft.

Property Crime Rate in 1997

National Rate = 4,311.9 Property Crimes per 100,000 Population*

ALPHA ORDER			RANK ORDER		
RANK	STATE	RATE	RANK	STATE	RATE
20	Alabama	4,325.3	1	Arizona	6,571.3
17	Alaska	4,571.4	2	Florida	6,248.2
1	Arizona	6,571.3	3	New Mexico	6,053.2
25	Arkansas	4,191.8	4	Oregon	5,825.3
30	California	4,067.1	5	Hawaii	5,745.0
21	Colorado	4,287.2	6	Utah	5,661.4
35	Connecticut	3,593.4	7	Louisiana	5,593.4
18	Delaware	4,460.4	8	Washington	5,485.6
2	Florida	6,248.2	9	Nevada	5,265.8
10	Georgia	5,185.1	10	Georgia	5,185.1
5	Hawaii	5,745.0	11	South Carolina	5,143.7
34	Idaho	3,668.4	12	Oklahoma	4,935.1
22	Illinois	4,279.7	13	North Carolina	4,884.5
31	Indiana	3,951.6	14	Texas	4,878.0
38	Iowa	3,505.8	15	Maryland	4,806.5
27	Kansas	4,154.3	16	Tennessee	4,722.1
46	Kentucky	2,810.1	17	Alaska	4,571.4
7	Louisiana	5,593.4	18	Delaware	4,460.4
44	Maine	3,011.0	19	Michigan	4,326.9
15	Maryland	4,806.5	20	Alabama	4,325.3
43	Massachusetts	3,031.0	21	Colorado	4,287.2
19	Michigan	4,326.9	22	Illinois	4,279.7
29	Minnesota	4,076.1	23	Montana	4,276.7
26	Mississippi	4,161.3	24	Missouri	4,237.1
24	Missouri	4,237.1	25	Arkansas	4,191.8
23	Montana	4,276.7	26	Mississippi	4,161.3
33	Nebraska	3,845.3	27	Kansas	4,154.3
9	Nevada	5,265.8	28	Ohio	4,079.2
49	New Hampshire	2,526.4	29	Minnesota	4,076.1
36	New Jersey	3,564.4	30	California	4,067.1
3	New Mexico	6,053.2	31	Indiana	3,951.6
41	New York	3,222.4	32	Wyoming	3,925.6
13	North Carolina	4,884.5	33	Nebraska	3,845.3
48	North Dakota	2,624.2	34	Idaho	3,668.4
28	Ohio	4,079.2	35	Connecticut	3,593.4
12	Oklahoma	4,935.1	36	New Jersey	3,564.4
4	Oregon	5,825.3	37	Virginia	3,530.9
45	Pennsylvania	2,989.4	38	Iowa	3,505.8
40	Rhode Island	3,320.9	39	Wisconsin	3,407.1
11	South Carolina	5,143.7	40	Rhode Island	3,320.9
42	South Dakota	3,047.6	41	New York	3,222.4
16	Tennessee	4,722.1	42	South Dakota	3,047.6
14	Texas	4,878.0	43	Massachusetts	3,031.0
6	Utah	5,661.4	44	Maine	3,011.0
47	Vermont	2,708.5	45	Pennsylvania	2,989.4
37	Virginia	3,530.9	46	Kentucky	2,810.1
8	Washington	5,485.6	47	Vermont	2,708.5
50	West Virginia	2,250.4	48	North Dakota	2,624.2
39	Wisconsin	3,407.1	49	New Hampshire	2,526.4
32	Wyoming	3,925.6	50	West Virginia	2,250.4
				District of Columbia	7,814.9

Source: Federal Bureau of Investigation
"Crime in the United States 1997" (Uniform Crime Reports, November 22, 1998)
*Property crimes are offenses of burglary, larceny-theft and motor vehicle theft.

Percent Change in Property Crime Rate: 1996 to 1997

National Percent Change = 3.1% Decrease*

ALPHA ORDER

RANK	STATE	PERCENT CHANGE
8	Alabama	1.7
30	Alaska	(3.2)
7	Arizona	2.1
13	Arkansas	0.4
44	California	(6.4)
50	Colorado	(9.1)
40	Connecticut	(5.8)
2	Delaware	5.5
29	Florida	(3.1)
47	Georgia	(8.6)
48	Hawaii	(8.9)
24	Idaho	(2.1)
31	Illinois	(3.4)
16	Indiana	(0.2)
5	Iowa	3.8
27	Kansas	(2.7)
20	Kentucky	(1.3)
37	Louisiana	(5.4)
46	Maine	(7.9)
43	Maryland	(6.3)
36	Massachusetts	(5.1)
32	Michigan	(3.5)
19	Minnesota	(1.2)
6	Mississippi	3.1
39	Missouri	(5.7)
20	Montana	(1.3)
34	Nebraska	(3.9)
9	Nevada	1.6
45	New Hampshire	(6.6)
42	New Jersey	(6.2)
4	New Mexico	5.1
37	New York	(5.4)
18	North Carolina	(1.1)
10	North Dakota	1.5
11	Ohio	1.3
25	Oklahoma	(2.4)
3	Oregon	5.3
28	Pennsylvania	(2.8)
48	Rhode Island	(8.9)
22	South Carolina	(1.4)
1	South Dakota	9.1
12	Tennessee	1.0
33	Texas	(3.7)
14	Utah	0.1
41	Vermont	(6.0)
26	Virginia	(2.6)
14	Washington	0.1
17	West Virginia	(1.0)
35	Wisconsin	(4.5)
23	Wyoming	(2.0)

RANK ORDER

RANK	STATE	PERCENT CHANGE
1	South Dakota	9.1
2	Delaware	5.5
3	Oregon	5.3
4	New Mexico	5.1
5	Iowa	3.8
6	Mississippi	3.1
7	Arizona	2.1
8	Alabama	1.7
9	Nevada	1.6
10	North Dakota	1.5
11	Ohio	1.3
12	Tennessee	1.0
13	Arkansas	0.4
14	Utah	0.1
14	Washington	0.1
16	Indiana	(0.2)
17	West Virginia	(1.0)
18	North Carolina	(1.1)
19	Minnesota	(1.2)
20	Kentucky	(1.3)
20	Montana	(1.3)
22	South Carolina	(1.4)
23	Wyoming	(2.0)
24	Idaho	(2.1)
25	Oklahoma	(2.4)
26	Virginia	(2.6)
27	Kansas	(2.7)
28	Pennsylvania	(2.8)
29	Florida	(3.1)
30	Alaska	(3.2)
31	Illinois	(3.4)
32	Michigan	(3.5)
33	Texas	(3.7)
34	Nebraska	(3.9)
35	Wisconsin	(4.5)
36	Massachusetts	(5.1)
37	Louisiana	(5.4)
37	New York	(5.4)
39	Missouri	(5.7)
40	Connecticut	(5.8)
41	Vermont	(6.0)
42	New Jersey	(6.2)
43	Maryland	(6.3)
44	California	(6.4)
45	New Hampshire	(6.6)
46	Maine	(7.9)
47	Georgia	(8.6)
48	Hawaii	(8.9)
48	Rhode Island	(8.9)
50	Colorado	(9.1)
	District of Columbia	(17.1)

Source: Federal Bureau of Investigation
   "Crime in the United States 1997" (Uniform Crime Reports, November 22, 1998)
*Property crimes are offenses of burglary, larceny-theft and motor vehicle theft.

Burglaries in 1997

National Total = 2,461,120 Burglaries*

ALPHA ORDER

ALPHA ORDER

RANK	STATE	BURGLARIES	% of USA
20	Alabama	43,786	1.8%
46	Alaska	4,276	0.2%
14	Arizona	60,077	2.4%
30	Arkansas	25,568	1.0%
1	California	299,240	12.2%
27	Colorado	30,994	1.3%
33	Connecticut	24,143	1.0%
43	Delaware	5,620	0.2%
2	Florida	213,926	8.7%
8	Georgia	81,320	3.3%
37	Hawaii	12,741	0.5%
40	Idaho	9,175	0.4%
5	Illinois	103,550	4.2%
16	Indiana	48,182	2.0%
34	Iowa	22,003	0.9%
31	Kansas	25,187	1.0%
29	Kentucky	26,638	1.1%
15	Louisiana	53,935	2.2%
41	Maine	8,241	0.3%
17	Maryland	47,918	1.9%
21	Massachusetts	40,491	1.6%
9	Michigan	80,726	3.3%
24	Minnesota	35,265	1.4%
26	Mississippi	32,429	1.3%
18	Missouri	46,900	1.9%
44	Montana	5,002	0.2%
39	Nebraska	9,813	0.4%
35	Nevada	21,975	0.9%
45	New Hampshire	4,612	0.2%
13	New Jersey	60,894	2.5%
32	New Mexico	25,126	1.0%
4	New York	118,306	4.8%
6	North Carolina	100,002	4.1%
50	North Dakota	2,300	0.1%
7	Ohio	94,972	3.9%
22	Oklahoma	40,015	1.6%
25	Oregon	33,507	1.4%
10	Pennsylvania	68,218	2.8%
42	Rhode Island	7,083	0.3%
19	South Carolina	46,322	1.9%
47	South Dakota	4,088	0.2%
11	Tennessee	62,899	2.6%
3	Texas	201,059	8.2%
36	Utah	18,335	0.7%
48	Vermont	3,611	0.1%
23	Virginia	38,475	1.6%
12	Washington	62,064	2.5%
38	West Virginia	10,647	0.4%
28	Wisconsin	29,503	1.2%
49	Wyoming	2,998	0.1%

RANK ORDER

RANK	STATE	BURGLARIES	% of USA
1	California	299,240	12.2%
2	Florida	213,926	8.7%
3	Texas	201,059	8.2%
4	New York	118,306	4.8%
5	Illinois	103,550	4.2%
6	North Carolina	100,002	4.1%
7	Ohio	94,972	3.9%
8	Georgia	81,320	3.3%
9	Michigan	80,726	3.3%
10	Pennsylvania	68,218	2.8%
11	Tennessee	62,899	2.6%
12	Washington	62,064	2.5%
13	New Jersey	60,894	2.5%
14	Arizona	60,077	2.4%
15	Louisiana	53,935	2.2%
16	Indiana	48,182	2.0%
17	Maryland	47,918	1.9%
18	Missouri	46,900	1.9%
19	South Carolina	46,322	1.9%
20	Alabama	43,786	1.8%
21	Massachusetts	40,491	1.6%
22	Oklahoma	40,015	1.6%
23	Virginia	38,475	1.6%
24	Minnesota	35,265	1.4%
25	Oregon	33,507	1.4%
26	Mississippi	32,429	1.3%
27	Colorado	30,994	1.3%
28	Wisconsin	29,503	1.2%
29	Kentucky	26,638	1.1%
30	Arkansas	25,568	1.0%
31	Kansas	25,187	1.0%
32	New Mexico	25,126	1.0%
33	Connecticut	24,143	1.0%
34	Iowa	22,003	0.9%
35	Nevada	21,975	0.9%
36	Utah	18,335	0.7%
37	Hawaii	12,741	0.5%
38	West Virginia	10,647	0.4%
39	Nebraska	9,813	0.4%
40	Idaho	9,175	0.4%
41	Maine	8,241	0.3%
42	Rhode Island	7,083	0.3%
43	Delaware	5,620	0.2%
44	Montana	5,002	0.2%
45	New Hampshire	4,612	0.2%
46	Alaska	4,276	0.2%
47	South Dakota	4,088	0.2%
48	Vermont	3,611	0.1%
49	Wyoming	2,998	0.1%
50	North Dakota	2,300	0.1%
	District of Columbia	6,963	0.3%

Source: Federal Bureau of Investigation
   "Crime in the United States 1997" (Uniform Crime Reports, November 22, 1998)
*Burglary is the unlawful entry of a structure to commit a felony or theft. Attempts are included.

Average Time Between Burglaries in 1997

National Rate = A Burglary Occurs Every 13 Seconds*

RANK	STATE	MINUTES.SECONDS
31	Alabama	12.00
5	Alaska	122.55
37	Arizona	8.45
21	Arkansas	20.34
50	California	1.46
24	Colorado	16.58
18	Connecticut	21.46
8	Delaware	93.31
49	Florida	2.28
43	Georgia	6.28
14	Hawaii	41.15
11	Idaho	57.17
46	Illinois	5.05
35	Indiana	10.55
17	Iowa	23.53
20	Kansas	20.52
22	Kentucky	19.44
36	Louisiana	9.45
10	Maine	63.47
34	Maryland	10.58
30	Massachusetts	12.59
42	Michigan	6.31
27	Minnesota	14.54
25	Mississippi	16.13
33	Missouri	11.13
7	Montana	105.05
12	Nebraska	53.34
16	Nevada	23.55
6	New Hampshire	113.58
38	New Jersey	8.38
19	New Mexico	20.55
47	New York	4.26
45	North Carolina	5.16
1	North Dakota	228.31
44	Ohio	5.32
29	Oklahoma	13.08
26	Oregon	15.41
41	Pennsylvania	7.42
9	Rhode Island	74.13
32	South Carolina	11.21
4	South Dakota	128.34
40	Tennessee	8.22
48	Texas	2.37
15	Utah	28.40
3	Vermont	145.34
28	Virginia	13.40
39	Washington	8.28
13	West Virginia	49.22
23	Wisconsin	17.49
2	Wyoming	175.19

RANK	STATE	MINUTES.SECONDS
1	North Dakota	228.31
2	Wyoming	175.19
3	Vermont	145.34
4	South Dakota	128.34
5	Alaska	122.55
6	New Hampshire	113.58
7	Montana	105.05
8	Delaware	93.31
9	Rhode Island	74.13
10	Maine	63.47
11	Idaho	57.17
12	Nebraska	53.34
13	West Virginia	49.22
14	Hawaii	41.15
15	Utah	28.40
16	Nevada	23.55
17	Iowa	23.53
18	Connecticut	21.46
19	New Mexico	20.55
20	Kansas	20.52
21	Arkansas	20.34
22	Kentucky	19.44
23	Wisconsin	17.49
24	Colorado	16.58
25	Mississippi	16.13
26	Oregon	15.41
27	Minnesota	14.54
28	Virginia	13.40
29	Oklahoma	13.08
30	Massachusetts	12.59
31	Alabama	12.00
32	South Carolina	11.21
33	Missouri	11.13
34	Maryland	10.58
35	Indiana	10.55
36	Louisiana	9.45
37	Arizona	8.45
38	New Jersey	8.38
39	Washington	8.28
40	Tennessee	8.22
41	Pennsylvania	7.42
42	Michigan	6.31
43	Georgia	6.28
44	Ohio	5.32
45	North Carolina	5.16
46	Illinois	5.05
47	New York	4.26
48	Texas	2.37
49	Florida	2.28
50	California	1.46
	District of Columbia	75.29

Source: Morgan Quitno Press using data from Federal Bureau of Investigation
"Crime in the United States 1997" (Uniform Crime Reports, November 22, 1998)
Burglary is the unlawful entry of a structure to commit a felony or theft. Attempts are included.

Percent Change in Number of Burglaries: 1996 to 1997

National Percent Change = 1.8% Decrease*

ALPHA ORDER

RANK	STATE	PERCENT CHANGE
14	Alabama	2.3
50	Alaska	(16.5)
6	Arizona	8.0
7	Arkansas	6.9
35	California	(4.2)
46	Colorado	(10.0)
48	Connecticut	(12.4)
33	Delaware	(3.6)
28	Florida	(2.3)
24	Georgia	(0.8)
21	Hawaii	(0.3)
4	Idaho	8.8
36	Illinois	(4.3)
13	Indiana	5.2
1	Iowa	16.1
20	Kansas	(0.2)
22	Kentucky	(0.4)
36	Louisiana	(4.3)
47	Maine	(11.4)
39	Maryland	(4.8)
40	Massachusetts	(5.6)
42	Michigan	(6.0)
23	Minnesota	(0.7)
12	Mississippi	5.4
27	Missouri	(2.1)
15	Montana	1.9
31	Nebraska	(3.3)
3	Nevada	12.4
43	New Hampshire	(8.9)
34	New Jersey	(3.7)
9	New Mexico	6.5
43	New York	(8.9)
18	North Carolina	1.5
2	North Dakota	15.5
16	Ohio	1.8
32	Oklahoma	(3.5)
11	Oregon	5.8
38	Pennsylvania	(4.4)
49	Rhode Island	(12.9)
29	South Carolina	(2.5)
19	South Dakota	0.3
17	Tennessee	1.6
25	Texas	(1.6)
5	Utah	8.1
43	Vermont	(8.9)
26	Virginia	(2.0)
10	Washington	6.1
8	West Virginia	6.7
30	Wisconsin	(2.8)
41	Wyoming	(5.8)

RANK ORDER

RANK	STATE	PERCENT CHANGE
1	Iowa	16.1
2	North Dakota	15.5
3	Nevada	12.4
4	Idaho	8.8
5	Utah	8.1
6	Arizona	8.0
7	Arkansas	6.9
8	West Virginia	6.7
9	New Mexico	6.5
10	Washington	6.1
11	Oregon	5.8
12	Mississippi	5.4
13	Indiana	5.2
14	Alabama	2.3
15	Montana	1.9
16	Ohio	1.8
17	Tennessee	1.6
18	North Carolina	1.5
19	South Dakota	0.3
20	Kansas	(0.2)
21	Hawaii	(0.3)
22	Kentucky	(0.4)
23	Minnesota	(0.7)
24	Georgia	(0.8)
25	Texas	(1.6)
26	Virginia	(2.0)
27	Missouri	(2.1)
28	Florida	(2.3)
29	South Carolina	(2.5)
30	Wisconsin	(2.8)
31	Nebraska	(3.3)
32	Oklahoma	(3.5)
33	Delaware	(3.6)
34	New Jersey	(3.7)
35	California	(4.2)
36	Illinois	(4.3)
36	Louisiana	(4.3)
38	Pennsylvania	(4.4)
39	Maryland	(4.8)
40	Massachusetts	(5.6)
41	Wyoming	(5.8)
42	Michigan	(6.0)
43	New Hampshire	(8.9)
43	New York	(8.9)
43	Vermont	(8.9)
46	Colorado	(10.0)
47	Maine	(11.4)
48	Connecticut	(12.4)
49	Rhode Island	(12.9)
50	Alaska	(16.5)
	District of Columbia	(29.2)

Source: Federal Bureau of Investigation
   "Crime in the United States 1997" (Uniform Crime Reports, November 22, 1998)
*Burglary is the unlawful entry of a structure to commit a felony or theft. Attempts are included.

Burglary Rate in 1997

National Rate = 919.6 Burglaries per 100,000 Population*

ALPHA ORDER

RANK	STATE	RATE
16	Alabama	1,013.8
35	Alaska	702.1
4	Arizona	1,318.9
17	Arkansas	1,013.4
20	California	927.4
27	Colorado	796.1
33	Connecticut	738.3
29	Delaware	767.8
1	Florida	1,459.8
12	Georgia	1,086.3
13	Hawaii	1,073.4
30	Idaho	758.3
22	Illinois	870.5
26	Indiana	821.7
28	Iowa	771.5
18	Kansas	970.6
36	Kentucky	681.6
6	Louisiana	1,239.3
37	Maine	663.5
19	Maryland	940.7
38	Massachusetts	661.8
25	Michigan	825.9
32	Minnesota	752.6
9	Mississippi	1,187.4
23	Missouri	868.2
46	Montana	569.1
42	Nebraska	592.2
5	Nevada	1,310.4
49	New Hampshire	393.2
31	New Jersey	756.2
2	New Mexico	1,452.4
39	New York	652.3
3	North Carolina	1,346.8
50	North Dakota	358.8
24	Ohio	849.0
8	Oklahoma	1,206.4
15	Oregon	1,033.2
47	Pennsylvania	567.5
34	Rhode Island	717.6
7	South Carolina	1,232.0
48	South Dakota	553.9
10	Tennessee	1,171.7
14	Texas	1,034.3
21	Utah	890.5
41	Vermont	613.1
44	Virginia	571.4
11	Washington	1,106.3
43	West Virginia	586.3
45	Wisconsin	570.7
40	Wyoming	624.6

RANK ORDER

RANK	STATE	RATE
1	Florida	1,459.8
2	New Mexico	1,452.4
3	North Carolina	1,346.8
4	Arizona	1,318.9
5	Nevada	1,310.4
6	Louisiana	1,239.3
7	South Carolina	1,232.0
8	Oklahoma	1,206.4
9	Mississippi	1,187.4
10	Tennessee	1,171.7
11	Washington	1,106.3
12	Georgia	1,086.3
13	Hawaii	1,073.4
14	Texas	1,034.3
15	Oregon	1,033.2
16	Alabama	1,013.8
17	Arkansas	1,013.4
18	Kansas	970.6
19	Maryland	940.7
20	California	927.4
21	Utah	890.5
22	Illinois	870.5
23	Missouri	868.2
24	Ohio	849.0
25	Michigan	825.9
26	Indiana	821.7
27	Colorado	796.1
28	Iowa	771.5
29	Delaware	767.8
30	Idaho	758.3
31	New Jersey	756.2
32	Minnesota	752.6
33	Connecticut	738.3
34	Rhode Island	717.6
35	Alaska	702.1
36	Kentucky	681.6
37	Maine	663.5
38	Massachusetts	661.8
39	New York	652.3
40	Wyoming	624.6
41	Vermont	613.1
42	Nebraska	592.2
43	West Virginia	586.3
44	Virginia	571.4
45	Wisconsin	570.7
46	Montana	569.1
47	Pennsylvania	567.5
48	South Dakota	553.9
49	New Hampshire	393.2
50	North Dakota	358.8
	District of Columbia	1,316.3

Source: Federal Bureau of Investigation
"Crime in the United States 1997" (Uniform Crime Reports, November 22, 1998)
*Burglary is the unlawful entry of a structure to commit a felony or theft. Attempts are included.

Percent Change in Burglary Rate: 1996 to 1997

National Percent Change = 2.7% Decrease*

RANK	STATE	PERCENT CHANGE
16	Alabama	1.2
50	Alaska	(16.7)
8	Arizona	5.0
6	Arkansas	6.3
39	California	(5.3)
47	Colorado	(11.6)
48	Connecticut	(12.3)
35	Delaware	(4.5)
31	Florida	(4.0)
24	Georgia	(2.6)
19	Hawaii	(0.6)
5	Idaho	6.9
37	Illinois	(4.7)
11	Indiana	4.8
1	Iowa	16.1
22	Kansas	(1.1)
21	Kentucky	(1.0)
34	Louisiana	(4.4)
46	Maine	(11.3)
38	Maryland	(5.2)
41	Massachusetts	(6.0)
42	Michigan	(7.8)
23	Minnesota	(1.3)
10	Mississippi	4.9
26	Missouri	(2.9)
14	Montana	1.9
29	Nebraska	(3.6)
3	Nevada	7.4
45	New Hampshire	(9.8)
35	New Jersey	(4.5)
7	New Mexico	5.5
43	New York	(8.6)
18	North Carolina	0.1
2	North Dakota	16.0
15	Ohio	1.6
30	Oklahoma	(3.9)
13	Oregon	4.5
33	Pennsylvania	(4.1)
49	Rhode Island	(12.7)
31	South Carolina	(4.0)
19	South Dakota	(0.6)
17	Tennessee	0.7
28	Texas	(3.2)
8	Utah	5.0
44	Vermont	(8.9)
25	Virginia	(2.8)
12	Washington	4.6
4	West Virginia	7.3
27	Wisconsin	(3.0)
40	Wyoming	(5.6)

RANK	STATE	PERCENT CHANGE
1	Iowa	16.1
2	North Dakota	16.0
3	Nevada	7.4
4	West Virginia	7.3
5	Idaho	6.9
6	Arkansas	6.3
7	New Mexico	5.5
8	Arizona	5.0
8	Utah	5.0
10	Mississippi	4.9
11	Indiana	4.8
12	Washington	4.6
13	Oregon	4.5
14	Montana	1.9
15	Ohio	1.6
16	Alabama	1.2
17	Tennessee	0.7
18	North Carolina	0.1
19	Hawaii	(0.6)
19	South Dakota	(0.6)
21	Kentucky	(1.0)
22	Kansas	(1.1)
23	Minnesota	(1.3)
24	Georgia	(2.6)
25	Virginia	(2.8)
26	Missouri	(2.9)
27	Wisconsin	(3.0)
28	Texas	(3.2)
29	Nebraska	(3.6)
30	Oklahoma	(3.9)
31	Florida	(4.0)
31	South Carolina	(4.0)
33	Pennsylvania	(4.1)
34	Louisiana	(4.4)
35	Delaware	(4.5)
35	New Jersey	(4.5)
37	Illinois	(4.7)
38	Maryland	(5.2)
39	California	(5.3)
40	Wyoming	(5.6)
41	Massachusetts	(6.0)
42	Michigan	(7.8)
43	New York	(8.6)
44	Vermont	(8.9)
45	New Hampshire	(9.8)
46	Maine	(11.3)
47	Colorado	(11.6)
48	Connecticut	(12.3)
49	Rhode Island	(12.7)
50	Alaska	(16.7)
	District of Columbia	(27.3)

Source: Federal Bureau of Investigation
   "Crime in the United States 1997" (Uniform Crime Reports, November 22, 1998)
*Burglary is the unlawful entry of a structure to commit a felony or theft. Attempts are included.

Larcenies and Thefts in 1997

National Total = 7,725,470 Larcenies and Thefts*

RANK	STATE	THEFTS	% of USA
24	Alabama	127,616	1.7%
46	Alaska	20,780	0.3%
12	Arizona	195,045	2.5%
32	Arkansas	72,253	0.9%
1	California	784,405	10.2%
25	Colorado	119,801	1.6%
29	Connecticut	78,821	1.0%
44	Delaware	23,312	0.3%
3	Florida	594,492	7.7%
8	Georgia	262,263	3.4%
37	Hawaii	48,984	0.6%
39	Idaho	32,784	0.4%
5	Illinois	350,140	4.5%
17	Indiana	158,442	2.1%
34	Iowa	71,301	0.9%
30	Kansas	76,125	1.0%
31	Kentucky	73,487	1.0%
16	Louisiana	163,114	2.1%
41	Maine	27,513	0.4%
15	Maryland	166,256	2.2%
26	Massachusetts	115,494	1.5%
7	Michigan	276,863	3.6%
20	Minnesota	137,872	1.8%
33	Mississippi	71,887	0.9%
19	Missouri	155,472	2.0%
40	Montana	30,411	0.4%
38	Nebraska	48,363	0.6%
36	Nevada	53,112	0.7%
43	New Hampshire	23,430	0.3%
13	New Jersey	184,979	2.4%
35	New Mexico	67,188	0.9%
4	New York	386,435	5.0%
10	North Carolina	238,228	3.1%
49	North Dakota	13,367	0.2%
6	Ohio	315,908	4.1%
27	Oklahoma	109,039	1.4%
21	Oregon	136,129	1.8%
9	Pennsylvania	246,892	3.2%
45	Rhode Island	21,499	0.3%
22	South Carolina	131,325	1.7%
47	South Dakota	17,545	0.2%
18	Tennessee	156,843	2.0%
2	Texas	645,451	8.4%
28	Utah	89,090	1.2%
50	Vermont	11,542	0.1%
14	Virginia	180,406	2.3%
11	Washington	213,823	2.8%
42	West Virginia	26,934	0.3%
23	Wisconsin	131,002	1.7%
48	Wyoming	15,198	0.2%

RANK	STATE	THEFTS	% of USA
1	California	784,405	10.2%
2	Texas	645,451	8.4%
3	Florida	594,492	7.7%
4	New York	386,435	5.0%
5	Illinois	350,140	4.5%
6	Ohio	315,908	4.1%
7	Michigan	276,863	3.6%
8	Georgia	262,263	3.4%
9	Pennsylvania	246,892	3.2%
10	North Carolina	238,228	3.1%
11	Washington	213,823	2.8%
12	Arizona	195,045	2.5%
13	New Jersey	184,979	2.4%
14	Virginia	180,406	2.3%
15	Maryland	166,256	2.2%
16	Louisiana	163,114	2.1%
17	Indiana	158,442	2.1%
18	Tennessee	156,843	2.0%
19	Missouri	155,472	2.0%
20	Minnesota	137,872	1.8%
21	Oregon	136,129	1.8%
22	South Carolina	131,325	1.7%
23	Wisconsin	131,002	1.7%
24	Alabama	127,616	1.7%
25	Colorado	119,801	1.6%
26	Massachusetts	115,494	1.5%
27	Oklahoma	109,039	1.4%
28	Utah	89,090	1.2%
29	Connecticut	78,821	1.0%
30	Kansas	76,125	1.0%
31	Kentucky	73,487	1.0%
32	Arkansas	72,253	0.9%
33	Mississippi	71,887	0.9%
34	Iowa	71,301	0.9%
35	New Mexico	67,188	0.9%
36	Nevada	53,112	0.7%
37	Hawaii	48,984	0.6%
38	Nebraska	48,363	0.6%
39	Idaho	32,784	0.4%
40	Montana	30,411	0.4%
41	Maine	27,513	0.4%
42	West Virginia	26,934	0.3%
43	New Hampshire	23,430	0.3%
44	Delaware	23,312	0.3%
45	Rhode Island	21,499	0.3%
46	Alaska	20,780	0.3%
47	South Dakota	17,545	0.2%
48	Wyoming	15,198	0.2%
49	North Dakota	13,367	0.2%
50	Vermont	11,542	0.1%
	District of Columbia	26,809	0.3%

Source: Federal Bureau of Investigation
    "Crime in the United States 1997" (Uniform Crime Reports, November 22, 1998)
*Larceny and theft is the unlawful taking of property without use of force, violence or fraud. Attempts are included.
Motor vehicle thefts are excluded.

Average Time Between Larcenies and Thefts in 1997

National Rate = A Larceny-Theft Occurs Every 4 Seconds*

ALPHA ORDER				RANK ORDER		
RANK	STATE	MINUTES.SECONDS		RANK	STATE	MINUTES.SECONDS
27	Alabama	4.07		1	Vermont	45.32
5	Alaska	25.17		2	North Dakota	39.19
39	Arizona	2.41		3	Wyoming	34.35
19	Arkansas	7.16		4	South Dakota	29.58
50	California	0.40		5	Alaska	25.17
26	Colorado	4.23		6	Rhode Island	24.27
22	Connecticut	6.40		7	Delaware	22.33
7	Delaware	22.33		8	New Hampshire	22.26
48	Florida	0.53		9	West Virginia	19.31
43	Georgia	2.00		10	Maine	19.06
14	Hawaii	10.44		11	Montana	17.17
12	Idaho	16.02		12	Idaho	16.02
46	Illinois	1.30		13	Nebraska	10.52
34	Indiana	3.19		14	Hawaii	10.44
17	Iowa	7.22		15	Nevada	9.54
21	Kansas	6.54		16	New Mexico	7.49
20	Kentucky	7.09		17	Iowa	7.22
35	Louisiana	3.13		18	Mississippi	7.19
10	Maine	19.06		19	Arkansas	7.16
36	Maryland	3.10		20	Kentucky	7.09
25	Massachusetts	4.33		21	Kansas	6.54
44	Michigan	1.54		22	Connecticut	6.40
31	Minnesota	3.49		23	Utah	5.54
18	Mississippi	7.19		24	Oklahoma	4.49
32	Missouri	3.23		25	Massachusetts	4.33
11	Montana	17.17		26	Colorado	4.23
13	Nebraska	10.52		27	Alabama	4.07
15	Nevada	9.54		28	Wisconsin	4.01
8	New Hampshire	22.26		29	South Carolina	4.00
38	New Jersey	2.50		30	Oregon	3.52
16	New Mexico	7.49		31	Minnesota	3.49
47	New York	1.22		32	Missouri	3.23
41	North Carolina	2.13		33	Tennessee	3.21
2	North Dakota	39.19		34	Indiana	3.19
45	Ohio	1.40		35	Louisiana	3.13
24	Oklahoma	4.49		36	Maryland	3.10
30	Oregon	3.52		37	Virginia	2.55
42	Pennsylvania	2.08		38	New Jersey	2.50
6	Rhode Island	24.27		39	Arizona	2.41
29	South Carolina	4.00		40	Washington	2.28
4	South Dakota	29.58		41	North Carolina	2.13
33	Tennessee	3.21		42	Pennsylvania	2.08
49	Texas	0.49		43	Georgia	2.00
23	Utah	5.54		44	Michigan	1.54
1	Vermont	45.32		45	Ohio	1.40
37	Virginia	2.55		46	Illinois	1.30
40	Washington	2.28		47	New York	1.22
9	West Virginia	19.31		48	Florida	0.53
28	Wisconsin	4.01		49	Texas	0.49
3	Wyoming	34.35		50	California	0.40
					District of Columbia	19.37

Source: Morgan Quitno Press using data from Federal Bureau of Investigation
    "Crime in the United States 1997" (Uniform Crime Reports, November 22, 1998)
*Larceny and theft is the unlawful taking of property without use of force, violence or fraud. Attempts are included.
Motor vehicle thefts are excluded.

Percent Change in Number of Larcenies and Thefts: 1996 to 1997

National Percent Change = 2.3% Decrease*

ALPHA ORDER

RANK	STATE	PERCENT CHANGE
6	Alabama	3.5
13	Alaska	1.1
5	Arizona	3.6
22	Arkansas	(1.0)
43	California	(5.5)
48	Colorado	(8.3)
32	Connecticut	(3.1)
2	Delaware	7.6
27	Florida	(1.8)
49	Georgia	(9.2)
50	Hawaii	(10.5)
33	Idaho	(3.2)
30	Illinois	(2.3)
24	Indiana	(1.5)
20	Iowa	(0.8)
31	Kansas	(2.6)
16	Kentucky	(0.2)
44	Louisiana	(5.9)
45	Maine	(6.9)
38	Maryland	(4.3)
35	Massachusetts	(3.4)
14	Michigan	0.0
19	Minnesota	(0.6)
4	Mississippi	3.7
46	Missouri	(7.9)
26	Montana	(1.7)
37	Nebraska	(3.9)
10	Nevada	1.6
40	New Hampshire	(4.8)
39	New Jersey	(4.6)
7	New Mexico	3.1
34	New York	(3.3)
15	North Carolina	(0.1)
18	North Dakota	(0.5)
10	Ohio	1.6
17	Oklahoma	(0.4)
3	Oregon	5.8
24	Pennsylvania	(1.5)
47	Rhode Island	(8.0)
12	South Carolina	1.3
1	South Dakota	13.0
8	Tennessee	2.9
28	Texas	(2.1)
9	Utah	1.8
40	Vermont	(4.8)
28	Virginia	(2.1)
21	Washington	(0.9)
40	West Virginia	(4.8)
36	Wisconsin	(3.6)
23	Wyoming	(1.4)

RANK ORDER

RANK	STATE	PERCENT CHANGE
1	South Dakota	13.0
2	Delaware	7.6
3	Oregon	5.8
4	Mississippi	3.7
5	Arizona	3.6
6	Alabama	3.5
7	New Mexico	3.1
8	Tennessee	2.9
9	Utah	1.8
10	Nevada	1.6
10	Ohio	1.6
12	South Carolina	1.3
13	Alaska	1.1
14	Michigan	0.0
15	North Carolina	(0.1)
16	Kentucky	(0.2)
17	Oklahoma	(0.4)
18	North Dakota	(0.5)
19	Minnesota	(0.6)
20	Iowa	(0.8)
21	Washington	(0.9)
22	Arkansas	(1.0)
23	Wyoming	(1.4)
24	Indiana	(1.5)
24	Pennsylvania	(1.5)
26	Montana	(1.7)
27	Florida	(1.8)
28	Texas	(2.1)
28	Virginia	(2.1)
30	Illinois	(2.3)
31	Kansas	(2.6)
32	Connecticut	(3.1)
33	Idaho	(3.2)
34	New York	(3.3)
35	Massachusetts	(3.4)
36	Wisconsin	(3.6)
37	Nebraska	(3.9)
38	Maryland	(4.3)
39	New Jersey	(4.6)
40	New Hampshire	(4.8)
40	Vermont	(4.8)
40	West Virginia	(4.8)
43	California	(5.5)
44	Louisiana	(5.9)
45	Maine	(6.9)
46	Missouri	(7.9)
47	Rhode Island	(8.0)
48	Colorado	(8.3)
49	Georgia	(9.2)
50	Hawaii	(10.5)
	District of Columbia	(14.6)

Source: Federal Bureau of Investigation
      "Crime in the United States 1997" (Uniform Crime Reports, November 22, 1998)
*Larceny and theft is the unlawful taking of property without use of force, violence or fraud. Attempts are included.
Motor vehicle thefts are excluded.

Larceny and Theft Rate in 1997

National Rate = 2,886.5 Larcenies and Thefts per 100,000 Population*

ALPHA ORDER			RANK ORDER		
RANK	STATE	RATE	RANK	STATE	RATE
21	Alabama	2,954.8	1	Utah	4,326.9
12	Alaska	3,412.2	2	Arizona	4,282.0
2	Arizona	4,282.0	3	Oregon	4,197.6
28	Arkansas	2,863.8	4	Hawaii	4,126.7
37	California	2,430.9	5	Florida	4,056.9
20	Colorado	3,077.3	6	New Mexico	3,883.7
38	Connecticut	2,410.4	7	Washington	3,811.5
17	Delaware	3,184.7	8	Louisiana	3,748.0
5	Florida	4,056.9	9	Georgia	3,503.4
9	Georgia	3,503.4	10	South Carolina	3,492.7
4	Hawaii	4,126.7	11	Montana	3,459.7
31	Idaho	2,709.4	12	Alaska	3,412.2
22	Illinois	2,943.3	13	Texas	3,320.4
32	Indiana	2,701.9	14	Oklahoma	3,287.3
36	Iowa	2,500.0	15	Maryland	3,263.8
24	Kansas	2,933.5	16	North Carolina	3,208.5
49	Kentucky	1,880.4	17	Delaware	3,184.7
8	Louisiana	3,748.0	18	Nevada	3,167.1
41	Maine	2,215.2	19	Wyoming	3,166.3
15	Maryland	3,263.8	20	Colorado	3,077.3
48	Massachusetts	1,887.8	21	Alabama	2,954.8
29	Michigan	2,832.6	22	Illinois	2,943.3
23	Minnesota	2,942.2	23	Minnesota	2,942.2
34	Mississippi	2,632.3	24	Kansas	2,933.5
27	Missouri	2,878.0	25	Tennessee	2,921.8
11	Montana	3,459.7	26	Nebraska	2,918.7
26	Nebraska	2,918.7	27	Missouri	2,878.0
18	Nevada	3,167.1	28	Arkansas	2,863.8
46	New Hampshire	1,997.4	29	Michigan	2,832.6
40	New Jersey	2,297.0	30	Ohio	2,824.1
6	New Mexico	3,883.7	31	Idaho	2,709.4
43	New York	2,130.6	32	Indiana	2,701.9
16	North Carolina	3,208.5	33	Virginia	2,679.0
44	North Dakota	2,085.3	34	Mississippi	2,632.3
30	Ohio	2,824.1	35	Wisconsin	2,533.9
14	Oklahoma	3,287.3	36	Iowa	2,500.0
3	Oregon	4,197.6	37	California	2,430.9
45	Pennsylvania	2,054.0	38	Connecticut	2,410.4
42	Rhode Island	2,178.2	39	South Dakota	2,377.4
10	South Carolina	3,492.7	40	New Jersey	2,297.0
39	South Dakota	2,377.4	41	Maine	2,215.2
25	Tennessee	2,921.8	42	Rhode Island	2,178.2
13	Texas	3,320.4	43	New York	2,130.6
1	Utah	4,326.9	44	North Dakota	2,085.3
47	Vermont	1,959.6	45	Pennsylvania	2,054.0
33	Virginia	2,679.0	46	New Hampshire	1,997.4
7	Washington	3,811.5	47	Vermont	1,959.6
50	West Virginia	1,483.1	48	Massachusetts	1,887.8
35	Wisconsin	2,533.9	49	Kentucky	1,880.4
19	Wyoming	3,166.3	50	West Virginia	1,483.1
				District of Columbia	5,067.9

Source: Federal Bureau of Investigation
    "Crime in the United States 1997" (Uniform Crime Reports, November 22, 1998)
*Larceny and theft is the unlawful taking of property without use of force, violence or fraud. Attempts are included.
Motor vehicle thefts are excluded.

Percent Change in Larceny and Theft Rate: 1996 to 1997

National Percent Change = 3.1% Decrease*

ALPHA ORDER

RANK	STATE	PERCENT CHANGE
5	Alabama	2.4
9	Alaska	0.8
10	Arizona	0.7
20	Arkansas	(1.5)
44	California	(6.7)
48	Colorado	(9.9)
29	Connecticut	(3.0)
2	Delaware	6.6
32	Florida	(3.5)
50	Georgia	(10.8)
49	Hawaii	(10.7)
40	Idaho	(4.9)
26	Illinois	(2.7)
23	Indiana	(1.8)
13	Iowa	(0.8)
31	Kansas	(3.4)
13	Kentucky	(0.8)
43	Louisiana	(5.9)
45	Maine	(6.8)
38	Maryland	(4.8)
34	Massachusetts	(3.8)
24	Michigan	(1.9)
17	Minnesota	(1.2)
4	Mississippi	3.2
47	Missouri	(8.7)
22	Montana	(1.7)
36	Nebraska	(4.2)
27	Nevada	(2.9)
42	New Hampshire	(5.7)
41	New Jersey	(5.4)
6	New Mexico	2.1
29	New York	(3.0)
20	North Carolina	(1.5)
11	North Dakota	0.0
8	Ohio	1.4
15	Oklahoma	(0.9)
3	Oregon	4.6
17	Pennsylvania	(1.2)
46	Rhode Island	(7.7)
12	South Carolina	(0.4)
1	South Dakota	12.0
7	Tennessee	2.0
33	Texas	(3.7)
16	Utah	(1.1)
38	Vermont	(4.8)
27	Virginia	(2.9)
25	Washington	(2.2)
37	West Virginia	(4.3)
34	Wisconsin	(3.8)
17	Wyoming	(1.2)

RANK ORDER

RANK	STATE	PERCENT CHANGE
1	South Dakota	12.0
2	Delaware	6.6
3	Oregon	4.6
4	Mississippi	3.2
5	Alabama	2.4
6	New Mexico	2.1
7	Tennessee	2.0
8	Ohio	1.4
9	Alaska	0.8
10	Arizona	0.7
11	North Dakota	0.0
12	South Carolina	(0.4)
13	Iowa	(0.8)
13	Kentucky	(0.8)
15	Oklahoma	(0.9)
16	Utah	(1.1)
17	Minnesota	(1.2)
17	Pennsylvania	(1.2)
17	Wyoming	(1.2)
20	Arkansas	(1.5)
20	North Carolina	(1.5)
22	Montana	(1.7)
23	Indiana	(1.8)
24	Michigan	(1.9)
25	Washington	(2.2)
26	Illinois	(2.7)
27	Nevada	(2.9)
27	Virginia	(2.9)
29	Connecticut	(3.0)
29	New York	(3.0)
31	Kansas	(3.4)
32	Florida	(3.5)
33	Texas	(3.7)
34	Massachusetts	(3.8)
34	Wisconsin	(3.8)
36	Nebraska	(4.2)
37	West Virginia	(4.3)
38	Maryland	(4.8)
38	Vermont	(4.8)
40	Idaho	(4.9)
41	New Jersey	(5.4)
42	New Hampshire	(5.7)
43	Louisiana	(5.9)
44	California	(6.7)
45	Maine	(6.8)
46	Rhode Island	(7.7)
47	Missouri	(8.7)
48	Colorado	(9.9)
49	Hawaii	(10.7)
50	Georgia	(10.8)
	District of Columbia	(12.3)

Source: Federal Bureau of Investigation
"Crime in the United States 1997" (Uniform Crime Reports, November 22, 1998)
Larceny and theft is the unlawful taking of property without use of force, violence or fraud. Attempts are included. Motor vehicle thefts are excluded.

Motor Vehicle Thefts in 1997

National Total = 1,353,707 Motor Vehicle Thefts*

ALPHA ORDER					RANK ORDER			
RANK	STATE	THEFTS	% of USA		RANK	STATE	THEFTS	% of USA
26	Alabama	15,407	1.1%		1	California	228,722	16.9%
42	Alaska	2,784	0.2%		2	Florida	107,195	7.9%
10	Arizona	44,201	3.3%		3	Texas	101,721	7.5%
34	Arkansas	7,938	0.6%		4	New York	79,697	5.9%
1	California	228,722	16.9%		5	Michigan	65,327	4.8%
23	Colorado	16,107	1.2%		6	Illinois	55,423	4.1%
28	Connecticut	14,541	1.1%		7	Ohio	45,419	3.4%
40	Delaware	3,718	0.3%		8	Georgia	44,572	3.3%
2	Florida	107,195	7.9%		9	Pennsylvania	44,213	3.3%
8	Georgia	44,572	3.3%		10	Arizona	44,201	3.3%
37	Hawaii	6,468	0.5%		11	New Jersey	41,165	3.0%
43	Idaho	2,429	0.2%		12	Tennessee	33,742	2.5%
6	Illinois	55,423	4.1%		13	Washington	31,855	2.4%
18	Indiana	25,099	1.9%		14	Maryland	30,668	2.3%
35	Iowa	6,682	0.5%		15	Massachusetts	29,452	2.2%
36	Kansas	6,491	0.5%		16	Missouri	26,517	2.0%
31	Kentucky	9,694	0.7%		17	Louisiana	26,374	1.9%
17	Louisiana	26,374	1.9%		18	Indiana	25,099	1.9%
45	Maine	1,642	0.1%		19	North Carolina	24,442	1.8%
14	Maryland	30,668	2.3%		20	Oregon	19,280	1.4%
15	Massachusetts	29,452	2.2%		21	Virginia	18,892	1.4%
5	Michigan	65,327	4.8%		22	Minnesota	17,869	1.3%
22	Minnesota	17,869	1.3%		23	Colorado	16,107	1.2%
32	Mississippi	9,328	0.7%		24	South Carolina	15,755	1.2%
16	Missouri	26,517	2.0%		25	Wisconsin	15,640	1.2%
44	Montana	2,179	0.2%		26	Alabama	15,407	1.1%
38	Nebraska	5,541	0.4%		27	Oklahoma	14,644	1.1%
29	Nevada	13,220	1.0%		28	Connecticut	14,541	1.1%
46	New Hampshire	1,593	0.1%		29	Nevada	13,220	1.0%
11	New Jersey	41,165	3.0%		30	New Mexico	12,407	0.9%
30	New Mexico	12,407	0.9%		31	Kentucky	9,694	0.7%
4	New York	79,697	5.9%		32	Mississippi	9,328	0.7%
19	North Carolina	24,442	1.8%		33	Utah	9,144	0.7%
47	North Dakota	1,154	0.1%		34	Arkansas	7,938	0.6%
7	Ohio	45,419	3.4%		35	Iowa	6,682	0.5%
27	Oklahoma	14,644	1.1%		36	Kansas	6,491	0.5%
20	Oregon	19,280	1.4%		37	Hawaii	6,468	0.5%
9	Pennsylvania	44,213	3.3%		38	Nebraska	5,541	0.4%
39	Rhode Island	4,195	0.3%		39	Rhode Island	4,195	0.3%
24	South Carolina	15,755	1.2%		40	Delaware	3,718	0.3%
48	South Dakota	858	0.1%		41	West Virginia	3,287	0.2%
12	Tennessee	33,742	2.5%		42	Alaska	2,784	0.2%
3	Texas	101,721	7.5%		43	Idaho	2,429	0.2%
33	Utah	9,144	0.7%		44	Montana	2,179	0.2%
49	Vermont	800	0.1%		45	Maine	1,642	0.1%
21	Virginia	18,892	1.4%		46	New Hampshire	1,593	0.1%
13	Washington	31,855	2.4%		47	North Dakota	1,154	0.1%
41	West Virginia	3,287	0.2%		48	South Dakota	858	0.1%
25	Wisconsin	15,640	1.2%		49	Vermont	800	0.1%
50	Wyoming	647	0.0%		50	Wyoming	647	0.0%
						District of Columbia	7,569	0.6%

Source: Federal Bureau of Investigation
    "Crime in the United States 1997" (Uniform Crime Reports, November 22, 1998)
*Includes the theft or attempted theft of a self-propelled vehicle. Excludes motorboats, construction equipment, airplanes and farming equipment.

Average Time Between Motor Vehicle Thefts in 1997

National Rate = A Motor Vehicle Theft Occurs Every 23 Seconds*

ALPHA ORDER				RANK ORDER		
RANK	STATE	MINUTES.SECONDS		RANK	STATE	MINUTES.SECONDS
25	Alabama	34.07		1	Wyoming	812.22
9	Alaska	188.47		2	Vermont	657.00
41	Arizona	11.53		3	South Dakota	612.35
17	Arkansas	66.13		4	North Dakota	455.28
50	California	2.18		5	New Hampshire	329.56
28	Colorado	32.38		6	Maine	320.06
23	Connecticut	36.09		7	Montana	241.13
11	Delaware	141.22		8	Idaho	216.23
49	Florida	4.54		9	Alaska	188.47
43	Georgia	11.47		10	West Virginia	159.54
14	Hawaii	81.16		11	Delaware	141.22
8	Idaho	216.23		12	Rhode Island	125.17
45	Illinois	9.29		13	Nebraska	94.52
33	Indiana	20.56		14	Hawaii	81.16
16	Iowa	78.40		15	Kansas	80.58
15	Kansas	80.58		16	Iowa	78.40
20	Kentucky	54.13		17	Arkansas	66.13
34	Louisiana	19.56		18	Utah	57.29
6	Maine	320.06		19	Mississippi	56.21
37	Maryland	17.08		20	Kentucky	54.13
36	Massachusetts	17.51		21	New Mexico	42.22
46	Michigan	8.03		22	Nevada	39.46
29	Minnesota	29.25		23	Connecticut	36.09
19	Mississippi	56.21		24	Oklahoma	35.53
35	Missouri	19.49		25	Alabama	34.07
7	Montana	241.13		26	Wisconsin	33.37
13	Nebraska	94.52		27	South Carolina	33.22
22	Nevada	39.46		28	Colorado	32.38
5	New Hampshire	329.56		29	Minnesota	29.25
40	New Jersey	12.46		30	Virginia	27.49
21	New Mexico	42.22		31	Oregon	27.16
47	New York	6.36		32	North Carolina	21.30
32	North Carolina	21.30		33	Indiana	20.56
4	North Dakota	455.28		34	Louisiana	19.56
44	Ohio	11.34		35	Missouri	19.49
24	Oklahoma	35.53		36	Massachusetts	17.51
31	Oregon	27.16		37	Maryland	17.08
41	Pennsylvania	11.53		38	Washington	16.30
12	Rhode Island	125.17		39	Tennessee	15.35
27	South Carolina	33.22		40	New Jersey	12.46
3	South Dakota	612.35		41	Arizona	11.53
39	Tennessee	15.35		41	Pennsylvania	11.53
48	Texas	5.10		43	Georgia	11.47
18	Utah	57.29		44	Ohio	11.34
2	Vermont	657.00		45	Illinois	9.29
30	Virginia	27.49		46	Michigan	8.03
38	Washington	16.30		47	New York	6.36
10	West Virginia	159.54		48	Texas	5.10
26	Wisconsin	33.37		49	Florida	4.54
1	Wyoming	812.22		50	California	2.18
					District of Columbia	69.26

Source: Morgan Quitno Press using data from Federal Bureau of Investigation
   "Crime in the United States 1997" (Uniform Crime Reports, November 22, 1998)
*Includes the theft or attempted theft of a self-propelled vehicle. Excludes motorboats, construction equipment, airplanes and farming equipment.

Percent Change in Number of Motor Vehicle Thefts: 1996 to 1997

National Percent Change = 2.9% Decrease*

ALPHA ORDER

RANK	STATE	PERCENT CHANGE
23	Alabama	(1.4)
37	Alaska	(7.0)
9	Arizona	7.7
17	Arkansas	1.1
35	California	(5.7)
11	Colorado	5.9
42	Connecticut	(9.2)
3	Delaware	18.1
12	Florida	3.3
31	Georgia	(3.6)
44	Hawaii	(9.6)
8	Idaho	9.0
34	Illinois	(4.6)
17	Indiana	1.1
2	Iowa	22.6
15	Kansas	1.6
33	Kentucky	(4.4)
32	Louisiana	(4.0)
38	Maine	(7.5)
50	Maryland	(15.0)
40	Massachusetts	(8.5)
27	Michigan	(2.8)
20	Minnesota	(0.3)
26	Mississippi	(2.1)
6	Missouri	10.5
28	Montana	(3.1)
24	Nebraska	(1.8)
3	Nevada	18.1
44	New Hampshire	(9.6)
48	New Jersey	(11.4)
1	New Mexico	24.4
47	New York	(11.3)
21	North Carolina	(0.5)
35	North Dakota	(5.7)
19	Ohio	(0.2)
39	Oklahoma	(8.1)
5	Oregon	13.3
43	Pennsylvania	(9.3)
41	Rhode Island	(8.7)
22	South Carolina	(0.6)
13	South Dakota	2.9
25	Tennessee	(2.0)
28	Texas	(3.1)
10	Utah	6.7
44	Vermont	(9.6)
16	Virginia	1.5
7	Washington	10.3
14	West Virginia	1.7
49	Wisconsin	(12.4)
30	Wyoming	(3.3)

RANK ORDER

RANK	STATE	PERCENT CHANGE
1	New Mexico	24.4
2	Iowa	22.6
3	Delaware	18.1
3	Nevada	18.1
5	Oregon	13.3
6	Missouri	10.5
7	Washington	10.3
8	Idaho	9.0
9	Arizona	7.7
10	Utah	6.7
11	Colorado	5.9
12	Florida	3.3
13	South Dakota	2.9
14	West Virginia	1.7
15	Kansas	1.6
16	Virginia	1.5
17	Arkansas	1.1
17	Indiana	1.1
19	Ohio	(0.2)
20	Minnesota	(0.3)
21	North Carolina	(0.5)
22	South Carolina	(0.6)
23	Alabama	(1.4)
24	Nebraska	(1.8)
25	Tennessee	(2.0)
26	Mississippi	(2.1)
27	Michigan	(2.8)
28	Montana	(3.1)
28	Texas	(3.1)
30	Wyoming	(3.3)
31	Georgia	(3.6)
32	Louisiana	(4.0)
33	Kentucky	(4.4)
34	Illinois	(4.6)
35	California	(5.7)
35	North Dakota	(5.7)
37	Alaska	(7.0)
38	Maine	(7.5)
39	Oklahoma	(8.1)
40	Massachusetts	(8.5)
41	Rhode Island	(8.7)
42	Connecticut	(9.2)
43	Pennsylvania	(9.3)
44	Hawaii	(9.6)
44	New Hampshire	(9.6)
44	Vermont	(9.6)
47	New York	(11.3)
48	New Jersey	(11.4)
49	Wisconsin	(12.4)
50	Maryland	(15.0)
	District of Columbia	(24.1)

Source: Federal Bureau of Investigation
    "Crime in the United States 1997" (Uniform Crime Reports, November 22, 1998)
*Includes the theft or attempted theft of a self-propelled vehicle. Excludes motorboats, construction equipment, airplanes and farming equipment.

Motor Vehicle Theft Rate in 1997

National Rate = 505.8 Motor Vehicle Thefts per 100,000 Population*

ALPHA ORDER

RANK ORDER

RANK	STATE	RATE
32	Alabama	356.7
20	Alaska	457.1
1	Arizona	970.4
36	Arkansas	314.6
5	California	708.8
28	Colorado	413.7
21	Connecticut	444.7
16	Delaware	507.9
3	Florida	731.5
10	Georgia	595.4
13	Hawaii	544.9
43	Idaho	200.7
19	Illinois	465.9
25	Indiana	428.0
42	Iowa	234.3
39	Kansas	250.1
40	Kentucky	248.1
8	Louisiana	606.0
49	Maine	132.2
9	Maryland	602.0
18	Massachusetts	481.4
6	Michigan	668.4
30	Minnesota	381.3
33	Mississippi	341.6
17	Missouri	490.9
41	Montana	247.9
34	Nebraska	334.4
2	Nevada	788.3
46	New Hampshire	135.8
15	New Jersey	511.2
4	New Mexico	717.2
24	New York	439.4
35	North Carolina	329.2
45	North Dakota	180.0
29	Ohio	406.0
23	Oklahoma	441.5
11	Oregon	594.5
31	Pennsylvania	367.8
26	Rhode Island	425.0
27	South Carolina	419.0
50	South Dakota	116.3
7	Tennessee	628.6
14	Texas	523.3
22	Utah	444.1
46	Vermont	135.8
38	Virginia	280.5
12	Washington	567.8
44	West Virginia	181.0
37	Wisconsin	302.5
48	Wyoming	134.8

RANK	STATE	RATE
1	Arizona	970.4
2	Nevada	788.3
3	Florida	731.5
4	New Mexico	717.2
5	California	708.8
6	Michigan	668.4
7	Tennessee	628.6
8	Louisiana	606.0
9	Maryland	602.0
10	Georgia	595.4
11	Oregon	594.5
12	Washington	567.8
13	Hawaii	544.9
14	Texas	523.3
15	New Jersey	511.2
16	Delaware	507.9
17	Missouri	490.9
18	Massachusetts	481.4
19	Illinois	465.9
20	Alaska	457.1
21	Connecticut	444.7
22	Utah	444.1
23	Oklahoma	441.5
24	New York	439.4
25	Indiana	428.0
26	Rhode Island	425.0
27	South Carolina	419.0
28	Colorado	413.7
29	Ohio	406.0
30	Minnesota	381.3
31	Pennsylvania	367.8
32	Alabama	356.7
33	Mississippi	341.6
34	Nebraska	334.4
35	North Carolina	329.2
36	Arkansas	314.6
37	Wisconsin	302.5
38	Virginia	280.5
39	Kansas	250.1
40	Kentucky	248.1
41	Montana	247.9
42	Iowa	234.3
43	Idaho	200.7
44	West Virginia	181.0
45	North Dakota	180.0
46	New Hampshire	135.8
46	Vermont	135.8
48	Wyoming	134.8
49	Maine	132.2
50	South Dakota	116.3
	District of Columbia	1,430.8

Source: Federal Bureau of Investigation
"Crime in the United States 1997" (Uniform Crime Reports, November 22, 1998)
*Includes the theft or attempted theft of a self-propelled vehicle. Excludes motorboats, construction equipment, airplanes and farming equipment.

Percent Change in Motor Vehicle Theft Rate: 1996 to 1997

National Percent Change = 3.8% Decrease*

ALPHA ORDER			RANK ORDER		
RANK	STATE	PERCENT CHANGE	RANK	STATE	PERCENT CHANGE
24	Alabama	(2.5)	1	New Mexico	23.2
37	Alaska	(7.3)	2	Iowa	22.6
9	Arizona	4.7	3	Delaware	17.0
18	Arkansas	0.5	4	Nevada	12.9
36	California	(6.8)	5	Oregon	12.0
10	Colorado	4.0	6	Missouri	9.6
43	Connecticut	(9.1)	7	Washington	8.7
3	Delaware	17.0	8	Idaho	7.0
14	Florida	1.5	9	Arizona	4.7
34	Georgia	(5.3)	10	Colorado	4.0
45	Hawaii	(9.9)	11	Utah	3.6
8	Idaho	7.0	12	West Virginia	2.3
32	Illinois	(5.0)	13	South Dakota	2.1
15	Indiana	0.7	14	Florida	1.5
2	Iowa	22.6	15	Indiana	0.7
15	Kansas	0.7	15	Kansas	0.7
32	Kentucky	(5.0)	17	Virginia	0.6
29	Louisiana	(4.1)	18	Arkansas	0.5
38	Maine	(7.5)	19	Ohio	(0.4)
50	Maryland	(15.4)	20	Minnesota	(0.9)
41	Massachusetts	(8.9)	21	North Carolina	(1.9)
30	Michigan	(4.6)	22	Nebraska	(2.1)
20	Minnesota	(0.9)	23	South Carolina	(2.2)
25	Mississippi	(2.6)	24	Alabama	(2.5)
6	Missouri	9.6	25	Mississippi	(2.6)
27	Montana	(3.1)	26	Tennessee	(2.9)
22	Nebraska	(2.1)	27	Montana	(3.1)
4	Nevada	12.9	27	Wyoming	(3.1)
46	New Hampshire	(10.4)	29	Louisiana	(4.1)
48	New Jersey	(12.1)	30	Michigan	(4.6)
1	New Mexico	23.2	30	Texas	(4.6)
47	New York	(11.1)	32	Illinois	(5.0)
21	North Carolina	(1.9)	32	Kentucky	(5.0)
34	North Dakota	(5.3)	34	Georgia	(5.3)
19	Ohio	(0.4)	34	North Dakota	(5.3)
40	Oklahoma	(8.6)	36	California	(6.8)
5	Oregon	12.0	37	Alaska	(7.3)
42	Pennsylvania	(9.0)	38	Maine	(7.5)
39	Rhode Island	(8.5)	39	Rhode Island	(8.5)
23	South Carolina	(2.2)	40	Oklahoma	(8.6)
13	South Dakota	2.1	41	Massachusetts	(8.9)
26	Tennessee	(2.9)	42	Pennsylvania	(9.0)
30	Texas	(4.6)	43	Connecticut	(9.1)
11	Utah	3.6	44	Vermont	(9.6)
44	Vermont	(9.6)	45	Hawaii	(9.9)
17	Virginia	0.6	46	New Hampshire	(10.4)
7	Washington	8.7	47	New York	(11.1)
12	West Virginia	2.3	48	New Jersey	(12.1)
49	Wisconsin	(12.5)	49	Wisconsin	(12.5)
27	Wyoming	(3.1)	50	Maryland	(15.4)
				District of Columbia	(22.1)

Source: Federal Bureau of Investigation
   "Crime in the United States 1997" (Uniform Crime Reports, November 22, 1998)
*Includes the theft or attempted theft of a self-propelled vehicle. Excludes motorboats, construction equipment, airplanes and farming equipment.

Crimes in Urban Areas in 1997

National Urban Total = 12,510,152 Crimes*

ALPHA ORDER

RANK	STATE	CRIMES	% of USA
20	Alabama	199,614	1.6%
41	Alaska	27,051	0.2%
11	Arizona	320,670	2.6%
31	Arkansas	105,096	0.8%
1	California	1,550,460	12.4%
24	Colorado	174,517	1.4%
27	Connecticut	126,871	1.0%
39	Delaware	33,894	0.3%
3	Florida	1,032,775	8.3%
8	Georgia	394,208	3.2%
35	Hawaii	53,410	0.4%
36	Idaho	39,515	0.3%
NA	Illinois**	NA	NA
18	Indiana	243,330	1.9%
32	Iowa	98,530	0.8%
NA	Kansas**	NA	NA
NA	Kentucky**	NA	NA
15	Louisiana	264,176	2.1%
40	Maine	33,256	0.3%
13	Maryland	280,688	2.2%
19	Massachusetts	224,793	1.8%
6	Michigan	454,123	3.6%
22	Minnesota	189,043	1.5%
30	Mississippi	107,181	0.9%
16	Missouri	244,594	2.0%
NA	Montana**	NA	NA
34	Nebraska	65,157	0.5%
33	Nevada	96,081	0.8%
NA	New Hampshire**	NA	NA
10	New Jersey	326,711	2.6%
29	New Mexico	113,717	0.9%
4	New York	690,805	5.5%
9	North Carolina	360,682	2.9%
44	North Dakota	15,206	0.1%
5	Ohio	483,956	3.9%
26	Oklahoma	171,021	1.4%
23	Oregon	188,769	1.5%
7	Pennsylvania	394,635	3.2%
37	Rhode Island	36,042	0.3%
21	South Carolina	194,952	1.6%
42	South Dakota	20,931	0.2%
14	Tennessee	273,771	2.2%
2	Texas	1,034,192	8.3%
28	Utah	117,492	0.9%
NA	Vermont**	NA	NA
17	Virginia	243,848	1.9%
12	Washington	315,966	2.5%
38	West Virginia	35,120	0.3%
25	Wisconsin	174,288	1.4%
43	Wyoming	17,576	0.1%

RANK ORDER

RANK	STATE	CRIMES	% of USA
1	California	1,550,460	12.4%
2	Texas	1,034,192	8.3%
3	Florida	1,032,775	8.3%
4	New York	690,805	5.5%
5	Ohio	483,956	3.9%
6	Michigan	454,123	3.6%
7	Pennsylvania	394,635	3.2%
8	Georgia	394,208	3.2%
9	North Carolina	360,682	2.9%
10	New Jersey	326,711	2.6%
11	Arizona	320,670	2.6%
12	Washington	315,966	2.5%
13	Maryland	280,688	2.2%
14	Tennessee	273,771	2.2%
15	Louisiana	264,176	2.1%
16	Missouri	244,594	2.0%
17	Virginia	243,848	1.9%
18	Indiana	243,330	1.9%
19	Massachusetts	224,793	1.8%
20	Alabama	199,614	1.6%
21	South Carolina	194,952	1.6%
22	Minnesota	189,043	1.5%
23	Oregon	188,769	1.5%
24	Colorado	174,517	1.4%
25	Wisconsin	174,288	1.4%
26	Oklahoma	171,021	1.4%
27	Connecticut	126,871	1.0%
28	Utah	117,492	0.9%
29	New Mexico	113,717	0.9%
30	Mississippi	107,181	0.9%
31	Arkansas	105,096	0.8%
32	Iowa	98,530	0.8%
33	Nevada	96,081	0.8%
34	Nebraska	65,157	0.5%
35	Hawaii	53,410	0.4%
36	Idaho	39,515	0.3%
37	Rhode Island	36,042	0.3%
38	West Virginia	35,120	0.3%
39	Delaware	33,894	0.3%
40	Maine	33,256	0.3%
41	Alaska	27,051	0.2%
42	South Dakota	20,931	0.2%
43	Wyoming	17,576	0.1%
44	North Dakota	15,206	0.1%
NA	Illinois**	NA	NA
NA	Kansas**	NA	NA
NA	Kentucky**	NA	NA
NA	Montana**	NA	NA
NA	New Hampshire**	NA	NA
NA	Vermont**	NA	NA
	District of Columbia	52,049	0.4%

Source: Morgan Quitno Press using data from Federal Bureau of Investigation
   "Crime in the United States 1997" (Uniform Crime Reports, November 22, 1998)
*Estimated rates for urban areas, defined by the F.B.I. as Metropolitan Statistical Areas and other cities outside such areas. National total includes those states listed as not available. Includes murder, rape, robbery, aggravated assault, burglary, larceny-theft and motor vehicle theft.
**Not available.

400

Urban Crime Rate in 1997

National Urban Rate = 5,314.0 Crimes per 100,000 Population*

ALPHA ORDER

RANK	STATE	RATE
21	Alabama	5,661.1
10	Alaska	6,482.8
2	Arizona	7,628.9
16	Arkansas	6,146.6
30	California	4,901.2
31	Colorado	4,896.4
36	Connecticut	4,112.0
22	Delaware	5,311.9
3	Florida	7,452.7
8	Georgia	6,556.5
17	Hawaii	6,067.4
31	Idaho	4,896.4
NA	Illinois**	NA
25	Indiana	5,064.5
26	Iowa	5,010.7
NA	Kansas**	NA
NA	Kentucky**	NA
4	Louisiana	7,202.5
39	Maine	3,738.3
19	Maryland	5,816.2
40	Massachusetts	3,680.2
24	Michigan	5,220.5
27	Minnesota	4,967.1
6	Mississippi	6,639.7
18	Missouri	5,844.8
NA	Montana**	NA
23	Nebraska	5,269.8
9	Nevada	6,483.7
NA	New Hampshire**	NA
37	New Jersey	4,057.0
1	New Mexico	7,932.9
38	New York	3,996.5
14	North Carolina	6,316.6
42	North Dakota	3,629.3
29	Ohio	4,910.8
13	Oklahoma	6,371.0
5	Oregon	6,934.3
43	Pennsylvania	3,598.5
41	Rhode Island	3,651.7
7	South Carolina	6,589.6
33	South Dakota	4,678.6
11	Tennessee	6,404.3
20	Texas	5,814.3
12	Utah	6,389.9
NA	Vermont**	NA
34	Virginia	4,308.7
15	Washington	6,200.1
44	West Virginia	3,386.1
35	Wisconsin	4,162.8
28	Wyoming	4,952.8

RANK ORDER

RANK	STATE	RATE
1	New Mexico	7,932.9
2	Arizona	7,628.9
3	Florida	7,452.7
4	Louisiana	7,202.5
5	Oregon	6,934.3
6	Mississippi	6,639.7
7	South Carolina	6,589.6
8	Georgia	6,556.5
9	Nevada	6,483.7
10	Alaska	6,482.8
11	Tennessee	6,404.3
12	Utah	6,389.9
13	Oklahoma	6,371.0
14	North Carolina	6,316.6
15	Washington	6,200.1
16	Arkansas	6,146.6
17	Hawaii	6,067.4
18	Missouri	5,844.8
19	Maryland	5,816.2
20	Texas	5,814.3
21	Alabama	5,661.1
22	Delaware	5,311.9
23	Nebraska	5,269.8
24	Michigan	5,220.5
25	Indiana	5,064.5
26	Iowa	5,010.7
27	Minnesota	4,967.1
28	Wyoming	4,952.8
29	Ohio	4,910.8
30	California	4,901.2
31	Colorado	4,896.4
31	Idaho	4,896.4
33	South Dakota	4,678.6
34	Virginia	4,308.7
35	Wisconsin	4,162.8
36	Connecticut	4,112.0
37	New Jersey	4,057.0
38	New York	3,996.5
39	Maine	3,738.3
40	Massachusetts	3,680.2
41	Rhode Island	3,651.7
42	North Dakota	3,629.3
43	Pennsylvania	3,598.5
44	West Virginia	3,386.1
NA	Illinois**	NA
NA	Kansas**	NA
NA	Kentucky**	NA
NA	Montana**	NA
NA	New Hampshire**	NA
NA	Vermont**	NA

District of Columbia   9,839.1

Source: Morgan Quitno Press using data from Federal Bureau of Investigation
    "Crime in the United States 1997" (Uniform Crime Reports, November 22, 1998)
*Estimated rates for urban areas, defined by the F.B.I. as Metropolitan Statistical Areas and other cities outside
such areas. National rate includes those states listed as not available. Includes murder, rape, robbery,
aggravated assault, burglary, larceny-theft and motor vehicle theft.
**Not available.

Percent of Crimes Occurring in Urban Areas in 1997

National Percent = 95.0% of Crimes*

ALPHA ORDER			RANK ORDER		
RANK	STATE	PERCENT	RANK	STATE	PERCENT
17	Alabama	94.5	1	Massachusetts	100.0
41	Alaska	84.2	1	New Jersey	100.0
5	Arizona	97.8	3	Rhode Island	99.9
34	Arkansas	88.3	4	California	98.8
4	California	98.8	5	Arizona	97.8
11	Colorado	96.4	6	Maryland	97.5
7	Connecticut	97.4	7	Connecticut	97.4
32	Delaware	90.1	7	New York	97.4
10	Florida	96.9	9	Texas	97.1
30	Georgia	90.9	10	Florida	96.9
44	Hawaii	74.7	11	Colorado	96.4
42	Idaho	83.2	12	Ohio	95.8
NA	Illinois**	NA	13	Pennsylvania	95.7
24	Indiana	92.9	14	New Mexico	95.2
31	Iowa	90.5	14	Utah	95.2
NA	Kansas**	NA	16	Washington	95.0
NA	Kentucky**	NA	17	Alabama	94.5
20	Louisiana	94.1	17	Michigan	94.5
38	Maine	85.5	17	Nevada	94.5
6	Maryland	97.5	20	Louisiana	94.1
1	Massachusetts	100.0	21	Missouri	94.0
17	Michigan	94.5	22	Oklahoma	93.8
29	Minnesota	91.4	23	Virginia	93.4
39	Mississippi	84.8	24	Indiana	92.9
21	Missouri	94.0	25	Oregon	92.8
NA	Montana**	NA	26	Tennessee	92.5
27	Nebraska	91.8	27	Nebraska	91.8
17	Nevada	94.5	28	Wisconsin	91.7
NA	New Hampshire**	NA	29	Minnesota	91.4
1	New Jersey	100.0	30	Georgia	90.9
14	New Mexico	95.2	31	Iowa	90.5
7	New York	97.4	32	Delaware	90.1
33	North Carolina	88.5	33	North Carolina	88.5
36	North Dakota	87.5	34	Arkansas	88.3
12	Ohio	95.8	35	Wyoming	87.6
22	Oklahoma	93.8	36	North Dakota	87.5
25	Oregon	92.8	37	South Dakota	87.4
13	Pennsylvania	95.7	38	Maine	85.5
3	Rhode Island	99.9	39	Mississippi	84.8
40	South Carolina	84.5	40	South Carolina	84.5
37	South Dakota	87.4	41	Alaska	84.2
26	Tennessee	92.5	42	Idaho	83.2
9	Texas	97.1	43	West Virginia	78.3
14	Utah	95.2	44	Hawaii	74.7
NA	Vermont**	NA	NA	Illinois**	NA
23	Virginia	93.4	NA	Kansas**	NA
16	Washington	95.0	NA	Kentucky**	NA
43	West Virginia	78.3	NA	Montana**	NA
28	Wisconsin	91.7	NA	New Hampshire**	NA
35	Wyoming	87.6	NA	Vermont**	NA
				District of Columbia	100.0

Source: Morgan Quitno Press using data from Federal Bureau of Investigation
"Crime in the United States 1997" (Uniform Crime Reports, November 22, 1998)
*Estimated percentages for urban areas, defined by the F.B.I. as Metropolitan Statistical Areas and other cities outside such areas. National percent includes those states listed as not available. Includes murder, rape, robbery, aggravated assault, burglary, larceny-theft and motor vehicle theft.
**Not available.

Crimes in Rural Areas in 1997

National Rural Total = 664,918 Crimes*

ALPHA ORDER

RANK	STATE	CRIMES	% of USA
23	Alabama	11,574	1.7%
36	Alaska	5,059	0.8%
29	Arizona	7,064	1.1%
22	Arkansas	13,956	2.1%
9	California	19,489	2.9%
30	Colorado	6,524	1.0%
38	Connecticut	3,415	0.5%
37	Delaware	3,718	0.6%
4	Florida	32,834	4.9%
2	Georgia	39,355	5.9%
13	Hawaii	18,082	2.7%
27	Idaho	7,980	1.2%
NA	Illinois**	NA	NA
11	Indiana	18,572	2.8%
25	Iowa	10,297	1.5%
NA	Kansas**	NA	NA
NA	Kentucky**	NA	NA
18	Louisiana	16,495	2.5%
34	Maine	5,640	0.8%
28	Maryland	7,281	1.1%
42	Massachusetts	55	0.0%
6	Michigan	26,456	4.0%
15	Minnesota	17,790	2.7%
10	Mississippi	19,271	2.9%
20	Missouri	15,487	2.3%
NA	Montana**	NA	NA
32	Nebraska	5,825	0.9%
35	Nevada	5,621	0.8%
NA	New Hampshire**	NA	NA
44	New Jersey	0	0.0%
33	New Mexico	5,766	0.9%
12	New York	18,523	2.8%
1	North Carolina	47,061	7.1%
41	North Dakota	2,174	0.3%
8	Ohio	21,049	3.2%
24	Oklahoma	11,237	1.7%
21	Oregon	14,559	2.2%
14	Pennsylvania	17,828	2.7%
43	Rhode Island	27	0.0%
3	South Carolina	35,685	5.4%
39	South Dakota	3,017	0.5%
7	Tennessee	22,102	3.3%
5	Texas	31,165	4.7%
31	Utah	5,955	0.9%
NA	Vermont**	NA	NA
16	Virginia	17,174	2.6%
17	Washington	16,500	2.5%
26	West Virginia	9,719	1.5%
19	Wisconsin	15,845	2.4%
40	Wyoming	2,492	0.4%

RANK ORDER

RANK	STATE	CRIMES	% of USA
1	North Carolina	47,061	7.1%
2	Georgia	39,355	5.9%
3	South Carolina	35,685	5.4%
4	Florida	32,834	4.9%
5	Texas	31,165	4.7%
6	Michigan	26,456	4.0%
7	Tennessee	22,102	3.3%
8	Ohio	21,049	3.2%
9	California	19,489	2.9%
10	Mississippi	19,271	2.9%
11	Indiana	18,572	2.8%
12	New York	18,523	2.8%
13	Hawaii	18,082	2.7%
14	Pennsylvania	17,828	2.7%
15	Minnesota	17,790	2.7%
16	Virginia	17,174	2.6%
17	Washington	16,500	2.5%
18	Louisiana	16,495	2.5%
19	Wisconsin	15,845	2.4%
20	Missouri	15,487	2.3%
21	Oregon	14,559	2.2%
22	Arkansas	13,956	2.1%
23	Alabama	11,574	1.7%
24	Oklahoma	11,237	1.7%
25	Iowa	10,297	1.5%
26	West Virginia	9,719	1.5%
27	Idaho	7,980	1.2%
28	Maryland	7,281	1.1%
29	Arizona	7,064	1.1%
30	Colorado	6,524	1.0%
31	Utah	5,955	0.9%
32	Nebraska	5,825	0.9%
33	New Mexico	5,766	0.9%
34	Maine	5,640	0.8%
35	Nevada	5,621	0.8%
36	Alaska	5,059	0.8%
37	Delaware	3,718	0.6%
38	Connecticut	3,415	0.5%
39	South Dakota	3,017	0.5%
40	Wyoming	2,492	0.4%
41	North Dakota	2,174	0.3%
42	Massachusetts	55	0.0%
43	Rhode Island	27	0.0%
44	New Jersey	0	0.0%
NA	Illinois**	NA	NA
NA	Kansas**	NA	NA
NA	Kentucky**	NA	NA
NA	Montana**	NA	NA
NA	New Hampshire**	NA	NA
NA	Vermont**	NA	NA
	District of Columbia	0	0.0%

Source: Federal Bureau of Investigation
    "Crime in the United States 1997" (Uniform Crime Reports, November 22, 1998)
*Estimated totals for rural areas, defined by the F.B.I. as other than Metropolitan Statistical Areas and other cities outside such areas. National total includes those states listed as not available. Includes murder, rape, robbery, aggravated assault, burglary, larceny-theft and motor vehicle theft.
**Not available.

Rural Crime Rate in 1997

National Rural Rate = 2,063.7 Crimes per 100,000 Population*

ALPHA ORDER				RANK ORDER		
RANK	STATE	RATE		RANK	STATE	RATE
35	Alabama	1,459.7		1	Hawaii	5,895.1
13	Alaska	2,638.7		2	South Carolina	4,452.1
19	Arizona	2,008.9		3	Florida	4,123.0
29	Arkansas	1,716.2		4	Delaware	3,958.3
6	California	3,074.5		5	Washington	3,211.2
21	Colorado	1,984.0		6	California	3,074.5
25	Connecticut	1,849.4		7	Nevada	2,880.9
4	Delaware	3,958.3		8	Oregon	2,795.7
3	Florida	4,123.0		9	North Carolina	2,744.2
12	Georgia	2,670.7		10	Maryland	2,716.8
1	Hawaii	5,895.1		11	Utah	2,703.1
22	Idaho	1,980.3		12	Georgia	2,670.7
NA	Illinois**	NA		13	Alaska	2,638.7
27	Indiana	1,753.1		14	Michigan	2,460.7
39	Iowa	1,162.7		15	Louisiana	2,411.0
NA	Kansas**	NA		16	New York	2,174.4
NA	Kentucky**	NA		17	Tennessee	2,021.8
15	Louisiana	2,411.0		18	Minnesota	2,021.3
32	Maine	1,600.5		19	Arizona	2,008.9
10	Maryland	2,716.8		20	Wyoming	1,991.5
42	Massachusetts	558.0		21	Colorado	1,984.0
14	Michigan	2,460.7		22	Idaho	1,980.3
18	Minnesota	2,021.3		23	New Mexico	1,944.6
28	Mississippi	1,725.6		24	Texas	1,886.4
37	Missouri	1,272.4		25	Connecticut	1,849.4
NA	Montana**	NA		26	Oklahoma	1,776.2
36	Nebraska	1,385.0		27	Indiana	1,753.1
7	Nevada	2,880.9		28	Mississippi	1,725.6
NA	New Hampshire**	NA		29	Arkansas	1,716.2
43	New Jersey	0.0		30	Pennsylvania	1,692.3
23	New Mexico	1,944.6		31	Wisconsin	1,611.6
16	New York	2,174.4		32	Maine	1,600.5
9	North Carolina	2,744.2		33	Virginia	1,598.2
41	North Dakota	979.2		34	Ohio	1,581.4
34	Ohio	1,581.4		35	Alabama	1,459.7
26	Oklahoma	1,776.2		36	Nebraska	1,385.0
8	Oregon	2,795.7		37	Missouri	1,272.4
30	Pennsylvania	1,692.3		38	West Virginia	1,247.9
43	Rhode Island	0.0		39	Iowa	1,162.7
2	South Carolina	4,452.1		40	South Dakota	1,038.1
40	South Dakota	1,038.1		41	North Dakota	979.2
17	Tennessee	2,021.8		42	Massachusetts	558.0
24	Texas	1,886.4		43	New Jersey	0.0
11	Utah	2,703.1		43	Rhode Island	0.0
NA	Vermont**	NA		NA	Illinois**	NA
33	Virginia	1,598.2		NA	Kansas**	NA
5	Washington	3,211.2		NA	Kentucky**	NA
38	West Virginia	1,247.9		NA	Montana**	NA
31	Wisconsin	1,611.6		NA	New Hampshire**	NA
20	Wyoming	1,991.5		NA	Vermont**	NA
					District of Columbia	0.0

Source: Morgan Quitno Press using data from Federal Bureau of Investigation
    "Crime in the United States 1997" (Uniform Crime Reports, November 22, 1998)
*Estimated rates for rural areas, defined by the F.B.I. as other than Metropolitan Statistical Areas and other cities outside such areas. National rate includes those states listed as not available. Includes murder, rape, robbery, aggravated assault, burglary, larceny-theft and motor vehicle theft.
**Not available.

Percent of Crimes Occurring in Rural Areas in 1997

National Percent = 5.0% of Crimes*

ALPHA ORDER

RANK	STATE	PERCENT
26	Alabama	5.5
4	Alaska	15.8
40	Arizona	2.2
11	Arkansas	11.7
41	California	1.2
34	Colorado	3.6
37	Connecticut	2.6
13	Delaware	9.9
35	Florida	3.1
15	Georgia	9.1
1	Hawaii	25.3
3	Idaho	16.8
NA	Illinois**	NA
21	Indiana	7.1
14	Iowa	9.5
NA	Kansas**	NA
NA	Kentucky**	NA
25	Louisiana	5.9
7	Maine	14.5
39	Maryland	2.5
43	Massachusetts	0.0
26	Michigan	5.5
16	Minnesota	8.6
6	Mississippi	15.2
24	Missouri	6.0
NA	Montana**	NA
18	Nebraska	8.2
26	Nevada	5.5
NA	New Hampshire**	NA
43	New Jersey	0.0
30	New Mexico	4.8
37	New York	2.6
12	North Carolina	11.5
9	North Dakota	12.5
33	Ohio	4.2
23	Oklahoma	6.2
20	Oregon	7.2
32	Pennsylvania	4.3
42	Rhode Island	0.1
5	South Carolina	15.5
8	South Dakota	12.6
19	Tennessee	7.5
36	Texas	2.9
30	Utah	4.8
NA	Vermont**	NA
22	Virginia	6.6
29	Washington	5.0
2	West Virginia	21.7
17	Wisconsin	8.3
10	Wyoming	12.4

RANK ORDER

RANK	STATE	PERCENT
1	Hawaii	25.3
2	West Virginia	21.7
3	Idaho	16.8
4	Alaska	15.8
5	South Carolina	15.5
6	Mississippi	15.2
7	Maine	14.5
8	South Dakota	12.6
9	North Dakota	12.5
10	Wyoming	12.4
11	Arkansas	11.7
12	North Carolina	11.5
13	Delaware	9.9
14	Iowa	9.5
15	Georgia	9.1
16	Minnesota	8.6
17	Wisconsin	8.3
18	Nebraska	8.2
19	Tennessee	7.5
20	Oregon	7.2
21	Indiana	7.1
22	Virginia	6.6
23	Oklahoma	6.2
24	Missouri	6.0
25	Louisiana	5.9
26	Alabama	5.5
26	Michigan	5.5
26	Nevada	5.5
29	Washington	5.0
30	New Mexico	4.8
30	Utah	4.8
32	Pennsylvania	4.3
33	Ohio	4.2
34	Colorado	3.6
35	Florida	3.1
36	Texas	2.9
37	Connecticut	2.6
37	New York	2.6
39	Maryland	2.5
40	Arizona	2.2
41	California	1.2
42	Rhode Island	0.1
43	Massachusetts	0.0
43	New Jersey	0.0
NA	Illinois**	NA
NA	Kansas**	NA
NA	Kentucky**	NA
NA	Montana**	NA
NA	New Hampshire**	NA
NA	Vermont**	NA
	District of Columbia	0.0

Source: Morgan Quitno Press using data from Federal Bureau of Investigation
   "Crime in the United States 1997" (Uniform Crime Reports, November 22, 1998)
*Estimated percentages for rural areas, defined by the F.B.I. as other than Metropolitan Statistical Areas and other
cities outside such areas. National percent includes those states listed as not available. Includes murder, rape,
robbery, aggravated assault, burglary, larceny-theft and motor vehicle theft.
**Not available.

Violent Crimes in Urban Areas in 1997

National Urban Total = 1,560,474 Violent Crimes*

<table>
<tr><td colspan="4">ALPHA ORDER</td><td colspan="4">RANK ORDER</td></tr>
<tr><th>RANK</th><th>STATE</th><th>CRIMES</th><th>% of USA</th><th>RANK</th><th>STATE</th><th>CRIMES</th><th>% of USA</th></tr>
<tr><td>20</td><td>Alabama</td><td>22,888</td><td>1.5%</td><td>1</td><td>California</td><td>254,596</td><td>16.3%</td></tr>
<tr><td>36</td><td>Alaska</td><td>3,464</td><td>0.2%</td><td>2</td><td>Florida</td><td>145,101</td><td>9.3%</td></tr>
<tr><td>18</td><td>Arizona</td><td>27,336</td><td>1.8%</td><td>3</td><td>New York</td><td>122,724</td><td>7.9%</td></tr>
<tr><td>30</td><td>Arkansas</td><td>11,865</td><td>0.8%</td><td>4</td><td>Texas</td><td>113,176</td><td>7.3%</td></tr>
<tr><td>1</td><td>California</td><td>254,596</td><td>16.3%</td><td>5</td><td>Michigan</td><td>55,133</td><td>3.5%</td></tr>
<tr><td>25</td><td>Colorado</td><td>13,672</td><td>0.9%</td><td>6</td><td>Pennsylvania</td><td>51,429</td><td>3.3%</td></tr>
<tr><td>29</td><td>Connecticut</td><td>12,348</td><td>0.8%</td><td>7</td><td>Ohio</td><td>47,643</td><td>3.1%</td></tr>
<tr><td>35</td><td>Delaware</td><td>4,160</td><td>0.3%</td><td>8</td><td>Maryland</td><td>42,185</td><td>2.7%</td></tr>
<tr><td>2</td><td>Florida</td><td>145,101</td><td>9.3%</td><td>9</td><td>Georgia</td><td>40,852</td><td>2.6%</td></tr>
<tr><td>9</td><td>Georgia</td><td>40,852</td><td>2.6%</td><td>10</td><td>North Carolina</td><td>40,405</td><td>2.6%</td></tr>
<tr><td>39</td><td>Hawaii</td><td>2,636</td><td>0.2%</td><td>11</td><td>New Jersey</td><td>39,673</td><td>2.5%</td></tr>
<tr><td>40</td><td>Idaho</td><td>2,404</td><td>0.2%</td><td>12</td><td>Massachusetts</td><td>39,398</td><td>2.5%</td></tr>
<tr><td>NA</td><td>Illinois**</td><td>NA</td><td>NA</td><td>13</td><td>Tennessee</td><td>39,075</td><td>2.5%</td></tr>
<tr><td>17</td><td>Indiana</td><td>27,767</td><td>1.8%</td><td>14</td><td>Louisiana</td><td>33,924</td><td>2.2%</td></tr>
<tr><td>32</td><td>Iowa</td><td>8,304</td><td>0.5%</td><td>15</td><td>South Carolina</td><td>30,522</td><td>2.0%</td></tr>
<tr><td>NA</td><td>Kansas**</td><td>NA</td><td>NA</td><td>16</td><td>Missouri</td><td>28,658</td><td>1.8%</td></tr>
<tr><td>NA</td><td>Kentucky**</td><td>NA</td><td>NA</td><td>17</td><td>Indiana</td><td>27,767</td><td>1.8%</td></tr>
<tr><td>14</td><td>Louisiana</td><td>33,924</td><td>2.2%</td><td>18</td><td>Arizona</td><td>27,336</td><td>1.8%</td></tr>
<tr><td>41</td><td>Maine</td><td>1,321</td><td>0.1%</td><td>19</td><td>Washington</td><td>23,719</td><td>1.5%</td></tr>
<tr><td>8</td><td>Maryland</td><td>42,185</td><td>2.7%</td><td>20</td><td>Alabama</td><td>22,888</td><td>1.5%</td></tr>
<tr><td>12</td><td>Massachusetts</td><td>39,398</td><td>2.5%</td><td>21</td><td>Virginia</td><td>21,421</td><td>1.4%</td></tr>
<tr><td>5</td><td>Michigan</td><td>55,133</td><td>3.5%</td><td>22</td><td>Oklahoma</td><td>17,112</td><td>1.1%</td></tr>
<tr><td>23</td><td>Minnesota</td><td>14,834</td><td>1.0%</td><td>23</td><td>Minnesota</td><td>14,834</td><td>1.0%</td></tr>
<tr><td>31</td><td>Mississippi</td><td>9,257</td><td>0.6%</td><td>24</td><td>New Mexico</td><td>13,782</td><td>0.9%</td></tr>
<tr><td>16</td><td>Missouri</td><td>28,658</td><td>1.8%</td><td>25</td><td>Colorado</td><td>13,672</td><td>0.9%</td></tr>
<tr><td>NA</td><td>Montana**</td><td>NA</td><td>NA</td><td>26</td><td>Oregon</td><td>13,625</td><td>0.9%</td></tr>
<tr><td>33</td><td>Nebraska</td><td>6,994</td><td>0.4%</td><td>27</td><td>Wisconsin</td><td>13,173</td><td>0.8%</td></tr>
<tr><td>28</td><td>Nevada</td><td>12,671</td><td>0.8%</td><td>28</td><td>Nevada</td><td>12,671</td><td>0.8%</td></tr>
<tr><td>NA</td><td>New Hampshire**</td><td>NA</td><td>NA</td><td>29</td><td>Connecticut</td><td>12,348</td><td>0.8%</td></tr>
<tr><td>11</td><td>New Jersey</td><td>39,673</td><td>2.5%</td><td>30</td><td>Arkansas</td><td>11,865</td><td>0.8%</td></tr>
<tr><td>24</td><td>New Mexico</td><td>13,782</td><td>0.9%</td><td>31</td><td>Mississippi</td><td>9,257</td><td>0.6%</td></tr>
<tr><td>3</td><td>New York</td><td>122,724</td><td>7.9%</td><td>32</td><td>Iowa</td><td>8,304</td><td>0.5%</td></tr>
<tr><td>10</td><td>North Carolina</td><td>40,405</td><td>2.6%</td><td>33</td><td>Nebraska</td><td>6,994</td><td>0.4%</td></tr>
<tr><td>44</td><td>North Dakota</td><td>480</td><td>0.0%</td><td>34</td><td>Utah</td><td>6,536</td><td>0.4%</td></tr>
<tr><td>7</td><td>Ohio</td><td>47,643</td><td>3.1%</td><td>35</td><td>Delaware</td><td>4,160</td><td>0.3%</td></tr>
<tr><td>22</td><td>Oklahoma</td><td>17,112</td><td>1.1%</td><td>36</td><td>Alaska</td><td>3,464</td><td>0.2%</td></tr>
<tr><td>26</td><td>Oregon</td><td>13,625</td><td>0.9%</td><td>37</td><td>Rhode Island</td><td>3,284</td><td>0.2%</td></tr>
<tr><td>6</td><td>Pennsylvania</td><td>51,429</td><td>3.3%</td><td>38</td><td>West Virginia</td><td>3,002</td><td>0.2%</td></tr>
<tr><td>37</td><td>Rhode Island</td><td>3,284</td><td>0.2%</td><td>39</td><td>Hawaii</td><td>2,636</td><td>0.2%</td></tr>
<tr><td>15</td><td>South Carolina</td><td>30,522</td><td>2.0%</td><td>40</td><td>Idaho</td><td>2,404</td><td>0.2%</td></tr>
<tr><td>42</td><td>South Dakota</td><td>1,213</td><td>0.1%</td><td>41</td><td>Maine</td><td>1,321</td><td>0.1%</td></tr>
<tr><td>13</td><td>Tennessee</td><td>39,075</td><td>2.5%</td><td>42</td><td>South Dakota</td><td>1,213</td><td>0.1%</td></tr>
<tr><td>4</td><td>Texas</td><td>113,176</td><td>7.3%</td><td>43</td><td>Wyoming</td><td>988</td><td>0.1%</td></tr>
<tr><td>34</td><td>Utah</td><td>6,536</td><td>0.4%</td><td>44</td><td>North Dakota</td><td>480</td><td>0.0%</td></tr>
<tr><td>NA</td><td>Vermont**</td><td>NA</td><td>NA</td><td>NA</td><td>Illinois**</td><td>NA</td><td>NA</td></tr>
<tr><td>21</td><td>Virginia</td><td>21,421</td><td>1.4%</td><td>NA</td><td>Kansas**</td><td>NA</td><td>NA</td></tr>
<tr><td>19</td><td>Washington</td><td>23,719</td><td>1.5%</td><td>NA</td><td>Kentucky**</td><td>NA</td><td>NA</td></tr>
<tr><td>38</td><td>West Virginia</td><td>3,002</td><td>0.2%</td><td>NA</td><td>Montana**</td><td>NA</td><td>NA</td></tr>
<tr><td>27</td><td>Wisconsin</td><td>13,173</td><td>0.8%</td><td>NA</td><td>New Hampshire**</td><td>NA</td><td>NA</td></tr>
<tr><td>43</td><td>Wyoming</td><td>988</td><td>0.1%</td><td>NA</td><td>Vermont**</td><td>NA</td><td>NA</td></tr>
<tr><td colspan="4"></td><td colspan="2">District of Columbia</td><td>10,708</td><td>0.7%</td></tr>
</table>

Source: Morgan Quitno Press using data from Federal Bureau of Investigation
    "Crime in the United States 1997" (Uniform Crime Reports, November 22, 1998)
*Estimated totals for urban areas, defined by the F.B.I. as Metropolitan Statistical Areas and other cities outside such areas. National total includes those states listed as not available. Violent crimes are offenses of murder, forcible rape, robbery and aggravated assault.
**Not available.

Urban Violent Crime Rate in 1997

National Urban Rate = 662.9 Violent Crimes per 100,000 Population*

ALPHA ORDER				RANK ORDER		
RANK	STATE	RATE		RANK	STATE	RATE
17	Alabama	649.1		1	Florida	1,047.1
8	Alaska	830.1		2	South Carolina	1,031.7
16	Arizona	650.3		3	New Mexico	961.4
12	Arkansas	693.9		4	Louisiana	924.9
9	California	804.8		5	Tennessee	914.1
33	Colorado	383.6		6	Maryland	874.1
31	Connecticut	400.2		7	Nevada	855.1
15	Delaware	652.0		8	Alaska	830.1
1	Florida	1,047.1		9	California	804.8
14	Georgia	679.5		10	New York	710.0
38	Hawaii	299.5		11	North Carolina	707.6
39	Idaho	297.9		12	Arkansas	693.9
NA	Illinois**	NA		13	Missouri	684.8
22	Indiana	577.9		14	Georgia	679.5
30	Iowa	422.3		15	Delaware	652.0
NA	Kansas**	NA		16	Arizona	650.3
NA	Kentucky**	NA		17	Alabama	649.1
4	Louisiana	924.9		18	Massachusetts	645.0
43	Maine	148.5		19	Oklahoma	637.5
6	Maryland	874.1		20	Texas	636.3
18	Massachusetts	645.0		21	Michigan	633.8
21	Michigan	633.8		22	Indiana	577.9
32	Minnesota	389.8		23	Mississippi	573.5
23	Mississippi	573.5		24	Nebraska	565.7
13	Missouri	684.8		25	Oregon	500.5
NA	Montana**	NA		26	New Jersey	492.6
24	Nebraska	565.7		27	Ohio	483.4
7	Nevada	855.1		28	Pennsylvania	469.0
NA	New Hampshire**	NA		29	Washington	465.4
26	New Jersey	492.6		30	Iowa	422.3
3	New Mexico	961.4		31	Connecticut	400.2
10	New York	710.0		32	Minnesota	389.8
11	North Carolina	707.6		33	Colorado	383.6
44	North Dakota	114.6		34	Virginia	378.5
27	Ohio	483.4		35	Utah	355.5
19	Oklahoma	637.5		36	Rhode Island	332.7
25	Oregon	500.5		37	Wisconsin	314.6
28	Pennsylvania	469.0		38	Hawaii	299.5
36	Rhode Island	332.7		39	Idaho	297.9
2	South Carolina	1,031.7		40	West Virginia	289.4
42	South Dakota	271.1		41	Wyoming	278.4
5	Tennessee	914.1		42	South Dakota	271.1
20	Texas	636.3		43	Maine	148.5
35	Utah	355.5		44	North Dakota	114.6
NA	Vermont**	NA		NA	Illinois**	NA
34	Virginia	378.5		NA	Kansas**	NA
29	Washington	465.4		NA	Kentucky**	NA
40	West Virginia	289.4		NA	Montana**	NA
37	Wisconsin	314.6		NA	New Hampshire**	NA
41	Wyoming	278.4		NA	Vermont**	NA
					District of Columbia	2,024.2

Source: Morgan Quitno Press using data from Federal Bureau of Investigation
    "Crime in the United States 1997" (Uniform Crime Reports, November 22, 1998)
*Estimated rates for urban areas, defined by the F.B.I. as Metropolitan Statistical Areas and other cities outside
such areas. National rate includes those states listed as not available. Violent crimes are offenses of murder,
forcible rape, robbery and aggravated assault.
**Not available.

Percent of Violent Crimes Occurring in Urban Areas in 1997

National Percent = 95.5% of Violent Crimes*

ALPHA ORDER

ALPHA ORDER

RANK	STATE	PERCENT
21	Alabama	93.9
39	Alaska	81.1
14	Arizona	96.2
33	Arkansas	89.3
4	California	98.8
9	Colorado	96.7
11	Connecticut	96.6
36	Delaware	83.8
9	Florida	96.7
31	Georgia	90.0
41	Hawaii	79.9
42	Idaho	77.4
NA	Illinois**	NA
28	Indiana	92.0
21	Iowa	93.9
NA	Kansas**	NA
NA	Kentucky**	NA
30	Louisiana	91.1
34	Maine	88.1
6	Maryland	97.8
1	Massachusetts	100.0
16	Michigan	95.6
23	Minnesota	93.7
44	Mississippi	72.3
29	Missouri	91.9
NA	Montana**	NA
13	Nebraska	96.3
18	Nevada	94.6
NA	New Hampshire**	NA
1	New Jersey	100.0
24	New Mexico	93.4
5	New York	98.3
32	North Carolina	89.6
35	North Dakota	85.9
6	Ohio	97.8
25	Oklahoma	92.2
19	Oregon	94.5
8	Pennsylvania	96.8
3	Rhode Island	99.8
38	South Carolina	82.0
37	South Dakota	83.3
25	Tennessee	92.2
11	Texas	96.6
17	Utah	95.0
NA	Vermont**	NA
27	Virginia	92.1
15	Washington	95.9
43	West Virginia	75.6
20	Wisconsin	94.2
40	Wyoming	80.7

RANK ORDER

RANK	STATE	PERCENT
1	Massachusetts	100.0
1	New Jersey	100.0
3	Rhode Island	99.8
4	California	98.8
5	New York	98.3
6	Maryland	97.8
6	Ohio	97.8
8	Pennsylvania	96.8
9	Colorado	96.7
9	Florida	96.7
11	Connecticut	96.6
11	Texas	96.6
13	Nebraska	96.3
14	Arizona	96.2
15	Washington	95.9
16	Michigan	95.6
17	Utah	95.0
18	Nevada	94.6
19	Oregon	94.5
20	Wisconsin	94.2
21	Alabama	93.9
21	Iowa	93.9
23	Minnesota	93.7
24	New Mexico	93.4
25	Oklahoma	92.2
25	Tennessee	92.2
27	Virginia	92.1
28	Indiana	92.0
29	Missouri	91.9
30	Louisiana	91.1
31	Georgia	90.0
32	North Carolina	89.6
33	Arkansas	89.3
34	Maine	88.1
35	North Dakota	85.9
36	Delaware	83.8
37	South Dakota	83.3
38	South Carolina	82.0
39	Alaska	81.1
40	Wyoming	80.7
41	Hawaii	79.9
42	Idaho	77.4
43	West Virginia	75.6
44	Mississippi	72.3
NA	Illinois**	NA
NA	Kansas**	NA
NA	Kentucky**	NA
NA	Montana**	NA
NA	New Hampshire**	NA
NA	Vermont**	NA

District of Columbia 100.0

Source: Morgan Quitno Press using data from Federal Bureau of Investigation
"Crime in the United States 1997" (Uniform Crime Reports, November 22, 1998)
Estimated percentages for urban areas, defined by the F.B.I. as Metropolitan Statistical Areas and other cities outside such areas. National percent includes those states listed as not available. Violent crimes are offenses of murder, forcible rape, robbery and aggravated assault.
**Not available.*

Violent Crimes in Rural Areas in 1997

National Rural Total = 74,299 Violent Crimes*

<table>
<tr><td colspan="4">ALPHA ORDER</td><td colspan="4">RANK ORDER</td></tr>
<tr><td>RANK</td><td>STATE</td><td>CRIMES</td><td>% of USA</td><td>RANK</td><td>STATE</td><td>CRIMES</td><td>% of USA</td></tr>
<tr><td>16</td><td>Alabama</td><td>1,491</td><td>2.0%</td><td>1</td><td>South Carolina</td><td>6,713</td><td>9.0%</td></tr>
<tr><td>27</td><td>Alaska</td><td>806</td><td>1.1%</td><td>2</td><td>Florida</td><td>4,895</td><td>6.6%</td></tr>
<tr><td>19</td><td>Arizona</td><td>1,075</td><td>1.4%</td><td>3</td><td>North Carolina</td><td>4,666</td><td>6.3%</td></tr>
<tr><td>18</td><td>Arkansas</td><td>1,428</td><td>1.9%</td><td>4</td><td>Georgia</td><td>4,556</td><td>6.1%</td></tr>
<tr><td>9</td><td>California</td><td>2,986</td><td>4.0%</td><td>5</td><td>Texas</td><td>3,950</td><td>5.3%</td></tr>
<tr><td>34</td><td>Colorado</td><td>467</td><td>0.6%</td><td>6</td><td>Mississippi</td><td>3,551</td><td>4.8%</td></tr>
<tr><td>35</td><td>Connecticut</td><td>433</td><td>0.6%</td><td>7</td><td>Louisiana</td><td>3,324</td><td>4.5%</td></tr>
<tr><td>28</td><td>Delaware</td><td>802</td><td>1.1%</td><td>8</td><td>Tennessee</td><td>3,314</td><td>4.5%</td></tr>
<tr><td>2</td><td>Florida</td><td>4,895</td><td>6.6%</td><td>9</td><td>California</td><td>2,986</td><td>4.0%</td></tr>
<tr><td>4</td><td>Georgia</td><td>4,556</td><td>6.1%</td><td>10</td><td>Missouri</td><td>2,534</td><td>3.4%</td></tr>
<tr><td>32</td><td>Hawaii</td><td>663</td><td>0.9%</td><td>11</td><td>Michigan</td><td>2,530</td><td>3.4%</td></tr>
<tr><td>31</td><td>Idaho</td><td>703</td><td>0.9%</td><td>12</td><td>Indiana</td><td>2,412</td><td>3.2%</td></tr>
<tr><td>NA</td><td>Illinois**</td><td>NA</td><td>NA</td><td>13</td><td>New York</td><td>2,166</td><td>2.9%</td></tr>
<tr><td>12</td><td>Indiana</td><td>2,412</td><td>3.2%</td><td>14</td><td>Virginia</td><td>1,828</td><td>2.5%</td></tr>
<tr><td>33</td><td>Iowa</td><td>537</td><td>0.7%</td><td>15</td><td>Pennsylvania</td><td>1,711</td><td>2.3%</td></tr>
<tr><td>NA</td><td>Kansas**</td><td>NA</td><td>NA</td><td>16</td><td>Alabama</td><td>1,491</td><td>2.0%</td></tr>
<tr><td>NA</td><td>Kentucky**</td><td>NA</td><td>NA</td><td>17</td><td>Oklahoma</td><td>1,448</td><td>1.9%</td></tr>
<tr><td>7</td><td>Louisiana</td><td>3,324</td><td>4.5%</td><td>18</td><td>Arkansas</td><td>1,428</td><td>1.9%</td></tr>
<tr><td>40</td><td>Maine</td><td>179</td><td>0.2%</td><td>19</td><td>Arizona</td><td>1,075</td><td>1.4%</td></tr>
<tr><td>25</td><td>Maryland</td><td>942</td><td>1.3%</td><td>20</td><td>Ohio</td><td>1,063</td><td>1.4%</td></tr>
<tr><td>42</td><td>Massachusetts</td><td>13</td><td>0.0%</td><td>21</td><td>Washington</td><td>1,005</td><td>1.4%</td></tr>
<tr><td>11</td><td>Michigan</td><td>2,530</td><td>3.4%</td><td>22</td><td>Minnesota</td><td>993</td><td>1.3%</td></tr>
<tr><td>22</td><td>Minnesota</td><td>993</td><td>1.3%</td><td>23</td><td>New Mexico</td><td>980</td><td>1.3%</td></tr>
<tr><td>6</td><td>Mississippi</td><td>3,551</td><td>4.8%</td><td>24</td><td>West Virginia</td><td>969</td><td>1.3%</td></tr>
<tr><td>10</td><td>Missouri</td><td>2,534</td><td>3.4%</td><td>25</td><td>Maryland</td><td>942</td><td>1.3%</td></tr>
<tr><td>NA</td><td>Montana**</td><td>NA</td><td>NA</td><td>26</td><td>Wisconsin</td><td>815</td><td>1.1%</td></tr>
<tr><td>37</td><td>Nebraska</td><td>271</td><td>0.4%</td><td>27</td><td>Alaska</td><td>806</td><td>1.1%</td></tr>
<tr><td>30</td><td>Nevada</td><td>724</td><td>1.0%</td><td>28</td><td>Delaware</td><td>802</td><td>1.1%</td></tr>
<tr><td>NA</td><td>New Hampshire**</td><td>NA</td><td>NA</td><td>29</td><td>Oregon</td><td>787</td><td>1.1%</td></tr>
<tr><td>44</td><td>New Jersey</td><td>0</td><td>0.0%</td><td>30</td><td>Nevada</td><td>724</td><td>1.0%</td></tr>
<tr><td>23</td><td>New Mexico</td><td>980</td><td>1.3%</td><td>31</td><td>Idaho</td><td>703</td><td>0.9%</td></tr>
<tr><td>13</td><td>New York</td><td>2,166</td><td>2.9%</td><td>32</td><td>Hawaii</td><td>663</td><td>0.9%</td></tr>
<tr><td>3</td><td>North Carolina</td><td>4,666</td><td>6.3%</td><td>33</td><td>Iowa</td><td>537</td><td>0.7%</td></tr>
<tr><td>41</td><td>North Dakota</td><td>79</td><td>0.1%</td><td>34</td><td>Colorado</td><td>467</td><td>0.6%</td></tr>
<tr><td>20</td><td>Ohio</td><td>1,063</td><td>1.4%</td><td>35</td><td>Connecticut</td><td>433</td><td>0.6%</td></tr>
<tr><td>17</td><td>Oklahoma</td><td>1,448</td><td>1.9%</td><td>36</td><td>Utah</td><td>342</td><td>0.5%</td></tr>
<tr><td>29</td><td>Oregon</td><td>787</td><td>1.1%</td><td>37</td><td>Nebraska</td><td>271</td><td>0.4%</td></tr>
<tr><td>15</td><td>Pennsylvania</td><td>1,711</td><td>2.3%</td><td>38</td><td>South Dakota</td><td>244</td><td>0.3%</td></tr>
<tr><td>43</td><td>Rhode Island</td><td>8</td><td>0.0%</td><td>39</td><td>Wyoming</td><td>237</td><td>0.3%</td></tr>
<tr><td>1</td><td>South Carolina</td><td>6,713</td><td>9.0%</td><td>40</td><td>Maine</td><td>179</td><td>0.2%</td></tr>
<tr><td>38</td><td>South Dakota</td><td>244</td><td>0.3%</td><td>41</td><td>North Dakota</td><td>79</td><td>0.1%</td></tr>
<tr><td>8</td><td>Tennessee</td><td>3,314</td><td>4.5%</td><td>42</td><td>Massachusetts</td><td>13</td><td>0.0%</td></tr>
<tr><td>5</td><td>Texas</td><td>3,950</td><td>5.3%</td><td>43</td><td>Rhode Island</td><td>8</td><td>0.0%</td></tr>
<tr><td>36</td><td>Utah</td><td>342</td><td>0.5%</td><td>44</td><td>New Jersey</td><td>0</td><td>0.0%</td></tr>
<tr><td>NA</td><td>Vermont**</td><td>NA</td><td>NA</td><td>NA</td><td>Illinois**</td><td>NA</td><td>NA</td></tr>
<tr><td>14</td><td>Virginia</td><td>1,828</td><td>2.5%</td><td>NA</td><td>Kansas**</td><td>NA</td><td>NA</td></tr>
<tr><td>21</td><td>Washington</td><td>1,005</td><td>1.4%</td><td>NA</td><td>Kentucky**</td><td>NA</td><td>NA</td></tr>
<tr><td>24</td><td>West Virginia</td><td>969</td><td>1.3%</td><td>NA</td><td>Montana**</td><td>NA</td><td>NA</td></tr>
<tr><td>26</td><td>Wisconsin</td><td>815</td><td>1.1%</td><td>NA</td><td>New Hampshire**</td><td>NA</td><td>NA</td></tr>
<tr><td>39</td><td>Wyoming</td><td>237</td><td>0.3%</td><td>NA</td><td>Vermont**</td><td>NA</td><td>NA</td></tr>
<tr><td></td><td></td><td></td><td></td><td></td><td>District of Columbia</td><td>0</td><td>0.0%</td></tr>
</table>

Source: Federal Bureau of Investigation
   "Crime in the United States 1997" (Uniform Crime Reports, November 22, 1998)
*Estimated totals for rural areas, defined by the F.B.I. as other than Metropolitan Statistical Areas and other cities outside such areas. National total includes those states listed as not available. Violent crimes are offenses of murder, forcible rape, robbery and aggravated assault.
**Not available.

Rural Violent Crime Rate in 1997

National Rural Rate = 230.6 Violent Crimes per 100,000 Population*

ALPHA ORDER

RANK ORDER

RANK	STATE	RATE		RANK	STATE	RATE
25	Alabama	188.0		1	Delaware	853.8
6	Alaska	420.4		2	South Carolina	837.5
12	Arizona	305.7		3	Florida	614.7
26	Arkansas	175.6		4	Louisiana	485.9
5	California	471.1		5	California	471.1
32	Colorado	142.0		6	Alaska	420.4
18	Connecticut	234.5		7	Nevada	371.1
1	Delaware	853.8		8	Maryland	351.5
3	Florida	614.7		9	New Mexico	330.5
11	Georgia	309.2		10	Mississippi	318.0
21	Hawaii	216.2		11	Georgia	309.2
27	Idaho	174.5		12	Arizona	305.7
NA	Illinois**	NA		13	Tennessee	303.1
20	Indiana	227.7		14	North Carolina	272.1
40	Iowa	60.6		15	New York	254.3
NA	Kansas**	NA		16	Texas	239.1
NA	Kentucky**	NA		17	Michigan	235.3
4	Louisiana	485.9		18	Connecticut	234.5
41	Maine	50.8		19	Oklahoma	228.9
8	Maryland	351.5		20	Indiana	227.7
33	Massachusetts	131.9		21	Hawaii	216.2
17	Michigan	235.3		22	Missouri	208.2
35	Minnesota	112.8		23	Washington	195.6
10	Mississippi	318.0		24	Wyoming	189.4
22	Missouri	208.2		25	Alabama	188.0
NA	Montana**	NA		26	Arkansas	175.6
39	Nebraska	64.4		27	Idaho	174.5
7	Nevada	371.1		28	Virginia	170.1
NA	New Hampshire**	NA		29	Pennsylvania	162.4
43	New Jersey	0.0		30	Utah	155.2
9	New Mexico	330.5		31	Oregon	151.1
15	New York	254.3		32	Colorado	142.0
14	North Carolina	272.1		33	Massachusetts	131.9
42	North Dakota	35.6		34	West Virginia	124.4
38	Ohio	79.9		35	Minnesota	112.8
19	Oklahoma	228.9		36	South Dakota	84.0
31	Oregon	151.1		37	Wisconsin	82.9
29	Pennsylvania	162.4		38	Ohio	79.9
43	Rhode Island	0.0		39	Nebraska	64.4
2	South Carolina	837.5		40	Iowa	60.6
36	South Dakota	84.0		41	Maine	50.8
13	Tennessee	303.1		42	North Dakota	35.6
16	Texas	239.1		43	New Jersey	0.0
30	Utah	155.2		43	Rhode Island	0.0
NA	Vermont**	NA		NA	Illinois**	NA
28	Virginia	170.1		NA	Kansas**	NA
23	Washington	195.6		NA	Kentucky**	NA
34	West Virginia	124.4		NA	Montana**	NA
37	Wisconsin	82.9		NA	New Hampshire**	NA
24	Wyoming	189.4		NA	Vermont**	NA
					District of Columbia	0.0

Source: Morgan Quitno Press using data from Federal Bureau of Investigation
"Crime in the United States 1997" (Uniform Crime Reports, November 22, 1998)
Estimated rates for rural areas, defined by the F.B.I. as other than Metropolitan Statistical Areas and other cities outside such areas. National rate includes those states listed as not available. Violent crimes are offenses of murder, forcible rape, robbery and aggravated assault.
**Not available.

Percent of Violent Crimes Occurring in Rural Areas in 1997

National Percent = 4.5% of Violent Crimes*

ALPHA ORDER				RANK ORDER		
RANK	STATE	PERCENT		RANK	STATE	PERCENT
23	Alabama	6.1		1	Mississippi	27.7
6	Alaska	18.9		2	West Virginia	24.4
31	Arizona	3.8		3	Idaho	22.6
12	Arkansas	10.7		4	Hawaii	20.1
41	California	1.2		5	Wyoming	19.3
35	Colorado	3.3		6	Alaska	18.9
33	Connecticut	3.4		7	South Carolina	18.0
9	Delaware	16.2		8	South Dakota	16.7
35	Florida	3.3		9	Delaware	16.2
14	Georgia	10.0		10	North Dakota	14.1
4	Hawaii	20.1		11	Maine	11.9
3	Idaho	22.6		12	Arkansas	10.7
NA	Illinois**	NA		13	North Carolina	10.4
17	Indiana	8.0		14	Georgia	10.0
23	Iowa	6.1		15	Louisiana	8.9
NA	Kansas**	NA		16	Missouri	8.1
NA	Kentucky**	NA		17	Indiana	8.0
15	Louisiana	8.9		18	Virginia	7.9
11	Maine	11.9		19	Oklahoma	7.8
38	Maryland	2.2		19	Tennessee	7.8
43	Massachusetts	0.0		21	New Mexico	6.6
29	Michigan	4.4		22	Minnesota	6.3
22	Minnesota	6.3		23	Alabama	6.1
1	Mississippi	27.7		23	Iowa	6.1
16	Missouri	8.1		25	Wisconsin	5.8
NA	Montana**	NA		26	Oregon	5.5
32	Nebraska	3.7		27	Nevada	5.4
27	Nevada	5.4		28	Utah	5.0
NA	New Hampshire**	NA		29	Michigan	4.4
43	New Jersey	0.0		30	Washington	4.1
21	New Mexico	6.6		31	Arizona	3.8
40	New York	1.7		32	Nebraska	3.7
13	North Carolina	10.4		33	Connecticut	3.4
10	North Dakota	14.1		33	Texas	3.4
38	Ohio	2.2		35	Colorado	3.3
19	Oklahoma	7.8		35	Florida	3.3
26	Oregon	5.5		37	Pennsylvania	3.2
37	Pennsylvania	3.2		38	Maryland	2.2
42	Rhode Island	0.2		38	Ohio	2.2
7	South Carolina	18.0		40	New York	1.7
8	South Dakota	16.7		41	California	1.2
19	Tennessee	7.8		42	Rhode Island	0.2
33	Texas	3.4		43	Massachusetts	0.0
28	Utah	5.0		43	New Jersey	0.0
NA	Vermont**	NA		NA	Illinois**	NA
18	Virginia	7.9		NA	Kansas**	NA
30	Washington	4.1		NA	Kentucky**	NA
2	West Virginia	24.4		NA	Montana**	NA
25	Wisconsin	5.8		NA	New Hampshire**	NA
5	Wyoming	19.3		NA	Vermont**	NA
				District of Columbia		0.0

Source: Morgan Quitno Press using data from Federal Bureau of Investigation
  "Crime in the United States 1997" (Uniform Crime Reports, November 22, 1998)
*Estimated percentages for rural areas, defined by the F.B.I. as other than Metropolitan Statistical Areas and other cities outside such areas. National percent includes those states listed as not available. Violent crimes are offenses of murder, forcible rape, robbery and aggravated assault.
**Not available.

411

Murders in Urban Areas in 1997

National Urban Total = 16,722 Murders*

ALPHA ORDER					RANK ORDER			
RANK	STATE		MURDERS	% of USA	RANK	STATE		MURDERS	% of USA

RANK	STATE	MURDERS	% of USA
15	Alabama	386	2.3%
36	Alaska	36	0.2%
16	Arizona	365	2.2%
22	Arkansas	194	1.2%
1	California	2,553	15.3%
26	Colorado	150	0.9%
27	Connecticut	121	0.7%
41	Delaware	14	0.1%
4	Florida	981	5.9%
11	Georgia	479	2.9%
37	Hawaii	34	0.2%
39	Idaho	21	0.1%
NA	Illinois**	NA	NA
14	Indiana	407	2.4%
32	Iowa	46	0.3%
NA	Kansas**	NA	NA
NA	Kentucky**	NA	NA
7	Louisiana	621	3.7%
40	Maine	18	0.1%
9	Maryland	486	2.9%
30	Massachusetts	119	0.7%
5	Michigan	723	4.3%
27	Minnesota	121	0.7%
21	Mississippi	214	1.3%
16	Missouri	365	2.2%
NA	Montana**	NA	NA
32	Nebraska	46	0.3%
23	Nevada	184	1.1%
NA	New Hampshire**	NA	NA
18	New Jersey	337	2.0%
27	New Mexico	121	0.7%
3	New York	1,077	6.4%
10	North Carolina	481	2.9%
44	North Dakota	4	0.0%
8	Ohio	506	3.0%
24	Oklahoma	182	1.1%
31	Oregon	78	0.5%
6	Pennsylvania	682	4.1%
38	Rhode Island	25	0.1%
19	South Carolina	236	1.4%
43	South Dakota	7	0.0%
12	Tennessee	443	2.6%
2	Texas	1,245	7.4%
34	Utah	45	0.3%
NA	Vermont**	NA	NA
13	Virginia	434	2.6%
20	Washington	220	1.3%
35	West Virginia	39	0.2%
25	Wisconsin	181	1.1%
42	Wyoming	10	0.1%

RANK	STATE	MURDERS	% of USA
1	California	2,553	15.3%
2	Texas	1,245	7.4%
3	New York	1,077	6.4%
4	Florida	981	5.9%
5	Michigan	723	4.3%
6	Pennsylvania	682	4.1%
7	Louisiana	621	3.7%
8	Ohio	506	3.0%
9	Maryland	486	2.9%
10	North Carolina	481	2.9%
11	Georgia	479	2.9%
12	Tennessee	443	2.6%
13	Virginia	434	2.6%
14	Indiana	407	2.4%
15	Alabama	386	2.3%
16	Arizona	365	2.2%
16	Missouri	365	2.2%
18	New Jersey	337	2.0%
19	South Carolina	236	1.4%
20	Washington	220	1.3%
21	Mississippi	214	1.3%
22	Arkansas	194	1.2%
23	Nevada	184	1.1%
24	Oklahoma	182	1.1%
25	Wisconsin	181	1.1%
26	Colorado	150	0.9%
27	Connecticut	121	0.7%
27	Minnesota	121	0.7%
27	New Mexico	121	0.7%
30	Massachusetts	119	0.7%
31	Oregon	78	0.5%
32	Iowa	46	0.3%
32	Nebraska	46	0.3%
34	Utah	45	0.3%
35	West Virginia	39	0.2%
36	Alaska	36	0.2%
37	Hawaii	34	0.2%
38	Rhode Island	25	0.1%
39	Idaho	21	0.1%
40	Maine	18	0.1%
41	Delaware	14	0.1%
42	Wyoming	10	0.1%
43	South Dakota	7	0.0%
44	North Dakota	4	0.0%
NA	Illinois**	NA	NA
NA	Kansas**	NA	NA
NA	Kentucky**	NA	NA
NA	Montana**	NA	NA
NA	New Hampshire**	NA	NA
NA	Vermont**	NA	NA
	District of Columbia	301	1.8%

Source: Morgan Quitno Press using data from Federal Bureau of Investigation
    "Crime in the United States 1997" (Uniform Crime Reports, November 22, 1998)
*Estimated totals for urban areas, defined by the F.B.I. as Metropolitan Statistical Areas and other cities outside such areas. National total includes those states listed as not available. Includes nonnegligent manslaughter.
**Not available.

Urban Murder Rate in 1997

National Urban Rate = 7.1 Murders per 100,000 Population*

ALPHA ORDER

RANK	STATE	RATE
5	Alabama	10.9
10	Alaska	8.6
8	Arizona	8.7
4	Arkansas	11.3
15	California	8.1
27	Colorado	4.2
29	Connecticut	3.9
40	Delaware	2.2
19	Florida	7.1
16	Georgia	8.0
29	Hawaii	3.9
36	Idaho	2.6
NA	Illinois**	NA
11	Indiana	8.5
39	Iowa	2.3
NA	Kansas**	NA
NA	Kentucky**	NA
1	Louisiana	16.9
41	Maine	2.0
7	Maryland	10.1
42	Massachusetts	1.9
14	Michigan	8.3
33	Minnesota	3.2
2	Mississippi	13.3
8	Missouri	8.7
NA	Montana**	NA
32	Nebraska	3.7
3	Nevada	12.4
NA	New Hampshire**	NA
27	New Jersey	4.2
12	New Mexico	8.4
22	New York	6.2
12	North Carolina	8.4
44	North Dakota	1.0
24	Ohio	5.1
21	Oklahoma	6.8
34	Oregon	2.9
22	Pennsylvania	6.2
37	Rhode Island	2.5
16	South Carolina	8.0
43	South Dakota	1.6
6	Tennessee	10.4
20	Texas	7.0
38	Utah	2.4
NA	Vermont**	NA
18	Virginia	7.7
25	Washington	4.3
31	West Virginia	3.8
25	Wisconsin	4.3
35	Wyoming	2.8

RANK ORDER

RANK	STATE	RATE
1	Louisiana	16.9
2	Mississippi	13.3
3	Nevada	12.4
4	Arkansas	11.3
5	Alabama	10.9
6	Tennessee	10.4
7	Maryland	10.1
8	Arizona	8.7
8	Missouri	8.7
10	Alaska	8.6
11	Indiana	8.5
12	New Mexico	8.4
12	North Carolina	8.4
14	Michigan	8.3
15	California	8.1
16	Georgia	8.0
16	South Carolina	8.0
18	Virginia	7.7
19	Florida	7.1
20	Texas	7.0
21	Oklahoma	6.8
22	New York	6.2
22	Pennsylvania	6.2
24	Ohio	5.1
25	Washington	4.3
25	Wisconsin	4.3
27	Colorado	4.2
27	New Jersey	4.2
29	Connecticut	3.9
29	Hawaii	3.9
31	West Virginia	3.8
32	Nebraska	3.7
33	Minnesota	3.2
34	Oregon	2.9
35	Wyoming	2.8
36	Idaho	2.6
37	Rhode Island	2.5
38	Utah	2.4
39	Iowa	2.3
40	Delaware	2.2
41	Maine	2.0
42	Massachusetts	1.9
43	South Dakota	1.6
44	North Dakota	1.0
NA	Illinois**	NA
NA	Kansas**	NA
NA	Kentucky**	NA
NA	Montana**	NA
NA	New Hampshire**	NA
NA	Vermont**	NA
	District of Columbia	56.9

Source: Morgan Quitno Press using data from Federal Bureau of Investigation
  "Crime in the United States 1997" (Uniform Crime Reports, November 22, 1998)
*Estimated rates for urban areas, defined by the F.B.I. as Metropolitan Statistical Areas and other cities outside
such areas. National rate includes those states listed as not available. Includes nonnegligent manslaughter.*
**Not available.*

Percent of Murders Occurring in Urban Areas in 1997

National Percent = 91.8% of Murders*

ALPHA ORDER

RANK	STATE	PERCENT	RANK	STATE	PERCENT
21	Alabama	90.6	1	Massachusetts	100.0
39	Alaska	66.7	1	New Jersey	100.0
8	Arizona	97.3	1	Rhode Island	100.0
4	California	99.0	4	California	99.0
13	Colorado	95.5	5	New York	98.5
7	Connecticut	97.6	6	Nevada	98.4
33	Delaware	77.8	7	Connecticut	97.6
9	Florida	96.9	8	Arizona	97.3
29	Georgia	85.1	9	Florida	96.9
36	Hawaii	72.3	10	Maryland	96.8
43	Idaho	53.8	11	Ohio	96.7
NA	Illinois**	NA	11	Pennsylvania	96.7
15	Indiana	94.7	13	Colorado	95.5
25	Iowa	88.5	14	Michigan	95.3
NA	Kansas**	NA	15	Indiana	94.7
NA	Kentucky**	NA	16	Minnesota	93.8
20	Louisiana	91.1	16	Texas	93.8
37	Maine	72.0	18	Nebraska	92.0
10	Maryland	96.8	19	Washington	91.3
1	Massachusetts	100.0	20	Louisiana	91.1
14	Michigan	95.3	21	Alabama	90.6
16	Minnesota	93.8	22	New Mexico	90.3
41	Mississippi	59.8	23	Utah	90.0
28	Missouri	85.7	24	Virginia	88.9
NA	Montana**	NA	25	Iowa	88.5
18	Nebraska	92.0	26	Wisconsin	88.3
6	Nevada	98.4	27	Tennessee	86.7
NA	New Hampshire**	NA	28	Missouri	85.7
1	New Jersey	100.0	29	Georgia	85.1
22	New Mexico	90.3	30	Oregon	82.1
5	New York	98.5	31	Oklahoma	79.5
32	North Carolina	78.3	32	North Carolina	78.3
39	North Dakota	66.7	33	Delaware	77.8
11	Ohio	96.7	34	Arkansas	77.6
31	Oklahoma	79.5	35	South Carolina	75.2
30	Oregon	82.1	36	Hawaii	72.3
11	Pennsylvania	96.7	37	Maine	72.0
1	Rhode Island	100.0	38	South Dakota	70.0
35	South Carolina	75.2	39	Alaska	66.7
38	South Dakota	70.0	39	North Dakota	66.7
27	Tennessee	86.7	41	Mississippi	59.8
16	Texas	93.8	42	Wyoming	58.8
23	Utah	90.0	43	Idaho	53.8
NA	Vermont**	NA	44	West Virginia	52.0
24	Virginia	88.9	NA	Illinois**	NA
19	Washington	91.3	NA	Kansas**	NA
44	West Virginia	52.0	NA	Kentucky**	NA
26	Wisconsin	88.3	NA	Montana**	NA
42	Wyoming	58.8	NA	New Hampshire**	NA
			NA	Vermont**	NA
				District of Columbia	100.0

Source: Morgan Quitno Press using data from Federal Bureau of Investigation
   "Crime in the United States 1997" (Uniform Crime Reports, November 22, 1998)

*Estimated percentages for urban areas, defined by the F.B.I. as Metropolitan Statistical Areas and other cities outside such areas. National percent includes those states listed as not available. Includes nonnegligent manslaughter.
**Not available.

Murders in Rural Areas in 1997

National Rural Total = 1,487 Murders*

ALPHA ORDER					RANK ORDER			
RANK	**STATE**	**MURDERS**	**% of USA**		**RANK**	**STATE**	**MURDERS**	**% of USA**
12	Alabama	40	2.7%		1	Mississippi	144	9.7%
21	Alaska	18	1.2%		2	North Carolina	133	8.9%
29	Arizona	10	0.7%		3	Georgia	84	5.6%
9	Arkansas	56	3.8%		4	Texas	82	5.5%
16	California	26	1.7%		5	South Carolina	78	5.2%
31	Colorado	7	0.5%		6	Tennessee	68	4.6%
38	Connecticut	3	0.2%		7	Louisiana	61	4.1%
36	Delaware	4	0.3%		7	Missouri	61	4.1%
15	Florida	31	2.1%		9	Arkansas	56	3.8%
3	Georgia	84	5.6%		10	Virginia	54	3.6%
27	Hawaii	13	0.9%		11	Oklahoma	47	3.2%
21	Idaho	18	1.2%		12	Alabama	40	2.7%
NA	Illinois**	NA	NA		13	Michigan	36	2.4%
18	Indiana	23	1.5%		13	West Virginia	36	2.4%
34	Iowa	6	0.4%		15	Florida	31	2.1%
NA	Kansas**	NA	NA		16	California	26	1.7%
NA	Kentucky**	NA	NA		17	Wisconsin	24	1.6%
7	Louisiana	61	4.1%		18	Indiana	23	1.5%
31	Maine	7	0.5%		18	Pennsylvania	23	1.5%
25	Maryland	16	1.1%		20	Washington	21	1.4%
42	Massachusetts	0	0.0%		21	Alaska	18	1.2%
13	Michigan	36	2.4%		21	Idaho	18	1.2%
30	Minnesota	8	0.5%		23	Ohio	17	1.1%
1	Mississippi	144	9.7%		23	Oregon	17	1.1%
7	Missouri	61	4.1%		25	Maryland	16	1.1%
NA	Montana**	NA	NA		25	New York	16	1.1%
36	Nebraska	4	0.3%		27	Hawaii	13	0.9%
38	Nevada	3	0.2%		27	New Mexico	13	0.9%
NA	New Hampshire**	NA	NA		29	Arizona	10	0.7%
42	New Jersey	0	0.0%		30	Minnesota	8	0.5%
27	New Mexico	13	0.9%		31	Colorado	7	0.5%
25	New York	16	1.1%		31	Maine	7	0.5%
2	North Carolina	133	8.9%		31	Wyoming	7	0.5%
41	North Dakota	2	0.1%		34	Iowa	6	0.4%
23	Ohio	17	1.1%		35	Utah	5	0.3%
11	Oklahoma	47	3.2%		36	Delaware	4	0.3%
23	Oregon	17	1.1%		36	Nebraska	4	0.3%
18	Pennsylvania	23	1.5%		38	Connecticut	3	0.2%
42	Rhode Island	0	0.0%		38	Nevada	3	0.2%
5	South Carolina	78	5.2%		38	South Dakota	3	0.2%
38	South Dakota	3	0.2%		41	North Dakota	2	0.1%
6	Tennessee	68	4.6%		42	Massachusetts	0	0.0%
4	Texas	82	5.5%		42	New Jersey	0	0.0%
35	Utah	5	0.3%		42	Rhode Island	0	0.0%
NA	Vermont**	NA	NA		NA	Illinois**	NA	NA
10	Virginia	54	3.6%		NA	Kansas**	NA	NA
20	Washington	21	1.4%		NA	Kentucky**	NA	NA
13	West Virginia	36	2.4%		NA	Montana**	NA	NA
17	Wisconsin	24	1.6%		NA	New Hampshire**	NA	NA
31	Wyoming	7	0.5%		NA	Vermont**	NA	NA
						District of Columbia	0	0.0%

Source: Federal Bureau of Investigation
   "Crime in the United States 1997" (Uniform Crime Reports, November 22, 1998)
*Estimated totals for rural areas, defined by the F.B.I. as other than Metropolitan Statistical Areas and other cities outside such areas. National total includes those states listed as not available. Includes nonnegligent manslaughter.
**Not available.

Rural Murder Rate in 1997

National Rural Rate = 4.6 Murders per 100,000 Population*

RANK	STATE	RATE
12	Alabama	5.0
3	Alaska	9.4
26	Arizona	2.8
7	Arkansas	6.9
21	California	4.1
31	Colorado	2.1
34	Connecticut	1.6
19	Delaware	4.3
23	Florida	3.9
10	Georgia	5.7
20	Hawaii	4.2
17	Idaho	4.5
NA	Illinois**	NA
29	Indiana	2.2
41	Iowa	0.7
NA	Kansas**	NA
NA	Kentucky**	NA
4	Louisiana	8.9
32	Maine	2.0
9	Maryland	6.0
42	Massachusetts	0.0
24	Michigan	3.3
39	Minnesota	0.9
1	Mississippi	12.9
12	Missouri	5.0
NA	Montana**	NA
37	Nebraska	1.0
35	Nevada	1.5
NA	New Hampshire**	NA
42	New Jersey	0.0
18	New Mexico	4.4
33	New York	1.9
5	North Carolina	7.8
39	North Dakota	0.9
36	Ohio	1.3
6	Oklahoma	7.4
24	Oregon	3.3
29	Pennsylvania	2.2
42	Rhode Island	0.0
2	South Carolina	9.7
37	South Dakota	1.0
8	Tennessee	6.2
12	Texas	5.0
28	Utah	2.3
NA	Vermont**	NA
12	Virginia	5.0
21	Washington	4.1
16	West Virginia	4.6
27	Wisconsin	2.4
11	Wyoming	5.6

RANK	STATE	RATE
1	Mississippi	12.9
2	South Carolina	9.7
3	Alaska	9.4
4	Louisiana	8.9
5	North Carolina	7.8
6	Oklahoma	7.4
7	Arkansas	6.9
8	Tennessee	6.2
9	Maryland	6.0
10	Georgia	5.7
11	Wyoming	5.6
12	Alabama	5.0
12	Missouri	5.0
12	Texas	5.0
12	Virginia	5.0
16	West Virginia	4.6
17	Idaho	4.5
18	New Mexico	4.4
19	Delaware	4.3
20	Hawaii	4.2
21	California	4.1
21	Washington	4.1
23	Florida	3.9
24	Michigan	3.3
24	Oregon	3.3
26	Arizona	2.8
27	Wisconsin	2.4
28	Utah	2.3
29	Indiana	2.2
29	Pennsylvania	2.2
31	Colorado	2.1
32	Maine	2.0
33	New York	1.9
34	Connecticut	1.6
35	Nevada	1.5
36	Ohio	1.3
37	Nebraska	1.0
37	South Dakota	1.0
39	Minnesota	0.9
39	North Dakota	0.9
41	Iowa	0.7
42	Massachusetts	0.0
42	New Jersey	0.0
42	Rhode Island	0.0
NA	Illinois**	NA
NA	Kansas**	NA
NA	Kentucky**	NA
NA	Montana**	NA
NA	New Hampshire**	NA
NA	Vermont**	NA
	District of Columbia	0.0

Source: Morgan Quitno Press using data from Federal Bureau of Investigation
    "Crime in the United States 1997" (Uniform Crime Reports, November 22, 1998)
*Estimated rates for rural areas, defined by the F.B.I. as other than Metropolitan Statistical Areas and other cities outside such areas. National rate includes those states listed as not available. Includes nonnegligent manslaughter.
**Not available.

Percent of Murders Occurring in Rural Areas in 1997

National Percent = 8.2% of Murders*

<table>
<tr><td colspan="3">ALPHA ORDER</td><td colspan="3">RANK ORDER</td></tr>
<tr><td>RANK</td><td>STATE</td><td>PERCENT</td><td>RANK</td><td>STATE</td><td>PERCENT</td></tr>
<tr><td>24</td><td>Alabama</td><td>9.4</td><td>1</td><td>West Virginia</td><td>48.0</td></tr>
<tr><td>5</td><td>Alaska</td><td>33.3</td><td>2</td><td>Idaho</td><td>46.2</td></tr>
<tr><td>37</td><td>Arizona</td><td>2.7</td><td>3</td><td>Wyoming</td><td>41.2</td></tr>
<tr><td>11</td><td>Arkansas</td><td>22.4</td><td>4</td><td>Mississippi</td><td>40.2</td></tr>
<tr><td>41</td><td>California</td><td>1.0</td><td>5</td><td>Alaska</td><td>33.3</td></tr>
<tr><td>32</td><td>Colorado</td><td>4.5</td><td>5</td><td>North Dakota</td><td>33.3</td></tr>
<tr><td>38</td><td>Connecticut</td><td>2.4</td><td>7</td><td>South Dakota</td><td>30.0</td></tr>
<tr><td>12</td><td>Delaware</td><td>22.2</td><td>8</td><td>Maine</td><td>28.0</td></tr>
<tr><td>36</td><td>Florida</td><td>3.1</td><td>9</td><td>Hawaii</td><td>27.7</td></tr>
<tr><td>16</td><td>Georgia</td><td>14.9</td><td>10</td><td>South Carolina</td><td>24.8</td></tr>
<tr><td>9</td><td>Hawaii</td><td>27.7</td><td>11</td><td>Arkansas</td><td>22.4</td></tr>
<tr><td>2</td><td>Idaho</td><td>46.2</td><td>12</td><td>Delaware</td><td>22.2</td></tr>
<tr><td>NA</td><td>Illinois**</td><td>NA</td><td>13</td><td>North Carolina</td><td>21.7</td></tr>
<tr><td>30</td><td>Indiana</td><td>5.3</td><td>14</td><td>Oklahoma</td><td>20.5</td></tr>
<tr><td>20</td><td>Iowa</td><td>11.5</td><td>15</td><td>Oregon</td><td>17.9</td></tr>
<tr><td>NA</td><td>Kansas**</td><td>NA</td><td>16</td><td>Georgia</td><td>14.9</td></tr>
<tr><td>NA</td><td>Kentucky**</td><td>NA</td><td>17</td><td>Missouri</td><td>14.3</td></tr>
<tr><td>25</td><td>Louisiana</td><td>8.9</td><td>18</td><td>Tennessee</td><td>13.3</td></tr>
<tr><td>8</td><td>Maine</td><td>28.0</td><td>19</td><td>Wisconsin</td><td>11.7</td></tr>
<tr><td>35</td><td>Maryland</td><td>3.2</td><td>20</td><td>Iowa</td><td>11.5</td></tr>
<tr><td>42</td><td>Massachusetts</td><td>0.0</td><td>21</td><td>Virginia</td><td>11.1</td></tr>
<tr><td>31</td><td>Michigan</td><td>4.7</td><td>22</td><td>Utah</td><td>10.0</td></tr>
<tr><td>28</td><td>Minnesota</td><td>6.2</td><td>23</td><td>New Mexico</td><td>9.7</td></tr>
<tr><td>4</td><td>Mississippi</td><td>40.2</td><td>24</td><td>Alabama</td><td>9.4</td></tr>
<tr><td>17</td><td>Missouri</td><td>14.3</td><td>25</td><td>Louisiana</td><td>8.9</td></tr>
<tr><td>NA</td><td>Montana**</td><td>NA</td><td>26</td><td>Washington</td><td>8.7</td></tr>
<tr><td>27</td><td>Nebraska</td><td>8.0</td><td>27</td><td>Nebraska</td><td>8.0</td></tr>
<tr><td>39</td><td>Nevada</td><td>1.6</td><td>28</td><td>Minnesota</td><td>6.2</td></tr>
<tr><td>NA</td><td>New Hampshire**</td><td>NA</td><td>28</td><td>Texas</td><td>6.2</td></tr>
<tr><td>42</td><td>New Jersey</td><td>0.0</td><td>30</td><td>Indiana</td><td>5.3</td></tr>
<tr><td>23</td><td>New Mexico</td><td>9.7</td><td>31</td><td>Michigan</td><td>4.7</td></tr>
<tr><td>40</td><td>New York</td><td>1.5</td><td>32</td><td>Colorado</td><td>4.5</td></tr>
<tr><td>13</td><td>North Carolina</td><td>21.7</td><td>33</td><td>Ohio</td><td>3.3</td></tr>
<tr><td>5</td><td>North Dakota</td><td>33.3</td><td>33</td><td>Pennsylvania</td><td>3.3</td></tr>
<tr><td>33</td><td>Ohio</td><td>3.3</td><td>35</td><td>Maryland</td><td>3.2</td></tr>
<tr><td>14</td><td>Oklahoma</td><td>20.5</td><td>36</td><td>Florida</td><td>3.1</td></tr>
<tr><td>15</td><td>Oregon</td><td>17.9</td><td>37</td><td>Arizona</td><td>2.7</td></tr>
<tr><td>33</td><td>Pennsylvania</td><td>3.3</td><td>38</td><td>Connecticut</td><td>2.4</td></tr>
<tr><td>42</td><td>Rhode Island</td><td>0.0</td><td>39</td><td>Nevada</td><td>1.6</td></tr>
<tr><td>10</td><td>South Carolina</td><td>24.8</td><td>40</td><td>New York</td><td>1.5</td></tr>
<tr><td>7</td><td>South Dakota</td><td>30.0</td><td>41</td><td>California</td><td>1.0</td></tr>
<tr><td>18</td><td>Tennessee</td><td>13.3</td><td>42</td><td>Massachusetts</td><td>0.0</td></tr>
<tr><td>28</td><td>Texas</td><td>6.2</td><td>42</td><td>New Jersey</td><td>0.0</td></tr>
<tr><td>22</td><td>Utah</td><td>10.0</td><td>42</td><td>Rhode Island</td><td>0.0</td></tr>
<tr><td>NA</td><td>Vermont**</td><td>NA</td><td>NA</td><td>Illinois**</td><td>NA</td></tr>
<tr><td>21</td><td>Virginia</td><td>11.1</td><td>NA</td><td>Kansas**</td><td>NA</td></tr>
<tr><td>26</td><td>Washington</td><td>8.7</td><td>NA</td><td>Kentucky**</td><td>NA</td></tr>
<tr><td>1</td><td>West Virginia</td><td>48.0</td><td>NA</td><td>Montana**</td><td>NA</td></tr>
<tr><td>19</td><td>Wisconsin</td><td>11.7</td><td>NA</td><td>New Hampshire**</td><td>NA</td></tr>
<tr><td>3</td><td>Wyoming</td><td>41.2</td><td>NA</td><td>Vermont**</td><td>NA</td></tr>
<tr><td></td><td></td><td></td><td></td><td>District of Columbia</td><td>0.0</td></tr>
</table>

Source: Morgan Quitno Press using data from Federal Bureau of Investigation
   "Crime in the United States 1997" (Uniform Crime Reports, November 22, 1998)
*Estimated percentages for rural areas, defined by the F.B.I. as other than Metropolitan Statistical Areas and other cities outside such areas. National percent includes those states listed as not available. Includes nonnegligent manslaughter.
**Not available.

Rapes in Urban Areas in 1997

National Urban Total = 88,154 Rapes*

ALPHA ORDER

RANK	STATE	RAPES	% of USA
24	Alabama	1,283	1.5%
39	Alaska	266	0.3%
21	Arizona	1,436	1.6%
26	Arkansas	928	1.1%
1	California	10,033	11.4%
18	Colorado	1,622	1.8%
32	Connecticut	722	0.8%
34	Delaware	385	0.4%
3	Florida	7,252	8.2%
11	Georgia	2,031	2.3%
41	Hawaii	257	0.3%
38	Idaho	277	0.3%
NA	Illinois**	NA	NA
13	Indiana	1,751	2.0%
33	Iowa	538	0.6%
NA	Kansas**	NA	NA
NA	Kentucky**	NA	NA
16	Louisiana	1,670	1.9%
42	Maine	218	0.2%
15	Maryland	1,712	1.9%
17	Massachusetts	1,647	1.9%
5	Michigan	4,186	4.7%
10	Minnesota	2,095	2.4%
30	Mississippi	863	1.0%
22	Missouri	1,386	1.6%
NA	Montana**	NA	NA
35	Nebraska	380	0.4%
28	Nevada	912	1.0%
NA	New Hampshire**	NA	NA
14	New Jersey	1,729	2.0%
31	New Mexico	799	0.9%
6	New York	3,944	4.5%
12	North Carolina	1,980	2.2%
43	North Dakota	131	0.1%
4	Ohio	4,420	5.0%
23	Oklahoma	1,370	1.6%
25	Oregon	1,153	1.3%
7	Pennsylvania	2,959	3.4%
36	Rhode Island	362	0.4%
20	South Carolina	1,515	1.7%
37	South Dakota	279	0.3%
8	Tennessee	2,790	3.2%
2	Texas	7,652	8.7%
29	Utah	902	1.0%
NA	Vermont**	NA	NA
19	Virginia	1,587	1.8%
9	Washington	2,697	3.1%
40	West Virginia	264	0.3%
27	Wisconsin	915	1.0%
44	Wyoming	129	0.1%

RANK ORDER

RANK	STATE	RAPES	% of USA
1	California	10,033	11.4%
2	Texas	7,652	8.7%
3	Florida	7,252	8.2%
4	Ohio	4,420	5.0%
5	Michigan	4,186	4.7%
6	New York	3,944	4.5%
7	Pennsylvania	2,959	3.4%
8	Tennessee	2,790	3.2%
9	Washington	2,697	3.1%
10	Minnesota	2,095	2.4%
11	Georgia	2,031	2.3%
12	North Carolina	1,980	2.2%
13	Indiana	1,751	2.0%
14	New Jersey	1,729	2.0%
15	Maryland	1,712	1.9%
16	Louisiana	1,670	1.9%
17	Massachusetts	1,647	1.9%
18	Colorado	1,622	1.8%
19	Virginia	1,587	1.8%
20	South Carolina	1,515	1.7%
21	Arizona	1,436	1.6%
22	Missouri	1,386	1.6%
23	Oklahoma	1,370	1.6%
24	Alabama	1,283	1.5%
25	Oregon	1,153	1.3%
26	Arkansas	928	1.1%
27	Wisconsin	915	1.0%
28	Nevada	912	1.0%
29	Utah	902	1.0%
30	Mississippi	863	1.0%
31	New Mexico	799	0.9%
32	Connecticut	722	0.8%
33	Iowa	538	0.6%
34	Delaware	385	0.4%
35	Nebraska	380	0.4%
36	Rhode Island	362	0.4%
37	South Dakota	279	0.3%
38	Idaho	277	0.3%
39	Alaska	266	0.3%
40	West Virginia	264	0.3%
41	Hawaii	257	0.3%
42	Maine	218	0.2%
43	North Dakota	131	0.1%
44	Wyoming	129	0.1%
NA	Illinois**	NA	NA
NA	Kansas**	NA	NA
NA	Kentucky**	NA	NA
NA	Montana**	NA	NA
NA	New Hampshire**	NA	NA
NA	Vermont**	NA	NA
	District of Columbia	218	0.2%

Source: Morgan Quitno Press using data from Federal Bureau of Investigation
"Crime in the United States 1997" (Uniform Crime Reports, November 22, 1998)
*Estimated totals for urban areas, defined by the F.B.I. as Metropolitan Statistical Areas and other cities outside such areas. National total includes those states listed as not available. Forcible rape is the carnal knowledge of a female forcibly and against her will. Attempts are included. However, statutory rape without force and other sex offenses are excluded. **Not available.

Urban Rape Rate in 1997

National Urban Rate = 37.4 Rapes per 100,000 Population*

ALPHA ORDER

RANK	STATE	RATE
22	Alabama	36.4
2	Alaska	63.7
28	Arizona	34.2
8	Arkansas	54.3
31	California	31.7
16	Colorado	45.5
41	Connecticut	23.4
5	Delaware	60.3
11	Florida	52.3
29	Georgia	33.8
34	Hawaii	29.2
27	Idaho	34.3
NA	Illinois**	NA
22	Indiana	36.4
36	Iowa	27.4
NA	Kansas**	NA
NA	Kentucky**	NA
16	Louisiana	45.5
40	Maine	24.5
25	Maryland	35.5
37	Massachusetts	27.0
15	Michigan	48.1
7	Minnesota	55.0
9	Mississippi	53.5
30	Missouri	33.1
NA	Montana**	NA
33	Nebraska	30.7
4	Nevada	61.5
NA	New Hampshire**	NA
44	New Jersey	21.5
6	New Mexico	55.7
42	New York	22.8
26	North Carolina	34.7
32	North Dakota	31.3
18	Ohio	44.9
13	Oklahoma	51.0
20	Oregon	42.4
37	Pennsylvania	27.0
21	Rhode Island	36.7
12	South Carolina	51.2
3	South Dakota	62.4
1	Tennessee	65.3
19	Texas	43.0
14	Utah	49.1
NA	Vermont**	NA
35	Virginia	28.0
10	Washington	52.9
39	West Virginia	25.5
43	Wisconsin	21.9
22	Wyoming	36.4

RANK ORDER

RANK	STATE	RATE
1	Tennessee	65.3
2	Alaska	63.7
3	South Dakota	62.4
4	Nevada	61.5
5	Delaware	60.3
6	New Mexico	55.7
7	Minnesota	55.0
8	Arkansas	54.3
9	Mississippi	53.5
10	Washington	52.9
11	Florida	52.3
12	South Carolina	51.2
13	Oklahoma	51.0
14	Utah	49.1
15	Michigan	48.1
16	Colorado	45.5
16	Louisiana	45.5
18	Ohio	44.9
19	Texas	43.0
20	Oregon	42.4
21	Rhode Island	36.7
22	Alabama	36.4
22	Indiana	36.4
22	Wyoming	36.4
25	Maryland	35.5
26	North Carolina	34.7
27	Idaho	34.3
28	Arizona	34.2
29	Georgia	33.8
30	Missouri	33.1
31	California	31.7
32	North Dakota	31.3
33	Nebraska	30.7
34	Hawaii	29.2
35	Virginia	28.0
36	Iowa	27.4
37	Massachusetts	27.0
37	Pennsylvania	27.0
39	West Virginia	25.5
40	Maine	24.5
41	Connecticut	23.4
42	New York	22.8
43	Wisconsin	21.9
44	New Jersey	21.5
NA	Illinois**	NA
NA	Kansas**	NA
NA	Kentucky**	NA
NA	Montana**	NA
NA	New Hampshire**	NA
NA	Vermont**	NA
	District of Columbia	41.2

Source: Morgan Quitno Press using data from Federal Bureau of Investigation
  "Crime in the United States 1997" (Uniform Crime Reports, November 22, 1998)
*Estimated rates for urban areas, defined by the F.B.I. as Metropolitan Statistical Areas and other cities outside
such areas. National rate includes those states listed as not available. Forcible rape is the carnal knowledge of
a female forcibly and against her will. Attempts are included. However, statutory rape without force and other sex
offenses are excluded. **Not available.

419

Percent of Rapes Occurring in Urban Areas in 1997

National Percent = 91.7% of Rapes*

ALPHA ORDER				RANK ORDER		
RANK	STATE	PERCENT		RANK	STATE	PERCENT
19	Alabama	91.9		1	Massachusetts	100.0
44	Alaska	66.0		1	New Jersey	100.0
9	Arizona	96.2		3	Rhode Island	99.7
33	Arkansas	84.5		4	California	98.5
4	California	98.5		5	Connecticut	97.6
8	Colorado	96.7		6	New York	96.8
5	Connecticut	97.6		6	Ohio	96.8
39	Delaware	80.9		8	Colorado	96.7
11	Florida	95.4		9	Arizona	96.2
29	Georgia	87.2		10	Texas	95.5
43	Hawaii	69.3		11	Florida	95.4
40	Idaho	79.1		12	Maryland	94.4
NA	Illinois**	NA		13	Wyoming	94.2
23	Indiana	90.8		14	Nebraska	93.6
16	Iowa	92.9		15	Washington	93.5
NA	Kansas**	NA		16	Iowa	92.9
NA	Kentucky**	NA		17	Louisiana	92.8
17	Louisiana	92.8		18	Utah	92.3
31	Maine	85.8		19	Alabama	91.9
12	Maryland	94.4		20	New Mexico	91.6
1	Massachusetts	100.0		21	Tennessee	91.3
35	Michigan	82.6		22	Missouri	90.9
32	Minnesota	85.7		23	Indiana	90.8
38	Mississippi	81.0		24	Nevada	90.7
22	Missouri	90.9		25	Oklahoma	90.3
NA	Montana**	NA		26	Pennsylvania	90.0
14	Nebraska	93.6		27	Oregon	88.3
24	Nevada	90.7		28	Wisconsin	87.3
NA	New Hampshire**	NA		29	Georgia	87.2
1	New Jersey	100.0		29	Virginia	87.2
20	New Mexico	91.6		31	Maine	85.8
6	New York	96.8		32	Minnesota	85.7
34	North Carolina	84.3		33	Arkansas	84.5
37	North Dakota	82.4		34	North Carolina	84.3
6	Ohio	96.8		35	Michigan	82.6
25	Oklahoma	90.3		36	South Carolina	82.5
27	Oregon	88.3		37	North Dakota	82.4
26	Pennsylvania	90.0		38	Mississippi	81.0
3	Rhode Island	99.7		39	Delaware	80.9
36	South Carolina	82.5		40	Idaho	79.1
41	South Dakota	78.2		41	South Dakota	78.2
21	Tennessee	91.3		42	West Virginia	74.4
10	Texas	95.5		43	Hawaii	69.3
18	Utah	92.3		44	Alaska	66.0
NA	Vermont**	NA		NA	Illinois**	NA
29	Virginia	87.2		NA	Kansas**	NA
15	Washington	93.5		NA	Kentucky**	NA
42	West Virginia	74.4		NA	Montana**	NA
28	Wisconsin	87.3		NA	New Hampshire**	NA
13	Wyoming	94.2		NA	Vermont**	NA
					District of Columbia	100.0

Source: Morgan Quitno Press using data from Federal Bureau of Investigation
     "Crime in the United States 1997" (Uniform Crime Reports, November 22, 1998)
*Estimated percentages for urban areas, defined by the F.B.I. as Metropolitan Statistical Areas and other cities outside such areas. National percent includes those states listed as not available. Forcible rape is the carnal knowledge of a female forcibly and against her will. Attempts are included. However, statutory rape without force and other sex offenses are excluded. **Not available.

420

Rapes in Rural Areas in 1997

National Rural Total = 7,968 Rapes*

ALPHA ORDER

RANK	STATE	RAPES	% of USA
25	Alabama	113	1.4%
20	Alaska	137	1.7%
34	Arizona	56	0.7%
14	Arkansas	170	2.1%
15	California	156	2.0%
35	Colorado	55	0.7%
40	Connecticut	18	0.2%
28	Delaware	91	1.1%
5	Florida	347	4.4%
8	Georgia	297	3.7%
24	Hawaii	114	1.4%
32	Idaho	73	0.9%
NA	Illinois**	NA	NA
13	Indiana	177	2.2%
36	Iowa	41	0.5%
NA	Kansas**	NA	NA
NA	Kentucky**	NA	NA
23	Louisiana	129	1.6%
37	Maine	36	0.5%
26	Maryland	102	1.3%
43	Massachusetts	0	0.0%
1	Michigan	884	11.1%
4	Minnesota	351	4.4%
11	Mississippi	202	2.5%
19	Missouri	139	1.7%
NA	Montana**	NA	NA
39	Nebraska	26	0.3%
27	Nevada	93	1.2%
NA	New Hampshire**	NA	NA
43	New Jersey	0	0.0%
32	New Mexico	73	0.9%
22	New York	131	1.6%
2	North Carolina	368	4.6%
38	North Dakota	28	0.4%
18	Ohio	146	1.8%
17	Oklahoma	147	1.8%
16	Oregon	153	1.9%
6	Pennsylvania	330	4.1%
42	Rhode Island	1	0.0%
7	South Carolina	322	4.0%
30	South Dakota	78	1.0%
9	Tennessee	266	3.3%
3	Texas	359	4.5%
31	Utah	75	0.9%
NA	Vermont**	NA	NA
10	Virginia	232	2.9%
12	Washington	188	2.4%
28	West Virginia	91	1.1%
21	Wisconsin	133	1.7%
41	Wyoming	8	0.1%

RANK ORDER

RANK	STATE	RAPES	% of USA
1	Michigan	884	11.1%
2	North Carolina	368	4.6%
3	Texas	359	4.5%
4	Minnesota	351	4.4%
5	Florida	347	4.4%
6	Pennsylvania	330	4.1%
7	South Carolina	322	4.0%
8	Georgia	297	3.7%
9	Tennessee	266	3.3%
10	Virginia	232	2.9%
11	Mississippi	202	2.5%
12	Washington	188	2.4%
13	Indiana	177	2.2%
14	Arkansas	170	2.1%
15	California	156	2.0%
16	Oregon	153	1.9%
17	Oklahoma	147	1.8%
18	Ohio	146	1.8%
19	Missouri	139	1.7%
20	Alaska	137	1.7%
21	Wisconsin	133	1.7%
22	New York	131	1.6%
23	Louisiana	129	1.6%
24	Hawaii	114	1.4%
25	Alabama	113	1.4%
26	Maryland	102	1.3%
27	Nevada	93	1.2%
28	Delaware	91	1.1%
28	West Virginia	91	1.1%
30	South Dakota	78	1.0%
31	Utah	75	0.9%
32	Idaho	73	0.9%
32	New Mexico	73	0.9%
34	Arizona	56	0.7%
35	Colorado	55	0.7%
36	Iowa	41	0.5%
37	Maine	36	0.5%
38	North Dakota	28	0.4%
39	Nebraska	26	0.3%
40	Connecticut	18	0.2%
41	Wyoming	8	0.1%
42	Rhode Island	1	0.0%
43	Massachusetts	0	0.0%
43	New Jersey	0	0.0%
NA	Illinois**	NA	NA
NA	Kansas**	NA	NA
NA	Kentucky**	NA	NA
NA	Montana**	NA	NA
NA	New Hampshire**	NA	NA
NA	Vermont**	NA	NA
	District of Columbia	0	0.0%

Source: Federal Bureau of Investigation
"Crime in the United States 1997" (Uniform Crime Reports, November 22, 1998)
*Estimated totals for rural areas, defined by the F.B.I. as other than Metropolitan Statistical Areas and other cities outside such areas. National total includes those states listed as not available. Forcible rape is the carnal knowledge of a female forcibly and against her will. Attempts are included. However, statutory rape without force and other sex offenses are excluded. **Not available.

Rural Rape Rate in 1997

National Rural Rate = 24.7 Rapes per 100,000 Population*

ALPHA ORDER

RANK	STATE	RATE
31	Alabama	14.3
3	Alaska	71.5
29	Arizona	15.9
22	Arkansas	20.9
15	California	24.6
27	Colorado	16.7
38	Connecticut	9.7
1	Delaware	96.9
5	Florida	43.6
23	Georgia	20.2
9	Hawaii	37.2
25	Idaho	18.1
NA	Illinois**	NA
27	Indiana	16.7
41	Iowa	4.6
NA	Kansas**	NA
NA	Kentucky**	NA
24	Louisiana	18.9
37	Maine	10.2
8	Maryland	38.1
42	Massachusetts	0.0
2	Michigan	82.2
7	Minnesota	39.9
25	Mississippi	18.1
35	Missouri	11.4
NA	Montana**	NA
40	Nebraska	6.2
4	Nevada	47.7
NA	New Hampshire**	NA
42	New Jersey	0.0
15	New Mexico	24.6
30	New York	15.4
21	North Carolina	21.5
33	North Dakota	12.6
36	Ohio	11.0
18	Oklahoma	23.2
13	Oregon	29.4
12	Pennsylvania	31.3
42	Rhode Island	0.0
6	South Carolina	40.2
14	South Dakota	26.8
17	Tennessee	24.3
19	Texas	21.7
11	Utah	34.0
NA	Vermont**	NA
20	Virginia	21.6
10	Washington	36.6
34	West Virginia	11.7
32	Wisconsin	13.5
39	Wyoming	6.4

RANK ORDER

RANK	STATE	RATE
1	Delaware	96.9
2	Michigan	82.2
3	Alaska	71.5
4	Nevada	47.7
5	Florida	43.6
6	South Carolina	40.2
7	Minnesota	39.9
8	Maryland	38.1
9	Hawaii	37.2
10	Washington	36.6
11	Utah	34.0
12	Pennsylvania	31.3
13	Oregon	29.4
14	South Dakota	26.8
15	California	24.6
15	New Mexico	24.6
17	Tennessee	24.3
18	Oklahoma	23.2
19	Texas	21.7
20	Virginia	21.6
21	North Carolina	21.5
22	Arkansas	20.9
23	Georgia	20.2
24	Louisiana	18.9
25	Idaho	18.1
25	Mississippi	18.1
27	Colorado	16.7
27	Indiana	16.7
29	Arizona	15.9
30	New York	15.4
31	Alabama	14.3
32	Wisconsin	13.5
33	North Dakota	12.6
34	West Virginia	11.7
35	Missouri	11.4
36	Ohio	11.0
37	Maine	10.2
38	Connecticut	9.7
39	Wyoming	6.4
40	Nebraska	6.2
41	Iowa	4.6
42	Massachusetts	0.0
42	New Jersey	0.0
42	Rhode Island	0.0
NA	Illinois**	NA
NA	Kansas**	NA
NA	Kentucky**	NA
NA	Montana**	NA
NA	New Hampshire**	NA
NA	Vermont**	NA
	District of Columbia	0.0

Source: Morgan Quitno Press using data from Federal Bureau of Investigation
   "Crime in the United States 1997" (Uniform Crime Reports, November 22, 1998)
*Estimated rates for rural areas, defined by the F.B.I. as other than Metropolitan Statistical Areas and other cities outside such areas. National rate includes those states listed as not available. Forcible rape is the carnal knowledge of a female forcibly and against her will. Attempts are included. However, statutory rape without force and other sex offenses are excluded. **Not available.

Percent of Rapes Occurring in Rural Areas in 1997

National Percent = 8.3% of Rapes*

ALPHA ORDER				RANK ORDER		
RANK	STATE	PERCENT		RANK	STATE	PERCENT
26	Alabama	8.1		1	Alaska	34.0
1	Alaska	34.0		2	Hawaii	30.7
36	Arizona	3.8		3	West Virginia	25.6
12	Arkansas	15.5		4	South Dakota	21.8
41	California	1.5		5	Idaho	20.9
37	Colorado	3.3		6	Delaware	19.1
40	Connecticut	2.4		7	Mississippi	19.0
6	Delaware	19.1		8	North Dakota	17.6
34	Florida	4.6		9	South Carolina	17.5
15	Georgia	12.8		10	Michigan	17.4
2	Hawaii	30.7		11	North Carolina	15.7
5	Idaho	20.9		12	Arkansas	15.5
NA	Illinois**	NA		13	Minnesota	14.3
22	Indiana	9.2		14	Maine	14.2
29	Iowa	7.1		15	Georgia	12.8
NA	Kansas**	NA		15	Virginia	12.8
NA	Kentucky**	NA		17	Wisconsin	12.7
28	Louisiana	7.2		18	Oregon	11.7
14	Maine	14.2		19	Pennsylvania	10.0
33	Maryland	5.6		20	Oklahoma	9.7
43	Massachusetts	0.0		21	Nevada	9.3
10	Michigan	17.4		22	Indiana	9.2
13	Minnesota	14.3		23	Missouri	9.1
7	Mississippi	19.0		24	Tennessee	8.7
23	Missouri	9.1		25	New Mexico	8.4
NA	Montana**	NA		26	Alabama	8.1
31	Nebraska	6.4		27	Utah	7.7
21	Nevada	9.3		28	Louisiana	7.2
NA	New Hampshire**	NA		29	Iowa	7.1
43	New Jersey	0.0		30	Washington	6.5
25	New Mexico	8.4		31	Nebraska	6.4
38	New York	3.2		32	Wyoming	5.8
11	North Carolina	15.7		33	Maryland	5.6
8	North Dakota	17.6		34	Florida	4.6
38	Ohio	3.2		35	Texas	4.5
20	Oklahoma	9.7		36	Arizona	3.8
18	Oregon	11.7		37	Colorado	3.3
19	Pennsylvania	10.0		38	New York	3.2
42	Rhode Island	0.3		38	Ohio	3.2
9	South Carolina	17.5		40	Connecticut	2.4
4	South Dakota	21.8		41	California	1.5
24	Tennessee	8.7		42	Rhode Island	0.3
35	Texas	4.5		43	Massachusetts	0.0
27	Utah	7.7		43	New Jersey	0.0
NA	Vermont**	NA		NA	Illinois**	NA
15	Virginia	12.8		NA	Kansas**	NA
30	Washington	6.5		NA	Kentucky**	NA
3	West Virginia	25.6		NA	Montana**	NA
17	Wisconsin	12.7		NA	New Hampshire**	NA
32	Wyoming	5.8		NA	Vermont**	NA
					District of Columbia	0.0

Source: Morgan Quitno Press using data from Federal Bureau of Investigation
  "Crime in the United States 1997" (Uniform Crime Reports, November 22, 1998)
*Estimated percentages for rural areas, defined by the F.B.I. as other than Metropolitan Statistical Areas and other cities outside such areas. National percent includes those states listed as not available. Forcible rape is the carnal knowledge of a female forcibly and against her will. Attempts are included. However, statutory rape without force and other sex offenses are excluded. **Not available.

Robberies in Urban Areas in 1997

National Urban Total = 492,118 Robberies*

ALPHA ORDER					RANK ORDER			

RANK	STATE	ROBBERIES	% of USA		RANK	STATE	ROBBERIES	% of USA
18	Alabama	6,776	1.4%		1	California	81,308	16.5%
39	Alaska	623	0.1%		2	New York	55,993	11.4%
17	Arizona	7,505	1.5%		3	Florida	40,020	8.1%
31	Arkansas	2,704	0.5%		4	Texas	30,317	6.2%
1	California	81,308	16.5%		5	Pennsylvania	18,660	3.8%
29	Colorado	3,228	0.7%		6	Ohio	17,602	3.6%
25	Connecticut	4,962	1.0%		7	Maryland	17,043	3.5%
34	Delaware	1,223	0.2%		8	New Jersey	16,957	3.4%
3	Florida	40,020	8.1%		9	Georgia	15,044	3.1%
9	Georgia	15,044	3.1%		10	Michigan	14,844	3.0%
35	Hawaii	1,214	0.2%		11	North Carolina	12,196	2.5%
41	Idaho	219	0.0%		12	Tennessee	11,303	2.3%
NA	Illinois**	NA	NA		13	Louisiana	10,204	2.1%
16	Indiana	7,615	1.5%		14	Missouri	8,328	1.7%
32	Iowa	1,572	0.3%		15	Virginia	8,185	1.7%
NA	Kansas**	NA	NA		16	Indiana	7,615	1.5%
NA	Kentucky**	NA	NA		17	Arizona	7,505	1.5%
13	Louisiana	10,204	2.1%		18	Alabama	6,776	1.4%
40	Maine	253	0.1%		19	Massachusetts	6,676	1.4%
7	Maryland	17,043	3.5%		20	Washington	6,655	1.4%
19	Massachusetts	6,676	1.4%		21	South Carolina	5,841	1.2%
10	Michigan	14,844	3.0%		22	Minnesota	5,324	1.1%
22	Minnesota	5,324	1.1%		23	Wisconsin	5,177	1.1%
27	Mississippi	3,407	0.7%		24	Nevada	5,021	1.0%
14	Missouri	8,328	1.7%		25	Connecticut	4,962	1.0%
NA	Montana**	NA	NA		26	Oregon	3,725	0.8%
36	Nebraska	1,080	0.2%		27	Mississippi	3,407	0.7%
24	Nevada	5,021	1.0%		28	Oklahoma	3,388	0.7%
NA	New Hampshire**	NA	NA		29	Colorado	3,228	0.7%
8	New Jersey	16,957	3.4%		30	New Mexico	2,938	0.6%
30	New Mexico	2,938	0.6%		31	Arkansas	2,704	0.5%
2	New York	55,993	11.4%		32	Iowa	1,572	0.3%
11	North Carolina	12,196	2.5%		33	Utah	1,383	0.3%
44	North Dakota	38	0.0%		34	Delaware	1,223	0.2%
6	Ohio	17,602	3.6%		35	Hawaii	1,214	0.2%
28	Oklahoma	3,388	0.7%		36	Nebraska	1,080	0.2%
26	Oregon	3,725	0.8%		37	West Virginia	718	0.1%
5	Pennsylvania	18,660	3.8%		38	Rhode Island	706	0.1%
38	Rhode Island	706	0.1%		39	Alaska	623	0.1%
21	South Carolina	5,841	1.2%		40	Maine	253	0.1%
42	South Dakota	169	0.0%		41	Idaho	219	0.0%
12	Tennessee	11,303	2.3%		42	South Dakota	169	0.0%
4	Texas	30,317	6.2%		43	Wyoming	79	0.0%
33	Utah	1,383	0.3%		44	North Dakota	38	0.0%
NA	Vermont**	NA	NA		NA	Illinois**	NA	NA
15	Virginia	8,185	1.7%		NA	Kansas**	NA	NA
20	Washington	6,655	1.4%		NA	Kentucky**	NA	NA
37	West Virginia	718	0.1%		NA	Montana**	NA	NA
23	Wisconsin	5,177	1.1%		NA	New Hampshire**	NA	NA
43	Wyoming	79	0.0%		NA	Vermont**	NA	NA
						District of Columbia	4,501	0.9%

Source: Morgan Quitno Press using data from Federal Bureau of Investigation
    "Crime in the United States 1997" (Uniform Crime Reports, November 22, 1998)
Estimated totals for urban areas, defined by the F.B.I. as Metropolitan Statistical Areas and other cities outside such areas. National total includes those states listed as not available. Robbery is the taking or attempting to take anything of value by force or threat of force.
**Not available.*

Urban Robbery Rate in 1997

National Urban Rate = 209.0 Robberies per 100,000 Population*

ALPHA ORDER				RANK ORDER		
RANK	STATE	RATE		RANK	STATE	RATE
15	Alabama	192.2		1	Maryland	353.1
25	Alaska	149.3		2	Nevada	338.8
18	Arizona	178.5		3	New York	323.9
24	Arkansas	158.1		4	Florida	288.8
7	California	257.0		5	Louisiana	278.2
34	Colorado	90.6		6	Tennessee	264.4
22	Connecticut	160.8		7	California	257.0
16	Delaware	191.7		8	Georgia	250.2
4	Florida	288.8		9	North Carolina	213.6
8	Georgia	250.2		10	Mississippi	211.1
28	Hawaii	137.9		11	New Jersey	210.6
42	Idaho	27.1		12	New Mexico	205.0
NA	Illinois**	NA		13	Missouri	199.0
23	Indiana	158.5		14	South Carolina	197.4
36	Iowa	79.9		15	Alabama	192.2
NA	Kansas**	NA		16	Delaware	191.7
NA	Kentucky**	NA		17	Ohio	178.6
5	Louisiana	278.2		18	Arizona	178.5
41	Maine	28.4		19	Michigan	170.6
1	Maryland	353.1		20	Texas	170.4
33	Massachusetts	109.3		21	Pennsylvania	170.2
19	Michigan	170.6		22	Connecticut	160.8
27	Minnesota	139.9		23	Indiana	158.5
10	Mississippi	211.1		24	Arkansas	158.1
13	Missouri	199.0		25	Alaska	149.3
NA	Montana**	NA		26	Virginia	144.6
35	Nebraska	87.3		27	Minnesota	139.9
2	Nevada	338.8		28	Hawaii	137.9
NA	New Hampshire**	NA		29	Oregon	136.8
11	New Jersey	210.6		30	Washington	130.6
12	New Mexico	205.0		31	Oklahoma	126.2
3	New York	323.9		32	Wisconsin	123.7
9	North Carolina	213.6		33	Massachusetts	109.3
44	North Dakota	9.1		34	Colorado	90.6
17	Ohio	178.6		35	Nebraska	87.3
31	Oklahoma	126.2		36	Iowa	79.9
29	Oregon	136.8		37	Utah	75.2
21	Pennsylvania	170.2		38	Rhode Island	71.5
38	Rhode Island	71.5		39	West Virginia	69.2
14	South Carolina	197.4		40	South Dakota	37.8
40	South Dakota	37.8		41	Maine	28.4
6	Tennessee	264.4		42	Idaho	27.1
20	Texas	170.4		43	Wyoming	22.3
37	Utah	75.2		44	North Dakota	9.1
NA	Vermont**	NA		NA	Illinois**	NA
26	Virginia	144.6		NA	Kansas**	NA
30	Washington	130.6		NA	Kentucky**	NA
39	West Virginia	69.2		NA	Montana**	NA
32	Wisconsin	123.7		NA	New Hampshire**	NA
43	Wyoming	22.3		NA	Vermont**	NA
					District of Columbia	850.9

Source: Morgan Quitno Press using data from Federal Bureau of Investigation
  "Crime in the United States 1997" (Uniform Crime Reports, November 22, 1998)
*Estimated rates for urban areas, defined by the F.B.I. as Metropolitan Statistical Areas and other cities outside
such areas. National rate includes those states listed as not available. Robbery is the taking or attempting to take
anything of value by force or threat of force.
**Not available.

Percent of Robberies Occurring in Urban Areas in 1997

National Percent = 98.8% of Robberies*

ALPHA ORDER				RANK ORDER		
RANK	STATE	PERCENT		RANK	STATE	PERCENT
30	Alabama	97.8		1	Massachusetts	100.0
34	Alaska	96.1		1	New Jersey	100.0
7	Arizona	99.4		3	Rhode Island	99.9
34	Arkansas	96.1		4	California	99.8
4	California	99.8		4	New York	99.8
6	Colorado	99.6		6	Colorado	99.6
9	Connecticut	99.3		7	Arizona	99.4
37	Delaware	93.1		7	Michigan	99.4
18	Florida	98.9		9	Connecticut	99.3
33	Georgia	97.2		9	Maryland	99.3
44	Hawaii	86.5		9	Pennsylvania	99.3
40	Idaho	92.4		9	Texas	99.3
NA	Illinois**	NA		9	Wisconsin	99.3
28	Indiana	98.1		14	Minnesota	99.1
21	Iowa	98.7		14	New Mexico	99.1
NA	Kansas**	NA		14	Ohio	99.1
NA	Kentucky**	NA		17	Nevada	99.0
29	Louisiana	98.0		18	Florida	98.9
23	Maine	98.4		19	Missouri	98.8
9	Maryland	99.3		19	Washington	98.8
1	Massachusetts	100.0		21	Iowa	98.7
7	Michigan	99.4		22	Nebraska	98.5
14	Minnesota	99.1		23	Maine	98.4
42	Mississippi	91.1		23	Tennessee	98.4
19	Missouri	98.8		25	Oklahoma	98.3
NA	Montana**	NA		25	South Dakota	98.3
22	Nebraska	98.5		27	Utah	98.2
17	Nevada	99.0		28	Indiana	98.1
NA	New Hampshire**	NA		29	Louisiana	98.0
1	New Jersey	100.0		30	Alabama	97.8
14	New Mexico	99.1		31	Oregon	97.7
4	New York	99.8		32	Virginia	97.6
36	North Carolina	95.2		33	Georgia	97.2
39	North Dakota	92.7		34	Alaska	96.1
14	Ohio	99.1		34	Arkansas	96.1
25	Oklahoma	98.3		36	North Carolina	95.2
31	Oregon	97.7		37	Delaware	93.1
9	Pennsylvania	99.3		38	Wyoming	92.9
3	Rhode Island	99.9		39	North Dakota	92.7
43	South Carolina	88.2		40	Idaho	92.4
25	South Dakota	98.3		41	West Virginia	91.8
23	Tennessee	98.4		42	Mississippi	91.1
9	Texas	99.3		43	South Carolina	88.2
27	Utah	98.2		44	Hawaii	86.5
NA	Vermont**	NA		NA	Illinois**	NA
32	Virginia	97.6		NA	Kansas**	NA
19	Washington	98.8		NA	Kentucky**	NA
41	West Virginia	91.8		NA	Montana**	NA
9	Wisconsin	99.3		NA	New Hampshire**	NA
38	Wyoming	92.9		NA	Vermont**	NA
					District of Columbia	100.0

Source: Morgan Quitno Press using data from Federal Bureau of Investigation
   "Crime in the United States 1997" (Uniform Crime Reports, November 22, 1998)
*Estimated percentages for urban areas, defined by the F.B.I. as Metropolitan Statistical Areas and other cities outside such areas. National percent includes those states listed as not available. Robbery is the taking or attempting to take anything of value by force or threat of force.
**Not available.

Robberies in Rural Areas in 1997

National Rural Total = 5,832 Robberies*

ALPHA ORDER

RANK	STATE	ROBBERIES	% of USA
12	Alabama	155	2.7%
32	Alaska	25	0.4%
28	Arizona	42	0.7%
17	Arkansas	110	1.9%
11	California	160	2.7%
37	Colorado	14	0.2%
29	Connecticut	37	0.6%
20	Delaware	91	1.6%
3	Florida	439	7.5%
4	Georgia	429	7.4%
9	Hawaii	189	3.2%
35	Idaho	18	0.3%
NA	Illinois**	NA	NA
14	Indiana	148	2.5%
34	Iowa	21	0.4%
NA	Kansas**	NA	NA
NA	Kentucky**	NA	NA
7	Louisiana	203	3.5%
39	Maine	4	0.1%
16	Maryland	114	2.0%
43	Massachusetts	0	0.0%
21	Michigan	90	1.5%
27	Minnesota	49	0.8%
5	Mississippi	334	5.7%
18	Missouri	102	1.7%
NA	Montana**	NA	NA
36	Nebraska	17	0.3%
26	Nevada	50	0.9%
NA	New Hampshire**	NA	NA
43	New Jersey	0	0.0%
31	New Mexico	28	0.5%
19	New York	101	1.7%
2	North Carolina	621	10.6%
40	North Dakota	3	0.1%
13	Ohio	153	2.6%
25	Oklahoma	58	1.0%
22	Oregon	86	1.5%
15	Pennsylvania	128	2.2%
42	Rhode Island	1	0.0%
1	South Carolina	783	13.4%
40	South Dakota	3	0.1%
10	Tennessee	184	3.2%
6	Texas	205	3.5%
32	Utah	25	0.4%
NA	Vermont**	NA	NA
8	Virginia	199	3.4%
23	Washington	79	1.4%
24	West Virginia	64	1.1%
29	Wisconsin	37	0.6%
38	Wyoming	6	0.1%

RANK ORDER

RANK	STATE	ROBBERIES	% of USA
1	South Carolina	783	13.4%
2	North Carolina	621	10.6%
3	Florida	439	7.5%
4	Georgia	429	7.4%
5	Mississippi	334	5.7%
6	Texas	205	3.5%
7	Louisiana	203	3.5%
8	Virginia	199	3.4%
9	Hawaii	189	3.2%
10	Tennessee	184	3.2%
11	California	160	2.7%
12	Alabama	155	2.7%
13	Ohio	153	2.6%
14	Indiana	148	2.5%
15	Pennsylvania	128	2.2%
16	Maryland	114	2.0%
17	Arkansas	110	1.9%
18	Missouri	102	1.7%
19	New York	101	1.7%
20	Delaware	91	1.6%
21	Michigan	90	1.5%
22	Oregon	86	1.5%
23	Washington	79	1.4%
24	West Virginia	64	1.1%
25	Oklahoma	58	1.0%
26	Nevada	50	0.9%
27	Minnesota	49	0.8%
28	Arizona	42	0.7%
29	Connecticut	37	0.6%
29	Wisconsin	37	0.6%
31	New Mexico	28	0.5%
32	Alaska	25	0.4%
32	Utah	25	0.4%
34	Iowa	21	0.4%
35	Idaho	18	0.3%
36	Nebraska	17	0.3%
37	Colorado	14	0.2%
38	Wyoming	6	0.1%
39	Maine	4	0.1%
40	North Dakota	3	0.1%
40	South Dakota	3	0.1%
42	Rhode Island	1	0.0%
43	Massachusetts	0	0.0%
43	New Jersey	0	0.0%
NA	Illinois**	NA	NA
NA	Kansas**	NA	NA
NA	Kentucky**	NA	NA
NA	Montana**	NA	NA
NA	New Hampshire**	NA	NA
NA	Vermont**	NA	NA
	District of Columbia	0	0.0%

Source: Federal Bureau of Investigation
   "Crime in the United States 1997" (Uniform Crime Reports, November 22, 1998)
*Estimated totals for rural areas, defined by the F.B.I. as other than Metropolitan Statistical Areas and other cities outside such areas. National total includes those states listed as not available. Robbery is the taking or attempting to take anything of value by force or threat of force.
**Not available.

Rural Robbery Rate in 1997

National Rural Rate = 18.1 Robberies per 100,000 Population*

ALPHA ORDER				RANK ORDER		
RANK	STATE	RATE		RANK	STATE	RATE
13	Alabama	19.5		1	South Carolina	97.7
20	Alaska	13.0		2	Delaware	96.9
23	Arizona	11.9		3	Hawaii	61.6
19	Arkansas	13.5		4	Florida	55.1
11	California	25.2		5	Maryland	42.5
35	Colorado	4.3		6	North Carolina	36.2
12	Connecticut	20.0		7	Mississippi	29.9
2	Delaware	96.9		8	Louisiana	29.7
4	Florida	55.1		9	Georgia	29.1
9	Georgia	29.1		10	Nevada	25.6
3	Hawaii	61.6		11	California	25.2
34	Idaho	4.5		12	Connecticut	20.0
NA	Illinois**	NA		13	Alabama	19.5
18	Indiana	14.0		14	Virginia	18.5
38	Iowa	2.4		15	Tennessee	16.8
NA	Kansas**	NA		16	Oregon	16.5
NA	Kentucky**	NA		17	Washington	15.4
8	Louisiana	29.7		18	Indiana	14.0
40	Maine	1.1		19	Arkansas	13.5
5	Maryland	42.5		20	Alaska	13.0
42	Massachusetts	0.0		21	Texas	12.4
29	Michigan	8.4		22	Pennsylvania	12.2
32	Minnesota	5.6		23	Arizona	11.9
7	Mississippi	29.9		23	New York	11.9
29	Missouri	8.4		25	Ohio	11.5
NA	Montana**	NA		26	Utah	11.3
36	Nebraska	4.0		27	New Mexico	9.4
10	Nevada	25.6		28	Oklahoma	9.2
NA	New Hampshire**	NA		29	Michigan	8.4
42	New Jersey	0.0		29	Missouri	8.4
27	New Mexico	9.4		31	West Virginia	8.2
23	New York	11.9		32	Minnesota	5.6
6	North Carolina	36.2		33	Wyoming	4.8
39	North Dakota	1.4		34	Idaho	4.5
25	Ohio	11.5		35	Colorado	4.3
28	Oklahoma	9.2		36	Nebraska	4.0
16	Oregon	16.5		37	Wisconsin	3.8
22	Pennsylvania	12.2		38	Iowa	2.4
42	Rhode Island	0.0		39	North Dakota	1.4
1	South Carolina	97.7		40	Maine	1.1
41	South Dakota	1.0		41	South Dakota	1.0
15	Tennessee	16.8		42	Massachusetts	0.0
21	Texas	12.4		42	New Jersey	0.0
26	Utah	11.3		42	Rhode Island	0.0
NA	Vermont**	NA		NA	Illinois**	NA
14	Virginia	18.5		NA	Kansas**	NA
17	Washington	15.4		NA	Kentucky**	NA
31	West Virginia	8.2		NA	Montana**	NA
37	Wisconsin	3.8		NA	New Hampshire**	NA
33	Wyoming	4.8		NA	Vermont**	NA
					District of Columbia	0.0

Source: Morgan Quitno Press using data from Federal Bureau of Investigation
"Crime in the United States 1997" (Uniform Crime Reports, November 22, 1998)
*Estimated rates for rural areas, defined by the F.B.I. as other than Metropolitan Statistical Areas and other cities outside such areas. National rate includes those states listed as not available. Robbery is the taking or attempting to take anything of value by force or threat of force.
**Not available.

Percent of Robberies Occurring in Rural Areas in 1997

National Percent = 1.2% of Robberies*

ALPHA ORDER				RANK ORDER		
RANK	STATE	PERCENT		RANK	STATE	PERCENT
15	Alabama	2.2		1	Hawaii	13.5
10	Alaska	3.9		2	South Carolina	11.8
37	Arizona	0.6		3	Mississippi	8.9
10	Arkansas	3.9		4	West Virginia	8.2
40	California	0.2		5	Idaho	7.6
39	Colorado	0.4		6	North Dakota	7.3
32	Connecticut	0.7		7	Wyoming	7.1
8	Delaware	6.9		8	Delaware	6.9
27	Florida	1.1		9	North Carolina	4.8
12	Georgia	2.8		10	Alaska	3.9
1	Hawaii	13.5		10	Arkansas	3.9
5	Idaho	7.6		12	Georgia	2.8
NA	Illinois**	NA		13	Virginia	2.4
17	Indiana	1.9		14	Oregon	2.3
24	Iowa	1.3		15	Alabama	2.2
NA	Kansas**	NA		16	Louisiana	2.0
NA	Kentucky**	NA		17	Indiana	1.9
16	Louisiana	2.0		18	Utah	1.8
21	Maine	1.6		19	Oklahoma	1.7
32	Maryland	0.7		19	South Dakota	1.7
43	Massachusetts	0.0		21	Maine	1.6
37	Michigan	0.6		21	Tennessee	1.6
29	Minnesota	0.9		23	Nebraska	1.5
3	Mississippi	8.9		24	Iowa	1.3
25	Missouri	1.2		25	Missouri	1.2
NA	Montana**	NA		25	Washington	1.2
23	Nebraska	1.5		27	Florida	1.1
28	Nevada	1.0		28	Nevada	1.0
NA	New Hampshire**	NA		29	Minnesota	0.9
43	New Jersey	0.0		29	New Mexico	0.9
29	New Mexico	0.9		29	Ohio	0.9
40	New York	0.2		32	Connecticut	0.7
9	North Carolina	4.8		32	Maryland	0.7
6	North Dakota	7.3		32	Pennsylvania	0.7
29	Ohio	0.9		32	Texas	0.7
19	Oklahoma	1.7		32	Wisconsin	0.7
14	Oregon	2.3		37	Arizona	0.6
32	Pennsylvania	0.7		37	Michigan	0.6
42	Rhode Island	0.1		39	Colorado	0.4
2	South Carolina	11.8		40	California	0.2
19	South Dakota	1.7		40	New York	0.2
21	Tennessee	1.6		42	Rhode Island	0.1
32	Texas	0.7		43	Massachusetts	0.0
18	Utah	1.8		43	New Jersey	0.0
NA	Vermont**	NA		NA	Illinois**	NA
13	Virginia	2.4		NA	Kansas**	NA
25	Washington	1.2		NA	Kentucky**	NA
4	West Virginia	8.2		NA	Montana**	NA
32	Wisconsin	0.7		NA	New Hampshire**	NA
7	Wyoming	7.1		NA	Vermont**	NA
					District of Columbia	0.0

Source: Morgan Quitno Press using data from Federal Bureau of Investigation
"Crime in the United States 1997" (Uniform Crime Reports, November 22, 1998)
*Estimated percentages for rural areas, defined by the F.B.I. as other than Metropolitan Statistical Areas and other cities outside such areas. National percent includes those states listed as not available. Robbery is the taking or attempting to take anything of value by force or threat of force.
**Not available.

Aggravated Assaults in Urban Areas in 1997

National Urban Total = 963,480 Aggravated Assaults*

RANK	STATE	ASSAULTS	% of USA
19	Alabama	14,443	1.5%
35	Alaska	2,539	0.3%
17	Arizona	18,030	1.9%
26	Arkansas	8,039	0.8%
1	California	160,702	16.7%
24	Colorado	8,672	0.9%
30	Connecticut	6,543	0.7%
36	Delaware	2,538	0.3%
2	Florida	96,848	10.1%
11	Georgia	23,298	2.4%
40	Hawaii	1,131	0.1%
39	Idaho	1,887	0.2%
NA	Illinois**	NA	NA
18	Indiana	17,994	1.9%
31	Iowa	6,148	0.6%
NA	Kansas**	NA	NA
NA	Kentucky**	NA	NA
14	Louisiana	21,429	2.2%
41	Maine	832	0.1%
12	Maryland	22,944	2.4%
6	Massachusetts	30,956	3.2%
5	Michigan	35,380	3.7%
27	Minnesota	7,294	0.8%
33	Mississippi	4,773	0.5%
16	Missouri	18,579	1.9%
NA	Montana**	NA	NA
32	Nebraska	5,488	0.6%
29	Nevada	6,554	0.7%
NA	New Hampshire**	NA	NA
15	New Jersey	20,650	2.1%
23	New Mexico	9,924	1.0%
4	New York	61,710	6.4%
8	North Carolina	25,748	2.7%
44	North Dakota	307	0.0%
9	Ohio	25,115	2.6%
21	Oklahoma	12,172	1.3%
25	Oregon	8,669	0.9%
7	Pennsylvania	29,128	3.0%
37	Rhode Island	2,191	0.2%
13	South Carolina	22,930	2.4%
43	South Dakota	758	0.1%
10	Tennessee	24,539	2.5%
3	Texas	73,962	7.7%
34	Utah	4,206	0.4%
NA	Vermont**	NA	NA
22	Virginia	11,215	1.2%
20	Washington	14,147	1.5%
38	West Virginia	1,981	0.2%
28	Wisconsin	6,900	0.7%
42	Wyoming	770	0.1%

RANK	STATE	ASSAULTS	% of USA
1	California	160,702	16.7%
2	Florida	96,848	10.1%
3	Texas	73,962	7.7%
4	New York	61,710	6.4%
5	Michigan	35,380	3.7%
6	Massachusetts	30,956	3.2%
7	Pennsylvania	29,128	3.0%
8	North Carolina	25,748	2.7%
9	Ohio	25,115	2.6%
10	Tennessee	24,539	2.5%
11	Georgia	23,298	2.4%
12	Maryland	22,944	2.4%
13	South Carolina	22,930	2.4%
14	Louisiana	21,429	2.2%
15	New Jersey	20,650	2.1%
16	Missouri	18,579	1.9%
17	Arizona	18,030	1.9%
18	Indiana	17,994	1.9%
19	Alabama	14,443	1.5%
20	Washington	14,147	1.5%
21	Oklahoma	12,172	1.3%
22	Virginia	11,215	1.2%
23	New Mexico	9,924	1.0%
24	Colorado	8,672	0.9%
25	Oregon	8,669	0.9%
26	Arkansas	8,039	0.8%
27	Minnesota	7,294	0.8%
28	Wisconsin	6,900	0.7%
29	Nevada	6,554	0.7%
30	Connecticut	6,543	0.7%
31	Iowa	6,148	0.6%
32	Nebraska	5,488	0.6%
33	Mississippi	4,773	0.5%
34	Utah	4,206	0.4%
35	Alaska	2,539	0.3%
36	Delaware	2,538	0.3%
37	Rhode Island	2,191	0.2%
38	West Virginia	1,981	0.2%
39	Idaho	1,887	0.2%
40	Hawaii	1,131	0.1%
41	Maine	832	0.1%
42	Wyoming	770	0.1%
43	South Dakota	758	0.1%
44	North Dakota	307	0.0%
NA	Illinois**	NA	NA
NA	Kansas**	NA	NA
NA	Kentucky**	NA	NA
NA	Montana**	NA	NA
NA	New Hampshire**	NA	NA
NA	Vermont**	NA	NA
	District of Columbia	5,688	0.6%

Source: Morgan Quitno Press using data from Federal Bureau of Investigation
   "Crime in the United States 1997" (Uniform Crime Reports, November 22, 1998)
*Estimated totals for urban areas, defined by the F.B.I. as Metropolitan Statistical Areas and other cities outside such areas. National total includes those states listed as not available. Aggravated assault is an attack for the purpose of inflicting severe bodily injury.
**Not available.

Urban Aggravated Assault Rate in 1997

National Urban Rate = 409.3 Aggravated Assaults per 100,000 Population*

RANK	STATE	RATE
18	Alabama	409.6
4	Alaska	608.5
16	Arizona	428.9
10	Arkansas	470.2
7	California	508.0
31	Colorado	243.3
36	Connecticut	212.1
20	Delaware	397.8
2	Florida	698.9
21	Georgia	387.5
42	Hawaii	128.5
32	Idaho	233.8
NA	Illinois**	NA
22	Indiana	374.5
25	Iowa	312.7
NA	Kansas**	NA
NA	Kentucky**	NA
5	Louisiana	584.2
43	Maine	93.5
9	Maryland	475.4
8	Massachusetts	506.8
19	Michigan	406.7
38	Minnesota	191.7
26	Mississippi	295.7
13	Missouri	444.0
NA	Montana**	NA
14	Nebraska	443.9
15	Nevada	442.3
NA	New Hampshire**	NA
29	New Jersey	256.4
3	New Mexico	692.3
23	New York	357.0
12	North Carolina	450.9
44	North Dakota	73.3
30	Ohio	254.8
11	Oklahoma	453.4
24	Oregon	318.5
28	Pennsylvania	265.6
34	Rhode Island	222.0
1	South Carolina	775.1
40	South Dakota	169.4
6	Tennessee	574.0
17	Texas	415.8
33	Utah	228.7
NA	Vermont**	NA
37	Virginia	198.2
27	Washington	277.6
39	West Virginia	191.0
41	Wisconsin	164.8
35	Wyoming	217.0

RANK	STATE	RATE
1	South Carolina	775.1
2	Florida	698.9
3	New Mexico	692.3
4	Alaska	608.5
5	Louisiana	584.2
6	Tennessee	574.0
7	California	508.0
8	Massachusetts	506.8
9	Maryland	475.4
10	Arkansas	470.2
11	Oklahoma	453.4
12	North Carolina	450.9
13	Missouri	444.0
14	Nebraska	443.9
15	Nevada	442.3
16	Arizona	428.9
17	Texas	415.8
18	Alabama	409.6
19	Michigan	406.7
20	Delaware	397.8
21	Georgia	387.5
22	Indiana	374.5
23	New York	357.0
24	Oregon	318.5
25	Iowa	312.7
26	Mississippi	295.7
27	Washington	277.6
28	Pennsylvania	265.6
29	New Jersey	256.4
30	Ohio	254.8
31	Colorado	243.3
32	Idaho	233.8
33	Utah	228.7
34	Rhode Island	222.0
35	Wyoming	217.0
36	Connecticut	212.1
37	Virginia	198.2
38	Minnesota	191.7
39	West Virginia	191.0
40	South Dakota	169.4
41	Wisconsin	164.8
42	Hawaii	128.5
43	Maine	93.5
44	North Dakota	73.3
NA	Illinois**	NA
NA	Kansas**	NA
NA	Kentucky**	NA
NA	Montana**	NA
NA	New Hampshire**	NA
NA	Vermont**	NA
	District of Columbia	1,075.2

Source: Morgan Quitno Press using data from Federal Bureau of Investigation
"Crime in the United States 1997" (Uniform Crime Reports, November 22, 1998)
*Estimated rates for urban areas, defined by the F.B.I. as Metropolitan Statistical Areas and other cities outside such areas. National rate includes those states listed as not available. Aggravated assault is an attack for the purpose of inflicting severe bodily injury.
**Not available.

Percent of Aggravated Assaults Occurring in Urban Areas in 1997

National Percent = 94.2% of Aggravated Assaults*

RANK	STATE	PERCENT		RANK	STATE	PERCENT
21	Alabama	92.4		1	Massachusetts	100.0
39	Alaska	80.2		1	New Jersey	100.0
15	Arizona	94.9		3	Rhode Island	99.7
30	Arkansas	88.0		4	California	98.4
4	California	98.4		5	Ohio	97.1
12	Colorado	95.7		6	Maryland	97.0
17	Connecticut	94.6		6	New York	97.0
38	Delaware	80.5		8	Nebraska	96.1
9	Florida	96.0		9	Florida	96.0
35	Georgia	86.1		10	Michigan	95.9
41	Hawaii	76.5		10	Pennsylvania	95.9
42	Idaho	76.1		12	Colorado	95.7
NA	Illinois**	NA		12	Texas	95.7
27	Indiana	89.7		14	Washington	95.2
19	Iowa	92.9		15	Arizona	94.9
NA	Kansas**	NA		16	Utah	94.7
NA	Kentucky**	NA		17	Connecticut	94.6
30	Louisiana	88.0		18	Oregon	94.2
34	Maine	86.3		19	Iowa	92.9
6	Maryland	97.0		20	Minnesota	92.6
1	Massachusetts	100.0		21	Alabama	92.4
10	Michigan	95.9		22	New Mexico	92.0
20	Minnesota	92.6		23	Nevada	91.9
44	Mississippi	62.4		24	Wisconsin	91.7
28	Missouri	89.3		25	Oklahoma	91.1
NA	Montana**	NA		26	Tennessee	89.8
8	Nebraska	96.1		27	Indiana	89.7
23	Nevada	91.9		28	Missouri	89.3
NA	New Hampshire**	NA		28	Virginia	89.3
1	New Jersey	100.0		30	Arkansas	88.0
22	New Mexico	92.0		30	Louisiana	88.0
6	New York	97.0		32	North Carolina	87.9
32	North Carolina	87.9		33	North Dakota	87.0
33	North Dakota	87.0		34	Maine	86.3
5	Ohio	97.1		35	Georgia	86.1
25	Oklahoma	91.1		36	South Dakota	82.6
18	Oregon	94.2		37	South Carolina	80.6
10	Pennsylvania	95.9		38	Delaware	80.5
3	Rhode Island	99.7		39	Alaska	80.2
37	South Carolina	80.6		40	Wyoming	78.1
36	South Dakota	82.6		41	Hawaii	76.5
26	Tennessee	89.8		42	Idaho	76.1
12	Texas	95.7		43	West Virginia	71.8
16	Utah	94.7		44	Mississippi	62.4
NA	Vermont**	NA		NA	Illinois**	NA
28	Virginia	89.3		NA	Kansas**	NA
14	Washington	95.2		NA	Kentucky**	NA
43	West Virginia	71.8		NA	Montana**	NA
24	Wisconsin	91.7		NA	New Hampshire**	NA
40	Wyoming	78.1		NA	Vermont**	NA

ALPHA ORDER / RANK ORDER

District of Columbia 100.0

Source: Morgan Quitno Press using data from Federal Bureau of Investigation "Crime in the United States 1997" (Uniform Crime Reports, November 22, 1998)
Estimated percentages for urban areas, defined by the F.B.I. as Metropolitan Statistical Areas and other cities outside such areas. National percent includes those states listed as not available. Aggravated assault is an attack for the purpose of inflicting severe bodily injury.
**Not available.*

432

Aggravated Assaults in Rural Areas in 1997

National Rural Total = 59,012 Aggravated Assaults*

ALPHA ORDER

RANK	STATE	ASSAULTS	% of USA
17	Alabama	1,183	2.0%
25	Alaska	626	1.1%
19	Arizona	967	1.6%
18	Arkansas	1,092	1.9%
9	California	2,644	4.5%
33	Colorado	391	0.7%
34	Connecticut	375	0.6%
27	Delaware	616	1.0%
2	Florida	4,078	6.9%
3	Georgia	3,746	6.3%
35	Hawaii	347	0.6%
28	Idaho	594	1.0%
NA	Illinois**	NA	NA
11	Indiana	2,064	3.5%
32	Iowa	469	0.8%
NA	Kansas**	NA	NA
NA	Kentucky**	NA	NA
6	Louisiana	2,931	5.0%
40	Maine	132	0.2%
24	Maryland	710	1.2%
42	Massachusetts	13	0.0%
13	Michigan	1,520	2.6%
29	Minnesota	585	1.0%
7	Mississippi	2,871	4.9%
10	Missouri	2,232	3.8%
NA	Montana**	NA	NA
37	Nebraska	224	0.4%
30	Nevada	578	1.0%
NA	New Hampshire**	NA	NA
44	New Jersey	0	0.0%
20	New Mexico	866	1.5%
12	New York	1,918	3.3%
4	North Carolina	3,544	6.0%
41	North Dakota	46	0.1%
22	Ohio	747	1.3%
16	Oklahoma	1,196	2.0%
31	Oregon	531	0.9%
15	Pennsylvania	1,230	2.1%
43	Rhode Island	6	0.0%
1	South Carolina	5,530	9.4%
39	South Dakota	160	0.3%
8	Tennessee	2,796	4.7%
5	Texas	3,304	5.6%
36	Utah	237	0.4%
NA	Vermont**	NA	NA
14	Virginia	1,343	2.3%
23	Washington	717	1.2%
21	West Virginia	778	1.3%
26	Wisconsin	621	1.1%
38	Wyoming	216	0.4%

RANK ORDER

RANK	STATE	ASSAULTS	% of USA
1	South Carolina	5,530	9.4%
2	Florida	4,078	6.9%
3	Georgia	3,746	6.3%
4	North Carolina	3,544	6.0%
5	Texas	3,304	5.6%
6	Louisiana	2,931	5.0%
7	Mississippi	2,871	4.9%
8	Tennessee	2,796	4.7%
9	California	2,644	4.5%
10	Missouri	2,232	3.8%
11	Indiana	2,064	3.5%
12	New York	1,918	3.3%
13	Michigan	1,520	2.6%
14	Virginia	1,343	2.3%
15	Pennsylvania	1,230	2.1%
16	Oklahoma	1,196	2.0%
17	Alabama	1,183	2.0%
18	Arkansas	1,092	1.9%
19	Arizona	967	1.6%
20	New Mexico	866	1.5%
21	West Virginia	778	1.3%
22	Ohio	747	1.3%
23	Washington	717	1.2%
24	Maryland	710	1.2%
25	Alaska	626	1.1%
26	Wisconsin	621	1.1%
27	Delaware	616	1.0%
28	Idaho	594	1.0%
29	Minnesota	585	1.0%
30	Nevada	578	1.0%
31	Oregon	531	0.9%
32	Iowa	469	0.8%
33	Colorado	391	0.7%
34	Connecticut	375	0.6%
35	Hawaii	347	0.6%
36	Utah	237	0.4%
37	Nebraska	224	0.4%
38	Wyoming	216	0.4%
39	South Dakota	160	0.3%
40	Maine	132	0.2%
41	North Dakota	46	0.1%
42	Massachusetts	13	0.0%
43	Rhode Island	6	0.0%
44	New Jersey	0	0.0%
NA	Illinois**	NA	NA
NA	Kansas**	NA	NA
NA	Kentucky**	NA	NA
NA	Montana**	NA	NA
NA	New Hampshire**	NA	NA
NA	Vermont**	NA	NA
	District of Columbia	0	0.0%

Source: Federal Bureau of Investigation
   "Crime in the United States 1997" (Uniform Crime Reports, November 22, 1998)
*Estimated totals for rural areas, defined by the F.B.I. as other than Metropolitan Statistical Areas and other cities outside such areas. National total includes those states listed as not available. Aggravated assault is an attack for the purpose of inflicting severe bodily injury.
**Not available.

Rural Aggravated Assault Rate in 1997

National Rural Rate = 183.2 Aggravated Assaults per 100,000 Population*

ALPHA ORDER

RANK	STATE	RATE
22	Alabama	149.2
6	Alaska	326.5
9	Arizona	275.0
26	Arkansas	134.3
5	California	417.1
29	Colorado	118.9
16	Connecticut	203.1
2	Delaware	655.8
3	Florida	512.1
13	Georgia	254.2
31	Hawaii	113.1
23	Idaho	147.4
NA	Illinois**	NA
18	Indiana	194.8
40	Iowa	53.0
NA	Kansas**	NA
NA	Kentucky**	NA
4	Louisiana	428.4
41	Maine	37.5
10	Maryland	264.9
27	Massachusetts	131.9
24	Michigan	141.4
35	Minnesota	66.5
11	Mississippi	257.1
20	Missouri	183.4
NA	Montana**	NA
39	Nebraska	53.3
7	Nevada	296.2
NA	New Hampshire**	NA
43	New Jersey	0.0
8	New Mexico	292.1
14	New York	225.2
15	North Carolina	206.7
42	North Dakota	20.7
37	Ohio	56.1
19	Oklahoma	189.0
33	Oregon	102.0
30	Pennsylvania	116.8
43	Rhode Island	0.0
1	South Carolina	689.9
38	South Dakota	55.1
12	Tennessee	255.8
17	Texas	200.0
32	Utah	107.6
NA	Vermont**	NA
28	Virginia	125.0
25	Washington	139.5
34	West Virginia	99.9
36	Wisconsin	63.2
21	Wyoming	172.6

RANK ORDER

RANK	STATE	RATE
1	South Carolina	689.9
2	Delaware	655.8
3	Florida	512.1
4	Louisiana	428.4
5	California	417.1
6	Alaska	326.5
7	Nevada	296.2
8	New Mexico	292.1
9	Arizona	275.0
10	Maryland	264.9
11	Mississippi	257.1
12	Tennessee	255.8
13	Georgia	254.2
14	New York	225.2
15	North Carolina	206.7
16	Connecticut	203.1
17	Texas	200.0
18	Indiana	194.8
19	Oklahoma	189.0
20	Missouri	183.4
21	Wyoming	172.6
22	Alabama	149.2
23	Idaho	147.4
24	Michigan	141.4
25	Washington	139.5
26	Arkansas	134.3
27	Massachusetts	131.9
28	Virginia	125.0
29	Colorado	118.9
30	Pennsylvania	116.8
31	Hawaii	113.1
32	Utah	107.6
33	Oregon	102.0
34	West Virginia	99.9
35	Minnesota	66.5
36	Wisconsin	63.2
37	Ohio	56.1
38	South Dakota	55.1
39	Nebraska	53.3
40	Iowa	53.0
41	Maine	37.5
42	North Dakota	20.7
43	New Jersey	0.0
43	Rhode Island	0.0
NA	Illinois**	NA
NA	Kansas**	NA
NA	Kentucky**	NA
NA	Montana**	NA
NA	New Hampshire**	NA
NA	Vermont**	NA

District of Columbia 0.0

Source: Morgan Quitno Press using data from Federal Bureau of Investigation
  "Crime in the United States 1997" (Uniform Crime Reports, November 22, 1998)
*Estimated rates for rural areas, defined by the F.B.I. as other than Metropolitan Statistical Areas and other cities outside such areas. National rate includes those states listed as not available. Aggravated assault is an attack for the purpose of inflicting severe bodily injury.
**Not available.

Percent of Aggravated Assaults Occurring in Rural Areas in 1997

National Percent = 5.8% of Aggravated Assaults*

<table>
<tr><td colspan="3">ALPHA ORDER</td><td colspan="3">RANK ORDER</td></tr>
<tr><td>RANK</td><td>STATE</td><td>PERCENT</td><td>RANK</td><td>STATE</td><td>PERCENT</td></tr>
<tr><td>24</td><td>Alabama</td><td>7.6</td><td>1</td><td>Mississippi</td><td>37.6</td></tr>
<tr><td>6</td><td>Alaska</td><td>19.8</td><td>2</td><td>West Virginia</td><td>28.2</td></tr>
<tr><td>30</td><td>Arizona</td><td>5.1</td><td>3</td><td>Idaho</td><td>23.9</td></tr>
<tr><td>14</td><td>Arkansas</td><td>12.0</td><td>4</td><td>Hawaii</td><td>23.5</td></tr>
<tr><td>41</td><td>California</td><td>1.6</td><td>5</td><td>Wyoming</td><td>21.9</td></tr>
<tr><td>32</td><td>Colorado</td><td>4.3</td><td>6</td><td>Alaska</td><td>19.8</td></tr>
<tr><td>28</td><td>Connecticut</td><td>5.4</td><td>7</td><td>Delaware</td><td>19.5</td></tr>
<tr><td>7</td><td>Delaware</td><td>19.5</td><td>8</td><td>South Carolina</td><td>19.4</td></tr>
<tr><td>36</td><td>Florida</td><td>4.0</td><td>9</td><td>South Dakota</td><td>17.4</td></tr>
<tr><td>10</td><td>Georgia</td><td>13.9</td><td>10</td><td>Georgia</td><td>13.9</td></tr>
<tr><td>4</td><td>Hawaii</td><td>23.5</td><td>11</td><td>Maine</td><td>13.7</td></tr>
<tr><td>3</td><td>Idaho</td><td>23.9</td><td>12</td><td>North Dakota</td><td>13.0</td></tr>
<tr><td>NA</td><td>Illinois**</td><td>NA</td><td>13</td><td>North Carolina</td><td>12.1</td></tr>
<tr><td>18</td><td>Indiana</td><td>10.3</td><td>14</td><td>Arkansas</td><td>12.0</td></tr>
<tr><td>26</td><td>Iowa</td><td>7.1</td><td>14</td><td>Louisiana</td><td>12.0</td></tr>
<tr><td>NA</td><td>Kansas**</td><td>NA</td><td>16</td><td>Missouri</td><td>10.7</td></tr>
<tr><td>NA</td><td>Kentucky**</td><td>NA</td><td>16</td><td>Virginia</td><td>10.7</td></tr>
<tr><td>14</td><td>Louisiana</td><td>12.0</td><td>18</td><td>Indiana</td><td>10.3</td></tr>
<tr><td>11</td><td>Maine</td><td>13.7</td><td>19</td><td>Tennessee</td><td>10.2</td></tr>
<tr><td>38</td><td>Maryland</td><td>3.0</td><td>20</td><td>Oklahoma</td><td>8.9</td></tr>
<tr><td>43</td><td>Massachusetts</td><td>0.0</td><td>21</td><td>Wisconsin</td><td>8.3</td></tr>
<tr><td>34</td><td>Michigan</td><td>4.1</td><td>22</td><td>Nevada</td><td>8.1</td></tr>
<tr><td>25</td><td>Minnesota</td><td>7.4</td><td>23</td><td>New Mexico</td><td>8.0</td></tr>
<tr><td>1</td><td>Mississippi</td><td>37.6</td><td>24</td><td>Alabama</td><td>7.6</td></tr>
<tr><td>16</td><td>Missouri</td><td>10.7</td><td>25</td><td>Minnesota</td><td>7.4</td></tr>
<tr><td>NA</td><td>Montana**</td><td>NA</td><td>26</td><td>Iowa</td><td>7.1</td></tr>
<tr><td>37</td><td>Nebraska</td><td>3.9</td><td>27</td><td>Oregon</td><td>5.8</td></tr>
<tr><td>22</td><td>Nevada</td><td>8.1</td><td>28</td><td>Connecticut</td><td>5.4</td></tr>
<tr><td>NA</td><td>New Hampshire**</td><td>NA</td><td>29</td><td>Utah</td><td>5.3</td></tr>
<tr><td>43</td><td>New Jersey</td><td>0.0</td><td>30</td><td>Arizona</td><td>5.1</td></tr>
<tr><td>23</td><td>New Mexico</td><td>8.0</td><td>31</td><td>Washington</td><td>4.8</td></tr>
<tr><td>38</td><td>New York</td><td>3.0</td><td>32</td><td>Colorado</td><td>4.3</td></tr>
<tr><td>13</td><td>North Carolina</td><td>12.1</td><td>32</td><td>Texas</td><td>4.3</td></tr>
<tr><td>12</td><td>North Dakota</td><td>13.0</td><td>34</td><td>Michigan</td><td>4.1</td></tr>
<tr><td>40</td><td>Ohio</td><td>2.9</td><td>34</td><td>Pennsylvania</td><td>4.1</td></tr>
<tr><td>20</td><td>Oklahoma</td><td>8.9</td><td>36</td><td>Florida</td><td>4.0</td></tr>
<tr><td>27</td><td>Oregon</td><td>5.8</td><td>37</td><td>Nebraska</td><td>3.9</td></tr>
<tr><td>34</td><td>Pennsylvania</td><td>4.1</td><td>38</td><td>Maryland</td><td>3.0</td></tr>
<tr><td>42</td><td>Rhode Island</td><td>0.3</td><td>38</td><td>New York</td><td>3.0</td></tr>
<tr><td>8</td><td>South Carolina</td><td>19.4</td><td>40</td><td>Ohio</td><td>2.9</td></tr>
<tr><td>9</td><td>South Dakota</td><td>17.4</td><td>41</td><td>California</td><td>1.6</td></tr>
<tr><td>19</td><td>Tennessee</td><td>10.2</td><td>42</td><td>Rhode Island</td><td>0.3</td></tr>
<tr><td>32</td><td>Texas</td><td>4.3</td><td>43</td><td>Massachusetts</td><td>0.0</td></tr>
<tr><td>29</td><td>Utah</td><td>5.3</td><td>43</td><td>New Jersey</td><td>0.0</td></tr>
<tr><td>NA</td><td>Vermont**</td><td>NA</td><td>NA</td><td>Illinois**</td><td>NA</td></tr>
<tr><td>16</td><td>Virginia</td><td>10.7</td><td>NA</td><td>Kansas**</td><td>NA</td></tr>
<tr><td>31</td><td>Washington</td><td>4.8</td><td>NA</td><td>Kentucky**</td><td>NA</td></tr>
<tr><td>2</td><td>West Virginia</td><td>28.2</td><td>NA</td><td>Montana**</td><td>NA</td></tr>
<tr><td>21</td><td>Wisconsin</td><td>8.3</td><td>NA</td><td>New Hampshire**</td><td>NA</td></tr>
<tr><td>5</td><td>Wyoming</td><td>21.9</td><td>NA</td><td>Vermont**</td><td>NA</td></tr>
<tr><td></td><td></td><td></td><td></td><td>District of Columbia</td><td>0.0</td></tr>
</table>

Source: Morgan Quitno Press using data from Federal Bureau of Investigation
"Crime in the United States 1997" (Uniform Crime Reports, November 22, 1998)
*Estimated percentages for rural areas, defined by the F.B.I. as other than Metropolitan Statistical Areas and other cities outside such areas. National percent includes those states listed as not available. Aggravated assault is an attack for the purpose of inflicting severe bodily injury.
**Not available.

Property Crimes in Urban Areas in 1997

National Urban Total = 10,949,678 Property Crimes*

ALPHA ORDER					RANK ORDER			
RANK	STATE		CRIMES	% of USA	RANK	STATE	CRIMES	% of USA
20	Alabama		176,726	1.6%	1	California	1,295,864	11.8%
41	Alaska		23,587	0.2%	2	Texas	921,016	8.4%
10	Arizona		293,334	2.7%	3	Florida	887,674	8.1%
31	Arkansas		93,231	0.9%	4	New York	568,081	5.2%
1	California		1,295,864	11.8%	5	Ohio	436,313	4.0%
25	Colorado		160,845	1.5%	6	Michigan	398,990	3.6%
27	Connecticut		114,523	1.0%	7	Georgia	353,356	3.2%
40	Delaware		29,734	0.3%	8	Pennsylvania	343,206	3.1%
3	Florida		887,674	8.1%	9	North Carolina	320,277	2.9%
7	Georgia		353,356	3.2%	10	Arizona	293,334	2.7%
35	Hawaii		50,774	0.5%	11	Washington	292,247	2.7%
36	Idaho		37,111	0.3%	12	New Jersey	287,038	2.6%
NA	Illinois**		NA	NA	13	Maryland	238,503	2.2%
18	Indiana		215,563	2.0%	14	Tennessee	234,696	2.1%
32	Iowa		90,226	0.8%	15	Louisiana	230,252	2.1%
NA	Kansas**		NA	NA	16	Virginia	222,427	2.0%
NA	Kentucky**		NA	NA	17	Missouri	215,936	2.0%
15	Louisiana		230,252	2.1%	18	Indiana	215,563	2.0%
39	Maine		31,935	0.3%	19	Massachusetts	185,395	1.7%
13	Maryland		238,503	2.2%	20	Alabama	176,726	1.6%
19	Massachusetts		185,395	1.7%	21	Oregon	175,144	1.6%
6	Michigan		398,990	3.6%	22	Minnesota	174,209	1.6%
22	Minnesota		174,209	1.6%	23	South Carolina	164,430	1.5%
30	Mississippi		97,924	0.9%	24	Wisconsin	161,115	1.5%
17	Missouri		215,936	2.0%	25	Colorado	160,845	1.5%
NA	Montana**		NA	NA	26	Oklahoma	153,909	1.4%
34	Nebraska		58,163	0.5%	27	Connecticut	114,523	1.0%
33	Nevada		83,410	0.8%	28	Utah	110,956	1.0%
NA	New Hampshire**		NA	NA	29	New Mexico	99,935	0.9%
12	New Jersey		287,038	2.6%	30	Mississippi	97,924	0.9%
29	New Mexico		99,935	0.9%	31	Arkansas	93,231	0.9%
4	New York		568,081	5.2%	32	Iowa	90,226	0.8%
9	North Carolina		320,277	2.9%	33	Nevada	83,410	0.8%
44	North Dakota		14,726	0.1%	34	Nebraska	58,163	0.5%
5	Ohio		436,313	4.0%	35	Hawaii	50,774	0.5%
26	Oklahoma		153,909	1.4%	36	Idaho	37,111	0.3%
21	Oregon		175,144	1.6%	37	Rhode Island	32,758	0.3%
8	Pennsylvania		343,206	3.1%	38	West Virginia	32,118	0.3%
37	Rhode Island		32,758	0.3%	39	Maine	31,935	0.3%
23	South Carolina		164,430	1.5%	40	Delaware	29,734	0.3%
42	South Dakota		19,718	0.2%	41	Alaska	23,587	0.2%
14	Tennessee		234,696	2.1%	42	South Dakota	19,718	0.2%
2	Texas		921,016	8.4%	43	Wyoming	16,588	0.2%
28	Utah		110,956	1.0%	44	North Dakota	14,726	0.1%
NA	Vermont**		NA	NA	NA	Illinois**	NA	NA
16	Virginia		222,427	2.0%	NA	Kansas**	NA	NA
11	Washington		292,247	2.7%	NA	Kentucky**	NA	NA
38	West Virginia		32,118	0.3%	NA	Montana**	NA	NA
24	Wisconsin		161,115	1.5%	NA	New Hampshire**	NA	NA
43	Wyoming		16,588	0.2%	NA	Vermont**	NA	NA
						District of Columbia	41,341	0.4%

Source: Morgan Quitno Press using data from Federal Bureau of Investigation
   "Crime in the United States 1997" (Uniform Crime Reports, November 22, 1998)
Estimated totals for urban areas, defined by the F.B.I. as Metropolitan Statistical Areas and other cities outside such areas. National total includes those states listed as not available. Property crimes are offenses of burglary, larceny-theft and motor vehicle theft.
**Not available.*

Urban Property Crime Rate in 1997

National Urban Rate = 4,651.2 Property Crimes per 100,000 Population*

ALPHA ORDER

RANK	STATE	RATE
20	Alabama	5,012.0
12	Alaska	5,652.6
1	Arizona	6,978.5
17	Arkansas	5,452.7
33	California	4,096.4
29	Colorado	4,512.8
36	Connecticut	3,711.8
24	Delaware	4,660.0
4	Florida	6,405.7
8	Georgia	5,877.1
9	Hawaii	5,768.0
25	Idaho	4,598.5
NA	Illinois**	NA
30	Indiana	4,486.6
26	Iowa	4,588.4
NA	Kansas**	NA
NA	Kentucky**	NA
5	Louisiana	6,277.6
37	Maine	3,589.8
21	Maryland	4,942.0
44	Massachusetts	3,035.2
27	Michigan	4,586.7
28	Minnesota	4,577.4
6	Mississippi	6,066.2
19	Missouri	5,160.0
NA	Montana**	NA
22	Nebraska	4,704.2
13	Nevada	5,628.6
NA	New Hampshire**	NA
38	New Jersey	3,564.4
2	New Mexico	6,971.4
41	New York	3,286.5
14	North Carolina	5,609.0
39	North Dakota	3,514.7
31	Ohio	4,427.4
11	Oklahoma	5,733.6
3	Oregon	6,433.8
42	Pennsylvania	3,129.6
40	Rhode Island	3,318.9
15	South Carolina	5,557.9
32	South Dakota	4,407.4
16	Tennessee	5,490.2
18	Texas	5,178.1
7	Utah	6,034.5
NA	Vermont**	NA
34	Virginia	3,930.2
10	Washington	5,734.6
43	West Virginia	3,096.7
35	Wisconsin	3,848.2
23	Wyoming	4,674.4

RANK ORDER

RANK	STATE	RATE
1	Arizona	6,978.5
2	New Mexico	6,971.4
3	Oregon	6,433.8
4	Florida	6,405.7
5	Louisiana	6,277.6
6	Mississippi	6,066.2
7	Utah	6,034.5
8	Georgia	5,877.1
9	Hawaii	5,768.0
10	Washington	5,734.6
11	Oklahoma	5,733.6
12	Alaska	5,652.6
13	Nevada	5,628.6
14	North Carolina	5,609.0
15	South Carolina	5,557.9
16	Tennessee	5,490.2
17	Arkansas	5,452.7
18	Texas	5,178.1
19	Missouri	5,160.0
20	Alabama	5,012.0
21	Maryland	4,942.0
22	Nebraska	4,704.2
23	Wyoming	4,674.4
24	Delaware	4,660.0
25	Idaho	4,598.5
26	Iowa	4,588.4
27	Michigan	4,586.7
28	Minnesota	4,577.4
29	Colorado	4,512.8
30	Indiana	4,486.6
31	Ohio	4,427.4
32	South Dakota	4,407.4
33	California	4,096.4
34	Virginia	3,930.2
35	Wisconsin	3,848.2
36	Connecticut	3,711.8
37	Maine	3,589.8
38	New Jersey	3,564.4
39	North Dakota	3,514.7
40	Rhode Island	3,318.9
41	New York	3,286.5
42	Pennsylvania	3,129.6
43	West Virginia	3,096.7
44	Massachusetts	3,035.2
NA	Illinois**	NA
NA	Kansas**	NA
NA	Kentucky**	NA
NA	Montana**	NA
NA	New Hampshire**	NA
NA	Vermont**	NA
	District of Columbia	7,814.9

Source: Morgan Quitno Press using data from Federal Bureau of Investigation
"Crime in the United States 1997" (Uniform Crime Reports, November 22, 1998)
*Estimated rates for urban areas, defined by the F.B.I. as Metropolitan Statistical Areas and other cities outside such areas. National rate includes those states listed as not available. Property crimes are offenses of burglary, larceny-theft and motor vehicle theft.
**Not available.

Percent of Property Crimes Occurring in Urban Areas in 1997

National Percent = 94.9% of Property Crimes*

ALPHA ORDER

RANK	STATE	PERCENT
17	Alabama	94.6
41	Alaska	84.7
5	Arizona	98.0
34	Arkansas	88.2
4	California	98.7
11	Colorado	96.4
6	Connecticut	97.5
30	Delaware	91.1
10	Florida	96.9
31	Georgia	91.0
44	Hawaii	74.5
42	Idaho	83.6
NA	Illinois**	NA
24	Indiana	93.0
32	Iowa	90.2
NA	Kansas**	NA
NA	Kentucky**	NA
17	Louisiana	94.6
39	Maine	85.4
7	Maryland	97.4
1	Massachusetts	100.0
20	Michigan	94.3
29	Minnesota	91.2
38	Mississippi	86.2
20	Missouri	94.3
NA	Montana**	NA
28	Nebraska	91.3
19	Nevada	94.5
NA	New Hampshire**	NA
1	New Jersey	100.0
14	New Mexico	95.4
8	New York	97.2
33	North Carolina	88.3
37	North Dakota	87.5
12	Ohio	95.6
22	Oklahoma	94.0
25	Oregon	92.7
13	Pennsylvania	95.5
3	Rhode Island	99.9
40	South Carolina	85.0
36	South Dakota	87.7
26	Tennessee	92.6
9	Texas	97.1
15	Utah	95.2
NA	Vermont**	NA
23	Virginia	93.5
16	Washington	95.0
43	West Virginia	78.6
27	Wisconsin	91.5
35	Wyoming	88.0

RANK ORDER

RANK	STATE	PERCENT
1	Massachusetts	100.0
1	New Jersey	100.0
3	Rhode Island	99.9
4	California	98.7
5	Arizona	98.0
6	Connecticut	97.5
7	Maryland	97.4
8	New York	97.2
9	Texas	97.1
10	Florida	96.9
11	Colorado	96.4
12	Ohio	95.6
13	Pennsylvania	95.5
14	New Mexico	95.4
15	Utah	95.2
16	Washington	95.0
17	Alabama	94.6
17	Louisiana	94.6
19	Nevada	94.5
20	Michigan	94.3
20	Missouri	94.3
22	Oklahoma	94.0
23	Virginia	93.5
24	Indiana	93.0
25	Oregon	92.7
26	Tennessee	92.6
27	Wisconsin	91.5
28	Nebraska	91.3
29	Minnesota	91.2
30	Delaware	91.1
31	Georgia	91.0
32	Iowa	90.2
33	North Carolina	88.3
34	Arkansas	88.2
35	Wyoming	88.0
36	South Dakota	87.7
37	North Dakota	87.5
38	Mississippi	86.2
39	Maine	85.4
40	South Carolina	85.0
41	Alaska	84.7
42	Idaho	83.6
43	West Virginia	78.6
44	Hawaii	74.5
NA	Illinois**	NA
NA	Kansas**	NA
NA	Kentucky**	NA
NA	Montana**	NA
NA	New Hampshire**	NA
NA	Vermont**	NA

District of Columbia 100.0

Source: Morgan Quitno Press using data from Federal Bureau of Investigation
   "Crime in the United States 1997" (Uniform Crime Reports, November 22, 1998)
*Estimated percentages for urban areas, defined by the F.B.I. as Metropolitan Statistical Areas and other cities outside such areas. National percent includes those states listed as not available. Property crimes are offenses of burglary, larceny-theft and motor vehicle theft.
**Not available.

Property Crimes in Rural Areas in 1997

National Rural Total = 590,619 Property Crimes*

ALPHA ORDER					RANK ORDER			
RANK	STATE		CRIMES	% of USA	RANK	STATE	CRIMES	% of USA
23	Alabama		10,083	1.7%	1	North Carolina	42,395	7.2%
36	Alaska		4,253	0.7%	2	Georgia	34,799	5.9%
30	Arizona		5,989	1.0%	3	South Carolina	28,972	4.9%
22	Arkansas		12,528	2.1%	4	Florida	27,939	4.7%
11	California		16,503	2.8%	5	Texas	27,215	4.6%
29	Colorado		6,057	1.0%	6	Michigan	23,926	4.1%
37	Connecticut		2,982	0.5%	7	Ohio	19,986	3.4%
38	Delaware		2,916	0.5%	8	Tennessee	18,788	3.2%
4	Florida		27,939	4.7%	9	Hawaii	17,419	2.9%
2	Georgia		34,799	5.9%	10	Minnesota	16,797	2.8%
9	Hawaii		17,419	2.9%	11	California	16,503	2.8%
27	Idaho		7,277	1.2%	12	New York	16,357	2.8%
NA	Illinois**		NA	NA	13	Indiana	16,160	2.7%
13	Indiana		16,160	2.7%	14	Pennsylvania	16,117	2.7%
25	Iowa		9,760	1.7%	15	Mississippi	15,720	2.7%
NA	Kansas**		NA	NA	16	Washington	15,495	2.6%
NA	Kentucky**		NA	NA	17	Virginia	15,346	2.6%
20	Louisiana		13,171	2.2%	18	Wisconsin	15,030	2.5%
33	Maine		5,461	0.9%	19	Oregon	13,772	2.3%
28	Maryland		6,339	1.1%	20	Louisiana	13,171	2.2%
42	Massachusetts		42	0.0%	21	Missouri	12,953	2.2%
6	Michigan		23,926	4.1%	22	Arkansas	12,528	2.1%
10	Minnesota		16,797	2.8%	23	Alabama	10,083	1.7%
15	Mississippi		15,720	2.7%	24	Oklahoma	9,789	1.7%
21	Missouri		12,953	2.2%	25	Iowa	9,760	1.7%
NA	Montana**		NA	NA	26	West Virginia	8,750	1.5%
32	Nebraska		5,554	0.9%	27	Idaho	7,277	1.2%
34	Nevada		4,897	0.8%	28	Maryland	6,339	1.1%
NA	New Hampshire**		NA	NA	29	Colorado	6,057	1.0%
44	New Jersey		0	0.0%	30	Arizona	5,989	1.0%
35	New Mexico		4,786	0.8%	31	Utah	5,613	1.0%
12	New York		16,357	2.8%	32	Nebraska	5,554	0.9%
1	North Carolina		42,395	7.2%	33	Maine	5,461	0.9%
41	North Dakota		2,095	0.4%	34	Nevada	4,897	0.8%
7	Ohio		19,986	3.4%	35	New Mexico	4,786	0.8%
24	Oklahoma		9,789	1.7%	36	Alaska	4,253	0.7%
19	Oregon		13,772	2.3%	37	Connecticut	2,982	0.5%
14	Pennsylvania		16,117	2.7%	38	Delaware	2,916	0.5%
43	Rhode Island		19	0.0%	39	South Dakota	2,773	0.5%
3	South Carolina		28,972	4.9%	40	Wyoming	2,255	0.4%
39	South Dakota		2,773	0.5%	41	North Dakota	2,095	0.4%
8	Tennessee		18,788	3.2%	42	Massachusetts	42	0.0%
5	Texas		27,215	4.6%	43	Rhode Island	19	0.0%
31	Utah		5,613	1.0%	44	New Jersey	0	0.0%
NA	Vermont**		NA	NA	NA	Illinois**	NA	NA
17	Virginia		15,346	2.6%	NA	Kansas**	NA	NA
16	Washington		15,495	2.6%	NA	Kentucky**	NA	NA
26	West Virginia		8,750	1.5%	NA	Montana**	NA	NA
18	Wisconsin		15,030	2.5%	NA	New Hampshire**	NA	NA
40	Wyoming		2,255	0.4%	NA	Vermont**	NA	NA
						District of Columbia	0	0.0%

Source: Federal Bureau of Investigation
   "Crime in the United States 1997" (Uniform Crime Reports, November 22, 1998)
*Estimated totals for rural areas, defined by the F.B.I. as other than Metropolitan Statistical Areas and other cities outside such areas. National total includes those states listed as not available. Property crimes are offenses of burglary, larceny-theft and motor vehicle theft.
**Not available.

Rural Property Crime Rate in 1997

National Rural Rate = 1,833.1 Property Crimes per 100,000 Population

ALPHA ORDER

RANK	STATE	RATE
36	Alabama	1,271.6
14	Alaska	2,218.3
22	Arizona	1,703.2
28	Arkansas	1,540.6
7	California	2,603.4
18	Colorado	1,842.0
24	Connecticut	1,614.9
4	Delaware	3,104.5
3	Florida	3,508.4
12	Georgia	2,361.5
1	Hawaii	5,679.0
19	Idaho	1,805.8
NA	Illinois**	NA
31	Indiana	1,525.4
38	Iowa	1,102.1
NA	Kansas**	NA
NA	Kentucky**	NA
15	Louisiana	1,925.2
26	Maine	1,549.7
11	Maryland	2,365.3
42	Massachusetts	426.1
13	Michigan	2,225.3
17	Minnesota	1,908.5
34	Mississippi	1,407.7
39	Missouri	1,064.2
NA	Montana**	NA
35	Nebraska	1,320.6
9	Nevada	2,509.8
NA	New Hampshire**	NA
43	New Jersey	0.0
25	New Mexico	1,614.1
16	New York	1,920.1
10	North Carolina	2,472.1
41	North Dakota	943.6
32	Ohio	1,501.5
27	Oklahoma	1,547.3
6	Oregon	2,644.6
29	Pennsylvania	1,529.9
43	Rhode Island	0.0
2	South Carolina	3,614.6
40	South Dakota	954.2
21	Tennessee	1,718.6
23	Texas	1,647.3
8	Utah	2,547.9
NA	Vermont**	NA
33	Virginia	1,428.1
5	Washington	3,015.6
37	West Virginia	1,123.5
30	Wisconsin	1,528.7
20	Wyoming	1,802.1

RANK ORDER

RANK	STATE	RATE
1	Hawaii	5,679.0
2	South Carolina	3,614.6
3	Florida	3,508.4
4	Delaware	3,104.5
5	Washington	3,015.6
6	Oregon	2,644.6
7	California	2,603.4
8	Utah	2,547.9
9	Nevada	2,509.8
10	North Carolina	2,472.1
11	Maryland	2,365.3
12	Georgia	2,361.5
13	Michigan	2,225.3
14	Alaska	2,218.3
15	Louisiana	1,925.2
16	New York	1,920.1
17	Minnesota	1,908.5
18	Colorado	1,842.0
19	Idaho	1,805.8
20	Wyoming	1,802.1
21	Tennessee	1,718.6
22	Arizona	1,703.2
23	Texas	1,647.3
24	Connecticut	1,614.9
25	New Mexico	1,614.1
26	Maine	1,549.7
27	Oklahoma	1,547.3
28	Arkansas	1,540.6
29	Pennsylvania	1,529.9
30	Wisconsin	1,528.7
31	Indiana	1,525.4
32	Ohio	1,501.5
33	Virginia	1,428.1
34	Mississippi	1,407.7
35	Nebraska	1,320.6
36	Alabama	1,271.6
37	West Virginia	1,123.5
38	Iowa	1,102.1
39	Missouri	1,064.2
40	South Dakota	954.2
41	North Dakota	943.6
42	Massachusetts	426.1
43	New Jersey	0.0
43	Rhode Island	0.0
NA	Illinois**	NA
NA	Kansas**	NA
NA	Kentucky**	NA
NA	Montana**	NA
NA	New Hampshire**	NA
NA	Vermont**	NA

District of Columbia   0.0

Source: Morgan Quitno Press using data from Federal Bureau of Investigation
    "Crime in the United States 1997" (Uniform Crime Reports, November 22, 1998)
Estimated rates for rural areas, defined by the F.B.I. as other than Metropolitan Statistical Areas and other cities outside such areas. National rate includes those states listed as not available. Property crimes are offenses of burglary, larceny-theft and motor vehicle theft.
**Not available.*

Percent of Property Crimes Occurring in Rural Areas in 1997

National Percent = 5.1% of Property Crimes*

RANK	STATE	PERCENT
27	Alabama	5.4
4	Alaska	15.3
40	Arizona	2.0
11	Arkansas	11.8
41	California	1.3
34	Colorado	3.6
39	Connecticut	2.5
15	Delaware	8.9
35	Florida	3.1
14	Georgia	9.0
1	Hawaii	25.5
3	Idaho	16.4
NA	Illinois**	NA
21	Indiana	7.0
13	Iowa	9.8
NA	Kansas**	NA
NA	Kentucky**	NA
27	Louisiana	5.4
6	Maine	14.6
38	Maryland	2.6
43	Massachusetts	0.0
24	Michigan	5.7
16	Minnesota	8.8
7	Mississippi	13.8
24	Missouri	5.7
NA	Montana**	NA
17	Nebraska	8.7
26	Nevada	5.5
NA	New Hampshire**	NA
43	New Jersey	0.0
31	New Mexico	4.6
37	New York	2.8
12	North Carolina	11.7
8	North Dakota	12.5
33	Ohio	4.4
23	Oklahoma	6.0
20	Oregon	7.3
32	Pennsylvania	4.5
42	Rhode Island	0.1
5	South Carolina	15.0
9	South Dakota	12.3
19	Tennessee	7.4
36	Texas	2.9
30	Utah	4.8
NA	Vermont**	NA
22	Virginia	6.5
29	Washington	5.0
2	West Virginia	21.4
18	Wisconsin	8.5
10	Wyoming	12.0

RANK	STATE	PERCENT
1	Hawaii	25.5
2	West Virginia	21.4
3	Idaho	16.4
4	Alaska	15.3
5	South Carolina	15.0
6	Maine	14.6
7	Mississippi	13.8
8	North Dakota	12.5
9	South Dakota	12.3
10	Wyoming	12.0
11	Arkansas	11.8
12	North Carolina	11.7
13	Iowa	9.8
14	Georgia	9.0
15	Delaware	8.9
16	Minnesota	8.8
17	Nebraska	8.7
18	Wisconsin	8.5
19	Tennessee	7.4
20	Oregon	7.3
21	Indiana	7.0
22	Virginia	6.5
23	Oklahoma	6.0
24	Michigan	5.7
24	Missouri	5.7
26	Nevada	5.5
27	Alabama	5.4
27	Louisiana	5.4
29	Washington	5.0
30	Utah	4.8
31	New Mexico	4.6
32	Pennsylvania	4.5
33	Ohio	4.4
34	Colorado	3.6
35	Florida	3.1
36	Texas	2.9
37	New York	2.8
38	Maryland	2.6
39	Connecticut	2.5
40	Arizona	2.0
41	California	1.3
42	Rhode Island	0.1
43	Massachusetts	0.0
43	New Jersey	0.0
NA	Illinois**	NA
NA	Kansas**	NA
NA	Kentucky**	NA
NA	Montana**	NA
NA	New Hampshire**	NA
NA	Vermont**	NA
	District of Columbia	0.0

Source: Morgan Quitno Press using data from Federal Bureau of Investigation
"Crime in the United States 1997" (Uniform Crime Reports, November 22, 1998)
*Estimated percentages for rural areas, defined by the F.B.I. as other than Metropolitan Statistical Areas and other cities outside such areas. National percent includes those states listed as not available. Property crimes are offenses of burglary, larceny-theft and motor vehicle theft.
**Not available.

Burglaries in Urban Areas in 1997

National Urban Total = 2,260,803 Burglaries*

ALPHA ORDER

RANK	STATE	BURGLARIES	% of USA
19	Alabama	39,632	1.8%
42	Alaska	2,984	0.1%
11	Arizona	58,033	2.6%
30	Arkansas	21,041	0.9%
1	California	292,739	12.9%
23	Colorado	29,692	1.3%
29	Connecticut	23,181	1.0%
40	Delaware	4,686	0.2%
2	Florida	204,549	9.0%
8	Georgia	70,756	3.1%
34	Hawaii	8,755	0.4%
38	Idaho	6,985	0.3%
NA	Illinois**	NA	NA
16	Indiana	43,310	1.9%
32	Iowa	18,661	0.8%
NA	Kansas**	NA	NA
NA	Kentucky**	NA	NA
14	Louisiana	49,982	2.2%
39	Maine	6,156	0.3%
15	Maryland	46,064	2.0%
18	Massachusetts	40,479	1.8%
7	Michigan	72,336	3.2%
24	Minnesota	29,658	1.3%
26	Mississippi	25,505	1.1%
17	Missouri	41,507	1.8%
NA	Montana**	NA	NA
35	Nebraska	8,567	0.4%
31	Nevada	20,640	0.9%
NA	New Hampshire**	NA	NA
10	New Jersey	60,894	2.7%
28	New Mexico	23,468	1.0%
4	New York	112,722	5.0%
6	North Carolina	81,828	3.6%
44	North Dakota	1,762	0.1%
5	Ohio	89,377	4.0%
21	Oklahoma	35,574	1.6%
25	Oregon	29,145	1.3%
9	Pennsylvania	62,677	2.8%
37	Rhode Island	7,080	0.3%
20	South Carolina	37,392	1.7%
41	South Dakota	3,120	0.1%
13	Tennessee	55,834	2.5%
3	Texas	190,126	8.4%
33	Utah	17,012	0.8%
NA	Vermont**	NA	NA
22	Virginia	34,176	1.5%
12	Washington	57,082	2.5%
36	West Virginia	7,516	0.3%
27	Wisconsin	24,531	1.1%
43	Wyoming	2,488	0.1%

RANK ORDER

RANK	STATE	BURGLARIES	% of USA
1	California	292,739	12.9%
2	Florida	204,549	9.0%
3	Texas	190,126	8.4%
4	New York	112,722	5.0%
5	Ohio	89,377	4.0%
6	North Carolina	81,828	3.6%
7	Michigan	72,336	3.2%
8	Georgia	70,756	3.1%
9	Pennsylvania	62,677	2.8%
10	New Jersey	60,894	2.7%
11	Arizona	58,033	2.6%
12	Washington	57,082	2.5%
13	Tennessee	55,834	2.5%
14	Louisiana	49,982	2.2%
15	Maryland	46,064	2.0%
16	Indiana	43,310	1.9%
17	Missouri	41,507	1.8%
18	Massachusetts	40,479	1.8%
19	Alabama	39,632	1.8%
20	South Carolina	37,392	1.7%
21	Oklahoma	35,574	1.6%
22	Virginia	34,176	1.5%
23	Colorado	29,692	1.3%
24	Minnesota	29,658	1.3%
25	Oregon	29,145	1.3%
26	Mississippi	25,505	1.1%
27	Wisconsin	24,531	1.1%
28	New Mexico	23,468	1.0%
29	Connecticut	23,181	1.0%
30	Arkansas	21,041	0.9%
31	Nevada	20,640	0.9%
32	Iowa	18,661	0.8%
33	Utah	17,012	0.8%
34	Hawaii	8,755	0.4%
35	Nebraska	8,567	0.4%
36	West Virginia	7,516	0.3%
37	Rhode Island	7,080	0.3%
38	Idaho	6,985	0.3%
39	Maine	6,156	0.3%
40	Delaware	4,686	0.2%
41	South Dakota	3,120	0.1%
42	Alaska	2,984	0.1%
43	Wyoming	2,488	0.1%
44	North Dakota	1,762	0.1%
NA	Illinois**	NA	NA
NA	Kansas**	NA	NA
NA	Kentucky**	NA	NA
NA	Montana**	NA	NA
NA	New Hampshire**	NA	NA
NA	Vermont**	NA	NA
	District of Columbia	6,963	0.3%

Source: Morgan Quitno Press using data from Federal Bureau of Investigation
   "Crime in the United States 1997" (Uniform Crime Reports, November 22, 1998)
*Estimated totals for urban areas, defined by the F.B.I. as Metropolitan Statistical Areas and other cities outside such areas. National total includes those states listed as not available. Burglary is the unlawful entry of a structure to commit a felony or theft. Attempts are included.
**Not available.

Urban Burglary Rate in 1997

National Urban Rate = 960.3 Burglaries per 100,000 Population*

RANK	STATE	RATE
13	Alabama	1,124.0
34	Alaska	715.1
6	Arizona	1,380.6
11	Arkansas	1,230.6
21	California	925.4
26	Colorado	833.1
30	Connecticut	751.3
31	Delaware	734.4
3	Florida	1,476.1
12	Georgia	1,176.8
17	Hawaii	994.6
25	Idaho	865.5
NA	Illinois**	NA
24	Indiana	901.4
20	Iowa	949.0
NA	Kansas**	NA
NA	Kentucky**	NA
7	Louisiana	1,362.7
38	Maine	692.0
19	Maryland	954.5
39	Massachusetts	662.7
27	Michigan	831.6
28	Minnesota	779.3
2	Mississippi	1,580.0
18	Missouri	991.9
NA	Montana**	NA
37	Nebraska	692.9
5	Nevada	1,392.8
NA	New Hampshire**	NA
29	New Jersey	756.2
1	New Mexico	1,637.1
40	New York	652.1
4	North Carolina	1,433.0
44	North Dakota	420.5
23	Ohio	906.9
8	Oklahoma	1,325.2
15	Oregon	1,070.6
43	Pennsylvania	571.5
33	Rhode Island	717.3
10	South Carolina	1,263.9
36	South Dakota	697.4
9	Tennessee	1,306.1
16	Texas	1,068.9
22	Utah	925.2
NA	Vermont**	NA
41	Virginia	603.9
14	Washington	1,120.1
32	West Virginia	724.7
42	Wisconsin	585.9
35	Wyoming	701.1

RANK	STATE	RATE
1	New Mexico	1,637.1
2	Mississippi	1,580.0
3	Florida	1,476.1
4	North Carolina	1,433.0
5	Nevada	1,392.8
6	Arizona	1,380.6
7	Louisiana	1,362.7
8	Oklahoma	1,325.2
9	Tennessee	1,306.1
10	South Carolina	1,263.9
11	Arkansas	1,230.6
12	Georgia	1,176.8
13	Alabama	1,124.0
14	Washington	1,120.1
15	Oregon	1,070.6
16	Texas	1,068.9
17	Hawaii	994.6
18	Missouri	991.9
19	Maryland	954.5
20	Iowa	949.0
21	California	925.4
22	Utah	925.2
23	Ohio	906.9
24	Indiana	901.4
25	Idaho	865.5
26	Colorado	833.1
27	Michigan	831.6
28	Minnesota	779.3
29	New Jersey	756.2
30	Connecticut	751.3
31	Delaware	734.4
32	West Virginia	724.7
33	Rhode Island	717.3
34	Alaska	715.1
35	Wyoming	701.1
36	South Dakota	697.4
37	Nebraska	692.9
38	Maine	692.0
39	Massachusetts	662.7
40	New York	652.1
41	Virginia	603.9
42	Wisconsin	585.9
43	Pennsylvania	571.5
44	North Dakota	420.5
NA	Illinois**	NA
NA	Kansas**	NA
NA	Kentucky**	NA
NA	Montana**	NA
NA	New Hampshire**	NA
NA	Vermont**	NA

District of Columbia 1,316.3

Source: Morgan Quitno Press using data from Federal Bureau of Investigation
    "Crime in the United States 1997" (Uniform Crime Reports, November 22, 1998)
*Estimated rates for urban areas, defined by the F.B.I. as Metropolitan Statistical Areas and other cities outside such areas. National rate includes those states listed as not available. Burglary is the unlawful entry of a structure to commit a felony or theft. Attempts are included.
**Not available.

Percent of Burglaries Occurring in Urban Areas in 1997

National Percent = 91.9% of Burglaries*

ALPHA ORDER				RANK ORDER		
RANK	STATE	PERCENT		RANK	STATE	PERCENT
19	Alabama	90.5		1	Massachusetts	100.0
43	Alaska	69.8		1	New Jersey	100.0
5	Arizona	96.6		1	Rhode Island	100.0
34	Arkansas	82.3		4	California	97.8
4	California	97.8		5	Arizona	96.6
8	Colorado	95.8		6	Maryland	96.1
7	Connecticut	96.0		7	Connecticut	96.0
31	Delaware	83.4		8	Colorado	95.8
9	Florida	95.6		9	Florida	95.6
27	Georgia	87.0		10	New York	95.3
44	Hawaii	68.7		11	Texas	94.6
40	Idaho	76.1		12	Ohio	94.1
NA	Illinois**	NA		13	Nevada	93.9
20	Indiana	89.9		14	New Mexico	93.4
29	Iowa	84.8		15	Utah	92.8
NA	Kansas**	NA		16	Louisiana	92.7
NA	Kentucky**	NA		17	Washington	92.0
16	Louisiana	92.7		18	Pennsylvania	91.9
41	Maine	74.7		19	Alabama	90.5
6	Maryland	96.1		20	Indiana	89.9
1	Massachusetts	100.0		21	Michigan	89.6
21	Michigan	89.6		22	Oklahoma	88.9
30	Minnesota	84.1		23	Tennessee	88.8
37	Mississippi	78.6		23	Virginia	88.8
25	Missouri	88.5		25	Missouri	88.5
NA	Montana**	NA		26	Nebraska	87.3
26	Nebraska	87.3		27	Georgia	87.0
13	Nevada	93.9		27	Oregon	87.0
NA	New Hampshire**	NA		29	Iowa	84.8
1	New Jersey	100.0		30	Minnesota	84.1
14	New Mexico	93.4		31	Delaware	83.4
10	New York	95.3		32	Wisconsin	83.1
35	North Carolina	81.8		33	Wyoming	83.0
38	North Dakota	76.6		34	Arkansas	82.3
12	Ohio	94.1		35	North Carolina	81.8
22	Oklahoma	88.9		36	South Carolina	80.7
27	Oregon	87.0		37	Mississippi	78.6
18	Pennsylvania	91.9		38	North Dakota	76.6
1	Rhode Island	100.0		39	South Dakota	76.3
36	South Carolina	80.7		40	Idaho	76.1
39	South Dakota	76.3		41	Maine	74.7
23	Tennessee	88.8		42	West Virginia	70.6
11	Texas	94.6		43	Alaska	69.8
15	Utah	92.8		44	Hawaii	68.7
NA	Vermont**	NA		NA	Illinois**	NA
23	Virginia	88.8		NA	Kansas**	NA
17	Washington	92.0		NA	Kentucky**	NA
42	West Virginia	70.6		NA	Montana**	NA
32	Wisconsin	83.1		NA	New Hampshire**	NA
33	Wyoming	83.0		NA	Vermont**	NA
				District of Columbia		100.0

Source: Morgan Quitno Press using data from Federal Bureau of Investigation
"Crime in the United States 1997" (Uniform Crime Reports, November 22, 1998)
*Estimated percentages for urban areas, defined by the F.B.I. as Metropolitan Statistical Areas and other cities outside such areas. National percent includes those states listed as not available. Burglary is the unlawful entry of a structure to commit a felony or theft. Attempts are included.
**Not available.

444

Burglaries in Rural Areas in 1997

National Rural Total = 200,317 Burglaries*

RANK	STATE	BURGLARIES	% of USA
22	Alabama	4,154	2.1%
35	Alaska	1,292	0.6%
29	Arizona	2,044	1.0%
18	Arkansas	4,527	2.3%
9	California	6,501	3.2%
34	Colorado	1,302	0.6%
38	Connecticut	962	0.5%
39	Delaware	934	0.5%
4	Florida	9,377	4.7%
3	Georgia	10,564	5.3%
23	Hawaii	3,986	2.0%
27	Idaho	2,190	1.1%
NA	Illinois**	NA	NA
17	Indiana	4,872	2.4%
25	Iowa	3,342	1.7%
NA	Kansas**	NA	NA
NA	Kentucky**	NA	NA
24	Louisiana	3,953	2.0%
28	Maine	2,085	1.0%
30	Maryland	1,854	0.9%
42	Massachusetts	12	0.0%
6	Michigan	8,390	4.2%
10	Minnesota	5,607	2.8%
8	Mississippi	6,924	3.5%
14	Missouri	5,393	2.7%
NA	Montana**	NA	NA
36	Nebraska	1,246	0.6%
32	Nevada	1,335	0.7%
NA	New Hampshire**	NA	NA
44	New Jersey	0	0.0%
31	New Mexico	1,658	0.8%
12	New York	5,584	2.8%
1	North Carolina	18,174	9.1%
40	North Dakota	538	0.3%
11	Ohio	5,595	2.8%
19	Oklahoma	4,441	2.2%
20	Oregon	4,362	2.2%
13	Pennsylvania	5,541	2.8%
43	Rhode Island	3	0.0%
5	South Carolina	8,930	4.5%
37	South Dakota	968	0.5%
7	Tennessee	7,065	3.5%
2	Texas	10,933	5.5%
33	Utah	1,323	0.7%
NA	Vermont**	NA	NA
21	Virginia	4,299	2.1%
15	Washington	4,982	2.5%
26	West Virginia	3,131	1.6%
16	Wisconsin	4,972	2.5%
41	Wyoming	510	0.3%

RANK	STATE	BURGLARIES	% of USA
1	North Carolina	18,174	9.1%
2	Texas	10,933	5.5%
3	Georgia	10,564	5.3%
4	Florida	9,377	4.7%
5	South Carolina	8,930	4.5%
6	Michigan	8,390	4.2%
7	Tennessee	7,065	3.5%
8	Mississippi	6,924	3.5%
9	California	6,501	3.2%
10	Minnesota	5,607	2.8%
11	Ohio	5,595	2.8%
12	New York	5,584	2.8%
13	Pennsylvania	5,541	2.8%
14	Missouri	5,393	2.7%
15	Washington	4,982	2.5%
16	Wisconsin	4,972	2.5%
17	Indiana	4,872	2.4%
18	Arkansas	4,527	2.3%
19	Oklahoma	4,441	2.2%
20	Oregon	4,362	2.2%
21	Virginia	4,299	2.1%
22	Alabama	4,154	2.1%
23	Hawaii	3,986	2.0%
24	Louisiana	3,953	2.0%
25	Iowa	3,342	1.7%
26	West Virginia	3,131	1.6%
27	Idaho	2,190	1.1%
28	Maine	2,085	1.0%
29	Arizona	2,044	1.0%
30	Maryland	1,854	0.9%
31	New Mexico	1,658	0.8%
32	Nevada	1,335	0.7%
33	Utah	1,323	0.7%
34	Colorado	1,302	0.6%
35	Alaska	1,292	0.6%
36	Nebraska	1,246	0.6%
37	South Dakota	968	0.5%
38	Connecticut	962	0.5%
39	Delaware	934	0.5%
40	North Dakota	538	0.3%
41	Wyoming	510	0.3%
42	Massachusetts	12	0.0%
43	Rhode Island	3	0.0%
44	New Jersey	0	0.0%
NA	Illinois**	NA	NA
NA	Kansas**	NA	NA
NA	Kentucky**	NA	NA
NA	Montana**	NA	NA
NA	New Hampshire**	NA	NA
NA	Vermont**	NA	NA
	District of Columbia	0	0.0%

Source: Federal Bureau of Investigation
"Crime in the United States 1997" (Uniform Crime Reports, November 22, 1998)
*Estimated totals for rural areas, defined by the F.B.I. as other than Metropolitan Statistical Areas and other cities outside such areas. National total includes those states listed as not available. Burglary is the unlawful entry of a structure to commit a felony or theft. Attempts are included.
**Not available.

Rural Burglary Rate in 1997

National Rural Rate = 621.7 Burglaries per 100,000 Population*

ALPHA ORDER				RANK ORDER		
RANK	STATE	RATE		RANK	STATE	RATE
28	Alabama	523.9		1	Hawaii	1,299.5
14	Alaska	673.9		2	Florida	1,177.5
22	Arizona	581.3		3	South Carolina	1,114.1
25	Arkansas	556.7		4	North Carolina	1,059.7
5	California	1,025.6		5	California	1,025.6
37	Colorado	396.0		6	Delaware	994.4
29	Connecticut	521.0		7	Washington	969.6
6	Delaware	994.4		8	Oregon	837.6
2	Florida	1,177.5		9	Michigan	780.3
10	Georgia	716.9		10	Georgia	716.9
1	Hawaii	1,299.5		11	Oklahoma	702.0
26	Idaho	543.5		12	Maryland	691.8
NA	Illinois**	NA		13	Nevada	684.2
31	Indiana	459.9		14	Alaska	673.9
38	Iowa	377.4		15	Texas	661.8
NA	Kansas**	NA		16	New York	655.5
NA	Kentucky**	NA		17	Tennessee	646.3
23	Louisiana	577.8		18	Minnesota	637.1
21	Maine	591.7		19	Mississippi	620.0
12	Maryland	691.8		20	Utah	600.5
42	Massachusetts	121.7		21	Maine	591.7
9	Michigan	780.3		22	Arizona	581.3
18	Minnesota	637.1		23	Louisiana	577.8
19	Mississippi	620.0		24	New Mexico	559.2
32	Missouri	443.1		25	Arkansas	556.7
NA	Montana**	NA		26	Idaho	543.5
40	Nebraska	296.3		27	Pennsylvania	526.0
13	Nevada	684.2		28	Alabama	523.9
NA	New Hampshire**	NA		29	Connecticut	521.0
43	New Jersey	0.0		30	Wisconsin	505.7
24	New Mexico	559.2		31	Indiana	459.9
16	New York	655.5		32	Missouri	443.1
4	North Carolina	1,059.7		33	Ohio	420.3
41	North Dakota	242.3		34	Wyoming	407.6
33	Ohio	420.3		35	West Virginia	402.0
11	Oklahoma	702.0		36	Virginia	400.1
8	Oregon	837.6		37	Colorado	396.0
27	Pennsylvania	526.0		38	Iowa	377.4
43	Rhode Island	0.0		39	South Dakota	333.1
3	South Carolina	1,114.1		40	Nebraska	296.3
39	South Dakota	333.1		41	North Dakota	242.3
17	Tennessee	646.3		42	Massachusetts	121.7
15	Texas	661.8		43	New Jersey	0.0
20	Utah	600.5		43	Rhode Island	0.0
NA	Vermont**	NA		NA	Illinois**	NA
36	Virginia	400.1		NA	Kansas**	NA
7	Washington	969.6		NA	Kentucky**	NA
35	West Virginia	402.0		NA	Montana**	NA
30	Wisconsin	505.7		NA	New Hampshire**	NA
34	Wyoming	407.6		NA	Vermont**	NA
					District of Columbia	0.0

Source: Morgan Quitno Press using data from Federal Bureau of Investigation
 "Crime in the United States 1997" (Uniform Crime Reports, November 22, 1998)
*Estimated rates for rural areas, defined by the F.B.I. as other than Metropolitan Statistical Areas and other cities outside such areas. National rate includes those states listed as not available. Burglary is the unlawful entry of a structure to commit a felony or theft. Attempts are included.
**Not available.

Percent of Burglaries Occurring in Rural Areas in 1997

National Percent = 8.1% of Burglaries*

<table>
<tr><td colspan="3">ALPHA ORDER</td><td colspan="3">RANK ORDER</td></tr>
<tr><td>RANK</td><td>STATE</td><td>PERCENT</td><td>RANK</td><td>STATE</td><td>PERCENT</td></tr>
<tr><td>26</td><td>Alabama</td><td>9.5</td><td>1</td><td>Hawaii</td><td>31.3</td></tr>
<tr><td>2</td><td>Alaska</td><td>30.2</td><td>2</td><td>Alaska</td><td>30.2</td></tr>
<tr><td>40</td><td>Arizona</td><td>3.4</td><td>3</td><td>West Virginia</td><td>29.4</td></tr>
<tr><td>11</td><td>Arkansas</td><td>17.7</td><td>4</td><td>Maine</td><td>25.3</td></tr>
<tr><td>41</td><td>California</td><td>2.2</td><td>5</td><td>Idaho</td><td>23.9</td></tr>
<tr><td>37</td><td>Colorado</td><td>4.2</td><td>6</td><td>South Dakota</td><td>23.7</td></tr>
<tr><td>38</td><td>Connecticut</td><td>4.0</td><td>7</td><td>North Dakota</td><td>23.4</td></tr>
<tr><td>14</td><td>Delaware</td><td>16.6</td><td>8</td><td>Mississippi</td><td>21.4</td></tr>
<tr><td>36</td><td>Florida</td><td>4.4</td><td>9</td><td>South Carolina</td><td>19.3</td></tr>
<tr><td>17</td><td>Georgia</td><td>13.0</td><td>10</td><td>North Carolina</td><td>18.2</td></tr>
<tr><td>1</td><td>Hawaii</td><td>31.3</td><td>11</td><td>Arkansas</td><td>17.7</td></tr>
<tr><td>5</td><td>Idaho</td><td>23.9</td><td>12</td><td>Wyoming</td><td>17.0</td></tr>
<tr><td>NA</td><td>Illinois**</td><td>NA</td><td>13</td><td>Wisconsin</td><td>16.9</td></tr>
<tr><td>25</td><td>Indiana</td><td>10.1</td><td>14</td><td>Delaware</td><td>16.6</td></tr>
<tr><td>16</td><td>Iowa</td><td>15.2</td><td>15</td><td>Minnesota</td><td>15.9</td></tr>
<tr><td>NA</td><td>Kansas**</td><td>NA</td><td>16</td><td>Iowa</td><td>15.2</td></tr>
<tr><td>NA</td><td>Kentucky**</td><td>NA</td><td>17</td><td>Georgia</td><td>13.0</td></tr>
<tr><td>29</td><td>Louisiana</td><td>7.3</td><td>17</td><td>Oregon</td><td>13.0</td></tr>
<tr><td>4</td><td>Maine</td><td>25.3</td><td>19</td><td>Nebraska</td><td>12.7</td></tr>
<tr><td>39</td><td>Maryland</td><td>3.9</td><td>20</td><td>Missouri</td><td>11.5</td></tr>
<tr><td>42</td><td>Massachusetts</td><td>0.0</td><td>21</td><td>Tennessee</td><td>11.2</td></tr>
<tr><td>24</td><td>Michigan</td><td>10.4</td><td>21</td><td>Virginia</td><td>11.2</td></tr>
<tr><td>15</td><td>Minnesota</td><td>15.9</td><td>23</td><td>Oklahoma</td><td>11.1</td></tr>
<tr><td>8</td><td>Mississippi</td><td>21.4</td><td>24</td><td>Michigan</td><td>10.4</td></tr>
<tr><td>20</td><td>Missouri</td><td>11.5</td><td>25</td><td>Indiana</td><td>10.1</td></tr>
<tr><td>NA</td><td>Montana**</td><td>NA</td><td>26</td><td>Alabama</td><td>9.5</td></tr>
<tr><td>19</td><td>Nebraska</td><td>12.7</td><td>27</td><td>Pennsylvania</td><td>8.1</td></tr>
<tr><td>32</td><td>Nevada</td><td>6.1</td><td>28</td><td>Washington</td><td>8.0</td></tr>
<tr><td>NA</td><td>New Hampshire**</td><td>NA</td><td>29</td><td>Louisiana</td><td>7.3</td></tr>
<tr><td>42</td><td>New Jersey</td><td>0.0</td><td>30</td><td>Utah</td><td>7.2</td></tr>
<tr><td>31</td><td>New Mexico</td><td>6.6</td><td>31</td><td>New Mexico</td><td>6.6</td></tr>
<tr><td>35</td><td>New York</td><td>4.7</td><td>32</td><td>Nevada</td><td>6.1</td></tr>
<tr><td>10</td><td>North Carolina</td><td>18.2</td><td>33</td><td>Ohio</td><td>5.9</td></tr>
<tr><td>7</td><td>North Dakota</td><td>23.4</td><td>34</td><td>Texas</td><td>5.4</td></tr>
<tr><td>33</td><td>Ohio</td><td>5.9</td><td>35</td><td>New York</td><td>4.7</td></tr>
<tr><td>23</td><td>Oklahoma</td><td>11.1</td><td>36</td><td>Florida</td><td>4.4</td></tr>
<tr><td>17</td><td>Oregon</td><td>13.0</td><td>37</td><td>Colorado</td><td>4.2</td></tr>
<tr><td>27</td><td>Pennsylvania</td><td>8.1</td><td>38</td><td>Connecticut</td><td>4.0</td></tr>
<tr><td>42</td><td>Rhode Island</td><td>0.0</td><td>39</td><td>Maryland</td><td>3.9</td></tr>
<tr><td>9</td><td>South Carolina</td><td>19.3</td><td>40</td><td>Arizona</td><td>3.4</td></tr>
<tr><td>6</td><td>South Dakota</td><td>23.7</td><td>41</td><td>California</td><td>2.2</td></tr>
<tr><td>21</td><td>Tennessee</td><td>11.2</td><td>42</td><td>Massachusetts</td><td>0.0</td></tr>
<tr><td>34</td><td>Texas</td><td>5.4</td><td>42</td><td>New Jersey</td><td>0.0</td></tr>
<tr><td>30</td><td>Utah</td><td>7.2</td><td>42</td><td>Rhode Island</td><td>0.0</td></tr>
<tr><td>NA</td><td>Vermont**</td><td>NA</td><td>NA</td><td>Illinois**</td><td>NA</td></tr>
<tr><td>21</td><td>Virginia</td><td>11.2</td><td>NA</td><td>Kansas**</td><td>NA</td></tr>
<tr><td>28</td><td>Washington</td><td>8.0</td><td>NA</td><td>Kentucky**</td><td>NA</td></tr>
<tr><td>3</td><td>West Virginia</td><td>29.4</td><td>NA</td><td>Montana**</td><td>NA</td></tr>
<tr><td>13</td><td>Wisconsin</td><td>16.9</td><td>NA</td><td>New Hampshire**</td><td>NA</td></tr>
<tr><td>12</td><td>Wyoming</td><td>17.0</td><td>NA</td><td>Vermont**</td><td>NA</td></tr>
<tr><td></td><td></td><td></td><td></td><td>District of Columbia</td><td>0.0</td></tr>
</table>

Source: Morgan Quitno Press using data from Federal Bureau of Investigation
    "Crime in the United States 1997" (Uniform Crime Reports, November 22, 1998)
*Estimated percentages for rural areas, defined by the F.B.I. as other than Metropolitan Statistical Areas and other
cities outside such areas. National percent includes those states listed as not available. Burglary is the unlawful
entry of a structure to commit a felony or theft. Attempts are included.
**Not available.

Larcenies and Thefts in Urban Areas in 1997

National Urban Total = 7,376,860 Larcenies and Thefts*

ALPHA ORDER

RANK	STATE	THEFTS	% of USA
21	Alabama	122,487	1.7%
41	Alaska	18,304	0.2%
11	Arizona	191,548	2.6%
30	Arkansas	65,233	0.9%
1	California	776,020	10.5%
24	Colorado	115,329	1.6%
28	Connecticut	77,048	1.0%
40	Delaware	21,445	0.3%
3	Florida	577,817	7.8%
7	Georgia	240,941	3.3%
35	Hawaii	36,430	0.5%
36	Idaho	28,209	0.4%
NA	Illinois**	NA	NA
17	Indiana	148,466	2.0%
29	Iowa	65,562	0.9%
NA	Kansas**	NA	NA
NA	Kentucky**	NA	NA
15	Louisiana	154,555	2.1%
37	Maine	24,485	0.3%
14	Maryland	162,074	2.2%
23	Massachusetts	115,470	1.6%
6	Michigan	262,724	3.6%
19	Minnesota	128,027	1.7%
32	Mississippi	64,292	0.9%
16	Missouri	148,792	2.0%
NA	Montana**	NA	NA
34	Nebraska	44,383	0.6%
33	Nevada	49,863	0.7%
NA	New Hampshire**	NA	NA
12	New Jersey	184,979	2.5%
31	New Mexico	64,449	0.9%
4	New York	376,228	5.1%
9	North Carolina	216,714	2.9%
44	North Dakota	11,974	0.2%
5	Ohio	302,649	4.1%
26	Oklahoma	104,524	1.4%
20	Oregon	127,800	1.7%
8	Pennsylvania	237,627	3.2%
39	Rhode Island	21,484	0.3%
25	South Carolina	113,571	1.5%
42	South Dakota	15,861	0.2%
18	Tennessee	146,941	2.0%
2	Texas	630,964	8.6%
27	Utah	85,096	1.2%
NA	Vermont**	NA	NA
13	Virginia	170,539	2.3%
10	Washington	204,234	2.8%
38	West Virginia	22,310	0.3%
22	Wisconsin	121,990	1.7%
43	Wyoming	13,537	0.2%

RANK ORDER

RANK	STATE	THEFTS	% of USA
1	California	776,020	10.5%
2	Texas	630,964	8.6%
3	Florida	577,817	7.8%
4	New York	376,228	5.1%
5	Ohio	302,649	4.1%
6	Michigan	262,724	3.6%
7	Georgia	240,941	3.3%
8	Pennsylvania	237,627	3.2%
9	North Carolina	216,714	2.9%
10	Washington	204,234	2.8%
11	Arizona	191,548	2.6%
12	New Jersey	184,979	2.5%
13	Virginia	170,539	2.3%
14	Maryland	162,074	2.2%
15	Louisiana	154,555	2.1%
16	Missouri	148,792	2.0%
17	Indiana	148,466	2.0%
18	Tennessee	146,941	2.0%
19	Minnesota	128,027	1.7%
20	Oregon	127,800	1.7%
21	Alabama	122,487	1.7%
22	Wisconsin	121,990	1.7%
23	Massachusetts	115,470	1.6%
24	Colorado	115,329	1.6%
25	South Carolina	113,571	1.5%
26	Oklahoma	104,524	1.4%
27	Utah	85,096	1.2%
28	Connecticut	77,048	1.0%
29	Iowa	65,562	0.9%
30	Arkansas	65,233	0.9%
31	New Mexico	64,449	0.9%
32	Mississippi	64,292	0.9%
33	Nevada	49,863	0.7%
34	Nebraska	44,383	0.6%
35	Hawaii	36,430	0.5%
36	Idaho	28,209	0.4%
37	Maine	24,485	0.3%
38	West Virginia	22,310	0.3%
39	Rhode Island	21,484	0.3%
40	Delaware	21,445	0.3%
41	Alaska	18,304	0.2%
42	South Dakota	15,861	0.2%
43	Wyoming	13,537	0.2%
44	North Dakota	11,974	0.2%
NA	Illinois**	NA	NA
NA	Kansas**	NA	NA
NA	Kentucky**	NA	NA
NA	Montana**	NA	NA
NA	New Hampshire**	NA	NA
NA	Vermont**	NA	NA
	District of Columbia	26,809	0.4%

Source: Morgan Quitno Press using data from Federal Bureau of Investigation
"Crime in the United States 1997" (Uniform Crime Reports, November 22, 1998)
*Estimated totals for urban areas, defined by the F.B.I. as Metropolitan Statistical Areas and other cities outside such areas. National total includes those states listed as not available. Larceny and theft is the unlawful taking of property without use of force, violence or fraud. Attempts are included. Motor vehicle thefts are excluded.
**Not available.

Urban Larceny and Theft Rate in 1997

National Urban Rate = 3,133.5 Larcenies and Thefts per 100,000 Population*

ALPHA ORDER

RANK	STATE	RATE
22	Alabama	3,473.7
5	Alaska	4,386.6
3	Arizona	4,557.0
14	Arkansas	3,815.2
38	California	2,453.1
29	Colorado	3,235.8
37	Connecticut	2,497.2
26	Delaware	3,360.9
7	Florida	4,169.7
10	Georgia	4,007.4
8	Hawaii	4,138.5
21	Idaho	3,495.4
NA	Illinois**	NA
30	Indiana	3,090.1
28	Iowa	3,334.1
NA	Kansas**	NA
NA	Kentucky**	NA
6	Louisiana	4,213.8
36	Maine	2,752.3
27	Maryland	3,358.3
44	Massachusetts	1,890.4
32	Michigan	3,020.2
25	Minnesota	3,363.9
11	Mississippi	3,982.8
18	Missouri	3,555.5
NA	Montana**	NA
17	Nebraska	3,589.6
24	Nevada	3,364.8
NA	New Hampshire**	NA
39	New Jersey	2,297.0
4	New Mexico	4,495.9
41	New York	2,176.6
16	North Carolina	3,795.3
35	North Dakota	2,857.9
31	Ohio	3,071.0
12	Oklahoma	3,893.8
1	Oregon	4,694.7
42	Pennsylvania	2,166.8
40	Rhode Island	2,176.7
13	South Carolina	3,838.8
20	South Dakota	3,545.3
23	Tennessee	3,437.4
19	Texas	3,547.4
2	Utah	4,628.1
NA	Vermont**	NA
33	Virginia	3,013.4
9	Washington	4,007.6
43	West Virginia	2,151.0
34	Wisconsin	2,913.7
15	Wyoming	3,814.7

RANK ORDER

RANK	STATE	RATE
1	Oregon	4,694.7
2	Utah	4,628.1
3	Arizona	4,557.0
4	New Mexico	4,495.9
5	Alaska	4,386.6
6	Louisiana	4,213.8
7	Florida	4,169.7
8	Hawaii	4,138.5
9	Washington	4,007.6
10	Georgia	4,007.4
11	Mississippi	3,982.8
12	Oklahoma	3,893.8
13	South Carolina	3,838.8
14	Arkansas	3,815.2
15	Wyoming	3,814.7
16	North Carolina	3,795.3
17	Nebraska	3,589.6
18	Missouri	3,555.5
19	Texas	3,547.4
20	South Dakota	3,545.3
21	Idaho	3,495.4
22	Alabama	3,473.7
23	Tennessee	3,437.4
24	Nevada	3,364.8
25	Minnesota	3,363.9
26	Delaware	3,360.9
27	Maryland	3,358.3
28	Iowa	3,334.1
29	Colorado	3,235.8
30	Indiana	3,090.1
31	Ohio	3,071.0
32	Michigan	3,020.2
33	Virginia	3,013.4
34	Wisconsin	2,913.7
35	North Dakota	2,857.9
36	Maine	2,752.3
37	Connecticut	2,497.2
38	California	2,453.1
39	New Jersey	2,297.0
40	Rhode Island	2,176.7
41	New York	2,176.6
42	Pennsylvania	2,166.8
43	West Virginia	2,151.0
44	Massachusetts	1,890.4
NA	Illinois**	NA
NA	Kansas**	NA
NA	Kentucky**	NA
NA	Montana**	NA
NA	New Hampshire**	NA
NA	Vermont**	NA
	District of Columbia	5,067.9

Source: Morgan Quitno Press using data from Federal Bureau of Investigation
  "Crime in the United States 1997" (Uniform Crime Reports, November 22, 1998)
*Estimated rates for urban areas, defined by the F.B.I. as Metropolitan Statistical Areas and other cities outside such areas. National rate includes those states listed as not available. Larceny and theft is the unlawful taking of property without use of force, violence or fraud. Attempts are included. Motor vehicle thefts are excluded.
**Not available.

Percent of Larcenies and Thefts Occurring in Urban Areas in 1997

National Percent = 95.5% of Larcenies and Thefts*

ALPHA ORDER				RANK ORDER		
RANK	STATE	PERCENT		RANK	STATE	PERCENT
13	Alabama	96.0		1	Massachusetts	100.0
40	Alaska	88.1		1	New Jersey	100.0
5	Arizona	98.2		3	Rhode Island	99.9
35	Arkansas	90.3		4	California	98.9
4	California	98.9		5	Arizona	98.2
11	Colorado	96.3		6	Connecticut	97.8
6	Connecticut	97.8		6	Texas	97.8
29	Delaware	92.0		8	Maryland	97.5
10	Florida	97.2		9	New York	97.4
31	Georgia	91.9		10	Florida	97.2
44	Hawaii	74.4		11	Colorado	96.3
42	Idaho	86.0		12	Pennsylvania	96.2
NA	Illinois**	NA		13	Alabama	96.0
25	Indiana	93.7		14	New Mexico	95.9
29	Iowa	92.0		14	Oklahoma	95.9
NA	Kansas**	NA		16	Ohio	95.8
NA	Kentucky**	NA		17	Missouri	95.7
21	Louisiana	94.8		18	Utah	95.5
39	Maine	89.0		18	Washington	95.5
8	Maryland	97.5		20	Michigan	94.9
1	Massachusetts	100.0		21	Louisiana	94.8
20	Michigan	94.9		22	Virginia	94.5
28	Minnesota	92.9		23	Nevada	93.9
37	Mississippi	89.4		23	Oregon	93.9
17	Missouri	95.7		25	Indiana	93.7
NA	Montana**	NA		25	Tennessee	93.7
32	Nebraska	91.8		27	Wisconsin	93.1
23	Nevada	93.9		28	Minnesota	92.9
NA	New Hampshire**	NA		29	Delaware	92.0
1	New Jersey	100.0		29	Iowa	92.0
14	New Mexico	95.9		31	Georgia	91.9
9	New York	97.4		32	Nebraska	91.8
33	North Carolina	91.0		33	North Carolina	91.0
36	North Dakota	89.6		34	South Dakota	90.4
16	Ohio	95.8		35	Arkansas	90.3
14	Oklahoma	95.9		36	North Dakota	89.6
23	Oregon	93.9		37	Mississippi	89.4
12	Pennsylvania	96.2		38	Wyoming	89.1
3	Rhode Island	99.9		39	Maine	89.0
41	South Carolina	86.5		40	Alaska	88.1
34	South Dakota	90.4		41	South Carolina	86.5
25	Tennessee	93.7		42	Idaho	86.0
6	Texas	97.8		43	West Virginia	82.8
18	Utah	95.5		44	Hawaii	74.4
NA	Vermont**	NA		NA	Illinois**	NA
22	Virginia	94.5		NA	Kansas**	NA
18	Washington	95.5		NA	Kentucky**	NA
43	West Virginia	82.8		NA	Montana**	NA
27	Wisconsin	93.1		NA	New Hampshire**	NA
38	Wyoming	89.1		NA	Vermont**	NA

District of Columbia — 100.0

Source: Morgan Quitno Press using data from Federal Bureau of Investigation
"Crime in the United States 1997" (Uniform Crime Reports, November 22, 1998)
*Estimated percentages for urban areas, defined by the F.B.I. as Metropolitan Statistical Areas and other cities outside such areas. National percent includes those states listed as not available. Larceny and theft is the unlawful taking of property without use of force, violence or fraud. Attempts are included. Motor vehicle thefts are excluded.
**Not available.

Larcenies and Thefts in Rural Areas in 1997

National Rural Total = 348,610 Larcenies and Thefts*

ALPHA ORDER

RANK	STATE	THEFTS	% of USA
24	Alabama	5,129	1.5%
36	Alaska	2,476	0.7%
32	Arizona	3,497	1.0%
21	Arkansas	7,020	2.0%
18	California	8,385	2.4%
28	Colorado	4,472	1.3%
38	Connecticut	1,773	0.5%
37	Delaware	1,867	0.5%
4	Florida	16,675	4.8%
2	Georgia	21,322	6.1%
8	Hawaii	12,554	3.6%
26	Idaho	4,575	1.3%
NA	Illinois**	NA	NA
10	Indiana	9,976	2.9%
23	Iowa	5,739	1.6%
NA	Kansas**	NA	NA
NA	Kentucky**	NA	NA
17	Louisiana	8,559	2.5%
34	Maine	3,028	0.9%
29	Maryland	4,182	1.2%
42	Massachusetts	24	0.0%
6	Michigan	14,139	4.1%
13	Minnesota	9,845	2.8%
20	Mississippi	7,595	2.2%
22	Missouri	6,680	1.9%
NA	Montana**	NA	NA
31	Nebraska	3,980	1.1%
33	Nevada	3,249	0.9%
NA	New Hampshire**	NA	NA
44	New Jersey	0	0.0%
35	New Mexico	2,739	0.8%
9	New York	10,207	2.9%
1	North Carolina	21,514	6.2%
41	North Dakota	1,393	0.4%
7	Ohio	13,259	3.8%
27	Oklahoma	4,515	1.3%
19	Oregon	8,329	2.4%
15	Pennsylvania	9,265	2.7%
43	Rhode Island	15	0.0%
3	South Carolina	17,754	5.1%
39	South Dakota	1,684	0.5%
11	Tennessee	9,902	2.8%
5	Texas	14,487	4.2%
30	Utah	3,994	1.1%
NA	Vermont**	NA	NA
12	Virginia	9,867	2.8%
14	Washington	9,589	2.8%
25	West Virginia	4,624	1.3%
16	Wisconsin	9,012	2.6%
40	Wyoming	1,661	0.5%

RANK ORDER

RANK	STATE	THEFTS	% of USA
1	North Carolina	21,514	6.2%
2	Georgia	21,322	6.1%
3	South Carolina	17,754	5.1%
4	Florida	16,675	4.8%
5	Texas	14,487	4.2%
6	Michigan	14,139	4.1%
7	Ohio	13,259	3.8%
8	Hawaii	12,554	3.6%
9	New York	10,207	2.9%
10	Indiana	9,976	2.9%
11	Tennessee	9,902	2.8%
12	Virginia	9,867	2.8%
13	Minnesota	9,845	2.8%
14	Washington	9,589	2.8%
15	Pennsylvania	9,265	2.7%
16	Wisconsin	9,012	2.6%
17	Louisiana	8,559	2.5%
18	California	8,385	2.4%
19	Oregon	8,329	2.4%
20	Mississippi	7,595	2.2%
21	Arkansas	7,020	2.0%
22	Missouri	6,680	1.9%
23	Iowa	5,739	1.6%
24	Alabama	5,129	1.5%
25	West Virginia	4,624	1.3%
26	Idaho	4,575	1.3%
27	Oklahoma	4,515	1.3%
28	Colorado	4,472	1.3%
29	Maryland	4,182	1.2%
30	Utah	3,994	1.1%
31	Nebraska	3,980	1.1%
32	Arizona	3,497	1.0%
33	Nevada	3,249	0.9%
34	Maine	3,028	0.9%
35	New Mexico	2,739	0.8%
36	Alaska	2,476	0.7%
37	Delaware	1,867	0.5%
38	Connecticut	1,773	0.5%
39	South Dakota	1,684	0.5%
40	Wyoming	1,661	0.5%
41	North Dakota	1,393	0.4%
42	Massachusetts	24	0.0%
43	Rhode Island	15	0.0%
44	New Jersey	0	0.0%
NA	Illinois**	NA	NA
NA	Kansas**	NA	NA
NA	Kentucky**	NA	NA
NA	Montana**	NA	NA
NA	New Hampshire**	NA	NA
NA	Vermont**	NA	NA
	District of Columbia	0	0.0%

Source: Federal Bureau of Investigation
"Crime in the United States 1997" (Uniform Crime Reports, November 22, 1998)
*Estimated totals for rural areas, defined by the F.B.I. as other than Metropolitan Statistical Areas and other cities outside such areas. National total includes those states listed as not available. Larceny and theft is the unlawful taking of property without use of force, violence or fraud. Attempts are included. Motor vehicle thefts are excluded.
**Not available.

Rural Larceny and Theft Rate in 1997

National Rural Rate = 1,082.0 Larcenies and Thefts per 100,000 Population*

ALPHA ORDER

RANK	STATE	RATE
37	Alabama	646.8
15	Alaska	1,291.4
22	Arizona	994.5
32	Arkansas	863.3
13	California	1,322.8
11	Colorado	1,360.0
23	Connecticut	960.2
4	Delaware	1,987.7
3	Florida	2,093.9
10	Georgia	1,447.0
1	Hawaii	4,092.9
19	Idaho	1,135.3
NA	Illinois**	NA
25	Indiana	941.7
36	Iowa	648.0
NA	Kansas**	NA
NA	Kentucky**	NA
17	Louisiana	1,251.0
33	Maine	859.3
9	Maryland	1,560.5
42	Massachusetts	243.5
14	Michigan	1,315.1
20	Minnesota	1,118.6
35	Mississippi	680.1
41	Missouri	548.8
NA	Montana**	NA
24	Nebraska	946.3
7	Nevada	1,665.2
NA	New Hampshire**	NA
43	New Jersey	0.0
26	New Mexico	923.8
18	New York	1,198.2
16	North Carolina	1,254.5
38	North Dakota	627.4
21	Ohio	996.1
34	Oklahoma	713.7
8	Oregon	1,599.4
30	Pennsylvania	879.5
43	Rhode Island	0.0
2	South Carolina	2,215.0
40	South Dakota	579.5
29	Tennessee	905.8
31	Texas	876.9
6	Utah	1,813.0
NA	Vermont**	NA
27	Virginia	918.2
5	Washington	1,866.2
39	West Virginia	593.7
28	Wisconsin	916.6
12	Wyoming	1,327.4

RANK ORDER

RANK	STATE	RATE
1	Hawaii	4,092.9
2	South Carolina	2,215.0
3	Florida	2,093.9
4	Delaware	1,987.7
5	Washington	1,866.2
6	Utah	1,813.0
7	Nevada	1,665.2
8	Oregon	1,599.4
9	Maryland	1,560.5
10	Georgia	1,447.0
11	Colorado	1,360.0
12	Wyoming	1,327.4
13	California	1,322.8
14	Michigan	1,315.1
15	Alaska	1,291.4
16	North Carolina	1,254.5
17	Louisiana	1,251.0
18	New York	1,198.2
19	Idaho	1,135.3
20	Minnesota	1,118.6
21	Ohio	996.1
22	Arizona	994.5
23	Connecticut	960.2
24	Nebraska	946.3
25	Indiana	941.7
26	New Mexico	923.8
27	Virginia	918.2
28	Wisconsin	916.6
29	Tennessee	905.8
30	Pennsylvania	879.5
31	Texas	876.9
32	Arkansas	863.3
33	Maine	859.3
34	Oklahoma	713.7
35	Mississippi	680.1
36	Iowa	648.0
37	Alabama	646.8
38	North Dakota	627.4
39	West Virginia	593.7
40	South Dakota	579.5
41	Missouri	548.8
42	Massachusetts	243.5
43	New Jersey	0.0
43	Rhode Island	0.0
NA	Illinois**	NA
NA	Kansas**	NA
NA	Kentucky**	NA
NA	Montana**	NA
NA	New Hampshire**	NA
NA	Vermont**	NA
	District of Columbia	0.0

Source: Morgan Quitno Press using data from Federal Bureau of Investigation
"Crime in the United States 1997" (Uniform Crime Reports, November 22, 1998)
*Estimated rates for rural areas, defined by the F.B.I. as other than Metropolitan Statistical Areas and other cities outside such areas. National rate includes those states listed as not available. Larceny and theft is the unlawful taking of property without use of force, violence or fraud. Attempts are included. Motor vehicle thefts are excluded.
**Not available.

452

Percent of Larcenies and Thefts Occurring in Rural Areas in 1997

National Percent = 4.5% of Larcenies and Thefts*

ALPHA ORDER			RANK ORDER		
RANK	STATE	PERCENT	RANK	STATE	PERCENT
32	Alabama	4.0	1	Hawaii	25.6
5	Alaska	11.9	2	West Virginia	17.2
40	Arizona	1.8	3	Idaho	14.0
10	Arkansas	9.7	4	South Carolina	13.5
41	California	1.1	5	Alaska	11.9
34	Colorado	3.7	6	Maine	11.0
38	Connecticut	2.2	7	Wyoming	10.9
15	Delaware	8.0	8	Mississippi	10.6
35	Florida	2.8	9	North Dakota	10.4
14	Georgia	8.1	10	Arkansas	9.7
1	Hawaii	25.6	11	South Dakota	9.6
3	Idaho	14.0	12	North Carolina	9.0
NA	Illinois**	NA	13	Nebraska	8.2
19	Indiana	6.3	14	Georgia	8.1
15	Iowa	8.0	15	Delaware	8.0
NA	Kansas**	NA	15	Iowa	8.0
NA	Kentucky**	NA	17	Minnesota	7.1
24	Louisiana	5.2	18	Wisconsin	6.9
6	Maine	11.0	19	Indiana	6.3
37	Maryland	2.5	19	Tennessee	6.3
43	Massachusetts	0.0	21	Nevada	6.1
25	Michigan	5.1	21	Oregon	6.1
17	Minnesota	7.1	23	Virginia	5.5
8	Mississippi	10.6	24	Louisiana	5.2
28	Missouri	4.3	25	Michigan	5.1
NA	Montana**	NA	26	Utah	4.5
13	Nebraska	8.2	26	Washington	4.5
21	Nevada	6.1	28	Missouri	4.3
NA	New Hampshire**	NA	29	Ohio	4.2
43	New Jersey	0.0	30	New Mexico	4.1
30	New Mexico	4.1	30	Oklahoma	4.1
36	New York	2.6	32	Alabama	4.0
12	North Carolina	9.0	33	Pennsylvania	3.8
9	North Dakota	10.4	34	Colorado	3.7
29	Ohio	4.2	35	Florida	2.8
30	Oklahoma	4.1	36	New York	2.6
21	Oregon	6.1	37	Maryland	2.5
33	Pennsylvania	3.8	38	Connecticut	2.2
42	Rhode Island	0.1	38	Texas	2.2
4	South Carolina	13.5	40	Arizona	1.8
11	South Dakota	9.6	41	California	1.1
19	Tennessee	6.3	42	Rhode Island	0.1
38	Texas	2.2	43	Massachusetts	0.0
26	Utah	4.5	43	New Jersey	0.0
NA	Vermont**	NA	NA	Illinois**	NA
23	Virginia	5.5	NA	Kansas**	NA
26	Washington	4.5	NA	Kentucky**	NA
2	West Virginia	17.2	NA	Montana**	NA
18	Wisconsin	6.9	NA	New Hampshire**	NA
7	Wyoming	10.9	NA	Vermont**	NA
				District of Columbia	0.0

Source: Morgan Quitno Press using data from Federal Bureau of Investigation
   "Crime in the United States 1997" (Uniform Crime Reports, November 22, 1998)
*Estimated percentages for rural areas, defined by the F.B.I. as other than Metropolitan Statistical Areas and other cities outside such areas. National percent includes those states listed as not available. Larceny and theft is the unlawful taking of property without use of force, violence or fraud. Attempts are included. Motor vehicle thefts are excluded. **Not available.

Motor Vehicle Thefts in Urban Areas in 1997

National Urban Total = 1,312,015 Motor Vehicle Thefts*

ALPHA ORDER

RANK	STATE	THEFTS	% of USA
23	Alabama	14,607	1.1%
38	Alaska	2,299	0.2%
7	Arizona	43,753	3.3%
32	Arkansas	6,957	0.5%
1	California	227,105	17.3%
22	Colorado	15,824	1.2%
25	Connecticut	14,294	1.1%
37	Delaware	3,603	0.3%
2	Florida	105,308	8.0%
9	Georgia	41,659	3.2%
34	Hawaii	5,589	0.4%
40	Idaho	1,917	0.1%
NA	Illinois**	NA	NA
17	Indiana	23,787	1.8%
33	Iowa	6,003	0.5%
NA	Kansas**	NA	NA
NA	Kentucky**	NA	NA
15	Louisiana	25,715	2.0%
41	Maine	1,294	0.1%
13	Maryland	30,365	2.3%
14	Massachusetts	29,446	2.2%
5	Michigan	63,930	4.9%
21	Minnesota	16,524	1.3%
31	Mississippi	8,127	0.6%
16	Missouri	25,637	2.0%
NA	Montana**	NA	NA
35	Nebraska	5,213	0.4%
28	Nevada	12,907	1.0%
NA	New Hampshire**	NA	NA
10	New Jersey	41,165	3.1%
29	New Mexico	12,018	0.9%
4	New York	79,131	6.0%
18	North Carolina	21,735	1.7%
42	North Dakota	990	0.1%
6	Ohio	44,287	3.4%
26	Oklahoma	13,811	1.1%
19	Oregon	18,199	1.4%
8	Pennsylvania	42,902	3.3%
36	Rhode Island	4,194	0.3%
27	South Carolina	13,467	1.0%
43	South Dakota	737	0.1%
11	Tennessee	31,921	2.4%
3	Texas	99,926	7.6%
30	Utah	8,848	0.7%
NA	Vermont**	NA	NA
20	Virginia	17,712	1.3%
12	Washington	30,931	2.4%
39	West Virginia	2,292	0.2%
24	Wisconsin	14,594	1.1%
44	Wyoming	563	0.0%

RANK ORDER

RANK	STATE	THEFTS	% of USA
1	California	227,105	17.3%
2	Florida	105,308	8.0%
3	Texas	99,926	7.6%
4	New York	79,131	6.0%
5	Michigan	63,930	4.9%
6	Ohio	44,287	3.4%
7	Arizona	43,753	3.3%
8	Pennsylvania	42,902	3.3%
9	Georgia	41,659	3.2%
10	New Jersey	41,165	3.1%
11	Tennessee	31,921	2.4%
12	Washington	30,931	2.4%
13	Maryland	30,365	2.3%
14	Massachusetts	29,446	2.2%
15	Louisiana	25,715	2.0%
16	Missouri	25,637	2.0%
17	Indiana	23,787	1.8%
18	North Carolina	21,735	1.7%
19	Oregon	18,199	1.4%
20	Virginia	17,712	1.3%
21	Minnesota	16,524	1.3%
22	Colorado	15,824	1.2%
23	Alabama	14,607	1.1%
24	Wisconsin	14,594	1.1%
25	Connecticut	14,294	1.1%
26	Oklahoma	13,811	1.1%
27	South Carolina	13,467	1.0%
28	Nevada	12,907	1.0%
29	New Mexico	12,018	0.9%
30	Utah	8,848	0.7%
31	Mississippi	8,127	0.6%
32	Arkansas	6,957	0.5%
33	Iowa	6,003	0.5%
34	Hawaii	5,589	0.4%
35	Nebraska	5,213	0.4%
36	Rhode Island	4,194	0.3%
37	Delaware	3,603	0.3%
38	Alaska	2,299	0.2%
39	West Virginia	2,292	0.2%
40	Idaho	1,917	0.1%
41	Maine	1,294	0.1%
42	North Dakota	990	0.1%
43	South Dakota	737	0.1%
44	Wyoming	563	0.0%
NA	Illinois**	NA	NA
NA	Kansas**	NA	NA
NA	Kentucky**	NA	NA
NA	Montana**	NA	NA
NA	New Hampshire**	NA	NA
NA	Vermont**	NA	NA
	District of Columbia	7,569	0.6%

Source: Morgan Quitno Press using data from Federal Bureau of Investigation
"Crime in the United States 1997" (Uniform Crime Reports, November 22, 1998)
*Estimated totals for urban areas, defined by the F.B.I. as Metropolitan Statistical Areas and other cities outside such areas. National total includes those states listed as not available. Motor vehicle theft includes the theft or attempted theft of a self-propelled vehicle. Excludes motorboats, construction equipment, airplanes and farming equipment. **Not available.

Urban Motor Vehicle Theft Rate in 1997

National Urban Rate = 557.3 Motor Vehicle Thefts per 100,000 Population*

<table>
<tr><td colspan="3">ALPHA ORDER</td><td colspan="3">RANK ORDER</td></tr>
<tr><th>RANK</th><th>STATE</th><th>RATE</th><th>RANK</th><th>STATE</th><th>RATE</th></tr>
<tr><td>32</td><td>Alabama</td><td>414.3</td><td>1</td><td>Arizona</td><td>1,040.9</td></tr>
<tr><td>17</td><td>Alaska</td><td>551.0</td><td>2</td><td>Nevada</td><td>871.0</td></tr>
<tr><td>1</td><td>Arizona</td><td>1,040.9</td><td>3</td><td>New Mexico</td><td>838.4</td></tr>
<tr><td>33</td><td>Arkansas</td><td>406.9</td><td>4</td><td>Florida</td><td>759.9</td></tr>
<tr><td>7</td><td>California</td><td>717.9</td><td>5</td><td>Tennessee</td><td>746.7</td></tr>
<tr><td>28</td><td>Colorado</td><td>444.0</td><td>6</td><td>Michigan</td><td>734.9</td></tr>
<tr><td>24</td><td>Connecticut</td><td>463.3</td><td>7</td><td>California</td><td>717.9</td></tr>
<tr><td>15</td><td>Delaware</td><td>564.7</td><td>8</td><td>Louisiana</td><td>701.1</td></tr>
<tr><td>4</td><td>Florida</td><td>759.9</td><td>9</td><td>Georgia</td><td>692.9</td></tr>
<tr><td>9</td><td>Georgia</td><td>692.9</td><td>10</td><td>Oregon</td><td>668.5</td></tr>
<tr><td>11</td><td>Hawaii</td><td>634.9</td><td>11</td><td>Hawaii</td><td>634.9</td></tr>
<tr><td>39</td><td>Idaho</td><td>237.5</td><td>12</td><td>Maryland</td><td>629.2</td></tr>
<tr><td>NA</td><td>Illinois**</td><td>NA</td><td>13</td><td>Missouri</td><td>612.6</td></tr>
<tr><td>21</td><td>Indiana</td><td>495.1</td><td>14</td><td>Washington</td><td>606.9</td></tr>
<tr><td>38</td><td>Iowa</td><td>305.3</td><td>15</td><td>Delaware</td><td>564.7</td></tr>
<tr><td>NA</td><td>Kansas**</td><td>NA</td><td>16</td><td>Texas</td><td>561.8</td></tr>
<tr><td>NA</td><td>Kentucky**</td><td>NA</td><td>17</td><td>Alaska</td><td>551.0</td></tr>
<tr><td>8</td><td>Louisiana</td><td>701.1</td><td>18</td><td>Oklahoma</td><td>514.5</td></tr>
<tr><td>44</td><td>Maine</td><td>145.5</td><td>19</td><td>New Jersey</td><td>511.2</td></tr>
<tr><td>12</td><td>Maryland</td><td>629.2</td><td>20</td><td>Mississippi</td><td>503.5</td></tr>
<tr><td>22</td><td>Massachusetts</td><td>482.1</td><td>21</td><td>Indiana</td><td>495.1</td></tr>
<tr><td>6</td><td>Michigan</td><td>734.9</td><td>22</td><td>Massachusetts</td><td>482.1</td></tr>
<tr><td>29</td><td>Minnesota</td><td>434.2</td><td>23</td><td>Utah</td><td>481.2</td></tr>
<tr><td>20</td><td>Mississippi</td><td>503.5</td><td>24</td><td>Connecticut</td><td>463.3</td></tr>
<tr><td>13</td><td>Missouri</td><td>612.6</td><td>25</td><td>New York</td><td>457.8</td></tr>
<tr><td>NA</td><td>Montana**</td><td>NA</td><td>26</td><td>South Carolina</td><td>455.2</td></tr>
<tr><td>31</td><td>Nebraska</td><td>421.6</td><td>27</td><td>Ohio</td><td>449.4</td></tr>
<tr><td>2</td><td>Nevada</td><td>871.0</td><td>28</td><td>Colorado</td><td>444.0</td></tr>
<tr><td>NA</td><td>New Hampshire**</td><td>NA</td><td>29</td><td>Minnesota</td><td>434.2</td></tr>
<tr><td>19</td><td>New Jersey</td><td>511.2</td><td>30</td><td>Rhode Island</td><td>424.9</td></tr>
<tr><td>3</td><td>New Mexico</td><td>838.4</td><td>31</td><td>Nebraska</td><td>421.6</td></tr>
<tr><td>25</td><td>New York</td><td>457.8</td><td>32</td><td>Alabama</td><td>414.3</td></tr>
<tr><td>35</td><td>North Carolina</td><td>380.6</td><td>33</td><td>Arkansas</td><td>406.9</td></tr>
<tr><td>40</td><td>North Dakota</td><td>236.3</td><td>34</td><td>Pennsylvania</td><td>391.2</td></tr>
<tr><td>27</td><td>Ohio</td><td>449.4</td><td>35</td><td>North Carolina</td><td>380.6</td></tr>
<tr><td>18</td><td>Oklahoma</td><td>514.5</td><td>36</td><td>Wisconsin</td><td>348.6</td></tr>
<tr><td>10</td><td>Oregon</td><td>668.5</td><td>37</td><td>Virginia</td><td>313.0</td></tr>
<tr><td>34</td><td>Pennsylvania</td><td>391.2</td><td>38</td><td>Iowa</td><td>305.3</td></tr>
<tr><td>30</td><td>Rhode Island</td><td>424.9</td><td>39</td><td>Idaho</td><td>237.5</td></tr>
<tr><td>26</td><td>South Carolina</td><td>455.2</td><td>40</td><td>North Dakota</td><td>236.3</td></tr>
<tr><td>42</td><td>South Dakota</td><td>164.7</td><td>41</td><td>West Virginia</td><td>221.0</td></tr>
<tr><td>5</td><td>Tennessee</td><td>746.7</td><td>42</td><td>South Dakota</td><td>164.7</td></tr>
<tr><td>16</td><td>Texas</td><td>561.8</td><td>43</td><td>Wyoming</td><td>158.7</td></tr>
<tr><td>23</td><td>Utah</td><td>481.2</td><td>44</td><td>Maine</td><td>145.5</td></tr>
<tr><td>NA</td><td>Vermont**</td><td>NA</td><td>NA</td><td>Illinois**</td><td>NA</td></tr>
<tr><td>37</td><td>Virginia</td><td>313.0</td><td>NA</td><td>Kansas**</td><td>NA</td></tr>
<tr><td>14</td><td>Washington</td><td>606.9</td><td>NA</td><td>Kentucky**</td><td>NA</td></tr>
<tr><td>41</td><td>West Virginia</td><td>221.0</td><td>NA</td><td>Montana**</td><td>NA</td></tr>
<tr><td>36</td><td>Wisconsin</td><td>348.6</td><td>NA</td><td>New Hampshire**</td><td>NA</td></tr>
<tr><td>43</td><td>Wyoming</td><td>158.7</td><td>NA</td><td>Vermont**</td><td>NA</td></tr>
<tr><td></td><td></td><td></td><td></td><td>District of Columbia</td><td>1,430.8</td></tr>
</table>

Source: Morgan Quitno Press using data from Federal Bureau of Investigation
   "Crime in the United States 1997" (Uniform Crime Reports, November 22, 1998)
*Estimated rates for urban areas, defined by the F.B.I. as Metropolitan Statistical Areas and other cities outside
such areas. National rate includes those states listed as not available. Motor vehicle theft includes the theft or
attempted theft of a self-propelled vehicle. Excludes motorboats, construction equipment, airplanes and farming
equipment. **Not available.

Percent of Motor Vehicle Thefts Occurring in Urban Areas in 1997

National Percent = 96.9% of Motor Vehicle Thefts*

ALPHA ORDER				RANK ORDER		
RANK	STATE	PERCENT		RANK	STATE	PERCENT
22	Alabama	94.8		1	Massachusetts	100.0
41	Alaska	82.6		1	New Jersey	100.0
6	Arizona	99.0		1	Rhode Island	100.0
34	Arkansas	87.6		4	California	99.3
4	California	99.3		4	New York	99.3
9	Colorado	98.2		6	Arizona	99.0
8	Connecticut	98.3		6	Maryland	99.0
18	Delaware	96.9		8	Connecticut	98.3
9	Florida	98.2		9	Colorado	98.2
29	Georgia	93.5		9	Florida	98.2
37	Hawaii	86.4		9	Texas	98.2
42	Idaho	78.9		12	Michigan	97.9
NA	Illinois**	NA		13	Nevada	97.6
22	Indiana	94.8		14	Louisiana	97.5
32	Iowa	89.8		14	Ohio	97.5
NA	Kansas**	NA		16	Washington	97.1
NA	Kentucky**	NA		17	Pennsylvania	97.0
14	Louisiana	97.5		18	Delaware	96.9
43	Maine	78.8		18	New Mexico	96.9
6	Maryland	99.0		20	Utah	96.8
1	Massachusetts	100.0		21	Missouri	96.7
12	Michigan	97.9		22	Alabama	94.8
31	Minnesota	92.5		22	Indiana	94.8
35	Mississippi	87.1		24	Tennessee	94.6
21	Missouri	96.7		25	Oregon	94.4
NA	Montana**	NA		26	Oklahoma	94.3
27	Nebraska	94.1		27	Nebraska	94.1
13	Nevada	97.6		28	Virginia	93.8
NA	New Hampshire**	NA		29	Georgia	93.5
1	New Jersey	100.0		30	Wisconsin	93.3
18	New Mexico	96.9		31	Minnesota	92.5
4	New York	99.3		32	Iowa	89.8
33	North Carolina	88.9		33	North Carolina	88.9
39	North Dakota	85.8		34	Arkansas	87.6
14	Ohio	97.5		35	Mississippi	87.1
26	Oklahoma	94.3		36	Wyoming	87.0
25	Oregon	94.4		37	Hawaii	86.4
17	Pennsylvania	97.0		38	South Dakota	85.9
1	Rhode Island	100.0		39	North Dakota	85.8
40	South Carolina	85.5		40	South Carolina	85.5
38	South Dakota	85.9		41	Alaska	82.6
24	Tennessee	94.6		42	Idaho	78.9
9	Texas	98.2		43	Maine	78.8
20	Utah	96.8		44	West Virginia	69.7
NA	Vermont**	NA		NA	Illinois**	NA
28	Virginia	93.8		NA	Kansas**	NA
16	Washington	97.1		NA	Kentucky**	NA
44	West Virginia	69.7		NA	Montana**	NA
30	Wisconsin	93.3		NA	New Hampshire**	NA
36	Wyoming	87.0		NA	Vermont**	NA

District of Columbia		100.0

Source: Morgan Quitno Press using data from Federal Bureau of Investigation
   "Crime in the United States 1997" (Uniform Crime Reports, November 22, 1998)
*Estimated percentages for urban areas, defined by the F.B.I. as Metropolitan Statistical Areas and other cities outside such areas. National percent includes those states listed as not available. Motor vehicle theft includes the theft or attempted theft of a self-propelled vehicle. Excludes motorboats, construction equipment, airplanes and farming equipment. **Not available.*

Motor Vehicle Thefts in Rural Areas in 1997

National Rural Total = 41,692 Motor Vehicle Thefts*

<table>
<tr><td colspan="4">ALPHA ORDER</td><td colspan="4">RANK ORDER</td></tr>
<tr><td>RANK</td><td>STATE</td><td>THEFTS</td><td>% of USA</td><td>RANK</td><td>STATE</td><td>THEFTS</td><td>% of USA</td></tr>
<tr><td>23</td><td>Alabama</td><td>800</td><td>1.9%</td><td>1</td><td>Georgia</td><td>2,913</td><td>7.0%</td></tr>
<tr><td>28</td><td>Alaska</td><td>485</td><td>1.2%</td><td>2</td><td>North Carolina</td><td>2,707</td><td>6.5%</td></tr>
<tr><td>29</td><td>Arizona</td><td>448</td><td>1.1%</td><td>3</td><td>South Carolina</td><td>2,288</td><td>5.5%</td></tr>
<tr><td>18</td><td>Arkansas</td><td>981</td><td>2.4%</td><td>4</td><td>Florida</td><td>1,887</td><td>4.5%</td></tr>
<tr><td>7</td><td>California</td><td>1,617</td><td>3.9%</td><td>5</td><td>Tennessee</td><td>1,821</td><td>4.4%</td></tr>
<tr><td>36</td><td>Colorado</td><td>283</td><td>0.7%</td><td>6</td><td>Texas</td><td>1,795</td><td>4.3%</td></tr>
<tr><td>37</td><td>Connecticut</td><td>247</td><td>0.6%</td><td>7</td><td>California</td><td>1,617</td><td>3.9%</td></tr>
<tr><td>40</td><td>Delaware</td><td>115</td><td>0.3%</td><td>8</td><td>Michigan</td><td>1,397</td><td>3.4%</td></tr>
<tr><td>4</td><td>Florida</td><td>1,887</td><td>4.5%</td><td>9</td><td>Minnesota</td><td>1,345</td><td>3.2%</td></tr>
<tr><td>1</td><td>Georgia</td><td>2,913</td><td>7.0%</td><td>10</td><td>Indiana</td><td>1,312</td><td>3.1%</td></tr>
<tr><td>21</td><td>Hawaii</td><td>879</td><td>2.1%</td><td>11</td><td>Pennsylvania</td><td>1,311</td><td>3.1%</td></tr>
<tr><td>27</td><td>Idaho</td><td>512</td><td>1.2%</td><td>12</td><td>Mississippi</td><td>1,201</td><td>2.9%</td></tr>
<tr><td>NA</td><td>Illinois**</td><td>NA</td><td>NA</td><td>13</td><td>Virginia</td><td>1,180</td><td>2.8%</td></tr>
<tr><td>10</td><td>Indiana</td><td>1,312</td><td>3.1%</td><td>14</td><td>Ohio</td><td>1,132</td><td>2.7%</td></tr>
<tr><td>24</td><td>Iowa</td><td>679</td><td>1.6%</td><td>15</td><td>Oregon</td><td>1,081</td><td>2.6%</td></tr>
<tr><td>NA</td><td>Kansas**</td><td>NA</td><td>NA</td><td>16</td><td>Wisconsin</td><td>1,046</td><td>2.5%</td></tr>
<tr><td>NA</td><td>Kentucky**</td><td>NA</td><td>NA</td><td>17</td><td>West Virginia</td><td>995</td><td>2.4%</td></tr>
<tr><td>25</td><td>Louisiana</td><td>659</td><td>1.6%</td><td>18</td><td>Arkansas</td><td>981</td><td>2.4%</td></tr>
<tr><td>31</td><td>Maine</td><td>348</td><td>0.8%</td><td>19</td><td>Washington</td><td>924</td><td>2.2%</td></tr>
<tr><td>34</td><td>Maryland</td><td>303</td><td>0.7%</td><td>20</td><td>Missouri</td><td>880</td><td>2.1%</td></tr>
<tr><td>42</td><td>Massachusetts</td><td>6</td><td>0.0%</td><td>21</td><td>Hawaii</td><td>879</td><td>2.1%</td></tr>
<tr><td>8</td><td>Michigan</td><td>1,397</td><td>3.4%</td><td>22</td><td>Oklahoma</td><td>833</td><td>2.0%</td></tr>
<tr><td>9</td><td>Minnesota</td><td>1,345</td><td>3.2%</td><td>23</td><td>Alabama</td><td>800</td><td>1.9%</td></tr>
<tr><td>12</td><td>Mississippi</td><td>1,201</td><td>2.9%</td><td>24</td><td>Iowa</td><td>679</td><td>1.6%</td></tr>
<tr><td>20</td><td>Missouri</td><td>880</td><td>2.1%</td><td>25</td><td>Louisiana</td><td>659</td><td>1.6%</td></tr>
<tr><td>NA</td><td>Montana**</td><td>NA</td><td>NA</td><td>26</td><td>New York</td><td>566</td><td>1.4%</td></tr>
<tr><td>32</td><td>Nebraska</td><td>328</td><td>0.8%</td><td>27</td><td>Idaho</td><td>512</td><td>1.2%</td></tr>
<tr><td>33</td><td>Nevada</td><td>313</td><td>0.8%</td><td>28</td><td>Alaska</td><td>485</td><td>1.2%</td></tr>
<tr><td>NA</td><td>New Hampshire**</td><td>NA</td><td>NA</td><td>29</td><td>Arizona</td><td>448</td><td>1.1%</td></tr>
<tr><td>44</td><td>New Jersey</td><td>0</td><td>0.0%</td><td>30</td><td>New Mexico</td><td>389</td><td>0.9%</td></tr>
<tr><td>30</td><td>New Mexico</td><td>389</td><td>0.9%</td><td>31</td><td>Maine</td><td>348</td><td>0.8%</td></tr>
<tr><td>26</td><td>New York</td><td>566</td><td>1.4%</td><td>32</td><td>Nebraska</td><td>328</td><td>0.8%</td></tr>
<tr><td>2</td><td>North Carolina</td><td>2,707</td><td>6.5%</td><td>33</td><td>Nevada</td><td>313</td><td>0.8%</td></tr>
<tr><td>38</td><td>North Dakota</td><td>164</td><td>0.4%</td><td>34</td><td>Maryland</td><td>303</td><td>0.7%</td></tr>
<tr><td>14</td><td>Ohio</td><td>1,132</td><td>2.7%</td><td>35</td><td>Utah</td><td>296</td><td>0.7%</td></tr>
<tr><td>22</td><td>Oklahoma</td><td>833</td><td>2.0%</td><td>36</td><td>Colorado</td><td>283</td><td>0.7%</td></tr>
<tr><td>15</td><td>Oregon</td><td>1,081</td><td>2.6%</td><td>37</td><td>Connecticut</td><td>247</td><td>0.6%</td></tr>
<tr><td>11</td><td>Pennsylvania</td><td>1,311</td><td>3.1%</td><td>38</td><td>North Dakota</td><td>164</td><td>0.4%</td></tr>
<tr><td>43</td><td>Rhode Island</td><td>1</td><td>0.0%</td><td>39</td><td>South Dakota</td><td>121</td><td>0.3%</td></tr>
<tr><td>3</td><td>South Carolina</td><td>2,288</td><td>5.5%</td><td>40</td><td>Delaware</td><td>115</td><td>0.3%</td></tr>
<tr><td>39</td><td>South Dakota</td><td>121</td><td>0.3%</td><td>41</td><td>Wyoming</td><td>84</td><td>0.2%</td></tr>
<tr><td>5</td><td>Tennessee</td><td>1,821</td><td>4.4%</td><td>42</td><td>Massachusetts</td><td>6</td><td>0.0%</td></tr>
<tr><td>6</td><td>Texas</td><td>1,795</td><td>4.3%</td><td>43</td><td>Rhode Island</td><td>1</td><td>0.0%</td></tr>
<tr><td>35</td><td>Utah</td><td>296</td><td>0.7%</td><td>44</td><td>New Jersey</td><td>0</td><td>0.0%</td></tr>
<tr><td>NA</td><td>Vermont**</td><td>NA</td><td>NA</td><td>NA</td><td>Illinois**</td><td>NA</td><td>NA</td></tr>
<tr><td>13</td><td>Virginia</td><td>1,180</td><td>2.8%</td><td>NA</td><td>Kansas**</td><td>NA</td><td>NA</td></tr>
<tr><td>19</td><td>Washington</td><td>924</td><td>2.2%</td><td>NA</td><td>Kentucky**</td><td>NA</td><td>NA</td></tr>
<tr><td>17</td><td>West Virginia</td><td>995</td><td>2.4%</td><td>NA</td><td>Montana**</td><td>NA</td><td>NA</td></tr>
<tr><td>16</td><td>Wisconsin</td><td>1,046</td><td>2.5%</td><td>NA</td><td>New Hampshire**</td><td>NA</td><td>NA</td></tr>
<tr><td>41</td><td>Wyoming</td><td>84</td><td>0.2%</td><td>NA</td><td>Vermont**</td><td>NA</td><td>NA</td></tr>
<tr><td></td><td></td><td></td><td></td><td></td><td>District of Columbia</td><td>0</td><td>0.0%</td></tr>
</table>

Source: Federal Bureau of Investigation
   "Crime in the United States 1997" (Uniform Crime Reports, November 22, 1998)
*Estimated totals for rural areas, defined by the F.B.I. as other than Metropolitan Statistical Areas and other cities outside such areas. National total includes those states listed as not available. Motor vehicle theft includes the theft or attempted theft of a self-propelled vehicle. Excludes motorboats, construction equipment, airplanes and farming equipment. **Not available.

Rural Motor Vehicle Theft Rate in 1997

National Rural Rate = 129.4 Motor Vehicle Thefts per 100,000 Population*

ALPHA ORDER

RANK	STATE	RATE
30	Alabama	100.9
4	Alaska	253.0
19	Arizona	127.4
24	Arkansas	120.6
3	California	255.1
33	Colorado	86.1
14	Connecticut	133.8
23	Delaware	122.4
5	Florida	237.0
7	Georgia	197.7
1	Hawaii	286.6
20	Idaho	127.1
NA	Illinois**	NA
22	Indiana	123.8
36	Iowa	76.7
NA	Kansas**	NA
NA	Kentucky**	NA
32	Louisiana	96.3
31	Maine	98.8
25	Maryland	113.1
41	Massachusetts	60.9
17	Michigan	129.9
12	Minnesota	152.8
28	Mississippi	107.5
38	Missouri	72.3
NA	Montana**	NA
35	Nebraska	78.0
10	Nevada	160.4
NA	New Hampshire**	NA
43	New Jersey	0.0
16	New Mexico	131.2
40	New York	66.4
11	North Carolina	157.8
37	North Dakota	73.9
34	Ohio	85.0
15	Oklahoma	131.7
6	Oregon	207.6
21	Pennsylvania	124.4
43	Rhode Island	0.0
2	South Carolina	285.5
42	South Dakota	41.6
9	Tennessee	166.6
27	Texas	108.6
13	Utah	134.4
NA	Vermont**	NA
26	Virginia	109.8
8	Washington	179.8
18	West Virginia	127.8
29	Wisconsin	106.4
39	Wyoming	67.1

RANK ORDER

RANK	STATE	RATE
1	Hawaii	286.6
2	South Carolina	285.5
3	California	255.1
4	Alaska	253.0
5	Florida	237.0
6	Oregon	207.6
7	Georgia	197.7
8	Washington	179.8
9	Tennessee	166.6
10	Nevada	160.4
11	North Carolina	157.8
12	Minnesota	152.8
13	Utah	134.4
14	Connecticut	133.8
15	Oklahoma	131.7
16	New Mexico	131.2
17	Michigan	129.9
18	West Virginia	127.8
19	Arizona	127.4
20	Idaho	127.1
21	Pennsylvania	124.4
22	Indiana	123.8
23	Delaware	122.4
24	Arkansas	120.6
25	Maryland	113.1
26	Virginia	109.8
27	Texas	108.6
28	Mississippi	107.5
29	Wisconsin	106.4
30	Alabama	100.9
31	Maine	98.8
32	Louisiana	96.3
33	Colorado	86.1
34	Ohio	85.0
35	Nebraska	78.0
36	Iowa	76.7
37	North Dakota	73.9
38	Missouri	72.3
39	Wyoming	67.1
40	New York	66.4
41	Massachusetts	60.9
42	South Dakota	41.6
43	New Jersey	0.0
43	Rhode Island	0.0
NA	Illinois**	NA
NA	Kansas**	NA
NA	Kentucky**	NA
NA	Montana**	NA
NA	New Hampshire**	NA
NA	Vermont**	NA
	District of Columbia	0.0

Source: Morgan Quitno Press using data from Federal Bureau of Investigation
"Crime in the United States 1997" (Uniform Crime Reports, November 22, 1998)
*Estimated rates for rural areas, defined by the F.B.I. as other than Metropolitan Statistical Areas and other cities outside such areas. National rate includes those states listed as not available. Motor vehicle theft includes the theft or attempted theft of a self-propelled vehicle. Excludes motorboats, construction equipment, airplanes and farming equipment. **Not available.

Percent of Motor Vehicle Thefts Occurring in Rural Areas in 1997

National Percent = 3.1% of Motor Vehicle Thefts*

ALPHA ORDER

RANK	STATE	PERCENT
22	Alabama	5.2
4	Alaska	17.4
38	Arizona	1.0
11	Arkansas	12.4
40	California	0.7
34	Colorado	1.8
37	Connecticut	1.7
26	Delaware	3.1
34	Florida	1.8
16	Georgia	6.5
8	Hawaii	13.6
3	Idaho	21.1
NA	Illinois**	NA
22	Indiana	5.2
13	Iowa	10.2
NA	Kansas**	NA
NA	Kentucky**	NA
30	Louisiana	2.5
2	Maine	21.2
38	Maryland	1.0
42	Massachusetts	0.0
33	Michigan	2.1
14	Minnesota	7.5
10	Mississippi	12.9
24	Missouri	3.3
NA	Montana**	NA
18	Nebraska	5.9
32	Nevada	2.4
NA	New Hampshire**	NA
42	New Jersey	0.0
26	New Mexico	3.1
40	New York	0.7
12	North Carolina	11.1
6	North Dakota	14.2
30	Ohio	2.5
19	Oklahoma	5.7
20	Oregon	5.6
28	Pennsylvania	3.0
42	Rhode Island	0.0
5	South Carolina	14.5
7	South Dakota	14.1
21	Tennessee	5.4
34	Texas	1.8
25	Utah	3.2
NA	Vermont**	NA
17	Virginia	6.2
29	Washington	2.9
1	West Virginia	30.3
15	Wisconsin	6.7
9	Wyoming	13.0

RANK ORDER

RANK	STATE	PERCENT
1	West Virginia	30.3
2	Maine	21.2
3	Idaho	21.1
4	Alaska	17.4
5	South Carolina	14.5
6	North Dakota	14.2
7	South Dakota	14.1
8	Hawaii	13.6
9	Wyoming	13.0
10	Mississippi	12.9
11	Arkansas	12.4
12	North Carolina	11.1
13	Iowa	10.2
14	Minnesota	7.5
15	Wisconsin	6.7
16	Georgia	6.5
17	Virginia	6.2
18	Nebraska	5.9
19	Oklahoma	5.7
20	Oregon	5.6
21	Tennessee	5.4
22	Alabama	5.2
22	Indiana	5.2
24	Missouri	3.3
25	Utah	3.2
26	Delaware	3.1
26	New Mexico	3.1
28	Pennsylvania	3.0
29	Washington	2.9
30	Louisiana	2.5
30	Ohio	2.5
32	Nevada	2.4
33	Michigan	2.1
34	Colorado	1.8
34	Florida	1.8
34	Texas	1.8
37	Connecticut	1.7
38	Arizona	1.0
38	Maryland	1.0
40	California	0.7
40	New York	0.7
42	Massachusetts	0.0
42	New Jersey	0.0
42	Rhode Island	0.0
NA	Illinois**	NA
NA	Kansas**	NA
NA	Kentucky**	NA
NA	Montana**	NA
NA	New Hampshire**	NA
NA	Vermont**	NA

District of Columbia   0.0

Source: Morgan Quitno Press using data from Federal Bureau of Investigation
  "Crime in the United States 1997" (Uniform Crime Reports, November 22, 1998)
*Estimated percentages for rural areas, defined by the F.B.I. as other than Metropolitan Statistical Areas and other cities outside such areas. National percent includes those states listed as not available. Motor vehicle theft includes the theft or attempted theft of a self-propelled vehicle. Excludes motorboats, construction equipment, airplanes and farming equipment. **Not available.

Crimes Reported at Universities and Colleges in 1997

National Total = 104,036 Reported Crimes*

ALPHA ORDER

RANK	STATE	CRIMES	% of USA
22	Alabama	1,526	1.5%
39	Alaska	308	0.3%
11	Arizona	3,491	3.4%
29	Arkansas	1,119	1.1%
1	California	14,263	13.7%
23	Colorado	1,459	1.4%
21	Connecticut	1,561	1.5%
35	Delaware	632	0.6%
7	Florida	4,296	4.1%
6	Georgia	4,676	4.5%
NA	Hawaii**	NA	NA
NA	Idaho**	NA	NA
NA	Illinois**	NA	NA
12	Indiana	3,214	3.1%
32	Iowa	679	0.7%
NA	Kansas**	NA	NA
NA	Kentucky**	NA	NA
15	Louisiana	2,828	2.7%
38	Maine	358	0.3%
14	Maryland	3,136	3.0%
9	Massachusetts	4,078	3.9%
8	Michigan	4,225	4.1%
27	Minnesota	1,265	1.2%
28	Mississippi	1,168	1.1%
26	Missouri	1,273	1.2%
NA	Montana**	NA	NA
31	Nebraska	766	0.7%
36	Nevada	630	0.6%
NA	New Hampshire**	NA	NA
13	New Jersey	3,155	3.0%
20	New Mexico	1,572	1.5%
3	New York	5,602	5.4%
4	North Carolina	4,996	4.8%
37	North Dakota	392	0.4%
5	Ohio	4,932	4.7%
24	Oklahoma	1,406	1.4%
NA	Oregon**	NA	NA
25	Pennsylvania	1,383	1.3%
34	Rhode Island	636	0.6%
16	South Carolina	2,209	2.1%
NA	South Dakota**	NA	NA
30	Tennessee	868	0.8%
2	Texas	9,225	8.9%
19	Utah	1,860	1.8%
NA	Vermont**	NA	NA
10	Virginia	4,048	3.9%
18	Washington	1,952	1.9%
33	West Virginia	645	0.6%
17	Wisconsin	2,012	1.9%
40	Wyoming	192	0.2%

RANK ORDER

RANK	STATE	CRIMES	% of USA
1	California	14,263	13.7%
2	Texas	9,225	8.9%
3	New York	5,602	5.4%
4	North Carolina	4,996	4.8%
5	Ohio	4,932	4.7%
6	Georgia	4,676	4.5%
7	Florida	4,296	4.1%
8	Michigan	4,225	4.1%
9	Massachusetts	4,078	3.9%
10	Virginia	4,048	3.9%
11	Arizona	3,491	3.4%
12	Indiana	3,214	3.1%
13	New Jersey	3,155	3.0%
14	Maryland	3,136	3.0%
15	Louisiana	2,828	2.7%
16	South Carolina	2,209	2.1%
17	Wisconsin	2,012	1.9%
18	Washington	1,952	1.9%
19	Utah	1,860	1.8%
20	New Mexico	1,572	1.5%
21	Connecticut	1,561	1.5%
22	Alabama	1,526	1.5%
23	Colorado	1,459	1.4%
24	Oklahoma	1,406	1.4%
25	Pennsylvania	1,383	1.3%
26	Missouri	1,273	1.2%
27	Minnesota	1,265	1.2%
28	Mississippi	1,168	1.1%
29	Arkansas	1,119	1.1%
30	Tennessee	868	0.8%
31	Nebraska	766	0.7%
32	Iowa	679	0.7%
33	West Virginia	645	0.6%
34	Rhode Island	636	0.6%
35	Delaware	632	0.6%
36	Nevada	630	0.6%
37	North Dakota	392	0.4%
38	Maine	358	0.3%
39	Alaska	308	0.3%
40	Wyoming	192	0.2%
NA	Hawaii**	NA	NA
NA	Idaho**	NA	NA
NA	Illinois**	NA	NA
NA	Kansas**	NA	NA
NA	Kentucky**	NA	NA
NA	Montana**	NA	NA
NA	New Hampshire**	NA	NA
NA	Oregon**	NA	NA
NA	South Dakota**	NA	NA
NA	Vermont**	NA	NA
	District of Columbia**	NA	NA

Source: Morgan Quitno Press using data from Federal Bureau of Investigation
"Crime in the United States 1997" (Uniform Crime Reports, November 22, 1998)
*Includes murder, rape, robbery, aggravated assault, burglary, larceny-theft and motor vehicle theft. Total is only for states shown separately. Many states had incomplete reports.
**Not available.

Crimes Reported at Universities and Colleges as a Percent of All Crimes in 1997

National Percent = 0.79% of Crimes*

ALPHA ORDER			RANK ORDER		
RANK	STATE	PERCENT	RANK	STATE	PERCENT
32	Alabama	0.72	1	North Dakota	2.26
20	Alaska	0.96	2	Massachusetts	1.81
15	Arizona	1.07	3	Rhode Island	1.76
23	Arkansas	0.94	4	Delaware	1.68
26	California	0.91	5	Virginia	1.55
29	Colorado	0.81	6	Utah	1.51
11	Connecticut	1.20	7	West Virginia	1.44
4	Delaware	1.68	8	New Mexico	1.32
38	Florida	0.40	9	Indiana	1.23
13	Georgia	1.08	9	North Carolina	1.23
NA	Hawaii**	NA	11	Connecticut	1.20
NA	Idaho**	NA	12	Maryland	1.09
NA	Illinois**	NA	13	Georgia	1.08
9	Indiana	1.23	13	Nebraska	1.08
33	Iowa	0.62	15	Arizona	1.07
NA	Kansas**	NA	16	Wisconsin	1.06
NA	Kentucky**	NA	17	Louisiana	1.01
17	Louisiana	1.01	18	Ohio	0.98
24	Maine	0.92	19	New Jersey	0.97
12	Maryland	1.09	20	Alaska	0.96
2	Massachusetts	1.81	20	South Carolina	0.96
27	Michigan	0.88	20	Wyoming	0.96
35	Minnesota	0.61	23	Arkansas	0.94
24	Mississippi	0.92	24	Maine	0.92
37	Missouri	0.49	24	Mississippi	0.92
NA	Montana**	NA	26	California	0.91
13	Nebraska	1.08	27	Michigan	0.88
33	Nevada	0.62	28	Texas	0.87
NA	New Hampshire**	NA	29	Colorado	0.81
19	New Jersey	0.97	30	New York	0.79
8	New Mexico	1.32	31	Oklahoma	0.77
30	New York	0.79	32	Alabama	0.72
9	North Carolina	1.23	33	Iowa	0.62
1	North Dakota	2.26	33	Nevada	0.62
18	Ohio	0.98	35	Minnesota	0.61
31	Oklahoma	0.77	36	Washington	0.59
NA	Oregon**	NA	37	Missouri	0.49
39	Pennsylvania	0.34	38	Florida	0.40
3	Rhode Island	1.76	39	Pennsylvania	0.34
20	South Carolina	0.96	40	Tennessee	0.29
NA	South Dakota**	NA	NA	Hawaii**	NA
40	Tennessee	0.29	NA	Idaho**	NA
28	Texas	0.87	NA	Illinois**	NA
6	Utah	1.51	NA	Kansas**	NA
NA	Vermont**	NA	NA	Kentucky**	NA
5	Virginia	1.55	NA	Montana**	NA
36	Washington	0.59	NA	New Hampshire**	NA
7	West Virginia	1.44	NA	Oregon**	NA
16	Wisconsin	1.06	NA	South Dakota**	NA
20	Wyoming	0.96	NA	Vermont**	NA
				District of Columbia**	NA

Source: Morgan Quitno Press using data from Federal Bureau of Investigation
   "Crime in the United States 1997" (Uniform Crime Reports, November 22, 1998)
*Includes murder, rape, robbery, aggravated assault, burglary, larceny-theft and motor vehicle theft. National percent is only for states shown separately. Many states had incomplete reports.
**Not available.

Violent Crimes Reported at Universities and Colleges in 1997

National Total = 2,511 Reported Violent Crimes*

<table>
<tr><td colspan="4">ALPHA ORDER</td><td colspan="4">RANK ORDER</td></tr>
<tr><td>RANK</td><td>STATE</td><td>CRIMES</td><td>% of USA</td><td>RANK</td><td>STATE</td><td>CRIMES</td><td>% of USA</td></tr>
<tr><td>18</td><td>Alabama</td><td>40</td><td>1.6%</td><td>1</td><td>California</td><td>391</td><td>15.6%</td></tr>
<tr><td>25</td><td>Alaska</td><td>29</td><td>1.2%</td><td>2</td><td>Texas</td><td>173</td><td>6.9%</td></tr>
<tr><td>14</td><td>Arizona</td><td>60</td><td>2.4%</td><td>3</td><td>North Carolina</td><td>161</td><td>6.4%</td></tr>
<tr><td>17</td><td>Arkansas</td><td>51</td><td>2.0%</td><td>4</td><td>Florida</td><td>129</td><td>5.1%</td></tr>
<tr><td>1</td><td>California</td><td>391</td><td>15.6%</td><td>5</td><td>Georgia</td><td>117</td><td>4.7%</td></tr>
<tr><td>29</td><td>Colorado</td><td>23</td><td>0.9%</td><td>5</td><td>Virginia</td><td>117</td><td>4.7%</td></tr>
<tr><td>26</td><td>Connecticut</td><td>26</td><td>1.0%</td><td>7</td><td>Maryland</td><td>114</td><td>4.5%</td></tr>
<tr><td>34</td><td>Delaware</td><td>13</td><td>0.5%</td><td>8</td><td>Louisiana</td><td>113</td><td>4.5%</td></tr>
<tr><td>4</td><td>Florida</td><td>129</td><td>5.1%</td><td>9</td><td>Massachusetts</td><td>110</td><td>4.4%</td></tr>
<tr><td>5</td><td>Georgia</td><td>117</td><td>4.7%</td><td>10</td><td>New York</td><td>94</td><td>3.7%</td></tr>
<tr><td>NA</td><td>Hawaii**</td><td>NA</td><td>NA</td><td>11</td><td>New Jersey</td><td>93</td><td>3.7%</td></tr>
<tr><td>NA</td><td>Idaho**</td><td>NA</td><td>NA</td><td>12</td><td>Ohio</td><td>91</td><td>3.6%</td></tr>
<tr><td>NA</td><td>Illinois**</td><td>NA</td><td>NA</td><td>13</td><td>Michigan</td><td>83</td><td>3.3%</td></tr>
<tr><td>16</td><td>Indiana</td><td>56</td><td>2.2%</td><td>14</td><td>Arizona</td><td>60</td><td>2.4%</td></tr>
<tr><td>36</td><td>Iowa</td><td>9</td><td>0.4%</td><td>15</td><td>South Carolina</td><td>58</td><td>2.3%</td></tr>
<tr><td>NA</td><td>Kansas**</td><td>NA</td><td>NA</td><td>16</td><td>Indiana</td><td>56</td><td>2.2%</td></tr>
<tr><td>NA</td><td>Kentucky**</td><td>NA</td><td>NA</td><td>17</td><td>Arkansas</td><td>51</td><td>2.0%</td></tr>
<tr><td>8</td><td>Louisiana</td><td>113</td><td>4.5%</td><td>18</td><td>Alabama</td><td>40</td><td>1.6%</td></tr>
<tr><td>40</td><td>Maine</td><td>2</td><td>0.1%</td><td>18</td><td>New Mexico</td><td>40</td><td>1.6%</td></tr>
<tr><td>7</td><td>Maryland</td><td>114</td><td>4.5%</td><td>20</td><td>Oklahoma</td><td>37</td><td>1.5%</td></tr>
<tr><td>9</td><td>Massachusetts</td><td>110</td><td>4.4%</td><td>21</td><td>Mississippi</td><td>36</td><td>1.4%</td></tr>
<tr><td>13</td><td>Michigan</td><td>83</td><td>3.3%</td><td>22</td><td>Pennsylvania</td><td>32</td><td>1.3%</td></tr>
<tr><td>28</td><td>Minnesota</td><td>24</td><td>1.0%</td><td>22</td><td>Utah</td><td>32</td><td>1.3%</td></tr>
<tr><td>21</td><td>Mississippi</td><td>36</td><td>1.4%</td><td>22</td><td>Wisconsin</td><td>32</td><td>1.3%</td></tr>
<tr><td>30</td><td>Missouri</td><td>21</td><td>0.8%</td><td>25</td><td>Alaska</td><td>29</td><td>1.2%</td></tr>
<tr><td>NA</td><td>Montana**</td><td>NA</td><td>NA</td><td>26</td><td>Connecticut</td><td>26</td><td>1.0%</td></tr>
<tr><td>37</td><td>Nebraska</td><td>7</td><td>0.3%</td><td>26</td><td>Washington</td><td>26</td><td>1.0%</td></tr>
<tr><td>32</td><td>Nevada</td><td>17</td><td>0.7%</td><td>28</td><td>Minnesota</td><td>24</td><td>1.0%</td></tr>
<tr><td>NA</td><td>New Hampshire**</td><td>NA</td><td>NA</td><td>29</td><td>Colorado</td><td>23</td><td>0.9%</td></tr>
<tr><td>11</td><td>New Jersey</td><td>93</td><td>3.7%</td><td>30</td><td>Missouri</td><td>21</td><td>0.8%</td></tr>
<tr><td>18</td><td>New Mexico</td><td>40</td><td>1.6%</td><td>31</td><td>Tennessee</td><td>19</td><td>0.8%</td></tr>
<tr><td>10</td><td>New York</td><td>94</td><td>3.7%</td><td>32</td><td>Nevada</td><td>17</td><td>0.7%</td></tr>
<tr><td>3</td><td>North Carolina</td><td>161</td><td>6.4%</td><td>33</td><td>West Virginia</td><td>16</td><td>0.6%</td></tr>
<tr><td>38</td><td>North Dakota</td><td>5</td><td>0.2%</td><td>34</td><td>Delaware</td><td>13</td><td>0.5%</td></tr>
<tr><td>12</td><td>Ohio</td><td>91</td><td>3.6%</td><td>35</td><td>Rhode Island</td><td>11</td><td>0.4%</td></tr>
<tr><td>20</td><td>Oklahoma</td><td>37</td><td>1.5%</td><td>36</td><td>Iowa</td><td>9</td><td>0.4%</td></tr>
<tr><td>NA</td><td>Oregon**</td><td>NA</td><td>NA</td><td>37</td><td>Nebraska</td><td>7</td><td>0.3%</td></tr>
<tr><td>22</td><td>Pennsylvania</td><td>32</td><td>1.3%</td><td>38</td><td>North Dakota</td><td>5</td><td>0.2%</td></tr>
<tr><td>35</td><td>Rhode Island</td><td>11</td><td>0.4%</td><td>39</td><td>Wyoming</td><td>3</td><td>0.1%</td></tr>
<tr><td>15</td><td>South Carolina</td><td>58</td><td>2.3%</td><td>40</td><td>Maine</td><td>2</td><td>0.1%</td></tr>
<tr><td>NA</td><td>South Dakota**</td><td>NA</td><td>NA</td><td>NA</td><td>Hawaii**</td><td>NA</td><td>NA</td></tr>
<tr><td>31</td><td>Tennessee</td><td>19</td><td>0.8%</td><td>NA</td><td>Idaho**</td><td>NA</td><td>NA</td></tr>
<tr><td>2</td><td>Texas</td><td>173</td><td>6.9%</td><td>NA</td><td>Illinois**</td><td>NA</td><td>NA</td></tr>
<tr><td>22</td><td>Utah</td><td>32</td><td>1.3%</td><td>NA</td><td>Kansas**</td><td>NA</td><td>NA</td></tr>
<tr><td>NA</td><td>Vermont**</td><td>NA</td><td>NA</td><td>NA</td><td>Kentucky**</td><td>NA</td><td>NA</td></tr>
<tr><td>5</td><td>Virginia</td><td>117</td><td>4.7%</td><td>NA</td><td>Montana**</td><td>NA</td><td>NA</td></tr>
<tr><td>26</td><td>Washington</td><td>26</td><td>1.0%</td><td>NA</td><td>New Hampshire**</td><td>NA</td><td>NA</td></tr>
<tr><td>33</td><td>West Virginia</td><td>16</td><td>0.6%</td><td>NA</td><td>Oregon**</td><td>NA</td><td>NA</td></tr>
<tr><td>22</td><td>Wisconsin</td><td>32</td><td>1.3%</td><td>NA</td><td>South Dakota**</td><td>NA</td><td>NA</td></tr>
<tr><td>39</td><td>Wyoming</td><td>3</td><td>0.1%</td><td>NA</td><td>Vermont**</td><td>NA</td><td>NA</td></tr>
<tr><td></td><td></td><td></td><td></td><td></td><td>District of Columbia**</td><td>NA</td><td>NA</td></tr>
</table>

Source: Morgan Quitno Press using data from Federal Bureau of Investigation
"Crime in the United States 1997" (Uniform Crime Reports, November 22, 1998)
*Includes murder, rape, robbery and aggravated assault. Total is only for states shown separately. Many states had incomplete reports.
**Not available.

Violent Crimes Reported at Universities and Colleges
As a Percent of All Violent Crimes in 1997
National Percent = 0.15% of Violent Crimes*

ALPHA ORDER

RANK	STATE	PERCENT
24	Alabama	0.16
2	Alaska	0.68
19	Arizona	0.21
6	Arkansas	0.38
27	California	0.15
24	Colorado	0.16
20	Connecticut	0.20
13	Delaware	0.26
36	Florida	0.09
13	Georgia	0.26
NA	Hawaii**	NA
NA	Idaho**	NA
NA	Illinois**	NA
22	Indiana	0.19
34	Iowa	0.10
NA	Kansas**	NA
NA	Kentucky**	NA
9	Louisiana	0.30
31	Maine	0.13
13	Maryland	0.26
10	Massachusetts	0.28
30	Michigan	0.14
27	Minnesota	0.15
10	Mississippi	0.28
38	Missouri	0.07
NA	Montana**	NA
34	Nebraska	0.10
31	Nevada	0.13
NA	New Hampshire**	NA
17	New Jersey	0.23
12	New Mexico	0.27
37	New York	0.08
7	North Carolina	0.36
1	North Dakota	0.89
22	Ohio	0.19
20	Oklahoma	0.20
NA	Oregon**	NA
39	Pennsylvania	0.06
8	Rhode Island	0.33
24	South Carolina	0.16
NA	South Dakota**	NA
40	Tennessee	0.04
27	Texas	0.15
4	Utah	0.47
NA	Vermont**	NA
3	Virginia	0.50
33	Washington	0.11
5	West Virginia	0.40
17	Wisconsin	0.23
16	Wyoming	0.24

RANK ORDER

RANK	STATE	PERCENT
1	North Dakota	0.89
2	Alaska	0.68
3	Virginia	0.50
4	Utah	0.47
5	West Virginia	0.40
6	Arkansas	0.38
7	North Carolina	0.36
8	Rhode Island	0.33
9	Louisiana	0.30
10	Massachusetts	0.28
10	Mississippi	0.28
12	New Mexico	0.27
13	Delaware	0.26
13	Georgia	0.26
13	Maryland	0.26
16	Wyoming	0.24
17	New Jersey	0.23
17	Wisconsin	0.23
19	Arizona	0.21
20	Connecticut	0.20
20	Oklahoma	0.20
22	Indiana	0.19
22	Ohio	0.19
24	Alabama	0.16
24	Colorado	0.16
24	South Carolina	0.16
27	California	0.15
27	Minnesota	0.15
27	Texas	0.15
30	Michigan	0.14
31	Maine	0.13
31	Nevada	0.13
33	Washington	0.11
34	Iowa	0.10
34	Nebraska	0.10
36	Florida	0.09
37	New York	0.08
38	Missouri	0.07
39	Pennsylvania	0.06
40	Tennessee	0.04
NA	Hawaii**	NA
NA	Idaho**	NA
NA	Illinois**	NA
NA	Kansas**	NA
NA	Kentucky**	NA
NA	Montana**	NA
NA	New Hampshire**	NA
NA	Oregon**	NA
NA	South Dakota**	NA
NA	Vermont**	NA
	District of Columbia**	NA

Source: Morgan Quitno Press using data from Federal Bureau of Investigation
   "Crime in the United States 1997" (Uniform Crime Reports, November 22, 1998)
*Includes murder, rape, robbery and aggravated assault. Total is only for states shown separately. Many states had incomplete reports.
**Not available.

Property Crimes Reported at Universities and Colleges in 1997

National Total = 101,525 Reported Property Crimes*

ALPHA ORDER

RANK	STATE	CRIMES	% of USA
22	Alabama	1,486	1.5%
39	Alaska	279	0.3%
11	Arizona	3,431	3.4%
29	Arkansas	1,068	1.1%
1	California	13,872	13.7%
23	Colorado	1,436	1.4%
20	Connecticut	1,535	1.5%
35	Delaware	619	0.6%
7	Florida	4,167	4.1%
6	Georgia	4,559	4.5%
NA	Hawaii**	NA	NA
NA	Idaho**	NA	NA
NA	Illinois**	NA	NA
12	Indiana	3,158	3.1%
32	Iowa	670	0.7%
NA	Kansas**	NA	NA
NA	Kentucky**	NA	NA
15	Louisiana	2,715	2.7%
38	Maine	356	0.4%
14	Maryland	3,022	3.0%
9	Massachusetts	3,968	3.9%
8	Michigan	4,142	4.1%
27	Minnesota	1,241	1.2%
28	Mississippi	1,132	1.1%
26	Missouri	1,252	1.2%
NA	Montana**	NA	NA
31	Nebraska	759	0.7%
36	Nevada	613	0.6%
NA	New Hampshire**	NA	NA
13	New Jersey	3,062	3.0%
21	New Mexico	1,532	1.5%
3	New York	5,508	5.4%
5	North Carolina	4,835	4.8%
37	North Dakota	387	0.4%
4	Ohio	4,841	4.8%
24	Oklahoma	1,369	1.3%
NA	Oregon**	NA	NA
25	Pennsylvania	1,351	1.3%
34	Rhode Island	625	0.6%
16	South Carolina	2,151	2.1%
NA	South Dakota**	NA	NA
30	Tennessee	849	0.8%
2	Texas	9,052	8.9%
19	Utah	1,828	1.8%
NA	Vermont**	NA	NA
10	Virginia	3,931	3.9%
18	Washington	1,926	1.9%
33	West Virginia	629	0.6%
17	Wisconsin	1,980	2.0%
40	Wyoming	189	0.2%

RANK ORDER

RANK	STATE	CRIMES	% of USA
1	California	13,872	13.7%
2	Texas	9,052	8.9%
3	New York	5,508	5.4%
4	Ohio	4,841	4.8%
5	North Carolina	4,835	4.8%
6	Georgia	4,559	4.5%
7	Florida	4,167	4.1%
8	Michigan	4,142	4.1%
9	Massachusetts	3,968	3.9%
10	Virginia	3,931	3.9%
11	Arizona	3,431	3.4%
12	Indiana	3,158	3.1%
13	New Jersey	3,062	3.0%
14	Maryland	3,022	3.0%
15	Louisiana	2,715	2.7%
16	South Carolina	2,151	2.1%
17	Wisconsin	1,980	2.0%
18	Washington	1,926	1.9%
19	Utah	1,828	1.8%
20	Connecticut	1,535	1.5%
21	New Mexico	1,532	1.5%
22	Alabama	1,486	1.5%
23	Colorado	1,436	1.4%
24	Oklahoma	1,369	1.3%
25	Pennsylvania	1,351	1.3%
26	Missouri	1,252	1.2%
27	Minnesota	1,241	1.2%
28	Mississippi	1,132	1.1%
29	Arkansas	1,068	1.1%
30	Tennessee	849	0.8%
31	Nebraska	759	0.7%
32	Iowa	670	0.7%
33	West Virginia	629	0.6%
34	Rhode Island	625	0.6%
35	Delaware	619	0.6%
36	Nevada	613	0.6%
37	North Dakota	387	0.4%
38	Maine	356	0.4%
39	Alaska	279	0.3%
40	Wyoming	189	0.2%
NA	Hawaii**	NA	NA
NA	Idaho**	NA	NA
NA	Illinois**	NA	NA
NA	Kansas**	NA	NA
NA	Kentucky**	NA	NA
NA	Montana**	NA	NA
NA	New Hampshire**	NA	NA
NA	Oregon**	NA	NA
NA	South Dakota**	NA	NA
NA	Vermont**	NA	NA
	District of Columbia**	NA	NA

Source: Morgan Quitno Press using data from Federal Bureau of Investigation
   "Crime in the United States 1997" (Uniform Crime Reports, November 22, 1998)
*Includes burglary, larceny-theft and motor vehicle theft. Total is only for states shown separately. Many states had incomplete reports.
**Not available.

Property Crimes at Universities and Colleges
As a Percent of All Property Crimes in 1997
National Percent = 0.88% of Property Crimes*

<table>
<tr><td colspan="3">ALPHA ORDER</td><td colspan="3">RANK ORDER</td></tr>
<tr><td>RANK</td><td>STATE</td><td>PERCENT</td><td>RANK</td><td>STATE</td><td>PERCENT</td></tr>
<tr><td>32</td><td>Alabama</td><td>0.80</td><td>1</td><td>North Dakota</td><td>2.30</td></tr>
<tr><td>23</td><td>Alaska</td><td>1.00</td><td>2</td><td>Massachusetts</td><td>2.14</td></tr>
<tr><td>15</td><td>Arizona</td><td>1.15</td><td>3</td><td>Rhode Island</td><td>1.91</td></tr>
<tr><td>22</td><td>Arkansas</td><td>1.01</td><td>4</td><td>Delaware</td><td>1.90</td></tr>
<tr><td>20</td><td>California</td><td>1.06</td><td>5</td><td>Virginia</td><td>1.65</td></tr>
<tr><td>30</td><td>Colorado</td><td>0.86</td><td>6</td><td>Utah</td><td>1.57</td></tr>
<tr><td>11</td><td>Connecticut</td><td>1.31</td><td>7</td><td>West Virginia</td><td>1.54</td></tr>
<tr><td>4</td><td>Delaware</td><td>1.90</td><td>8</td><td>New Mexico</td><td>1.46</td></tr>
<tr><td>38</td><td>Florida</td><td>0.46</td><td>9</td><td>Indiana</td><td>1.36</td></tr>
<tr><td>14</td><td>Georgia</td><td>1.17</td><td>10</td><td>North Carolina</td><td>1.33</td></tr>
<tr><td>NA</td><td>Hawaii**</td><td>NA</td><td>11</td><td>Connecticut</td><td>1.31</td></tr>
<tr><td>NA</td><td>Idaho**</td><td>NA</td><td>12</td><td>Maryland</td><td>1.23</td></tr>
<tr><td>NA</td><td>Illinois**</td><td>NA</td><td>13</td><td>Nebraska</td><td>1.19</td></tr>
<tr><td>9</td><td>Indiana</td><td>1.36</td><td>14</td><td>Georgia</td><td>1.17</td></tr>
<tr><td>34</td><td>Iowa</td><td>0.67</td><td>15</td><td>Arizona</td><td>1.15</td></tr>
<tr><td>NA</td><td>Kansas**</td><td>NA</td><td>16</td><td>Louisiana</td><td>1.12</td></tr>
<tr><td>NA</td><td>Kentucky**</td><td>NA</td><td>16</td><td>Wisconsin</td><td>1.12</td></tr>
<tr><td>16</td><td>Louisiana</td><td>1.12</td><td>18</td><td>South Carolina</td><td>1.11</td></tr>
<tr><td>27</td><td>Maine</td><td>0.95</td><td>19</td><td>New Jersey</td><td>1.07</td></tr>
<tr><td>12</td><td>Maryland</td><td>1.23</td><td>20</td><td>California</td><td>1.06</td></tr>
<tr><td>2</td><td>Massachusetts</td><td>2.14</td><td>20</td><td>Ohio</td><td>1.06</td></tr>
<tr><td>26</td><td>Michigan</td><td>0.98</td><td>22</td><td>Arkansas</td><td>1.01</td></tr>
<tr><td>35</td><td>Minnesota</td><td>0.65</td><td>23</td><td>Alaska</td><td>1.00</td></tr>
<tr><td>23</td><td>Mississippi</td><td>1.00</td><td>23</td><td>Mississippi</td><td>1.00</td></tr>
<tr><td>37</td><td>Missouri</td><td>0.55</td><td>23</td><td>Wyoming</td><td>1.00</td></tr>
<tr><td>NA</td><td>Montana**</td><td>NA</td><td>26</td><td>Michigan</td><td>0.98</td></tr>
<tr><td>13</td><td>Nebraska</td><td>1.19</td><td>27</td><td>Maine</td><td>0.95</td></tr>
<tr><td>33</td><td>Nevada</td><td>0.69</td><td>27</td><td>Texas</td><td>0.95</td></tr>
<tr><td>NA</td><td>New Hampshire**</td><td>NA</td><td>29</td><td>New York</td><td>0.94</td></tr>
<tr><td>19</td><td>New Jersey</td><td>1.07</td><td>30</td><td>Colorado</td><td>0.86</td></tr>
<tr><td>8</td><td>New Mexico</td><td>1.46</td><td>31</td><td>Oklahoma</td><td>0.84</td></tr>
<tr><td>29</td><td>New York</td><td>0.94</td><td>32</td><td>Alabama</td><td>0.80</td></tr>
<tr><td>10</td><td>North Carolina</td><td>1.33</td><td>33</td><td>Nevada</td><td>0.69</td></tr>
<tr><td>1</td><td>North Dakota</td><td>2.30</td><td>34</td><td>Iowa</td><td>0.67</td></tr>
<tr><td>20</td><td>Ohio</td><td>1.06</td><td>35</td><td>Minnesota</td><td>0.65</td></tr>
<tr><td>31</td><td>Oklahoma</td><td>0.84</td><td>36</td><td>Washington</td><td>0.63</td></tr>
<tr><td>NA</td><td>Oregon**</td><td>NA</td><td>37</td><td>Missouri</td><td>0.55</td></tr>
<tr><td>39</td><td>Pennsylvania</td><td>0.38</td><td>38</td><td>Florida</td><td>0.46</td></tr>
<tr><td>3</td><td>Rhode Island</td><td>1.91</td><td>39</td><td>Pennsylvania</td><td>0.38</td></tr>
<tr><td>18</td><td>South Carolina</td><td>1.11</td><td>40</td><td>Tennessee</td><td>0.33</td></tr>
<tr><td>NA</td><td>South Dakota**</td><td>NA</td><td>NA</td><td>Hawaii**</td><td>NA</td></tr>
<tr><td>40</td><td>Tennessee</td><td>0.33</td><td>NA</td><td>Idaho**</td><td>NA</td></tr>
<tr><td>27</td><td>Texas</td><td>0.95</td><td>NA</td><td>Illinois**</td><td>NA</td></tr>
<tr><td>6</td><td>Utah</td><td>1.57</td><td>NA</td><td>Kansas**</td><td>NA</td></tr>
<tr><td>NA</td><td>Vermont**</td><td>NA</td><td>NA</td><td>Kentucky**</td><td>NA</td></tr>
<tr><td>5</td><td>Virginia</td><td>1.65</td><td>NA</td><td>Montana**</td><td>NA</td></tr>
<tr><td>36</td><td>Washington</td><td>0.63</td><td>NA</td><td>New Hampshire**</td><td>NA</td></tr>
<tr><td>7</td><td>West Virginia</td><td>1.54</td><td>NA</td><td>Oregon**</td><td>NA</td></tr>
<tr><td>16</td><td>Wisconsin</td><td>1.12</td><td>NA</td><td>South Dakota**</td><td>NA</td></tr>
<tr><td>23</td><td>Wyoming</td><td>1.00</td><td>NA</td><td>Vermont**</td><td>NA</td></tr>
<tr><td></td><td></td><td></td><td></td><td>District of Columbia**</td><td>NA</td></tr>
</table>

Source: Morgan Quitno Press using data from Federal Bureau of Investigation
    "Crime in the United States 1997" (Uniform Crime Reports, November 22, 1998)
*Includes burglary, larceny-theft and motor vehicle theft. Total is only for states shown separately. Many states had incomplete reports.
**Not available.

Crimes in 1993

National Total = 14,144,800 Crimes*

ALPHA ORDER

RANK	STATE	CRIMES	% of USA
22	Alabama	204,274	1.4%
45	Alaska	33,352	0.2%
16	Arizona	292,513	2.1%
32	Arkansas	116,612	0.8%
1	California	2,015,265	14.2%
25	Colorado	197,085	1.4%
28	Connecticut	152,392	1.1%
44	Delaware	34,105	0.2%
3	Florida	1,142,338	8.1%
8	Georgia	428,367	3.0%
37	Hawaii	73,566	0.5%
41	Idaho	42,258	0.3%
5	Illinois	657,129	4.6%
20	Indiana	255,090	1.8%
33	Iowa	108,239	0.8%
29	Kansas	125,924	0.9%
30	Kentucky	123,509	0.9%
15	Louisiana	294,061	2.1%
43	Maine	39,077	0.3%
13	Maryland	303,187	2.1%
14	Massachusetts	294,224	2.1%
6	Michigan	516,788	3.7%
24	Minnesota	198,125	1.4%
31	Mississippi	116,775	0.8%
19	Missouri	266,694	1.9%
42	Montana	40,188	0.3%
38	Nebraska	66,162	0.5%
36	Nevada	85,842	0.6%
46	New Hampshire	32,681	0.2%
11	New Jersey	378,257	2.7%
34	New Mexico	101,260	0.7%
4	New York	1,010,176	7.1%
10	North Carolina	392,555	2.8%
50	North Dakota	17,909	0.1%
7	Ohio	497,465	3.5%
27	Oklahoma	171,058	1.2%
26	Oregon	174,812	1.2%
9	Pennsylvania	394,136	2.8%
40	Rhode Island	44,990	0.3%
21	South Carolina	215,060	1.5%
48	South Dakota	21,151	0.1%
17	Tennessee	267,164	1.9%
2	Texas	1,161,031	8.2%
35	Utah	97,415	0.7%
47	Vermont	22,881	0.2%
18	Virginia	267,135	1.9%
12	Washington	312,793	2.2%
39	West Virginia	46,093	0.3%
23	Wisconsin	204,244	1.4%
49	Wyoming	19,566	0.1%

RANK ORDER

RANK	STATE	CRIMES	% of USA
1	California	2,015,265	14.2%
2	Texas	1,161,031	8.2%
3	Florida	1,142,338	8.1%
4	New York	1,010,176	7.1%
5	Illinois	657,129	4.6%
6	Michigan	516,788	3.7%
7	Ohio	497,465	3.5%
8	Georgia	428,367	3.0%
9	Pennsylvania	394,136	2.8%
10	North Carolina	392,555	2.8%
11	New Jersey	378,257	2.7%
12	Washington	312,793	2.2%
13	Maryland	303,187	2.1%
14	Massachusetts	294,224	2.1%
15	Louisiana	294,061	2.1%
16	Arizona	292,513	2.1%
17	Tennessee	267,164	1.9%
18	Virginia	267,135	1.9%
19	Missouri	266,694	1.9%
20	Indiana	255,090	1.8%
21	South Carolina	215,060	1.5%
22	Alabama	204,274	1.4%
23	Wisconsin	204,244	1.4%
24	Minnesota	198,125	1.4%
25	Colorado	197,085	1.4%
26	Oregon	174,812	1.2%
27	Oklahoma	171,058	1.2%
28	Connecticut	152,392	1.1%
29	Kansas	125,924	0.9%
30	Kentucky	123,509	0.9%
31	Mississippi	116,775	0.8%
32	Arkansas	116,612	0.8%
33	Iowa	108,239	0.8%
34	New Mexico	101,260	0.7%
35	Utah	97,415	0.7%
36	Nevada	85,842	0.6%
37	Hawaii	73,566	0.5%
38	Nebraska	66,162	0.5%
39	West Virginia	46,093	0.3%
40	Rhode Island	44,990	0.3%
41	Idaho	42,258	0.3%
42	Montana	40,188	0.3%
43	Maine	39,077	0.3%
44	Delaware	34,105	0.2%
45	Alaska	33,352	0.2%
46	New Hampshire	32,681	0.2%
47	Vermont	22,881	0.2%
48	South Dakota	21,151	0.1%
49	Wyoming	19,566	0.1%
50	North Dakota	17,909	0.1%
	District of Columbia	67,979	0.5%

Source: Federal Bureau of Investigation
"Crime in the United States 1993" (Uniform Crime Reports, December 4, 1994)
Revised national total. Includes murder, rape, robbery, aggravated assault, burglary, larceny-theft and motor vehicle theft.

Percent Change in Number of Crimes: 1993 to 1997

National Percent Change = 6.9% Decrease*

ALPHA ORDER			RANK ORDER		
RANK	STATE	PERCENT CHANGE	RANK	STATE	PERCENT CHANGE
18	Alabama	3.4	1	Utah	26.7
33	Alaska	(3.7)	2	Nevada	18.5
7	Arizona	12.0	3	New Mexico	18.0
21	Arkansas	2.1	4	Oregon	16.3
47	California	(22.1)	5	South Dakota	13.2
42	Colorado	(8.1)	6	Idaho	12.4
45	Connecticut	(14.5)	7	Arizona	12.0
9	Delaware	10.3	8	Tennessee	10.7
38	Florida	(6.7)	9	Delaware	10.3
23	Georgia	1.2	10	Mississippi	8.3
30	Hawaii	(2.8)	11	Nebraska	7.3
6	Idaho	12.4	12	South Carolina	7.2
39	Illinois	(6.9)	13	Oklahoma	6.5
19	Indiana	2.7	14	Washington	6.3
24	Iowa	0.5	15	Pennsylvania	4.6
37	Kansas	(6.0)	16	Minnesota	4.4
26	Kentucky	(1.1)	17	North Carolina	3.9
34	Louisiana	(4.6)	18	Alabama	3.4
25	Maine	(0.5)	19	Indiana	2.7
35	Maryland	(5.0)	20	Wyoming	2.6
48	Massachusetts	(23.6)	21	Arkansas	2.1
41	Michigan	(7.0)	22	Ohio	1.5
16	Minnesota	4.4	23	Georgia	1.2
10	Mississippi	8.3	24	Iowa	0.5
28	Missouri	(2.5)	25	Maine	(0.5)
32	Montana	(3.6)	26	Kentucky	(1.1)
11	Nebraska	7.3	27	Virginia	(2.3)
2	Nevada	18.5	28	Missouri	(2.5)
36	New Hampshire	(5.3)	29	West Virginia	(2.7)
44	New Jersey	(13.6)	30	Hawaii	(2.8)
3	New Mexico	18.0	31	North Dakota	(3.0)
50	New York	(29.8)	32	Montana	(3.6)
17	North Carolina	3.9	33	Alaska	(3.7)
31	North Dakota	(3.0)	34	Louisiana	(4.6)
22	Ohio	1.5	35	Maryland	(5.0)
13	Oklahoma	6.5	36	New Hampshire	(5.3)
4	Oregon	16.3	37	Kansas	(6.0)
15	Pennsylvania	4.6	38	Florida	(6.7)
46	Rhode Island	(19.8)	39	Illinois	(6.9)
12	South Carolina	7.2	39	Wisconsin	(6.9)
5	South Dakota	13.2	41	Michigan	(7.0)
8	Tennessee	10.7	42	Colorado	(8.1)
43	Texas	(8.2)	43	Texas	(8.2)
1	Utah	26.7	44	New Jersey	(13.6)
49	Vermont	(27.2)	45	Connecticut	(14.5)
27	Virginia	(2.3)	46	Rhode Island	(19.8)
14	Washington	6.3	47	California	(22.1)
29	West Virginia	(2.7)	48	Massachusetts	(23.6)
39	Wisconsin	(6.9)	49	Vermont	(27.2)
20	Wyoming	2.6	50	New York	(29.8)
				District of Columbia	(23.4)

Source: Morgan Quitno Press using data from Federal Bureau of Investigation
   "Crime in the United States" (Uniform Crime Reports, 1993 and 1997 editions)
*Includes murder, rape, robbery, aggravated assault, burglary, larceny-theft and motor vehicle theft.

Crime Rate in 1993

National Rate = 5,484.4 Crimes per 100,000 Population*

ALPHA ORDER

RANK	STATE	RATE
26	Alabama	4,878.8
16	Alaska	5,567.9
2	Arizona	7,431.7
28	Arkansas	4,810.7
4	California	6,456.9
18	Colorado	5,526.8
31	Connecticut	4,650.4
27	Delaware	4,872.1
1	Florida	8,351.0
8	Georgia	6,193.0
6	Hawaii	6,277.0
43	Idaho	3,845.1
15	Illinois	5,617.9
34	Indiana	4,465.1
42	Iowa	3,846.4
24	Kansas	4,975.3
45	Kentucky	3,259.7
3	Louisiana	6,846.6
46	Maine	3,153.9
10	Maryland	6,106.5
25	Massachusetts	4,893.9
19	Michigan	5,452.5
36	Minnesota	4,386.2
35	Mississippi	4,418.3
23	Missouri	5,095.4
30	Montana	4,790.0
38	Nebraska	4,117.1
9	Nevada	6,180.1
48	New Hampshire	2,905.0
29	New Jersey	4,800.8
7	New Mexico	6,266.1
17	New York	5,551.3
14	North Carolina	5,652.3
49	North Dakota	2,820.3
33	Ohio	4,485.3
20	Oklahoma	5,294.3
13	Oregon	5,765.6
44	Pennsylvania	3,271.4
32	Rhode Island	4,499.0
12	South Carolina	5,903.4
47	South Dakota	2,958.2
21	Tennessee	5,239.5
5	Texas	6,439.1
22	Utah	5,237.4
41	Vermont	3,972.4
39	Virginia	4,115.5
11	Washington	5,952.3
50	West Virginia	2,532.6
40	Wisconsin	4,054.1
37	Wyoming	4,163.0

RANK ORDER

RANK	STATE	RATE
1	Florida	8,351.0
2	Arizona	7,431.7
3	Louisiana	6,846.6
4	California	6,456.9
5	Texas	6,439.1
6	Hawaii	6,277.0
7	New Mexico	6,266.1
8	Georgia	6,193.0
9	Nevada	6,180.1
10	Maryland	6,106.5
11	Washington	5,952.3
12	South Carolina	5,903.4
13	Oregon	5,765.6
14	North Carolina	5,652.3
15	Illinois	5,617.9
16	Alaska	5,567.9
17	New York	5,551.3
18	Colorado	5,526.8
19	Michigan	5,452.5
20	Oklahoma	5,294.3
21	Tennessee	5,239.5
22	Utah	5,237.4
23	Missouri	5,095.4
24	Kansas	4,975.3
25	Massachusetts	4,893.9
26	Alabama	4,878.8
27	Delaware	4,872.1
28	Arkansas	4,810.7
29	New Jersey	4,800.8
30	Montana	4,790.0
31	Connecticut	4,650.4
32	Rhode Island	4,499.0
33	Ohio	4,485.3
34	Indiana	4,465.1
35	Mississippi	4,418.3
36	Minnesota	4,386.2
37	Wyoming	4,163.0
38	Nebraska	4,117.1
39	Virginia	4,115.5
40	Wisconsin	4,054.1
41	Vermont	3,972.4
42	Iowa	3,846.4
43	Idaho	3,845.1
44	Pennsylvania	3,271.4
45	Kentucky	3,259.7
46	Maine	3,153.9
47	South Dakota	2,958.2
48	New Hampshire	2,905.0
49	North Dakota	2,820.3
50	West Virginia	2,532.6
	District of Columbia	11,761.1

Source: Federal Bureau of Investigation
   "Crime in the United States 1993" (Uniform Crime Reports, December 4, 1994)
*Revised national rate. Includes murder, rape, robbery, aggravated assault, burglary, larceny-theft and motor vehicle theft.

Percent Change in Crime Rate: 1993 to 1997

National Percent Change = 10.2% Decrease*

RANK	STATE	PERCENT CHANGE
16	Alabama	0.2
29	Alaska	(5.3)
25	Arizona	(3.2)
21	Arkansas	(1.9)
47	California	(24.6)
45	Colorado	(15.9)
42	Connecticut	(14.3)
5	Delaware	5.5
41	Florida	(12.9)
33	Georgia	(6.5)
27	Hawaii	(4.0)
12	Idaho	2.1
37	Illinois	(8.5)
17	Indiana	0.0
20	Iowa	(0.8)
36	Kansas	(8.3)
28	Kentucky	(4.1)
31	Louisiana	(5.8)
19	Maine	(0.7)
34	Maryland	(7.4)
48	Massachusetts	(24.9)
40	Michigan	(9.8)
14	Minnesota	0.6
8	Mississippi	4.8
30	Missouri	(5.5)
35	Montana	(8.0)
9	Nebraska	4.0
21	Nevada	(1.9)
38	New Hampshire	(9.1)
44	New Jersey	(15.5)
2	New Mexico	10.2
50	New York	(29.5)
24	North Carolina	(2.8)
26	North Dakota	(3.9)
13	Ohio	0.7
11	Oklahoma	3.8
4	Oregon	8.7
7	Pennsylvania	4.9
46	Rhode Island	(18.8)
10	South Carolina	3.9
3	South Dakota	9.7
6	Tennessee	5.2
43	Texas	(14.9)
1	Utah	14.5
49	Vermont	(28.8)
31	Virginia	(5.8)
18	Washington	(0.4)
23	West Virginia	(2.5)
39	Wisconsin	(9.3)
15	Wyoming	0.4

RANK	STATE	PERCENT CHANGE
1	Utah	14.5
2	New Mexico	10.2
3	South Dakota	9.7
4	Oregon	8.7
5	Delaware	5.5
6	Tennessee	5.2
7	Pennsylvania	4.9
8	Mississippi	4.8
9	Nebraska	4.0
10	South Carolina	3.9
11	Oklahoma	3.8
12	Idaho	2.1
13	Ohio	0.7
14	Minnesota	0.6
15	Wyoming	0.4
16	Alabama	0.2
17	Indiana	0.0
18	Washington	(0.4)
19	Maine	(0.7)
20	Iowa	(0.8)
21	Arkansas	(1.9)
21	Nevada	(1.9)
23	West Virginia	(2.5)
24	North Carolina	(2.8)
25	Arizona	(3.2)
26	North Dakota	(3.9)
27	Hawaii	(4.0)
28	Kentucky	(4.1)
29	Alaska	(5.3)
30	Missouri	(5.5)
31	Louisiana	(5.8)
31	Virginia	(5.8)
33	Georgia	(6.5)
34	Maryland	(7.4)
35	Montana	(8.0)
36	Kansas	(8.3)
37	Illinois	(8.5)
38	New Hampshire	(9.1)
39	Wisconsin	(9.3)
40	Michigan	(9.8)
41	Florida	(12.9)
42	Connecticut	(14.3)
43	Texas	(14.9)
44	New Jersey	(15.5)
45	Colorado	(15.9)
46	Rhode Island	(18.8)
47	California	(24.6)
48	Massachusetts	(24.9)
49	Vermont	(28.8)
50	New York	(29.5)
	District of Columbia	(16.3)

Source: Morgan Quitno Press using data from Federal Bureau of Investigation
"Crime in the United States" (Uniform Crime Reports, 1993 and 1997 editions)
*Includes murder, rape, robbery, aggravated assault, burglary, larceny-theft and motor vehicle theft.

Violent Crimes in 1993

National Total = 1,926,020 Violent Crimes*

ALPHA ORDER

RANK	STATE	CRIMES	% of USA
18	Alabama	32,676	1.7%
39	Alaska	4,557	0.2%
19	Arizona	28,142	1.5%
30	Arkansas	14,381	0.7%
1	California	336,381	17.5%
24	Colorado	20,229	1.1%
28	Connecticut	14,949	0.8%
38	Delaware	4,801	0.2%
3	Florida	164,975	8.6%
9	Georgia	50,019	2.6%
43	Hawaii	3,061	0.2%
42	Idaho	3,097	0.2%
5	Illinois	112,260	5.8%
20	Indiana	27,941	1.5%
35	Iowa	9,159	0.5%
32	Kansas	12,564	0.7%
25	Kentucky	17,530	0.9%
14	Louisiana	45,600	2.4%
44	Maine	1,558	0.1%
10	Maryland	49,540	2.6%
12	Massachusetts	48,393	2.5%
6	Michigan	75,021	3.9%
29	Minnesota	14,778	0.8%
34	Mississippi	11,467	0.6%
16	Missouri	38,963	2.0%
47	Montana	1,489	0.1%
37	Nebraska	5,450	0.3%
33	Nevada	12,157	0.6%
45	New Hampshire	1,550	0.1%
11	New Jersey	49,390	2.6%
27	New Mexico	15,024	0.8%
2	New York	195,352	10.1%
13	North Carolina	47,178	2.4%
50	North Dakota	522	0.0%
7	Ohio	55,915	2.9%
23	Oklahoma	20,512	1.1%
26	Oregon	15,254	0.8%
8	Pennsylvania	50,295	2.6%
40	Rhode Island	4,017	0.2%
17	South Carolina	37,281	1.9%
46	South Dakota	1,490	0.1%
15	Tennessee	39,047	2.0%
4	Texas	137,419	7.1%
36	Utah	5,599	0.3%
49	Vermont	658	0.0%
22	Virginia	24,160	1.3%
21	Washington	27,040	1.4%
41	West Virginia	3,793	0.2%
31	Wisconsin	13,321	0.7%
48	Wyoming	1,345	0.1%

RANK ORDER

RANK	STATE	CRIMES	% of USA
1	California	336,381	17.5%
2	New York	195,352	10.1%
3	Florida	164,975	8.6%
4	Texas	137,419	7.1%
5	Illinois	112,260	5.8%
6	Michigan	75,021	3.9%
7	Ohio	55,915	2.9%
8	Pennsylvania	50,295	2.6%
9	Georgia	50,019	2.6%
10	Maryland	49,540	2.6%
11	New Jersey	49,390	2.6%
12	Massachusetts	48,393	2.5%
13	North Carolina	47,178	2.4%
14	Louisiana	45,600	2.4%
15	Tennessee	39,047	2.0%
16	Missouri	38,963	2.0%
17	South Carolina	37,281	1.9%
18	Alabama	32,676	1.7%
19	Arizona	28,142	1.5%
20	Indiana	27,941	1.5%
21	Washington	27,040	1.4%
22	Virginia	24,160	1.3%
23	Oklahoma	20,512	1.1%
24	Colorado	20,229	1.1%
25	Kentucky	17,530	0.9%
26	Oregon	15,254	0.8%
27	New Mexico	15,024	0.8%
28	Connecticut	14,949	0.8%
29	Minnesota	14,778	0.8%
30	Arkansas	14,381	0.7%
31	Wisconsin	13,321	0.7%
32	Kansas	12,564	0.7%
33	Nevada	12,157	0.6%
34	Mississippi	11,467	0.6%
35	Iowa	9,159	0.5%
36	Utah	5,599	0.3%
37	Nebraska	5,450	0.3%
38	Delaware	4,801	0.2%
39	Alaska	4,557	0.2%
40	Rhode Island	4,017	0.2%
41	West Virginia	3,793	0.2%
42	Idaho	3,097	0.2%
43	Hawaii	3,061	0.2%
44	Maine	1,558	0.1%
45	New Hampshire	1,550	0.1%
46	South Dakota	1,490	0.1%
47	Montana	1,489	0.1%
48	Wyoming	1,345	0.1%
49	Vermont	658	0.0%
50	North Dakota	522	0.0%
	District of Columbia	16,888	0.9%

Source: Federal Bureau of Investigation
   "Crime in the United States 1993" (Uniform Crime Reports, December 4, 1994)
*Revised national total. Violent crimes are offenses of murder, forcible rape, robbery and aggravated assault.

Percent Change in Number of Violent Crimes: 1993 to 1997

National Percent Change = 15.1% Decrease*

ALPHA ORDER

RANK	STATE	PERCENT CHANGE
47	Alabama	(25.4)
25	Alaska	(6.3)
15	Arizona	1.0
26	Arkansas	(7.6)
46	California	(23.4)
49	Colorado	(30.1)
36	Connecticut	(14.5)
14	Delaware	3.4
30	Florida	(9.1)
31	Georgia	(9.2)
7	Hawaii	7.8
16	Idaho	0.3
28	Illinois	(8.7)
6	Indiana	8.0
20	Iowa	(3.5)
38	Kansas	(15.5)
48	Kentucky	(29.3)
40	Louisiana	(18.3)
21	Maine	(3.7)
33	Maryland	(12.9)
41	Massachusetts	(18.6)
45	Michigan	(23.1)
8	Minnesota	7.1
3	Mississippi	11.7
43	Missouri	(19.9)
44	Montana	(22.0)
1	Nebraska	33.3
4	Nevada	10.2
35	New Hampshire	(14.3)
42	New Jersey	(19.7)
18	New Mexico	(1.7)
50	New York	(36.1)
23	North Carolina	(4.5)
8	North Dakota	7.1
33	Ohio	(12.9)
32	Oklahoma	(9.5)
24	Oregon	(5.5)
11	Pennsylvania	5.7
39	Rhode Island	(18.0)
17	South Carolina	(0.1)
19	South Dakota	(2.2)
5	Tennessee	8.6
37	Texas	(14.8)
2	Utah	22.8
8	Vermont	7.1
22	Virginia	(3.8)
27	Washington	(8.6)
13	West Virginia	4.7
12	Wisconsin	5.0
29	Wyoming	(8.9)

RANK ORDER

RANK	STATE	PERCENT CHANGE
1	Nebraska	33.3
2	Utah	22.8
3	Mississippi	11.7
4	Nevada	10.2
5	Tennessee	8.6
6	Indiana	8.0
7	Hawaii	7.8
8	Minnesota	7.1
8	North Dakota	7.1
8	Vermont	7.1
11	Pennsylvania	5.7
12	Wisconsin	5.0
13	West Virginia	4.7
14	Delaware	3.4
15	Arizona	1.0
16	Idaho	0.3
17	South Carolina	(0.1)
18	New Mexico	(1.7)
19	South Dakota	(2.2)
20	Iowa	(3.5)
21	Maine	(3.7)
22	Virginia	(3.8)
23	North Carolina	(4.5)
24	Oregon	(5.5)
25	Alaska	(6.3)
26	Arkansas	(7.6)
27	Washington	(8.6)
28	Illinois	(8.7)
29	Wyoming	(8.9)
30	Florida	(9.1)
31	Georgia	(9.2)
32	Oklahoma	(9.5)
33	Maryland	(12.9)
33	Ohio	(12.9)
35	New Hampshire	(14.3)
36	Connecticut	(14.5)
37	Texas	(14.8)
38	Kansas	(15.5)
39	Rhode Island	(18.0)
40	Louisiana	(18.3)
41	Massachusetts	(18.6)
42	New Jersey	(19.7)
43	Missouri	(19.9)
44	Montana	(22.0)
45	Michigan	(23.1)
46	California	(23.4)
47	Alabama	(25.4)
48	Kentucky	(29.3)
49	Colorado	(30.1)
50	New York	(36.1)
	District of Columbia	(36.6)

Source: Morgan Quitno Press using data from Federal Bureau of Investigation
"Crime in the United States" (Uniform Crime Reports, 1993 and 1997 editions)
*Violent crimes are offenses of murder, forcible rape, robbery and aggravated assault.

Violent Crime Rate in 1993

National Rate = 746.8 Violent Crimes per 100,000 Population*

ALPHA ORDER

RANK	STATE	RATE
12	Alabama	780.4
15	Alaska	760.8
18	Arizona	715.0
23	Arkansas	593.3
2	California	1,077.8
24	Colorado	567.3
31	Connecticut	456.2
19	Delaware	685.9
1	Florida	1,206.0
17	Georgia	723.1
43	Hawaii	261.2
41	Idaho	281.8
7	Illinois	959.7
29	Indiana	489.1
38	Iowa	325.5
28	Kansas	496.4
30	Kentucky	462.7
4	Louisiana	1,061.7
48	Maine	125.7
6	Maryland	997.8
10	Massachusetts	804.9
11	Michigan	791.5
37	Minnesota	327.2
32	Mississippi	433.9
16	Missouri	744.4
46	Montana	177.5
36	Nebraska	339.1
9	Nevada	875.2
47	New Hampshire	137.8
22	New Jersey	626.9
8	New Mexico	929.7
3	New York	1,073.5
20	North Carolina	679.3
50	North Dakota	82.2
26	Ohio	504.1
21	Oklahoma	634.8
27	Oregon	503.1
33	Pennsylvania	417.5
34	Rhode Island	401.7
5	South Carolina	1,023.4
44	South Dakota	208.4
13	Tennessee	765.8
14	Texas	762.1
39	Utah	301.0
49	Vermont	114.2
35	Virginia	372.2
25	Washington	514.6
44	West Virginia	208.4
42	Wisconsin	264.4
40	Wyoming	286.2

RANK ORDER

RANK	STATE	RATE
1	Florida	1,206.0
2	California	1,077.8
3	New York	1,073.5
4	Louisiana	1,061.7
5	South Carolina	1,023.4
6	Maryland	997.8
7	Illinois	959.7
8	New Mexico	929.7
9	Nevada	875.2
10	Massachusetts	804.9
11	Michigan	791.5
12	Alabama	780.4
13	Tennessee	765.8
14	Texas	762.1
15	Alaska	760.8
16	Missouri	744.4
17	Georgia	723.1
18	Arizona	715.0
19	Delaware	685.9
20	North Carolina	679.3
21	Oklahoma	634.8
22	New Jersey	626.9
23	Arkansas	593.3
24	Colorado	567.3
25	Washington	514.6
26	Ohio	504.1
27	Oregon	503.1
28	Kansas	496.4
29	Indiana	489.1
30	Kentucky	462.7
31	Connecticut	456.2
32	Mississippi	433.9
33	Pennsylvania	417.5
34	Rhode Island	401.7
35	Virginia	372.2
36	Nebraska	339.1
37	Minnesota	327.2
38	Iowa	325.5
39	Utah	301.0
40	Wyoming	286.2
41	Idaho	281.8
42	Wisconsin	264.4
43	Hawaii	261.2
44	South Dakota	208.4
44	West Virginia	208.4
46	Montana	177.5
47	New Hampshire	137.8
48	Maine	125.7
49	Vermont	114.2
50	North Dakota	82.2
	District of Columbia	2,921.8

Source: Federal Bureau of Investigation
"Crime in the United States 1993" (Uniform Crime Reports, December 4, 1994)
Revised national rate. Violent crimes are offenses of murder, forcible rape, robbery and aggravated assault.

Percent Change in Violent Crime Rate: 1993 to 1997

National Percent Change = 18.2% Decrease*

ALPHA ORDER				RANK ORDER		
RANK	STATE	PERCENT CHANGE		RANK	STATE	PERCENT CHANGE
47	Alabama	(27.7)		1	Nebraska	29.3
19	Alaska	(7.8)		2	Utah	11.0
29	Arizona	(12.8)		3	Mississippi	8.1
26	Arkansas	(11.2)		4	Hawaii	6.4
46	California	(25.9)		5	North Dakota	6.1
50	Colorado	(36.0)		6	Pennsylvania	5.9
31	Connecticut	(14.3)		7	Indiana	5.2
13	Delaware	(1.2)		8	West Virginia	4.9
33	Florida	(15.1)		9	Vermont	4.8
35	Georgia	(16.1)		10	Minnesota	3.2
4	Hawaii	6.4		11	Tennessee	3.1
22	Idaho	(8.9)		12	Wisconsin	2.3
23	Illinois	(10.2)		13	Delaware	(1.2)
7	Indiana	5.2		14	South Carolina	(3.2)
16	Iowa	(4.8)		15	Maine	(3.9)
37	Kansas	(17.6)		16	Iowa	(4.8)
48	Kentucky	(31.5)		17	South Dakota	(5.3)
39	Louisiana	(19.4)		18	Virginia	(7.3)
15	Maine	(3.9)		19	Alaska	(7.8)
34	Maryland	(15.2)		20	New Mexico	(8.2)
40	Massachusetts	(20.0)		21	Nevada	(8.7)
44	Michigan	(25.5)		22	Idaho	(8.9)
10	Minnesota	3.2		23	Illinois	(10.2)
3	Mississippi	8.1		24	North Carolina	(10.6)
43	Missouri	(22.4)		25	Wyoming	(10.8)
45	Montana	(25.6)		26	Arkansas	(11.2)
1	Nebraska	29.3		27	Oregon	(11.7)
21	Nevada	(8.7)		28	Oklahoma	(11.9)
38	New Hampshire	(17.9)		29	Arizona	(12.8)
42	New Jersey	(21.4)		30	Ohio	(13.6)
20	New Mexico	(8.2)		31	Connecticut	(14.3)
49	New York	(35.9)		32	Washington	(14.4)
24	North Carolina	(10.6)		33	Florida	(15.1)
5	North Dakota	6.1		34	Maryland	(15.2)
30	Ohio	(13.6)		35	Georgia	(16.1)
28	Oklahoma	(11.9)		36	Rhode Island	(17.0)
27	Oregon	(11.7)		37	Kansas	(17.6)
6	Pennsylvania	5.9		38	New Hampshire	(17.9)
36	Rhode Island	(17.0)		39	Louisiana	(19.4)
14	South Carolina	(3.2)		40	Massachusetts	(20.0)
17	South Dakota	(5.3)		41	Texas	(20.9)
11	Tennessee	3.1		42	New Jersey	(21.4)
41	Texas	(20.9)		43	Missouri	(22.4)
2	Utah	11.0		44	Michigan	(25.5)
9	Vermont	4.8		45	Montana	(25.6)
18	Virginia	(7.3)		46	California	(25.9)
32	Washington	(14.4)		47	Alabama	(27.7)
8	West Virginia	4.9		48	Kentucky	(31.5)
12	Wisconsin	2.3		49	New York	(35.9)
25	Wyoming	(10.8)		50	Colorado	(36.0)
					District of Columbia	(30.7)

Source: Morgan Quitno Press using data from Federal Bureau of Investigation
   "Crime in the United States" (Uniform Crime Reports, 1993 and 1997 editions)
*Violent crimes are offenses of murder, forcible rape, robbery and aggravated assault.

Murders in 1993

National Total = 24,526 Murders*

ALPHA ORDER

RANK	STATE	MURDERS	% of USA
16	Alabama	484	2.0%
39	Alaska	54	0.2%
21	Arizona	339	1.4%
25	Arkansas	247	1.0%
1	California	4,096	16.7%
28	Colorado	206	0.8%
28	Connecticut	206	0.8%
42	Delaware	35	0.1%
5	Florida	1,224	5.0%
9	Georgia	789	3.2%
40	Hawaii	45	0.2%
43	Idaho	32	0.1%
4	Illinois	1,332	5.4%
17	Indiana	430	1.8%
36	Iowa	66	0.3%
30	Kansas	161	0.7%
24	Kentucky	249	1.0%
7	Louisiana	874	3.6%
48	Maine	20	0.1%
12	Maryland	632	2.6%
26	Massachusetts	233	1.0%
6	Michigan	933	3.8%
31	Minnesota	155	0.6%
20	Mississippi	357	1.5%
13	Missouri	590	2.4%
44	Montana	25	0.1%
37	Nebraska	63	0.3%
32	Nevada	144	0.6%
46	New Hampshire	23	0.1%
18	New Jersey	418	1.7%
34	New Mexico	130	0.5%
2	New York	2,420	9.9%
10	North Carolina	785	3.2%
50	North Dakota	11	0.0%
11	Ohio	667	2.7%
22	Oklahoma	273	1.1%
33	Oregon	140	0.6%
8	Pennsylvania	823	3.4%
41	Rhode Island	39	0.2%
19	South Carolina	377	1.5%
45	South Dakota	24	0.1%
15	Tennessee	521	2.1%
3	Texas	2,147	8.8%
38	Utah	58	0.2%
47	Vermont	21	0.1%
14	Virginia	539	2.2%
23	Washington	271	1.1%
35	West Virginia	126	0.5%
27	Wisconsin	222	0.9%
49	Wyoming	16	0.1%

RANK ORDER

RANK	STATE	MURDERS	% of USA
1	California	4,096	16.7%
2	New York	2,420	9.9%
3	Texas	2,147	8.8%
4	Illinois	1,332	5.4%
5	Florida	1,224	5.0%
6	Michigan	933	3.8%
7	Louisiana	874	3.6%
8	Pennsylvania	823	3.4%
9	Georgia	789	3.2%
10	North Carolina	785	3.2%
11	Ohio	667	2.7%
12	Maryland	632	2.6%
13	Missouri	590	2.4%
14	Virginia	539	2.2%
15	Tennessee	521	2.1%
16	Alabama	484	2.0%
17	Indiana	430	1.8%
18	New Jersey	418	1.7%
19	South Carolina	377	1.5%
20	Mississippi	357	1.5%
21	Arizona	339	1.4%
22	Oklahoma	273	1.1%
23	Washington	271	1.1%
24	Kentucky	249	1.0%
25	Arkansas	247	1.0%
26	Massachusetts	233	1.0%
27	Wisconsin	222	0.9%
28	Colorado	206	0.8%
28	Connecticut	206	0.8%
30	Kansas	161	0.7%
31	Minnesota	155	0.6%
32	Nevada	144	0.6%
33	Oregon	140	0.6%
34	New Mexico	130	0.5%
35	West Virginia	126	0.5%
36	Iowa	66	0.3%
37	Nebraska	63	0.3%
38	Utah	58	0.2%
39	Alaska	54	0.2%
40	Hawaii	45	0.2%
41	Rhode Island	39	0.2%
42	Delaware	35	0.1%
43	Idaho	32	0.1%
44	Montana	25	0.1%
45	South Dakota	24	0.1%
46	New Hampshire	23	0.1%
47	Vermont	21	0.1%
48	Maine	20	0.1%
49	Wyoming	16	0.1%
50	North Dakota	11	0.0%
	District of Columbia	454	1.9%

Source: Federal Bureau of Investigation
   "Crime in the United States 1993" (Uniform Crime Reports, December 4, 1994)
*Includes nonnegligent manslaughter.

Percent Change in Number of Murders: 1993 to 1997

National Percent Change = 25.8% Decrease*

ALPHA ORDER				RANK ORDER		
RANK	**STATE**	**PERCENT CHANGE**		**RANK**	**STATE**	**PERCENT CHANGE**
19	Alabama	(12.0)		1	Montana	68.0
11	Alaska	0.0		2	Nevada	29.9
5	Arizona	10.6		3	Maine	25.0
9	Arkansas	1.2		4	Idaho	21.9
41	California	(37.0)		5	Arizona	10.6
35	Colorado	(23.8)		6	Wyoming	6.3
43	Connecticut	(39.8)		7	Hawaii	4.4
46	Delaware	(48.6)		8	New Mexico	3.1
25	Florida	(17.3)		9	Arkansas	1.2
37	Georgia	(28.6)		10	Mississippi	0.3
7	Hawaii	4.4		11	Alaska	0.0
4	Idaho	21.9		11	Indiana	0.0
26	Illinois	(17.7)		13	Tennessee	(1.9)
11	Indiana	0.0		14	Kansas	(3.7)
31	Iowa	(21.2)		15	Wisconsin	(7.7)
14	Kansas	(3.7)		16	Kentucky	(8.4)
16	Kentucky	(8.4)		17	Virginia	(9.5)
34	Louisiana	(22.0)		18	Washington	(11.1)
3	Maine	25.0		19	Alabama	(12.0)
29	Maryland	(20.6)		20	Utah	(13.8)
47	Massachusetts	(48.9)		21	Pennsylvania	(14.3)
27	Michigan	(18.6)		22	Oklahoma	(16.1)
24	Minnesota	(16.8)		23	South Carolina	(16.7)
10	Mississippi	0.3		24	Minnesota	(16.8)
36	Missouri	(27.8)		25	Florida	(17.3)
1	Montana	68.0		26	Illinois	(17.7)
29	Nebraska	(20.6)		27	Michigan	(18.6)
2	Nevada	29.9		28	New Jersey	(19.4)
38	New Hampshire	(30.4)		29	Maryland	(20.6)
28	New Jersey	(19.4)		29	Nebraska	(20.6)
8	New Mexico	3.1		31	Iowa	(21.2)
48	New York	(54.8)		32	Ohio	(21.6)
33	North Carolina	(21.8)		33	North Carolina	(21.8)
45	North Dakota	(45.5)		34	Louisiana	(22.0)
32	Ohio	(21.6)		35	Colorado	(23.8)
22	Oklahoma	(16.1)		36	Missouri	(27.8)
39	Oregon	(32.1)		37	Georgia	(28.6)
21	Pennsylvania	(14.3)		38	New Hampshire	(30.4)
40	Rhode Island	(35.9)		39	Oregon	(32.1)
23	South Carolina	(16.7)		40	Rhode Island	(35.9)
50	South Dakota	(58.3)		41	California	(37.0)
13	Tennessee	(1.9)		42	Texas	(38.2)
42	Texas	(38.2)		43	Connecticut	(39.8)
20	Utah	(13.8)		44	West Virginia	(40.5)
49	Vermont	(57.1)		45	North Dakota	(45.5)
17	Virginia	(9.5)		46	Delaware	(48.6)
18	Washington	(11.1)		47	Massachusetts	(48.9)
44	West Virginia	(40.5)		48	New York	(54.8)
15	Wisconsin	(7.7)		49	Vermont	(57.1)
6	Wyoming	6.3		50	South Dakota	(58.3)
					District of Columbia	(33.7)

Source: Morgan Quitno Press using data from Federal Bureau of Investigation
    "Crime in the United States" (Uniform Crime Reports, 1993 and 1997 editions)
*Includes nonnegligent manslaughter.

Murder Rate in 1993

National Rate = 9.5 Murders Per 100,000 Population*

ALPHA ORDER

ALPHA ORDER

RANK	STATE	RATE
7	Alabama	11.6
17	Alaska	9.0
19	Arizona	8.6
14	Arkansas	10.2
4	California	13.1
30	Colorado	5.8
28	Connecticut	6.3
33	Delaware	5.0
18	Florida	8.9
8	Georgia	11.4
39	Hawaii	3.8
46	Idaho	2.9
8	Illinois	11.4
23	Indiana	7.5
47	Iowa	2.3
27	Kansas	6.4
26	Kentucky	6.6
1	Louisiana	20.3
50	Maine	1.6
5	Maryland	12.7
36	Massachusetts	3.9
16	Michigan	9.8
41	Minnesota	3.4
2	Mississippi	13.5
10	Missouri	11.3
45	Montana	3.0
36	Nebraska	3.9
12	Nevada	10.4
48	New Hampshire	2.0
31	New Jersey	5.3
22	New Mexico	8.0
3	New York	13.3
10	North Carolina	11.3
49	North Dakota	1.7
29	Ohio	6.0
20	Oklahoma	8.4
34	Oregon	4.6
25	Pennsylvania	6.8
36	Rhode Island	3.9
13	South Carolina	10.3
41	South Dakota	3.4
14	Tennessee	10.2
6	Texas	11.9
44	Utah	3.1
40	Vermont	3.6
21	Virginia	8.3
32	Washington	5.2
24	West Virginia	6.9
35	Wisconsin	4.4
41	Wyoming	3.4

RANK ORDER

RANK	STATE	RATE
1	Louisiana	20.3
2	Mississippi	13.5
3	New York	13.3
4	California	13.1
5	Maryland	12.7
6	Texas	11.9
7	Alabama	11.6
8	Georgia	11.4
8	Illinois	11.4
10	Missouri	11.3
10	North Carolina	11.3
12	Nevada	10.4
13	South Carolina	10.3
14	Arkansas	10.2
14	Tennessee	10.2
16	Michigan	9.8
17	Alaska	9.0
18	Florida	8.9
19	Arizona	8.6
20	Oklahoma	8.4
21	Virginia	8.3
22	New Mexico	8.0
23	Indiana	7.5
24	West Virginia	6.9
25	Pennsylvania	6.8
26	Kentucky	6.6
27	Kansas	6.4
28	Connecticut	6.3
29	Ohio	6.0
30	Colorado	5.8
31	New Jersey	5.3
32	Washington	5.2
33	Delaware	5.0
34	Oregon	4.6
35	Wisconsin	4.4
36	Massachusetts	3.9
36	Nebraska	3.9
36	Rhode Island	3.9
39	Hawaii	3.8
40	Vermont	3.6
41	Minnesota	3.4
41	South Dakota	3.4
41	Wyoming	3.4
44	Utah	3.1
45	Montana	3.0
46	Idaho	2.9
47	Iowa	2.3
48	New Hampshire	2.0
49	North Dakota	1.7
50	Maine	1.6
	District of Columbia	78.5

Source: Federal Bureau of Investigation
"Crime in the United States 1993" (Uniform Crime Reports, December 4, 1994)
Includes nonnegligent manslaughter.

Percent Change in Murder Rate: 1993 to 1997

National Percent Change = 28.4% Decrease*

ALPHA ORDER				RANK ORDER		
RANK	STATE	PERCENT CHANGE		RANK	STATE	PERCENT CHANGE
19	Alabama	(14.7)		1	Montana	60.0
7	Alaska	(1.1)		2	Maine	25.0
12	Arizona	(4.7)		3	Idaho	10.3
9	Arkansas	(2.9)		4	Nevada	7.7
41	California	(38.9)		5	Hawaii	5.3
37	Colorado	(31.0)		6	Wyoming	2.9
42	Connecticut	(39.7)		7	Alaska	(1.1)
46	Delaware	(50.0)		8	Indiana	(2.7)
30	Florida	(22.5)		9	Arkansas	(2.9)
38	Georgia	(34.2)		10	Mississippi	(3.0)
5	Hawaii	5.3		11	New Mexico	(3.8)
3	Idaho	10.3		12	Arizona	(4.7)
24	Illinois	(19.3)		13	Kansas	(6.3)
8	Indiana	(2.7)		14	Tennessee	(6.9)
27	Iowa	(21.7)		15	Wisconsin	(9.1)
13	Kansas	(6.3)		16	Kentucky	(12.1)
16	Kentucky	(12.1)		17	Pennsylvania	(13.2)
32	Louisiana	(22.7)		18	Virginia	(13.3)
2	Maine	25.0		19	Alabama	(14.7)
29	Maryland	(22.0)		20	Washington	(17.3)
47	Massachusetts	(51.3)		21	Minnesota	(17.6)
25	Michigan	(20.4)		22	Oklahoma	(17.9)
21	Minnesota	(17.6)		23	South Carolina	(18.4)
10	Mississippi	(3.0)		24	Illinois	(19.3)
36	Missouri	(30.1)		25	Michigan	(20.4)
1	Montana	60.0		26	New Jersey	(20.8)
33	Nebraska	(23.1)		27	Iowa	(21.7)
4	Nevada	7.7		27	Ohio	(21.7)
35	New Hampshire	(30.0)		29	Maryland	(22.0)
26	New Jersey	(20.8)		30	Florida	(22.5)
11	New Mexico	(3.8)		31	Utah	(22.6)
48	New York	(54.9)		32	Louisiana	(22.7)
34	North Carolina	(26.5)		33	Nebraska	(23.1)
45	North Dakota	(47.1)		34	North Carolina	(26.5)
27	Ohio	(21.7)		35	New Hampshire	(30.0)
22	Oklahoma	(17.9)		36	Missouri	(30.1)
40	Oregon	(37.0)		37	Colorado	(31.0)
17	Pennsylvania	(13.2)		38	Georgia	(34.2)
39	Rhode Island	(35.9)		39	Rhode Island	(35.9)
23	South Carolina	(18.4)		40	Oregon	(37.0)
50	South Dakota	(58.8)		41	California	(38.9)
14	Tennessee	(6.9)		42	Connecticut	(39.7)
44	Texas	(42.9)		43	West Virginia	(40.6)
31	Utah	(22.6)		44	Texas	(42.9)
49	Vermont	(58.3)		45	North Dakota	(47.1)
18	Virginia	(13.3)		46	Delaware	(50.0)
20	Washington	(17.3)		47	Massachusetts	(51.3)
43	West Virginia	(40.6)		48	New York	(54.9)
15	Wisconsin	(9.1)		49	Vermont	(58.3)
6	Wyoming	2.9		50	South Dakota	(58.8)
					District of Columbia	(27.5)

Source: Morgan Quitno Press using data from Federal Bureau of Investigation
"Crime in the United States" (Uniform Crime Reports, 1993 and 1997 editions)
*Includes nonnegligent manslaughter.

Rapes in 1993

National Total = 106,010 Rapes*

ALPHA ORDER

RANK	STATE	RAPES	% of USA
26	Alabama	1,471	1.4%
38	Alaska	502	0.5%
25	Arizona	1,488	1.4%
30	Arkansas	1,028	1.0%
1	California	11,766	11.1%
21	Colorado	1,633	1.5%
35	Connecticut	800	0.8%
37	Delaware	539	0.5%
3	Florida	7,359	6.9%
11	Georgia	2,448	2.3%
41	Hawaii	394	0.4%
42	Idaho	388	0.4%
7	Illinois	4,046	3.8%
13	Indiana	2,234	2.1%
36	Iowa	686	0.6%
31	Kansas	1,016	1.0%
27	Kentucky	1,301	1.2%
20	Louisiana	1,817	1.7%
44	Maine	329	0.3%
15	Maryland	2,185	2.1%
17	Massachusetts	2,006	1.9%
4	Michigan	6,740	6.4%
23	Minnesota	1,588	1.5%
29	Mississippi	1,125	1.1%
19	Missouri	1,894	1.8%
47	Montana	234	0.2%
40	Nebraska	447	0.4%
32	Nevada	846	0.8%
39	New Hampshire	499	0.5%
14	New Jersey	2,215	2.1%
33	New Mexico	842	0.8%
6	New York	5,008	4.7%
12	North Carolina	2,379	2.2%
50	North Dakota	149	0.1%
5	Ohio	5,444	5.1%
22	Oklahoma	1,592	1.5%
24	Oregon	1,554	1.5%
9	Pennsylvania	3,195	3.0%
46	Rhode Island	286	0.3%
18	South Carolina	1,905	1.8%
45	South Dakota	318	0.3%
10	Tennessee	2,544	2.4%
2	Texas	9,922	9.4%
34	Utah	829	0.8%
48	Vermont	229	0.2%
16	Virginia	2,083	2.0%
8	Washington	3,384	3.2%
43	West Virginia	365	0.3%
28	Wisconsin	1,269	1.2%
49	Wyoming	161	0.2%

RANK ORDER

RANK	STATE	RAPES	% of USA
1	California	11,766	11.1%
2	Texas	9,922	9.4%
3	Florida	7,359	6.9%
4	Michigan	6,740	6.4%
5	Ohio	5,444	5.1%
6	New York	5,008	4.7%
7	Illinois	4,046	3.8%
8	Washington	3,384	3.2%
9	Pennsylvania	3,195	3.0%
10	Tennessee	2,544	2.4%
11	Georgia	2,448	2.3%
12	North Carolina	2,379	2.2%
13	Indiana	2,234	2.1%
14	New Jersey	2,215	2.1%
15	Maryland	2,185	2.1%
16	Virginia	2,083	2.0%
17	Massachusetts	2,006	1.9%
18	South Carolina	1,905	1.8%
19	Missouri	1,894	1.8%
20	Louisiana	1,817	1.7%
21	Colorado	1,633	1.5%
22	Oklahoma	1,592	1.5%
23	Minnesota	1,588	1.5%
24	Oregon	1,554	1.5%
25	Arizona	1,488	1.4%
26	Alabama	1,471	1.4%
27	Kentucky	1,301	1.2%
28	Wisconsin	1,269	1.2%
29	Mississippi	1,125	1.1%
30	Arkansas	1,028	1.0%
31	Kansas	1,016	1.0%
32	Nevada	846	0.8%
33	New Mexico	842	0.8%
34	Utah	829	0.8%
35	Connecticut	800	0.8%
36	Iowa	686	0.6%
37	Delaware	539	0.5%
38	Alaska	502	0.5%
39	New Hampshire	499	0.5%
40	Nebraska	447	0.4%
41	Hawaii	394	0.4%
42	Idaho	388	0.4%
43	West Virginia	365	0.3%
44	Maine	329	0.3%
45	South Dakota	318	0.3%
46	Rhode Island	286	0.3%
47	Montana	234	0.2%
48	Vermont	229	0.2%
49	Wyoming	161	0.2%
50	North Dakota	149	0.1%
	District of Columbia	324	0.3%

Source: Federal Bureau of Investigation
   "Crime in the United States 1993" (Uniform Crime Reports, December 4, 1994)
*Revised national total. Forcible rape is the carnal knowledge of a female forcibly and against her will. Assaults or attempts to commit rape by force or threat of force are included. However, statutory rape without force and other sex offenses are excluded.

Percent Change in Number of Rapes: 1993 to 1997

National Percent Change = 9.3% Decrease*

ALPHA ORDER				RANK ORDER		
RANK	STATE	PERCENT CHANGE		RANK	STATE	PERCENT CHANGE
23	Alabama	(5.1)		1	Minnesota	54.0
44	Alaska	(19.7)		2	Rhode Island	26.9
15	Arizona	0.3		3	Tennessee	20.1
9	Arkansas	6.8		4	Nevada	18.8
31	California	(13.4)		5	Utah	17.9
14	Colorado	2.7		6	South Dakota	12.3
26	Connecticut	(7.5)		7	Illinois	9.1
29	Delaware	(11.7)		8	Kansas	8.3
12	Florida	3.3		9	Arkansas	6.8
22	Georgia	(4.9)		10	North Dakota	6.7
25	Hawaii	(5.8)		11	New Mexico	3.6
28	Idaho	(9.8)		12	Florida	3.3
7	Illinois	9.1		13	Pennsylvania	2.9
32	Indiana	(13.7)		14	Colorado	2.7
35	Iowa	(15.6)		15	Arizona	0.3
8	Kansas	8.3		16	Kentucky	0.2
16	Kentucky	0.2		17	Louisiana	(1.0)
17	Louisiana	(1.0)		18	North Carolina	(1.3)
47	Maine	(22.8)		19	West Virginia	(2.7)
38	Maryland	(17.0)		20	South Carolina	(3.6)
40	Massachusetts	(17.9)		21	Oklahoma	(4.7)
48	Michigan	(24.8)		22	Georgia	(4.9)
1	Minnesota	54.0		23	Alabama	(5.1)
24	Mississippi	(5.3)		24	Mississippi	(5.3)
43	Missouri	(19.5)		25	Hawaii	(5.8)
49	Montana	(26.9)		26	Connecticut	(7.5)
27	Nebraska	(9.2)		27	Nebraska	(9.2)
4	Nevada	18.8		28	Idaho	(9.8)
45	New Hampshire	(20.8)		29	Delaware	(11.7)
46	New Jersey	(21.9)		30	Virginia	(12.7)
11	New Mexico	3.6		31	California	(13.4)
41	New York	(18.6)		32	Indiana	(13.7)
18	North Carolina	(1.3)		33	Washington	(14.7)
10	North Dakota	6.7		34	Wyoming	(14.9)
37	Ohio	(16.1)		35	Iowa	(15.6)
21	Oklahoma	(4.7)		36	Oregon	(16.0)
36	Oregon	(16.0)		37	Ohio	(16.1)
13	Pennsylvania	2.9		38	Maryland	(17.0)
2	Rhode Island	26.9		39	Wisconsin	(17.4)
20	South Carolina	(3.6)		40	Massachusetts	(17.9)
6	South Dakota	12.3		41	New York	(18.6)
3	Tennessee	20.1		42	Texas	(19.3)
42	Texas	(19.3)		43	Missouri	(19.5)
5	Utah	17.9		44	Alaska	(19.7)
50	Vermont	(31.9)		45	New Hampshire	(20.8)
30	Virginia	(12.7)		46	New Jersey	(21.9)
33	Washington	(14.7)		47	Maine	(22.8)
19	West Virginia	(2.7)		48	Michigan	(24.8)
39	Wisconsin	(17.4)		49	Montana	(26.9)
34	Wyoming	(14.9)		50	Vermont	(31.9)
					District of Columbia	(32.7)

Source: Morgan Quitno Press using data from Federal Bureau of Investigation
    "Crime in the United States" (Uniform Crime Reports, 1993 and 1997 editions)
*Forcible rape is the carnal knowledge of a female forcibly and against her will. Assaults or attempts to commit rape by force or threat of force are included. However, statutory rape without force and other sex offenses are excluded.

Rape Rate in 1993

National Rate = 41.1 Rapes per 100,000 Population*

ALPHA ORDER

RANK	STATE	RATE
31	Alabama	35.1
1	Alaska	83.8
25	Arizona	37.8
20	Arkansas	42.4
26	California	37.7
14	Colorado	45.8
47	Connecticut	24.4
2	Delaware	77.0
7	Florida	53.8
28	Georgia	35.4
36	Hawaii	33.6
29	Idaho	35.3
32	Illinois	34.6
24	Indiana	39.1
47	Iowa	24.4
22	Kansas	40.1
33	Kentucky	34.3
21	Louisiana	42.3
44	Maine	26.6
18	Maryland	44.0
37	Massachusetts	33.4
3	Michigan	71.1
30	Minnesota	35.2
19	Mississippi	42.6
27	Missouri	36.2
41	Montana	27.9
42	Nebraska	27.8
5	Nevada	60.9
17	New Hampshire	44.4
40	New Jersey	28.1
9	New Mexico	52.1
43	New York	27.5
33	North Carolina	34.3
49	North Dakota	23.5
13	Ohio	49.1
12	Oklahoma	49.3
10	Oregon	51.3
45	Pennsylvania	26.5
39	Rhode Island	28.6
8	South Carolina	52.3
16	South Dakota	44.5
11	Tennessee	49.9
6	Texas	55.0
15	Utah	44.6
23	Vermont	39.8
38	Virginia	32.1
4	Washington	64.4
50	West Virginia	20.1
46	Wisconsin	25.2
33	Wyoming	34.3

RANK ORDER

RANK	STATE	RATE
1	Alaska	83.8
2	Delaware	77.0
3	Michigan	71.1
4	Washington	64.4
5	Nevada	60.9
6	Texas	55.0
7	Florida	53.8
8	South Carolina	52.3
9	New Mexico	52.1
10	Oregon	51.3
11	Tennessee	49.9
12	Oklahoma	49.3
13	Ohio	49.1
14	Colorado	45.8
15	Utah	44.6
16	South Dakota	44.5
17	New Hampshire	44.4
18	Maryland	44.0
19	Mississippi	42.6
20	Arkansas	42.4
21	Louisiana	42.3
22	Kansas	40.1
23	Vermont	39.8
24	Indiana	39.1
25	Arizona	37.8
26	California	37.7
27	Missouri	36.2
28	Georgia	35.4
29	Idaho	35.3
30	Minnesota	35.2
31	Alabama	35.1
32	Illinois	34.6
33	Kentucky	34.3
33	North Carolina	34.3
33	Wyoming	34.3
36	Hawaii	33.6
37	Massachusetts	33.4
38	Virginia	32.1
39	Rhode Island	28.6
40	New Jersey	28.1
41	Montana	27.9
42	Nebraska	27.8
43	New York	27.5
44	Maine	26.6
45	Pennsylvania	26.5
46	Wisconsin	25.2
47	Connecticut	24.4
47	Iowa	24.4
49	North Dakota	23.5
50	West Virginia	20.1
	District of Columbia	56.1

Source: Federal Bureau of Investigation
   "Crime in the United States 1993" (Uniform Crime Reports, December 4, 1994)
*Revised national rate. Forcible rape is the carnal knowledge of a female forcibly and against her will. Assaults or attempts to commit rape by force or threat of force are included. However, statutory rape without force and other sex offenses are excluded.

Percent Change in Rape Rate: 1993 to 1997

National Percent Change = 12.7% Decrease*

ALPHA ORDER

RANK	STATE	PERCENT CHANGE
23	Alabama	(8.0)
41	Alaska	(21.0)
27	Arizona	(13.2)
10	Arkansas	2.6
31	California	(16.2)
17	Colorado	(5.9)
21	Connecticut	(7.4)
28	Delaware	(15.6)
16	Florida	(3.5)
26	Georgia	(12.1)
19	Hawaii	(6.8)
35	Idaho	(18.1)
5	Illinois	7.2
29	Indiana	(15.9)
32	Iowa	(16.8)
7	Kansas	5.7
13	Kentucky	(2.6)
12	Louisiana	(2.4)
44	Maine	(22.9)
37	Maryland	(19.1)
39	Massachusetts	(19.5)
48	Michigan	(27.0)
1	Minnesota	48.3
24	Mississippi	(8.5)
43	Missouri	(22.1)
49	Montana	(30.1)
25	Nebraska	(11.9)
11	Nevada	(1.6)
46	New Hampshire	(24.1)
45	New Jersey	(23.5)
15	New Mexico	(3.3)
36	New York	(18.2)
22	North Carolina	(7.9)
8	North Dakota	5.5
33	Ohio	(16.9)
20	Oklahoma	(7.3)
42	Oregon	(21.4)
9	Pennsylvania	3.4
2	Rhode Island	28.7
18	South Carolina	(6.5)
4	South Dakota	8.8
3	Tennessee	14.0
47	Texas	(25.1)
6	Utah	6.5
50	Vermont	(33.4)
29	Virginia	(15.9)
40	Washington	(20.2)
14	West Virginia	(3.0)
38	Wisconsin	(19.4)
33	Wyoming	(16.9)

RANK ORDER

RANK	STATE	PERCENT CHANGE
1	Minnesota	48.3
2	Rhode Island	28.7
3	Tennessee	14.0
4	South Dakota	8.8
5	Illinois	7.2
6	Utah	6.5
7	Kansas	5.7
8	North Dakota	5.5
9	Pennsylvania	3.4
10	Arkansas	2.6
11	Nevada	(1.6)
12	Louisiana	(2.4)
13	Kentucky	(2.6)
14	West Virginia	(3.0)
15	New Mexico	(3.3)
16	Florida	(3.5)
17	Colorado	(5.9)
18	South Carolina	(6.5)
19	Hawaii	(6.8)
20	Oklahoma	(7.3)
21	Connecticut	(7.4)
22	North Carolina	(7.9)
23	Alabama	(8.0)
24	Mississippi	(8.5)
25	Nebraska	(11.9)
26	Georgia	(12.1)
27	Arizona	(13.2)
28	Delaware	(15.6)
29	Indiana	(15.9)
29	Virginia	(15.9)
31	California	(16.2)
32	Iowa	(16.8)
33	Ohio	(16.9)
33	Wyoming	(16.9)
35	Idaho	(18.1)
36	New York	(18.2)
37	Maryland	(19.1)
38	Wisconsin	(19.4)
39	Massachusetts	(19.5)
40	Washington	(20.2)
41	Alaska	(21.0)
42	Oregon	(21.4)
43	Missouri	(22.1)
44	Maine	(22.9)
45	New Jersey	(23.5)
46	New Hampshire	(24.1)
47	Texas	(25.1)
48	Michigan	(27.0)
49	Montana	(30.1)
50	Vermont	(33.4)

District of Columbia   (26.6)

Source: Morgan Quitno Press using data from Federal Bureau of Investigation
   "Crime in the United States" (Uniform Crime Reports, 1993 and 1997 editions)
*Forcible rape is the carnal knowledge of a female forcibly and against her will. Assaults or attempts to commit rape by force or threat of force are included. However, statutory rape without force and other sex offenses are excluded.

Robberies in 1993

National Total = 659,870 Robberies*

ALPHA ORDER

ALPHA ORDER

RANK	STATE	ROBBERIES	% of USA
21	Alabama	6,677	1.0%
42	Alaska	733	0.1%
23	Arizona	6,412	1.0%
33	Arkansas	3,027	0.5%
1	California	126,436	19.2%
27	Colorado	4,160	0.6%
22	Connecticut	6,447	1.0%
36	Delaware	1,307	0.2%
3	Florida	48,913	7.4%
11	Georgia	17,154	2.6%
37	Hawaii	1,214	0.2%
46	Idaho	186	0.0%
4	Illinois	44,584	6.8%
19	Indiana	6,845	1.0%
35	Iowa	1,517	0.2%
32	Kansas	3,128	0.5%
31	Kentucky	3,425	0.5%
14	Louisiana	12,182	1.8%
45	Maine	264	0.0%
8	Maryland	21,582	3.3%
16	Massachusetts	10,563	1.6%
7	Michigan	22,601	3.4%
25	Minnesota	5,092	0.8%
30	Mississippi	3,683	0.6%
13	Missouri	12,654	1.9%
44	Montana	272	0.0%
40	Nebraska	890	0.1%
26	Nevada	4,724	0.7%
43	New Hampshire	307	0.0%
6	New Jersey	23,319	3.5%
34	New Mexico	2,237	0.3%
2	New York	102,122	15.5%
12	North Carolina	13,364	2.0%
49	North Dakota	53	0.0%
10	Ohio	21,373	3.2%
28	Oklahoma	3,935	0.6%
29	Oregon	3,930	0.6%
9	Pennsylvania	21,563	3.3%
39	Rhode Island	1,011	0.2%
20	South Carolina	6,825	1.0%
47	South Dakota	107	0.0%
15	Tennessee	11,224	1.7%
5	Texas	40,469	6.1%
38	Utah	1,090	0.2%
50	Vermont	52	0.0%
17	Virginia	9,216	1.4%
18	Washington	7,204	1.1%
41	West Virginia	782	0.1%
24	Wisconsin	5,714	0.9%
48	Wyoming	81	0.0%

RANK ORDER

RANK	STATE	ROBBERIES	% of USA
1	California	126,436	19.2%
2	New York	102,122	15.5%
3	Florida	48,913	7.4%
4	Illinois	44,584	6.8%
5	Texas	40,469	6.1%
6	New Jersey	23,319	3.5%
7	Michigan	22,601	3.4%
8	Maryland	21,582	3.3%
9	Pennsylvania	21,563	3.3%
10	Ohio	21,373	3.2%
11	Georgia	17,154	2.6%
12	North Carolina	13,364	2.0%
13	Missouri	12,654	1.9%
14	Louisiana	12,182	1.8%
15	Tennessee	11,224	1.7%
16	Massachusetts	10,563	1.6%
17	Virginia	9,216	1.4%
18	Washington	7,204	1.1%
19	Indiana	6,845	1.0%
20	South Carolina	6,825	1.0%
21	Alabama	6,677	1.0%
22	Connecticut	6,447	1.0%
23	Arizona	6,412	1.0%
24	Wisconsin	5,714	0.9%
25	Minnesota	5,092	0.8%
26	Nevada	4,724	0.7%
27	Colorado	4,160	0.6%
28	Oklahoma	3,935	0.6%
29	Oregon	3,930	0.6%
30	Mississippi	3,683	0.6%
31	Kentucky	3,425	0.5%
32	Kansas	3,128	0.5%
33	Arkansas	3,027	0.5%
34	New Mexico	2,237	0.3%
35	Iowa	1,517	0.2%
36	Delaware	1,307	0.2%
37	Hawaii	1,214	0.2%
38	Utah	1,090	0.2%
39	Rhode Island	1,011	0.2%
40	Nebraska	890	0.1%
41	West Virginia	782	0.1%
42	Alaska	733	0.1%
43	New Hampshire	307	0.0%
44	Montana	272	0.0%
45	Maine	264	0.0%
46	Idaho	186	0.0%
47	South Dakota	107	0.0%
48	Wyoming	81	0.0%
49	North Dakota	53	0.0%
50	Vermont	52	0.0%
	District of Columbia	7,107	1.1%

Source: Federal Bureau of Investigation
"Crime in the United States 1993" (Uniform Crime Reports, December 4, 1994)
*Revised national total. Robbery is the taking or attempting to take anything of value by force or threat of force.

Percent Change in Number of Robberies: 1993 to 1997

National Percent Change = 24.5% Decrease*

RANK	STATE	PERCENT CHANGE
14	Alabama	3.8
30	Alaska	(11.6)
7	Arizona	17.7
25	Arkansas	(7.0)
48	California	(35.6)
37	Colorado	(22.1)
38	Connecticut	(22.5)
18	Delaware	0.5
35	Florida	(17.3)
28	Georgia	(9.8)
8	Hawaii	15.6
5	Idaho	27.4
42	Illinois	(25.7)
9	Indiana	13.4
12	Iowa	5.0
39	Kansas	(22.6)
15	Kentucky	3.5
33	Louisiana	(14.6)
20	Maine	(2.7)
36	Maryland	(20.5)
49	Massachusetts	(36.8)
46	Michigan	(33.9)
11	Minnesota	5.5
17	Mississippi	1.6
45	Missouri	(33.4)
47	Montana	(34.2)
6	Nebraska	23.3
10	Nevada	7.3
29	New Hampshire	(10.7)
43	New Jersey	(27.3)
3	New Mexico	32.6
50	New York	(45.1)
23	North Carolina	(4.1)
39	North Dakota	(22.6)
34	Ohio	(16.9)
31	Oklahoma	(12.4)
22	Oregon	(3.0)
32	Pennsylvania	(12.9)
44	Rhode Island	(30.1)
21	South Carolina	(2.9)
1	South Dakota	60.7
16	Tennessee	2.3
41	Texas	(24.6)
4	Utah	29.2
2	Vermont	51.9
27	Virginia	(9.0)
24	Washington	(6.5)
19	West Virginia	0.0
26	Wisconsin	(8.8)
13	Wyoming	4.9

RANK	STATE	PERCENT CHANGE
1	South Dakota	60.7
2	Vermont	51.9
3	New Mexico	32.6
4	Utah	29.2
5	Idaho	27.4
6	Nebraska	23.3
7	Arizona	17.7
8	Hawaii	15.6
9	Indiana	13.4
10	Nevada	7.3
11	Minnesota	5.5
12	Iowa	5.0
13	Wyoming	4.9
14	Alabama	3.8
15	Kentucky	3.5
16	Tennessee	2.3
17	Mississippi	1.6
18	Delaware	0.5
19	West Virginia	0.0
20	Maine	(2.7)
21	South Carolina	(2.9)
22	Oregon	(3.0)
23	North Carolina	(4.1)
24	Washington	(6.5)
25	Arkansas	(7.0)
26	Wisconsin	(8.8)
27	Virginia	(9.0)
28	Georgia	(9.8)
29	New Hampshire	(10.7)
30	Alaska	(11.6)
31	Oklahoma	(12.4)
32	Pennsylvania	(12.9)
33	Louisiana	(14.6)
34	Ohio	(16.9)
35	Florida	(17.3)
36	Maryland	(20.5)
37	Colorado	(22.1)
38	Connecticut	(22.5)
39	Kansas	(22.6)
39	North Dakota	(22.6)
41	Texas	(24.6)
42	Illinois	(25.7)
43	New Jersey	(27.3)
44	Rhode Island	(30.1)
45	Missouri	(33.4)
46	Michigan	(33.9)
47	Montana	(34.2)
48	California	(35.6)
49	Massachusetts	(36.8)
50	New York	(45.1)
	District of Columbia	(36.7)

Source: Morgan Quitno Press using data from Federal Bureau of Investigation
"Crime in the United States" (Uniform Crime Reports, 1993 and 1997 editions)
Robbery is the taking or attempting to take anything of value by force or threat of force.

Robbery Rate in 1993

National Rate = 255.9 Robberies per 100,000 Population*

ALPHA ORDER

RANK	STATE	RATE
22	Alabama	159.5
30	Alaska	122.4
21	Arizona	162.9
28	Arkansas	124.9
3	California	405.1
33	Colorado	116.7
14	Connecticut	196.7
18	Delaware	186.7
5	Florida	357.6
9	Georgia	248.0
36	Hawaii	103.6
47	Idaho	16.9
4	Illinois	381.2
32	Indiana	119.8
41	Iowa	53.9
29	Kansas	123.6
38	Kentucky	90.4
8	Louisiana	283.6
45	Maine	21.3
2	Maryland	434.7
20	Massachusetts	175.7
11	Michigan	238.5
35	Minnesota	112.7
24	Mississippi	139.3
10	Missouri	241.8
43	Montana	32.4
40	Nebraska	55.4
6	Nevada	340.1
44	New Hampshire	27.3
7	New Jersey	296.0
25	New Mexico	138.4
1	New York	561.2
16	North Carolina	192.4
50	North Dakota	8.3
15	Ohio	192.7
31	Oklahoma	121.8
27	Oregon	129.6
19	Pennsylvania	179.0
37	Rhode Island	101.1
17	South Carolina	187.3
48	South Dakota	15.0
13	Tennessee	220.1
12	Texas	224.4
39	Utah	58.6
49	Vermont	9.0
23	Virginia	142.0
26	Washington	137.1
42	West Virginia	43.0
34	Wisconsin	113.4
46	Wyoming	17.2

RANK ORDER

RANK	STATE	RATE
1	New York	561.2
2	Maryland	434.7
3	California	405.1
4	Illinois	381.2
5	Florida	357.6
6	Nevada	340.1
7	New Jersey	296.0
8	Louisiana	283.6
9	Georgia	248.0
10	Missouri	241.8
11	Michigan	238.5
12	Texas	224.4
13	Tennessee	220.1
14	Connecticut	196.7
15	Ohio	192.7
16	North Carolina	192.4
17	South Carolina	187.3
18	Delaware	186.7
19	Pennsylvania	179.0
20	Massachusetts	175.7
21	Arizona	162.9
22	Alabama	159.5
23	Virginia	142.0
24	Mississippi	139.3
25	New Mexico	138.4
26	Washington	137.1
27	Oregon	129.6
28	Arkansas	124.9
29	Kansas	123.6
30	Alaska	122.4
31	Oklahoma	121.8
32	Indiana	119.8
33	Colorado	116.7
34	Wisconsin	113.4
35	Minnesota	112.7
36	Hawaii	103.6
37	Rhode Island	101.1
38	Kentucky	90.4
39	Utah	58.6
40	Nebraska	55.4
41	Iowa	53.9
42	West Virginia	43.0
43	Montana	32.4
44	New Hampshire	27.3
45	Maine	21.3
46	Wyoming	17.2
47	Idaho	16.9
48	South Dakota	15.0
49	Vermont	9.0
50	North Dakota	8.3
	District of Columbia	1,229.6

Source: Federal Bureau of Investigation
"Crime in the United States 1993" (Uniform Crime Reports, December 4, 1994)
Revised national rate. Robbery is the taking or attempting to take anything of value by force or threat of force.

Percent Change in Robbery Rate: 1993 to 1997

National Percent Change = 27.3% Decrease*

ALPHA ORDER

RANK	STATE	PERCENT CHANGE
13	Alabama	0.6
29	Alaska	(13.1)
12	Arizona	1.7
23	Arkansas	(10.7)
48	California	(37.7)
41	Colorado	(28.6)
35	Connecticut	(22.3)
19	Delaware	(3.9)
37	Florida	(22.8)
33	Georgia	(16.7)
7	Hawaii	14.1
6	Idaho	16.0
40	Illinois	(27.0)
8	Indiana	10.5
9	Iowa	3.7
39	Kansas	(24.5)
14	Kentucky	0.3
32	Louisiana	(15.7)
17	Maine	(2.8)
36	Maryland	(22.5)
49	Massachusetts	(37.9)
46	Michigan	(35.9)
11	Minnesota	1.8
16	Mississippi	(1.7)
45	Missouri	(35.4)
47	Montana	(37.0)
4	Nebraska	19.5
25	Nevada	(11.1)
30	New Hampshire	(14.3)
42	New Jersey	(28.9)
3	New Mexico	23.8
50	New York	(44.9)
22	North Carolina	(10.3)
38	North Dakota	(22.9)
34	Ohio	(17.6)
31	Oklahoma	(14.7)
21	Oregon	(9.3)
28	Pennsylvania	(12.7)
43	Rhode Island	(29.2)
20	South Carolina	(5.9)
1	South Dakota	55.3
17	Tennessee	(2.8)
44	Texas	(30.0)
5	Utah	16.7
2	Vermont	48.9
26	Virginia	(12.3)
27	Washington	(12.5)
15	West Virginia	0.2
24	Wisconsin	(11.0)
10	Wyoming	2.9

RANK ORDER

RANK	STATE	PERCENT CHANGE
1	South Dakota	55.3
2	Vermont	48.9
3	New Mexico	23.8
4	Nebraska	19.5
5	Utah	16.7
6	Idaho	16.0
7	Hawaii	14.1
8	Indiana	10.5
9	Iowa	3.7
10	Wyoming	2.9
11	Minnesota	1.8
12	Arizona	1.7
13	Alabama	0.6
14	Kentucky	0.3
15	West Virginia	0.2
16	Mississippi	(1.7)
17	Maine	(2.8)
17	Tennessee	(2.8)
19	Delaware	(3.9)
20	South Carolina	(5.9)
21	Oregon	(9.3)
22	North Carolina	(10.3)
23	Arkansas	(10.7)
24	Wisconsin	(11.0)
25	Nevada	(11.1)
26	Virginia	(12.3)
27	Washington	(12.5)
28	Pennsylvania	(12.7)
29	Alaska	(13.1)
30	New Hampshire	(14.3)
31	Oklahoma	(14.7)
32	Louisiana	(15.7)
33	Georgia	(16.7)
34	Ohio	(17.6)
35	Connecticut	(22.3)
36	Maryland	(22.5)
37	Florida	(22.8)
38	North Dakota	(22.9)
39	Kansas	(24.5)
40	Illinois	(27.0)
41	Colorado	(28.6)
42	New Jersey	(28.9)
43	Rhode Island	(29.2)
44	Texas	(30.0)
45	Missouri	(35.4)
46	Michigan	(35.9)
47	Montana	(37.0)
48	California	(37.7)
49	Massachusetts	(37.9)
50	New York	(44.9)

District of Columbia (30.8)

Source: Morgan Quitno Press using data from Federal Bureau of Investigation
"Crime in the United States" (Uniform Crime Reports, 1993 and 1997 editions)
*Robbery is the taking or attempting to take anything of value by force or threat of force.

Aggravated Assaults in 1993

National Total = 1,135,610 Aggravated Assaults*

ALPHA ORDER				RANK ORDER			
RANK	STATE	ASSAULTS	% of USA	RANK	STATE	ASSAULTS	% of USA
16	Alabama	24,044	2.1%	1	California	194,083	17.1%
38	Alaska	3,268	0.3%	2	Florida	107,479	9.5%
19	Arizona	19,903	1.8%	3	New York	85,802	7.6%
27	Arkansas	10,079	0.9%	4	Texas	84,881	7.5%
1	California	194,083	17.1%	5	Illinois	62,298	5.5%
23	Colorado	14,230	1.3%	6	Michigan	44,747	3.9%
31	Connecticut	7,496	0.7%	7	Massachusetts	35,591	3.1%
39	Delaware	2,920	0.3%	8	Louisiana	30,727	2.7%
2	Florida	107,479	9.5%	9	North Carolina	30,650	2.7%
10	Georgia	29,628	2.6%	10	Georgia	29,628	2.6%
43	Hawaii	1,408	0.1%	11	Ohio	28,431	2.5%
42	Idaho	2,491	0.2%	12	South Carolina	28,174	2.5%
5	Illinois	62,298	5.5%	13	Maryland	25,141	2.2%
20	Indiana	18,432	1.6%	14	Tennessee	24,758	2.2%
32	Iowa	6,890	0.6%	15	Pennsylvania	24,714	2.2%
29	Kansas	8,259	0.7%	16	Alabama	24,044	2.1%
24	Kentucky	12,555	1.1%	17	Missouri	23,825	2.1%
8	Louisiana	30,727	2.7%	18	New Jersey	23,438	2.1%
47	Maine	945	0.1%	19	Arizona	19,903	1.8%
13	Maryland	25,141	2.2%	20	Indiana	18,432	1.6%
7	Massachusetts	35,591	3.1%	21	Washington	16,181	1.4%
6	Michigan	44,747	3.9%	22	Oklahoma	14,712	1.3%
30	Minnesota	7,943	0.7%	23	Colorado	14,230	1.3%
34	Mississippi	6,302	0.6%	24	Kentucky	12,555	1.1%
17	Missouri	23,825	2.1%	25	Virginia	12,322	1.1%
46	Montana	958	0.1%	26	New Mexico	11,815	1.0%
36	Nebraska	4,050	0.4%	27	Arkansas	10,079	0.9%
33	Nevada	6,443	0.6%	28	Oregon	9,630	0.8%
48	New Hampshire	721	0.1%	29	Kansas	8,259	0.7%
18	New Jersey	23,438	2.1%	30	Minnesota	7,943	0.7%
26	New Mexico	11,815	1.0%	31	Connecticut	7,496	0.7%
3	New York	85,802	7.6%	32	Iowa	6,890	0.6%
9	North Carolina	30,650	2.7%	33	Nevada	6,443	0.6%
50	North Dakota	309	0.0%	34	Mississippi	6,302	0.6%
11	Ohio	28,431	2.5%	35	Wisconsin	6,116	0.5%
22	Oklahoma	14,712	1.3%	36	Nebraska	4,050	0.4%
28	Oregon	9,630	0.8%	37	Utah	3,622	0.3%
15	Pennsylvania	24,714	2.2%	38	Alaska	3,268	0.3%
40	Rhode Island	2,681	0.2%	39	Delaware	2,920	0.3%
12	South Carolina	28,174	2.5%	40	Rhode Island	2,681	0.2%
45	South Dakota	1,041	0.1%	41	West Virginia	2,520	0.2%
14	Tennessee	24,758	2.2%	42	Idaho	2,491	0.2%
4	Texas	84,881	7.5%	43	Hawaii	1,408	0.1%
37	Utah	3,622	0.3%	44	Wyoming	1,087	0.1%
49	Vermont	356	0.0%	45	South Dakota	1,041	0.1%
25	Virginia	12,322	1.1%	46	Montana	958	0.1%
21	Washington	16,181	1.4%	47	Maine	945	0.1%
41	West Virginia	2,520	0.2%	48	New Hampshire	721	0.1%
35	Wisconsin	6,116	0.5%	49	Vermont	356	0.0%
44	Wyoming	1,087	0.1%	50	North Dakota	309	0.0%
					District of Columbia	9,003	0.8%

Source: Federal Bureau of Investigation
   "Crime in the United States 1993" (Uniform Crime Reports, December 4, 1994)
*Revised national total. Aggravated assault is an attack for the purpose of inflicting severe bodily injury.

Percent Change in Number of Aggravated Assaults: 1993 to 1997

National Percent Change = 10.0% Decrease*

ALPHA ORDER

RANK	STATE	PERCENT CHANGE		RANK	STATE	PERCENT CHANGE
48	Alabama	(35.0)		1	Nebraska	41.0
20	Alaska	(3.2)		2	Vermont	29.5
24	Arizona	(4.6)		3	Wisconsin	23.0
35	Arkansas	(9.4)		4	Pennsylvania	22.8
41	California	(15.8)		5	Utah	22.7
49	Colorado	(36.3)		6	Mississippi	21.3
27	Connecticut	(7.7)		7	North Dakota	14.2
12	Delaware	8.0		8	Nevada	10.7
26	Florida	(6.1)		9	Tennessee	10.4
29	Georgia	(8.7)		10	West Virginia	9.5
13	Hawaii	5.0		11	Indiana	8.8
18	Idaho	(0.4)		12	Delaware	8.0
14	Illinois	2.5		13	Hawaii	5.0
11	Indiana	8.8		14	Illinois	2.5
21	Iowa	(4.0)		15	Maine	2.0
42	Kansas	(15.9)		16	Virginia	1.9
50	Kentucky	(41.8)		17	South Carolina	1.0
46	Louisiana	(20.7)		18	Idaho	(0.4)
15	Maine	2.0		19	Minnesota	(0.8)
25	Maryland	(5.9)		20	Alaska	(3.2)
40	Massachusetts	(13.0)		21	Iowa	(4.0)
43	Michigan	(17.5)		22	North Carolina	(4.4)
19	Minnesota	(0.8)		23	Oregon	(4.5)
6	Mississippi	21.3		24	Arizona	(4.6)
39	Missouri	(12.7)		25	Maryland	(5.9)
45	Montana	(19.7)		26	Florida	(6.1)
1	Nebraska	41.0		27	Connecticut	(7.7)
8	Nevada	10.7		28	Washington	(8.1)
36	New Hampshire	(10.8)		29	Georgia	(8.7)
38	New Jersey	(11.9)		29	New Mexico	(8.7)
29	New Mexico	(8.7)		31	Ohio	(9.0)
47	New York	(25.8)		31	Texas	(9.0)
22	North Carolina	(4.4)		33	Oklahoma	(9.1)
7	North Dakota	14.2		34	Wyoming	(9.3)
31	Ohio	(9.0)		35	Arkansas	(9.4)
33	Oklahoma	(9.1)		36	New Hampshire	(10.8)
23	Oregon	(4.5)		37	South Dakota	(11.8)
4	Pennsylvania	22.8		38	New Jersey	(11.9)
44	Rhode Island	(18.1)		39	Missouri	(12.7)
17	South Carolina	1.0		40	Massachusetts	(13.0)
37	South Dakota	(11.8)		41	California	(15.8)
9	Tennessee	10.4		42	Kansas	(15.9)
31	Texas	(9.0)		43	Michigan	(17.5)
5	Utah	22.7		44	Rhode Island	(18.1)
2	Vermont	29.5		45	Montana	(19.7)
16	Virginia	1.9		46	Louisiana	(20.7)
28	Washington	(8.1)		47	New York	(25.8)
10	West Virginia	9.5		48	Alabama	(35.0)
3	Wisconsin	23.0		49	Colorado	(36.3)
34	Wyoming	(9.3)		50	Kentucky	(41.8)
					District of Columbia	(36.8)

Source: Morgan Quitno Press using data from Federal Bureau of Investigation
"Crime in the United States" (Uniform Crime Reports, 1993 and 1997 editions)
*Aggravated assault is an attack for the purpose of inflicting severe bodily injury.

Aggravated Assault Rate in 1993

National Rate = 440.3 Aggravated Assaults per 100,000 Population*

<table>
<tr><td colspan="3">ALPHA ORDER</td><td colspan="3">RANK ORDER</td></tr>
<tr><td>RANK</td><td>STATE</td><td>RATE</td><td>RANK</td><td>STATE</td><td>RATE</td></tr>
<tr><td>7</td><td>Alabama</td><td>574.3</td><td>1</td><td>Florida</td><td>785.7</td></tr>
<tr><td>8</td><td>Alaska</td><td>545.6</td><td>2</td><td>South Carolina</td><td>773.4</td></tr>
<tr><td>11</td><td>Arizona</td><td>505.7</td><td>3</td><td>New Mexico</td><td>731.1</td></tr>
<tr><td>22</td><td>Arkansas</td><td>415.8</td><td>4</td><td>Louisiana</td><td>715.4</td></tr>
<tr><td>5</td><td>California</td><td>621.8</td><td>5</td><td>California</td><td>621.8</td></tr>
<tr><td>23</td><td>Colorado</td><td>399.0</td><td>6</td><td>Massachusetts</td><td>592.0</td></tr>
<tr><td>36</td><td>Connecticut</td><td>228.7</td><td>7</td><td>Alabama</td><td>574.3</td></tr>
<tr><td>21</td><td>Delaware</td><td>417.1</td><td>8</td><td>Alaska</td><td>545.6</td></tr>
<tr><td>1</td><td>Florida</td><td>785.7</td><td>9</td><td>Illinois</td><td>532.6</td></tr>
<tr><td>20</td><td>Georgia</td><td>428.3</td><td>10</td><td>Maryland</td><td>506.4</td></tr>
<tr><td>45</td><td>Hawaii</td><td>120.1</td><td>11</td><td>Arizona</td><td>505.7</td></tr>
<tr><td>37</td><td>Idaho</td><td>226.7</td><td>12</td><td>Tennessee</td><td>485.5</td></tr>
<tr><td>9</td><td>Illinois</td><td>532.6</td><td>13</td><td>Michigan</td><td>472.1</td></tr>
<tr><td>26</td><td>Indiana</td><td>322.6</td><td>14</td><td>New York</td><td>471.5</td></tr>
<tr><td>33</td><td>Iowa</td><td>244.8</td><td>15</td><td>Texas</td><td>470.8</td></tr>
<tr><td>25</td><td>Kansas</td><td>326.3</td><td>16</td><td>Nevada</td><td>463.9</td></tr>
<tr><td>24</td><td>Kentucky</td><td>331.4</td><td>17</td><td>Oklahoma</td><td>455.3</td></tr>
<tr><td>4</td><td>Louisiana</td><td>715.4</td><td>18</td><td>Missouri</td><td>455.2</td></tr>
<tr><td>47</td><td>Maine</td><td>76.3</td><td>19</td><td>North Carolina</td><td>441.3</td></tr>
<tr><td>10</td><td>Maryland</td><td>506.4</td><td>20</td><td>Georgia</td><td>428.3</td></tr>
<tr><td>6</td><td>Massachusetts</td><td>592.0</td><td>21</td><td>Delaware</td><td>417.1</td></tr>
<tr><td>13</td><td>Michigan</td><td>472.1</td><td>22</td><td>Arkansas</td><td>415.8</td></tr>
<tr><td>41</td><td>Minnesota</td><td>175.8</td><td>23</td><td>Colorado</td><td>399.0</td></tr>
<tr><td>34</td><td>Mississippi</td><td>238.4</td><td>24</td><td>Kentucky</td><td>331.4</td></tr>
<tr><td>18</td><td>Missouri</td><td>455.2</td><td>25</td><td>Kansas</td><td>326.3</td></tr>
<tr><td>46</td><td>Montana</td><td>114.2</td><td>26</td><td>Indiana</td><td>322.6</td></tr>
<tr><td>32</td><td>Nebraska</td><td>252.0</td><td>27</td><td>Oregon</td><td>317.6</td></tr>
<tr><td>16</td><td>Nevada</td><td>463.9</td><td>28</td><td>Washington</td><td>307.9</td></tr>
<tr><td>48</td><td>New Hampshire</td><td>64.1</td><td>29</td><td>New Jersey</td><td>297.5</td></tr>
<tr><td>29</td><td>New Jersey</td><td>297.5</td><td>30</td><td>Rhode Island</td><td>268.1</td></tr>
<tr><td>3</td><td>New Mexico</td><td>731.1</td><td>31</td><td>Ohio</td><td>256.3</td></tr>
<tr><td>14</td><td>New York</td><td>471.5</td><td>32</td><td>Nebraska</td><td>252.0</td></tr>
<tr><td>19</td><td>North Carolina</td><td>441.3</td><td>33</td><td>Iowa</td><td>244.8</td></tr>
<tr><td>50</td><td>North Dakota</td><td>48.7</td><td>34</td><td>Mississippi</td><td>238.4</td></tr>
<tr><td>31</td><td>Ohio</td><td>256.3</td><td>35</td><td>Wyoming</td><td>231.3</td></tr>
<tr><td>17</td><td>Oklahoma</td><td>455.3</td><td>36</td><td>Connecticut</td><td>228.7</td></tr>
<tr><td>27</td><td>Oregon</td><td>317.6</td><td>37</td><td>Idaho</td><td>226.7</td></tr>
<tr><td>38</td><td>Pennsylvania</td><td>205.1</td><td>38</td><td>Pennsylvania</td><td>205.1</td></tr>
<tr><td>30</td><td>Rhode Island</td><td>268.1</td><td>39</td><td>Utah</td><td>194.7</td></tr>
<tr><td>2</td><td>South Carolina</td><td>773.4</td><td>40</td><td>Virginia</td><td>189.8</td></tr>
<tr><td>42</td><td>South Dakota</td><td>145.6</td><td>41</td><td>Minnesota</td><td>175.8</td></tr>
<tr><td>12</td><td>Tennessee</td><td>485.5</td><td>42</td><td>South Dakota</td><td>145.6</td></tr>
<tr><td>15</td><td>Texas</td><td>470.8</td><td>43</td><td>West Virginia</td><td>138.5</td></tr>
<tr><td>39</td><td>Utah</td><td>194.7</td><td>44</td><td>Wisconsin</td><td>121.4</td></tr>
<tr><td>49</td><td>Vermont</td><td>61.8</td><td>45</td><td>Hawaii</td><td>120.1</td></tr>
<tr><td>40</td><td>Virginia</td><td>189.8</td><td>46</td><td>Montana</td><td>114.2</td></tr>
<tr><td>28</td><td>Washington</td><td>307.9</td><td>47</td><td>Maine</td><td>76.3</td></tr>
<tr><td>43</td><td>West Virginia</td><td>138.5</td><td>48</td><td>New Hampshire</td><td>64.1</td></tr>
<tr><td>44</td><td>Wisconsin</td><td>121.4</td><td>49</td><td>Vermont</td><td>61.8</td></tr>
<tr><td>35</td><td>Wyoming</td><td>231.3</td><td>50</td><td>North Dakota</td><td>48.7</td></tr>
<tr><td></td><td></td><td></td><td></td><td>District of Columbia</td><td>1,557.6</td></tr>
</table>

Source: Federal Bureau of Investigation
"Crime in the United States 1993" (Uniform Crime Reports, December 4, 1994)
*Revised national rate. Aggravated assault is an attack for the purpose of inflicting severe bodily injury.

488

Percent Change in Aggravated Assault Rate: 1993 to 1997

National Percent Change = 13.2% Decrease*

ALPHA ORDER

RANK	STATE	PERCENT CHANGE
48	Alabama	(37.0)
18	Alaska	(4.7)
41	Arizona	(17.5)
30	Arkansas	(13.0)
43	California	(18.6)
49	Colorado	(41.7)
20	Connecticut	(7.5)
12	Delaware	3.3
29	Florida	(12.3)
38	Georgia	(15.6)
11	Hawaii	3.7
23	Idaho	(9.6)
14	Illinois	0.8
9	Indiana	6.0
19	Iowa	(5.2)
42	Kansas	(18.0)
50	Kentucky	(43.6)
45	Louisiana	(21.8)
13	Maine	1.7
21	Maryland	(8.3)
33	Massachusetts	(14.5)
44	Michigan	(20.0)
17	Minnesota	(4.4)
5	Mississippi	17.4
37	Missouri	(15.4)
46	Montana	(23.4)
1	Nebraska	36.8
21	Nevada	(8.3)
33	New Hampshire	(14.5)
31	New Jersey	(13.8)
36	New Mexico	(14.7)
47	New York	(25.6)
25	North Carolina	(10.6)
6	North Dakota	13.1
24	Ohio	(9.8)
28	Oklahoma	(11.5)
26	Oregon	(10.7)
3	Pennsylvania	23.2
40	Rhode Island	(17.0)
16	South Carolina	(2.1)
35	South Dakota	(14.6)
10	Tennessee	4.9
38	Texas	(15.6)
7	Utah	10.8
2	Vermont	26.7
15	Virginia	(1.7)
32	Washington	(13.9)
8	West Virginia	9.7
4	Wisconsin	19.9
27	Wyoming	(11.2)

RANK ORDER

RANK	STATE	PERCENT CHANGE
1	Nebraska	36.8
2	Vermont	26.7
3	Pennsylvania	23.2
4	Wisconsin	19.9
5	Mississippi	17.4
6	North Dakota	13.1
7	Utah	10.8
8	West Virginia	9.7
9	Indiana	6.0
10	Tennessee	4.9
11	Hawaii	3.7
12	Delaware	3.3
13	Maine	1.7
14	Illinois	0.8
15	Virginia	(1.7)
16	South Carolina	(2.1)
17	Minnesota	(4.4)
18	Alaska	(4.7)
19	Iowa	(5.2)
20	Connecticut	(7.5)
21	Maryland	(8.3)
21	Nevada	(8.3)
23	Idaho	(9.6)
24	Ohio	(9.8)
25	North Carolina	(10.6)
26	Oregon	(10.7)
27	Wyoming	(11.2)
28	Oklahoma	(11.5)
29	Florida	(12.3)
30	Arkansas	(13.0)
31	New Jersey	(13.8)
32	Washington	(13.9)
33	Massachusetts	(14.5)
33	New Hampshire	(14.5)
35	South Dakota	(14.6)
36	New Mexico	(14.7)
37	Missouri	(15.4)
38	Georgia	(15.6)
38	Texas	(15.6)
40	Rhode Island	(17.0)
41	Arizona	(17.5)
42	Kansas	(18.0)
43	California	(18.6)
44	Michigan	(20.0)
45	Louisiana	(21.8)
46	Montana	(23.4)
47	New York	(25.6)
48	Alabama	(37.0)
49	Colorado	(41.7)
50	Kentucky	(43.6)

	District of Columbia	(31.0)

Source: Morgan Quitno Press using data from Federal Bureau of Investigation
    "Crime in the United States" (Uniform Crime Reports, 1993 and 1997 editions)
*Aggravated assault is an attack for the purpose of inflicting severe bodily injury.

Property Crimes in 1993

National Total = 12,218,800 Property Crimes*

ALPHA ORDER				RANK ORDER			
RANK	STATE	CRIMES	% of USA	RANK	STATE	CRIMES	% of USA
25	Alabama	171,598	1.4%	1	California	1,678,884	13.7%
46	Alaska	28,795	0.2%	2	Texas	1,023,612	8.4%
13	Arizona	264,371	2.2%	3	Florida	977,363	8.0%
32	Arkansas	102,231	0.8%	4	New York	814,824	6.7%
1	California	1,678,884	13.7%	5	Illinois	544,869	4.5%
24	Colorado	176,856	1.4%	6	Michigan	441,767	3.6%
28	Connecticut	137,443	1.1%	7	Ohio	441,550	3.6%
45	Delaware	29,304	0.2%	8	Georgia	378,348	3.1%
3	Florida	977,363	8.0%	9	North Carolina	345,377	2.8%
8	Georgia	378,348	3.1%	10	Pennsylvania	343,841	2.8%
37	Hawaii	70,505	0.6%	11	New Jersey	328,867	2.7%
41	Idaho	39,161	0.3%	12	Washington	285,753	2.3%
5	Illinois	544,869	4.5%	13	Arizona	264,371	2.2%
20	Indiana	227,149	1.9%	14	Maryland	253,647	2.1%
33	Iowa	99,080	0.8%	15	Louisiana	248,461	2.0%
29	Kansas	113,360	0.9%	16	Massachusetts	245,831	2.0%
30	Kentucky	105,979	0.9%	17	Virginia	242,975	2.0%
15	Louisiana	248,461	2.0%	18	Tennessee	228,117	1.9%
43	Maine	37,519	0.3%	19	Missouri	227,731	1.9%
14	Maryland	253,647	2.1%	20	Indiana	227,149	1.9%
16	Massachusetts	245,831	2.0%	21	Wisconsin	190,923	1.6%
6	Michigan	441,767	3.6%	22	Minnesota	183,347	1.5%
22	Minnesota	183,347	1.5%	23	South Carolina	177,779	1.5%
31	Mississippi	105,308	0.9%	24	Colorado	176,856	1.4%
19	Missouri	227,731	1.9%	25	Alabama	171,598	1.4%
42	Montana	38,699	0.3%	26	Oregon	159,558	1.3%
38	Nebraska	60,712	0.5%	27	Oklahoma	150,546	1.2%
36	Nevada	73,685	0.6%	28	Connecticut	137,443	1.1%
44	New Hampshire	31,131	0.3%	29	Kansas	113,360	0.9%
11	New Jersey	328,867	2.7%	30	Kentucky	105,979	0.9%
35	New Mexico	86,236	0.7%	31	Mississippi	105,308	0.9%
4	New York	814,824	6.7%	32	Arkansas	102,231	0.8%
9	North Carolina	345,377	2.8%	33	Iowa	99,080	0.8%
50	North Dakota	17,387	0.1%	34	Utah	91,816	0.8%
7	Ohio	441,550	3.6%	35	New Mexico	86,236	0.7%
27	Oklahoma	150,546	1.2%	36	Nevada	73,685	0.6%
26	Oregon	159,558	1.3%	37	Hawaii	70,505	0.6%
10	Pennsylvania	343,841	2.8%	38	Nebraska	60,712	0.5%
40	Rhode Island	40,973	0.3%	39	West Virginia	42,300	0.3%
23	South Carolina	177,779	1.5%	40	Rhode Island	40,973	0.3%
48	South Dakota	19,661	0.2%	41	Idaho	39,161	0.3%
18	Tennessee	228,117	1.9%	42	Montana	38,699	0.3%
2	Texas	1,023,612	8.4%	43	Maine	37,519	0.3%
34	Utah	91,816	0.8%	44	New Hampshire	31,131	0.3%
47	Vermont	22,223	0.2%	45	Delaware	29,304	0.2%
17	Virginia	242,975	2.0%	46	Alaska	28,795	0.2%
12	Washington	285,753	2.3%	47	Vermont	22,223	0.2%
39	West Virginia	42,300	0.3%	48	South Dakota	19,661	0.2%
21	Wisconsin	190,923	1.6%	49	Wyoming	18,221	0.1%
49	Wyoming	18,221	0.1%	50	North Dakota	17,387	0.1%
					District of Columbia	51,091	0.4%

Source: Federal Bureau of Investigation
"Crime in the United States 1993" (Uniform Crime Reports, December 4, 1994)
*Revised national total. Property crimes are offenses of burglary, larceny-theft and motor vehicle theft.

Percent Change in Number of Property Crimes: 1993 to 1997

National Percent Change = 5.6% Decrease*

ALPHA ORDER

RANK	STATE	PERCENT CHANGE
10	Alabama	8.9
31	Alaska	(3.3)
7	Arizona	13.2
20	Arkansas	3.5
47	California	(21.8)
39	Colorado	(5.6)
45	Connecticut	(14.5)
8	Delaware	11.4
40	Florida	(6.3)
23	Georgia	2.6
31	Hawaii	(3.3)
6	Idaho	13.3
41	Illinois	(6.6)
24	Indiana	2.0
25	Iowa	0.9
38	Kansas	(4.9)
19	Kentucky	3.6
28	Louisiana	(2.0)
27	Maine	(0.3)
35	Maryland	(3.5)
48	Massachusetts	(24.6)
36	Michigan	(4.3)
18	Minnesota	4.2
13	Mississippi	7.9
26	Missouri	0.5
30	Montana	(2.9)
16	Nebraska	4.9
3	Nevada	19.8
37	New Hampshire	(4.8)
44	New Jersey	(12.7)
2	New Mexico	21.4
50	New York	(28.3)
15	North Carolina	5.0
31	North Dakota	(3.3)
22	Ohio	3.3
12	Oklahoma	8.7
4	Oregon	18.4
17	Pennsylvania	4.5
46	Rhode Island	(20.0)
11	South Carolina	8.8
5	South Dakota	14.4
9	Tennessee	11.1
42	Texas	(7.4)
1	Utah	27.0
49	Vermont	(28.2)
29	Virginia	(2.1)
14	Washington	7.7
34	West Virginia	(3.4)
43	Wisconsin	(7.7)
21	Wyoming	3.4

RANK ORDER

RANK	STATE	PERCENT CHANGE
1	Utah	27.0
2	New Mexico	21.4
3	Nevada	19.8
4	Oregon	18.4
5	South Dakota	14.4
6	Idaho	13.3
7	Arizona	13.2
8	Delaware	11.4
9	Tennessee	11.1
10	Alabama	8.9
11	South Carolina	8.8
12	Oklahoma	8.7
13	Mississippi	7.9
14	Washington	7.7
15	North Carolina	5.0
16	Nebraska	4.9
17	Pennsylvania	4.5
18	Minnesota	4.2
19	Kentucky	3.6
20	Arkansas	3.5
21	Wyoming	3.4
22	Ohio	3.3
23	Georgia	2.6
24	Indiana	2.0
25	Iowa	0.9
26	Missouri	0.5
27	Maine	(0.3)
28	Louisiana	(2.0)
29	Virginia	(2.1)
30	Montana	(2.9)
31	Alaska	(3.3)
31	Hawaii	(3.3)
31	North Dakota	(3.3)
34	West Virginia	(3.4)
35	Maryland	(3.5)
36	Michigan	(4.3)
37	New Hampshire	(4.8)
38	Kansas	(4.9)
39	Colorado	(5.6)
40	Florida	(6.3)
41	Illinois	(6.6)
42	Texas	(7.4)
43	Wisconsin	(7.7)
44	New Jersey	(12.7)
45	Connecticut	(14.5)
46	Rhode Island	(20.0)
47	California	(21.8)
48	Massachusetts	(24.6)
49	Vermont	(28.2)
50	New York	(28.3)
	District of Columbia	(19.1)

Source: Morgan Quitno Press using data from Federal Bureau of Investigation
"Crime in the United States" (Uniform Crime Reports, 1993 and 1997 editions)
*Property crimes are offenses of burglary, larceny-theft and motor vehicle theft.

Property Crime Rate in 1993

National Rate = 4,737.6 Property Crimes per 100,000 Population*

ALPHA ORDER

RANK	STATE	RATE
30	Alabama	4,098.4
17	Alaska	4,807.2
2	Arizona	6,716.7
26	Arkansas	4,217.5
8	California	5,379.1
14	Colorado	4,959.5
27	Connecticut	4,194.2
28	Delaware	4,186.3
1	Florida	7,145.0
6	Georgia	5,469.8
3	Hawaii	6,015.8
42	Idaho	3,563.3
20	Illinois	4,658.2
36	Indiana	3,976.0
43	Iowa	3,521.0
22	Kansas	4,478.8
46	Kentucky	2,797.0
4	Louisiana	5,784.9
44	Maine	3,028.2
12	Maryland	5,108.7
32	Massachusetts	4,089.0
18	Michigan	4,661.0
33	Minnesota	4,059.0
34	Mississippi	3,984.4
25	Missouri	4,351.0
21	Montana	4,612.5
40	Nebraska	3,778.0
10	Nevada	5,304.9
47	New Hampshire	2,767.2
29	New Jersey	4,174.0
9	New Mexico	5,336.4
23	New York	4,477.8
13	North Carolina	4,973.0
49	North Dakota	2,738.1
35	Ohio	3,981.2
19	Oklahoma	4,659.4
11	Oregon	5,262.5
45	Pennsylvania	2,853.9
31	Rhode Island	4,097.3
16	South Carolina	4,880.0
48	South Dakota	2,749.8
24	Tennessee	4,473.8
5	Texas	5,677.0
15	Utah	4,936.3
38	Vermont	3,858.2
41	Virginia	3,743.3
7	Washington	5,437.7
50	West Virginia	2,324.2
39	Wisconsin	3,789.7
37	Wyoming	3,876.8

RANK ORDER

RANK	STATE	RATE
1	Florida	7,145.0
2	Arizona	6,716.7
3	Hawaii	6,015.8
4	Louisiana	5,784.9
5	Texas	5,677.0
6	Georgia	5,469.8
7	Washington	5,437.7
8	California	5,379.1
9	New Mexico	5,336.4
10	Nevada	5,304.9
11	Oregon	5,262.5
12	Maryland	5,108.7
13	North Carolina	4,973.0
14	Colorado	4,959.5
15	Utah	4,936.3
16	South Carolina	4,880.0
17	Alaska	4,807.2
18	Michigan	4,661.0
19	Oklahoma	4,659.4
20	Illinois	4,658.2
21	Montana	4,612.5
22	Kansas	4,478.8
23	New York	4,477.8
24	Tennessee	4,473.8
25	Missouri	4,351.0
26	Arkansas	4,217.5
27	Connecticut	4,194.2
28	Delaware	4,186.3
29	New Jersey	4,174.0
30	Alabama	4,098.4
31	Rhode Island	4,097.3
32	Massachusetts	4,089.0
33	Minnesota	4,059.0
34	Mississippi	3,984.4
35	Ohio	3,981.2
36	Indiana	3,976.0
37	Wyoming	3,876.8
38	Vermont	3,858.2
39	Wisconsin	3,789.7
40	Nebraska	3,778.0
41	Virginia	3,743.3
42	Idaho	3,563.3
43	Iowa	3,521.0
44	Maine	3,028.2
45	Pennsylvania	2,853.9
46	Kentucky	2,797.0
47	New Hampshire	2,767.2
48	South Dakota	2,749.8
49	North Dakota	2,738.1
50	West Virginia	2,324.2
	District of Columbia	8,839.3

Source: Federal Bureau of Investigation
"Crime in the United States 1993" (Uniform Crime Reports, December 4, 1994)
*Revised national rate. Property crimes are offenses of burglary, larceny-theft and motor vehicle theft.

Percent Change in Property Crime Rate: 1993 to 1997

National Percent Change = 9.0% Decrease*

ALPHA ORDER

RANK	STATE	PERCENT CHANGE
8	Alabama	5.5
31	Alaska	(4.9)
25	Arizona	(2.2)
20	Arkansas	(0.6)
47	California	(24.4)
42	Colorado	(13.6)
44	Connecticut	(14.3)
5	Delaware	6.5
41	Florida	(12.6)
32	Georgia	(5.2)
30	Hawaii	(4.5)
12	Idaho	2.9
38	Illinois	(8.1)
20	Indiana	(0.6)
19	Iowa	(0.4)
35	Kansas	(7.2)
17	Kentucky	0.5
28	Louisiana	(3.3)
20	Maine	(0.6)
34	Maryland	(5.9)
48	Massachusetts	(25.9)
35	Michigan	(7.2)
18	Minnesota	0.4
11	Mississippi	4.4
26	Missouri	(2.6)
37	Montana	(7.3)
14	Nebraska	1.8
23	Nevada	(0.7)
39	New Hampshire	(8.7)
45	New Jersey	(14.6)
2	New Mexico	13.4
49	New York	(28.0)
24	North Carolina	(1.8)
29	North Dakota	(4.2)
13	Ohio	2.5
6	Oklahoma	5.9
4	Oregon	10.7
10	Pennsylvania	4.7
46	Rhode Island	(18.9)
9	South Carolina	5.4
3	South Dakota	10.8
7	Tennessee	5.6
43	Texas	(14.1)
1	Utah	14.7
50	Vermont	(29.8)
33	Virginia	(5.7)
16	Washington	0.9
27	West Virginia	(3.2)
40	Wisconsin	(10.1)
15	Wyoming	1.3

RANK ORDER

RANK	STATE	PERCENT CHANGE
1	Utah	14.7
2	New Mexico	13.4
3	South Dakota	10.8
4	Oregon	10.7
5	Delaware	6.5
6	Oklahoma	5.9
7	Tennessee	5.6
8	Alabama	5.5
9	South Carolina	5.4
10	Pennsylvania	4.7
11	Mississippi	4.4
12	Idaho	2.9
13	Ohio	2.5
14	Nebraska	1.8
15	Wyoming	1.3
16	Washington	0.9
17	Kentucky	0.5
18	Minnesota	0.4
19	Iowa	(0.4)
20	Arkansas	(0.6)
20	Indiana	(0.6)
20	Maine	(0.6)
23	Nevada	(0.7)
24	North Carolina	(1.8)
25	Arizona	(2.2)
26	Missouri	(2.6)
27	West Virginia	(3.2)
28	Louisiana	(3.3)
29	North Dakota	(4.2)
30	Hawaii	(4.5)
31	Alaska	(4.9)
32	Georgia	(5.2)
33	Virginia	(5.7)
34	Maryland	(5.9)
35	Kansas	(7.2)
35	Michigan	(7.2)
37	Montana	(7.3)
38	Illinois	(8.1)
39	New Hampshire	(8.7)
40	Wisconsin	(10.1)
41	Florida	(12.6)
42	Colorado	(13.6)
43	Texas	(14.1)
44	Connecticut	(14.3)
45	New Jersey	(14.6)
46	Rhode Island	(18.9)
47	California	(24.4)
48	Massachusetts	(25.9)
49	New York	(28.0)
50	Vermont	(29.8)

District of Columbia ..... (11.6)

Source: Morgan Quitno Press using data from Federal Bureau of Investigation
"Crime in the United States" (Uniform Crime Reports, 1993 and 1997 editions)
*Property crimes are offenses of burglary, larceny-theft and motor vehicle theft.

Burglaries in 1993

National Total = 2,834,800 Burglaries*

ALPHA ORDER

RANK	STATE	BURGLARIES	% of USA
21	Alabama	45,578	1.6%
47	Alaska	4,893	0.2%
15	Arizona	57,684	2.0%
32	Arkansas	26,646	0.9%
1	California	414,182	14.6%
25	Colorado	36,011	1.3%
28	Connecticut	32,052	1.1%
43	Delaware	6,244	0.2%
2	Florida	251,063	8.9%
9	Georgia	90,423	3.2%
37	Hawaii	13,310	0.5%
42	Idaho	7,350	0.3%
5	Illinois	118,788	4.2%
19	Indiana	48,677	1.7%
34	Iowa	20,562	0.7%
30	Kansas	28,655	1.0%
31	Kentucky	28,041	1.0%
14	Louisiana	58,768	2.1%
41	Maine	8,909	0.3%
16	Maryland	56,246	2.0%
13	Massachusetts	60,220	2.1%
8	Michigan	93,143	3.3%
24	Minnesota	38,147	1.3%
26	Mississippi	33,985	1.2%
18	Missouri	53,673	1.9%
44	Montana	5,992	0.2%
39	Nebraska	10,662	0.4%
35	Nevada	17,293	0.6%
45	New Hampshire	5,795	0.2%
10	New Jersey	76,738	2.7%
33	New Mexico	22,966	0.8%
4	New York	181,709	6.4%
6	North Carolina	105,270	3.7%
50	North Dakota	2,370	0.1%
7	Ohio	97,394	3.4%
23	Oklahoma	39,903	1.4%
29	Oregon	31,072	1.1%
11	Pennsylvania	70,125	2.5%
40	Rhode Island	10,409	0.4%
20	South Carolina	47,695	1.7%
48	South Dakota	3,927	0.1%
12	Tennessee	60,299	2.1%
3	Texas	233,913	8.3%
36	Utah	14,708	0.5%
46	Vermont	5,036	0.2%
22	Virginia	43,338	1.5%
17	Washington	56,083	2.0%
38	West Virginia	10,904	0.4%
27	Wisconsin	33,400	1.2%
49	Wyoming	3,023	0.1%

RANK ORDER

RANK	STATE	BURGLARIES	% of USA
1	California	414,182	14.6%
2	Florida	251,063	8.9%
3	Texas	233,913	8.3%
4	New York	181,709	6.4%
5	Illinois	118,788	4.2%
6	North Carolina	105,270	3.7%
7	Ohio	97,394	3.4%
8	Michigan	93,143	3.3%
9	Georgia	90,423	3.2%
10	New Jersey	76,738	2.7%
11	Pennsylvania	70,125	2.5%
12	Tennessee	60,299	2.1%
13	Massachusetts	60,220	2.1%
14	Louisiana	58,768	2.1%
15	Arizona	57,684	2.0%
16	Maryland	56,246	2.0%
17	Washington	56,083	2.0%
18	Missouri	53,673	1.9%
19	Indiana	48,677	1.7%
20	South Carolina	47,695	1.7%
21	Alabama	45,578	1.6%
22	Virginia	43,338	1.5%
23	Oklahoma	39,903	1.4%
24	Minnesota	38,147	1.3%
25	Colorado	36,011	1.3%
26	Mississippi	33,985	1.2%
27	Wisconsin	33,400	1.2%
28	Connecticut	32,052	1.1%
29	Oregon	31,072	1.1%
30	Kansas	28,655	1.0%
31	Kentucky	28,041	1.0%
32	Arkansas	26,646	0.9%
33	New Mexico	22,966	0.8%
34	Iowa	20,562	0.7%
35	Nevada	17,293	0.6%
36	Utah	14,708	0.5%
37	Hawaii	13,310	0.5%
38	West Virginia	10,904	0.4%
39	Nebraska	10,662	0.4%
40	Rhode Island	10,409	0.4%
41	Maine	8,909	0.3%
42	Idaho	7,350	0.3%
43	Delaware	6,244	0.2%
44	Montana	5,992	0.2%
45	New Hampshire	5,795	0.2%
46	Vermont	5,036	0.2%
47	Alaska	4,893	0.2%
48	South Dakota	3,927	0.1%
49	Wyoming	3,023	0.1%
50	North Dakota	2,370	0.1%
	District of Columbia	11,534	0.4%

Source: Federal Bureau of Investigation
"Crime in the United States 1993" (Uniform Crime Reports, December 4, 1994)
*Burglary is the unlawful entry of a structure to commit a felony or theft. Attempts are included.

Percent Change in Number of Burglaries: 1993 to 1997

National Percent Change = 13.2% Decrease*

ALPHA ORDER

RANK	STATE	PERCENT CHANGE
19	Alabama	(3.9)
34	Alaska	(12.6)
9	Arizona	4.1
20	Arkansas	(4.0)
46	California	(27.8)
38	Colorado	(13.9)
45	Connecticut	(24.7)
29	Delaware	(10.0)
40	Florida	(14.8)
30	Georgia	(10.1)
21	Hawaii	(4.3)
2	Idaho	24.8
36	Illinois	(12.8)
13	Indiana	(1.0)
7	Iowa	7.0
33	Kansas	(12.1)
23	Kentucky	(5.0)
28	Louisiana	(8.2)
25	Maine	(7.5)
40	Maryland	(14.8)
49	Massachusetts	(32.8)
37	Michigan	(13.3)
26	Minnesota	(7.6)
22	Mississippi	(4.6)
34	Missouri	(12.6)
42	Montana	(16.5)
27	Nebraska	(8.0)
1	Nevada	27.1
43	New Hampshire	(20.4)
44	New Jersey	(20.6)
5	New Mexico	9.4
50	New York	(34.9)
23	North Carolina	(5.0)
18	North Dakota	(3.0)
15	Ohio	(2.5)
11	Oklahoma	0.3
6	Oregon	7.8
16	Pennsylvania	(2.7)
48	Rhode Island	(32.0)
17	South Carolina	(2.9)
9	South Dakota	4.1
8	Tennessee	4.3
39	Texas	(14.0)
3	Utah	24.7
47	Vermont	(28.3)
31	Virginia	(11.2)
4	Washington	10.7
14	West Virginia	(2.4)
32	Wisconsin	(11.7)
12	Wyoming	(0.8)

RANK ORDER

RANK	STATE	PERCENT CHANGE
1	Nevada	27.1
2	Idaho	24.8
3	Utah	24.7
4	Washington	10.7
5	New Mexico	9.4
6	Oregon	7.8
7	Iowa	7.0
8	Tennessee	4.3
9	Arizona	4.1
9	South Dakota	4.1
11	Oklahoma	0.3
12	Wyoming	(0.8)
13	Indiana	(1.0)
14	West Virginia	(2.4)
15	Ohio	(2.5)
16	Pennsylvania	(2.7)
17	South Carolina	(2.9)
18	North Dakota	(3.0)
19	Alabama	(3.9)
20	Arkansas	(4.0)
21	Hawaii	(4.3)
22	Mississippi	(4.6)
23	Kentucky	(5.0)
23	North Carolina	(5.0)
25	Maine	(7.5)
26	Minnesota	(7.6)
27	Nebraska	(8.0)
28	Louisiana	(8.2)
29	Delaware	(10.0)
30	Georgia	(10.1)
31	Virginia	(11.2)
32	Wisconsin	(11.7)
33	Kansas	(12.1)
34	Alaska	(12.6)
34	Missouri	(12.6)
36	Illinois	(12.8)
37	Michigan	(13.3)
38	Colorado	(13.9)
39	Texas	(14.0)
40	Florida	(14.8)
40	Maryland	(14.8)
42	Montana	(16.5)
43	New Hampshire	(20.4)
44	New Jersey	(20.6)
45	Connecticut	(24.7)
46	California	(27.8)
47	Vermont	(28.3)
48	Rhode Island	(32.0)
49	Massachusetts	(32.8)
50	New York	(34.9)
	District of Columbia	(39.6)

Source: Morgan Quitno Press using data from Federal Bureau of Investigation
"Crime in the United States" (Uniform Crime Reports, 1993 and 1997 editions)
*Burglary is the unlawful entry of a structure to commit a felony or theft. Attempts are included.

Burglary Rate in 1993

National Rate = 1,099.2 Burglaries per 100,000 Population*

ALPHA ORDER			RANK ORDER		
RANK	STATE	RATE	RANK	STATE	RATE
18	Alabama	1,088.6	1	Florida	1,835.4
35	Alaska	816.9	2	North Carolina	1,515.8
3	Arizona	1,465.5	3	Arizona	1,465.5
17	Arkansas	1,099.3	4	New Mexico	1,421.2
6	California	1,327.0	5	Louisiana	1,368.3
24	Colorado	1,009.8	6	California	1,327.0
28	Connecticut	978.1	7	South Carolina	1,309.2
30	Delaware	892.0	8	Georgia	1,307.3
1	Florida	1,835.4	9	Texas	1,297.3
8	Georgia	1,307.3	10	Mississippi	1,285.8
14	Hawaii	1,135.7	11	Nevada	1,245.0
41	Idaho	668.8	12	Oklahoma	1,235.0
23	Illinois	1,015.5	13	Tennessee	1,182.6
33	Indiana	852.0	14	Hawaii	1,135.7
38	Iowa	730.7	15	Maryland	1,132.8
16	Kansas	1,132.2	16	Kansas	1,132.2
37	Kentucky	740.1	17	Arkansas	1,099.3
5	Louisiana	1,368.3	18	Alabama	1,088.6
39	Maine	719.0	19	Washington	1,067.2
15	Maryland	1,132.8	20	Rhode Island	1,040.9
25	Massachusetts	1,001.7	21	Missouri	1,025.5
27	Michigan	982.7	22	Oregon	1,024.8
34	Minnesota	844.5	23	Illinois	1,015.5
10	Mississippi	1,285.8	24	Colorado	1,009.8
21	Missouri	1,025.5	25	Massachusetts	1,001.7
40	Montana	714.2	26	New York	998.6
43	Nebraska	663.5	27	Michigan	982.7
11	Nevada	1,245.0	28	Connecticut	978.1
49	New Hampshire	515.1	29	New Jersey	974.0
29	New Jersey	974.0	30	Delaware	892.0
4	New Mexico	1,421.2	31	Ohio	878.1
26	New York	998.6	32	Vermont	874.3
2	North Carolina	1,515.8	33	Indiana	852.0
50	North Dakota	373.2	34	Minnesota	844.5
31	Ohio	878.1	35	Alaska	816.9
12	Oklahoma	1,235.0	36	Utah	790.8
22	Oregon	1,024.8	37	Kentucky	740.1
47	Pennsylvania	582.0	38	Iowa	730.7
20	Rhode Island	1,040.9	39	Maine	719.0
7	South Carolina	1,309.2	40	Montana	714.2
48	South Dakota	549.2	41	Idaho	668.8
13	Tennessee	1,182.6	42	Virginia	667.7
9	Texas	1,297.3	43	Nebraska	663.5
36	Utah	790.8	44	Wisconsin	663.0
32	Vermont	874.3	45	Wyoming	643.2
42	Virginia	667.7	46	West Virginia	599.1
19	Washington	1,067.2	47	Pennsylvania	582.0
46	West Virginia	599.1	48	South Dakota	549.2
44	Wisconsin	663.0	49	New Hampshire	515.1
45	Wyoming	643.2	50	North Dakota	373.2
				District of Columbia	1,995.5

Source: Federal Bureau of Investigation
   "Crime in the United States 1993" (Uniform Crime Reports, December 4, 1994)
*Burglary is the unlawful entry of a structure to commit a felony or theft. Attempts are included.

Percent Change in Burglary Rate: 1993 to 1997

National Percent Change = 16.3% Decrease*

RANK	STATE	PERCENT CHANGE
19	Alabama	(6.9)
31	Alaska	(14.1)
25	Arizona	(10.0)
22	Arkansas	(7.8)
47	California	(30.1)
42	Colorado	(21.2)
45	Connecticut	(24.5)
29	Delaware	(13.9)
41	Florida	(20.5)
37	Georgia	(16.9)
17	Hawaii	(5.5)
1	Idaho	13.4
32	Illinois	(14.3)
15	Indiana	(3.6)
3	Iowa	5.6
32	Kansas	(14.3)
23	Kentucky	(7.9)
24	Louisiana	(9.4)
20	Maine	(7.7)
38	Maryland	(17.0)
49	Massachusetts	(33.9)
36	Michigan	(16.0)
27	Minnesota	(10.9)
20	Mississippi	(7.7)
35	Missouri	(15.3)
39	Montana	(20.3)
26	Nebraska	(10.7)
4	Nevada	5.3
44	New Hampshire	(23.7)
43	New Jersey	(22.4)
6	New Mexico	2.2
50	New York	(34.7)
28	North Carolina	(11.1)
16	North Dakota	(3.9)
14	Ohio	(3.3)
11	Oklahoma	(2.3)
8	Oregon	0.8
12	Pennsylvania	(2.5)
48	Rhode Island	(31.1)
18	South Carolina	(5.9)
7	South Dakota	0.9
9	Tennessee	(0.9)
39	Texas	(20.3)
2	Utah	12.6
46	Vermont	(29.9)
34	Virginia	(14.4)
5	Washington	3.7
10	West Virginia	(2.1)
29	Wisconsin	(13.9)
13	Wyoming	(2.9)

RANK	STATE	PERCENT CHANGE
1	Idaho	13.4
2	Utah	12.6
3	Iowa	5.6
4	Nevada	5.3
5	Washington	3.7
6	New Mexico	2.2
7	South Dakota	0.9
8	Oregon	0.8
9	Tennessee	(0.9)
10	West Virginia	(2.1)
11	Oklahoma	(2.3)
12	Pennsylvania	(2.5)
13	Wyoming	(2.9)
14	Ohio	(3.3)
15	Indiana	(3.6)
16	North Dakota	(3.9)
17	Hawaii	(5.5)
18	South Carolina	(5.9)
19	Alabama	(6.9)
20	Maine	(7.7)
20	Mississippi	(7.7)
22	Arkansas	(7.8)
23	Kentucky	(7.9)
24	Louisiana	(9.4)
25	Arizona	(10.0)
26	Nebraska	(10.7)
27	Minnesota	(10.9)
28	North Carolina	(11.1)
29	Delaware	(13.9)
29	Wisconsin	(13.9)
31	Alaska	(14.1)
32	Illinois	(14.3)
32	Kansas	(14.3)
34	Virginia	(14.4)
35	Missouri	(15.3)
36	Michigan	(16.0)
37	Georgia	(16.9)
38	Maryland	(17.0)
39	Montana	(20.3)
39	Texas	(20.3)
41	Florida	(20.5)
42	Colorado	(21.2)
43	New Jersey	(22.4)
44	New Hampshire	(23.7)
45	Connecticut	(24.5)
46	Vermont	(29.9)
47	California	(30.1)
48	Rhode Island	(31.1)
49	Massachusetts	(33.9)
50	New York	(34.7)
	District of Columbia	(34.0)

Source: Morgan Quitno Press using data from Federal Bureau of Investigation
   "Crime in the United States" (Uniform Crime Reports, 1993 and 1997 editions)
*Burglary is the unlawful entry of a structure to commit a felony or theft. Attempts are included.

Larcenies and Thefts in 1993

National Total = 7,820,909 Larcenies and Thefts*

RANK	STATE	THEFTS	% of USA
25	Alabama	111,878	1.4%
45	Alaska	21,201	0.3%
14	Arizona	172,689	2.2%
33	Arkansas	67,767	0.9%
1	California	945,407	12.1%
23	Colorado	124,787	1.6%
28	Connecticut	85,876	1.1%
46	Delaware	20,853	0.3%
3	Florida	603,784	7.7%
8	Georgia	246,849	3.2%
36	Hawaii	51,912	0.7%
40	Idaho	29,795	0.4%
5	Illinois	360,730	4.6%
17	Indiana	154,016	2.0%
30	Iowa	73,148	0.9%
29	Kansas	76,538	1.0%
32	Kentucky	69,745	0.9%
16	Louisiana	163,334	2.1%
42	Maine	26,945	0.3%
15	Maryland	163,471	2.1%
21	Massachusetts	136,548	1.7%
7	Michigan	290,333	3.7%
22	Minnesota	129,727	1.7%
34	Mississippi	62,467	0.8%
18	Missouri	145,392	1.9%
39	Montana	30,641	0.4%
37	Nebraska	46,811	0.6%
38	Nevada	46,137	0.6%
44	New Hampshire	23,153	0.3%
12	New Jersey	195,876	2.5%
35	New Mexico	56,723	0.7%
4	New York	481,166	6.2%
10	North Carolina	220,071	2.8%
50	North Dakota	14,073	0.2%
6	Ohio	295,880	3.8%
27	Oklahoma	95,111	1.2%
26	Oregon	110,878	1.4%
9	Pennsylvania	220,683	2.8%
43	Rhode Island	24,101	0.3%
24	South Carolina	117,553	1.5%
48	South Dakota	14,915	0.2%
20	Tennessee	137,683	1.8%
2	Texas	664,862	8.5%
31	Utah	72,603	0.9%
47	Vermont	16,423	0.2%
13	Virginia	181,104	2.3%
11	Washington	205,701	2.6%
41	West Virginia	28,456	0.4%
19	Wisconsin	139,148	1.8%
49	Wyoming	14,470	0.2%

RANK	STATE	THEFTS	% of USA
1	California	945,407	12.1%
2	Texas	664,862	8.5%
3	Florida	603,784	7.7%
4	New York	481,166	6.2%
5	Illinois	360,730	4.6%
6	Ohio	295,880	3.8%
7	Michigan	290,333	3.7%
8	Georgia	246,849	3.2%
9	Pennsylvania	220,683	2.8%
10	North Carolina	220,071	2.8%
11	Washington	205,701	2.6%
12	New Jersey	195,876	2.5%
13	Virginia	181,104	2.3%
14	Arizona	172,689	2.2%
15	Maryland	163,471	2.1%
16	Louisiana	163,334	2.1%
17	Indiana	154,016	2.0%
18	Missouri	145,392	1.9%
19	Wisconsin	139,148	1.8%
20	Tennessee	137,683	1.8%
21	Massachusetts	136,548	1.7%
22	Minnesota	129,727	1.7%
23	Colorado	124,787	1.6%
24	South Carolina	117,553	1.5%
25	Alabama	111,878	1.4%
26	Oregon	110,878	1.4%
27	Oklahoma	95,111	1.2%
28	Connecticut	85,876	1.1%
29	Kansas	76,538	1.0%
30	Iowa	73,148	0.9%
31	Utah	72,603	0.9%
32	Kentucky	69,745	0.9%
33	Arkansas	67,767	0.9%
34	Mississippi	62,467	0.8%
35	New Mexico	56,723	0.7%
36	Hawaii	51,912	0.7%
37	Nebraska	46,811	0.6%
38	Nevada	46,137	0.6%
39	Montana	30,641	0.4%
40	Idaho	29,795	0.4%
41	West Virginia	28,456	0.4%
42	Maine	26,945	0.3%
43	Rhode Island	24,101	0.3%
44	New Hampshire	23,153	0.3%
45	Alaska	21,201	0.3%
46	Delaware	20,853	0.3%
47	Vermont	16,423	0.2%
48	South Dakota	14,915	0.2%
49	Wyoming	14,470	0.2%
50	North Dakota	14,073	0.2%
	District of Columbia	31,495	0.4%

Source: Federal Bureau of Investigation
"Crime in the United States 1993" (Uniform Crime Reports, December 4, 1994)
*Larceny and theft is the unlawful taking of property without use of force, violence or fraud. Attempts are included.
Motor vehicle thefts are excluded.

Percent Change in Number of Larcenies and Thefts: 1993 to 1997

National Percent Change = 1.2% Decrease*

ALPHA ORDER

ALPHA ORDER			RANK ORDER	

RANK	STATE	PERCENT CHANGE	RANK	STATE	PERCENT CHANGE
8	Alabama	14.1	1	Oregon	22.8
34	Alaska	(2.0)	2	Utah	22.7
10	Arizona	12.9	3	New Mexico	18.4
18	Arkansas	6.6	4	South Dakota	17.6
48	California	(17.0)	5	Mississippi	15.1
38	Colorado	(4.0)	5	Nevada	15.1
45	Connecticut	(8.2)	7	Oklahoma	14.6
12	Delaware	11.8	8	Alabama	14.1
33	Florida	(1.5)	9	Tennessee	13.9
20	Georgia	6.2	10	Arizona	12.9
42	Hawaii	(5.6)	11	Pennsylvania	11.9
14	Idaho	10.0	12	Delaware	11.8
36	Illinois	(2.9)	13	South Carolina	11.7
25	Indiana	2.9	14	Idaho	10.0
35	Iowa	(2.5)	15	North Carolina	8.3
31	Kansas	(0.5)	16	Missouri	6.9
21	Kentucky	5.4	17	Ohio	6.8
29	Louisiana	(0.1)	18	Arkansas	6.6
26	Maine	2.1	19	Minnesota	6.3
27	Maryland	1.7	20	Georgia	6.2
47	Massachusetts	(15.4)	21	Kentucky	5.4
39	Michigan	(4.6)	22	Wyoming	5.0
19	Minnesota	6.3	23	Washington	3.9
5	Mississippi	15.1	24	Nebraska	3.3
16	Missouri	6.9	25	Indiana	2.9
32	Montana	(0.8)	26	Maine	2.1
24	Nebraska	3.3	27	Maryland	1.7
5	Nevada	15.1	28	New Hampshire	1.2
28	New Hampshire	1.2	29	Louisiana	(0.1)
42	New Jersey	(5.6)	30	Virginia	(0.4)
3	New Mexico	18.4	31	Kansas	(0.5)
49	New York	(19.7)	32	Montana	(0.8)
15	North Carolina	8.3	33	Florida	(1.5)
40	North Dakota	(5.0)	34	Alaska	(2.0)
17	Ohio	6.8	35	Iowa	(2.5)
7	Oklahoma	14.6	36	Illinois	(2.9)
1	Oregon	22.8	36	Texas	(2.9)
11	Pennsylvania	11.9	38	Colorado	(4.0)
46	Rhode Island	(10.8)	39	Michigan	(4.6)
13	South Carolina	11.7	40	North Dakota	(5.0)
4	South Dakota	17.6	41	West Virginia	(5.3)
9	Tennessee	13.9	42	Hawaii	(5.6)
36	Texas	(2.9)	42	New Jersey	(5.6)
2	Utah	22.7	44	Wisconsin	(5.9)
50	Vermont	(29.7)	45	Connecticut	(8.2)
30	Virginia	(0.4)	46	Rhode Island	(10.8)
23	Washington	3.9	47	Massachusetts	(15.4)
41	West Virginia	(5.3)	48	California	(17.0)
44	Wisconsin	(5.9)	49	New York	(19.7)
22	Wyoming	5.0	50	Vermont	(29.7)
				District of Columbia	(14.9)

Source: Morgan Quitno Press using data from Federal Bureau of Investigation
"Crime in the United States" (Uniform Crime Reports, 1993 and 1997 editions)
*Larceny and theft is the unlawful taking of property without use of force, violence or fraud. Attempts are included.
Motor vehicle thefts are excluded.

Larceny and Theft Rate in 1993

National Rate = 3,032.4 Larcenies and Thefts per 100,000 Population*

ALPHA ORDER

RANK	STATE	RATE
35	Alabama	2,672.0
11	Alaska	3,539.4
3	Arizona	4,387.4
28	Arkansas	2,795.7
21	California	3,029.1
13	Colorado	3,499.4
38	Connecticut	2,620.6
23	Delaware	2,979.0
2	Florida	4,413.9
10	Georgia	3,568.7
1	Hawaii	4,429.4
32	Idaho	2,711.1
18	Illinois	3,084.0
34	Indiana	2,695.9
39	Iowa	2,599.4
22	Kansas	3,024.0
48	Kentucky	1,840.7
6	Louisiana	3,802.9
45	Maine	2,174.7
15	Maryland	3,292.5
43	Massachusetts	2,271.3
20	Michigan	3,063.2
26	Minnesota	2,872.0
42	Mississippi	2,363.5
30	Missouri	2,777.8
9	Montana	3,652.1
25	Nebraska	2,912.9
14	Nevada	3,321.6
47	New Hampshire	2,058.0
40	New Jersey	2,486.1
12	New Mexico	3,510.1
37	New York	2,644.2
17	North Carolina	3,168.8
44	North Dakota	2,216.2
36	Ohio	2,667.7
24	Oklahoma	2,943.7
8	Oregon	3,656.9
49	Pennsylvania	1,831.7
41	Rhode Island	2,410.1
16	South Carolina	3,226.8
46	South Dakota	2,086.0
33	Tennessee	2,700.2
7	Texas	3,687.3
5	Utah	3,903.4
27	Vermont	2,851.2
29	Virginia	2,790.1
4	Washington	3,914.4
50	West Virginia	1,563.5
31	Wisconsin	2,762.0
19	Wyoming	3,078.7

RANK ORDER

RANK	STATE	RATE
1	Hawaii	4,429.4
2	Florida	4,413.9
3	Arizona	4,387.4
4	Washington	3,914.4
5	Utah	3,903.4
6	Louisiana	3,802.9
7	Texas	3,687.3
8	Oregon	3,656.9
9	Montana	3,652.1
10	Georgia	3,568.7
11	Alaska	3,539.4
12	New Mexico	3,510.1
13	Colorado	3,499.4
14	Nevada	3,321.6
15	Maryland	3,292.5
16	South Carolina	3,226.8
17	North Carolina	3,168.8
18	Illinois	3,084.0
19	Wyoming	3,078.7
20	Michigan	3,063.2
21	California	3,029.1
22	Kansas	3,024.0
23	Delaware	2,979.0
24	Oklahoma	2,943.7
25	Nebraska	2,912.9
26	Minnesota	2,872.0
27	Vermont	2,851.2
28	Arkansas	2,795.7
29	Virginia	2,790.1
30	Missouri	2,777.8
31	Wisconsin	2,762.0
32	Idaho	2,711.1
33	Tennessee	2,700.2
34	Indiana	2,695.9
35	Alabama	2,672.0
36	Ohio	2,667.7
37	New York	2,644.2
38	Connecticut	2,620.6
39	Iowa	2,599.4
40	New Jersey	2,486.1
41	Rhode Island	2,410.1
42	Mississippi	2,363.5
43	Massachusetts	2,271.3
44	North Dakota	2,216.2
45	Maine	2,174.7
46	South Dakota	2,086.0
47	New Hampshire	2,058.0
48	Kentucky	1,840.7
49	Pennsylvania	1,831.7
50	West Virginia	1,563.5
	District of Columbia	5,449.0

Source: Federal Bureau of Investigation
   "Crime in the United States 1993" (Uniform Crime Reports, December 4, 1994)
*Larceny and theft is the unlawful taking of property without use of force, violence or fraud. Attempts are included.
Motor vehicle thefts are excluded.

Percent Change in Larceny and Theft Rate: 1993 to 1997

National Percent Change = 4.8% Decrease*

ALPHA ORDER				RANK ORDER		
RANK	STATE	PERCENT CHANGE		RANK	STATE	PERCENT CHANGE
7	Alabama	10.6		1	Oregon	14.8
30	Alaska	(3.6)		2	South Dakota	14.0
26	Arizona	(2.4)		3	Pennsylvania	12.1
15	Arkansas	2.4		4	Oklahoma	11.7
49	California	(19.7)		5	Mississippi	11.4
46	Colorado	(12.1)		6	Utah	10.8
41	Connecticut	(8.0)		7	Alabama	10.6
11	Delaware	6.9		7	New Mexico	10.6
42	Florida	(8.1)		9	South Carolina	8.2
25	Georgia	(1.8)		9	Tennessee	8.2
38	Hawaii	(6.8)		11	Delaware	6.9
22	Idaho	(0.1)		12	Ohio	5.9
33	Illinois	(4.6)		13	Missouri	3.6
20	Indiana	0.2		14	Wyoming	2.8
31	Iowa	(3.8)		15	Arkansas	2.4
29	Kansas	(3.0)		15	Minnesota	2.4
17	Kentucky	2.2		17	Kentucky	2.2
24	Louisiana	(1.4)		18	Maine	1.9
18	Maine	1.9		19	North Carolina	1.3
23	Maryland	(0.9)		20	Indiana	0.2
47	Massachusetts	(16.9)		20	Nebraska	0.2
39	Michigan	(7.5)		22	Idaho	(0.1)
15	Minnesota	2.4		23	Maryland	(0.9)
5	Mississippi	11.4		24	Louisiana	(1.4)
13	Missouri	3.6		25	Georgia	(1.8)
36	Montana	(5.3)		26	Arizona	(2.4)
20	Nebraska	0.2		27	Washington	(2.6)
34	Nevada	(4.7)		28	New Hampshire	(2.9)
28	New Hampshire	(2.9)		29	Kansas	(3.0)
40	New Jersey	(7.6)		30	Alaska	(3.6)
7	New Mexico	10.6		31	Iowa	(3.8)
48	New York	(19.4)		32	Virginia	(4.0)
19	North Carolina	1.3		33	Illinois	(4.6)
37	North Dakota	(5.9)		34	Nevada	(4.7)
12	Ohio	5.9		35	West Virginia	(5.1)
4	Oklahoma	11.7		36	Montana	(5.3)
1	Oregon	14.8		37	North Dakota	(5.9)
3	Pennsylvania	12.1		38	Hawaii	(6.8)
44	Rhode Island	(9.6)		39	Michigan	(7.5)
9	South Carolina	8.2		40	New Jersey	(7.6)
2	South Dakota	14.0		41	Connecticut	(8.0)
9	Tennessee	8.2		42	Florida	(8.1)
45	Texas	(10.0)		43	Wisconsin	(8.3)
6	Utah	10.8		44	Rhode Island	(9.6)
50	Vermont	(31.3)		45	Texas	(10.0)
32	Virginia	(4.0)		46	Colorado	(12.1)
27	Washington	(2.6)		47	Massachusetts	(16.9)
35	West Virginia	(5.1)		48	New York	(19.4)
43	Wisconsin	(8.3)		49	California	(19.7)
14	Wyoming	2.8		50	Vermont	(31.3)
					District of Columbia	(7.0)

Source: Morgan Quitno Press using data from Federal Bureau of Investigation
   "Crime in the United States" (Uniform Crime Reports, 1993 and 1997 editions)
*Larceny and theft is the unlawful taking of property without use of force, violence or fraud. Attempts are included. Motor vehicle thefts are excluded.

Motor Vehicle Thefts in 1993

National Total = 1,563,100 Motor Vehicle Thefts*

<table>
<tr><td colspan="4"><u>ALPHA ORDER</u></td><td colspan="4"><u>RANK ORDER</u></td></tr>
<tr><td>RANK</td><td>STATE</td><td>THEFTS</td><td>% of USA</td><td>RANK</td><td>STATE</td><td>THEFTS</td><td>% of USA</td></tr>
<tr><td>27</td><td>Alabama</td><td>14,142</td><td>0.9%</td><td>1</td><td>California</td><td>319,295</td><td>20.4%</td></tr>
<tr><td>41</td><td>Alaska</td><td>2,701</td><td>0.2%</td><td>2</td><td>New York</td><td>151,949</td><td>9.7%</td></tr>
<tr><td>12</td><td>Arizona</td><td>33,998</td><td>2.2%</td><td>3</td><td>Texas</td><td>124,837</td><td>8.0%</td></tr>
<tr><td>33</td><td>Arkansas</td><td>7,818</td><td>0.5%</td><td>4</td><td>Florida</td><td>122,516</td><td>7.8%</td></tr>
<tr><td>1</td><td>California</td><td>319,295</td><td>20.4%</td><td>5</td><td>Illinois</td><td>65,351</td><td>4.2%</td></tr>
<tr><td>24</td><td>Colorado</td><td>16,058</td><td>1.0%</td><td>6</td><td>Michigan</td><td>58,291</td><td>3.7%</td></tr>
<tr><td>20</td><td>Connecticut</td><td>19,515</td><td>1.2%</td><td>7</td><td>New Jersey</td><td>56,253</td><td>3.6%</td></tr>
<tr><td>42</td><td>Delaware</td><td>2,207</td><td>0.1%</td><td>8</td><td>Pennsylvania</td><td>53,033</td><td>3.4%</td></tr>
<tr><td>4</td><td>Florida</td><td>122,516</td><td>7.8%</td><td>9</td><td>Massachusetts</td><td>49,063</td><td>3.1%</td></tr>
<tr><td>11</td><td>Georgia</td><td>41,076</td><td>2.6%</td><td>10</td><td>Ohio</td><td>48,276</td><td>3.1%</td></tr>
<tr><td>37</td><td>Hawaii</td><td>5,283</td><td>0.3%</td><td>11</td><td>Georgia</td><td>41,076</td><td>2.6%</td></tr>
<tr><td>45</td><td>Idaho</td><td>2,016</td><td>0.1%</td><td>12</td><td>Arizona</td><td>33,998</td><td>2.2%</td></tr>
<tr><td>5</td><td>Illinois</td><td>65,351</td><td>4.2%</td><td>13</td><td>Maryland</td><td>33,930</td><td>2.2%</td></tr>
<tr><td>17</td><td>Indiana</td><td>24,456</td><td>1.6%</td><td>14</td><td>Tennessee</td><td>30,135</td><td>1.9%</td></tr>
<tr><td>36</td><td>Iowa</td><td>5,370</td><td>0.3%</td><td>15</td><td>Missouri</td><td>28,666</td><td>1.8%</td></tr>
<tr><td>32</td><td>Kansas</td><td>8,167</td><td>0.5%</td><td>16</td><td>Louisiana</td><td>26,359</td><td>1.7%</td></tr>
<tr><td>31</td><td>Kentucky</td><td>8,193</td><td>0.5%</td><td>17</td><td>Indiana</td><td>24,456</td><td>1.6%</td></tr>
<tr><td>16</td><td>Louisiana</td><td>26,359</td><td>1.7%</td><td>18</td><td>Washington</td><td>23,969</td><td>1.5%</td></tr>
<tr><td>46</td><td>Maine</td><td>1,665</td><td>0.1%</td><td>19</td><td>North Carolina</td><td>20,036</td><td>1.3%</td></tr>
<tr><td>13</td><td>Maryland</td><td>33,930</td><td>2.2%</td><td>20</td><td>Connecticut</td><td>19,515</td><td>1.2%</td></tr>
<tr><td>9</td><td>Massachusetts</td><td>49,063</td><td>3.1%</td><td>21</td><td>Virginia</td><td>18,533</td><td>1.2%</td></tr>
<tr><td>6</td><td>Michigan</td><td>58,291</td><td>3.7%</td><td>22</td><td>Wisconsin</td><td>18,375</td><td>1.2%</td></tr>
<tr><td>26</td><td>Minnesota</td><td>15,473</td><td>1.0%</td><td>23</td><td>Oregon</td><td>17,608</td><td>1.1%</td></tr>
<tr><td>30</td><td>Mississippi</td><td>8,856</td><td>0.6%</td><td>24</td><td>Colorado</td><td>16,058</td><td>1.0%</td></tr>
<tr><td>15</td><td>Missouri</td><td>28,666</td><td>1.8%</td><td>25</td><td>Oklahoma</td><td>15,532</td><td>1.0%</td></tr>
<tr><td>44</td><td>Montana</td><td>2,066</td><td>0.1%</td><td>26</td><td>Minnesota</td><td>15,473</td><td>1.0%</td></tr>
<tr><td>39</td><td>Nebraska</td><td>3,239</td><td>0.2%</td><td>27</td><td>Alabama</td><td>14,142</td><td>0.9%</td></tr>
<tr><td>29</td><td>Nevada</td><td>10,255</td><td>0.7%</td><td>28</td><td>South Carolina</td><td>12,531</td><td>0.8%</td></tr>
<tr><td>43</td><td>New Hampshire</td><td>2,183</td><td>0.1%</td><td>29</td><td>Nevada</td><td>10,255</td><td>0.7%</td></tr>
<tr><td>7</td><td>New Jersey</td><td>56,253</td><td>3.6%</td><td>30</td><td>Mississippi</td><td>8,856</td><td>0.6%</td></tr>
<tr><td>34</td><td>New Mexico</td><td>6,547</td><td>0.4%</td><td>31</td><td>Kentucky</td><td>8,193</td><td>0.5%</td></tr>
<tr><td>2</td><td>New York</td><td>151,949</td><td>9.7%</td><td>32</td><td>Kansas</td><td>8,167</td><td>0.5%</td></tr>
<tr><td>19</td><td>North Carolina</td><td>20,036</td><td>1.3%</td><td>33</td><td>Arkansas</td><td>7,818</td><td>0.5%</td></tr>
<tr><td>47</td><td>North Dakota</td><td>944</td><td>0.1%</td><td>34</td><td>New Mexico</td><td>6,547</td><td>0.4%</td></tr>
<tr><td>10</td><td>Ohio</td><td>48,276</td><td>3.1%</td><td>35</td><td>Rhode Island</td><td>6,463</td><td>0.4%</td></tr>
<tr><td>25</td><td>Oklahoma</td><td>15,532</td><td>1.0%</td><td>36</td><td>Iowa</td><td>5,370</td><td>0.3%</td></tr>
<tr><td>23</td><td>Oregon</td><td>17,608</td><td>1.1%</td><td>37</td><td>Hawaii</td><td>5,283</td><td>0.3%</td></tr>
<tr><td>8</td><td>Pennsylvania</td><td>53,033</td><td>3.4%</td><td>38</td><td>Utah</td><td>4,505</td><td>0.3%</td></tr>
<tr><td>35</td><td>Rhode Island</td><td>6,463</td><td>0.4%</td><td>39</td><td>Nebraska</td><td>3,239</td><td>0.2%</td></tr>
<tr><td>28</td><td>South Carolina</td><td>12,531</td><td>0.8%</td><td>40</td><td>West Virginia</td><td>2,940</td><td>0.2%</td></tr>
<tr><td>48</td><td>South Dakota</td><td>819</td><td>0.1%</td><td>41</td><td>Alaska</td><td>2,701</td><td>0.2%</td></tr>
<tr><td>14</td><td>Tennessee</td><td>30,135</td><td>1.9%</td><td>42</td><td>Delaware</td><td>2,207</td><td>0.1%</td></tr>
<tr><td>3</td><td>Texas</td><td>124,837</td><td>8.0%</td><td>43</td><td>New Hampshire</td><td>2,183</td><td>0.1%</td></tr>
<tr><td>38</td><td>Utah</td><td>4,505</td><td>0.3%</td><td>44</td><td>Montana</td><td>2,066</td><td>0.1%</td></tr>
<tr><td>49</td><td>Vermont</td><td>764</td><td>0.0%</td><td>45</td><td>Idaho</td><td>2,016</td><td>0.1%</td></tr>
<tr><td>21</td><td>Virginia</td><td>18,533</td><td>1.2%</td><td>46</td><td>Maine</td><td>1,665</td><td>0.1%</td></tr>
<tr><td>18</td><td>Washington</td><td>23,969</td><td>1.5%</td><td>47</td><td>North Dakota</td><td>944</td><td>0.1%</td></tr>
<tr><td>40</td><td>West Virginia</td><td>2,940</td><td>0.2%</td><td>48</td><td>South Dakota</td><td>819</td><td>0.1%</td></tr>
<tr><td>22</td><td>Wisconsin</td><td>18,375</td><td>1.2%</td><td>49</td><td>Vermont</td><td>764</td><td>0.0%</td></tr>
<tr><td>50</td><td>Wyoming</td><td>728</td><td>0.0%</td><td>50</td><td>Wyoming</td><td>728</td><td>0.0%</td></tr>
<tr><td></td><td></td><td></td><td></td><td></td><td>District of Columbia</td><td>8,062</td><td>0.5%</td></tr>
</table>

Source: Federal Bureau of Investigation
"Crime in the United States 1993" (Uniform Crime Reports, December 4, 1994)
*Revised national total. Includes the theft or attempted theft of a self-propelled vehicle. Excludes motorboats, construction equipment, airplanes and farming equipment.

Percent Change in Number of Motor Vehicle Thefts: 1993 to 1997

National Percent Change = 13.4% Decrease*

ALPHA ORDER

RANK	STATE	PERCENT CHANGE
20	Alabama	8.9
26	Alaska	3.1
6	Arizona	30.0
29	Arkansas	1.5
47	California	(28.4)
30	Colorado	0.3
44	Connecticut	(25.5)
4	Delaware	68.5
38	Florida	(12.5)
21	Georgia	8.5
10	Hawaii	22.4
13	Idaho	20.5
40	Illinois	(15.2)
27	Indiana	2.6
9	Iowa	24.4
43	Kansas	(20.5)
14	Kentucky	18.3
31	Louisiana	0.1
32	Maine	(1.4)
36	Maryland	(9.6)
49	Massachusetts	(40.0)
16	Michigan	12.1
15	Minnesota	15.5
23	Mississippi	5.3
35	Missouri	(7.5)
22	Montana	5.5
3	Nebraska	71.1
7	Nevada	28.9
46	New Hampshire	(27.0)
45	New Jersey	(26.8)
2	New Mexico	89.5
50	New York	(47.6)
12	North Carolina	22.0
11	North Dakota	22.2
34	Ohio	(5.9)
33	Oklahoma	(5.7)
19	Oregon	9.5
41	Pennsylvania	(16.6)
48	Rhode Island	(35.1)
8	South Carolina	25.7
24	South Dakota	4.8
17	Tennessee	12.0
42	Texas	(18.5)
1	Utah	103.0
25	Vermont	4.7
28	Virginia	1.9
5	Washington	32.9
18	West Virginia	11.8
39	Wisconsin	(14.9)
37	Wyoming	(11.1)

RANK ORDER

RANK	STATE	PERCENT CHANGE
1	Utah	103.0
2	New Mexico	89.5
3	Nebraska	71.1
4	Delaware	68.5
5	Washington	32.9
6	Arizona	30.0
7	Nevada	28.9
8	South Carolina	25.7
9	Iowa	24.4
10	Hawaii	22.4
11	North Dakota	22.2
12	North Carolina	22.0
13	Idaho	20.5
14	Kentucky	18.3
15	Minnesota	15.5
16	Michigan	12.1
17	Tennessee	12.0
18	West Virginia	11.8
19	Oregon	9.5
20	Alabama	8.9
21	Georgia	8.5
22	Montana	5.5
23	Mississippi	5.3
24	South Dakota	4.8
25	Vermont	4.7
26	Alaska	3.1
27	Indiana	2.6
28	Virginia	1.9
29	Arkansas	1.5
30	Colorado	0.3
31	Louisiana	0.1
32	Maine	(1.4)
33	Oklahoma	(5.7)
34	Ohio	(5.9)
35	Missouri	(7.5)
36	Maryland	(9.6)
37	Wyoming	(11.1)
38	Florida	(12.5)
39	Wisconsin	(14.9)
40	Illinois	(15.2)
41	Pennsylvania	(16.6)
42	Texas	(18.5)
43	Kansas	(20.5)
44	Connecticut	(25.5)
45	New Jersey	(26.8)
46	New Hampshire	(27.0)
47	California	(28.4)
48	Rhode Island	(35.1)
49	Massachusetts	(40.0)
50	New York	(47.6)
	District of Columbia	(6.1)

Source: Morgan Quitno Press using data from Federal Bureau of Investigation
   "Crime in the United States" (Uniform Crime Reports, 1993 and 1997 editions)
*Includes the theft or attempted theft of a self-propelled vehicle. Excludes motorboats, construction equipment,
airplanes and farming equipment.

503

Motor Vehicle Theft Rate in 1993

National Rate = 606.1 Motor Vehicle Thefts per 100,000 Population*

ALPHA ORDER

RANK	STATE	RATE
31	Alabama	337.8
21	Alaska	450.9
3	Arizona	863.8
34	Arkansas	322.5
1	California	1,023.0
23	Colorado	450.3
13	Connecticut	595.5
35	Delaware	315.3
2	Florida	895.7
14	Georgia	593.8
22	Hawaii	450.8
44	Idaho	183.4
17	Illinois	558.7
26	Indiana	428.1
43	Iowa	190.8
33	Kansas	322.7
40	Kentucky	216.2
12	Louisiana	613.7
48	Maine	134.4
9	Maryland	683.4
5	Massachusetts	816.1
11	Michigan	615.0
30	Minnesota	342.6
32	Mississippi	335.1
18	Missouri	547.7
38	Montana	246.2
41	Nebraska	201.6
6	Nevada	738.3
42	New Hampshire	194.0
7	New Jersey	714.0
27	New Mexico	405.1
4	New York	835.0
36	North Carolina	288.5
47	North Dakota	148.7
25	Ohio	435.3
19	Oklahoma	480.7
16	Oregon	580.7
24	Pennsylvania	440.2
10	Rhode Island	646.3
29	South Carolina	344.0
50	South Dakota	114.5
15	Tennessee	591.0
8	Texas	692.3
39	Utah	242.2
49	Vermont	132.6
37	Virginia	285.5
20	Washington	456.1
45	West Virginia	161.5
28	Wisconsin	364.7
46	Wyoming	154.9

RANK ORDER

RANK	STATE	RATE
1	California	1,023.0
2	Florida	895.7
3	Arizona	863.8
4	New York	835.0
5	Massachusetts	816.1
6	Nevada	738.3
7	New Jersey	714.0
8	Texas	692.3
9	Maryland	683.4
10	Rhode Island	646.3
11	Michigan	615.0
12	Louisiana	613.7
13	Connecticut	595.5
14	Georgia	593.8
15	Tennessee	591.0
16	Oregon	580.7
17	Illinois	558.7
18	Missouri	547.7
19	Oklahoma	480.7
20	Washington	456.1
21	Alaska	450.9
22	Hawaii	450.8
23	Colorado	450.3
24	Pennsylvania	440.2
25	Ohio	435.3
26	Indiana	428.1
27	New Mexico	405.1
28	Wisconsin	364.7
29	South Carolina	344.0
30	Minnesota	342.6
31	Alabama	337.8
32	Mississippi	335.1
33	Kansas	322.7
34	Arkansas	322.5
35	Delaware	315.3
36	North Carolina	288.5
37	Virginia	285.5
38	Montana	246.2
39	Utah	242.2
40	Kentucky	216.2
41	Nebraska	201.6
42	New Hampshire	194.0
43	Iowa	190.8
44	Idaho	183.4
45	West Virginia	161.5
46	Wyoming	154.9
47	North Dakota	148.7
48	Maine	134.4
49	Vermont	132.6
50	South Dakota	114.5
	District of Columbia	1,394.8

Source: Federal Bureau of Investigation
   "Crime in the United States 1993" (Uniform Crime Reports, December 4, 1994)
*Revised national rate. Includes the theft or attempted theft of a self-propelled vehicle. Excludes motorboats, construction equipment, airplanes and farming equipment.

Percent Change in Motor Vehicle Theft Rate: 1993 to 1997

National Percent Change = 16.5% Decrease*

RANK	STATE	PERCENT CHANGE
19	Alabama	5.6
24	Alaska	1.4
12	Arizona	12.3
31	Arkansas	(2.4)
47	California	(30.7)
33	Colorado	(8.1)
44	Connecticut	(25.3)
4	Delaware	61.1
41	Florida	(18.3)
26	Georgia	0.3
9	Hawaii	20.9
15	Idaho	9.4
39	Illinois	(16.6)
27	Indiana	0.0
6	Iowa	22.8
42	Kansas	(22.5)
10	Kentucky	14.8
28	Louisiana	(1.3)
29	Maine	(1.6)
36	Maryland	(11.9)
49	Massachusetts	(41.0)
16	Michigan	8.7
14	Minnesota	11.3
22	Mississippi	1.9
35	Missouri	(10.4)
25	Montana	0.7
3	Nebraska	65.9
17	Nevada	6.8
46	New Hampshire	(30.0)
45	New Jersey	(28.4)
2	New Mexico	77.0
50	New York	(47.4)
11	North Carolina	14.1
8	North Dakota	21.0
32	Ohio	(6.7)
34	Oklahoma	(8.2)
20	Oregon	2.4
38	Pennsylvania	(16.4)
48	Rhode Island	(34.2)
7	South Carolina	21.8
23	South Dakota	1.6
18	Tennessee	6.4
43	Texas	(24.4)
1	Utah	83.4
20	Vermont	2.4
30	Virginia	(1.8)
5	Washington	24.5
13	West Virginia	12.1
40	Wisconsin	(17.1)
37	Wyoming	(13.0)

RANK	STATE	PERCENT CHANGE
1	Utah	83.4
2	New Mexico	77.0
3	Nebraska	65.9
4	Delaware	61.1
5	Washington	24.5
6	Iowa	22.8
7	South Carolina	21.8
8	North Dakota	21.0
9	Hawaii	20.9
10	Kentucky	14.8
11	North Carolina	14.1
12	Arizona	12.3
13	West Virginia	12.1
14	Minnesota	11.3
15	Idaho	9.4
16	Michigan	8.7
17	Nevada	6.8
18	Tennessee	6.4
19	Alabama	5.6
20	Oregon	2.4
20	Vermont	2.4
22	Mississippi	1.9
23	South Dakota	1.6
24	Alaska	1.4
25	Montana	0.7
26	Georgia	0.3
27	Indiana	0.0
28	Louisiana	(1.3)
29	Maine	(1.6)
30	Virginia	(1.8)
31	Arkansas	(2.4)
32	Ohio	(6.7)
33	Colorado	(8.1)
34	Oklahoma	(8.2)
35	Missouri	(10.4)
36	Maryland	(11.9)
37	Wyoming	(13.0)
38	Pennsylvania	(16.4)
39	Illinois	(16.6)
40	Wisconsin	(17.1)
41	Florida	(18.3)
42	Kansas	(22.5)
43	Texas	(24.4)
44	Connecticut	(25.3)
45	New Jersey	(28.4)
46	New Hampshire	(30.0)
47	California	(30.7)
48	Rhode Island	(34.2)
49	Massachusetts	(41.0)
50	New York	(47.4)

District of Columbia   2.6

Source: Morgan Quitno Press using data from Federal Bureau of Investigation
   "Crime in the United States" (Uniform Crime Reports, 1993 and 1997 editions)
*Includes the theft or attempted theft of a self-propelled vehicle. Excludes motorboats, construction equipment, airplanes and farming equipment.

Hate Crimes in 1997

National Total = 8,049 Reported Hate Crimes*

<u>ALPHA ORDER</u>

RANK	STATE	HATE CRIMES	% of USA
46	Alabama	0	0.0%
39	Alaska	10	0.1%
8	Arizona	330	4.1%
46	Arkansas	0	0.0%
1	California	1,831	22.7%
15	Colorado	113	1.4%
15	Connecticut	113	1.4%
22	Delaware	58	0.7%
19	Florida	93	1.2%
31	Georgia	45	0.6%
NA	Hawaii**	NA	NA
29	Idaho	46	0.6%
6	Illinois	339	4.2%
21	Indiana	62	0.8%
24	Iowa	55	0.7%
24	Kansas	55	0.7%
28	Kentucky	48	0.6%
41	Louisiana	4	0.0%
23	Maine	57	0.7%
9	Maryland	321	4.0%
5	Massachusetts	441	5.5%
4	Michigan	461	5.7%
11	Minnesota	214	2.7%
46	Mississippi	0	0.0%
14	Missouri	157	2.0%
38	Montana	15	0.2%
42	Nebraska	3	0.0%
31	Nevada	45	0.6%
NA	New Hampshire**	NA	NA
3	New Jersey	694	8.6%
37	New Mexico	24	0.3%
2	New York	853	10.6%
34	North Carolina	42	0.5%
45	North Dakota	2	0.0%
10	Ohio	265	3.3%
35	Oklahoma	41	0.5%
17	Oregon	105	1.3%
13	Pennsylvania	168	2.1%
33	Rhode Island	43	0.5%
20	South Carolina	71	0.9%
36	South Dakota	34	0.4%
29	Tennessee	46	0.6%
7	Texas	333	4.1%
27	Utah	49	0.6%
42	Vermont	3	0.0%
17	Virginia	105	1.3%
12	Washington	190	2.4%
42	West Virginia	3	0.0%
26	Wisconsin	50	0.6%
40	Wyoming	6	0.1%

<u>RANK ORDER</u>

RANK	STATE	HATE CRIMES	% of USA
1	California	1,831	22.7%
2	New York	853	10.6%
3	New Jersey	694	8.6%
4	Michigan	461	5.7%
5	Massachusetts	441	5.5%
6	Illinois	339	4.2%
7	Texas	333	4.1%
8	Arizona	330	4.1%
9	Maryland	321	4.0%
10	Ohio	265	3.3%
11	Minnesota	214	2.7%
12	Washington	190	2.4%
13	Pennsylvania	168	2.1%
14	Missouri	157	2.0%
15	Colorado	113	1.4%
15	Connecticut	113	1.4%
17	Oregon	105	1.3%
17	Virginia	105	1.3%
19	Florida	93	1.2%
20	South Carolina	71	0.9%
21	Indiana	62	0.8%
22	Delaware	58	0.7%
23	Maine	57	0.7%
24	Iowa	55	0.7%
24	Kansas	55	0.7%
26	Wisconsin	50	0.6%
27	Utah	49	0.6%
28	Kentucky	48	0.6%
29	Idaho	46	0.6%
29	Tennessee	46	0.6%
31	Georgia	45	0.6%
31	Nevada	45	0.6%
33	Rhode Island	43	0.5%
34	North Carolina	42	0.5%
35	Oklahoma	41	0.5%
36	South Dakota	34	0.4%
37	New Mexico	24	0.3%
38	Montana	15	0.2%
39	Alaska	10	0.1%
40	Wyoming	6	0.1%
41	Louisiana	4	0.0%
42	Nebraska	3	0.0%
42	Vermont	3	0.0%
42	West Virginia	3	0.0%
45	North Dakota	2	0.0%
46	Alabama	0	0.0%
46	Arkansas	0	0.0%
46	Mississippi	0	0.0%
NA	Hawaii**	NA	NA
NA	New Hampshire**	NA	NA
	District of Columbia	6	0.1%

Source: Federal Bureau of Investigation
"Crime in the United States 1997" (Uniform Crime Reports, November 22, 1998)
Figures are for reporting law enforcement agencies. Participating agencies covered 83 percent of the U.S. population. Sixty percent of the incidents were motivated by racial bias; 15 percent by religious bias; 14 percent by sexual-orientation bias; and 11 percent by ethnicity/national origin bias.
**Not available.

Rate of Hate Crimes in 1997

National Reported Rate = 3.6 Hate Crimes per 100,000 Population*

ALPHA ORDER			RANK ORDER		
RANK	STATE	RATE	RANK	STATE	RATE
44	Alabama	0.0	1	New Jersey	8.6
16	Alaska	3.9	2	South Dakota	8.4
4	Arizona	7.7	3	Delaware	7.9
44	Arkansas	0.0	4	Arizona	7.7
10	California	5.7	5	Massachusetts	7.3
21	Colorado	2.9	6	Michigan	7.1
9	Connecticut	5.8	7	Illinois	6.5
3	Delaware	7.9	8	Maryland	6.3
40	Florida	0.6	9	Connecticut	5.8
NA	Georgia**	NA	10	California	5.7
NA	Hawaii**	NA	11	New York	4.8
17	Idaho	3.8	12	Maine	4.6
7	Illinois	6.5	12	Minnesota	4.6
25	Indiana	2.0	14	Rhode Island	4.4
25	Iowa	2.0	15	Missouri	4.0
NA	Kansas**	NA	16	Alaska	3.9
28	Kentucky	1.9	17	Idaho	3.8
43	Louisiana	0.1	18	Ohio	3.7
12	Maine	4.6	19	Washington	3.5
8	Maryland	6.3	20	Oregon	3.2
5	Massachusetts	7.3	21	Colorado	2.9
6	Michigan	7.1	22	Nevada	2.7
12	Minnesota	4.6	23	Utah	2.4
44	Mississippi	0.0	24	New Mexico	2.2
15	Missouri	4.0	25	Indiana	2.0
28	Montana	1.9	25	Iowa	2.0
34	Nebraska	1.4	25	Tennessee	2.0
22	Nevada	2.7	28	Kentucky	1.9
NA	New Hampshire**	NA	28	Montana	1.9
1	New Jersey	8.6	28	South Carolina	1.9
24	New Mexico	2.2	31	Wyoming	1.8
11	New York	4.8	32	Texas	1.7
40	North Carolina	0.6	33	Virginia	1.6
42	North Dakota	0.4	34	Nebraska	1.4
18	Ohio	3.7	34	Pennsylvania	1.4
36	Oklahoma	1.2	36	Oklahoma	1.2
20	Oregon	3.2	37	Vermont	1.0
34	Pennsylvania	1.4	37	Wisconsin	1.0
14	Rhode Island	4.4	39	West Virginia	0.8
28	South Carolina	1.9	40	Florida	0.6
2	South Dakota	8.4	40	North Carolina	0.6
25	Tennessee	2.0	42	North Dakota	0.4
32	Texas	1.7	43	Louisiana	0.1
23	Utah	2.4	44	Alabama	0.0
37	Vermont	1.0	44	Arkansas	0.0
33	Virginia	1.6	44	Mississippi	0.0
19	Washington	3.5	NA	Georgia**	NA
39	West Virginia	0.8	NA	Hawaii**	NA
37	Wisconsin	1.0	NA	Kansas**	NA
31	Wyoming	1.8	NA	New Hampshire**	NA
				District of Columbia	1.1

Source: Morgan Quitno Press using data from Federal Bureau of Investigation
   "Crime in the United States 1997" (Uniform Crime Reports, November 22, 1998)
*Figures are for reporting law enforcement agencies. Rates calculated using only the population of reporting jurisdictions. Participating agencies covered 83 percent of the U.S. population. Sixty percent of the incidents were motivated by racial bias; 15 percent by religious bias; 14 percent by sexual-orientation bias; and 11 percent by ethnicity/national origin bias. **Not available.

Criminal Victimization in 1997

Each year the Bureau of Justice Statistics conducts the National Criminal Victimization Survey (NCVS). Unlike the FBI's Uniform Crime Reports which collects crime data from law enforcement agencies, the NCVS information is obtained through interviews with victims of crime. In 1997, approximately 43,400 households were represented and 80,000 people age 12 or older were interviewed.

Type of Crime	Number of Victimizations	Victimization Rates*
All crimes	34,788,000	NA
Personal crimes	8,971,000	40.8
Crimes of violence	8,614,000	39.2
Completed violence**	2,679,000	12.2
Attempted/threatened violence	5,935,000	27.0
Rape/Sexual Assault	311,000	1.4
Rape/attempted rape	194,000	0.9
Rape	115,000	0.5
Attempted rape	79,000	0.4
Sexual assault	117,000	0.5
Robbery	944,000	4.3
Completed/property taken	607,000	2.8
With injury	243,000	1.1
Without injury	363,000	1.7
Attempted to take property	337,000	1.5
With injury	73,000	0.3
Without injury	265,000	1.2
Assault	7,359,000	33.5
Aggravated	1,883,000	8.6
With injury	595,000	2.7
Threatened with weapon	1,288,000	5.9
Simple	5,476,000	24.9
With minor injury	1,258,000	5.7
Without injury	4,218,000	19.2
Personal theft**	357,000	1.6
Property crimes	25,817,000	248.3
Household burglary	4,635,000	44.6
Completed	3,893,000	37.4
Forcible entry	1,497,000	14.4
Unlawful entry without force	2,396,000	23.0
Attempted forcible entry	742,000	7.1
Motor vehicle theft	1,433,000	13.8
Completed	1,007,000	9.7
Attempted	426,000	4.1
Theft	19,749,000	189.9
Completed**	18,960,000	182.3
Less than $50	7,218,000	69.4
$50-$249	6,680,000	64.2
$250 or more	3,955,000	38.0
Attempted	789,000	7.6

Source: U.S. Department of Justice, Bureau of Justice Statistics
  "Criminal Victimization 1997: Changes 1996-97 with Trends 1993-97" (Bulletin, December 1998, NCJ-173385)
*Rates are per 1,000 persons age 12 or older or per 1,000 households. In 1997, there were 219,839,110 persons age 12 or older and 103,988,670 households. **Completed violent crimes include rape, sexual assault, robbery with or without injury, aggravated assault with injury, and simple assault with minor injury. The NCVS is based on interviews with victims and thus cannot measure murder. Personal theft includes pick pocketing, purse snatching and attempted purse snatching not shown separately. Completed theft includes thefts with unknown losses.

VII. APPENDIX

Population in 1998

National Total = 270,298,524*

ALPHA ORDER					RANK ORDER			
RANK	**STATE**	**POPULATION**	**% of USA**		**RANK**	**STATE**	**POPULATION**	**% of USA**
23	Alabama	4,351,999	1.6%		1	California	32,666,550	12.1%
48	Alaska	614,010	0.2%		2	Texas	19,759,614	7.3%
21	Arizona	4,668,631	1.7%		3	New York	18,175,301	6.7%
33	Arkansas	2,538,303	0.9%		4	Florida	14,915,980	5.5%
1	California	32,666,550	12.1%		5	Illinois	12,045,326	4.5%
24	Colorado	3,970,971	1.5%		6	Pennsylvania	12,001,451	4.4%
29	Connecticut	3,274,069	1.2%		7	Ohio	11,209,493	4.1%
45	Delaware	743,603	0.3%		8	Michigan	9,817,242	3.6%
4	Florida	14,915,980	5.5%		9	New Jersey	8,115,011	3.0%
10	Georgia	7,642,207	2.8%		10	Georgia	7,642,207	2.8%
41	Hawaii	1,193,001	0.4%		11	North Carolina	7,546,493	2.8%
40	Idaho	1,228,684	0.5%		12	Virginia	6,791,345	2.5%
5	Illinois	12,045,326	4.5%		13	Massachusetts	6,147,132	2.3%
14	Indiana	5,899,195	2.2%		14	Indiana	5,899,195	2.2%
30	Iowa	2,862,447	1.1%		15	Washington	5,689,263	2.1%
32	Kansas	2,629,067	1.0%		16	Missouri	5,438,559	2.0%
25	Kentucky	3,936,499	1.5%		17	Tennessee	5,430,621	2.0%
22	Louisiana	4,368,967	1.6%		18	Wisconsin	5,223,500	1.9%
39	Maine	1,244,250	0.5%		19	Maryland	5,134,808	1.9%
19	Maryland	5,134,808	1.9%		20	Minnesota	4,725,419	1.7%
13	Massachusetts	6,147,132	2.3%		21	Arizona	4,668,631	1.7%
8	Michigan	9,817,242	3.6%		22	Louisiana	4,368,967	1.6%
20	Minnesota	4,725,419	1.7%		23	Alabama	4,351,999	1.6%
31	Mississippi	2,752,092	1.0%		24	Colorado	3,970,971	1.5%
16	Missouri	5,438,559	2.0%		25	Kentucky	3,936,499	1.5%
44	Montana	880,453	0.3%		26	South Carolina	3,835,962	1.4%
38	Nebraska	1,662,719	0.6%		27	Oklahoma	3,346,713	1.2%
36	Nevada	1,746,898	0.6%		28	Oregon	3,281,974	1.2%
42	New Hampshire	1,185,048	0.4%		29	Connecticut	3,274,069	1.2%
9	New Jersey	8,115,011	3.0%		30	Iowa	2,862,447	1.1%
37	New Mexico	1,736,931	0.6%		31	Mississippi	2,752,092	1.0%
3	New York	18,175,301	6.7%		32	Kansas	2,629,067	1.0%
11	North Carolina	7,546,493	2.8%		33	Arkansas	2,538,303	0.9%
47	North Dakota	638,244	0.2%		34	Utah	2,099,758	0.8%
7	Ohio	11,209,493	4.1%		35	West Virginia	1,811,156	0.7%
27	Oklahoma	3,346,713	1.2%		36	Nevada	1,746,898	0.6%
28	Oregon	3,281,974	1.2%		37	New Mexico	1,736,931	0.6%
6	Pennsylvania	12,001,451	4.4%		38	Nebraska	1,662,719	0.6%
43	Rhode Island	988,480	0.4%		39	Maine	1,244,250	0.5%
26	South Carolina	3,835,962	1.4%		40	Idaho	1,228,684	0.5%
46	South Dakota	738,171	0.3%		41	Hawaii	1,193,001	0.4%
17	Tennessee	5,430,621	2.0%		42	New Hampshire	1,185,048	0.4%
2	Texas	19,759,614	7.3%		43	Rhode Island	988,480	0.4%
34	Utah	2,099,758	0.8%		44	Montana	880,453	0.3%
49	Vermont	590,883	0.2%		45	Delaware	743,603	0.3%
12	Virginia	6,791,345	2.5%		46	South Dakota	738,171	0.3%
15	Washington	5,689,263	2.1%		47	North Dakota	638,244	0.2%
35	West Virginia	1,811,156	0.7%		48	Alaska	614,010	0.2%
18	Wisconsin	5,223,500	1.9%		49	Vermont	590,883	0.2%
50	Wyoming	480,907	0.2%		50	Wyoming	480,907	0.2%
						District of Columbia	523,124	0.2%

Source: U.S. Bureau of the Census
   Press Release (CB98-242, December 31, 1998)
*Includes armed forces residing in each state.

Population in 1997

National Total = 267,743,595*

ALPHA ORDER

RANK	STATE	POPULATION	% of USA
23	Alabama	4,322,113	1.6%
48	Alaska	609,655	0.2%
21	Arizona	4,553,249	1.7%
33	Arkansas	2,523,186	0.9%
1	California	32,182,118	12.0%
25	Colorado	3,892,029	1.5%
28	Connecticut	3,267,240	1.2%
46	Delaware	735,143	0.3%
4	Florida	14,677,181	5.5%
10	Georgia	7,489,982	2.8%
41	Hawaii	1,192,057	0.4%
40	Idaho	1,208,865	0.5%
6	Illinois	11,989,352	4.5%
14	Indiana	5,864,847	2.2%
30	Iowa	2,854,330	1.1%
32	Kansas	2,601,437	1.0%
24	Kentucky	3,910,366	1.5%
22	Louisiana	4,353,646	1.6%
39	Maine	1,241,895	0.5%
19	Maryland	5,094,924	1.9%
13	Massachusetts	6,114,440	2.3%
8	Michigan	9,779,984	3.7%
20	Minnesota	4,687,408	1.8%
31	Mississippi	2,731,644	1.0%
16	Missouri	5,408,455	2.0%
44	Montana	878,730	0.3%
38	Nebraska	1,657,009	0.6%
37	Nevada	1,678,691	0.6%
42	New Hampshire	1,172,140	0.4%
9	New Jersey	8,058,384	3.0%
36	New Mexico	1,723,965	0.6%
3	New York	18,146,200	6.8%
11	North Carolina	7,430,675	2.8%
47	North Dakota	640,965	0.2%
7	Ohio	11,192,932	4.2%
27	Oklahoma	3,321,611	1.2%
29	Oregon	3,243,272	1.2%
5	Pennsylvania	12,011,278	4.5%
43	Rhode Island	987,263	0.4%
26	South Carolina	3,788,119	1.4%
45	South Dakota	737,755	0.3%
17	Tennessee	5,371,693	2.0%
2	Texas	19,385,699	7.2%
34	Utah	2,065,001	0.8%
49	Vermont	588,632	0.2%
12	Virginia	6,737,489	2.5%
15	Washington	5,614,151	2.1%
35	West Virginia	1,815,231	0.7%
18	Wisconsin	5,201,226	1.9%
50	Wyoming	480,043	0.2%

RANK ORDER

RANK	STATE	POPULATION	% of USA
1	California	32,182,118	12.0%
2	Texas	19,385,699	7.2%
3	New York	18,146,200	6.8%
4	Florida	14,677,181	5.5%
5	Pennsylvania	12,011,278	4.5%
6	Illinois	11,989,352	4.5%
7	Ohio	11,192,932	4.2%
8	Michigan	9,779,984	3.7%
9	New Jersey	8,058,384	3.0%
10	Georgia	7,489,982	2.8%
11	North Carolina	7,430,675	2.8%
12	Virginia	6,737,489	2.5%
13	Massachusetts	6,114,440	2.3%
14	Indiana	5,864,847	2.2%
15	Washington	5,614,151	2.1%
16	Missouri	5,408,455	2.0%
17	Tennessee	5,371,693	2.0%
18	Wisconsin	5,201,226	1.9%
19	Maryland	5,094,924	1.9%
20	Minnesota	4,687,408	1.8%
21	Arizona	4,553,249	1.7%
22	Louisiana	4,353,646	1.6%
23	Alabama	4,322,113	1.6%
24	Kentucky	3,910,366	1.5%
25	Colorado	3,892,029	1.5%
26	South Carolina	3,788,119	1.4%
27	Oklahoma	3,321,611	1.2%
28	Connecticut	3,267,240	1.2%
29	Oregon	3,243,272	1.2%
30	Iowa	2,854,330	1.1%
31	Mississippi	2,731,644	1.0%
32	Kansas	2,601,437	1.0%
33	Arkansas	2,523,186	0.9%
34	Utah	2,065,001	0.8%
35	West Virginia	1,815,231	0.7%
36	New Mexico	1,723,965	0.6%
37	Nevada	1,678,691	0.6%
38	Nebraska	1,657,009	0.6%
39	Maine	1,241,895	0.5%
40	Idaho	1,208,865	0.5%
41	Hawaii	1,192,057	0.4%
42	New Hampshire	1,172,140	0.4%
43	Rhode Island	987,263	0.4%
44	Montana	878,730	0.3%
45	South Dakota	737,755	0.3%
46	Delaware	735,143	0.3%
47	North Dakota	640,965	0.2%
48	Alaska	609,655	0.2%
49	Vermont	588,632	0.2%
50	Wyoming	480,043	0.2%
	District of Columbia	529,895	0.2%

Source: U.S. Bureau of the Census
   Press Release (CB98-242, December 31, 1998)
*Includes armed forces residing in each state. This updates earlier 1997 population estimates.

Population in 1993

National Total = 257,746,103*

ALPHA ORDER

RANK	STATE	POPULATION	% of USA
22	Alabama	4,191,879	1.6%
48	Alaska	596,906	0.2%
23	Arizona	3,993,563	1.5%
33	Arkansas	2,423,980	0.9%
1	California	31,124,200	12.1%
26	Colorado	3,562,064	1.4%
27	Connecticut	3,269,944	1.3%
46	Delaware	700,112	0.3%
4	Florida	13,712,052	5.3%
11	Georgia	6,895,071	2.7%
40	Hawaii	1,163,835	0.5%
42	Idaho	1,100,328	0.4%
6	Illinois	11,718,133	4.5%
14	Indiana	5,700,920	2.2%
30	Iowa	2,820,625	1.1%
32	Kansas	2,538,069	1.0%
24	Kentucky	3,793,694	1.5%
21	Louisiana	4,285,622	1.7%
39	Maine	1,236,178	0.5%
19	Maryland	4,943,092	1.9%
13	Massachusetts	6,008,044	2.3%
8	Michigan	9,523,247	3.7%
20	Minnesota	4,523,560	1.8%
31	Mississippi	2,635,647	1.0%
16	Missouri	5,237,813	2.0%
44	Montana	840,052	0.3%
37	Nebraska	1,612,336	0.6%
38	Nevada	1,382,223	0.5%
41	New Hampshire	1,122,141	0.4%
9	New Jersey	7,873,468	3.1%
36	New Mexico	1,615,385	0.6%
2	New York	18,139,051	7.0%
10	North Carolina	6,948,740	2.7%
47	North Dakota	637,315	0.2%
7	Ohio	11,063,366	4.3%
28	Oklahoma	3,229,393	1.3%
29	Oregon	3,034,869	1.2%
5	Pennsylvania	12,022,460	4.7%
43	Rhode Island	997,817	0.4%
25	South Carolina	3,634,842	1.4%
45	South Dakota	722,550	0.3%
17	Tennessee	5,082,456	2.0%
3	Texas	18,009,031	7.0%
34	Utah	1,872,018	0.7%
49	Vermont	573,837	0.2%
12	Virginia	6,466,977	2.5%
15	Washington	5,248,735	2.0%
35	West Virginia	1,816,508	0.7%
18	Wisconsin	5,055,710	2.0%
50	Wyoming	469,065	0.2%

RANK ORDER

RANK	STATE	POPULATION	% of USA
1	California	31,124,200	12.1%
2	New York	18,139,051	7.0%
3	Texas	18,009,031	7.0%
4	Florida	13,712,052	5.3%
5	Pennsylvania	12,022,460	4.7%
6	Illinois	11,718,133	4.5%
7	Ohio	11,063,366	4.3%
8	Michigan	9,523,247	3.7%
9	New Jersey	7,873,468	3.1%
10	North Carolina	6,948,740	2.7%
11	Georgia	6,895,071	2.7%
12	Virginia	6,466,977	2.5%
13	Massachusetts	6,008,044	2.3%
14	Indiana	5,700,920	2.2%
15	Washington	5,248,735	2.0%
16	Missouri	5,237,813	2.0%
17	Tennessee	5,082,456	2.0%
18	Wisconsin	5,055,710	2.0%
19	Maryland	4,943,092	1.9%
20	Minnesota	4,523,560	1.8%
21	Louisiana	4,285,622	1.7%
22	Alabama	4,191,879	1.6%
23	Arizona	3,993,563	1.5%
24	Kentucky	3,793,694	1.5%
25	South Carolina	3,634,842	1.4%
26	Colorado	3,562,064	1.4%
27	Connecticut	3,269,944	1.3%
28	Oklahoma	3,229,393	1.3%
29	Oregon	3,034,869	1.2%
30	Iowa	2,820,625	1.1%
31	Mississippi	2,635,647	1.0%
32	Kansas	2,538,069	1.0%
33	Arkansas	2,423,980	0.9%
34	Utah	1,872,018	0.7%
35	West Virginia	1,816,508	0.7%
36	New Mexico	1,615,385	0.6%
37	Nebraska	1,612,336	0.6%
38	Nevada	1,382,223	0.5%
39	Maine	1,236,178	0.5%
40	Hawaii	1,163,835	0.5%
41	New Hampshire	1,122,141	0.4%
42	Idaho	1,100,328	0.4%
43	Rhode Island	997,817	0.4%
44	Montana	840,052	0.3%
45	South Dakota	722,550	0.3%
46	Delaware	700,112	0.3%
47	North Dakota	637,315	0.2%
48	Alaska	596,906	0.2%
49	Vermont	573,837	0.2%
50	Wyoming	469,065	0.2%
	District of Columbia	577,180	0.2%

Source: U.S. Bureau of the Census
  Press Release (CB98-242, December 31, 1998)
Includes armed forces residing in each state. This updates earlier 1993 population estimates.

Urban Population in 1997

National Total = 235,417,876 Urban Population*

ALPHA ORDER

RANK	STATE	POPULATION	% of USA
23	Alabama	3,526,080	1.5%
43	Alaska	417,274	0.2%
17	Arizona	4,203,368	1.8%
30	Arkansas	1,709,823	0.7%
1	California	31,634,109	13.4%
22	Colorado	3,564,174	1.5%
24	Connecticut	3,085,347	1.3%
40	Delaware	638,071	0.3%
4	Florida	13,857,647	5.9%
10	Georgia	6,012,432	2.6%
38	Hawaii	880,272	0.4%
39	Idaho	807,024	0.3%
NA	Illinois**	NA	NA
15	Indiana	4,804,593	2.0%
28	Iowa	1,966,385	0.8%
NA	Kansas**	NA	NA
NA	Kentucky**	NA	NA
21	Louisiana	3,667,853	1.6%
37	Maine	889,613	0.4%
14	Maryland	4,826,004	2.0%
9	Massachusetts	6,108,143	2.6%
7	Michigan	8,698,839	3.7%
20	Minnesota	3,805,888	1.6%
31	Mississippi	1,614,247	0.7%
19	Missouri	4,184,806	1.8%
NA	Montana**	NA	NA
34	Nebraska	1,236,418	0.5%
32	Nevada	1,481,886	0.6%
NA	New Hampshire**	NA	NA
8	New Jersey	8,053,000	3.4%
33	New Mexico	1,433,492	0.6%
3	New York	17,285,135	7.3%
11	North Carolina	5,710,065	2.4%
42	North Dakota	418,980	0.2%
6	Ohio	9,854,927	4.2%
27	Oklahoma	2,684,350	1.1%
26	Oregon	2,722,238	1.2%
5	Pennsylvania	10,966,505	4.7%
36	Rhode Island	987,000	0.4%
25	South Carolina	2,958,477	1.3%
41	South Dakota	447,381	0.2%
16	Tennessee	4,274,810	1.8%
2	Texas	17,786,892	7.6%
29	Utah	1,838,700	0.8%
NA	Vermont**	NA	NA
12	Virginia	5,659,402	2.4%
13	Washington	5,096,175	2.2%
35	West Virginia	1,037,173	0.4%
18	Wisconsin	4,186,814	1.8%
44	Wyoming	354,867	0.2%

RANK ORDER

RANK	STATE	POPULATION	% of USA
1	California	31,634,109	13.4%
2	Texas	17,786,892	7.6%
3	New York	17,285,135	7.3%
4	Florida	13,857,647	5.9%
5	Pennsylvania	10,966,505	4.7%
6	Ohio	9,854,927	4.2%
7	Michigan	8,698,839	3.7%
8	New Jersey	8,053,000	3.4%
9	Massachusetts	6,108,143	2.6%
10	Georgia	6,012,432	2.6%
11	North Carolina	5,710,065	2.4%
12	Virginia	5,659,402	2.4%
13	Washington	5,096,175	2.2%
14	Maryland	4,826,004	2.0%
15	Indiana	4,804,593	2.0%
16	Tennessee	4,274,810	1.8%
17	Arizona	4,203,368	1.8%
18	Wisconsin	4,186,814	1.8%
19	Missouri	4,184,806	1.8%
20	Minnesota	3,805,888	1.6%
21	Louisiana	3,667,853	1.6%
22	Colorado	3,564,174	1.5%
23	Alabama	3,526,080	1.5%
24	Connecticut	3,085,347	1.3%
25	South Carolina	2,958,477	1.3%
26	Oregon	2,722,238	1.2%
27	Oklahoma	2,684,350	1.1%
28	Iowa	1,966,385	0.8%
29	Utah	1,838,700	0.8%
30	Arkansas	1,709,823	0.7%
31	Mississippi	1,614,247	0.7%
32	Nevada	1,481,886	0.6%
33	New Mexico	1,433,492	0.6%
34	Nebraska	1,236,418	0.5%
35	West Virginia	1,037,173	0.4%
36	Rhode Island	987,000	0.4%
37	Maine	889,613	0.4%
38	Hawaii	880,272	0.4%
39	Idaho	807,024	0.3%
40	Delaware	638,071	0.3%
41	South Dakota	447,381	0.2%
42	North Dakota	418,980	0.2%
43	Alaska	417,274	0.2%
44	Wyoming	354,867	0.2%
NA	Illinois**	NA	NA
NA	Kansas**	NA	NA
NA	Kentucky**	NA	NA
NA	Montana**	NA	NA
NA	New Hampshire**	NA	NA
NA	Vermont**	NA	NA
	District of Columbia	529,000	0.2%

Source: Morgan Quitno Press using data from Federal Bureau of Investigation
     "Crime in the United States 1997" (Uniform Crime Reports, November 22, 1998)
*Estimated totals for urban areas, defined by the F.B.I. as Metropolitan Statistical Areas and other cities outside
such areas. National total includes states not shown separately.
**Not available.

Rural Population in 1997

National Total = 32,219,124 Rural Population*

ALPHA ORDER

RANK	STATE	POPULATION	% of USA
19	Alabama	792,920	2.5%
38	Alaska	191,726	0.6%
29	Arizona	351,632	1.1%
16	Arkansas	813,177	2.5%
22	California	633,891	2.0%
30	Colorado	328,826	1.0%
39	Connecticut	184,653	0.6%
41	Delaware	93,929	0.3%
18	Florida	796,353	2.5%
3	Georgia	1,473,568	4.6%
31	Hawaii	306,728	1.0%
27	Idaho	402,976	1.3%
NA	Illinois**	NA	NA
10	Indiana	1,059,407	3.3%
13	Iowa	885,615	2.7%
NA	Kansas**	NA	NA
NA	Kentucky**	NA	NA
21	Louisiana	684,147	2.1%
28	Maine	352,387	1.1%
34	Maryland	267,996	0.8%
42	Massachusetts	9,857	0.0%
8	Michigan	1,075,161	3.3%
14	Minnesota	880,112	2.7%
6	Mississippi	1,116,753	3.5%
5	Missouri	1,217,194	3.8%
NA	Montana**	NA	NA
26	Nebraska	420,582	1.3%
37	Nevada	195,114	0.6%
NA	New Hampshire**	NA	NA
43	New Jersey	0	0.0%
32	New Mexico	296,508	0.9%
15	New York	851,865	2.6%
1	North Carolina	1,714,935	5.3%
35	North Dakota	222,020	0.7%
4	Ohio	1,331,073	4.1%
23	Oklahoma	632,650	2.0%
24	Oregon	520,762	1.6%
11	Pennsylvania	1,053,495	3.3%
43	Rhode Island	0	0.0%
17	South Carolina	801,523	2.5%
33	South Dakota	290,619	0.9%
7	Tennessee	1,093,190	3.4%
2	Texas	1,652,108	5.1%
36	Utah	220,300	0.7%
NA	Vermont**	NA	NA
9	Virginia	1,074,598	3.3%
25	Washington	513,825	1.6%
20	West Virginia	778,827	2.4%
12	Wisconsin	983,186	3.1%
40	Wyoming	125,133	0.4%

RANK ORDER

RANK	STATE	POPULATION	% of USA
1	North Carolina	1,714,935	5.3%
2	Texas	1,652,108	5.1%
3	Georgia	1,473,568	4.6%
4	Ohio	1,331,073	4.1%
5	Missouri	1,217,194	3.8%
6	Mississippi	1,116,753	3.5%
7	Tennessee	1,093,190	3.4%
8	Michigan	1,075,161	3.3%
9	Virginia	1,074,598	3.3%
10	Indiana	1,059,407	3.3%
11	Pennsylvania	1,053,495	3.3%
12	Wisconsin	983,186	3.1%
13	Iowa	885,615	2.7%
14	Minnesota	880,112	2.7%
15	New York	851,865	2.6%
16	Arkansas	813,177	2.5%
17	South Carolina	801,523	2.5%
18	Florida	796,353	2.5%
19	Alabama	792,920	2.5%
20	West Virginia	778,827	2.4%
21	Louisiana	684,147	2.1%
22	California	633,891	2.0%
23	Oklahoma	632,650	2.0%
24	Oregon	520,762	1.6%
25	Washington	513,825	1.6%
26	Nebraska	420,582	1.3%
27	Idaho	402,976	1.3%
28	Maine	352,387	1.1%
29	Arizona	351,632	1.1%
30	Colorado	328,826	1.0%
31	Hawaii	306,728	1.0%
32	New Mexico	296,508	0.9%
33	South Dakota	290,619	0.9%
34	Maryland	267,996	0.8%
35	North Dakota	222,020	0.7%
36	Utah	220,300	0.7%
37	Nevada	195,114	0.6%
38	Alaska	191,726	0.6%
39	Connecticut	184,653	0.6%
40	Wyoming	125,133	0.4%
41	Delaware	93,929	0.3%
42	Massachusetts	9,857	0.0%
43	New Jersey	0	0.0%
43	Rhode Island	0	0.0%
NA	Illinois**	NA	NA
NA	Kansas**	NA	NA
NA	Kentucky**	NA	NA
NA	Montana**	NA	NA
NA	New Hampshire**	NA	NA
NA	Vermont**	NA	NA
	District of Columbia	0	0.0%

Source: Morgan Quitno Press using data from Federal Bureau of Investigation
"Crime in the United States 1997" (Uniform Crime Reports, November 22, 1998)
*Estimated totals for rural areas, defined by the F.B.I. as other than Metropolitan Statistical Areas and other cities outside such areas. National total includes states not shown separately.
**Not available.

Population 10 to 17 Years Old in 1997

National Total = 30,639,951

ALPHA ORDER

RANK	STATE	POPULATION	% of USA
23	Alabama	483,599	1.6%
46	Alaska	84,231	0.3%
22	Arizona	542,265	1.8%
34	Arkansas	304,755	1.0%
1	California	3,623,251	11.8%
24	Colorado	460,891	1.5%
31	Connecticut	342,335	1.1%
48	Delaware	77,280	0.3%
4	Florida	1,515,538	4.9%
9	Georgia	868,191	2.8%
42	Hawaii	126,621	0.4%
39	Idaho	166,540	0.5%
5	Illinois	1,370,656	4.5%
13	Indiana	679,036	2.2%
29	Iowa	346,724	1.1%
32	Kansas	321,546	1.0%
25	Kentucky	443,208	1.4%
20	Louisiana	554,435	1.8%
40	Maine	144,511	0.5%
21	Maryland	549,550	1.8%
17	Massachusetts	625,056	2.0%
8	Michigan	1,140,230	3.7%
19	Minnesota	589,947	1.9%
30	Mississippi	346,603	1.1%
15	Missouri	648,845	2.1%
43	Montana	113,712	0.4%
36	Nebraska	210,040	0.7%
38	Nevada	186,478	0.6%
41	New Hampshire	136,809	0.4%
10	New Jersey	845,725	2.8%
35	New Mexico	227,172	0.7%
3	New York	1,913,295	6.2%
11	North Carolina	815,139	2.7%
47	North Dakota	80,926	0.3%
7	Ohio	1,299,090	4.2%
27	Oklahoma	412,737	1.3%
28	Oregon	375,479	1.2%
6	Pennsylvania	1,312,396	4.3%
44	Rhode Island	103,401	0.3%
26	South Carolina	428,276	1.4%
45	South Dakota	95,016	0.3%
18	Tennessee	592,123	1.9%
2	Texas	2,424,274	7.9%
33	Utah	310,443	1.0%
49	Vermont	69,860	0.2%
12	Virginia	721,936	2.4%
14	Washington	661,396	2.2%
37	West Virginia	198,715	0.6%
16	Wisconsin	643,086	2.1%
50	Wyoming	66,532	0.2%

RANK ORDER

RANK	STATE	POPULATION	% of USA
1	California	3,623,251	11.8%
2	Texas	2,424,274	7.9%
3	New York	1,913,295	6.2%
4	Florida	1,515,538	4.9%
5	Illinois	1,370,656	4.5%
6	Pennsylvania	1,312,396	4.3%
7	Ohio	1,299,090	4.2%
8	Michigan	1,140,230	3.7%
9	Georgia	868,191	2.8%
10	New Jersey	845,725	2.8%
11	North Carolina	815,139	2.7%
12	Virginia	721,936	2.4%
13	Indiana	679,036	2.2%
14	Washington	661,396	2.2%
15	Missouri	648,845	2.1%
16	Wisconsin	643,086	2.1%
17	Massachusetts	625,056	2.0%
18	Tennessee	592,123	1.9%
19	Minnesota	589,947	1.9%
20	Louisiana	554,435	1.8%
21	Maryland	549,550	1.8%
22	Arizona	542,265	1.8%
23	Alabama	483,599	1.6%
24	Colorado	460,891	1.5%
25	Kentucky	443,208	1.4%
26	South Carolina	428,276	1.4%
27	Oklahoma	412,737	1.3%
28	Oregon	375,479	1.2%
29	Iowa	346,724	1.1%
30	Mississippi	346,603	1.1%
31	Connecticut	342,335	1.1%
32	Kansas	321,546	1.0%
33	Utah	310,443	1.0%
34	Arkansas	304,755	1.0%
35	New Mexico	227,172	0.7%
36	Nebraska	210,040	0.7%
37	West Virginia	198,715	0.6%
38	Nevada	186,478	0.6%
39	Idaho	166,540	0.5%
40	Maine	144,511	0.5%
41	New Hampshire	136,809	0.4%
42	Hawaii	126,621	0.4%
43	Montana	113,712	0.4%
44	Rhode Island	103,401	0.3%
45	South Dakota	95,016	0.3%
46	Alaska	84,231	0.3%
47	North Dakota	80,926	0.3%
48	Delaware	77,280	0.3%
49	Vermont	69,860	0.2%
50	Wyoming	66,532	0.2%
	District of Columbia	40,051	0.1%

Source: U.S. Bureau of the Census
   "State Population Estimates by Age" (http://www.census.gov/population/www/estimates/stagesex.html)

Total Area of States in Square Miles in 1998

National Total = 3,717,796 Square Miles*

ALPHA ORDER

RANK	STATE	MILES	% of USA
30	Alabama	52,237	1.41%
1	Alaska	615,230	16.55%
6	Arizona	114,006	3.07%
28	Arkansas	53,182	1.43%
3	California	158,869	4.27%
8	Colorado	104,100	2.80%
48	Connecticut	5,544	0.15%
49	Delaware	2,396	0.06%
23	Florida	59,928	1.61%
24	Georgia	58,977	1.59%
47	Hawaii	6,459	0.17%
14	Idaho	83,574	2.25%
25	Illinois	57,918	1.56%
38	Indiana	36,420	0.98%
26	Iowa	56,276	1.51%
15	Kansas	82,282	2.21%
37	Kentucky	40,411	1.09%
31	Louisiana	49,651	1.34%
39	Maine	33,741	0.91%
42	Maryland	12,297	0.33%
45	Massachusetts	9,241	0.25%
11	Michigan	96,705	2.60%
12	Minnesota	86,943	2.34%
32	Mississippi	48,286	1.30%
21	Missouri	69,709	1.88%
4	Montana	147,046	3.96%
16	Nebraska	77,358	2.08%
7	Nevada	110,567	2.97%
44	New Hampshire	9,283	0.25%
46	New Jersey	8,215	0.22%
5	New Mexico	121,598	3.27%
27	New York	53,989	1.45%
29	North Carolina	52,672	1.42%
18	North Dakota	70,704	1.90%
34	Ohio	44,828	1.21%
20	Oklahoma	69,903	1.88%
10	Oregon	97,132	2.61%
33	Pennsylvania	46,058	1.24%
50	Rhode Island	1,231	0.03%
40	South Carolina	31,189	0.84%
17	South Dakota	77,121	2.07%
36	Tennessee	42,146	1.13%
2	Texas	267,277	7.19%
13	Utah	84,904	2.28%
43	Vermont	9,615	0.26%
35	Virginia	42,326	1.14%
19	Washington	70,637	1.90%
41	West Virginia	24,231	0.65%
22	Wisconsin	65,499	1.76%
9	Wyoming	97,818	2.63%

RANK ORDER

RANK	STATE	MILES	% of USA
1	Alaska	615,230	16.55%
2	Texas	267,277	7.19%
3	California	158,869	4.27%
4	Montana	147,046	3.96%
5	New Mexico	121,598	3.27%
6	Arizona	114,006	3.07%
7	Nevada	110,567	2.97%
8	Colorado	104,100	2.80%
9	Wyoming	97,818	2.63%
10	Oregon	97,132	2.61%
11	Michigan	96,705	2.60%
12	Minnesota	86,943	2.34%
13	Utah	84,904	2.28%
14	Idaho	83,574	2.25%
15	Kansas	82,282	2.21%
16	Nebraska	77,358	2.08%
17	South Dakota	77,121	2.07%
18	North Dakota	70,704	1.90%
19	Washington	70,637	1.90%
20	Oklahoma	69,903	1.88%
21	Missouri	69,709	1.88%
22	Wisconsin	65,499	1.76%
23	Florida	59,928	1.61%
24	Georgia	58,977	1.59%
25	Illinois	57,918	1.56%
26	Iowa	56,276	1.51%
27	New York	53,989	1.45%
28	Arkansas	53,182	1.43%
29	North Carolina	52,672	1.42%
30	Alabama	52,237	1.41%
31	Louisiana	49,651	1.34%
32	Mississippi	48,286	1.30%
33	Pennsylvania	46,058	1.24%
34	Ohio	44,828	1.21%
35	Virginia	42,326	1.14%
36	Tennessee	42,146	1.13%
37	Kentucky	40,411	1.09%
38	Indiana	36,420	0.98%
39	Maine	33,741	0.91%
40	South Carolina	31,189	0.84%
41	West Virginia	24,231	0.65%
42	Maryland	12,297	0.33%
43	Vermont	9,615	0.26%
44	New Hampshire	9,283	0.25%
45	Massachusetts	9,241	0.25%
46	New Jersey	8,215	0.22%
47	Hawaii	6,459	0.17%
48	Connecticut	5,544	0.15%
49	Delaware	2,396	0.06%
50	Rhode Island	1,231	0.03%
	District of Columbia	68	0.00%

Source: U.S. Bureau of the Census
"1990 Census of Population and Housing" (Series CPH-1)
*Total of land and water area. These totals are revised. Excludes territorial water which was included in previous reports.

IX. SOURCES

Administrative Office of the U.S. Courts
Statistics Division
One Columbus Circle, NE
Washington, DC 20544
202-273-2290
www.uscourts.gov

American Correctional Association
4380 Forbes Blvd.
Lanham, MD 20706-4322
800-222-5646
www.corrections.com/aca

Bureau of the Census
3 Silver Hill & Suitland Roads
Suitland, MD 20746
301-457-2794
www.census.gov

Bureau of Justice Assistance Clearinghouse
2277 Research Boulevard
Box 6000
Rockville, MD 20850
800-688-4252
www.ojp.usdoj.gov/BJA/

Bureau of Justice Statistics Clearinghouse
810 Seventh Street, NW
Washington, DC 20531
202-307-0765
www.ojp.usdoj.gov/bjs/

Drugs and Crime Clearinghouse of the Office of National Drug Control Policy
Box 6000
Rockville, MD 20849-6000
800-666-3332
www.whitehousedrugpolicy.gov

Federal Bureau of Investigation
J. Edgar Hoover FBI Building
935 Pennsylvania Avenue, NW
Washington, DC 20535
202-324-3000
Internet: http://www.fbi.gov

Juvenile Justice Clearinghouse
Box 6000
Rockville, MD 20849-6000
800-638-8736
www.ncjrs.org/ojjhome.htm

National Archive of Crime and Justice Programs
Inter-University Consortium for Political
  and Social Research
P.O. Box 1248
Ann Arbor, MI 48106
800-999-0960
www.icpsr.umich.edu/NACJD/home.html

National Association of State Alcohol and Drug Abuse Directors, Inc.
808 17th Street, NW
Suite 410
Washington, DC 20006
202-293-0090
www.nasadad.org

National Center for State Courts
300 Newport Avenue
Williamsburg, VA 23185
757-253-2000
www.ncsc.dni.us/

National Institute of Justice
810 Seventh Street, NW.
Washington, DC 20531
(202) 307-2942
www.ojp.usdoj.gov/nij

National Clearinghouse on Child Abuse and Neglect
330 C Street, SW
Washington, DC 20447
800-394-3366
www.calib.com/nccanch/

National Criminal Justice Reference Service (NCJRS)
Box 6000
Rockville, MD 20849-6000
800-851-3420
www.ncjrs.org

Substance Abuse and Mental Health Services Administration
U.S. Department of Health and Human Services
5600 Fishers Lane
Rockville, MD 20857
301-468-2600
www.samhsa.gov

Victims of Crime Resource Center
810 Seventh Street, NW.
Washington, DC 20531
800-627-6872
www.ojp.usdoj.gov/ovc/

X. INDEX

X. INDEX (continued)

X. INDEX (continued)

X. INDEX (continued)

CHAPTER INDEX

HOW TO USE THIS INDEX

Place left thumb on the outer edge of this page. To locate the desired entry, fold back the remaining page edges and align the index edge mark with the appropriate page edge mark.

Other books by Morgan Quitno Press:

- *State Statistical Trends (monthly journal)*
- *State Rankings 1999 ($49.95)*
- *Health Care State Rankings 1999 ($49.95)*
- *City Crime Rankings, 5th Edition ($37.95)*

Call toll free: 1-800-457-0742 or
visit us at www.morganquitno.com